Get Connected.

FEATURES

Guided Examples

Problem Solution

- General model for analyzing labor variances:

AH x AR	AH x SR	SH x SR
140 hrs	140 hrs x $25	126 hrs x $25

Labor Rate Variance

Calculation:
126 standard hours + 14 unfavorable efficiency variance hours

Step 3 – Calculate the actual hours used for the units produced. The labor efficiency variance was 14 hours unfavorable.

1:27 / 2:39 CC

Guided Examples give you a narrated, animated, step-by-step walkthrough of an exercise similar to the one you've been assigned by your instructor, allowing you to identify, review, and reinforce the concepts and activities covered in class.

Intelligent Response Technology

Intelligent Response Technology (IRT) is *Connect Accounting's* new student interface for end-of-chapter assessment content. Intelligent Response Technology provides a general journal application that looks and feels more like what you would find in a general ledger software package, improves answer acceptance to reduce student frustration with formatting issues (such as rounding), and, for select questions, provides an expanded table that guides students through the process of solving the problem.

view transaction list   view general journal

Journal Entry Worksheet

1 2 3 4 5 6 7

Two-thirds of the work related to $12,000 cash received in advance is performed this period.

Transaction	General Journal	Debit	Credit
a.	Unearned fee revenue	12,000	
	fe		12,000
	Fee revenue		
	Unearned fee revenue		

*Enter debits before credits

done   clear transaction   record transaction

Get Engaged.

e-Books

Connect Plus includes a media-rich e-Book that allows you to share your notes with your students. Your students can insert and review their own notes, highlight the text, search for specific information, and interact with media resources. Using an e-Book with *Connect Plus* gives your students a complete digital solution that allows them to access their materials from any computer.

Lecture Capture

Make your classes available anytime, anywhere. With simple, one-click recording, students can search for a word or phrase and be taken to the exact place in your lecture that they need to review.

Accounting

Tenth Edition

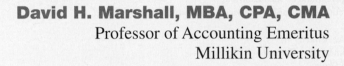

Accounting

What the Numbers Mean

David H. Marshall, MBA, CPA, CMA
Professor of Accounting Emeritus
Millikin University

**Wayne W. McManus, LLM, JD, MS,
MBA, CFA, CPA, CMA, CIA**
Professor of Accounting and Law
International College of the Cayman Islands

Daniel F. Viele, MS, CPA, CMA
Professor of Accounting
Associate Vice President for Academic Affairs
Webster University

McGraw-Hill
Irwin

ACCOUNTING: WHAT THE NUMBERS MEAN, TENTH EDITION
Published by McGraw-Hill/Irwin, a business unit of The McGraw-Hill Companies, Inc., 1221 Avenue of the
Americas, New York, NY, 10020. Copyright © 2014 by The McGraw-Hill Companies, Inc. All rights reserved.
Printed in the United States of America. Previous editions © 2011, 2008, and 2007. No part of this publication
may be reproduced or distributed in any form or by any means, or stored in a database or retrieval system,
without the prior written consent of The McGraw-Hill Companies, Inc., including, but not limited to, in any
network or other electronic storage or transmission, or broadcast for distance learning.

Some ancillaries, including electronic and print components, may not be available to customers outside the
United States.

This book is printed on acid-free paper.

Printed in China

2 3 4 5 6 7 8 9 0 CTP/CTP 1 0 9 8 7 6 5 4

ISBN   978-0-07-802529-7
MHID   0-07-802529-X

Senior Vice President, Products & Markets: *Kurt L. Strand*
Vice President, Content Production & Technology Services: *Kimberly Meriwether David*
Director: *Tim Vertovec*
Executive Brand Manager: *Steve Schuetz*
Executive Director of Development: *Ann Torbert*
Development Editor II: *Megan Shultz*
Director of Digital Content: *Patricia Plumb*
Digital Development Editor: *Julie Hankins*
Senior Marketing Manager: *Michelle Heaster*
Senior Project Manager: *Diane L. Nowaczyk*
Senior Buyer: *Michael R. McCormick*
Senior Designer: *Matt Diamond*
Cover Designer: *Kay Lieberherr*
Cover Image: *Superstock*
Senior Content Licensing Specialist: *Jeremy Cheshareck*
Senior Media Project Manager: *Susan Lombardi*
Media Project Manager: *Ron Nelms*
Typeface: *10.5/12 Times Roman*
Compositor: *MPS Limited*
Printer: *CTPS*

Library of Congress Cataloging-in-Publication Data

Marshall, David H.
    Accounting : what the numbers mean / David H. Marshall, Wayne W. McManus, Daniel F. Viele.—
10th ed.
        p. cm.
    Includes index.
    ISBN-13: 978-0-07-802529-7 (alk. paper)
    ISBN-10: 0-07-802529-X (alk. paper)
    1. Accounting. 2. Managerial accounting. I. McManus, Wayne W. II. Viele, Daniel F. III. Title.
HF5636.M37 2014
657—dc23

                                                                              2012041059

The Internet addresses listed in the text were accurate at the time of publication. The inclusion of a website does
not indicate an endorsement by the authors or McGraw-Hill, and McGraw-Hill does not guarantee the accuracy
of the information presented at these sites.

www.mhhe.com

Meet the Authors

David H. Marshall is Professor of Accounting Emeritus at Millikin University. He taught at Millikin, a small, independent university located in Decatur, Illinois, for 25 years. He taught courses in accounting, finance, computer information systems, and business policy, and was recognized as an outstanding teacher. The draft manuscript of this book was written in 1986 and used in a one-semester course that was developed for the non-business major. Subsequently supplemented with cases, it was used in the business core accounting principles and managerial accounting courses. Concurrently, a one-credit hour accounting laboratory taught potential accounting majors the mechanics of the accounting process. Prior to his teaching career, Marshall worked in public accounting and industry and he earned an MBA from Northwestern University. Professor Marshall's interests outside academia include community service, woodturning, sailing, and travel.

Wayne W. McManus makes his home in Grand Cayman, Cayman Islands, BWI, where he worked in the private banking sector for several years and is now a semi-retired consultant. He maintains an ongoing relationship with the International College of the Cayman Islands as an adjunct Professor of Accounting and Law and as a member of the College's Board of Trustees. McManus now offers the Cayman CPA Review course through the Financial Education Institute Ltd. and several professional development courses through the Chamber of Commerce. He earned an MS in accounting from Illinois State University, an MBA from the University of Kansas, a law degree from Northern Illinois University, and a master's of law in taxation from the University of Missouri–Kansas City. He serves as an independent director and chairman of the audit committee for Endeavour Mining Corp. (EDV on the TSX exchange). He is an active member of the Cayman Islands Society of Professional Accountants and the local chapter of the CFA Institute. Professor McManus volunteers as a "professional" Santa each December, enjoys travel, golf, and scuba diving, and is an audio/video enthusiast.

Daniel F. Viele is Professor of Accounting and currently serves as Associate Vice President for Academic Affairs at Webster University. He teaches courses in financial, managerial, and cost accounting, as well as accounting information systems. He has developed and taught numerous online graduate courses, and for his leadership role in pioneering online teaching and learning, the university presented him with a Presidential Recognition Award. Professor Viele's students and colleagues have also cited his dedication to teaching and innovative use of technology, and in 2002 Webster awarded him its highest honor—the Kemper Award for Teaching Excellence. Prior to joining Webster University in 1998, he served as a systems consultant to the graphics arts industry, and his previous teaching experience includes 10 years at Millikin University with Professor Marshall. Professor Viele holds an MS in Accounting from Colorado State University and has completed the Information Systems Faculty Development Institute at the University of Minnesota and the Advanced Information Systems Faculty Development Institute at Indiana University. He is a member of the American Accounting Association and the Institute of Management Accountants, where he has served as President of the Sangamon Valley Chapter and as a member of the National Board of Directors. Professor Viele enjoys sports of all kinds, boating, and a good book.

Preface

Welcome to the Tenth Edition of *Accounting: What the Numbers Mean*. We are confident that this text and supplemental resources will permit the achievement of understanding the basics of financial reporting by corporations and other enterprises.

Accounting has become known as the language of business. Financial statements result from the accounting process and are used by owners/investors, employees, creditors, and regulators in their planning, controlling, and decision-making activities as they evaluate the achievement of an organization's objectives. Active study of this text will allow you to acquire command of the language and help you become an informed user of accounting information.

Accounting issues are likely to touch the majority of career paths in today's economy. Students whose principal academic interests are not in accounting, but who are interested in other areas of business or nonbusiness areas, such as engineering, behavioral sciences, public administration, and prelaw programs, will benefit from the approach used in this book. Individuals aspiring to an MBA degree or other graduate programs that focus on administration and management, who do not have an undergraduate business degree, will benefit from a course using this text.

Accounting: What the Numbers Mean takes the user through the basics: what accounting information is, how it is developed, how it is used, and what it means. Financial statements are examined to learn what they do and do not communicate, enhancing the student's decision-making and problem-solving abilities from a user perspective. Achieving expertise in the preparation of financial statements is not an objective of this text. In short, we have designed these materials to assist those who wish to learn "what the numbers mean" without concentrating on the mechanical aspects of the accounting process.

Best wishes for successful use of the information presented here.

David H. Marshall

Wayne W. McManus

Daniel F. Viele

Putting the Pieces Together

Named after a Chinese word meaning "sparrow," mah-jongg is a centuries-old game of skill. The object of the game is to collect different tiles; players win points by accumulating different combinations of pieces and creating patterns. We've chosen mah-jongg tiles as our cover image for the tenth edition of *Accounting: What the Numbers Mean* because the authors show students how to put the pieces together and understand their relationship to one another to see the larger pattern. By focusing on the meaning of the numbers used in financial statements, students develop the crucial decision-making and problem-solving skills needed to succeed in any professional environment.

Marshall continues to be the market-leading text for the Survey of Accounting course, helping students to succeed through clear and concise writing, a conceptual focus, and unparalleled technology support.

Clear

Instructors and students alike have praised *Accounting: What the Numbers Mean* for its effectiveness in explaining difficult and important accounting concepts to all students, not just future accountants. Instructors consistently point out that students find this text much less intimidating and easier to follow than others they have used.

Concise

In concentrating on the basics—what accounting information is, what it means, and how it is used—*Accounting: What the Numbers Mean* does not overwhelm students with encyclopedic detail. The emphasis on discovering what financial statements communicate and how to better use them (as well as other pieces of accounting information) facilitates student comprehension of the big picture.

Conceptual

Accounting: What the Numbers Mean focuses on helping students understand the meaning of the numbers in financial statements, their relationship to each other, and how they are used in evaluation, planning, and control. Technical details are minimized wherever possible, allowing instructors to highlight the function of financial statements, as opposed to their formation.

Technology

To meet the evolving needs of instructors and students, the tenth edition features a far more extensive technology support package than ever before. An expanded Online Learning Center includes a wealth of self-study material for students. McGraw-Hill's *Connect Accounting* lets instructors assign, collect, and grade homework online. In addition, McGraw-Hill's *Connect Accounting Plus* gives students the ability to work with an integrated eBook while managing and completing homework online.

What Makes *Accounting: What the Numbers Mean* Such a *Powerful Learning Tool?*

Fiscal Year

A firm's **fiscal year** is the annual period used for reporting to owners, the government, and others. Many firms select the calendar year as their fiscal year, but other 12-month periods can also be selected. Some firms select a reporting period ending on a date when inventories will be relatively low or business activity will be slow because this facilitates the process of preparing financial statements.

Many firms select fiscal periods that relate to the pace of their business activity. Food retailers, for example, have a weekly operating cycle, and many of these firms select a 52-week fiscal year (with a 53-week fiscal year every five or six years so their year-end remains near the same date every year). Campbell Soup Company has adopted this strategy; note, on page 715 in the appendix, that Campbell's fiscal year ends on the Sunday nearest July 31 each year. (The next 53-week year will end on August 3, 2014).

For internal reporting purposes, many firms use periods other than the month (e.g., 13 four-week periods). Such firms wish to maintain the same number of operating days in each period so that comparisons between the same periods of different years can be made without having to consider differences in the number of operating days in the respective periods.

Business in Practice

Campbell's

---

2. What does it mean to refer to a balance sheet for the year ended August 31, 2014?
3. What does it mean when a balance sheet has been prepared for an organization?

What Does It Mean?
Answers on pages 56–57

This is a difficult but important concept to grasp, so please consider the following example: Assume that Cruisers, Inc., sells a boat to a customer for $2,000 and uses the FIFO assumption. For argument's sake, assume that the cost of goods sold for this boat is $1,500 (taken from the beginning inventory); yet the current cost of replacing the boat has recently increased to $1,850, and the tax rate is 30 percent. The income tax owed by Cruisers, Inc., from this sale would be $150, computed as ($2,000 − $1,500) × 30%, and when this amount is added to the cost of replacing the boat, the company hasn't had any positive net cash flow! However, on the income statement, net income would be $350 ($2,000 − $1,500 − $150).

Study Suggestion

The IFRS Approach

The LIFO inventory cost flow assumption is not permitted under international financial reporting standards. The primary reason for the disallowance of LIFO appears to be that international standards have a strong balance sheet measurement focus and efforts have been made to eliminate accounting methods such as LIFO that do not support this so-called "balance sheet approach." As discussed in the following sections, during inflationary times LIFO assigns to inventory the costs of the oldest items acquired by the company, thus causing balance sheet values to become "outdated" as the company grows. As you study this material, think about what the implications would be for U.S. companies if the LIFO cost flow assumption were no longer available as a reporting alternative under U.S. GAAP.

FYI

The Activity Based Costing Association (ABCA) is an association of companies and organizations with activity-based costing interests. The association conducts benchmarking studies to identify practices that improve the overall operations of the members. ABCA's mission is to identify "best in class" activity-based costing processes, which lead member companies to exceptional performance when implemented. See www.abcbenchmarking.com for additional information about the objectives, services, and activities of the association.

APPENDIX

Excerpts from 2011 Annual Report of Campbell Soup Company

- **Business in Practice**
  Throughout each chapter, these boxes highlight and discuss various business practices and their impact on financial statements. Seeing the real-world impact of these business practices helps students more completely understand financial statements in general.

- **What Does It Mean?**
  As students progress through each chapter, *What Does It Mean?* questions prompt students to self-test their understanding following coverage of key topics. *What Does It Mean?* answers are provided in the end-of-chapter section.

- **Study Suggestion**
  Here the authors offer advice and tips to students to help them better grasp specific chapter concepts.

- **The IFRS Approach**
  New to this edition, these boxes highlight some of the key differences between U.S. generally accepted accounting principles and International Financial Reporting Standards.

- **FYI**
  These boxes direct students' attention to a wide variety of helpful resources available on the Internet for a fresh perspective on how the concepts they've just learned in the managerial chapters are applied in a modern context.

- **Campbell's 2011 Annual Report**
  Excerpts from Campbell Soup Company's annual report are included as an appendix at the back of the book. Frequent references to this material are made in the financial chapters of the text. The Campbell's icon is located in the margins next to relevant text and requires the student to call upon this real-world resource. The inclusion of annual report data piques student interest and provides valuable hands-on experience.

More great pedagogy *to guide student learning, and* extensive end-of-chapter material *to challenge students in* applying what they have learned.

- **Chapter Summaries and Key Terms and Concepts** promote greater retention of important points and definitions as well as facilitate review.

- **Demonstration Problems** drive students to the Marshall/McManus/Viele Online Learning Center (www .mhhe.com/marshall10e) to view a fully worked-out problem with solution.

- **Self-Study Material** is an additional online resource located on the Online Learning Center (www.mhhe.com/ marshall10e). The quizzes help students test their knowledge and understanding of chapter concepts. Results are tabulated and can be routed to multiple e-mail addresses if necessary.

- **Self-Study Quizzes** feature multiple-choice and matching questions. Answers for this section are given on the final page of each chapter.

- **Mini-Exercises** are new to this edition and are designed to be used as simple in-class demos to highlight key relationships and calculations or as simple take-home assignments.

- **Exercises** give students a chance to practice using the knowledge gained from working through the chapter material.

- **Problems** challenge students to apply what they have learned. Specific problems are tied to the Campbell's 2011 Annual Report, excerpts of which are included at the back of the text, bringing a strong, real-world flavor to the assignment material.

- **Cases** allow students to think analytically about topics from the chapter and apply them to business decisions.

- **A Continuous Case** is provided for Chapters 4, 6, 8 and 11 to allow the student to link concepts learned in earlier chapters to what they learn in later chapters. It also allows for an understanding of how the material works together to form a larger picture.

- **Icons** identify exercises, problems, and cases involving Excel Templates, the Campbell's 2011 Annual Report, and *Connect Accounting.*

McGraw-Hill *Connect Plus Accounting* is a complete online assignment, learning, and textbook assessment solution that connects your students with the tools and resources needed to achieve success through faster learning, more efficient studying, and higher retention of knowledge. Key features found in *Connect Plus Accounting* include:

Intelligent Response Technology

Intelligent Response Technology is *Connect Accounting's* new student interface for end-of-chapter assessment content. Intelligent Response Technology provides a general journal application that looks and feels more like what you would find in a general ledger software package, improves answer acceptance to reduce student frustration with formatting issues (such as rounding), and, for select questions, provides an expanded table that guides students through the process of solving the problem.

Connect Accounting helps students learn more efficiently by providing feedback and practice material when they need it, where they need it. *Connect* grades homework automatically and gives immediate feedback on any questions students may have missed.

Integrated eBooks

Connect Plus includes a media-rich eBook. With it, you can share your notes with your students, and they can insert their own notes, highlight the text, search for specific information, and review their materials. Using an eBook with *Connect* gives your students a complete digital solution that allows them to access their materials from any computer. And over time, as more and more students use mobile devices, our eBooks will even enable them to learn on the go.

Guided Examples

Guided Examples provide narrated, animated, and step-by-step walkthroughs of algorithmic versions of assigned exercises in *Connect Accounting,* allowing the student to identify, review, or reinforce the concepts and activities covered in class. Guided Examples provide immediate feedback and focus on the areas where students need the most guidance.

Student Resource Library

The *Connect Accounting* Student Study Center gives access to additional resources such as recorded lectures, online practice materials, an eBook, and more.

The integrated solutions for *Accounting: What the Numbers Mean, 10e,* have been proven to help you achieve your course goals of improving student readiness, enhancing student engagement, and increasing their comprehension of content. Marshall continues to be the market-leading text for the Survey of Accounting course, helping students to succeed through clear and concise writing, a conceptual focus, and unparalleled technology support. The Marshall solution employs the use of current companies and instant feedback on practice problems to help students engage with course materials, comprehend the content, and achieve higher outcomes in the course.

McGraw-Hill *Connect* provides many valuable learning resources to students, including **Guided Examples.** These narrated and animated videos are available to students as they work through homework assignments and can be viewed anytime, anywhere. Finally, our new **Intelligent Response Technology**-based content offers students an intelligent homework experience that helps them stay focused on learning instead of navigating the technology.

Simple Assignment Management and Smart Grading

With *Connect Plus Accounting,* creating assignments is easier than ever, so you can spend more time teaching and less time managing. *Connect Accounting* enables you to:

* Create and deliver assignments easily with select end-of-chapter questions and test bank items.
* Go paperless with the eBook and online submission and grading of student assignments.
* Have assignments scored automatically, giving students immediate feedback on their work and side-by-side comparisons with correct answers.
* Reinforce classroom concepts with practice tests and instant quizzes.

Student Reporting

Connect Accounting keeps instructors informed about how each student, section, and class is performing, allowing for more productive use of lecture and office hours. The reporting function enables you to:

- View scored work immediately and track individual or group performance with assignment and grade reports.
- Access an instant view of student or class performance relative to learning objectives.
- Collect data and generate reports required by many accreditation organizations, such as AACSB and AICPA.
- Identify low-performance students with the "At Risk" student report.

Instructor Library

The *Connect Accounting* Instructor Library is your repository for additional resources to improve student engagement in and out of class. You can select and use any asset that enhances your lecture. The *Connect Accounting* Instructor Library includes: access to the eBook version of the text, PowerPoint files, Solutions Manual, Instructor Resource Manual, and Test Bank.

Tegrity: Lectures 24/7

Make your classes available anytime, anywhere. With simple one-click recording, instructors can record lectures, presentations, and step-by-step problem solutions with Tegrity. Using Tegrity with *Connect Accounting,* instructors can post recordings directly to *Connect* for student viewing. Students can also search for a word or phrase and be taken to the exact place in your lecture that they need to review.

To learn more about Tegrity, watch a two-minute Flash demo at **http://tegritycampus.mhhe.com**.

McGraw-Hill Customer Experience Group Contact Information

At McGraw-Hill, we understand that getting the most from new technology can be challenging. That's why our services don't stop after you purchase our products. You can e-mail our Product Specialists 24 hours a day to get product training online. Or you can search our knowledge bank of Frequently Asked Questions on our support website. For Customer Support, call 800-331-5094 or visit **www.mhhe.com/support**. One of our Technical Support Analysts will be able to assist you in a timely fashion.

How Can Text-Related Web Resources Enrich My Course?

Online Learning Center (OLC)

We offer an Online Learning Center (OLC) that follows *Accounting: What the Numbers Mean* chapter by chapter. It doesn't require any building or maintenance on your part. It's ready to go the moment you and your students type in the URL: www.mhhe.com/marshall10e

As students study and learn from *Accounting: What the Numbers Mean,* they can visit the Student Edition of the OLC Website to work with a multitude of helpful tools:

- Interactive Chapter Quizzes
- PowerPoint Presentations
- Excel Problems
- Study Guide
- Demonstration Problems
- Odd-Problem Solutions

A secured Instructor Edition stores essential course materials to save you prep time before class. Everything you need to run a lively classroom and an efficient course is included. All resources available to students, plus . . .

- Instructor's Resource Manual
- Solutions Manual
- Solutions to Excel Problems
- Test Bank
- Guided Examples
- PowerPoint Presentations
- Web-Enhanced Solutions
- End-of-Chapter Conversion Guide

The OLC Website also serves as a doorway to other technology solutions, like course management systems.

The **Best** of **Both Worlds**

Online Course Management

McGraw-Hill Higher Education and Blackboard Have Teamed Up. What Does This Mean for You?

1. **Single sign-on.** Now you and your students can access McGraw-Hill's *Connect*™ and Create™ right from within your Blackboard course—all with one single sign-on.
2. **Deep integration of content and tools.** You get single sign-on with *Connect* and Create, you also get integration of McGraw-Hill content and content engines right in Blackboard. Whether you're choosing a book for your course or building *Connect* assignments, all the tools you need are right where you want them—inside Blackboard.
3. **One grade book.** Keeping several grade books and manually synchronizing grades in Blackboard is no longer necessary. When a student completes an integrated *Connect* assignment, the grade for that assignment automatically (and instantly) feeds your Blackboard grade center.
4. **A solution for everyone.** Whether your institution is already using Blackboard or you just want to try Blackboard on your own, we have a solution for you. McGraw-Hill and Blackboard can now offer you easy access to industry-leading technology and content, whether your campus hosts it, or we do. Be sure to ask your local McGraw-Hill representative for details.

McGraw-Hill Campus™

McGraw-Hill Campus™ is a new one-stop teaching and learning experience available to users of any learning management system. This complimentary integration allows faculty and students to enjoy single sign-on (SSO) access to all McGraw-Hill Higher Education materials and synchronized grade-book with our award-winning McGraw-Hill *Connect* platform. McGraw-Hill Campus provides faculty with instant access to all McGraw-Hill Higher Education teaching materials (eTextbooks, test banks, PowerPoint slides, animations and learning objects, and so on), allowing them to browse, search, and use any instructor ancillary content in our vast library at no additional cost to the instructor or students. Students enjoy SSO access to a variety of free (quizzes, flash cards, narrated presentations, and so on) and subscription-based products (McGraw-Hill *Connect*). With this integration enabled, faculty and students will never need to create another account to access McGraw-Hill products and services. For more information on McGraw-Hill Campus, please visit our website at **www.mhcampus.com**.

CourseSmart

CourseSmart is a new way to find and buy eTextbooks. CourseSmart has the largest selection of eTextbooks available anywhere, offering thousands of the most commonly adopted textbooks from a wide variety of higher education publishers. CourseSmart eTextbooks are available in one standard online reader with full text search, notes, highlighting, and email tools for sharing between classmates. Visit **www.CourseSmart.com** for more information on ordering.

Online Learning Center (OLC)

www.mhhe.com/marshall10e

More and more students are studying online. That's why we offer an Online Learning Center (OLC) that follows *Accounting: What the Numbers Mean* chapter by chapter. It doesn't require any building or maintenance on your part. It's ready to go the moment you and your students enter in the URL.

As your students study, they can refer to the OLC website and access

- Check Figures and Odd-Problem Solutions
- Digital Text Images
- Self-Grading Quizzes
- PowerPoint Presentations
- Excel Problems
- Study Guide
- Demonstration Problems

A **secured Instructor Resource Center** stores your essential course materials to save you prep time before class. The Instructor's Resource Manual, Solutions Manual, Test Bank, and PowerPoint presentations are now just a couple of clicks away.

Instructor Supplements

Connect Accounting
MHID: 0-07-751583-8
ISBN: 978-0-07-751583-6

Connect Plus Accounting
MHID: 0-07-751585-4
ISBN: 978-0-07-751585-0

Instructor's Manual
(Available on the password-protected Instructor OLC)
This supplement contains the lecture notes to help with classroom presentation. It contains useful suggestions for presenting key concepts and ideas.

Solutions Manual
(Available on the password-protected Instructor OLC)
This supplement contains completely worked-out solutions to all assignment material and a general discussion of the use of group exercises. In addition, the manual contains suggested course outlines and a listing of exercises, problems, and cases scaled according to difficulty.

Test Bank
(Available on the password-protected Instructor OLC)
Hundreds of questions are organized by chapter and include multiple-choice problems. This edition of the test bank includes worked-out solutions, and all items have been tied to AACSB-AICPA and Bloom's standards.

Computerized Test Bank
(Available on the password-protected Instructor OLC)
This test bank utilizes McGraw-Hill's EZ Test software to quickly create customized exams. This user-friendly program allows instructors to sort questions by format, edit existing questions, or add new ones. It also can scramble questions for multiple versions of the same test.

PowerPoint® Presentations
(Prepared by Jon A. Booker, Charles W. Caldwell, Susan Galbreath, and Cynthia J. Rooney)
Presentations allow for revision of lecture slides.

Assurance of Learning Ready

Many educational institutions today are focused on the notion of assurance of learning, an important element of some accreditation standards. *Accounting: What the Numbers Mean* is designed specifically to support your assurance of learning initiatives with a simple, yet powerful solution. Each test bank question for *Accounting: What the Numbers Mean* maps to a specific chapter learning objective listed in the text. You can use our test bank software, EZ Test Online or *Connect Accounting* to easily query for learning objectives that directly relate to the learning objectives for your course. You can then use the reporting features of EZ Test to aggregate student results in similar fashion, making the collection and presentation of assurance of learning data simple and easy.

AACSB Statement

The McGraw-Hill Companies is a proud corporate member of AACSB International. Understanding the importance and value of AACSB accreditation, *Accounting: What the Numbers Mean* recognizes the curricula guidelines detailed in the AACSB standards for business accreditation by connecting selected questions in the test bank to the six general knowledge and skill guidelines in the AACSB standards. The statements contained in *Accounting: What the Numbers Mean* are provided only as a guide for the users of this textbook. The AACSB leaves content coverage and assessment within the purview of individual schools, the mission of the school, and the faculty. While *Accounting: What the Numbers Mean* and the teaching package make no claim of any specific AACSB qualification or evaluation, we have within *Accounting: What the Numbers Mean* labeled select questions according to the six general knowledge and skills areas.

Enhancements for This Edition

Chapter 1:
- Overall chapter content revisions for clarity and general updates.
- Refocused chapter learning objectives to align with Bloom's Taxonomy.
- New discussion of the *FASB Accounting Standards Codification* and the role of *Accounting Standards Updates (ASUs)*.
- Updated references to Campbell's annual report information.
- Expanded discussion of international financial reporting issues with emphasis on the progress made in recent years to achieve convergence of IFRS and U.S. GAAP.
- Streamlined discussion of the Conceptual Framework project with an integration of *FASB Concepts Statement No. 8* and the removal of the "Highlights" of *Concepts Statement No. 1* exhibit.
- Further clarification provided in the Plan of the Book section including a new "Resources for Students" subsection, highlighting the key features offered on our text's website.
- General update of all Exercises.
- Complete revision of all even-numbered Exercises.

Chapter 2:
- Overall chapter content revisions for clarity and general updates.
- Refocused chapter learning objectives to align with Bloom's Taxonomy.
- Updated terminology used in the financial statements from Owners' Equity to Stockholders' Equity to reflect the text's emphasis on corporate financial reporting.
- Updated references to Campbell's annual report information.
- Deleted the Cash Flows versus Accrual Accounting "Business in Practice" box, as well as the "Business on the Internet" box to improve the chapter's efficiency.
- New Mini-Exercises (6) to emphasize computational-type learning objectives.
- General update of all Exercises, Problems, and Cases.

- Complete revision of all even-numbered Exercises and Problems.
- New guided example video demonstrations.

Chapter 3:
- Overall chapter content revisions for clarity and general updates.
- Refocused chapter learning objectives to align with Bloom's Taxonomy.
- Deleted the "Business on the Internet" box to improve the chapter's efficiency.
- Integration of Campbell's annual report information for the financial and graphical analyses of profitability and liquidity trends.
- New Mini-Exercises (6) to emphasize computational-type learning objectives.
- New "Focus company" Case on the analysis of liquidity and profitability measures.
- General update of all Exercises, Problems, and Cases.
- Complete revision of all even-numbered Exercises and Problems.
- New guided example video demonstrations.

Chapter 4:
- Overall chapter content revisions for clarity and general updates.
- Refocused chapter learning objectives to align with Bloom's Taxonomy.
- Deleted the "Business on the Internet" box to improve the chapter's efficiency.
- Updated references to Campbell's annual report information.
- New Mini-Exercises (4) to emphasize computational-type learning objectives.
- General update of all Exercises, Problems, and Cases.
- Complete revision of all even-numbered Exercises and Problems.
- New guided example video demonstrations.

Chapter 5:
- Overall chapter content revisions for clarity and general updates.
- Refocused chapter learning objectives to align with Bloom's Taxonomy.

- Integration and analysis of Campbell's annual report information for the accounting and presentation of current assets including cash, accounts receivable, and inventories.
- Reduced coverage of Short-Term Marketable Securities, deleted The Impact of Inventory Quantity Changes section, and deleted the Deferred Assets section to improve the chapter's efficiency.
- New "The IFRS Approach" boxes (3) highlighting key differences between U.S. GAAP and IFRS with respect to the valuation and reporting of inventories.
- Simplified the discussion of inventory errors by including an illustration of "as reported" and "as corrected" data over a two-year period for self-correcting errors.
- New Mini-Exercises (6) to emphasize computational-type learning objectives.
- New "Focus company" Case on accounts receivable and inventory disclosures.
- General update of all Exercises, Problems, and Cases.
- Complete revision of all even-numbered Exercises and Problems.
- New guided example video demonstrations.

Chapter 6:
- Overall chapter content revisions for clarity and general updates.
- Refocused chapter learning objectives to align with Bloom's Taxonomy.
- Integration and analysis of Campbell's annual report information for the accounting and presentation of property, plant, and equipment, and other noncurrent assets.
- New "The IFRS Approach" boxes (2) highlighting key differences between U.S. GAAP and IFRS with respect to the valuation and reporting of property, plant, and equipment.
- New Focus on the Big Picture "Study Suggestion" box.
- New Mini-Exercises (6) to emphasize computational-type learning objectives.
- New "Focus company" Case on property, plant, and equipment disclosures.
- General update of all Exercises, Problems, and Cases.

- Complete revision of all even-numbered Exercises and Problems.
- New guided example video demonstrations.

Chapter 7:
- Overall chapter content revisions for clarity and general updates.
- Refocused chapter learning objectives to align with Bloom's Taxonomy.
- Integration and analysis of Campbell's annual report information for the accounting and presentation of liabilities.
- Deleted the Gross and Net Methods of Recording Purchases "Business in Practice" box, deleted the "Business on the Internet" box, and streamlined the Bond Discount and Premium exhibit to improve the chapter's efficiency.
- New Mini-Exercises (4) to emphasize computational-type learning objectives.
- New "Focus company" Case on noncurrent liability disclosures.
- General update of all Exercises, Problems, and Cases.
- Complete revision of all even-numbered Exercises and Problems.
- New guided example video demonstrations.

Chapter 8:
- Overall chapter content revisions for clarity and general updates.
- Refocused chapter learning objectives to align with Bloom's Taxonomy.
- Integration and analysis of Campbell's annual report information for the accounting and presentation of stockholders' equity.
- New Mini-Exercises (4) to emphasize computational-type learning objectives.
- New "Focus company" Case on stockholders' equity disclosures.
- General update of all Exercises, Problems, and Cases.
- Complete revision of all even-numbered Exercises and Problems.
- New guided example video demonstrations.

Chapter 9:
- Overall chapter content revisions for clarity and general updates.
- Refocused chapter learning objectives to align with Bloom's Taxonomy.

Enhancements for This Edition

- Deleted the "Business on the Internet" box to improve the chapter's efficiency.
- Integration and analysis of Campbell's annual report information for the presentation and disclosure of income statement and statement of cash flows data.
- New "The IFRS Approach" boxes (3) highlighting key differences between U.S. GAAP and IFRS with respect to the valuation of revenues, expenses, gains, and losses.
- New Mini-Exercises (4) to emphasize computational-type learning objectives.
- New "Focus company" Cases (2) on income statement and statement of cash flows analysis.
- General update of all Exercises, Problems, and Cases.
- Complete revision of all even-numbered Exercises and Problems.
- New guided example video demonstrations.

Chapter 10:
- Chapter title changed to reflect updated terminology, with "Notes to the Financial Statements" replacing "Explanatory Notes."
- Overall chapter content revisions for clarity and general updates.
- Refocused chapter learning objectives to align with Bloom's Taxonomy.
- Corporate Governance discussion updated with references to the impact of the financial crisis of 2007–2008 and the key provisions of the Dodd–Frank Act of 2010.
- "Financial Shenanigans" exhibit expanded to include new categories and content.
- Deleted "Study Suggestion" box to improve the chapter's efficiency.
- Integration and analysis of Campbell's annual report information for the Notes to the Financial Statements section of the chapter.
- "Non-GAAP Financial Measures" described within the Management Discussion and Analysis section.
- New Mini-Exercises (2) to emphasize computational-type learning objectives.
- New "Focus company" Case to find various accounting policy disclosures.

- General update of all Exercises, Problems, and Cases.
- Complete revision of all even-numbered Exercises and Problems.
- New guided example video demonstrations.

Chapter 11:
- Overall chapter content revisions for clarity and general updates.
- Refocused chapter learning objectives to align with Bloom's Taxonomy.
- Deleted "Study Suggestion" box to improve the chapter's efficiency.
- Integration and analysis of Campbell's annual report information for the performance of financial ratio analysis.
- New Mini-Exercises (4) to emphasize computational-type learning objectives.
- New "Focus company" Case on financial statement analysis.
- General update of all Exercises, Problems, and Cases.
- Complete revision of all even-numbered Exercises and Problems.
- New guided example video demonstrations.

Chapter 12:
- Overall chapter content revisions for clarity and general updates.
- Refocused chapter learning objectives to align with Bloom's Taxonomy.
- Enhanced graphic and presentation of Expanded Contribution Margin Model.
- New Mini-Exercises (6) to emphasize computational-type learning objectives.
- General update of all Exercises, Problems, and Cases.
- Complete revision of all even-numbered Exercises and Problems.
- New guided example video demonstrations.

Chapter 13:
- Overall chapter content revisions for clarity and general updates.
- Refocused chapter learning objectives to align with Bloom's Taxonomy.
- Enhanced graphic of the Cost Accumulation and Assignment process.

- Integration and analysis of Campbell's annual report information for manufacturing inventories, cost of products sold, and operating income performance.
- Conversion of "Business on the Internet" boxes to "FYI" boxes.
- New Mini-Exercises (6) to emphasize computational-type learning objectives.
- General update of all Exercises, Problems, and Cases.
- Complete revision of all even-numbered Exercises and Problems.
- New guided example video demonstrations.

Chapter 14:
- Overall chapter content revisions for clarity and general updates.
- Refocused chapter learning objectives to align with Bloom's Taxonomy.
- Conversion of "Business on the Internet" boxes to "FYI" boxes.
- New Mini-Exercises (6) to emphasize computational-type learning objectives.
- General update of all Exercises, Problems, and Cases.
- Complete revision of all even-numbered Exercises and Problems.
- New guided example video demonstrations.

Chapter 15:
- Overall chapter content revisions for clarity and general updates.
- Refocused chapter learning objectives to align with Bloom's Taxonomy.
- Revised complete presentation order of Standard Cost Variance Analysis in order to provide for a more natural conceptual flow.

- Created new graphical summary overview of the budget variance illustration.
- Conversion of "Business on the Internet" boxes to "FYI" boxes.
- New Mini-Exercises (6) to emphasize computational-type learning objectives.
- General update of all Exercises, Problems, and Cases.
- Complete revision of all even-numbered Exercises and Problems.
- New guided example video demonstrations.

Chapter 16:
- Overall chapter content revisions for clarity and general updates.
- Refocused chapter learning objectives to align with Bloom's Taxonomy.
- Enhanced graphical relationship presentation of the PV of expected cash flows, NPV, and IRR.
- Conversion of "Business on the Internet" boxes to "FYI" boxes.
- New Mini-Exercises (6) to emphasize computational-type learning objectives.
- General update of all Exercises, Problems, and Cases.
- Complete revision of all even-numbered Exercises and Problems.
- New guided example video demonstrations.

Epilogue:
- Overall content revisions for clarity and additions for current updates.
- New graphic updating IFRS adoption around the world.
- New graphics and presentation of accounting as an information system.
- Conversion of "Business on the Internet" boxes to "FYI" boxes.

Acknowledgments

The task of creating and revising a textbook is not accomplished by the work of the authors alone. Thoughtful feedback from reviewers is integral to the development process and gratitude is extended to all who have participated in earlier reviews of *Accounting: What the Numbers Mean* as well as to our most recent panel of reviewers. Your help in identifying strengths to further develop and areas of weakness to improve was invaluable to us. We are grateful to the following for their comments and constructive criticisms that helped us with development of the tenth edition, and previous editions:

Janet Adeyiga, *Hampton University*

Gary Adna Ames, *Brigham Young University–Idaho*

Sharon Agee, *Rollins College*

Vernon Allen, *Central Florida Community College*

Tim Alzheimer, *Montana State University*

David Anderson, *Louisiana State University*

Susan Anderson, *North Carolina A&T State University*

Florence Atiase, *University of Texas–Austin*

Benjamin Bae, *Virginia Commonwealth University*

Linda T. Bartlett, *Bessemer State Technical College*

Jean Beaulieu, *Westminster College*

Robert Beebe, *Morrisville State College*

Jekabs Bikis, *Dallas Baptist University*

David Bilker, *Temple University*

Scott Butler, *Dominican University of California*

Marci L. Butterfield, *University of Utah*

Sandra Byrd, *Southwest Missouri State University*

Harlow Callander, *University of St. Thomas*

John Callister, *Cornell University*

Sharon Campbell, *University of North Alabama*

Elizabeth D. Capener, *Dominican University of CA*

Kay Carnes, *Gonzaga University*

Thomas J. Casey, *DeVry University*

Royce E. Chaffin, *University of West Georgia*

James Crockett, *University of Southern Mississippi*

Alan B. Czyzewski, *Indiana State University*

Weldon Terry Dancer, *Arkansas State University*

Thomas D'Arrigo, *Manhattan College*

Patricia Davis, *Keystone College*

Francis Dong, *DeVry University*

Martha Doran, *San Diego State University*

Robert Dunn, *Columbus State University*

Marthanne Edwards, *Colorado State University*

Craig Ehlert, *Montana State University–Bozeman*

John A. Elfrink, *Central Missouri State University*

Robert C. Elmore, *Tennessee Tech University*

Leslie Fletcher, *Georgia Southern University*

Norman Foy, *Mercy College*

Randy Frye, *Saint Francis University*

Harry E Gallatin, *Indiana State University*

Regan Garey, *Immaculata University*

Terrie Gehman, *Elizabethtown College*

Daniel Gibbons, *Waubonsee Community College*

Louis Gingerella, *Rensselaer–Hartford*

Dan Goldzband, *University of California–San Diego*

Kyle L. Grazier, *University of Michigan*

Alice M. Handlang, *Southern Christian University*

Betty S. Harper, *Middle Tennessee State University*

Elaine Henry, *Rutgers University*

William Hood, *Central Michigan University*

Fred Hughes, *Faulkner University*

Kim Hurt, *Central Community College*

Lori Jacobson, *North Idaho College*

Linda L. Kadlecek, *Central Arizona College*

Zulfiqar Khan, *Benedictine University*

Charles Kile, *Middle Tennessee State University*

Nancy Kelly, *Middlesex Community College*

Ronald W. Kilgore, *University of Tennessee*

Bert Luken, *Wilmington College–Cincinnati*

Anna Lusher, *West Liberty State College*

Suneel Maheshwari, *Marshall University*

Gwen McFadden, *North Carolina A&T State University*

Tammy Metzke, *Milwaukee Area Technical College*

Melanie Middlemist, *Colorado State University*

Richard Monbrod, *DeVry University*

Murat Neset Tanju, *University of Alabama–Birmingham*

Eugene D. O'Donnell, *Harcum College*

William A. O'Toole, *Defiance College*

Sandra Owen, *Indiana University–Bloomington*

Carol Pace, *Grayson County College*

Robert Patterson, *Penn State–Erie*

Robert M. Peevy, *Tarleton State University*

Craig Pence, *Highland Community College*

Candace Person, *University of California–San Diego Extension*

David H. Peters, *Southeastern University*

Ronald Picker, *St. Mary of the Woods College*

Martha Pointer, *East Tennessee State University*

James Pofal, *University of Wisconsin–Oshkosh*

Shirley Powell, *Arkansas State University–Beebe*

Barbara Powers-Ingram, *Wytheville Community College*

M. Jeff Quinlan, *Madison College*

John Rush, *Illinois College*

Robert W. Rutledge, *Texas State University*

Robert E. Rosacker, *The University of South Dakota*

Paul Schwin, *Tiffin University*

Raymond Shaffer, *Youngstown State University*

Erin Sims, *DeVry University*

Forest E. Stegelin, *University of Georgia*

Mark Steadman, *East Tennessee State University*

Charles Smith, *Iowa Western Community College*

Ray Sturm, *University of Central Florida*

John Suroviak, *Pacific University*

Linda Tarrago, *Hillsborough Community College*

Judith A. Toland, *Bucks County Community College*

Catherine Traynor, *Northern Illinois University*

Michael Vasilou, *DeVry University*

David Verduzco, *University of Texas–Austin*

Joseph Vesci, *Immaculata University*

William Ward, *Mid-Continent University*

Kortney White, *Arkansas State University–State University*

Dennis Wooten, *Erie Community College–North*

We Are Grateful . . . Although the approach to the material and the scope of coverage in this text are the results of our own conclusions, truly new ideas are rare. The authors whose textbooks we have used in the past have influenced many of our ideas for particular accounting and financial management explanations. Likewise, students and colleagues through the years have helped us clarify illustrations and teaching techniques. Many of the users of the first nine editions—both teachers and students—have offered comments and constructive criticisms that have been encouraging and helpful. All of this input is greatly appreciated. We extend special thanks to Helen Roybark of Radford University for her careful accuracy check of the text manuscript and solutions manual and ancillaries, and Jon A. Booker and Charles W. Caldwell of Tennessee Technological University, Cynthia J. Rooney of the University of New Mexico, and Susan C. Galbreath of Lipscomb University for a thorough revision of the PowerPoint presentations. Finally, we wish to thank our many colleagues at McGraw-Hill, who for more than 20 years have provided exceptional editorial assistance and product development guidance. Your collective efforts have helped to shape every aspect of this text, and it continues to be a pleasure to work with such a fine group of publishing professionals.

David H. Marshall   Wayne W. McManus   Daniel F. Viele

Brief Contents

Contents

1 Accounting—Present and Past

The worldwide financial and credit crisis that came to a head in the fall of 2008 was precipitated by many factors. Not the least of these factors were greed, inadequate market regulatory supervision, and an excess of "financial engineering" involved in the creation of financial instruments which almost defied understanding even by sophisticated investors. This crisis was preceded in the first decade of the century by the bankruptcy filings of two large, publicly owned corporations that resulted in billions of dollars of losses by thousands of stockholders. In 2001 it had been Enron Corporation, and a few months later, WorldCom, Inc. In each case a number of factors caused the precipitous fall in the value of the firms' stock. The most significant factor was probably the loss of investor confidence in each company's financial reports and other disclosures reported to stockholders and other regulatory bodies, including the Securities and Exchange Commission.

The Enron and WorldCom debacles, and other widely publicized breakdowns of corporate financial reporting, resulted in close scrutiny of such reporting by the accounting profession itself and also by the U.S. Congress and other governing bodies. The accounting practices that were criticized generally involved complex transactions.

Also contributing to the issue were aggressive attempts by some executives to avoid the spirit of sound accounting even though many of the reporting practices in question were not specifically forbidden by existing accounting pronouncements. To be sure, the financial reporting requirements faced by companies whose securities are publicly traded have now become more strenuously scrutinized under the Sarbanes–Oxley Act of 2002 (SOX) and the watchful eye of the Public Company Accounting Oversight Board (PCAOB), which is the regulatory body created under SOX to oversee the activities of the auditing profession and further protect the public interest. These enhanced regulatory efforts have helped to increase the transparency of the financial reporting process and the understandability of financial statements. Although the financial crisis that disrupted the financial world in 2008 has not been directly blamed on financial accounting or auditing weaknesses, some accounting and financial reporting practices have been severely criticized. This book will briefly address some of the more troublesome technical issues faced by the accounting profession today, but the elaborate attempts to embellish the financial image of the companies in question go well beyond the fundamentals described in the following pages.

The objective of this text is to present enough fundamentals of accounting to permit the nonaccountant to understand the financial statements of an organization operating in our society and to understand how financial information can be used in the management planning, control, and decision-making processes. Although usually expressed in the context of profit-seeking business enterprises, most of the material is equally applicable to not-for-profit social service and governmental organizations.

Accounting is sometimes called the *language of business*, and it is appropriate for people who are involved in the economic activities of our society—and that is just about everyone—to know at least enough of this language to be able to make decisions and informed judgments about those economic activities.

LEARNING OBJECTIVES (LO)

After studying this chapter you should understand and be able to

LO 1-1   Explain the definition of *accounting*.

LO 1-2   Identify who the users of accounting information are and explain why they find accounting information useful.

LO 1-3   Identify the variety of professional services that accountants provide.

LO 1-4   Summarize the development of accounting from a broad historical perspective.

LO 1-5   Explain the role that the Financial Accounting Standards Board (FASB) plays in the development of financial accounting standards.

LO 1-6   Generalize about how financial reporting standards evolve.

LO 1-7   Identify the key elements of ethical behavior for a professional accountant.

LO 1-8   Summarize the reasons for the FASB's Conceptual Framework project.

LO 1-9   Summarize the objective of general purpose financial reporting.

LO 1-10   Describe the plan of the book.

What Is Accounting?

In a broad sense, **accounting** is the process of identifying, measuring, and communicating economic information about an organization for the purpose of making decisions and informed judgments. (Accountants frequently use the term **entity** instead of *organization* because it is more inclusive.)

This definition of accounting can be expressed schematically as follows:

Accounting is the process of:

LO 1
Explain the definition of *accounting*.

$$\left.\begin{array}{c} \text{Identifying} \\ \text{Measuring} \\ \text{Communicating} \end{array}\right\} \quad \begin{array}{c} \text{Economic information} \\ \text{about an entity} \end{array} \quad \rightarrow \quad \begin{array}{c} \text{For decisions and} \\ \text{informed judgments} \end{array}$$

Exhibit 1-1

Users and Uses of
Accounting Information

LO 2
Identify who the users
of accounting informa-
tion are and explain why
they find accounting
information useful.

User	Decision/Informed Judgment Made
Management	When performing its functions of planning, directing, and controlling, management makes many decisions and informed judgments. For example, when considering the expansion of a product line, planning involves identifying and measuring costs and benefits; directing involves communicating the strategies selected; and controlling involves identifying, measuring, and communicating the results of the product line expansion during and after its implementation.
Investors/ shareholders	When considering whether to invest in the common stock of a company, **investors** use accounting information to help assess the amounts, timing, and uncertainty of future cash returns on their investment.
Creditors/ suppliers	When determining how much merchandise to ship to a customer before receiving payment, **creditors** assess the probability of collection and the risks of late (or non-) payment. Banks also become creditors when they make loans and thus have similar needs for accounting information.
Employees	When planning for retirement, employees assess the company's ability to offer long-term job prospects and an attractive retirement benefits package.
SEC (Securities and Exchange Commission)	When reviewing for compliance with SEC regulations, analysts determine whether financial statements issued to investors fully disclose all required information.

Who makes these decisions and informed judgments? Users of accounting information include the management of the entity or organization; the owners of the organization (who are frequently not involved in the management process); potential investors in and creditors of the organization; employees; and various federal, state, and local governmental agencies that are concerned with regulatory and tax matters. Exhibit 1-1 describes some of the users and uses of accounting information. Pause, and try to think of at least one other decision or informed judgment that each of these users might make from the economic information that could be communicated about an entity.

Accounting information is required for just about every kind of organization. When accounting is mentioned, most people initially think of the information needs and reporting requirements of business firms, but not-for-profit social service organizations, governmental units, educational institutions, social clubs, political committees, and other groups all require accounting for their economic activities as well.

Accounting is frequently perceived as something that others do, rather than as the process of providing information that supports decisions and informed judgments. Relatively few people actually become accountants, but almost all people use accounting information. The principal objective of this text is to help you become an informed user of accounting information, rather than to prepare you to become an accountant. However, the essence of this user orientation provides a solid foundation for students who choose to seek a career in accounting.

If you haven't already experienced the lack of understanding or confusion that results from looking at one or more financial statements, you have been spared one of life's frustrations. Certainly during your formal business education and early during your employment experience, you will be presented with financial data. Being an informed user means knowing how to use those data as information.

The following sections introduce the major areas of practice within the accounting discipline and will help you understand the types of work done by professional accountants within each of these broad categories. The following Business in Practice discussion highlights career opportunities in accounting.

---

1. What does it mean to state that the accounting process should support decisions and informed judgments?

What Does It Mean?

Answer on page 25

Business in
Practice

Career Opportunities in Accounting

Because accounting is a profession, most entry-level positions require a bachelor of science degree with a major in accounting. Individuals are encouraged to achieve CPA licensure as quickly as feasible. Persons who work hard and smart can expect to attain high professional levels in their careers. The major employers of accountants include public accounting firms, industrial firms, government, and not-for-profit organizations.

Public Accounting

The work done by public accountants varies significantly depending on whether they are employed by a local, regional, or international CPA firm. Small local firms concentrate on the bookkeeping, accounting, tax return, and financial planning needs of individuals and small businesses. These firms need generalists who can adequately serve in a variety of capacities. The somewhat larger, regional firms offer a broad range of professional services but concentrate on the performance of audits (frequently referred to as *attestation* or *compliance services*), corporate tax returns, and management advisory services. They often hire experienced financial and industry specialists to serve particular client needs, in addition to recruiting well-qualified recent graduates.

The large, international CPA firms also perform auditing, tax, and consulting services. Their principal clients are large domestic and international corporations. The "Big 4" CPA firms are PricewaterhouseCoopers, Deloitte Touche Tohmatsu, Ernst & Young, and KPMG International. These firms dominate the market in terms of total revenues, number of corporate audit clients, and number of offices, partners, and staff members. These international firms generally recruit outstanding graduates and highly experienced CPAs and encourage the development of specialized skills by their personnel. (*Visit any of the Big 4 websites for detailed information regarding career opportunities in public accounting:* www.pwc.com, www.deloitte.com, www.ey.com, or www.kpmg.com.)

Industrial Accounting

More accountants are employed in industry than in public accounting because of the vast number of manufacturing, merchandising, and service firms of all sizes. In addition to using the services of public accounting firms, these firms employ cost and management accountants, as well as financial accountants. Many accountants in industry start working in this environment right out of school; others get their start in public accounting as auditors but move to industry after getting at least a couple of years of experience.

Government and Not-for-Profit Accounting

Opportunities for accounting professionals in the governmental and not-for-profit sectors of the economy are constantly increasing. In the United States, literally thousands of state and local government reporting entities touch the lives of every citizen. Likewise, accounting specialists are employed by colleges and universities, hospitals, and voluntary health and welfare organizations such as the American Red Cross, United Way, and Greenpeace.

Financial Accounting

LO 3

Identify the variety of professional services that accountants provide.

Financial accounting generally refers to the process that results in the preparation and reporting of financial statements for an entity. As will be explained in more detail, financial statements present the financial position of an entity at a point in time, the results of the entity's operations for some period of time, the **cash flow** activities for the same period, and other information (the notes to the financial statements or financial review) about the entity's financial resources, obligations, owners' interests, and operations.

Financial accounting is primarily oriented toward the external user. The financial statements are directed to individuals who are not in a position to be aware of the day-to-day financial and operating activities of the entity. Financial accounting is also primarily concerned with the historical results of an entity's performance. Financial statements reflect what has happened in the past. Although readers may want to project past activities and their results into future performance, financial statements are not a crystal ball. Many corporate annual reports refer to the historical nature of financial accounting information to emphasize the fact that users must make their own judgments about a firm's future prospects.

Bookkeeping procedures are used to accumulate the financial results of many of an entity's activities, and these procedures are part of the financial accounting process. Bookkeeping procedures have been thoroughly systematized using manual, mechanical, and computer techniques. Although these procedures support the financial accounting process, they are only a part of the process.

Financial accounting is done by accounting professionals who have generally earned a bachelor's degree with a major in accounting. The financial accountant is employed by an entity to use her or his expertise, analytical skills, and judgment in the many activities that are necessary for the preparation of financial statements. The title **controller** is used to designate the chief accounting officer of a corporation. The controller is usually responsible for both the financial and managerial accounting functions of the organization (as discussed later). Sometimes the title *comptroller* (the Old English spelling) is used for this position.

An individual earns the **Certified Public Accountant (CPA)** professional designation by fulfilling certain education and experience requirements and passing a comprehensive four-part examination. A uniform CPA exam is given nationally, although it is administered by individual states.[1] Some states require that candidates have accounting work experience before sitting for the exam. A total of 54 of the 55 U.S. jurisdictions, including all 50 states, have now enacted legislation increasing the educational requirements for CPA candidates from 120 semester hours of college study, or a bachelor's degree, to a minimum of 150 semester hours of college study to be granted licensure as a CPA.[2] Twenty-nine of these states allow candidates to sit for the CPA exam with 120 hours, but require 150 hours for certification.[3] The American Institute of Certified Public Accountants (AICPA), the national professional organization of CPAs, has also endorsed this movement by requiring that an individual CPA

---

[1] Since 2004, CPA candidates have been allowed to schedule their own exam dates; they may sit for one part at a time because the examination is now computer-based. The former "pencil and paper" CPA exam has become a relic of the past.

[2] The U.S. Virgin Islands is the only jurisdiction that has not enacted the 150-hour education requirement as this text goes to print. See www.aicpa.org/Advocacy/State/DownloadableDocuments/SumState150Req.pdf for the effective date of the legislation in your state.

[3] See www.becker.com/accounting/cpaexamreview/state for state-by-state details.

wishing to become a member must have met the 150-hour requirement. This increase in the educational requirements for becoming a CPA and for joining the AICPA reflects the increasing demands placed on accounting professionals to be both broadly educated and technically competent. Practicing CPAs work in all types of organizations, but as explained later, a CPA who expresses an auditor's opinion about an entity's financial statements must be licensed by the jurisdiction/state in which she or he performs the auditing service.

Managerial Accounting/Cost Accounting

Managerial accounting is concerned with the use of economic and financial information to plan and control many activities of the entity and to support the management decision-making process. **Cost accounting** is a subset of managerial accounting that relates to the determination and accumulation of product, process, or service costs. Managerial accounting and cost accounting have primarily an internal orientation, as opposed to the primarily external orientation of financial accounting. Many of the same data used in or generated by the financial accounting process are used in managerial and cost accounting, but the data are more likely to be used in a future-oriented way, such as in the preparation of budgets. A detailed discussion of the similarities and differences between financial and managerial accounting is provided in Chapter 12 and highlighted in Exhibit 12-1.

Managerial accountants and cost accountants are professionals who have usually earned a bachelor's degree with a major in accounting. Their work frequently involves close coordination with the production, marketing, and finance functions of the entity. The **Certified Management Accountant (CMA)** designation can be earned by a management accountant or cost accountant by passing a broad two-part examination. The CMA examination is given in a computer-based format using only objective questions.

Auditing—Public Accounting

Many entities have their financial statements reviewed or examined by an independent third party. In most cases, an audit (examination) is required by securities laws if the stock or bonds of a company are owned and publicly traded by investors. **Public accounting** firms and individual CPAs provide this **auditing** service, which constitutes an important part of the accounting profession.

The result of an audit is the **independent auditor's report.** The report usually has four relatively brief paragraphs. The first paragraph identifies the financial statements that were audited, explains that the statements are the responsibility of the company's management, and states that the auditor's responsibility is to express an opinion about the financial statements. The second paragraph explains that the audit was conducted "in accordance with the standards of the Public Company Accounting Oversight Board (United States)" and describes briefly what those standards require and what work is involved in performing an audit. (In effect, they require the application of **generally accepted auditing standards,** or **GAAS.**) The third paragraph contains the auditor's opinion, which is usually that the named statements "present fairly, in all material respects" the financial position of the entity and the results of its operations and cash flows for the identified periods "in conformity with U.S. generally accepted accounting principles." This is an unqualified, or "clean," opinion. Occasionally the opinion will be qualified with respect to fair presentation, departure from **generally accepted**

accounting principles (GAAP), or the auditor's inability to perform certain auditing procedures. Similarly, an explanatory paragraph may be added to an unqualified opinion regarding the firm's ability to continue as a going concern (that is, as a viable economic entity) when substantial doubt exists. An unqualified opinion is not a clean bill of health about either the current financial condition or the future prospects of the entity. Readers must reach their own judgments about these and other matters after studying the **annual report,** which includes the financial statements and the notes to the financial statements, as well as management's extensive discussion and analysis. A final paragraph makes reference to the auditors' opinion about the effectiveness of the company's internal control over financial reporting. The entire auditors' report is further discussed in Chapter 10.

Auditors who work in public accounting are professional accountants who usually have earned at least a bachelor's degree with a major in accounting. The auditor may work for a public accounting firm (a few firms have several thousand partners and professional staff) or as an individual practitioner. Most auditors seek and earn the CPA designation; the firm partner or individual practitioner who actually signs the audit opinion must be a licensed CPA in the state in which she or he practices. To be licensed, the CPA must satisfy the character, education, examination, and experience requirements of the state or other jurisdiction.

To see an example of the independent auditors' report, refer to page 753 of the 2011 annual report of Campbell Soup Company, which is reproduced in the appendix.

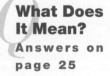

What Does It Mean?

Answers on page 25

2. What does it mean to work in public accounting?
3. What does it mean to be a CPA?

Internal Auditing

Organizations with many plant locations or activities involving many financial transactions employ professional accountants to do **internal auditing.** In many cases, the internal auditor performs functions much like those of the external auditor/public accountant, but perhaps on a smaller scale. For example, internal auditors may be responsible for reviewing the financial statements of a single plant or for analyzing the operating efficiency of an entity's activities. The qualifications of an internal auditor are similar to those of any other professional accountant. In addition to having the CPA and the CMA designation, the internal auditor may have also passed the examination to become a Certified Internal Auditor (CIA).

Governmental and Not-for-Profit Accounting

Governmental units at the municipal, state, and federal levels and not-for-profit entities such as colleges and universities, hospitals, and voluntary health and welfare organizations require the same accounting functions to be performed as do other accounting entities. Religious organizations, labor unions, trade associations, performing arts organizations, political parties, libraries, museums, country clubs, and many other not-for-profit organizations employ accountants with similar educational qualifications as those employed in business and public accounting.

Income Tax Accounting

The growing complexity of federal, state, municipal, and foreign income tax laws has led to a demand for professional accountants who are specialists in various aspects of taxation. Tax practitioners often develop specialties in the taxation of individuals, partnerships, corporations, trusts and estates, or in international tax law issues. These accountants work for corporations, public accounting firms, governmental units, and other entities. Many tax accountants have bachelor's degrees and are CPAs; some have a master's degree in accounting or taxation or are attorneys as well.

How Has Accounting Developed?

Accounting has developed over time in response to the needs of users of financial statements for financial information to support decisions and informed judgments such as those mentioned in Exhibit 1-1 and others that you were challenged to identify. Even though an aura of exactness is conveyed by the numbers in financial statements, a great deal of judgment and approximation is involved in determining the numbers to be reported. Although broad generally accepted principles of accounting exist, different accountants may reach different but often equally legitimate conclusions about how to account for a particular transaction or event. A brief review of the history of the development of accounting principles may make this often confusing state of affairs a little easier to understand.

LO 4
Summarize the development of accounting from a broad historical perspective.

Early History

It is not surprising that evidence of record keeping for economic events has been found in the earliest civilizations. Dating back to the clay tablets used by Mesopotamians in about 3000 B.C. to record tax receipts, accounting has responded to the information needs of users. In 1494, Luca Pacioli, a Franciscan monk and mathematics professor, published the first known text to describe a comprehensive double-entry bookkeeping system. Modern bookkeeping systems (as discussed in Chapter 4) have evolved directly from Pacioli's "method of Venice" system, which was developed in response to the needs of the Italian mercantile trading practices in that period.

The Industrial Revolution generated the need for large amounts of capital to finance the enterprises that supplanted individual craftsmen. This need resulted in the corporate form of organization marked by absentee owners, or investors, who entrusted their money to managers. It followed that investors required reports from the corporate managers showing the entity's financial position and results of operations. In mid-19th-century England, the independent (external) audit function added credence to financial reports. As British capital was invested in a growing U.S. economy in the late 19th century, British-chartered accountants and accounting methods came to the United States. However, no group was legally authorized to establish financial reporting standards. This led to alternative methods of reporting financial condition and results of operations, which resulted in confusion and, in some cases, outright fraud.

The Accounting Profession in the United States

Accounting professionals in this country organized themselves in the early 1900s and worked hard to establish certification laws, standardized audit procedures, and other attributes of a profession. However, not until 1932–1934 did the American

Institute of Accountants (predecessor of today's American Institute of Certified Public Accountants—AICPA) and the New York Stock Exchange agree on five broad principles of accounting. This was the first formal accounting standard-setting activity. The accounting, financial reporting, and auditing weaknesses related to the 1929 stock market crash gave impetus to this effort.

The Securities Act of 1933 and the Securities Exchange Act of 1934 apply to securities offered for sale in interstate commerce. These laws had a significant effect on the standard-setting process because they gave the **Securities and Exchange Commission (SEC)** the authority to establish accounting principles to be followed by companies whose securities had to be registered with the SEC. The SEC still has this authority, but the standard-setting process has been delegated to other organizations over the years. Between 1939 and 1959, the Committee on Accounting Procedure of the American Institute of Accountants issued 51 *Accounting Research Bulletins* that dealt with accounting principles. This work was done without a common conceptual framework for financial reporting. Each bulletin dealt with a specific issue in a relatively narrow context, and alternative methods of reporting the results of similar transactions remained.

In 1959, the Accounting Principles Board (APB) replaced the Committee on Accounting Procedure as the standard-setting body. The APB was an arm of the AICPA, and although it was given resources and directed to engage in more research than its predecessor, its early efforts intensified the controversies that existed. The APB did issue 39 *Opinions* on serious accounting issues, but it failed to develop a conceptual underpinning for accounting and financial reporting.

Financial Accounting Standard Setting at the Present Time

LO 5

Explain the role that the FASB plays in the development of financial accounting standards.

In 1973, as a result of congressional and other criticism of the accounting standard-setting process being performed by an arm of the AICPA, the **Financial Accounting Foundation (FAF)** was created as a more independent entity. The foundation established the **Financial Accounting Standards Board (FASB)** as the authoritative standard-setting body within the accounting profession. The FASB embarked on a project called the Conceptual Framework of Financial Accounting and Reporting and issued eight *Statements of Financial Accounting Concepts* through September 2012.

Concurrently with its Conceptual Framework project, the FASB issued 168 ***Statements of Financial Accounting Standards* (SFAS)** that established standards of accounting and reporting for particular issues, much as its predecessors did. Effective in July 2009, however, all such FASB standards were superseded by the *FASB Accounting Standards Codification* (**FASB Codification**). Essentially, the FASB Codification reorganized divergent sources of U.S. GAAP in a more accessible and researchable format. The FASB Codification now represents a single source of U.S. GAAP. Changes to the Codification are communicated through an *Accounting Standards Update* (**Update** or **ASU**), regardless of the form in which such guidance may have been issued prior to the release of the FASB Codification. Although such Updates do in fact amend the FASB Codification, the FASB does not consider ASUs as authoritative in their own right. A total of 58 ASUs had been issued through the end of 2011.

Alternative ways of accounting for and reporting the effects of similar transactions still exist. In many aspects of financial reporting, the accountant still must use judgment in selecting between equally acceptable alternatives. To make sense of financial statements, one must understand the impact of the accounting methods used by a firm, relative to alternative methods that were not selected. Subsequent chapters will describe many of these alternatives and the impact that various accounting choices have on financial statements. For example, Chapter 5 discusses the effects of the first-in, first-out inventory cost flow assumption in comparison to the last-in, first-out and the weighted-average assumptions. Likewise, Chapter 6 discusses the difference between the straight-line and accelerated methods of depreciating long-lived assets. Although such terminology may not be meaningful to you at this time, you should understand that the FASB has sanctioned each of these alternative methods of accounting for inventory and depreciation, and that the methods selected can significantly affect a firm's reported profits.

The FASB does not set standards in a vacuum. An open, due process procedure is followed. The FASB invites input from any individual or organization that cares to provide ideas and viewpoints about the particular standard under consideration. Among the many professional accounting and financial organizations that regularly present suggestions to the FASB, in addition to the AICPA and the SEC, are the **International Accounting Standards Board (IASB),** the American Accounting Association, the Institute of Management Accountants, Financial Executives International, and the Chartered Financial Analysts Institute.

The accounting and auditing standard-setting processes were heavily criticized as a result of the Enron and WorldCom collapses and the accounting and reporting problems of other companies that came to light in 2001 and early 2002. In July 2002, President George W. Bush signed into law the most significant legislation affecting the accounting profession since 1933: the Sarbanes–Oxley Act (SOX) of 2002. Essentially, the act created a five-member **Public Company Accounting Oversight Board (PCAOB),** which has the authority to set and enforce auditing, attestation, quality control, and ethics (including independence) standards for public companies. It is also empowered to inspect the auditing operations of public accounting firms that audit public companies as well as impose disciplinary sanctions for violations of the Board's rules, securities laws, and professional auditing standards. The impact of SOX on financial reporting has been far-reaching and will be explored in some detail in Chapter 10, which addresses corporate governance and disclosure issues.

The point of this discussion is to emphasize that financial accounting and reporting practices are not based on a set of inflexible rules to be mastered and blindly followed. The reality is that financial reporting practices have evolved over time in response to the changing needs of society, and are still evolving. In recent years, financial instruments and business transactions have become increasingly complex, and are now being used with greater frequency by firms of all sizes. The FASB has thus been hard pressed to develop appropriate standards to adequately address emerging accounting issues in a timely manner. Moreover, many recent ASUs appear to be more like rules than the judgmental application of fair guidelines. Don't worry about any critical reviews you may read concerning new FASB Codification updates; instead, keep your eye on the big picture. Your objective is to learn enough about the fundamentals of financial accounting and reporting practices to be neither awed nor confounded by the overall presentation of financial data.

LO 6
Generalize about how financial reporting standards evolve.

---

4. What does it mean to state that generally accepted accounting principles are not a set of rules to be blindly followed?
5. What does it mean when the Financial Accounting Standards Board issues a new *Accounting Standards Update?*

What Does It Mean?
Answers on page 25

Standards for Other Types of Accounting

Because managerial/cost accounting is oriented primarily to internal use, it is presumed that internal users will know about the accounting practices being followed by their firms. As a result, the accounting profession has not regarded the development of internal reporting standards for use by management as an important issue. Instead, individual companies are generally allowed to self-regulate with respect to internal reporting matters. One significant exception is accounting for the cost of work done under government contracts. Over the years, various governmental agencies have issued directives prescribing the procedures to be followed by government contractors. During the 1970–1980 period, the **Cost Accounting Standards Board (CASB)** operated as a governmental body to establish standards applicable to government contracts. Congress abolished the CASB in 1981, although its standards remained in effect. In 1988, Congress reestablished the CASB as an independent body within the Office of Federal Procurement Policy. The CASB now has authority to establish cost accounting standards for government contracts in excess of $700,000, provided that the contractor or subcontractor is performing a total of $7.5 million or more in all such contracts. Since 1995, CASB standards also have applied to colleges and universities that receive major federal research funds.

In the auditing/public accounting area, auditing standards are established by the Auditing Standards Board, a technical committee of the AICPA, unless superseded or amended by the PCAOB. The SEC has had input into this process, and over the years a number of auditing standards and procedures have been issued. One of the most important of these standards requires the auditor to be *independent* of the client whose financial statements are being audited. Yet the auditor's judgment is still very important in the auditing process. Because of this, critics of the accounting profession often raise questions concerning the independence of CPA firms in the auditing process (see Business in Practice—Auditor Independence). It is worth repeating here that an unqualified auditor's opinion does not constitute a clean bill of health about either the current financial condition of or the future prospects for the entity. It is up to the readers of the financial statements to reach their own judgments about these and other matters after studying the firm's annual report, which includes the financial statements and notes to the financial statements.

In 1984, the **Governmental Accounting Standards Board (GASB)** was established to develop guidelines for financial accounting and reporting by state and local governmental units. The GASB operates under the auspices of the Financial Accounting Foundation, which is also the parent organization of the FASB. The GASB is attempting to unify practices of the nation's many state and municipal entities, thus providing investors and taxpayers with a better means of comparing financial data of the issuers of state and municipal securities. In the absence of a GASB standard for a particular activity or transaction occurring in both the public and private sectors, governmental entities will continue to use FASB standards for guidance. The GASB had issued 68 standards and 5 Concepts Statements by September 2012.

The United States Internal Revenue Code and related regulations and the various state and local tax laws specify the rules to be followed in determining an entity's income tax liability. Although quite specific and complicated, the code and regulations provide rules of law to be followed. In income tax matters, accountants use their judgment and expertise to design transactions so that the entity's overall income tax liability is minimized. In addition, accountants prepare or help prepare tax returns, and may represent clients whose returns are being reviewed or challenged by taxing authorities.

Auditor Independence

Certified public accountants have traditionally provided auditing, tax, and consulting services designed to meet a broad range of client needs. In recent years, the consultancy area of practice has expanded considerably, especially among the Big 4 international CPA firms. Consulting services commonly offered include financial advisory services, assurance (risk management) services, and information systems design and installation services. Until recent years, it was not unusual for a CPA firm to provide such services to its audit clients.

In the opinion of some observers, including the SEC, having the auditing firm involved in the development of information and accounting systems raises the possibility and appearance of a conflict of interest. Such a conflict might arise if the auditors are reluctant to challenge the results of a system from which the amounts shown on an audit client's financial statements were derived. The appearance of independence could be further affected by the fact that consulting fees frequently exceed the auditing fees generated from many corporate clients.

For several years prior to the Enron case, the SEC and the AICPA discussed the impact of auditors' consulting practices on auditor independence. To help achieve independence in fact and in appearance, several auditing firms split off their consulting practices, thus making them separate entities. However, when it was learned that Arthur Andersen had earned considerably more in consulting fees from Enron than it had earned in auditing fees, and that this situation prevailed for many auditing firms, there was strong pressure to require all auditing firms to divest their consulting practices. As discussed in Chapter 10, SOX now prohibits auditors from performing a variety of nonaudit services for financial statement audit clients. Clearly, the issue of auditor independence has acquired "hot button" status, and it is likely to remain under close scrutiny for the foreseeable future.

International Accounting Standards

Accounting standards in individual countries have evolved in response to the unique user needs and cultural attributes of each country. Thus, despite the development of a global marketplace, accounting standards in one country may differ significantly from those in another country. In 1973, the International Accounting Standards Committee (IASC) was formed by accountancy bodies in Australia, Canada, France, Germany, Japan, Mexico, the Netherlands, the United Kingdom and Ireland, and the United States to create and promote worldwide acceptance and observation of accounting and financial reporting standards. In 2001 the International Accounting Standards Board (IASB) was formed in a restructuring effort and has since assumed all responsibilities previously carried out by the IASC, which was disbanded at that time. The IFRS Foundation, based in London, is the legal entity under which the IASB operates as an independent, not-for-profit private sector organization.

The goal of the IASB is to develop a single set of high-quality, understandable, enforceable, and globally accepted financial reporting standards based upon clearly articulated principles. The IASB and its predecessor organization had issued 41 International Accounting Standards (IAS) and 13 **International Financial Reporting Standards (IFRS)** by September 2012, with much of this progress coming in recent years. As a result, all major nations have now established time lines to converge with or adopt IFRS standards in the near future.

The IASB and the FASB have been working together since 2002 to achieve convergence of IFRS and U.S. GAAP. The principal difference between IFRS and U.S. GAAP is that U.S. standards have been increasingly based on detailed rules whereas

Exhibit 1-2

Websites for Accounting
Organizations

American Institute of Certified Public Accountants: www.aicpa.org

Financial Accounting Standards Board: www.fasb.org

Government Accounting Standards Board: www.gasb.org

Institute of Internal Auditors: www.theiia.org

Institute of Management Accountants: www.imanet.org

IFRS Foundation and the International Accounting Standards Board: www.ifrs.org

Public Company Accounting Oversight Board: www.pcaob.org

Securities and Exchange Commission: www.sec.gov

IFRS standards require companies to follow broad principles, which can result in "situational" accounting that can lead to financial reporting differences between companies having similar transactions. With this in mind, the two boards continue to work closely on nearly a dozen joint projects designed to improve both IFRS and U.S. GAAP, and ultimately make the standards fully compatible. Through these projects—some covering major components of the financial statements such as financial instruments, leases, and revenue recognition issues—the boards intend to improve financial reporting to investors while also aligning U.S. and international standards.

In November 2008, the SEC issued a "Roadmap" discussion paper for a possible path to the adoption of IFRS standards in the United States. In May 2011, the SEC released a more detailed proposal for the FASB to change U.S. GAAP over a defined period of perhaps five to seven years by endorsing, and thereby incorporating, individual IFRS standards into U.S. GAAP. Under this proposal, the FASB would continue as the U.S. standard setter, and would participate in the development of new standards, but the nature of its role would differ from what it is today. Rather than acting as the principal standard setter for new standards, the FASB would provide input and support to the IASB in its mission to develop high-quality, global standards. Moreover, because of the FASB's active participation in the process, it is expected that U.S. modifications to new IFRS standards would be avoidable except in rare instances. The FASB is now developing a transition plan to effect the necessary changes over the next five to seven years.

Although it is appropriate to follow the progress of the SEC convergence proposal, this text explains and illustrates only those current U.S. financial accounting and reporting standards that are necessary for you to gain a comprehension of the "big picture"—what the numbers mean. However, where appropriate, IFRS standards currently in effect and under development are identified in text boxes titled "The IFRS Approach." These text boxes contain brief explanations of the relevant international standards. A variety of hot topic issues affecting the accounting profession, such as those mentioned here, are discussed further in the Epilogue, "Accounting—The Future."

Exhibit 1-2 lists the website addresses of various accounting organizations. You are encouraged to visit these sites for more information about each one.

The **IFRS**

Approach

**What Does
It Mean?**

Answer on
page 25

6. What does it mean that the FASB and IASB have been working together to achieve convergence?

Ethics and the Accounting Profession

One characteristic frequently associated with any profession is that those practicing the profession acknowledge the importance of an ethical code. This is especially important in the accounting profession because so much of an accountant's work involves providing information to support the informed judgments and decisions made by users of accounting information.

The American Institute of Certified Public Accountants (AICPA) and the Institute of Management Accountants (IMA) have both published ethics codes. The *Code of Professional Conduct,* most recently amended in 2011, was adopted by the membership of the AICPA. The organization's bylaws state that members shall conform to the rules of the Code or be subject to disciplinary action by the AICPA. Although it doesn't have the same enforcement mechanism, the IMA's *Statement of Ethical Professional Practice* calls on management accountants to maintain the highest standards of ethical conduct as they fulfill their obligations to the organizations they serve, their profession, the public, and themselves.

Both codes of conduct identify integrity and objectivity as two key elements of ethical behavior for a professional accountant. Having **integrity** means being honest and forthright in dealings and communications with others; **objectivity** means impartiality and freedom from conflict of interest. An accountant who lacks integrity and/or objectivity cannot be relied on to produce complete and relevant information with which to make an informed judgment or decision.

Other elements of ethical behavior include independence, competence, and acceptance of an obligation to serve the best interests of the employer, the client, and the public. **Independence** is related to objectivity and is especially important to the auditor, who must be independent both in appearance and in fact. Having competence means having the knowledge and professional skills to adequately perform the work assigned. Accountants should recognize that the nature of their work requires an understanding of the obligation to serve those who will use the information communicated by them.

In the recent past, incidents involving allegations that accountants have violated their ethical codes by being dishonest, biased, and/or incompetent have been highly publicized. The fact that some of these allegations have been proved true should not be used to condemn all accountants. The profession has used these rare circumstances to reaffirm that the public and the profession expect accountants to exhibit a very high level of ethical behavior. In this sense, are accountants really any different from those involved in any other endeavor?

LO 7
Identify the key elements of ethical behavior for a professional accountant.

---

7. What does it mean to state that ethical behavior includes being objective and independent?

What Does It Mean?
Answer on page 25

The Conceptual Framework

Various accounting standards have existed for many years. But it wasn't until the mid-1970s that the FASB began the process of identifying a structure or framework of financial accounting concepts. New users of financial statements can benefit from an overview of these concepts because they provide the foundation for understanding

LO 8
Summarize the reasons for the FASB's Conceptual Framework project.

Business in
Practice

Business Ethics

Events like the 2008–2009 global economic crisis have highlighted the necessity of sound ethical practices across the business world. An indication of the breadth of this concern is the development of the term *stakeholder* to refer to the many entities—owners, managers, employees, customers, suppliers, communities, and even competitors—who have a stake in the way an organization conducts its activities. Another indicator of this concern is that business ethics and corporate social responsibility issues are merging into a single broad area of interest.

This concern is international in scope and is attracting political attention. In 2011 the Caux Round Table (CRT) celebrated its 17th year of leadership in corporate business ethics after publishing its *Principles for Business,* in 1994, which attempts to express a worldwide standard for ethical and socially responsible corporate behavior. Another influential organization is Business for Social Responsibility (BSR), a U.S.-based global resource for companies seeking to sustain their commercial success in ways that demonstrate respect for ethical values and for people, communities, and the environment. For more information, visit www.cauxroundtable.org or www.bsr.org.

The Foreign Corrupt Practices Act of 1977, as amended by the International Anti-Bribery and Fair Competition Act of 1998, has certainly contributed to a management focus on ethical behavior—although government regulation, in and of itself, tends to curtail only the most abusive ethical violations. As early as 1987, a private sector commission was convened in response to perceived weaknesses in corporate financial reporting practices. This resulted in a series of recommendations to the SEC that publicly owned corporations include in their annual reports disclosures about how the company fulfills its responsibilities for achieving a broadly defined set of internal control objectives related to safeguarding assets, authorizing transactions, and reporting properly. (See the Business in Practice discussion of internal control in Chapter 5.) Section 404 of the Sarbanes–Oxley Act of 2002 now requires all SEC-regulated companies to include in their annual reports a report by management on the effectiveness of the company's internal control over financial reporting. The auditor that audits the company's financial statements included in the annual report is required to attest to and report on management's assessment of internal controls. Many companies provide further disclosures in their annual reports concerning their corporate code of conduct or ethics and whistle-blowing systems. Within the accounting profession, it is generally accepted that an organization's integrity and ethical values bear directly on the effectiveness of its internal control system.

Researchers are beginning to demonstrate that well-constructed ethical and social programs can contribute to profitability by helping to attract customers, raise employee morale and productivity, and strengthen trust relationships within the organization. Indeed, organizations that are committed to ethical quality often institute structures and procedures (such as codes of conduct) to encourage decency. Ethics codes vary from generalized value statements and credos to detailed discussions of global ethical policy. Johnson & Johnson's "Our Credo" is perhaps the most frequently cited corporate ethics statement, and rightfully so (see www.jnj.com).

For a list of the 100 Best Corporate Citizens as determined by one observer of the corporate scene, see www.thecro.com. Incidentally, Campbell's was ranked 8th and McGraw-Hill was ranked 16th on the 2012 list, which also included IBM, Intel, Microsoft, and Nike in the top 10.

For additional guidance, check out US SIF (formerly the Social Investment Forum), which offers comprehensive information, contacts, and resources on socially responsible investing (see www.ussif.org).

It is never too early to understand and refine your own value system and to sharpen your awareness of the ethical dimensions of your activities; and don't be surprised if you are asked to literally "sign on" to an employer's code of conduct.

The following websites reference other sites dealing with business ethics:

www.ethicsworld.org

www.scu.edu/ethics (then click on *Business Ethics*)

financial accounting reports. The FASB issued eight *Statements of Financial Accounting Concepts* through September 2012, the first six of which were issued between 1978 and 1985. These statements represent a great deal of effort by the FASB, and progress made on this project has not come easily.

In concert with their efforts to converge U.S. and international accounting standards, the FASB and IASB have undertaken a project to improve and converge their respective Conceptual Frameworks as well. In September 2010, *FASB Concepts Statement No. 8*, "Conceptual Framework for Financial Reporting," was issued; it included two chapters of the new Conceptual Framework and superseded *FASB Concepts Statements No. 1* and *No. 2*. In *Concepts Statement No. 8*, the FASB made the following assertions:[4]

> Concepts Statements are not part of the *FASB Accounting Standards Codification*, which is the source of authoritative GAAP recognized by the FASB to be applied by nongovernmental entities. Rather, Concepts Statements describe concepts that will underlie guidance on future accounting practices and in due course will serve as a basis for evaluating existing guidance and practices.
>
> Establishment of objectives and identification of fundamental concepts will not directly solve accounting and reporting problems. Rather, objectives give direction, and concepts are tools for solving problems.
>
> The Board itself is likely to be the most direct beneficiary of the guidance provided by Concepts Statements. They will guide the Board in developing accounting and reporting guidance by providing the Board with a common foundation and basic reasoning on which to consider merits of alternatives.

Summary of *Concepts Statement No. 8*, Chapter 1: "The Objective of General Purpose Financial Reporting"

To set the stage more completely for your study of financial accounting, it is appropriate to have an overview of the foundational building blocks of financial reporting, as expressed in Chapter 1 of *Concepts Statement No. 8*. (To gain a comprehensive understanding of the author summary that follows, you may want to download the full text of *Concepts Statement No. 8* from the FASB's website.)

LO 9
Summarize the objective of general purpose financial reporting.

Financial reporting is done for individual firms, or entities, rather than for industries or the economy as a whole. It is aimed primarily at meeting the needs of external users of accounting information who would not otherwise have access to the firm's records. Investors, creditors, and financial advisers are the primary users who create

At this point, it is unlikely that you will fully grasp and retain all of the details expressed here. Don't try to memorize these summary highlights! Instead, read through this material to get a basic understanding of what the accounting profession is "gearing toward." That way, as specific applications of these concepts are presented later in the course, you will have a basis for comparison, and you won't be surprised very often.

Study
Suggestion

---

[4] FASB, *Statement of Financial Accounting Concepts No. 8*, Preface (Stamford, CT, 2010). Copyright © the Financial Accounting Foundation, High Ridge Park, Stamford, CT 06905, U.S.A. Excerpted with permission. Copies of the complete document are available from the FASB.

the demand for accounting information. Financial reporting is designed to meet the needs of users by providing information that is relevant to making rational investment and credit decisions and other informed judgments. The users of accounting information are assumed to be reasonably astute in business and financial reporting practices. However, each user reads the financial statements with her or his own judgment and biases and must be willing to take responsibility for her or his own decision making.

Most users are on the outside looking in. For its own use, management can prescribe the information it wants. Reporting for *internal* planning, control, and decision making need not be constrained by financial reporting requirements—thus the Concepts Statements are not directed at internal (i.e., managerial) uses of accounting information.

Financial accounting is historical scorekeeping; it is not future-oriented. Although the future is unknown, it is likely to be influenced by the past. To the extent that accounting information provides a fair basis for the evaluation of past performance, it may be helpful in assessing an entity's future prospects. However, financial reports are not the sole source of information about an entity. For example, a potential employee might want to know about employee turnover rates, which are not disclosed in the financial reporting process. The information reported in financial accounting relates primarily to past transactions and events that can be measured in dollars and cents.

Financial accounting information is developed and used at a cost, and the benefit to the user of accounting information should exceed the cost of providing it.

Many of the objectives of financial reporting relate to the presentation of earnings and cash flow information. Investors and creditors are interested in making judgments about the firm's profitability and whether or not they are likely to receive payment of amounts owed to them. The user may ask, "How much profit did the firm earn during the year ended December 31, 2013?" or "What was the net cash inflow from operating the firm for the year?" Users understand that cash has to be received from somewhere before the firm can pay principal and interest to its creditors or dividends to its investors. A primary objective of financial reporting is to provide timely information about a firm's earnings and cash flow.

Financial reporting includes detailed notes and other disclosures.

Accrual accounting—to be explained in more detail later—involves accounting for the effect of an economic activity, or transaction, on an entity when the activity has occurred, rather than when the cash receipt or payment takes place. Thus, the company for which you work reports a cost for your wages in the month in which you do the work, even though you may not be paid until the next month. Earnings information is reported on the accrual basis rather than the cash basis because past performance can be measured more accurately under accrual accounting. In the process of measuring a firm's accrual accounting earnings, some costs applicable to one year's results of operations may have to be estimated; for example, product warranty costs applicable to 2013 may not be finally determined until 2016. Reporting an approximately correct amount in 2013 is obviously preferable to recording nothing at all until 2016, when the precise amount is known.

In addition to providing information about earnings and cash flows, financial reporting should provide information to help users assess the relative strengths and weaknesses of a firm's financial position. The user may ask, "What economic resources does the firm own? How much does the firm owe? What caused these amounts to change over time?" Financial accounting does not attempt to directly measure the value of a firm, although it can be used to facilitate the efforts of those attempting to achieve such an objective. The numbers reported in a firm's financial statements do not change just because the market price of its stock changes.

Financial accounting standards are still evolving; with each new update to the FASB Codification, accounting procedures are modified to mirror new developments in the business world as well as current views and theories of financial reporting. At times, the FASB finds it difficult to keep pace with the ever-changing economic activities addressed by its ASUs. Fortunately, however, such efforts have resulted in improved financial reporting practices each step along the way.

Students of accounting should be aware that the how-to aspects of accounting are not static; the accounting discipline is relatively young in comparison to other professions and is in constant motion. Perhaps the most important outcome of the conceptual framework project is the sense that the profession now has a blueprint in place that will carry financial reporting into the future.

---

8. What does it mean to state that the objectives of financial reporting given in *Statement of Financial Accounting Concepts No. 8* provide a framework for this text?

What Does It Mean?

Answer on page 25

Objectives of Financial Reporting for Nonbusiness Organizations

At the outset of this chapter, it was stated that the material to be presented, although usually to be expressed in the context of profit-seeking business enterprises, would also be applicable to not-for-profit social service and governmental organizations. The FASB's "Highlights" of *Concepts Statement No. 4,* "Objectives of Financial Reporting by Nonbusiness Organizations," states, "Based on its study, the Board believes that the objectives of general-purpose external financial reporting for government-sponsored entities (for example, hospitals, universities, or utilities) engaged in activities that are not unique to government should be similar to those of business enterprises or other nonbusiness organizations engaged in similar activities."[5] *Statement 6* amended *Statement 2* by affirming that the qualitative characteristics described in *Statement 2* apply to the information about both business enterprises and not-for-profit organizations.

The objectives of financial reporting for nonbusiness organizations focus on providing information for resource providers (such as taxpayers to governmental entities and donors to charitable organizations), rather than investors. Information is provided about the economic resources, obligations, net resources, and performance of an organization during a period of time. Thus, even though nonbusiness organizations have unique characteristics that distinguish them from profit-oriented businesses, the information characteristics of the financial reporting process for each type of organization are similar.

It will be appropriate to remember the gist of the preceding objectives as individual accounting and financial statement issues are encountered in subsequent chapters and are related to real-world situations.

---

[5] FASB, *Statement of Financial Accounting Concepts No. 4* (Stamford, CT, 1980). Copyright © the Financial Accounting Standards Board, High Ridge Park, Stamford, CT 06905, U.S.A. Excerpted with permission. Copies of the complete document are available from the FASB.

Plan of the Book

LO 10

Describe the plan of the book.

This text is divided into two main parts. Chapters 2 through 11, which comprise the first part of the book, are devoted to financial accounting topics. The remaining chapters, Chapters 12 through 16, provide an in-depth look at managerial accounting.

As you study the topics that lie ahead, the authors believe it will be to your advantage to be aware of the organizational strategy that we followed in writing this book. In general, the coverage of each topic begins with a "big picture" designed to put the topic in perspective relative to its role in financial accounting and reporting (Chapters 2 through 11) and managerial analysis and decision making (Chapters 12 through 16). The text coverage is limited in detail and is designed to provide a broad, "high spot" understanding of the material and a foundation for further learning in a more advanced academic environment or experiential setting. You are quite likely to encounter certain situations in practice that do not follow exactly this textbook's descriptions of accounting practices. Yet we are confident that your own thoughtful study, and practical input from others who do accounting-related work and use its results, will permit you to refine your knowledge and use this material effectively.

Chapter 2, which kicks off our discussion of financial accounting, describes financial statements, presents a model of how they are interrelated, and briefly summarizes key accounting concepts and principles. This is a "big picture" chapter; later chapters elaborate on most of the material introduced here. This chapter also includes four Business in Practice features. As you have seen from the features in this chapter, these are brief explanations of business practices that make some of the ideas covered in the text easier to understand.

Chapter 3 describes some of the basic analytical tools that allow financial statement users to make fundamental interpretations of a company's financial position and results of operations. This is a "big picture" chapter that just scratches the surface of financial statement analysis; a more complete explanation of the key financial statement relationships is presented in subsequent chapters. Understanding the basic relationships presented here permits a better comprehension of the impact of alternative accounting methods discussed in Chapters 4 through 10. However, because Chapter 11 presents a more comprehensive treatment of financial statement analysis, some instructors may prefer to cover the Chapter 3 material with that of Chapter 11.

Chapter 4 describes the bookkeeping process and presents a powerful transaction analysis model. Using this model, the financial statement user can understand the effect of any transaction on the statements, and many of the judgments based on the statements. You will not be asked to learn bookkeeping in this chapter.

Chapters 5 through 9 examine specific financial statement elements. Chapter 5 describes the accounting for short-term *(current)* assets, including cash, accounts and notes receivable, inventory, and prepaid items. Chapter 6 describes the accounting for long-term assets, including land, buildings and equipment, and a variety of intangible assets and natural resources. Chapter 7 discusses the accounting issues related to current and long-term liabilities, including accounts and notes payable, bonds payable, and deferred income taxes. Chapter 8 deals with the components of stockholders' equity, including common stock, preferred stock, retained earnings, and treasury stock. Chapter 9 presents a comprehensive view of the income statement and the statement of cash flows.

Chapter 10 covers corporate governance issues as well as the notes to the financial statements, and Chapter 11 concludes our look at financial accounting with a detailed discussion of financial statement analysis. The financial accounting chapters frequently make reference to Campbell Soup Company's 2011 annual report, appropriate elements of which are reproduced in the appendix. You should refer to those financial statements and notes, as well as other company financial reports you may have, to get acquainted with actual applications of the issues being discussed in the text.

Following Chapter 11, we turn our focus to managerial accounting topics. Chapter 12 presents the "big picture" of managerial accounting. It contrasts financial and managerial accounting, introduces key managerial accounting terminology, and illustrates cost behavior patterns by describing various applications of cost–volume–profit analysis, including the calculation of a firm's break-even point in units and sales dollars. Chapter 13 describes the principal cost accounting systems used in business today, with emphasis on the cost accumulation and assignment activities carried out by most firms. Chapter 14 illustrates many aspects of a typical firm's operating budget, including the sales forecast, production and purchases budgets, and the cash budget, as well as the development and use of standard costs for planning purposes. Chapter 15 concentrates on cost analysis for control; it highlights a number of performance reporting techniques and describes the analysis of variances for raw materials, direct labor, and manufacturing overhead. Chapter 16 concludes our discussion of managerial accounting with an overview of short-run versus long-run decision making, including a demonstration of the payback, net present value, and internal rate of return techniques used to support capital budgeting decisions.

An epilogue titled "Accounting—The Future" (with no homework problems!) reemphasizes the evolutionary nature of the accounting discipline and calls students' attention to a world of possibilities that remains to be explored in the future.

Resources for Students

The solutions to the odd-numbered exercises and problems of each chapter are provided for your convenience on the text website at www.mhhe.com/marshall10e. These homework assignments serve as additional illustrations of the material presented in the chapters. Each even-numbered exercise or problem is similar to the odd-numbered item that precedes it. We recommend that before working on an even-numbered exercise or problem you attempt to work out the preceding item in writing, using the solution to check your work only if you really don't know how to proceed.

Other features of our text website include: check figures for the end-of-chapter exercises and problems, study guide questions and answers, self-study quizzes, PowerPoint presentations of the key ideas introduced in each chapter, study outlines, and downloadable problem materials in Excel format. A complete e-book of this text is accessible online to students who have entered their registration codes or have otherwise purchased access to the premium content area of our site.

Use each chapter's learning objectives, "What Does It Mean?" questions, summary, and glossary of key terms and concepts to help manage your learning. With reasonable effort, you will achieve your objective of becoming an effective user of accounting information to support the related informed judgments and decisions you will make throughout your life.

Summary

Accounting is the process of identifying, measuring, and communicating economic information about an entity for the purpose of making decisions and informed judgments.

Users of financial statements include management, investors, creditors, employees, and government agencies. Decisions made by users relate to, among other things, entity operating results, investment and credit questions, employment characteristics, and compliance with laws. Financial statements support these decisions because they communicate important financial information about the entity.

The major classifications of accounting include financial accounting, managerial accounting/cost accounting, auditing/public accounting, internal auditing, governmental and not-for-profit accounting, and income tax accounting.

Accounting has developed over time in response to the information needs of users of financial statements. Financial accounting standards have been established by different organizations over the years. These standards have become increasingly complex in recent times, and in some cases are extremely specific almost to the point of being statutelike. As a result, interest in converging U.S. financial reporting standards with International Financial Reporting Standards, which are more general and flow from broad principles, has increased greatly. The Securities and Exchange Commission, the Financial Accounting Standards Board, and the International Accounting Standards Board have been working on a project that promises to make the existing financial reporting standards fully compatible as soon as possible. Currently in the United States, the FASB is the standard-setting body for financial accounting. Other organizations are involved in establishing standards for cost accounting, auditing, governmental accounting, and income tax accounting.

Integrity, objectivity, independence, and competence are several characteristics of ethical behavior required of a professional accountant. High standards of ethical conduct are appropriate for all people, but professional accountants have a special responsibility because so many people make decisions and informed judgments using information provided by the accounting process.

The Financial Accounting Standards Board has issued several *Statements of Financial Accounting Concepts* resulting from the Conceptual Framework project that began in the late 1970s and still receives considerable attention today. These statements describe concepts and relations that will underlie future financial accounting standards and practices and will in due course serve as a basis for evaluating existing standards and practices. Efforts are under way to ensure that the FASB and IASB Conceptual Frameworks will be converged similarly to the way in which their respective accounting standards are expected to be converged in the near-term future.

Highlights of the Concepts Statement dealing with the objectives of financial reporting provide that financial information should be useful to investor and creditor concerns about the cash flows of the enterprise, the resources and obligations of the enterprise, and the profit of the enterprise. Financial accounting is not designed to directly measure the value of a business enterprise.

The objectives of financial reporting for nonbusiness enterprises are not significantly different from those for business enterprises, except that resource providers, rather than investors, are concerned about performance results, rather than profit.

The book starts with the big picture of financial accounting and then moves to some of the basic financial interpretations made from accounting data. An overview of the bookkeeping process is followed by a discussion of specific financial statement elements and notes to the financial statements. The financial accounting material ends with a chapter focusing on financial statement analysis and use of the data developed from analysis. The managerial accounting chapters focus on the development and use of financial information for managerial planning, control, and decision making.

Key Terms and Concepts

accounting (p. 3)   The process of identifying, measuring, and communicating economic information about an organization for the purpose of making decisions and informed judgments.

Accounting Standards Update (**Update** or **ASU**) **(p. 10)**   A transient document which communicates the details of specific amendments to the FASB Codification, and explains the basis for the Board's decisions. Although ASUs update the FASB Codification, the FASB does not consider Updates as authoritative in their own right.

accrual accounting (p. 18)   Accounting that recognizes revenues and expenses as they occur, even though the cash receipt from the revenue or the cash disbursement related to the expense may occur before or after the event that causes revenue or expense recognition.

annual report (p. 8)   A document distributed to shareholders and other interested parties that contains the financial statements, notes to the financial statements, and management's discussion and analysis of financial and operating factors that affected the firm together with the report of the external auditor's examination of the financial statements.

auditing (p. 7)   The process of examining the financial statements of an entity by an independent third party with the objective of expressing an opinion about the fairness of the presentation of the entity's financial position, results of operations, changes in financial position, and cash flows. The practice of auditing is less precisely referred to as *public accounting*.

bookkeeping (p. 6)   Procedures that are used to keep track of financial transactions and accumulate the results of an entity's financial activities.

cash flow (p. 6)   Cash receipts or disbursements of an entity.

Certified Management Accountant (CMA) (p. 7)   Professional designation earned by passing a broad, two-part examination and meeting certain experience requirements. Examination topics include budgeting, performance management, cost management, financial statement analysis, corporate finance, decision analysis, and professional ethics.

Certified Public Accountant (CPA) (p. 6)   A professional designation earned by fulfilling certain education and experience requirements, in addition to passing a comprehensive, four-part examination. Examination topics include financial accounting theory and practice, income tax accounting, managerial accounting, governmental and not-for-profit accounting, auditing, business law, and other aspects of the business environment.

controller (p. 6)   The job title of the person who is the chief accounting officer of an organization. The controller is usually responsible for both the financial and managerial accounting functions. Sometimes referred to as *comptroller*.

cost accounting (p. 7)   A subset of managerial accounting that relates to the determination and accumulation of product, process, or service costs.

Cost Accounting Standards Board (CASB) (p. 12)   A group authorized by the U.S. Congress to establish cost accounting standards for government contractors.

creditor (p. 4)   An organization or individual who lends to the entity. Examples include suppliers who ship merchandise to the entity prior to receiving payment for their goods and banks that lend cash to the entity.

entity (p. 3)   An organization, individual, or a group of organizations or individuals for which accounting services are performed.

FASB Accounting Standards Codification **(FASB Codification) (p. 10)**   An advanced user-accessible computer application that systemized and reorganized many divergent elements of U.S. GAAP into one composite structure permitting users to review, study, and research topics. The Codification presents U.S. GAAP in a uniform and logical order, with approximately 90 major accounting topics. Since July 2009, the FASB Codification has represented a single source of all U.S. GAAP.

financial accounting (p. 6)   Accounting that focuses on reporting an entity's financial position at a point in time and/or its results of operations and cash flows for a period of time.

Financial Accounting Foundation (FAF) (p. 10)   An organization composed of people from the public accounting profession, businesses, and the public that is responsible for the funding of and appointing members to the Financial Accounting Standards Board and the Governmental Accounting Standards Board.

Financial Accounting Standards Board (FASB) (p. 10)   The body responsible for establishing U.S. generally accepted accounting principles.

generally accepted accounting principles (GAAP) (pp. 7–8)   Pronouncements of the Financial Accounting Standards Board (FASB) and its predecessors that constitute appropriate accounting for various transactions used for reporting financial position and results of operations to investors and creditors. Since July 2009, the FASB Codification has represented a single source of U.S. GAAP.

generally accepted auditing standards (GAAS) (p. 7)   Standards for auditing that are established by the Auditing Standards Board of the American Institute of Certified Public Accountants unless superseded or amended by the PCAOB.

Governmental Accounting Standards Board (GASB) (p. 12)   Established by the Financial Accounting Foundation to develop guidelines for financial accounting and reporting by state and local governmental units.

independence (p. 15)   The personal characteristic of an accountant, especially an auditor, that refers to both appearing and in fact being objective and impartial.

independent auditor's report (p. 7)   The report accompanying audited financial statements that explains briefly the auditor's responsibility and the extent of work performed. The report includes an opinion about whether the information contained in the financial statements is presented fairly in accordance with generally accepted accounting principles.

integrity (p. 15)   The personal characteristic of honesty, including being forthright in dealings and communications with others.

internal auditing (p. 8)   The practice of auditing within a company by employees of the company.

International Accounting Standards Board (IASB) (p. 11)   Standard-setting body responsible for the development of International Financial Reporting Standards (IFRS), permitted or required by more than 100 countries.

International Financial Reporting Standards (IFRS) (p. 13)   Pronouncements of the International Accounting Standards Board that are considered to be a "principles-based" set of standards in that they establish broad rules as well as dictating specific treatments. Many of the standards forming part of IFRS are known by the older name of International Accounting Standards (IAS).

investor (p. 4)   An organization or individual who has an ownership interest in the firm. For corporations, referred to as *stockholder* or *shareholder*.

managerial accounting (p. 7)   Accounting that is concerned with the internal use of economic and financial information to plan and control many of the activities of an entity and to support the management decision-making process.

objectivity (p. 15)   The personal characteristic of impartiality, including freedom from conflict of interest.

public accounting (p. 7)   The segment of the accounting profession that provides auditing, income tax accounting, and management consulting services to clients.

Public Company Accounting Oversight Board (PCAOB) (p. 11)   Established in 2002 with authority to set and enforce auditing and ethics standards for public companies and their auditing firms; affiliated with the SEC.

Securities and Exchange Commission (SEC) (p. 10)   A unit of the federal government that is responsible for establishing regulations and ensuring full disclosure to investors about companies and their securities that are traded in interstate commerce.

***Statements of Financial Accounting Standards* (SFAS) (p. 10)**   Pronouncements of the Financial Accounting Standards Board that formerly constituted generally accepted accounting principles. Effective in July 2009, the SFAS series was superseded by the *FASB Accounting Standards Codification.*

---

1. It means that accounting is a service activity that helps many different users of accounting information who use the information in many ways.

2. It means to perform professional services for clients principally in the areas of auditing, income taxes, management consulting, and/or accounting systems evaluation and development.

3. It means that the individual has met the education and experience requirements, and has passed the examination to qualify for a license as a Certified Public Accountant.

4. It means that generally accepted accounting principles sometimes permit alternative ways of accounting for identical transactions, thus requiring professional judgment, and that these principles are still evolving.

5. It means that the FASB has completed an extensive process of research and development, including receiving input from interested individuals and organizations, and has made an authoritative pronouncement (i.e., an Update to the FASB Codification) that defines accounting and reporting for a specific activity or transaction and becomes a generally accepted accounting principle.

6. It means that the FASB is committed to working with the IASB to ensure that a solution can be reached whereby U.S. accounting standards will eventually be merged with international accounting standards.

7. It means that the individual is impartial, free from conflict of interest, and will not receive a personal gain from the activity in which she or he is involved.

8. It means that the accounting and financial reporting topics explained in the financial accounting part of this text should:
   a. Relate to external financial reporting.
   b. Support business and economic decisions.
   c. Provide information about cash flows.
   d. Focus on earnings based on accrual accounting.
   e. Not seek to directly measure the value of a business enterprise.
   f. Report information that is subject to evaluation by individual financial statement users.

ANSWERS TO
What Does It Mean?

Self-Study Material

Visit the text website at <u>www.mhhe.com/marshall10e</u> to take on online self-study quiz for this chapter.

Matching Following is a list of the key terms and concepts introduced in the chapter, along with a list of corresponding definitions. Match the appropriate letter for the key term or concept to each definition provided (items 1–10). Note that not all key terms and concepts will be used. Answers are provided at the end of this chapter.

a.	Accounting	p.	Generally accepted accounting principles
b.	Entity		
c.	Financial accounting	q.	Internal auditing
d.	Bookkeeping	r.	Securities and Exchange Commission
e.	Certified Public Accountant		
f.	Managerial accounting	s.	Financial Accounting Foundation
g.	Cost accounting		
h.	Certified Management Accountant	t.	Financial Accounting Standards Board
i.	Auditing	u.	*FASB Accounting Standards Codification*
j.	Public accounting		
k.	Certified Internal Auditor	v.	Cost Accounting Standards Board
l.	Generally accepted auditing standards	w.	Governmental Accounting Standards Board
m.	Cash flows	x.	Accrual accounting
n.	Controller	y.	Integrity
o.	Independence	z.	Objectivity

_____ **1.** The process of identifying, measuring, and communicating economic information about an organization for the purpose of making decisions or informed judgments.

_____ **2.** Accounting that recognizes revenues and expenses as they occur, even though cash receipts from revenues and cash disbursements related to expenses may occur before or after the event that causes revenue or expense recognition.

_____ **3.** The process of examining the financial statements of an entity by an independent third party with the objective of expressing an opinion about the fairness of the presentation of the entity's financial position, results of operations, changes in financial position, and cash flows.

_____ **4.** Procedures that are used to keep track of an entity's financial transactions and to accumulate the results of its operations.

_____ **5.** An advanced user-accessible computer application that has systemized and reorganized many divergent elements of U.S. GAAP into a single source.

_____ **6.** Accounting that is concerned with the use of economic and financial information to plan and control the activities of an entity and to support the management decision-making process.

_____ **7.** An organization, individual, or group of organizations or individuals for which accounting services are performed.

_____**8.** A unit of the federal government that is responsible for establishing regulations and ensuring that full disclosure is made to investors about large companies and their securities traded in interstate commerce.

_____**9.** The body responsible for establishing U.S. generally accepted accounting principles.

_____**10.** The personal characteristic of honesty, including being forthright in dealings and communications with others.

_____

Multiple Choice For each of the following questions, circle the best response. Answers are provided at the end of this chapter.

1. Common examples of "users" of the accounting information related to an organization include

    a. the management of the organization.

    b. investors and creditors.

    c. employees.

    d. the Securities and Exchange Commission.

    e. all of the above.

2. As it relates to financial reporting, which of the following is _not_ required of an accounting entity?

    a. A financial statement presenting the amount that the entity expects to earn next year.

    b. A financial statement presenting the financial position of the entity at a point in time.

    c. A financial statement presenting the results of the entity's operations for a period of time.

    d. A financial statement summarizing the entity's cash flows for a period of time.

3. In _SFAC No. 8,_ which of the following ideas is _not_ expressed?

    a. Information largely reflects financial effects of past transactions and events.

    b. Financial information must always be accurate because it is the only source of information available to decision makers.

    c. The objectives of financial reporting stem primarily from the needs of external users who lack the authority to demand the information they want from management.

    d. The objectives are directed toward the common interests of many user groups, not just investors and creditors.

4. Which of the following ideas is expressed in _SFAC No. 8_?

    a. Financial reporting is not an end in itself but is intended to provide useful information to decision makers.

    b. The objectives of financial reporting are subject to changes in the economic, legal, political, and social environments.

    c. Information pertains to business entities rather than industries or the economy as a whole.

    d. Approximate rather than exact measures must sometimes be used.

    e. All of these ideas are expressed in _SFAC No. 8._

5. Which of the following statements related to the origins and traditions of auditing is the most appropriate description?

   a. Auditing has always followed a codified set of rules designed to detect and report fraud.

   b. Little judgment has traditionally been required on the auditor's part because either the numbers a firm reports are correct or they're not.

   c. Auditing evolved as a response to the needs of absentee owners of large corporations who had entrusted their money with managers they could not directly control.

   d. In the early 1920s auditors became unified in their efforts, and generally accepted auditing procedures were consistently followed to the point that financial statements were considered quite reliable.

6. Examples of how investors, creditors, and others commonly use reported earnings figures and the related information about the elements of financial statements include all of the following except

   a. estimating the number of employees the firm will hire during the next year.

   b. evaluating management's past performance.

   c. predicting future earnings.

   d. assessing the risks of future cash flows.

   e. all of the above are examples of how these data are used.

connect | ACCOUNTING   Exercises

All applicable Exercises are available with McGraw-Hill's *Connect*™ *Accounting*.

Exercise 1.1   Obtain an annual report Throughout this course, you will be asked to relate the material being studied to actual financial statements. After you complete this course, you will be able to use an organization's financial statements to make decisions and informed judgments about that organization. The purpose of this assignment is to provide the experience of obtaining a company's annual report. You may wish to refer to the financial statements in the report during the rest of the course.

Required:

Obtain the most recently issued annual report of a publicly owned manufacturing or merchandising corporation of your choice. Do not select a bank, insurance company, financial institution, or public utility. It would be appropriate to select a firm that you know something about or have an interest in.

Type www.firmname.com or use a search engine to locate your company's website and then scan your firm's home page for information about annual report ordering. If you don't see a direct link to *Investor Relations* or *Investors* on the home page, look for links such as *Our Company, About Us,* or *Site Map* that may lead you to *SEC Filings, Financial Information,* or *Annual Reports.* Most companies allow you to save or print an Adobe Acrobat version of their annual reports.

Exercise 1.2   Read and outline an article The accounting profession is frequently in the news, **LO 4** not always in the most positive light. The purpose of this assignment is to increase your awareness of an issue facing the profession.

Required:

Find, read, outline, and prepare to discuss a brief article from a general audience or business audience publication about accounting and/or the accounting profession. The article should have been published within the past eight months and should relate to accounting or the accounting profession in general; it should *not* be about some technical accounting issue. The appropriate search terms to use are "accountants," "accounting," and/or "accounting (specific topic)."

Your ideas about accounting Write a paragraph describing your perceptions of what accounting is all about and the work that accountants do.

Exercise 1.3
LO 3

Your expectations for this course Write a statement identifying the expectations you have for this course.

Exercise 1.4
LO 10

Identify factors in an ethical decision Jennifer Rankine is an accountant for a local manufacturing company. Jennifer's good friend, Mike Bortolotto, has been operating a retail sporting goods store for about a year. The store has been moderately successful, and Mike needs a bank loan to help finance the next stage of his store's growth. He has asked Jennifer to prepare financial statements that the banker will use to help decide whether to grant the loan. Mike has proposed that the fee he will pay for Jennifer's accounting work should be contingent upon his receiving the loan.

Exercise 1.5
LO 7

Required:

What factors should Jennifer consider when making her decision about whether to prepare the financial statements for Mike's store?

Identify information used in making an informed decision Charlie and Maribelle Brown have owned and operated a retail furniture store for more than 30 years. They have employed an independent CPA during this time to prepare various sales tax, payroll tax, and income tax returns, as well as financial statements for themselves and the bank from which they have borrowed money from time to time. They are considering selling the store but are uncertain about how to establish an asking price.

Exercise 1.6
LO 2

Required:

What type of information is likely to be included in the material prepared by the CPA that may help the Browns establish an asking price for the store?

Auditor independence Using the search engine you are most comfortable with, identify at least five sources on the general topic of auditor independence. Write a brief memo to provide an update on the current status of the auditor independence standard-setting process. The Business in Practice box on page 13 should serve as the starting point for this exercise. *Note: You might find it useful to contrast the opinions expressed by any of the Big 4 accounting firms to those expressed by nonaccounting professionals.*

Exercise 1.7
LO 6

Find financial information From the set of financial statements acquired for E1.1, determine the following:

Exercise 1.8

a. Who is the chief financial officer?
b. What are the names of the directors?

    c.   Which firm conducted the audit? Have the auditors reviewed the entire report?

    d.   What are the names of the financial statements provided?

    e.   How many pages of notes accompany the financial statements?

    f.   In addition to the financial statements, are there other reports? If so, what are they?

Answers to Self-Study Material

Matching: 1. a, 2. x, 3. i, 4. d, 5. u, 6. f, 7. b, 8. r, 9. t, 10. y

Multiple choice: 1. e, 2. a, 3. b, 4. e, 5. c, 6. a

2

Financial Statements and Accounting Concepts/Principles

Financial statements are the product of the financial accounting process. They are the means of communicating economic information about the entity to individuals who want to make decisions and informed judgments about the entity's financial position, results of operations, and cash flows. Although each of the four principal financial statements has a unique purpose, they are interrelated, and all must be considered in order to get a complete financial picture of the reporting entity.

Users cannot make meaningful interpretations of financial statement data without understanding the concepts and principles that relate to the entire financial accounting process. It is also important for users to understand that these concepts and principles are broad in nature; they do not constitute an inflexible set of rules, but instead serve as guidelines for the development of sound financial reporting practices.

LEARNING OBJECTIVES (LO)

After studying this chapter you should understand and be able to

LO 2-1 Explain what transactions are.

LO 2-2 Identify and explain the kind of information reported in each financial statement and describe how financial statements are related to each other.

LO 2-3 Explain the meaning and usefulness of the accounting equation.

LO 2-4 Explain the meaning of each of the captions on the financial statements illustrated in this chapter.

LO 2-5 Identify and explain the broad, generally accepted concepts and principles that apply to the accounting process.

LO 2-6 Discuss why investors must carefully consider cash flow information in conjunction with accrual accounting results.

LO 2-7 Identify and explain several limitations of financial statements.

LO 2-8 Describe what a corporation's annual report is and why it is issued.

Financial Statements

From Transactions to Financial Statements

An entity's financial statements are the end product of a process that starts with **transactions** between the entity and other organizations and individuals. Transactions are economic interchanges between entities: for example, a sale/purchase, or a receipt of cash by a borrower and the payment of cash by a lender. The flow from transactions to financial statements can be illustrated as follows:

LO 1
Explain what transactions are.

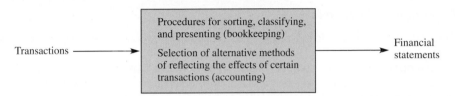

1. What does it mean to say that there has been an accounting transaction between you and your school? Give an example of such a transaction.

What Does It Mean?
Answer on page 56

Transactions are summarized in **accounts,** and accounts are further summarized in the financial statements. In this sense, transactions can be seen as the bricks that build the financial statements. By learning about the form, content, and relationships among financial statements in this chapter, you will better understand the process of building those results—bookkeeping and transaction analysis—described in Chapter 4 and subsequent chapters.

Current generally accepted accounting principles and auditing standards require that the financial statements of an entity show the following for the reporting period:

Financial position at the end of the period.

Earnings for the period.

Cash flows during the period.

Investments by and distributions to owners (i.e., stockholders) during the period.

The financial statements that satisfy these requirements are, respectively, the:

Balance sheet (or statement of financial position).

Income statement (or statement of earnings, or profit and loss statement, or statement of operations).

Statement of cash flows.

Statement of changes in stockholders' equity (or statement of changes in capital stock and/or statement of changes in retained earnings).

In addition to the financial statements themselves, the annual report will probably include several accompanying notes (sometimes called the financial review) that include explanations of the accounting policies and detailed information about many of the amounts and captions shown on the financial statements. These notes are designed to assist the reader of the financial statements by disclosing as much relevant supplementary information as the company and its auditors deem necessary and appropriate. For Campbell Soup Company, the notes to the 2011 financial statements are shown in the "Notes to Consolidated Financial Statements" section on pages 715–750 of the annual report in the appendix. One of this text's objectives is to enable you to read, interpret, and understand financial statement footnotes. Chapter 10 describes the notes to the financial statements in detail.

Business in
Practice

Organizing a Business

There are three principal forms of business organization: proprietorship, partnership, and corporation.

A **proprietorship** is an activity conducted by an individual. Operating as a proprietorship is the easiest way to get started in a business activity. Other than the possibility of needing a local license, there aren't any formal prerequisites to beginning operations. Besides being easy to start, a proprietorship has the advantage, according to many people, that the owner is his or her own boss. A principal disadvantage of the proprietorship is that the owner's liability for business debts is not limited by the assets of the business. For example, if the business fails, and if, after all available business assets have been used to pay business debts, the business creditors are still owed money, the owner's personal assets can be claimed by business creditors. Another disadvantage is that the individual proprietor may have difficulty raising the money needed to provide the capital base that will be required if the business is to grow substantially. Because of the ease of getting started, every year many business activities begin as proprietorships.

The **partnership** is essentially a group of proprietors who have banded together. The unlimited liability characteristic of the proprietorship still exists, but with several partners the ability of the firm to raise capital may be improved. Income earned from partnership activities is taxed at the individual partner level; the partnership itself is not a tax-paying entity. Accountants, attorneys, and other professionals frequently operate their firms as partnerships. In recent years, many large professional partnerships, including the Big 4 accounting firms, have been operating under *limited liability partnership* (LLP) rules, which shield individual partners from unlimited personal liability.

Most large businesses, and many new businesses, use the corporate form of organization. Note that "Inc." in the name of our example business, Main Street Stores, Inc., is an abbreviation for *incorporated* and means that the firm was legally organized as a corporation. The owners of the corporation are called **stockholders** (or shareholders). They have invested funds in the corporation and received shares of **stock** as evidence of their ownership. Stockholders' liability is limited to the amount invested; creditors cannot seek recovery of losses from the personal assets of stockholders. Large amounts of capital can frequently be raised by selling shares of stock to many individuals. It is also possible for all of the stock of a corporation to be owned by a single individual. A stockholder can usually sell his or her shares to other investors or buy more shares from other stockholders if a change in ownership interest is desired. A **corporation** is formed by having a charter and bylaws prepared and registered with the appropriate office in 1 of the 50 states. The cost of forming a corporation is usually greater than that of starting a proprietorship or forming a partnership. A major disadvantage of the corporate form of business is that corporations are taxpaying entities. Thus, any income distributed to stockholders has been taxed first as income of the corporation and then is taxed a second time as income of the individual stockholders.

A form of organization that has been approved in many states is the *limited liability company* (LLC). For accounting and legal purposes, this type of organization is treated as a corporation even though some of the formalities of the corporate form of organization are not present. Stockholders of small corporations may find that banks and major creditors usually require the personal guarantees of the principal stockholders as a condition for granting credit to the corporation. Therefore, the limited liability of the corporate form may be, in the case of small corporations, more theoretical than real.

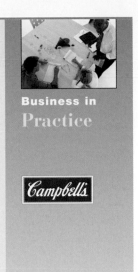

Fiscal Year

A firm's **fiscal year** is the annual period used for reporting to owners, the government, and others. Many firms select the calendar year as their fiscal year, but other 12-month periods can also be selected. Some firms select a reporting period ending on a date when inventories will be relatively low or business activity will be slow because this facilitates the process of preparing financial statements.

Many firms select fiscal periods that relate to the pace of their business activity. Food retailers, for example, have a weekly operating cycle, and many of these firms select a 52-week fiscal year (with a 53-week fiscal year every five or six years so their year-end remains near the same date every year). Campbell Soup Company has adopted this strategy; note, on page 715 in the appendix, that Campbell's fiscal year ends on the Sunday nearest July 31 each year. (The next 53-week year will end on August 3, 2014).

For internal reporting purposes, many firms use periods other than the month (e.g., 13 four-week periods). Such firms wish to maintain the same number of operating days in each period so that comparisons between the same periods of different years can be made without having to consider differences in the number of operating days in the respective periods.

Financial Statements Illustrated

To illustrate financial statements, we present an example of what they might look like for a simple retail business. Main Street Store, Inc., was organized as a corporation and began business during September 2013 (see Business in Practice—Organizing a Business). The company buys clothing and accessories from distributors and manufacturers and sells these items from a rented building. The financial statements of Main Street Store, Inc., at August 31, 2014, and for the fiscal year (see Business in Practice—Fiscal Year) ended on that date are presented in Exhibits 2-1 through 2-4.

As you look at these financial statements, you will probably have several questions concerning the nature of specific accounts and how the numbers are computed. For now, concentrate on the explanations and definitions that are appropriate and inescapable, and notice especially the characteristics of each financial statement. Many of your questions about specific accounts will be answered in subsequent chapters that explain the individual statements and their components in detail.

LO 2
Identify and explain the kind of information reported in each financial statement and describe how the statements are related to each other.

Explanations and Definitions

Balance Sheet. The **balance sheet** is a listing of the organization's assets, liabilities, and stockholders' equity (often referred to simply as *owners' equity*) *at a point in time.* In this sense, the balance sheet is like a snapshot of the organization's financial position, frozen at a specific point in time. The balance sheet is sometimes called the **statement of financial position** because it summarizes the entity's resources (assets), obligations (liabilities), and owners' claims (stockholders' equity). The balance sheet for Main Street Store, Inc., at August 31, 2014, the end of the firm's first year of operations, is illustrated in Exhibit 2-1.

Notice the two principal sections of the balance sheet that are shown side by side: (1) assets and (2) liabilities and stockholders' equity. Observe that the dollar total of $320,000 is the same for each side. This equality is sometimes referred to as the

LO 3
Explain the meaning and usefulness of the accounting equation.

Exhibit 2-1

Balance Sheet

MAIN STREET STORE, INC.
Balance Sheet
August 31, 2014

Assets		Liabilities and Stockholders' Equity	
Current assets:		Current liabilities:	
Cash	$ 34,000	Accounts payable	$ 35,000
Accounts receivable	80,000	Other accrued liabilities	12,000
Merchandise inventory	170,000	Short-term debt	20,000
Total current assets	$284,000	Total current liabilities	$ 67,000
Plant and equipment:		Long-term debt	50,000
Equipment	40,000	Total liabilities	$117,000
Less: Accumulated		Stockholders' equity	203,000
depreciation	(4,000)	Total liabilities and	
Total assets	$320,000	stockholders' equity	$320,000

accounting equation or the **balance sheet equation.** It is the equality, or balance, of these two amounts from which the term *balance sheet* is derived.

$$\text{Assets} = \text{Liabilities} + \text{Stockholders' equity}$$
$$\$320,000 = \$117,000 + \$203,000$$

Now we will provide some of those appropriate and inescapable definitions and explanations:

"**Assets** are probable future economic benefits obtained or controlled by a particular entity as a result of past transactions or events."[1] In brief, assets represent the amount of resources controlled (which ordinarily means owned) by the entity. Assets are often tangible; they can be seen and handled (like cash, merchandise inventory, or equipment), or evidence of their existence can be observed (such as a customer's acknowledgment of receipt of merchandise and the implied promise to pay the amount due when agreed upon—an account receivable).

"**Liabilities** are probable future sacrifices of economic benefits arising from present obligations of a particular entity to transfer assets or provide services to other entities in the future as a result of past transactions or events."[2] In brief, liabilities are amounts *owed* to other entities. For example, the accounts payable arose because suppliers shipped merchandise to Main Street Store, Inc., and this merchandise will be paid for at some point in the future. In other words, the supplier has a "claim" against the merchandise until it is paid for and thus has become a creditor of the firm by supplying merchandise on account.

Stockholders' equity (often referred to as **owners' equity**) is the ownership right of the stockholder(s) of the entity in the assets that remain after deducting the liabilities. (A car or house owner refers to his or her **equity** as the market value of the car or house less the loan or mortgage balance.) Stockholders' equity is sometimes

---

[1] FASB, *Statement of Financial Accounting Concepts No. 6*, "Elements of Financial Statements" (Stamford, CT, 1985), para. 25. Copyright © by the Financial Accounting Standards Board, High Ridge Park, Stamford, CT 06905, U.S.A. Quoted with permission. Copies of the complete document are available from the FASB.

[2] Ibid., para. 35.

referred to as **net assets.** This can be shown by rearranging the basic accounting equation:

$$\text{Assets} - \text{Liabilities} = \text{Stockholders' equity}$$
$$\text{Net assets} = \text{Stockholders' equity}$$

Another term sometimes used when referring to stockholders' equity is **net worth.** However, this term is misleading because it implies that the net assets are "worth" the amount reported on the balance sheet as stockholders' equity. *Financial statements prepared in accordance with generally accepted accounting principles do not purport to show the current market value of the entity's assets, except in a few restricted cases.*

---

2. What does it mean to refer to a balance sheet for the year ended August 31, 2014?

3. What does it mean when a balance sheet has been prepared for an organization?

What Does It Mean?

Answers on pages 56–57

Each of the individual assets and liabilities reported by Main Street Stores, Inc., warrants a brief explanation. Each account (*caption* in the financial statements) will be discussed in more detail in later chapters. Your task at this point is to achieve a broad understanding of each account and to make sense of its classification as an asset or liability.

Cash represents cash on hand and in the bank or banks used by Main Street Store, Inc. If the firm had made any temporary cash investments to earn interest, these marketable securities probably would be shown as a separate asset because these funds are not as readily available as cash.

Accounts receivable represent amounts due from customers who have purchased merchandise on credit and who have agreed to pay within a specified period or when billed by Main Street Store, Inc.

Merchandise inventory represents the cost to Main Street Store, Inc., of the merchandise that it has acquired but not yet sold.

Equipment represents the cost to Main Street Store, Inc., of the display cases, racks, shelving, and other store equipment purchased and installed in the rented building in which it operates. The building is not shown as an asset because Main Street Store, Inc., does not own it.

Accumulated depreciation represents the portion of the cost of the equipment that is estimated to have been used up in the process of operating the business. Note that one-tenth ($4,000/$40,000) of the cost of the equipment has been depreciated. From this relationship, one might assume that the equipment is estimated to have a useful life of 10 years because this is the balance sheet at the end of the firm's first year of operations. **Depreciation** in accounting is the process of spreading the cost of an asset over its useful life to the entity—it is *not* an attempt to recognize the economic loss in value of an asset because of its age or use.

Accounts payable represent amounts owed to suppliers of merchandise inventory that was purchased on credit and will be paid within a specific period of time.

Other **accrued liabilities** represent amounts owed to various creditors, including any wages owed to employees for services provided to Main Street Store, Inc., through August 31, 2014, the balance sheet date.

LO 4

Explain the meaning of each of the captions on the financial statements illustrated in Exhibits 2-1 through 2-4.

Short-term debt represents amounts borrowed, probably from banks, that will be repaid within one year of the balance sheet date.

Long-term debt represents amounts borrowed from banks or others that will not be repaid within one year from the balance sheet date.

Stockholders' equity, shown as a single amount in Exhibit 2-1, is explained in more detail later in this chapter in the discussion of the statement of changes in stockholders' equity.

Notice that in Exhibit 2-1 some assets and liabilities are classified as "current." **Current assets** are cash and other assets that are likely to be converted into cash or used to benefit the entity within one year, and **current liabilities** are those liabilities that are likely to be paid with cash within one year of the balance sheet date. In this example, it is expected that the accounts receivable from the customers of Main Street Store, Inc., will be collected within a year and that the merchandise inventory will be sold within a year of the balance sheet date. This time-frame classification is important and, as will be explained later, is used in assessing the entity's ability to pay its obligations when they come due.

To summarize, the balance sheet is a listing of the entity's assets, liabilities, and stockholders' equity. A balance sheet can be prepared as of any date but is most frequently prepared as of the end of a fiscal reporting period (e.g., month-end or year-end). The balance sheet as of the end of one period is the balance sheet as of the beginning of the next period. This can be illustrated on a time line as follows:

8/31/13	Fiscal 2014	8/31/14
Balance sheet		Balance sheet
A = L + SE		A = L + SE

On the time line, Fiscal 2014 refers to the 12 months during which the entity carried out its economic activities.

Income Statement.   The principal purpose of the **income statement,** or **statement of earnings,** or **profit and loss statement,** or **statement of operations,** is to answer the question "Did the entity operate at a **profit** for the period of time under consideration?" The question is answered by first reporting **revenues** from the entity's operating activities (such as selling merchandise) and then subtracting the **expenses** incurred in generating those revenues and operating the entity. **Gains** and **losses** are also reported on the income statement. Gains and losses result from nonoperating activities, rather than from the day-to-day operating activities that generate revenues and expenses. The income statement reports results for *a period of time,* in contrast to the balance sheet focus on a single date. In this sense, the income statement is more like a movie than a snapshot; it depicts the results of activities that have occurred during a period of time.

The income statement for Main Street Store, Inc., for the year ended August 31, 2014, is presented in Exhibit 2-2. Notice that the statement starts with **net sales** (which are revenues) and that the various expenses are subtracted to arrive at **net income** in total and per share of common stock outstanding. Net income is the profit for the period; if expenses exceed net sales, a net loss results. The reasons for reporting earnings per share of common stock outstanding, and the calculation of this amount, will be explained in Chapter 9.

Now look at the individual captions on the income statement. Each warrants a brief explanation, which will be expanded in subsequent chapters. Your task at this point is to make sense of how each item influences the determination of net income.

Net sales represent the amount of sales of merchandise to customers, less the amount of sales originally recorded but canceled because the merchandise was

Exhibit 2-2

Income Statement

MAIN STREET STORE, INC. Income Statement For the Year Ended August 31, 2014	
Net sales	$1,200,000
Cost of goods sold	850,000
Gross profit	$ 350,000
Selling, general, and administrative expenses	311,000
Income from operations	$ 39,000
Interest expense	9,000
Income before taxes	$ 30,000
Income taxes	12,000
Net income	$ 18,000
Earnings per share of common stock outstanding	$ 1.80

subsequently returned by customers for one reason or another (wrong size, spouse didn't want it, and so on). The sales amount is frequently called *sales revenue,* or just *revenue.* Revenue results from selling a product or service to a customer.

Cost of goods sold represents the total cost of merchandise removed from inventory and delivered to customers as a result of sales. This is shown as a separate expense because of its significance and because of the desire to show gross profit as a separate item. Frequently used synonyms are *cost of sales* and *cost of products sold.*

Gross profit is the difference between net sales and cost of goods sold and represents the seller's maximum amount of "cushion" from which all other expenses of operating the business must be met before it is possible to have net income. Gross profit (sometimes referred to as *gross margin*) is shown as a separate item because it is significant to both management and nonmanagement readers of the income statement. The uses made of this amount will be explained in subsequent chapters.

Selling, general, and administrative expenses represent the operating expenses of the entity. In some income statements, these expenses will not be lumped together as in Exhibit 2-2 but will be reported separately for each of several operating expense categories, such as wages, advertising, and depreciation.

Income from operations represents one of the most important measures of the firm's activities. Income from operations (or *operating income* or *earnings from operations*) can be related to the assets available to the firm to obtain a useful measure of management's performance. A method of doing this is explained in Chapter 3.

Interest expense represents the cost of using borrowed funds. This item is reported separately because it is a function of how assets are financed, not how assets are used.

Income taxes are shown after all of the other income statement items have been reported because income taxes (often captioned as *income tax expense* or *provision for income taxes*) are a function of the firm's income before taxes.

Earnings per share of common stock outstanding is reported as a separate item at the bottom of the income statement because of its significance in evaluating the market value of a share of common stock. This measure, which is often referred to simply as *EPS,* will be explained in more detail in Chapter 9.

To review, the income statement summarizes the entity's income- (or loss-) producing activities *for a period of time.* Transactions that affect the income statement will also affect the balance sheet. For example, a sale made for cash increases sales revenue on the income statement and increases cash, an asset on the balance sheet. Likewise, wages earned by employees during the last week of the current year to be paid early in the next year are an expense of the current year. These wages will be deducted from revenues in the income statement and are considered a liability reported on the balance sheet at the end of the year. Thus, the income statement is a link between the balance sheets at the beginning and end of the year. How this link is made is explained in the next section, which describes the statement of changes in stockholders' equity. The time line presented earlier can be expanded as follows:

8/31/13	Fiscal 2014	8/31/14
Balance sheet	Income statement for the year	Balance sheet
	Revenues	
	− Expenses	
A = L + SE	Net income	A = L + SE

Statement of Changes in Stockholders' Equity. The **statement of changes in stockholders' equity** (sometimes called the *statement of changes in owners' equity*), or **statement of changes in capital stock,** or **statement of changes in retained earnings,** like the income statement, has a *period of time* orientation. This statement shows the detail of stockholders' equity and explains the changes that occurred in the components of stockholders' equity during the year.

Exhibit 2-3 illustrates this statement for Main Street Store, Inc., for the year ended August 31, 2014. Remember that these are the results of Main Street Store's first year of operations, so the beginning-of-the-year balances are zero. On subsequent years' statements, the beginning-of-the-year amount is the ending balance from the prior year.

Notice in Exhibit 2-3 that stockholders' equity is made up of two principal components: **paid-in capital** and **retained earnings.** These items are briefly explained here and are discussed in more detail in Chapter 8.

Paid-in capital represents the total amount invested in the entity by the owners—in this case, the stockholders. When the stock issued to the owners has a **par value** (see Business in Practice—Par Value), there will usually be two categories of paid-in capital: common stock and additional paid-in capital.

Common stock reflects the number of shares authorized by the corporation's charter, the number of shares that have been issued to stockholders, and the number of shares

Exhibit 2-3

Statement of Changes in Stockholders' Equity

MAIN STREET STORE, INC.
Statement of Changes in Stockholders' Equity
For the Year Ended August 31, 2014

Paid-In Capital:		
Beginning balance	$	–0–
Common stock, par value, $10; 50,000 shares authorized,		
10,000 shares issued and outstanding.		100,000
Additional paid-in capital		90,000
Balance, August 31, 2014		$190,000
Retained Earnings:		
Beginning balance	$	–0–
Net income for the year		18,000
Less: Cash dividends of $.50 per share.		(5,000)
Balance, August 31, 2014		$ 13,000
Total stockholders' equity.		$203,000

Par Value

Par value is a relic from the past that has, for all practical purposes, lost its significance. The par value of common stock is an arbitrary value assigned when the corporation is organized. Par value bears no relationship to the fair market value of a share of stock (except that a corporation may not issue its stock for less than par value). Many firms issue stock with a par value of a nominal amount, such as $1. Campbell Soup Company's capital stock has a par value of $0.0375 per share. (See page 712 in the appendix.) Because of investor confusion about the significance of par value, most states now permit corporations to issue no-par-value stock. Some state laws permit a firm to assign a stated value to its no-par-value stock, in which case the stated value operates as a par value.

Business in *Practice*

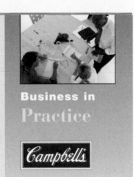

that are held by the stockholders. When the common stock has a par value or stated value, the amount shown for common stock in the financial statements will always be the par value or stated value multiplied by the number of shares issued. If the common stock does not have a par value or stated value, the amount shown for common stock in the financial statements will be the total amount invested by the stockholders.

Additional paid-in capital is the difference between the total amount invested by the stockholders and the par value or stated value of the stock. (If no-par-value stock without a stated value is issued, there won't be any additional paid-in capital because the total amount paid in, or invested, by the stockholders will be shown as common stock.)

Retained earnings is the second principal category of stockholders' equity, and it represents the cumulative net income of the entity that has been retained for use in the business. **Dividends** are distributions of earnings that have been made to the stockholders, so these reduce retained earnings. If retained earnings has a negative balance because cumulative losses and dividends have exceeded cumulative net income, this part of stockholders' equity is referred to as an *accumulated deficit,* or simply *deficit.*

Note that in Exhibit 2-3 the net income for the year of $18,000 added to retained earnings is the amount of net income reported in Exhibit 2-2. The retained earnings section of the statement of changes in stockholders' equity is where the link (known as *articulation*) between the balance sheet and income statement is made. The time-line model is thus expanded and modified as follows:

Notice that the total stockholders' equity reported in Exhibit 2-3 agrees with the stockholders' equity shown on the balance sheet in Exhibit 2-1. Most balance sheets include the amount of common stock, additional paid-in capital, and retained earnings within the stockholders' equity section. Changes that occur in these components of stockholders' equity are likely to be shown in a separate statement so that users of the financial statements can learn what caused these important balance sheet elements to change.

Statement of Cash Flows.   The purpose of the **statement of cash flows** is to identify the sources and uses of cash during the year. This objective is accomplished by reporting the changes in all of the other balance sheet items. Because of the equality that exists between assets and liabilities plus stockholders' equity, the total of the changes in every other asset and each liability and element of stockholders' equity will equal the change in cash. The statement of cash flows is described in detail in Chapter 9. For now, make sense of the three principal activity groups that cause cash to change, and see how the amounts on this statement relate to the balance sheet in Exhibit 2-1.

The statement of cash flows for Main Street Store, Inc., for the year ended August 31, 2014, is illustrated in Exhibit 2-4. Notice that this statement, like the income statement and statement of changes in stockholders' equity, is *for a period of time.* Notice also the three activity categories: operating activities, investing activities, and financing activities.

Cash flows from operating activities are shown first, and net income is the starting point for this measure of cash flow. Using net income also directly relates the income statement (see Exhibit 2-2) to the statement of cash flows. Next, reconciling items are considered (i.e., items that must be added to or subtracted from net income to arrive at cash flows from operating activities).

Depreciation expense is added back to net income because, even though it was deducted as an expense in determining net income, *depreciation expense did not*

Exhibit 2-4	
Statement of Cash Flows	

MAIN STREET STORE, INC. **Statement of Cash Flows** **For the Year Ended August 31, 2014**	
Cash Flows from Operating Activities:	
Net income.	$ 18,000
Add (deduct) items not affecting cash:	
Depreciation expense	4,000
Increase in accounts receivable	(80,000)
Increase in merchandise inventory	(170,000)
Increase in current liabilities	67,000
Net cash used by operating activities.	$(161,000)
Cash Flows from Investing Activities:	
Cash paid for equipment	$ (40,000)
Cash Flows from Financing Activities:	
Cash received from issue of long-term debt	$ 50,000
Cash received from sale of common stock	190,000
Payment of cash dividend on common stock	(5,000)
Net cash provided by financing activities	$ 235,000
Net increase in cash for the year.	$ 34,000

require the use of cash. Remember—depreciation in accounting is the process of spreading the cost of an asset over its estimated useful life.

The increase in accounts receivable is deducted because this reflects sales revenues, included in net income, that have not yet been collected in cash.

The increase in merchandise inventory is deducted because cash was spent to acquire the increase in inventory.

The increase in current liabilities is added because cash has not yet been paid for this amount of products and services that have been received during the current fiscal period.

Cash flows from investing activities show the cash used to purchase long-lived assets. You should find the increase in equipment in the balance sheet (Exhibit 2-1), which shows the cost of the equipment owned at August 31, 2014. Because this is the first year of the firm's operations, the equipment purchase required the use of $40,000 during the year.

Cash flows from financing activities include amounts raised from the sale of long-term debt and common stock, and dividends paid on common stock. You should find each of these financing amounts in the balance sheet (Exhibit 2-1) or the statement of changes in stockholders' equity (Exhibit 2-3). For example, the $190,000 received from the sale of stock is shown on the statement of changes in stockholders' equity (Exhibit 2-3) as the increase in paid-in capital during the year.

The net increase in cash for the year of $34,000 is the amount of cash in the August 31, 2014, balance sheet. Check this out. This should make sense because the firm started its business during September 2013, so it had no cash to begin with.

The statement of cash flows results in a further expansion and modification of the time-line model:

What Does It Mean?

Answers on page 57

4. What does it mean when a stockholder says that she needs to look at her firm's set of four financial statements to fully understand its financial position and results of operations?

5. What does it mean when a company that has a high net income doesn't have enough cash to pay its bills?

Comparative Statements in Subsequent Years

The financial statements presented on the previous pages for Main Street Store, Inc., show data as of August 31, 2014, and for the year then ended. Because this was the first year of the firm's operations, comparative financial statements are not possible. In subsequent years, however, comparative statements for the current year and the prior year should be presented so that users of the data can more easily spot changes in the firm's financial position and in its results of operations. Some companies present data for two prior years in their financial statements. Most companies will include selected data from their balance sheets and income statements for at least 5 years, and sometimes for up to 25 years, as supplementary information in their annual report to stockholders. Campbell Soup Company's five-year selected financial data, which appear on page 709 in the appendix, illustrate the firm's consistency and financial stability.

Illustration of Financial Statement Relationships

Exhibit 2-5 uses the financial statements of Main Street Store, Inc., to illustrate the financial statement relationships just discussed. Note that in Exhibit 2-5, the August 31, 2013, balance sheet has no amounts because Main Street Store, Inc., started business in September 2013. As you study this exhibit, note especially that net income for the year was an increase in retained earnings and is one of the reasons retained earnings changed during the year.

In subsequent chapters, the relationship between the balance sheet and income statement will be presented using the following diagram:

Balance sheet	Income Statement
Assets = Liabilities + Stockholders' equity	← Net Income = Revenues − Expenses

The arrow from net income in the income statement to stockholders' equity in the balance sheet indicates that net income affects retained earnings, which is a component of stockholders' equity.

The following examples also illustrate the relationships within and between the principal financial statements. Using the August 31, 2014, Main Street Store, Inc., data for assets and liabilities in the balance sheet equation of A = L + SE, stockholders' equity at August 31, 2014, can be calculated:

$$A = L + SE$$
$$\$320,000 = \$117,000 + SE$$
$$\$203,000 = SE$$

Remember, other terms for stockholders' equity are *owners' equity* and *net assets*. This is shown clearly in the previous calculation because stockholders' equity is the difference between assets and liabilities.

Exhibit 2-5 Financial Statement Relationships

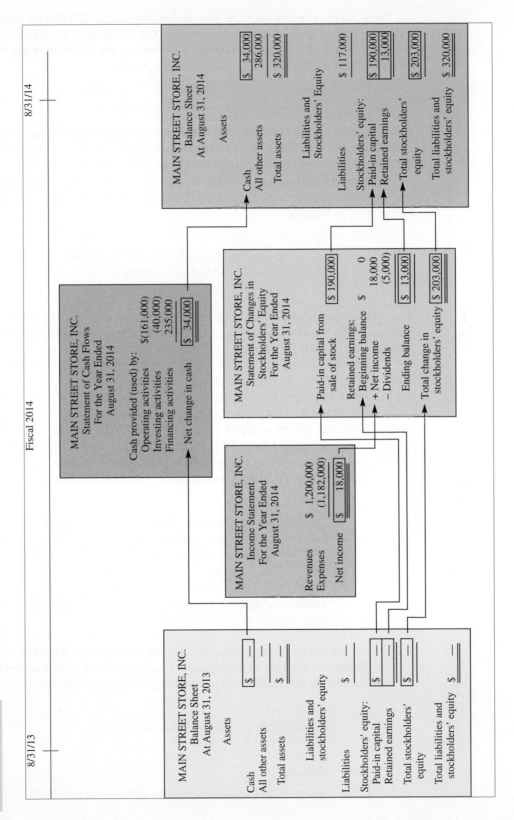

Now suppose that during the year ended August 31, 2015, total assets increased $10,000, and total liabilities decreased $3,000. What was stockholders' equity at the end of the year? There are two ways of solving the problem. First, focus on the changes in the elements of the balance sheet equation:

$$A \quad = \quad L \quad + SE$$
Change: $+ 10,000 = -3,000 + ?$

It is clear that for the equation to stay in balance, stockholders' equity must have increased by $13,000. Because stockholders' equity was $203,000 at the beginning of the year, it must have been $216,000 at the end of the year.

The second approach to solving the problem is to calculate the amount of assets and liabilities at the end of the year and then solve for stockholders' equity at the end of the year, as follows:

$$A \quad = \quad L \quad + \quad SE$$
Beginning: $320,000 = 117,000 + 203,000$
Change: $\quad +10,000 = -3,000 + \quad ?$
End: $\quad 330,000 = 114,000 + \quad ?$

The ending stockholders' equity or net assets is $330,000 - \$114,000 = \$216,000$. Because ending stockholders' equity is $216,000, it increased $13,000 during the year from August 31, 2014, to August 31, 2015.

Assume that during the year ended August 31, 2015, the stockholders invested an additional $8,000 in the firm and that dividends of $6,000 were declared. How much net income did the firm have for the year ended August 31, 2015? Recall that net income is one of the items that affects the retained earnings component of stockholders' equity. What else affects retained earnings? That's right—dividends. Because stockholders' equity increased from $203,000 to $216,000 during the year, and the items causing that change were net income, dividends, and the additional investment by the stockholders, the amount of net income can be calculated as follows:

Stockholders' equity, beginning of year............	$203,000
Increase in paid-in capital from additional investment by stockholders..................	8,000
Net income..................................	?
Dividends	−6,000
Stockholders' equity, end of year	$216,000

Solving for the unknown shows that net income was equal to $11,000.

An alternative solution to determine net income for the year involves focusing on just the *changes* in stockholders' equity during the year, as follows:

Increase in paid-in capital from additional investment by stockholders....................	$ 8,000
Net income....................................	?
Dividends	−6,000
Change in stockholders' equity for the year	$13,000

Again, solving for the unknown, we find that net income was equal to $11,000.

The important points to remember here are:

- The balance sheet shows the amounts of assets, liabilities, and stockholders' equity at a point in time.
- The balance sheet equation must always be in balance.
- The income statement shows net income for a period of time.
- The retained earnings component of stockholders' equity changes over a period of time as a result of the firm's net income (or loss) and dividends for that period of time.

---

6. What does it mean to say that the balance sheet must be in balance after every transaction even though a lot of transactions affect the income statement?

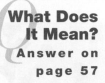

What Does It Mean?
Answer on page 57

Accounting Concepts and Principles

To understand the kinds of decisions and informed judgments that can be made from the financial statements, it is appropriate to understand some of the broad concepts and principles of accounting that have become generally accepted for financial accounting and reporting purposes. The terms *concepts* and *principles* are used interchangeably here. Some of these ideas relate directly to the financial accounting concepts introduced in Chapter 1, and others relate to the broader notion of generally accepted accounting principles. Again, it is important to recognize that these concepts and principles are more like practices that have been generally agreed upon over time than hard-and-fast rules or basic laws such as those encountered in the physical sciences.

These concepts and principles can be related to the basic model of the flow of data from transactions to financial statements illustrated earlier and shown here:

LO 5

Identify and explain the broad, generally accepted concepts and principles that apply to the accounting process.

This chapter, titled "Financial Statements and Accounting Concepts/Principles," presents two sets of interrelated topics that are themselves related. As illustrated in Exhibit 2-5, individual financial statements are most meaningful when considered as part of an integrated set of financial statements presented by a firm. Likewise, the individual concepts and principles discussed in this section of the chapter are most meaningful when considered in relation to each other. The challenge that lies ahead (in the financial accounting part of this book) is for you to see logical connections between the end-product financial statements and the underlying concepts and principles upon which they are based. Our suggestion? Bookmark Exhibit 2-5 on page 45 and the concepts/principles model shown on page 47. Learn the terminology presented in each of these illustrations and refer back to these pages as you encounter difficulties in subsequent chapters. You will be surprised at how far this basic knowledge will carry you.

Business in
Practice

Parent and Subsidiary Corporations

It is not unusual for a corporation that wants to expand its operations to form a separate corporation to carry out its plans. In such a case, the original corporation owns all of the stock of the new corporation; it has become the "parent" of a **"subsidiary."** One parent may have several subsidiaries, and the subsidiaries themselves may be parents of subsidiaries. It is not necessary for the parent to own 100 percent of the stock of another corporation for the parent–subsidiary relationship to exist. If one corporation owns more than half of the stock of another, it is presumed that the majority owner can exercise enough control to create a parent–subsidiary relationship. When a subsidiary is not wholly owned, the other stockholders of the subsidiary are referred to as *minority stockholders,* and their ownership rights are referred to as the *noncontrolling interest.*

In most instances, the financial statements issued by the parent corporation will include the assets, liabilities, revenues, expenses, and gains and losses of the subsidiaries. Financial statements that reflect the financial position, results of operations, and cash flows of a parent and one or more subsidiaries are called *consolidated financial statements.*

The fact that one corporation is a subsidiary of another is frequently transparent to the general public. For example, Frito-Lay Company, Quaker Oats Company, and Tropicana Products, Inc., are all subsidiaries of PepsiCo Inc., but that relationship is usually irrelevant to consumers of each company's products.

Concepts/Principles Related to the Entire Model

The basic accounting equation described earlier in this chapter is the mechanical key to the entire financial accounting process because the equation must be in balance after every transaction has been recorded in the accounting records. The method for recording transactions and maintaining this balance will be illustrated in Chapter 4.

Accounting entity refers to the entity for which the financial statements are being prepared. The entity can be a proprietorship, partnership, corporation, or even a group of corporations (see Business in Practice—Parent and Subsidiary Corporations). The entity for which the accounting is being done is defined by the accountant; even though the entities may be related (such as an individual and the business she owns), the accounting is done for the defined entity.

The **going concern concept** refers to the presumption that the entity will continue to operate in the future—that it is not being liquidated. This continuity assumption is necessary because the amounts shown on the balance sheet for various assets do not reflect the liquidation value of those assets.

Concepts/Principles Related to Transactions

In the United States, the dollar is the *unit of measurement* for all transactions. No adjustment is made for changes in the purchasing power of the dollar. No attempt is made to reflect qualitative economic factors in the measurement of transactions.

The *cost principle* refers to the fact that transactions are recorded at their original (historical) cost to the entity as measured in dollars. For example, if a parcel of land were purchased by a firm for $8,600 even though an appraisal showed the land to be worth $10,000, the purchase transaction would be reflected in the accounting records and financial statements at its cost of $8,600. If the land is still owned and being used 15 years later, even though its market value has increased to $80,000, it continues to be reported in the balance sheet at its original cost of $8,600.

Objectivity refers to accountants' desire to have a given transaction recorded the same way in all situations. This objective is facilitated by using the dollar as the unit of measurement and by applying the cost principle. As previously stressed, there are transactions for which the exercise of professional judgment could result in alternative recording results. These alternatives will be illustrated in subsequent chapters.

Concepts/Principles Related to Bookkeeping Procedures and the Accounting Process

These concepts/principles relate to the *accounting period*—that is, the period of time selected for reporting results of operations and changes in financial position. Financial position will be reported at the end of this period (and the balance sheet at the beginning of the period will probably be included with the financial statements). For most entities, the accounting period will be one year in length.

Matching revenue and expense is necessary if the results of the firm's operations are to reflect accurately its economic activities during the period. The **matching concept** does not mean that revenues and expenses for a period are equal. Revenue is not earned without effort (businesses do not receive birthday gifts), and expenses are the measure of the economic efforts exerted to generate revenues. A fair presentation of the results of a firm's operations during a period of time requires that all expenses incurred in generating that period's revenues be deducted from the revenues earned. This results in an accurate measure of the net income or net loss for the period. This seems like common sense, but as we shall see, there are alternative methods of determining some of the expenses to be recognized in any given period. This concept of matching revenue and expense is very important and will be referred to again and again as accounting practices are discussed in the following chapters.

Revenue is recognized at the time of sale, which is when title to the product being sold passes from the seller to the buyer or when the services involved in the transaction have been performed. Passing of legal ownership (title) is the critical event, not the cash payment from buyer to seller.

Accrual accounting uses the *accrual concept* and results in recognizing revenue at the point of sale and recognizing expenses as they are incurred, even though the cash receipt or payment occurs at another time or in another accounting period. Thus, many activities of the firm will involve two transactions: one that recognizes the revenue or expense and the other that reflects the receipt or payment of cash. The use of accrual procedures accomplishes much of the matching of revenues and expenses because most transactions between business firms (and between many firms and individuals) involve purchase/sale at one point in time and cash payment/receipt at some other point.

LO 6

Discuss why investors must carefully consider cash flow information in conjunction with accrual accounting results.

The financial statement user relies on these concepts and principles related to the accounting period when making judgments and informed decisions about an entity's financial position and results of operations.

What Does It Mean?

Answers on page 57

7. What does matching of revenue and expense in the income statement mean?
8. What does the accrual concept mean?

Concepts/Principles Related to Financial Statements

Consistency in financial reporting is essential if meaningful trend comparisons are to be made using an entity's financial statements for several years. It is inappropriate to change from one generally accepted alternative of accounting for a particular type of transaction to another generally accepted method, unless both the fact that the change has been made and the effect of the change on the financial statements are explicitly described in the financial statements or the accompanying notes to the financial statements.

Full disclosure means that the financial statements and notes should include all necessary information to prevent a reasonably astute user of the financial statements from being misled. This is a tall order—one that the Securities and Exchange Commission (SEC) has helped to define over the years. This requirement for full disclosure is one reason that the notes to the financial statements are usually considered an integral part of the financial statements.

Materiality means that absolute exactness, even if that idea could be defined, is not necessary in the amounts shown in the financial statements. Because of the numerous estimates involved in accounting, amounts reported in financial statements may be approximate, but they will not be "wrong" enough to be misleading. The financial statements of publicly owned corporations usually show amounts rounded to the nearest thousand, hundred thousand, or even million dollars. This rounding does not impair the informational content of the financial statements and probably makes them easier to read. A management concept related to materiality is the cost–benefit relationship. Just as a manager would not spend $500 to get $300 worth of information, the incremental benefit of increased accuracy in accounting estimates is frequently not worth the cost of achieving the increased accuracy.

Conservatism in accounting relates to making judgments and estimates that result in lower profits and asset valuation estimates rather than higher profits and asset valuation estimates. Accountants try to avoid wishful thinking or pie-in-the-sky estimates that could result in overstating profits for a current period. This is not to say that accountants always look at issues from a gloom-and-doom viewpoint; rather, they seek to be realistic but are conservative when in doubt.

Limitations of Financial Statements

LO 7

Identify and explain several limitations of financial statements.

Financial statements report quantitative economic information; they do not reflect qualitative economic variables. Thus, the value to the firm of a management team or of the morale of the workforce is not included as a balance sheet asset because it cannot be objectively measured. Such qualitative attributes of the firm are frequently relevant to the decisions and informed judgments that the financial statement user is making, but they are not communicated in the financial statements. It's unfortunate that the accounting process does not capture these kinds of data because often a company's human resources and information resources are its most valuable assets. Many highly valued Internet and high-tech companies have little, if any, fixed assets or inventory— sometimes the "product" they intend to offer comes in the form of a service that has not yet made it through the research, design, and testing phases. In fact, a common saying about such companies is that their assets "walk out the door every night." The accounting profession is not yet comfortable with the idea of trying to measure these kinds of intangible assets, even though fairly reliable appraisal techniques are available, such as those endorsed in the Uniform Standards of Professional Appraisal Practice (USPAP).

As already emphasized, the cost principle requires assets to be recorded at their original cost. The balance sheet does not generally show the current market value or the replacement cost of the assets. Some assets are reported at the lower of their cost or market value, and in some cases market value may be reported parenthetically, but asset values are not generally increased to reflect current value. For example, the trademark of a firm has virtually no cost; its value has developed over the years as the firm has successfully met customers' needs. Thus, trademarks usually are excluded from the balance sheet listing of assets even though they clearly have economic value to the firm.

Estimates are used in many areas of accounting; when the estimate is made, about the only fact known is that the estimate is probably not equal to the "true" amount. It is hoped that the estimate is near the true amount (the concept of materiality); it usually is. For example, recognizing depreciation expense involves estimating both the useful life to the entity of the asset being depreciated and the probable salvage value of the asset to the entity when it is disposed of. The original cost minus the salvage value is the amount to be depreciated or recognized as expense over the asset's life. Estimates also must be made to determine pension expense, warranty costs, and numerous other expense and revenue items to be reflected in the current year's income statement because they relate to the economic activity of the current year. These estimates also affect balance sheet accounts. So even though the balance sheet balances to the penny, do not be misled by this aura of exactness. Accountants do their best to make their estimates as accurate as possible, but estimates are still estimates.

The principle of consistency suggests that an entity should not change from one generally accepted method of accounting for a particular item to another generally accepted method of accounting for the same item, but it is possible that two firms operating in the same industry may follow different methods. This means that *comparability* between firms may not be appropriate, or if comparisons are made, the effects of any differences between the accounting methods followed by the firms must be understood.

Related to the use of the original cost principle is the fact that financial statements are not adjusted to show the impact of inflation. Land acquired by a firm 50 years ago is still reported at its original cost, even though it may have a significantly higher current value because of inflation. Likewise, depreciation expense and the cost of goods sold—both significant expense elements of the income statement of many firms— reflect original cost, not replacement cost. This weakness is not significant when the rate of inflation is low, but the usefulness of financial statements is seriously impaired when the inflation rate rises to double digits.

Financial statements do not reflect **opportunity cost,** which is an economic concept relating to income forgone because an opportunity to earn income was not pursued. For example, if an individual or organization maintains a non–interest-bearing checking account balance that is $300 more than that required to avoid any service charges, the opportunity cost associated with that $300 is the interest that could otherwise be earned on the money if it had been invested. Financial accounting does not give formal recognition to opportunity cost; however, financial managers should be aware of the concept as they plan the utilization of the firm's resources.

What Does It Mean?

Answer on page 57

9. What does it mean when some investors state that a corporation's published financial statements don't tell the whole story about a firm's financial position and results of operations?

The Corporation's Annual Report

LO 8

Describe what a corporation's annual report is and why it is issued.

The annual report is the document distributed (or made available electronically) to shareholders that contains the reporting firm's financial statements for the fiscal year, together with the report of the external auditor's examination of the financial statements. The annual report document can be as simple as a transmittal letter from the president or chairman of the board of directors along with the financial statements, or as fancy as a glossy, 100-page booklet that showcases the firm's products, services, and personnel, as well as its financial results.

In addition to the financial statements described here and the notes to the financial statements described more fully in Chapter 10, some other financial data are usually included in the annual report. Highlights for the year, including net revenues, diluted earnings per share, and return on average stockholders' equity, often appear inside the front cover or elsewhere toward the front of the report. Most firms also include a historical summary of certain financial data for at least the past five years. This summary usually is located near the back of the annual report.

The vast majority of U.S. publicly traded companies now include within their annual reports the entire 10-K report that is filed with the SEC each year. As a result, the appendix material for Campbell Soup Company's 2011 annual report excludes certain disclosures that are not heavily referenced in this text, such as the Management's Discussion and Analysis section. To obtain a complete copy of Campbell's current annual report, please visit www.campbellsoup.com. Click on "Our Company" in the upper left corner of the home page and then click on "Investor Center," "Financial Information," and "Annual Reports" to reach the relevant Adobe Acrobat files that can be saved and/or printed. Many specific aspects of Campbell's annual report will be referred to in subsequent chapters.

Demonstration Problem

Visit the text website at www.mhhe.com/marshall10e **to view a demonstration problem for this chapter.**

Summary

Financial statements communicate economic information that helps individuals make decisions and informed judgments.

The bookkeeping and accounting processes result in an entity's numerous transactions with other entities being reflected in the financial statements. The financial statements presented by an entity are the balance sheet, income statement, statement of changes in stockholders' equity, and statement of cash flows.

The balance sheet is a listing of the entity's assets, liabilities, and stockholders' equity at a point in time. Assets are probable future economic benefits (things or claims against others) controlled by the entity. Liabilities are amounts owed by the entity. An entity's stockholders' equity is the difference between its assets and liabilities. This relationship is known as the *accounting equation*. Current assets are cash and those assets likely to be converted to cash or used to benefit the entity within one year of the balance sheet date, such as accounts receivable and inventories. Current liabilities are expected to be paid or otherwise satisfied within one year of the balance sheet date. The balance sheet as of the end of a fiscal period is also the balance sheet as of the beginning of the next fiscal period.

The income statement reports the results of an entity's operating activities for a period of time. Revenues are reported first, and expenses are subtracted to arrive at net income or net loss for the period.

The statement of changes in stockholders' equity describes changes in paid-in capital and retained earnings during the period. Retained earnings are increased by the amount of net income and decreased by dividends to stockholders (and by any net loss for the period). It is through retained earnings that the income statement is linked to the balance sheet.

The statement of cash flows summarizes the impact on cash of the entity's operating, investing, and financing activities during the period. The bottom line of this financial statement is the change in cash from the amount shown in the balance sheet at the beginning of the period (e.g., fiscal year) to that shown in the balance sheet at the end of the period.

Financial statements usually are presented on a comparative basis so users can easily spot significant changes in an entity's financial position (balance sheet) and results of operations (income statement).

The financial statements are interrelated. Net income for the period (from the income statement) is added to retained earnings, a part of stockholders' equity (in the balance sheet). The statement of changes in stockholders' equity explains the difference between the amounts of stockholders' equity at the beginning and the end of the fiscal period. The statement of cash flows explains the change in the amount of cash from the beginning to the end of the fiscal period.

Accounting concepts and principles reflect generally accepted practices that have evolved over time. They can be related to a schematic model of the flow of data from transactions to the financial statements. Pertaining to the entire model are the accounting entity concept, the accounting equation, and the going concern concept.

Transactions are recorded in currency units (e.g., the U.S. dollar) without regard to purchasing power changes. Thus transactions are recorded at an objectively determinable original cost amount.

The concepts and principles for the accounting period involve recognizing revenue when a sale of a product or service is made and then relating to that revenue all of the expenses incurred in generating the revenue of the period. This matching of revenues and expenses is a crucial and fundamental concept to understand if accounting itself is to be understood. The accrual concept is used to implement the matching concept by recognizing revenues when earned and expenses when incurred, regardless of whether cash is received or paid in the same fiscal period.

The concepts of consistency, full disclosure, materiality, and conservatism relate primarily to financial statement presentation.

There are limitations to the information presented in financial statements. These limitations are related to the concepts and principles that have become generally accepted. Thus subjective qualitative factors, current values, the impact of inflation, and opportunity cost are not usually reflected in financial statements. In addition, many financial statement amounts involve the use of estimates. Permissible alternative accounting practices may mean that interfirm comparisons are not appropriate.

Corporations and other organizations include financial statements in an annual report made available to stockholders, employees, potential investors, and others interested in the entity. Refer to the financial statements on pages 711–714 of the Campbell Soup Company annual report in the appendix, as well as to the financial statements of other annual reports, to see how the material discussed in this chapter applies to real companies.

Key Terms and Concepts

account (p. 33)   A record in which transactions affecting individual assets, liabilities, stockholders' equity, revenues, and expenses are recorded.

accounting equation (p. 36)   Assets = Liabilities + Stockholders' equity (A = L + SE). The fundamental relationship represented by the balance sheet and the foundation of the bookkeeping process.

accounts payable (p. 37)   A liability representing an amount payable to another entity, usually because of the purchase of merchandise or services on credit.

accounts receivable (p. 37)   An asset representing a claim against another entity, usually arising from selling goods or services on credit.

accrual accounting (p. 49)   Accounting that recognizes revenues and expenses as they occur, even though the cash receipt from the revenue or the cash disbursement related to the expense may occur before or after the event that causes revenue or expense recognition.

accrued liabilities (p. 37)   Amounts that are owed by an entity on the balance sheet date.

accumulated depreciation (p. 37)   The sum of the depreciation expense that has been recognized over time. Accumulated depreciation is a contra asset—an amount that is subtracted from the cost of the related asset on the balance sheet.

additional paid-in capital (p. 41)   The excess of the amount received from the sale of stock over the par value of the shares sold.

assets (p. 36)   Probable future economic benefits obtained or controlled by an entity as a result of past transactions or events.

balance sheet (p. 35)   The financial statement that is a listing of the entity's assets, liabilities, and stockholders' equity at a point in time. Sometimes this statement is called the *statement of financial position*.

balance sheet equation (p. 36)   Another term for *accounting equation*.

cash (p. 37)   An asset on the balance sheet that represents the amount of cash on hand and balances in bank accounts maintained by the entity.

common stock (p. 40)   The class of stock that represents residual ownership of the corporation.

corporation (p. 34)   A form of organization in which ownership is evidenced by shares of stock owned by stockholders; its features, such as limited liability of the stockholders, make this the principal form of organization for most business activity.

cost of goods sold (p. 39)   Cost of merchandise sold during the period; an expense deducted from net sales to arrive at gross profit. Frequently used synonyms are *cost of sales* and *cost of products sold.*

current assets (p. 38)   Cash and those assets that are likely to be converted to cash or used to benefit the entity within one year of the balance sheet date.

current liabilities (p. 38)   Those liabilities due to be paid within one year of the balance sheet date.

depreciation (p. 37)   The accounting process of recognizing the cost of an asset that is used up over its useful life to the entity.

depreciation expense (p. 42)   The expense recognized in a fiscal period for the depreciation of an asset.

dividend (p. 41)   A distribution of earnings to the stockholders of a corporation.

earnings per share of common stock outstanding (p. 39)   Net income available to the common stockholders divided by the average number of shares of common stock outstanding during the period. Usually referred to simply as *EPS.*

equity (p. 36)   The ownership right associated with an asset. See *stockholders' equity.*

expenses (p. 38)   Outflows or other using up of assets or incurring a liability during a period from delivering or producing goods, rendering services, or carrying out other activities that constitute the entity's major operations.

fiscal year (p. 35)   The annual period used for reporting to owners.

gains (p. 38)   Increases in net assets from incidental transactions that are not revenues or investments by owners.

going concern concept (p. 48)   A presumption that the entity will continue in existence for the indefinite future.

gross profit (p. 39)   Net sales less cost of goods sold. Sometimes called *gross margin.*

income from operations (p. 39)   The difference between gross profit and operating expenses. Also referred to as *operating income.*

income statement (p. 38)   The financial statement that summarizes the entity's revenues, expenses, gains, and losses for a period of time and thereby reports the entity's results of operations for that period of time.

liabilities (p. 36)   Probable future sacrifices of economic benefits arising from present obligations of a particular entity to transfer assets or provide services to other entities in the future as a result of past transactions or events.

losses (p. 38)   Decreases in net assets from incidental transactions that are not expenses or distributions to owners.

matching concept (p. 49)   The concept that expenses incurred in generating revenues should be deducted from revenues earned during the period for which results are being reported.

merchandise inventory (p. 37)   Items held by an entity for sale to customers in the normal course of business.

net assets (p. 37)   The difference between assets and liabilities; also referred to as *stockholders' equity* or *owners' equity.*

net income (p. 38)   The excess of revenues and gains over expenses and losses for a fiscal period.

net sales (p. 38)   Gross sales, less sales discounts and sales returns and allowances.

net worth (p. 37)   Another term for *net assets* or *stockholders' equity* or *owners' equity,* but not as appropriate because the term *worth* may be misleading.

opportunity cost (p. 52)   An economic concept relating to income forgone because an opportunity to earn income was not pursued.

owners' equity (p. 36)   Another term for *stockholders' equity*. The owners' claim in the assets of the entity. Sometimes called *net assets;* the difference between assets and liabilities.

paid-in capital (p. 40)   The amount invested in the entity by the stockholders.

par value (p. 40)   An arbitrary value assigned to a share of stock when the corporation is organized. Sometimes used to refer to the stated value or face amount of a security.

partnership (p. 34)   A form of organization indicating ownership by two or more individuals or corporations without the limited liability and other features of a corporation.

profit (p. 38)   The excess of revenues and gains over expenses and losses for a fiscal period; another term for *net income*.

profit and loss statement (p. 38)   Another term for *income statement*.

proprietorship (p. 34)   A form of organization indicating individual ownership without the limited liability and other features of a corporation.

retained earnings (p. 40)   Cumulative net income that has not been distributed to the stockholders of a corporation as dividends.

revenues (p. 38)   Inflows of cash or increases in other assets, or the settlement of liabilities during a period, from delivering or producing goods, rendering services, or performing other activities that constitute the entity's major operations.

statement of cash flows (p. 42)   The financial statement that explains why cash changed during a fiscal period. Cash flows from operating, investing, and financing activities are shown.

statement of changes in capital stock (p. 40)   The financial statement that summarizes changes during a fiscal period in capital stock and additional paid-in capital. This information may be included in the statement of changes in stockholders' equity.

statement of changes in retained earnings (p. 40)   The financial statement that summarizes the changes during a fiscal period in retained earnings. This information may be included in the statement of changes in stockholders' equity.

statement of changes in stockholders' equity (p. 40)   The financial statement that summarizes the changes during a fiscal period in capital stock, additional paid-in capital, retained earnings, and other elements of stockholders' equity.

statement of earnings (p. 38)   Another term for *income statement;* it shows the revenues, expenses, gains, and losses for a period of time and thereby the entity's results of operations for that period of time.

statement of financial position (p. 35)   Another term for *balance sheet;* a listing of the entity's assets, liabilities, and stockholders' equity at a point in time.

statement of operations (p. 38)   Another term for *income statement*.

stock (p. 34)   The evidence of ownership of a corporation.

stockholders (p. 34)   The owners of a corporation's stock; sometimes called *shareholders*.

stockholders' equity (p. 36)   The stockholders' claim in the assets of the entity. Sometimes called *owners' equity* or *net assets*; the difference between assets and liabilities.

subsidiary (p. 48)   A corporation whose stock is more than 50 percent owned by another corporation.

transactions (p. 33)   Economic interchanges between entities that are accounted for and reflected in financial statements.

ANSWERS TO
What Does
It Mean?

1. It means that there has been some sort of economic interchange; for example, you have agreed to pay tuition in exchange for classes.
2. It means the person doing this is really mixed up because the balance sheet presents data as of a point in time. It's a balance sheet *as of* August 31, 2014.

3. It means that the organization's financial position *at a point in time* has been determined and summarized.

4. It means that each individual financial statement provides unique information but focuses on only a part of the big picture, so all four statements need to be reviewed to achieve a full understanding of the firm's financial position and results of operations.

5. It means that revenues have been earned from selling products or providing services but that the accounts receivable from those revenues have not yet been collected—or if the receivables have been collected, the cash has been used for some purpose other than paying bills.

6. It means that transactions affecting the income statement also affect the stockholders' equity section of the balance sheet as well as the asset and/or liability sections of the balance sheet.

7. It means that all expenses incurred in generating revenue for the period are subtracted from those revenues to determine net income. Matching does not mean that revenues equal expenses.

8. It means that revenues and expenses are recognized in the accounting period in which they are earned or incurred, even though cash may be received or paid in a different accounting period.

9. It means that there may be both qualitative (for example, workforce morale) and quantitative (for example, opportunity cost) factors that are not reflected in the financial statements.

Self-Study Material

Visit the text website at www.mhhe.com/marshall10e to take an online self-study quiz for this chapter.

Matching Following is a list of the key terms and concepts introduced in the chapter, along with a list of corresponding definitions. Match the appropriate letter for the key term or concept to each definition provided (items 1–15). Note that not all key terms and concepts will be used. Answers are provided at the end of this chapter.

a.	Accumulated depreciation	i.	Gains
b.	Balance sheet	j.	Losses
c.	Accrued liabilities	k.	Net sales
d.	Current assets	l.	Cost of goods sold
e.	Current liabilities	m.	Gross profit
f.	Merchandise inventory	n.	Income from operations
g.	Revenues	o.	Net income
h.	Expenses	p.	Earnings per share of common stock

q. Paid-in capital
r. Common stock
s. Additional paid-in capital
t. Retained earnings
u. Dividends
v. Par value

w. Going concern concept
x. Matching concept
y. Accrual concept
z. Opportunity cost
aa. Annual report
bb. Income statement

_____ 1. The difference between the total amount invested by the stockholders and the par value or stated value of the stock issued.

_____ 2. Outflows or using up of assets or incurrence of liabilities during a period from delivering or producing goods, rendering services, or carrying out other activities that constitute the entity's major operations.

_____ 3. The financial statement that is a list of the entity's assets, liabilities, and stockholders' equity at a point in time.

_____ 4. A document distributed to stockholders that contains the financial statements for the fiscal year of the reporting firm with the report of the external auditor's examination of the financial statements.

_____ 5. A distribution of earnings to the stockholders of a corporation.

_____ 6. An arbitrary value assigned to a share of stock when the corporation is organized.

_____ 7. Net income available to the common stockholders divided by the average number of shares of common stock outstanding during the period.

_____ 8. Items held by an entity for sale to potential customers in the normal course of business.

_____ 9. Inflows of cash or increases in other assets, or settlement of liabilities during a period from delivering or producing goods, rendering services, or other activities that constitute the entity's major operations.

_____10. Cash and those assets likely to be converted to cash or used to benefit the entity within one year of the balance sheet date.

_____11. Cumulative net income that has not been distributed to the stockholders of a corporation as dividends.

_____12. The difference between gross profit and operating expenses. Also referred to as *operating income* and *earnings from operations*.

_____13. Increases in net assets from incidental transactions and other events affecting an entity during a period except those that result from revenues or investments by owners.

_____14. A presumption that the entity will continue in existence for the indefinite future.

_____15. Net sales less cost of goods sold.

Multiple Choice For each of the following questions, circle the best response. Answers are provided at the end of this chapter.

1. Which of the following is *not* a correct expression of the accounting equation?
   a. Assets − Liabilities = Stockholders' equity
   b. Net assets = Liabilities + Stockholders' equity

    c. Assets = Liabilities + Stockholders' equity

    d. Net assets = Stockholders' equity

2. Partnerships, as contrasted with corporations, can be characterized as being relatively

    a. easier to form, less risky to be an owner of, and easier to raise large amounts of capital for.

    b. easier to form, more risky to be an owner of, and harder to raise large amounts of capital for.

    c. harder to form, more risky to be an owner of, and harder to raise large amounts of capital for.

    d. harder to form, less risky to be an owner of, and easier to raise large amounts of capital for.

    e. none of the above.

3. The stockholders' equity section of a balance sheet contains two major components:

    a. Common Stock and Additional Paid-in Capital.

    b. Paid-in Capital and Retained Earnings.

    c. Common Stock and Retained Earnings.

    d. Net Income and Dividends.

    e. Additional Paid-in Capital and Net Income.

4. Which of the following accounts is *not* an asset?

    a. Cash.   *d.* Equipment.

    b. Inventory.   *e.* Land.

    c. Accounts Payable.

5. Which of the following financial statement descriptions is *inaccurate?*

    a. Balance Sheet—shows the organization's financial position for a period of time.

    b. Income Statement—shows what the organization's earnings were for a period time.

    c. Statement of Cash Flows—shows what the organization's receipts and disbursements were for a period of time.

    d. Statement of Stockholders' Equity—shows the investments by and distributions to stockholders for a period of time.

    e. All of the above descriptions are accurate.

6. If total assets were $21,000 and total liabilities were $12,000 at the beginning of the year, and if net income for the year was $5,000, how much was total stockholders' equity at the end of the year?

    a. $4,000.   *c.* $9,000.

    b. $5,000.   *d.* $14,000.

7. At the beginning of the year, stockholders' equity totaled $119,000. During the year, net income was $35,000 and dividends of $29,000 were declared and paid. How much was stockholders' equity at the end of the year?

    a. $113,000.   *c.* $148,000.

    b. $125,000.   *d.* $154,000.

8. The principle stating that all expenses incurred while earning revenues should be identified with the revenues when they are earned and reported for the same time period is the

    a. cost principle.   *d.* matching principle.

    b. revenue principle.   *e.* timing principle.

    c. expense principle.

9. Corporate annual reports do *not* ordinarily include

    a. a transmittal letter from the president or chairman of the board of directors.

    b. financial statements for the most recent year.

    c. explanatory notes and comments about the financial statements.

    d. the internal auditor's report and opinion about the financial statements.

    e. a historical summary of selected financial data for the past five years or more.

10. Which of these is *not* a limitation of financial statements?

    a. Qualitative data are not reflected in financial statements.

    b. Market values of assets are not generally reported.

    c. Estimates are commonly used and are sometimes inaccurate.

    d. It may be difficult to compare firms in the same industry because they often use different accounting methods.

    e. All of the above are limitations of financial statements.

connect | ACCOUNTING   Mini-Exercises

All applicable Mini-Exercises are available with McGraw-Hill's *Connect™ Accounting*.

Mini-Exercise 2.1
LO 2, 3

Understanding financial statement relationships Total assets were $48,000 and total liabilities were $27,000 at the beginning of the year. Net income for the year was $8,000, and dividends of $2,000 were declared and paid during the year.

Required:
Calculate total stockholders' equity at the end of the year.

Mini-Exercise 2.2
LO 2, 3

Understanding financial statement relationships Stockholders' equity totaled $82,000 at the beginning of the year. During the year, net income was $12,000, dividends of $3,000 were declared and paid, and $10,000 of common stock was issued at par value.

Required:
Calculate total stockholders' equity at the end of the year.

Mini-Exercise 2.3
LO 2, 3

Understanding income statement relationships During the year, net sales were $125,000; gross profit was $50,000; net income was $20,000; income tax expense was $5,000; and selling, general, and administrative expenses were $22,000.

Required:
Calculate cost of goods sold, income from operations, income before taxes, and interest expense. *(Hint: Exhibit 2-2 may be used as a solution model.)*

Mini-Exercise 2.4
LO 2, 3

Understanding income statement relationships During the year, cost of goods sold was $40,000; income from operations was $38,000; income tax expense was

$8,000; interest expense was $6,000; and selling, general, and administrative expenses were $22,000.

Required:

Calculate net sales, gross profit, income before taxes, and net income. *(Hint: Exhibit 2-2 may be used as a solution model.)*

Identify accounts by category Listed here are a number of accounts: Land, Common stock, Merchandise inventory, Equipment, Cost of goods sold, Accounts receivable, Interest expense, Supplies, Long-term debt, Cash, Sales, Accounts payable, Buildings, Retained earnings.

Required:

Which of the accounts listed above are not assets? How would you categorize each of these nonasset accounts?

Mini-Exercise 2.5

LO 2, 4

Identify accounts by statement Listed here are a number of accounts: Income tax expense, Accumulated depreciation, Notes payable, Land, Sales, Common stock, Cost of goods sold, Equipment, Accounts receivable, Rent expense, Supplies, Buildings, Service revenue, Cash.

Required:

Which of the accounts listed above would appear on a company's income statement?

Mini-Exercise 2.6

LO 2, 4

Exercises

All applicable Exercises are available with McGraw-Hill's *Connect™ Accounting*.

Identify accounts by category and financial statement(s) Listed here are a number of financial statement captions. Indicate in the spaces to the right of each caption the category of each item and the financial statement(s) on which the item can usually be found. Use the following abbreviations:

Exercise 2.7

LO 2, 4

Category		Financial Statement	
Asset	A	Balance sheet	BS
Liability	L	Income statement	IS
Stockholders' equity	SE		
Revenue	R		
Expense	E		
Gain	G		
Loss	LS		

Cash	_____	_____
Accounts payable	_____	_____
Common stock	_____	_____
Depreciation expense	_____	_____
Net sales	_____	_____
Income tax expense	_____	_____
Short-term investments	_____	_____
Gain on sale of land	_____	_____
Retained earnings	_____	_____
Dividends payable	_____	_____
Accounts receivable	_____	_____
Short-term debt	_____	_____

Exercise 2.8

LO 2, 4

Identify accounts by category and financial statement(s) Listed here are a number of financial statement captions. Indicate in the spaces to the right of each caption the category of each item and the financial statement(s) on which the item can usually be found. Use the following abbreviations:

Category		Financial Statement	
Asset	A	Balance sheet	BS
Liability	L	Income statement	IS
Stockholders' equity	SE		
Revenue	R		
Expense	E		
Gain	G		
Loss	LS		

Accumulated depreciation	_____	_____
Long-term debt	_____	_____
Equipment	_____	_____
Loss on sale of short-term investments	_____	_____
Net income	_____	_____
Merchandise inventory	_____	_____
Other accrued liabilities	_____	_____
Dividends paid	_____	_____
Cost of goods sold	_____	_____
Additional paid-in capital	_____	_____
Interest income	_____	_____
Selling expenses	_____	_____

Exercise 2.9

LO 2, 3

Understanding financial statement relationships The information presented here represents selected data from the December 31, 2013, balance sheets and income statements for the year then ended for three firms:

	Firm A	Firm B	Firm C
Total assets, 12/31/13	$420,000	$540,000	$325,000
Total liabilities, 12/31/13	215,000	145,000	?
Paid-in capital, 12/31/13	75,000	?	40,000
Retained earnings, 12/31/13	?	310,000	?
Net income for 2013	?	83,000	113,000
Dividends declared and paid during 2013 . . .	50,000	19,000	65,000
Retained earnings, 1/1/13	78,000	?	42,000

Required:

Calculate the missing amounts for each firm.

Exercise 2.10

LO 2, 3

Understanding financial statement relationships The information presented here represents selected data from the December 31, 2013, balance sheets and income statements for the year then ended for three firms:

	Firm A	Firm B	Firm C
Total assets, 12/31/13.................	?	$870,000	$310,000
Total liabilities, 12/31/13	$160,000	?	150,000
Paid-in capital, 12/31/13...............	110,000	118,000	90,000
Retained earnings, 12/31/13............	?	372,000	?
Net income for 2013	136,000	220,000	51,000
Dividends declared and paid during 2013 ...	24,000	?	33,000
Retained earnings, 1/1/13...............	100,000	248,000	?

Required:

Calculate the missing amounts for each firm.

Calculate retained earnings From the following data, calculate the retained earnings balance as of December 31, 2013:

Exercise 2.11

LO 2, 3

Retained earnings, December 31, 2012...........................	$311,800
Cost of equipment purchased during 2013........................	32,400
Net loss for the year ended December 31, 2013....................	4,700
Dividends declared and paid in 2013	18,500
Decrease in cash balance from January 1, 2013, to December 31, 2013 ..	13,600
Decrease in long-term debt in 2013	14,800

Calculate retained earnings From the following data, calculate the retained earnings balance as of December 31, 2012:

Exercise 2.12

LO 2, 3

Retained earnings, December 31, 2013	$420,600
Decrease in total liabilities during 2013	91,600
Gain on the sale of buildings during 2013.........................	32,200
Dividends declared and paid in 2013	9,000
Proceeds from sale of common stock in 2013	98,800
Net income for the year ended December 31, 2013................	45,200

Calculate dividends using the accounting equation At the beginning of its current fiscal year, Willie Corp.'s balance sheet showed assets of $12,400 and liabilities of $7,000. During the year, liabilities decreased by $1,200. Net income for the year was $3,000, and net assets at the end of the year were $6,000. There were no changes in paid-in capital during the year.

Exercise 2.13

LO 2, 3

Required:

Calculate the dividends, if any, declared during the year.

(Hint: Set up an accounting equation for the beginning of the year, changes during the year, and at the end of the year. Enter known data and solve for the unknowns.)

Here is a possible worksheet format:

					SE	
	A	=	L	+	PIC	+ RE
Beginning:		=		+		+
Changes:	_____	=	_____	+	_____	+ _____
Ending:		=		+		+

Exercise 2.14
LO 2, 3

Calculate net income (or loss) using the accounting equation At the beginning of the current fiscal year, the balance sheet for Davis Co. showed liabilities of $640,000. During the year liabilities decreased by $36,000, assets increased by $130,000, and paid-in capital increased from $60,000 to $384,000. Dividends declared and paid during the year were $50,000. At the end of the year, stockholders' equity totaled $858,000.

Required:

Calculate net income (or loss) for the year.

(Hint: Set up an accounting equation for the beginning of the year, changes during the year, and at the end of the year. Enter known data and solve for the unknowns. Remember, net income [or loss] may not be the only item affecting retained earnings.)

 Problems

All applicable Problems are available with McGraw-Hill's *Connect*™ *Accounting*.

Problem 2.15
LO 2, 3, 6

Calculate cash available upon liquidation of business Circle-Square, Ltd., is in the process of liquidating and going out of business. The firm's balance sheet shows $22,800 in cash, accounts receivable of $114,200, inventory totaling $61,400, plant and equipment of $265,000, and total liabilities of $305,600. It is estimated that the inventory can be disposed of in a liquidation sale for 80 percent of its cost, all but 5 percent of the accounts receivable can be collected, and plant and equipment can be sold for $190,000.

Required:

Calculate the amount of cash that would be available to the owners if the accounts receivable are collected, the other assets are sold as described, and the liabilities are paid off in full.

Problem 2.16
LO 2, 3, 6

Calculate cash available upon liquidation of business Kimber Co. is in the process of liquidating and going out of business. The firm's accountant has provided the following balance sheet and additional information:

Assets		
Cash	$ 36,800	
Accounts receivable	125,200	
Merchandise inventory.	229,400	
Total current assets		$391,400
Land	$ 102,000	
Buildings & equipment.	686,000	
Less: Accumulated depreciation	(390,000)	
Total land, buildings, & equipment		398,000
Total assets		$789,400

(continued)

Liabilities and Stockholders' Equity

Accounts payable	$ 93,400	
Notes payable	117,000	
Total current liabilities		$210,400
Long-term debt		129,600
Total liabilities		$340,000
Stockholders' Equity		
Common stock, no par	$220,000	
Retained earnings	229,400	
Total stockholders' equity		449,400
Total liabilities and stockholders' equity		$789,400

It is estimated that all but 12 percent of the accounts receivable can be collected, and that the merchandise inventory can be disposed of in a liquidation sale for 85 percent of its cost. Buildings and equipment can be sold at $80,000 above book value (the difference between original cost and accumulated depreciation shown on the balance sheet), and the land can be sold at its current appraisal value of $130,000. In addition to the liabilities included in the balance sheet, $4,800 is owed to employees for their work since the last pay period, and interest of $10,500 has accrued on notes payable and long-term debt.

Required:

a. Calculate the amount of cash that will be available to the stockholders if the accounts receivable are collected, the other assets are sold as described, and all liabilities and other claims are paid in full.

b. Briefly explain why the amount of cash available to stockholders (computed in part *a*) is different from the amount of total stockholders' equity shown in the balance sheet.

Understanding and analyzing financial statement relationships—sales/ service organization Pope's Garage had the following accounts and amounts in its financial statements on December 31, 2013. Assume that all balance sheet items reflect account balances at December 31, 2013, and that all income statement items reflect activities that occurred during the year then ended.

Problem 2.17
LO 2, 3, 4

Accounts receivable	$ 33,000
Depreciation expense	12,000
Land	27,000
Cost of goods sold	90,000
Retained earnings	59,000
Cash	9,000
Equipment	71,000
Supplies	6,000
Accounts payable	23,000
Service revenue	20,000
Interest expense	4,000
Common stock	10,000
Income tax expense	12,000
Accumulated depreciation	45,000
Long-term debt	40,000
Supplies expense	14,000
Merchandise inventory	31,000
Sales revenue	140,000

Required:

a. Calculate the total current assets at December 31, 2013.

b. Calculate the total liabilities and stockholders' equity at December 31, 2013.

c. Calculate the earnings from operations (operating income) for the year ended December 31, 2013.

d. Calculate the net income (or loss) for the year ended December 31, 2013.

e. What was the average income tax rate for Pope's Garage for 2013?

f. If $16,000 of dividends had been declared and paid during the year, what was the January 1, 2013, balance of retained earnings?

Problem 2.18

LO 2, 3, 4

Understanding and analyzing financial statement relationships—merchandising organization Gary's TV had the following accounts and amounts in its financial statements on December 31, 2013. Assume that all balance sheet items reflect account balances at December 31, 2013, and that all income statement items reflect activities that occurred during the year then ended.

Interest expense	$ 18,000
Paid-in capital	40,000
Accumulated depreciation	12,000
Notes payable (long-term)	140,000
Rent expense	36,000
Merchandise inventory	420,000
Accounts receivable	96,000
Depreciation expense	6,000
Land	64,000
Retained earnings	450,000
Cash	72,000
Cost of goods sold	880,000
Equipment	36,000
Income tax expense	120,000
Accounts payable	46,000
Sales revenue	1,240,000

Required:

a. Calculate the difference between current assets and current liabilities for Gary's TV at December 31, 2013.

b. Calculate the total assets at December 31, 2013.

c. Calculate the earnings from operations (operating income) for the year ended December 31, 2013.

d. Calculate the net income (or loss) for the year ended December 31, 2013.

e. What was the average income tax rate for Gary's TV for 2013?

f. If $128,000 of dividends had been declared and paid during the year, what was the January 1, 2013, balance of retained earnings?

Problem 2.19

LO 2, 3, 4

Prepare an income statement, balance sheet, and statement of changes in stockholders' equity; analyze results The information on the following page was obtained from the records of Breanna, Inc.:

Accounts receivable	$ 10,000
Accumulated depreciation.	52,000
Cost of goods sold	128,000
Income tax expense	8,000
Cash	65,000
Sales.	200,000
Equipment.	120,000
Selling, general, and administrative expenses	34,000
Common stock (9,000 shares)	90,000
Accounts payable	15,000
Retained earnings, 1/1/13.	23,000
Interest expense	6,000
Merchandise inventory	37,000
Long-term debt.	40,000
Dividends declared and paid during 2013	12,000

Except as otherwise indicated, assume that all balance sheet items reflect account balances at December 31, 2013, and that all income statement items reflect activities that occurred during the year ended December 31, 2013. There were no changes in paid-in capital during the year.

Required:

a. Prepare an income statement and statement of changes in stockholders' equity for the year ended December 31, 2013, and a balance sheet at December 31, 2013, for Breanna, Inc.

 Based on the financial statements that you have prepared for part **a**, answer the questions in parts **b–e**. Provide brief explanations for each of your answers and state any assumptions you believe are necessary to ensure that your answers are correct.

b. What is the company's average income tax rate?

c. What interest rate is charged on long-term debt?

d. What is the par value per share of common stock?

e. What is the company's dividend policy (i.e., what proportion of the company's earnings are used for dividends)?

Prepare an income statement, balance sheet, and statement of changes in stockholders' equity; analyze results The following information was obtained from the records of Shae, Inc.:

Problem 2.20

LO 2, 3, 4

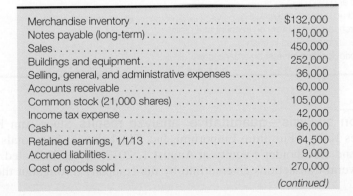

Merchandise inventory	$132,000
Notes payable (long-term)	150,000
Sales.	450,000
Buildings and equipment.	252,000
Selling, general, and administrative expenses	36,000
Accounts receivable	60,000
Common stock (21,000 shares)	105,000
Income tax expense	42,000
Cash	96,000
Retained earnings, 1/1/13	64,500
Accrued liabilities.	9,000
Cost of goods sold	270,000
	(continued)

Accumulated depreciation.	108,000
Interest expense	24,000
Accounts payable	45,000
Dividends declared and paid during 2013	19,500

Except as otherwise indicated, assume that all balance sheet items reflect account balances at December 31, 2013, and that all income statement items reflect activities that occurred during the year ended December 31, 2013. There were no changes in paid-in capital during the year.

Required:

a. Prepare an income statement and statement of changes in stockholders' equity for the year ended December 31, 2013, and a balance sheet at December 31, 2013, for Shae, Inc.

Based on the financial statements that you have prepared for part **a**, answer the questions in parts **b–e**. Provide brief explanations for each of your answers and state any assumptions you believe are necessary to ensure that your answers are correct.

b. What is the company's average income tax rate?

c. What interest rate is charged on long-term debt?

d. What is the par value per share of common stock?

e. What is the company's dividend policy (i.e., what proportion of the company's earnings is used for dividends)?

Problem 2.21

LO 2, 3

Transaction analysis—nonquantitative Indicate the effect of each of the following transactions on total assets, total liabilities, and total stockholders' equity. Use + for increase, − for decrease, and (NE) for no effect. The first transaction is provided as an illustration.

		Assets	Liabilities	Stockholders' Equity
a.	Borrowed cash on a bank loan.	+	+	NE
b.	Paid an account payable			
c.	Sold common stock			
d.	Purchased merchandise inventory on account.			
e.	Declared and paid dividends.			
f.	Collected an account receivable.			
g.	Sold merchandise inventory on account at a profit. . .			
h.	Paid operating expenses in cash			
i.	Repaid principal and interest on a bank loan			

Problem 2.22

LO 2, 3, 6

Transaction analysis—quantitative; analyze results Stacy-Ann Kelly owns and operates Kelly's Furniture Emporium, Inc. The balance sheet totals for assets, liabilities, and stockholder's equity at August 1, 2013, are as indicated. Described here are several transactions entered into by the company throughout the month of August.

Required:

a. Indicate the amount and effect (+ or −) of each transaction on total assets, total liabilities, and total stockholder's equity, and then compute the new totals for each category. The first transaction is provided as an illustration.

	Assets =	Liabilities +	Stockholder's Equity
August 1, 2013, totals.	$350,000	$275,000	$75,000
August 3, borrowed $12,000 in cash from the bank.	+ 12,000	+ 12,000	
New totals	$362,000	$287,000	$75,000
August 7, bought merchandise inventory valued at $19,000 on account.			
New totals			
August 10, paid $7,000 cash for operating expenses.			
New totals			
August 14, received $50,000 in cash from sales of merchandise that had cost $33,000.			
New totals			
August 17, paid $14,000 owed on accounts payable			
New totals			
August 21, collected $17,000 of accounts receivable			
New totals			
August 24, repaid $10,000 to the bank plus $200 interest.			
New totals			
August 29, paid Stacy-Ann Kelly a cash dividend of $5,000.			
New totals			

b. What was the amount of net income (or loss) during August? How much were total revenues and total expenses during August?

c. What were the net changes during the month of August in total assets, total liabilities, and total stockholder's equity?

d. Explain to Stacy-Ann Kelly which transactions caused the net change in her stockholder's equity during August.

e. Explain why dividend payments are not an expense, but interest is an expense.

f. Explain why the money borrowed from the bank increased assets but did not increase net income.

g. Explain why paying off accounts payable and collecting accounts receivable do not affect net income.

Complete the balance sheet A partially completed balance sheet for Blue Co., Inc., as of October 31, 2013, is presented on the following page. Where amounts are shown for various items, the amounts are correct.

Problem 2.23
LO 2, 3, 5

Assets		Liabilities and Stockholders' Equity	
Cash.................... $ 700		Note payable........................ $ _____	
Accounts receivable .... _____		Accounts payable...................	3,400
Land..................... _____			
Automobile .... _____		Total liabilities..................... $ _____	
Less: Accumulated		Stockholders' equity	
depreciation............ _____		Common stock.................... $ 8,000	
		Retained earnings .... _____	
		Total stockholders' equity .... $ _____	
Total assets............... $ _____		Total liabilities + stockholders' equity .... $ _____	

Required:

Using the following data, complete the balance sheet.

a. Blue Co.'s records show that current and former customers owe the firm a total of $4,000; $600 of this amount has been due for more than a year from two customers who are now bankrupt.

b. The automobile, which is still being used in the business, cost $18,000 new; a used car dealer's Blue Book shows that it is now worth $10,000. Management estimates that the car has been used for one-third of its total potential use.

c. The land cost Blue Co. $11,000; it was recently assessed for real estate tax purposes at a value of $15,000.

d. Blue Co.'s president isn't sure of the amount of the note payable, but he does know that he signed a note.

e. Since Blue Co. was formed, net income has totaled $33,000, and dividends to stockholders have totaled $19,500.

Problem 2.24

LO 2, 3, 5, 6

Complete the balance sheet using cash flow data Following is a partially completed balance sheet for Epsico, Inc., at December 31, 2013, together with comparative data for the year ended December 31, 2012. From the statement of cash flows for the year ended December 31, 2013, you determine the following:

Net income for the year ended December 31, 2013, was $78.

Dividends paid during the year ended December 31, 2013, were $24.

Cash increased $24 during the year ended December 31, 2013.

The cost of new equipment acquired during 2013 was $45; no equipment was disposed of.

There were no transactions affecting the land account during 2013, but it is estimated that the fair market value of the land at December 31, 2013, is $126.

Required:

Complete the balance sheet at December 31, 2013.

EPSICO, INC.
Balance Sheets
December 31, 2013 and 2012

Assets	2013	2012	Liabilities and Stockholders' Equity	2013	2012
Current assets:			Current liabilities:		
Cash	$	$ 90	Note payable	$147	$ 120
Accounts receivable	378	360	Accounts payable	369	330
Inventory	723	690			
Total current assets	$	$1,140	Total current liabilities	$516	$ 450
			Long-term debt		240
Land	$	$ 75	Total liabilities	$	$ 690
Equipment		1,125	**Stockholders' Equity**		
Less: Accumulated			Common stock	$600	$ 600
depreciation	(540)	(480)	Retained earnings		570
Total land & equipment	$	$ 720	Total stockholders' equity	$	$1,170
Total assets	$	$1,860	Total liabilities and stockholders' equity	$	$1,860

Understanding income statement relationships—Levi Strauss & Co.

Problem 2.25
LO 2, 4

The following selected data are adapted from the November 27, 2011, and November 28, 2010, consolidated balance sheets and income statements for the years then ended for Levi Strauss & Co. and Subsidiaries. All amounts are reported in thousands.

	2011	2010
Net revenues.	$4,761,566	$?
Cost of goods sold	?	2,187,726
Gross profit	2,292,239	2,222,923
Selling, general, and administrative expenses	?	1,841,562
Operating income	?	?
Interest expense and other expenses, net	133,566	145,763
Income before income taxes	202,827	?
Income tax expense	?	86,152
Net income	$ 135,112	$ 149,446
As at November 27 and 28, respectively:		
Total assets	$3,279,555	$?
Total liabilities	3,429,384	3,335,077
Total stockholders' deficit	?	(199,828)

Required:
Calculate the missing amounts for each year.

Problem 2.26

LO 2, 4

Understanding income statement relationships—Apple Inc. Selected data from the September 24, 2011, and September 25, 2010, consolidated balance sheets and income statements for the years then ended for Apple Inc. follow. All amounts are reported in millions.

	2011	2010
Net sales.	$108,249	$65,225
Cost of sales.	64,431	39,541
Research and development expenses.	2,429	1,782
Selling, general, and administrative expenses	7,599	5,517
Operating income	?	?
Other income, net	?	155
Provision for income taxes.	8,283	?
Net income	$ 25,922	$14,013

Required:

a. Calculate the amount of Apple's gross profit for each year. Has gross profit as a percentage of sales changed significantly during the past year?

b. Calculate the amount of Apple's operating income for each year. Has operating income as a percentage of sales changed significantly during the past year?

c. After completing parts **a** and **b**, calculate the other missing amounts for each year.

connect **Case**
|ACCOUNTING

All applicable Cases are available with McGraw-Hill's *Connect*™ *Accounting.*

Case 2.27

LO 2, 4, 6, 7

Prepare a personal balance sheet and projected income statement; explain financial statement relationships.

Required:

a. Prepare a personal balance sheet for yourself as of today. Work at identifying your assets and liabilities; use rough estimates for amounts.

b. Prepare a projected income statement for yourself for the current semester. Work at identifying your revenues and expenses, again using rough estimates for amounts.

c. Explain how your projected income statement for the semester is likely to impact your financial position (i.e., balance sheet) at the end of the semester. *(Note: You are not required to prepare a projected balance sheet.)*

d. Identify the major sources (and uses) of cash that you are expecting to receive (and spend) this semester. *(Note: You are not required to prepare a projected statement of cash flows.)*

e. Give three possible explanations why a full-time college student might incur a substantial net loss during the fall semester of her junior year, yet have more cash at the end of the semester than she had at the beginning.

Answers to Self-Study Material

Matching: 1. s, 2. h, 3. b, 4. aa, 5. u, 6. v, 7. p, 8. f, 9. g, 10. d, 11. t, 12. n, 13. i, 14. w, 15. m
Multiple choice 1. b, 2. b, 3. b, 4. c, 5. a, 6. d, 7. b, 8. d, 9. d, 10. e

3 Fundamental Interpretations Made from Financial Statement Data

Chapter 2 presented an overview of the financial statements that result from the financial accounting process. It is now appropriate to preview some of the interpretations made by financial statement users to support their decisions and informed judgments. Understanding the uses of accounting information will make development of that information more meaningful. Current and potential stockholders are interested in making their own assessments of management's stewardship of the resources made available by the owners. For example, judgments about profitability will affect the investment decision. Creditors assess the entity's ability to repay loans and pay for products and services. These assessments of profitability and debt-paying ability involve interpreting the relationships among amounts reported in the financial statements. Most of these relationships will be referred to in subsequent chapters. They are introduced now to illustrate how management's financial objectives for the firm are quantified so that you may begin to understand what the numbers mean. Likewise, these concepts will prepare you to better understand the impact of alternative accounting methods on financial statements when accounting alternatives are explained in subsequent chapters.

This chapter introduces some fundamental financial statement analysis concepts and tools. Chapter 11, Financial Statement Analysis, is a comprehensive explanation of how to use financial statement data to analyze a firm's financial condition and results of operations. You will better understand topics in that chapter after you have studied the financial accounting material in Chapters 5 through 10.

LEARNING OBJECTIVES (LO)

After studying this chapter you should understand and be able to

LO 3-1   Discuss why financial statement ratios are important.

LO 3-2   Explain the importance and show the calculation of return on investment.

LO 3-3   Illustrate how to calculate and interpret margin and turnover using the DuPont model.

LO 3-4   Explain the importance and show the calculation of return on equity.

LO 3-5   Explain the meaning of liquidity and discuss why it is important.

LO 3-6   Discuss the significance and calculation of working capital, the current ratio, and the acid-test ratio.

LO 3-7   Generalize about how trend analysis can be used most effectively.

Study

Suggestion

The authors have found that learning about the basics of profitability and liquidity measures in Chapter 3 is important for several reasons. (1) It introduces you to the "big picture" of real-world financial reporting before getting into the accounting details presented in subsequent chapters; (2) it demonstrates the relevance of studying financial accounting; (3) it encourages you to think about the impact of transactions on the financial statements; and (4) it provides a perspective that you can use in the homework assignments for Chapters 4–11. It is important that you attempt to understand the *business implications* of ROI, ROE, and the current ratio in particular.

Keep in mind that there are no singular, unchangeable rules that universally apply to the definitions of the data used in financial ratio analysis. While the illustrations presented in this text endeavor to use the most commonly applied financial statement components, individual firms and financial analysts may define certain ratio components in a slightly (or even dramatically) different manner than is illustrated here. Presumably, there are sound and logical reasons for any such variations that you may encounter in practice. As a user of financial statement data, you should understand the reasons for those variations and the effects that any unique definition may have on ratio results relative to a more traditional definition for that same ratio.

Financial Ratios and Trend Analysis

The large dollar amounts reported in the financial statements of many companies, and the varying sizes of companies, make ratio analysis the only sensible method of evaluating various financial characteristics of a company. Students frequently are awed by the number of ratio measurements commonly used in financial management and sometimes are intimidated by the mere thought of calculating a ratio. Be neither awed nor intimidated! A ratio is simply the relationship between two numbers; the name of virtually every financial ratio describes the numbers to be related and usually how the ratio is calculated. As you study this material, concentrate on understanding why the ratio is considered important and work to understand the meaning of the ratio. If you do these things, you should avoid much of the stress associated with understanding financial ratios.

In most cases a single ratio does not describe very much about the company whose statements are being studied. Much more meaningful analysis is accomplished when the *trend* of a particular ratio over several time periods is examined. Of course, consistency in financial reporting and in defining the ratio components is crucial if the trend is to be meaningful.

Most industry and trade associations publish industry average ratios based on aggregated data compiled by the associations from reports submitted by association members. Comparison of an individual company's ratio with the comparable industry ratio is frequently made as a means of assessing a company's relative standing in its industry. However, a comparison of a company with its industry that is based on a single observation may not be very meaningful because the company may use a financial accounting alternative that is different from that used by the rest of the industry. **Trend analysis** results in a much more meaningful comparison because even though the data used in

LO 1

Discuss why financial statement ratios are important.

the ratio may have been developed under different financial accounting alternatives, internal consistency within each of the trends will permit useful trend comparisons.

Trend analysis is described later in this chapter, but this brief example illustrates the process: Suppose a student's grade point average for last semester was 3.5 on a 4.0 scale. That GPA may be interesting, but it says little about the student's work. However, suppose you learn that this student's GPA was 1.9 four semesters ago, 2.7 three semesters ago, and 3.0 two semesters ago. The upward trend of grades suggests that the student is working "smarter and harder." This conclusion would be reinforced if you knew that the average GPA for all students in this person's class was 2.9 for each of the four semesters. You still don't know everything about the individual student's academic performance, but the comparative trend data let you make a more informed judgment than was possible with just the grades from one semester.

What Does It Mean?

Answer on page 90

1. What does it mean to state that the trend of data is frequently more important than the data themselves?

Return on Investment

LO 2

Explain the importance and show the calculation of return on investment.

Imagine that you are presented with two investment alternatives. Each investment will be made for one year, and each investment is equally risky. At the end of the year you will get your original investment back, plus income of $75 from investment A and $90 from investment B. Which investment alternative would you choose? The answer seems so obvious that you believe the question is loaded, so you hesitate to answer—a sensible response. But why is this a trick question? A little thought should make you think of a question to which you need an answer before you can select between investment A and investment B. Your question? "How much money would I have to invest in either alternative?" If the amount to be invested is the same, for example $1,000, then clearly you would select investment B because your income would be greater than that earned on investment A for the same amount invested. If the amount to be invested in investment B is more than that required for investment A, you would have to calculate the **rate of return** on each investment to choose the more profitable alternative.

Rate of return is calculated by dividing the amount of return (the income of $75 or $90 in the preceding example) by the amount of the investment. For example, using an investment of $1,000 for each alternative:

Investment A:

$$\text{Rate of return} = \frac{\text{Amount of return}}{\text{Amount invested}} = \frac{\$75}{\$1,000} = 7.5\%$$

Investment B:

$$\text{Rate of return} = \frac{\text{Amount of return}}{\text{Amount invested}} = \frac{\$90}{\$1,000} = 9\%$$

Your intuitive selection of investment B as the better investment is confirmed by the fact that its rate of return is higher than that of investment A.

The example situation assumed that each of the investments would be made for one year. Remember that unless otherwise specified, rate of return calculations assume that the time period of the investment and return is one year.

The rate of return calculation is derived from the interest calculation you probably learned many years ago. Recall that:

$$\text{Interest} = \text{Principal} \times \text{Rate} \times \text{Time}$$

Interest is the income or expense from investing or borrowing money.

Principal is the amount invested or borrowed.

Rate is the **interest rate** per year expressed as a percentage.

Time is the length of time the funds are invested or borrowed, expressed in years.

Note that when time is assumed to be one year, that term of the equation becomes 1/1 or 1, and it disappears. Thus, the rate of return calculation is simply a rearranged interest calculation that solves for the annual interest rate.

Return to the example situation and assume that the amounts required to be invested are $500 for investment A and $600 for investment B. Now which alternative would you select on the basis of rate of return? You should have made these calculations:

Investment A:

$$\text{Rate of return} = \frac{\text{Amount of return}}{\text{Amount invested}} = \frac{\$75}{\$500} = 15\%$$

Investment B:

$$\text{Rate of return} = \frac{\text{Amount of return}}{\text{Amount invested}} = \frac{\$90}{\$600} = 15\%$$

All other things being equal (and they seldom are except in textbook illustrations), you would be indifferent with respect to the alternatives available to you because each has a rate of return of 15% (per year).

Rate of return and riskiness related to an investment go hand in hand. **Risk** relates to the range of possible outcomes from an activity. The wider the range of possible outcomes, the greater the risk. An investment in a bank savings account is less risky than an investment in the stock of a corporation because the investor is virtually assured of receiving her or his principal and interest from the savings account, but the market value of stock may fluctuate widely even over a short period. Thus, the investor antici- pates a higher rate of return from the stock investment than from the savings account as compensation for taking on additional risk. Yet the greater risk of the stock investment means that the actual rate of return earned could be considerably less (even negative) or much greater than the interest earned on the savings account. Market prices for products and commodities, as well as stock prices, reflect this basic risk–reward relationship. For now, understand that the higher the rate of return of one investment relative to another, the greater the risk associated with the higher return investment.

Rate of return is a universally accepted measure of profitability. Because it is a ratio, profitability of unequal investments can be compared, and risk–reward relation- ships can be evaluated. Bank advertisements for certificates of deposit feature the in- terest rate, or rate of return, that will be earned by the depositor. All investors evaluate the profitability of an investment by making a rate of return calculation.

Return on investment (ROI) is the label usually assigned to the rate of return calculation made using data from financial statements. This ratio is sometimes re- ferred to as the **return on assets (ROA).** There are many ways of defining both the amount of return and the amount invested. For now we use net income as the amount of return and use average total assets during the year as the amount invested. It is not appropriate to use total assets as reported on a single year-end balance sheet because that is the total at one point in time: the balance sheet date. Net income was earned during the entire fiscal year, so it should be related to the assets that were used during

Exhibit 3-1   Condensed Balance Sheets and Income Statement of Cruisers, Inc.

CRUISERS, INC. **Comparative Condensed Balance Sheets** **September 30, 2014 and 2013**			**CRUISERS, INC.** **Condensed Income Statement** **For the Year Ended** **September 30, 2014**	
	2014	**2013**		
Current assets:				
Cash and marketable securities.......	$ 22,286	$ 16,996	Net sales	$611,873
Accounts receivable	42,317	39,620	Cost of goods sold.......	428,354
Inventories.......................	53,716	48,201	Gross margin	$183,519
Total current assets	$118,319	$104,817	Operating expenses	122,183
Other assets......................	284,335	259,903	Income from operations ...	$ 61,336
Total assets	$402,654	$364,720	Interest expense.........	6,400
Current liabilities	$ 57,424	$ 51,400	Income before taxes......	$ 54,936
Other liabilities	80,000	83,000	Income taxes	20,026
Total liabilities....................	$137,424	$134,400	Net income.............	$ 34,910
Stockholders' equity................	265,230	230,320	Earnings per share	$1.21
Total liabilities and stockholders' equity....	$402,654	$364,720		

the entire year. Average assets used during the year usually are estimated by averaging the assets reported at the beginning of the year (the prior year-end balance sheet total) and assets reported at the end of the year. Recall from Chapter 2 that the income statement for the year is the link between the beginning and ending balance sheets. If seasonal fluctuations in total assets are significant (the materiality concept) and if quarter-end or month-end balance sheets are available, a more refined average asset calculation may be made.

The ROI of a firm is significant to most financial statement readers because it describes the rate of return management was able to earn on the assets that it had available to use during the year. Investors especially will make decisions and informed judgments about the quality of management and the relative profitability of a company based on ROI. Many financial analysts (these authors included) believe that ROI is the most meaningful measure of a company's profitability. Knowing net income alone is not enough; *an informed judgment about the firm's profitability requires relating net income to the assets used to generate that net income.*

The condensed balance sheets and income statement of Cruisers, Inc., a hypothetical company, are presented in Exhibit 3-1. Using these data, the company's ROI calculation is illustrated here:

From the firm's balance sheets:

Total assets, September 30, 2013..................... $364,720

Total assets, September 30, 2014..................... $402,654

From the firm's income statement for the year ended September 30, 2014:

Net income .... $ 34,910

$$\text{Return on investment} = \frac{\text{Net income}}{\text{Average total assets}}$$

$$= \frac{\$34,910}{(\$364,720 + \$402,654)/2} = 9.1\%$$

Some financial analysts prefer to use income from operations (or earnings before interest and income taxes) and average operating assets in the ROI calculation. They believe that excluding interest expense, income taxes, and assets not used in operations provides a better measure of the operating results of the firm. With these refinements, the ROI formula would be:

$$\text{Return on investment} = \frac{\text{Operating income}}{\text{Average operating assets}}$$

Other analysts will make similar adjustments to arrive at the amounts used in the ROI calculation. Consistency in the definition of terms is more important than the definition itself because the trend of ROI will be more significant for decision making than the absolute result of the ROI calculation for any one year. However, it is appropriate to understand the definitions used in any ROI results you see.

---

2. What does it mean to express economic performance as a rate of return?
3. What does it mean to say that return on investment (ROI) is one of the most meaningful measures of financial performance?

What Does It Mean?
Answers on page 90

The DuPont Model: An Expansion of the ROI Calculation

Financial analysts at E.I. DuPont de Nemours & Co. are credited with developing the **DuPont model,** an expansion of the basic ROI calculation, in the late 1930s. They reasoned that profitability from sales and utilization of assets to generate sales revenue were both important factors to be considered when evaluating a company's overall profitability. One popular adaptation of their model introduces total sales revenue into the ROI calculation as follows:

LO 3
Illustrate how to calculate and interpret margin and turnover using the DuPont model.

$$\text{Return on investment} = \frac{\text{Net income}}{\text{Sales}} \times \frac{\text{Sales}}{\text{Average total assets}}$$

The first term, net income/sales, is **margin.** The second term, sales/average total assets, is **asset turnover,** or simply **turnover.** Of course the sales quantities cancel out algebraically, but they are introduced to this version of the ROI model because of their significance. *Margin* emphasizes that from every dollar of sales revenue, some amount must work its way to the bottom line (net income) if the company is to be profitable. *Turnover* relates to the efficiency with which the firm's assets are used in the revenue-generating process.

Another quick quiz will illustrate the significance of turnover. Many of us look forward to a 40-hour-per-week job, generally thought of as five 8-hour days. Imagine a company's factory operating on such a schedule—one shift per day, five days per week. What percentage of the available time is that factory operating? You may have answered 33% or one-third of the time because eight hours is one-third of a day. But what about Saturday and Sunday? In fact there are 21 shifts available in a week (7 days × 3 shifts per day), so a factory operating 5 shifts per week is being used only 5/21 of the time—less than 25%. The factory is idle more than 75% of the time! And as

Study

Suggestion

As a rule of thumb, do not place much reliance on rules of thumb! Do not try to memorize them. Instead you should understand that ratio comparisons are often difficult to make. Firms within a given industry may vary considerably over time in terms of their relative scale of operations, life cycle stage of development, market segmentation strategies, cost and capital structures, selected accounting methods, or a number of other economic factors; cross-industry ratio comparisons are even more problematic. Thus, the rules of thumb provided in this chapter are intended merely to serve as points of reference; they are not based on empirical evidence unless otherwise indicated.

you can imagine, many of the occupancy costs (real estate taxes, utilities, insurance) are incurred whether or not the plant is in use. This explains why many firms operate their plants on a two-shift, three-shift, or even seven-day basis rather than building additional plants—it allows them to increase their level of production and thereby expand sales volume without expanding their investment in assets. The higher costs associated with multiple-shift operations (like late-shift premiums for workers and additional shipping costs relative to shipping from multiple locations closer to customers) will increase the company's operating expenses, thereby lowering net income and decreasing margin. Yet the multiple-shift company's overall ROI will be higher if turnover is increased proportionately more than margin is reduced, which is likely to be the case.

Calculation of ROI using the DuPont model is illustrated here, using data from the financial statements of Cruisers, Inc., in Exhibit 3-1:

From the firm's balance sheets:	
Total assets, September 30, 2013.	$364,720
Total assets, September 30, 2014.	$402,654
From the firm's income statement for the year ended September 30, 2014:	
Net sales	$611,873
Net income	$ 34,910

$$\text{Return on investment} = \text{Margin} \times \text{Turnover}$$
$$= \frac{\text{Net income}}{\text{Sales}} \times \frac{\text{Sales}}{\text{Average total assets}}$$
$$= \frac{\$34,910}{\$611,873} \times \frac{\$611,873}{(\$364,720 + \$402,654) / 2}$$
$$= 5.7\% \times 1.6$$
$$= 9.1\%$$

The significance of the DuPont model is that it has led top management in many organizations to consider utilization of assets, including keeping investment in assets as low as feasible, to be just as important to overall performance as generating profit from sales.

A rule of thumb useful for putting ROI in perspective is that for most American merchandising and manufacturing companies, average ROI based on net income normally ranges between 8% and 12% during stable economic times. Average ROI based on operating income (earnings before interest and taxes) for the same set of firms is typically between 10% and 15%. Average margin, based on net income, ranges from about 5% to 10%. Using operating income, average margin tends to range from 10%

to 15%. Asset turnover is usually about 1.0 to 1.5 but often ranges as high as 3.0, depending on the operating characteristics of the firm and its industry. The ranges given here are rather wide and are intended to suggest only that a firm with ROI and component values consistently beyond these ranges is exceptional.

---

4. What does it mean when the straightforward ROI calculation is expanded by using margin and turnover?

What Does It Mean?

Answer on page 90

Return on Equity

Recall that the balance sheet equation is:

$$\text{Assets} = \text{Liabilities} + \text{Stockholders' equity}$$

LO 4
Explain the importance and show the calculation of return on equity.

The return on investment calculation relates net income (perhaps adjusted for interest, income taxes, or other items) to assets. Assets (perhaps adjusted to exclude nonoperating assets or other items) represent the amount invested to generate earnings. As the balance sheet equation indicates, the investment in assets can result from either amounts borrowed from creditors (liabilities) or amounts invested by the owners. Stockholders (and others) are interested in expressing the profits of the firm as a rate of return on the amount of stockholders' equity; this is called **return on equity (ROE),** and it is calculated as follows:

$$\text{Return on equity} = \frac{\text{Net income}}{\text{Average stockholders' equity}}$$

Return on equity usually is calculated using average stockholders' equity during the period for which the net income was earned for the same reason that average assets is used in the ROI calculation; net income is earned over a period of time, so it should be related to the stockholders' equity over that same period.

Calculation of ROE is illustrated here using data from the financial statements of Cruisers, Inc., in Exhibit 3-1:

From the firm's balance sheets:	
Total stockholders' equity, September 30, 2013	$230,320
Total stockholders' equity, September 30, 2014	$265,230
From the firm's income statement for the year ended September 30, 2014:	
Net income	$ 34,910

$$
\begin{aligned}
\text{Return on equity} &= \frac{\text{Net income}}{\text{Average stockholders' equity}} \\
&= \frac{\$34,910}{(\$230,320 + \$265,230) / 2} \\
&= \$34,910 / \$247,775 \\
&= 14.1\%
\end{aligned}
$$

A rule of thumb for putting ROE in perspective is that average ROE for most American merchandising and manufacturing companies has historically ranged from 10% to 15%.

Keep in mind that return on equity is a special application of the rate of return concept. ROE is important to current stockholders and prospective investors because it relates earnings to stockholders' investment—that is, the stockholders' equity in the assets of the entity. Adjustments to both net income and average stockholders' equity are sometimes made in an effort to improve the comparability of ROE results between firms, and some of these will be explained later in the text. For now, you should understand that both return on investment and return on equity are fundamental measures of the profitability of a firm and that the data for making these calculations come from the firm's financial statements.

What Does It Mean?
Answer on page 90

5. What does it mean when return on equity is used to evaluate a firm's financial performance?

LO 5
Explain the meaning of liquidity and discuss why it is important.

Working Capital and Measures of Liquidity

Liquidity refers to a firm's ability to meet its current obligations and is measured by relating its current assets and current liabilities as reported on the balance sheet. **Working capital** is the excess of a firm's current assets over its current liabilities. Current assets are cash and other assets that are likely to be converted to cash within a year (principally accounts receivable and merchandise inventories). Current liabilities are obligations that are expected to be paid within a year, including loans, accounts payable, and other accrued liabilities (such as wages payable, interest payable, and rent payable). Most financially healthy firms have positive working capital. Even though a firm is not likely to have cash on hand at any point in time equal to its current liabilities, it will expect to collect accounts receivable or sell merchandise inventory and then collect the resulting accounts receivable in time to pay the liabilities when they are scheduled for payment. Of course, in the process of converting inventories to cash, the firm will be purchasing additional merchandise for its inventory, and the suppliers will want to be assured of collecting the amounts due according to the previously agreed provisions for when payment is due.

Liquidity is measured in three principal ways:

$$\text{Working capital} = \text{Current assets} - \text{Current liabilities}$$

$$\text{Current ratio} = \frac{\text{Current assets}}{\text{Current liabilities}}$$

$$\text{Acid-test ratio} = \frac{\text{Cash (including temporary cash investments)} + \text{Accounts receivable}}{\text{Current liabilities}}$$

The dollar amount of a firm's working capital is not as significant as the ratio of its current assets to current liabilities because the amount can be misleading unless it is related to another quantity (how large is large?). Therefore the *trend* of a company's **current ratio** is most useful in judging its current bill-paying ability. The **acid-test ratio,** also known as the *quick ratio,* is a more conservative short-term measure of liquidity because merchandise inventories are excluded from the computation. This ratio provides information about an almost worst-case situation—the firm's ability to meet its current obligations even if none of the inventory can be sold.

The liquidity measure calculations shown here use September 30, 2014, data from the balance sheet of Cruisers, Inc., in Exhibit 3-1:

LO 6

Discuss the significance and calculation of working capital, the current ratio, and the acid-test ratio.

$$\text{Working capital} = \text{Current assets} - \text{Current liabilities}$$
$$= \$118,319 - \$57,424$$
$$= \$60,895$$

$$\text{Current ratio} = \frac{\text{Current assets}}{\text{Current liabilities}} = \frac{\$118,319}{\$57,424} = 2.1$$

$$\text{Acid-test ratio} = \frac{\text{Cash (including temporary cash investments)} + \text{Accounts receivable}}{\text{Current liabilities}}$$
$$= \frac{\$22,286 + \$42,317}{\$57,424}$$
$$= 1.1$$

As a general rule, a current ratio of 2.0 and an acid-test ratio of 1.0 are considered indicative of adequate liquidity. From these data, it can be concluded that Cruisers, Inc., has a high degree of liquidity; it should not have any trouble meeting its current obligations as they become due.

In terms of debt-paying ability, the higher the current ratio, the better. Yet an overly high current ratio sometimes can be a sign that the company has not made the most productive use of its assets. In recent years many large, well-managed corporations have made efforts to streamline operations by reducing their current ratios to the 1.0–1.5 range or even lower, with corresponding reductions in their acid-test ratios. So what motivates this practice? It's clear that investments in cash, accounts receivable, and inventories are being minimized because these current assets tend to be the least productive assets employed by the company. For example, what kind of ROI is earned on accounts receivable or inventory? Very little, if any. Funds freed up by reducing a company's investment in working capital items can be used to purchase new production equipment or to expand marketing efforts for existing product lines.

Remember, however, that judgments based on the results of any of these calculations using data from a single balance sheet are not as meaningful as the trend of the results over several periods. It is also important to note the composition of working capital and to understand the impact on the ratios of equal changes in current assets and current liabilities. As the following illustration shows, if a short-term bank loan were repaid just before the balance sheet date, working capital would not change (because current assets and current liabilities would each decrease by the same amount), but the current ratio (and the acid-test ratio) would change:

	Before Loan Repayment	After $20,000 Loan Repaid
Current assets.	$200,000	$180,000
Current liabilities	100,000	80,000
Working capital	$100,000	$100,000
Current ratio	2.0	2.25

If a new loan for $20,000 were then taken out just after the balance sheet date, the level of the firm's liquidity at the balance sheet date as expressed by the current ratio would have been overstated. Thus, liquidity measures should be viewed with a healthy dose of skepticism because the timing of short-term borrowings and repayments is entirely within the control of management.

Business in
Practice

Establishing a Credit Relationship

Most transactions between businesses, and many transactions between individuals and businesses, are credit transactions. That is, the sale of the product or provision of the service is completed sometime before payment is made by the purchaser. Usually, before delivering the product or service, the seller wants to have some assurance that the bill will be paid when due. This involves determining that the buyer is a good **credit risk.**

Individuals usually establish credit by submitting to the potential creditor a completed credit application, which includes information about employment, salary, bank accounts, liabilities, and other credit relationships (such as charge accounts) established. Most credit grantors are looking for a good record of timely payments on existing credit accounts; this is why an individual's first credit account is usually the most difficult to obtain. Potential credit grantors also may check an individual's credit record as maintained by one or more of the three national credit bureaus in the United States.

Businesses seeking credit may follow a procedure similar to that used by individuals. Alternatively, they may provide financial statements and names of firms with which a credit relationship has been established. A newly organized firm may have to pay for its purchases in advance or on delivery **(COD)** until it has been in operation for several months, and then the seller may set a relatively low credit limit for sales on credit. Once a record is established of having paid bills when due, the credit limit will be raised. After a firm has been in operation for a year or more, its credit history may be reported by the Dun & Bradstreet credit reporting service—a type of national credit bureau to which many companies subscribe. Even after a credit relationship has been established, it is not unusual for a firm to continue providing financial statements to its principal creditors.

Measures of liquidity are used primarily by potential creditors who are seeking to judge their prospects of being paid promptly if they enter a creditor relationship with the firm whose liquidity is being analyzed (see Business in Practice—Establishing a Credit Relationship).

The statement of cash flows also is useful in assessing the reasons for a firm's liquidity (or illiquidity). Recall that this financial statement identifies the reasons for the change in a firm's cash during the period (usually a year) by reporting the changes during the period in noncash balance sheet items.

What Does It Mean?
Q
Answer on page 90

6. What does it mean to say that the financial position of a firm is liquid?

Illustration of Trend Analysis

LO 7
Generalize about how trend analysis can be used most effectively.

Trend analysis of return on investment, return on equity, and working capital and liquidity measures is illustrated in the following tables and exhibits. The data in these illustrations come primarily from the financial statements in the 2011 annual report of Campbell Soup Company, reproduced in the appendix.

Campbell Soup Company (Profitability* and Liquidity Data,† 2007–2011)	**Table 3-1**				
	2011	**2010**	**2009**	**2008**	**2007**
Margin (net earnings‡/net sales)	10.4	11.0	9.7	14.6	11.6
Turnover (net sales/average total assets).	1.18	1.24	1.21	1.24	0.97
ROI (net earnings/average total assets).	12.4	13.7	11.7	18.0	12.0
ROE (net earnings/average total equity)	79.5	101.7	71.7	89.0	55.7
Year-end position (in millions):					
Current assets.	$1,963	$1,687	$1,551	$1,693	$1,518
Current liabilities.	1,989	2,065	1,628	2,403	2,030
Working capital	(26)	(378)	(77)	(710)	(450)
Current ratio	0.99	0.82	0.95	0.70	0.75

*Profitability calculations were made from the data presented in the five-year selected financial data.

†Liquidity calculations were made from the data presented in the balance sheets of this and prior annual reports.

‡In 2011, "Net earnings" was $802, whereas "Net earnings attributable to Campbell Soup Company" was $805; the latter amount is used in these calculations. These two amounts were the same for all of the other years (2007–2010).

Source: Campbell Soup Company, 2011 Annual Report, pp. 12, 34–35.

The data in Table 3-1 come from the five-year "selected financial data" of Campbell's 2011 annual report (see page 709 in the appendix) and from balance sheets of prior annual reports. The data in Table 3-1 are presented graphically in Exhibits 3-2 through 3-4. Note that the sequence of the years in the table is opposite from that of the years in the graphs. Tabular data are frequently presented so the most recent year is closest to the captions of the table. Graphs of time series data usually flow from left to right. In any event, it is necessary to notice and understand the captions of both tables and graphs.

The graph in Exhibit 3-2 illustrates that the ROI and ROE results varied significantly during the five-year period presented. ROI and ROE rose dramatically during the year ended August 3, 2008 and then fell considerably during fiscal 2009. The global financial crisis that took hold in the fourth quarter of 2008 (after Campbell's 2008 fiscal year-end

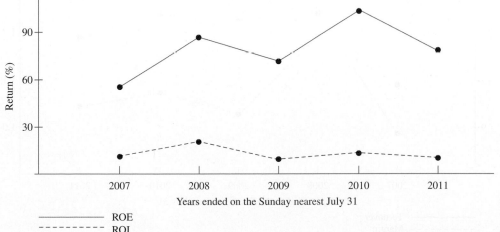

Campbell Soup Company, Return on Investment (ROI) and Return on Equity (ROE), 2007–2011   **Exhibit 3-2**

had ended) negatively impacted the company's 2009 reported results. However, in 2010, Campbell's stockholders were rewarded with another uptick in ROE. Unfortunately, this was promptly followed by a decline in both ROI and ROE during 2011. With such varied results from year to year, the trend in the profitability data is obviously quite difficult to interpret without understanding more about the company's operations.

As the graphs in Exhibit 3-2 illustrate, Campbell's ROI trend was clearly more stable than its ROE trend during the five-year period from 2007 to 2011, as is typically the case for many companies. A firm's asset growth from year to year tends to be well planned and thus is likely to generate more consistency in the ROI results than would equity growth, which is much harder to predict and control. In recent years, Campbell's total assets have been approximately 5 to 7 times larger than the company's total equity due to the presence of substantial amounts of debt on the company's balance sheet. As a direct result of Campbell's aggressive use of *financial leverage* (i.e., taking the risk of borrowing funds from creditors on a long-term basis to enhance the return to stockholders), ROE ranged from an astonishing 51.7% to 101.7% during the five-year period depicted in the graph. Suffice it to say, stockholder returns of this magnitude are highly unusual for a mature company such as Campbell's, although competitive consumer goods companies such as Hershey's and Kellogg's have recently reported unusually high ROE results as well.

Not only do these ROE results represent a staggering five-year return to Campbell's stockholders, but they also present some difficulties in making meaningful comparisons of the company's ROI and ROE trends. In Exhibit 3-2, the vertical scale spans a range from 11.7% (ROI for 2009) to the high data point of 101.7% (ROE for 2010). By using such a heavily compressed vertical scale, the variation of the actual data points for ROI (from 11.7% to 18%) becomes lost in the flattened-out graphical representation. Yet the "big picture" is that Campbell's has consistently provided a satisfying ROI to all resource providers while also providing abnormally high returns to its stockholders. This feat is even more impressive given that the company performed admirably not only during the mild recessionary times of 2007 but also through the most difficult economic downturn since the Great Depression, from late 2008 until mid-2010.

Exhibit 3-3 illustrates that Campbell's turnover has been remarkably stable in recent years, other than the temporary low in 2007, which was a peak year for the company's

Exhibit 3-3   Campbell Soup Company, Margin and Turnover, 2007–2011

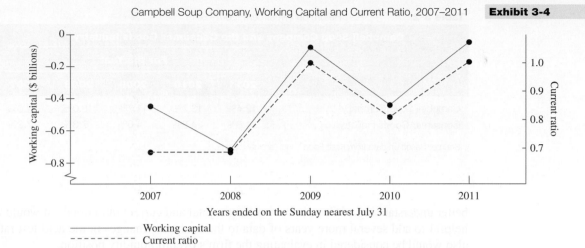

Campbell Soup Company, Working Capital and Current Ratio, 2007–2011   **Exhibit 3-4**

Working capital
Current ratio

Years ended on the Sunday nearest July 31

average total assets; the higher than usual denominator that year reduced turnover. Note that the range of turnover results during this period, 0.97–1.24, is not significant in absolute terms, and excluding the 0.97 data point for 2007, the range narrowed to a virtual flat-line representation of 1.18–1.24 during the final four years presented.

The trend in margin is more difficult to interpret. Margin spiked in 2008, and has shown considerably more variability than has the stable turnover trend. Yet even in 2009, which represents the low point in the data depicted in Exhibit 3-3, Campbell's margin was a healthy 9.7%, so what appears to be an overall downward trend is certainly no cause for alarm.

The overall trend in Campbell's liquidity during this period is not difficult to determine, although it is perhaps difficult to understand. As illustrated in Exhibit 3-4, Campbell's maintained a consistent current ratio in the range of 0.70–0.99 throughout the five-year period, meaning that current liabilities exceeded current assets in all years presented. Working capital peaked at ($26) million in 2011 and reached a low point of ($710) million in 2008. Yet it is highly unlikely that Campbell Soup Company has ever failed to meet any significant debt obligation in a timely manner. The tight manner in which the working capital and current ratio graphs mimic each other's progress suggests that Campbell's keeps a very close eye on these important relationships.

Campbell's clearly adheres to contemporary working capital management techniques, which suggest that investments in current assets (especially cash, accounts receivable, and inventories) ought to be minimized to the greatest extent possible. Likewise, management appears to take a similar view that it is perfectly acceptable to carry significant levels of current liabilities, as long as cash is readily available to pay all obligations as they fall due. As discussed on page 83, funds freed up by reducing one's investment in working capital items can be used, for example, to purchase new production equipment or to expand marketing efforts for existing product lines.

Large-scale multinational corporations often invest significant time and resources to develop sophisticated cash management systems that will help to facilitate the timely movement of funds and ensure that the company maximizes the utilization of its cash resources. Lines of credit are often arranged with major banks throughout the world as well, to provide for emergency cash needs. Although Campbell Soup Company may appear to be on the verge of a cash crisis, it's more likely that its working capital management team has carefully guided the company at every step along the way. To gain a

Table 3-2   Return on Investment, 2007–2011

Campbell Soup Company and the Consumer Goods Industry					
	For the Year				
	2011	**2010**	**2009**	**2008**	**2007**
Campbell Soup Company	12.4%	13.7%	11.7%	18.0%	12.0%
Consumer Goods industry	4.8%	4.8%	4.0%	7.3%	7.2%

Source: Based on data from Kraft Foods, Inc., annual reports.

better understanding of Campbell's working capital and current ratio trends, it would be helpful to add several more years of data to the analysis. Changes in the acid-test ratio also would be considered in evaluating the firm's overall liquidity position.

Table 3-2 summarizes industry data based on disclosures provided in the annual reports of Kraft Foods, Inc., during the past several years. These data are graphed in Exhibit 3-5 against the corresponding data from Campbell Soup Company, which is classified in the consumer goods industry. The story of the graph is that although Campbell's has been consistently outperforming the industry since 2007, its results have mirrored those of the industry.

All the graphs presented in this chapter use an arithmetic vertical scale. This means that the distance between values shown on the vertical axis is the same. So if the data being plotted increase at a constant rate over the period of time shown on the horizontal scale, the plot will be a line that curves upward more and more steeply. Many analysts prefer to plot data that will change significantly over time (a company's sales, for example) on a graph that has a logarithmic vertical scale. This is called a **semilogarithmic graph** because the horizontal scale is still arithmetic. The intervals between years, for example, will be equal. The advantage of a semilogarithmic presentation is that a constant rate of growth results in a straight-line plot. Extensive use of semilog graphs is made for data presented in the financial press, such as *The Wall Street Journal, The Financial Times, Fortune,* and *BusinessWeek.*

Exhibit 3-5   Campbell Soup Company and Consumer Goods Industry, Return on Investment, 2007–2011

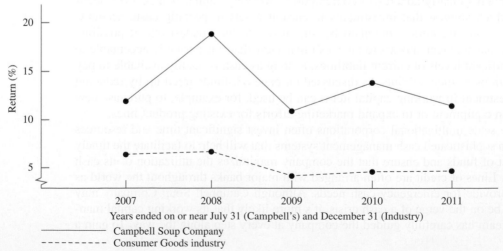

Years ended on or near July 31 (Campbell's) and December 31 (Industry)

——————— Campbell Soup Company
– – – – – – – – Consumer Goods industry

7. What does it mean when the trend of a company's ROE is consistently higher by an approximately equal amount than the trend of ROE for the industry of which the company is a part?

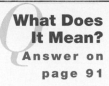
What Does It Mean?

Answer on page 91

Demonstration Problem

Visit the text website at www.mhhe.com/marshall10e to view a demonstration problem for this chapter.

Summary

Financial statement users express financial statement data in ratio format to facilitate making informed judgments and decisions. Users are especially interested in the trend of a company's ratios over time and the comparison of the company's ratio trends with those of its industry as a whole.

The rate of return on investment is a universally accepted measure of profitability. Rate of return is calculated by dividing the amount of return, or profit, by the amount invested. Rate of return is expressed as an annual percentage rate.

Return on investment (ROI) is one of the most important measures of profitability because it relates the income earned during a period to the assets that were invested to generate those earnings. The DuPont model for calculating ROI expands the basic model by introducing sales to calculate margin (net income/sales) and asset turnover (sales/ average assets); ROI equals margin × turnover. *Margin* describes the profit from each dollar of sales, and *turnover* expresses the sales-generating capacity (utilization efficiency) of the firm's assets. This financial ratio is often referred to as *return on assets (ROA)*.

Return on equity (ROE) relates net income earned for the year to the average stockholders' equity for the year. This rate of return measure is important to current and prospective owners/stockholders because it relates earnings to the stockholders' investment.

Creditors are interested in an entity's liquidity—that is, its ability to pay its liabilities when due. The amount of working capital, the current ratio, and the acid-test ratio are measures of liquidity. These calculations are made using the amounts of current assets and current liabilities reported in the balance sheet.

When ratio trend data are plotted graphically, it is easy to determine the significance of ratio changes and to evaluate a firm's performance. However, it is necessary to pay attention to how graphs are constructed because the visual image presented can be influenced by the scales used.

Key Terms and Concepts

acid-test ratio (p. 82)   The ratio of the sum of cash (including temporary cash investments) and accounts receivable to current liabilities. A primary measure of a firm's liquidity.

asset turnover (p. 79)   The quotient of sales divided by average assets for the year or other fiscal period.

COD (p. 84) Cash on delivery, or collect on delivery.

credit risk (p. 84) The risk that an entity to which credit has been extended will not pay the amount due on the date set for payment.

current ratio (p. 82) The ratio of current assets to current liabilities. A primary measure of a firm's liquidity.

DuPont model (p. 79) An expansion of the return on investment calculation to margin $\times$ turnover.

interest (p. 77) The income or expense from investing or borrowing money.

interest rate (p. 77) The percentage amount used, together with principal and time, to calculate interest.

liquidity (p. 82) Refers to a firm's ability to meet its current financial obligations.

margin (p. 79) The percentage of net income to net sales. Sometimes margin is calculated using operating income or other intermediate subtotals of the income statement. The term also can refer to the *amount* of gross profit, operating income, or net income.

principal (p. 77) The amount of money invested or borrowed.

rate of return (p. 76) A percentage calculated by dividing the amount of return on an investment for a period of time by the average amount invested for the period. A primary measure of profitability.

return on assets (ROA) (p. 77) A synonym for *return on investment (ROI)*.

return on equity (ROE) (p. 81) The percentage of net income divided by average stockholders' equity for the fiscal period in which the net income was earned; frequently referred to as *ROE*. A primary measure of a firm's profitability.

return on investment (ROI) (p. 77) The rate of return on an investment; frequently referred to as *ROI*. Sometimes referred to as *return on assets* or *ROA*. A primary measure of a firm's profitability.

risk (p. 77) A concept that describes the range of possible outcomes from an action. The greater the range of possible outcomes, the greater the risk.

semilogarithmic graph (p. 88) A graph format in which the vertical axis is a logarithmic scale.

trend analysis (p. 75) Evaluation of the trend of data over time.

turnover (p. 79) The quotient of sales divided by the average assets for the year or some other fiscal period. A descriptor, such as total asset, inventory, or plant and equipment, usually precedes the turnover term. A measure of the efficiency with which assets are used to generate sales.

working capital (p. 82) The difference between current assets and current liabilities. A measure of a firm's liquidity.

ANSWERS TO
What Does It Mean?

1. It means that almost everything is relative, so comparison of individual and group trends is important when making judgments about performance.

2. It means that the economic outcome (the amount of return) is related to the input (the investment) utilized to produce the return.

3. It means that investors and others can evaluate the economic performance of a firm, and make comparisons between firms, by using this ratio.

4. It means that a better understanding of ROI is achieved by knowing about the profitability from sales (margin) and the efficiency with which assets have been used (turnover) to generate sales.

5. It means that the focus is changed from return on total assets to return on the portion of total assets provided by the stockholders of the firm.

6. It means that the firm has enough cash, or is likely to soon collect enough cash, to pay its liabilities that are now, or soon will be, due for payment.

7. It means that the company is following the industry; it does not necessarily mean that the company is doing better than the industry because the company's higher ROE may be caused by its use of different accounting practices than those used by other firms in the industry.

Self-Study Material

Visit the text website at www.mhhe.com/marshall10e to take an online self-study quiz for this chapter.

Matching Following are a number of the key terms and concepts introduced in the chapter, along with a list of corresponding definitions. Match the appropriate letter for the key term or concept to each definition provided (items 1–10). Note that not all key terms and concepts will be used. Answers are provided at the end of this chapter.

a.	Ratio	j.	Turnover
b.	Trend analysis	k.	Return on equity
c.	Rate of return	l.	Working capital
d.	Interest	m.	Liquidity
e.	Principal	n.	Current ratio
f.	Risk	o.	Acid-test ratio
g.	Return on investment	p.	Credit risk
h.	DuPont model	q.	Collect on delivery
i.	Margin		

_____ 1. The percentage of net income to net sales.

_____ 2. The amount of money invested or borrowed.

_____ 3. The difference between current assets and current liabilities.

_____ 4. The percentage of net income divided by average stockholders' equity for the fiscal period in which the net income was earned.

_____ 5. An indication of a firm's ability to meet its current financial obligations.

_____ 6. The quotient of sales divided by the average assets for the year or some other fiscal period.

_____ 7. Evaluation of data patterns over time.

_____ 8. The income or expense from investing or borrowing money.

_____ 9. A calculation of return on investment made by multiplying margin by turnover.

_____10. The ratio of the sum of cash (including temporary cash investments) and accounts receivable to current liabilities.

Multiple Choice For each of the following questions, circle the best response. Answers are provided at the end of this chapter.

1. Return on investment (ROI) can be described or computed in each of the following ways *except*

    a. Amount invested / Amount of return = ROI.

    b. Net income / Average total assets = ROI.

    c. (Net income / Sales) × (Sales / Average total assets) = ROI.

    d. Margin × Turnover = ROI.

2. Working capital includes all of the following accounts *except*

    a. Accounts Payable.

    b. Cash.

    c. Accumulated Depreciation.

    d. Merchandise Inventory.

3. Which of the following would *not* decrease working capital?

    a. A decrease in Cash.

    b. An increase in Accounts Payable.

    c. An increase in Merchandise Inventory.

    d. A decrease in Accounts Receivable.

4. Assume that Kulpa Company has a current ratio of 0.7. Which of the following transactions would increase this ratio?

    a. Purchasing merchandise inventory on credit.

    b. Selling merchandise inventory at cost for cash.

    c. Collecting accounts receivable in cash.

    d. Paying off accounts payable with cash.

The following data apply to Questions 5–8:

BAREFOOT INDUSTRIES Balance Sheet and Income Statement Data At December 31, 2013, and for the Year Then Ended	
Assets	
Cash	$ 400
Accounts receivable	440
Merchandise inventory	360
Land	100
Equipment	300
Accumulated depreciation	(100)
Liabilities and Stockholders' Equity	
Accounts payable	$ 300
Notes payable, short-term	500
Long-term debt	200
Common stock	100
Retained earnings	400
Income Statement	
Sales	$3,000
Cost of goods sold	(2,000)
Gross profit	1,000
Selling expenses	(500)
Income taxes	(200)
Net income	300

5. The current ratio is
   a. 1.05.   c. 1.55.
   b. 1.5.   d. 2.0.
6. The acid-test ratio is
   a. 1.05.   c. 1.55.
   b. 1.5.   d. 2.0.
7. The amount of working capital that would remain if $400 of land was purchased on January 1, 2014, with the use of $200 cash and $200 of long-term debt is
   a. $200.   c. $600.
   b. $400.   d. $900.
8. Assume that both total assets and total stockholders' equity were the same on December 31, 2012, as on December 31, 2013. The margin, ROI, ROE, and turnover are
   a. 10%, 20%, 60%, 2.0.
   b. 10%, 20%, 75%, 1.5.
   c. 30%, 15%, 60%, 2.0.
   d. 30%, 15%, 75%, 1.5.

Mini-Exercises

All applicable Mini-Exercises are available with McGraw-Hill's *Connect*™ *Accounting*.

ROI analysis using the DuPont model Firm J has net income of $72,000, sales of $960,000, and average total assets of $480,000.

Mini-Exercise 3.1
LO 3

Required:
Calculate Firm J's margin, turnover, and return on investment (ROI).

ROI analysis using the DuPont model Firm K has a margin of 16%, turnover of 1.2, and sales of $1,500,000.

Mini-Exercise 3.2
LO 3

Required:
Calculate Firm K's net income, average total assets, and return on investment (ROI).

Calculate ROE Firm L had net assets at the end of the year of $365,000. The only transactions affecting stockholders' equity during the year were net income of $56,000 and dividends of $26,000.

Mini-Exercise 3.3
LO 4

Required:
Calculate Firm L's average stockholders' equity and return on equity (ROE).

Calculate average total assets, net income, ROI, and ROE Firm M has a margin of 9%, turnover of 1.6, sales of $800,000, and average stockholders' equity of $360,000.

Mini-Exercise 3.4
LO 3, 4

Required:
Calculate Firm M's average total assets, net income, return on investment (ROI), and return on equity (ROE).

Mini-Exercise 3.5
LO 6

Calculate current liabilities and working capital Firm N has a current ratio of 2.6 and current assets of $150,800.

Required:
Calculate Firm N's current liabilities and working capital.

Mini-Exercise 3.6
LO 6

Calculate working capital and current ratio Firm O has accounts receivable of $31,000, cash of $14,600, property, plant, and equipment of $320,000, merchandise inventory of $43,200, accounts payable of $22,100, other accrued liabilities of $7,500, common stock of $250,000, and retained earnings of $129,200.

Required:
Calculate Firm N's working capital and current ratio.

connect
|ACCOUNTING

Exercises

All applicable Exercises are available with McGraw-Hill's *Connect*™ *Accounting*.

Exercise 3.7
LO 2

Compare investment alternatives Two acquaintances have approached you about investing in business activities in which each is involved. Nateisha is seeking $2,800 and Tian needs $3,600. One year from now your original investment will be returned, along with $252 income from Nateisha or $306 income from Tian. You can make only one investment.

Required:
a.   Which investment would you prefer? Why? Round your percentage answer to two decimal places.
b.   What other factors should you consider before making either investment?

Exercise 3.8
LO 2

Compare investment alternatives A friend has $5,000 that has been saved from her part-time job. She will need her money, plus any interest earned on it, in six months and has asked for your help in deciding whether to put the money in a bank savings account at 4.5% interest or to lend it to Simone. Simone has promised to repay $5,250 after six months.

Required:
a.   Calculate the interest earned on the savings account for six months.
b.   Calculate the rate of return if the money is lent to Simone. Round your percentage answer to two decimal places.
c.   Which alternative would you recommend? Explain your answer.

Exercise 3.9
LO 2

Compare investment alternatives You have two investment opportunities. One will have a 10% rate of return on an investment of $5,000; the other will have an 11% rate of return on principal of $7,000. You would like to take advantage of the higher-yielding investment but have only $5,000 available.

Required:
What is the maximum rate of interest that you would pay to borrow the $2,000 needed to take advantage of the higher yield?

Compare investment alternatives You have accumulated $12,000 and are looking for the best rate of return that can be earned over the next year. A bank savings account will pay 5%. A one-year bank certificate of deposit will pay 8%, but the minimum investment is $15,000.

Exercise 3.10
LO 2

Required:
a. Calculate the amount of return you would earn if the $12,000 were invested for one year at 5%.
b. Calculate the net amount of return you would earn if $3,000 were borrowed at a cost of 15%, and then $15,000 were invested for one year at 8%.
c. Calculate the net rate of return on your investment of $12,000 if you accept the strategy of part **b.**
d. In addition to the amount of investment required and the rate of return offered, what other factors would you normally consider before making an investment decision such as the one described in this exercise?

ROI analysis using the DuPont model

Exercise 3.11
LO 3

a. Firm A has a margin of 12%, sales of $600,000, and ROI of 18%. Calculate the firm's average total assets.
b. Firm B has net income of $78,000, turnover of 1.3, and average total assets of $950,000. Calculate the firm's sales, margin, and ROI. Round your percentage answer to one decimal place.
c. Firm C has net income of $132,000, turnover of 2.1, and ROI of 7.37%. Calculate the firm's margin. Round your percentage answer to one decimal place.

ROI analysis using the DuPont model

Exercise 3.12
LO 3

a. Firm D has net income of $66,640, sales of $2,380,000, and average total assets of $680,000. Calculate the firm's margin, turnover, and ROI.
b. Firm E has net income of $300,000, sales of $5,000,000, and ROI of 12%. Calculate the firm's turnover and average total assets.
c. Firm F has ROI of 17.4%, average total assets of $2,700,000, and turnover of 1.2. Calculate the firm's sales, margin, and net income. Round your answers to the nearest whole numbers.

Calculate ROE At the beginning of the year, the net assets of Carby Co. were $346,800. The only transactions affecting stockholders' equity during the year were net income of $42,300 and dividends of $12,000.

Exercise 3.13
LO 4

Required:
Calculate Carby Co.'s return on equity (ROE) for the year. Round your percentage answer to one decimal place.

Calculate margin, net income, and ROE For the year ended December 31, 2013, Ebanks, Inc., earned an ROI of 12%. Sales for the year were $150 million, and average asset turnover was 2.5. Average stockholders' equity was $50 million.

Exercise 3.14
LO 3, 4

Required:
a. Calculate Ebanks, Inc.'s margin and net income.
b. Calculate Ebanks, Inc.'s return on equity.

Exercise 3.15

LO 6

Effect of transactions on working capital and current ratio Management of Rivers Co. anticipates that its year-end balance sheet will show current assets of $12,639 and current liabilities of $7,480. Management is considering paying $3,850 of accounts payable before year-end even though payment isn't due until later.

Required:

a. Calculate the firm's working capital and current ratio under each situation. Would you recommend early payment of the accounts payable? Why? Round your current ratio answer to two decimal places.

b. Assume that Rivers Co. had negotiated a short-term bank loan of $5,000 that can be drawn down either before or after the end of the year. Calculate working capital and the current ratio at year-end under each situation, assuming that early payment of accounts payable is not made. When would you recommend that the loan be taken? Why? Round your current ratio answer to two decimal places.

Exercise 3.16

LO 6

Effect of transactions on working capital and current ratio Evans, Inc., had current liabilities at April 30 of $120,500. The firm's current ratio at that date was 1.8.

Required:

a. Calculate the firm's current assets and working capital at April 30.

b. Assume that management paid $30,125 of accounts payable on April 29. Calculate the current ratio and working capital at April 30 as if the April 29 payment had not been made. Round your current ratio answer to two decimal places.

c. Explain the changes, if any, to working capital and the current ratio that would be caused by the April 29 payment.

Problems

All applicable Problems are available with McGraw-Hill's *Connect™ Accounting.*

Problem 3.17

LO 3, 4, 6

Campbell's

Calculate profitability measures using annual report data Using data from the financial statements of Campbell Soup Company in the appendix, calculate:

a. ROI for 2011. Round your percentage answer to one decimal place.

b. ROE for 2011. Round your percentage answer to one decimal place.

c. Working capital at July 31, 2011, and August 1, 2010.

d. Current ratio at July 31, 2011, and August 1, 2010. Round your answers to two decimal places.

e. Acid-test ratio at July 31, 2011, and August 1, 2010. Round your answers to two decimal places.

Note: Visit www.campbellsoup.com to update this problem with data from the most recent annual report.

Problem 3.18

LO 3, 4, 6

Calculate profitability and liquidity measures Presented here are the comparative balance sheets of Hames, Inc., at December 31, 2014 and 2013. Sales for the year ended December 31, 2014, totaled $870,000.

HAMES, INC. Balance Sheets December 31, 2014 and 2013		
	2014	**2013**
Assets		
Cash	$31,500	$28,500
Accounts receivable	117,000	108,000
Merchandise inventory	154,500	148,500
Total current assets	$303,000	$285,000
Land	75,000	60,000
Plant and equipment	187,500	165,000
Less: Accumulated depreciation	(97,500)	(90,000)
Total assets	$468,000	$420,000
Liabilities		
Short-term debt	$27,000	$ 25,500
Accounts payable	84,000	72,000
Other accrued liabilities	30,000	27,000
Total current liabilities	$141,000	$124,500
Long-term debt	33,000	45,000
Total liabilities	$174,000	$169,500
Stockholders' Equity		
Common stock, no par, 100,000 shares authorized, 40,000 and 25,000 shares issued, respectively	$111,000	$ 88,500
Retained earnings:		
Beginning balance	$162,000	$127,500
Net income for the year	51,000	42,000
Dividends for the year	(30,000)	(7,500)
Ending balance	$183,000	$162,000
Total stockholders' equity	$294,000	$250,500
Total liabilities and stockholders' equity	$468,000	$420,000

Required:

a. Calculate ROI for 2014. Round your percentage answer to two decimal places.

b. Calculate ROE for 2014. Round your percentage answer to one decimal place.

c. Calculate working capital at December 31, 2014.

d. Calculate the current ratio at December 31, 2014. Round your answer to two decimal places.

e. Calculate the acid-test ratio at December 31, 2014. Round your answer to two decimal places.

f. Assume that on December 31, 2014, the treasurer of Hames, Inc., decided to pay $22,500 of accounts payable. Explain what impact, if any, this payment will have on the answers you calculated for parts **a–d** (increase, decrease, or no effect).

g. Assume that instead of paying $22,500 of accounts payable on December 31, 2014, Hames, Inc., collected $22,500 of accounts receivable. Explain what impact, if any, this receipt will have on the answers you calculated for parts **a–d** (increase, decrease, or no effect).

Problem 3.19

LO 6

Calculate and analyze liquidity measures Following are the current asset and current liability sections of the balance sheets for Freedom, Inc., at January 31, 2014 and 2013 (in millions):

	January 31, 2014	January 31, 2013
Current Assets		
Cash.	$ 5	$ 2
Accounts receivable	3	6
Inventories.	6	10
Total current assets	$14	$18
Current Liabilities		
Note payable.	$ 3	$ 3
Accounts payable	4	1
Other accrued liabilities	2	2
Total current liabilities	$ 9	$ 6

Required:

a. Calculate the working capital and current ratio at each balance sheet date. Round your current ratio answers to two decimal places.

b. Evaluate the firm's liquidity at each balance sheet date.

c. Assume that the firm operated at a loss during the year ended January 31, 2014. How could cash have increased during the year?

Problem 3.20

LO 6

Calculate and analyze liquidity measures Following are the current asset and current liability sections of the balance sheets for Calketch, Inc., at August 31, 2014 and 2013 (in millions):

	August 31, 2014	August 31, 2013
Current Assets		
Cash	$ 18	$ 36
Marketable securities.	42	60
Accounts receivable	78	48
Inventories.	108	48
Total current assets	$246	$192
Current Liabilities		
Note payable.	$ 18	$ 48
Accounts payable	60	84
Other accrued liabilities	54	42
Total current liabilities	$132	$174

Required:

a. Calculate the working capital and current ratio at each balance sheet date. Round your current ratio answers to two decimal places.

b. Describe the change in the firm's liquidity from 2013 to 2014.

Problem 3.21

LO 3

Applications of ROI using the DuPont model; manufacturing versus service firm Manyops, Inc., is a manufacturing firm that has experienced strong competition in its traditional business. Management is considering joining the trend to the "service economy" by eliminating its manufacturing operations and concentrating on providing specialized maintenance services to other manufacturers. Management of Manyops, Inc., has had a target ROI of 15% on an asset base that has averaged $6 million. To achieve this ROI, average asset turnover of 2 was required. If the company shifts its operations from manufacturing to providing maintenance services, it is estimated that average assets will decrease to $1 million.

Required:

a. Calculate net income, margin, and sales required for Manyops, Inc., to achieve its target ROI as a manufacturing firm.

b. Assume that the average margin of maintenance service firms is 2.5%, and that the average ROI for such firms is 15%. Calculate the net income, sales, and asset turnover that Manyops, Inc., will have if the change to services is made and the firm is able to earn an average margin and achieve a 15% ROI.

ROI analysis using the DuPont model Charlie's Furniture Store has been in business for several years. The firm's owners have described the store as a "high-price, high-service" operation that provides lots of assistance to its customers. Margin has averaged a relatively high 40% per year for several years, but turnover has been a relatively low 0.3 based on average total assets of $3,000,000. A discount furniture store is about to open in the area served by Charlie's, and management is considering lowering prices to compete effectively.

Problem 3.22
LO 3

*e**X**cel*

Required:

a. Calculate current sales and ROI for Charlie's Furniture Store.

b. Assuming that the new strategy would reduce margin to 24%, and assuming that average total assets would stay the same, calculate the sales that would be required to have the same ROI as Charlie's currently earns.

c. Suppose you presented the results of your analysis in parts **a** and **b** of this problem to Charlie, and he replied, "What are you telling me? If I reduce my prices as planned, then I have to practically double my sales volume to earn the same return?" Given the results of your analysis, how would you react to Charlie?

d. Now suppose Charlie says, "You know, I'm not convinced that lowering prices is my only option in staying competitive. What if I were to increase my marketing effort? I'm thinking about kicking off a new advertising campaign after conducting more extensive market research to better identify who my target customer groups are." In general, explain to Charlie what the likely impact of a successful strategy of this nature would be on margin, turnover, and ROI.

e. Think of an alternative strategy that might help Charlie maintain the competitiveness of his business. Explain the strategy, and then describe the likely impact of this strategy on margin, turnover, and ROI.

Cases

All applicable Cases are available with McGraw-Hill's *Connect*™ *Accounting*.

Focus company—analysis of liquidity and profitability measures In Exercise 1-1, you were asked to obtain a recent annual report of a company that you were interested in reviewing throughout this term.

Case 3.23
LO 3, 4, 6, 7

Required:

a. Please locate the five-year (or longer) selected financial data (usually in the management discussion and analysis section of the annual report), or use your focus company's income statement and balance sheet data to calculate as many of the following ratios and results as possible:

1. Working capital
2. Current ratio
3. Margin
4. Turnover
5. ROI
6. ROE

b. Briefly describe your perception of your focus company's liquidity and profitability based on your calculation and review of these ratios and results.

Case 3.24
LO 3, 4, 6, 7

Analysis of liquidity and profitability measures of Apple Inc. The following summarized data (amounts in millions) are taken from the September 24, 2011, and September 25, 2010, comparative financial statements of Apple Inc., a manufacturer of personal computers, portable digital music players, and mobile communications devices, along with a variety of related software, services, peripherals, and networking solutions:

(Amounts Expressed in Millions) For the Fiscal Years Ended September 24 and September 25, respectively:	2011	2010
Net sales	$108,249	$ 65,225
Costs of sales	64,431	39,541
Operating income	33,790	18,385
Net income	$ 25,922	$ 14,013
At Year End:		
Assets		
Current assets:		
Cash and cash equivalents.	$ 9,815	$ 11,261
Short-term marketable securities	16,137	14,359
Accounts receivable, net	5,369	5,510
Inventories.	776	1,051
Deferred tax assets.	2,014	1,636
Vendor nontrade receivables	6,348	4,414
Other current assets.	4,529	3,447
Total current assets.	44,988	41,678
Long-term marketable securities.	55,618	25,391
Property, plant, and equipment, net.	7,777	4,768
Goodwill	896	741
Acquired intangible assets, net.	3,536	342
Other assets..	3,556	2,263
Total assets.	$116,371	$ 75,183
Liabilities and Shareholders' Equity		
Current liabilities:		
Accounts payable	$ 14,632	$ 12,015
Accrued expenses	9,247	5,723
Deferred revenue	4,091	2,984
Total current liabilities	27,970	20,722
Deferred revenue—noncurrent.	1,686	1,139
Other noncurrent liabilities..	10,100	5,531
Total liabilities	39,756	27,392
Shareholders' equity:		
Common stock, no par value, 1,800,000 shares authorized; 929,277 and 915,970 shares issued and outstanding, respectively.	13,331	10,668
Retained earnings..	62,841	37,169
Accumulated other comprehensive income (loss)	443	(46)
Total shareholders' equity.	76,615	47,791
Total liabilities and shareholders' equity.	$116,371	$ 75,183

At September 26, 2009, total assets were $47,501 and total shareholders' equity was $31,640.

Required:

a. Calculate Apple Inc.'s working capital, current ratio, and acid-test ratio at September 24, 2011, and September 25, 2010. Round your ratio answers to one decimal place.

b. Calculate Apple's ROE for the years ended September 24, 2011, and September 25, 2010. Round your percentage answers to one decimal place.

c. Calculate Apple's ROI, showing margin and turnover, for the years ended September 24, 2011, and September 25, 2010. Round your turnover calculations to two decimal places. Round your margin and ROI percentages to one decimal place.

d. Evaluate the company's overall liquidity and profitability.

Optional continuation of Case 3.24—trend analysis

The following historical data were derived from Apple Inc.'s consolidated financial statements (in millions):

Note: Past data are not necessarily indicative of the results of future operations.

	2011	2010	2009	2008	2007
Net sales	$108,249	$65,225	$42,905	$37,491	$24,578
Net income	25,922	14,013	8,235	6,119	3,495
Cash, cash equivalents, and marketable securities	81,570	51,011	33,992	24,490	15,386
Total assets	116,371	75,183	53,851	36,171	24,878
Shareholders' equity	76,615	47,791	27,832	22,297	14,531
Long-term debt obligations*	10,100	5,531	3,502	1,745	687

*Apple Inc. did not have any long-term debt during the five years ended September 24, 2011. Long-term obligations exclude noncurrent deferred revenue.

e. Calculate Apple Inc.'s total liabilities for each year presented above.

f. Are the trends expressed in these data generally consistent with each other?

g. In your opinion, which of these trends would be most meaningful to a potential investor in common stock of Apple Inc.? Which trend would be least meaningful?

h. What other data (trend or otherwise) would you like to have access to before making an investment in Apple Inc.?

Analysis of liquidity and profitability measures of Dell Inc. The following data (amounts in millions) are taken from the February 3, 2012, and January 28, 2011, comparative financial statements of Dell Inc., a direct marketer and distributor of personal computers (PCs) and PC-related products:

Case 3.25
LO 3, 4, 6, 7

DELL INC. Consolidated Statements of Income		
	Fiscal Year Ended	
	February 3, 2012	**January 28, 2011**
Net revenue	$62,071	$61,494
Cost of net revenue	48,260	50,098
Gross margin	13,811	11,396

(continued)

	Fiscal Year Ended	
	February 3, 2012	January 28, 2011
Operating expenses:		
Selling, general, and administrative	8,524	7,302
Research, development, and engineering	856	661
Total operating expenses	9,380	7,963
Operating income	4,431	3,433
Interest and other, net	(191)	(83)
Income before income taxes	4,240	3,350
Income tax provision	748	715
Net income	$3,492	$2,635

DELL INC.
Consolidated Statements of Financial Position

	February 3, 2012	January 28, 2011
Assets		
Current assets:		
Cash and cash equivalents	$13,852	$13,913
Short-term investments	966	452
Accounts receivable, net	6,476	6,493
Short-term financing receivables, net	3,327	3,643
Inventories, net	1,404	1,301
Other current assets	3,423	3,219
Total current assets	29,448	29,021
Property, plant, and equipment, net	2,124	1,953
Long-term investments	3,404	704
Long-term financing receivables, net	1,372	799
Goodwill	5,838	4,365
Purchased intangible assets, net	1,857	1,495
Other noncurrent assets	490	262
Total assets	$44,533	$38,599
Liabilities and Stockholders' Equity		
Current liabilities:		
Short-term debt	$ 2,867	$ 851
Accounts payable	11,656	11,293
Accrued and other	3,934	4,181
Short-term deferred services revenue	3,544	3,158
Total current liabilities	22,001	19,483
Long-term debt	6,387	5,146
Long-term deferred services revenue	3,836	3,518
Other noncurrent liabilities	3,392	2,686
Total liabilities	35,616	30,833
Stockholders' equity:		
Common stock and capital in excess of $.01 par value; shares authorized: 7,000; shares issued: 3,369 respectively; shares outstanding: 1,761 and 1,918, respectively	12,187	11,797
Treasury stock, at cost; 1,154 and 976 shares, respectively	(31,445)	(28,704)
Retained earnings	28,236	24,744
Accumulated other comprehensive loss	(61)	(71)
Total stockholders' equity	8,917	7,766
Total liabilities and equity	$44,533	$38,599

At January 30, 2010, total assets were $33,652 and total stockholders' equity was $5,641.

a. Calculate Dell, Inc.'s, working capital, current ratio, and acid-test ratio at February 3, 2012, and January 28, 2011. Round your ratio answers to two decimal places.

b. Calculate Dell's ROE for the years ended February 3, 2012, and January 28, 2011. Round your ratio answers to two decimal places, and your percentage answers to one decimal place.

c. Calculate Dell's ROI, showing margin and turnover, for the years ended February 3, 2012, and January 28, 2011. Round your ratio answers to two decimal places and your percentage answers to one decimal place.

d. Evaluate the company's overall liquidity and profitability.

e. Dell, Inc., did not declare or pay any dividends during the years ended February 3, 2012, or January 28, 2011. What do you suppose is the primary reason for this?

Optional continuation of Case 3.25—trend analysis

The following historical data were derived from Dell, Inc.'s, consolidated financial statements (in millions):

Note: Past data are not necessarily indicative of the results of future operations.

	2012	2011	2010	2009	2008
Net revenues	$62,071	$61,494	$59,902	$61,101	$61,133
Net income	3,492	2,635	1,433	2,478	2,947
Total assets	44,533	38,599	33,652	26,500	27,561
Long-term debt	6,387	5,146	3,417	1,898	362

f. Are the trends expressed in these data generally consistent with each other?

g. In your opinion, which of these trends would be most meaningful to a potential investor in common stock of Dell, Inc.? Which trend would be least meaningful?

h. What other data (trend or otherwise) would you like to have access to before making an investment in Dell, Inc.?

Answers to Self-Study Material

Matching: 1. i, 2. e, 3. l, 4. k, 5. m, 6. j, 7. b, 8. d, 9. h, 10. o
Multiple choice: 1. a, 2. c, 3. c, 4. a, 5. b, 6. a, 7. a, 8. a

4

The Bookkeeping Process and Transaction Analysis

To understand how different transactions affect the financial statements and in turn make sense of the information in the financial statements, it is necessary to understand the mechanical operation of the bookkeeping process. The principal objectives of this chapter are to explain this mechanical process and to introduce a method of analyzing the effects of a transaction on the financial statements.

LEARNING OBJECTIVES (LO)

After studying this chapter you should understand and be able to

LO 4-1   Illustrate the expansion of the basic accounting equation to include revenues and expenses.

LO 4-2   Describe how the expanded accounting equation stays in balance after every transaction.

LO 4-3   Describe how the income statement is linked to the balance sheet through stockholders' equity.

LO 4-4   Explain the meaning of the bookkeeping terms *journal, ledger, T-account, account balance, debit, credit,* and *closing the books.*

LO 4-5   Explain why the bookkeeping system is a mechanical adaptation of the expanded accounting equation.

LO 4-6   Analyze a transaction, prepare a journal entry, and determine the effects of the transaction on the financial statements.

LO 4-7   Apply the five questions of transaction analysis.

The Bookkeeping/Accounting Process

The bookkeeping/accounting process begins with **transactions** (economic interchanges between entities that are accounted for and reflected in financial statements) and culminates in the financial statements. This flow was illustrated in Chapter 2 as follows:

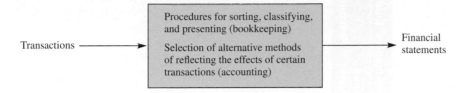

This chapter presents an overview of bookkeeping procedures. Your objective is not to become a bookkeeper but to learn enough about the mechanical process of bookkeeping so you will be able to determine the effects of any transaction on the financial statements. This ability is crucial to the process of making informed judgments and decisions from the financial statements. Bookkeepers (and accountants) use some special terms to describe the bookkeeping process, and you will have to learn these terms. Once you understand the language of bookkeeping, you will see that the process is quite straightforward.

The Balance Sheet Equation—A Mechanical Key

You now know that the balance sheet equation expresses the equality between an entity's assets and the claims to those assets:

$$\text{Assets} = \text{Liabilities} + \text{Stockholders' equity}$$

For present illustration purposes, let us consider a firm without liabilities. What do you suppose happens to the amounts in the equation if the entity operates at a profit? Well, assets (perhaps cash) increase, and if the equation is to balance (and it must), then clearly stockholders' equity must also increase. Yes, profits increase stockholders' equity, and to keep the equation in balance, assets will increase and/or liabilities will decrease. Every financial transaction that is accounted for will cause a change somewhere in the balance sheet equation, and the equation will remain in balance after every transaction.

You have already seen that a firm's net income (profit) or loss is the difference between the revenues and expenses reported on its income statement (Exhibit 2-2). Likewise, you have seen that net income from the income statement is reported as one of the factors causing a change in the retained earnings part of the statement of changes in stockholders' equity (Exhibit 2-3). The other principal element of stockholders' equity is the amount of capital invested by the owners/stockholders—that is, the paid-in capital of Exhibit 2-3. Given these components of stockholders' equity, it is possible to modify the basic balance sheet equation as follows:

LO 1

Illustrate the expansion of the basic accounting equation to include revenues and expenses.

$$\text{Assets} = \text{Liabilities} + \text{Stockholders' equity}$$
$$\text{Assets} = \text{Liabilities} + \text{Paid-in capital} + \text{Retained earnings}$$
$$\text{Assets} = \text{Liabilities} + \text{Paid-in capital} + \begin{array}{c}\text{Retained}\\\text{earnings}\\\text{(beginning}\\\text{of period)}\end{array} + \begin{array}{c}\text{Revenues}\\\text{(during the}\\\text{period)}\end{array} - \begin{array}{c}\text{Expenses}\\\text{(during the}\\\text{period)}\end{array}$$

To illustrate the operation of this equation and the effect of several transactions, study how the following transactions are reflected in Exhibit 4-1. Note that in the exhibit some

Exhibit 4-1   Transaction Summary (in thousands)

Transaction	Cash	+ Accounts Receivable	+ Merchandise Inventory	+ Equipment	= Notes Payable	+ Accounts Payable	+ Paid-In Capital	+ Retained Earnings	+ Revenue	+ Expenses
1.	+30						+30			
2.	−25			+25						
3.	+15				+15					
4.	−10		+20			+10				
5.	+2	+5		−7						
6.	+5	−5								
Total	17	0	20	18	15	10	30			
7. Revenues		+20							+20	
7. Expenses			−12							−12
8.						+3				−3
Total	17	20	8	18	15	13	30	+5	+20	−15

specific assets and liabilities have been identified within those general categories, and a column has been established for each. All dollar amounts are expressed in thousands.

Transactions

1. Investors organized the firm and invested $30, thus becoming the initial group of stockholders. (In this example the broad category *Paid-In Capital* is used rather than *Common Stock* and, possibly, *Additional Paid-In Capital.* There isn't any beginning balance in Retained Earnings because the firm is just getting started.)
2. Equipment costing $25 was purchased for cash.
3. The firm borrowed $15 from a bank.
4. Merchandise costing $20 was purchased for inventory; $10 cash was paid and $10 of the cost was charged on account.
5. Equipment that cost $7 was sold for $7; $2 was received in cash, and $5 will be received later.
6. The $5 account receivable from the sale of equipment was collected.

Each column of the exhibit has been totaled after transaction (6). Does the total of all the asset columns equal the total of all the liability and stockholders' equity columns? (They'd better be equal!)

The firm hasn't had any revenue or expense transactions yet, and it's hard to make a profit without them, so the transactions continue:

7. The firm sold merchandise inventory that had cost $12 for a selling price of $20; the sale was made **on account** (that is, on credit), and the customer will pay later. Notice that in Exhibit 4-1 this transaction is shown on two lines; one reflects the revenue of $20 and the other reflects the expense, or cost of the merchandise sold, of $12.
8. Wages of $3 earned by the firm's employees are accrued. This means that the expense is recorded even though it has not yet been paid. The wages have been earned by employees (the expense has been incurred) and are owed but have not yet been paid; they will be paid in the next accounting period. The accrual is made in this period so that revenues and expenses of the current period will be matched (the matching concept), and net income will reflect the economic results of this period's activities.

Again, each column of the exhibit has been totaled, and the total of all the asset columns equals the total of all the liability and stockholders' equity columns. If the accounting period were to end after transaction (8), the income statement would report net income of $5, and the balance sheet would show total stockholders' equity of $35. Simplified financial statements for Exhibit 4-1 data after transaction (8) are presented in Exhibit 4-2 on the next page.

LO 2
Describe how the expanded accounting equation stays in balance after every transaction.

---

1. What does it mean to determine "what kind of account" an account is?

What Does It Mean?
Answer on page 126

Exhibit 4-2

Financial Statements for
Exhibit 4-1 Data
(in thousands)

Exhibit 4-1 Data Income Statement for Transactions (1) through (8)		Exhibit 4-1 Data Statement of Changes in Retained Earnings	
Revenues	$20	Beginning balance	$ 0
Expenses	(15)	Net income	5
		Dividends	(0)
Net income	$ 5	Ending balance	$ 5

Exhibit 4-1 Data Balance Sheet after Transaction (8)			
Assets		**Liabilities**	
Cash	$17	Notes payable	$15
Accounts receivable	20	Accounts payable	13
Merchandise inventory	8	Total liabilities	$28
Total current assets	$45	**Stockholders' Equity**	
Equipment	18	Paid-in capital	$30
		Retained earnings	5
		Total stockholders' equity	$35
		Total liabilities & stockholders' equity	
Total assets	$63	equity	$63

LO 3

Describe how the
income statement is
linked to the balance
sheet through stock-
holders' equity.

Notice especially in Exhibit 4-2 how net income on the income statement gets into the balance sheet via the retained earnings section of stockholders' equity. In the equation of Exhibit 4-1, revenues and expenses were treated as a part of stockholders' equity to keep the equation in balance. For financial reporting purposes, however, revenues and expenses are shown in the income statement. In order to have the balance sheet balance, it is necessary that net income be reflected in the balance sheet, and this is done in retained earnings. If any retained earnings are distributed to the stockholders as a dividend, the dividend does not show on the income statement but is a deduction from retained earnings, shown in the statement of changes in retained earnings. This is so because a dividend is not an expense (it is not incurred in the process of generating revenue). A *dividend* is a distribution of earnings to the stockholders of the firm.

What you have just learned is the essence of the bookkeeping process. Transactions are analyzed to determine which asset, liability, or stockholders' equity category is affected and how each is affected. The amount of the effect is recorded, the amounts are totaled, and financial statements are prepared.

Bookkeeping Jargon and Procedures

LO 4

Explain the meaning
of the bookkeeping
terms *journal, ledger,
T-account, account
balance, debit, credit,*
and *closing the books.*

Because of the complexity of most business operations, and the frequent need to refer to past transactions, a bookkeeping system has evolved to facilitate the record-keeping process. The system may be manual or computerized, but the general features are virtually the same.

Transactions are initially recorded in a **journal**. A journal (derived from the French word *jour,* meaning *day*) is a day-by-day, or chronological, record of transactions. Transactions are then recorded in—**posted** to—a **ledger**. The ledger serves the function of

Bookkeeping Language in Everyday English

Many bookkeeping and accounting terms have found their way into the language, especially in the business context. *Debit* and *credit* are no exceptions to this, and some brief examples may stress the left–right definition. The terms *debit* and *credit* are used by banks to describe additions to or subtractions from an individual's checking account. For example, your account is credited for interest earned and is debited for a service charge or for the cost of checks that are furnished to you. From the bank's perspective, your account is a liability; that is, the bank owes you the balance in your account. Interest earned by your account increases that liability of the bank; hence, the interest is credited. Service charges reduce your claim on the bank—its liability to you—so those are debits from the bank's perspective. Perhaps because of these effects on a checking or savings account balance, many people think that debit is a synonym for bad, and that credit means good. In certain contexts these synonyms may be appropriate, but they do not apply in accounting.

A synonym for debit that is used in accounting is *charge.* To **charge** an account is to make a debit entry to the account. This usage carries over to the terminology used when merchandise or services are purchased on credit; that is, they are received now and will be paid for later. This arrangement is frequently called a *charge account* because from the seller's perspective, an asset (accounts receivable) is increasing as a result of the transaction, and assets increase with a debit entry. The fact that a credit card is used and that this is called a *credit transaction* may refer to the increase in the purchaser's liability.

Exhibit 4-1, but rather than having a large sheet with a column for each asset, liability, and stockholders' equity category, there is an account for each category. In a manual bookkeeping system, each account is a separate page in a book, much like a loose-leaf binder. Accounts are arranged in a sequence to facilitate the posting process. Usually the sequence is assets, liabilities, stockholders' equity, revenues, and expenses. A **chart of accounts** serves as an index to the ledger, and each account is numbered to facilitate the frequent written references that are made to it.

The account format that has been used for several hundred years looks like a "T." (In the illustration shown on the next page, notice the T under the captions for Assets, Liabilities, and Stockholders' Equity.) On one side of the T, additions to the account are recorded, and on the other side of the T, subtractions are recorded. The **account balance** at any point in time is the arithmetic difference between the prior balance and the additions and subtractions. This is the same as in Exhibit 4-1 where the account balance shown after transactions (6) and (8) is the sum of the prior balance, plus the additions, minus the subtractions.

To facilitate making reference to account entries and **balances** (and to confuse neophytes), the left side of a **T-account** is called the *debit* side, and the right side of a T-account is called the *credit* side. In bookkeeping and accounting, **debit** and **credit** mean left and right, respectively, and nothing more (see Business in Practice—Bookkeeping Language in Everyday English). A record of a transaction involving a posting to the left side of an account is called a *debit entry.* An account that has a balance on its right side is said to have a *credit balance.*

The beauty of the bookkeeping system is that debit and credit entries to accounts, and account balances, are set up so that if debits equal credits, the balance sheet equation will be in balance. The key to this is that asset accounts will normally have a debit balance: Increases in assets are recorded as debit entries to these accounts, and

LO 5

Explain why the bookkeeping system is a mechanical adaptation of the expanded accounting equation.

decreases in assets are recorded as credit entries to these accounts. For liabilities and stockholders' equity accounts, the opposite will be true:

Assets		=	Liabilities		+	Stockholders' Equity	
Debit	*Credit*		*Debit*	*Credit*		*Debit*	*Credit*
Increases	Decreases		Decreases	Increases		Decreases	Increases
+	−		−	+		−	+
Normal balance				Normal balance			Normal balance

It is no coincidence that the debit and credit system of normal balances coincides with the balance sheet presentation illustrated earlier. In fact, most of the balance sheets illustrated so far have been presented in what is known as the *account format.* An alternative approach is to use the *report format,* in which assets are shown above liabilities and stockholders' equity.

Entries to revenue and expense accounts follow a pattern that is consistent with entries to other stockholders' equity accounts. Revenues are increases in stockholders' equity, so revenue accounts normally will have a credit balance and will increase with credit entries. Expenses are decreases in stockholders' equity, so expense accounts normally will have a debit balance and will increase with debit entries. Gains and losses are recorded like revenues and expenses, respectively.

The debit or credit behavior of accounts for assets, liabilities, stockholders' equity, revenues, and expenses is summarized in the following illustration:

Account Name	
Debit side	*Credit* side
Normal balance for:	Normal balance for:
Assets	Liabilities
Expenses	Stockholders' equity
	Revenues
Debit entries increase:	Credit entries increase:
Assets	Liabilities
Expenses	Stockholders' equity
	Revenues
Debit entries decrease:	Credit entries decrease:
Liabilities	Assets
Stockholders' equity	Expenses
Revenues	

Referring to the transactions that were illustrated in Exhibit 4-1, a bookkeeper would say that in transaction (1), which was the investment of $30 in the firm by the stockholders, Cash was debited—it increased—and Paid-In Capital was credited, each for $30. Transaction (2), the purchase of equipment for $25 cash, would be described as a $25 debit to Equipment and a $25 credit to Cash. Pretend that you are a bookkeeper and describe the remaining transactions of that illustration.

The bookkeeper would say, after transaction (8) has been recorded, that the Cash account has a debit balance of $17, the Notes Payable account has a credit balance of $15, and the Expense account has a debit balance of $15. (There was only one expense account in the example; usually there will be a separate account for each category of expense and each category of revenue.) What kind of balance do the other accounts have after transaction (8)?

The journal was identified earlier as the chronological record of the firm's transactions. The journal is also the place where transactions are first recorded, and it is sometimes referred to as the *book of original entry.* The **journal entry** format is a useful and convenient way of describing the effect of a transaction on the accounts involved, and will be used in subsequent chapters of this text, so it is introduced now and is worth learning now.

The general format of the journal entry is:

Date	Dr. Account Name . . . . Cr. Account Name.	Amount	Amount

Notice these characteristics of the journal entry:

- The date is recorded to provide a cross-reference to the transaction. In many of our examples, a transaction reference number will be used instead of a date; the point is that a cross-reference is provided.

- The name of the account to be debited and the debit amount are to the left of the name of the account to be credited and the credit amount. Remember, debit means *left* and credit means *right.*

- The abbreviations *Dr.* and *Cr.* are used for debit and credit, respectively. These identifiers are frequently omitted from the journal entry to reduce writing time and because the indenting practice is universally followed and understood.

It is possible for a journal entry to have more than one debit account and amount and/or more than one credit account and amount. The only requirement of a journal entry is that the total of the debit amounts equal the total of the credit amounts. Frequently there will be a brief explanation of the transaction beneath the journal entry, especially if the **entry** is not self-explanatory.

The journal entry for transaction (1) of Exhibit 4-1 would appear as follows:

(1)	Dr. Cash. . . . . Cr. Paid-In Capital . . . . To record an investment in the firm by the stockholders.	30	30

Technically, the journal entry procedure illustrated here is a *general journal entry.* Most bookkeeping systems also use specialized journals, but they are still books of original entry, recording transactions chronologically, involving various accounts, and resulting in entries in which debits equal credits. If you understand the basic general journal entry just illustrated, you will be able to understand a specialized journal if you ever see one.

Transactions generate **source documents,** such as an invoice from a supplier, a copy of a credit purchase made by a customer, a check stub, or a tape printout of the totals from a cash register's activity for a period. These source documents are the raw materials used in the bookkeeping process and support the journal entry.

The following flowchart illustrates the bookkeeping process that we have explored:

Although information systems technology has made it financially feasible for virtually all businesses to automate their accounting functions (see Business in Practice—Accounting Information Systems and Data Protection), many small firms continue to rely on manual processing techniques. Understanding basic bookkeeping terminology and appreciating how transactions are recorded will help you understand any accounting software you may encounter.

What Does It Mean?

Answers on page 126

2. What does it mean when an account has a debit balance?
3. What does it mean to say that asset and expense accounts normally have debit balances?
4. What does it mean when a liability, stockholders' equity, or revenue account is credited?

Understanding the Effects of Transactions on the Financial Statements

LO 6

Analyze a transaction, prepare a journal entry, and determine the effects of the transaction on the financial statements.

T-accounts and journal entries are models used by accountants to explain and understand the effects of transactions on the financial statements. These models are frequently difficult for a nonaccountant to use because one must know what kind of account (asset, liability, stockholders' equity, revenue, or expense) is involved, where in the financial statements (balance sheet or income statement) the account is found, and how the account is affected by the debit or credit characteristic of the transaction.

An alternative to the T-account and journal entry models that should be useful to you is the horizontal financial statement relationship model first introduced in Chapter 2. The **horizontal model** is as follows:

Balance sheet	Income Statement
Assets = Liabilities + Stockholders' equity	← Net Income = Revenues − Expenses

The key to using this model is to keep the balance sheet in balance. The arrow from net income in the income statement to stockholders' equity in the balance sheet indicates that net income affects retained earnings, which is a component of stockholders' equity. For a transaction affecting both the balance sheet and income statement, the balance sheet will balance when the income statement effect on stockholders' equity is considered. In this model, the account name is entered under the appropriate financial statement category, and the dollar effect of the transaction on that account is entered

Business in
Practice

Accounting Information Systems and Data Protection

A wide variety of accounting software products have been developed, ranging from off-the-shelf systems that support the basic bookkeeping needs of individuals and small businesses (see quickbooks.intuit.com or na.sage.com/sage-50-accounting-us) to full-scale accounting systems designed for businesses with more complex informational needs (see generally na.sage.com or search for "Microsoft Dynamics SL") to customized, comprehensive enterprisewide resource planning systems used by large multinational corporations (see sap.com or oracle.com).

The methodology for evaluating and selecting a system should focus on matching the decision-making requirements of the business across its functional areas (finance, production, marketing, human resources, and information services) with the functionality and scalability of the software. Important elements to consider include the initial investment and ongoing cost, hardware and human resource requirements, system performance expectations, supplier reliability and service levels, and implementation and training procedures in light of the existing accounting system. Many firms use a structured methodology referred to as the *System Life Cycle (SLC)* to identify their organizational needs and system requirements. The SLC includes phases for planning, analysis, design, implementation, and use of the system.

Reviews of accounting system software products appear regularly in computer and accounting periodicals. Product information is available at supplier websites and normally includes downloadable demos. Online review services such as ctsguides.com or 2020software.com are also available to provide insight into the functionality, cost, and service levels of various systems.

In any computerized system, transaction information should be entered only once. For an individual, this may be when a check is written. For a business, this may be when an order is placed with a supplier or when an order is received from a customer. Such processes are often automated, as with the bar code scanners used to record sales and inventory transactions at retail stores. By linking business systems electronically, the initial recording of a transaction can be extended from a seller's system to the systems used by its suppliers and/or customers. For example, once a purchase order is entered into the purchasing system, it may also automatically update the supplier's system for the sales transaction.

To be certain, the majority of e-commerce activity today is represented by these business-to-business transactions, and nobody doubts that the Internet economy has dramatically reduced many of the "data-capturing" costs of doing business. Unfortunately, the data security risks associated with doing business in the electronic age are significant and cannot be ignored. Corporate management must learn to prioritize information assets and to safeguard them against the dangers associated with cyberfraud, viruses, computer crime, and breaches of trust by employees. Disaster prevention and recovery plans should be in place and should include access firewalls, intrusion detection systems within the network architecture, audit logs of system usage, timely virus protection updates, and insurance policies that cover hacker invasions. In today's business environment, the integrity of the accounting information system must be carefully protected to ensure that transaction data can be used to develop relevant and reliable information that supports the management planning, control, and decision-making processes.

with a plus or minus sign below the account name. For example, the journal entry shown earlier, which records the investment of $30 in the firm by the stockholders, would be shown in this horizontal model as follows:

Balance sheet		Income Statement
Assets = Liabilities + Stockholders' equity		← Net Income = Revenues − Expenses
Cash	Paid-in Capital	
+ 30	+30	

To further illustrate the model's use, assume a transaction in which the firm paid $12 for advertising. The effect on the financial statements is:

Balance sheet	Income Statement
Assets = Liabilities + Stockholders' equity	← Net Income = Revenues − Expenses
Cash −12	Advertising Expense −12

The journal entry would be:

Dr. Advertising Expense	12	
Cr. Cash.		12

Notice that in the horizontal model the amount of advertising expense is shown with a minus sign. This is so because the expense reduces net income, which reduces stockholders' equity. A plus or minus sign is used in the context of each financial statement equation (A = L + SE, and NI = R − E). Thus, a minus sign for expenses means that net income is reduced (expenses are greater), not that expenses are lower.

It is possible that a transaction can affect two accounts in a single balance sheet or income statement category. For example, assume a transaction in which a firm collects $40 that was owed to it by a customer for services performed in a prior period. The effect of this transaction is shown as follows:

Balance sheet	Income Statement
Assets = Liabilities + Stockholders' equity	← Net Income = Revenues − Expenses
Cash +40 Accounts Receivable −40	

The journal entry would be:

Dr. Cash	40	
Cr. Accounts Receivable.		40

It is also possible for a transaction to affect more than two accounts. For example, assume a transaction in which a firm provided $60 worth of services to a client, $45 of which was collected when the services were provided and $15 of which will be collected later. Here is the effect on the financial statements:

Balance sheet	Income Statement
Assets = Liabilities + Stockholders' equity	← Net Income = Revenues − Expenses
Cash +45 Accounts Receivable +15	Service Revenues +60

The journal entry would be:

Dr.	Cash	45	
Dr.	Accounts Receivable.	15	
	Cr. Service Revenues		60

Recall that revenues and expenses from the income statement are increases and decreases, respectively, to stockholders' equity. Thus, the horizontal model and its two financial statement equations can be combined into this single equation:

$$\text{Assets} = \text{Liabilities} + \text{Stockholders' equity} + \text{Revenues} - \text{Expenses}$$

Notice that as the balance sheet equation (Assets = Liabilities + Stockholders' equity) is expanded to include the results of the income statement (Net income = Revenues − Expenses), the model includes each of the five broad categories of accounts. Remember that dividends reduce retained earnings, which is part of the stockholders' equity term. A separate "Dividends" term has not been included in the model because dividends are not considered a separate account category. Note that the operational equal sign in the horizontal model is the one between assets and liabilities. You can check that a transaction recorded in the horizontal model keeps the balance sheet in balance by mentally (or actually) putting an equal sign between assets and liabilities as you use the model to record transaction amounts.

Spend some time now becoming familiar with the horizontal model (by working Exercise 4.5, for example) so it will be easier for you to understand the effects on the financial statements of transactions that you will encounter later in this book and in the "real world." As a financial statement user (as opposed to a financial statement preparer), you will find that the horizontal model is an easily used tool. With practice, you will become proficient at understanding how an amount shown on either the balance sheet or income statement probably affected other parts of the financial statements when it was recorded.

---

5. What does it mean when "the books are in balance"?

What Does It Mean?
Answer on page 126

Adjustments

After the end of the accounting period, bookkeepers normally have to record an **adjustment** to certain account balances to reflect **accrual** accounting in the financial statements. As discussed in Chapters 1 and 2, accrual accounting recognizes revenues and expenses as they occur, even though the cash receipt from the revenue or the cash disbursement related to the expense may occur before or after the event that causes revenue or expense recognition. Although prepared after the end of the accounting period (when all of the necessary information has been gathered), adjustments are dated and recorded as of the end of the period.

Adjustments result in revenues and expenses being reported in the appropriate fiscal period. For example, revenue may be *earned* in fiscal 2013 from selling a product or providing a service, and the customer/client may not pay until fiscal 2014. (Most firms pay for products purchased or services received within a week to a month after receiving the product or service.) It is also likely that some expenses *incurred* in fiscal 2013 will not be paid until fiscal 2014. (Utility costs and employee wages are examples.) Alternatively, it is possible that an entity will receive cash from a customer/client for a product or service in fiscal 2012, and the product will not be sold or the service provided until fiscal 2013. (Subscription fees and insurance premiums are usually received in advance.) Likewise, the entity may pay for an item in fiscal 2012, but the expense applies to fiscal 2013. (Insurance premiums and rent are usually paid in advance.) These alternative activities are illustrated on the following time line:

Fiscal 2012	12/31/12	Fiscal 2013	12/31/13	Fiscal 2014
Cash received		Product sold or service provided and revenue earned		Cash received
Cash paid		Expense incurred		Cash paid

There are two categories of adjustments:

1. *Accruals*—Transactions for which cash has not yet been received or paid, but the effect of which must be recorded in the accounts (at the end of the accounting period) to accomplish a matching of revenues and expenses and accurate financial statements.

2. *Reclassifications*—The initial recording of a transaction, although a true reflection of the transaction at the time, does not result in assigning revenues to the period in which they were earned or expenses to the period in which they were incurred. As a result, an amount must be reclassified from one account to another (at the end of the accounting period) to reflect the appropriate balance in each account.

The first type of adjustment is illustrated by the accrual of wages expense and wages payable. For example, work performed by employees during March, for which they will be paid in April, results in wages expense to be included in the March income statement and a wages payable liability to be included in the March 31 balance sheet. To illustrate this accrual, assume that employees earned $60 in March that will be paid to them in April. Using the horizontal model, the **accrued** wages adjustment has the following effect on the financial statements:

Balance sheet	Income Statement
Assets = Liabilities + Stockholders' equity	← Net Income = Revenues − Expenses
Wages Payable +60	Wages Expense −60

The journal entry would be:

Dr. Wages Expense.................................... 60	
Cr. Wages Payable	60

Thus, the March 31 balance sheet will reflect the wages payable liability, and the income statement for March will include all of the wages expense incurred during March. Again note that the recognition of the expense of $60 is shown with a minus sign because as expenses increase, net income and stockholders' equity (retained earnings) decrease. The balance sheet remains in balance after this adjustment because the $60 increase in liabilities is offset by the $60 decrease in stockholders' equity. When the wages are paid in April, both the Cash and Wages Payable accounts will be decreased. (Wages Expense will not be affected by the cash payment entry because it was already affected when the accrual was made.)

Similar adjustments are made to accrue revenues (such as for services performed but not yet billed or for interest earned but not yet received) and other expenses including various operating expenses, interest expense, and income tax expense.

The effect on the financial statements, using the horizontal model, of accruing $50 of interest income that has been earned but not yet received is shown as follows:

Balance Sheet	Income Statement
Assets = Liabilities + Stockholders' equity	← Net Income = Revenues − Expenses
Interest Receivable +50	Interest Income +50

The journal entry would be:

Dr. Interest Receivable	50	
Cr. Interest Income		50

An example of the second kind of adjustment is the reclassification for supplies. If the purchase of supplies at a cost of $100 during February was initially recorded as an increase in the Supplies (asset) account (and a decrease in Cash), the cost of supplies used during February must be removed from the asset account and recorded as Supplies Expense. Assuming that supplies costing $35 were used during February, the reclassification adjustment would be reflected in the horizontal model as follows:

Balance Sheet	Income Statement
Assets = Liabilities + Stockholders' equity	← Net Income = Revenues − Expenses
Supplies −35	Supplies Expense −35

The journal entry would be:

Dr. Supplies Expense	35	
Cr. Supplies		35

Conversely, if the purchase of supplies during February at a cost of $100 was originally recorded as an increase in Supplies Expense for February, the cost of supplies still on hand at the end of February ($65, if supplies costing $35 were used during February) must be removed from the Supplies Expense account and recorded as an asset. The reclassification adjustment for the $65 of supplies still on hand at the end of February would be reflected in the horizontal model as follows:

Balance Sheet	Income Statement
Assets = Liabilities + Stockholders' equity	← Net Income = Revenues − Expenses
Supplies +65	Supplies Expense +65

The journal entry would be:

Dr. Supplies...	65	
Cr. Supplies Expense		65

What's going on here? Supplies costing $100 were originally recorded as an expense (a minus 100 in the expense column offset by a minus 100 of cash in the asset column). The expense for February should be only $35 because $65 of the supplies are still on hand at the end of February, so Supplies Expense is adjusted to $35 by showing a plus $65 in the expense column. The model is kept in balance by increasing Supplies in the asset column by $65.

Adjustments for prepaid insurance (insurance premiums paid in a fiscal period before the insurance expense has been incurred) and revenues received in advance (cash received from customers before the service has been performed or the product has been sold) are also reclassification adjustments.

Generally speaking, every adjustment affects both the balance sheet and the income statement. That is, if one part of the entry—either the debit or the credit—affects the balance sheet, the other part affects the income statement. The result of adjustments is to make both the balance sheet at the end of the accounting period and the income statement for the accounting period more accurate. That is, asset and liability account balances are appropriately stated, all revenues earned during the period are reported, and all expenses incurred in generating those revenues are subtracted to arrive at net income. By properly applying the matching concept, the entity's ROI, ROE, and liquidity calculations will be valid measures of results of operations and financial position.

After the year-end adjustments have been posted to the ledger accounts, account balances are determined. The financial statements are prepared using the account balance amounts, which usually are summarized to a certain extent. For example, if the company has only one ledger account for cash, the balance in that account is shown on the balance sheet as Cash. If the company has several separate selling expense accounts (e.g., Advertising Expense, Salesforce Travel Expense, and Salesforce Commissions), these account balances are added together to get the selling expense amount shown on the income statement.

This entire process is called **closing the books** and usually takes at least several working days to complete. At the end of the fiscal year for a large, publicly owned company, a period from 4 to 10 weeks may be required to close the books and prepare the financial statements because of the complexities involved, including the annual audit by the firm's public accountants. (See Business in Practice—The Closing Process.)

It should be clear that the bookkeeping process itself is procedural and that the same kinds and sequence of activities are repeated each fiscal period. These procedures and the sequence are system characteristics that make mechanization and computerization feasible. Mechanical bookkeeping system aids were developed many years ago. Today many computer programs use transaction data as input and with minimal operator intervention complete the bookkeeping procedures and prepare financial statements. Accounting knowledge and judgment are as necessary as ever, however, to ensure that transactions are initially recorded in an appropriate manner, required adjustments are made, and the output of the computer processing is sensible.

---

6. What does it mean when a revenue or expense must be accrued?
7. What does it mean when an adjustment must be made?

What Does It Mean?
Answers on pages 126–127

Transaction Analysis Methodology

The key to being able to understand the effect of any transaction on the financial statements is having the ability to analyze the transaction. **Transaction analysis methodology** involves answering five questions:

LO 7
Apply the five questions of transaction analysis.

1. What's going on?
2. What accounts are affected?
3. How are they affected?
4. Does the balance sheet balance? (Do the debits equal the credits?)
5. Does my analysis make sense?

   1. *What's going on?* To analyze any transaction, it is necessary to understand the transaction—that is, to understand the activity that is taking place between the entity for which the accounting is being done and the other entity involved in the transaction. This is why most elementary accounting texts, including this one, explain many business practices. It is impossible to understand the effect of a transaction on the financial statements if the basic activity being accounted for is not understood.

   2. *What accounts are affected?* This question is frequently answered by the answer to "What's going on?" because the specific account names are often included in that explanation. This question may be answered by a process of elimination. First think about whether one of the accounts is an asset, liability, stockholders' equity, revenue, or expense; then apply that same logic to the other account(s) involved in the transaction. From the broad categories identified, it is usually possible to identify the specific accounts affected.

   3. *How are they affected?* Answer this question with the word *increasing* or *decreasing*, and then, if you are using the journal entry or T-account model, translate to *debit* or *credit*. Accountants learn to think directly in debit and credit terms after much more practice than you will probably have. Note that you can avoid the debit/credit issue by using the horizontal model.

   4. *Does the balance sheet balance?* If the horizontal model is being used, it is possible to determine easily that the balance sheet equation is in balance by observing the arithmetic sign and the amounts involved in the transaction. Remember that the operational equal sign in the model is between assets and liabilities. Alternatively, the journal entry for the transaction can be written, or T-accounts can be sketched, and the equality of the debits and credits can be verified. You know by

The Closing Process

From a business perspective, the closing process allows a firm to complete one accounting year and begin another. Once the year-end financial statements have been prepared, managers and financial analysts can evaluate the firm's relative profitability, liquidity, or other measures in relation to key competitors, industry performance measures, or the firm's own financial past.

From a bookkeeping perspective, the closing process simply *transfers* the year-end balances of all income statement accounts (revenues, expenses, gains, and losses that have accumulated during the year) to the retained earnings account, which is part of stockholders' equity on the balance sheet. In addition, if any dividends declared during the year were accumulated in a separate "dividends" account, the balance in that account is also closed to retained earnings.

This is nothing new! The following diagram, with slight modifications from the version presented in Chapter 2, illustrates the *articulation* between the income statement for the year and the balance sheet at the end of the year:

How is the closing process accomplished? Mechanically, the credit balances in all revenue and gain accounts must be reduced to zero by *debiting* each of these accounts for amounts equal to their respective year-end adjusted balances. Conversely, the debit balances in all expense and loss accounts, as well as dividends, are eliminated by *crediting* each account to close out its year-end adjusted balance. The difference between net income earned and dividends declared during the year goes to retained earnings—it's that simple:

now that if the balance sheet equation is not in balance, or if the debits do not equal the credits, your analysis of the transaction is wrong!

5. *Does my analysis make sense?* This is the most important question, and it involves standing back from the trees to look at the forest. You must determine whether the horizontal model effects or the journal entry that results from your analysis causes changes in account balances and the financial statements that are consistent with your understanding of what's going on. If the analysis doesn't make sense to you, go back to question number 1 and start again.

Application of this five-question transaction analysis routine is illustrated in Exhibit 4-3. You are learning transaction analysis to better understand how the amounts reported on financial statements got there, which in turn will improve your ability to make decisions and informed judgments from those statements.

Exhibit 4-3

Transaction Analysis

Situation:
On September 1, 2013, Cruisers, Inc., borrowed $2,500 from its bank; a note was signed providing that the loan principal, plus interest, was to be repaid in 10 months.

Required:
Analyze the transaction and prepare a journal entry, or use the horizontal model, to record the transaction.

Solution:
Analysis of transaction:
What's going on? The firm signed a note at the bank and is receiving cash from the bank.
What accounts are affected? Notes Payable (a liability) and Cash (an asset).
How are they affected? Notes Payable is increasing and Cash is increasing.
Does the balance sheet balance? Using the horizontal model, the effect of the loan transaction on the financial statements is:

Balance Sheet	Income Statement
Assets = Liabilities + Stockholders' equity	← Net Income = Revenues − Expenses
Cash Notes Payable +2,500 +2,500	

Yes, the balance sheet does balance; assets and liabilities each increased by $2,500. The journal entry for this transaction, in which debits equal credits, is:

Sept. 1, 2013	Dr. Cash	2,500	
	Cr. Notes Payable		2,500
	Bank loan received.		

Does my analysis make sense? Yes, because a balance sheet prepared immediately after this transaction will show an increased amount of cash and the liability to the bank. The interest associated with the loan is not reflected in this entry because at this point Cruisers, Inc., has not incurred any interest expense, nor does the firm owe any interest; if the loan were to be immediately repaid, there would not be any interest due to the bank. Interest expense and the liability for the interest payable will be recorded as adjustments over the life of the loan.

To get a preview of things to come, let's look at how the interest would be accrued each month (the expense and liability have been incurred, but the liability has not yet been paid) and at how the ultimate repayment of the loan and accrued interest

(continued)

Exhibit 4-3

would be recorded. Assume that the interest rate on the note is 12% (remember, an interest rate is an annual rate unless otherwise specified). Interest expense for one month would be calculated as follows:

$$\text{Annual interest} = \text{Principal} \times \text{Annual rate} \times \text{Time (in years)}$$
$$\text{Monthly interest} = \text{Principal} \times \text{Annual rate} \times \text{Time/12}$$
$$= \$2,500 \times .12 \times 1/12$$
$$= \$25$$

It is appropriate that the monthly financial statements of Cruisers, Inc., reflect accurately the firm's interest expense for the month and its interest payable liability at the end of the month. To achieve this accuracy, an adjustment would need to be made at the end of every month of the 10-month life of the note. The effects of each of the monthly adjustments would be as shown here:

Balance Sheet	Income Statement
Assets = Liabilities + Stockholders' equity	← Net Income = Revenues − Expenses
Interest Payable +25	Interest Expense −25

Remember, a minus sign for expenses means that net income is reduced as expenses are increased, not that expenses are reduced.

Here is the entry to record this monthly adjustment:

Each month-end	Dr. Interest Expense	25	
	Cr. Interest Payable		25
	To accrue monthly interest on bank loan.		

As explained earlier, if the two financial statement equations are combined into the single equation

$$\text{Assets} = \text{Liabilities} + \text{Stockholders' equity} + \text{Revenues} - \text{Expenses}$$

the equation's balance will be preserved after each transaction or adjustment.

At the end of the 10th month, when the loan and accrued interest are paid, the following effects on the financial statements occur:

Balance Sheet	Income Statement
Assets = Liabilities + Stockholders' equity	← Net Income = Revenues − Expenses
Cash Notes Payable −2,750 −2,500 Interest Payable −250	

The entry to record this transaction is:

June 30, 2014	Dr. Notes Payable..................	2,500	
	Dr. Interest Payable	250	
	Cr. Cash..................		2,750
	Payment of bank loan and accrued interest.		

Apply the five questions of transaction analysis to both the monthly interest expense/interest payable accrual and to the payment. Also think about the effect of each of these entries on the financial statements. What is happening to net income each month? What has happened to net income for the 10 months?

Transaction analysis methodology and knowledge about the arithmetic operation of a T-account can be used to understand the activity that is recorded in an account. For example, assume that the Interest Receivable account shows the following activity for a month:

Interest Receivable			
Beginning balance	2,400		
		Transactions	1,700
Month-end adjustment	1,300		
Ending balance	2,000		

What transactions caused the credit to this account? Because the credit to this asset account represents a reduction in the account balance, the question can be rephrased as "What transaction would cause Interest Receivable to decrease?" The answer: Receipt of cash from entities that owed this firm interest. What is the month-end adjustment that caused the debit to the account? The rephrased question is "What causes Interest Receivable to increase?" The answer: Accrual of interest income that was earned this month but not yet received.

Using the horizontal model, the financial statement effects of this transaction and adjustment are:

Balance Sheet	Income Statement
Assets = Liabilities + Stockholders' equity	← Net Income = Revenues − Expenses
Transaction: Cash +1,700 Interest Receivable −1,700	
Adjustment: Interest Receivable +1,300	Interest Income +1,300

Here are the journal entries to record this transaction and adjustment:

Dr. Cash	1,700	
Cr. Interest Receivable		1,700
Dr. Interest Receivable	1,300	
Cr. Interest Income		1,300

The T-account format is a useful way of visualizing the effect of transactions and adjustments on the account balance. In addition, because of the arithmetic operation of the T-account (beginning balance +/− transactions and adjustments = ending balance), if all of the amounts except one are known, the unknown amount can be calculated.

You should invest practice and study time to learn to use transaction analysis procedures and to understand the horizontal model, journal entries, and T-accounts because these tools are used in subsequent chapters to describe the impact of transactions on the financial statements. Although these models are part of the bookkeeper's "tool kit," you are not learning them to become a bookkeeper—you are learning them to become an informed user of financial statements.

What Does It Mean?

Answers on page 127

8. What does it mean to analyze a transaction?
9. What does it mean to use a T-account to determine which activities have affected the account during a period?

Demonstration Problem

Visit the text website at www.mhhe.com/marshall10e to view a demonstration problem for this chapter.

Summary

Financial statements result from the bookkeeping (procedures for sorting, classifying, and presenting the effects of a transaction) and accounting (the selection of alternative methods of reflecting the effects of certain transactions) processes. Bookkeeping procedures for recording transactions are built on the framework of the accounting equation (Assets = Liabilities + Stockholders' equity), which must be kept in balance.

The income statement is linked to the balance sheet through the retained earnings component of stockholders' equity. Revenues and expenses of the income statement are really subparts of retained earnings that are reported separately as net income (or net loss) for a fiscal period. Net income (or net loss) is then added to (or subtracted from) the retained earnings balance at the beginning of the fiscal period in the process of determining retained earnings at the end of the fiscal period. Dividends are a subtraction in the process of determining the ending retained earnings balance.

Bookkeeping procedures involve establishing an account for each asset, liability, stockholders' equity element, revenue, and expense. Accounts can be represented by a T; the left side is the debit side and the right side is the credit side. Transactions are recorded in journal entry format:

Dr. Account Name.............................	Amount	
Cr. Account Name.............................		Amount

The journal entry is the source of amounts recorded in an account. The ending balance in an account is the positive difference between the debit and credit amounts recorded in the account, including the beginning balance. Asset and expense accounts normally have a debit balance; liability, stockholders' equity, and revenue accounts normally have a credit balance.

The horizontal model is an easy and meaningful way of understanding the effect of a transaction on the balance sheet and/or income statement. The representation of the horizontal model is:

Balance Sheet	Income Statement
Assets = Liabilities + Stockholders' equity	← Net Income = Revenues − Expenses

The key to using this model is to keep the balance sheet in balance. The arrow from net income in the income statement to stockholders' equity in the balance sheet indicates that net income affects retained earnings, which is a component of stockholders' equity. For a transaction affecting both the balance sheet and the income statement, the balance sheet will balance when the income statement effect on stockholders' equity is considered. In this model, the account name is entered under the appropriate financial statement category, and the dollar effect of the transaction on that account is entered with a plus or minus sign below the account name. The horizontal model can be shortened to this single equation:

$$\text{Assets} = \text{Liabilities} + \text{Stockholders' equity} + \text{Revenues} - \text{Expenses}$$

Adjustments describe accruals or reclassifications rather than transactions. Adjustments usually affect both a balance sheet account and an income statement account. Adjustments are part of accrual accounting, and they are required to achieve a matching of revenue and expense so that the financial statements reflect accurately the financial position and results of operations of the entity.

Transaction analysis is the process of determining how a transaction affects the financial statements. Transaction analysis involves asking and answering five questions:

1. What's going on?
2. What accounts are affected?
3. How are they affected?
4. Does the balance sheet balance? (Do the debits equal the credits?)
5. Does my analysis make sense?

Transactions can be initially recorded in virtually any way that makes sense at the time. Prior to the preparation of period-end financial statements, a reclassification adjustment can be made to reflect the appropriate asset/liability and expense/revenue recognition with respect to the accounts affected by the transaction (e.g., purchase of supplies) and subsequent activities (e.g., use of supplies).

Key Terms and Concepts

account balance (p. 109)   The arithmetic sum of the additions and subtractions to an account through a given date.

accrual (p. 115)   The process of recognizing revenue that has been earned but not collected, or an expense that has been incurred but not paid.

accrued (p. 116)   Describes revenue that has been earned and a related asset that will be collected, or an expense that has been incurred and a related liability that will be paid.

adjustment (p. 115)   An entry usually made during the process of "closing the books" that results in more accurate financial statements. Adjustments involve accruals and reclassifications. Adjustments are sometimes made at the end of interim periods, such as month-end or quarter-end, as well.

balance (p. 109)   See *account balance*.

charge (p. 109)   In bookkeeping, a synonym for *debit*.

chart of accounts (p. 109)   An index of the accounts contained in a ledger.

closing the books (p. 118)   The process of posting transactions, adjustments, and closing entries to the ledger and preparing the financial statements.

credit (p. 109)   The right side of an account. A decrease in asset and expense accounts; an increase in liability, stockholders' equity, and revenue accounts.

debit (p. 109) The left side of an account. An increase in asset and expense accounts; a decrease in liability, stockholders' equity, and revenue accounts.

entry (p. 111) A journal entry or a posting to an account.

horizontal model (p. 112) A representation of the balance sheet and income statement relationship that is useful for understanding the effects of transactions and adjustments on the financial statements. The model is:

Balance Sheet	Income Statement
Assets = Liabilities + Stockholders' equity	← Net Income = Revenues − Expenses

journal (p. 108) A chronological record of transactions.

journal entry (p. 111) A description of a transaction in a format that shows the debit account(s) and amount(s) and credit account(s) and amount(s).

ledger (p. 108) A book or file of accounts.

on account (p. 107) Used to describe a purchase or sale transaction for which cash will be paid or received at a later date. A "credit" transaction.

post (p. 108) The process of recording a transaction in the respective ledger accounts using a journal entry as the source of the information recorded.

source document (p. 111) Evidence of a transaction that supports the journal entry recording the transaction.

T-account (p. 109) An account format with a debit (left) side and a credit (right) side.

transaction analysis methodology (p. 119) The process of answering five questions to ensure that a transaction is understood:

1. What's going on?
2. What accounts are affected?
3. How are they affected?
4. Does the balance sheet balance? (Do the debits equal the credits?)
5. Does my analysis make sense?

transactions (p. 105) Economic interchanges between entities that are accounted for and reflected in financial statements.

**ANSWERS TO
What Does
It Mean?**

1. It means that you are being asked to determine whether the account is for an asset, liability, stockholders' equity element, revenue, or expense. Frequently the account classification is included in the account title. In other cases, it is necessary to understand what transactions affect the account.

2. It means that the sum of the debit entries from transactions affecting the account, plus any beginning debit balance in the account, is larger than the sum of any credit entries from transactions affecting the account plus any beginning credit balance in the account.

3. It means that because the balance of these accounts is increased by a debit entry, an asset or expense account will usually have a debit balance.

4. It means that a transaction results in increasing the balance of these kinds of accounts.

5. It means that the sum of all accounts with debit balances in the ledger equals the sum of all accounts with credit balances in the ledger.

6. It means that revenue has been earned by selling a product or providing a service, or that an expense has been incurred, but that cash has not been received (from a

revenue) or paid (for an expense) so an account receivable or an account payable, respectively, must be recognized.

7. It means that a more accurate income statement—matching of revenue and expense—and a more accurate balance sheet will result from the accrual or reclassification accomplished by the adjustment.

8. It means that the effect of the transaction on the affected accounts and financial statement categories is determined.

9. It means that by sketching a T and using arithmetic, if any three of the following are known—balance at the beginning of the period, total debits during the period, total credits during the period, or balance at the end of the period—the fourth can be calculated. The kinds of transactions or adjustments most likely to have affected the account are determined by knowing what the account is used for.

Self-Study Material

Visit the text website at www.mhhe.com/marshall10e to take an online self-study quiz for this chapter.

Matching Following are a number of the key terms and concepts introduced in the chapter, along with a list of corresponding definitions. Match the appropriate letter for the key term or concept to each definition provided (items 1–15). Note that not all key terms and concepts will be used. Answers are provided at the end of this chapter.

a. Balance sheet equation
b. Transactions
c. On account
d. Accrued (or accrual)
e. Journal
f. Post (posting)
g. Ledger
h. Account
i. Chart of accounts
j. T-account
k. Account balance

l. Debit
m. Credit
n. Entry
o. Balance
p. Charge
q. Journal entry
r. Source document
s. Adjusting journal entry
t. Closing the books
u. Transaction analysis methodology

_____ 1. The process of answering five questions to ensure that a transaction is understood. The questions are:
(1) What's going on?
(2) What accounts are affected?
(3) How are they affected?
(4) Does the balance sheet balance? (Do the debits equal the credits?)
(5) Does my analysis make sense?

_____ **2.** The left side of an account; an increase in asset and expense accounts or a decrease in liability, stockholders' equity, and revenue accounts.

_____ **3.** Economic interchanges between entities that are accounted for and reflected in financial statements.

_____ **4.** A chronological record of transactions.

_____ **5.** A journal entry usually made during the process of closing the books that results in more accurate financial statements.

_____ **6.** Assets = Liabilities + Stockholders' Equity (A = L + SE) expresses the fundamental structure of the balance sheet and is the basis of bookkeeping procedures.

_____ **7.** Used to describe a purchase or sale for which cash will be paid or received at a later date. A "credit" transaction.

_____ **8.** The process of recording a transaction in the respective ledger accounts using a journal entry as the source of information recorded.

_____ **9.** A record of transactions arranged by account name.

_____ **10.** The arithmetic sum of the additions and subtractions to an account through a given date.

_____ **11.** An index of the accounts contained in a ledger.

_____ **12.** The right side of an account; a decrease in asset and expense accounts or an increase in liability, stockholders' equity, and revenue accounts.

_____ **13.** Evidence of a transaction that supports the journal entry recording the transaction.

_____ **14.** The process of posting transactions and adjustments to the ledger and preparing the financial statements.

_____ **15.** Recognition that an amount has been earned (or is owed) but has not been received (or paid).

Multiple Choice For each of the following questions, circle the best response. Answers are provided at the end of this chapter.

1. Retained Earnings is *not*
   a. increased by net income.
   b. decreased by expenses.
   c. increased by revenues.
   d. decreased by dividends declared.
   e. decreased by gains and losses.

2. Which of the following transactions resulted in a $35,000 increase in assets and a $35,000 increase in liabilities?
   a. Collected accounts receivable of $35,000.
   b. Paid accounts payable of $35,000.
   c. Purchased land for $50,000, paying $15,000 in cash as a down payment and signing a note payable for the balance.
   d. Purchased on account, and used, $35,000 worth of office supplies during the period.
   e. Reclassified a $35,000 account receivable as a note receivable when the customer failed to pay on time.

3. Which of the following is *not* a correct expression of the accounting equation?

   a. Assets = Liabilities + Stockholders' Equity.

   b. Assets = Liabilities − Stockholders' Equity.

   c. Assets = Liabilities + Paid-In Capital + Retained Earnings.

   d. Assets = Liabilities + Paid-In Capital + Revenues − Expenses.

   e. Assets − Liabilities = Stockholders' Equity.

4. Normal account balances are as follows:

   a. Cash, Accounts Receivable, and Service Revenues are debits.

   b. Interest Expense, Wages Payable, and Retained Earnings are credits.

   c. Merchandise Inventory, Cost of Goods Sold, and Equipment are debits.

   d. Accumulated Depreciation, Cash, and Merchandise Inventory are debits.

   e. None of the above.

5. Which of the following is *not* an example of a source document?

   a. Purchase invoice.

   b. Chart of accounts.

   c. Cash register tape printout.

   d. Receipt from sales register at the point of purchase.

   e. Check stub.

6. Comparison of the balance sheet of Kohl Company at the end of 2014 with its balance sheet at the end of 2013 showed that total assets had decreased by $34,500 and stockholders' equity had increased by $7,500. The change in liabilities during the year was

   a. a decrease of $42,000.   d. an increase of $42,000.

   b. an increase of $27,000.   e. none of the above.

   c. a decrease of $27,000.

7. Total assets remain the same when

   a. depreciation expense is recorded.

   b. common stock is issued for cash.

   c. an account payable is paid to a creditor.

   d. an account receivable is reclassified as a note receivable.

   e. dividends are paid to common stockholders.

8. Which of the following groups of accounts all have debit balances?

   a. Land, Equipment, and Paid-In Capital.

   b. Accounts Receivable, Merchandise Inventory, and Salary Expense.

   c. Notes Receivable, Dividends Payable, and Interest Expense.

   d. Accounts Receivable, Accumulated Depreciation, and Buildings.

   e. None of the above.

9. If equipment is acquired by paying $12,000 in cash and issuing a $7,000 note payable,

   a. total assets are decreased by $12,000.

   b. total assets are increased by $19,000.

   c. total assets are increased by $7,000.

   d. total stockholders' equity is decreased by $12,000.

   e. total stockholders' equity is decreased by $7,000.

10. Credits are used to record

    a. decreases to assets and increases to expenses, liabilities, revenues, and stockholders' equity.

    b. decreases to assets and expenses and increases to liabilities, revenues, and stockholders' equity.

    c. increases to assets and decreases to expenses, liabilities, and stockholders' equity.

    d. increases to assets and expenses and decreases to revenues, liabilities, and stockholders' equity.

    e. decreases to assets and stockholders' equity and increases to liabilities, expenses, and revenues.

connect |ACCOUNTING

Mini-Exercises

All applicable Mini-Exercises are available with McGraw-Hill's *Connect™ Accounting.*

Mini-Exercise 4.1

LO 2, 6, 7

Record transactions and adjustments The transactions and adjustments related to the first month of operations of Zoe Amelia Corp. were as follows:

  a. Issued common stock to the initial stockholders in exchange for their cash investment.

  b. Signed a lease for office space and paid the first three months of rent in advance.

  c. Purchased office equipment and shelving for cash.

  d. Purchased merchandise inventory; made a partial payment in cash, and agreed to pay the balance within 30 days.

  e. Sold merchandise inventory on account for an amount greater than the cost of the inventory sold.

  f. Paid employees for the first two weeks of the month.

  g. At the end of the month, accrued wages owed to employees for the second two weeks of the month.

  h. Recognized rent expense for one month of the payment of rent in advance in transaction **b** (as a reclassification adjusting entry).

Required:

Enter the following column headings across the top of a sheet of paper:

Transaction/ Adjustment	A	=	L	+	SE	Net Income

Enter the transaction/adjustment in the first column, and show the effect, if any, of the transaction entry or adjusting entry on the appropriate balance sheet category or on net income by indicating the account name(s) affected and whether each is an addition ($+$) or subtraction ($-$). Items that affect net income should not be shown as affecting stockholders' equity.

Mini-Exercise 4.2

LO 2, 6, 7

Record transactions and adjustments The transactions and adjustments related to the second month of operations of Zoe Amelia Corp. were as follows:

  a. Paid wages that had been accrued at the end of the prior month.

  b. Collected accounts receivable from sales recorded in the prior month.

  c. Paid accounts payable owed for purchases made in the prior month.

  d. Borrowed cash from a local bank on a short-term promissory note.

  e. Purchased merchandise inventory for cash.

f. Incurred and paid utilities expense for the month.

g. At the end of the month, accrued interest on the short-term promissory note recorded in transaction **d.**

h. Recognized rent expense for one month of the three-month payment of rent in advance made in the prior month (as a reclassification adjusting entry).

Required:

Enter the following column headings across the top of a sheet of paper:

Transaction/ Adjustment	A	=	L	+	SE	Net Income

Enter the transaction/adjustment in the first column, and show the effect, if any, of the transaction entry or adjusting entry on the appropriate balance sheet category or on net income by indicating the account name(s) affected and whether each is an addition (+) or subtraction (−). Items that affect net income should not be shown as affecting stockholders' equity.

Transaction analysis using T-accounts

a. Accounts Payable had a balance of $3,000 at the beginning of the month and $3,400 at the end of the month. During the month, purchases on account amounted to $6,100. Calculate the payments to suppliers during the month.

b. Accounts Receivable had a balance of $21,400 at the beginning of the month and $19,800 at the end of the month. Cash collected from customers totaled $76,000 during the month. Calculate credit sales during the month, assuming that all sales were made on account.

Mini-Exercise 4.3
LO 6, 7

Required:

Solve for the missing amounts using a T-account for the balance sheet accounts in each situation. Assume that there is only one debit entry and one credit entry in the account during the month.

Transaction analysis using T-accounts

a. The Supplies account had a balance of $1,200 at the beginning of the month and $1,600 at the end of the month. The cost of supplies purchased during the month was $3,900. Calculate the cost of supplies used during the month.

b. Wages Payable had a balance of $5,800 at the end of the month. During the month, $28,000 of wages were paid to employees. Wages expense accrued during the month totaled $29,500. Calculate Wages Payable at the beginning of the month.

Mini-Exercise 4.4
LO 6, 7

Required:

Solve for the missing amounts using a T-account for the balance sheet accounts in each situation. Assume that there is only one debit entry and one credit entry in the account during the month.

Exercises

connect
|ACCOUNTING

All applicable Exercises are available with McGraw-Hill's *Connect*™ *Accounting.*

Record transactions and calculate financial statement amounts The transactions relating to the formation of Blue Co. Stores, Inc., and its first month of

Exercise 4.5
LO 2, 6, 7

operations follow. Prepare an answer sheet with the columns shown. Record each transaction in the appropriate columns of your answer sheet. Show the amounts involved and indicate how each account is affected (+ or −). After all transactions have been recorded, calculate the total assets, liabilities, and stockholders' equity at the end of the month and calculate the amount of net income for the month.

a. The firm was organized and the stockholders invested cash of $8,000.

b. The firm borrowed $5,000 from the bank; a short-term note was signed.

c. Display cases and other store equipment costing $1,750 were purchased for cash. The original list price of the equipment was $1,900, but a discount was received because the seller was having a sale.

d. A store location was rented, and $1,400 was paid for the first month's rent.

e. Inventory of $15,000 was purchased; $9,000 cash was paid to the suppliers, and the balance will be paid within 30 days.

f. During the first week of operations, merchandise that had cost $4,000 was sold for $6,500 cash.

g. A newspaper ad costing $100 was arranged for; it ran during the second week of the store's operations. The ad will be paid for in the next month.

h. Additional inventory costing $4,200 was purchased; cash of $1,200 was paid, and the balance is due in 30 days.

i. In the last three weeks of the first month, sales totaled $13,500, of which $9,600 was sold on account. The cost of the goods sold totaled $9,000.

j. Employee wages for the month totaled $1,850; these will be paid during the first week of the next month.

k. The firm collected a total of $3,160 from the sales on account recorded in transaction i.

l. The firm paid a total of $4,720 of the amount owed to suppliers from transaction e.

Answer sheet:

				Assets = Liabilities + Stockholders' equity						
	Accounts	Merchandise			Notes	Accounts	Paid-In	Retained		
Transaction	Cash + Receivable +	Inventory	+ Equipment	= Payable +	Payable	+ Capital +	Earnings +	Revenues − Expenses		

Optional continuation of Exercise 4.5

Prepare an income statement and balance sheet After you have completed parts **a** through **l** in Exercise 4.5, prepare an income statement for Blue Co. Stores, Inc., for the month presented and a balance sheet at the end of the month using the captions shown on the answer sheet.

Exercise 4.6
LO 2, 6, 7

Record transactions and calculate financial statement amounts The following are the transactions relating to the formation of Cardinal Mowing Services, Inc., and its first month of operations. Prepare an answer sheet with the columns shown. Record each transaction in the appropriate columns of your answer sheet. Show the amounts involved and indicate how each account is affected (+ or −). After all transactions have been recorded, calculate the total assets, liabilities, and stockholders' equity at the end of the month and calculate the amount of net income for the month.

a. The firm was organized and the initial stockholders invested cash of $3,000.

b. The company borrowed $4,500 from a relative of one of the initial stockholders; a short-term note was signed.

c. Two zero-turn lawn mowers costing $2,400 each and a professional trimmer costing $650 were purchased for cash. The original list price of each mower was $3,050, but a discount was received because the seller was having a sale.

d. Gasoline, oil, and several packages of trash bags were purchased for cash of $450.

e. Advertising flyers announcing the formation of the business and a newspaper ad were purchased. The cost of these items, $850, will be paid in 30 days.

f. During the first two weeks of operations, 47 lawns were mowed. The total revenue for this work was $3,525; $2,325 was collected in cash, and the balance will be received within 30 days.

g. Employees were paid $2,100 for their work during the first two weeks.

h. Additional gasoline, oil, and trash bags costing $550 were purchased for cash.

i. In the last two weeks of the first month, revenues totaled $4,600, of which $1,875 was collected.

j. Employee wages for the last two weeks totaled $2,550; these will be paid during the first week of the next month.

k. It was determined that at the end of the month the cost of the gasoline, oil, and trash bags still on hand was $150.

l. Customers paid a total of $750 due from mowing services provided during the first two weeks. The revenue for these services was recognized in transaction **f**.

Answer sheet:

			Assets = Liabilities + Stockholders' equity							
		Accounts			Notes	Accounts	Paid-In	Retained		
Transaction	Cash +	Receivable +	Supplies +	Equipment	= Payable +	Payable	+ Capital +	Earnings +	Revenues −	Expenses

Prepare an income statement and balance sheet After you have completed parts **a** through **l** in Exercise 4.6, prepare an income statement for Cardinal Mowing Services, Inc., for the month presented and a balance sheet at the end of the month using the captions shown on the answer sheet.

Optional continuation of Exercise 4.6

Write journal entries Write the journal entry(ies) for each of the transactions of Exercise 4.5.

Exercise 4.7
LO 6

Write journal entries Write the journal entry(ies) for each of the transactions of Exercise 4.6.

Exercise 4.8
LO 6

Record transactions and adjustments Prepare an answer sheet with the column headings shown after the following list of transactions. Record the effect, if any, of the transaction entry or adjusting entry on the appropriate balance sheet category or on the income statement by entering the account name and amount and indicating whether it is an addition (+) or subtraction (−). Column headings reflect the expanded balance sheet equation; items that affect net income should not be shown as affecting stockholders' equity. The first transaction is provided as an illustration.

(Note: As an alternative to using the columns, you may write the journal entry for each transaction or adjustment.)

Exercise 4.9
LO 2, 6, 7

a. During the month, the Supplies (asset) account was debited $1,800 for supplies purchased. The cost of supplies used during the month was $1,400. Record the adjustment to properly reflect the amount of supplies used and supplies still on hand at the end of the month.

b. An insurance premium of $480 was paid for the coming year. Prepaid Insurance was debited.

c. Wages of $3,200 were paid for the current month.

d. Interest income of $250 was received for the current month.

e. Accrued $700 of commissions payable to sales staff for the current month.

f. Accrued $130 of interest expense at the end of the month.

g. Received $2,100 on accounts receivable accrued at the end of the prior month.

h. Purchased $600 of merchandise inventory from a supplier on account.

i. Paid $160 of interest expense for the month.

j. Accrued $800 of wages at the end of the current month.

k. Paid $500 of accounts payable.

Transaction/ Adjustment	Assets	Liabilities	Stockholders' Equity	Net Income
a.	Supplies −1,400			Supplies Exp. −1,400
				(Note: An increase to Supplies Expense decreases Net Income.)

Exercise 4.10

LO 2, 6, 7

Record transactions and adjustments Prepare an answer sheet with the column headings shown after the following list of transactions. Record the effect, if any, of the transaction entry or adjusting entry on the appropriate balance sheet category or on the income statement by entering the account name and amount and indicating whether it is an addition (+) or subtraction (−). Column headings reflect the expanded balance sheet equation; items that affect net income should not be shown as affecting stockholders' equity. The first transaction is provided as an illustration.

(Note: As an alternative to using the columns, you may write the journal entry for each transaction or adjustment.)

a. During the month, Supplies Expense was debited $2,600 for supplies purchased. The cost of supplies used during the month was $1,900. Record the adjustment to properly reflect the amount of supplies used and supplies still on hand at the end of the month.

b. During the month, the board of directors declared a cash dividend of $14,400, payable next month.

c. Employees were paid $10,500 in wages for their work during the first three weeks of the month.

d. Employee wages of $3,600 for the last week of the month have not been recorded.

e. Revenues from services performed during the month totaled $22,200. Of this amount, $9,300 was received in cash and the balance is expected to be received within 30 days.

f. A contract was signed with a newspaper for a $1,200 advertisement; the ad ran during this month but will not be paid for until next month.

g. Merchandise that cost $4,650 was sold for $8,700. Of this amount, $3,300 was received in cash and the balance is expected to be received within 30 days.

h. Independent of transaction **a**, assume that during the month, supplies were purchased at a cost of $1,230 and debited to the Supplies (asset) account. A total of $990 of supplies were used during the month. Record the adjustment to properly reflect the amount of supplies used and supplies still on hand at the end of the month.

i. Interest of $540 has been earned on a note receivable but has not yet been received.

j. Issued 1,200 shares of $10 par value common stock for $26,400 in cash.

Transaction/ Adjustment	Assets	Liabilities	Stockholders' Equity	Net Income
a.	Supplies +700			Supplies Exp. +700
				(Note: A decrease to Supplies Expense increases Net Income.)

Record transactions and adjustments Enter the following column headings across the top of a sheet of paper:

Exercise 4.11
LO 2, 6, 7

Transaction/ Adjustment	Assets	Liabilities	Stockholders' Equity	Net Income

Enter the transaction/adjustment letter in the first column and show the effect, if any, of the transaction entry or adjusting entry on the appropriate balance sheet category or on the income statement by entering the amount and indicating whether it is an addition (+) or a subtraction (−). Column headings reflect the expanded balance sheet equation; items that affect net income should not be shown as affecting stockholders' equity. In some cases, only one column may be affected because all of the specific accounts affected by the transaction are included in that category. Transaction **a** has been completed as an illustration.

(Note: As an alternative to using the columns, you may write the journal entry for each transaction or adjustment.)

a. Provided services to a client on account; revenues totaled $550.

b. Paid an insurance premium of $360 for the coming year. An asset, Prepaid Insurance, was debited.

c. Recognized insurance expense for one month from the premium transaction in **b** via a reclassification adjusting entry.

d. Paid $800 of wages accrued at the end of the prior month.

e. Paid $2,600 of wages for the current month.

f. Accrued $600 of wages at the end of the current month.

g. Received cash of $1,500 on accounts receivable accrued at the end of the prior month.

Transaction/ Adjustment	Assets	Liabilities	Stockholders' Equity	Net Income
a.	+550			+550

Exercise 4.12
LO 2, 6, 7

e**X**cel

Record transactions and adjustments Enter the following column headings across the top of a sheet of paper:

Transaction/ Adjustment	Assets	Liabilities	Stockholders' Equity	Net Income

Enter the transaction/adjustment letter in the first column and show the effect, if any, of the transaction entry or adjustment on the appropriate balance sheet category or on the income statement by entering the amount and indicating whether it is an addition ($+$) or a subtraction ($-$). Column headings reflect the expanded balance sheet equation; items that affect net income should not be shown as affecting stockholders' equity. In some cases, only one column may be affected because all of the specific accounts affected by the transaction are included in that category. Transaction **a** has been completed as an illustration.

(Note: As an alternative to using the columns, you may write the journal entry for each transaction or adjustment.)

a. During the month, Supplies Expense was debited $5,200 for supplies purchased. The cost of supplies used during the month was $3,800. Record the adjustment to properly reflect the amount of supplies used and supplies still on hand at the end of the month.

b. Independent of transaction **a**, assume that during the month, Supplies (asset) was debited $5,200 for supplies purchased. The total cost of supplies used during the month was $3,800. Record the adjustment to properly reflect the amount of supplies used and supplies still on hand at the end of the month.

c. Received $3,400 of cash from clients for services provided during the current month.

d. Paid $1,900 of accounts payable.

e. Received $1,500 of cash from clients for revenues accrued at the end of the prior month.

f. Received $800 of interest income accrued at the end of the prior month.

g. Received $1,650 of interest income for the current month.

h. Accrued $740 of interest income earned in the current month.

i. Paid $4,200 of interest expense for the current month.

j. Accrued $1,480 of interest expense at the end of the current month.

k. Accrued $3,200 of commissions payable to sales staff for the current month.

Transaction/ Adjustment	Assets	Liabilities	Stockholders' Equity	Net Income
a.	+1,400			+1,400

Exercise 4.13
LO 3

Calculate retained earnings On February 1, 2013, the balance of the retained earnings account of Blue Power Corporation was $630,000. Revenues for February totaled $123,000, of which $115,000 was collected in cash. Expenses for February totaled $131,000, of which $108,000 was paid in cash. Dividends declared and paid during February were $12,000.

Required:
Calculate the retained earnings balance at February 28, 2013.

Cash receipts versus revenues During the month of April, Riley Co. had cash receipts from customers of $680,000. Expenses totaled $624,000, and accrual basis net income was $168,000. There were no gains or losses during the month.

Exercise 4.14
LO 6, 7

Required:

a. Calculate the revenues for Riley Co. for April.

b. Explain why cash receipts from customers can be different from revenues.

Notes receivable—interest accrual and collection On April 1, 2013, Tabor Co. received a $6,000 note from a customer in settlement of a $6,000 account receivable from that customer. The note bore interest at the rate of 15% per annum, and the note plus interest was payable March 31, 2014.

Exercise 4.15
LO 6, 7

Required:

Use the horizontal model to show the effects of each of these transactions and adjustments:

a. Receipt of the note on April 1, 2013.

b. The accrual of interest at December 31, 2013.

c. The collection of the note and interest on March 31, 2014.

(Note: As an alternative to using the horizontal model, write the journal entries to show each of these transactions and adjustments.)

Notes payable—interest accrual and payment Proco had an account payable of $84,000 due to Shirmoo, Inc., one of its suppliers. The amount was due to be paid on January 31. Proco did not have enough cash on hand then to pay the amount due, so Proco's treasurer called Shirmoo's treasurer and agreed to sign a note payable for the amount due. The note was dated February 1, had an interest rate of 7% per annum, and was payable with interest on May 31.

Exercise 4.16
LO 6, 7

Required:

Use the horizontal model to show the effects of each of these transactions and adjustments for Proco on

a. February 1, to show that the account payable had been changed to a note payable.

b. March 31, to accrue interest expense for February and March.

c. May 31, to record payment of the note and all of the interest due to Shirmoo.

(Note: As an alternative to using the horizontal model, write the journal entries to show each of these transactions and adjustments.)

Effect of adjustments on net income Assume that Cater Co.'s accountant neglected to record the payroll expense accrual adjustment at the end of October.

Exercise 4.17
LO 6, 7

Required:

a. Explain the effect of this omission on net income reported for October.

b. Explain the effect of this omission on net income reported for November.

c. Explain the effect of this omission on total net income for the two months of October and November taken together.

d. Explain why the accrual adjustment should have been recorded as of October 31.

Exercise 4.18

LO 6, 7

Effects of adjustments A bookkeeper prepared the year-end financial statements of Giftwrap, Inc. The income statement showed net income of $237,000, and the balance sheet showed ending retained earnings of $910,000. The firm's accountant reviewed the bookkeeper's work and determined that adjustments should be made that would increase revenues by $50,000 and increase expenses by $84,000.

Required:

Calculate the amounts of net income and retained earnings after the preceding adjustments are recorded.

Exercise 4.19

LO 6, 7

T-account analysis Answer these questions that are related to the following Interest Payable T-account:

a. What is the amount of the February 28 adjustment?
b. What account would most likely have been credited for the amount of the February transactions?
c. What account would most likely have been debited for the amount of the February 28 adjustment?
d. Why would this adjusting entry have been made?

Interest Payable			
		February 1 balance	1,200
February transactions	1,500	February 28 adjustment	?
		February 28 balance	2,100

Exercise 4.20

LO 6, 7

Transaction analysis using T-accounts This exercise provides practice in understanding the operation of T-accounts and transaction analysis. For each situation, you must solve for a missing amount. Use a T-account for the balance sheet account, show in a horizontal model, or prepare journal entries for the information provided. In each case, there is only one debit entry and one credit entry in the account during the month.

Example:

Accounts Payable had a balance of $6,000 at the beginning of the month and $5,400 at the end of the month. During the month, payments to suppliers amounted to $16,000. Calculate the purchases on account during the month.

Solution:

Accounts Payable							
	Beginning balance	6,000	Dr. Accounts Payable 16,000		Dr. Inventory	15,400	
Payment 16,000	Purchase	?=15,400	Cr. Cash	16,000	Cr. Accounts Payable	15,400	
	Ending balance	5,400	Payments to suppliers.		Purchases on account.		

a. Accounts Receivable had a balance of $16,200 at the beginning of the month and $6,600 at the end of the month. Credit sales totaled $90,000 during the month. Calculate the cash collected from customers during the month, assuming that all sales were made on account.

b. The Supplies account had a balance of $5,840 at the beginning of the month and $7,760 at the end of the month. The cost of supplies used during the month was $25,280. Calculate the cost of supplies purchased during the month.

c. Wages Payable had a balance of $7,600 at the beginning of the month. During the month, $31,000 of wages were paid to employees. Wages Expense accrued during the month totaled $39,000. Calculate the balance of Wages Payable at the end of the month.

Problems

All applicable Problems are available with McGraw-Hill's *Connect*™ *Accounting.*

Record transactions and adjustments Use the horizontal model, or write the journal entry, for each of the following transactions and adjustments that occurred during the first year of operations at Kissick Co.

Problem 4.21
LO 2, 6, 7

a. Issued 200,000 shares of $5-par-value common stock for $1,000,000 in cash.

b. Borrowed $500,000 from Oglesby National Bank and signed a 12% note due in two years.

c. Incurred and paid $380,000 in salaries for the year.

d. Purchased $640,000 of merchandise inventory on account during the year.

e. Sold inventory costing $580,000 for a total of $910,000, all on credit.

f. Paid rent of $110,000 on the sales facilities during the first 11 months of the year.

g. Purchased $150,000 of store equipment, paying $50,000 in cash and agreeing to pay the difference within 90 days.

h. Paid the entire $100,000 owed for store equipment, and $620,000 of the amount due to suppliers for credit purchases previously recorded.

i. Incurred and paid utilities expense of $36,000 during the year.

j. Collected $825,000 in cash from customers during the year for credit sales previously recorded.

k. At year-end, accrued $60,000 of interest on the note due to Oglesby National Bank.

l. At year-end, accrued $10,000 of past-due December rent on the sales facilities.

Prepare an income statement and balance sheet from transaction data

Problem 4.22
LO 1

a. Based on your answers to Problem 4.21, prepare an income statement (ignoring income taxes) for Kissick Co.'s first year of operations and a balance sheet as of the end of the year. *(Hint: You may find it helpful to prepare T-accounts for each account affected by the transactions.)*

b. Provide a brief written evaluation of Kissick Co.'s results from operations for the year and its financial position at the end of the year. In your opinion, what are the likely explanations for the company's net loss?

Problem 4.23

LO 6, 7

Calculate income from operations and net income Selected information taken from the financial statements of Verbeke Co. for the year ended December 31, 2013, follows:

Gross profit	$412,000
General and administrative expenses.	83,000
Net cash used by investing activities	106,000
Dividends paid.	51,000
Interest expense	61,000
Net sales.	741,000
Advertising expense	76,000
Accounts payable	101,000
Income tax expense	38,000
Other selling expenses.	42,000

a.   Calculate income from operations (operating income) for the year ended December 31, 2013. *(Hint: You may wish to review Exhibit 2-2.)*

b.   Calculate net income for the year ended December 31, 2013.

Problem 4.24

LO 6, 7

Calculate income from operations and net income Selected information taken from the financial statements of Fordstar Co. for the year ended December 31, 2013, follows:

Net cash provided by operations	$ 49,000
Cost of goods sold	155,000
Selling, general, and administrative expenses	62,000
Accounts payable.	45,000
Dividends paid.	68,000
Research and development expenses	15,000
Merchandise inventory.	39,000
Provision for income taxes.	420,000
Net sales	32,000
Interest expense	

a.   Calculate income from operations (operating income) for the year ended December 31, 2013. *(Hint: You may wish to review Exhibit 2-2.)*

b.   Calculate net income for the year ended December 31, 2013.

Problem 4.25

LO 6, 7

Alternative adjustments—supplies On January 10, 2013, the first day of the spring semester, the cafeteria of The Defiance College purchased for cash enough paper napkins to last the entire 16-week semester. The total cost was $2,400.

Required:

Use the horizontal model to show the effects of recording the following:

a.   The purchase of the paper napkins, assuming that the purchase was initially recorded as an expense.

b.   At January 31, it was estimated that the cost of the paper napkins used during the first three weeks of the semester totaled $475. Use the horizontal model to show the adjustments that should be made as of January 31 so that the appropriate amount of expense will be shown in the income statement for the month of January.

c.   Use the horizontal model to show the effects of the alternative way of recording the initial purchase of napkins.

d. Use the horizontal model to show the effects of the adjustment that should occur at January 31 if the initial purchase had been recorded as in **c**.

e. Consider the effects that entries **a** and **b** would have on the financial statements of The Defiance College. Compare these effects to those that would be caused by entries **c** and **d**. Are there any differences between these alternative sets of entries on the
  1. Income statement for the month of January?
  2. Balance sheet at January 31?

(Note: As an alternative to using the horizontal model, write the journal entries to show each of these transactions and adjustments.)

Alternative adjustments—rent Calco, Inc., rents its store location. Rent is $3,000 per month, payable quarterly in advance. On July 1, a check for $9,000 was issued to the landlord for the July–September quarter.

Problem 4.26
LO 6, 7

Required:
Use the horizontal model to show the effects on the financial statements of Calco, Inc.:

a. To record the payment, assuming that all $9,000 is initially recorded as Rent Expense.

b. To record the adjustment that would be appropriate at July 31 if your entry in **a** had been made.

c. To record the initial payment as Prepaid Rent.

d. To record the adjustment that would be appropriate at July 31 if your entry in **c** had been made.

e. To record the adjustment that would be appropriate at August 31 and September 30, regardless of how the initial payment had been recorded (and assuming that the July 31 adjustment had been made).

f. If you were supervising the bookkeeper, how would you suggest that the July 1 payment be recorded? Explain your answer.

(Note: As an alternative to using the horizontal model, write the journal entries to show each of these transactions and adjustments.)

Analyze several accounts using Campbell Soup Company **annual report data** Set up a horizontal model in the following format:

Problem 4.27
LO 6, 7

	Assets			Liabilities	Revenues		Expenses
				Payable to		Cost of	Marketing,
	Cash and Cash	Accounts		Suppliers and	Net	Products	Selling, and
	Equivalents	Receivable	Inventories	Others	Sales	Sold	Administrative
Beginning balance							
Net sales							
Cost of products sold							
Marketing, selling, and administrative expenses							
Purchases on account							
Collections of accounts receivable							
Payments to suppliers and others							
Ending balance							

Required:

a. Enter the beginning (August 1, 2010) and ending (July 31, 2011) account balances for Accounts Receivable, Inventories, and Payable to Suppliers and Others. Find these amounts on the balance sheet for Campbell Soup Company in the appendix.

b. From the income statement for Campbell Soup Company for the year ended July 31, 2011, in the appendix, record the following transactions in the model:

   1. Net Sales, assuming that all sales were made on account.

   2. Cost of Products Sold, assuming that all costs were transferred from inventories.

   3. Marketing, Selling, and Administrative Expenses, assuming all of these expenses were accrued in the Payable to Suppliers and Others liability category as they were incurred.
   (Hint: Campbell's General, Selling, and Administrative Expenses are contained in two separate captions. Note that Payable to Suppliers and Others is another term for Accounts Payable.)

c. Assuming that the only other transactions affecting these balance sheet accounts were those described next, calculate the amount of each transaction:

   1. Purchases of inventories on account.

   2. Collections of accounts receivable.

   3. Payments to suppliers and others.

Problem 4.28

LO 6, 7

Make corrections and adjustments to income statement and balance sheet Big Blue Rental Corp. provides rental agent services to apartment building owners. Big Blue Rental Corp.'s preliminary income statement for August 2013, and its August 31, 2013, preliminary balance sheet, did not reflect the following.

a. Rental commissions of $500 had been earned in August but had not yet been received from or billed to building owners.

b. When supplies are purchased, their cost is recorded as an asset. As supplies are used, a record of those used is kept. The record sheet shows that $360 of supplies were used in August.

c. Interest on the note payable is to be paid on May 31 and November 30. Interest for August has not been accrued—that is, it has not yet been recorded. (The Interest Payable of $80 on the balance sheet is the amount of the accrued liability at July 31.) The interest rate on this note is 10%.

d. Wages of $260 for the last week of August have not been recorded.

e. The Rent Expense of $1,020 represents rent for August, September, and October, which was paid early in August.

f. Interest of $280 has been earned on notes receivable but has not yet been received.

g. Late in August, the board of directors met and declared a cash dividend of $2,800, payable September 10. Once declared, the dividend is a liability of the corporation until it is paid.

BIG BLUE RENTAL CORP.
Income Statement
August 2013

	Preliminary	Adjustments/Corrections Debit	Credit	Final
Commissions revenue..................................	$ 9,000	$	$	$
Interest revenue	1,700			
Total revenue...	$10,700	$	$	$
Rent expense..	$ 1,020	$	$	$
Wages expense	2,380			
Supplies expense...	—			
Interest expense	—			
Total expenses	$ 3,400	$	$	$
Net income...	$ 7,300	$	$	$

BIG BLUE RENTAL CORP.
Balance Sheet
August 31, 2013

	Preliminary	Adjustments/Corrections Debit	Credit	Final
Assets				
Cash..	$ 800	$	$	$
Notes receivable	26,000			
Commissions receivable	—			
Interest receivable	—			
Prepaid rent	—			
Supplies..	1,300			
Total assets	$ 28,100	$	$	$
Liabilities and Stockholders' Equity				
Accounts payable	$ 240	$	$	$
Notes payable...	4,800			
Interest payable	80			
Wages payable	—			
Dividends payable.......................................	—			
Total liabilities...	$ 5,120	$	$	$
Paid-in capital	$ 4,800	$	$	$
Retained earnings:				
Balance, August 1....................................	$ 10,880	$	$	$
Net income...	7,300			
Dividends	—			
Balance, August 31	$ 18,180	$	$	$
Total stockholders' equity........................	$ 22,980	$	$	$
Total liabilities and stockholders' equity	$ 28,100	$	$	$

Required:

a. Using the columns provided on the income statement and balance sheet for Big Blue Rental Corp., make the appropriate adjustments/corrections to the statements, and enter the correct amount in the Final column. Key your adjustments/corrections with the letter of the item in the preceding list. Captions/account names that you will have to use are on the statements. *(Hint: Use the five questions of transaction analysis. What is the relationship between net income and the balance sheet?)*

b. Consider the entries that you have recorded in your answer to part **a**. Using these items as examples, explain why adjusting entries normally have an effect on both the balance sheet and the income statement.

c. Explain why the Cash account on the balance sheet is not usually affected by adjustments. In your answer, identify the types of activities and/or events that normally cause the need for adjustments to be recorded. Give at least one example of an adjustment (other than those provided in the problem data).

Cases

All applicable Cases are available with McGraw-Hill's *Connect*™ *Accounting*.

Case 4.29

LO 6, 7

Capstone analytical review of Chapters 2–4. Calculate liquidity and profitability measures and explain various financial statement relationships for a realty firm DeBauge Realtors, Inc., is a realty firm owned by Jeff and Kristi DeBauge. The DeBauge family owns 100% of the corporation's stock. The following summarized data (in thousands) are taken from the December 31, 2013, financial statements:

For the Year Ended December 31, 2013:	
Commissions revenue	$142
Cost of services provided	59
Advertising expense	28
Operating income	$ 55
Interest expense	5
Income tax expense	16
Net income	$ 34

At December 31, 2013:	
Assets	
Cash and short-term investments	$ 30
Accounts receivable, net	40
Property, plant, and equipment, net	125
Total assets	$195
Liabilities and Stockholders' Equity	
Accounts payable	$ 90
Income taxes payable	5
Notes payable (long term)	50
Paid-in capital	20
Retained earnings	30
Total liabilities and stockholders' equity	$195

At December 31, 2012, total assets were $205 and total stockholders' equity was $50. There were no changes in notes payable or paid-in capital during 2013.

Required:

a. What particular expense do you suppose accounts for the largest portion of the $59 cost of services provided?

b. The cost of services provided amount includes all operating expenses (i.e., selling, general, and administrative expenses) except advertising expense. What do you suppose the primary reason was for DeBauge Realtors, Inc., to separate advertising from other operating expenses?

c. Calculate the effective interest rate on the notes payable for DeBauge Realtors, Inc.

d. Calculate the company's average income tax rate. (*Hint: You must first determine the earnings before taxes.*)

e. Calculate the amount of dividends declared and paid to Jeff and Kristi DeBauge during the year ended December 31, 2013. (*Hint: Do a T-account analysis of retained earnings.*) What is the company's dividend policy? (What proportion of the company's earnings are distributed as dividends?)

f. DeBauge Realtors, Inc., was organized and operates as a corporation rather than a partnership. What is the primary advantage of the corporate form of business to a realty firm? What is the primary disadvantage of the corporate form?

g. Explain why the amount of income tax expense is different from the amount of income taxes payable.

h. Calculate the amount of working capital and the current ratio at December 31, 2013. Assess the company's overall liquidity.

i. Calculate ROI (including margin and turnover) and ROE for the year ended December 31, 2013. Explain why these single measures may not be very meaningful for this firm.

Capstone analytical review of Chapters 2–4. Calculate liquidity and profitability measures and explain various financial statement relationships for an excavation contractor Gerrard Construction Co. is an excavation contractor. The following summarized data (in thousands) are taken from the December 31, 2013, financial statements:

Case 4.30

LO 6, 7

For the Year Ended December 31, 2013:	
Net revenues	$32,200
Cost of services provided	11,400
Depreciation expense	6,500
Operating income	$14,300
Interest expense	3,800
Income tax expense	3,200
Net income	$ 7,300

(continued)

At December 31, 2013:	
Assets	
Cash and short-term investments	$ 2,800
Accounts receivable, net	9,800
Property, plant, and equipment, net	77,400
Total assets	$90,000
Liabilities and Stockholders' Equity	
Accounts payable	$ 1,500
Income taxes payable	1,600
Notes payable (long term)	47,500
Paid-in capital	10,000
Retained earnings	29,400
Total liabilities and stockholders' equity	$90,000

At December 31, 2012, total assets were $82,000 and total stockholders' equity was $32,600. There were no changes in notes payable or paid-in capital during 2013.

Required:

a. The cost of services provided amount includes all operating expenses (selling, general, and administrative expenses) except depreciation expense. What do you suppose the primary reason was for management to separate depreciation from other operating expenses? From a conceptual point of view, should depreciation be considered a "cost" of providing services?

b. Why do you suppose the amounts of depreciation expense and interest expense are so high for Gerrard Construction Co.? To which specific balance sheet accounts should a financial analyst relate these expenses?

c. Calculate the company's average income tax rate. *(Hint: You must first determine the earnings before taxes.)*

d. Explain why the amount of income tax expense is different from the amount of income taxes payable.

e. Calculate the amount of total current assets. Why do you suppose this amount is so low, relative to total assets?

f. Why doesn't the company have a Merchandise Inventory account?

g. Calculate the amount of working capital and the current ratio at December 31, 2013. Assess the company's overall liquidity.

h. Calculate ROI (including margin and turnover) and ROE for the year ended December 31, 2013. Assess the company's overall profitability. What additional information would you like to have to increase the validity of this assessment?

i. Calculate the amount of dividends declared and paid during the year ended December 31, 2013. *(Hint: Do a T-account analysis of retained earnings.)*

Answers to Self-Study Material

Matching: 1. u, 2. l, 3. b, 4. e, 5. s, 6. a, 7. c, 8. f, 9. g, 10. k, 11. i, 12. m, 13. r, 14. t, 15. d

Multiple choice: 1. e, 2. c, 3. b, 4. c, 5. b, 6. a, 7. d, 8. b, 9. c, 10. b

5 Accounting for and Presentation of Current Assets

Current assets include cash and other assets that are expected to be converted to cash or used up within one year, or an **operating cycle,** whichever is longer. An entity's operating cycle is the average time it takes to convert an investment in inventory back to cash. This is illustrated in the following diagram:

Cash   is used to purchase finished goods or raw materials and labor used to manufacture

     ➤ ***Inventory,***   which is held until sold, usually on account, resulting in

         ➤ ***Accounts Receivable,***   which must then be collected to increase

For most firms, the normal operating cycle is less than one year. As you learn more about each of the current assets discussed in this chapter, keep in mind that a shorter operating cycle permits a lower investment in current assets. This results in an increase in turnover, which in turn increases return on investment (ROI). Many firms attempt to reduce their operating cycle and increase overall profitability by trying to sell inventory and collect accounts receivable as quickly as possible.

Current asset captions usually seen in a balance sheet are:

Cash and Cash Equivalents

Short-Term Marketable Securities

Accounts and Notes Receivable

Inventories

Prepaid Expenses or Other Current Assets

Refer to the Consolidated Balance Sheets of Campbell Soup Company on page 712 of the appendix. Note that Campbell's current assets at July 31, 2011, total $1,963 million and account for 29 percent of the company's total assets. Look at the components of current assets. Notice that Cash and Cash Equivalents, Accounts Receivable, and Inventories are the largest current asset amounts. Now refer to the balance sheets in other annual reports that you may have and examine the composition of current assets. Do they differ significantly from Campbell's balance sheet? The objective of this chapter is to permit you to make sense of the current asset presentation of any balance sheet.

---

1. What does it mean when an asset is referred to as a current asset?

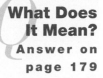

What Does It Mean?
Answer on page 179

LEARNING OBJECTIVES (LO)

After studying this chapter you should understand and be able to

LO 5-1   Explain what is included in the cash and cash equivalents amount reported on the balance sheet.

LO 5-2   Describe the key features of a system of internal control and explain why internal controls are important.

LO 5-3   Explain the bank reconciliation procedure.

LO 5-4   Explain how short-term marketable securities are reported on the balance sheet.

LO 5-5   Discuss how accounts receivable are reported on the balance sheet, including the valuation allowances for estimated uncollectible accounts and estimated cash discounts.

LO 5-6   Explain how notes receivable and related accrued interest are reported on the balance sheet.

LO 5-7   Explain how inventories are reported on the balance sheet.

LO 5-8   Discuss the alternative inventory cost flow assumptions and generalize about their respective effects on the income statement and balance sheet when price levels are changing.

LO 5-9   Discuss the impact of inventory errors on the balance sheet and income statement.

LO 5-10   Explain what prepaid expenses are and how they are reported on the balance sheet.

Chapters 5 through 9 are organized around the financial statements, starting with the asset side of the balance sheet in Chapters 5 and 6, moving over to the liability and stockholders' equity side in Chapters 7 and 8, and then on to the income statement and statement of cash flows in Chapter 9. Exhibit 5-1 highlights the balance sheet accounts covered in detail in this chapter and shows the income statement and statement of cash flows components affected by these accounts.

Exhibit 5-1

Financial Statements—
The Big Picture

Balance Sheet

Current Assets	Chapter	*Current Liabilities*	Chapter
Cash and cash equivalents	5, 9	Short-term debt	7
Short-term marketable securities	5	Current maturities of long-term debt	7
Accounts receivable	5, 9	Accounts payable	7
Notes receivable	5	Unearned revenue or deferred credits	7
Inventories	5, 9	Payroll taxes and other withholdings	7
Prepaid expenses	5	Other accrued liabilities	7
Noncurrent Assets		*Noncurrent Liabilities*	
Land	6	Long-term debt	7
Buildings and equipment	6	Deferred tax liabilities	7
Assets acquired by capital lease	6	Other long-term liabilities	7
Intangible assets	6	*Stockholders' Equity*	
Natural resources	6	Common stock	8
Other noncurrent assets	6	Preferred stock	8
		Additional paid-in capital	8
		Retained earnings	8
		Treasury stock	8
		Accumulated other comprehensive income (loss)	8

Income Statement

	Chapter
Sales	5, 9
Cost of goods sold	5, 9
Gross profit (or gross margin)	5, 9
Selling, general, and administrative expenses	5, 6, 9
Income from operations	9
Gains (losses) on sale of assets	6, 9
Interest income	5, 9
Interest expense	7, 9
Income tax expense	7, 9
Unusual items	9
Net income	5, 6, 7, 8, 9
Earnings per share	9

Statement of Cash Flows

Operating Activities	Chapter
Net income	5, 6, 7, 8, 9
Depreciation expense	6, 9
(Gains) losses on sale of assets	6, 9
(Increase) decrease in current assets	5, 9
Increase (decrease) in current liabilities	7, 9
Investing Activities	
Proceeds from sale of property, plant, and equipment	6, 9
Purchase of property, plant, and equipment	6, 9
Financing Activities	
Proceeds from long-term debt*	7, 9
Repayment of long-term debt*	7, 9
Issuance of common stock and/or preferred stock	8, 9
Purchase of treasury stock	8, 9
Payment of dividends	8, 9

Primary topics of this chapter.

Other affected financial statement components.

*May include short-term debt items as well.

Petty Cash Funds

Although most of an entity's cash disbursements should be made by check for security and record-keeping purposes, a petty cash fund could be used for small payments for which writing a check would be inconvenient. For example, postage due, **collect on delivery (COD)** charges, or the cost of an urgently needed office supply item often is paid from the petty cash fund to avoid the delay and expense associated with creating a check.

The petty cash fund is an **imprest account,** which means that the sum of the cash on hand in the petty cash box and the receipts in support of disbursements (called *petty cash vouchers*) should equal the amount initially put in the petty cash fund.

Periodically (usually at the end of the accounting period) the petty cash fund is reimbursed to bring the cash in the fund back to the original amount. It is at this time that the expenses paid through the fund are recognized in the accounts.

The amount of the petty cash fund is included in the cash amount reported on the entity's balance sheet.

Business in Practice

Cash and Cash Equivalents

The vast majority of publicly traded corporations report their most liquid assets in the *cash* and *cash equivalents* category. **Cash** includes money on hand in change funds, **petty cash** funds (see Business in Practice—Petty Cash Funds), undeposited receipts (including currency, checks, money orders, and bank drafts), and any funds immediately available to the firm in its bank accounts ("demand deposits" such as checking and savings accounts). **Cash equivalents** are short-term investments readily convertible into cash with a minimal risk of price change due to interest rate movements.

Because cash on hand or in checking accounts earns little if any interest, management of just about every organization will develop a cash management system to permit investment of cash balances not currently required for the entity's operation. The broad objective of the cash management program is to maximize earnings by having as much cash as feasible invested for the longest possible time. Cash managers are interested in minimizing investment risks, and this is accomplished by investing in U.S. Treasury securities, securities of agencies of the federal government, bank certificates of deposit, money market mutual funds, and commercial paper. (**Commercial paper** is like an IOU issued by a very creditworthy corporation.) Securities selected for investment usually will have a maturity date that is within a few months of the investment date and that corresponds to the time when the cash manager thinks the cash will be needed. Cash equivalents included with cash on the balance sheets of Campbell Soup Company are defined as "all highly liquid debt instruments purchased with a maturity of three months or less" (see page 715 in the appendix).

In addition to an organization's cash management system, policies to minimize the chances of customer theft and employee embezzlement also will be developed. These are part of the **internal control system** (see Business in Practice—The Internal Control System), which is designed to help safeguard all of an entity's assets, including cash.

LO 1
Explain what is included in the cash and cash equivalents amount reported on the balance sheet.

LO 2
Describe the key features of a system of internal control and explain why internal controls are important.

---

2. What does it mean to have an effective system of internal control?

What Does It Mean?
Answer on page 179

The Internal Control System

Internal control is broadly defined as a process, established by an entity's board of directors, management, and other personnel, designed to provide reasonable assurance that objectives are achieved with respect to:

1. The effectiveness and efficiency of the operations of the organization.

2. The reliability of the organization's financial reporting.

3. The organization's compliance with applicable laws and regulations.

Internal controls relate to every level of the organization, and the tone established by the board of directors and top management establishes the control environment. Ethical considerations expressed in the organization's code of conduct and social responsibility activities are a part of this overall tone. Although the system of internal control is frequently discussed in the context of the firm's accounting system, it is equally applicable to every activity of the firm, and it is appropriate for everyone to understand the need for and significance of internal controls.

Internal control policies and procedures sometimes are classified as financial controls and administrative controls.

Financial controls, which are related to the concept of *separation of duties,* include a series of checks and balances ensuring that more than one person is involved in a transaction from beginning to end. For example, most organizations require that checks be signed by someone other than the person who prepares them. The check signer is expected to review the documents supporting the disbursement and to raise questions about unusual items. Another internal control requires the credit manager who authorizes the write-off of an account receivable to have that write-off approved by another officer of the firm. Likewise, a bank teller or cashier who has made a mistake in initially recording a transaction must have a supervisor approve the correction.

Administrative controls are frequently included in policy and procedure manuals and are reflected in management reviews of reports of operations and activities. For example, a firm's credit policy might specify that no customer is to have an account receivable balance in excess of $10,000 until the customer has had a clean payment record for at least one year. The firm's internal auditors might periodically review the accounts receivable detail to determine whether this policy is being followed. In addition to *limit* (or *reasonableness*) *tests* such as this, administrative controls also ensure the proper *authorization of transactions* before they are entered into. For example, a firm may require its credit department to conduct a thorough evaluation of a new customer's credit history prior to approving a sales order prepared by a salesperson.

The system of internal control does not exist because top management thinks that the employees are dishonest. Internal controls provide a framework within which employees can operate, knowing that their work is being performed in a way that is consistent with the desires of top management. To the extent that temptation is removed from a situation that might otherwise lead to an employee's dishonest act, the system of internal control provides an even more significant benefit.

The Bank Reconciliation as a Control over Cash

Many transactions either directly or indirectly affect the receipt or payment of cash. For instance, a sale of merchandise on account normally leads to a cash receipt when the account receivable is collected. Likewise, a purchase of inventory on account results in a cash payment when the account payable is paid. In fact, cash (in one form or another) is eventually involved in the settlement of virtually all business affairs.

As a result of the high volume of cash transactions and the ease with which money can be exchanged, it is appropriate to design special controls to help safeguard cash. At a minimum, all cash received should be deposited in the company's bank account at the end of each business day, and all cash payments (other than petty cash disbursements) should be made from the company's bank account using prenumbered checks. Using this simple control system, a duplicate record of each cash transaction is automatically maintained—one by the company and the other by the bank.

To determine the amount of cash available in the bank, it is appropriate that the Cash account balance as shown in the general ledger (or your checkbook) be reconciled with the balance reported by the bank. The **bank reconciliation** process, which you do (or should do) for your own checking account, involves bringing into agreement the account balance reported by the bank on the bank statement with the account balance in the ledger. The balances might differ for two reasons: timing differences and errors.

Timing differences arise because the company knows about some transactions affecting the cash balance about which the bank is not yet aware, or the bank has recorded some transactions about which the company is not yet aware. The most common timing differences involve:

LO 3
Explain the bank reconciliation procedure.

Deposits in transit, which have been recorded in the company's Cash account but which have not yet been added to the company's balance in the bank's records. From the company's point of view, the deposit in transit represents cash on hand because it has been received. In the bank reconciliation process, deposits in transit are added to the bank's indicated (prereconciled) balance.

Outstanding checks, which have been recorded as credits (reductions) to the company's cash balance, but which have not yet been presented to the bank for payment. From the company's point of view, outstanding checks should not be included in its cash balance because its intent was to disburse cash when it issued the checks. In the reconciliation process, outstanding checks are subtracted from the bank's indicated balance.

Bank service charges against the company's account, and interest income added to the company's balance during the period by the bank. The bank service charge and interest income should be recognized by the company in the period incurred or earned, respectively, because both of these items affect the cash balance at the end of the period. In the reconciliation process, bank service charges are subtracted from the company's indicated balance; interest income is added to the company's indicated balance.

NSF (not sufficient funds) checks, which are checks that have "bounced" from the maker's bank because the account did not have enough funds to cover the check. Because the company that received the check recorded it as a cash receipt and added the check amount to the balance of its Cash account, it is necessary to establish an account receivable for the amount due from the maker of the NSF check. In the reconciliation process, NSF checks are subtracted from the company's indicated balance.

Errors, which can be made by either the company or the bank, are detected in what may be a trial-and-error process if the book balance and bank balance do not reconcile after timing differences have been recognized. Finding errors is a tedious process involving verification of the timing difference amounts (e.g., double-checking the makeup and total of the list of outstanding checks), verifying the debits and credits to the company's ledger account, and verifying the arithmetic and amounts included on the bank statement. If the error is in the recording of cash transactions on the company's books, an appropriate journal entry must be made to correct the error. If the bank has made the error, the bank is notified but no change is made to the Cash account balance. In the reconciliation process, an addition or subtraction is made to correct the error on the side that made the error (either the bank or the company).

There are a number of ways of mechanically setting up the bank reconciliation. The reverse side of the bank statement usually has a reconciliation format printed on it. Many computer-based bookkeeping systems contain a bank reconciliation module that can facilitate the bank reconciliation process. When the bank statement lists returned checks in numerical order, the process is made even easier. A simple and clear technique for setting up the reconciliation is illustrated in Exhibit 5-2.

Even in today's world of electronic banking, the need to reconcile checking accounts on a regular basis retains its importance. Although deposits are now recorded instantaneously in many e-banking systems, checks still take time to clear, banks still charge fees for their services, and NSF checks and errors are every bit as likely to occur as in older systems.

What Does It Mean?

Answer on page 179

3. What does it mean to reconcile a bank account?

Short-Term Marketable Securities

LO 4

Explain how short-term marketable securities are reported on the balance sheet.

As emphasized in the discussion of cash and cash equivalents, a firm's ROI can be improved by developing a cash management program that involves investing cash balances over and above those required for day-to-day operations in **short-term marketable securities.** An integral part of the cash management program is the forecast of cash receipts and disbursements (forecasting, or budgeting, is discussed in Chapter 14). Recall from Chapter 2 that current assets are defined as *cash and other assets that are likely to be converted into cash or used to benefit the entity within one year of the balance sheet date.* Thus, any debt investments that mature beyond one year from the balance sheet date, and any equity securities that management has the ability and intent to hold for more than one year from the balance sheet date, would be reported as "long-term marketable securities."

Balance Sheet Valuation

Short-term marketable debt securities that fall in the *held-to-maturity* category are reported on the balance sheet at the entity's *cost,* which is usually about the same as market value, because of their high quality and the short time until maturity. The majority of investments made by most firms are of this variety because the excess cash available for investment will soon be needed to meet working capital obligations. If an entity owns marketable debt securities that are not likely to be converted to cash

Exhibit 5-2

A Bank Reconciliation
Illustrated

Assumptions:

- The balance in the Cash account of Cruisers, Inc., at September 30 was $4,614.58.
- The bank statement showed a balance of $5,233.21 as of September 30.
- Included with the bank statement were notices that the bank had deducted a service charge of $42.76 and had credited the account with interest of $28.91 earned on the average daily balance.
- An NSF check for $35.00 from a customer was returned with the bank statement.
- A comparison of deposits recorded in the Cash account with those shown on the bank statement showed that the September 30 deposit of $859.10 was not on the bank statement. This is not surprising because the September 30 deposit was put in the bank's night depository on the evening of September 30.
- A comparison of the record of checks issued with the checks returned in the bank statement showed that the amount of outstanding checks was $1,526.58.

Reconciliation as of September 30:

From Bank Records		From Company's Books	
Indicated balance	$5,233.21	Indicated balance	$4,614.58
Add: Deposit in transit	859.10	Add: Interest earned	28.91
		Less: Service charge	(42.76)
Less: Outstanding checks	(1,526.58)	NSF check	(35.00)
Reconciled balance	$4,565.73	Reconciled balance	$4,565.73

The balance in the company's general ledger account before reconciliation (the "Indicated balance") must be adjusted to the reconciled balance. Using the horizontal model, the effect of this adjustment on the financial statements is:

Balance Sheet	Income Statement	
Asset = Liabilities + Stockholders' equity	← Net income = Revenues − Expenses	
Accounts Receivable +35.00 Cash −48.85	Interest Income +28.91	Service Charge Expense −42.76

The journal entry to reflect this adjustment is:

Dr.	Service Charge Expense	42.76	
Dr.	Accounts Receivable	35.00	
Cr.	Interest Income		28.91
Cr.	Cash		48.85

Alternatively, a separate adjustment could be made for each reconciling item. The amount from this particular bank account to be included in the cash amount shown on the balance sheet for September 30 is $4,565.73. There would not be an adjustment for the reconciling items that affect the bank balance because those items have already been recorded on the company's books.

within a few months of the balance sheet date, or marketable equity securities that are subject to significant fluctuation in market value (like common and preferred stock), the balance sheet valuation and related accounting become more complex. Debt and equity securities that fall in the *trading* and *available-for-sale* categories are reported at *market value,* and any unrealized gains or losses are recognized. This is an application of the matching concept because the change in market value is reflected in the fiscal period in which it occurs.

What Does It Mean?

Answer on page 180

4. What does it mean to invest cash in short-term marketable securities?

Interest Accrual

Of course, it is appropriate that interest income on short-term marketable debt securities be accrued as earned so that both the balance sheet and income statement more accurately reflect the financial position at the end of the period and results of operations for the period. The asset involved is called *Interest Receivable,* and *Interest Income* is the income statement account. Here is the effect of the interest accrual on the financial statements:

Balance Sheet	Income Statement
Assets = Liabilities + Stockholders' equity	← Net income = Revenues − Expenses
+ Interest Receivable	+ Interest Income

The accrual is made with the following entry:

Dr.	Interest Receivable	xx	
	Cr. Interest Income.		xx

The amount in the Interest Receivable account is combined with other receivables in the current asset section of the balance sheet.

What Does It Mean?

Answer on page 180

5. What does it mean when interest income from marketable securities must be accrued?

Accounts Receivable

Recall from the Campbell Soup Company balance sheet that Accounts Receivable was a significant current asset category at July 31, 2011. Accounts receivable from customers for merchandise and services delivered are reported at **net realizable value**—the amount that is expected to be received from customers in settlement of their obligations. Two factors will cause this amount to differ from the amount of the receivable originally recorded: bad debts and cash discounts.

Bad Debts/Uncollectible Accounts

Whenever a firm permits its customers to purchase merchandise or services on credit, it knows that some of the customers will not pay. Even a thorough check of the potential customer's credit rating and history of payments to other suppliers will not ensure that the customer will pay in the future. Although some bad debt losses are inevitable when a firm makes credit sales, internal control policies and procedures exist in most firms to keep losses at a minimum and to ensure that every reasonable effort is made to collect all amounts that are due to the firm. Some companies, however, willingly accept high credit risk customers and know that they will experience high bad debt losses. These firms maximize their ROI by having a very high margin and requiring a down payment that equals or approaches the cost of the item being sold. Sales volume is higher than it would be if credit standards were tougher; thus, even though bad debts are relatively high, all or most of the product cost is recovered, and bad debt losses are more than offset by the profits from greater sales volume.

LO 5
Discuss how accounts receivable are reported on the balance sheet, including the valuation allowances for estimated uncollectible accounts and estimated cash discounts.

Based on recent collection experience, tempered by the current state of economic affairs of the industry in which a firm is operating, credit managers can estimate with a high degree of accuracy the probable **bad debts expense** (or **uncollectible accounts expense**) of the firm. Many firms estimate bad debts based on a simplified assumption about the collectibility of all credit sales made during a period (percentage of credit sales method). Other firms perform a detailed analysis and aging of their year-end accounts receivable to estimate the net amount most likely to be collected (aging of receivables method). For instance, a firm may choose the following age categories and estimated collection percentages: 0–30 days (98%), 31–60 days (95%), 61–120 days (85%), and 121–180 days (60%). The firm also may have an administrative internal control policy requiring that all accounts more than six months overdue be immediately turned over to a collection agency. Such a policy is likely to increase the probability of collecting these accounts, facilitate the collection efforts for other overdue accounts, and reduce the overall costs of managing accounts receivable. The success of any bad debts estimation technique ultimately depends on the careful application of professional judgment, using the best available information.

When the amount of accounts receivable estimated to be uncollectible has been determined, a **valuation adjustment** can be recorded to reduce the **carrying value** of the asset and recognize the bad debt expense. The effect of this adjustment on the financial statements is:

Balance Sheet	Income Statement
Assets = Liabilities + Stockholders' equity	← Net income = Revenues − Expenses
− Allowance for Bad Debts	− Bad Debts Expense

Here is the adjustment:

Dr.   Bad Debts Expense (or Uncollectible Accounts Expense).
      Cr.   Allowance for Bad Debts (or Allowance for
      Uncollectible Accounts) . . . .
	xx
	
	xx

In bookkeeping language, the **Allowance for Uncollectible Accounts** or **Allowance for Bad Debts** account is considered a **contra asset** because it is reported as a subtraction from an asset in the balance sheet. The debit and credit mechanics of a contra asset account are the opposite of those of an asset account; that is, a contra asset increases with credit entries and decreases with debit entries, and it normally has a credit balance. The presentation of the Allowance for Bad Debts in the current asset section of the balance sheet (using assumed amounts) is

Accounts receivable	$10,000
Less: Allowance for bad debts	(500)
Net accounts receivable	$ 9,500

or, as more commonly reported,

Accounts receivable, less allowance for bad debts of $500	$9,500

The Allowance for Bad Debts account communicates to financial statement readers that an estimated portion of the total amount of accounts receivable is expected to become uncollectible. So why not simply reduce the Accounts Receivable account directly for estimated bad debts? The problem with this approach is that the firm hasn't yet determined *which* customers will not pay—only that *some* will not pay. Before accounts receivable can be reduced, the firm must be able to identify which specific accounts need to be written off as uncollectible. Throughout the year, as specific accounts are determined to be uncollectible, they are written off against the allowance account. The effect of this entry on the financial statements follows:

Balance Sheet	Income Statement
Assets = Liabilities + Stockholders' equity	← Net income = Revenues – Expenses

− Accounts
   Receivable
 	
+ Allowance
   for Bad Debts	

The write-off entry is:

Dr. Allowance for Bad Debts. . . . . Cr. Accounts Receivable	xx xx

Note that the **write-off** of an account receivable has no effect on the income statement, nor should it. The expense was recognized in the year in which the revenue from the transaction with this customer was recognized. The write-off entry removes from

Accounts Receivable an amount that is never expected to be collected. Also note that the write-off of an account will not affect the net accounts receivable reported on the balance sheet because the financial statement effects on the asset (Accounts Receivable) and the contra asset (Allowance for Bad Debts) are offsetting. Assume that $100 of the accounts receivable in the previous example was written off. The balance sheet presentation now would be

Accounts receivable	$9,900
Less: Allowance for bad debts.	(400)
Net accounts receivable.	$9,500

Providing for bad debts expense in the same year in which the related sales revenue is recognized is an application of the matching concept. The Allowance for Bad Debts (or Allowance for Uncollectible Accounts) account is a **valuation account,** and its credit balance is subtracted from the debit balance of Accounts Receivable to arrive at the amount of net receivables reported in the Current Asset section of the balance sheet. This procedure results in stating Accounts Receivable at the amount expected to be collected (net realizable value). If an appropriate allowance for bad debts is not provided, Accounts Receivable and net income will be overstated, and the ROI, ROE, and liquidity measures will be distorted. The amount of the allowance usually is reported parenthetically in the Accounts Receivable caption on the balance sheet, or possibly in a schedule in the notes to the financial statements, so that financial statement users can evaluate the credit and collection practices of the firm.

---

6. What does it mean that the Allowance for Bad Debts account is a contra asset?

What Does It Mean?
Answer on page 180

Cash Discounts

To encourage prompt payment, many firms permit their customers to deduct up to 2 percent of the amount owed if the bill is paid within a stated period—usually 10 days—of the date of the sale (usually referred to as the *invoice date*). Most firms' **credit terms** provide that if the invoice is not paid within the discount period, it must be paid in full within 30 days of the invoice date. These credit terms are abbreviated as 2/10, n30. The *2/10* refers to the discount terms, and the *n30* means that the full amount of the invoice is due within 30 days. To illustrate, assume that Cruisers, Inc., has credit sales terms of 2/10, n30. On April 8 Cruisers, Inc., made a $5,000 sale to Mount Marina. Mount Marina has the option of paying $4,900 (5,000 − [2% × $5,000]) by April 18 or paying $5,000 by May 8.

Like most firms, Mount Marina will probably take advantage of the **cash discount** because it represents a high rate of return (see Business in Practice—Cash Discounts). The discount is clearly a cost to the seller because the selling firm will not receive the full amount of the account receivable resulting from the sale. The accounting treatment

Cash Discounts

Cash discounts for prompt payment represent a significant cost to the seller and a benefit to the purchaser. Not only do they encourage prompt payment, they also represent an element of the pricing decision and will be considered when evaluating the selling prices of competitors.

Converting the discount to an annual return on investment will illustrate its significance. Assume that an item sells for $100, with credit terms of 2/10, n30. If the invoice is paid by the 10th day, a $2 discount is taken, and the payor (purchaser) gives up the use of the $98 paid for 20 days because the alternative is to keep the money for another 20 days and then pay $100 to the seller. In effect, by choosing not to make payment within the 10-day discount period, the purchaser is "borrowing" $98 from the seller for 20 additional days at a cost of $2. The return on investment for 20 days is $2/$98, or slightly more than 2 percent; however, there are 18 available 20-day periods in a year (360 days/20 days), so the annualized return on investment is over 36 percent! Very few firms are able to earn this high an ROI on their principal activities. For this reason, most firms have a rigidly followed internal control policy of taking all cash discounts possible.

One of the facts that credit-rating agencies and credit grantors want to know about a firm when evaluating its liquidity and creditworthiness is whether the firm consistently takes cash discounts. If it does not, that is a signal either that the management doesn't understand their significance or that the firm can't borrow money at a lower interest rate to earn the higher rate from the cash discount. Either of these reasons indicates a potentially poor credit risk.

Clearly the purchaser's benefit is the seller's burden. So why do sellers allow cash discounts if they represent such a high cost? The principal reasons are to encourage prompt payment and to be competitive. Obviously, however, cash discounts represent a cost that must be covered for the firm to be profitable.

for estimated cash discounts is similar to that illustrated for estimated bad debts. Cash discounts on sales usually are subtracted from Sales in the income statement to arrive at the net sales amount that is reported because the discount is in effect a reduction of the selling price. On the balance sheet, it is appropriate to reduce Accounts Receivable by an allowance for estimated cash discounts that will be taken by customers when they pay within the discount period. Estimated cash discounts are recognized in the fiscal period in which the sales are made, based on past experience with cash discounts taken.

Notes Receivable

LO 6
Explain how notes receivable and related accrued interest are reported on the balance sheet.

If a firm has an account receivable from a customer that developed difficulties paying its balance when due, the firm may convert that account receivable to a **note receivable.** Here is the effect of this transaction on the financial statements:

Balance Sheet	Income Statement
Assets = Liabilities + Stockholders' equity	← Net income = Revenues − Expenses
− Accounts Receivable + Notes Receivable	

The entry to reflect this transaction is:

Dr.	Notes Receivable...............................	xx	
	Cr. Accounts Receivable		xx

One asset has been exchanged for another. Does the entry make sense?

A note receivable differs from an account receivable in several ways. A note is a formal document that includes specific provisions with respect to its maturity date (when it is to be paid), agreements or *covenants* made by the borrower (such as to supply financial statements to the lender or refrain from paying dividends until the note is repaid), identification of security or **collateral** pledged by the borrower to support the loan, penalties to be assessed if it is not paid on the maturity date, and, most important, the interest rate associated with the loan. Although some firms assess an interest charge or service charge on invoice amounts that are not paid when due, this practice is unusual for regular transactions between firms. Thus, if an account receivable is not going to be paid promptly, the seller will ask the customer to sign a note so that interest can be earned on the overdue account.

Retail firms often use notes to facilitate sales transactions for which the initial credit period exceeds 60 or 90 days, such as an installment plan for equipment sales. In such cases, Notes Receivable (rather than Accounts Receivable) is increased at the point of sale, even though the seller may provide interest-free financing for a period of time.

Under other circumstances, a firm may lend money to another entity and take a note from that entity; for example, a manufacturer may lend money to a distributor that is also a customer or potential customer in order to help the distributor build its business. Such a transaction is another rearrangement of assets: Cash is decreased and Notes Receivable is increased.

Interest Accrual

If interest is to be paid at the maturity of the note (a common practice), it is appropriate that the holder of the note accrue interest income, usually monthly. This is appropriate because interest income has been earned, and accruing the revenue and increasing interest receivable result in more accurate monthly financial statements. The financial statement effects of doing this are the same as that for interest accrued on short-term marketable securities:

Balance Sheet	Income Statement
Assets = Liabilities + Stockholders' equity	← Net income = Revenues − Expenses
+ Interest Receivable	+ Interest Income

The adjustment is:

Dr. Interest Receivable................................		xx	
Cr. Interest Income			xx

This accrual entry reflects interest income that has been earned in the period and increases current assets by the amount earned but not yet received.

Interest Receivable is frequently combined with Notes Receivable in the balance sheet for reporting purposes. Amounts to be received within a year of the balance sheet date are classified as current assets. If the note has a maturity date beyond a year, it will be classified as a noncurrent asset.

It is appropriate to recognize any probable loss from uncollectible notes and interest receivable just as is done for accounts receivable, and the bookkeeping process is the same. Cash discounts do not apply to notes, so there is no discount valuation allowance.

Inventories

LO 7

Explain how inventories are reported on the balance sheet.

For service organizations, inventories consist mainly of office supplies and other items of relatively low value that will be used up within the organization, rather than being offered for sale to customers. As illustrated in Chapter 4, recording the purchase and use of supplies is a straightforward process, although year-end adjustments are usually necessary to improve the accuracy of the accounting records.

For merchandising and manufacturing firms, the sale of inventory in the ordinary course of business provides the major, ongoing source of operating revenue. Cost of Goods Sold (Campbell's uses the equally acceptable synonymous term Cost of Products Sold) is usually the largest expense that is subtracted from Sales in determining net income, and, not surprisingly, inventories represent the most significant current asset for many such firms. At Campbell Soup Company, inventories account for 39 percent of current assets and 11 percent of total assets.[1] For Wal-Mart Stores, Inc., 74 percent of current assets and 21 percent of total assets are tied up in inventories.[2] Can you think of some possible explanations for these varying results? Obviously not all firms (and not all industries) have the same inventory needs because of differences in their respective products, markets, customers, and distribution systems. Moreover, some firms do a better job than others of managing their inventory by turning it over quickly to enhance ROI. What other factors might cause the relative size of inventories to vary among firms?

Although inventory management practices are diverse, the accounting treatment for inventory items is essentially the same for all firms. Just as warehouse bins and store shelves hold inventory until the product is sold to the customer, the inventory accounts of a firm hold the *cost* of a product until that cost is released to the income statement to be subtracted from (matched with) the revenue from the sale. The cost of a purchased or manufactured product is recorded as an asset and carried in the asset account until the product is sold (or becomes worthless or is lost or stolen), at which point the cost becomes an expense to be reported in the income statement. The cost of an item purchased for inventory includes not only the invoice price paid to the supplier but also other costs associated with the purchase of the item, such as freight and material handling charges. Cost is reduced by the amount of any cash discount allowed on the purchase. The income statement caption used to report this expense is Cost of Goods Sold. Here are the effects of purchase and sale transactions on the financial statements:

Balance Sheet	Income Statement
Assets = Liabilities + Stockholders' equity	← Net income = Revenues − Expenses

Purchase of inventory:
   + Inventory + Accounts
                Payable
 	
Recognize cost of goods sold:
   − Inventory
	− Cost of Goods Sold

---

[1] Data based on Campbell Soup Company's Form 10-K filing for the year ended July 31, 2011.

[2] Data based on Wal-Mart Stores, Inc.'s, annual report for the year ended January 31, 2012.

Balance Sheet		Income Statement	
Inventory (asset)		*Cost of Goods Sold (expenses)*	
Purchases of merchandise for resale increase Inventory (credit to Accounts Payable or Cash)	When merchandise is sold, the cost flows from the Inventory asset account to ⟶	the Cost of Goods Sold expense account	

Exhibit 5-3

Flow of Costs from Inventory to Cost of Goods Sold

The entries are:

```
Dr. Inventory..........................................        xx
      Cr.  Accounts Payable (or Cash) .....................              xx
      Purchase of inventory.
Dr. Cost of Goods Sold................................        xx
      Cr.  Inventory.......................................              xx
      To transfer cost of item sold to income statement.
```

Recognizing cost of goods sold is a process of accounting for the *flow of costs* from the Inventory (asset) account of the balance sheet to the Cost of Goods Sold (expense) account of the income statement. T-accounts also can be used to illustrate this flow of costs, as shown in Exhibit 5-3. Of course the sale of merchandise also generates revenue, but *recognizing revenue is a separate transaction* involving Accounts Receivable (or Cash) and the Sales Revenue accounts. The following discussion focuses only on the accounting for the cost of the inventory sold.

Inventory Cost Flow Assumptions

Accounting for inventories is one of the areas in which alternative generally accepted practices can result in major differences between the assets and expenses reported by companies that otherwise might be alike in all respects. It is therefore important to study this material carefully to appreciate the impact of inventory methods on a firm's financial statements.

The inventory accounting alternative selected by an entity relates to the assumption about how costs flow from the Inventory account to the Cost of Goods Sold account. There are four principal alternative **cost flow assumptions:**

1. Specific identification.
2. Weighted average.
3. First-in, first-out (FIFO) (pronounced FIE-FOE).
4. Last-in, first-out (LIFO) (pronounced LIE-FOE).

It is important to recognize that these are *cost flow assumptions* and that FIFO and LIFO do not refer to the physical flow of product. Thus, it is possible for a firm to have a FIFO physical flow (a grocery store usually tries to accomplish this) and to use the LIFO cost flow assumption.

LO 8

Discuss the alternative inventory cost flow assumptions and generalize about their respective effects on the income statement and balance sheet when price levels are changing.

The IFRS

Approach

The LIFO inventory cost flow assumption is not permitted under international financial reporting standards. The primary reason for the disallowance of LIFO appears to be that international standards have a strong balance sheet measurement focus and efforts have been made to eliminate accounting methods such as LIFO that do not support this so-called "balance sheet approach." As discussed in the following sections, during inflationary times LIFO assigns to inventory the costs of the oldest items acquired by the company, thus causing balance sheet values to become "outdated" as the company grows. As you study this material, think about what the implications would be for U.S. companies if the LIFO cost flow assumption were no longer available as a reporting alternative under U.S. GAAP.

The **specific identification** alternative links cost and physical flow. When an item is sold, the cost of that specific item is determined from the firm's records, and that amount is transferred from the Inventory account to Cost of Goods Sold. The amount of ending inventory is the cost of the items held in inventory at the end of the year. This alternative is appropriate for a firm dealing with specifically identifiable products, such as automobiles, that have an identifying serial number and are purchased and sold by specific unit. This assumption is not practical for a firm having many inventory items that are not easily identified individually.

The **weighted-average** alternative is applied to individual items of inventory. It involves calculating the average cost of the items in the beginning inventory plus purchases made during the year. Then this average is used to determine the cost of goods sold and the carrying value of ending inventory. This method is illustrated in Exhibit 5-4. Notice that the average cost is not a simple average of the unit costs but

Exhibit 5-4

Inventory Cost Flow Alternatives Illustrated

Situation:

On September 1, 2013, the inventory of Cruisers, Inc., consisted of five Model OB3 boats. Each boat had cost $1,500. During the year ended August 31, 2014, 40 boats were purchased on the dates and at the costs that follow. During the year, 37 boats were sold.

Date of Purchase	Number of Boats	Cost per Boat	Total Cost
September 1, 2013 (beginning inventory)	5	$1,500	$ 7,500
November 7, 2013	8	1,600	12,800
March 12, 2014	12	1,650	19,800
May 22, 2014	10	1,680	16,800
July 28, 2014	6	1,700	10,200
August 30, 2014	4	1,720	6,880
Total of boats available for sale	45		$73,980
Number of boats sold	37		
Number of boats in August 31, 2014, inventory . . .	8		

Required:

Determine the ending inventory amount at August 31, 2014, and the cost of goods sold for the year then ended, using the weighted-average, FIFO, and LIFO cost flow assumptions.

(continued)

Exhibit 5-4

Solution:

a. Weighted-average cost flow assumption:

$$\text{Weighted-average cost} = \frac{\text{Total cost of boats available for sale}}{\text{Number of boats available for sale}}$$

$$= \frac{\$73,980}{45}$$

$$= \$1,644 \text{ per boat}$$

Cost of ending inventory = $1,644 × 8 = $13,152

Cost of goods sold = $1,644 × 37 = $60,828

b. FIFO cost flow assumption:

The cost of ending inventory is the cost of the eight boats most recently purchased:

4 boats purchased August 30, 2014, @1,720 ea	=	$ 6,880
4 boats purchased July 28, 2014, @1,700 ea	=	6,800
Cost of 8 boats in ending inventory		$13,680

The cost of 37 boats sold is the sum of the costs for the first 37 boats purchased:

Beginning inventory	5 boats @ $1,500 =	$ 7,500
November 7, 2013, purchase	8 boats @ 1,600 =	12,800
March 12, 2014, purchase	12 boats @ 1,650 =	19,800
May 22, 2014, purchase	10 boats @ 1,680 =	16,800
July 28, 2014, purchase*	2 boats @ 1,700 =	3,400
Cost of goods sold		$60,300

*Applying the FIFO cost flow assumption, the cost of two of the six boats purchased this date is transferred from Inventory to Cost of Goods Sold.

Note that the cost of goods sold also could have been calculated by subtracting the ending inventory amount from the total cost of the boats available for sale:

Total cost of boats available for sale	$73,980
Less cost of boats in ending inventory	(13,680)
Cost of goods sold	$60,300

c. LIFO cost flow assumption:

The cost of ending inventory is the cost of the first eight boats purchased:

5 boats in beginning inventory @ $1,500 ea	=	$ 7,500
3 boats purchased November 7, 2013, @ $1,600 ea	=	4,800
Cost of 8 boats in ending inventory	=	$12,300

The cost of the 37 boats sold is the sum of costs for the last 37 boats purchased:

August 30, 2014, purchase	4 boats @ $1,720 =	$ 6,880
July 28, 2014, purchase	6 boats @ 1,700 =	10,200
May 22, 2014, purchase	10 boats @ 1,680 =	16,800
March 12, 2014, purchase	12 boats @ 1,650 =	19,800
November 7, 2013, purchase†	5 boats @ 1,600 =	8,000
Cost of goods sold		$61,680

†Applying the LIFO cost flow assumption, the cost of five of the eight boats purchased this date is transferred from Inventory to Cost of Goods Sold.

Note that the cost of goods sold also could have been calculated by subtracting the ending inventory amount from the total cost of the boats available for sale:

Total cost of boats available for sale	$73,980
Less cost of boats in ending inventory	(12,300)
Cost of goods sold	$61,680

is instead an average weighted by the number of units in beginning inventory and each purchase.

First-in, first-out, or **FIFO,** means more than first-in, first-out; it means that the first costs *in to inventory* are the first costs *out to cost of goods sold.* The first cost in is the cost of the inventory on hand at the beginning of the fiscal year. The effect of this inventory cost flow assumption is to transfer to the Cost of Goods Sold account the oldest costs incurred (for the quantity of merchandise sold) and to leave in the Inventory asset account the most recent costs of merchandise purchased or manufactured (for the quantity of merchandise in ending inventory). This cost flow assumption is also illustrated in Exhibit 5-4.

Last-in, first-out, or **LIFO,** is an alternative cost flow assumption opposite to FIFO. Remember, we are thinking about cost flow, not physical flow, and it is possible for a firm to have a FIFO physical flow (like the grocery store) and still use the LIFO cost flow assumption. Under LIFO, the most recent costs incurred for merchandise purchased or manufactured are transferred to the income statement (as Cost of Goods Sold) when items are sold, and the inventory on hand at the balance sheet date is costed at the oldest costs, including those used to value the beginning inventory. This cost flow assumption is also illustrated in Exhibit 5-4.

The way these cost flow assumptions are applied depends on the inventory accounting system in use. The two systems—*periodic* and *perpetual*—are described later in this chapter. Exhibit 5-4 uses the periodic system.

To recap the results of the three alternatives presented in Exhibit 5-4:

Cost Flow Assumption	Cost of Ending Inventory	Costs of Goods Sold
Weighted average	$13,152	$60,828
FIFO	13,680	60,300
LIFO	12,300	61,680

Although the differences between amounts seem small in this illustration, under real-world circumstances with huge amounts of inventory the differences often become large and are thus considered to be material (the materiality concept). Why do the differences occur? Because, as you probably have noticed, the cost of the boats purchased changed over time. If the cost had not changed, there would not have been any difference in the ending inventory and cost of goods sold among the three alternatives. But in practice, costs do change. Notice that the amounts resulting from the weighted-average cost flow assumption are between those for FIFO and LIFO; this is to be expected. Weighted-average results will never be outside the range of amounts resulting from FIFO and LIFO.

The crucial point to understand about the inventory cost flow assumption issue is the impact on cost of goods sold, operating income, and net income of the alternative assumptions. Naturally a company's ROI, ROE, and measures of liquidity are also impacted by its choice of inventory cost flow assumptions (Table 5-1 summarizes the cost flow assumptions most commonly used in practice). Because of the importance of the inventory valuation to a firm's measures of profitability and liquidity, the impact of alternative cost flow assumptions must be understood if these measures are to be used effectively in making judgments and informed decisions—especially if comparisons are made between entities.

	Number of Companies
Methods:	
Not disclosed	55
First-in, first-out (FIFO)	316
Last-in, first-out (LIFO)	166
Average cost	113
Other	110
Use of LIFO:	
All inventories	4
50% or more of inventories	83
Less than 50% of inventories	54
Not determinable	25
Companies using LIFO	166

Table 5-1

Inventory Cost Flow Assumptions Used by 500 Publicly Owned Industrial and Merchandising Corporations—2010

Source: Reprinted with permission from *Accounting Trends and Techniques,* Table 2-4, copyright © 2011 by American Institute of Certified Public Accountants, Inc.

---

7. What does it mean to identify the inventory cost flow assumption?

What Does It Mean? Answer on page 180

The Impact of Changing Costs (Inflation/Deflation)

It is important to understand how the inventory cost flow assumption used by a firm interacts with the direction of cost changes to affect both inventory and cost of goods sold. *In times of rising costs,* LIFO results in lower ending inventory and higher cost of goods sold than FIFO. These changes occur because the LIFO assumption results in most recent, and higher, costs being transferred to cost of goods sold. When purchase costs are falling, the opposite is true. These relationships are illustrated graphically in Exhibit 5-5 on the next page.

The graphs in Exhibit 5-5 are helpful in understanding the relative impact on cost of goods sold and ending inventory when costs move in one direction. Of course, in the real world, costs rise and fall over time, and the impact of a strategy chosen during a period of rising costs will reverse when costs decline. Thus, in the mid-1980s some firms that had switched to LIFO during a prior inflationary period began to experience falling costs. These firms then reported higher profits under LIFO than they would have under FIFO.

Selecting an Inventory Cost Flow Assumption

What factors influence the selection of a cost flow assumption? When rates of inflation were relatively low and the conventional wisdom was that they would always be low, most financial managers selected the FIFO cost flow assumption because that resulted in slightly lower cost of goods sold and hence higher net income. Financial managers have a strong motivation to report higher, rather than lower, net income to

Exhibit 5-5

Effect of Changing
Costs on Inventory and
Cost of Goods Sold
under FIFO and LIFO

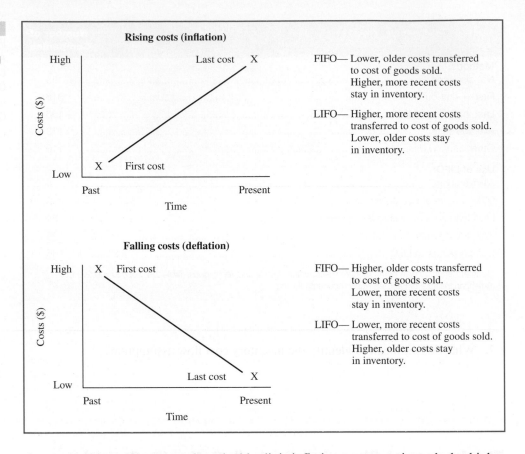

Rising costs (inflation)

FIFO— Lower, older costs transferred
to cost of goods sold.
Higher, more recent costs
stay in inventory.

LIFO— Higher, more recent costs
transferred to cost of goods sold.
Lower, older costs stay
in inventory.

Falling costs (deflation)

FIFO— Higher, older costs transferred
to cost of goods sold.
Lower, more recent costs
stay in inventory.

LIFO— Lower, more recent costs
transferred to cost of goods sold.
Higher, older costs stay
in inventory.

the stockholders. However, when double-digit inflation was experienced, the higher net income from the FIFO assumption also resulted in higher income taxes—which, of course, managers prefer not to experience. But why would this occur? When the FIFO cost flow assumption is used during a period of rapidly rising costs, **inventory profits,** or **phantom profits,** result. Under FIFO, the release of older, lower costs to the income statement results in higher profits than if current costs were to be recognized. Taxes must be paid on these profits, and because the current cost of replacing merchandise sold is much higher than the old cost, users of financial statements can be misled about the firm's real economic profitability. See the nearby Study Suggestion, which illustrates this unusual situation with a numerical example.

To avoid inventory profits (and to decrease taxes), many firms changed from FIFO to LIFO for at least part of their inventories during the years of high inflation. (Generally accepted accounting principles do not require that the same cost flow assumption be used for all inventories.) This change to LIFO resulted in higher cost of goods sold than FIFO and lower profits, lower taxes, and (in the opinion of some analysts) more realistic financial reporting of net income. Note, however, that even though net income under LIFO may better reflect a matching of revenues (which also usually rise on a per unit basis during periods of inflation) and costs of merchandise sold, the inventory amount on the balance sheet will be reported at older, lower costs. Thus, under LIFO the balance sheet will not reflect current costs for items in inventory. This is consistent with the original cost concept and underscores the fact that balance sheet amounts do not reflect current values of most assets. It also suggests that, in reality, the use of LIFO only delays the recognition of inventory profits, although this delay can

This is a difficult but important concept to grasp, so please consider the following example: Assume that Cruisers, Inc., sells a boat to a customer for $2,000 and uses the FIFO assumption. For argument's sake, assume that the cost of goods sold for this boat is $1,500 (taken from the beginning inventory); yet the current cost of replacing the boat has recently increased to $1,850, and the tax rate is 30 percent. The income tax owed by Cruisers, Inc., from this sale would be $150, computed as ($2,000 − $1,500) × 30%, and when this amount is added to the cost of replacing the boat, the company hasn't had any positive net cash flow! However, on the income statement, net income would be $350 ($2,000 − $1,500 − $150).

Study
Suggestion

be long-term if prices continue to rise and LIFO inventory layers are not eliminated through liquidations.

But what about consistency—the concept that requires whatever accounting alternative selected for one year to be used for subsequent financial reporting? With respect to the inventory cost flow assumption, the Internal Revenue Service permits a one-time, one-way change from FIFO to LIFO. (Note that if a firm decides to use the LIFO cost flow assumption for tax purposes, federal income tax law requires that LIFO also must be used for financial reporting purposes. This tax requirement, referred to as the *LIFO conformity rule,* is a constraint that does not exist in other areas where alternative accounting methods exist.) When a change in methods is made, the effect of the change on both the balance sheet inventory amount and cost of goods sold must be disclosed, so financial statement users can evaluate the impact of the change on the firm's financial position and results of operations.

Look back at Table 5-1, which reports the methods used to determine inventory cost by 500 industrial and merchandising corporations whose annual reports are reviewed and summarized by the AICPA. It is significant that many companies use at least two methods and that only four companies use LIFO for all inventories. The mix of inventory cost flow assumptions used in practice emphasizes the complex ramifications of selecting a cost flow assumption.

---

8. What does it mean to say that net income includes inventory profits?

What Does It Mean?
Answer on page 180

There is obviously a conflict between international financial reporting standards, which do not allow the use of LIFO, and the LIFO conformity rule, which requires that firms using LIFO for tax purposes must also use LIFO for financial reporting purposes. Thus, under current federal income tax law, it seems clear that a U.S. company using LIFO for tax purposes will be in violation of the LIFO conformity rule if it issues financial statements under IFRS. As IFRS and U.S. GAAP convergence becomes a reality in the next few years, this issue will become even more relevant and will require a pragmatic solution.

The IFRS

Approach

Inventory Accounting System Alternatives

The system to account for inventory cost flow is often quite complex in practice because most firms have hundreds or thousands of inventory items. There are two principal **inventory accounting systems:** perpetual and periodic.

In a **perpetual inventory system,** a record is made of every purchase and every sale, and a continuous record of the quantity and cost of each item of inventory is maintained. Computers have made perpetual inventory systems feasible for an increasingly large number of small to medium-sized retail organizations that were forced in previous years to use periodic systems. Advances in the use of product bar coding and scanning devices at cash registers, as well as radio frequency identification tags, have lowered the costs of maintaining perpetual records. The accounting issues involved with a perpetual system are easy to understand (see Business in Practice—The Perpetual Inventory System) once you have learned how the alternative cost flow assumptions are applied in a periodic system (refer to Exhibit 5-4 if you need a review).

In a **periodic inventory system,** a count of the inventory on hand (taking a **physical inventory**) is made periodically—frequently at the end of the fiscal year—and the cost of the inventory on hand, based on the cost flow assumption being used, is determined and subtracted from the sum of the beginning inventory and purchases to determine the cost of goods sold. This calculation is illustrated with the following **cost of goods sold model,** using data from the FIFO cost flow assumption of Exhibit 5-4:

Beginning inventory	$ 7,500
Purchases	66,480
Cost of goods available for sale	$73,980
Less: Ending inventory	(13,680)
Cost of goods sold	$60,300

The examples in Exhibit 5-4 use the periodic inventory system. Although less detailed record keeping is needed for the periodic system than for the perpetual system, the efforts involved in counting and costing the inventory on hand are still significant.

Even when a perpetual inventory system is used, it is appropriate to periodically verify that the quantity of an item shown by the perpetual inventory record to be on hand is the quantity actually on hand. Bookkeeping errors and theft or mysterious disappearance will cause differences between the recorded and actual quantities of inventory items. When differences are found, it is appropriate to reflect these as inventory losses, or corrections to cost of goods sold, as appropriate. If the losses are significant, management probably would authorize an investigation to determine the cause of the loss and develop recommendations for strengthening the system of internal control over inventories.

This discussion of accounting for inventories has focused on the products available for sale to the entity's customers. A retail firm would use the term **merchandise inventory** to describe this inventory category; a manufacturing firm would use the term **finished goods inventory.** Besides finished goods inventory, a manufacturing firm will have two other broad inventory categories: raw materials and work in process. In a manufacturing firm, the **Raw Materials Inventory** account is used to hold the costs of raw materials until the materials are released to the factory floor, at which time the costs are transferred to the **Work in Process Inventory** account. Direct labor costs (wages of production workers) and factory overhead costs (e.g., factory utilities, maintenance costs for production equipment, and the depreciation of factory buildings and equipment) are also recorded in the Work in Process Inventory account. These

The Perpetual Inventory System

Under a perpetual inventory system, the cost flow assumption used by the firm is applied on a day-to-day basis as sales are recorded, rather than at the end of the year (or month). This allows the firm to record increases to Cost of Goods Sold and decreases to Inventory on a daily basis. This makes sense from a matching perspective because the sale of inventory is what triggers the cost of goods sold. The following financial statement effects occur at the point of sale:

Business in
Practice

Balance Sheet	Income Statement
Assets = Liabilities + Stockholders' equity	← Net income = Revenues − Expenses

Record sale of goods:
+ Accounts
  Receivable
  (or Cash)
	+ Sales

Recognize cost of goods sold:
− Inventory
	− Cost of
	  Goods
	  Sold

The entries to reflect these transactions are:

```
Dr.  Accounts Receivable (or Cash) . . . . . . . . . . . . . . . . . . . . .   xx
     Cr.  Sales . . . . . . . . . . . . . . . . . . . . . . . . . . . . . . . . . . . . . . .        xx
Dr.  Cost of Goods Sold . . . . . . . . . . . . . . . . . . . . . . . . . . . . .   xx
     Cr.  Inventory . . . . . . . . . . . . . . . . . . . . . . . . . . . . . . . . . . . .        xx
```

Thus, a continuous (or perpetual) record is maintained of the inventory account balance. Under FIFO, the periodic and perpetual systems will always produce the same results for ending inventory and cost of goods sold. Why would this be the case? Even though the FIFO rules are applied at different points in time—at the end of the year (or month) with periodic, and daily with perpetual—the first-in cost will remain in inventory until the next item of inventory is sold. Once first in, always first in, and costs flow from Inventory to Cost of Goods Sold based strictly on the chronological order of purchase transactions. The results are the same under either system because whenever the question "What was the first-in cost?" is asked (daily or monthly), the answer is the same.

Under LIFO, when the question "What was the last-in cost?" is asked, the answer will change each time a new item of inventory is purchased. In a perpetual system, the last-in costs must be determined on a daily basis so that cost of goods sold can be recorded as sales transactions occur; the cost of the most recently purchased inventory items is assigned to Cost of Goods Sold each day. But as soon as new items of inventory are purchased, the last-in costs are redefined accordingly. This differs from the periodic approach to applying the LIFO rules. In a periodic system, the last-in costs are assumed to relate only to those inventory items that are purchased toward the end of the year (or month), even though some of the sales transactions occurred earlier in the year (or month).

The weighted-average method becomes a "moving" average under the perpetual system. As with the LIFO method, when the question "What was the average cost of inventory?" is asked, the answer is likely to change each time new inventory items are purchased.

costs, *incurred in making the product,* as opposed to costs of selling the product or administering the company generally, are appropriately related to the inventory items being produced and become part of the product cost to be accounted for as an asset (inventory) until the product is sold. Accounting for production costs is a large part of cost accounting, a topic that will be explored in more detail in Chapter 13.

The effects of inventory errors on cost of goods sold and gross profit are difficult to reason through. Two alternative approaches to solving this difficult problem in your head are to use T-accounts for Inventory and Cost of Goods Sold or to use the cost of goods sold model. The captions for the model are (a) Beginning inventory, (b) Cost of goods purchased or manufactured, (c) Cost of goods available for sale, (d) Ending inventory, and (e) Cost of goods sold. Under either approach, you would:

1. Plug in the "as reported" results for each year.

2. Make the necessary corrections to these amounts to determine the "as corrected" results.

3. Compare your results—before and after the corrections—to determine the effects of the error(s).

Inventory Errors

LO 9

Discuss the impact of inventory errors on the balance sheet and income statement.

Errors in the amount of ending inventory have a direct dollar-for-dollar effect on cost of goods sold and net income. This direct link between inventory amounts and reported profit or loss causes independent auditors, income tax auditors, and financial analysts to look closely at reported inventory amounts. The following T-account diagram illustrates this link:

Balance Sheet	**Income Statement**
Inventory (asset)	*Cost of Goods Sold (expense)*

Beginning balance		
Cost of goods purchased or manufactured	Cost of goods sold ⟶	Cost of goods sold
Ending balance		

When the periodic inventory system is used, a great deal of effort is made to ensure that the ending inventory count and valuation are as accurate as possible because inventory errors can have a significant impact on both the balance sheet and the income statement for each period affected. As illustrated in Exhibit 5-6, this type of error "washes out" over the two periods taken together (*total* net income is not affected by the error) assuming that the inventory at the end of the second period is counted correctly. Check this out by adding together the total net income for 2013 and 2014 before and after the error is corrected in Exhibit 5-6.

What Does It Mean?

Answer on page 180

9. What does it mean to say that an error in the ending inventory of the current accounting period has an equal but opposite effect on the net income of the subsequent accounting period?

To illustrate the effects of inventory errors, assume that Sample Co. reported the following comparative results:

Exhibit 5-6

Inventory Errors
Illustrated

	As Reported	
For the year ended December 31:	**2013**	**2014**
Sales	$500,000	$500,000
Cost of goods sold.......................................	300,000	300,000
Gross profit..	$200,000	$200,000
Operating expenses.....................................	100,000	100,000
Net income (ignoring income taxes).............	$100,000	$100,000

In early 2015, it was determined that ending inventory on the December 31, 2013, balance sheet was overstated by $10,000 due to the double counting of certain inventory items. All of the inventory items in question were sold during 2014, so the December 31, 2014, inventory count was done correctly and thus the 2014 inventory amount was correct as reported.

As corrected for the effects of the inventory error that occurred at December 31, 2013, Sample Co.'s comparative results would be reported as follows:

	As Corrected	
For the year ended December 31:	**2013**	**2014**
Sales	$500,000	$500,000
Cost of goods sold.......................................	310,000	290,000
Gross profit..	$190,000	$210,000
Operating expenses.....................................	100,000	100,000
Net income (ignoring income taxes).............	$ 90,000	$110,000

Note that by overstating ending inventory by $10,000 in 2013, cost of goods sold was understated by the same amount ($300,000 as reported rather than $310,000 as corrected). By understating cost of goods sold in 2013, gross profit was overstated ($200,000 rather than $190,000), with a corresponding overstatement of net income in 2013 by the same $10,000 amount.

In 2014, the effects of the 2013 ending inventory error were all reversed because the ending inventory on December 31, 2013, became the beginning inventory on January 1, 2014. By overstating beginning inventory, the cost of goods available for sale was overstated, causing cost of goods sold in 2014 to be overstated ($300,000 as reported rather than $290,000 as corrected). By overstating cost of goods sold, gross profit was understated in 2014 ($200,000 rather than $210,000) and net income was understated by the same $10,000 amount.

Balance Sheet Valuation at the Lower of Cost or Market

Inventory carrying values on the balance sheet are reported at the **lower of cost or market.** This reporting is an application of accounting conservatism. The "cost" of lower of cost or market is determined as described in the preceding pages. Inventory is initially recorded for the purchase price (or for the cost of goods manufactured) to the firm. The firm's cost flow assumption (FIFO, LIFO, or weighted average) is then applied to determine the "cost" of ending inventory, which is the amount ordinarily

The IFRS Approach

Under international accounting standards, inventories are initially recorded at cost. For financial reporting purposes, inventories are valued at the lower of cost or net realizable value. Net realizable value is the estimated selling price in the ordinary course of business less the estimated costs of completion and estimated selling expenses.

shown as the carrying value of inventory on the balance sheet. However, this "cost" amount must be compared to the market value of the firm's inventory to ensure that the inventory (an asset) is not overvalued for financial reporting purposes. The "market" of lower of cost or market is generally the replacement cost of the inventory on the balance sheet date. If market value is lower than cost, then a loss is reported in the accounting period in which the decline in inventory value occurred. The lower-of-cost-or-market determination can be made with respect to individual items of inventory, broad categories of inventory, or to the inventory as a whole.

Prepaid Expenses and Other Current Assets

LO 10

Explain what prepaid expenses are and how they are reported on the balance sheet.

Other current assets are principally **prepaid expenses**—that is, expenses that have been paid in the current fiscal period but that will not be subtracted from revenue until a subsequent fiscal period. This is the opposite of an accrual and is referred to in accounting and bookkeeping jargon as a *deferral* or *deferred charge* (or *deferred debit* because *charge is a bookkeeping synonym for debit*). An example of a **deferred charge** transaction is a premium payment to an insurance company. It is standard business practice to pay an insurance premium at the beginning of the period of insurance coverage. Assume that a one-year casualty insurance premium of $1,800 is paid on November 1, 2013. At December 31, 2013, insurance coverage for two months has been received, and it is appropriate to recognize the cost of that coverage as an expense. However, the cost of coverage for the next 10 months should be deferred—that is, not shown as an expense but reported as **prepaid insurance,** an asset. Usual bookkeeping practice is to record the premium payment transaction as an increase in the Prepaid Insurance asset account and then to transfer a portion of the premium to the Insurance Expense account as the expense is incurred. Using the horizontal model, this transaction and the adjustment affect the financial statements as follows:

Balance Sheet	Income Statement
Assets = Liabilities + Stockholders' equity	← Net income = Revenues − Expenses
Payment of premium for the year: Cash −1,800	
Prepaid Insurance +1,800	
Recognition of expense for two months: Prepaid Insurance −300	Insurance Expense −300

The journal entries are:

Nov. 1	Dr. Prepaid Insurance	1,800	
	Cr. Cash................................		1,800
	Payment of one-year premium.		
Dec. 31	Dr. Insurance Expense..........................	300	
	Cr. Prepaid Insurance		300
	Insurance expense for two months incurred.		

The balance in the Prepaid Insurance asset account at December 31 would be $1,500, which represents the premium for the next 10 months' coverage that has already been paid and will be transferred to Insurance Expense over the next 10 months.

Other expenses that could be prepaid and included in this category of current assets include rent, office supplies, postage, and travel expense advances to salespeople and other employees. The key to deferring these expenses is that they can be objectively associated with a benefit to be received in a future period. Advertising expenditures are not properly deferred because determining objectively how much of the benefit of advertising was received in the current period and how much of the benefit will be received in future periods is impossible. As with advertising expenditures, research and development costs are not deferred but are instead treated as expenses in the year incurred. The accountant's principal concerns are that the prepaid item be a properly deferred expense and that it will be used up, and become an expense, within the one-year time frame for classification as a current asset.

---

10. What does it mean to defer an expense?

What Does It Mean?
Answer on page 180

Demonstration Problem

Visit the text website at www.mhhe.com/marshall10e to view a demonstration problem for this chapter.

Summary

This chapter has discussed the accounting for and the presentation of the following balance sheet current assets and related income statement accounts:

Balance Sheet		Income Statement
Assets = Liabilities + Stockholders' equity		← Net income = Revenues − Expenses
Cash		
Marketable Securities		
Interest Receivable		Interest Income
Accounts Receivable		Sales Revenue
(Allowance for Bad Debts)		Bad Debts Expense
Inventory		Cost of Goods Sold
Prepaid Expenses		Operating Expenses

The amount of cash reported on the balance sheet represents the cash available to the company as of the close of business on the balance sheet date. Cash available in bank accounts is determined by reconciling the bank statement balance with the company's book balance. Reconciling items are caused by timing differences (such as deposits in transit or outstanding checks) and errors.

Petty cash funds are used as a convenience for making small disbursements of cash. Well-managed companies temporarily invest excess cash in short-term marketable securities to earn interest income. Cash managers invest in short-term, low-risk securities that are not likely to have a widely fluctuating market value. Marketable securities that will be held until maturity are reported in the balance sheet at cost; securities that may be traded or that are available for sale are reported at market value.

Accounts receivable are valued in the balance sheet at the amount expected to be collected, referred to as the *net realizable value*. This valuation principle, as well as the matching concept, requires that the estimated losses from uncollectible accounts be recognized in the fiscal period in which the receivable arose. A valuation adjustment recognizing bad debts expense and using the Allowance for Bad Debts account accomplishes this. When a specific account receivable is determined to be uncollectible, it is written off against the allowance account.

Many businesses encourage customers to pay their bills promptly by allowing a cash discount if the bill is paid within a specified period, such as 10 days. Cash discounts are classified in the income statement as a deduction from sales revenue. It is appropriate to reduce accounts receivable with an allowance for estimated cash discounts, which accomplishes the same objectives associated with the allowance for bad debts.

Organizations have a system of internal control to promote the effectiveness and efficiency of the organization's operations, the reliability of the organization's financial reporting, and the organization's compliance with applicable laws and regulations.

Notes receivable usually have a longer term than accounts receivable, and they bear interest. The accounting for notes receivable is similar to that for accounts receivable.

Accounting for inventories involves selecting and applying a cost flow assumption that determines the assumed pattern of cost flow from the Inventory asset account to the Cost of Goods Sold expense account. The alternative cost flow assumptions under U.S. GAAP are specific identification; weighted-average; FIFO; and LIFO. LIFO is not permitted under international financial reporting standards. The assumed cost flow will probably differ from the physical flow of the product. When price levels change, different cost flow assumptions result in different cost of goods sold amounts in the income statement and different Inventory account balances in the balance sheet. Because of the significance of inventories in most balance sheets and the direct relationship between inventory and cost of goods sold, accurate accounting for inventories must be achieved if the financial statements are to be meaningful.

Prepaid expenses (or deferred charges) arise in the accrual accounting process. To achieve an appropriate matching of revenue and expense, amounts prepaid for insurance, rent, and other similar items should be recorded as assets (rather than expenses) until the period in which the benefits of such payments are received.

Refer to the Campbell Soup Company balance sheet and related notes in the appendix, and to other financial statements you may have, and observe how current assets are presented.

Key Terms and Concepts

administrative controls (p. 152)   Features of the internal control system that emphasize adherence to management's policies and operating efficiency.

Allowance for Uncollectible Accounts (or Allowance for Bad Debts) (p. 158)   The valuation allowance that results in accounts receivable being reduced by the amount not expected to be collected.

bad debts expense (or uncollectible accounts expense) (p. 157)   An estimated expense, recognized in the fiscal period of the sale, representing accounts receivable that are not expected to be collected.

bank reconciliation (p. 153)   The process of bringing into agreement the balance in the Cash account in the company's ledger and the balance reported by the bank on the bank statement.

bank service charge (p. 153)   The fee charged by a bank for maintaining the company's checking account.

carrying value (p. 157)   The balance of the ledger account (net of related contra accounts, if any) of an asset, liability, or stockholders' equity account. Sometimes referred to as *book value*.

cash (p. 151)   A company's most liquid asset; includes money in change funds, petty cash, undeposited receipts such as currency, checks, bank drafts, and money orders, and funds immediately available in bank accounts.

cash discount (p. 160)   A discount offered for prompt payment.

cash equivalents (p. 151)   Short-term, highly liquid investments that can be readily converted into cash with a minimal risk of price change due to interest rate movements; examples include U.S. Treasury securities, bank CDs, money market funds, and commercial paper.

collateral (p. 161)   Assets of a borrower that can be used to satisfy the obligation if payment is not made when due.

collect on delivery (COD) (p. 151)   A requirement that an item be paid for when it is delivered. Sometimes COD is defined as *"cash" on delivery*.

commercial paper (p. 151)   A short-term security usually issued by a large, creditworthy corporation.

contra asset (p. 158)   An account that normally has a credit balance that is subtracted from a related asset on the balance sheet.

cost flow assumption (p. 163)   An assumption made for accounting purposes that identifies how costs flow from the Inventory account to the Cost of Goods Sold account. Alternatives include specific identification; weighted average; first-in, first-out; and last-in, first-out.

cost of goods sold model (p. 170)   The way to calculate cost of goods sold when the periodic inventory system is used. The model is

Beginning inventory
+ Purchases
Cost of goods available for sale
− Ending inventory
= Cost of goods sold

credit terms (p. 160)   A seller's policy with respect to when payment of an invoice is due and what cash discount (if any) is allowed.

deferred charge (p. 174)   An expenditure made in one fiscal period that will be recognized as an expense in a future fiscal period. Another term for a *prepaid expense.*

deposit in transit (p. 153)   A bank deposit that has been recorded in the company's cash account but that does not appear on the bank statement because the bank received the deposit after the date of the statement.

financial controls (p. 152)   Features of the internal control system that emphasize accuracy of bookkeeping and financial statements and protection of assets.

finished goods inventory (p. 170)   The term used primarily by manufacturing firms to describe inventory ready for sale to customers.

first-in, first-out (FIFO) (p. 166)   The inventory cost flow assumption that the first costs in to inventory are the first costs out to cost of goods sold.

imprest account (p. 151)   An asset account that has a constant balance in the ledger; cash on hand and vouchers (as receipts for payments) add up to the account balance. Used especially for petty cash funds.

internal control system (p. 151)   Policies and procedures designed to provide reasonable assurance that objectives are achieved with respect to

1. The effectiveness and efficiency of the operations of the organization.

2. The reliability of the organization's financial reporting.

3. The organization's compliance with applicable laws and regulations.

inventory accounting system (p. 170)   The method used to account for the movement of items in to inventory and out to cost of goods sold. The alternatives are the periodic system and the perpetual system.

inventory profits (p. 168)   Profits that result from using the FIFO cost flow assumption rather than LIFO during periods of inflation. Sometimes called *phantom profits.*

last-in, first-out (LIFO) (p. 166)   The inventory cost flow assumption that the last costs in to inventory are the first costs out to cost of goods sold.

lower of cost or market (p. 173)   A valuation process that may result in an asset being reported at an amount less than cost.

merchandise inventory (p. 170)   The term used primarily by retail firms to describe inventory ready for sale to customers.

net realizable value (p. 157)   The amount of funds expected to be received upon sale or liquidation of an asset. For accounts receivable, the amount expected to be collected from customers after allowing for bad debts and estimated cash discounts.

note receivable (p. 160)   A formal document (usually interest bearing) that supports the financial claim of one entity against another.

NSF (not sufficient funds) check (p. 153)   A check returned by the maker's bank because there were not enough funds in the account to cover the check.

operating cycle (p. 148)   The average time needed for a firm to convert an amount invested in inventory back to cash. For most firms, the operating cycle is measured as the average number of days to produce and sell inventory, plus the average number of days to collect accounts receivable.

outstanding check (p. 153) A check that has been recorded as a cash disbursement by the company but that has not yet been processed by the bank.

periodic inventory system (p. 170) A system of accounting for the movement of items in to inventory and out to cost of goods sold that involves periodically making a physical count of the inventory on hand.

perpetual inventory system (p. 170) A system of accounting for the movement of items in to inventory and out to cost of goods sold that involves keeping a continuous record of items received, items sold, inventory on hand, and cost of goods sold.

petty cash (p. 151) A fund used for small payments for which writing a check is inconvenient.

phantom profits (p. 168) See *inventory profits*.

physical inventory (p. 170) The process of counting the inventory on hand and determining its cost based on the inventory cost flow assumption being used.

prepaid expenses (p. 174) Expenses that have been paid in the current fiscal period but that will not be subtracted from revenues until a subsequent fiscal period when the benefits are received. Usually a current asset. Another term for *deferred charge*.

prepaid insurance (p. 174) An asset account that represents an expenditure made in one fiscal period for insurance that will be recognized as an expense in a subsequent fiscal period to which the coverage applies.

raw materials inventory (p. 170) An asset account that accumulates the costs of materials ready for the production process.

short-term marketable securities (p. 154) Investments made with cash not needed for current operations.

specific identification (p. 164) The inventory cost flow assumption that matches cost flow with physical flow.

uncollectible accounts expense (p. 157) See *bad debts expense*.

valuation account (p. 159) A contra account that reduces the carrying value of an asset to a net realizable value that is less than cost.

valuation adjustment (p. 157) An adjustment that results in an asset being reported at a net realizable value that is less than cost.

weighted average (p. 164) The inventory cost flow assumption that is based on an average of the cost of beginning inventory plus the cost of purchases during the year, weighted by the quantity of items at each cost.

work in process inventory (p. 170) An asset account that accumulates the costs (raw materials, direct labor, and manufacturing overhead) of items that are in the process of being manufactured.

write-off (p. 158) The process of removing a specific account receivable that is not expected to be collected from the Accounts Receivable account. Also used generically to describe the reduction of an asset and the related recognition of an expense or loss.

1. It means that the asset is cash, or it is an asset that is expected to be converted to cash or used up in the operating activities of the entity within one year.

2. It means that from the board of directors down through the organization, the policies and procedures related to effectiveness and efficiency of operations, reliability of financial reporting, and compliance with laws and regulations are understood and followed.

3. It means that the balance in the Cash account in the ledger has been brought into agreement with the balance on the bank statement by recognizing timing differences and errors.

ANSWERS TO
What Does
It Mean?

4. It means that cash not immediately required for use by the entity is invested temporarily to earn a return and thus increase the entity's ROI and ROE.

5. It means that interest has not been received by the entity for part of the period for which funds have been invested even though the interest has been earned, so interest receivable and interest income are recognized by an adjustment.

6. It means that the estimate of accounts receivable that will not be collected is subtracted from the total accounts receivable because it isn't yet known which specific accounts receivable will not be collected.

7. It means to identify the method used to transfer the cost of an item sold from the Inventory asset account in the balance sheet to the Cost of Goods Sold expense account in the income statement. This is different from the physical flow, which describes the physical movement of product from storeroom to customer. The alternative inventory cost flow assumptions are FIFO, LIFO, weighted-average cost, and specific identification.

8. It means that because of applying a particular inventory cost flow assumption (usually FIFO), net income is higher than what it would have been if an alternative cost flow assumption had been used (usually LIFO).

9. It means that an ending inventory error affects cost of goods sold on the income statement for two consecutive periods. Because ending inventory of one period is beginning inventory of the next period, the over/understatement of cost of goods sold in one period will be reversed in the next period.

10. It means to delay the income statement recognition of an expense until a future period to which it is applicable. Even though a cash payment has been made, the expense has not yet been incurred. An asset account is established for the prepaid expense.

Self-Study Material

Visit the text website at www.mhhe.com/marshall10e to take an online self-study quiz for this chapter.

Matching I Following are a number of the key terms and concepts introduced in the chapter, along with a list of corresponding definitions. Match the appropriate letter for the key term or concept to each definition provided (items 1–10). Note that not all key terms and concepts will be used. Answers are provided at the end of this chapter.

a.   Petty cash
b.   Bank reconciliation
c.   Deposit in transit
d.   Outstanding check
e.   Bank service charge
f.   Not sufficient funds (NSF) check

g.   Imprest account
h.   Short-term marketable securities
i.   Commercial paper
j.   Perpetual system
k.   Cash discount
l.   Credit terms

m.	Notes receivable	q.	First-in, first-out (FIFO)
n.	Collateral	r.	Last-in, first-out (LIFO)
o.	Cost flow assumption	s.	Weighted average
p.	Specific identification	t.	Periodic system

_____ **1.** The inventory cost flow assumption based on an average of the cost of beginning inventory and the cost of purchases during the year (taking into account the quantity of items at each cost).

_____ **2.** A formal document that supports the claim of one entity against another for an amount owed.

_____ **3.** A check returned by the maker's bank because the account did not have enough funds to cover the check.

_____ **4.** A check that has been recorded as a cash disbursement by the company but that has not yet been processed by the bank.

_____ **5.** A system of accounting for the movement of items into inventory and out to cost of goods sold that involves a continuous record of items received and items sold.

_____ **6.** Investments made with cash not needed for current operations.

_____ **7.** The process of bringing into agreement the balance in the Cash account in the company's ledger and the balance reported on the bank statement.

_____ **8.** A short-term security usually issued by a large, creditworthy corporation.

_____ **9.** A bank deposit that has been recorded in the company's Cash account but that does not appear on the bank statement because the bank received the deposit after the date of the statement.

_____**10.** The fee charged by a bank for maintaining the company's checking account.

Matching II Following are a number of the key terms and concepts introduced in the chapter, along with a list of corresponding definitions. Match the appropriate letter for the key term or concept to each definition provided (items 1–10). Note that not all key terms and concepts will be used. Answers are provided at the end of this chapter.

a.	Contra asset	i.	Administrative controls
b.	Aging of accounts receivable	j.	Prepaid insurance
c.	Bad Debts Expense (or Uncollectible Accounts Expense)	k.	Physical inventory
		l.	Lower of cost or market
d.	Allowance for Bad Debts (or Allowance for Uncollectible Accounts)	m.	Inventory profits (or phantom profits)
		n.	Finished Goods Inventory
e.	Valuation account	o.	Raw Materials Inventory
f.	Write-off	p.	Work in Process Inventory
g.	Internal control system	q.	Prepaid expenses
h.	Financial controls	r.	Deferral

_____ **1.** A valuation process that may result in an asset being reported at an amount less than cost.

_____ **2.** The process of removing an account receivable that is not expected to be collected from the Accounts Receivable account. Also used generically to describe the reduction of an asset and the related recognition of an expense.

_____ **3.** Expenses that have been paid in the current fiscal period but that will not be subtracted from revenue until a subsequent fiscal period. Usually a current asset.

_____ **4.** The valuation allowance that results in accounts receivable being reduced by the amount not expected to be collected.

_____ **5.** Increases in net income that result from using the FIFO cost flow assumption rather than LIFO during periods of inflation.

_____ **6.** Features of the internal control system that emphasize accuracy of book-keeping and financial statements, and protection of assets.

_____ **7.** The process of counting the inventory on hand and determining its cost based on the inventory cost flow assumption being used.

_____ **8.** Inventory account for the costs (raw materials, direct labor, and manufacturing overhead) of items that are in the process of being manufactured.

_____ **9.** The process of estimating the appropriate allowance for uncollectible accounts by classifying accounts according to the length of time they have been on the books.

_____**10.** Inventory ready for sale to customers.

Multiple Choice For each of the following questions, circle the best response. Answers are provided at the end of this chapter.

1. All of the following are typically classified as current assets *except*

    a. Marketable Securities.

    b. Accounts Receivable.

    c. Cash.

    d. Equipment.

    e. Notes Receivable.

2. Internal control systems involve a series of checks and balances that separate each of the functional duties involved in processing a transaction, and are normally designed to do all of the following *except*

    a. promote accuracy and reliability of the company's records and financial statements.

    b. safeguard and protect a company's assets against improper or unauthorized use.

    c. prevent groups of employees from committing collusive acts of fraud.

    d. encourage employees to adhere to the company's prescribed policies and procedures.

    e. provide an environment that is conducive to efficient operation of the organization.

3. Bank reconciliations often result in the recording of adjusting (or correcting) entries affecting the cash account on the books of the company involved. Which of the following items would *not* cause such an adjustment?

    a. Bank service charges.

    b. Outstanding checks.

    c. Notes collected on behalf of the company by the bank.

    d. Errors made in recording amounts of checks written.

    e. Not sufficient funds checks.

4. Regarding bank reconciliations, which of the following is true?

    a. Deposits in transit are added to the bank balance.

    b. Service charges are subtracted from the bank balance.

    c. Interest earned on notes collected by the bank is not a reconciling item (only the note itself is a reconciling item).

    d. NSF checks result in the recognition of bad debts expense on the books.

    e. Outstanding checks are subtracted from the book balance.

5. Inventories

    a. represent a major portion of the property, plant, and equipment assets for many firms.

    b. are recorded as debits to assets when purchased and as debits to expenses when used.

    c. must be accounted for using either the LIFO or FIFO method.

    d. are not an important component of working capital for most firms.

    e. decrease ROI because they use cash.

6. LIFO

    a. is the only method of inventory costing that is allowed for tax purposes.

    b. assigns the highest dollar amount to ending inventory when prices are rising.

    c. is used in inflationary times to improve net income.

    d. is required for financial reporting purposes by firms that use it for tax purposes.

    e. presents the best approximation of the underlying value of inventory on the balance sheet.

7. When comparing its effects to LIFO during an inflationary time, the effects of FIFO are to

    a. decrease net income and decrease total assets.

    b. decrease net income and increase total assets.

    c. increase net income and decrease total assets.

    d. increase net income and increase total assets.

8. As contrasted with the periodic inventory system, the perpetual system

    a. shows higher ending inventory and lower cost of goods sold in all cases.

    b. does not require a continuous record of all purchases and sales made during the period.

    c. is easier to use and does not often require the use of computers.

    d. provides better information for management to control unauthorized use and theft of inventory.

9. Assuming that ending inventory is counted correctly at the end of 2014, an error in the physical count of ending inventory at the end of 2013 will have had an effect on all of the following *except*

    a. cost of goods sold in the year of the error (2013).

    b. total assets in the year of the error (2013).

    c. cost of goods sold in the year after the error (2014).

    d. total assets in the year after the error (2014).

10. On July 31, 2013, the Prepaid Insurance account for St. Bede Abbey Press had a balance of $3,600, which was recorded that day for the payment of a five-year insurance premium. On December 31, 2013, at the end of the fiscal year, St. Bede would make the following adjusting entry:

a.	Insurance expense	300	
	Prepaid insurance........................		300
b.	Insurance expense	600	
	Prepaid insurance........................		600
c.	Prepaid insurance	3,300	
	Insurance expense........................		3,300
d.	Prepaid insurance	3,000	
	Insurance expense........................		3,000

connect
|ACCOUNTING

Mini-Exercises

All applicable Mini-Exercises are available with McGraw-Hill's *Connect*™ *Accounting.*

**Mini-Exercise
5.1
LO 3**

Bank reconciliation The balance in Happ, Inc.'s general ledger Cash account was $12,430 at September 30, before reconciliation. The September 30 balance shown in the bank statement was $11,130. Reconciling items included deposits in transit, $1,200; bank service charges, $70; NSF check written by a customer and returned with the bank statement, $450; outstanding checks, $380; and interest credited to the account during September but not recorded on the company's books, $30.

Required:

Prepare a bank reconciliation as of September 30 for Happ, Inc.

**Mini-Exercise
5.2
LO 3**

Bank reconciliation adjustment Refer to Mini-Exercise 5.1.

Required:

a. Show the reconciling items in a horizontal model, or write the adjusting journal entry (or entries) that should be prepared to reflect the reconciling items for Happ, Inc., at September 30.

b. What is the amount of cash to be included in the September 30 balance sheet for the company's bank account?

**Mini-Exercise
5.3
LO 5**

Accounts receivable, bad debts, credit sales, and cash collections analysis At the beginning of the year, accounts receivable were $144,000 and the allowance for bad debts was $11,500. During the year, sales (all on account) were $600,000, cash collections were $580,0000, bad debts expense totaled $14,200, and $12,000 of accounts receivable were written off as bad debts.

Required:

Calculate the balances at the end of the year for the Accounts Receivable and Allowance for Bad Debts accounts. (*Hint: Use T-accounts to analyze each of these accounts, plug in the amounts that you know, and solve for the ending balances.*)

Bad debts analysis—Allowance account The Allowance for Bad Debts account had a balance of $5,300 at the beginning of the year and $6,100 at the end of the year. During the year (including the year-end adjustment), bad debts expense of $9,400 was recognized.

Mini-Exercise 5.4
LO 5

Required:

Calculate the total amount of past-due accounts receivable that were written off as uncollectible during the year. *(Hint: Make a T-account for the Allowance for Bad Debts account, plug in the amounts that you know, and solve for the missing amount.)*

Cost flow assumptions—FIFO and LIFO using a periodic system Sales during the year were 500 units. Beginning inventory was 200 units at a cost of $5 per unit. Purchase 1 was 250 units at $6 per unit. Purchase 2 was 400 units at $7 per unit.

Mini-Exercise 5.5
LO 7, 8

Required:

Calculate cost of goods sold and ending inventory under the following cost flow assumptions (using a periodic inventory system):

a. FIFO
b. LIFO

Cost flow assumptions—FIFO and LIFO using a periodic system The beginning inventory was 300 units at a cost of $10 per unit. Goods available for sale during the year were 1,300 units at a total cost of $14,400. In May, 600 units were purchased at a total cost of $6,600. The only other purchase transaction occurred during October. Ending inventory was 550 units.

Mini-Exercise 5.6
LO 7, 8

Required:

a. Calculate the number of units purchased in October and the cost per unit purchased in October.
b. Calculate cost of goods sold and ending inventory under the following cost flow assumptions (using a periodic inventory system):
   1. FIFO
   2. LIFO

Exercises

All applicable Exercises are available with McGraw-Hill's *Connect*™ *Accounting*.

Bank reconciliation Prepare a bank reconciliation as of October 31 from the following information:

Exercise 5.7
LO 3

a. The October 31 cash balance in the general ledger is $844.
b. The October 31 balance shown on the bank statement is $373.
c. Checks issued but not returned with the bank statement were No. 462 for $13 and No. 483 for $50.
d. A deposit made late on October 31 for $450 is included in the general ledger balance but not in the bank statement balance.
e. Returned with the bank statement was a notice that a customer's check for $75 that was deposited on October 25 had been returned because the customer's account was overdrawn.

f.   During a review of the checks that were returned with the bank statement, it was noted that the amount of Check No. 471 was $65 but that in the company's records supporting the general ledger balance, the check had been erroneously recorded as a payment of an account payable in the amount of $56.

Exercise 5.8
LO 3

Bank reconciliation Prepare a bank reconciliation as of August 31 from the following information:

a.   The August 31 balance shown on the bank statement is $4,905.

b.   There is a deposit in transit of $630 at August 31.

c.   Outstanding checks at August 31 totaled $945.

d.   Interest credited to the account during August but not recorded on the company's books amounted to $54.

e.   A bank charge of $28 for checks was made to the account during August. Although the company was expecting a charge, its amount was not known until the bank statement arrived.

f.   In the process of reviewing the canceled checks, it was determined that a check issued to a supplier in payment of accounts payable of $759 had been recorded as a disbursement of $579.

g.   The August 31 balance in the general ledger Cash account, before reconciliation, is $4,744.

Exercise 5.9
LO 3

Bank reconciliation adjustment

a.   Show the reconciling items in a horizontal model or write the adjusting journal entry (or entries) that should be prepared to reflect the reconciling items of Exercise 5.7.

b.   What is the amount of cash to be included in the October 31 balance sheet for the bank account reconciled in Exercise 5.7?

Exercise 5.10
LO 3

Bank reconciliation adjustment

a.   Show the reconciling items in a horizontal model or write the adjusting journal entry (or entries) that should be prepared to reflect the reconciling items of Exercise 5.8.

b.   What is the amount of cash to be included in the August 31 balance sheet for the bank account reconciled in Exercise 5.8?

Exercise 5.11
LO 5

Bad debts analysis—Allowance account On January 1, 2013, the balance in Tabor Co.'s Allowance for Bad Debts account was $13,400. During the first 11 months of the year, bad debts expense of $21,462 was recognized. The balance in the Allowance for Bad Debts account at November 30, 2013, was $9,763.

Required:

a.   What was the total of accounts written off during the first 11 months? *(Hint: Make a T-account for the Allowance for Bad Debts account.)*

b.   As the result of a comprehensive analysis, it is determined that the December 31, 2013, balance of the Allowance for Bad Debts account should be $9,500. Show the adjustment required in the horizontal model or in journal entry format.

c. During a conversation with the credit manager, one of Tabor's sales representatives learns that a $1,230 receivable from a bankrupt customer has not been written off but was considered in the determination of the appropriate year-end balance of the Allowance for Bad Debts account balance. Write a brief explanation to the sales representative explaining the effect that the write-off of this account receivable would have had on 2013 net income.

Bad debts analysis—Allowance account On January 1, 2013, the balance in Kubera Co.'s Allowance for Bad Debts account was $4,860. During the year, a total of $11,950 of delinquent accounts receivable was written off as bad debts. The balance in the Allowance for Bad Debts account at December 31, 2013, was $5,240.

Exercise 5.12
LO 5

Required:

a. What was the total amount of bad debts expense recognized during the year? *(Hint: Make a T-account for the Allowance for Bad Debts account.)*

b. As a result of a comprehensive analysis, it is determined that the December 31, 2013, balance of Allowance for Bad Debts should be $11,600. Show in the horizontal model or in journal entry format the adjustment required.

Cash discounts—ROI Annual credit sales of Nadak Co. total $340 million. The firm gives a 2% cash discount for payment within 10 days of the invoice date; 90% of Nadak's accounts receivable are paid within the discount period.

Exercise 5.13
LO 5

Required:

a. What is the total amount of cash discounts allowed in a year?

b. Calculate the approximate annual rate of return on investment that Nadak Co.'s cash discount terms represent to customers who take the discount.

Cash discounts—ROI

Exercise 5.14
LO 5

a. Calculate the approximate annual rate of return on investment of the following cash discount terms:
    1. 1/15, n30.
    2. 2/10, n60.
    3. 1/10, n90.

b. Which of these terms, if any, is not likely to be a significant incentive to the customer to pay promptly? Explain your answer.

Notes receivable—interest accrual and collection Agrico, Inc., accepted a 10-month, 13.8% (annual rate), $4,500 note from one of its customers on June 15; interest is payable with the principal at maturity.

Exercise 5.15
LO 6

Required:

a. Use the horizontal model or write the journal entry to record the interest earned by Agrico during its fiscal year ended October 31.

b. Use the horizontal model or write the journal entry to record collection of the note and interest at maturity.

Exercise 5.16

LO 6

Notes receivable—interest accrual and collection Husemann Co.'s assets include notes receivable from customers. During fiscal 2013, the amount of notes receivable averaged $138,750, and the interest rate of the notes averaged 4.8%.

Required:

a. Calculate the amount of interest income earned by Husemann Co. during fiscal 2013 and show in the horizontal model or write a journal entry that accrues the interest income earned from the notes.

b. If the balance in the Interest Receivable account increased by $1,500 from the beginning to the end of the fiscal year, how much interest receivable was collected during the fiscal year? Use the horizontal model, a T-account, or write the journal entry to show the collection of this amount.

Exercise 5.17

LO 7, 8

LIFO versus FIFO—matching and balance sheet impact Proponents of the LIFO inventory cost flow assumption argue that this costing method is superior to the alternatives because it results in better matching of revenue and expense.

Required:

a. Explain why "better matching" occurs with LIFO.

b. What is the impact on the carrying value of inventory in the balance sheet when LIFO rather than FIFO is used during periods of inflation?

Exercise 5.18

LO 7, 8

LIFO versus FIFO—impact on ROI Mannisto, Inc., uses the FIFO inventory cost flow assumption. In a year of rising costs and prices, the firm reported net income of $1,920,000 and average assets of $12,000,000. If Mannisto had used the LIFO cost flow assumption in the same year, its cost of goods sold would have been $320,000 more than under FIFO, and its average assets would have been $320,000 less than under FIFO.

Required:

a. Calculate the firm's ROI under each cost flow assumption.

b. Suppose that two years later costs and prices were falling. Under FIFO, net income and average assets were $2,304,000 and $14,400,000, respectively. If LIFO had been used through the years, inventory values would have been $400,000 less than under FIFO, and current year cost of goods sold would have been $160,000 less than under FIFO. Calculate the firm's ROI under each cost flow assumption.

Exercise 5.19

LO 10

Prepaid expenses—insurance

a. Use the horizontal model or write the journal entry to record the payment of a one-year insurance premium of $3,000 on March 1.

b. Use the horizontal model or write the adjusting entry that will be made at the end of every month to show the amount of insurance premium "used" that month.

c. Calculate the amount of prepaid insurance that should be reported on the August 31 balance sheet with respect to this policy.

d. If the premium had been $6,000 for a two-year period, how should the prepaid amount at August 31 of the first year be reported on the balance sheet?

e. Why are prepaid expenses reflected as an asset instead of being recorded as an expense in the accounting period in which the item is paid?

Prepaid expenses—rent

(Note: See Problem 7.25 for the related unearned revenue accounting.)
On November 1, 2013, Wenger Co. paid its landlord $37,800 in cash as an advance rent payment on its store location. The six-month lease period ends on April 30, 2014, at which time the contract may be renewed.

Required:

a. Use the horizontal model or write the journal entry to record the six-month advance rent payment on November 1, 2013.

b. Use the horizontal model or write the adjusting entry that will be made at the end of every month to show the amount of rent "used" during the month.

c. Calculate the amount of prepaid rent that should be reported on the December 31, 2013, balance sheet with respect to this lease.

d. If the advance payment made on November 1, 2013, had covered an 18-month lease period at the same amount of rent per month, how should Wenger Co. report the prepaid amount on its December 31, 2013, balance sheet

Transaction analysis—various accounts

Prepare an answer sheet with the column headings shown here. For each of the following transactions or adjustments, indicate the effect of the transaction or adjustment on the appropriate balance sheet category and on net income by entering for each account affected the account name and amount and indicating whether it is an addition (+) or a subtraction (−). Transaction **a** has been done as an illustration. Net income is *not* affected by every transaction. In some cases only one column may be affected because all of the specific accounts affected by the transaction are included in that category.

	Current Assets	Current Liabilities	Stockholders' Equity	Net Income
a. Accrued interest income of $15 on a note receivable.	Interest Receivable + 15			Interest Income + 15

b. Determined that the Allowance for Bad Debts account balance should be increased by $2,200.

c. Recognized bank service charges of $30 for the month.

d. Received $25 cash for interest accrued in a prior month.

e. Purchased five units of a new item of inventory on account at a cost of $35 each. Perpetual inventory is maintained.

f. Purchased 10 more units of the same item at a cost of $38 each. Perpetual inventory is maintained.

g. Sold eight of the items purchased (in **e** and **f**) and recognized the cost of goods sold using the FIFO cost flow assumption. Perpetual inventory is maintained.

Transaction analysis—various accounts

Prepare an answer sheet with the column headings shown here. For each of the following transactions or adjustments, indicate the effect of the transaction or adjustment on the appropriate balance sheet category and on net income by entering for each account affected the account name and amount and indicating whether it is an addition (+) or a subtraction (−). Transaction **a** has been done as an illustration. Net income is *not* affected by every transaction. In some cases only one column may be affected because all of the specific accounts affected by the transaction are included in that category.

	Current Assets	Current Liabilities	Stockholders' Equity	Net Income
a. Accrued interest income of $15 on a note receivable.	Interest Receivable + 15			Interest Income + 15

b. Determined that the Allowance for Bad Debts account balance should be decreased by $4,800 because expense during the year had been overestimated.

c. Wrote off an account receivable of $2,160.

d. Received cash from a customer in full payment of an account receivable of $750 that was paid within the 2% discount period. A Cash Discount Allowance account is maintained.

e. Purchased eight units of a new item of inventory on account at a cost of $60 each. Perpetual inventory is maintained.

f. Purchased 17 more units of the above item at a cost of $57 each. Perpetual inventory is maintained.

g. Sold 20 of the items purchased (in **e** and **f**) and recognized the cost of goods sold using the LIFO cost flow assumption. Perpetual inventory is maintained.

h. Paid a one-year insurance premium of $720 that applied to the next fiscal year.

i. Recognized insurance expense related to the preceding policy during the first month of the fiscal year to which it applied.

Exercise 5.23
LO 5, 6, 7

Transaction analysis—various accounts Prepare an answer sheet with the column headings shown here. For each of the following transactions or adjustments, indicate the effect of the transaction or adjustment on the appropriate balance sheet category and on net income by entering for each account affected the account name and amount and indicating whether it is an addition (+) or a subtraction (−). Transaction **a** has been done as an illustration. Net income is *not* affected by every transaction. In some cases only one column may be affected because all of the specific accounts affected by the transaction are included in that category.

	Current Assets	Current Liabilities	Stockholders' Equity	Net Income
a. Accrued interest income of $15 on a note receivable.	Interest Receivable + 15			Interest Income + 15

b. Recorded estimated bad debts in the amount of $700.

c. Wrote off an overdue account receivable of $520.

d. Converted a customer's $1,200 overdue account receivable into a note.

e. Accrued $48 of interest earned on the note (in **d**).

f. Collected the accrued interest (in **e**).

g. Recorded $4,000 of sales, 80% of which were on account.

h. Recognized cost of goods sold in the amount of $3,200.

Transaction analysis—various accounts Prepare an answer sheet with the column headings shown here. For each of the following transactions or adjustments, indicate the effect of the transaction or adjustment on the appropriate balance sheet category and on net income by entering for each account affected the account name and amount and indicating whether it is an addition (+) or a subtraction (−). Transaction a has been done as an illustration. Net income is *not* affected by every transaction. In some cases only one column may be affected because all of the specific accounts affected by the transaction are included in that category.

Exercise 5.24
LO 7, 8, 10

	Current Assets	Current Liabilities	Stockholders' Equity	Net Income
a. Accrued interest income of $15 on a note receivable.	Interest Receivable + 15			Interest Income + 15

b. Paid $5,600 in cash as an advance rent payment for a short-term lease that covers the next four months.

c. Recorded an adjustment at the end of the first month (in **b**) to show the amount of rent "used" in the month.

d. Inventory was acquired on account and recorded for $1,640. Perpetual inventory is maintained.

e. It was later determined that the amount of inventory acquired on account (in **d**) was erroneously recorded. The actual amount purchased was only $1,460. No payments have been made. Record the correction of this error.

f. Purchased 12 units of inventory at a cost of $80 each and then 8 more units of the same inventory item at $88 each. Perpetual inventory is maintained.

g. Sold 15 of the items purchased (in **f**) for $120 each and received the entire amount in cash. Record the sales transaction and the cost of goods sold using the LIFO cost flow assumption. Perpetual inventory is maintained.

h. Assume the same facts (in **g**) except that the company uses the FIFO cost flow assumption. Record only the cost of goods sold.

i. Assume the same facts (in **g**) except that the company uses the weighted-average cost flow assumption. Record only the cost of goods sold.

j. Explain why the sales transaction in **h** and **i** would be recorded in exactly the same way it was in **g**.

Problems

All applicable Problems are available with McGraw-Hill's *Connect*™ *Accounting.*

Problem 5.25
LO 3

Bank reconciliation—compute Cash account balance and bank statement balance before reconciling items Beckett Co. received its bank statement for the month ending June 30, 2013, and reconciled the statement balance to the June 30, 2013, balance in the Cash account. The reconciled balance was determined to be $4,800. The reconciliation recognized the following items:

1. Deposits in transit were $2,100.
2. Outstanding checks totaled $3,000.
3. Bank service charges shown as a deduction on the bank statement were $50.
4. An NSF check from a customer for $400 was included with the bank statement. Beckett Co. had not been previously notified that the check had been returned NSF.
5. Included in the canceled checks was a check actually written for $890. However, it had been recorded as a disbursement of $980.

Required:

a. What was the balance in Beckett Co.'s Cash account before recognizing any of the preceding reconciling items?

b. What was the balance shown on the bank statement before recognizing any of the preceding reconciling items?

Problem 5.26
LO 3

Bank reconciliation—compute Cash account balance and bank statement balance before reconciling items Branson Co. received its bank statement for the month ending May 31, 2013, and reconciled the statement balance to the May 31, 2013, balance in the Cash account. The reconciled balance was determined to be $9,300. The reconciliation recognized the following items:

1. A deposit made on May 31 for $5,100 was included in the Cash account balance but not in the bank statement balance.
2. Checks issued but not returned with the bank statement were No. 673 for $1,470 and No. 687 for $2,550.
3. Bank service charges shown as a deduction on the bank statement were $120.
4. Interest credited to Branson Co.'s account but not recorded on the company's books amounted to $72.
5. Returned with the bank statement was a "debit memo" stating that a customer's check for $960 that had been deposited on May 23 had been returned because the customer's account was overdrawn.
6. During a review of the checks that were returned with the bank statement, it was noted that the amount of check No. 681 was $480 but that in the company's records supporting the Cash account balance, the check had been erroneously recorded in the amount of $48.

Required:

a. What was the balance in Branson Co.'s Cash account before recognizing any of these reconciling items?

b. What was the balance shown on the bank statement before recognizing any of these reconciling items?

Bad debts analysis—Allowance account and financial statement effect The following is a portion of the current assets section of the balance sheets of Avanti's, Inc., at December 31, 2014 and 2013:

	12/31/14	12/31/13
Accounts receivable, less allowance for bad debts of $9,500 and $17,900, respectively	$173,200	$236,400

Required:

a. If $11,800 of accounts receivable were written off during 2014, what was the amount of bad debts expense recognized for the year? *(Hint: Use a T-account model of the Allowance account, plug in the three amounts that you know, and solve for the unknown.)*

b. The December 31, 2014, Allowance account balance includes $3,100 for a past due account that is not likely to be collected. This account has *not* been written off. *If it had been written off,* what would have been the effect of the write-off on
   1. Working capital at December 31, 2014?
   2. Net income and ROI for the year ended December 31, 2014?

c. What do you suppose was the level of Avanti's sales in 2014, compared to 2013? Explain your answer.

Bad debts analysis—Allowance account and financial statement effects The following is a portion of the current asset section of the balance sheets of HiROE Co., at December 31, 2014 and 2013:

	December 31, 2014	December 31, 2013
Accounts receivable, less allowance for uncollectible accounts of $27,000 and $9,000, respectively	$453,000	$361,000

Required:

a. Describe how the allowance amount at December 31, 2014, was most likely determined.

b. If bad debts expense for 2014 totaled $24,000, what was the amount of accounts receivable written off during the year? *(Hint: Use the T-account model of the Allowance account, plug in the three amounts that you know, and solve for the unknown.)*

c. The December 31, 2014, Allowance account balance includes $10,500 for a past due account that is not likely to be collected. This account has *not* been written off. *If it had been written off,* what would have been the effect of the write-off on
   1. Working capital at December 31, 2014?
   2. Net income and ROI for the year ended December 31, 2014?

d. What do you suppose was the level of HiROE's sales in 2014, compared to 2013? Explain your answer.

e. Calculate the ratio of the Allowance for Uncollectible Accounts balance to the Accounts Receivable balance at December 31, 2013, and 2014. What factors might have caused the change in this ratio?

Problem 5.29

LO 5

Analysis of accounts receivable and allowance for bad debts—determine beginning balances A portion of the current assets section of the December 31, 2014, balance sheet for Carr Co. is presented here:

Accounts receivable	$50,000	
Less: Allowance for bad debts	(7,000)	$43,000

The company's accounting records revealed the following information for the year ended December 31, 2014:

Sales (all on account)	$400,000
Cash collections from customers	410,000
Accounts written off	15,000
Bad debts expense (accrued at 12/31/14)	12,000

Required:
Using the information provided for 2014, calculate the net realizable value of accounts receivable at December 31, 2013, and prepare the appropriate balance sheet presentation for Carr Co., as of that point in time. *(Hint: Use T-accounts to analyze the Accounts Receivable and Allowance for Bad Debts accounts. Remember that you are solving for the beginning balance of each account.)*

Problem 5.30

LO 5

Analysis of accounts receivable and allowance for bad debts—determine ending balances A portion of the current assets section of the December 31, 2013, balance sheet for Gibbs Co. is presented here:

Accounts receivable	$315,000	
Less: Allowance for bad debts	(45,000)	$270,000

The company's accounting records revealed the following information for the year ended December 31, 2014:

Sales (all on account)	$2,400,000
Cash collections from customers	2,175,000
Accounts written off	52,500
Bad debts expense (accrued at 12/31/14)	82,500

Required:
Calculate the net realizable value of accounts receivable at December 31, 2014, and prepare the appropriate balance sheet presentation for Gibbs Co., as of that point in time. *(Hint: Use T-accounts to analyze the Accounts Receivable and Allowance for Bad Debts accounts.)*

Problem 5.31

LO 7, 8

Cost flow assumptions—FIFO and LIFO using a periodic system Mower-Blower Sales Co. started business on January 20, 2013. Products sold were snow blowers and lawn mowers. Each product sold for $700. Purchases during 2013 were as follows:

	Blowers	Mowers
January 21	20 @ $400	
February 3	40 @ 390	
February 28	30 @ 380	
March 13	20 @ 380	
April 6		20 @ $420
May 22		40 @ 430
June 3		40 @ 440
June 20		60 @ 460
August 15		20 @ 430
September 20		20 @ 420
November 7	20 @ 400	

The December 31, 2013, inventory included 10 blowers and 25 mowers. Assume the company uses a periodic inventory system.

Required:

a. What will be the *difference* between ending inventory valuation at December 31, 2013, under the FIFO and LIFO cost flow assumptions? *(Hint: Compute ending inventory under each method, and then compare results.)*

b. If the cost of mowers had increased to $480 each by December 1, and if management had purchased 30 mowers at that time, which cost flow assumption was probably being used by the firm? Explain your answer.

Cost flow assumptions—FIFO, LIFO, and weighted average using a periodic system The following data are available for Sellco for the fiscal year ended on January 31, 2014:

Problem 5.32
LO 7, 8

Sales	3,200 units
Beginning inventory	1,000 units @ $4
Purchases, in chronological order.	1,200 units @ $5
	1,600 units @ $6
	800 units @ $8

Required:

a. Calculate cost of goods sold and ending inventory under the following cost flow assumptions (using a periodic inventory system):
   1. FIFO.
   2. LIFO.
   3. Weighted average. Round the unit cost answer to two decimal places and ending inventory to the nearest $10.

b. Assume that net income using the weighted-average cost flow assumption is $116,000. Calculate net income under FIFO and LIFO.

Problem 5.33

LO 7, 8

Cost flow assumptions—FIFO and LIFO using periodic and perpetual systems The inventory records of Kuffel Co. reflected the following information for the year ended December 31, 2013:

Date	Transaction	Number of Units	Unit Cost	Total Cost
1/1	Beginning inventory	150	$30	$4,500
1/24	Purchase	70	33	2,310
2/22	Sale	(100)	—	—
3/7	Purchase	90	35	3,150
4/10	Purchase	140	36	5,040
6/11	Sale	(100)	—	—
9/28	Purchase	50	38	1,900
12/4	Sale	(100)	—	—

Required:

a. Assume that Kuffel Co. uses a periodic inventory system. Calculate cost of goods sold and ending inventory under FIFO and LIFO.

b. Assume that Kuffel Co. uses a perpetual inventory system. Calculate cost of goods sold and ending inventory under FIFO and LIFO.

c. Explain why the FIFO results for cost of goods sold and ending inventory are the same in your answers to parts **a** and **b**, but the LIFO results are different.

Problem 5.34

LO 7, 8

Cost flow assumptions—FIFO and LIFO using periodic and perpetual systems The inventory records of Cushing, Inc., reflected the following information for the year ended December 31, 2013:

	Number of Units	Unit Cost	Total Cost
Inventory, January 1	100	$13	$1,300
Purchases:			
May 30	160	15	2,400
September 28	200	16	3,200
Goods available for sale	460		$6,900
Sales:			
April 10	(70)		
June 11	(150)		
November 1	(190)		
Inventory, December 31	50		

Required:

a. Assume that Cushing, Inc., uses a periodic inventory system. Calculate cost of goods sold and ending inventory under FIFO and LIFO.

b. Assume that Cushing, Inc., uses a perpetual inventory system. Calculate cost of goods sold and ending inventory under FIFO and LIFO.

c. Explain why the FIFO results for cost of goods sold and ending inventory are the same in your answers to parts **a** and **b**, but the LIFO results are different.

d. Explain why the results from the LIFO periodic calculations in part **a** cannot possibly represent the actual physical flow of inventory items.

Effects of inventory errors

a. If the beginning balance of the Inventory account and the cost of items purchased or made during the period are correct, but an error resulted in overstating the firm's ending inventory balance by $5,000, how would the firm's cost of goods sold be affected? Explain your answer by drawing T-accounts for the Inventory and Cost of Goods Sold accounts and entering amounts that illustrate the difference between correctly stating and overstating the ending inventory balance.

b. If management wanted to understate profits, would ending inventory be understated or overstated? Explain your answer.

Problem 5.35
LO 7

Effects of inventory errors Following are condensed income statements for Uncle Bill's Home Improvement Center for the years ended December 31, 2014, and 2013:

Problem 5.36
LO 7

	2014	2013
Sales	$811,800	$785,400
Cost of goods sold	(606,900)	(540,600)
Gross profit	$204,900	$244,800
Operating expenses	(155,550)	(142,050)
Net income (ignoring income taxes)	$ 49,350	$102,750

Uncle Bill was concerned about the operating results for 2014 and asked his recently hired accountant, "If sales increased in 2014, why was net income less than half of what it was in 2013?" In February of 2015, Uncle Bill got his answer: "The ending inventory reported in 2013 was overstated by $35,250 for merchandise that we were holding on consignment on behalf of Kirk's Servistar. We still keep some of their appliances in stock, but the value of these items was not included in the 2014 inventory count because we don't own them."

a. Recast the 2013 and 2014 income statements to take into account the correction of the 2013 ending inventory error.

b. Calculate the combined net income for 2013 and 2014 before and after the correction of the error. Explain to Uncle Bill why the error was corrected in 2014 before it was actually discovered in 2015.

c. What effect, if any, will the error have on net income and stockholders' equity in 2015?

Cases

All applicable Cases are available with McGraw-Hill's *Connect*™ *Accounting*.

Focus company—accounts receivable and inventory disclosures In Exercise 1.1, you were asked to obtain the most recent annual report of a company that you were interested in reviewing throughout this term.

Case 5.37
LO 5, 7, 8

Required:

Please review the note disclosures provided in your focus company's annual report and discuss what you've learned about how your company's accounts receivable and inventory are accounted for and presented.

Case 5.38

LO 5, 7

Comparative analysis of current asset structures The 2011 annual reports of Pearson plc and The McGraw-Hill Companies, Inc., two publishing and information services companies, included the following selected data as at December 31, 2011, and 2010:

PEARSON PLC		
(Amounts in millions)	**2011**	**2010**
Inventories...	£ 407	£ 429
Trade and other receivables, net of provision for bad and doubtful debts, and anticipated future sales returns of £102 in 2011 and £83 in 2010........	1,386	1,337
Financial assets—Marketable securities..	9	18
Cash and cash equivalents...	1,369	1,736
Total current assets	£3,171	£3,520

THE McGRAW-HILL COMPANIES, INC.		
(Amounts in millions)	**2011**	**2010**
Cash and equivalents	$ 944	$1,526
Short-term investments	29	22
Accounts receivable, net of allowance for doubtful accounts and sales returns of $242 in 2011 and $275 in 2010	1,045	973
Inventories...	263	275
Deferred income taxes...	260	281
Prepaid and other current assets..	138	298
Total current assets	$2,679	$3,375

Required:

a. Do you notice anything unusual about the data presented for Pearson? Comment specifically about some of the difficulties you would expect to encounter when comparing financial statement data of a U.S.-based company to data of a non–U.S.-based company.

b. Review the current asset data presented for each company. Comment briefly about your first impressions concerning the relative composition of current assets within each company.

c. Pearson's revenues are derived from educational publishing (68%) including Prentice Hall and Addison-Wesley, business and technology publishing (7%), FT *(Financial Times)* Group (7%), and Penguin books (18%). McGraw-Hill's revenues are derived from educational publishing (37%), S&P credit ratings (28%), S&P capital IQ and research indexes (22%), and C&C (commodities and commercial, 13%), including J.D. Power & Associates and other professional media outlets. How can these data help you make sense of your observations in part **b**?

Answers to Self-Study Material

Matching I: 1. s, 2. m, 3. f, 4. d, 5. j, 6. h, 7. b, 8. i, 9. c, 10. e
Matching II: 1. l, 2. f, 3. q, 4. d, 5. m, 6. h, 7. k, 8. p, 9. b, 10. n
Multiple choice: 1. d, 2. c, 3. b, 4. a, 5. b, 6. d, 7. d, 8. d, 9. d, 10. a

Accounting for and Presentation of Property, Plant, and Equipment, and Other Noncurrent Assets

Noncurrent assets include land, buildings, and equipment (less accumulated depreciation); intangible assets such as leaseholds, patents, trademarks, and goodwill; and natural resources. The presentation of property, plant, and equipment, and other noncurrent assets on the consolidated balance sheets of Campbell Soup Company, on page 712 of the appendix, appears straightforward. However, several business and accounting matters are involved in understanding this presentation. The objective of this chapter is to show you how to make sense of the noncurrent assets section of any balance sheet.

The primary issues related to the accounting for noncurrent assets are:

1. Accounting for the acquisition of assets.
2. Accounting for the use (depreciation) of assets.
3. Accounting for maintenance and repair costs.
4. Accounting for the disposition of assets.

LEARNING OBJECTIVES (LO)

After studying this chapter you should understand and be able to

LO 6-1   Explain how the cost of land, buildings, and equipment is reported on the balance sheet.

LO 6-2   Discuss how the terms *capitalize* and *expense* are used with respect to property, plant, and equipment.

LO 6-3   Describe alternative methods of calculating depreciation for financial accounting purposes and compare the relative effects of each on the income statement and the balance sheet.

LO 6-4   Describe the accounting treatment of repair and maintenance expenditures.

LO 6-5   Explain why depreciation for income tax purposes is an important concern of taxpayers and how tax depreciation differs from financial accounting depreciation.

LO 6-6   Describe the effect on the financial statements of the disposition of noncurrent assets, either by sale or abandonment.

LO 6-7   Describe the difference between an operating lease and a capital lease.

LO 6-8   Explain the similarities in the financial statement effects of buying an asset compared to using a capital lease to acquire the rights to an asset.

LO 6-9   Discuss the meaning of various intangible assets, how their values are measured, and how their costs are reflected in the income statement.

LO 6-10   Explain the role of time value of money concepts in financial reporting and their usefulness in decision making.

Exhibit 6-1 on the next page highlights the balance sheet accounts covered in detail in this chapter and shows the income statement and statement of cash flows components affected by these accounts.

Land

Land owned and used in the operations of the firm is shown on the balance sheet at its original cost. All ordinary and necessary costs the firm incurs to get the land ready for its intended use are considered part of the original cost. These costs include the purchase price of the land, title fees, legal fees, and other costs related to the acquisition. If a firm purchases land with a building on it and razes the building so that a new one can be built to the firm's specifications, then the costs of the land, old building, and razing (less any salvage proceeds) all become part of the cost of the land and are *capitalized* (see Business in Practice—Capitalizing versus Expensing) because all of these costs were incurred to get the land ready for its intended use.

LO 1

Explain how the cost of land is reported on the balance sheet.

---

1.   What does it mean to capitalize an expenditure?

What Does It Mean? **Answer on page 231**

Land acquired for investment purposes or for some potential future but undefined use is classified as a separate noncurrent and nonoperating asset. This asset is reported at its original cost. A land development company would treat land under development as inventory, and all development costs would be included in the asset carrying value. As lots are sold, the costs are transferred from inventory to cost of goods sold.

Because land is not "used up," no accounting depreciation is associated with land.

When land is sold, the difference between the selling price and cost will be a gain or loss to be reported in the income statement of the period in which the sale occurred. For example, if a parcel of land on which Cruisers, Inc., had once operated a plant is sold this year for a price of $140,000 and the land had cost $6,000 when it was acquired 35 years earlier, the effect of this transaction on the financial statements would be:

Balance Sheet	Income Statement
Assets = Liabilities + Stockholders' equity	←Net income = Revenues − Expenses
Cash + 140,000 Land − 6,000	Gain on Sale of Land + 134,000

Exhibit 6-1

Financial Statements—
The Big Picture

Balance Sheet			
Current Assets	Chapter	**Current Liabilities**	Chapter
Cash and cash equivalents	5, 9	Short-term debt	7
Short-term marketable securities	5	Current maturities of long-term debt	7
Accounts receivable	5, 9	Accounts payable	7
Notes receivable	5	Unearned revenue or deferred credits	7
Inventories	5, 9	Payroll taxes and other withholdings	7
Prepaid expenses	5	Other accrued liabilities	7
Noncurrent Assets		**Noncurrent Liabilities**	
Land	6	Long-term debt	7
Buildings and equipment	6	Deferred tax liabilities	7
Assets acquired by capital lease	6	Other long-term liabilities	7
Intangible assets	6	**Stockholders' Equity**	
Natural resources	6	Common stock	8
Other noncurrent assets	6	Preferred stock	8
		Additional paid-in capital	8
		Retained earnings	8
		Treasury stock	8
		Accumulated other comprehensive income (loss)	8
		Noncontrolling interest	8

Income Statement		Statement of Cash Flows	
Sales	5, 9	**Operating Activities**	
Cost of goods sold	5, 9	Net income	5, 6, 7, 8, 9
Gross profit (or gross margin)	5, 9	Depreciation expense	6, 9
Selling, general, and administrative expenses	5, 6, 9	(Gains) losses on sale of assets	6, 9
Income from operations	9	(Increase) decrease in current assets	5, 9
Gains (losses) on sale of assets	6, 9	Increase (decrease) in current liabilities	7, 9
Interest income	5, 9	**Investing Activities**	
Interest expense	7, 9	Proceeds from sale of property, plant, and equipment	6, 9
Income tax expense	7, 9	Purchase of property, plant, and equipment	6, 9
Unusual items	9	**Financing Activities**	
Net income	5, 6, 7, 8, 9	Proceeds from long-term debt*	7, 9
Earnings per share	9	Repayment of long-term debt*	7, 9
		Issuance of common stock and/or preferred stock	8, 9
		Purchase of treasury stock	8, 9
		Payment of dividends	8, 9

Primary topics of this chapter.

Other affected financial statement components.

*May include short-term debt items as well.

Capitalizing versus Expensing

An expenditure involves using an asset (usually cash) or incurring a liability to acquire goods, services, or other economic benefits. Whenever a firm buys something, it has made an expenditure. All expenditures must be accounted for as either assets (**capitalizing** an expenditure) or expenses (**expensing** an expenditure). Although this jargon applies to any expenditure, it is most prevalent in discussions about property, plant, and equipment.

Expenditures should be capitalized if the item acquired will have an economic benefit to the entity that extends beyond the end of the current fiscal year. However, expenditures for preventive maintenance and normal repairs, even though they are needed to maintain the usefulness of the asset over a number of years, are expensed as incurred. The capitalize versus expense issue is resolved by applying the matching concept, under which costs incurred in generating revenues are subtracted from revenues in the period in which the revenues are earned.

When an expenditure is capitalized, plant assets increase. If the asset is depreciable—and all plant assets except land are depreciable—depreciation expense is recognized over the estimated useful life of the asset. If the expenditure is expensed, then the full cost is reflected in the current period's income statement. There is a broad gray area between expenditures that are clearly assets and those that are obviously expenses. This gray area leads to differences of opinion that have a direct impact on the net income reported across fiscal periods.

The materiality concept (see Chapter 2) is often applied to the issue of accounting for capital expenditures. Generally speaking, most accountants will expense items that are not material. Thus, the cost of a $25 wastebasket may be expensed, rather than capitalized and depreciated, even though the wastebasket clearly has a useful life of many years and should theoretically be accounted for as a capital asset.

Another factor that influences the capitalize versus expense decision is the potential income tax reduction in the current year that results from expensing. Although depreciation would be claimed (and income taxes reduced) over the life of a capitalized expenditure, many managers prefer the immediate income tax reduction that results from expensing.

This capitalize versus expense issue is another area in which accountants' judgments can have a significant effect on an entity's financial position and results of operations. Explanations in this text will reflect sound accounting theory. However, recognize that in practice there may be some deviation from theory.

Business in
Practice

LO 2
Discuss how the terms *capitalize* and *expense* are used with respect to property, plant, and equipment.

The entry for this transaction is:

Dr.	Cash	140,000	
	Cr. Land		6,000
	Cr. Gain on Sale of Land		134,000

Because land is carried on the books at original cost, the unrealized holding gain that had gradually occurred was ignored from an accounting perspective by Cruisers, Inc., until it sold the land (and realized the gain). Thus, the financial statements for each of the years between purchase and sale would *not* have reflected the increasing value of the land. Instead, the entire $134,000 gain will be reported in this year's income statement. The gain will not be included with operating income; it will be highlighted in the income statement as a nonrecurring, nonoperating item (usually reported as an element of "other income or expense"), so financial statement users will not be led to expect a similar gain in future years.

The original cost valuation of land (and all other categories of noncurrent assets discussed in this chapter) is often criticized for understating asset values on the balance sheet and for failing to provide proper matching on the income statement. Cruisers, Inc., management would have known that its land was appreciating in value over time, but this appreciation would not have been reflected on the balance sheet. The accounting profession defends the *cost principle* based on its reliability, consistency, and conservatism. To record land at fair value would involve appraisals or other subjective estimates of value that could not be verified until an exchange transaction (sale) occurred. Although approximate fair value would be more relevant than original cost for decision makers, original cost is the basis for accounting for noncurrent assets. You should be aware of this important limitation of the noncurrent asset information shown in balance sheets.

What Does It Mean?

Answer on page 231

2. What does it mean to state that balance sheet values do not represent current fair values of long-lived assets?

Buildings and Equipment

Cost of Assets Acquired

LO 1

Explain how the cost of buildings and equipment is reported on the balance sheet.

Buildings and equipment are recorded at their original cost, which is the purchase price plus all the ordinary and necessary costs incurred to get the building or equipment ready to use in the operations of the firm. "Construction in Progress," or some similar description, is often used to accumulate the costs of facilities that are being constructed to the firm's specifications until the completed assets are placed in service. Interest costs associated with loans used to finance the construction of a building are capitalized until the building is put into operation. Installation and shakedown costs (costs associated with adjusting and preparing the equipment to be used in production) incurred for a new piece of equipment should be capitalized. If a piece of equipment is made by a firm's own employees, all of the material, labor, and overhead costs that would ordinarily be recorded as inventory costs (were the machine being made for an outside customer) should be capitalized as equipment costs. Such costs are capitalized because they are directly related to assets that will be used by the firm over several accounting periods and are not related only to current period earnings.

The IFRS

Approach

One of the principal differences between U.S. GAAP and IFRS lies in the balance sheet valuation of noncurrent assets and liabilities. Under U.S. GAAP, most of a firm's noncurrent assets (i.e., property, plant, and equipment) are recorded at original cost. Once recorded, except in rare instances, original cost remains the amount associated with any given noncurrent asset and is likewise the amount used as the base on which depreciation expense is calculated.

International standards focus, instead, on fair value, which may be more than or less than original cost at any point in time. Under IFRS, most noncurrent assets must be revalued on a regular basis, perhaps annually. Revaluation may be applied to an entire class of assets or to individual asset categories. Revaluation increases are recorded as increases in the noncurrent asset's carrying value (on the debit side of the entry) and as increases in "Accumulated other comprehensive income (loss)" within stockholders' equity (on the credit side). Revaluation decreases are recorded in just the opposite manner, as reductions both in "Accumulated other comprehensive income (loss)" and in the relevant noncurrent asset's carrying value. Not surprisingly, significant disclosures are required under IFRS concerning any such revaluations.

Exhibit 6-2

Basket Purchase
Allocation Illustrated

Situation:

Cruisers, Inc., acquired a parcel of land, along with a building and some production equipment, from a bankrupt competitor for $200,000 in cash. Current fair values reported by an independent appraiser were land, $20,000; building, $170,000; and equipment, $60,000.

Allocation of Acquisition Cost:

Asset	Appraised Fair Value	Percent of Total*	Cost Allocation		
Land	$ 20,000	8%	$200,000 ×	8% =	$ 16,000
Building	170,000	68%	$200,000 ×	68% =	136,000
Equipment	60,000	24%	$200,000 ×	24% =	48,000
	$250,000	100%			$200,000

*$20,000/$250,000 = 8%; $170,000/$250,000 = 68%; $60,000/$250,000 = 24%.

Effect of the Acquisition on the Financial Statements:

Balance Sheet	Income Statement
Assets = Liabilities + Stockholders' equity	←Net income = Revenues − Expenses
Land + 16,000 Building + 136,000 Equipment + 48,000 Cash − 200,000	

Entry to Record the Acquisition:

```
Dr.  Land . . . . . . . . . . . . . . . . . . . . . . . . . . . . . . . . . . . . . . . . . . . .      16,000
Dr.  Building . . . . . . . . . . . . . . . . . . . . . . . . . . . . . . . . . . . . . . . . .     136,000
Dr.  Equipment . . . . . . . . . . . . . . . . . . . . . . . . . . . . . . . . . . . . . .      48,000
      Cr.   Cash . . . . . . . . . . . . . . . . . . . . . . . . . . . . . . . . . . . . . . . . .              200,000
```

Original cost is not usually difficult to determine, but when two or more noncurrent assets are acquired in a single transaction for a lump-sum purchase price, the cost of each asset acquired must be measured and recorded separately. In such cases, an allocation of the "basket" purchase price is made to the individual assets acquired based on relative appraisal values on the date of acquisition. Exhibit 6-2 illustrates this allocation process and the related accounting.

Depreciation for Financial Accounting Purposes

In financial accounting, depreciation is an application of the matching concept. The original cost of noncurrent assets represents the *prepaid* cost of economic benefits that will be received in future years. To the extent that an asset is "used up" in the operations of the entity, a portion of the asset's cost should be subtracted from the revenues that were generated through the use of the asset. Thus, the depreciation process involves an allocation of the cost of an asset to the years in which the benefits of the asset are expected to be received. Depreciation is *not* an attempt to recognize a loss in fair value or any difference between the original cost and replacement cost of an asset. In fact, the fair value of noncurrent assets may actually increase as they are used—but appreciation is not presently recorded (as discussed in the land section of this chapter). Depreciation expense is recorded in each fiscal period, and its effect on the financial statements is shown below:

Balance Sheet	Income Statement
Assets = Liabilities + Stockholders' equity	←Net income = Revenues − Expenses
−Accumulated Depreciation	−Depreciation Expense

The adjusting entry to record depreciation is:

Dr. Depreciation Expense	xx	
Cr. Accumulated Depreciation.		xx

Accumulated depreciation is another contra asset, and the balance in this account is the cumulative total of all the depreciation expense that has been recorded over the life of the asset up to the balance sheet date. It is classified with the related asset on the balance sheet as a subtraction from the cost of the asset. The difference between the cost of an asset and the accumulated depreciation on that asset is the **net book value** (carrying value) of the asset. The balance sheet presentation of a building asset and its related Accumulated Depreciation account (using assumed amounts) looks like this:

Building.	$100,000
Less: Accumulated depreciation	(15,000)
Net book value of building	$ 85,000

or, as more commonly reported, like this:

Building, less accumulated depreciation of $15,000. . . . . $85,000

With either presentation, the user can determine how much of the cost has been recognized as expense since the asset was acquired—which would not be possible if the Building account was directly reduced for the amount depreciated each year. This is why a contra asset account is used for accumulated depreciation.

Note that cash is not involved in the depreciation expense entry. The entity's Cash account was affected when the asset was purchased or as it is being paid for if a liability was incurred when the asset was acquired. The fact that depreciation expense does not affect cash is important in understanding the statement of cash flows, which identifies the sources and uses of a firm's cash during a fiscal period.

There are several alternative methods of calculating depreciation expense for financial accounting purposes. Each involves spreading the amount to be depreciated, which is the asset's cost minus its estimated salvage value, over the asset's estimated useful life to the entity. The depreciation method selected does not affect the total depreciation expense to

Straight-line depreciation

Accelerated depreciation

Exhibit 6-3

Depreciation Expense
Patterns

be recognized over the life of the asset; however, different methods result in different patterns of depreciation expense by fiscal period. There are two broad categories of depreciation calculation methods: the straight-line methods and accelerated methods. Depreciation expense patterns resulting from these alternatives are illustrated in Exhibit 6-3.

---

3. What does it mean to say that depreciation expense does not affect cash?

What Does It Mean?
Answer on page 231

Accelerated depreciation methods result in greater depreciation expense and lower net income than straight-line depreciation during the early years of the asset's life. During the later years of the asset's life, annual depreciation expense using accelerated methods is less than it would be using straight-line depreciation, and net income is higher.

Which method is used, and why? For reporting to stockholders, most firms use the **straight-line depreciation method** because in the early years of an asset's life it results in lower depreciation expense and hence higher reported net income than accelerated depreciation. In later years, when accelerated depreciation is less than straight-line depreciation, *total* depreciation expense using the straight-line method will still be less than under an accelerated method if the amount invested in new assets has grown each year. Such a regular increase in depreciable assets is not unusual for firms that are growing, assuming that prices of new and replacement equipment are rising.

The specific depreciation calculation methods are

LO 3

Describe alternative methods of calculating depreciation for financial accounting purposes and compare the relative effects of each on the income statement and the balance sheet.

Straight-line

Straight-line.

Units-of-production.

Accelerated

Declining-balance.

Sum-of-the-years'-digits.

The straight-line, units-of-production, and declining-balance depreciation calculation methods are illustrated in Exhibit 6-4 on the next page.[1]

---

[1] The sum-of-the-years'-digits method is not illustrated because it is seldom used in practice.

Exhibit 6-4

Depreciation Calculation Methods

Assumptions:

Cruisers, Inc., purchased a molding machine at the beginning of 2013 at a cost of $22,000. The machine is estimated to have a useful life to Cruisers, Inc., of five years and an estimated salvage value of $2,000. It is estimated that the machine will produce 200 boat hulls before it wears out.

a. Straight-line depreciation:

$$\text{Annual depreciation expense} = \frac{\text{Cost} - \text{Estimated salvage value}}{\text{Estimated useful life}}$$

$$= \frac{\$22,000 - \$2,000}{5 \text{ years}}$$

$$= \$4,000$$

Alternatively, a straight-line depreciation rate could be determined and multiplied by the amount to be depreciated:

$$\text{Straight-line depreciation rate} = \frac{1}{\text{Life in years}} = \frac{1}{5} = 20\%$$

$$\text{Annual depreciation expense} = 20\% \times \$20,000 = \$4,000$$

b. Units-of-production depreciation:

$$\text{Depreciation expense per unit produced} = \frac{\text{Cost} - \text{Estimated salvage value}}{\text{Estimated total units to be made}}$$

$$= \frac{\$22,000 - \$2,000}{200 \text{ hulls}}$$

$$= \$100$$

Each year's depreciation expense would be $100 multiplied by the number of hulls produced.

c. Declining-balance depreciation:

$$\text{Annual depreciation expense} = \text{Double the straight-line depreciation rate}$$
$$\times \text{Asset's net book value at beginning of year}$$

$$\text{Straight-line depreciation rate} = \frac{1}{\text{Life in years}} = \frac{1}{5} = 20\%$$

Double the straight-line depreciation rate is 40%.

	Net Book Value at Beginning of Year		Factor		Depreciation Expense for the Year	Accumulated Depreciation	Net Book Value at End of Year
2013	$22,000	×	0.4	=	$8,800	$ 8,800	$13,200
2014	13,200	×	0.4	=	5,280	14,080	7,920
2015	7,920	×	0.4	=	3,168	17,248	4,752
2016	4,752	×	0.4	=	1,901	19,149	2,851
2017	2,851	×	0.4	=	851*	20,000	2,000

Recap of depreciation expense by year and method:

	Straight-Line	Declining Balance
2013	$ 4,000	$ 8,800
2014	4,000	5,280
2015	4,000	3,168
2016	4,000	1,901
2017	4,000	851
Total.	$20,000	$20,000

*Depreciation expense at the end of the asset's life is equal to an amount that will cause the net book value to equal the asset's estimated salvage value.

Note that the total depreciation expense for the five years is the same for both methods; it is the pattern of the expense that differs. Because depreciation is an expense, the effect on operating income of the alternative methods will be opposite; 2013 operating income will be higher if the straight-line method is used and lower if the declining-balance method is used.

   Depreciation calculations using the straight-line, units-of-production, and sum-of-the-years'-digits methods involve determining the amount to be depreciated by subtracting the estimated salvage value from the cost of the asset. Salvage value is considered in the declining-balance method only near the end of the asset's life when salvage value becomes the target for net book value.

   The declining-balance calculation illustrated in Exhibit 6-4 is known as *double-declining balance* because the depreciation rate used is double the straight-line rate. In some instances the rate used is 1.5 times the straight-line rate; this is referred to as *150% declining-balance depreciation.* Whatever rate is used, a constant percentage is applied each year to the declining balance of the net book value.

   Although many firms will use a single depreciation method for all of their depreciable assets, the consistency concept is applied to the depreciation method used for a particular asset acquired in a particular year. Thus, it is possible for a firm to use an accelerated depreciation method for some of its assets and the straight-line method for other assets. Differences can even occur between similar assets purchased in the same or different years. To make sense of the income statement and balance sheet, it is necessary to find out from the notes to the financial statements which depreciation methods are used (see page 715 of Campbell's annual report in the appendix).

   Table 6-1 summarizes the depreciation methods used for stockholder reporting purposes by 500 large firms.

   The estimates made of useful life and salvage value are educated guesses to be sure, but accountants, frequently working with engineers, can estimate these factors with great accuracy. A firm's experience and equipment replacement practices are considered in the estimating process. For income tax purposes (see Business in Practice—Depreciation for Income Tax Purposes), the useful life of various depreciable assets is determined by the Internal Revenue Code, which also specifies that salvage values are to be ignored.

   In practice, a number of technical accounting challenges must be considered in calculating depreciation. These include part-year depreciation for assets acquired or disposed of during a year, changes in estimated salvage value and/or useful life after the asset has been depreciated for some time, asset improvements (or *betterments*), and asset grouping to facilitate the depreciation calculation. These are beyond the scope of this text; your task is to understand the alternative calculation methods and the different effect of each on both depreciation expense in the income statement and accumulated depreciation (and net book value) on the balance sheet.

Methods	Number of Companies
Straight-line	492
Declining-balance	10
Sum-of-the-years'-digits	2
Accelerated method—not specified	13
Units of production	15
Group/Composite	4

Table 6-1

Depreciation Calculation Methods Used by 500 Publicly Owned Industrial and Merchandising Corporations—2010

Source: *Accounting Trends and Techniques,* Table 3–4, copyright © 2011 by American Institute of Certified Public Accountants, Inc. Reprinted with permission.

The IFRS Approach

International financial reporting standards provide that Property, Plant and Equipment (P,P&E) should be recognized as an asset when it is probable that (1) future economic benefits associated with the asset will flow to the entity and (2) the cost of the asset can be measured reliably. When the cost model is used, each element of P,P&E that is significant in relation to the total balance sheet valuation must be depreciated separately. The depreciation method for each element should reflect the pattern in which the asset's economic benefits are likely to be consumed by the entity. When the initial measurement of cost is based on U.S. GAAP, revaluation should be carried out regularly so that asset carrying amounts do not differ materially from fair values at the balance sheet date.

What Does It Mean?

Answers on page 231

4. What does it mean to use an accelerated depreciation method?
5. What does it mean to refer to the tax benefit of depreciation expense?

Repair and Maintenance Expenditures

LO 4
Describe the accounting treatment of repair and maintenance expenditures.

Routine repair costs and preventive maintenance expenditures are clearly expenses of the period in which they are incurred. There is a gray area with respect to some maintenance expenditures, however, and accountants' judgments may differ. If a maintenance expenditure will extend the useful life and/or increase the salvage value of an asset beyond that used in the original depreciation calculation, it is appropriate that the expenditure be capitalized and that the remaining depreciable cost of the asset be depreciated over the asset's remaining useful life.

In practice, most accountants decide in favor of expensing rather than capitalizing for several reasons. Revising the depreciation calculation data is frequently time-consuming with little perceived benefit. Because depreciation involves estimates of useful life and salvage value to begin with, revising those estimates without overwhelming evidence that they are significantly in error is an exercise of questionable value. For income tax purposes, most taxpayers would rather have a deductible expense now (expensing) rather than later (capitalizing and depreciating).

Because of the possibility that net income could be affected either favorably or unfavorably by inconsistent judgments about the accounting for repair and maintenance expenditures, auditors (internal and external) and the Internal Revenue Service usually look closely at these expenditures when they are reviewing a firm's reported results.

What Does It Mean?

Answer on page 231

6. What does it mean to prefer expensing repair and maintenance expenditures rather than capitalizing them?

Depreciation for Income Tax Purposes

Depreciation is a deductible expense for income tax purposes. Although depreciation expense does not directly affect cash, it does reduce taxable income. Therefore, most firms would like their deductible depreciation expense to be as large an amount as possible because this means lower taxable income and lower taxes payable. The Internal Revenue Code has permitted taxpayers to use an accelerated depreciation calculation method for many years. Estimated useful life is generally the most significant factor (other than calculation method) affecting the amount of depreciation expense, and for many years this was a contentious issue between taxpayers and the Internal Revenue Service.

In 1981, the Internal Revenue Code was amended to permit use of the **Accelerated Cost Recovery System (ACRS),** frequently pronounced "acres," for depreciable assets placed in service after 1980. The ACRS rules simplified the determination of useful life and allowed rapid write-off patterns similar to the declining-balance methods, so most firms started using ACRS for tax purposes. Unlike the LIFO inventory cost flow assumption (which, if selected, must be used for both financial reporting and income tax determination purposes), there is no requirement that "book" (financial statement) and tax depreciation calculation methods be the same. Most firms continued to use straight-line depreciation for book purposes.

ACRS used relatively short, and arbitrary, useful lives, and ignored salvage value. The intent was more to permit relatively quick "cost recovery" and thus encourage investment than it was to recognize traditional depreciation expense. For example, ACRS permitted the write-off of most machinery and equipment over three to five years.

In the Tax Reform Act of 1986 Congress changed the original ACRS provisions. The system has since been referred to as the **Modified Accelerated Cost Recovery System (MACRS).** Recovery periods were lengthened, additional categories for classifying assets were created, and the method of calculating the depreciation deduction was specified. Cost recovery periods are specified based on the type of asset and its class life, as defined in the Internal Revenue Code. Most machinery and equipment is depreciated using the double-declining-balance method, but the 150% declining-balance method is required for some longer-lived assets, and the straight-line method is specified for buildings.

In addition to the MACRS rules, small businesses benefit from a special relief provision that allows certain depreciable assets to be treated as immediate expense deductions as they are purchased. An annual election can be made to expense as much as $125,000 (for the 2012 tax year) of the cost of qualifying depreciable property purchased for use in a trade or business, subject to certain limitations and phaseouts.* The immediate deduction promotes administrative convenience by eliminating the need for extensive depreciation schedules for small purchases.

The use of ACRS for book depreciation was discouraged because of the arbitrarily short lives involved. MACRS lives are closer to actual useful lives, but basing depreciation expense for financial accounting purposes on tax law provisions, which are subject to frequent change, is not appropriate. Yet many small to medium-size business organizations yield to the temptation to do so. Such decisions are based on the inescapable fact that tax depreciation schedules must be maintained to satisfy Internal Revenue Service rules, and therefore the need to keep separate schedules for financial reporting is avoided.

*The maximum amount allowed to be expensed under this provision of the tax law will be reduced to $25,000 for years beginning after 2012.

Business in
Practice

LO 5
Explain why depreciation for income tax purposes is an important concern of taxpayers and how tax depreciation differs from financial accounting depreciation.

Disposal of Depreciable Assets

When a depreciable asset is sold or scrapped, both the asset and its related accumulated depreciation account must be removed from the books. For example, scrapping a fully depreciated piece of equipment, for which no salvage value had been estimated, would produce the following financial statement effects:

Balance Sheet	Income Statement
Assets = Liabilities + Stockholders' equity	←Net income = Revenues − Expenses
− Equipment + Accumulated Depreciation	

The entry would be:

LO 6

Describe the effect on the financial statements of the disposition of noncurrent assets, either by sale or abandonment.

Dr. Accumulated Depreciation xx	
Cr. Equipment	xx

Note that this entry does not affect *total* assets or any other parts of the financial statements.

When the asset being disposed of has a positive net book value, either because a salvage value was estimated or because it has not reached the end of its estimated useful life to the firm, a gain or loss on the disposal will result unless the asset is sold for a price that is equal to the net book value. For example, if equipment that cost $6,000 new has a net book value equal to its estimated salvage value of $900 and is sold for $1,200, the following financial statement effects would occur:

Balance Sheet	Income Statement
Assets = Liabilities + Stockholders' equity	←Net income = Revenues − Expenses
Cash + 1,200 Accumulated Depreciation + 5,100 Equipment − 6,000	Gain on Sale of Equipment + 300

Here is the entry to record the sale of equipment:

Dr. Cash.	1,200	
Dr. Accumulated Depreciation	5,100*	
Cr. Equipment		6,000
Cr. Gain on Sale of Equipment		300
Sold equipment.		

*Net book value = Cost − Accumulated depreciation

900 = 6,000 − Accumulated depreciation

Accumulated depreciation = 5,100

Alternatively, assume that the equipment had to be scrapped without receiving any proceeds. The effect of this entry on the financial statements looks like this:

Balance Sheet	Income Statement
Assets = Liabilities + Stockholders' equity	←Net income = Revenues − Expenses
Accumulated Depreciation + 5,100 Equipment − 6,000	Loss on Disposal of Equipment − 900

You will have no difficulty with the preceding material if you can learn to apply the following formula:

$$
\begin{aligned}
&\text{Sales price (of the fixed asset)}\\
&\underline{-\text{ Net book value (original cost }-\text{ accumulated depreciation)}}\\
&=\text{Gain (if the difference is positive) or loss (if negative)}
\end{aligned}
$$

Study

Suggestion

The entry would be:

Dr.	Accumulated Depreciation	5,100	
Dr.	Loss on Disposal of Equipment	900	
	Cr. Equipment		6,000
	Scrapped equipment.		

The gain or loss on the disposal of a depreciable asset is, in effect, a correction of the total depreciation expense that has been recorded over the life of the asset. If salvage value and useful life estimates had been correct, the net book value of the asset would be equal to the **proceeds** (if any) received from its sale or disposal. Depreciation expense is never adjusted retroactively, so the significance of these gains or losses gives the financial statement user a basis for judging the accuracy of the accountant's estimates of salvage value and useful life. Gains or losses on the disposal of depreciable assets are not part of the operating income of the entity. If significant, they will be reported separately as elements of other income or expense. If not material, they will be reported with miscellaneous other income.

Assets Acquired by Capital Lease

Many firms will lease, or rent, assets rather than purchase them. An **operating lease** is an agreement for the use of an asset that does not involve any attributes of ownership. For example, the renter (lessee) of a car from Hertz or Avis (the lessor) must return the

LO 7
Describe the difference between an operating lease and a capital lease.

Focus on the "Big Picture"

A number of technical financial accounting topics are presented in this text at an overview level to provide a basic, user-oriented exposure to the key financial statement accounts and captions that you are likely to encounter at some point in your life as an investor, creditor, or employee of a large, publicly traded company. In this chapter, the accounting for assets acquired by capital lease and for goodwill represent two such examples. Likewise, brief references were made to the "Accumulated other comprehensive income (loss)" caption, which is reported as an element of stockholders' equity on the balance sheet; this important topic is described in Chapter 8. The authors believe that for students to understand "what the numbers mean," an exposure to these (and similar) types of accounts and captions is not only appropriate but essential, as they represent key components of the modern-day language of accounting and financial reporting. Your attention should be focused on understanding the essential nature of any such "technical" topics as you encounter them, specifically as to how they relate to the "big picture" financial statement model (A = L + SE, and NI = R − E) that you learned in Chapter 2.

Study

Suggestion

car at the end of the lease term. Therefore, assets rented under an operating lease are not reflected on the lessee's balance sheet, and the rent expense involved is reported in the income statement as an operating expense.

A **capital lease** (or *financing lease*) results in the lessee (renter) assuming virtually all of the benefits and risks of ownership of the leased asset. For example, the lessee of a car from an automobile dealership may sign a noncancelable lease agreement with a term of five years requiring monthly payments sufficient to cover the cost of the car, plus interest and administrative costs. A lease is a capital lease if it has *any* of the following characteristics:

1. It transfers ownership of the asset to the lessee.
2. It permits the lessee to purchase the asset for a nominal sum (a bargain purchase price) at the end of the lease period.
3. The lease term is at least 75 percent of the economic life of the asset.
4. The **present value** of the lease payments is at least 90 percent of the fair value of the asset. (Please refer to the appendix at the end of this chapter if you are not familiar with the present value concept.)

LO 8

Explain the similarities in the financial statement effects of buying an asset compared to using a capital lease to acquire the rights to an asset.

The economic impact of a capital lease isn't really any different from buying the asset outright and signing a note payable that will be paid off, with interest, over the life of the asset. Therefore, it is appropriate that the asset and related liability be reflected in the lessee's balance sheet. In the lessee's income statement, the cost of the leased asset will be reflected as depreciation expense, rather than rent expense, and the financing cost will be shown as interest expense.

Prior to a FASB standard issued in 1976, many companies did not record assets acquired under a capital lease because they did not want to reflect the related lease liability in their balance sheet. This practice is known as *off-balance-sheet financing* and is deemed inappropriate because the full disclosure concept would be violated were it to be allowed.

Assets acquired by capital lease now are included with purchased assets on the balance sheet. The amount recorded as the cost of the asset involved in a capital lease, and as the related lease liability, is the present value of the lease payments to be made, based on the interest rate used by the lessor to determine the periodic lease payments. Here are the effects of capital lease transactions on the financial statements using the horizontal model:

Balance Sheet	Income Statement
Assets = Liabilities + Stockholders' equity	←Net income = Revenues − Expenses
1. Date of acquisition: + Equipment + Capital Lease Liability	

2. Annual depreciation expense:
− Accumulated
   Depreciation
	− Depreciation
	   Expense

3. Annual lease payments:
− Cash   − Capital
               Lease Liability
	− Interest
	   Expense

The entries to record capital lease transactions are as follows:

1. Date of acquisition.
   Dr. Equipment.................................... xx
       Cr. Capital Lease Liability........................ xx
2. Annual depreciation expense.
   Dr. Depreciation Expense......................... xx
       Cr. Accumulated Depreciation xx
3. Annual lease payments.
   Dr. Interest Expense.............................. xx
   Dr. Capital Lease Liability.......................... xx
       Cr. Cash xx

The first entry shows the asset acquisition and the related financial obligation that has been incurred. The second shows depreciation expense in the same way it is recorded for purchased assets. The third shows the lease payment effect on cash, reflects the interest expense for the period on the amount that has been borrowed (in effect) from the lessor, and reduces the lease liability by what is really a payment on the principal of a loan from the lessor.

To illustrate the equivalence of capital lease payments and a long-term loan, assume that a firm purchased a computer system at a cost of $217,765 and borrowed the money by giving a note payable that had an annual interest rate of 10 percent and that required payments of $50,000 per year for six years. Using the horizontal model, the following is the effect on the financial statements:

Balance Sheet	Income Statement
Assets = Liabilities + Stockholders' equity	←Net income = Revenues − Expenses
Equipment Note + 217,765 Payable + 217,765	

The purchase would be recorded using the following entry:

Dr. Equipment.................................... 217,765
    Cr. Note Payable 217,765

Each year the firm will accrue and pay interest expense on the note, and make principal payments, as shown in the following table:

Year	Principal Balance at Beginning of Year	Interest at 10%	Payment Applied to Principal ($50,000 − Interest)	Principal Balance at End of Year
1 . . .	$217,765	$21,776	$28,224	$189,541
2 . . .	189,541	18,954	31,046	158,495
3 . . .	158,495	15,849	34,151	124,344
4 . . .	124,344	12,434	37,566	86,778
5 . . .	86,778	8,677	41,323	45,455
6 . . .	45,455	4,545	45,455	–0–

After six years, the note will have been fully paid.

If the firm were to lease the computer system and agree to make annual lease payments of $50,000 for six years instead of borrowing the money and buying the computer system outright, the financial statements should reflect the transaction in essentially the same way. This will happen because the present value of all of the lease payments (which include principal and interest) is $217,765. (Referring to Table 6-5 in the appendix to this chapter, in the 10% column and six-period row, the factor is 4.3553. This factor multiplied by the $50,000 annual lease payment is $217,765.) Using the horizontal model, the following is the effect on the financial statements:

Balance Sheet		Income Statement
Assets = Liabilities + Stockholders' equity		←Net income = Revenues − Expenses

Equipment   Capital
+ 217,765   Lease
       Liability
       + 217,765		

The entry at the beginning of the lease will be:

Dr. Equipment..................................	217,765	
Cr. Capital Lease Liability		217,765

Each year the principal portion of the lease payment will reduce the capital lease liability, and the interest portion will be recognized as an expense. In addition, the equipment will be depreciated each year. Thus, liabilities on the balance sheet and expenses in the income statement will be the same as under the borrow and purchase alternative.

Again, the significance of capital lease accounting is that the economic impact of capital leasing isn't really any different from buying the asset outright; the impact on the financial statements shouldn't differ either.

What Does It Mean?

Answer on page 232

7. What does it mean to acquire an asset with a capital lease?

Intangible Assets

LO 9

Discuss the meaning of various intangible assets, how their values are measured, and how their costs are reflected in the income statement.

Intangible assets are long-lived assets that differ from property, plant, and equipment that have been purchased outright or acquired under a capital lease—either because the asset is represented by a contractual right or because the asset results from a purchase transaction but is not physically identifiable. Examples of the first type of intangible asset are leaseholds, licenses, franchises, brand names, customer lists/relationships, patents, copyrights, and trademarks; the second type of intangible asset is known as *goodwill*.

Just as the cost of plant and equipment is transferred to expense over time through accounting depreciation, the cost of most intangibles is also expensed over time. **Amortization,** which means spreading an amount over time, is the term used to describe the process of allocating the cost of an intangible asset from the balance sheet to the income statement as an expense. The cost of tangible assets is depreciated; the cost of intangible assets is amortized. The terms are different, but the process is the same. Most intangibles are amortized on a straight-line basis based on the useful life to the entity. Although the Accumulated Amortization account is sometimes used, amortization expense is usually recorded as a direct reduction in the carrying value of the related intangible asset. Thus, the effect of periodic amortization on the financial statements would be as follows:

Balance Sheet	Income Statement
Assets = Liabilities + Stockholders' equity	←Net income = Revenues − Expenses
− Intangible Asset	− Amortization Expense

The entry would be:

Dr. Amortization Expense............................	xx	
Cr. Intangible Asset		xx

Amortization expense is usually included with depreciation expense in the income statement. Note that neither depreciation expense nor amortization expense involves a cash disbursement; cash is disbursed when the asset is acquired or, if a loan is used to finance the acquisition, when the loan payments are made.

Leasehold Improvements

When the tenant of an office building makes modifications to the office space, such as having private offices constructed, the cost of these modifications is a capital expenditure to be amortized over their useful life to the tenant or over the life of the lease, whichever is shorter. The concept is the same as that applying to buildings or equipment, but the terminology is different. Entities that use rented facilities extensively, such as smaller shops or retail store chains that operate in shopping malls, may have a significant amount of **leasehold improvements.**

Patents, Trademarks, and Copyrights

A **patent** is a monopoly license granted by the government giving the owner control of the use or sale of an invention for a period of 20 years. A **trademark** (or trade name), when registered with the Federal Trade Commission, can be used only by the entity that owns it or by another entity that has secured permission from the owner. A trademark has an unlimited life, but it can be terminated by lack of use. A **copyright** is a protection granted to writers and artists that is designed to prevent unauthorized copying of printed or recorded material. A copyright is granted for a period of time equal to the life of the writer or artist, plus 70 years.

To the extent that an entity has incurred some cost in obtaining a patent, trademark, or copyright, that cost should be capitalized and amortized over its estimated remaining useful life to the entity or its statutory life, whichever is shorter. The cost of developing a patent, trademark, or copyright is not usually significant. Most intangible assets in this category arise when one firm purchases a patent, trademark, or copyright from another entity. An intangible that becomes very valuable because of the success of a product (like "Coke") cannot be assigned a value and recorded as an asset while it continues to be owned by the entity that created it. In some cases a firm will include a caption for trademarks, or another intangible asset, on its balance sheet and report a nominal cost of $1 just to communicate to financial statement users that it has this type of asset.

License fees or royalties earned from an intangible asset owned by a firm are reported as operating revenues in the income statement. Likewise, license fees or royalty expenses incurred by a firm using an intangible asset owned by another entity are operating expenses.

Goodwill

Goodwill results from the purchase of one firm by another for a price that is greater than the fair value of the net assets acquired. (Recall from Chapter 2 that *net assets* means total assets minus total liabilities.) Why would one firm be willing to pay more for a business than the fair value of the inventory, plant, and equipment, and other assets being acquired? Because the purchasing firm does not see the transaction as the purchase of assets but instead evaluates the transaction as the purchase of *profits*. The purchaser will be willing to pay such an amount because the profits expected to be earned from the investment will generate an adequate return on the investment. If the firm being purchased has been able to earn a greater than average rate of return on its invested net assets, the owners of that firm will be able to command a price for the firm that is greater than the fair value of its net assets. This greater than average return may result from excellent management, a great location, unusual customer loyalty, a unique product or service, or a combination of these and other factors.

When one firm purchases another, the purchase price is first assigned to the net assets acquired, which includes physical assets and intangible assets. The cost recorded for these net assets is their fair value, usually determined by appraisal. This cost then becomes the basis for depreciating or amortizing the assets, or for determining cost of goods sold if inventory is involved. To the extent that the total price exceeds the fair value of the net assets acquired, the excess is recorded as goodwill. For example, assume that Cruisers, Inc., purchased a business by paying $1,000,000 in cash and assuming a note payable liability of $100,000. The fair value of the net assets acquired was $700,000, assigned as follows: Inventory, $250,000; Land, $150,000; Buildings, $400,000; and Notes Payable, $100,000. Here is the effect of this transaction on the financial statements:

Balance Sheet	Income Statement
Assets = Liabilities + Stockholders' equity	←Net income = Revenues − Expenses
Inventory + 250,000 Notes Payable + 100,000	
Land + 150,000	
Buildings + 400,000	
Goodwill + 300,000	
Cash − 1,000,000	

The entry would be:

Dr. Inventory	250,000	
Dr. Land	150,000	
Dr. Buildings	400,000	
Dr. Goodwill	300,000	
Cr. Notes Payable		100,000
Cr. Cash		1,000,000

Goodwill is an intangible asset and is *not* amortized. Instead goodwill must be tested annually for impairment. If the book value of goodwill does not exceed its fair value, goodwill is not considered impaired. However, if the book value of goodwill *does* exceed its fair value, an impairment loss is recorded equal to that excess. Although the details of this test are more appropriate for an advanced accounting course, the financial statement effects of an impairment loss are straightforward. In the preceding Cruisers, Inc., example, assume that three years after the business was acquired, the fair value of the resulting goodwill of $300,000 was determined to be only $180,000. Here would be the effects on the financial statements of the impairment loss adjustment:

Balance Sheet	Income Statement
Assets = Liabilities + Stockholders' equity	←Net income = Revenues − Expenses
Goodwill − 120,000	Goodwill Impairment Loss − 120,000

The entry for the impairment loss would be:

Dr. Goodwill impairment loss	120,000	
Cr. Goodwill		120,000

Goodwill impairment loss is generally reported as a separate line item within operating income on the income statement. Once goodwill is considered to be impaired and has been written down to its impaired fair value, no subsequent upward adjustments are permitted for recoveries of fair value. In the preceding example, $180,000 would become the new book value for goodwill, and this amount would be compared to the fair value of goodwill in future years to determine if further impairment has occurred.

The prior examples provide a basic illustration of the recording of goodwill and subsequent impairment losses, if any, by an acquiring firm. One way of describing goodwill is to say that—in theory at least—it is the present value of the greater than average earnings on the net assets of the acquired firm, discounted for the period they are expected to last, at the acquiring firm's desired return on investment. In fact, when analysts at the acquiring firm are calculating the price to offer for the firm to be acquired, they use a lot of present value analysis.

Some critics suggest that goodwill is a fictitious asset that should be written off immediately against the firm's retained earnings. Others point out that it is at best a "different" asset that must be evaluated carefully when it is encountered. However, if goodwill is included in the assets used in the return on investment calculation, the ROI measure will reflect management's ability to earn a return on this asset.

What Does It Mean?
Answer on page 232

8. What does it mean when goodwill results from the acquisition of another firm?

Natural Resources

Accounting for natural resource assets, such as coal deposits, crude oil reserves, timber, and mineral deposits, parallels that for depreciable assets. **Depletion,** rather than depreciation, is the term for the using up of natural resources, but the concepts are exactly the same, even though depletion usually involves considerably more complex estimates.

For example, when a firm pays for the right to drill for oil or mine for coal, the cost of that right and the costs of developing the well or mine are capitalized. The cost is then reflected in the income statement as Depletion Expense, which is matched with the revenue resulting from the sale of the natural resource. Depletion usually is recognized on a straight-line basis, based on geological and engineering estimates of the quantity of the natural resource to be recovered. Thus, if $100 million was the cost of a mine that held an estimated 20 million tons of coal, the depletion cost would be $5 per ton. In most cases the cost of the asset is credited, or reduced directly, in the Depletion Expense entry instead of using an Accumulated Depletion account.

In practice, estimating depletion expense is very complex. Depletion expense allowed for federal income tax purposes frequently differs from that recognized for financial accounting purposes because, from time to time, tax laws have been used to provide special incentives to develop natural resources.

Other Noncurrent Assets

Long-term investments, notes receivable that mature more than a year after the balance sheet date, long-term deferred income tax assets, and other noncurrent assets are included in this category. At such time as they become current (receivable within one year), they will be reclassified to the current asset section of the balance sheet. The explanatory notes accompanying the financial statements will include appropriate explanations about these assets if they are significant.

Demonstration Problem

Visit the text website at www.mhhe.com/marshall10e **to view a demonstration problem for this chapter.**

Summary

This chapter has discussed the accounting for and presentation of the following balance sheet noncurrent asset and related income statement accounts:

Balance Sheet	Income Statement
Assets = Liabilities + Stockholders' equity	←Net income = Revenues − Expenses
Land	Gain on or Loss on sale* sale*
Purchased Buildings/ Equipment	Repair and Maintenance Expense
Leased Capital Buildings/ Lease Equipment Liability	Interest Expense
(Accumulated Depreciation)	Depreciation Expense
Natural Resources	Depletion Expense
Intangible Assets	Amortization Expense
*For any noncurrent asset.	

Property, plant, and equipment owned by the entity are reported on the balance sheet at their original cost, less (for depreciable assets) accumulated depreciation.

Expenditures representing the cost of acquiring an asset that will benefit the entity for more than the current fiscal period are capitalized. Routine repair and maintenance costs are expensed in the fiscal period in which they are incurred.

Accounting depreciation is the process of spreading the cost of an asset to the fiscal periods in which the asset is used. Depreciation does not affect cash, nor is it an attempt to recognize a loss in the market value of an asset.

Depreciation expense can be calculated several ways. The calculations result in a depreciation expense pattern that is straight-line or accelerated. Straight-line methods are usually used for book purposes, and accelerated methods (based on the Modified Accelerated Cost Recovery System specified in the Internal Revenue Code) are usually used for income tax purposes.

When a depreciable asset is disposed of, both the asset and its related accumulated depreciation are removed from the accounts. A gain or loss normally results, depending on the relationship of any cash (and/or other assets) received in the transaction to the net book value of the asset disposed of.

When the use of an asset is acquired in a capital lease transaction, the asset and related lease liability are reported on the balance sheet. The cost of the asset is the present value of the lease payments, calculated using the interest rate used by the lessor to determine the periodic lease payments. The asset is depreciated, and interest expense related to the lease is recorded.

Intangible assets are represented by a contractual right or are not physically identifiable. The cost of most intangible assets is spread over the useful life to the entity of the intangible asset and is called *amortization expense*. Intangible assets include leasehold improvements, patents, trademarks, copyrights, and goodwill.

Goodwill is not amortized but is tested annually for impairment. The cost of natural resources is recognized as *depletion expense,* which is allocated to the natural resources recovered.

Refer to the Campbell Soup Company balance sheet and related notes in the appendix, and to other financial statements you may have, and observe how information about property, plant, and equipment, and other noncurrent assets is presented.

Appendix TO CHAPTER SIX

Time Value of Money

LO 10

Explain the role of time value of money concepts in financial reporting and their usefulness in decision making.

Two financial behaviors learned early in life are that money saved or invested at compound interest can yield large returns, and that given the choice of paying a bill sooner or later it can be financially beneficial to pay later. The first of these situations involves future value and the second is an application of present value; both are time value of money applications.

Future Value

Future value refers to the amount accumulated when interest on an investment is compounded for a given number of periods. *Compounding* refers to the practice of calculating interest for a period on the sum of the principal and interest accumulated at the beginning of the period (thus, interest is earned on interest). For example, if $1,000 is invested in a savings account earning interest at the rate of 10% compounded annually, and if the account is left alone for four years, the results shown in the following table will occur:

Year	Principal at Beginning of Year	Interest Earned at 10%	Principal at End of Year
1	$1,000	$100	$1,100
2	1,100	110	1,210
3	1,210	121	1,331
4	1,331	133	1,464

This is a familiar concept. This process can be illustrated on a time line as follows:

There is a formula for calculating future value, and many computer program packages and business calculators include a future value function. Table 6-2 presents future value factors for a range of interest rates and compounding periods. Note in Table 6-2

Factors for Calculating the Future Value of $1 | **Table 6-2**

No. of										
					Interest Rate					
Periods	2%	4%	6%	8%	10%	12%	14%	16%	18%	20%
1	1.020	1.040	1.060	1.080	1.100	1.120	1.140	1.160	1.180	1.200
2	1.040	1.082	1.124	1.166	1.210	1.254	1.300	1.346	1.392	1.440
3	1.061	1.125	1.191	1.260	1.331	1.405	1.482	1.561	1.643	1.728
4	1.082	1.170	1.262	1.360	1.464	1.574	1.689	1.811	1.939	2.074
5	1.104	1.217	1.338	1.469	1.611	1.762	1.925	2.100	2.288	2.488
10	1.219	1.480	1.791	2.159	2.594	3.106	3.707	4.411	5.234	6.192
15	1.346	1.801	2.397	3.172	4.177	5.474	7.138	9.266	11.974	15.407
20	1.486	2.191	3.207	4.661	6.727	9.646	13.743	19.461	27.393	38.338
30	1.811	3.243	5.743	10.063	17.449	29.960	50.950	85.850	143.371	237.376
40	2.208	4.801	10.286	21.725	45.259	93.051	188.884	378.721	750.378	1469.772
50	2.692	7.107	18.420	46.902	117.391	289.002	700.233	1670.704	3927.357	9100.438

Factors for Calculating the Future Value of an Annuity of $1 in Arrears | **Table 6-3**

No. of										
					Interest Rate					
Periods	2%	4%	6%	8%	10%	12%	14%	16%	18%	20%
1	1.000	1.000	1.000	1.000	1.000	1.000	1.000	1.000	1.000	1.000
2	2.020	2.040	2.060	2.080	2.100	2.120	2.140	2.160	2.180	2.200
3	3.060	3.122	3.184	3.246	3.310	3.374	3.440	3.506	3.572	3.640
4	4.112	4.246	4.375	4.506	4.641	4.779	4.921	5.066	5.215	5.368
5	5.204	5.416	5.637	5.867	6.105	6.353	6.610	6.877	7.154	7.442
10	10.950	12.006	13.181	14.487	15.937	17.549	19.337	21.321	23.521	25.959
15	17.293	20.024	23.276	27.152	31.772	37.280	43.842	51.660	60.965	72.035
20	24.297	29.778	36.786	45.762	57.275	72.052	91.025	115.380	146.628	186.688
30	40.568	56.085	79.058	113.283	164.494	241.333	356.787	530.312	790.948	1181.882
40	60.402	95.026	154.762	259.057	442.593	767.091	1342.025	2360.757	4163.213	7343.858
50	84.579	152.667	290.336	573.770	1163.909	2400.018	4994.521	10435.649	21813.094	45497.191

that the factor for 10% and four periods is 1.464. This factor is multiplied by the beginning principal to get the future value. The future value of $1,000 at 10% for four periods is $1,464, as shown in the time line illustration.

Future Value of an Annuity

Sometimes a savings or investment pattern involves adding an amount equal to the initial investment on a regular basis. This is called an **annuity.** When the investment is made at the end of each compounding period, a usual practice, the annuity is in arrears. The future value of an annuity is simply the sum of the future value of each individual investment. Table 6-3 presents the future value factors for a range of interest rates and compounding periods for an annuity in arrears. Note that the factor for an annuity in arrears at 10% for two periods is 2.100. This is the future value of an amount invested at the end of the first period after one more period, plus the amount of the investment at the end of the second period. What is the future value of an annuity in arrears of $200 invested at 12% (at the end of each year) for 10 years? How does this compare to the future value of a single amount of $200 invested for 10 years?

Present Value

Whereas future value focuses on the value at some point in the future of an amount invested today, present value focuses on the value today of an amount to be paid or received at some point in the future. Present value is another application of compound interest that is of great significance in accounting and business practice. Organizations and individuals are frequently confronted with the choice of paying for a purchase today or at a later date. Intuition suggests that all other things being equal, it would be better to pay later because in the meantime the cash not spent today could be invested to earn interest. This reflects the fact that money has value over time. Of course other things aren't always equal, and sometimes the choice is between paying one amount—say $1,000—today and a larger amount—say $1,100—a year later. Or in the opposite case, the choice may be between receiving $1,000 today or $1,100 a year from now. Present value analysis is used to determine which of these alternatives is financially preferable.

Present value concepts are well established in financial reporting, having been used traditionally in the valuation of assets and liabilities that characteristically involve far-distant cash flows. In 2000, the Financial Accounting Standards Board extended its Conceptual Framework project to embrace the present value concept more formally as a fundamental accounting measurement technique.[2] Per the FASB,

> The objective of using present value in an accounting measurement is to capture, to the extent possible, the economic difference between sets of estimated future cash flows. Without present value, a $1,000 cash flow due tomorrow and a $1,000 cash flow due in 10 years appear the same. Because present value distinguishes between cash flows that otherwise might appear similar, a measurement based on the present value of estimated future cash flows provides more relevant information than a measurement based on the undiscounted sum of those cash flows.[3]

Present value analysis involves looking at the same compound interest concept from the opposite perspective. Using data in the compound interest table developed earlier, you can say that the present value of $1,464 to be received four years from now, assuming an interest rate of 10% compounded annually, is $1,000. On a time-line representation, the direction of the arrow indicating the time perspective is reversed:

If someone owed you $1,464 to be paid four years from now, and if you were to agree with your debtor that 10% was a fair interest rate for that period, you would both be satisfied to settle the debt for $1,000 today. Alternatively, if you owed $1,464 payable

[2] See FASB,*Statement of Financial Accounting Concepts No. 7,* "Using Cash Flow Information and Present Value in Accounting Measurements" (Stamford, CT, 2000). Copyright © the Financial Accounting Standards Board, High Ridge Park, Stamford, CT 06905, U.S.A. Excerpted with permission. Copies of the complete document are available from the FASB.

[3] FASB, *Statement of Financial Accounting Concepts No. 7,* "Highlights" (Stamford, CT, 2000). The FASB cautions that highlights are best understood in the context of the full statement.

Using Financial Calculators

Most undergraduate and graduate business students will be encouraged by their faculty members to purchase and use a financial calculator, such as the Texas Instruments BAII Plus or the Hewlett-Packard 10BII+ or 12c, to solve present value problems. Such calculators are a viable alternative to using the present value tables provided in this text. If you recently acquired a financial calculator and are having trouble getting started, several online tutorials are available to assist you. A quick Google search for "financial calculators" will yield some interesting results, including a number of proprietary financial calculator models that have been developed to solve a variety of common business problems. Although the use of a financial calculator may make your job as a student easier, it is important to learn the basics of present value analysis in the "old-fashioned" way by referring to present value tables. This will help you appreciate the impact that the selected interest rate, compounding frequency, and number of years have on present value calculations.

Business in
Practice

Understanding Present Value Tables

Take a moment now to glance at Tables 6-4 and 6-5 and learn how they are constructed. Notice that for any given number of periods, the factors shown in the annuity table represent cumulative totals of the factors shown in the present value of $1 table. Check this out by adding together the single amount factors for periods 1, 2, and 3 in the 4% column of Table 6-4 and comparing your result to the annuity factor shown for three periods at 4% in Table 6-5. In both cases, your answer should be 2.7751. Notice also (by scanning across the tables) that for any given number of periods, the higher the discount (interest) rate, the lower the present value. This makes sense when you remember that present values operate in a manner opposite to future values. The higher the interest rate, the greater the future value—and the lower the present value. Now scan down Table 6-4 and notice that for any given interest rate, the present value of $1 decreases as more periods are added. The same effects are also present in Table 6-5 but cannot be visualized because the annuity factors represent cumulative totals; yet for each additional period, a smaller amount is added to the previous annuity factor.

Study
Suggestion

four years from now, both you and your creditor would be satisfied to settle the debt for $1,000 today (still assuming agreement on the 10% interest rate). That is because $1,000 invested at 10% interest compounded annually will grow to $1,464 in four years. Stated differently, the future value of $1,000 at 10% interest in four years is $1,464, and the present value of $1,464 in four years at 10% is $1,000.

Present value analysis involves determining the present amount that is equivalent to an amount to be paid or received in the future, recognizing that money has value over time. The time value of money is represented by the interest that can be earned on money over an investment period. In present value analysis, **discount rate** is a term frequently used for *interest rate*. In our example, the present value of $1,464, discounted at 10% for four years, is $1,000. Thus, the *time value of money* in this example is represented by the $464 in interest that is being charged to the borrower for the use of money over the four-year period.

Present value analysis does not directly recognize the effects of inflation, although inflationary expectations will influence the discount rate used in the present value calculation. Generally, the higher the inflationary expectations, the higher the discount rate used in present value analysis.

Present Value of an Annuity

The preceding example deals with the present value of a *single amount* to be received or paid in the future. Some transactions involve receiving or paying the same amount each period for a number of periods. This sort of receipt or payment pattern is referred to as an *annuity*. The present value of an annuity is simply the sum of the present value of each of the annuity payment amounts.

There are formulas and computer program functions for calculating the present value of a single amount and the present value of an annuity (see Business in Practice—Using Financial Calculators). In all cases, the amount to be received or paid in the future, the discount rate, and the number of years (or other time periods) are used in the present value calculation. Table 6-4 presents factors for calculating the present

Table 6-4   Factors for Calculating the Present Value of $1

No. of Periods	\multicolumn{10}{c}{Discount Rate}
	2%	4%	6%	8%	10%	12%	14%	16%	18%	20%
1	0.980	0.9615	0.9434	0.9259	0.9091	0.8929	0.8772	0.8621	0.8475	0.8333
2	0.961	0.9246	0.8900	0.8573	0.8264	0.7972	0.7695	0.7432	0.7182	0.6944
3	0.942	0.8890	0.8396	0.7938	0.7513	0.7118	0.6750	0.6407	0.6086	0.5787
4	0.924	0.8548	0.7921	0.7350	0.6830	0.6355	0.5921	0.5523	0.5158	0.4823
5	0.906	0.8219	0.7473	0.6806	0.6209	0.5674	0.5194	0.4761	0.4371	0.4019
6	0.888	0.7903	0.7050	0.6302	0.5645	0.5066	0.4556	0.4104	0.3704	0.3349
7	0.871	0.7599	0.6651	0.5835	0.5132	0.4523	0.3996	0.3538	0.3139	0.2791
8	0.853	0.7307	0.6274	0.5403	0.4665	0.4039	0.3506	0.3050	0.2660	0.2326
9	0.837	0.7026	0.5919	0.5002	0.4241	0.3606	0.3075	0.2630	0.2255	0.1938
10	0.820	0.6756	0.5584	0.4632	0.3855	0.3220	0.2697	0.2267	0.1911	0.1615
11	0.804	0.6496	0.5268	0.4289	0.3505	0.2875	0.2366	0.1954	0.1619	0.1346
12	0.788	0.6246	0.4970	0.3971	0.3186	0.2567	0.2076	0.1685	0.1372	0.1122
13	0.773	0.6006	0.4688	0.3677	0.2897	0.2292	0.1821	0.1452	0.1163	0.0935
14	0.758	0.5775	0.4423	0.3405	0.2633	0.2046	0.1597	0.1252	0.0985	0.0779
15	0.743	0.5553	0.4173	0.3152	0.2394	0.1827	0.1401	0.1079	0.0835	0.0649
16	0.728	0.5339	0.3936	0.2919	0.2176	0.1631	0.1229	0.0930	0.0708	0.0541
17	0.714	0.5134	0.3714	0.2703	0.1978	0.1456	0.1078	0.0802	0.0600	0.0451
18	0.700	0.4936	0.3503	0.2502	0.1799	0.1300	0.0946	0.0691	0.0508	0.0376
19	0.686	0.4746	0.3305	0.2317	0.1635	0.1161	0.0829	0.0596	0.0431	0.0313
20	0.673	0.4564	0.3118	0.2145	0.1486	0.1037	0.0728	0.0514	0.0365	0.0261
21	0.660	0.4388	0.2942	0.1987	0.1351	0.0926	0.0638	0.0443	0.0309	0.0217
22	0.647	0.4220	0.2775	0.1839	0.1228	0.0826	0.0560	0.0382	0.0262	0.0181
23	0.634	0.4057	0.2618	0.1703	0.1117	0.0738	0.0491	0.0329	0.0222	0.0151
24	0.622	0.3901	0.2470	0.1577	0.1015	0.0659	0.0431	0.0284	0.0188	0.0126
25	0.610	0.3751	0.2330	0.1460	0.0923	0.0588	0.0378	0.0245	0.0160	0.0105
30	0.552	0.3083	0.1741	0.0994	0.0573	0.0334	0.0196	0.0116	0.0070	0.0042
35	0.500	0.2534	0.1301	0.0676	0.0356	0.0189	0.0102	0.0055	0.0030	0.0017
40	0.453	0.2083	0.0972	0.0460	0.0221	0.0107	0.0053	0.0026	0.0013	0.0007
45	0.410	0.1712	0.0727	0.0313	0.0137	0.0061	0.0027	0.0013	0.0006	0.0003
50	0.372	0.1407	0.0543	0.0213	0.0085	0.0035	0.0014	0.0006	0.0003	0.0001

Factors for Calculating the Present Value of an Annuity of $1   **Table 6-5**

No. of Periods	Discount Rate									
	2%	4%	6%	8%	10%	12%	14%	16%	18%	20%
1	0.980	0.9615	0.9434	0.9259	0.9091	0.8929	0.8772	0.8621	0.8475	0.8333
2	1.942	1.8861	1.8334	1.7833	1.7355	1.6901	1.6467	1.6052	1.5656	1.5278
3	2.884	2.7751	2.6730	2.5771	2.4869	2.4018	2.3216	2.2459	2.1743	2.1065
4	3.808	3.6299	3.4651	3.3121	3.1699	3.0373	2.9137	2.7982	2.6901	2.5887
5	4.713	4.4518	4.2124	3.9927	3.7908	3.6048	3.4331	3.2743	3.1272	2.9906
6	5.601	5.2421	4.9173	4.6229	4.3553	4.1114	3.8887	3.6847	3.4976	3.3255
7	6.472	6.0021	5.5824	5.2064	4.8684	4.5638	4.2883	4.0386	3.8115	3.6046
8	7.325	6.7327	6.2098	5.7466	5.3349	4.9676	4.6389	4.3436	4.0776	3.8372
9	8.162	7.4353	6.8017	6.2469	5.7590	5.3282	4.9464	4.6065	4.3030	4.0310
10	8.983	8.1109	7.3601	6.7101	6.1446	5.6502	5.2161	4.8332	4.4941	4.1925
11	9.787	8.7605	7.8869	7.1390	6.4951	5.9377	5.4527	5.0286	4.6560	4.3271
12	10.575	9.3851	8.3838	7.5361	6.8137	6.1944	5.6603	5.1971	4.7932	4.4392
13	11.348	9.9856	8.8527	7.9038	7.1034	6.4235	5.8424	5.3423	4.9095	4.5327
14	12.106	10.5631	9.2950	8.2442	7.3667	6.6282	6.0021	5.4675	5.0081	4.6106
15	12.849	11.1184	9.7122	8.5595	7.6061	6.8109	6.1422	5.5755	5.0916	4.6755
16	13.578	11.6523	10.1059	8.8514	7.8237	6.9740	6.2651	5.6685	5.1624	4.7296
17	14.292	12.1657	10.4773	9.1216	8.0216	7.1196	6.3729	5.7487	5.2223	4.7746
18	14.992	12.6593	10.8276	9.3719	8.2014	7.2497	6.4674	5.8178	5.2732	4.8122
19	15.678	13.1339	11.1581	9.6036	8.3649	7.3658	6.5504	5.8775	5.3162	4.8435
20	16.351	13.5903	11.4699	9.8181	8.5136	7.4694	6.6231	5.9288	5.3527	4.8696
21	17.011	14.0292	11.7641	10.0168	8.6487	7.5620	6.6870	5.9731	5.3837	4.8913
22	17.658	14.4511	12.0416	10.2007	8.7715	7.6446	6.7429	6.0113	5.4099	4.9094
23	18.292	14.8568	12.3034	10.3711	8.8832	7.7184	6.7921	6.0442	5.4321	4.9245
24	18.914	15.2470	12.5504	10.5288	8.9847	7.7843	6.8351	6.0726	5.4509	4.9371
25	19.523	15.6221	12.7834	10.6748	9.0770	7.8431	6.8729	6.0971	5.4669	4.9476
30	22.396	17.2920	13.7648	11.2578	9.4269	8.0552	7.0027	6.1772	5.5168	4.9789
35	24.999	18.6646	14.4982	11.6546	9.6442	8.1755	7.0700	6.2153	5.5386	4.9915
40	27.355	19.7928	15.0463	11.9246	9.7791	8.2438	7.1050	6.2335	5.5482	4.9966
45	29.490	20.7200	15.4558	12.1084	9.8628	8.2825	7.1232	6.2421	5.5523	4.9986
50	31.424	21.4822	15.7619	12.2335	9.9148	8.3045	7.1327	6.2463	5.5541	4.9995

value of $1 (single amount), and Table 6-5 gives the factors for the present value of an annuity of $1 for several discount rates and number of periods.

To find the present value of any amount, the appropriate factor from the table is multiplied by the amount to be received or paid in the future. Using the data from the initial example just described, we can calculate the present value of $1,464 to be received four years from now, based on a discount rate of 10%:

$1,464 × 0.6830 (from the 10% column, four-period row
of Table 6-4) = $1,000 (rounded)

What is the present value of a lottery prize of $1,000,000, payable in 20 annual installments of $50,000 each, assuming a discount (interest) rate of 12%? Here is the time line representation of this situation:

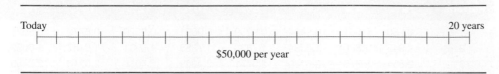

The present value of this annuity is calculated by multiplying the annuity amount ($50,000) by the annuity factor from Table 6-5. The solution is:

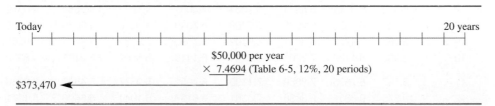

Although the answer of $373,470 shouldn't make the winner feel less fortunate, she certainly has not become an instant millionaire in present value terms. The lottery authority needs to deposit only $373,470 today in an account earning 12% interest to be able to pay the winner $50,000 per year for 20 years beginning a year from now. What is the present value of the same lottery prize assuming that 8% was the appropriate discount rate? What if a 16% interest rate was used? (Take a moment to calculate these amounts.) Imagine how the wife of *The Born Loser* comic strip character must have felt upon learning that he had won a million dollars—payable at $1 per year for a million years! As these examples point out, the present value of future cash flows is directly affected by both the chosen discount rate and the relevant time frame.

Let's look at another example. Assume you have accepted a job from a company willing to pay you a signing bonus, and you must now choose between three alternative payment plans. The plan A bonus is $3,000 payable today. The plan B bonus is $4,000 payable three years from today. The plan C bonus is three annual payments of $1,225 each (an annuity) with the first payment to be made one year from today. Assuming a discount rate of 8%, which bonus should you accept? The solution requires calculation of the present value of each bonus. Here is the timeline approach:

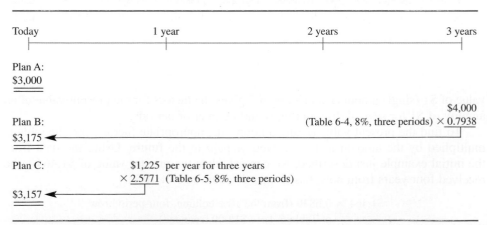

Bonus plan B has the highest present value and for that reason would be the plan selected based on present value analysis.

Impact of Compounding Frequency

The frequency with which interest is compounded affects both future value and present value. You would prefer to have the interest on your savings account compounded monthly, weekly, or even daily, rather than annually, because you will earn more interest the more frequently compounding occurs. This is recognized in present value calculations by converting the annual discount rate to a discount rate per compounding period by dividing the annual rate by the number of compounding periods per year. Likewise, the number of periods is adjusted by multiplying the number of years involved by the number of compounding periods per year. For example, the present value of $1,000 to be received or paid six years from now, at a discount rate of 16% compounded annually, is $410.40 (the factor 0.4104 from the 16% column, six-period row of Table 6-4, multiplied by $1,000). If interest were compounded quarterly, or four times per year, the present value calculation uses the factor from the 4% column (16% per year/four periods per year), and the 24-period row (six years × four periods per year), which is 0.3901. Thus, the present value of $1,000 to be received or paid in six years, compounding interest quarterly, is $390.10. Here is the time-line approach:

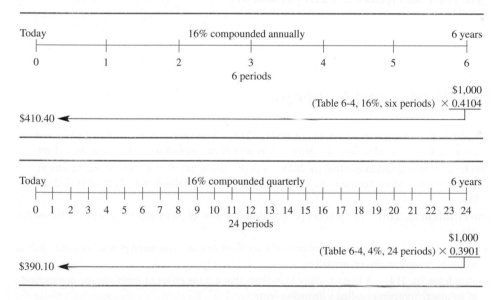

You can make sense of the fact that the present value of a single amount is lower the more frequent the compounding by visualizing what you could do with either $410.40 or $390.10 if you were to receive the amount today rather than receiving $1,000 in six years. Each amount could be invested at 16%, but interest would compound on the $410.40 only once a year, while interest on the $390.10 would compound every three months. Even though you start with different amounts, you'll still have $1,000 after six years. Test your comprehension of this calculation process by verifying that the present value of an annual annuity of $100 for 10 years, discounted at an annual rate of 16%, is $483.32, and that the present value of $50 paid every six months for 10 years, discounted at the same annual rate (which is an 8% semiannual rate), is $490.91. The present value of an annuity is greater the more frequent the compounding because the annuity amount is paid or received sooner than when the compounding period is longer.

Many of these ideas may seem complicated to you now, but your common sense will affirm the results of present value analysis. Remember that $1 in your hands today is worth more than $1 to be received tomorrow or a year from today. This explains why firms are interested in speeding up the collection of accounts receivable and other cash inflows. Of course, the opposite logic applies to cash payments, which explains why firms will defer the payment of accounts payable whenever possible. The prevailing attitude is "We're better off with the cash in our hands than in the hands of our customers or suppliers." Several applications of present value analysis to business transactions will be illustrated in subsequent chapters. By making the initial investment of time now, you will understand these ideas more quickly later.

What Does It Mean? Answers on page 232

9. What does it mean to say that money has value over time?
10. What does it mean to talk about the present value of an amount of money to be received or spent in the future?
11. What does it mean to receive an annuity?

Key Terms and Concepts

Accelerated Cost Recovery System (ACRS) (p. 211) The method prescribed in the Internal Revenue Code for calculating the depreciation deduction; applicable to the years 1981–1986.

accelerated depreciation method (p. 207) A depreciation calculation method that results in greater depreciation expense in the early periods of an asset's life than in the later periods of its life.

amortization (p. 216) The process of spreading the cost of an intangible asset over its useful life.

annuity (p. 223) The receipt or payment of a constant amount over fixed periods of time, such as monthly, semiannually, or annually.

capital lease (p. 214) A lease, usually long-term, that has the effect of financing the acquisition of an asset. Sometimes called a *financing lease.*

capitalizing (p. 203) To record an expenditure as an asset as opposed to expensing the expenditure.

copyright (p. 217) An amortizable intangible asset represented by the legally granted protection against unauthorized copying of a creative work.

declining-balance depreciation method (p. 208) An accelerated depreciation method in which the declining net book value of the asset is multiplied by a constant rate.

depletion (p. 220) The accounting process recognizing that the cost of a natural resource asset is used up as the natural resource is consumed.

discount rate (p. 225) The interest rate used in a present value calculation.

expensing (p. 203) To record an expenditure as an expense, as opposed to capitalizing the expenditure.

future value (p. 222)   The amount that a present investment will be worth at some point in the future, assuming a specified interest rate and the reinvestment of interest in each period that it is earned.

goodwill (p. 218)   A nonamortizable intangible asset arising from the purchase of a business for more than the fair value of the net assets acquired. Goodwill is the present value of the expected earnings of the acquired business in excess of the earnings that would represent an average return on investment, discounted at the investor's required rate of return for the expected duration of the excess earnings.

intangible asset (p. 216)   A long-lived asset represented by a contractual right, or an asset that is not physically identifiable.

leasehold improvement (p. 217)   An amortizable intangible asset represented by the cost of improvements made to a leasehold by the lessee.

Modified Accelerated Cost Recovery System (MACRS) (p. 211)   The method prescribed in the Internal Revenue Code for calculating the depreciation deduction; applicable to years after 1986.

net book value (p. 206)   The difference between the cost of an asset and the accumulated depreciation related to the asset. Sometimes called *carrying value.*

operating lease (p. 213)   A lease that does not involve any attributes of ownership.

patent (p. 217)   An amortizable intangible asset represented by a government-sanctioned monopoly over the use of a product or process.

present value (p. 214)   The value now of an amount to be received or paid at some future date, recognizing an interest (or discount) rate for the period from the present to the future date.

proceeds (p. 213)   The amount of cash (or equivalent value) received in a transaction.

straight-line depreciation method (p. 207)   Calculation of periodic depreciation expense by dividing the amount to be depreciated by the number of periods over which the asset is to be depreciated.

trademark (p. 217)   An amortizable intangible asset represented by a right to the exclusive use of an identifying mark.

units-of-production depreciation method (p. 208)   A depreciation method based on periodic use and life expressed in terms of asset utilization.

ANSWERS TO What Does It Mean?

1. It means that the expenditure is recorded as an asset rather than an expense. If the asset is a depreciable asset, depreciation expense will be recognized over the useful life—to the entity—of the asset.

2. It means that the assets are reported at their original cost, less accumulated depreciation, if applicable. These net book values are likely to be less than fair values.

3. It means that cash is not paid out for depreciation expense. Depreciation expense results from spreading the cost of an asset to expense over the useful life—to the entity—of the asset. Cash is reduced when the asset is purchased or when payments are made on a loan that was obtained when the asset was purchased.

4. It means that relative to straight-line depreciation, more depreciation expense is recognized in the early years of an asset's life and less is recognized in the later years of an asset's life.

5. It means that because depreciation expense is deducted to arrive at taxable income, income taxes are lowered by the tax rate multiplied by the amount of depreciation expense claimed for income tax purposes.

6. It means that, relative to a practice of capitalizing these expenditures, taxable income of the current year will be lower and less time will be spent making depreciation expense calculations than if the expenditures were capitalized.

7. It means that rather than paying cash for the asset when it is acquired, or instead of borrowing funds to pay for the asset, the entity agrees to make payments to the lessor, or a finance company, of specified amounts over a specified period. The agreement is called a lease, but it is really an installment loan agreement.

8. It means that the acquiring firm paid more than the fair value of the net assets acquired because of the potential for earning an above-average return on its investment.

9. It means that money could be invested to earn a return—as interest income—if it were invested for a period of time.

10. It means that the future amount has a value today that is equal to the amount that would have to be invested at a given rate of return to grow to the future amount. Present value is less than future value.

11. It means that the same amount will be received each period for a number of periods. For example, large lottery winnings are frequently received as an annuity—that is, equal amounts over 20 years.

Self-Study Material

Visit the text website at www.mhhe.com/marshall10e to take an online self-study quiz for this chapter.

Matching Following are a number of the key terms and concepts introduced in the chapter, along with a list of corresponding definitions. Match the appropriate letter for the key term or concept to each definition provided (items 1–15). Note that not all key terms and concepts will be used. Answers are provided at the end of this chapter.

a.	Capitalize	k.	Present value
b.	Depletion	l.	Discount rate
c.	Net book value	m.	Annuity
d.	Depreciation	n.	Intangible asset
e.	Units-of-production depreciation	o.	Leasehold
f.	Straight-line depreciation	p.	Patent
g.	Declining-balance depreciation	q.	Trademark
h.	Modified Accelerated Cost Recovery System (MACRS)	r.	Goodwill
		s.	Amortization
i.	Operating lease	t.	Leasehold improvement
j.	Capital lease	u.	Copyright

____ **1.** The receipt or payment of a constant amount over some period of time.

____ **2.** The process of spreading the cost of an intangible asset over its useful life.

____ **3.** An intangible asset represented by the legally granted protection against unauthorized copying of a creative work.

_____ **4.** The value now of an amount to be received or paid at some future point, recognizing an interest (or discount) rate for the period.

_____ **5.** An accelerated depreciation method in which the amount to be depreciated is multiplied by a rate that declines each year.

_____ **6.** The accounting process recognizing that the cost of a natural resource asset is used up as the natural resource is consumed.

_____ **7.** An intangible asset arising from the purchase of a business for more than the fair value of the net assets acquired.

_____ **8.** A depreciation method based on periodic use and life expressed in terms of asset utilization.

_____ **9.** An intangible asset represented by the right to use property that is not owned.

_____**10.** The difference between the cost of an asset and the accumulated depreciation related to the asset.

_____**11.** An intangible asset represented by a government-sanctioned monopoly over the use of a product or process.

_____**12.** The interest rate used in a present value calculation.

_____**13.** An accelerated depreciation method prescribed in the Internal Revenue Code and used for income tax purposes.

_____**14.** A lease that has the effect of financing the acquisition of an asset; a "financing lease."

_____**15.** Calculation of periodic depreciation expense by dividing the amount to be depreciated by the number of periods over which the asset is to be depreciated.

Multiple Choice For each of the following questions, circle the best response. Answers are provided at the end of this chapter.

1. The Buildings account should be increased (debited) for the purchase or construction price of the building, plus

    a. any ordinary and necessary costs incurred to get the building ready for use.

    b. any interest costs incurred on amounts borrowed to finance the building during its construction.

    c. any installation and inspection costs incurred to get the building ready for use.

    d. any material, labor, and overhead costs incurred by an entity in the construction of its own building.

    e. all of the above.

2. A firm wishing to minimize the amount reported for taxable income and maximize the amount reported as net income in the year in which a new long-term asset is placed in service would

    a. use straight-line depreciation for both book and tax purposes.

    b. use an accelerated depreciation method for both book and tax purposes.

    c. use straight-line depreciation on the books and an accelerated method for tax purposes.

    d. use an accelerated depreciation method on the books and straight-line depreciation for tax purposes.

3. The entry to record depreciation on long-term assets

    a. decreases total assets and increases net income.

    b. decreases current assets and increases net income.

    c. decreases total assets and decreases net income.

    d. increases total assets and increases net income.

    e. increases total assets and decreases net income.

4. Which depreciation method results in equal depreciation expense amounts for each year of an asset's useful life?

    a. Units-of-production.

    b. Straight-line.

    c. Double-declining-balance.

    d. MACRS.

5. Expenditures incurred on long-term assets after they have been placed in service are either capitalized or expensed. Which of the following statements concerning such expenditures is true?

    a. Capitalized amounts represent future economic benefits that extend beyond one year.

    b. Expensed amounts benefit no more than three future years.

    c. Capitalized amounts decrease net income for the entire amount in the year of the expenditure.

    d. Expensed amounts are added to the net book value of the related asset.

    e. Immaterial amounts should always be capitalized.

6. Depreciation on assets such as equipment and machinery is recorded because of the

    a. cost principle.

    b. matching principle.

    c. unit of measurement assumption.

    d. conservatism constraint.

    e. going concern concept.

7. All of the following are examples of intangible assets *except*

    a. leaseholds.

    b. goodwill.

    c. trademarks.

    d. oil reserves.

    e. patents.

8. With some simple adjustments, an annuity table for present values can be used to compute the present value of a series of future payments, even if

    a. the amounts involved vary from year to year.

    b. the payment periods are quarterly rather than yearly.

    c. the payment periods are interrupted for a few years and later continued.

    d. the amounts involved are paid at different times during different years.

9. The lessee's entry to record a periodic cash lease payment on a capital lease results in

    a. an increase in total liabilities and an increase in net income.

    b. an increase in total liabilities and a decrease in net income.

     c. a decrease in total liabilities and a decrease in net income.

     d. a decrease in total liabilities and an increase in net income.

10. If you were to win $1,000,000 in a lottery today, which of the following payment patterns would you find most attractive?

     a. $1 per year for 1 million years.

     b. $200,000 per year for 5 years.

     c. $50,000 per year for 20 years.

     d. $25,000 per quarter for 10 years.

     e. $2,000 per week for 500 weeks.

Mini-Exercises

All applicable Mini-Exercises are available with McGraw-Hill's *Connect™ Accounting*.

Basket purchase allocation Minott Jewelers, Ltd., purchased store fixtures, display cases, and a maximum-security commercial safe for a lump-sum price of $14,000 from a bankrupt competitor. Appraised values were as follows: store fixtures, $6,000; display cases, $9,000; commercial safe, $5,000.

Mini-Exercise 6.1
LO 1

Required:
What cost should be recorded for the commercial safe?

Capitalizing versus expensing Riley Holdings Corp. incurred the following expenditures: $3,100 cost to replace the transmission in a company-owned vehicle; $16,400 cost of annual property insurance on the company's production facilities; $13,800 cost to develop and register a design patent; $62,200 cost to add a security and monitoring system to the company's distribution center; $400 cost to repair paint damage on a company-owned vehicle caused by normal wear and tear.

Mini-Exercise 6.2
LO 2

Required:
Which, if any, of these expenditures should be capitalized?

Depreciation calculation methods Gandolfi Construction Co. purchased a used CAT 336DL earth mover at a cost of $325,000 in January 2013. The company's estimated useful life of this heavy equipment is 10 years, and the estimated salvage value is $75,000.

Mini-Exercise 6.3
LO 3

Required:

a. Using straight-line depreciation, calculate the depreciation expense to be recognized for 2013, the first year of the equipment's life, and calculate the equipment's net book value at December 31, 2015, after the third year of the equipment's life.

b. Using declining-balance depreciation at twice the straight-line rate, calculate the depreciation expense for the third year of the equipment's life.

Effect of depreciation on ROI Refer to the information presented in Mini-Exercise 6.3. Assume that Gandolfi Construction Co. calculated depreciation expense for the CAT 336DL earth mover on the straight-line method and reported $480,000 of net income for the year ended December 31, 2013. The company's average total assets for 2013 were $3,000,000.

Mini-Exercise 6.4
LO 3

Required:

a. Calculate Gandolfi's ROI for the year ended December 31, 2013.

b. Calculate what Gandolfi's ROI would have been for the year ended December 31, 2013, had the company used the double-declining-balance depreciation method for the CAT 336DL earth mover.

Mini-Exercise
6.5
LO 9

Goodwill Raider Co. recently acquired all of Lost Arc, Inc.'s net assets in a business acquisition. The cash purchase price was $6.3 million. Lost Arc, Inc.'s assets and liabilities had the following appraised values immediately prior to the acquisition: land, $1.2 million; buildings, $2.9 million; inventory, $1.7 million; long-term notes payable, for which Raider Co. assumes payment responsibilities, $1.0 million.

Required:

How much goodwill will result from this transaction?

Mini-Exercise
6.6
LO 10

Present value calculations Congratulations! You have just won $500 million in the largest Powerball jackpot payoff ever! You will receive payments of $25,000,000 per year for the next 20 years.

Required:

Using a present value table, your calculator, or a computer program present value function, calculate the present value of your lottery winnings, assuming an interest rate of 8%.

connect
|ACCOUNTING

Exercises

All applicable Exercises are available with McGraw-Hill's *Connect™ Accounting.*

Exercise 6.7
LO 1

Basket purchase allocation Dorsey Co. has expanded its operations by purchasing a parcel of land with a building on it from Bibb Co. for $90,000. The appraised value of the land is $20,000, and the appraised value of the building is $80,000.

Required:

a. Assuming that the building is to be used in Dorsey Co.'s business activities, what cost should be recorded for the land?

b. Explain why, for income tax purposes, management of Dorsey Co. would want as little of the purchase price as possible allocated to land.

c. Assuming that the building is razed at a cost of $10,000 so the land can be used for employee parking, what cost should Dorsey Co. record for the land?

d. Explain why Dorsey Co. allocated the cost of assets acquired based on appraised values at the purchase date rather than on the original cost of the land and building to Bibb Co.

Exercise 6.8
LO 1

Basket purchase allocation Crow Co. purchased some of the machinery of Hare, Inc., a bankrupt competitor, at a liquidation sale for a total cost of $50,400. Crow's cost of moving and installing the machinery totaled $4,800. The following data are available:

Item	Hare's Net Book Value on the Date of Sale	List Price of Same Item If New	Appraiser's Estimate of Fair Value
Punch press	$30,240	$54,000	$36,000
Lathe	24,192	27,000	18,000
Welder	6,048	9,000	6,000

Required:

a. Calculate the amount that should be recorded by Crow Co. as the cost of each piece of equipment.

b. Which of the following alternatives should be used as the depreciable life for Crow Co.'s depreciation calculation? Explain your answer.

> The remaining useful life to Hare, Inc.
>
> The life of a new machine.
>
> The useful life of the asset to Crow Co.

Capitalizing versus expensing For each of the following expenditures, indicate the type of account (asset or expense) in which the expenditure should be recorded. Explain your answers.

Exercise 6.9
LO 2

a. $15,000 annual cost of routine repair and maintenance expenditures for a fleet of delivery vehicles.

b. $6,000,000 cost to develop a coal mine, from which an estimated 1 million tons of coal can be extracted.

c. $124,000 cost to replace the roof on a building.

d. $70,000 cost of a radio and television advertising campaign to introduce a new product line.

e. $4,000 cost of grading and leveling land so that a building can be constructed.

Capitalizing versus expensing For each of the following expenditures, indicate the type of account (asset or expense) in which the expenditure should be recorded. Explain your answers.

Exercise 6.10
LO 2

a. $800 for repairing damage that resulted from the careless unloading of a new machine.

b. $7,200 cost of designing and registering a trademark.

c. $3,700 in legal fees incurred to perform a title search for the acquisition of land.

d. $1,200 cost of patching a leak in the roof of a building.

e. $95,000 cost of salaries paid to the research and development staff.

Effect of depreciation on ROI Alpha, Inc., and Beta Co. are sheet metal processors that supply component parts for consumer product manufacturers. Alpha, Inc., has been in business since 1980 and is operating in its original plant facilities. Much of its equipment was acquired in the 1980s. Beta Co. was started two years ago and acquired its building and equipment then. Each firm has about the same sales revenue, and material and labor costs are about the same for each firm. What would you expect Alpha's ROI to be relative to the ROI of Beta Co.? Explain your answer. What are the implications of this ROI difference for a firm seeking to enter an established industry?

Exercise 6.11
LO 3

Exercise 6.12

LO 3

Financial statement effects of depreciation—straight-line versus acceler-ated methods Assume that a company chooses an accelerated method of calculating depreciation expense for financial statement reporting purposes for an asset with a five-year life.

Required:

State the effect (higher, lower, no effect) of accelerated depreciation relative to straight-line depreciation on

a. Depreciation expense in the first year.

b. The asset's net book value after two years.

c. Cash flows from operations (excluding income taxes).

Exercise 6.13

LO 3

Depreciation calculation methods Millco, Inc., acquired a machine that cost $400,000 early in 2013. The machine is expected to last for eight years, and its estimated salvage value at the end of its life is $60,000.

Required:

a. Using straight-line depreciation, calculate the depreciation expense to be recognized in the first year of the machine's life and calculate the accumulated depreciation after the fifth year of the machine's life.

b. Using declining-balance depreciation at twice the straight-line rate, calculate the depreciation expense for the third year of the machine's life.

c. What will be the net book value of the machine at the end of its eighth year of use before it is disposed of, under each depreciation method?

Exercise 6.14

LO 3

eXcel

Depreciation calculation methods Kleener Co. acquired a new delivery truck at the beginning of its current fiscal year. The truck cost $52,000 and has an estimated useful life of four years and an estimated salvage value of $8,000.

Required:

a. Calculate depreciation expense for each year of the truck's life using
   1. Straight-line depreciation.
   2. Double-declining-balance depreciation.

b. Calculate the truck's net book value at the end of its third year of use under each depreciation method.

c. Assume that Kleener Co. had no more use for the truck after the end of the third year and that at the beginning of the fourth year it had an offer from a buyer who was willing to pay $12,400 for the truck. Should the depreciation method used by Kleener Co. affect the decision to sell the truck?

Exercise 6.15

LO 10

Present value calculations Using a present value table, your calculator, or a computer program present value function, calculate the present value of

a. A car down payment of $3,000 that will be required in two years, assuming an interest rate of 10%.

b. A lottery prize of $6 million to be paid at the rate of $300,000 per year for 20 years, assuming an interest rate of 10%.

c. The same annual amount as in part **b**, but assuming an interest rate of 14%.

d. A capital lease obligation that calls for the payment of $8,000 per year for 10 years, assuming a discount rate of 8%.

Present value calculations—effects of compounding frequency, discount rates, and time periods Using a present value table, your calculator, or a computer program present value function, verify that the present value of $100,000 to be received in five years at an interest rate of 16%, compounded annually, is $47,610. Calculate the present value of $100,000 for each of the following items (parts **a–f**) using these facts, except

Exercise 6.16
LO 10

a.   Interest is compounded semiannually.

b.   Interest is compounded quarterly.

c.   A discount rate of 12% is used.

d.   A discount rate of 20% is used.

e.   The cash will be received in three years.

f.   The cash will be received in seven years.

Goodwill effect on ROI Assume that fast-food restaurants generally provide an ROI of 15%, but that such a restaurant near a college campus has an ROI of 18% because its relatively large volume of business generates an above-average turnover (sales/assets). The replacement value of the restaurant's plant and equipment is $200,000. If you were to invest that amount in a restaurant elsewhere in town, you could expect a 15% ROI.

Exercise 6.17
LO 9

Required:

a.   Would you be willing to pay more than $200,000 for the restaurant near the campus? Explain your answer.

b.   If you purchased the restaurant near the campus for $240,000 and the fair value of the assets you acquired was $200,000, what balance sheet accounts would be used to record the cost of the restaurant?

Goodwill—effect on ROI and operating income Goodwill arises when one firm acquires the net assets of another firm and pays more for those net assets than their current fair value. Suppose that Target Co. had operating income of $180,000 and net assets with a fair value of $600,000. Takeover Co. pays $900,000 for Target Co.'s net assets and business activities.

Exercise 6.18
LO 9

Required:

a.   How much goodwill will result from this transaction?

b.   Calculate the ROI for Target Co. based on its present operating income and the fair value of its net assets.

c.   Calculate the ROI that Takeover Co. will earn if the operating income of the acquired net assets continues to be $180,000.

d.   What reasons can you think of to explain why Takeover Co. is willing to pay $300,000 more than fair value for the net assets acquired from Target Co.?

Transaction analysis—various accounts Prepare an answer sheet with the column headings that follow. For each of the following transactions or adjustments, indicate the effect of the transaction or adjustment on assets, liabilities, and net income by entering for each account affected the account name and amount and indicating whether it is an addition (+) or a subtraction (−). Transaction **a** has been done as an

Exercise 6.19
LO 6, 8, 9

illustration. Net income is *not* affected by every transaction. In some cases, only one column may be affected because all of the specific accounts affected by the transaction are included in that category.

		Assets	Liabilities	Net Income
a.	Recorded $200 of depreciation expense.	Accumulated Depreciation −200		Depreciation Expense −200

b. Sold land that had originally cost $9,000 for $14,000 in cash.

c. Acquired a new machine under a capital lease. The present value of future lease payments, discounted at 10%, was $12,000.

d. Recorded the first annual payment of $2,000 for the leased machine (in part **c**).

e. Recorded a $6,000 payment for the cost of developing and registering a trademark.

f. Recognized periodic amortization for the trademark (in part **e**) using a 40-year useful life.

g. Sold used production equipment for $16,000 in cash. The equipment originally cost $40,000, and the accumulated depreciation account has an unadjusted balance of $22,000. It was determined that a $1,000 year-to-date depreciation entry must be recorded before the sale transaction can be recorded. Record the adjustment and the sale.

Exercise 6.20

LO 3, 4, 6, 8

Transaction analysis—various accounts Prepare an answer sheet with the following column headings. For each of the following transactions or adjustments, indicate the effect of the transaction or adjustment on assets, liabilities, and net income by entering for each account affected the account name and amount and indicating whether it is an addition (+) or a subtraction (−). Transaction **a** has been done as an illustration. Net income is *not* affected by every transaction. In some cases, only one column may be affected because all of the specific accounts affected by the transaction are included in that category.

		Assets	Liabilities	Net Income
a.	Recorded $200 of depreciation expense.	Accumulated Depreciation −200		Depreciation Expense −200

b. Sold land that had originally cost $39,000 for $34,200 in cash.

c. Recorded a $204,000 payment for the cost of developing and registering a patent.

d. Recognized periodic amortization for the patent (in part **c**) using the maximum statutory useful life.

e. Capitalized $9,600 of cash expenditures made to extend the useful life of production equipment.

f. Expensed $5,400 of cash expenditures incurred for routine maintenance of production equipment.

g. Sold a used machine for $27,000 in cash. The machine originally cost $90,000 and had been depreciated for the first two years of its five-year useful life using the double-declining-balance method. *(Hint: You must compute the balance of the accumulated depreciation account before you can record the sale.)*

h. Purchased a business for $960,000 in cash. The fair values of the net assets acquired were as follows: Land, $120,000; Buildings, $600,000; Equipment, $300,000; and Long-Term Debt, $210,000.

Problems

All applicable Problems are available with McGraw-Hill's *Connect™ Accounting*.

Capitalizing versus expensing—effect on ROI and operating income During the first month of its current fiscal year, Green Co. incurred repair costs of $20,000 on a machine that had five years of remaining depreciable life. The repair cost was inappropriately capitalized. Green Co. reported operating income of $160,000 for the current year.

Problem 6.21
LO 2, 4

Required:

a. Assuming that Green Co. took a full year's straight-line depreciation expense in the current year, calculate the operating income that should have been reported for the current year.

b. Assume that Green Co.'s total assets at the end of the prior year and at the end of the current year were $940,000 and $1,020,000, respectively. Calculate ROI (based on operating income) for the current year using the originally reported data and then using corrected data.

c. Explain the effect on ROI of subsequent years if the error is not corrected.

Capitalizing versus expensing—effect on ROI Early in January 2013, Tellco, Inc., acquired a new machine and incurred $300,000 of interest, installation, and overhead costs that should have been capitalized but were expensed. The company earned net operating income of $3,000,000 on average total assets of $24,000,000 for 2013. Assume that the total cost of the new machine will be depreciated over 10 years using the straight-line method.

Problem 6.22
LO 2, 4

Required:

a. Calculate the ROI for Tellco, Inc., for 2013.

b. Calculate the ROI for Tellco, Inc., for 2013, assuming that the $300,000 had been capitalized and depreciated over 10 years using the straight-line method. *(Hint: There is an effect on net operating income and average assets.)*

c. Given your answers to **a** and **b**, why would the company want to account for this expenditure as an expense?

d. Assuming that the $300,000 is capitalized, what will be the effect on ROI for 2014 and subsequent years, compared to expensing the interest, installation, and overhead costs in 2013? Explain your answer.

Depreciation calculation methods—partial year Freedom Co. purchased a new machine on July 2, 2013, at a total installed cost of $44,000. The machine has an estimated life of five years and an estimated salvage value of $6,000.

Problem 6.23
LO 3

Required:

a. Calculate the depreciation expense for each year of the *asset's life* using:
1. Straight-line depreciation.
2. Double-declining-balance depreciation.
3. 150% declining-balance depreciation.

b. How much depreciation expense should be recorded by Freedom Co. for its fiscal year ended December 31, 2013, under each of the three methods? *(Note: The machine will have been used for one-half of its first year of life.)*

c. Calculate the accumulated depreciation and net book value of the machine at December 31, 2014, under each of the three methods.

Problem 6.24

LO 3

Partial-year depreciation calculations—straight-line and double-declining-balance methods Porter, Inc., acquired a machine that cost $360,000 on October 1, 2013. The machine is expected to have a four-year useful life and an estimated salvage value of $40,000 at the end of its life. Porter, Inc., uses the calendar year for financial reporting. Depreciation expense for one-fourth of a year was recorded in 2013.

Required:

a. Using the straight-line depreciation method, calculate the depreciation expense to be recognized in the income statement for the year ended December 31, 2015, and the balance of the Accumulated Depreciation account as of December 31, 2015. *(Note: This is the third calendar year in which the asset has been used.)*

b. Using the double-declining-balance depreciation method, calculate the depreciation expense for the year ended December 31, 2015, and the net book value of the machine at that date.

Problem 6.25

LO 3

Identify depreciation methods used Grove Co. acquired a production machine on January 1, 2013, at a cost of $240,000. The machine is expected to have a four-year useful life, with a salvage value of $40,000. The machine is capable of producing 50,000 units of product in its lifetime. Actual production was as follows: 11,000 units in 2013; 16,000 units in 2014; 14,000 units in 2015; and 9,000 units in 2016.

Following is the comparative balance sheet presentation of the *net book value* of the production machine at December 31 for each year of the asset's life, using three alternative depreciation methods (items **a–c**):

Production Machine, Net of Accumulated Depreciation

Depreciation Method?	At December 31			
	2016	2015	2014	2013
a. _____	40,000	76,000	132,000	196,000
b. _____	40,000	40,000	60,000	120,000
c. _____	40,000	90,000	140,000	190,000

Required:

Identify the depreciation method used for each of the preceding comparative balance sheet presentations (items **a–c**). If a declining-balance method is used, be sure to indicate the percentage (150% or 200%). *(Hint: Read the balance sheet from right to left to determine how much has been depreciated each year. Remember that December 31, 2013, is the end of the first year.)*

Identify depreciation methods used Moyle Co. acquired a machine on January 1, 2013, at a cost of $800,000. The machine is expected to have a five-year useful life, with a salvage value of $50,000. The machine is capable of producing 300,000 units of product in its lifetime. Actual production was as follows: 60,000 units in 2013; 40,000 units in 2014; 80,000 units in 2015; 50,000 units in 2016; and 70,000 units in 2017.

Problem 6.26
LO 3

Required:

Identify the depreciation method that would result in each of the following annual credit amount patterns to accumulated depreciation. If a declining-balance method is used, indicate the percentage (150% or 200%). *(Hint: What do the amounts shown for each year represent?)*

a.

Accumulated Depreciation	
320,000	12/31/13
192,000	12/31/14
115,200	12/31/15
69,120	12/31/16
41,472	12/31/17

c.

Accumulated Depreciation	
150,000	12/31/13
150,000	12/31/14
150,000	12/31/15
150,000	12/31/16
150,000	12/31/17

b.

Accumulated Depreciation	
150,000	12/31/13
100,000	12/31/14
200,000	12/31/15
125,000	12/31/16
175,000	12/31/17

d.

Accumulated Depreciation	
240,000	12/31/13
168,000	12/31/14
117,600	12/31/15
82,320	12/31/16
57,624	12/31/17

Determine depreciation method used and date of asset acquisition; record disposal of asset The balance sheets of Tully Corp. showed the following at December 31, 2014, and 2013:

Problem 6.27
LO 3, 6

	December 31, 2014	December 31, 2013
Machine, less accumulated depreciation of $80,000 at December 31, 2014, and $50,000 at December 31, 2013.	$60,000	$90,000

Required:

a. If there have not been any purchases, sales, or other transactions affecting this machine account since the machine was first acquired, what is the amount of depreciation expense for 2014?

b. Assume the same facts as in part **a,** and assume that the estimated useful life of the machine is four years and the estimated salvage value is $20,000. Determine

    1. What the original cost of the machine was.

    2. What depreciation method is apparently being used. Explain your answer.

    3. When the machine was acquired.

c. Assume that the machine is sold on December 31, 2014, for $47,200. Use the horizontal model (or write the journal entry) to show the effect of the sale of the machine.

Problem 6.28
LO 3, 6

Determine depreciation method used and date of asset acquisition; record disposal of asset
The balance sheets of HiROE, Inc., showed the following at December 31, 2014, and 2013:

	December 31, 2014	December 31, 2013
Machine, less accumulated depreciation of $425,250 at December 31, 2014, and $303,750 at December 31, 2013.	$546,750	$668,250

Required:

a. If there have not been any purchases, sales, or other transactions affecting this equipment account since the equipment was first acquired, what is the amount of the depreciation expense for 2014?

b. Assume the same facts as in part **a,** and assume that the estimated useful life of the equipment to HiROE, Inc., is eight years and that there is no estimated salvage value. Determine:

    1. What the original cost of the equipment was.

    2. What depreciation method is apparently being used. Explain your answer.

    3. When the equipment was acquired.

c. Assume that this equipment account represents the cost of 10 identical machines. Calculate the gain or loss on the sale of one of the machines on January 2, 2015, for $60,750. Use the horizontal model (or write the journal entry) to show the effect of the sale of the machine.

Problem 6.29
LO 7, 8, 10

Accounting for capital leases
On January 1, 2013, Carey, Inc., entered into a noncancelable lease agreement, agreeing to pay $3,500 at the end of each year for four years to acquire a new computer system having a market value of $10,200. The expected useful life of the computer system is also four years, and the computer will be depreciated on a straight-line basis with no salvage value. The interest rate used by the lessor to determine the annual payments was 14%. Under the terms of the lease, Carey, Inc., has an option to purchase the computer for $1 on January 1, 2017.

Required:

a. Explain why Carey, Inc., should account for this lease as a capital lease rather than an operating lease. *(Hint: Determine which of the four criteria for capitalizing a lease have been met.)*

b. Show in a horizontal model or write the entry that Carey, Inc., should make on January 1, 2013. Round your answer to the nearest $10. *(Hint: First determine the present value of future lease payments using Table 6-5.)*

c. Show in a horizontal model or write the entry that Carey, Inc., should make on December 31, 2013, to record the first annual lease payment of $3,500. Do not round your answers. *(Hint: Based on your answer to part b, determine the appropriate amounts for interest and principal.)*

d. What expenses (include amounts) should be recognized for this lease on the income statement for the year ended December 31, 2013?

e. Explain why the accounting for an asset acquired under a capital lease isn't really any different than the accounting for an asset that was purchased with money borrowed on a long-term loan.

Accounting for capital leases versus purchased assets Ambrose Co. has the option of purchasing a new delivery truck for $42,300 in cash or leasing the truck for $9,150 per year, payable at the end of each year for six years. The truck also has a useful life of six years and will be depreciated on a straight-line basis with no salvage value. The interest rate used by the lessor to determine the annual payments was 8%.

Problem 6.30
LO 7, 8, 10

Required:

a. Assume that Ambrose Co. purchased the delivery truck and signed a six-year, 8% note payable for $42,300 in satisfaction of the purchase price. Show in a horizontal model or write the entry that Ambrose should make to record the purchase transaction.

b. Assume instead that Ambrose Co. agreed to the terms of the lease. Show in a horizontal model or write the entry that Ambrose should make to record the capital lease transaction. Round your answer up to the nearest $1. *(Hint: First determine the present value of future lease payments using Table 6-5.)*

c. Show in a horizontal model or write the entry that Ambrose Co. should make at the end of the year to record the first annual lease payment of $9,150. Do not round your answers.*(Hint: Based on your answer to part b, determine the appropriate amounts for interest and principal.)*

d. What expenses (include amounts) should Ambrose Co. recognize on the income statement for the first year of the lease?

e. How much would the annual payments be for the note payable signed by Ambrose Co. in part **a**?*(Hint: Use the present value of an annuity factor from Table 6-5.)*

Present value calculation—capital lease Renter Co. acquired the use of a machine by agreeing to pay the manufacturer of the machine $1,500 per year for 10 years. At the time the lease was signed, the interest rate for a 10-year loan was 12%.

Problem 6.31
LO 8, 10

Required:

a. Use the appropriate factor from Table 6-5 to calculate the amount that Renter Co. could have paid at the beginning of the lease to buy the machine outright.

b. What causes the difference between the amount you calculated in part **a** and the total of $15,000 ($1,500 per year for 10 years) that Renter Co. will pay under the terms of the lease?

c. What is the appropriate amount of cost to be reported in Renter Co.'s balance sheet (at the time the lease was signed) with respect to this asset?

Problem 6.32

LO 10

eXcel

Present value calculations Using a present value table, your calculator, or a computer program present value function, answer the following questions:

Required:

a. What is the present value of nine annual cash payments of $12,000, to be paid at the end of each year using an interest rate of 6%?

b. What is the present value of $45,000 to be paid at the end of 20 years, using an interest rate of 18%?

c. How much cash must be deposited in a savings account as a single amount in order to accumulate $900,000 at the end of 12 years, assuming that the account will earn 10% interest?

d. How much cash must be deposited in a savings account (as a single amount) in order to accumulate $150,000 at the end of seven years, assuming that the account will earn 12% interest?

e. Assume that a machine was purchased for $180,000. Cash of $60,000 was paid, and a four-year, 8% note payable was signed for the balance.

   1. Use the horizontal model, or write the journal entry, to show the purchase of the machine as described.

   2. How much is the equal annual payment of principal and interest due at the end of each year? Round your answer to the nearest $1.

   3. What is the total amount of interest expense that will be reported over the life of the note? Round your answer to the nearest $1.

   4. Use the horizontal model, or write the journal entries, to show the equal annual payments of principal and interest due at the end of each year.

connect
|ACCOUNTING

Cases

All applicable Cases are available with McGraw-Hill's *Connect*™ *Accounting.*

Case 6.33

LO 1

Focus company—property, plant, and equipment disclosures In Exercise 1.1, you were asked to obtain the most recent annual report of a company that you were interested in reviewing throughout this term.

Required:

Please review the note disclosures provided in your focus company's annual report and discuss what you've learned about how your company's

a. Property, plant, and equipment is

   1. Depreciated.

   2. Accounted for and presented.

b. Other noncurrent assets are described and reported.

Financial statement effects of depreciation methods Answer the following questions using data from the Campbell Soup Company annual report in the appendix:

Required:

a. Find the discussion of Property, Plant, and Equipment and depreciation methods used by Campbell's on page 715. Explain why the particular method is used for the purpose described. What method do you think the company uses for income tax purposes?

b. Calculate the ratio of the depreciation and amortization expense for 2011 reported on page 713 in the Consolidated Statements of Cash Flows to the total cost (*not* net book value) of plant assets reported in the schedule shown on page 747.

c. Based on the ratio calculated in part **b** and the depreciation method being used by Campbell's, what is the average useful life being used for its depreciation calculation?

d. Assume that the use of an accelerated depreciation method would have resulted in 25% more accumulated depreciation than reported at July 31, 2011, and that Campbell's Retained Earnings account would have been affected by the entire difference. By what percentage would this have reduced the retained earnings amount reported at July 31, 2011?

Capstone analytical review of Chapters 5–6. Analyzing accounts receivable, property, plant, and equipment, and other related accounts (*Note: Please refer to Case 4.30 on pages 145–146 for the financial statement data needed for the analysis of this case. You should also review the solution to Case 4.30, provided by your instructor, before attempting to complete this case.*)

You have been approached by Gary Gerrard, President and CEO of Gerrard Construction Co., who would like your advice on a number of business and accounting related matters.

Your conversation with Mr. Gerrard, which took place in February 2014, proceeded as follows:

Mr. Gerrard: "The accounts receivable shown on the balance sheet for 2013 are nearly $10 million and the funny thing is, we just collected a bunch of the big accounts in early December but had to reinvest most of that money in new equipment. At one point last year, more than $20 million of accounts were outstanding! I had to put some pressure on our regular clients who keep falling behind. Normally, I don't bother with collections, but this is our main source of cash flows. My daughter Anna deals with collections and she's just too nice to people. I keep telling her that the money is better off in our hands than in someone else's! Can you have a look at our books? Some of these clients are really getting on my nerves."

Your reply: "That does seem like a big problem. I'll look at your accounts receivable details and get back to you with some of my ideas and maybe some questions you can help me with. What else did you want to ask me about?"

Mr. Gerrard: "The other major problem is with our long-term asset management. We don't have much in the way of buildings, just this office you're sitting in and the service garage where we keep most of the earthmoving equipment. That's where the expense of running this business comes in. I've always said that I'd rather see a dozen guys standing around leaning against shovels than to see one piece of equipment sit idle for even an hour of daylight! There is nothing complicated about doing 'dirt work,' but we've got one piece of equipment that would cost over $2 million to replace at today's prices. And that's just it—either you spend a fortune on maintenance or else you're constantly in the market for the latest and greatest new 'Cat.'"

Your reply: "So how can I help?"

Mr. Gerrard: "Now that you know a little about our business, I'll have my son Nathan show you the equipment records. He's our business manager. We've got to sell and replace some of our light-duty trucks. We need to get a handle on the value of some of the older equipment. What the books say, and what it's really worth, are two different things. I'd like to know what the accounting consequences of selling various pieces of equipment would be because I don't want to be selling anything at a loss."

Your reply: "Thanks, Gary. I'll have a chat with Anna and Nathan and get back to you."

After your discussion with Anna, you analyzed the accounts receivable details and prepared the following aging schedule:

Number of Days Outstanding	Number of Accounts Outstanding	Total Amount Outstanding
0–30	20	$2,240,000
31–60	9	1,600,000
61–120	6	1,320,000
121–180	4	1,080,000
>180	11	3,560,000

You've noted that Gerrard Construction Co. has not written off any accounts receivable as uncollectible during the past several years. The Allowance for Bad Debts account is included in the chart of accounts but has never been used. No cash discounts have been offered to customers, and the company does not employ a collection agency. Reminder invoices are sent to customers with outstanding balances at the end of every quarter.

After your discussion with Nathan, you analyzed the equipment records related to the three items that the company wishes to sell at this time:

Item Description	Date of Purchase	Cost	Accumulated Depreciation	Book Value	Estimated Market Value
2003 Ford F550	Mar 2003	$ 57,200	$ 38,600	$ 18,600	$ 14,000
2005 Cat DR9	June 2005	510,000	272,100	237,900	295,000
2007 Cat 345B L II	Sept 2007	422,700	226,500	196,200	160,000

Nathan explained that Gerrard Construction Co. uses the units-of-production depreciation method and estimates usage on the basis of hours in service for earthmoving equipment and miles driven for all on-road vehicles. You have recalculated the annual depreciation adjustments through December 31, 2013, and are satisfied that the company has made the proper entries. The estimated market values were recently obtained through the services of a qualified, independent appraiser whom you had recommended to Nathan.

Required:

a. Explain what Mr. Gerrard meant when he said, "I keep telling her that the money is better off in our hands than in someone else's!"

b. What is your overall reaction concerning Gerrard Construction Co.'s management of accounts receivable? What suggestions would you make to Mr. Gerrard that may prove helpful in the collection process?

c. What accounting advice would you give concerning the accounts receivable balance of $9,800,000 at December 31, 2013?

d. What impact (increase, decrease, or no effect) would any necessary adjustment(s) have on the company's working capital and current ratio? (Note that these items were computed in part **g** of C4.30 and do not need to be recomputed now.)

e. Explain what Mr. Gerrard meant when he said, "We need to get a handle on the value of some of the older equipment. What the books say, and what it's really worth, are two different things."

f. Use the horizontal model, or write the journal entries, to show the effect of selling each of the three assets for their respective estimated market values. Partial-year depreciation adjustments for 2014 can be ignored.

g. Explain to Mr. Gerrard why his statement that "I don't want to be selling anything at a loss" does not make economic sense.

Answers to Self-Study Material

Matching: 1. m, 2. s, 3. u, 4. k, 5. g, 6. b, 7. r, 8. e, 9. o, 10. c, 11. p, 12. l, 13. h, 14. j, 15. f

Multiple choice: 1. e, 2. c, 3. c, 4. b, 5. a, 6. b, 7. d, 8. b, 9. c, 10. b

7

Accounting for and Presentation of Liabilities

Liabilities are obligations of the entity or, as defined by the FASB, "probable future sacrifices of economic benefits arising from present obligations of a particular entity to transfer assets or provide services to other entities in the future as a result of past transactions or events."[1] Note that liabilities are recorded only for *present* obligations that are the result of past transactions or events that will require the probable *future* sacrifice of resources. Thus, the following items would not yet be recorded as liabilities: (1) negotiations for the possible purchase of inventory, (2) increases in the replacement cost of assets due to inflation, and (3) contingent losses on unsettled lawsuits against the entity unless the loss becomes *probable* and can be reasonably estimated.

Most liabilities that meet the above definition arise because credit has been obtained in the form of a loan (notes payable) or in the normal course of business—for example, when a supplier ships merchandise before payment is made (accounts payable) or when an employee works one week not expecting to be paid until the next week (wages payable). As has been illustrated in previous chapters, many liabilities are recorded in the accrual process that matches revenues and expenses. The term *accrued expenses* is used on some balance sheets to describe these liabilities, but this is shorthand for *liabilities resulting from the accrual of expenses.* If you keep in mind that revenues and expenses are reported only on the income statement, you will not be confused by this mixing of terms. Current liabilities are those that must be paid or otherwise satisfied within a year of the balance sheet date; noncurrent liabilities are those that will be paid or satisfied more than a year after the balance sheet date. Liability captions usually seen in a balance sheet are:

Current Liabilities:
Accounts Payable
Short-Term Debt (Notes Payable)
Current Maturities of Long-Term Debt
Unearned Revenue or Deferred Credits
Other Accrued Liabilities

---

[1]FASB, *Statement of Financial Accounting Concepts No. 6,* "Elements of Financial Statements" (Stamford, CT, 1985), para. 35. Copyright © by the Financial Accounting Standards Board, High Ridge Park, Stamford, CT 06905, U.S.A. Quoted with permission. Copies of the complete document are available from the FASB.

Noncurrent Liabilities:

Long-Term Debt (Bonds Payable)
Deferred Tax Liabilities

Noncontrolling (Minority) Interest in Subsidiaries

The order in which liabilities are presented within the current and noncurrent categories is a function of liquidity (how soon the debt becomes due) and management preference.

Review the liabilities section of the Campbell Soup Company consolidated balance sheets on page 712 of the annual report in the appendix. Note that most of these captions have to do with debt, accrued liabilities, and income taxes. The business and accounting practices relating to these items make up a major part of this chapter. Some of the most significant and controversial issues that the FASB has addressed in recent years, including accounting for income taxes, accounting for pensions, and consolidation of subsidiaries, relate to the liability section of the balance sheet. A principal reason for the interest generated by these topics is that the recognition of a liability usually involves recognizing an expense as well. Expenses reduce net income, and lower net income means lower ROI. Keep these relationships in mind as you study this chapter.

LEARNING OBJECTIVES (LO)

After studying this chapter you should understand and be able to

LO 7-1 Show the financial statement presentation of short-term debt and current maturities of long-term debt.

LO 7-2 Illustrate the difference between interest calculated on a straight basis and on a discount basis.

LO 7-3 Discuss what unearned revenues are and how they are presented in the balance sheet.

LO 7-4 Describe the accounting for an employer's liability for payroll and payroll taxes.

LO 7-5 Discuss the importance of making estimates for certain accrued liabilities and show how these items are presented in the balance sheet.

LO 7-6 Explain what financial leverage is and how it is provided by long-term debt.

LO 7-7 Describe the different characteristics of a bond, which is the formal document representing most long-term debt.

LO 7-8 Describe why bond discount or premium arises and how it is accounted for.

LO 7-9 Explain what deferred tax liabilities are and why they arise.

LO 7-10 Explain what noncontrolling interest is, why it arises, and what it means in the balance sheet.

Exhibit 7-1 on the next page highlights the balance sheet accounts covered in detail in this chapter and shows the income statement and statement of cash flows components affected by these accounts.

Exhibit 7-1

Financial Statements—
The Big Picture

Balance Sheet

Current Assets	Chapter	Current Liabilities	Chapter
Cash and cash equivalents	5, 9	Short-term debt	7
Short-term marketable securities	5	Current maturities of long-term debt	7
Accounts receivable	5, 9	Accounts payable	7
Notes receivable	5	Unearned revenue or deferred credits	7
Inventories	5, 9	Payroll taxes and other withholdings	7
Prepaid expenses	5	Other accrued liabilities	7
Noncurrent Assets		**Noncurrent Liabilities**	
Land	6	Long-term debt	7
Buildings and equipment	6	Deferred tax liabilities	7
Assets acquired by capital lease	6	Other noncurrent liabilities	7
Intangible assets	6	**Stockholders' Equity**	
Natural resources	6	Common stock	8
Other noncurrent assets	6	Preferred stock	8
		Additional paid-in capital	8
		Retained earnings	8
		Treasury stock	8
		Accumulated other comprehensive income (loss)	8
		Noncontrolling interest	8

Income Statement

	Chapter
Sales	5, 9
Cost of goods sold	5, 9
Gross profit (or gross margin)	5, 9
Selling, general, and administrative expenses	5, 6, 9
Income from operations	9
Gains (losses) on sale of assets	6, 9
Interest income	5, 9
Interest expense	7, 9
Income tax expense	7, 9
Unusual items	9
Net income	5, 6, 7, 8, 9
Earnings per share	9

Statement of Cash Flows

	Chapter
Operating Activities	
Net income	5, 6, 7, 8, 9
Depreciation expense	6, 9
(Gains) losses on sale of assets	6, 9
(Increase) decrease in current assets	5, 9
Increase (decrease) in current liabilities	7, 9
Investing Activities	
Proceeds from sale of property, plant, and equipment	6, 9
Purchase of property, plant, and equipment	6, 9
Financing Activities	
Proceeds from long-term debt*	7, 9
Repayment of long-term debt*	7, 9
Issuance of common stock and/or preferred stock	8, 9
Purchase of treasury stock	8, 9
Payment of dividends	8, 9

Primary topics of this chapter.

Other affected financial statement components.

*May include short-term debt items as well.

Current Liabilities

Short-Term Debt

Most firms experience seasonal fluctuations during the year in the demand for their products or services. For instance, a firm like Cruisers, Inc., a manufacturer of small boats, is likely to have greater demand for its product during the spring and early summer than in the winter. To use its production facilities most efficiently, Cruisers, Inc., will plan to produce boats on a level basis throughout the year. This means that during the fall and winter seasons, its inventory of boats will be increased in order to have enough product on hand to meet spring and summer demand. To finance this inventory increase and keep its payments to suppliers and employees current, Cruisers, Inc., will obtain a **working capital loan** from its bank. This type of short-term loan is made with the expectation that it will be repaid from the collection of accounts receivable that will be generated by the sale of inventory. The short-term loan usually has a **maturity date** specifying when the loan is to be repaid. Sometimes a firm will negotiate a **revolving line of credit** with its bank. The credit line represents a predetermined maximum loan amount, but the firm has flexibility in the timing and amount borrowed. There may be a specified repayment schedule or an agreement that all amounts borrowed will be repaid by a particular date. Whatever the specific loan arrangement may be, the borrowing has the following effect on the financial statements:

Balance Sheet	Income Statement
Assets = Liabilities + Stockholders' equity	←Net income = Revenues − Expenses
+ Cash + Short-Term Debt	

LO 1

Show the financial statement presentation of short-term debt and current maturities of long-term debt.

The entry to record the loan is:

```
Dr.  Cash ...............................................      xx
     Cr.  Short-Term Debt ...............................              xx
Borrowed money from bank.
```

The short-term debt resulting from this type of transaction is sometimes called a **note payable.** The note is a formal promise to pay a stated amount at a stated date, usually with interest at a stated rate and sometimes secured by collateral.

Interest expense is associated with almost any borrowing, and it is appropriate to record interest expense for each fiscal period during which the money is borrowed. The alternative methods of calculating interest are explained in Business in Practice—Interest Calculation Methods.

Prime rate is the term frequently used to express the interest rate on short-term loans. The prime rate is established by the lender, presumably for its most credit-worthy borrowers, but is in reality just a benchmark rate. The prime rate is raised or lowered by the lender in response to credit market forces. The borrower's rate may be expressed as "prime plus 1," for example, which means that the interest rate for the borrower will be the prime rate plus 1 percent. It is quite possible for the interest rate to change during the term of the loan, in which case a separate calculation of interest is made for each period having a different rate.

Interest Calculation Methods

Lenders calculate interest on either a straight (interest-bearing, or simple interest) basis or on a discount (non-interest-bearing) basis. The straight calculation involves charging interest on the money actually available to the borrower for the length of time it was borrowed. Interest on a **discount loan** is based on the principal amount of the loan, but the interest is subtracted from the principal at the beginning of the loan, and only the difference is made available to the borrower. In effect, the borrower pays the interest in advance. Assume that $1,000 is borrowed for one year at an interest rate of 12 percent.

Straight Interest

The **interest calculation—straight basis** is made as follows:

$$\text{Interest} = \text{Principal} \times \text{Rate} \times \text{Time (in years)}$$
$$= \$1,000 \times 0.12 \times 1$$
$$= \$120$$

At the maturity date of the note, the borrower will repay the principal of $1,000 plus the interest owed of $120. The borrower's *effective interest rate*—the **annual percentage rate (APR)**—is 12 percent:

$$\text{APR} = \text{Interest paid} / [\text{Money available to use} \times \text{Time (in years)}]$$
$$= \$120 / \$1,000 \times 1$$
$$= 12\%$$

This is another application of the present value concept described in Chapter 6. The amount of the liability on the date the money is borrowed is the present value of the amount to be repaid in the future, calculated at the effective interest rate—which is the rate of return desired by the lender. To illustrate, the amount to be repaid in one year is $1,120, the sum of the $1,000 principal plus the $120 of interest. From Table 6-4, the factor in the 12% column and one-period row is 0.8929; $1,120 × 0.8929 = $1,000 (rounded). These relationships are illustrated on the following time line:

1/1/13		12/31/13
$1,000 Principal borrowed	Interest = $1,000 × 0.12 × 1 year = $120	$1,120 Principal and interest repaid

For a loan on which interest is calculated on a straight basis, interest is accrued each period. Here is the effect of this accrual on the financial statements:

Balance Sheet	Income Statement
Assets = Liabilities + Stockholders' equity	←Net income = Revenues − Expenses
+ Interest Payable	− Interest Expense

Discount

The **interest calculation—discount basis** is made as just illustrated except that the interest amount is subtracted from the loan principal, and the borrower receives the difference. In this case, the loan proceeds would be $880 ($1,000 − $120). At the maturity of the note, the borrower will pay just the principal of $1,000 because the interest of $120 has already been paid—it was subtracted from the principal amount when the loan was obtained. These relationships are illustrated on the following time line:

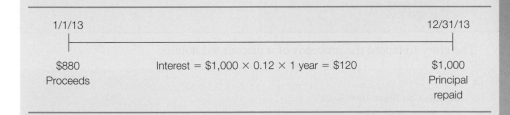

Because the full principal amount is not available to the borrower, the effective interest rate (APR) on a discount basis is much higher than the rate used in the lending agreement to calculate the interest:

$$APR = \text{Interest paid}/[\text{Money available to use} \times \text{Time (in years)}]$$
$$= \$120 / \$880 \times 1$$
$$= 13.6\%$$

Applying present value analysis, the carrying value of the liability on the date the money is borrowed represents the amount to be repaid, $1,000, multiplied by the present value factor for 13.6% for one year. The factor is 0.8803 and although it is not explicitly shown in Table 6-4, it can be derived approximately by **interpolating** between the factors for 12% and 14%.

An *installment loan* is repaid periodically over the life of the loan, so only about half of the proceeds (on average) are available for use throughout the life of the loan. Thus, the effective interest rate is about twice that of a *term loan* requiring a lump-sum repayment of principal at the maturity date.

In the final analysis, it isn't important whether interest is calculated using the straight method or the discount method, or whether an installment loan or term loan is arranged; what is important is the APR, or effective interest rate. The borrower's objective is to keep the APR (which must be disclosed in accordance with federal truth in lending laws) to a minimum.

The entry to record accrued interest is as follows:

Interest Payable is a current liability because it will be paid within a year of the balance sheet date. It may be disclosed in a separate caption or included with other accrued liabilities in the current liability section of the balance sheet.

For a loan on which interest is calculated on a discount basis, the amount of cash **proceeds** represents the initial carrying value of the liability. Using the data from the discount example in the Business in Practice box, the effect on the financial statements of the borrower is:

Balance Sheet	Income Statement
Assets = Liabilities + Stockholders' equity	←Net income = Revenues − Expenses

Cash   Short-Term
+ 880   Debt
         + 1,000
 	
         Discount on
         Short-term Debt
         − 120	

The entry to record the proceeds of a discounted note is:

Dr.	Cash	880	
Dr.	Discount on Short-Term Debt..........................	120	
	Cr. Short-Term Debt		1,000

The Discount on Short-Term Debt account is a **contra liability,** classified as a reduction of Short-Term Debt on the balance sheet. As interest expense is incurred, the Discount on Short-Term Debt is amortized as follows:

Balance Sheet	Income Statement
Assets = Liabilities + Stockholders' equity	←Net income = Revenues − Expenses
+ Discount on Short-Term Debt	− Interest Expense

The entry is:

Dr.	Interest Expense	xx	
	Cr. Discount on Short-Term Debt......................		xx

The amortization of the discount to interest expense affects neither cash nor interest payable. Net income decreases as interest expense is recorded, and the carrying value of short-term debt increases as the discount is amortized.

What Does It Mean?
Answer on page 277

1. What does it mean to borrow money on a discount basis?

Current Maturities of Long-Term Debt

When funds are borrowed on a long-term basis (a topic to be discussed later in this chapter), it is not unusual for principal repayments to be required on an installment basis; every year a portion of the debt matures and is to be repaid by the borrower. Any portion of a long-term borrowing (e.g., Notes Payable or Bonds Payable) that is to be repaid within a year of the balance sheet date is reclassified from the noncurrent liability section of the balance sheet to the **Current Maturities of Long-Term Debt** account. These amounts are reported in the current liability section but separately from short-term debt because the liability arose from a long-term borrowing transaction. Interest payable on long-term debt is classified with other interest payable and may be combined with other accrued liabilities for reporting purposes.

Accounts Payable

Amounts owed to suppliers for goods and services that have been provided to the entity on credit are the principal components of **accounts payable.** Unlike accounts receivable, which are reported net of estimated cash discounts expected to be taken, accounts payable to suppliers that permit a cash discount for prompt payment are not usually reduced by the amount of the cash discount expected to be taken. This treatment is supported by the materiality concept because the amount involved is not likely to have a significant effect on the financial position or results of the operations of the firm. However, accounts payable for firms that record purchases net of anticipated cash discounts will be reported at the amount expected to be paid.

Purchase transactions for which a cash discount is allowed are recorded using either the *gross* or *net* method. The difference between the two is the timing of the recognition of cash discounts. The gross method results in recognizing cash discounts only when invoices are paid within the discount period. The net method recognizes cash discounts when purchases are initially recorded, under the assumption that all discounts will be taken; an expense is then recognized if a discount is not taken.

Unearned Revenue or Deferred Credits

Customers often pay for services or even products before the service or product is delivered. An entity collecting cash in advance of earning the related revenue records **unearned revenue,** or a **deferred credit,** which is included in current liabilities. Unearned revenues must then be allocated to the fiscal periods in which the services are performed or the products are delivered, in accordance with the matching concept. The accounting for revenue received in advance was discussed in the context of the adjustments presented in Chapter 4. To illustrate, assume that a magazine publisher requires a subscriber to pay in advance for a subscription. Here are the financial statement effects of this transaction and the subsequent adjustment:

LO 3
Discuss what unearned revenues are and how they are presented in the balance sheet.

Balance Sheet	Income Statement
Assets = Liabilities + Stockholders' equity	←Net income = Revenues − Expenses
Cash received with subscription:	
+ Cash + Unearned Subscription Revenue	
Adjustments in fiscal period in which revenue is earned (magazines delivered):	
− Unearned Subscription Revenue	+ Subscription Revenue

The entry to record this transaction is:

Dr. Cash xx
  Cr. Unearned Subscription Revenue.   xx

The entry to record the adjustment for revenue earned during the fiscal period would be:

Dr. Unearned Subscription Revenue	xx	
Cr. Subscription Revenue		xx

As you think about this situation, you should understand that it is the opposite of the prepaid expense/deferred charge transaction described in Chapter 5 (see pages 174–175). In that kind of transaction, cash was *paid* in the current period, and *expense* was recognized in subsequent periods. Unearned revenue/deferred credit transactions involve the *receipt* of cash in the current period and the recognition of *revenue* in subsequent periods.

Deposits received from customers are also accounted for as deferred credits. If the deposit is an advance payment for a product or service, the deposit is transferred from a liability account to a revenue account when the product or service is delivered. Or, for example, if the deposit is received as security for a returnable container, when the container is returned the refund of the customer's deposit reduces (is a credit to) cash and eliminates (is a debit to) the liability.

Unearned revenues/deferred credits are usually classified with other accrued liabilities in the current liability section of the balance sheet.

Payroll Taxes and Other Withholdings

LO 4

Describe the accounting for an employer's liability for payroll and payroll taxes.

The total wages earned by employees for a payroll period, including bonuses and overtime pay, are referred to as their **gross pay,** which represents the employer's Wages Expense for the period. From this amount, several *deductions* are subtracted to arrive at the **net pay** (*take-home pay*) that each employee will receive, which represents the employer's Wages Payable (or Accrued Payroll). The largest deductions are normally for federal and state income tax withholdings and **FICA tax** withholdings, but employees frequently make voluntary contributions for hospitalization insurance, contributory pension plans, union dues, the United Way, and a variety of other items. Employers are responsible for remitting payment to the appropriate entities on behalf of their employees for each amount withheld. Thus, a separate liability account (e.g., Federal Income Taxes Withheld) normally is used for each applicable item. Here is the effect of this transaction on the financial statements:

Balance Sheet	Income Statement
Assets = Liabilities + Stockholders' equity	←Net income = Revenues − Expenses
+ Wages payable + Withholding Liabilities	− Wages Expense

The entry to record a firm's payroll obligation is:

Dr. Wages Expense (for gross pay)	xx	
Cr. Wages Payable (or Accrued Payroll, for net pay)		xx
Cr. Withholding Liabilities (various descriptions)		xx

When the withholdings are paid, both cash and the appropriate withholding liability are reduced.

Most employers are also subject to federal and state *payroll* taxes based on the amount of compensation paid to their employees. These taxes, assessed directly against the employer, include federal and state unemployment taxes and the employer's share of FICA tax. Employer taxes are appropriately recognized when compensation expense is accrued. This involves recognizing payroll tax expense and a related liability. The effect of this transaction on the financial statements is:

Balance Sheet	Income Statement
Assets = Liabilities + Stockholders' equity	←Net income = Revenues − Expenses
+ Payroll Taxes Payable	− Payroll Tax Expense

The entry to record a firm's payroll tax obligation is:

Dr. Payroll Tax Expense	xx	
Cr. Payroll Taxes Payable (or Accrued Payroll Taxes)		xx

When the taxes are paid, both cash and the liability are reduced.

The liabilities for accrued payroll, payroll withholdings, and accrued payroll taxes are usually classified with other accrued liabilities in the current liability section of the balance sheet.

Other Accrued Liabilities

As just discussed, this caption normally includes the accrued payroll accounts as well as most unearned revenue/deferred credit accounts. Accrued property taxes, accrued interest (if not reported separately), estimated warranty liabilities, and other accrued expenses such as advertising and insurance obligations are often included in this description. This is another application of the matching principle. Each of these items represents an expense that has been incurred but not yet paid. The expense is recognized and the liability is shown so that the financial statements present a more complete summary of the results of operations (income statement) and financial position (balance sheet) than would be presented without the accrual.

To illustrate the accrual of property taxes, assume that Cruisers, Inc., operates in a city in which real estate tax bills for one year are not issued until April of the following year and are payable in July. Thus, an adjustment must be made on December 31, 2013, to record the estimated property tax expense for the year then ended. The effect of this adjustment on the financial statements follows:

LO 5

Discuss the importance of making estimates for certain accrued liabilities and show how these items are presented in the balance sheet.

Balance Sheet	Income Statement
Assets = Liabilities + Stockholders' equity	←Net income = Revenues − Expenses
+ Property Taxes Payable	− Property Tax Expense

The entry is:

Dr. Property Taxes Expense	xx	
Cr. Property Taxes Payable.		xx

When the tax bill is received at some point in April 2014, the payable account must be adjusted to reflect the amount actually owed in July. The adjustment also affects the current year's property tax expense account. The liability and expense amounts reported in the previous year are not adjusted because the estimate was based on the best information available at the time.

A firm's estimated liability under product warranty or performance guarantees is another example of an accrued liability. It is appropriate to recognize the estimated warranty expense that will be incurred on a product in the same period in which the revenue from the sale is recorded. Although the expense and liability must be estimated, recent experience and statistical analysis can be used to develop accurate estimates. The following financial statement effects occur in the fiscal periods in which the product is sold and the warranty is honored:

Balance Sheet	Income Statement
Assets = Liabilities + Stockholders' equity	←Net income = Revenues − Expenses

Fiscal period in which product is sold:
 	
        + Estimated
          Warranty
          Liability
 	
Fiscal period in which warranty is honored:
 	
− Cash   − Estimated
  and/or   Warranty
  Repair   Liability
  Parts
  Inventory
	− Warranty
	                   Expense

Here is the entry to accrue the estimated warranty liability in the fiscal period in which the product is sold:

Dr. Warranty Expense.....................................	xx	
Cr. Estimated Warranty Liability		xx

The entry to record actual warranty cost in the fiscal period in which the warranty is honored is:

Dr. Estimated Warranty Liability	xx	
Cr. Cash (or Repair Parts Inventory)....................		xx

The accrual for income taxes is usually shown separately because of its significance. The current liability for income taxes is related to the long-term liability for deferred taxes; both are discussed later in this chapter.

What Does It Mean?
Answer on page 277

2. What does it mean to be concerned that an entity's liabilities are not understated?

Noncurrent Liabilities

Long-Term Debt

A corporation's *capital structure* is the mix of debt and stockholders' equity that is used to finance the acquisition of the firm's assets. For many nonfinancial firms, **long-term debt** accounts for up to half of the firm's capital structure. One of the advantages of using debt is that interest expense is deductible in calculating taxable income, whereas dividends (distributions of earnings to stockholders) are not tax deductible. Thus, debt usually has a lower economic cost to the firm than stockholders' equity. For example, assume a firm has an average tax rate of 30 percent and issues long-term debt with an interest rate of 10 percent. The firm's after-tax cost of debt is only 7 percent, which is probably less than the return sought by stockholders. Another reason for using debt is to obtain favorable financial leverage. **Financial leverage** refers to the difference between the rate of return earned on assets (ROI) and the rate of return earned on stockholders' equity (ROE). This difference results from the fact that the interest cost of debt is usually a fixed percentage, which is not a function of the return on assets. Thus, if the firm can borrow money at an interest cost of 10 percent and use money to buy assets on which it earns a return greater than 10 percent, the stockholders will have a greater return on their equity (ROE) than if they had provided all of the funds themselves. In other words, financial leverage relates to the use of borrowed money to enhance the return to stockholders. This is illustrated in Exhibit 7-2 on the next page.

This simplified illustration shows positive financial leverage. If a firm earns a lower return on investment than the interest rate on borrowed funds, financial leverage will be negative and ROE will be less than ROI. Financial leverage adds risk to the firm because if the firm does not earn enough to pay the interest on its debt, the debtholders can ultimately force the firm into bankruptcy.

Financial leverage is discussed in greater detail in Chapter 11. For now you should understand that the use of long-term debt with a fixed interest cost usually results in ROE being different from ROI. Whether financial leverage is good or bad for the stockholders depends on the relationship between ROI and the interest rate on long-term debt.

LO 6
Explain what financial leverage is and how it is provided by long-term debt.

---

3. What does it mean to say that financial leverage has been used effectively?
4. What does it mean that the more financial leverage a firm has, the greater the risk to stockholders and creditors?

What Does It Mean?
Answers on page 277

Recall the discussion and illustration of capital lease liabilities in Chapter 6. Lease payments that are due more than a year from the balance sheet date are included in long-term debt and recorded at the present value of future lease payments.

Most long-term debt, however, is issued in the form of bonds. A **bond** or **bond payable** is a formal document, usually issued in denominations of $1,000. Bond prices, both when the bonds are issued and later when they are bought and sold in the market, are expressed as a percentage of the bond's **face amount**—the principal amount printed on the face of the bond. A $1,000 face amount bond that has a market value of $1,000 is priced at 100. (This means 100 percent; usually the term *percent* is neither written nor stated.) A $1,000 bond trading at 102.5 can be purchased for $1,025; such a bond priced at 96 has a market value of $960. When a bond has a market value greater than its face

LO 7
Describe the different characteristics of a bond, which is the formal document representing most long-term debt.

Exhibit 7-2

Financial Leverage

Assumptions:

Two firms have the same assets and operating income. Current liabilities and income taxes are ignored for simplification. The firm without financial leverage has, by definition, no long-term debt. The firm with financial leverage has a capital structure that is 40% long-term debt with an interest rate of 10% and 60% stockholders' equity. Return on investment and return on equity follow for each firm.

Note that the return-on-investment calculation has been modified from the model introduced in Chapter 3. ROI is based on income from operations and total assets rather than net income and total assets. Income from operations (which is net income before interest expense) is used because the interest expense reflects a financing decision, not an operating result. Thus, ROI becomes an evaluation of the operating activities of the firm.

Firm without Leverage		**Firm with Leverage**	
Balance Sheet:		**Balance Sheet:**	
Assets	$10,000	Assets	$10,000
Liabilities.	$ 0	Liabilities (10% interest) . .	$ 4,000
Stockholders' equity	10,000	Stockholders' equity	6,000
Total liabilities and stockholders' equity	$10,000	Total liabilities and stockholders' equity	$10,000

Income Statement:		**Income Statement:**	
Income from operations. . .	$ 1,200	Income from operations. .	$ 1,200
Interest expense	0	Interest expense	400
Net income	$ 1,200	Net income	$ 800

ROI and ROE Calculations:

Return on investment (ROI = Income from operations / Assets)

$$\text{ROI} = \$1,200 / \$10,000 \qquad\qquad \text{ROI} = \$1,200 / \$10,000$$
$$= 12\% \qquad\qquad\qquad\qquad\qquad = 12\%$$

Return on equity (ROE = Net income / Stockholders' equity)

$$\text{ROE} = \$1,200 / \$10,000 \qquad\qquad \text{ROE} = \$800 / \$6,000$$
$$= 12\% \qquad\qquad\qquad\qquad\qquad = 13.3\%$$

Analysis:

In this case, ROI is the same for both firms because the operating results did not differ—each firm was able to earn 12% on the assets it had available to use. What differed was the way in which the assets were financed (capital structure). The firm with financial leverage has a higher return on stockholders' equity because it was able to borrow money at a cost of 10% and use the money to buy assets on which it earned 12%. Thus ROE will be higher than ROI for a firm with positive financial leverage. The excess return on borrowed funds is the reward to stockholders for taking the risk of borrowing money at a fixed cost.

Bond Market Basics

Bonds are long-term lending agreements between the issuing company (borrower) and the bondholder (lender). Many bonds are traded in highly regulated public securities markets such as the New York Bond Exchange. As with most lending arrangements, bonds essentially represent an exchange of cash flows between the parties—bondholders provide a lump sum of cash in exchange for periodic (usually semiannual) fixed-rate interest payments throughout the term of the bond and the return of principal at the bond's maturity. Bond prices vary over time and are influenced by the creditworthiness of the issuing company as well as broad economic factors affecting the overall economy, especially interest rates. What happens to the value of a bond as market interest rates rise? Recall from Chapter 6 that as interest (discount) rates increase, the present value of the future cash flows decreases, which is to say that bond prices fall as market interest rates rise. The opposite is true when market interest rates fall—bond prices rise.

To learn more about bonds, see www.investopedia.com/university/bonds for a tutorial about bond markets, including how to read a bond table. For a more detailed analysis of the bond market, including commentary from traders, academics, and other bond market experts, visit www.investinginbonds.com.

Business in Practice

You can get a fundamental understanding of the *accounting* for bonds payable, including the amortization of discount or premium, without fighting through the mechanics of present value analysis as it relates to *bond pricing:* Just remember that present value analysis is necessary to determine the *amount* of discount or premium when bonds are issued. Once the bond's issue price is determined (the bond may be priced at 96 or 102.5, for example), the difference between the issue price and 100 must be amortized against interest expense over the life of the bond. Present value analysis is included in our examples to illustrate the appropriate conceptual basis for bond pricing, but it can be deemphasized when considering the accounting aspects of bonds.

Study Suggestion

amount, it is trading at a premium; the amount of the **bond premium** is the excess of its market value over its face amount. A **bond discount** is the excess of the face amount over market value. See the Business in Practice—Bond Market Basics box, including the referenced websites, for a primer on the mechanics of bond pricing.

Accounting and financial reporting considerations for bonds can be classified into three categories: the original issuance of bonds, the recognition of interest expense, and the accounting for bond retirements or conversions.

Original issuance of bonds payable. If a bond is issued at its face amount, the effect on the financial statements is straightforward:

Balance Sheet	Income Statement
Assets = Liabilities + Stockholders' equity	←Net income = Revenues − Expenses
+ Cash + Bonds Payable	

The journal entry is:

Dr. Cash	xx	
Cr. Bonds Payable................................		xx
Issuance of bonds at face amount.		

As was the case with short-term notes payable, the bonds payable liability is reported at the present value of amounts to be paid in the future with respect to the bonds, discounted at the return on investment desired by the lender (bondholder). For example, assume that a 10 percent bond with a 10-year maturity is issued to investors who desire a 10 percent return on their investment. The issuer of the bonds provides two cash flow components to the investors in the bonds: the annual interest payments and the payment of principal at maturity. Note that the interest cash flow is an annuity because the same amount is paid each period. Using present value factors from Tables 6-4 and 6-5, here are the present values:

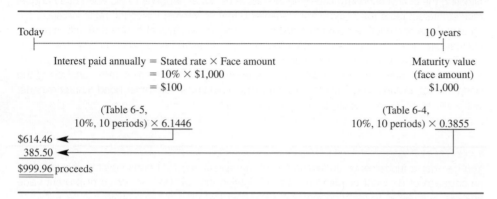

Today   10 years

Interest paid annually = Stated rate × Face amount   Maturity value
                       = 10% × $1,000   (face amount)
                       = $100 $1,000

            (Table 6-5,   (Table 6-4,
        10%, 10 periods) × 6.1446   10%, 10 periods) × 0.3855

$614.46
 385.50
$999.96 proceeds

The present value of the liability is the sum of the discounted principal and interest payments. Except for a rounding difference in the present value factors, this sum is the same as the face amount of the bonds.

Because of the mechanics involved in a bond issue, there is usually a time lag between the establishment of the interest rate to be printed on the face of the bond and the actual issue date. During this time lag, market interest rates will fluctuate and the market rate on the issue date probably will differ from the **stated rate** (or **coupon rate**) used to calculate interest payments to bondholders. This difference in interest rates causes the proceeds (cash received) from the sale of the bonds to be more or less than the face amount; the bonds are issued at a premium or discount, respectively. This is illustrated in Exhibit 7-3.

What Does It Mean?

Answer on page 277

5. What does it mean to say that a bond is a fixed-income investment?

Recognition of interest expense on bonds payable.   Because bond premium or discount arises from a difference between the bond's stated interest rate and the market interest rate, it should follow that the premium or discount will affect the issuing firm's interest expense. Bond discount really represents additional interest expense to be recognized over the life of the bonds. The interest that will be paid (based on the stated rate) is less than the interest that would be paid if it were based on the market

As already illustrated, the amount the investor is willing to pay for the bond is the present value of the cash flows to be received from the investment, discounted at the investor's desired rate of return (market interest rate).

Exhibit 7-3
Bond Discount and Premium

LO 8
Describe why bond discount or premium arises and how it is accounted for.

Assumptions:
Cruisers, Inc., issues a 10%, $1,000 bond when market interest rates are 12%. The bond will mature in eight years. Interest is paid semiannually.

Required:
Calculate the proceeds *(selling price)* of the bond and the premium or discount to be recognized.

Solution:
Note that the interest is an annuity because the same amount is paid each period. Because the interest is paid semiannually, it is appropriate to recognize semiannual compounding in the present value calculation. This is accomplished by using the number of semiannual periods in the life of the bonds. Because the bonds mature in eight years, there are 16 semiannual periods. However, the interest rate per semiannual period is half of the annual interest rate. To be consistent, the same approach is used to calculate the present value of the principal. Thus, the solution uses factors from the 6% column (one-half the investors' desired ROI) and the 16-period row (twice the term of the bonds in years) of the present value tables. Using present value factors from Tables 6-4 and 6-5, here are the present values:

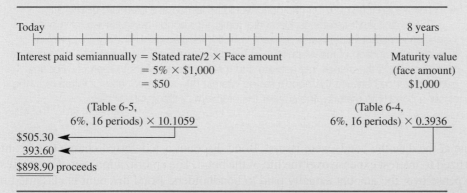

The proceeds received by Cruisers, Inc., as well as the amount invested by the buyer of the bond, are the sum of the present value of the interest payments and the present value of the principal amount. Because this sum is less than the face amount, the bond is priced at a discount.

This illustration demonstrates two important points about the process of calculating the proceeds from a bond issue:

1. The *stated interest rate* of the bond, adjusted for compounding frequency, is used to calculate the amount of interest paid each payment period; this is the annuity amount ($50 in this case) used in the calculation of the present value of the interest.

2. The *market interest rate* (or the investors' desired ROI), adjusted for the compounding frequency, is the discount rate used in the present value calculations.

In this illustration, the market interest rate is higher than the bond's stated interest rate; thus, the investor would pay sufficiently less than the face amount of the bond, such that the $50 to be received each six months and the $1,000 to be received at maturity will provide a market rate of return.

(continued)

Exhibit 7-3

The issuance of the $1,000 bond by Cruisers, Inc., will have the following effect on the financial statements:

Balance Sheet	Income Statement
Assets = Liabilities + Stockholders' equity	←Net income = Revenues − Expenses
Cash Bonds Payable + 898.90 + 1,000 Discount on Bonds Payable − 101.10	

The entry to record the issuance of the bond is:

```
Dr.  Cash...........................................    898.90
Dr.  Discount on Bonds Payable .......................   101.10
     Cr.  Bonds Payable................................              1,000.00
Issued bond at a discount.
```

If the market rate is less than the stated interest rate on the bond, the opposite will be true (the investor will be willing to pay a premium over the face amount of the bond). Use the above model to prove to yourself that if the market interest rate is 12%, then a 13% stated rate, $1,000 face amount, 10-year bond on which interest is paid semiannually would be issued for $1,057.34 (the bond would be issued at a premium of $57.34).

This exhibit illustrates the fundamental reason for bonds being issued for a price (or having a market value) that is different from the face amount. The actual premium or discount is a function of the magnitude of the difference between the stated interest rate of the bond and the market interest rate and the number of years to maturity. For any given difference between the bond's stated interest rate and the market interest rate, the closer a bond is to maturity, the smaller the premium or discount will be.

rate at the date the bonds were issued. Bond discount is a deferred charge that is amortized to interest expense over the life of the bond. The amortization increases interest expense over the amount actually paid to bondholders. Bond discount is classified in the balance sheet as a contra account to the Bonds Payable liability. Bond premium is a deferred credit that is amortized to interest expense, and its effect is to reduce interest expense below the amount actually paid to bondholders. Bond premium is classified in the balance sheet as an addition to the Bonds Payable liability.

Whether a bond is issued at a premium or a discount, the bond's carrying value will converge to its face amount over the life of the bond as the premium or discount is amortized:

Carrying value $

$1,050

$1,000 (face)   Premium amortization
Discount amortization

$950

0 (issuance)   Time   20 years (maturity)

The financial statement effects of recording the interest accrual, interest payment, and discount or premium amortization are as follows:

Balance Sheet	Income Statement
Assets = Liabilities + Stockholders' equity	←Net income = Revenues − Expenses
Interest accrual (each fiscal period, perhaps monthly):	

+ Interest
          Payable
	− Interest
	    Expense

Interest payment (periodically, perhaps semiannually):	
− Cash − Interest Payable	
Amortization (each time interest is accrued):	
Discount	

+ Discount
      on Bonds
      Payable
	− Interest
	    Expense
	(An increase in interest expense)

Premium	

− Premium
      on Bonds
      Payable
	+ Interest
	    Expense
	(A decrease in interest expense)

These entries record the financial statement effects:

```
Dr.   Interest Expense . . . . . . . . . . . . . . . . . . . . . . . . . . . . . . . . . .      xx
      Cr.   Interest Payable . . . . . . . . . . . . . . . . . . . . . . . . . . . . . . .            xx
      Interest accrual (each fiscal period, perhaps monthly).
Dr.   Interest Payable . . . . . . . . . . . . . . . . . . . . . . . . . . . . . . . . . .      xx
      Cr.   Cash . . . . . . . . . . . . . . . . . . . . . . . . . . . . . . . . . . . . . . .            xx
      Interest payment (periodically, perhaps semiannually).
Dr.   Interest Expense . . . . . . . . . . . . . . . . . . . . . . . . . . . . . . . . . .      xx
      Cr.   Discount on Bonds Payable . . . . . . . . . . . . . . . . . . . . . . .            xx
      Amortization of discount (each time interest is accrued).
Dr.   Premium on Bonds Payable . . . . . . . . . . . . . . . . . . . . . . . . . .      xx
      Cr.   Interest Expense . . . . . . . . . . . . . . . . . . . . . . . . . . . . . . .            xx
      Amortization of premium (each time interest is accrued).
```

Discount or premium usually is amortized on a straight-line basis over the life of the bonds because the amounts involved are often immaterial. However, it is more appropriate to use a compound interest method that results in amortization related to the carrying value (face amount plus unamortized premium or minus unamortized discount) of the bonds. This is referred to as the *effective interest method* and is used when the amount of discount or premium amortization is deemed material. When the effective interest method is used, amortization is smallest in the first year of the bond's life, and it increases in each subsequent year.

Retirements and conversions of bonds payable. Bonds payable are reported on the balance sheet at their carrying value. Sometimes this amount is referred to as the **book value** of the bonds. As discount is amortized over the life of a bond, the carrying value of the bond increases. At the maturity date, the bond's carrying value is equal to its face amount because the bond discount has been fully amortized. Likewise, as premium is amortized, the carrying value of the bond decreases until it equals the face amount at maturity. Thus, when bonds are paid off (or retired) at maturity, the effect on the financial statements is:

Balance Sheet	Income Statement
Assets = Liabilities + Stockholders' equity	←Net income = Revenues − Expenses
+ Cash − Bonds Payable	

The entry is:

Dr. Bonds Payable	xx
Cr. Cash.	xx

Most bonds are **callable bonds;** this means the issuer may pay off the bonds before the scheduled maturity date. Bonds will be called if market interest rates have dropped below the rate being paid on the bonds and the firm can save interest costs by issuing new bonds at a lower rate. Likewise, if the firm has cash that will not be needed in operations in the immediate future, it can redeem the bonds and save more interest expense than could be earned (as interest income) by investing the excess cash. A **call premium** usually is paid to bondholders if the bond is called; that is, bondholders receive more than the face amount of the bond because they must reinvest the proceeds, usually at a lower interest rate than was being earned on the called bonds.

If the bonds are called or redeemed prior to maturity, it is appropriate to write off the unamortized balance of premium or discount as part of the transaction. Because a call premium usually is involved in an early retirement of bonds, a loss on the retirement usually will be recognized—although a gain on the retirement is also possible. Here are the financial statement effects of recording an early retirement of $100,000 face amount bonds having a book value of $95,000 by redeeming them for a total payment of $102,000:

Balance Sheet	Income Statement
Assets = Liabilities + Stockholders' equity	←Net income = Revenues − Expenses

Cash   Bonds Payable
− 102,000 − 100,000
 	
         Discount on
         Bonds Payable
         + 5,000
	Loss on
	Retirement
	of Bonds
	− 7,000

The entry is:

Dr. Bonds Payable	100,000	
Dr. Loss on Retirement of Bonds	7,000	
Cr. Cash.		102,000
Cr. Discount on Bonds Payable		5,000

The gain or loss on the retirement of the bonds is reported as other income or expense in the income statement. The gain or loss is not considered part of operating income or interest expense. The firm is willing to retire the bonds and recognize the loss because it will save, in future interest expense, more than the loss incurred.

Additional bond terminology.   A discussion of bonds involves quite a bit of specialized terminology and although you need not master it all to understand the financial statement impact of bond transactions, it is relevant to understanding bonds.

The contract between the issuer of the bonds and the bondholders is the **bond indenture,** and it is frequently administered by a third party, the **trustee of bonds**—often a bank trust department. Bonds are issued in one of two forms: **registered bonds** and **coupon bonds.**

The name and address of the owner of a registered bond are known to the issuer, and interest payments are mailed to the bondholder on a quarterly, semiannual, or annual basis, as called for in the indenture. The owner of a coupon bond is not known to the issuer; the bondholder receives interest by clipping a coupon on the interest payment date and depositing it in her or his bank account. The coupon is then sent to the trustee and is honored as though it were a check. Coupon bonds are no longer issued because federal income tax regulations have been changed to require interest payers to report the names and Social Security numbers of payees, but coupon bonds issued prior to that regulation are still outstanding.

Bonds are also classified according to the security, or collateral, that is pledged by the issuer. **Debenture bonds** (or **debentures**) are bonds that are secured only by the general credit of the issuer and, thus, are considered to be unsecured debt securities because they are not secured by specific assets. **Mortgage bonds** are secured by a lien against real estate owned by the issuer. **Collateral trust bonds** are secured by the pledge of securities or other intangible property. Details of bond categories would be found in the notes to the financial statements.

Another classification of bonds relates to when the bonds mature. **Term bonds** require a lump-sum repayment of the face amount of the bond at the maturity date. **Serial bonds** are repaid in installments. The installments may or may not be equal in amount; the first installment is usually scheduled for a date several years after the issuance of the bonds. **Convertible bonds** may be converted into stock of the issuer corporation at the option of the bondholder. The number of shares of stock into which a bond is convertible is established when the bond is issued, but the conversion feature may not become effective for several years. If the stock price has risen substantially while the bonds have been outstanding, bondholders may elect to receive shares of stock with the anticipation that the stock will be worth more than the face amount of the bonds when the bonds mature.

The specific characteristics, the interest rate, and the maturity date usually are included in a bond's description. For example, you may hear or read about long-term debt described as Cruisers, Inc.'s, 12 percent convertible debentures due in 2027, callable after 2014 at 102, or its 12.5 percent First Mortgage Serial Bonds with maturities from 2013 to 2023.

---

6. What does it mean when a bond is referred to as a debenture bond?
7. What does it mean when bond market values change in the opposite direction from market interest rate changes?
8. What does it mean when a bond is issued at a premium?

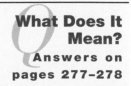

What Does It Mean?
Answers on pages 277–278

Deferred Tax Liabilities

LO 9

Explain what deferred
tax liabilities are and
why they arise.

Deferred tax liabilities are provided for temporary differences between income tax and financial statement recognition of revenues and expenses. Deferred tax liabilities are normally long-term and represent income taxes that are expected to be paid more than a year after the balance sheet date. For many firms, deferred income taxes are one of the most significant liabilities shown on the balance sheet. These amounts arise from the accounting process of matching revenues and expenses; a liability is recognized for the probable future tax consequences of events that have taken place up to the balance sheet date. For example, some revenues that have been earned and recognized for accounting (book) purposes during the current fiscal year may not be taxable until the following year. Likewise, some expenses (such as depreciation) may be deductible for tax purposes before they are recorded in determining book income. These temporary differences between book income and taxable income cause deferred tax liabilities that are postponed until future years.

The most significant temporary difference item resulting in a deferred income tax liability for most firms relates to depreciation expense. As previously explained, a firm may use straight-line depreciation for financial reporting and use the Modified Accelerated Cost Recovery System (prescribed by the Internal Revenue Code) for income tax determination. Thus, depreciation deductions for tax purposes are taken earlier than depreciation expense is recognized for book purposes. Of course, this temporary difference will eventually reverse; over the life of the asset, the same total amount of book and tax depreciation will be reported. Although the calculations involved are complicated, the effect on the financial statements of accruing income taxes when an increase in the deferred income tax liability is required is straightforward:

Balance Sheet	Income Statement
Assets = Liabilities + Stockholders' equity	←Net income = Revenues − Expenses
+ Income Taxes Payable + Deferred Tax Liabilities	− Income Tax Expense

The entry is:

Dr.	Income Tax Expense.	xx	
	Cr. Income Taxes Payable.		xx
	Cr. Deferred Tax Liabilities.		xx
To accrue current and deferred income taxes.			

If income tax rates do not decrease, the deferred income tax liability of most firms will increase over time. As firms grow, more and more depreciable assets are acquired, and price-level increases cause costs for (new) replacement assets to be higher than the cost of (old) assets being replaced. Thus, the temporary difference between book and tax depreciation grows each year because the excess of book depreciation over

Current Assets	Noncurrent Assets	Current Liabilities	Noncurrent Liabilities
331	232	138	314

Source: *Accounting Trends and Techniques,* Tables 2-5, 2-10, 2-12, and 2-14, copyright © 2011, by American Institute of Certified Public Accountants, Inc. Reprinted with permission.

Table 7-1

Reporting Frequency of Deferred Income Taxes by Category for 500 Publicly Owned Industrial and Merchandising Corporations—2010

income tax depreciation for older assets is more than offset by the excess of tax depreciation over book depreciation for newer assets. Accordingly, some accountants have questioned the appropriateness of showing deferred taxes as a liability because in the aggregate the balance of this account has grown larger and larger for many firms and therefore never seems to actually become payable. They argue that deferred tax liabilities—if recorded at all—should be recorded at the present value of future cash flows discounted at an appropriate interest rate. Otherwise, the amounts shown on the balance sheet will overstate the obligation to pay future taxes.

Most deferred income taxes result from the temporary difference between book and tax depreciation expense, but there are other temporary differences as well. When the temporary difference involves an expense that is recognized for financial accounting purposes before it is deductible for tax purposes, a deferred tax asset can arise. For example, an estimated warranty liability is shown on the balance sheet and warranty expense is reported in the income statement in the year the firm sells a warranted product, but the tax deduction is not allowed until an actual warranty expenditure is made. Because this temporary difference will cause taxable income to be lower in future years, a deferred tax asset is reported. As illustrated in Table 7-1, the number of companies reporting deferred tax assets now actually exceeds the number of companies reporting deferred tax liabilities, although some companies may have both but choose to offset one against the other for financial reporting purposes.

Accounting for deferred tax items is an extremely complex issue that has caused a great deal of debate within the accounting profession. Major changes in accounting for deferred income taxes have occurred in recent years as accounting standards have evolved in response to the needs of financial statement users.

9. What does it mean when a company has a deferred income tax liability?

What Does It Mean?
Answer on page 278

Other Noncurrent Liabilities

Frequently included in this balance sheet category are obligations to pension plans and other employee benefit plans, including deferred compensation and bonus plans. Expenses of these plans are accrued and reflected in the income statement of the fiscal period in which the benefit is earned by the employee. Because benefits are frequently conditional upon continued employment, future salary levels, and other factors, actuaries and other experts estimate the expense to be reported in a given fiscal period. The employer's pension expense will also depend on the ROI earned on funds invested in the pension or other benefit plan trust accounts over time. Because of the many significant factors that must be estimated in the expense and liability calculations, accounting for pension plans is a complex topic that has been controversial over the years. In 2006, the FASB issued an accounting standard to increase the uniformity of accounting for pensions. A significant provision of the standard requires the recognition of the overfunded (asset) or underfunded (liability) status of a defined benefit pension plan on the balance sheet. The funded status is measured as the difference between the plan assets at fair value and the projected benefit obligation, which is the present value of all future amounts expected to be paid to current plan participants and retirees.

An issue closely related to pensions is the accounting for postretirement benefit plans other than pensions. These plans provide medical, hospitalization, life insurance, and other benefits to retired employees. The 2006 standard that requires balance sheet recognition of an asset (for overfunded) or liability (for underfunded) pension plans applies to other postretirement benefit plans as well, although for pragmatic reasons the reporting entity's benefit obligation is measured in a different manner. Prior standards for both pension and other postretirement plans had relegated information about the overfunded or underfunded status of such plans to the notes to the financial statements. The present standard is believed to provide a better matching of revenues and expenses, a more appropriate balance sheet presentation, and more consistent and understandable note disclosures.

Another item included with other long-term liabilities of some firms is the estimated liability under lawsuits in progress and product warranty programs. The liability is reflected at its estimated amount, and the related expense is reported in the income statement of the period in which the expense was incurred or the liability was identified. Sometimes the term *reserve* is used to describe these items, as in "reserve for product warranty claims." However, the term *reserve* is misleading because this amount refers to an estimated liability, not an amount of money that has been set aside to meet the liability.

Explain what noncontrolling interest is, why it arises, and what it means in the balance sheet.

The last caption formerly seen in the long-term liability section of many balance sheets (in 2008 and previous years) was **noncontrolling interest** in subsidiaries (frequently called **minority interest**). A subsidiary is a corporation that is more than 50 percent owned by the firm for which the financial statements have been prepared. (See Business in Practice—Parent and Subsidiary Corporations in Chapter 2 for more discussion about a subsidiary.) The financial statements of the parent company and its subsidiaries are combined through a process known as *consolidation*. The resulting financial statements are referred to as the **consolidated financial statements** of the parent and its subsidiary(ies). In consolidation, most of the assets and liabilities of the parent and subsidiary are added together. Reciprocal amounts (such as a parent's account receivable from a subsidiary and the subsidiary's account payable to the parent) are eliminated, or offset. The parent's investment in the subsidiary (an asset) is offset against the stockholders' equity of the subsidiary. Noncontrolling interest arises if the subsidiary is not 100 percent owned by the parent company because the parent's investment will be less than the total stockholders' equity of the subsidiary. Noncontrolling interest is the equity of the other (minority) stockholders in the net assets of the subsidiary. This amount does not represent what the parent company would have to pay to acquire the rest of the stock of the subsidiary, nor is it a liability in the true sense of the term. The noncontrolling interest reported on a consolidated balance sheet is included because all of the subsidiary's assets and liabilities (except those eliminated to avoid double counting) have been added to the parent company's assets and liabilities, but only the parent company's share of the subsidiary's stockholders' equity is represented in the consolidated stockholders' equity total. To keep the balance sheet in balance, the noncontrolling stockholders' portion of stockholders' equity of the subsidiary must be shown.

Although it was usually included with noncurrent liabilities in most consolidated balance sheets in 2008 and previous years, some accountants believed that noncontrolling (minority) interest should have been shown as a separate item between liabilities and stockholders' equity because this amount is not really a liability representing a fixed claim against the consolidated entity. In December 2007, the FASB issued a standard that took this position one step further by requiring that noncontrolling interest be reported within equity, but separate from the parent company's equity, in the consolidated balance sheets of all reporting entities beginning in 2009. The financial reporting and presentation issues concerning noncontrolling interest are discussed further and illustrated in Chapters 8 and 9. For now, simply understand that this item is no longer reported as a liability, although some financial analysts may continue to treat it as though it were.

Contingent Liabilities

Contingencies are potential gains or losses, the determination of which depends on one or more future events. **Contingent liabilities** are potential claims on a company's resources arising from such things as pending litigation, environmental hazards, casualty losses to property, and product warranties, to name just a few. But when should a firm recognize a loss and record the related liability on its books due to a mere contingency? Only in cases where the following two conditions have been met: First, it must be *probable* that the loss will be confirmed by a future transaction or event; and second, the amount of the loss must be *reasonably estimable*. Using product warranties as an example, you learned in this chapter that a firm's annual warranty expense is normally recorded based on estimates made by management. Why are contingent warranty claims recorded as liabilities? Because it is probable that future warranty claims will have to be paid, and the amount of such claims can be estimated with reasonable accuracy at the time the original sales transaction (with the attached product warranty) is made.

Application of these conditions can become difficult in practice, especially with respect to litigation and environmental contingencies, so the note disclosures in annual reports must be carefully analyzed to determine the adequacy of management's estimates. The tobacco and firearms industries, for example, have been battling increasingly complex litigation in recent years, the final outcome of which may not be determinable for years or even decades to come.

Because of accounting conservatism, gain contingencies are not recognized in the financial statements; companies may, however, disclose the nature of a gain contingency in the notes to the financial statements (including estimated amounts), but only where the gain is highly likely to occur.

Demonstration Problem

Visit the text website at www.mhhe.com/marshall10e to view a demonstration problem for this chapter.

Summary

This chapter has discussed the accounting for and presentation of the following liabilities and related income statement accounts. Contra liabilities and reductions of expense accounts are shown in parentheses:

Balance Sheet	Income Statement
Assets = Liabilities + Stockholder's equity	←Net income = Revenues − Expenses
Current Liabilities	
Short-Term Debt	Interest Expense
(Discount on Short-Term Debt)	Interest Expense
Current Maturities of Long-Term Debt	
Accounts Payable	
Unearned Revenue	Revenue
Other Accrued Liabilities	Various Expenses
Long-Term Liabilities:	
Bonds Payable	Interest Expense
(Discount on Bonds Payable)	Interest Expense
Premium on Bonds Payable	(Interest Expense)
Deferred Tax Liabilities	Income Tax Expense

Liabilities are obligations of the entity. Most liabilities arise because funds have been borrowed or an obligation is recognized as a result of the accrual accounting process. Current liabilities are those that are expected to be paid within a year of the balance sheet date. Noncurrent, or long-term, liabilities are expected to be paid more than a year after the balance sheet date.

Short-term debt, such as a bank loan, is obtained to provide cash for seasonal buildup of inventory. The loan is expected to be repaid when the inventory is sold and the accounts receivable from the sale are collected. The interest cost of short-term debt sometimes is calculated on a discount basis.

Long-term debt principal payments that will be made within a year of the balance sheet date are classified as a current liability.

Accounts payable represents amounts owed to suppliers of inventories and other resources. Some accounts payable are subject to a cash discount if paid within a time frame specified by the supplier. The internal control system of most entities will attempt to encourage adherence to the policy of taking all cash discounts offered.

Unearned revenue, other deferred credits, and other accrued liabilities arise primarily because of accrual accounting procedures that result in the recognition of expenses/revenues in the fiscal period in which they are incurred/earned. Many of these liabilities are estimated because the actual liability isn't known when the financial statements are prepared.

Long-term debt is a significant part of the capital structure of many firms. Funds are borrowed, rather than invested by the owners, because the firm expects to take advantage of the financial leverage associated with debt. If borrowed money can be invested to earn a higher return (ROI) than the interest cost, the return on the stockholders' investment (ROE) will be greater than ROI. However, the opposite is also true. Leverage adds to the risk associated with an investment in an entity.

Long-term debt frequently is issued in the form of bonds payable. Bonds have a stated interest rate (that is almost always a fixed percentage), a face amount or principal, and a maturity date when the principal must be paid. Because the interest rate on a bond is fixed, changes in the market rate of interest result in fluctuations in the market value of the bond. As market interest rates rise, bond prices fall, and vice versa. The market value of a bond is the present value of the interest payments and maturity value, discounted at the market interest rate. When bonds are issued and the market rate at the date of issue is different from the stated rate of the bond, a premium or discount results. Both bond premium and discount are amortized to interest expense over the life of the bond. Premium amortization reduces interest expense below the amount of interest paid. Discount amortization increases interest expense over the amount of interest paid. A bond sometimes is retired before its maturity date because market interest rates have dropped significantly below the stated interest rate of the bond. For the issuer, early retirement of bonds can result in a gain but usually results in a loss.

Deferred income taxes result from temporary differences between book and taxable income. The most significant temporary difference is caused by the different depreciation methods used for each purpose. The amount of deferred income tax liability is the amount of income tax expected to be paid in future years, based on tax rates expected to apply in future years multiplied by the total amount of temporary differences.

Other long-term liabilities may relate to pension obligations, other postretirement benefit plan obligations, warranty obligations, or estimated liabilities under lawsuits in process. Noncontrolling interest, formerly reported as a long-term liability, is now reported within equity but separate from the parent company's equity, as discussed further in Chapters 8 and 9.

Refer to the Campbell Soup Company balance sheet and related notes in the appendix, and to other financial statements you may have, and observe how information about liabilities is presented.

Key Terms and Concepts

account payable (p. 257) A liability representing an amount payable to another entity, usually because of the purchase of merchandise or a service on credit.

annual percentage rate (APR) (p. 254) The effective (true) annual interest rate on a loan.

bond or **bond payable (p. 261)** A long-term liability with a stated interest rate and maturity date, usually issued in denominations of $1,000.

bond discount (p. 263) The excess of the face amount of a bond over the market value of a bond (the proceeds of the issue).

bond indenture (p. 269) The formal agreement between the borrower and investor(s) in bonds.

bond premium (p. 263)   The excess of the market value of a bond (the proceeds of a bond issue) over the face amount of the bond(s) issued.

book value (p. 267)   The balance of the ledger account (including related contra accounts, if any), for an asset, liability, or stockholders' equity account. Sometimes referred to as *carrying value.*

call premium (p. 268)   An amount paid in excess of the face amount of a bond when the bond is repaid prior to its established maturity date.

callable bonds (p. 268)   Bonds that can be redeemed by the issuer, at its option, prior to the maturity date.

collateral trust bond (p. 269)   A bond secured by the pledge of securities or other intangible property.

consolidated financial statements (p. 272)   Financial statements resulting from the combination of parent and subsidiary company financial statements.

contingent liability (p. 273)   A potential claim on a company's resources (i.e., loss) that depends on future events; must be *probable* and *reasonably estimable* to be recorded as a liability on the balance sheet.

contra liability (p. 256)   An account that normally has a debit balance that is subtracted from a related liability on the balance sheet.

convertible bonds (p. 269)   Bonds that can be converted to common stock of the issuer at the bondholder's option.

coupon bond (p. 269)   A bond for which the owner's name and address are not known by the issuer and/or trustee. Interest is received by clipping interest coupons that are attached to the bond and submitting them to the issuer.

coupon rate (p. 264)   The rate used to calculate the interest payments on a bond. Sometimes called *stated rate.*

current maturity of long-term debt (p. 257)   Principal payments on long-term debt that are scheduled to be paid within one year of the balance sheet date.

debenture bonds or **debentures (p. 269)**   Bonds secured by the general credit of the issuer but not secured by specific assets.

deferred credit (p. 257)   An account with a credit balance that will be recognized as a revenue (or as an expense reduction) in a future period. See *unearned revenue.*

deferred tax liability (p. 270)   A long-term liability that arises because of temporary differences between when an item (principally depreciation expense) is recognized for book and tax purposes.

discount loan (p. 254)   A loan on which interest is paid at the beginning of the loan period.

face amount (p. 261)   The principal amount of a bond.

FICA tax (p. 258)   Federal Insurance Contribution Act tax used to finance federal programs for old age and disability benefits (Social Security) and health insurance (Medicare).

financial leverage (p. 261)   The use of debt (with a fixed interest rate) that causes a difference between return on investment and return on equity.

gross pay (p. 258)   The total earnings of an employee for a payroll period.

interest calculation—discount basis (p. 255)   Interest calculation in which the interest (called *discount*) is subtracted from the principal to determine the amount of money (the proceeds) made available to the borrower. Only the principal is repaid at the maturity date because the interest is, in effect, prepaid.

interest calculation—straight basis (p. 254)   Interest calculation in which the principal is the amount of money made available to the borrower. Principal and interest are normally repaid by the borrower at the maturity date, although interest may be paid on an interim basis as well.

interpolating (p. 255)   A mathematical term to describe the process of *interpreting* and *relating* two factors from a (present value) table to approximate a third factor not shown in the table.

long-term debt (p. 261) A liability that will be paid more than one year from the balance sheet date.

maturity date (p. 253) The date when a loan is scheduled to be repaid.

minority interest (p. 272) Another term for *noncontrolling interest.*

mortgage bond (p. 269) A bond secured by a lien on real estate.

net pay (p. 258) Gross pay less payroll deductions; the amount the employer is obligated to pay to the employee.

noncontrolling interest (p. 272) The portion of equity in a less than 100 percent owned subsidiary not attributable, directly or indirectly, to the parent company; frequently called *minority interest.* Reported within equity, but separate from the parent company's equity, in the consolidated balance sheet; previously reported as a liability by most companies.

note payable (p. 253) A liability that arises from issuing a note; a formal promise to pay a stated amount at a stated date, usually with interest at a stated rate and sometimes secured by collateral. Can be short-term or long-term.

prime rate (p. 253) The interest rate charged by banks on loans to large and most creditworthy customers; a benchmark interest rate.

proceeds (p. 255) The amount of cash received in a transaction.

registered bond (p. 269) A bond for which the owner's name and address are recorded by the issuer and/or trustee.

revolving line of credit (p. 253) A loan on which regular payments are to be made but which can be quickly increased up to a predetermined limit as additional funds must be borrowed.

serial bond (p. 269) A bond that is to be repaid in installments.

stated rate (p. 264) The rate used to calculate the amount of interest payments on a bond. Sometimes called *coupon rate.*

term bond (p. 269) A bond that is to be repaid in one lump sum at the maturity date.

trustee of bonds (p. 269) The agent who coordinates activities between the bond issuer and the investors in bonds.

unearned revenue (p. 257) A liability arising from receipt of cash before the related revenue has been earned. See *deferred credit.*

working capital loan (p. 253) A short-term loan that is expected to be repaid from collections of accounts receivable.

---

1. It means that interest on the loan is subtracted from the principal of the loan and the difference is actually made available for the borrower's use.

2. It means that if liabilities are understated, it is most likely that expenses are also understated and net income is overstated.

3. It means that borrowed funds have been invested to earn a greater rate of return than the interest rate being paid on the borrowed funds.

4. It means that if the firm cannot earn a greater rate of return than the interest rate being paid on borrowed funds, its chances of not being able to repay the debt and of going bankrupt are greater than if it had less financial leverage.

5. It means that the interest rate used to calculate interest payments on the bond is fixed and does not change as market interest rates change.

6. It means that the bond is secured by the general credit of the issuer, not specific assets.

ANSWERS TO
What Does It Mean?

7. It means that as market interest rates rise, the present value of the fixed interest return on the bond falls, so the market value of the bond falls.

8. It means that the bond has been issued for more than its face amount because the stated interest rate is greater than the market interest rate on the issue date.

9. It means that the firm's deductions for income tax purposes have been greater than expenses subtracted in arriving at net income for book purposes; so when tax deductions become less than book expenses, more income tax will be payable than income taxes based on book net income.

Self-Study Material

Visit the text website at www.mhhe.com/marshall10e to take an online self-study quiz for this chapter.

Matching I Following are a number of the key terms and concepts introduced in the chapter, along with a list of corresponding definitions. Match the appropriate letter for the key term or concept to each definition provided (items 1–10). Note that not all key terms and concepts will be used. Answers are provided at the end of this chapter.

a. Working capital loan
b. Maturity date
c. Revolving line of credit
d. Straight interest
e. Discount interest
f. Annual percentage rate (APR)
g. Prime rate
h. Bond discount
i. Current maturities of long-term debt

j. Mortgage bond
k. Collateral trust bond
l. Serial bond
m. Callable
n. Call premium
o. Convertible bond
p. Face amount of bond
q. Stated interest rate
r. Bond premium

_____ **1.** The interest rate used to calculate the amount of interest payable on a bond. Sometimes called the *coupon rate*.

_____ **2.** A loan on which regular payments are to be made but which can be increased up to a predetermined limit as additional funds need to be borrowed.

_____ **3.** A short-term loan that is expected to be repaid from collections of accounts receivable.

_____ **4.** The interest rate charged by banks on loans to large and most creditworthy customers; a benchmark interest rate.

_____ **5.** The date when a loan is scheduled to be repaid.

_____ **6.** A bond secured by the pledge of securities or other intangible property.

_____ **7.** Principal payments on long-term debt that are scheduled to be paid within one year of the balance sheet date.

_____ **8.** The principal amount of a bond.

_____ **9.** An amount paid in excess of the face amount of a bond when the bond is repaid prior to its established maturity date.

_____ **10.** Refers to the bond issuer's right to redeem bonds prior to the established maturity date, or to a corporation's right to redeem its preferred stock.

Matching II Following are a number of the key terms and concepts introduced in the chapter, along with a list of corresponding definitions. Match the appropriate letter for the key term or concept to each definition provided (items 1–10). Note that not all key terms and concepts will be used. Answers are provided at the end of this chapter.

a.	Accounts payable	i.	Registered bonds
b.	Unearned revenue	j.	Contra liability
c.	Debenture bond	k.	Proceeds
d.	Long-term debt	l.	Carrying value
e.	Leverage	m.	Coupon bond
f.	Bond payable	n.	Deferred tax liabilities
g.	Bond indenture	o.	Consolidated financial
h.	Trustee of bonds		statements

_____ **1.** A bond for which the owner's name and address are recorded by the issuer and/or trustee.

_____ **2.** A liability arising from receipt of cash before the related revenue has been earned.

_____ **3.** The agent who coordinates activities between the bond issuer and the investor in bonds.

_____ **4.** A long-term liability with a stated interest rate and maturity date, usually in denominations of $1,000.

_____ **5.** The amount of cash received in a transaction.

_____ **6.** A bond for which the owner's name and address are not known by the issuer and/or trustee. Interest is received by clipping and submitting to the issuer interest coupons that are attached to the bond.

_____ **7.** The use of borrowed money on which the interest cost is different from the rate of return on the investment of the borrowed funds.

_____ **8.** A long-term liability that arises because of timing differences in the recognition of items (principally depreciation expense) for book purposes and tax purposes.

_____ **9.** An account that normally has a debit balance and that is subtracted from a related liability on the balance sheet.

_____ **10.** A bond secured by the general credit of the issuer and not secured by specific assets.

Multiple Choice For each of the following questions, circle the best response. Answers are provided at the end of this chapter.

1. All of the following are examples of "accrued expense" types of liabilities except the liability for

  _a._ short-term notes taken out at a bank during the year.

  _b._ payroll taxes owed by the employer for the year.

  _c._ property taxes owed to local governments for the year.

  _d._ salaries and wages owed to employees at the end of the year.

  _e._ estimated product warranty costs on products sold during the year.

2. When choosing between issuing common stock and issuing bonds, managers of corporations should take into account

    a. the tax advantages to the company of deducting the interest cost of bonds.

    b. the demands placed on their company by stockholders who expect to be paid quarterly dividends.

    c. the risks associated with having to make fixed interest payments on bonds at predetermined times.

    d. the impact that the choice will have on their company's financial leverage.

    e. all of the above.

3. The recognition of liabilities *often* results in

    a. the recognition of expenses.

    b. a more conservative representation of financial position.

    c. a decrease in net income.

    d. a decrease in ROI.

    e. all of the above.

4. The Discount on Short-Term Debt account

    a. is a contra liability account.

    b. reduces the total amount of liabilities reported on the balance sheet.

    c. is often netted against the liability account to which it relates for financial reporting purposes.

    d. is amortized to interest expense over the life of the liability to which it relates.

    e. all of the above.

5. Which of the following is *not* typically classified as a current liability?

    a. Accounts Payable.

    b. Notes Payable.

    c. Bonds Payable.

    d. Unearned Subscription Revenue.

    e. Interest Payable

6. All of the following give rise to a liability *except*

    a. money borrowed from a bank.

    b. interest costs resulting from the passage of time.

    c. employees working before being paid.

    d. products sold with warranties.

    e. negotiations to make a purchase on credit.

7. The *carrying value* of a bond in the liability section of the balance sheet will

    a. increase over time as the Premium on Bonds Payable account is amortized.

    b. increase over time as a bond issued at a discount reaches maturity.

    c. increase over time as a bond issued at par reaches maturity.

    d. decrease over time as the Discount on Bonds Payable account is amortized.

    e. increase over time as Interest Expense on the bond is accrued each year.

8. Kasap, Inc., has been authorized to issue $30 million of 14%, 20-year bonds payable. Interest will be paid on a semiannual basis on June 30 and December 31

each year. At the date the bonds were to be issued, the market rate of interest for this quality of bond was 14.7%. On the basis of these facts, it might be expected that

   a. Kasap, Inc., will not be able to sell the bonds because it offers less interest than is paid on similar bonds in the market.

   b. because of legal considerations, the bonds will be issued at par and investors will be paid the 14.7% market rate of interest.

   c. the bonds will be issued at a discount.

   d. the bonds will be issued at a premium.

   e. based on the facts presented, the issue price is indeterminable.

9. Evan and Michelle ask what should be done in their records in relation to the $1,900 they owe (but have not paid) Greenview County for property taxes on their farm at the end of 2013. You would respond by describing the journal entry they should record, which includes a $1,900

   a. decrease (credit) to Cash.

   b. increase (debit) to Cash.

   c. decrease (debit) to Property Taxes Payable.

   d. increase (debit) to Property Taxes Expense.

   e. increase (credit) to Property Taxes Revenue.

10. The accounting for deferred income taxes is a controversial topic because

   a. it is sometimes unclear whether deferred income taxes will ever have to be paid by companies that continue to grow (in total assets).

   b. estimating future tax rates that should be used in current calculations is difficult because changes in the tax code are difficult to project.

   c. price-level increases have caused the replacement cost of assets to be higher than the original costs of assets being replaced.

   d. new temporary differences originating on assets being purchased during the current year are often larger in dollar amount than old temporary differences reversing on assets purchased in prior years.

   e. all of the above.

Mini-Exercises

All applicable Mini-Exercises are available with McGraw-Hill's *Connect*™ *Accounting*.

Unearned revenues—rent On December 1, 2013, an advance rent payment of $12,900, representing a three-month prepayment for the months of December, January, and February, was received in cash from the company's tenant.

Mini-Exercise 7.1

LO 3

Required:

Use the horizontal model (or write the journal entries) to record the effects of the following items:

a. The three months of rent collected in advance on December 1, 2013.

b. The adjustment that will be made at the end of each month to show the amount of rent "earned" during the month.

**Mini-Exercise
7.2
LO 4**

Other accrued liabilities—payroll For the payroll period ended on June 25, 2013, gross pay was $14,300, net pay was $10,200, FICA tax withholdings were $1,000, income tax withholdings were $2,500, and medical insurance contributions were $600.

Required:

Use the horizontal model (or write the journal entry) to show the effects of the payroll accrual on June 25, 2013.

**Mini-Exercise
7.3
LO 5**

Other accrued liabilities—warranties The balance of the Estimated Warranty Liability account was $12,500 on January 1, 2013, and $17,200 on December 31, 2013. Based on an analysis of warranty claims during the past several years, this year's warranty provision was established at 1.5% of sales, and sales during the year were $1,300,000.

Required:

a. What amount of warranty expense will appear on the income statement for the year ended December 31, 2013?

b. What were the actual costs of servicing products under warranty during the year?

**Mini-Exercise
7.4
LO 8**

Bonds payable—various issues On July 1, 2013, $6 million face amount of 7%, 10-year bonds were issued. The bonds pay interest on an annual basis on June 30 each year. The market interest rates were slightly higher than 7% when the bonds were sold.

Required:

a. How much interest will be paid annually on these bonds?

b. Were the bonds issued at a premium or discount? Explain.

c. Will the annual interest expense on these bonds be more than, equal to, or less than the amount of interest paid each year? Explain your answer.

---

connect
|ACCOUNTING

Exercises

All applicable Exercises are available with McGraw-Hill's *Connect™ Accounting.*

**Exercise 7.5
LO 2**

Notes payable—discount basis On April 15, 2013, Powell, Inc., obtained a six-month working capital loan from its bank. The face amount of the note signed by the treasurer was $300,000. The interest rate charged by the bank was 9%. The bank made the loan on a discount basis.

Required:

a. Calculate the loan proceeds made available to Powell and use the horizontal model (or write the journal entry) to show the effect of signing the note and the receipt of the cash proceeds on April 15, 2013.

b. Calculate the amount of interest expense applicable to this loan during the fiscal year ended June 30, 2013.

c. What is the amount of the current liability related to this loan to be shown in the June 30, 2013, balance sheet?

Notes payable—discount basis On August 1, 2013, Colombo Co.'s treasurer signed a note promising to pay $120,000 on December 31, 2013. The proceeds of the note were $114,000.

Exercise 7.6
LO 2

Required:

a. Calculate the discount rate used by the lender.
b. Calculate the effective interest rate (APR) on the loan.
c. Use the horizontal model (or write the journal entry) to show the effects of
    1. Signing the note and the receipt of the cash proceeds on August 1, 2013.
    2. Recording interest expense for the month of September.
    3. Repaying the note on December 31, 2013.

Other accrued liabilities—payroll taxes At March 31, 2013, the end of the first year of operations at Jaryd, Inc., the firm's accountant neglected to accrue payroll taxes of $4,800 that were applicable to payrolls for the year then ended.

Exercise 7.7
LO 4

Required:

a. Use the horizontal model (or write the journal entry) to show the effect of the accrual that should have been made as of March 31, 2013.
b. Determine the income statement and balance sheet effects of not accruing payroll taxes at March 31, 2013.
c. Assume that when the payroll taxes were paid in April 2013, the payroll tax expense account was charged. Assume that at March 31, 2014, the accountant again neglected to accrue the payroll tax liability, which was $5,000 at that date. Determine the income statement and balance sheet effects of not accruing payroll taxes at March 31, 2014.

Other accrued liabilities—real estate taxes Karysa Co. operates in a city in which real estate tax bills for one year are issued in May of the subsequent year. Thus, tax bills for 2013 are issued in May 2014 and are payable in July 2014.

Exercise 7.8
LO 5

Required:

a. Explain how the amount of tax expense for calendar 2013 and the amount of taxes payable (if any) at December 31, 2013, can be determined.
b. Use the horizontal model (or write the journal entry) to show the effect of accruing 2013 taxes of $6,400 at December 31, 2013.
c. Assume that the actual tax bill, received in May 2014, was for $6,800. Use the horizontal model (or write the journal entry) to show the effects of the appropriate adjustment to the amount previously accrued.
d. Karysa Co.'s real estate taxes have been increasing at the rate of 10% annually. Determine the income statement and balance sheet effects of not accruing 2013 taxes at December 31, 2013 (assuming that taxes in **b** are not accrued).

Other accrued liabilities—warranties Kohl Co. provides warranties for many of its products. The January 1, 2013, balance of the Estimated Warranty Liability account was $70,400. Based on an analysis of warranty claims during the past several years, this year's warranty provision was established at 0.4% of sales. During 2013, the actual cost of servicing products under warranty was $31,200, and sales were $7,200,000.

Exercise 7.9
LO 5

Required:

a. What amount of Warranty Expense will appear on Kohl Co.'s income statement for the year ended December 31, 2013?

b. What amount will be reported in the Estimated Warranty Liability account on the December 31, 2013, balance sheet?

Exercise 7.10

LO 5

Other accrued liabilities—warranties Prist Co. had not provided a warranty on its products, but competitive pressures forced management to add this feature at the beginning of 2013. Based on an analysis of customer complaints made over the past two years, the cost of a warranty program was estimated at 0.3% of sales. During 2013, sales totaled $3,450,000. Actual costs of servicing products under warranty totaled $9,700.

Required:

a. Use the horizontal model (or a T-account of the Estimated Warranty Liability) to show the effect of having the warranty program during 2013.

b. What type of accrual adjustment should be made at the end of 2013?

c. Describe how the amount of the accrual adjustment could be determined.

Exercise 7.11

LO 3

Unearned revenues—customer deposits Coolfroth Brewing Company distributes its products in an aluminum keg. Customers are charged a deposit of $50 per keg; deposits are recorded in the Keg Deposits account.

Required:

a. Where on the balance sheet will the Keg Deposits account be found? Explain your answer.

b. Use the horizontal model (or write the journal entry) to show the effect of giving a keg deposit refund to a customer.

c. A keg use analyst who works for Coolfroth estimates that 200 kegs for which deposits were received during the year will never be returned. What accounting, if any, would be appropriate for the deposits associated with these kegs?

d. Describe the accounting that would be appropriate for the cost of the kegs that are purchased and used by Coolfroth Brewing Company, including how to account for unreturned kegs.

Exercise 7.12

LO 3

Unearned revenues—ticket sales Kirkland Theater sells season tickets for six events at a price of $378. For the 2013 season, 1,200 season tickets were sold.

Required:

a. Use the horizontal model (or write the journal entry) to show the effect of the sale of the season tickets.

b. Use the horizontal model (or write the journal entry) to show the effect of presenting an event.

c. Where on the balance sheet would the account balance representing funds received for performances not yet presented be classified?

Exercise 7.13

LO 8

Bonds payable—record issuance and premium amortization Kaye Co. issued $1 million face amount of 11%, 20-year bonds on April 1, 2013. The bonds pay interest on an annual basis on March 31 each year.

Required:

a. Assume that market interest rates were slightly lower than 11% when the bonds were sold. Would the proceeds from the bond issue have been more than, less than, or equal to the face amount? Explain.

b. Independent of your answer to part **a**, assume that the proceeds were $1,080,000. Use the horizontal model (or write the journal entry) to show the effect of issuing the bonds.

c. Calculate the interest expense that Kaye Co. will show with respect to these bonds in its income statement for the fiscal year ended September 30, 2013, assuming that the premium of $80,000 is amortized on a straight-line basis.

Bonds payable—record issuance and discount amortization Coley Co. issued $15 million face amount of 9%, 10-year bonds on June 1, 2013. The bonds pay interest on an annual basis on May 31 each year.

Exercise 7.14
LO 8

Required:

a. Assume that the market interest rates were slightly higher than 9% when the bonds were sold. Would the proceeds from the bond issue have been more than, less than, or equal to the face amount? Explain.

b. Independent of your answer to part **a**, assume that the proceeds were $14,820,000. Use the horizontal model (or write the journal entry) to show the effect of issuing the bonds.

c. Calculate the interest expense that Coley Co. will show with respect to these bonds in its income statement for the fiscal year ended September 30, 2013, assuming that the discount of $180,000 is amortized on a straight-line basis.

Bonds payable—calculate market value On August 1, 2005, Bonnie purchased $15,000 of Huber Co.'s 10%, 20-year bonds at face value. Huber Co. has paid the semiannual interest due on the bonds regularly. On August 1, 2013, market rates of interest had fallen to 8%, and Bonnie is considering selling the bonds.

Exercise 7.15
LO 8

Required:

Using the present value tables in Chapter 6, calculate the market value of Bonnie's bonds on August 1, 2013.

Bonds payable—calculate market value On March 1, 2008, Matt purchased $189,000 of Lawson Co.'s 8%, 20-year bonds at face value. Lawson Co. has paid the annual interest due on the bonds regularly. On March 1, 2013, market interest rates had risen to 12%, and Matt is considering selling the bonds.

Exercise 7.16
LO 8

Required:

Using the present value tables in Chapter 6, calculate the market value of Matt's bonds on March 1, 2013.

Bonds payable—various issues Reynolds Co. issued $40 million face amount of 11% bonds when market interest rates were 10.92% for bonds of similar risk and other characteristics.

Exercise 7.17
LO 8

Required:

a. How much interest will be paid annually on these bonds?

b. Were the bonds issued at a premium or discount? Explain your answer.

c. Will the annual interest expense on these bonds be more than, equal to, or less than the amount of interest paid each year? Explain your answer.

Exercise 7.18

LO 8

Bonds payable—various issues Atom Endeavour Co. issued $500 million face amount of 9% bonds when market interest rates were 9.14% for bonds of similar risk and other characteristics.

Required:

a. How much interest will be paid annually on these bonds?

b. Were the bonds issued at a premium or discount? Explain your answer.

c. Will the annual interest expense on these bonds be more than, equal to, or less than the amount of interest paid each year? Explain your answer.

Exercise 7.19

LO 9

Deferred income tax liability The difference between the amounts of book and tax depreciation expense, as well as the desire to report income tax expense that is related to book income before taxes, causes a long-term deferred income tax liability to be reported on the balance sheet. The amount of this liability reported on the balance sheets of many firms has been increasing over the years, creating the impression that the liability will never be paid. Why has the amount of the deferred income tax liability risen steadily for many firms?

Exercise 7.20

LO 6

Financial leverage A firm issues long-term debt with an effective interest rate of 10%, and the proceeds of this debt issue can be invested to earn an ROI of 12%. What effect will this financial leverage have on the firm's ROE relative to having the same amount of funds invested by the owners/stockholders?

Exercise 7.21

LO 4, 5, 8

Transaction analysis—various accounts Enter the following column headings across the top of a sheet of paper:

Transaction/ Adjustment	Current Assets	Current Liabilities	Long-Term Debt	Net Income

Enter the transaction/adjustment letter in the first column and show the effect, if any, of each of the transactions/adjustments on the appropriate balance sheet category or on the income statement by entering the amount and indicating whether it is an addition (+) or a subtraction (−). You may also write the journal entries to record each transaction/adjustment.

a. Wages of $867 for the last three days of the fiscal period have not been accrued.

b. Interest of $170 on a bank loan has not been accrued.

c. Interest on bonds payable has not been accrued for the current month. The company has outstanding $240,000 of 8.5% bonds.

d. The discount related to the bonds in part **c** has not been amortized for the current month. The current month amortization is $50.

e. Product warranties were honored during the month; parts inventory items valued at $830 were sent to customers making claims, and cash refunds of $410 were also made.

f. During the fiscal period, advance payments from customers totaling $1,500 were received and recorded as sales revenues. The items will not be delivered to the customers until the next fiscal period. Record the appropriate adjustment.

Transaction analysis—various accounts Enter the following column headings across the top of a sheet of paper:

Exercise 7.22
LO 4, 5, 8

Transaction/ Adjustment	Current Assets	Current Liabilities	Long-Term Debt	Net Income

Enter the transaction/adjustment letter in the first column, and show the effect, if any, of each of the transactions/adjustments on the appropriate balance sheet category or on the income statement by entering the amount and indicating whether it is an addition (+) or a subtraction (−). You may also write the journal entries to record each transaction/adjustment.

a. Wages of $1,325 accrued at the end of the prior fiscal period were paid this fiscal period.

b. Real estate taxes of $3,550 applicable to the current period have not been accrued.

c. Interest on bonds payable has not been accrued for the current month. The company has outstanding $420,000 of 7.5% bonds.

d. The premium related to the bonds in part **c** has not been amortized for the current month. The current-month amortization is $110.

e. Based on past experience with its warranty program, the estimated warranty expense for the current period should be 0.2% of sales of $612,000.

f. Analysis of the company's income taxes indicates that taxes currently payable are $93,000 and that the deferred tax liability should be increased by $34,000.

Transaction analysis—various accounts Enter the following column headings across the top of a sheet of paper:

Exercise 7.23
LO 1, 2, 5, 8, 9

Transaction/ Adjustment	Current Assets	Noncurrent Assets	Current Liabilities	Noncurrent Liabilities	Stockholders' Equity	Net Income

Enter the transaction/adjustment letter in the first column and show the effect, if any, of each transaction/adjustment on the appropriate balance sheet category or on net income by entering for each category affected the account name and amount, and indicating whether it is an addition (+) or a subtraction (−). Items that affect net income should not also be shown as affecting stockholders' equity. You may also write the journal entries to record each transaction/adjustment.

a. Income tax expense of $700 for the current period is accrued. Of the accrual, $200 represents deferred tax liabilities.

b. Bonds payable with a face amount of $5,000 are issued at a price of 99.

c. Of the proceeds from the bonds in part **b**, $3,000 is used to purchase land for future expansion.

d. Because of warranty claims, finished goods inventory costing $64 is sent to customers to replace defective products.

e. A three-month, 12% note payable with a face amount of $20,000 was signed. The bank made the loan on a discount basis.

f. The next installment of a long-term serial bond requiring an annual principal repayment of $35,000 will become due within the current year.

Exercise 7.24
LO 5, 8

Transaction analysis—various accounts Enter the following column headings across the top of a sheet of paper:

Transaction/Adjustment	Current Assets	Noncurrent Assets	Current Liabilities	Noncurrent Liabilities	Stockholders' Equity	Net Income

Enter the transaction/adjustment letter in the first column and show the effect, if any, of each transaction/adjustment on the appropriate balance sheet category or on net income by entering for each category affected the account name and amount, and indicating whether it is an addition (+) or a subtraction (−). Items that affect net income should *not* also be shown as affecting stockholders' equity. You may also write the journal entries to record each transaction/adjustment.

a. Recorded the financing (capital) lease of a truck. The present value of the lease payments is $65,000; the total of the lease payments to be made is $78,000.

b. Recorded the company's payroll for the month. Gross pay was $7,200, net pay was $5,100, and various withholding liability accounts were credited for the difference.

c. Issued $21,000 of bonds payable at a price of 103.

d. Adjusted the estimated liability under a warranty program by reducing previously accrued warranty expense by $4,200.

e. Retired bonds payable with a carrying value of $12,000 by calling them at a redemption value of 101.

f. Accrued estimated health care costs for retirees; $18,000 is expected to be paid within a year, and $155,000 is expected to be paid in more than a year.

 Problems

All applicable Problems are available with McGraw-Hill's *Connect*™ *Accounting.*

Problem 7.25
LO 3

Unearned revenues—rent *(Note: See Exercise 5.20 for the related prepaid expense accounting.)* On November 1, 2013, Gordon Co. collected $37,800 in cash from its tenant as an advance rent payment on its store location. The six-month lease period ends on April 30, 2014, at which time the contract may be renewed.

Required:

a. Use the horizontal model (or write the journal entries) to record the effects of the following items for Gordon Co.:

   1. The six months of rent collected in advance on November 1, 2013.

   2. The adjustment that will be made at the end of each month to show the amount of rent "earned" during the month.

b. Calculate the amount of unearned rent that should be shown on the December 31, 2013, balance sheet with respect to this lease.

c. Suppose the advance collection received on November 1, 2013, covered an 18-month lease period at the same amount of rent per month. How should Gordon Co. report the unearned rent amount on its December 31, 2013, balance sheet?

Unearned revenues—subscription fees Evans Ltd. publishes a monthly newsletter for retail marketing managers and requires its subscribers to pay $75 in advance for a one-year subscription. During the month of September 2013, Evans Ltd. sold 200 one-year subscriptions and received payments in advance from all new subscribers. Only 120 of the new subscribers paid their fees in time to receive the September newsletter; the other subscriptions began with the October newsletter.

Problem 7.26
LO 3

Required:

a. Use the horizontal model (or write the journal entries) to record the effects of the following items:

   1. Subscription fees received in advance during September 2013.

   2. Subscription revenue earned during September 2013.

b. Calculate the amount of subscription revenue earned by Evans Ltd. during the year ended December 31, 2013, for these 200 subscriptions.

Optional continuation of Problem 7.26—lifetime subscription offer *(Note: This is an analytical assignment involving the use of present value tables and accounting estimates. Only the first sentence in Problem 7.26 applies to this continuation of the problem.)* Evans Ltd. is now considering the possibility of offering a lifetime membership option to its subscribers. Under this proposal, subscribers could receive the monthly newsletter throughout their lives by paying a flat fee of $900. The one-year subscription rate of $75 would continue to apply to new and existing subscribers who choose to subscribe on an annual basis. Assume that the average age of Evans Ltd.'s current subscribers is 38 and their average life expectancy is 78 years. Evans Ltd.'s average interest rate on long-term debt is 12%.

c. Using the information given, determine whether it would be profitable for Evans Ltd. to sell lifetime subscriptions. *(Hint: Calculate the present value of a lifetime membership for an average subscriber using the appropriate table in Chapter 6.)*

d. What additional factors should Evans Ltd. consider in determining whether to offer a lifetime membership option? Explain your answer as specifically as possible.

Other accrued liabilities—payroll The following summary data for the payroll period ended on November 14, 2012, are available for Brac Construction Ltd.:

Problem 7.27
LO 4

Gross pay	$?
FICA tax withholdings	?
Income tax withholdings	13,760
Medical insurance contributions	1,120
Union dues	640
Total deductions	21,640
Net pay	58,360

Required:

a. Calculate the missing amounts and then determine the FICA tax withholding percentage.

b. Use the horizontal model (or write the journal entry) to show the effects of the payroll accrual.

Problem 7.28

LO 4

Other accrued liabilities—payroll and payroll taxes The following summary data for the payroll period ended December 27, 2012, are available for Cayman Coating Co.:

Gross pay	$86,000
FICA tax withholdings	?
Income tax withholdings	10,320
Group hospitalization insurance	1,270
Employee contributions to pension plan	?
Total deductions	19,825
Net pay	?

Additional information

- For employees, FICA tax rates for 2012 were 5.65% on the first $110,100 of each employee's annual earnings and 1.45% on any earnings in excess of $110,100. However, no employees had accumulated earnings for the year in excess of the $110,100 limit.

- For employers, FICA tax rates for 2012 were 7.65% on the first $110,100 of each employee's annual earnings and 1.45% on any earnings in excess of $110,100.

- The federal and state unemployment compensation tax rates are 0.6% and 5.4%, respectively. These rates are levied against the employer for the first $7,000 of each employee's annual earnings. Only $9,000 of the gross pay amount for the December 27, 2012, pay period was owed to employees who were still under the annual limit.

Required:

Assuming that Cayman Coating Co.'s payroll for the last week of the year is to be paid on January 3, 2013, use the horizontal model (or write the journal entry) to record the effects of the December 27, 2012, entries for

a. Accrued payroll.

b. Accrued payroll taxes.

Problem 7.29

LO 7

Bonds payable—convertible O'Kelley Co. has outstanding $2 million face amount of 12% bonds that were issued on January 1, 2005, for $2 million. The 20-year bonds were issued in $1,000 denominations and mature on December 31, 2024. Each $1,000 bond is convertible at the bondholder's option into five shares of $10 par value common stock.

Required:

a. Under what circumstances would O'Kelley Co.'s bondholders consider converting the bonds?

b. Assume that the market price of O'Kelley Co.'s common stock is now $215 and that a bondholder elects to convert 400 $1,000 bonds. Use the horizontal model (or write the journal entry) to show the effect of the conversion on O'Kelley Co.'s financial statements.

Bonds payable—callable Hurley Co. has outstanding $30 million face amount of 15% bonds that were issued on January 1, 2001, for $29,250,000. The 20-year bonds mature on December 31, 2020, and are callable at 102 (that is, they can be paid off at any time by paying the bondholders 102% of the face amount).

Problem 7.30
LO 7

Required:

a. Under what circumstances would Hurley Co. managers consider calling the bonds?

b. Assume that the bonds are called on December 31, 2013. Use the horizontal model (or write the journal entry) to show the effect of the retirement of the bonds. *(Hint: Calculate the amount paid to bondholders; then determine how much of the bond discount would have been amortized prior to calling the bonds; and then calculate the gain or loss on retirement.)*

Bonds payable—calculate issue price and amortize discount On January 1, 2013, Drennen, Inc., issued $3 million face amount of 10-year, 14% stated rate bonds when market interest rates were 12%. The bonds pay semiannual interest each June 30 and December 31 and mature on December 31, 2022.

Problem 7.31
LO 8

Required:

a. Using the present value tables in Chapter 6, calculate the proceeds (issue price) of Drennen, Inc.'s, bonds on January 1, 2013, assuming that the bonds were sold to provide a market rate of return to the investor.

b. Assume instead that the proceeds were $2,950,000. Use the horizontal model (or write the journal entry) to record the payment of semiannual interest and the related discount amortization on June 30, 2013, assuming that the discount of $50,000 is amortized on a straight-line basis.

c. If the discount in part **b** were amortized using the compound interest method, would interest expense for the year ended December 31, 2013, be more than, less than, or equal to the interest expense reported using the straight-line method of discount amortization? Explain.

Bonds payable—calculate issue price and amortize premium On January 1, 2013, Learned, Inc., issued $90 million face amount of 20-year, 14% stated rate bonds when market interest rates were 16%. The bonds pay interest semiannually each June 30 and December 31 and mature on December 31, 2032.

Problem 7.32
LO 8

Required:

a. Using the present value tables in Chapter 6, calculate the proceeds (issue price) of Learned, Inc.'s, bonds on January 1, 2013, assuming that the bonds were sold to provide a market rate of return to the investor.

b. Assume instead that the proceeds were $93,000,000. Use the horizontal model (or write the journal entry) to record the payment of semiannual interest and the related premium amortization on June 30, 2013, assuming that the premium of $3,000,000 is amortized on a straight-line basis.

c. If the premium in part **b** were amortized using the compound interest method, would interest expense for the year ended December 31, 2013, be more than, less than, or equal to the interest expense reported using the straight-line method of premium amortization? Explain.

d. In reality, the difference between the stated interest rate and the market rate would be substantially less than 2%. The dramatic difference in this problem was designed so that you could use present value tables to answer part **a**. What causes the stated rate to be different from the market rate, and why is the difference likely to be much less than depicted in this problem?

connect
|ACCOUNTING

Cases

All applicable Cases are available with McGraw-Hill's *Connect™ Accounting*.

Case 7.33
LO 7, 9

Focus company—noncurrent liability disclosures In Exercise 1.1, you were asked to obtain the most recent annual report of a company that you were interested in reviewing throughout this term.

Required:

Please review the note disclosures provided in your focus company's annual report and identify at least three items being reported as noncurrent liabilities. Discuss what you've learned about these items and how they are presented on the balance sheet.

Case 7.34
LO 1, 5, 7, 8

Other accrued liabilities—interest *(Note: This is an analytical assignment involving the interpretation of financial statement disclosures.)* A review of the accounting records at Corless Co. revealed the following information concerning the company's liabilities that were outstanding at December 31, 2014, and 2013, respectively:

Debt (Thousands)	2014	Year-End Interest Rate	2013	Year-End Interest Rate
Short-term debt:				
Working capital loans	$250	8%	$190	7%
Current maturities of				
long-term debt	80	6%	80	6%
Long-term debt:				
Debenture bonds due in 2031	400	9%	400	9%
Serial bonds due in equal				
annual installments	240	6%	320	6%

Required:

a. Corless Co. has not yet made an adjustment to accrue the interest expense related to its *working capital loans* for the year ended December 31, 2014. Assume that the amount of interest to be accrued can be accurately estimated using an average-for-the-year interest rate applied to the average liability balance. Use the horizontal model (or write the journal entry) to record the effect of the 2014 interest accrual for working capital loans.

b. Note that the dollar amount and interest rate of the *current maturities of long-term debt* have not changed from 2013 to 2014. Does this mean that the $80,000 amount owed at the end of 2013 still has not been paid as of

December 31, 2014? *(Hint: Explain your answer with reference to other information provided in the problem.)*

c. Assume that the *debenture bonds* were originally issued at their face amount. However, the market rate of interest for bonds of similar risk has decreased significantly in recent years and is 7% at December 31, 2014. If the debenture bonds were both callable by Corless Co. and convertible by its bondholders, which event is more likely to occur? Explain your answer.

d. Assume the same facts as in part **c**. Would the market value of Corless Co.'s debenture bonds be more than or less than the $400,000 reported amount? Is this good news or bad news to the management of Corless Co.?

e. When the Serial Bonds account decreased during the year, what other account was affected, and how was it affected? Use the horizontal model (or write the journal entry) to record the effect of this transaction.

Analysis of long-term debt Assume that Home and Office City, Inc., provided the following comparative data concerning long-term debt in the notes to its 2014 annual report (amounts in millions):

Case 7.35

LO 5, 7, 8

	December 31, 2014	December 31, 2013
3¼% Convertible Subordinated Notes, due October 1, 2015; converted into shares of common stock of the Company at a conversion price of $15.3611 per share in October 2013	$ —	$1,103
6½% Senior Notes, due September 15, 2018; interest payable semiannually on March 15 and September 15 beginning in 2014	500	—
Commercial Paper; weighted average interest rate of 4.8% at January 1, 2013	—	246
Capital Lease Obligations; payable in varying installments through January 31, 2041.	216	180
Installment Notes Payable; interest imputed at rates between 5.2% and 10.0%; payable in varying installments through 2032	45	27
Unsecured Bank Loan; floating interest rate averaging 6.05% in fiscal 2014 and 5.90% in fiscal 2013; payable in August 2016.	15	15
Variable-Rate Industrial Revenue Bonds; secured by letters of credit or land; interest rates averaging 2.9% during fiscal 2014 and 3.8% during fiscal 2013; payable in varying installments through 2024	3	9
Total long-term debt.	$779	$1,580
Less current installments	29	14
Long-term debt, excluding current installments	$750	$1,566

Required:

a. As indicated, Home and Office City's 3¼% Convertible Subordinated Notes were converted into shares of common stock in October 2013. How many shares of stock were issued in conversion of these notes?

b. Regarding the 6½% Senior Notes, Home and Office City, Inc., also disclosed that "The Company, at its option, may redeem all or any portion of the Senior Notes by notice to the holder. The Senior Notes are redeemable at a redemption price, plus accrued interest, equal to the greater of (1) 100% of the principal amount of the Senior Notes to be redeemed or (2) the sum of the present values of the remaining scheduled payments of principal and interest on the Senior Notes to maturity."

Redeemable fixed-rate notes, such as those described here, are similar to callable term bonds. Thinking of the 6½% Senior Notes on this basis, would it have been *possible* for Home and Office City, Inc., to redeem ("call") these notes for an amount

1. Below face value (at a discount)?
2. Above face value (at a premium)?
3. Equal to face value (at par)?

What circumstances would have been most likely to prompt Home and Office City to redeem these notes?

c. Recall from the discussion of Cash and Cash Equivalents in Chapter 5 that commercial paper is like an IOU issued by a very creditworthy corporation. Home and Office City's note disclosures concerning commercial paper reveal that "The company has a backup credit facility with a consortium of banks for up to $800 million. The credit facility contains various restrictive covenants, none of which is expected to materially impact the company's liquidity or capital resources."

What do you think is meant by this statement?

d. What other information would you have wanted to know about Home and Office City's "Capital Lease Obligations" when making an assessment of the company's overall liquidity and leverage?

e. Regarding the "Installment Notes Payable," what is meant by "interest *imputed* at rates between 5.2% and 10%"?

f. Why do you suppose that Home and Office City's "Unsecured Bank Loan" was immaterial in relation to the company's total long-term debt?

g. Note that the "current installments" due on Home and Office City's long-term debt were immaterial in amount for both years presented. Based on the data presented in this case, explain why this is likely to change over the next five years.

Answers to Self-Study Material

Matching I: 1. q, 2. c, 3. a, 4. g, 5. b, 6. k, 7. i, 8. p, 9. n, 10. m
Matching II: 1. i, 2. b, 3. h, 4. f, 5. k, 6. m, 7. e, 8. n, 9. j, 10. c
Multiple choice: 1. a, 2. e, 3. e, 4. e, 5. c, 6. e, 7. b, 8. c, 9. d, 10. e

8

Accounting for and Presentation of Stockholders' Equity

Stockholders' equity is the claim of the entity's owners/stockholders to the assets shown in the balance sheet. Another term for stockholders' equity is *net assets,* which is assets minus liabilities. Neither the liabilities nor the elements of stockholders' equity are specifically identifiable with particular assets, although certain assets may be pledged as collateral for some liabilities.

The specific terminology used to identify stockholders' equity depends on the form of the entity's legal organization. For an individual proprietorship, the term **proprietor's capital,** or *capital,* perhaps combined with the owner's name, is frequently used. For example, in the balance sheet of a single proprietorship owned by Taneisha Ford, stockholders' equity would be labeled Taneisha Ford, Capital. For a partnership, **partners' capital** is the term used, and sometimes the capital account balance of each partner is shown on the balance sheet. In both proprietorships and partnerships, no distinction is made between invested (or paid-in) capital and retained earnings (or earned capital).

Because the corporate form of organization is used for firms that account for most of the business activity in our economy, this text focuses on corporate stockholders' equity. As explained in Chapter 2, there are two principal components of corporate stockholders' equity: paid-in capital and retained earnings. The financial statements of many small businesses that use the corporate form of organization are likely to show in stockholders' equity only capital stock (which is paid-in capital) and retained earnings. However, as shown by the "shareowners' equity" section

of the Consolidated Balance Sheets of Campbell Soup Company on page 712 of the appendix, the stockholders' equity section can become quite complex. The stockholders' equity section of the balance sheets in other annual reports that you have may appear equally complex. Stockholders' equity captions usually seen in a balance sheet are:

1. Paid-in capital:
   a. Preferred stock (sometimes issued)
   b. Common stock (always issued)
   c. Additional paid-in capital
2. Retained earnings (Accumulated deficit if negative)
3. Accumulated other comprehensive income (loss)
4. Less: Treasury stock

	August 31	
	2014	**2013**
Stockholders' equity:		
Paid-in capital:		
Preferred stock, 6%, $100 par value, cumulative, callable at $102, 5,000 shares authorized, issued, and outstanding	$ 500,000	$ 500,000
Common stock, $2 par value, 1,000,000 shares authorized, 244,800 shares issued at August 31, 2014, and 200,000 shares issued at August 31, 2013	489,600	400,000
Additional paid-in capital	3,322,400	2,820,000
Total paid-in capital	$4,312,000	$3,720,000
Retained earnings	2,828,000	2,600,000
Accumulated other comprehensive income (loss)	50,000	(100,000)
Less: Common stock in treasury, at cost; 1,000 shares at August 31, 2014	(12,000)	—
Total stockholders' equity	$7,178,000	$6,220,000

Exhibit 8-1

Stockholders' Equity Section of Racers, Inc., Balance Sheets at August 31, 2014, and 2013

5.   Noncontrolling interest (which is actually the equity interest held by *nonowners* of the reporting entity)

The objective of this chapter is to permit you to make sense of the stockholders' equity presentation of any balance sheet. You will also learn about many characteristics of stockholders' equity that are relevant to personal investment decisions. A brief overview of personal investing is provided as an appendix to this chapter. For the purposes of our discussion, the stockholders' equity section of the balance sheets of Racers, Inc., in Exhibit 8-1 will be explained.

LEARNING OBJECTIVES (LO)

After studying this chapter you should understand and be able to

LO 8-1   Describe the characteristics of common stock and show how common stock is presented in the balance sheet.

LO 8-2   Explain what preferred stock is, discuss what its advantages and disadvantages to the corporation are, and show how it is presented in the balance sheet.

LO 8-3   Describe the accounting for a cash dividend and explain the dates involved in dividend transactions.

LO 8-4   Describe what stock dividends and stock splits are and discuss why each is used.

LO 8-5   Recognize what the components of accumulated other comprehensive income (loss) are and explain why these items appear in stockholders' equity.

LO 8-6   Explain what treasury stock is, discuss why it is acquired, and show how treasury stock transactions affect stockholders' equity.

LO 8-7   Show how stockholders' equity transactions for the year are reported in the financial statements.

LO 8-8   Discuss how the presence of a noncontrolling interest affects the presentation of consolidated financial statements.

Exhibit 8-2 highlights the balance sheet accounts covered in detail in this chapter and shows the income statement and statement of cash flows components affected by these accounts.

Paid-In Capital

The captions shown in the paid-in capital category of stockholders' equity (common stock, preferred stock, and additional paid-in capital) represent amounts invested in the corporation by stockholders and are sometimes referred to as *contributed capital*. On the other hand, the retained earnings (or earned capital) category of stockholders' equity represents the entity's cumulative earnings (net income over the life of the entity) less any dividends paid. Naturally, stockholders are interested in the relationship between paid-in capital and retained earnings. The higher the Retained Earnings account balance relative to paid-in capital amounts, the better—because retained earnings reflect, in part, management's ability to earn a return on invested (paid-in) amounts. However, a large retained earnings balance also may lead stockholders to pressure management and the board of directors to pay higher dividends. Remember to keep the distinction between paid-in capital and retained earnings in mind when interpreting the stockholders' equity section of any balance sheet.

Common Stock

LO 1
Describe the characteristics of common stock and show how common stock is presented in the balance sheet.

As already explained, **common stock** (called **capital stock** at times, especially when no other classes of stock are authorized) represents residual ownership. Common stockholders are the ultimate owners of the corporation; they have claim to all assets that remain in the entity after all liabilities and preferred stock claims (described in the next section) have been satisfied. In the case of bankruptcy or forced liquidation, this residual claim may not have any value because the liabilities and preferred stock claims may exceed the amount realized from the assets in liquidation. In this severe case, the liability of the common stockholders is limited to the amount they have invested in the stock; common stockholders cannot be forced by creditors and/or preferred stockholders to invest additional amounts to make up their losses. In the more positive (and usual) case, common stockholders prosper because the profits of the firm exceed the fixed claims of creditors (interest) and preferred stockholders (preferred dividends). All of these profits accrue to common stockholders—there is no upper limit to the value of their ownership interest. Of course it is the market value of common stock that reflects the public perception of profitability (or lack thereof) and ultimate dividend-paying capability of the corporation. However, as residual owners, common stockholders are not entitled to receive any specific dividend amount and may not receive any dividends at all in some years.

Common stockholders have the right and obligation to elect members to the corporation's board of directors. The election process can take one of two forms, as described in Business in Practice—Electing Directors. The board of directors hires corporate officers, and the officers execute strategies for achieving corporate objectives. Some officers may also be directors **(inside directors),** but current practice is that most boards are made up primarily of **independent directors** (individuals not

Exhibit 8-2

Financial Statements—
The Big Picture

Balance Sheet

Current Assets	Chapter	Current Liabilities	Chapter
Cash and cash equivalents	5, 9	Short-term debt	7
Short-term marketable securities	5	Current maturities of long-term debt	7
Accounts receivable	5, 9	Accounts payable	7
Notes receivable	5	Unearned revenue or deferred credits	7
Inventories	5, 9	Payroll taxes and other withholdings	7
Prepaid expenses	5	Other accrued liabilities	7
Noncurrent Assets		**Noncurrent Liabilities**	
Land	6	Long-term debt	7
Buildings and equipment	6	Deferred tax liabilities	7
Assets acquired by capital lease	6	Other long-term liabilities	7
Intangible assets	6	**Stockholders' Equity**	
Natural resources	6	Common stock	8
Other noncurrent assets	6	Preferred stock	8
		Additional paid-in capital	8
		Retained earnings	8
		Treasury stock	8
		Accumulated other comprehensive income (loss)	8
		Noncontrolling interest	8

Income Statement

	Chapter
Sales	5, 9
Cost of goods sold	5, 9
Gross profit (or gross margin)	5, 9
Selling, general, and administrative expenses	5, 6, 9
Income from operations	9
Gains (losses) on sale of assets	6, 9
Interest income	5, 9
Interest expense	7, 9
Income tax expense	7, 9
Unusual items	9
Net income	5, 6, 7, 8, 9
Earnings per share	9

Statement of Cash Flows

	Chapter
Operating Activities	
Net income	5, 6, 7, 8, 9
Depreciation expense	6, 9
(Gains) losses on sale of assets	6, 9
(Increase) decrease in current assets	5, 9
Increase (decrease) in current liabilities	7, 9
Investing Activities	
Proceeds from sale of property, plant, and equipment	6, 9
Purchase of property, plant, and equipment	6, 9
Financing Activities	
Proceeds from long-term debt*	7, 9
Repayment of long-term debt*	7, 9
Issuance of common stock and/or preferred stock	8, 9
Purchase of treasury stock	8, 9
Payment of dividends	8, 9

Primary topics of this chapter.
Other affected financial statement components.
*May include short-term debt items as well.

Electing Directors

Directors are elected by a **cumulative voting** procedure or on a slate basis. Under cumulative voting, each stockholder is entitled to cast a number of votes equal to the number of shares owned multiplied by the number of directors to be elected. Thus, if five directors are to be elected, the owner of 100 shares of common stock is entitled to 500 votes; all 500 can be cast for one candidate or 100 can be cast for each of five candidates or they can be cast in any combination between these extremes. In **slate voting** the common stockholder is entitled to one vote for each share owned, but that vote is applied to an entire slate of candidates.

In most cases the voting method doesn't affect the outcome. A committee of the board of directors nominates director candidates (equal to the number of directors to be elected), a proxy committee made up of members of the board seeks proxies from the stockholders, and the required number of nominees is duly elected. Occasionally, however, an outside group challenges the existing board; under these circumstances the election can be exciting. Each group nominates director candidates and solicits stockholder votes. Under slate voting, the successful group will be the one that gets a majority of the vote; that group's entire slate will be elected. Of course controlling 50.1 percent of the voting shares will ensure success. Under cumulative voting, however, it is possible for a minority group of stockholders to concentrate their votes on one or two of their own candidates, thus making it easier to secure representation on the board of directors. For example, if five directors are to be elected, the votes of approximately 17 percent of the outstanding common stock are required to elect one director.

Many people, especially proponents of corporate democracy, favor cumulative voting. Some states require corporations organized under their laws to have cumulative voting for directors. Yet corporations often prefer to maintain a slate voting practice because this method makes getting a seat on the board more difficult for corporate raiders and others. Another tactic designed to reduce an outsider's chance of securing a director position is to provide for rolling terms. For example, for a nine-member board, three directors will be elected each year for a three-year term. Thus, even with cumulative voting, the votes of many more shares are required to elect one director than would be required if all nine directors were elected each year.

employed by the firm and, thus, also referred to as **outside directors**) who can bring an independent viewpoint to the considerations and deliberations of the board.

Common stockholders also must approve changes to the corporate charter (for example, when the number of shares of stock authorized is changed so that additional shares can be sold to raise more capital) and may have to approve transactions such as mergers or divestitures.

Common stock can have **par value** or it can be of a no-par-value variety. When it is used, par value is usually a nominal amount assigned to each share when the corporation is organized. In today's business world, par value has virtually no economic significance with respect to common stock. In most states, the par value of the issued shares represents the **legal capital** of the corporation. Most state corporation laws provide that stock with par value cannot be issued for a price less than par value, and they provide that total stockholders' equity cannot be reduced to less than legal capital by the distribution of dividends or the purchase from stockholders of previously issued shares of stock. If the stock has par value, the amount reported in the balance sheet in the Common Stock account will be the par value multiplied by the number of shares issued. Any difference between par value and the amount realized from the sale of the stock is recorded as additional paid-in capital. Some firms assign a **stated value** to the common stock, which is essentially par value by another name. If a firm issues true no-par-value stock, then the total amount received from the sale of the shares is recorded as common stock. Campbell Soup Company's capital stock has a par value of $0.0375 per share (see page 712 in the appendix).

A survey of the 2010 annual reports of 500 publicly owned merchandising and manufacturing companies indicated that only 53 companies had no-par-value common stock. Of those 53 companies, 5 had an assigned or stated value per share.[1]

To illustrate the sale of common stock, assume that during the year ended August 31, 2014, Racers, Inc., sold 40,000 additional shares of its $2 par value common stock at a price of $13 per share. The effect of this stock issue on the financial statements of Racers, Inc., was:

Balance Sheet		Income Statement
Assets = Liabilities + Stockholders' equity		←Net income = Revenues − Expenses
Cash + 520,000 (40,000 shares × $13)	Common Stock + 80,000 (40,000 shares × $2)	
	Additional Paid-In Capital + 440,000 (40,000 shares × $11)	

The entry to record this transaction follows:

Dr. Cash (40,000 shares × $13)	520,000	
Cr. Common Stock (40,000 shares × $2)		80,000
Cr. Additional Paid-In Capital (40,000 shares $11)		440,000

Refer to Exhibit 8-1 and notice that common stock and additional paid-in capital increased during 2014 (the remaining portion of these increases will be explained in the stock dividends section of this chapter).

On the balance sheet the number of shares *authorized, issued,* and *outstanding* will be disclosed. The number of **authorized shares** is stated in the corporate charter that is filed with the state of incorporation according to its laws regarding corporate organization. This represents the maximum number of shares that the corporation is legally approved to issue; an increase in the number of authorized shares requires shareholder approval. The number of **issued shares** is the number of shares of stock that have actually been transferred from the corporation to shareholders. Issued shares are ordinarily *sold* to stockholders for cash, although it is possible to issue stock in exchange for other assets or for services. The number of **outstanding shares** will be less than the number of issued shares if the firm has **treasury stock.** As explained in more detail later in this chapter, treasury stock is a firm's own stock that has been acquired by the firm from its stockholders. The relationship between these terms and the balance sheet disclosure required for each is summarized in Exhibit 8-3. The difference between the number of shares authorized and the number of shares issued represents the potential for additional shares to be issued.

The common stock of many firms has a **preemptive right,** which gives present shareholders the right to purchase additional shares from any new share issuances in proportion to their present percentage of ownership. The preemptive right is usually

---

[1]AICPA, *Accounting Trends and Techniques* (New York, 2011), Table 5-4.

Exhibit 8-3

Balance Sheet Disclosure for Shares of Stock

Terminology	Number of Shares Disclosed	Dollar Amount Disclosed
Shares authorized	Number specified in the corporate charter (maximum approved to be issued)	None
Shares issued	Number of shares that have been issued to stockholders (usually by sale)	Number of shares × par or stated value per share or If no par or stated value, total amount received from sale of shares
Shares outstanding	Number of shares still held by stockholders (shares issued less treasury shares)	None
Treasury stock	Number of issued shares that have been repurchased by the corporation from stockholders and not formally retired	Cost of treasury stock owned by corporation

most significant in smaller, closely held corporations (those with only a few stockholders) in which existing stockholders want to prevent their ownership interest from being diluted. Even though they are not ordinarily bound by a preemptive right provision, many large corporations offer existing stockholders the right to purchase additional shares when more capital is needed. This maintains stockholder loyalty and can be a relatively inexpensive way to raise capital.

What Does It Mean?

Answers on page 323

1. What does it mean when common stock is referred to as part of paid-in capital?
2. What does it mean when the common stock of a corporation has a par value?
3. What does it mean when a corporation has treasury stock?

Preferred Stock

LO 2

Explain what preferred stock is, discuss what its advantages and disadvantages to the corporation are, and show how it is presented in the balance sheet.

Preferred stock is a class of paid-in capital that is different from common stock in that preferred stock has several debtlike features and a limited claim on assets in the event of liquidation. Also, in most cases preferred stock does not have a voting privilege. (Common stock represents residual equity—it has claim to all assets remaining after the liabilities and preferred stock claims have been met in the liquidation of the corporation.) Historically preferred stock has been viewed as having less risk than common stock. In the early years of the Industrial Revolution, when firms sought to raise the large amounts of capital required to finance factories and railroads, investors were more willing to acquire preferred stock in a firm than take the risks associated with common stock ownership. As firms have prospered and many investors have experienced the rewards of common stock ownership, preferred stock has become a less significant factor in the capital structure of many manufacturing, merchandising, and service firms. However, utilities and financial corporations continue to issue preferred stock.

The preferences for preferred stock, relative to common stock, relate to dividends and to the priority of claims on assets in the event of liquidation of the corporation. A **dividend** is a distribution of the earnings of the corporation to its owners/stockholders. The dividend requirement of preferred stock must be satisfied before a dividend can be paid to the common stockholders. Most preferred stock issues call for a quarterly or semiannual dividend, which must be kept current if there is to be a dividend on the common stock. The amount of the dividend is expressed in dollars and cents or as a percentage of the par value of the preferred stock. As shown in Exhibit 8-1, the preferred stock of Racers, Inc., is referred to as "6%, $100 par value." This means that each share of preferred stock is entitled to an annual dividend of $6 (6% × $100). The same dividend result could have been accomplished by creating a $6 cumulative preferred stock. The terms of the stock issue will specify whether the dividend is to be paid at the rate of $1.50 per quarter, $3 semiannually, or $6 annually.

Preferred stock issues, including that of Racers, Inc., usually provide a **cumulative dividend,** which means that if any dividend payments are not made to preferred stockholders, then the total amount of these missed dividends (or dividends in *arrears* from prior periods) must be paid subsequently before any dividends can be paid to the common stockholders. Occasionally preferred stock issues have **participating dividends,** which means that after the common stockholders have received a specified dividend, any further dividends are shared by the preferred and common stockholders in a specified ratio. Calculation of preferred stock dividend amounts is illustrated in Exhibit 8-4.

A preferred stock issue's claim on the assets in the event of liquidation (**liquidating value**) or redemption (**redemption value**) is an amount specified when the preferred stock is issued. If the preferred stock has a par value, the liquidating value or redemption value usually is equal to the par value or the par value plus a slight premium. If the preferred stock has no par value, then the liquidating value or redemption value is a stated amount. In either case, the claim in liquidation must be fulfilled before the common stockholders receive anything. However, once the liquidating claim is met, the preferred stockholders will not receive any additional amounts.

Exhibit 8-4

Illustration of Preferred Stock Dividend Calculation

Case 1:
6%, $100 par value cumulative preferred stock, 50,000 shares authorized, issued, and outstanding. Dividend payable semiannually, no dividends in arrears.
Semiannual preferred dividend amount:

$$6\% \times \$100 \times 50,000 \text{ shares outstanding} \times 1/2 \text{ year} = \$150,000$$

Case 2:
$4.50, $75 par value cumulative preferred stock, 50,000 shares authorized and issued, 40,000 shares outstanding (there are 10,000 shares of treasury stock). Dividend payable quarterly, no dividends in arrears.
Quarterly preferred dividend amount:

$$\$4.50 \times 40,000 \text{ shares outstanding} \times 1/4 \text{ year} = \$45,000$$

Case 3:
8%, $50 par value cumulative preferred stock, 100,000 shares authorized, 60,000 shares issued, 54,000 shares outstanding (there are 6,000 shares of treasury stock). Dividend payable annually. Dividends were not paid in prior two years.
Dividend required in current year to pay dividends in arrears and current year's preferred dividend:

$$8\% \times \$50 \times 54,000 \text{ shares outstanding} \times 3 \text{ years} = \$648,000$$

Exhibit 8-5

Comparison of
Preferred Stock and
Bonds Payable

Preferred Stock	Bonds Payable
Similarities	
• Dividend is (usually) a fixed claim to income.	• Interest is a fixed claim to income.
• Liquidating or redemption value is a fixed claim to assets.	• Maturity value is a fixed claim to assets.
• Is usually callable and may be convertible.	• Is usually callable and may be convertible.
Differences	
• Dividend may be skipped, even though it usually must be caught up before dividends can be paid on the common stock.	• Interest must be paid or firm faces legal action, possibly leading to bankruptcy.
• No maturity date.	• Principal must be paid at maturity.
• Dividends are not an expense and are not deductible for income tax purposes.	• Interest is an expense and is deductible for income tax purposes.

Callable preferred stock is redeemable (usually at a slight premium over par) at the option of the corporation. **Convertible preferred stock** may be exchanged for common stock of the corporation at the option of the stockholder at a conversion rate (such as six shares of common stock for each share of preferred stock) established when the preferred stock is authorized. For many firms the call and conversion features of preferred stock cannot be exercised for a number of years after the authorization (or issue) date of the stock; such restrictions are specified in the stock certificate. Note in Exhibit 8-1 that the preferred stock of Racers, Inc., is callable at a price of $102.

You probably have noticed that preferred stock has some of the same characteristics as bonds payable. Exhibit 8-5 summarizes the principal similarities and differences of the two. The tax deductibility of interest expense causes many financial managers to prefer debt to preferred stock. After all, they reason, if a fixed amount is going to have to be paid out regularly, it might as well be in the form of deductible interest rather than nondeductible preferred dividends. (As explained in Chapter 7, the after-tax cost of bonds paying 10 percent interest is only 7 percent for a corporation with an average tax rate of 30 percent.) Most investors also prefer bonds because the interest owed to them is a fixed claim that must be paid, but preferred stock dividends may be skipped, even though any arrearage may have to be paid before dividends can be paid on common stock. Of 500 publicly owned industrial and merchandising companies whose annual reports for 2010 were reviewed by the AICPA, only 28 had preferred stock outstanding.[2]

From a creditors' point of view, preferred stock reduces the risk associated with financial leverage (introduced in Chapter 7). Utilities and financial firms (such as banks, insurance companies, and finance companies) frequently have a significant portion of their stockholders' equity represented by preferred stock. This is because a significant proportion of the capital requirements of these firms is provided by investors who prefer the relative security of preferred stock rather than debt and/or common stock.

The balance sheet disclosures for preferred stock include the following:

The par value and dividend rate (or the amount of the annual dividend requirement).

The liquidation or redemption value.

---

[2]Ibid., Table 5-5.

The number of shares authorized by the corporate charter.

The number of shares issued.

The number of shares outstanding.

Any difference between the number of shares issued and the number of shares outstanding is caused by shares held in the firm's treasury, referred to as *treasury stock*. In addition, the amount of any preferred dividends that have been missed (that are in arrears) will be disclosed in the notes to the financial statements.

---

4. What does it mean when a corporation has preferred stock?

What Does It Mean?

Answer on page 323

Additional Paid-In Capital

As has already been illustrated, **additional paid-in capital** is a stockholders' equity category that reflects the excess of the amount received from the sale of preferred or common stock over par value. (Remember that the amount in the Common or Preferred Stock account is equal to the par value per share multiplied by the number of shares issued, or the total amount received from the sale of no-par-value stock.) The Additional Paid-In Capital account is also used for other relatively uncommon capital transactions that cannot be reflected in the Common or Preferred Stock accounts or that should not be reflected in Retained Earnings. **Capital in excess of par value** (or stated value) and *capital surplus* are terms sometimes used to describe additional paid-in capital. The latter term was widely used many years ago before the term *surplus* fell into disfavor because of its connotation as something "extra" and because uninformed financial statement readers might think that this amount was somehow available for dividends.

To summarize and emphasize, the paid-in capital of a corporation represents the amount invested by the stockholders. If par value stock is involved, paid-in capital includes separate accounts to record the par value and additional paid-in capital components. If no-par-value stock is issued, paid-in capital is represented by the stock accounts alone.

Retained Earnings

Retained earnings reflect the cumulative earnings of the corporation that have been retained for use in the business rather than disbursed to the stockholders as dividends. *Retained earnings are not cash!* Retained earnings are increased by the firm's net income, and the accrual basis of accounting results in a net income amount that is different from the operating cash flows during a fiscal period. To the extent that operating results increase cash, that cash may be used for operating, investing, or financing activities.

Virtually the only factors affecting retained earnings are net income or loss reported on the income statement, and dividends. (Remember that all revenue, expense, gain, and loss accounts reported on the income statement are indirect changes to the

Retained Earnings account on the balance sheet. As these items are recorded throughout the year, retained earnings are, in effect, increased for revenues and gains and decreased for expenses and losses.)

Under certain very restricted circumstances, generally accepted accounting principles permit direct adjustments of retained earnings for the correction of errors (referred to as *prior period adjustments*). For example, if a firm neglected to include a significant amount of inventory in its year-end physical count and this error was not discovered until the following year, a direct adjustment to inventory and retained earnings would be appropriate. Likewise, retained earnings is adjusted for the retrospective application to prior periods' financial statements of most changes in accounting principles. For example, if a company changes from the LIFO to FIFO cost flow assumption, the financial statements of all prior years will be restated as if the FIFO method had always been in use. Such restatements require direct adjustments to retained earnings as well as other affected accounts. However, new information about an estimate made in a prior year (such as for depreciation or bad debts) does not warrant a direct entry to retained earnings because the amounts reported would have reflected the best information available at the time.

Accounting principles emphasize that the income statement is to reflect all transactions affecting stockholders' equity except for the following:

1. Dividends to stockholders (which are a reduction in retained earnings).
2. Transactions involving the corporation's own stock (which are reflected in the paid-in capital section of the balance sheet).
3. Prior period adjustments for the correction of errors (which are direct adjustments to retained earnings).
4. Most changes from one generally accepted accounting principle to another generally accepted accounting principle (which are direct adjustments to retained earnings).
5. The four main components of accumulated other comprehensive income (which are accounted for within a separate category in stockholders' equity as explained later in this chapter).

If the Retained Earnings account has a negative balance because cumulative losses and dividends have exceeded cumulative net income, this account is referred to as an **accumulated deficit.**

Cash Dividends

LO 3

Describe the accounting for a cash dividend and explain the dates involved in dividend transactions.

For a corporation to pay a cash dividend, it must meet several requirements: The firm must have retained earnings (although some state corporation laws permit dividends in excess of retained earnings if certain conditions are met), the board of directors must declare the dividend, and the firm must have enough cash to pay the dividend. If the firm has agreed in a bond indenture or other loan covenant to maintain certain minimum standards of financial health (perhaps a current ratio of at least 1.5:1.0), the dividend must not cause any of these measures to fall below their agreed-upon levels. From both the corporation's and the stockholders' perspectives, several key dates are related to the dividend (see Business in Practice—Dividend Dates on page 308). Once the board of directors has declared the dividend, it becomes a legally enforceable liability of the corporation. The effects on the financial statements of recording the declaration and subsequent payment of a cash dividend are as follows:

Balance Sheet	Income Statement
Assets = Liabilities + Stockholders' equity	←Net income = Revenues − Expenses
Declaration date 　　　+ Dividends　− Retained 　　　Payable　　　Earnings *Payment date* 　− Cash　− Dividends 　　　　　Payable	

The journal entries follow:

On the declaration date:
Dr. Retained Earnings xx
　　Cr. Dividends Payable . . . . 　　xx

On the payment date:
Dr. Dividends Payable xx
　　Cr. Cash . . . . 　　xx

Note that *dividends are not an expense* and do not appear on the income statement. Dividends are a distribution of earnings of the corporation to its stockholders and are treated as a direct reduction of retained earnings. If a balance sheet is dated between the date the dividend is declared and the date it is paid, the Dividends Payable account will be included in the current liability section of the balance sheet.

What Does It Mean?
Answer on page 323

5. What does it mean when a corporation's board of directors has declared a cash dividend?

Stock Dividends and Stock Splits

LO 4
Describe what stock dividends and stock splits are and discuss why each is used.

In addition to a cash dividend, or sometimes instead of a cash dividend, a corporation may issue a **stock dividend**. A stock dividend is the issuance of additional shares of common stock to the existing stockholders in proportion to the number of shares each currently owns. It is expressed as a percentage; for example, a 5 percent stock dividend would result in the issuance of 5 percent of the previously issued shares. A stockholder who owns 100 shares would receive 5 additional shares of stock, but her proportionate ownership interest in the firm would not change. (Fractional shares are not issued, so an owner of 90 shares would receive 4 shares and cash equal to the market value of half of a share.)

The motivation for a stock dividend is usually to maintain the loyalty of stockholders when the firm does not have enough cash to pay (or increase) the cash dividend. Although many stockholders like to receive a stock dividend, such a distribution is not income to the stockholders. To understand why there is no income to stockholders, the impact of the stock dividend must be understood from the issuing corporation's point of view. A stock dividend does not cause any change in either assets or liabilities; therefore, it cannot affect *total* stockholders' equity. However, additional shares of stock are issued, and the Common Stock account must be increased by the number of shares issued multiplied

Business in
Practice

Dividend Dates

Three dates applicable to every dividend are the declaration date, the record date, and the payment date. In addition, there will be an ex-dividend date applicable to companies whose stock is publicly traded. There is no reason that the declaration, record, and payment dates for a closely held company couldn't be the same date.

The **declaration date** is the date on which the board of directors declares the dividend and it becomes a legal liability to be paid. The **record date** is used to determine who receives the dividend; the person listed on the stockholder records of the corporation on the record date is considered the owner of the shares. The stockholder of record is the person to whom the check is made payable and mailed to on the **payment date**. If shares have been sold privately but the ownership change has not yet been noted on the corporation's records, the prior stockholder (the one in the records) receives the dividend (and may have to settle with the new owner, depending on their agreement with respect to the dividend). The **ex-dividend date** relates to this issue of who receives the dividend. When the stock of a publicly traded company is bought or sold, the seller has a settlement period of two business days in which to deliver the stock certificate. The buyer also has two business days to pay for the purchase. Thus, the stock trades "ex-dividend" two business days before the record date to give the corporation a chance to increase the accuracy of its ownership records. On the ex-dividend date, the stock trades without the dividend (the seller retains the right to receive the dividend if the stock is sold on or after the ex-dividend date). If the stock is sold before the ex-dividend date, the buyer is entitled to receive the dividend. All other things being equal, the price of the stock in the market falls by the amount of the dividend on the ex-dividend date.

There is no specific requirement dealing with the number of days that should elapse between the declaration, record, and payment dates for publicly traded stocks. It is not unusual for two to four weeks to elapse between each date.

by par value per share. Because the issuance of shares is called a *dividend,* it is also appropriate for the Retained Earnings account to be reduced. The amount of the reduction in retained earnings is the number of dividend shares issued multiplied by the market price per share. Any difference between market price and par value is recorded in the Additional Paid-In Capital account. If the shares are without par value, then the Common Stock account is increased by the market value of the dividend shares issued.

To illustrate the effects of a stock dividend transaction, assume that during the year ended August 31, 2014, Racers, Inc., issued a 2 percent stock dividend on its $2 par value common stock when the market price was $15 per share. Refer back to Exhibit 8-1 and assume further that the stock dividend occurred at some point after the additional 40,000 shares of common stock had been issued. Thus, a total of 4,800 dividend shares were issued (2% × 240,000 shares previously issued). Using the horizontal model, here is the effect on the financial statements:

Balance Sheet	Income Statement
Assets = Liabilities + Stockholders' equity	←Net income = Revenues − Expenses
Retained Earnings − 72,000 (4,800 shares × $15)	
Common Stock + 9,600 (4,800 shares × $2)	
Additional Paid-In Capital + 62,400 (4,800 shares × $13)	

The entry to record this transaction follows:

Dr.	Retained Earnings (4,800 shares × $15)	72,000	
	Cr. Common Stock (4,800 shares × $2).		9,600
	Cr. Additional Paid-In Capital (4,800 shares × $13).		62,400

Note that the stock dividend affects *only* the stockholders' equity of the firm. *Capitalizing retained earnings* is the term sometimes used to refer to the effect of a stock dividend transaction because the dividend permanently transfers some retained earnings to paid-in capital. The income statement is not affected because the transaction is between the corporation and its stockholders (who own the corporation); no gain or loss can result from a capital transaction.

If the stock dividend percentage is more than 20 to 25 percent, only the par value or stated value of the additional common shares issued is transferred from retained earnings to common stock.

What happens to the market value of a share of stock when a firm issues a stock dividend? Is the share owner any wealthier? As already explained, nothing happens to the firm's assets, liabilities, or earning power as a result of the stock dividend; so the *total* market value of the firm should not change. Because more shares of stock are now outstanding and the total market value of all the shares remains the same, the market value of each share will drop. This is why the stock dividend does not represent income to the stockholder. However, under some circumstances the market value per share of the common stock will not settle at its theoretically lower value. This will be true especially if the cash dividend per share is not adjusted to reflect the stock dividend. Thus, if the firm had been paying a cash dividend of $1 per share before the stock dividend, and the same cash dividend rate of $1 per share is continued, there has been an effective increase in the dividend rate simply because each shareholder now owns more shares; the stock price will probably rise to reflect this "good news" to investors.

Sometimes the managers of a firm want to lower the market price of the firm's common stock by a significant amount because they believe that a stock trading in a price range of $20 to $60 per share is a more popular investment than a stock priced at more than $60 per share. A **stock split** will accomplish this objective. A stock split involves issuing additional shares to existing stockholders and, if the stock has a par value, the par value is typically reduced proportionately. For example, if a firm had 60,000 shares of $10 par value stock outstanding, with stock trading in the market at a price of $80 per share, a 4-for-1 stock split would involve issuing 3 additional shares to each stockholder for each share owned. Then the stockholder who had owned 200 shares would receive an additional 600 shares, bringing the total shares owned to 800. As in the case of a stock dividend, nothing has happened to the assets or liabilities of the firm, so nothing can happen to stockholders' equity. The total market value of the company would not change, but the market price of each share would fall. (Compare the results of 60,000 shares × $80 to 240,000 shares × $20.) No accounting entry is required for a stock split. However, the common stock caption of stockholders' equity indicates the drop in par value per share (if appropriate) and the proportionate increase in the number of shares authorized, issued, and outstanding. If the corporation has used no-par-value stock, only the number of shares changes.

Sometimes a stock split is accomplished in the form of a very large (perhaps 100 percent) stock dividend. As explained earlier, when this happens only the par or stated value of the additional shares issued is transferred from Retained Earnings to the Common Stock account. There is no adjustment to the par value of the stock.

A *reverse stock split* is unusual but may occur when the market price of a firm's common stock has settled at a lower level than management thinks appropriate. Say that a stock is trading at $15 per share, and historically it has traded in the $50 to $70 range. A 1-for-4 reverse stock split would reduce the number of shares outstanding to 25 percent of the prereverse split quantity, and the market price per share would increase by a factor of 4, or to $60 in this case. Again, no accounting entries are required for this event, but par value would increase by a factor of 4 and the number of shares authorized, issued, and outstanding would decrease by a factor of 4. The use of reverse splits is extremely uncommon in practice, although this method of price adjustment has been used in the technology sector from time to time. For example, Atari Corp. had a 1-for-10 reverse stock split in 2007, and Motorola Solutions, Inc.'s shareholders approved a 1-for-7 reverse stock split in 2010.

What Does It Mean?

Answers on page 323

6. What does it mean when a corporation's board of directors has declared a stock dividend on the common stock?
7. What does it mean when a corporation has a stock split?

Accumulated Other Comprehensive Income (Loss)

LO 5

Recognize what the components of accumulated other comprehensive income (loss) are and explain why these items appear in stockholders' equity.

At first glance it may seem surprising to find the word *income* in the stockholders' equity section of the balance sheet. To put the *comprehensive income* concept into perspective, think back to Chapter 2, where the link between the income statement and balance sheet was first established. Recall that net income is added to retained earnings within the stockholders' equity section of the balance sheet at the end of each accounting period. This is done through the closing process described in Chapter 4, which emphasizes that income statement accounts are temporary in nature—that is, revenues, gains, expenses, and losses are (in effect) subcategories of stockholders' equity that are "closed" to retained earnings at the end of the accounting period. The balance sheet equation (A = L + SE) and the horizontal model (where net income points back to stockholders' equity) both reinforce this fundamental relationship: *All items of income (or loss) ultimately affect stockholders' equity on the balance sheet.* This is the reason the word *income* appears in this section of the balance sheet.

Up until now, stockholders' equity has been described as being composed of two distinct categories: paid-in capital (*contributed* capital such as common and preferred stock) and retained earnings (*earned* capital from cumulative net income in excess of dividends paid). Unfortunately the line between these two is often blurry—and at times neither category adequately describes certain changes in stockholders' equity. The FASB and its predecessors have debated for years over which items should be included in "net income" for the period (and therefore added to retained earnings) and which items should be accounted for directly within the stockholders' equity section of the balance sheet. As a result, several exceptions to the preceding dichotomy were carved out over the years, resulting in a wide array of financial reporting practices among real-world companies.

To improve comparability between firms, the FASB issued *Statement of Financial Accounting Standards No. 130,* "Reporting Comprehensive Income," in 1997, which defined the term *comprehensive income (loss)* as including all nonshareholder changes in equity. These changes, as amended by subsequent FASB *Accounting Standards Codification Updates* (see ASC 220), include the following classifications:

1. Net income (as reported on the income statement).
2. Cumulative foreign currency translation adjustments.
3. Unrealized gains or losses on available-for-sale investments.
4. Changes during the period in certain pension or other postretirement benefit items.
5. Gains or losses on certain derivative instruments.

A new category of stockholders' equity, referred to as **accumulated other comprehensive income (loss),** was established to include items 2 through 5 (as amended) from the preceding list; each of these items is reported net of related income taxes. Firms are allowed considerable flexibility in *how* other comprehensive income is reported in the financial statements. Alternatives range from extending the income statement to append this information, to reporting line-item details within the stockholders' equity section of the balance sheet (or in a separate statement of stockholders' equity), to reporting only the net accumulated other comprehensive income or loss in the balance sheet and disclosing line-item details in the notes to the financial statements. Campbell's reports the net amount in its balance sheet and provides line-item details in its statement of equity (see pages 712 and 714 in the 2011 annual report in the appendix).

Note that the common characteristic of the four primary items that comprise other comprehensive income is that each involves *unrealized* changes in stockholders' equity. Because the accounting treatment accorded to each item is essentially the same, only the cumulative foreign currency translation adjustments will be explained here.

Cumulative foreign currency translation adjustment. When the financial statements of a foreign subsidiary are consolidated with those of its U.S. parent company, the financial statements of the subsidiary, originally expressed in the currency of the country in which it operates, must be converted to U.S. dollars. The conversion process is referred to as *foreign currency translation*. Because of the mechanics used in the translation process and because exchange rates fluctuate over time, a debit or credit difference between the translated value of the subsidiary's assets and liabilities and the translated value of the subsidiary's stockholders' equity arises in the translation and consolidation process. Prior to 1981, this debit or credit difference was reported as a loss or gain in the consolidated income statement. Because of large gyrations in exchange rates, a firm might have reported a large translation gain in one year and an equally large translation loss in the next year. The translation gain or loss had a material effect on reported results but did not have a significant economic impact because the gain or loss was never actually realized. The difference between

Exhibit 8-6   Statement of Changes in Stockholders' Equity

RACERS, INC.
Statement of Changes in Stockholders' Equity
For the Year Ended August 31, 2014

	Preferred Stock		Common Stock		Additional Paid-In Capital $	Retained Earnings $	Accumulated Other Comprehensive Income (Loss) $	Common Treasury Stock	
	No. of Shares	$	No. of Shares	$				No. of Shares	$
Balance, August 31, 2013	5,000	$500,000	200,000	$400,000	$2,820,000	$2,600,000	$(100,000)	—	—
Sale of common stock			40,000	80,000	440,000				
Purchase of common treasury stock								1,000	$12,000
Net income						390,000			
Cash dividends:									
Preferred stock						(30,000)			
Common stock						(60,000)			
Stock dividend:									
2% on 240,000 shares when market value was $15 per share			4,800	9,600	62,400	(72,000)			
Net movement in cumulative foreign currency translation adjustment							150,000		
Balance, August 31, 2014	5,000	$500,000	244,800	$489,600	$3,322,400	$2,828,000	$ 50,000	1,000	$12,000

the value of the subsidiaries as measured in U.S. dollars versus foreign currency units will never be realized unless the foreign subsidiaries are sold. Therefore, the FASB issued an accounting standard that required firms to report the translation gain or loss as a separate account within stockholders' equity rather than as a gain or loss in the income statement. The effect of this accounting standard was to make reported net income more meaningful and to highlight as a separate item in stockholders' equity the cumulative translation adjustment. (This 1981 FASB standard is still in effect, but the cumulative translation gain or loss is now reported as a component of the "accumulated other comprehensive income (loss)" in stockholders' equity.) To the extent that exchange rates of the U.S. dollar rise and fall relative to the foreign currencies involved, the amount of this **cumulative foreign currency translation adjustment** will fluctuate over time. This treatment of the translation adjustment is consistent with the going concern concept because as long as the entity continues to operate with foreign subsidiaries, the translation adjustment will not be realized.

As shown in Exhibits 8-1 and 8-6, the $100,000 accumulated other comprehensive loss for Racers, Inc., became a $50,000 accumulated gain as a result of a $150,000 net movement in the cumulative foreign currency translation adjustment during the year ended August 31, 2014.

Treasury Stock

LO 6
Explain what treasury stock is, discuss why it is acquired, and show how treasury stock transactions affect stockholders' equity.

Many corporations will, from time to time, purchase shares of their own stock. Any class of stock that is outstanding can be acquired as treasury stock. Rather than being retired, this stock is held for future use for employee stock purchase plans or acquisitions of other companies or even to be resold for cash if additional capital is needed. Sometimes treasury stock is acquired as a defensive move to thwart a takeover by another company, and frequently treasury shares are purchased with excess cash because the market price is low and the company wishes to shrink the supply of its own stock in the market. Whatever the motivation, the purchase of treasury stock is in effect a partial liquidation of the firm because the firm's assets are used to reduce the number of shares of stock outstanding. For this reason, treasury stock is not reflected in the balance sheet as an asset; it is reported as a contra stockholders' equity account (that is, treasury stock is deducted from the sum of paid-in capital and retained earnings).

Because treasury stock transactions are capital transactions (between the corporation and its stockholders), the income statement is never affected by the purchase or sale of treasury stock. When treasury stock is acquired, it is recorded at cost. When treasury stock is sold or issued, any difference between its cost and the consideration received is recorded in the Additional Paid-In Capital account. As can be seen in Exhibit 8-1, Racers, Inc., purchased 1,000 shares of its own common stock at a total cost of $12,000 during the year ended August 31, 2014. The effect of this transaction on the financial statements was:

Balance Sheet		Income Statement
Assets = Liabilities + Stockholders' equity		←Net income = Revenues − Expenses
Cash − 12,000	Treasury Stock (A contra stockholders' equity account) − 12,000	

The entry to record this purchase looks like this:

Dr. Treasury Stock.	12,000	
Cr. Cash.		12,000
Purchase of 1,000 shares of treasury stock at a cost of $12 per share.		

If 500 shares of this treasury stock were sold at a price of $15 per share in fiscal 2015, the effect on the financial statements of recording the sale would be:

Balance Sheet		Income Statement
Assets = Liabilities + Stockholders' equity		←Net income = Revenues − Expenses
Cash + 7,500	Treasury Stock + 6,000 Additional Paid-In Capital + 1,500	

Here would be the entry:

Dr. Cash	7,500	
Cr. Treasury Stock.		6,000
Cr. Additional Paid-In Capital		1,500
Sale of 500 shares of treasury stock at a price of $15 per share.		

Cash dividends are not paid on treasury stock. However, if state law allows, stock dividends are issued on treasury stock, and stock splits affect treasury stock. For many firms, the dollar amount reported for treasury stock represents a significant reduction in total stockholders' equity. Because treasury stock purchases are recorded at the market price per share, it is not uncommon to find a negative amount reported for total paid-in capital. Why? Let's say that 1,000 shares of common stock were issued in 1984 at the prevailing market price of $15 per share. These shares remained outstanding until 2013, when 300 shares were purchased as treasury stock for $80 per share. The $15,000 historical cost of common stock would now be offset by a $24,000 reduction for treasury stock. Many successful real-world corporations, such as Coca-Cola, McDonald's, General Electric, and ExxonMobil, reported negative paid-in capital in 2011 because of recently purchased treasury stock. Coca-Cola's $31.3 billion of treasury stock was 2.6 times greater than its common stock and additional paid-in capital combined. The primary culprit in this accounting anomaly is the cost principle. In recent years many such firms have curtailed their plans to issue new shares while also becoming active market participants in the previously issued shares of their own common stock. This strategy protects existing stockholders from the potential dilution of their ownership interests. Moreover, because treasury stock purchases do not affect net income, ROE is increased due to the reduction in stockholders' equity caused by recording treasury stock purchases.

To summarize and emphasize, you should understand that cash dividends are not paid on treasury stock because the company cannot pay a dividend to itself. However, stock dividends are issued on treasury stock, and stock splits affect treasury stock.

Exhibit 8-7

Statement of Changes in Retained Earnings

RACERS, INC. Statement of Changes in Retained Earnings For the Year Ended August 31, 2014	
Retained earnings balance, beginning of year	$2,600,000
Add: Net income	390,000
Less: Cash dividends:	
Preferred stock	(30,000)
Common stock	(60,000)
2% stock dividend on common stock	(72,000)
Retained earnings balance, end of year	$2,828,000

What this means, in practical terms, is that cash dividends are based on the number of shares outstanding, whereas stock dividends and stock splits are based on the number of shares previously issued.

Reporting Changes in Stockholders' Equity Accounts

It is appropriate that the reasons for changes to any stockholders' equity account during a fiscal period be presented in the balance sheet, in a separate statement of changes in stockholders' equity, or in the notes to the financial statements. One possible format for a statement of changes in stockholders' equity is presented for Racers, Inc., in Exhibit 8-6. (Amounts for net income and dividends on common stock are assumed. You should prove to yourself the amount of the cash dividends on the preferred stock.) Alternative formats may be used.

Even if there are no changes to the paid-in capital accounts and there is no treasury stock or foreign subsidiary, an analysis of retained earnings is presented. This can be done in a separate statement, as illustrated for Racers, Inc., in Exhibit 8-7, or by appending the beginning balance, dividend, and ending balance information to the bottom of the income statement, which then becomes a combined statement of income and retained earnings.

Note that Campbell's presents Consolidated Statements of Equity on page 714 of its 2011 annual report in the appendix. What approach is used in the other annual reports that you have?

LO 7

Show how stockholders' equity transactions for the year are reported in the financial statements.

Noncontrolling Interest

As discussed in Chapter 7 (see pages 272–273), a noncontrolling interest, sometimes called a minority interest, is the portion of equity in a subsidiary not attributable, directly or indirectly, to the parent company (reporting entity). As per the FASB's requirements in *Statement of Financial Accounting Standards No. 160*, "Noncontrolling Interest in Consolidated Financial Statements" (see FASB ASC 810), the ownership interests in subsidiaries held by parties other than the parent must be clearly identified, labeled, and presented in the consolidated balance sheet within equity, but separate from the parent's equity. The effect of this standard is to create, for financial reporting purposes, a new classification scheme allowing the balance sheet model to be *thought of* as being expanded as follows:

LO 8

Discuss how the presence of a noncontrolling interest affects the presentation of consolidated financial statements.

$$\text{Assets} = \text{Liabilities} + (\text{Stockholders' Equity} + \text{Nonowners' Equity})$$

Exhibit 8-8

Equity Section of
Racers, Inc., Consoli-
dated Balance Sheet at
August 31, 2014

RACERS, INC.
Consolidated Balance Sheet
August 31, 2014

Assets:	
Total assets	$12,950,000
Liabilities:	
Total liabilities	$ 5,510,000
Equity:	
Racers, Inc.'s Stockholders' Equity:	
Preferred stock 6%, $100 par value	$ 500,000
Common stock, $1 par value	489,600
Additional paid-in capital	3,322,400
Retained earnings	2,828,000
Accumulated other comprehensive income (loss)	50,000
Less: Common stock in treasury, at cost	(12,000)
Total Racers, Inc., stockholders' equity	$ 7,178,000
Noncontrolling interest	$ 262,000
Total equity	$ 7,440,000
Total liabilities and equity	$12,950,000

Because noncontrolling interest must be reported as an equity item, although it represents the interests of the minority shareholders in parent-controlled subsidiaries, the use of captions such as "Stockholders' Equity" or "Shareholders' Equity" as the lead description for this section of the consolidated balance sheet is no longer appropriate. As shown in Exhibit 8-8 for Racers, Inc. (using assumed amounts for total assets, total liabilities, and noncontrolling interest), the use of the term "Equity" for this section of the consolidated balance sheet provides the most appropriate presentation when noncontrolling interest must be reported.

Note that in the presentation of the equity section of Racers, Inc.'s, consolidated balance sheet, no subtotal is shown for Total Paid-In Capital. Many companies will, however, continue to categorize the parent company's stockholders' equity section into the paid-in capital and earned capital components.

As the noncontrolling interest caption shown in the consolidated balance sheet actually represents the equity interest held by *nonowners* of the reporting entity, no account for this item appears within the parent company's chart of accounts; it represents a balancing item that is created during the consolidation process each year as the financial statements of the parent company and subsidiary companies are combined. Thus, your primary focus should be on understanding how the presence of noncontrolling interest affects the presentation of consolidated financial statements, rather than how to account for this particular item.

The Statement of Changes in Stockholders' Equity for Racers, Inc., as depicted in Exhibit 8-6, would be renamed the Consolidated Statement of Changes in Equity, reflecting the fact that both owners' and nonowners' equity is represented. Of course, a column for noncontrolling interest would be added as well (normally as the rightmost column), and the parent company's equity accounts would be separately identified and totaled, so that the reader could clearly distinguish the parent company's equity from the noncontrolling interest equity.

8. What does it mean when noncontrolling interest is reported in the consolidated balance sheet?

What Does It Mean?
Answer on page 323

Owners' Equity for Other Types of Entities

Proprietorships and Partnerships

The discussion in this chapter has focused on the owners' equity of corporations, which is referred to as *stockholders' equity.* Neither proprietorships nor partnerships (single and multiple-owner unincorporated businesses, respectively) issue stock, and a distinction between invested capital and retained earnings is not usually made. Owners' equity of these firms is usually referred to as *capital,* as in "Tiger Woods, Capital" in the case of a proprietorship, or as "Partners' Capital" in the case of a partnership. For a small partnership, the capital account balance of each partner may be listed separately in the balance sheet. For a partnership with many partners, the capital interest of each may be expressed in "units" or "shares" representing proportional interest, but these shares do not carry the same legal rights as capital stock of a corporation. In fact, partnership shares are frequently used *only* for profit and loss distribution purposes; each partner ordinarily has an equal voice in the management of the firm. The partnership agreement will normally specify how the profits and losses of the partnership are to be allocated to individual partners. Distributions to the owner or owners during the year, including any salaries paid to the proprietor or partners, are treated as reductions of owners' equity rather than expenses. These amounts are frequently accumulated in a "drawing" account, which is similar to the dividends account for a corporation. The statement of changes in owners' equity for the year reports the beginning capital balance, additional capital investments, net income or loss for the year, and capital withdrawals (drawings) to arrive at the ending capital balance.

Not-for-Profit and Governmental Organizations

These types of organizations do not have owners who have *direct* financial interests in the entities. The financial reporting requirements are therefore focused on resource providers (such as taxpayers or donors), rather than investors. Owners' equity in these organizations is referred to as *fund balance.* Because individual resource providers do not have specific claims against the organization's assets, capital accounts are inappropriate, and net income is not reported for most funds. There is usually an operating (or current) fund, and there are frequently several restricted funds for enhancing accountability for certain assets. For example, a university would account for tuition income and operating expenses in its current fund. Money that is donated for student scholarships is accounted for in a restricted fund to help ensure that it is used for its intended purpose. Other funds frequently used are an endowment fund, loan fund, plant fund, and debt retirement fund. The transactions that affect these funds are nonoperating in nature, and specific accountability is required. The statement of owners' equity is called the *statement of changes in fund balances,* which summarizes the activities of each fund. Changes during the year include the excess (or deficiency) of operating revenues over (under) operating expenditures; increases from contributions, grants, or other support; decreases from nonoperating transactions; and transfers to and from other funds. This statement is similar in purpose and content to the statement of stockholders' equity of a corporation and is just as easy to understand.

Demonstration Problem

Visit the text website at www.mhhe.com/marshall10e **to view a demonstration problem for this chapter.**

Summary

This chapter has described the accounting for and presentation of the following stockholders' equity accounts. (Note that except for the fact that net income is added to retained earnings, transactions affecting stockholders' equity do not affect the income statement.)

Balance Sheet	Income Statement
Assets = Liabilities + Stockholders' equity	←Net income = Revenues − Expenses
Preferred Stock	
Common Stock	
Additional Paid-In Capital	
Retained Earnings	←Net income
Accumulated Other Comprehensive Income (Loss)	
(Treasury Stock)	
Noncontrolling Interest	

Stockholders' equity is also referred to as *net assets*. For single proprietorships and partnerships, the term *capital* is frequently used instead of stockholders' equity. For a corporation, the components of stockholders' equity are paid-in capital, retained earnings, accumulated other comprehensive income (loss), and treasury stock.

Paid-in capital always includes common stock and may include preferred stock and additional paid-in capital. Common stock represents the basic ownership of the corporation. Common stock may have a par value or may have no par value. Additional paid-in capital represents the difference between the par (or stated) value of common stock issued and the total amount paid in to the corporation when the stock was issued. Additional paid-in capital is sometimes given the more descriptive caption *capital in excess of par (or stated) value*. If no-par-value common stock has no stated value, the total amount paid in to the corporation when the stock was issued is reported as the dollar amount of common stock. The principal right and obligation of the common stockholders is to elect the board of directors of the corporation. Voting for directors can be on either a cumulative basis or a slate basis.

Preferred stock is different from common stock in that preferred has a prior claim to dividends and a prior claim on assets when the corporation is liquidated. In most cases, preferred stock does not have a voting privilege. Preferred stock is in some respects similar to bonds payable. However, the most significant difference between the two is that interest on bonds is a tax-deductible expense, whereas dividends on preferred stock are a nondeductible distribution of the corporation's earnings.

Retained earnings represent the cumulative earnings reinvested in the business. If earnings are not reinvested, they are distributed to stockholders as dividends. Retained earnings are not cash. The Retained Earnings account is increased by net income and decreased by dividends (and by a net loss).

Dividends are declared by the board of directors and paid to stockholders as of the record date. Although cash dividends can be paid with any frequency, quarterly or semiannual dividend payments are most common. Stock dividends represent the issuance of additional shares of stock to stockholders in proportion to the number of shares owned on the record date. Stock dividends do not affect the assets, liabilities, or total stockholders' equity of the firm but do transfer an amount of retained earnings to paid-in capital. Stock dividends are expressed as a percentage of the number of predividend shares issued, and that percentage is usually relatively small (less than 20 percent).

Stock splits also involve issuing additional shares of stock to stockholders in proportion to the number of shares owned on the record date—but usually result in at least doubling the number of shares held by each stockholder. Stock splits are expressed as a ratio of the number of shares held after the split to the number held before the split (for example, 2 for 1). The reason for (and effect of) a stock split is to reduce the market value per share of the stock. Reverse stock splits occur on occasion for just the opposite reason—to increase market value per share of the issuer's stock.

The cumulative foreign currency translation adjustment is an amount reported in stockholders' equity of corporations having foreign subsidiaries. The adjustment arises in the process of translating the financial statements of subsidiaries (expressed in foreign currency units) to U.S. dollars. Because exchange rates can fluctuate widely, net income could be distorted if this adjustment were reported in the income statement. To avoid this distortion, the adjustment is reported in stockholders' equity as a component of accumulated other comprehensive income (loss).

Treasury stock is the corporation's own stock that has been purchased from stockholders and is being held in the treasury for future reissue or other use. Treasury stock is reported as a contra stockholders' equity account. When treasury stock is reissued at a price different from its cost, no gain or loss is recognized, but paid-in capital is affected.

Noncontrolling interest, sometimes called minority interest, is the portion of equity in a subsidiary not owned by the parent company (reporting entity). This item must be presented in the consolidated balance sheet within equity, but separate from the parent's equity.

Stockholders' equity captions usually seen in a balance sheet include these:

1. Paid-In capital:
   a. Preferred stock (sometimes issued)
   b. Common stock (always issued)
   c. Additional paid-in capital
2. Retained earnings (accumulated deficit if negative)
3. Accumulated other comprehensive income (loss)
4. Less: Treasury stock
5. Noncontrolling interest (which is actually the equity interest held by *nonowners* of the reporting entity)

It is possible that a firm may have only common stock (sometimes called *capital stock*) and retained earnings as components of stockholders' equity.

Changes in stockholders' equity (and sometimes nonowners' equity) usually are reported in a comprehensive statement that summarizes the changes of each element of equity. However, if there have not been significant changes in paid-in capital accounts, a statement of changes in retained earnings may be presented by itself. Sometimes the statement of changes in retained earnings is combined with the income statement.

Proprietorships, partnerships, and not-for-profit organizations report changes in equity using terminology unique to each type of entity. In the final analysis, the purpose of this statement for these entities is the same as for corporations: to explain the change in net assets of the entity during the reporting period.

Refer to Campbell Soup Company's balance sheets and the statements of equity in the appendix, and to other financial statements you may have, and observe how information about stockholders' equity is presented.

Appendix TO CHAPTER EIGHT

Personal Investing

An exciting milestone in any individual's financial life is the beginning of a personal investment program in stocks, bonds, and other securities. A number of questions about one's capability to accept the risks involved must be answered before an investment plan is put into action; it is appropriate for most people to consult a trusted financial adviser to help them understand and answer those questions and to establish a sensible plan.

One investment medium appropriate for many people is an investment company, or mutual fund. Investors purchase shares of the mutual fund, which uses the money received from investors to purchase shares of common stock, preferred stock, and/or bonds. In essence, each investor owns a share of the portfolio of securities owned by the mutual fund. Shares in some mutual funds are purchased through a registered representative employed by a brokerage firm, and in other cases the investor purchases shares directly from the mutual fund. You should understand that not all mutual funds are alike in their operating and investing objectives. Thus, an individual investor should carefully define her own objectives and *then* select a fund that invests in a portfolio of securities consistent with her own views. Whether dealing through a broker or directly with the mutual fund, an investor will receive a prospectus that describes the fund, the costs related to investing in the fund, its operating and investment policies, and the risks to which an investment is exposed.

An alternative method of investing is to make direct purchases of specific corporate securities. This is usually done by opening an account with a brokerage firm, although an employee can invest in the stock of his own employer through a 401(k) plan without having to go through a broker. By taking this approach, the investor has direct ownership of individual stocks and bonds rather than an interest in a portfolio of securities owned by a mutual fund. A prospectus describing the securities purchased and risks involved is *not* furnished when an investor acquires previously issued shares traded on a stock exchange or in the over-the-counter market.

A full discussion of investment characteristics, risks, and alternatives is beyond the scope of this book. It is appropriate to understand the terminology, concepts, and financial reporting practices described here before starting an investment program. Online investing is perhaps the quickest, easiest, and most affordable way to get started. Check out some of the investing sites listed in Exhibit 8-9, especially the Motley Fool site, to learn more about the investing process.

1. **Motley Fool** Popular financial forum aims to inform, entertain, and help people make money. Check out portfolios and stock ideas, and get a broker. Offers extensive guides to a host of issues in the realm of personal finance. It's fun and it's free! www.fool.com

2. *Fortune* Online edition of this magazine features an extensive section for investors. Track and analyze up to 150 stocks in a free portfolio. Brief profiles of the 500 leading companies in the United States, including stock quotes, charts, and financial statements. Also access to the Global 500. www.fortune.com

3. *Bloomberg Businessweek* Find selected articles from the American and Asian editions of the popular magazine and access *Bloomberg Businessweek*. www.businessweek.com

4. **CNN Money** Get an at-a-glance update on the major U.S. markets, including Dow and Nasdaq indicators, and check on market movers. www.money.cnn.com /data/us_markets

5. **BigCharts** U.S. investment charting site. Find research on more than 24,000 stocks, mutual funds, and indexes, with intraday historical charts and quotes. www.bigcharts.com

6. **Dow Jones & Company** Home page of large publisher of business news and information. Details on products and services, including *The Wall Street Journal*. www.dowjones.com

7. **Bloomberg** Large compendium of global business and financial news. Descriptions of media products and services. www.bloomberg.com

8. **New York Stock Exchange** Offers stock prices, listing information and links to national and international listed companies, a market summary, and guidelines for investors. www.nyse.com

9. **Nasdaq** Provides listed company information, investor resources, a tour, a summary of market activity and indexes, and a glossary of market terms. www.nasdaq.com

10. **Standard & Poor's** Read about the Financial Information Service and Ratings Service. See daily closing values of listed securities. www.standardandpoors.com

Exhibit 8-9
A Sampling of Investing Websites

Key Terms and Concepts

accumulated deficit (p. 306) Retained earnings with a negative (debit) balance.

accumulated other comprehensive income (loss) (p. 311) A category of stockholders' equity for financial reporting purposes that includes a firm's cumulative foreign currency translation adjustments, unrealized gains or losses on available-for-sale marketable securities, changes during the period in certain pension or other postretirement benefit items, and gains (losses) on certain derivative instruments.

additional paid-in capital (p. 305) The excess of the amount received from the sale of stock over the par (or stated) value of the shares sold.

authorized shares (p. 301) The number of shares of a class of stock allowed to be issued per the corporation's charter. The maximum number of shares the corporation can legally issue.

callable preferred stock (p. 304) Preferred stock that can be redeemed by the corporation at its option.

capital in excess of par value (p. 305) Another term for *additional paid-in capital*.

capital stock (p. 298) The generic term for stock issued by a corporation.

common stock (p. 298)   The class of stock that represents residual ownership of the corporation.

convertible preferred stock (p. 304)   Preferred stock that can be converted to common stock of the corporation at the option of the stockholder.

cumulative dividend (p. 303)   A feature of preferred stock that requires any missed dividends to be paid before dividends are paid on common stock.

cumulative foreign currency translation adjustment (p. 313)   A component of stockholders' equity arising from the translation of foreign subsidiary financial statements.

cumulative voting (p. 300)   A system of voting for the directors of a firm in which the total number of votes that can be cast among one or more candidates is equal to the number of shares of stock owned, multiplied by the number of directors to be elected.

declaration date (p. 308)   The date on which a dividend is approved by the board of directors and becomes a legal liability of the company.

dividend (p. 303)   A distribution of earnings to the owners/stockholders of a corporation.

ex-dividend date (p. 308)   The date on and after which (up to the record date) the buyer of a publicly traded stock will not receive a dividend that has been declared.

independent director (p. 298)   A member of the firm's board of directors who is not an officer or employee of the firm; also referred to as *outside director*.

inside director (p. 298)   A member of the firm's board of directors who is also an officer or employee of the firm.

issued shares (p. 301)   The number of shares of a class of stock that has been issued (usually sold) to stockholders.

legal capital (p. 300)   An amount associated with the capital stock that has been issued by a corporation. Legal capital is generally the par value or stated value of the shares issued.

liquidating value (p. 303)   The stated claim of preferred stock in the event the corporation is liquidated. Sometimes called *redemption value*.

outside director (p. 300)   A member of the firm's board of directors who is not an officer or employee of the firm; another name for *independent director*.

outstanding shares (p. 301)   The number of shares of a class of stock held by stockholders.

par value (p. 300)   An arbitrary value assigned to a share of stock when the corporation is organized. Sometimes used to refer to the stated value or face amount of a security.

participating dividend (p. 303)   A feature of preferred stock that provides a right to preferred stockholders to receive additional dividends at a specified ratio after a base amount of dividends has been paid to common stockholders.

partners' capital (p. 296)   The owners' equity in a partnership.

payment date (p. 308)   The date a dividend is paid.

preemptive right (p. 301)   The right of a stockholder to purchase shares from any additional sales of shares in proportion to the stockholder's present percentage of ownership.

preferred stock (p. 302)   The class of stock representing an ownership interest with certain preferences relative to common stock, usually including a priority claim to dividends.

proprietor's capital (p. 296)   The owners' equity of an individual proprietorship.

record date (p. 308)   The date used to determine the stockholders who will receive a dividend.

redemption value (p. 303)   The stated claim of preferred stock in the event the corporation is liquidated. Sometimes called *liquidating value*.

retained earnings (p. 305)   Cumulative net income that has not been distributed to the owners/stockholders of a corporation as dividends.

slate voting (p. 300)   A system of voting for the directors of a firm in which votes equal to the number of shares owned are cast for a single slate of candidates.

stated value (p. 300)   An arbitrary value assigned to shares of no-par-value stock.

stock dividend (p. 307)   A distribution of additional shares to existing stockholders in proportion to their existing holdings. The additional shares issued usually amount to less than 20 percent of the previously issued shares.

stock split (p. 309)   A distribution of additional shares to existing stockholders in proportion to their existing holdings. The additional shares issued usually amount to 100 percent or more of the previously issued shares.

treasury stock (p. 301)   Shares of a firm's previously issued stock that have been reacquired by the firm.

ANSWERS TO
What Does It Mean?

1. It means that common stock has been issued to stockholders in exchange for their investment of capital in the corporation. The capital has not been earned; it has been paid in by the stockholders.

2. It means that an arbitrary amount has been assigned as a value for each share of common stock. This arbitrarily assigned value has no effect on the market value of each share of common stock.

3. It means that the corporation has reacquired from stockholders some previously issued shares of stock.

4. It means that the corporation has issued some stock that has many characteristics similar to those of bonds. Relative to common stock, preferred stock has a priority claim to dividends and to assets in the event of liquidation.

5. It means that the corporation has retained earnings from its operations and cash that the directors want to distribute to the stockholders.

6. It means that the corporation has retained earnings from its operations and that the directors want to transfer some of the retained earnings to paid-in capital rather than distribute cash to the stockholders.

7. It means that the corporation's board of directors wants to lower the market value of each share of common stock. This occurs because the corporation doesn't receive anything for the additional shares issued, so the total market value of the company is split among more shares than were outstanding before the stock split.

8. It means that the ownership interests in subsidiaries held by parties other than the parent must be clearly identified, labeled, and presented in the consolidated balance sheet within equity, but separate from the parent's equity.

Self-Study Material

Visit the text website at www.mhhe.com/marshall10e to take an online self-study quiz for this chapter.

Matching I Following are a number of the key terms and concepts introduced in the chapter, along with a list of corresponding definitions. Match the appropriate letter for the key term or concept to each definition provided (items 1–10). Note that not all key terms and concepts will be used. Answers are provided at the end of this chapter.

a. Proprietor's capital	j. Participating preferred stock
b. Partners' capital	k. Callable preferred stock
c. Common stock	l. Convertible preferred stock
d. Capital stock	m. Liquidating or redemption value
e. Inside director	n. Legal capital
f. Outside director	o. No-par-value
g. Cumulative voting	p. Stated value
h. Slate voting	q. Accumulated deficit
i. Par value	r. Retained earnings

_____ **1.** An arbitrary value assigned to a share of stock when the corporation is organized. Sometimes used to refer to the stated value or face amount of a security.

_____ **2.** A class of preferred stock providing that the preferred stockholders share in additional dividends in a specified ratio after a base amount of dividends has been paid on the common stock.

_____ **3.** A system of voting for directors of a firm in which votes equal to the number of shares owned are cast for a single slate of candidates.

_____ **4.** A member of the firm's board of directors who is not also an officer or employee of the firm.

_____ **5.** The stated claim of preferred stock in the event that the corporation is liquidated.

_____ **6.** An arbitrary value assigned to shares of no-par-value stock.

_____ **7.** Cumulative net income that has not been distributed to the owners/stockholders of a corporation as dividends.

_____ **8.** The owners' equity of a partnership.

_____ **9.** Retained earnings with a negative (debit) balance.

_____**10.** The class of stock that represents residual ownership of the corporation.

Matching II Following are a number of the key terms and concepts introduced in the chapter, along with a list of corresponding definitions. Match the appropriate letter for the key term or concept to each definition provided (items 1–10). Note that not all key terms and concepts will be used. Answers are provided at the end of this chapter.

a. Accumulated other comprehensive income (loss)	j. Cumulative dividend
b. Additional paid-in capital	k. Dividend declaration date
c. Authorized (shares of stock)	l. Dividend record date
d. Issued (shares of stock)	m. Dividend payment date
e. Outstanding (shares of stock)	n. Ex-dividend date
f. Treasury stock	o. Stock dividend
g. Preemptive right	p. Stock split
h. Preferred stock	q. Cumulative foreign currency translation adjustment
i. Dividend	

_____ **1.** A feature of preferred stock requiring that any missed dividends be paid before dividends can be paid on common stock.

_____ **2.** The difference between the total amount invested by the owners/stockholders and the par value or stated value of the stock issued. Often called *capital in excess of par value (or stated value).*

_____ **3.** Shares of a firm's stock that have been reacquired by the firm.

_____ **4.** The number of shares of a class of stock that have been sold to stockholders.

_____ **5.** The class of stock representing ownership of a corporation that has certain preferences relative to the common stock, usually including a priority claim to dividends.

_____ **6.** The right of a stockholder to purchase shares from any additional shares sold in proportion to the stockholder's present percentage of ownership.

_____ **7.** The date used to determine the stockholders who will receive a dividend.

_____ **8.** A distribution of additional shares to existing stockholders in proportion to their existing holdings. The additional shares issued usually amount to 100% or more of the previously issued shares.

_____ **9.** The number of shares of a class of stock held by stockholders.

_____**10.** A distribution of earnings to the owners/stockholders of a corporation.

Multiple Choice For each of the following questions, circle the best response. Answers are provided at the end of this chapter.

1. Which of the following classifications would represent the largest number of shares of common stock?

   a. Issued shares.

   b. Outstanding shares.

   c. Treasury shares.

   d. Authorized shares.

   e. Unissued shares.

2. Treasury stock involves shares that are

   a. authorized but not yet issued.

   b. authorized, issued, and outstanding.

   c. issued and outstanding but not yet authorized.

   d. not yet authorized.

   e. authorized and issued but not currently outstanding.

3. Gurwell Corporation declared a 10% stock dividend. Retained earnings should be capitalized for an amount equal to the number of shares to be distributed multiplied by the

   a. par value per share.

   b. book value per share.

   c. market value per share.

   d. stated value per share.

   e. lower of cost or market value per share.

4. Which of the following is *not* true about a 10% stock dividend?

   a. Retained earnings decrease.

   b. Paid-in capital increases.

   c. Par value decreases.

  d. Information concerning the market value of the stock is needed to record the stock dividend journal entry.

  e. Total stockholders' equity remains the same.

5. The Retained Earnings balance of Jayhawk Company at December 31, 2013, was $23,000. The December 31, 2014, balance of Retained Earnings was $31,000. Dividends of $3,000 were paid during 2014. The only other change in the Retained Earnings account was due to net income. The net income of Jayhawk Company during 2014 was

  a. $5,000.

  b. $8,000.

  c. $11,000.

  d. $14,000.

  e. $20,000.

6. Which of the following would *not* affect total retained earnings? Assume that it is the end of the fiscal year and that the books have been closed.

  a. Cash dividends.

  b. Net income.

  c. Stock dividends.

  d. Stock splits.

  e. All of the above would affect total retained earnings.

7. Similarities between preferred stock and long-term debt (bonds) include all of the following *except*

  a. each has a fixed claim to annual income (dividends and interest, respectively).

  b. each has a fixed claim on assets (liquidating value and principal amount, respectively).

  c. each allows the corporation a tax deduction (dividends and interest, respectively).

  d. each may be callable and/or convertible.

  e. All of the above are similarities between preferred stock and long-term debt (bonds).

8. Which of the following is normally a contra stockholders' equity account?

  a. Retained Earnings.

  b. Treasury Stock.

  c. Preferred Stock.

  d. Additional Paid-In Capital.

  e. None of the above.

9. The annual per share dividend requirement of an 8%, $150 par value preferred stock that was issued for $160 is

  a. $8.00.

  b. $12.00.

  c. $12.80.

  d. $15.00.

  e. $16.00.

10. Which of the following does *not* appear in the stockholders' equity section of a balance sheet?

   a. Preferred Stock.

   b. Bonds Payable.

   c. Additional Paid-In Capital.

   d. Accumulated Other Comprehensive Income (Loss).

   e. Treasury Stock.

Mini-Exercises

All applicable Mini-Exercises are available with McGraw-Hill's *Connect™ Accounting.*

Common stock—issuance and dividend transactions Altuve Co. was incorporated on January 1, 2013, at which time 500,000 shares of $1 par value common stock were authorized, and 210,000 of these shares were issued for $15 per share. Net income for the year ended December 31, 2013, was $2,400,000. Altuve Co.'s board of directors declared dividends of $4 per share of common stock on December 31, 2013, payable on February 7, 2014.

Mini-Exercise 8.1
LO 1, 3

Required:

Use the horizontal model (or write the entry) to show the effects of

a. The issuance of common stock on January 1, 2013.

b. The declaration of dividends on December 31, 2013.

c. The payment of dividends on February 7, 2014.

Preferred stock—calculate dividend amounts Spike & Jones Ltd. did not pay dividends on its 7.5%, $100 par value cumulative preferred stock during 2012 or 2013. Since 2006, 125,000 shares of this stock have been outstanding. Spike & Jones Ltd. has been profitable in 2014 and is considering a cash dividend on its common stock that would be payable in December 2014.

Mini-Exercise 8.2
LO 2

Required:

Calculate the amount of dividends that would have to be paid on the preferred stock before a cash dividend could be paid to the common stockholders.

Effects of a stock split Assume that you own 1,200 shares of $10 par value common stock and the company has a 5-for-1 stock split when the market price per share is $70.

Mini-Exercise 8.3
LO 4

Required:

a. How many shares of common stock will you own after the stock split?

b. What will probably happen to the market price per share of the stock?

c. What will probably happen to the par value per share of the stock?

Treasury stock transactions On April 10, 2013, Amelia, Inc., purchased 500 shares of its own common stock in the market for $24 per share. On September 28, 2013, the company sold 300 of these shares in the open market at a price of $27 per share.

Mini-Exercise 8.4
LO 6

Required:

Use the horizontal model (or write the entry) to show the effects on Amelia, Inc.'s financial statements of

a. The purchase of the treasury stock on April 10, 2013.
b. The sale of the treasury stock on September 28, 2013.

Exercises

All applicable Exercises are available with McGraw-Hill's *Connect*™ *Accounting*.

Exercise 8.5 **Review exercise—calculate net income** At the beginning of the current fiscal year, the balance sheet of Hughey, Inc., showed stockholders' equity of $520,000. During the year, liabilities increased by $21,000 to $234,000; paid-in capital increased by $40,000 to $175,000; and assets increased by $260,000. Dividends declared and paid during the year were $55,000.

Required:

Calculate net income or loss for the year. *(Hint: Set up the accounting equation for beginning balances, changes during the year, and ending balances; then solve for missing amounts.)*

	A	=	L	+	PIC	+	RE
					SE		
Beginning	$	=		+		+	
Changes		=		+		+	
Ending		=		+		+	

Exercise 8.6 **Review exercise—calculate net income** At the beginning of the current fiscal year, the balance sheet of Cummings Co. showed liabilities of $438,000. During the year, liabilities decreased by $72,000; assets increased by $154,000; and paid-in capital increased by $20,000 to $380,000. Dividends declared and paid during the year were $124,000. At the end of the year, stockholders' equity totaled $758,000.

Required:

Calculate net income or loss for the year using the same format as shown in Exercise 8.5.

Exercise 8.7 **Review exercise—calculate retained earnings** From the following data, calculate the Retained Earnings balance as of December 31, 2014:

Retained earnings, December 31, 2013	$346,400
Cost of buildings purchased during 2014	41,800
Net income for the year ended December 31, 2014	56,900
Dividends declared and paid in 2014	32,500
Increase in cash balance from January 1, 2014, to December 31, 2014	23,000
Increase in long-term debt in 2014	44,600

Review exercise—calculate retained earnings From the following data, calculate the Retained Earnings balance as of December 31, 2013:

Exercise 8.8

Retained earnings, December 31, 2014..	$245,200
Net decrease in total assets during 2014	37,400
Net increase in accounts receivable in 2014	8,600
Dividends declared and paid in 2014...	33,600
Proceeds from issuance of bonds during 2014...	88,400
Net loss for the year ended December 31, 2014..	23,000

Common stock balance sheet disclosure The balance sheet caption for common stock is the following:

Exercise 8.9

LO 1

Common stock, $5 par value, 2,000,000 shares authorized, 1,400,000 shares issued, 1,250,000 shares outstanding	$?

Required:

a. Calculate the dollar amount that will be presented opposite this caption.

b. Calculate the total amount of a cash dividend of $0.15 per share.

c. What accounts for the difference between issued shares and outstanding shares?

Common stock—calculate issue price and dividend amount The balance sheet caption for common stock is the following:

Exercise 8.10

LO 1

Common stock without par value, 1,000,000 shares authorized, 200,000 shares issued, and 180,000 shares outstanding	$2,600,000

Required:

a. Calculate the average price at which the shares were issued.

b. If these shares had been assigned a stated value of $1 each, show how the caption here would be different.

c. If a cash dividend of $0.60 per share were declared, calculate the total amount of cash that would be paid to stockholders.

d. What accounts for the difference between issued shares and outstanding shares?

Preferred stock—calculate dividend amounts Calculate the annual cash dividends required to be paid for each of the following preferred stock issues:

Exercise 8.11

LO 2

Required:

a. $3.75 cumulative preferred, no par value; 200,000 shares authorized, 161,522 shares issued. (The treasury stock caption of the stockholders' equity section of the balance sheet indicates that 43,373 shares of this preferred stock issue are owned by the company.)

b. 6%, $40 par value preferred, 100,000 shares authorized, 85,400 shares issued, and 73,621 shares outstanding.

c. 11.4% cumulative preferred, $100 stated value, $104 liquidating value; 50,000 shares authorized, 43,200 shares issued, 37,600 shares outstanding.

Exercise 8.12
LO 2

Preferred stock—calculate dividend amounts Calculate the cash dividends required to be paid for each of the following preferred stock issues:

Required:

a. The semiannual dividend on 7% cumulative preferred, $50 par value, 40,000 shares authorized, issued, and outstanding.

b. The annual dividend on $4.20 cumulative preferred, 500,000 shares authorized, 160,000 shares issued, 137,400 shares outstanding. Last year's dividend has not been paid.

c. The quarterly dividend on 9.5% cumulative preferred, $100 stated value, $103 liquidating value, 120,000 shares authorized, 108,000 shares issued and outstanding. No dividends are in arrears.

Exercise 8.13
LO 2

Preferred stock—calculate dividend amounts Maliha, Inc., did not pay dividends on its $6.50, $50 par value, cumulative preferred stock during 2012 or 2013. Since 2008, 22,000 shares of this stock have been outstanding. Maliha, Inc., has been profitable in 2014 and is considering a cash dividend on its common stock that would be payable in December 2014.

Required:

Calculate the amount of dividends that would have to be paid on the preferred stock before a cash dividend could be paid to the common stockholders.

Exercise 8.14
LO 2

Preferred stock—calculate dividend amounts Qamar, Inc., did not pay dividends in 2012 or 2013, even though 50,000 shares of its 7.5%, $50 par value cumulative preferred stock were outstanding during those years. The company has 600,000 shares of $2 par value common stock outstanding.

Required:

a. Calculate the annual dividend per share obligation on the preferred stock.

b. Calculate the amount that would be received by an investor who has owned 700 shares of preferred stock and 8,000 shares of common stock since 2011 if a $0.40 per share dividend on the common stock is paid at the end of 2014.

Exercise 8.15
LO 3

Dividend dates—market price effects Blanker, Inc., has paid a regular quarterly cash dividend of $0.50 per share for several years. The common stock is publicly traded. On February 21 of the current year, Blanker's board of directors declared the regular first-quarter dividend of $0.50 per share payable on March 30 to stockholders of record on March 15.

Required:

As a result of this dividend action, state what you would expect to happen to the market price of the common stock of Blanker, Inc., on each of the following dates. Explain your answers.

a. February 21.   **b.** March 13.

c. March 15.   **d.** March 30.

Ex-dividend date—market price effect Find a list of common stock ex-dividend date data. (You can go, via Google, to stocks—wsj.com. Select the reference which is labeled *Market Data;* then move your cursor over *U.S. Stocks* and select *Dividends* under the Stocks and Trading Statistics category. Scroll down until you see the Dividend Declarations Table, which includes the relevant ex-dividend dates. Select several stocks, preferably of large and well-known companies.) Go to a stock listing on the ex-dividend date and determine what happened to the market price of a share of stock on that date. Does this price action make sense? Explain your answer.

Exercise 8.16
LO 3

Requirements for declaring dividends Knight, Inc., expects to incur a loss for the current year. The chairperson of the board of directors wants to have a cash dividend so that the company's record of having paid a dividend during every year of its existence will continue. What factors will determine whether or not the board can declare a dividend?

Exercise 8.17
LO 3

Interpret dividend information from an annual report Refer to the Campbell Soup Company annual report in the appendix. From the table of quarterly financial information on page 749 and the Selected Financial Data (Five-Year Review—Consolidated) on page 709, find the information relating to cash dividends on common stock.

Exercise 8.18
LO 3

Required:
a. How frequently are cash dividends paid?
b. What has been the pattern of the cash dividend amount per share relative to the pattern of earnings per share?
c. Calculate the rate of change in the annual dividend per share for each of the years from 2008 through 2011.

e**X**cel

Cash dividends versus stock dividends Under what circumstances would you (as an investor) prefer to receive cash dividends rather than stock dividends? Under what circumstances would you prefer stock dividends to cash dividends?

Exercise 8.19
LO 4

Calculate stock dividend shares and cash dividend amounts Assume that you own 4,000 shares of Blueco, Inc.'s, common stock and that you currently receive cash dividends of $0.84 per share per year.

Exercise 8.20
LO 4

Required:
a. If Blueco, Inc., declared a 5% stock dividend, how many shares of common stock would you receive as a dividend?
b. Calculate the cash dividend per share amount to be paid after the stock dividend that would result in the same total cash dividend (as was received before the stock dividend).
c. If the cash dividend remained at $0.84 per share after the stock dividend, what per share cash dividend amount without a stock dividend would have accomplished the same total cash dividend?
d. Why would a company have a dividend policy of paying a $0.10 per share cash dividend and issuing a 5% stock dividend every year?

Effects of a stock split Assume that you own 500 shares of $10 par value common stock of a company and the company has a 2-for-1 stock split when the market price per share is $40.

Exercise 8.21
LO 4

Required:

a. How many shares of common stock will you own after the stock split?

b. What will probably happen to the market price per share of the stock?

c. What will probably happen to the par value per share of the stock?

Exercise 8.22
LO 4

Stock splits versus stock dividends Assume that you own 500 shares of common stock of a company, that you have been receiving cash dividends of $6 per share per year, and that the company has a 3-for-2 stock split.

Required:

a. How many shares of common stock will you own after the stock split?

b. What new cash dividend per share amount will result in the same total dividend income as you received before the stock split?

c. What stock dividend percentage could have accomplished the same end result as the 3-for-2 stock split?

connect
|ACCOUNTING

Problems

All applicable Problems are available with McGraw-Hill's *Connect*™ *Accounting.*

Problem 8.23
LO 1, 2

Common and preferred stock—issuances and dividends Homestead Oil Corp. was incorporated on January 1, 2013, and issued the following stock for cash:

800,000 shares of no-par common stock were authorized; 150,000 shares were issued on January 1, 2013, at $19 per share.

200,000 shares of $100 par value, 9.5% cumulative, preferred stock were authorized, and 60,000 shares were issued on January 1, 2013, at $122 per share.

Net income for the years ended December 31, 2013 and 2014, was $1,300,000 and $2,800,000, respectively.

No dividends were declared or paid during 2013. However, on December 28, 2014, the board of directors of Homestead declared dividends of $1,800,000, payable on February 12, 2015, to holders of record as of January 19, 2015.

Required:

a. Use the horizontal model (or write the entry) to show the effects of
   1. The issuance of common stock and preferred stock on January 1, 2013.
   2. The declaration of dividends on December 28, 2014.
   3. The payment of dividends on February 12, 2015.

b. Of the total amount of dividends declared during 2014, how much will be received by preferred shareholders?

Problem 8.24
LO 1, 2

Common and preferred stock—issuances and dividends Permabilt Corp. was incorporated on January 1, 2013, and issued the following stock for cash:

4,000,000 shares of no-par common stock were authorized; 1,250,000 shares were issued on January 1, 2013, at $35 per share.

1,500,000 shares of $100 par value, 8.5% cumulative, preferred stock were authorized, and 640,000 shares were issued on January 1, 2013, at $105 per share.

Net income for the years ended December 31, 2013, 2014, and 2015, was $18,400,000, $24,600,000, and $28,750,000, respectively.

No dividends were declared or paid during 2013 or 2014. However, on December 17, 2015, the board of directors of Permabilt Corp. declared dividends of $42,300,000, payable on February 9, 2016, to holders of record as of January 4, 2016.

Required:

a. Use the horizontal model (or write the entry) to show the effects of
   1. The issuance of common stock and *preferred* stock on January 1, 2013.
   2. The declaration of dividends on December 17, 2015.
   3. The payment of dividends on February 9, 2016.
b. Of the total amount of dividends declared during 2015, how much will be received by preferred shareholders?

Treasury stock transactions On May 4, 2013, Docker, Inc., purchased 800 shares of its own common stock in the market at a price of $18.25 per share. On September 19, 2013, 600 of these shares were sold in the open market at a price of $19.50 per share. There were 36,200 shares of Docker common stock outstanding prior to the May 4 purchase of treasury stock. A $0.35 per share cash dividend on the common stock was declared and paid on June 15, 2013.

Problem 8.25
LO 6

Required:

Use the horizontal model (or write the entry) to show the effects on Docker's financial statements of

a. The purchase of the treasury stock on May 4, 2013.
b. The declaration and payment of the cash dividend on June 15, 2013.
c. The sale of the treasury stock on September 19, 2013.

Treasury stock transactions On January 1, 2013, Metco, Inc., reported 622,100 shares of $3 par value common stock as being issued and outstanding. On March 15, 2013, Metco, Inc., purchased for its treasury 5,200 shares of its common stock at a price of $64 per share. On August 10, 2013, 1,900 of these treasury shares were sold for $76 per share. Metco's directors declared cash dividends of $2.10 per share during the second quarter and again during the fourth quarter, payable on June 30, 2013, and December 31, 2013, respectively. A 3% stock dividend was issued at the end of the year. There were no other transactions affecting common stock during the year.

Problem 8.26
LO 6

Required:

a. Use the horizontal model (or write the entry) to show the effect of the treasury stock purchase on March 15, 2013.
b. Calculate the total amount of the cash dividends paid in the second quarter.
c. Use the horizontal model (or write the entry) to show the effect of the sale of the treasury stock on August 10, 2013.
d. Calculate the total amount of cash dividends paid in the fourth quarter.
e. Calculate the number of shares of stock issued in the stock dividend.

Problem 8.27
LO 1, 2, 4, 6

Transaction analysis—various accounts Enter the following column headings across the top of a sheet of paper:

Transaction	Cash	Other Assets	Liabilities	Paid-In Capital	Retained Earnings	Treasury Stock	Net Income

Enter the transaction letter in the first column and show the effect (if any) of each of the following transactions on each financial statement category by entering a plus (+) or minus (−) sign and the amount in the appropriate column. Do not show items that affect net income in the retained earnings column. You may also write the entries to record each transaction.

a. Sold 4,100 shares of $50 par value 9% preferred stock at par.
b. Declared the annual dividend on the preferred stock.
c. Purchased 650 shares of preferred stock for the treasury at $54 per share.
d. Issued 2,000 shares of $1 par value common stock in exchange for land valued at $113,000.
e. Sold 300 shares of the treasury stock purchased in transaction **c** for $58 per share.
f. Split the common stock 2 for 1.

Problem 8.28
LO 1, 2, 4, 6

Transaction analysis—various accounts Enter the following column headings across the top of a sheet of paper:

Transaction	Cash	Other Assets	Liabilities	Paid-In Capital	Retained Earnings	Treasury Stock	Net Income

Enter the transaction letter in the first column and show the effect (if any) of each of the following transactions on each financial statement category by entering a plus (+) or minus (–) sign and the amount in the appropriate column. Do not show items that affect net income in the retained earnings column. You may also write the entries to record these transactions. You should assume that the transactions occurred in the same chronological sequence as listed here:

a. Sold 1,700 shares of $50 par value preferred stock at $52.50 per share.
b. Declared the annual cash dividend of $4.10 per share on common stock. There were 9,300 shares of $1 par value common stock issued and outstanding throughout the year.
c. Issued 2,500 shares of $50 par value preferred stock in exchange for a building when the market price of preferred stock was $54 per share.
d. Purchased 700 shares of preferred stock for the treasury at a price of $56 per share.
e. Sold 250 shares of the preferred stock held in treasury (see **d**) for $57 per share.
f. Declared and issued a 15% stock dividend on the $1 par value common stock when the market price per share was $36.

Problem 8.29
LO 1, 2, 4, 6

Transaction analysis—various accounts Enter the following column headings across the top of a sheet of paper:

Transaction	Cash	Other Assets	Liabilities	Paid-In Capital	Retained Earnings	Treasury Stock	Net Income

Enter the transaction letter in the first column and show the effect (if any) of each of the following transactions on each financial statement category by entering a plus (+) or minus (−) sign and the amount in the appropriate column. Do not show items that affect net income in the retained earnings column. You may also write the entries to record these transactions. You should assume that the transactions occurred in this chronological sequence and that 40,000 shares of previously issued common stock remain outstanding. *(Hint: Remember to consider appropriate effects of previous transactions.)*

a. Sold 5,000 previously unissued shares of $1 par value common stock for $18 per share.

b. Issued 1,000 shares of previously unissued 8% cumulative preferred stock, $40 par value, in exchange for land and a building appraised at $40,000.

c. Declared and paid the annual cash dividend on the preferred stock issued in transaction **b**.

d. Purchased 250 shares of common stock for the treasury at a total cost of $4,750.

e. Declared a cash dividend of $0.15 per share on the common stock outstanding.

f. Sold 130 shares of the treasury stock purchased in transaction **d** at a price of $20 per share.

g. Declared and issued a 3% stock dividend on the common stock issued when the market value per share of common stock was $21.

h. Split the common stock 3 for 1.

Transaction analysis—various accounts Enter the following column headings across the top of a sheet of paper:

Problem 8.30
LO 1, 2, 4, 6

Transaction	Cash	Other Assets	Liabilities	Paid-In Capital	Retained Earnings	Treasury Stock	Net Income

Enter the transaction letter in the first column and show the effect (if any) of each of the following transactions on each financial statement category by entering a plus (+) or minus (−) sign and the amount in the appropriate column. Do not show items that affect net income in the retained earnings column. You may also write the entries to record these transactions. You should assume that the transactions occurred in the listed chronological sequence and that no stock had been previously issued. *(Hint: Remember to consider appropriate effects of previous transactions.)*

a. Issued 3,000 shares of $100 par value preferred stock at par.

b. Issued 4,800 shares of $100 par value preferred stock in exchange for land that had an appraised value of $612,000.

c. Issued 34,000 shares of $5 par value common stock for $24 per share.

d. Purchased 14,000 shares of common stock for the treasury at $27 per share.

e. Sold 9,000 shares of the treasury stock purchased in transaction **d** for $29 per share.

f. Declared a cash dividend of $3.50 per share on the preferred stock outstanding, to be paid early next year.

g. Declared and issued a 12% stock dividend on the common stock when the market price per share of common stock was $30.

Problem 8.31

LO 1, 2, 3, 6, 7

Comprehensive problem—calculate missing amounts, dividends, total shares, and per share information Allyn, Inc., has the following stockholders' equity section in its November 30, 2013, balance sheet:

Paid-In capital:	
12% preferred stock, $60 par value, 1,500 shares	
authorized, issued, and outstanding..	$?
Common stock, $8 par value, 100,000 shares	
authorized, ? shares issued, ? shares outstanding..	240,000
Additional paid-in capital on common stock..	540,000
Additional paid-in capital from treasury stock	13,000
Retained earnings...	97,000
Less: Treasury stock, at cost (2,000 shares of common)..	(18,000)
Total stockholders' equity...	$?

Required:

a. Calculate the amount of the total annual dividend requirement on preferred stock.

b. Calculate the amount that should be shown on the balance sheet for preferred stock.

c. Calculate the number of shares of common stock that are issued and the number of shares of common stock that are outstanding.

d. On January 1, 2013, the firm's balance sheet showed common stock of $210,000 and additional paid-in capital on common stock of $468,750. The only transaction affecting these accounts during 2013 was the sale of common stock. Calculate the number of shares that were sold and the selling price per share.

e. Describe the transaction that resulted in the additional paid-in capital from treasury stock.

f. The retained earnings balance on January 1, 2013, was $90,300. Net income for the past 11 months has been $24,000. Preferred stock dividends for all of 2013 have been declared and paid. Calculate the amount of dividends on common stock during the first 11 months of 2013.

Problem 8.32

LO 1, 2, 3, 4, 6, 7

Comprehensive problem—calculate missing amounts, issue price, net income, and dividends; interpret stock dividend and split Bacon, Inc., has the following stockholders' equity section in its May 31, 2013, comparative balance sheets:

	May 31, 2013	April 30, 2013
Paid-In capital:		
Preferred stock, $120 par value, 9%, cumulative,		
100,000 shares authorized, 70,000 shares issued		
and outstanding	$ 8,400,000	$ 8,400,000
Common stock, $5 par value, 500,000 shares		
authorized, 300,000 and 270,000 shares		
issued, respectively	?	1,350,000
Additional paid-in capital	12,990,000	11,610,000
Retained earnings	18,100,000	17,320,000
Less: Treasury common stock, at cost; 36,000 shares		
and 34,000 shares, respectively	(2,202,000)	(2,074,000)
Total stockholders' equity	$?	$36,606,000

Required:

a. Calculate the amount that should be shown on the balance sheet for common stock at May 31, 2013.

b. The only transaction affecting additional paid-in capital during the month of May was the sale of additional common stock. At what price per share were the additional shares sold?

c. What was the average cost per share of the common stock purchased for the treasury during the month?

d. During May, dividends on preferred stock equal to one-half of the 2013 dividend requirement were declared and paid. There were no common dividends declared or paid in May. Calculate net income for May.

e. Assume that on June 1 the board of directors declared a cash dividend of $0.30 per share on the outstanding shares of common stock. The dividend will be payable on July 15 to stockholders of record on June 15.
   1. Calculate the total amount of the dividend.
   2. Explain the impact this action will have on the June 30 balance sheet and on the income statement for June.

f. Assume that on June 1 the market value of the common stock was $66 per share and that the board of directors declared a 5% stock dividend on the issued shares of common stock. Use the horizontal model (or write the entry) to show the issuance of the stock dividend.

g. Assume that instead of the stock dividend described in **f**, the board of directors authorized a 2-for-1 stock split on June 1 when the market price of the common stock was $66 per share.
   1. What will be the par value, and how many shares of common stock will be authorized after the split?
   2. What will be the market price per share of common stock after the split?
   3. How many shares of common stock will be in the treasury after the split?

h. By how much will total stockholders' equity change as a result of
   1. The stock dividend described in part **f**?
   2. The stock split described in part **g**?

connect | **Cases**
|ACCOUNTING

All applicable Cases are available with McGraw-Hill's *Connect™ Accounting*.

Case 8.33

LO 1, 2, 5, 6, 8

Focus company—stockholders' equity disclosures   In Exercise 1.1, you were asked to obtain the most recent annual report of a company that you were interested in reviewing throughout this term.

Required:

Please review the note disclosures provided in your focus company's annual report and identify at least three items being reported as stockholders' equity items. Discuss what you've learned about these items and how they are presented on the balance sheet.

Case 8.34

LO 1, 2, 6, 7

Analytical case (part 1)—calculate missing stockholders' equity amounts for 2013 *(Note: The information presented in this case is also used for Case 8.35. For now you can ignore the 2014 column in the balance sheet; all disclosures presented here relate to the June 30, 2013, balance sheet.)* DeZurik Corp. had the following stockholders' equity section in its June 30, 2013, balance sheet (in thousands, except share and per share amounts):

	June 30 (in thousands)	
	2014	2013
Paid-in capital:		
$4.50 Preferred stock, $ _?_ par value, cumulative, 200,000 shares authorized, 96,000 shares issued and outstanding	_____	$ 5,760
Common stock, $5 par value, 4,000,000 shares authorized, 3,280,000 shares issued, 3,000,000 shares outstanding	_____	_____
Additional paid-in capital on common stock	_____	22,960
Retained earnings	_____	_____
Less: Treasury common stock, at cost, _?_ shares	_____	_____
Total stockholders' equity	$66,168	$60,000

Required:

a. Calculate the par value per share of preferred stock and determine the preferred stock dividend percentage.

b. Calculate the amount that should be shown on the balance sheet for common stock at June 30, 2013.

c. What was the average issue price of common stock shown on the June 30, 2013, balance sheet?

d. How many shares of treasury stock does DeZurik Corp. own at June 30, 2013?

e. Assume that the treasury shares were purchased for $18 per share. Calculate the amount that should be shown on the balance sheet for treasury stock at June 30, 2013.

f. Calculate the retained earnings balance at June 30, 2013, after you have completed parts **a–e**. *(Hint: Keep in mind that Treasury Stock is a contra account.)*

g. (Optional) Review the solutions to parts **a–f** of this case on the website for this book at www.mhhe.com/marshall10e. Assume that the Retained Earnings balance on July 1, 2012, was $19,200 (in thousands) and that net income for the year ended June 30, 2013, was $1,152 (in thousands). The 2013 preferred dividends were paid in full, and no other dividend transactions were recorded during the year. Verify that the amount shown in the solution to part **f** is correct. *(Hint: Prepare a statement of retained earnings or do a T-account analysis to determine the June 30, 2013, balance.)*

Analytical case (part 2)—prepare stockholders' equity amounts and disclosures for 2014 using transaction information *(Note: You should review the solution to Case 8.34, provided by your instructor, before attempting to complete this case.)* The transactions affecting the stockholders' equity accounts of DeZurik Corp. for the year ended June 30, 2014, are summarized here:

Case 8.35
LO 1, 2, 4, 6, 9

1. 320,000 shares of common stock were issued at $14.25 per share.

2. 80,000 shares of treasury (common) stock were sold for $18 per share.

3. Net income for the year was $1,280 (in thousands).

4. The fiscal 2014 preferred dividends were paid in full. Assume that all 96,000 shares were outstanding throughout the year ended June 30, 2014.

5. A cash dividend of $.20 per share was declared and paid to common stockholders. Assume that transactions 1 and 2 occurred before the dividend was declared.

6. The preferred stock was split 2 for 1 on June 30, 2014. *(Note: This transaction had no effect on transaction 4.)*

Required:

a. Calculate the *dollar amounts* that DeZurik Corp. would report for each stockholders' equity caption on its June 30, 2014, balance sheet after recording the effects of transactions 1–6. Note that total stockholders' equity at June 30, 2014, is provided as a check figure. *(Hint: To determine the Retained Earnings balance, begin with the June 30, 2013, balance of $19,920 (in thousands) as determined in Case 8.34, and then make adjustments for the effects of transactions 3–5.)*

b. Indicate how the stockholders' equity caption details for DeZurik Corp. would change for the June 30, 2014, balance sheet, as compared to the disclosures shown in Case 8.34 for the 2013 balance sheet.

c. What was the average issue price of common stock shown on the June 30, 2014, balance sheet?

Capstone analytical review of Chapters 6–8. Analyzing capital leases, notes payable, preferred stock, and common stock *(Note: Please refer to Case 4.30 on pages 145–146 for the financial statement data needed for the analysis of this case. You should also review the solution to Case 4.30, provided by your instructor, before attempting to complete this case.)* Your conversation with Mr. Gerrard, which took place in February 2014 (see Case 6.35), continued as follows:

Case 8.36

Mr. Gerrard: I've been talking with my accountant about our capital expansion needs, which will be considerable during the next couple of years. To stay in a strong competitive position, we're constantly buying new pieces of earthmoving equipment and replacing machinery that has become obsolete. What it all comes down to is financing, and it's not easy to raise $10 million to $20 million all at once. There are a number of options, including dealer financing, but the interest rates offered by banks are usually lower.

Your reply: From reviewing your balance sheet, I can see that you've got a lot of notes payable already. How is your relationship with your bank?

Mr. Gerrard: Actually we use several banks and we have an excellent credit history, so getting the money is not a major problem. The problem is that we already owe more than $40 million on all of those notes and I don't want to get overextended.

Your reply: Have you considered long-term leases?

Mr. Gerrard: Yes. This is essentially how dealer financing works. Usually it is arranged as a lease with an option to buy the equipment after a number of years. We've been actively looking into this with our Cat dealer for a couple of scrapers that we need to put on a big job immediately. I can show you one of the contracts involved.

Your reply: OK, I'll have a look at the contract, but this sounds like a long-term capital lease.

Mr. Gerrard: Yes, I think that's what my accountant called it. What matters most to me is that we get the equipment in place ASAP; but if you could explain what the accounting implications would be of entering into these types of arrangements, that might put me at ease about it.

Your reply: No problem; will do. It would impact both your balance sheet and income statement, but in most respects a long-term capital lease is treated very much like a long-term note payable with a bank. I'll give you a memo about it. But what about looking into other sources of equity financing? Have you considered any of these options?

Mr. Gerrard: We're a family business and want to keep it that way. Our shares are publicly traded, but we're owned mostly by family members and employees. We've got a lot of retained earnings, but that's not the same thing as cash, you know. Should we be issuing bonds?

Your reply: Issuing bonds is possible, but I was thinking more on the lines of preferred stock. Are you familiar with this option?

Mr. Gerrard: Oh sure. That's the cologne I wear! But other than that, I don't know much about it. Isn't preferred stock a lot like bonds payable?

Your reply: Maybe this is something else I should include in my memo: an explanation of the differences between common stock, preferred stock, and bonds payable.

Mr. Gerrard: Yes, please do.

Required:

a. When discussing capital leases with Mr. Gerrard, you commented, "It would impact both your balance sheet and income statement, but in most respects a long-term capital lease is treated very much like a long-term note payable with a bank." Explain the accounting treatment of capital leases as compared to the accounting treatment of notes payable in terms that a nonaccountant could easily understand. Include in your answer both the balance sheet and income statement effects of capital leases. *(Note: You do not need to make reference to the four criteria for capitalizing a lease.)*

b. Assume you have reviewed the contract Mr. Gerrard provided concerning the dealer financing agreement for the purchase of two new scrapers. You have determined that the lease agreement would qualify as a capital lease. The present value of the lease payments would be $2 million. Use the horizontal model, or write the journal entry, to show Mr. Gerrard how this lease would affect the financial statements of Gerrard Construction Co.

c. Explain what Mr. Gerrard meant by his statement "We've got a lot of retained earnings, but that's not the same thing as cash, you know." Review the balance sheet at December 31, 2013, provided in Case 4.30. In which assets are most of the company's retained earnings invested?

d. Explain to Mr. Gerrard what the similarities and differences are between bonds payable, preferred stock, and common stock.

e. Why would you recommend to Mr. Gerrard that his company consider issuing $10 million to $20 million of preferred stock rather than bonds payable? *(Hint: Review the company's balance sheet provided in Case 4.30 in the context of your present conversation with Mr. Gerrard.)*

Answers to Self-Study Material

Matching I: 1. i, 2. j, 3. h, 4. f, 5. m, 6. p, 7. r, 8. b, 9. q, 10. c
Matching II: 1. j, 2. b, 3. f, 4. d, 5. h, 6. g, 7. l, 8. p, 9. e, 10. i
Multiple choice: 1. d, 2. e, 3. c, 4. c, 5. c, 6. d, 7. c, 8. b, 9. b, 10. b

9

The Income Statement and the Statement of Cash Flows

The income statement answers some of the most important questions that users of the financial statements have: What were the financial results of the firm's operations for the fiscal period? How much profit (or loss) did the firm have? Are sales increasing relative to cost of goods sold and other operating expenses? Many income statement accounts were introduced in Chapters 5 to 8 when transactions also affecting asset and liability accounts were explained. However, because of the significance of the net income figure to managers, stockholders, potential investors, and others, it is appropriate to focus on the form and content of this financial statement.

The Consolidated Statements of Earnings of Campbell Soup Company are shown on page 711 in the appendix. This page of the annual report has been reproduced as Exhibit 9-1. Note that comparative statements for the years ended on the Sunday nearest to July 31 of 2011, 2010, and 2009 are presented. This permits the reader of the statement to assess quickly the recent trend of these important data.

As you might expect, Campbell's income statement starts with "net sales." What in popular jargon is referred to as the *bottom line,* or "net income," is reported as "net earnings attributable to Campbell Soup Company." Before arriving at this amount, subtotals are also provided for "earnings before interest and taxes," "earnings before taxes," "earnings from continuing operations," and "net earnings." The significance of the "per share" data will be discussed later in this chapter. The principal objective of the first part of this chapter is to permit you to make sense of any income statement.

The second part of this chapter explores the statement of cash flows in more detail than presented in Chapter 2. Remember that this statement explains the change in the firm's cash from the beginning to the end of the fiscal period by summarizing the cash effects of the firm's operating, investing, and financing activities during the period. The statement of cash flows gives investors a chance to go beyond income statement numbers and determine whether those results are consistent with what is happening in the principal cash flow categories. For example, the first hints of financial difficulties of dot-com highfliers and Enron Corporation were visible in this financial statement.

Campbell's Consolidated Statements of Cash Flows are presented on page 713 in the appendix for each of the past three years. Notice that the subtotal captions describe the activities—operating, investing, and financing—that caused cash to be provided and used during these years. Pay more attention to these three "big picture" items than to the detailed captions and amounts within each

Income Statement   **Exhibit 9-1**

CAMPBELL SOUP COMPANY **Consolidated Statements of Earnings** **(dollars in millions)**			
Three Years Ended July 31, 2011	**2011**	**2010**	**2009**
Net sales	$7,719	$7,676	$7,586
Costs and expenses:			
Cost of products sold	4,616	4,526	4,558
Marketing and selling expenses.............................	1,007	1,058	1,077
Administrative expenses	612	605	591
Research and development expenses	129	123	114
Other expenses (income)...................................	13	4	61
Restructuring charges	63	12	—
Total costs and expenses.....................................	6,440	6,328	6,401
Earnings before interest and taxes	**1,279**	**1,348**	**1,185**
Interest expense..	122	112	110
Interest income..	11	6	4
Earnings before taxes......................................	1,168	1,242	1,079
Taxes on earnings..	366	398	347
Earnings from continuing operations........................	802	844	732
Earnings from discontinued operations......................	—	—	4
Net earnings	**802**	**844**	**736**
Less: Net earnings (loss) attributable to noncontrolling interests	(3)	—	—
Net earnings attributable to Campbell Soup Company...........	**$ 805**	**$ 844**	**$ 736**
Per Share—Basic			
Earnings from continuing operations attributable to Campbell Soup Company	$ 2.44	$ 2.44	$ 2.05
Earnings from discontinued operations attributable to Campbell Soup Company	—	—	0.01
Net earnings attributable to Campbell Soup Company...........	**$ 2.44**	**$ 2.44**	**$ 2.06**
Weighted average shares outstanding—basic	326	340	352
Per Share—Assuming Dilution			
Earnings from continuing operations attributable to Campbell Soup Company	$ 2.42	$ 2.42	$ 2.03
Earnings from discontinued operations attributable to Campbell Soup Company	—	—	0.01
Net earnings attributable to Campbell Soup Company...........	**$ 2.42**	**$ 2.42**	**$ 2.05**
Weighted average shares outstanding—assuming dilution	329	343	354

The sum of individual per share amounts does not equal due to rounding.

category. Notice, however, that Campbell's uses a substantial amount of cash each year to purchase plant assets (an investing activity) and to pay dividends (a financing activity). As explained later, these are both signs of a financially healthy firm—especially if the firm can cover these payments from its cash flows provided by operating activities. Did Campbell's do this for each year presented?

The income statement and statement of cash flows report what has happened for a *period of time* (usually, but not necessarily, for the fiscal year ended on the balance sheet date). The balance sheet, remember, is focused on a single *point in time*—usually the end of the fiscal year—but one can be prepared as of any date.

What Does It Mean?
Answer on page 373

1. What does it mean when net income is referred to as the "bottom line"?

LEARNING OBJECTIVES (LO)

After studying this chapter you should understand and be able to

LO 9-1   Explain what revenue is and what the two criteria are that permit revenue recognition.

LO 9-2   Describe how cost of goods sold is determined under both perpetual and periodic inventory accounting systems.

LO 9-3   Discuss the significance of gross profit and describe how the gross profit ratio is calculated and used.

LO 9-4   Identify the principal categories and components of "other operating expenses" and show how these items are reported on the income statement.

LO 9-5   Explain what "income from operations" includes and discuss why this income statement subtotal is significant to managers and financial analysts.

LO 9-6   Describe the components of the earnings per share calculation and discuss the reasons for some of the refinements made in that calculation.

LO 9-7   Compare and contrast the alternative income statement presentation models.

LO 9-8   Discuss the meaning and significance of each of the unusual items that may appear on the income statement.

LO 9-9   Describe the purpose and outline the general format of the statement of cash flows.

LO 9-10   Illustrate the difference between the direct and indirect methods of presenting cash flows from operating activities.

LO 9-11   Summarize why the statement of cash flows is significant to financial analysts and investors.

Exhibit 9-2 highlights the income statement and statement of cash flows components that are covered in detail in this chapter. Income statement transactions are often centered on the matching concept, and thus have a direct effect on most of the firm's

Balance Sheet				
Current Assets	Chapter	**Current Assets**		Chapter
Cash and cash equivalents	5, 9	Short-term debt		7
Short-term marketable securities	5	Current maturities of		
Accounts receivable	5, 9	long-term debt		7
Notes receivable	5	Accounts payable		7
Inventories	5, 9	Unearned revenue or		
Prepaid expenses	5	deferred credits		7
Noncurrent Assets		Payroll taxes and other		
Land	6	withholdings		7
Buildings and equipment	6	Other accrued liabilities		7
Assets acquired by capital lease	6	**Noncurrent Liabilities**		
Intangible assets	6	Long-term debt		7
Natural resources	6	Deferred tax liabilities		7
Other noncurrent assets	6	Other long-term liabilities		7
		Stockholders' Equity		
		Common stock		8
		Preferred stock		8
		Additional paid-in capital		8
		Retained earnings		8
		Accumulated other comprehensive		
		income (loss)		8
		Treasury stock		8
		Noncontrolling interest		8

Exhibit 9-2

Financial Statements—
The Big Picture

Income Statement		Statement of Cash Flows	
Sales	5, 9	**Operating Activities**	
Cost of goods sold	5, 9	Net income	5, 6, 7, 8, 9
Gross profit (or gross margin)	5, 9	Depreciation expense	6, 9
Selling, general, and		(Gains) losses on sale	
administrative expenses	5, 6, 9	of assets	6, 9
Income from operations	9	(Increase) decrease in	
Gains (losses) on sale		current assets	5, 9
of assets	6, 9	Increase (decrease) in	
Interest income	5, 9	current liabilities	7, 9
Interest expense	7, 9	**Investing Activities**	
Income tax expense	7, 9	Proceeds from sale of property,	
Unusual items	9	plant, and equipment	6, 9
Net income	5, 6, 7, 8, 9	Purchase of property, plant,	
Earnings per share	9	and equipment	6, 9
		Financing Activities	
		Proceeds from long-term debt*	7, 9
		Repayment of long-term debt*	7, 9
		Issuance of common stock	
		and/or preferred stock	8, 9
		Purchase of treasury stock	8, 9
		Payment of dividends	8, 9

Primary topics of this chapter.
Other affected financial statement components.
*May include short-term debt items as well.

current assets, especially accounts receivable and inventory. The preparation of the statement of cash flows requires analysis of the changes during the year to each and every balance sheet account, with cash as the focal point.

Income Statement

Revenues

LO 1

Explain what revenue is and what the two criteria are that permit revenue recognition.

The FASB defines **revenues** as "inflows or other enhancements of assets of an entity or settlements of its liabilities (or a combination of both) from delivering or producing goods, rendering services, or other activities that constitute the entity's ongoing major or central operations."[1] In its simplest and most straightforward application, this definition means that when a firm sells a product or provides a service to a client or customer and receives cash, creates an account receivable, or satisfies an obligation, the firm has revenue. Most revenue transactions fit this simple and straightforward situation. Revenues generally are measured by the amount of cash received or expected to be received from the transaction. If the cash is not expected to be received within a year, then the revenue usually is measured by the present value of the amount expected to be received.

In *Concepts Statement No. 5* the FASB expands on the preceding definition of revenues to provide guidance in applying the fundamental criteria involved in recognizing revenue. To be recognized, revenues must be realized or realizable and earned. Sometimes one of these criteria is more important than the other.

Realization means that the product or service has been exchanged for cash, claims to cash, or an asset that is readily convertible to a known amount of cash or claims to cash. Thus, the expectation that the product or service provided by the firm will result in a cash receipt has been fulfilled.

Earned means that the entity has completed, or substantially completed, the activities it must perform to be entitled to the revenue benefits (the increase in cash or some other asset, or the satisfaction of a liability).

The realization and earned criteria for recognizing revenue usually are satisfied when the product or merchandise being sold is delivered to the customer or when the service is provided. Thus, revenue from selling and servicing activities is commonly recognized when the sale is made, which means when the product is delivered or when the service is provided to the customer. Here is the effect on the financial statements:

Balance Sheet	Income Statement
Assets = Liabilities + Stockholders' equity	←Net income = Revenues − Expenses
+ Cash, or Accounts Receivable	+ Sales or Service Revenue

The typical entry would be:

Dr.	Cash (or Accounts Receivable)	xx	
	Cr. Sales (or Service Revenue)		xx

---

[1]FASB, *Statement of Financial Accounting Concepts No. 6,* "Elements of Financial Statements" (Stamford, CT, 1985), para. 78. Copyright © by the Financial Accounting Standards Board, High Ridge Park, Stamford, CT 06905, U.S.A. Quoted with permission. Copies of the complete document are available from the FASB.

An example of a situation in which the *earned* criterion is more significant than the realization criterion is a magazine publishing company that receives cash at the beginning of a subscription period. In this case revenue is recognized as earned by delivery of the magazine. On the other hand, if a product is delivered or a service is provided without any expectation of receiving an asset or satisfying a liability (such as when a donation is made), there is no revenue to be recognized because the *realization* criterion has not been fulfilled.

When revenues are related to the use of assets over a period of time—such as the renting of property or the lending of money—they are earned as time passes and are recognized based on the contractual prices that have been established in advance.

Some agricultural products, precious metals, and marketable securities have readily determinable prices and can be sold without significant effort. Where this is the case, revenues (and some gains or losses) may be recognized when production is completed or when prices of the assets change. These are unusual situations, however, and exceptions to the rule that an arm's-length exchange (i.e., sales transaction) must occur to meet the realization and earned criteria.

Due to the increasing complexity of many business activities and other newly developed transactions, a number of revenue recognition problems have arisen over the years. Therefore, the FASB and its predecessors within the American Institute of Certified Public Accountants have issued numerous pronouncements about revenue recognition issues for various industries and transactions. As a result, revenue recognition is straightforward an overwhelming proportion of the time. However, because they are the key to the entire income statement, revenues that are misstated (usually on the high side) can lead to significantly misleading financial statements. Accordingly, management and internal auditors often design internal control procedures to help promote the accuracy of the revenue recognition process of the firm.

Sales is the term used to describe the revenues of firms that sell purchased or manufactured products. In the normal course of business, some sales transactions will be subsequently voided because the customer returns the merchandise for credit or for a refund. In some cases, rather than have a shipment returned (especially if it is only slightly damaged or defective and is still usable by the customer), the seller will make an allowance on the amount billed and reduce the account receivable from the customer for the allowance amount. If the customer has already paid, a refund is made. These **sales returns and allowances** are accounted for separately for internal control and analysis purposes but are subtracted from the gross sales amount to arrive at **net sales.** In addition, if the firm allows cash discounts for prompt payment, total sales discounts are also subtracted from gross sales for reporting purposes. A fully detailed

The guidance on revenue recognition under U.S. GAAP is significantly more extensive than that provided under IFRS and tends to be industry-specific, whereas IFRS takes a broad principles-based approach to be applied across all entities and industries. As a result, the timing of revenue recognition may be different in several instances, with revenue potentially being recognized earlier under IFRS. Under U.S. GAAP, revenue is not recognized until the amount is either fixed or determinable. Thus, contingent amounts are not recognized as revenue until the contingency has been resolved. IFRS looks instead to the probability of economic benefits associated with the transaction flowing to the entity and the ability to reliably measure the amount of revenue in question, including any contingent revenue. Under IFRS, revenue is recognized based on the best reliable estimate available at the time of the transaction, even if the amount is not yet considered fixed or determinable.

The IFRS

Approach

income statement prepared for use within the company might have the following revenue section captions:

Sales	$
Less: Sales returns and allowances	( )
Less: Sales discounts	( )
Net sales	$

Net sales, or net revenues, is the first caption usually seen in the income statement of a merchandising or manufacturing company (as illustrated in Exhibit 9-1). Many companies provide a detailed calculation of the net sales amount in the accompanying notes of the annual report.

Firms that generate significant amounts of revenue from providing services in addition to (or instead of) selling a product will label the revenue source appropriately in the income statement. Thus, a leasing company might report Rental and Service Revenues as the lead item on its income statement, or a consulting service firm might show Fee Revenues or simply Fees. If a firm has several types of revenue, the amount of each could be shown if each amount is significant and is judged by the accountant to increase the usefulness of the income statement.

From a legal perspective, the sale of a product involves the passing of title (i.e., ownership rights) in the product from the seller to the purchaser. The point at which title passes usually is specified by the shipment terms (see Business in Practice—Shipping Terms). This issue becomes especially significant in two situations. The first involves shipments made near the end of a fiscal period. The shipping terms will determine whether revenue is recognized in the period in which the shipment was made or in the subsequent period when the shipment is received by the customer. Achieving an accurate "sales cutoff" may be important to the accuracy of the financial statements if the period-end shipments are material in amount. The second situation relates to any

Business in
Practice

Shipping Terms

Many products are shipped from the seller to the buyer instead of being picked up by the buyer at the time of sale. **Shipping terms** define the owner of products while they are in transit. **FOB destination** and **FOB shipping point** are the terms used. (FOB means *free on board* and is jargon that has carried over from the days when much merchandise was shipped by boat.) When an item is shipped FOB destination, the seller owns the product until it is accepted by the buyer at the buyer's designated location. Thus, title to merchandise shipped FOB destination passes from seller to buyer when the merchandise is received by the buyer. FOB shipping point means that the buyer accepts ownership of the product at the seller's shipping location.

Shipping terms also describe which party to the transaction is to *incur* the shipping cost. The *seller* incurs the freight cost for shipments made FOB destination; the *buyer* incurs the cost of shipments made FOB shipping point. *Payment* of the freight cost is another issue, however. The freight cost for products shipped **freight prepaid** is paid by the seller; when a shipment arrives **freight collect**, the buyer pays the freight cost. Ordinarily items shipped FOB destination will have freight prepaid, and items shipped FOB shipping point will be shipped freight collect. However, depending on freight company policies or other factors, an item having shipping terms of FOB destination may be shipped freight collect, or vice versa. If this happens, the firm paying the freight subsequently collects the amount paid to the freight company from the other firm, which *incurred* the freight cost under the shipping terms.

loss of or damage to the merchandise while it is in transit from the seller to the buyer. The legal owner of the merchandise, as determined by the shipping terms, is the one who suffers the loss. Of course, this party may seek to recover the amount of the loss from the party responsible for the damage (usually a third-party shipping company).

For certain sales transactions, a firm may take more than a year to construct the item being sold (for example, a cruise ship builder or a manufacturer of complex custom machinery). In these circumstances, delaying revenue recognition until the product has been delivered may result in the reporting of misleading income statement information for a number of years. Because these items are being manufactured under a contract with the buyer that specifies a price, it is possible to recognize revenue (and costs and profits) under what is known as the **percentage-of-completion method.** If, based on engineers' analyses and other factors, 40 percent of a job has been completed in the current year, 40 percent of the expected revenue (and 40 percent of the expected costs) will be recognized in the current year.

Companies should disclose any unusual revenue recognition methods, such as the percentage-of-completion method, in the notes accompanying the financial statements. Because profits will be directly affected by revenue, the user of the financial statements must be alert to, and understand the effect of, any revenue recognition method that differs from the usual and generally accepted practice of recognizing revenue when the product or service has been delivered to the customer (see Business in Practice—Revenue Recognition Practices of Dot-Com Companies for a glimpse at some of the questionable practices employed in recent years).

Gains, which are increases in an entity's net assets resulting from incidental transactions or nonoperating activities, are usually not included with revenues at the beginning of the income statement. Gains are reported as other income after the firm's operating expenses have been shown and income from operations has been reported. Interest income is an example of an "other income" item. The reporting of gains will be explained in more detail later in this chapter.

Revenue Recognition Practices of Dot-Com Companies

Rapidly rising stock values of dot-com companies during the late 1990s seemed to run contrary to traditional value measures such as the price/earnings ratio because many of these companies had no earnings. Financial analysts and investors used revenue growth as a key benchmark. That focus tempted many firms to record revenues in ways that stretched generally accepted revenue recognition practices and bordered on reporting misleading results. Some of these practices were:

Business in
Practice

Recognizing revenue too soon: Revenue was recognized when orders were received but before they were shipped, or revenue was recorded from future software upgrades before the upgrades had been completed, or revenue was recognized from software licenses when a contract was signed rather than over the life of the contract.

Overstating revenue from reselling: When a product or service was resold without ever having been owned by the reseller, revenue was recognized for the full amount charged to the purchaser rather than just for the reseller's markup.

As a result of such questionable practices, the Securities and Exchange Commission (SEC) issued a staff accounting bulletin on revenue recognition in late 1999 that generally delayed the recognition of revenue into future quarters for certain dot-com companies and caused several affected companies to restate prior year earnings. Historically, more than half of all SEC accounting fraud cases have involved revenue hoaxes, so the heightened scrutiny of software company practices did not come as a surprise to many financial analysts.

Expenses

The FASB defines **expenses** as "outflows or other using up of assets or incurrences of liabilities (or a combination of both) from delivering or producing goods, rendering services, or carrying out other activities that constitute the entity's ongoing major or central operations."[2] Some expenses (cost of goods sold is an example) are recognized concurrently with the revenues to which they relate. This is another application of the **matching principle,** which has been previously described and emphasized. Some expenses (administrative salaries, for example) are recognized in the period in which they are incurred because the benefit of the expense is used up simultaneously or soon after incurrence. Other expenses (depreciation, for example) result from an allocation of the cost of an asset to the periods that are expected to benefit from its use. In each of these categories, expenses are recognized in accordance with the matching principle because they are incurred to support the revenue-generating process. The amount of an expense is measured by the cash or other asset used up to obtain the economic benefit it represents. When the outflow of cash related to the expense will not occur within a year, it is appropriate to recognize the present value of the future cash flow as the amount of the expense.

Most of the time, identifying expenses to be recognized in the current period's income statement is straightforward. Cost of goods sold, compensation of employees, uncollectible accounts receivable, utilities consumed, and depreciation of long-lived assets are all examples. In other cases (research and development costs and advertising expense, for example), the impact of the expenditure on the revenues of future periods is not readily determinable. For these types of expenditures, there is no sound method of matching the expenditure with the revenues that may be earned over several periods. To avoid the necessity of making arbitrary allocations, all advertising and R&D expenditures are recorded as expenses in the period incurred under U.S. GAAP. This approach is justified by the objectivity and conservatism concepts.

Other types of expense involve complex recognition and measurement issues; income tax expense and pension expense are just two examples. Recall the discussion of these topics in Chapter 7 when the liabilities related to these expenses were discussed.

Losses, which are decreases in an entity's net assets resulting from incidental transactions or nonoperating activities, are not included with expenses. Losses are reported after income from operations, as discussed later in this chapter.

The discussion of expenses in this chapter follows the sequence in which expenses are presented in most income statements.

The IFRS

Approach

Under IFRS, all research expenditures are recorded as expenses in the period incurred but development costs must be capitalized as intangible assets once the technical and commercial feasibility of the asset being developed for sale or use has been established.

---

[2]Ibid., para. 80.

Cost of Goods Sold

Cost of goods sold (sometimes called "cost of products sold" as is the case for Campbell Soup Company) is the most significant expense for many manufacturing and merchandising companies. Recall from your study of the accounting for inventories in Chapter 5 that the **inventory cost flow assumption** (FIFO, LIFO, weighted average) being used by the firm affects this expense. **Inventory shrinkage** (the term that describes inventory losses from obsolescence, errors, and theft) usually is included in cost of goods sold unless the amount involved is material. In that case the inventory loss would be reported separately as a loss after operating income has been reported.

Determination of the cost of goods sold amount is a function of the inventory cost flow assumption and the inventory accounting system (periodic or perpetual) used to account for inventories. Recall that under a perpetual system, a record is made of every purchase and every sale, and a continuous record of the quantity and cost of each item is maintained. When an item is sold, its cost (as determined according to the cost flow assumption) is transferred from the inventory asset to the cost of goods sold expense with the following effect on the financial statements:

LO 2
Describe how cost of goods sold is determined under both perpetual and periodic inventory accounting systems.

Balance Sheet	Income Statement
Assets = Liabilities + Stockholders' equity	←Net income = Revenues − Expenses
− Inventory	− Cost of Goods Sold

Here is the entry:

Dr.	Cost of Goods Sold	xx	
	Cr. Inventory.		xx

The key point about a perpetual inventory system is that cost is determined when the item is sold. As you can imagine, a perpetual inventory system requires much data processing but can give management a great deal of information about which inventory items are selling well and which are not. Advances in point-of-sale technologies (such as standard bar code scanners used by retail stores) have allowed even small merchandising firms to achieve perpetual inventories. Some systems are even tied in with the firms' suppliers so that when inventory falls to a certain level, a reorder is automatically placed. Under any type of perpetual system, regular counts of specific inventory items will be made on a cycle basis during the year, and actual quantities on hand will be compared to the computer record of the quantity on hand. This is an internal control procedure designed to determine whether the perpetual system is operating accurately and to trigger an investigation of significant differences.

In a periodic inventory system, a count of the inventory on hand *(taking a physical inventory)* is made periodically—frequently at the end of a fiscal year—and the cost of inventory on hand (determined according to the cost flow assumption) is determined. This cost is then subtracted from the sum of the cost of the beginning inventory (that is, the ending inventory of the prior period) and the cost of the merchandise purchased during the current period. (A manufacturing firm uses the cost of goods manufactured—discussed in Chapter 13—rather than purchases.) This **cost of goods sold model** is illustrated here using 2011 data from the Campbell Soup Company financial statements in the appendix. Can you find the inventory and cost of goods sold amounts in the appendix? The unknown amounts for net purchases and goods available for sale have been solved for in the model using these known amounts. All amounts are in millions of dollars:

Cost of beginning inventory	$ 724
+ Net purchases (cost of goods manufactured)	4,659
= Cost of goods available for sale	$5,383
− Cost of ending inventory	(767)
= Cost of goods (products) sold	$4,616

The amounts shown for cost of goods sold, inventory, and net purchases include the price paid to the supplier, plus all ordinary and necessary costs related to the purchase transaction (such as freight and material handling charges). Cost is reduced by the amount of any cash discount allowed on the purchase. When the periodic inventory system is used, freight charges, purchase discounts, and **purchase returns and allowances** (the purchaser's side of the sales return and allowance transaction) are usually recorded in separate accounts, and each account balance is classified with purchases. Thus, the net purchases amount is made up of the following:

Purchases	$
Add: Freight charges	
Less: Purchase discounts	( )
Less: Purchase returns and allowances	( )
Net purchases	$

Although the periodic system may require a less complicated recordkeeping system than the perpetual system, the need to take a complete physical inventory to determine accurately the cost of goods sold is a disadvantage. Also, although it can be estimated or developed from special analysis, inventory shrinkage (losses from theft, errors, and so on) is not really known when the periodic system is used because these losses are included in the total cost of goods sold.

Note that selling and administrative expenses (discussed later in the Operating Expenses section of this chapter) are not included as part of cost of goods sold.

Gross Profit or Gross Margin

LO 3

Discuss the significance of gross profit and describe how the gross profit ratio is calculated and used.

The difference between sales revenue and cost of goods sold is **gross profit,** or **gross margin.** Using data from Exhibit 9-1, here is the income statement for Campbell Soup Company to this point:

CAMPBELL SOUP COMPANY **Consolidated Statements of Earnings** **(dollars in millions)**			
Three Years Ended July 31, 2011	**2011**	**2010**	**2009**
Net sales	$7,719	$7,676	$7,586
Cost of products sold	4,616	4,526	4,558
Gross margin	$3,103	$3,150	$3,028

CAMPBELL SOUP COMPANY Gross Profit Ratio—2011 (dollars in millions)	
Net sales (or net revenues)	$7,719
Cost of products sold (or cost of goods sold)	4,616
Gross profit (or gross margin)	$3,103

$$\text{Gross profit ratio} = \text{Gross profit}/\text{Net sales}$$
$$= \$3,103/\$7,719$$
$$= 40.2\%$$

Exhibit 9-3

Gross Profit Ratio

When the amount of gross profit is expressed as a percentage of the sales amount, the resulting **gross profit ratio** (or **gross margin ratio**) is an especially important statistic for managers of manufacturing and merchandising firms. The calculation of the gross profit ratio for Campbell Soup Company for 2011 is illustrated in Exhibit 9-3.

Because the gross profit ratio is a measure of the amount of each sales dollar that is available to cover operating expenses and profit, one of its principal uses by the manager is to estimate whether the firm is operating at a level of sales that will lead to profitability in the current period. The manager knows from experience that if the firm is to be profitable, a certain gross profit ratio and level of sales must be achieved. Sales can be determined daily from cash register tapes or sales invoice records, and that amount then can be multiplied by the estimated gross profit ratio to determine the estimated gross profit amount. This amount can be related to estimated operating expenses to estimate the firm's income from operations. In many cases, just knowing the amount of sales is enough to be able to estimate whether the firm has reached profitability. This is especially true for firms that have virtually the same gross profit ratio for every item sold. However, if the gross profit ratio differs by class of merchandise (and it usually does), then the proportion of the sales of each class to total sales (the **sales mix**) must be considered when estimating total gross profit. For example, assume that Campbell's has average gross profit ratios of 50 percent on simple meals (including condensed and ready-to-serve soups, broths, and sauces), 40 percent on baked snacks (including cookies, crackers, and biscuits), and 30 percent on beverages. If the sales mix changes frequently, then the sales of each product category must be considered to estimate total gross profit anticipated for any given month.

The gross profit ratio can be used to estimate cost of goods sold and ending inventory for periods in which a physical inventory has not been taken, as illustrated in Exhibit 9-4. This is the process used to estimate the amount of inventory lost in a fire, flood, or other natural disaster. Note that the key to the calculation is the estimated gross profit ratio. Many firms prepare quarterly (or monthly) income statements for internal reporting purposes and use this estimation technique to avoid the cost and business interruptions associated with an inventory count.

Another important use of the gross profit ratio is to set selling prices. If the manager knows the gross profit ratio required to achieve profitability at a given level of sales, the cost of the item can be divided by the complement of the gross profit ratio (or the cost of goods sold ratio) to determine the selling price. This is illustrated in Exhibit 9-5. Of course competitive pressures, the manufacturer's recommended selling price, and other factors will also influence the price finally established, but the

Exhibit 9-4

Using the Gross
Profit Ratio to Estimate
Ending Inventory and
Cost of Goods Sold

Assumptions:
A firm expects to have a gross profit ratio of 30% for the current fiscal year. Beginning inventory is known because it is the amount of the physical inventory taken at the end of the prior fiscal year. Net sales and net purchases are known from the accounting records of the current fiscal year.
    Here is the model (with assumed known data entered):

Net sales..................................	$100,000	100%
Cost of goods sold:		
Beginning inventory	$ 19,000	
Net purchases...........................	63,000	
Cost of goods available for sale..............	$ 82,000	
Less: Ending inventory......................	?	
Cost of goods sold	$?	
Gross profit..............................	$?	30%

Calculation of estimated ending inventory:

Gross profit = 30% × $100,000 = $30,000
Cost of goods sold = $100,000 − $30,000 = $70,000
Ending inventory = $82,000 − $70,000 = $12,000

desired gross profit ratio and the item's cost are frequently the starting points in the pricing decision.

The gross profit ratio required to achieve profitability will vary among firms as a result of their operating strategies. For example, a discount store seeks a high sales volume and a low level of operating expenses, so a relatively low gross profit ratio is accepted. A boutique, on the other hand, has a relatively low sales volume and higher operating expenses and needs a relatively high gross profit ratio to achieve profitability.

Even though gross profit and the gross profit ratio are widely used internally by the managers of the firm, many companies (including Campbell's) do not present gross profit as a separate item in their published income statements. However, cost of goods sold usually is shown as a separate item. Thus, the user of the income statement can make the calculation for comparative and other evaluation purposes.

Exhibit 9-5

Using Desired Gross
Profit Ratio to Set
Selling Price

Assumptions:
A retail store's cost for a particular carpet is $8 per square yard, and the store owners have a 20% desired gross profit ratio. What selling price per square yard should be established for this product?

Selling price = Cost of product/(1 − Desired gross profit ratio)
          = $8/(1 − 0.2)
          = $10

Proof:

Calculated selling price...............................	$10 per square yard
Cost of product	8 per square yard
Gross profit..	$ 2 per square yard

Gross profit ratio = Gross profit/Selling price
             = $2/$10
             = 20%

Operating Expenses

LO 4

Identify the principal categories and components of "other operating expenses" and show how these items are reported on the income statement.

The principal categories of other **operating expenses** frequently reported on the income statement are

Selling expenses.

General and administrative expenses.

Research and development expenses.

These categories can be combined in a variety of ways for financial reporting purposes. For instance, Campbell's uses three principal categories: "Marketing and selling expenses," "Administrative expenses," and "Research and development expenses."

The financial statement footnotes will sometimes provide detailed disclosure of the nature and amount of expense items that are combined with others in the income statement. However, management often reports certain operating expenses as separate items to highlight their significance. Common examples include repair and maintenance, research and development, and advertising. Total depreciation and amortization expense is frequently reported as a separate item on the income statement (or disclosed in the notes to the financial statements) because these expenses do not result in the disbursement of cash. The total of depreciation and amortization expense also appears in the statement of cash flows, as will be illustrated later in this chapter. Note that Campbell's includes a separate line item for restructuring charges (discussed on pages 723–725 in the notes to the consolidated financial statements in Campbell's annual report in the appendix).

Income from Operations

The difference between gross profit and operating expenses represents **income from operations** (or **operating income**), as shown in the following partial income statement from Exhibit 9-1:

LO 5

Explain what "income from operations" includes and discuss why this income statement subtotal is significant to managers and financial analysts.

CAMPBELL SOUP COMPANY Consolidated Statements of Earnings (dollars in millions)			
Three Years Ended July 31, 2011	**2011**	**2010**	**2009**
Net sales.	$7,719	$7,676	$7,586
Costs and expenses:			
Cost of products sold	4,616	4,526	4,558
Marketing and selling expenses	1,007	1,058	1,077
Administrative expenses	612	605	591
Research and development expenses	129	123	114
Other expenses (income)	13	4	61
Restructuring charges	63	12	—
Total costs and expenses	6,440	6,328	6,401
Earnings before interest and taxes	**1,279**	**1,348**	**1,185**

Although only an intermediate subtotal on the income statement, income from operations (reported as "Earnings before interest and taxes" by Campbell's) is frequently interpreted as the most appropriate measure of management's ability to utilize the firm's operating assets. Income from operations normally *excludes* the effects of interest expense, interest income, gains and losses, income taxes, and other nonoperating transactions. Thus, many investors prefer to use income from operations data (rather than net income data) to make a "cleaner" assessment of the firm's profitability trend. As discussed in Chapter 3, income from operations is frequently used in the return on investment calculation, which relates operating income to average operating assets.

Although operating income is commonly used as a proxy for net income, investors must pay careful attention to the items that are included in the determination of this important subtotal. In recent years, for example, many firms have reported items such as "restructuring charges" and "asset impairment losses" as operating expenses because the corporate downsizing efforts that lead to such write-offs have been occurring more frequently. Yet other firms report these items in the "other income and expenses" category, which is shown as a *nonoperating* item. Of course, it also is permissible (and quite common) to simply subtract total expenses from total revenues to arrive at net income without indicating a separate amount for income from operations.

Managers of firms that do not report income from operations as a separate item believe that other income and expense items (such as gains and losses) should receive as much attention in the evaluation process as revenues and expenses from the firm's principal operations. After all, nonoperating items do exist and do affect overall profitability. There is no single best presentation for all firms; this is another area in which the accountant's judgment is used to select among equally acceptable financial reporting alternatives.

Other Income and Expenses

Other income and expenses are reported after income from operations. These nonoperating items include interest expense, interest income, gains, and losses.

Interest expense is the item of other income and expenses most frequently identified separately. Most financial statement users want to know the amount of this expense because it represents a contractual obligation that cannot be avoided. As discussed in Chapter 7, interest expense is associated with financial leverage. The more a firm borrows, the more interest expense it incurs, and the higher its financial leverage. Although this may lead to a greater ROE for stockholders, it also increases the riskiness of their investment.

Interest income earned from excess cash that has been temporarily invested is not ordinarily subtracted from interest expense. Interest income is reported as a separate item if it is material in amount relative to other nonoperating items. The full disclosure principle is applied to determine the extent of the details reported in this section of the income statement. Significant items that would facilitate the reader's understanding of net income or loss are separately identified, either in the statement itself or in the notes. Items that are not significant are combined in an "other" or "miscellaneous" category. Examples of nonoperating gains or losses are those resulting from litigation, the sale or disposal of depreciable assets (including plant closings), and inventory obsolescence losses; also shown here are items that are unusual or infrequent, but not both.

Income before Income Taxes and Income Tax Expense

The income statement usually has a subtotal labeled "**Income before income taxes**," followed by the caption "Income taxes" or "Provision for income taxes" and the amount of this expense. Some income statements do not use the "Income before income taxes" caption; income taxes are simply listed as another expense in these statements. There will be a note disclosure of the details of the income tax expense calculation because this is required by generally accepted accounting principles.

---

2. What does it mean to look at the trend of the major subtotals on an income statement?

What Does It Mean?
Answer on page 373

Net Income and Earnings per Share

Net income (or net loss), sometimes called the *bottom line,* is the arithmetic sum of the revenues and gains minus the expenses and losses. Because net income increases retained earnings, which usually is a prerequisite to dividends, stockholders and potential investors are especially interested in net income. Reinforce your understanding of information presented in the income statement by referring again to Exhibit 9-1 and by studying the structure of income statements in other annual reports you may have.

To facilitate interpretation of net income (or loss), it also is reported on a per share of common stock basis. Reported are **basic earnings per share** and, if the firm has issued stock options or convertible securities (long-term debt or preferred stock that is convertible into common stock), **diluted earnings per share.** Basic EPS and diluted EPS (if appropriate) are presented both for income from continuing operations or income before extraordinary items (discussed later in this chapter) and for net income. Basic earnings per share is calculated by dividing net income by the average number of shares of common stock outstanding during the year. Two principal complications in the calculation should be understood. First, a weighted-average number of shares of common stock is used. This is sensible because if shares are issued early in the year, the proceeds from their sale have been used longer in the income-generating process than the proceeds from shares issued later in the year. For illustration purposes, the weighting basis used is the number of months each block of shares has been outstanding. The weighted-average calculation is illustrated in Exhibit 9-6.

LO 6
Describe the components of the earnings per share calculation and discuss the reasons for some of the refinements made in that calculation.

Assumptions:

On September 1, 2013, the beginning of its fiscal year, Cruisers, Inc., had 200,000 shares of common stock outstanding.

On December 3, 2013, 40,000 additional shares were issued for cash.

On June 28, 2014, 15,000 shares of common stock were acquired as treasury stock (and are no longer outstanding).

Weighted-average calculation:

Period	Number of Months	Number of Shares Outstanding	Months × Shares
9/1–12/3....................	3	200,000	600,000
12/3–6/28..................	7	240,000	1,680,000
6/28–8/31..................	2	225,000	450,000
Totals..........................	12		2,730,000

Weighted-average number of shares outstanding = $2,730,000 /12
= 227,500

Exhibit 9-6
Weighted-Average Shares Outstanding Calculation

The other complication in the EPS calculation arises when a firm has preferred stock outstanding. Remember that preferred stock is entitled to its dividend before dividends can be paid on common stock. Because of this prior claim to earnings, the amount of the preferred stock dividend requirement is subtracted from net income to arrive at the numerator in the calculation of earnings per share of common stock outstanding. Recall that dividends are not expenses, so the preferred stock dividend requirement is not shown as a deduction in the income statement. To illustrate the basic EPS calculation, assume that Cruisers, Inc., had net income of $1,527,000 for the year ended August 31, 2014, and had 80,000 shares of a 7 percent, $50 par value preferred stock outstanding during the year. Using the weighted-average number of shares of common stock outstanding from Exhibit 9-6, the earnings per share of common stock would be calculated as follows:

Net income	$1,527,000
Less preferred stock dividend requirement	
(7% × $50 par value × 80,000 shares outstanding) . . .	280,000
Net income available for common stock	$1,247,000

$$\begin{array}{l}\text{Basic earnings} \\ \text{per share of} \\ \text{common stock outstanding}\end{array} = \dfrac{\begin{array}{c}\text{Net income available for} \\ \text{common stock}\end{array}}{\begin{array}{c}\text{Weighted-average number of shares of} \\ \text{common stock outstanding}\end{array}}$$

$$= \$1,247,000/227,500$$
$$= \$5.48$$

Because of their significance, earnings per share amounts are reported on the income statement just below the amount of net income.

As stated previously, in addition to the basic earnings per share, a firm may be required to report *diluted earnings per share*. If the firm has issued long-term debt or preferred stock that is convertible into common stock, it is possible that the conversion of the debt or preferred stock could reduce basic earnings per share of common stock outstanding. This can happen because the increase in net income available for common stock (if interest expense is reduced, or preferred dividends are not required) is proportionately less than the number of additional common shares issued in the conversion. If a firm has a stock option plan (see Chapter 10), the issuance of additional shares pursuant to the plan has the potential of reducing basic earnings per share. Other incentive and financing arrangements may also require issuance of additional shares, which may similarly decrease basic earnings per share. The reduction in basic earnings per share of common stock is referred to as **dilution.** The effect of the potential dilution is reported on the income statement by showing diluted earnings per share of common stock as well as basic earnings per share. Campbell's diluted earnings per share of $2.42 for 2011 represented a potential dilution of just $0.02 per share due to the potentially dilutive effects of stock options and other share-based payment awards. Refer to pages 711 and 726–727 in Campbell's annual report in the appendix for details.

The income statement presentation of net income and EPS follows. Data are from the previous Cruisers, Inc., illustrations, which have no discontinued operations or extraordinary items. Note that the diluted earnings per share amount is assumed for illustration:

Net income	$1,527,000
Basic earnings per share of common stock	$ 5.48
Diluted earnings per share of common stock.	$ 5.27

If there are any *unusual items* on the income statement (discussed later in this chapter), the per share amount of each item is disclosed, and EPS is the sum of EPS before the unusual items and the per share amounts of the unusual items. This is done for both basic and diluted EPS data.

---

3. What does it mean when earnings per share are subject to dilution?

What Does It Mean?
Answer on page 373

Income Statement Presentation Alternatives

There are two principal alternative presentations of income statement data: the **single-step format** and the **multiple-step format.** These are illustrated in Exhibit 9-7 using hypothetical data for Cruisers, Inc., for fiscal years 2013 and 2014. (Examples of the unusual items that may appear on the income statement will be discussed in the next section of this chapter and illustrated in Exhibit 9-8.)

You may notice an inconsistency in the use of parentheses in the single-step and multiple-step formats in Exhibit 9-7. No parentheses are used in the single-step format; the user is expected to know by reading the captions which items to add and which to subtract in the calculation of net income. In the multiple-step format the caption for "Other income (expense)" indicates that *in this section of the statement,* items without parentheses are added and items in parentheses are subtracted. In other parts of the statement, the caption indicates the arithmetic operation. With either format, the statement reader must be alert to make sense of the information presented in the statement.

The gradual trend during the past several decades has been for more companies to use the multiple-step income statement format. A survey of the year 2010 annual reports of 500 publicly owned industrial and merchandising companies indicated that only 87 companies continued to use the single-step format.[3] This trend apparently reflects the increasing complexity of business activities and the demand for more detailed information.

LO 7
Compare and contrast the alternative income statement presentation models.

Unusual Items Sometimes Seen on an Income Statement

One way investors and potential investors use the income statement is to predict probable results of future operations from the results of current operations. Nonrecurring transactions that affect the predictive process are highlighted and reported separately from the results of recurring transactions. The reporting of unusual items also facilitates users' comparisons of net income for the current year with that of prior years.

LO 8
Discuss the meaning and significance of each of the unusual items that may appear on the income statement.

---

[3]AICPA, *Accounting Trends and Techniques* (New York, 2011), Table 3-1.

Exhibit 9-7

Income Statement
Format Alternatives

I. Single-step format:

CRUISERS, INC., AND SUBSIDIARIES Consolidated Income Statement For the Years Ended August 31, 2014 and 2013 (000 omitted)		
	2014	**2013**
Net sales	$77,543	$62,531
Cost of goods sold.	48,077	39,870
Selling expenses	13,957	10,590
General and administrative expenses	9,739	8,191
Interest expense.	3,378	2,679
Other income, net	385	193
Income before taxes.	$ 2,777	$ 1,394
Provision for income taxes	1,250	630
Net income.	$ 1,527	$ 764
Basic earnings per share of common stock	$ 5.48	$ 2.42

II. Multiple-step format:

CRUISERS, INC., AND SUBSIDIARIES Consolidated Income Statement For the Years Ended August 31, 2014 and 2013 (000 omitted)		
	2014	**2013**
Net sales	$77,543	$62,531
Cost of goods sold.	48,077	39,870
Gross profit.	$29,466	$22,661
Selling, general, and administrative expenses	23,696	18,781
Income from operations	$ 5,770	$ 3,880
Other income (expense):		
Interest expense	(3,378)	(2,679)
Other income, net.	385	193
Income before taxes	$ 2,777	$ 1,394
Provision for income taxes	1,250	630
Net income.	$ 1,527	$ 764
Basic earnings per share of common stock	$ 5.48	$ 2.42

The principal difference between these two formats is that the multiple-step format provides subtotals for gross profit and income from operations. As previously discussed, each of these amounts is useful in evaluating the performance of the firm, and proponents of the multiple-step format believe that it is appropriate to highlight these amounts.

Two frequently encountered unusual items relate to discontinued operations and extraordinary items. Another caption sometimes seen on an income statement relates to the noncontrolling (minority) interest in earnings of subsidiaries. *When any of these items affects income tax expense, the amount disclosed in the income statement is the amount of the item net of the income tax effect.* Each of these unusual items is discussed in the following paragraphs.

Discontinued operations. When a segment, or major portion of a business, is disposed of, it is appropriate to disclose separately the impact that the discontinued operation has had on the current operations of the firm, as well as its impact on any previous year results that are shown for comparative purposes. This separate disclosure is made to help users of the financial statements understand how future income statements may differ because the firm will be operating without the disposed business segment. This is accomplished by reporting the income or loss, after income taxes, of the discontinued operation separately after a subtotal amount labeled **income from continuing operations.** (Income from continuing operations is the income after income taxes of continuing operations.) By reporting discontinued operations as a separate item, net of taxes, all of the effects of the discontinued business segment are excluded from the revenues, expenses, gains, and losses of continuing operations. This presentation is illustrated in Exhibit 9-8. Note that earnings per share data are also reported separately for discontinued operations. If Cruisers, Inc., had issued dilutive securities or stock options, the impact of the discontinued operations on diluted EPS data would also have been reported.

---

4. What does it mean when income or loss from discontinued operations is shown in the income statement?

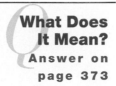

What Does It Mean?

Answer on page 373

Under either the single-step or multiple-step format (see Exhibit 9-7), the "Income before taxes" caption would be shown as "Income from *continuing operations* before taxes," and the rest of the income statement would appear as follows:

Exhibit 9-8

Income Statement Presentation of Unusual Items *(continued from Exhibit 9-7)*

	2014	2013
Income from continuing operations before taxes	$ 2,777	$1,394
Provision for income taxes	1,250	630
Income from continuing operations.	$ 1,527	$ 764
Discontinued operations, net of income taxes:		
Loss from operations	(162)	(122)
Loss on disposal.	(79)	—
Loss from discontinued operations.	$ (241)	(122)
Earnings before extraordinary item	$ 1,286	$ 642
Extraordinary item:		
Gain on termination of pension plan, net of income taxes	357	—
Net income.	$ 1,643	$ 642
Basic earnings per share of common stock outstanding:		
Continuing operations.	$ 5.48	$ 2.42
Discontinued operations:		
Loss from operations.	(0.71)	(0.61)
Loss on disposal	(0.35)	—
Extraordinary item.	1.57	—
Net income.	$ 5.99	$ 1.81

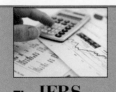

The IFRS

Approach

Under IFRS, there is no distinction between revenues/gains or expenses/losses on the income statement. Extraordinary items are not recognized separately and reported net of tax, but instead are included with other revenues and expenses within operating income.

Extraordinary items. A transaction that is unusual in nature and occurs infrequently qualifies for reporting as an **extraordinary item** if the amount involved has a significant after-tax income statement effect. The reason for such separate reporting is to emphasize that the item is extraordinary and that the income statements for subsequent years are not likely to include this kind of item. Examples of extraordinary items are pension plan terminations, some litigation settlements, and utilization of tax loss carryforwards. The financial effects of natural disasters such as hurricanes, earthquakes, and major floods or fires are also accounted for as extraordinary items.

When an extraordinary item is reported, basic and diluted (if applicable) earnings per share of common stock outstanding are reported for income before the extraordinary item, for the extraordinary item, and for net income (after the extraordinary item). This presentation is also illustrated in Exhibit 9-8 for basic EPS (it is assumed that Cruisers, Inc., has no dilutive securities or stock options).

Noncontrolling interest in earnings of subsidiaries. As explained in Chapters 7 and 8, the financial statements of a subsidiary are consolidated with those of the parent even though the parent owns less than 100 percent of the stock of the subsidiary. The consolidated income statement includes all of the revenues, expenses, gains, and losses of the subsidiary. However, only the parent company's equity in the subsidiary's earnings should be included in the *bottom line*, **net income attributable to (parent company name)** caption (sometimes referred to as *net income attributable to controlling interest*). The amount of **net income attributable to noncontrolling interest** must also be clearly identified and presented on the face of the consolidated income statement, and is normally subtracted from net income as follows:

$$
\begin{aligned}
& \text{Revenues} \\
&- \underline{\text{Expenses}} \\
&= \text{Net income} \\
&- \underline{\text{Net income attributable to noncontrolling interest}} \\
&= \text{Net income attributable to (parent company name)}
\end{aligned}
$$

Earnings-per-share amounts reported in consolidated financial statements are based on net income attributable to the parent.

Study

Suggestion

A wide variety of financial statement presentation alternatives for "unusual items" is encountered in practice, depending on the specific combination of items reported by any given company. Do not attempt to memorize the specific captions used in Exhibit 9-8 to describe these nonrecurring items. Instead, focus on the nature of each item and consider why it is reported *after* income from operations.

Statement of Cash Flows

Content and Format of the Statement

The **statement of cash flows** is a required financial statement that illustrates how accounting evolves to meet the requirements of users of financial statements. The importance of understanding the cash flows of an entity has been increasingly emphasized over the years. The accrual basis income statement is not designed to present cash flows from operations, and except for related revenues and expenses, it shows no information about cash flows from investing and financing activities.

LO 9

Describe the purpose and outline the general format of the statement of cash flows.

The primary purpose of the statement of cash flows is to provide relevant information about the cash receipts and cash payments of an enterprise during a period. The statement shows why cash (including short-term investments that are essentially equivalent to cash) changed during the period by reporting net cash provided or used by operating activities, investing activities, and financing activities.

Cash flows from operating activities.   There are two alternative approaches to presenting the operating activities section of the statement of cash flows: the *direct method presentation* and the *indirect method presentation*. The direct method involves listing each major class of cash receipts transactions and cash disbursements transactions for each of the three activity areas. The operating activity transactions include cash received from customers, cash paid to merchandise or raw material suppliers, cash paid to employees for salaries and wages, cash paid for other operating expenses, cash payments of interest, and cash payments for taxes. A direct method statement of cash flows is illustrated in Section I of Exhibit 9-9. *Notice that under the direct method, each of the captions reported on the statement explains how much cash was received or paid during the year for that item.* For this reason the FASB encourages enterprises to use the direct method.

LO 10

Illustrate the difference between the direct and indirect methods of presenting cash flows from operating activities.

The indirect method explains cash flows from operating activities by explaining the change in each noncash operating account in the balance sheet. A statement of cash flows prepared this way shows net income as the first source of operating cash. However, net income is determined on the accrual basis and must be adjusted for revenues and expenses that do not affect cash. The most significant noncash income statement item is usually total depreciation and amortization expense. Here are the effects of these transactions on the financial statements:

Balance Sheet	Income Statement
Assets = Liabilities + Stockholders' equity	← Net income = Revenues − Expenses
− Accumulated Depreciation	− Depreciation Expense
− Intangible Asset	− Amortization Expense

The entries to record these items are:

Dr. Depreciation Expense..................................	xx	
Cr. Accumulated Depreciation		xx

Dr. Amortization Expense..................................	xx	
Cr. Intangible Asset..................................		xx

Exhibit 9-9

Statement of Cash
Flows

I. Direct method:

	2014	2013
CRUISERS, INC., AND SUBSIDIARIES		
Consolidated Statements of Cash Flows		
For the Years Ended August 31, 2014 and 2013		
(000 omitted)		
Cash Flows from Operating Activities:		
Cash received from customers	$ 74,929	$ 63,021
Cash paid to suppliers.	46,784	38,218
Payments for compensation of employees	17,137	16,267
Other operating expenses paid	3,873	4,002
Interest paid.	3,675	2,703
Taxes paid	1,037	532
Net cash provided by operating activities.	$ 2,423	$ 1,299
Cash Flows from Investing Activities:		
Proceeds from sale of land	$ —	$ 200
Investment in plant and equipment	(1,622)	(1,437)
Net cash used for investing activities	$ (1,622)	$ (1,237)
Cash Flows from Financing Activities:		
Additional long-term borrowing	$ 7,350	$ 6,680
Payment of long-term debt	(3,268)	(3,053)
Purchase of treasury stock	(1,537)	(1,226)
Payment of dividends on common stock.	(2,863)	(2,610)
Net cash used for financing activities.	$ (318)	$ (209)
Increase (decrease) in cash	$ 483	$ (147)
Cash balance, August 31, 2013 and 2012	276	423
Cash balance, August 31, 2014 and 2013	$ 759	$ 276
Reconciliation of Net Income and Net Cash Provided by Operating Activities:		
Net income	$ 1,527	$ 764
Add (deduct) items not affecting cash:		
Depreciation expense.	926	835
Gain on sale of land	—	(161)
Increase in accounts receivable	(30)	(44)
Increase in inventories	(21)	(168)
Increase in current liabilities	16	66
Other (net)	5	7
Net cash provided by operating activities	$ 2,423	$ 1,299

(continued)

Because the depreciation and amortization expense amounts do not affect cash, these items are added back to net income to determine more accurately the amount of cash generated from operations. Other income statement items that need to be considered in a similar way include:

- Income tax expense not currently payable (that is, deferred income taxes resulting from temporary differences in the recognition of revenues and expenses for book and tax purposes).

II. Indirect method:

Exhibit 9-9

CRUISERS, INC., AND SUBSIDIARIES
Consolidated Statements of Cash Flows
For the Years Ended August 31, 2014 and 2013
(000 omitted)

	2014	2013
Cash Flows from Operating Activities:		
Net income	$ 1,527	$ 764
Add (deduct) items not affecting cash:		
Depreciation expense	926	835
Gain on sale of land	—	(161)
Increase in accounts receivable	(730)	(644)
Increase in inventories	(521)	(368)
Increase in current liabilities	866	716
Other (net)	355	157
Net cash provided by operating activities	$ 2,423	$ 1,299
Cash Flows from Investing Activities:		
Proceeds from sale of land	$ —	$ 200
Investment in plant and equipment	(1,622)	(1,437)
Net cash used for investing activities	$ (1,622)	$ (1,237)
Cash Flows from Financing Activities:		
Additional long-term borrowing	$ 7,350	$ 6,680
Payment of long-term debt	(3,268)	(3,053)
Purchase of treasury stock	(1,537)	(1,226)
Payment of dividends on common stock	(2,863)	(2,610)
Net cash used for financing activities	$ (318)	$ (209)
Increase (decrease) in cash	$ 483	$ (147)
Cash balance, August 31, 2013 and 2012	276	423
Cash balance, August 31, 2014 and 2013	$ 759	$ 276

- Gains or losses on the sale or abandonment of assets. The *proceeds* from the sale, not the gain or loss, affect cash. Losses are added back to net income, and gains are subtracted from net income. The sale proceeds are reported as an investing activity, as described later.

- Increases (or decreases) to interest expense that result from the amortization of discount (or premium) on bonds payable. Discount amortization is added back to net income, and premium amortization is subtracted from net income.

Changes in the noncash operating accounts must also be shown. Thus, increases in current assets and decreases in current liabilities are reported as operating uses of cash. Conversely, decreases in current assets and increases in current liabilities are reported as operating sources of cash. An indirect method statement of cash flows is illustrated in Section II of Exhibit 9-9.

Note that the difference between the two methods is only in the presentation of cash flows from operating activities. When the direct method format is used, a separate schedule is required to reconcile net income reported on the income statement with net cash provided by operating activities. This reconciliation is in the form of the

Business in
Practice

Understanding Cash Flow Relationships: Indirect Method

As indicated by the AICPA study, most firms report the statement of cash flows using the indirect method. The primary reason for this preference is that no separate accounting procedures are needed for companies to accumulate cash flow data when the indirect method is used. The statement of cash flows normally is prepared using balance sheet and income statement data and other information readily available from the company's accounting records. However, the operating activities information reported under the direct method is not so readily determinable, and the cost of generating this information can be prohibitive.

The primary objective of the operating activities section of the statement of cash flows (indirect method) is to determine the net cash provided by operating activities. Although net income is determined on an accrual basis, it is ordinarily the most accurate proxy for operating cash flows and thus serves as the starting point in the calculation of this important amount. *Note, however, that none of the adjustments shown in the operating activities section (indirect method) explains how much cash was actually received or paid during the year!* The only operating activity items that convey independent meaning are the amounts shown for net income and net cash provided by operating activities. Review the operating activities section of Exhibit 9-9 for the indirect method. Notice, for example, that accounts receivable increased during both years presented. Does this explain how much cash was received from the collection of accounts receivable during these years? (No, but the direct method shows these amounts.) Once you understand this, the adjustment process for the indirect method can be thought of in a rather mechanical fashion.

Net income is initially assumed to generate operating cash, and this assumption is then adjusted for the effects of noncash (or nonoperating) income statement items. As already explained, the amounts shown for depreciation and amortization expense will be added back to net income each year because cash is never paid for these expenses. Similar adjustments would be made to remove the effects of noncash revenues or to remove the effects of most nonoperating transactions included in net income (such as gains or losses from the sale of long-term assets). Once these income statement adjustments are made, the current (*operating*) accounts on the balance sheet must be analyzed to determine their effects on cash during the year. To simplify the analysis, assume that all changes in account balances from the beginning to the end of the year are attributable to cash transactions. For example, if inventory (a current asset) increased during the year, then cash must have decreased (to pay for the increase in inventory). The financial statement effect of this assumed transaction would be as shown in the horizontal model representation presented on the following page.

indirect method presentation of net cash provided by operating activities. A survey of the annual reports of 500 publicly owned industrial and merchandising companies for the year 2010 indicated that 492 firms used the indirect method presentation, whereas only 8 companies used the direct method presentation.[4] Business in Practice—Understanding Cash Flow Relationships: Indirect Method explains the cash flow relationships under the indirect method in more detail.

Cash flows from investing and financing activities. Investing activities relate primarily to the purchase and sale of noncurrent assets. Cash is often used for the acquisition of assets such as land, buildings, or equipment during the year (these investments are sometimes called *capital additions*). Investments in debt or equity securities of other entities are also shown as investing uses. Likewise, cash received from the sale of noncurrent assets is shown as an investing source of cash. The lending of money and subsequent collection of loans are considered investing activities as well.

---

[4]AICPA, *Accounting Trends and Techniques* (New York, 2011), Table 6-2.

Balance Sheet	Income Statement
Assets = Liabilities + Stockholders' equity	←Net income = Revenues − Expenses
+ Inventory − Cash	

The entry is:

Dr. Inventory	xx	
Cr. Cash...		xx

Likewise, if accounts payable (a current liability) increased during the year, then cash was not spent and the flow of cash thus increased, as illustrated by the following assumed transaction:

Balance Sheet	Income Statement
Assets = Liabilities + Stockholders' equity	←Net income = Revenues − Expenses
+ Cash + Accounts Payable	

The entry is:

Dr. Cash...	xx	
Cr. Accounts Payable		xx

In a similar way, decreases in current asset accounts are assumed to increase cash (for example, the collection of an accounts receivable), and decreases in current liability accounts are assumed to decrease cash (for example, the payment of an account payable). Of course these are only assumptions, but by assuming that cash is involved on the opposite side of every transaction, you will understand the nature of each of the adjustments made within the operating activities section of the statement of cash flows.

Financing activities relate primarily to changes during the year in nonoperating liabilities (such as bonds payable) and in stockholders' equity accounts other than net income (loss), which is treated as an operating activity. Thus, the issuance of bonds or common stock will result in a financing source of cash, and the retirement of bonds will be reported as a financing use. Cash dividends and treasury stock transactions also are reported as financing activities because they affect stockholders' equity.

Interpreting the Statement of Cash Flows

The statement of cash flows focuses on cash receipts and cash payments during the period, so the first question to be answered is "Did the company's cash balance increase or decrease during the period?" The answer is usually found near the bottom of the statement. In the annual report of a publicly owned corporation, comparative statements for the most recent and prior two years will be presented, and the change in each of the years can be noted. If the change in the cash balance during a year has been significant (for example, more than 10 percent of the beginning cash balance), the

LO 11

Summarize why the statement of cash flows is significant to financial analysts and investors.

financial statement user will try to understand the reasons for the change by focusing on the relative totals of each of the three categories of cash flows—operating activities, investing activities, and financing activities. Even if the change in the cash balance during a year is not significant, the relationship between these broad categories will be observed.

A firm should have a positive cash flow provided by operating activities. If operating activities do not generate cash, the firm will have to seek outside funding to finance its day-to-day activities, as well as its investment requirements. Although negative cash flow from operating activities might apply to a firm just starting up, it would be a sign of possible financial weakness for a mature company.

Virtually all financially healthy firms have growth in revenues as a financial objective. This growth usually requires increasing capacity to manufacture or sell products or provide services. Thus, a principal investing activity is the acquisition of plant and equipment. The total cash used for investing activities is compared to the total cash provided by operating activities. If cash provided by operating activities exceeds cash used for investing activities, the indication is that the firm is generating the cash it needs to finance its growth, and that is probably positive. If the cash used for investing activities exceeds the cash provided by operating activities, the difference will have to be provided by financing activities or come from the cash balance carried forward from the prior year. This is not necessarily negative because investment requirements in any one year may be unusually high. If, however, cash used for investing activities exceeds cash provided by operating activities year after year, and the difference is provided from financing activities, a question about the firm's ability to generate additional funds from financing activities must be raised.

Financing activities include the issue and repayment of debt, the sale of stock and purchase of treasury stock, and the payment of dividends on stock. For most companies, it would be desirable to have annual cash dividends covered by the excess of cash provided from operating activities over cash used for investing activities.

After the big picture of the entity's cash flows has been obtained, it may be necessary to look at the details of each category of cash flows for clues that will explain the overall change. For example, if cash flows provided by operating activities are less than cash used for investing activities or if operating cash flows are decreasing even though profits are increasing, accounts receivable and/or inventories may be increasing at a higher rate than sales. This is a signal that the firm may have liquidity problems that would not necessarily be reflected by the change in working capital, the current ratio, or the acid-test ratio. These liquidity measures include other items besides cash, and the firm's inability to collect its accounts receivable and/or sell its inventory may artificially increase current assets and distort these relationships. Of course other interpretations of this same trend might also be possible, but the trend itself might not have been observed without a careful analysis of cash flow data.

The details of an entity's investing activities frequently describe its growth strategy. Besides investing in more plant and equipment, some firms acquire capacity by purchasing other companies or by investing in the securities of other companies. Occasionally a firm will sell some of its plant and equipment, in which case cash is provided. The reasons for and consequences of such a sale of assets are of interest to the financial statement user.

To illustrate these interpretation techniques, refer to Campbell's Consolidated Statements of Cash Flows on page 713 in the annual report in the appendix. Note that a large add-back is made to net income each year for depreciation and amortization because cash is not disbursed for these expense items. Note also that the net cash provided by operating activities exceeded net income by a substantial amount for each of the three years presented. Net cash provided by operating activities also exceeded the cash used for investing activities in all three years—a relationship generally considered desirable. Purchases of plant assets represented Campbell's primary investment activity for each year presented. Financing activities likewise resulted in a net use of cash in all three years, with treasury stock purchases consistently accounting for the largest cash outlay. Cash dividends were paid in slightly increased amounts each year, reflecting a slow but steady growth rate. The company's debt transactions were largely offsetting in 2009, although substantial cash inflows were provided by net borrowings in 2010 and 2011. The overall picture for Campbell's is good; net cash provided by operating activities is covering all of the firm's investing and financing requirements and is creating a surplus of cash for new investment opportunities.

The statement of cash flows provides useful information for owners, managers, employees, suppliers, potential investors, and others interested in the economic activities of the entity. This statement provides information that is difficult, if not impossible, to obtain from the other three financial statements alone.

---

5. What does it mean when the statement of cash flows shows a negative amount of cash provided by operating activities?
6. What does it mean when cash used for investing activities is greater than cash generated from operating activities?

What Does It Mean?

Answers on page 373

Demonstration Problem

Visit the text website at www.mhhe.com/marshall10e to view a demonstration problem for this chapter.

Summary

This chapter has described the income statement and the statement of cash flows. The income statement summarizes the results of the firm's profit-generating or loss-generating activities for a fiscal period. The statement of cash flows explains the change in the firm's cash from the beginning to the end of the fiscal period by summarizing the cash effects of the firm's operating, investing, and financing activities during the period.

Revenues are reported at the beginning of the income statement. Revenues result from the sale of a product or the provision of a service, not necessarily from the receipt of cash. The revenues of most manufacturing and merchandising firms are called *sales*. Net sales, which is gross sales minus sales returns and allowances and cash discounts, is usually the first caption of the income statement. Service entities will describe the source of their revenues (such as rental fees or consulting fees).

Expenses are subtracted from revenues in the income statement. A significant expense for many firms is cost of goods sold. The actual calculation of cost of goods sold is determined by the system used to account for inventories. With a perpetual inventory system, cost can be determined and recognized when a product is sold. With a periodic inventory system, cost of goods sold is calculated at the end of the fiscal period using beginning and ending inventory amounts and the purchases (or cost of goods manufactured) amount. Sometimes cost of goods sold is reported separately and subtracted from net sales to arrive at gross profit or gross margin in what is called a *multiple-step income statement presentation*. Other firms will include cost of goods sold with operating expenses in a single-step income statement presentation.

Gross profit (or gross margin) is frequently expressed as a ratio. The gross profit ratio can be used to monitor profitability, set selling prices, and estimate ending inventory and cost of goods sold.

Selling, general, and administrative expenses are the costs of operating the firm. They are deducted from gross profit to arrive at operating income, an important measure of management performance.

Interest expense is usually shown as a separate item in the other income and expense category of the income statement. Other significant gains or losses will also be identified.

Income before income taxes is frequently reported as a subtotal before income tax expense is shown because taxes are a function of all items reported to this point in the income statement.

To facilitate users' comparisons of net income with that of prior years and to provide a basis for future expectations, income or loss from discontinued operations and extraordinary items are reported separately in the income statement and on a per share basis.

Net income attributable to noncontrolling interests is reported separately from net income (or net earnings) attributable to the reporting entity; the latter amount is reported in total and on a per share of outstanding common stock basis. If there is potential dilution from convertible debt, convertible preferred stock, or stock options, diluted earnings per share will also be reported.

The statement of cash flows shows the change in cash during the year and reports cash provided from or used by operating activities, investing activities, and financing activities.

The determination of cash flows from operating activities is essentially a conversion of the accrual accounting income statement to a cash basis income statement. The principal reasons net income doesn't affect cash directly are that not all accounts receivable from sales are collected in the fiscal period of the sale and not all of the expenses reported in the income statement result in the disbursement of cash in the fiscal period in which the expenses are incurred.

Investing activities include purchases of plant and equipment, investments in other companies, loans made to other entities, and the sale or collection of these assets.

Financing activities include issuance and redemption of bonds and stock, including treasury stock transactions, and cash dividends on stock.

There are two presentation formats for the statement of cash flows. The difference between the two is in the presentation of cash flows from operating activities. Most entities use the indirect method.

Interpretation of the statement of cash flows involves observing the relationship between the three broad categories of cash flows (operating activities, investing activities, and financing activities) and the change in the cash balance for the year. It is desirable to have cash provided from operating activities that is equal to or greater than cash used for investing activities, although large investment requirements in any one year may cause a reduction in the beginning-of-the-year cash balance. Cash can also be raised from financing activities to offset large investment requirements. The detailed activities of each cash flow category will be reviewed to assess their effect on the overall cash position of the firm. The statement of cash flows provides important information that is not easily obtained from the other financial statements.

Refer to the income statement and statement of cash flows for Campbell Soup Company in the appendix, and to these statements in other annual reports you may have, to observe content and presentation alternatives.

Key Terms and Concepts

basic earnings per share (p. 357)   Net income available to common stockholders divided by the weighted average number of shares of common stock outstanding during the period.

cost of goods sold (p. 351)   Cost of merchandise sold during the period; an expense deducted from net sales to arrive at gross profit.

cost of goods sold model (p. 351)   The formula for calculating cost of goods sold by adding beginning inventory and purchases and subtracting ending inventory.

diluted earnings per share (p. 357)   An amount less than basic earnings per share that assumes that additional shares of common stock have been issued pursuant to convertible debt, convertible preferred stock, and/or stock option plans.

dilution (p. 358)   The reduction in "earnings per share of common stock" that may occur if convertible securities are actually converted to common stock and/or if additional shares of common stock are issued pursuant to a stock option plan.

earned (p. 346)   A revenue recognition criterion that relates to completion of the revenue-generating activity.

expenses (p. 350)   Outflows or other using up of assets or incurrences of liabilities during a period from delivering or producing goods, rendering services, or carrying out other activities that constitute the entity's major operations.

extraordinary item (p. 362)   A gain or loss from a transaction that both is unusual in nature and occurs infrequently; it is reported separately in the income statement and shown net of taxes.

FOB destination (p. 348)   The shipping term that means that title passes from seller to buyer when the merchandise arrives at its destination.

FOB shipping point (p. 348)   The shipping term that means that title passes from seller to buyer when the merchandise leaves the seller's premises.

freight collect (p. 348)   A freight payment alternative meaning that freight is payable when the merchandise arrives at its destination.

freight prepaid (p. 348)   A freight payment alternative meaning that freight is paid by the shipper.

gains (p. 349)   Increases in net assets from incidental transactions and other events affecting an entity during a period except those that result from revenues or investments by owners.

gross margin (p. 352)   Another term for *gross profit*.

gross margin ratio (p. 353)   Another term for *gross profit ratio*.

gross profit (p. 352)   The difference between net sales and cost of goods sold. Sometimes called *gross margin*.

gross profit ratio (p. 353)   The ratio of gross profit to net sales. Sometimes called *gross margin ratio*.

income before income taxes (p. 356)   An income statement subtotal on which income tax expense is based.

income from continuing operations (p. 361)   An income statement subtotal that is presented before income or loss from discontinued operations.

income from operations (p. 355)   The difference between gross profit and operating expenses. Also called *operating income*.

inventory cost flow assumption (p. 351)   The application of FIFO, LIFO, weighted-average, or specific identification procedures to determine the cost of goods sold.

inventory shrinkage (p. 351)   Inventory losses resulting from theft, deterioration, and record-keeping errors.

losses (p. 350)   Decreases in net assets from incidental transactions and other events affecting an entity during a period except those that result from expenses or distributions to owners.

matching principle (p. 350)   The concept that expenses incurred in generating revenues should be "matched" against revenues earned during some period of time, usually one year, in determining net income or loss for the period.

multiple-step format (p. 359)   An income statement format that includes subtotals for gross profit, operating income, and income before taxes.

net income (p. 357)   The excess of revenues and gains over expenses and losses for a fiscal period.

net income attributable to noncontrolling interest (p. 362)   An income statement item representing the noncontrolling (minority) stockholders' share of the earnings of a subsidiary that have been included in the consolidated income statement.

net income attributable to (parent company name) (p. 362)   Net income, less "net income attributable to noncontrolling interest" in the consolidated income statement: for example, "Net income attributable to Racers, Inc." Sometimes referred to as *net income attributable to controlling interest*.

net sales (p. 347)   Gross sales, less sales discounts and sales returns and allowances.

operating expenses (p. 355)   Expenses, other than cost of goods sold, incurred in the day-to-day activities of the entity.

operating income (p. 355)   The difference between gross profit and operating expenses. Also referred to as *income from operations*.

other income and expenses (p. 356)   An income statement category that includes interest expense, interest income, and gain or loss items not related to the principal operating activities of the entity.

percentage-of-completion method (p. 349)   A method of recognizing revenue based on the completion percentage of a long-term construction project.

purchase returns and allowances (p. 352)   Reductions in purchases from products returned to the supplier or adjustments in the purchase cost.

realization (p. 346)   A revenue recognition criterion that relates to the receipt of cash or a claim to cash in exchange for the product or service.

revenues (p. 346)   Inflows of cash or increases in other assets, or settlement of liabilities, during a period from delivering or producing goods, rendering services, or performing other activities that constitute the entity's major operations.

sales (p. 347)   Revenues resulting from the sale of product.

sales mix (p. 353)   The proportion of total sales represented by various products or categories of products.

sales returns and allowances (p. 347)   Reductions in sales from product returns or adjustments in selling price.

shipping terms (p. 348)   The description of the point at which title passes from seller to buyer.

single-step format (p. 359)   An income statement format that excludes subtotals such as gross profit and operating income.

statement of cash flows (p. 363)   The financial statement that explains why cash changed during a fiscal period. Cash flows from operating, investing, and financing activities are shown in the statement.

1. It means that although net income is not the literal bottom line on the income statement, many financial statement users consider it the most important amount on the income statement.

2. It means that to have the "big picture" of the entity's results, one must look at more than the amounts opposite one or two captions. It is especially important to be aware of unusual items that may appear on the income statement.

3. It means that additional shares of common stock may be issued because of the existence of convertible bonds, convertible preferred stock, or stock options. Issuance of shares for these items could reduce earnings per share of common stock and the market value of the common stock.

4. It means that future income statements will not be affected by the results of the discontinued operations and that by highlighting this item it should be possible for a financial statement user to make adjustments when anticipating future results for the firm.

5. It means that the firm has not generated cash from its operations—a situation that should not exist for long. To keep operating, the firm will need to have generated cash from investing or financing activities and/or used cash on hand at the beginning of the reporting period.

6. It means that during the year, the firm may have made some significant investments financed by creditors or owners and/or used cash on hand at the beginning of the reporting period.

ANSWERS TO
What Does It Mean?

Self-Study Material

Visit the text website at www.mhhe.com/marshall10e to take an online self-study quiz for this chapter.

Matching I Following are a number of the key terms and concepts introduced in the chapter, along with a list of corresponding definitions. Match the appropriate letter for the key term or concept to each definition provided (items 1–10). Note that not all key terms and concepts will be used. Answers are provided at the end of this chapter.

a.	Revenues	l.	Gross profit (or gross margin)
b.	Realization	m.	Gross profit ratio (or gross margin ratio)
c.	Earned		
d.	Sales	n.	Sales mix
e.	Sales returns and allowances	o.	Operating expenses
f.	Net sales	p.	Income from operations
g.	Shipping terms	q.	Gains
h.	FOB destination	r.	Income before income taxes
i.	FOB shipping point	s.	Net income
j.	Freight prepaid	t.	Income before extraordinary items
k.	Freight collect		

_____ **1.** Reductions in sales from product returns or adjustments in selling price.

_____ **2.** A freight payment alternative meaning that freight is payable when the merchandise arrives at its destination.

_____ **3.** The difference between gross profit and operating expenses.

_____ **4.** The description of when title passes and whether buyer or seller is responsible for freight charges.

_____ **5.** The difference between net sales and cost of goods sold.

_____ **6.** A revenue recognition criterion that relates to the receipt of cash in exchange for the product or service.

_____ **7.** Increases in net assets from incidental transactions and other events affecting an entity during a period except those that result from revenues or investments by owners.

_____ **8.** The shipping term for passage of title from seller to buyer when the merchandise leaves the seller's premises.

_____ **9.** Gross sales less sales discounts and sales returns and allowances.

_____ **10.** The shipping term for passage of title from seller to buyer when the merchandise arrives at its destination.

Matching II Following are a number of the key terms and concepts introduced in the chapter, along with a list of corresponding definitions. Match the appropriate letter for the key term or concept to each definition provided (items 1–10). Note that not all key terms and concepts will be used. Answers are provided at the end of this chapter.

a. Percentage of completion method
b. Physical inventory
c. Expenses
d. Cost of goods sold
e. Matching principle
f. Inventory cost flow assumption
g. Inventory shrinkage
h. Perpetual system
i. Periodic system
j. Cost of goods sold model

k. Dilution
l. Basic earnings per share
m. Diluted earnings per share
n. Extraordinary item
o. Discontinued operations
p. Net income attributable to non-controlling interest
q. Single-step format
r. Multiple-step format
s. Statement of cash flows

_____ **1.** The financial statement that explains why cash changed during the fiscal period.

_____ **2.** Inventory losses resulting from theft, deterioration, and recordkeeping errors.

_____ **3.** Outflows or other using up of assets or incurrence of a liability during a period from delivering or producing goods, rendering services, or carrying out other activities that constitute the entity's major operations.

_____ **4.** A gain or loss from a transaction that both is unusual in nature and occurs infrequently, and is reported separately on the income statement net of taxes.

_____ **5.** An income statement format that includes subtotals for gross profit, operating income, and income before taxes.

_____ **6.** An expense deducted from net sales to arrive at gross profit.

_____ **7.** The reduction in earnings per share of common stock that can occur if convertible securities are actually converted to common stock.

_____ **8.** An income statement item representing the noncontrolling stockholders' share of the earnings of a subsidiary that have been included in the consolidated income statement.

_____ **9.** Achieves a fair presentation of the results of a firm's operations during a period by requiring the deduction of all expenses incurred in generating that period's revenues from the revenues earned in the period.

_____**10.** Net income available to the common stockholders divided by the average number of shares of common stock outstanding during the period.

Multiple Choice For each of the following questions, circle the best responses. Answers are provided at the end of this chapter.

1. All of the following are appropriate revenue accounts *except*

    a. Fees.

    b. Sales.

    c. Gross Profit.

    d. Service Revenues.

    e. Interest Revenues.

2. Extraordinary items include all of the following *except*

    a. utilization of tax loss carryforwards.

    b. litigation settlements.

    c. earthquake losses.

    d. All of the above are examples of extraordinary items.

3. Michael sells Melissa his grand piano and wishes to avoid both the cost of shipping it and the risk of loss while the piano is in transit. He should send the piano

    a. FOB shipping point, freight collect.

    b. FOB shipping point, freight prepaid.

    c. FOB destination, freight collect.

    d. FOB destination, freight prepaid.

4. The periodic and perpetual inventory systems share the following similarity:

    a. The Cost of Goods Sold account is adjusted daily as sales are made under both systems.

    b. The Purchases account is used under both systems.

    c. Both systems can be used in conjunction with any of the cost flow assumptions (FIFO, LIFO, or weighted average).

    d. Under both systems, it is necessary to estimate gross profit ratios for sales made during the most recent month.

    e. The cost of purchases is determined by an annual physical count under both systems.

5. Bublitz Company had net sales of $700,000 for fiscal 2013, cost of goods sold of $413,000, and interest expense amounting to $112,000. What would be the estimated gross profit for 2014 if sales were $800,000 or if sales were $1,100,000?

   a. $200,000 or $275,000, respectively.

   b. $275,000 or $575,000, respectively.

   c. $328,000 or $451,000, respectively.

   d. $387,000 or $687,000, respectively.

   e. $472,000 or $649,000, respectively.

6. Because of their importance to financial statement users, certain expenses are normally reported as separate items on the income statement (especially when significant in amount). Which of the following expenses is *not* normally reported as a separate item?

   a. Advertising Expense.

   b. Cost of Goods Sold.

   c. Interest Expense.

   d. Income Tax Expense.

7. Earnings per share calculations are required on the income statement for

   a. cost of goods sold, depreciation expense, and income from continuing operations.

   b. discontinued operations, depreciation expense, and net income.

   c. extraordinary items, income from continuing operations, and discontinued operations.

   d. income tax expense, extraordinary items, and net income.

   e. cost of goods sold, discontinued operations, and extraordinary items.

8. In what circumstance is it proper to recognize revenues before a sales transaction has occurred?

   a. When management has a policy to do so.

   b. When the conservatism principle applies.

   c. When the going concern principle requires the recognition of revenues for cash payments received in advance from customers.

   d. When the ultimate sales of the goods is assured because the products have readily determinable prices and can be sold without significant effort.

   e. When it is certain that competitors will raise their prices in the near future.

9. Which of the following is *not* one of the three broad categories presented in the statement of cash flows?

   a. Financing activities.

   b. Operating activities.

   c. Income activities.

   d. Investing activities.

10. Which of the following transactions would *not* be shown under the operating activities category of the statement of cash flows (using the direct method)?

   a. Cash received from customers.

   b. Cash paid to purchase land.

   c. Cash paid for interest and taxes.

   d. Cash paid to merchandise suppliers.

   e. Cash paid to employees for salaries.

Mini-Exercises

All applicable Mini-Exercises are available with McGraw-Hill's *Connect*™ *Accounting*.

Gross profit calculations Net sales for the year were $900,000 and cost of goods sold was $558,000 for the company's existing products. A new product is presently under development and will have an expected selling price of not more than $60 per unit in order to remain competitive with similar products in the marketplace.

Mini-Exercise 9.1
LO 3

Required:

a. Calculate gross profit and the gross profit ratio for the year.

b. What is the maximum cost per unit that can be incurred to manufacture the new product so that the product can be priced competitively and will not result in a reduction to the company's gross profit ratio?

Calculate operating income and net income Selling, general, and administrative expenses were $132,000; net sales were $600,000; interest expense was $14,200; research and development expenses were $63,000; net cash provided by operating activities was $159,300; net income was $33,600; income tax expense was $15,200; cost of goods sold was $330,000.

Mini-Exercise 9.2
LO 5

Required:

a. Calculate operating income for the period.

b. Calculate net income for the period.

Calculate basic EPS Net income was $329,550 for the year. Throughout the year the company had outstanding 18,000 shares of $2.50, $50 par value preferred stock and 105,000 shares of common stock.

Mini-Exercise 9.3
LO 7

Required:

Calculate basic earnings per share of common stock for the year.

Calculate cash flows from operations—indirect method Net income was $44,700; accounts receivable decreased by $12,000; inventory increased by $7,200; proceeds from the issuance of long-term debt were $15,000; accounts payable decreased by $4,100; equipment purchases were $50,000; depreciation and amortization expense was $22,500.

Mini-Exercise 9.4
LO 10

Required:

Calculate the net cash provided (used) by operating activities for the period.

Exercises

All applicable Exercises are available with McGraw-Hill's *Connect*™ *Accounting*.

Calculate earned revenues Big Blue University has a fiscal year that ends on June 30. The 2013 summer session of the university runs from June 9 through July 28. Total tuition paid by students for the summer session amounted to $112,000.

Exercise 9.5
LO 1

Required:

a. How much revenue should be reflected in the fiscal year ended June 30, 2013? Explain your answer.

b. Would your answer to part **a** be any different if the university had a tuition refund policy that no tuition would be refunded after the end of the third week of summer session classes? Explain your answer.

Exercise 9.6
LO 1

Calculate earned revenues Kirkland Theater sells season tickets for six events at a price of $240. In pricing the tickets, the planners assigned the leadoff event a value of $60 because the program was an expensive symphony orchestra. The last five events were priced equally; 1,500 season tickets were sold for the 2013 season.

Required:

a. Calculate the theater's earned revenue after the first three events have been presented.

b. About 95% of the season ticket holders attended the first event. Subsequent events were attended by about 80% of the season ticket holders. To what extent, if any, should the attendance data impact revenue recognition? Explain your answer.

Exercise 9.7
LO 2

Effects of inventory error If the ending inventory of a firm is overstated by $50,000, by how much and in what direction (overstated or understated) will the firm's operating income be misstated? *(Hint: Use the cost of goods sold model, enter hypothetically "correct" data, and then reflect the effects of the ending inventory error and determine the effect on cost of goods sold.)*

Exercise 9.8
LO 2

Effects of inventory error Assume that the ending inventory of a merchandising firm is overstated by $40,000.

Required:

a. By how much and in what direction (overstated or understated) will the firm's cost of goods sold be misstated?

b. If this error is not corrected, what effect will it have on the subsequent period's operating income?

c. If this error is not corrected, what effect will it have on the total operating income of the two periods (the period in which there is an error and the subsequent period) combined?

Exercise 9.9
LO 2, 3

Calculate gross profit ratio and cost of goods sold Refer to the consolidated statements of earnings on page 711 of the Campbell Soup Company annual report in the appendix.

Required:

a. Calculate the gross profit ratio for each of the past three years.

b. Assume that Campbell's net sales for the first four months of 2012 totaled $2.7 billion. Calculate an estimated cost of goods sold and gross profit for the four months.

Exercise 9.10
LO 2, 3

Calculate gross profit, cost of goods sold, and selling price MBI, Inc., had sales of $250 million for fiscal 2013. The company's gross profit ratio for that year was 37.2%.

Required:

a. Calculate the gross profit and cost of goods sold for MBI, Inc., for fiscal 2013.

b. Assume that a new product is developed and that it will cost $2,669 to manufacture. Calculate the selling price that must be set for this new product if its gross profit ratio is to be the same as the average achieved for all products for fiscal 2013.

c. From a management viewpoint, what would you do with this information?

Operating income versus net income If you were interested in evaluating the profitability of a company and could have only limited historical data, would you prefer to know operating income or net income for the past five years? Explain your answer.

Exercise 9.11
LO 5

Operating income versus net income Refer to the selected financial data (five-year financial summary) on page 709 of the Campbell Soup Company annual report in the appendix.

Exercise 9.12
LO 5

Campbell's

Required:

Compare the trend of the operating income (earnings before interest and taxes) data with the trend of net income (net earnings attributable to Campbell Soup Company) data from 2007 through 2011. Which series of data is more meaningful? Explain your answer.

Calculate basic EPS Ringmeup, Inc., had net income of $111,250 for the year ended December 31, 2013. At the beginning of the year, 40,000 shares of common stock were outstanding. On May 1, an additional 10,000 shares were issued. On December 1, the company purchased 5,000 shares of its own common stock and held them as treasury stock until the end of the year. No other changes in common shares outstanding occurred during the year. During the year, Ringmeup, Inc., paid the annual dividend on the 8,000 shares of 3.5%, $100 par value preferred stock that were outstanding the entire year.

Exercise 9.13
LO 7

Required:

Calculate basic earnings per share of common stock for the year ended December 31, 2013.

Calculate basic EPS, and explain the EPS effect of convertible preferred Thrifty Co. reported net income of $790,800 for its fiscal year ended January 31, 2014. At the beginning of that fiscal year, 100,000 shares of common stock were outstanding. On October 31, 2013, an additional 30,000 shares were issued. No other changes in common shares outstanding occurred during the year. Also during the year, the company paid the annual dividend on the 40,000 shares of 6%, $50 par value preferred stock that were outstanding the entire year.

Exercise 9.14
LO 7

Required:

a. Calculate basic earnings per share of common stock for the year ended January 31, 2014.

b. If Thrifty Co.'s preferred stock were convertible into common stock, what additional calculation would be required?

Accrual to cash flows For each of the following items, calculate the cash sources or cash uses that should be recognized on the statement of cash flows for Baldin Co. for the year ended December 31, 2013:

Exercise 9.15
LO 10

a. Sales on account (all are collectible) amounted to $760,000, and accounts receivable decreased by $24,000. How much cash was collected from customers?

b. Income tax expense for the year was $148,000, and income taxes payable decreased by $34,000. How much cash was paid for income taxes?

c. Cost of goods sold amounted to $408,000, accounts payable increased by $19,000, and inventories increased by $14,000. How much cash was paid to suppliers?

d. The net book value of buildings increased by $240,000. No buildings were sold, and depreciation expense for the year was $190,000. How much cash was paid to purchase buildings?

Exercise 9.16

LO 10

Cash flows to accrual For each of the following items, calculate the amount of revenue or expense that should be recognized on the income statement for Pelkey Co. for the year ended December 31, 2013:

a. Cash collected from customers during the year amounted to $412,000, and accounts receivable increased by $25,000. How much were sales on account for the year ended December 31, 2013?

b. Cash payments for income taxes during the year were $166,000, and income taxes payable increased by $14,000. How much was income tax expense?

c. Cash paid to suppliers during the year amounted to $243,000, accounts payable decreased by $27,300, and inventories decreased by $16,000. How much was cost of goods sold?

d. The net book value of buildings increased by $95,000. No buildings were sold, and a new building costing $170,000 was purchased during the year. How much was depreciation expense?

Exercise 9.17

LO 6, 7

Income statement format and EPS disclosures Refer to the consolidated statements of earnings on page 711 of the Campbell Soup Company annual report in the appendix.

Required:

a. Does Campbell's use the single-step format or the multiple-step format? Which format do you prefer? Explain your answer.

b. Refer to the basic and diluted earnings per share data on page 711 and the related note disclosures on pages 726–727. Explain why this disclosure is appropriate.

Exercise 9.18

LO 11

Statement of cash flows analysis Refer to the consolidated statements of cash flows on page 713 of the Campbell Soup Company annual report in the appendix.

Required:

a. Identify the two most significant sources of cash from operating activities during 2011. How much of a cash source amount do these items represent?

b. What was the firm's most significant investing activity during 2011, and how much cash did this activity use or generate?

c. Identify the two most significant financing activities during 2011. What was the net effect on cash of these items?

Problems

All applicable Problems are available with McGraw-Hill's *Connect™ Accounting.*

Calculate operating income and net income The following information is available from the accounting records of Manahan Co. for the year ended December 31, 2013:

Problem 9.19
LO 5

Net cash provided by financing activities	$112,000
Dividends paid	18,000
Extraordinary loss from flood, net of tax savings of $35,000	105,000
Income tax expense	26,000
Other selling expenses	13,000
Net sales	644,000
Advertising expense	45,000
Accounts receivable	62,000
Cost of goods sold	368,000
General and administrative expenses	143,000

Required:

a. Calculate the operating income for Manahan Co. for the year ended December 31, 2013.

b. Calculate the company's net income for 2013.

Calculate operating income and net income The following information is available from the accounting records of Spenser Co. for the year ended December 31, 2013:

Problem 9.20
LO 5

Selling, general, and administrative expenses	$102,000
Accounts payable	170,000
Extraordinary gain from lawsuit settlement, net of tax expense of $14,000	52,000
Research and development expenses	74,000
Loss from discontinued operations, net of tax savings of $10,000	34,000
Provision for income taxes	35,000
Net sales	979,000
Interest expense	128,000
Net cash provided by operations	296,000
Cost of goods sold	544,000

Required:

a. Calculate the operating income for Spenser Co. for the year ended December 31, 2013.

b. Calculate the company's net income for 2013.

Use gross profit ratio to calculate inventory loss Franklin Co. has experienced gross profit ratios for 2013, 2012, and 2011 of 33%, 30%, and 31%, respectively. On April 3, 2014, the firm's plant and all of its inventory were destroyed by a tornado.

Problem 9.21
LO 3

Accounting records for 2014, which were available because they were stored in a protected vault, showed the following:

Sales from January 1 thru April 2	$142,680
January 1 inventory amount	63,590
Purchases of inventory from	
January 1 thru April 2	118,652

Required:

Calculate the amount of the insurance claim to be filed for the inventory destroyed in the tornado. *(Hint: Use the cost of goods sold model and a gross profit ratio that will result in the largest claim.)*

Problem 9.22

LO 3

Use gross profit ratio to calculate inventory loss On April 8, 2013, a flood destroyed the warehouse of Stuco Distributing Co. From the waterlogged records of the company, management was able to determine that the firm's gross profit ratio had averaged 40% for the past several years and that the inventory at the beginning of the year was $314,200. It also was determined that during the year until the date of the flood, sales had totaled $638,400 and purchases totaled $355,140.

Required:

Calculate the amount of inventory loss from the flood.

Problem 9.23

LO 10

Cash flows from operations—indirect method The financial statements of Simon Co. include the following items (amounts in thousands):

Income Statement	For the Year Ended December 31, 2014
Net income	$420
Depreciation and amortization expense	320

	At December 31	
Balance Sheets	2014	2013
Accounts receivable	$125	$170
Inventory	170	150
Accounts payable	80	90
Income taxes payable	50	15

Required:

a. Calculate the net cash flow provided by operations for Simon Co. for the year ended December 31, 2014.

b. Explain why net income is different from the net cash provided by operations.

Prepare a statement of cash flows—indirect method The financial statements of Pouchie Co. included the following information for the year ended December 31, 2013 (amounts in millions):

Problem 9.24
LO 10

Depreciation and amortization expense	$260
Cash dividends declared and paid.	330
Purchase of equipment	820
Net income	384
Beginning cash balance.	120
Proceeds of common stock issued	148
Proceeds from sale of building (at book value)	212
Accounts receivable increase.	16
Ending cash balance	40
Inventory decrease	38
Accounts payable increase	44

Required:
Complete the following statement of cash flows, using the indirect method:

POUCHIE CO. Statement of Cash Flows For the Year Ended December 31, 2013	
Cash Flows from Operating Activities:	
Net income	$ 384
Add (deduct) items not affecting cash:	
_____	
_____	
_____	
_____	
Net cash provided (used) by operating activities.	$
Cash Flows from Investing Activities:	
_____	
_____	
Net cash provided (used) by investing activities	$
Cash Flows from Financing Activities:	
_____	
_____	
Net cash provided (used) by financing activities	$
Net increase (decrease) in cash for the year.	$
Cash balance, January 1, 2013	120
Cash balance, December 31, 2013	$ 40

Cash flows from operating, investing, and financing activities—direct method The following information is available from Bromfield Co.'s accounting records for the year ended December 31, 2013 (amounts in millions):

Problem 9.25
LO 10

Cash dividends declared and paid	$ 340
Interest and taxes paid	90
Collections from customers	1,350
Payment of long-term debt	220
Purchase of land and buildings	170
Cash paid to suppliers and employees	810
Issuance of preferred stock	300
Proceeds from the sale of equipment	40

Required:

a. Calculate the net cash provided (used) by operating activities for Bromfield Co. for the year ended December 31, 2013.

b. Calculate the net cash provided (used) by investing activities.

c. Calculate the net cash provided (used) by financing activities.

d. Calculate the net increase (decrease) in cash for the year.

Problem 9.26

LO 10

Cash flows from operating, investing, and financing activities—direct method The following information is available from Gray Co.'s accounting records for the year ended December 31, 2013 (amounts in millions):

Cash dividends declared and paid	$1,050
Retirement of bonds payable at maturity	600
Interest and taxes paid	450
Proceeds of common stock issued	1,650
Proceeds from the sale of land	375
Collections from customers	9,525
Cash paid to suppliers and employees	?
Purchase of buildings and equipment	?

Required:

a. The net cash provided by operating activities for Gray Co. for the year ended December 31, 2013, is $3,675 million. Calculate the cash paid to suppliers and employees.

b. The increase in cash for the year was $750 million. Calculate the amount of cash used to purchase buildings and equipment. Your answer to part **a** should be considered in your calculation. *(Hint: Set up a model of the statement of cash flows to determine the net cash provided [used] by operating and investing activities, and then solve for the missing amounts.)*

Problem 9.27

LO 10, 11

Complete balance sheet and prepare a statement of cash flows—indirect method Following is a partially completed balance sheet for Hoeman, Inc., at December 31, 2014, together with comparative data for the year ended December 31, 2013. From the statement of cash flows for the year ended December 31, 2014, you determine the following:

• Net income for the year ended December 31, 2014, was $94,000.

• Dividends paid during the year ended December 31, 2014, were $67,000.

- Accounts receivable decreased $10,000 during the year ended December 31, 2014.
- The cost of new buildings acquired during 2014 was $125,000.
- No buildings were disposed of during 2014.
- The land account was not affected by any transactions during the year, but the fair value of the land at December 31, 2014, was $178,000.

HOEMAN, INC.
Comparative Balance Sheets
At December 31, 2014 and 2013

	2014	2013
Assets		
Current assets:		
Cash	$ 52,000	$ 46,000
Accounts receivable		134,000
Inventory	156,000	176,000
Total current assets	$	$ 356,000
Land	$	140,000
Buildings		290,000
Less: Accumulated depreciation	(120,000)	(105,000)
Total land and buildings	$	$ 325,000
Total assets	$	$ 681,000
Liabilities		
Current liabilities:		
Accounts payable	$	$ 197,000
Note payable	155,000	124,000
Total current liabilities	$ 322,000	$ 321,000
Long-term debt	$	$ 139,000
Stockholders' Equity		
Common stock	$ 50,000	$ 45,000
Retained earnings		176,000
Total stockholders' equity	$	$ 221,000
Total liabilities and stockholders' equity	$	$ 681,000

Required:

a. Complete the December 31, 2014, balance sheet. (*Hint: Long-term debt is the last number to compute to make the balance sheet balance.*)

b. Prepare a statement of cash flows for the year ended December 31, 2014, using the indirect method.

Complete balance sheet and prepare a statement of changes in retained earnings Following is a statement of cash flows (indirect method) for Hartford, Inc., for the year ended December 31, 2014. Also shown is a partially completed comparative balance sheet as of December 31, 2014 and 2013:

Problem 9.28
LO 10, 11

HARTFORD, INC.
Statement of Cash Flows
For the Year Ended December 31, 2014

Cash Flows from Operating Activities:

Net income		$ 27,000
Add (deduct) items not affecting cash:		
Depreciation expense		135,000
Decrease in accounts receivable		69,000
Increase in inventory		(21,000)
Increase in notes payable		36,000
Decrease in accounts payable		(18,000)
Net cash provided by operating activities		$ 228,000

Cash Flows from Investing Activities:

Purchase of equipment		$(150,000)
Purchase of buildings		(144,000)
Net cash used by investing activities		$(294,000)

Cash Flows from Financing Activities:

Proceeds from short-term debt		$ 15,000
Cash used for retirement of long-term debt		(75,000)
Proceeds from issuance of common stock		30,000
Payment of cash dividends on common stock		(9,000)
Net cash used by financing activities		$ (39,000)
Net decrease in cash for the year		$(105,000)

HARTFORD, INC.
Comparative Balance Sheets
At December 31, 2014 and 2013

	2014	2013
Assets		
Current assets:		
Cash	$	$ 264,000
Accounts receivable		219,000
Inventory	168,000	
Total current assets	$	$
Land	$	$ 120,000
Buildings and equipment	780,000	
Less: Accumulated depreciation		(369,000)
Total land, buildings, and equipment	$	$
Total assets	$	$
Liabilities		
Current liabilities:		
Accounts payable	$	$ 87,000
Short-term debt	96,000	
Notes payable		108,000
Total current liabilities	$	$
Long-term debt	$ 255,000	$
Stockholders' Equity		
Common stock	$ 120,000	$
Retained earnings		
Total stockholders' equity	$	$
Total liabilities and stockholders' equity	$	$

Required:

a. Complete the December 31, 2014 and 2013, balance sheets.

b. Prepare a statement of changes in retained earnings for the year ended December 31, 2014.

Prepare balance sheet and retained earnings statement using statement of cash flows data Following are a statement of cash flows (indirect method) for Harris, Inc., for the year ended December 31, 2014, and the firm's balance sheet at December 31, 2013:

Problem 9.29
LO 10, 11

HARRIS, INC. Statement of Cash Flows For the Year Ended December 31, 2014	
Cash Flows from Operating Activities:	
Net income	$ 13,000
Add (deduct) items not affecting cash:	
Depreciation expense	29,000
Increase in accounts receivable	(6,000)
Decrease in merchandise inventory	30,000
Increase in accounts payable	3,000
Net cash provided by operating activities	$ 69,000
Cash Flows from Investing Activities:	
Purchase of buildings	(90,000)
Proceeds from sale of land at its cost	7,000
Net cash used by investing activities	$(83,000)
Cash Flows from Financing Activities:	
Payment of short-term debt	(4,000)
Payment of notes payable	(9,000)
Proceeds from issuance of long-term debt	15,000
Proceeds from issuance of common stock	8,000
Payment of cash dividends on common stock	(5,000)
Net cash provided by financing activities	$ 5,000
Net decrease in cash for the year	$ (9,000)

HARRIS, INC. Balance Sheet At December 31, 2013	
Assets	
Cash	$ 15,000
Accounts receivable	61,000
Merchandise inventory	76,000
Total current assets	$152,000
Land	34,000
Buildings	118,000
Less: Accumulated depreciation	(72,000)
Total land and buildings	$ 80,000
Total assets	$232,000
	(continued)

Liabilities	
Accounts payable	$ 58,000
Short-term debt	16,000
Notes payable	33,000
Total current liabilities	$107,000
Long-term debt	50,000
Stockholders' Equity	
Common stock, no par	$ 20,000
Retained earnings	55,000
Total stockholders' equity	$ 75,000
Total liabilities and stockholders' equity	$232,000

Required:

a. Using the preceding information, prepare the balance sheet for Harris, Inc., at December 31, 2014.

b. Prepare a statement of changes in retained earnings for the year ended December 31, 2014.

Problem 9.30

LO 10, 11

Prepare statement of cash flows (indirect method) using balance sheet data Following are comparative balance sheets for Millco, Inc., at January 31 and February 28, 2014:

MILLCO, INC. Balance Sheets February 28 and January 31, 2014		
	February 28	**January 31**
Assets		
Cash	$ 84,000	$ 74,000
Accounts receivable	128,000	106,000
Merchandise inventory	162,000	188,000
Total current assets	$ 374,000	$ 368,000
Plant and equipment:		
Production equipment	332,000	304,000
Less: Accumulated depreciation	(48,000)	(42,000)
Total assets	$ 658,000	$ 630,000
Liabilities		
Accounts payable	$ 74,000	$ 82,000
Short-term debt	88,000	88,000
Other accrued liabilities	42,000	48,000
Total current liabilities	$ 204,000	$ 218,000
Long-term debt	66,000	92,000
Total liabilities	$ 270,000	$ 310,000
Stockholders' Equity		
Common stock, no par value, 80,000 shares authorized, 60,000 and 56,000 shares issued, respectively	$ 208,000	$ 192,000
Retained earnings:		
Beginning balance	$ 128,000	$ 86,000
Net income for month	72,000	58,000
Dividends	(20,000)	(16,000)
Ending balance	$ 180,000	$ 128,000
Total stockholders' equity	$ 388,000	$ 320,000
Total liabilities and stockholders' equity	$ 658,000	$ 630,000

Required:

Prepare a statement of cash flows that explains the change that occurred in cash during the month. You may assume that the change in each balance sheet amount is due to a single event (for example, the change in the amount of production equipment is not the result of both a purchase and sale of equipment). *(Hints: What is the purpose of the statement of cash flows? How is this purpose accomplished?)* Use the space to the right of the January 31 data to enter the difference between the February 28 and January 31 amounts of each balance sheet item; these are the amounts that will be in your solution.

Cases

All applicable Cases are available with McGraw-Hill's *Connect*™ *Accounting.*

Focus company—income statement analysis In Exercise 1.1, you were asked to obtain the most recent annual report of a company that you were interested in reviewing throughout this term.

Case 9.31

LO 3, 5, 7, 8

Required:

a. Which method, single-step or multiple-step, is used in the statement?

b. What are the captions of the intermediate profit amounts reported by this company that are *not* reported by Campbell Soup Company?

c. Calculate the gross profit ratio for each of the years reported. Briefly evaluate the trend of these results.

d. Is operating income increasing or decreasing for the years reported?

e. Does the company report any unusual items? If so, what are the effects of these items on net income and earnings per share?

Focus company—statement of cash flows analysis In Exercise 1.1, you were asked to obtain the most recent annual report of a company that you were interested in reviewing throughout this term.

Case 9.32

LO 9, 10, 11

Required:

a. Which method, direct or indirect, is used in the statement?

b. List the principal sources and uses of cash for this firm.

c. Evaluate the change in cash. Has the firm generated most of its cash requirements from operations, or has it borrowed extensively? Has the firm's uses of cash been balanced between investments and dividends?

d. Have there been significant treasury stock transactions?

e. Has the cash balance been increasing or decreasing? What seem to be the implications of this pattern for dividends?

Using cash flow information—The Coca-Cola Company Following are comparative statements of cash flows, as reported by The Coca-Cola Company in its 2011 annual report:

Case 9.33

LO 11

THE COCA-COLA COMPANY AND SUBSIDIARIES Consolidated Statements of Cash Flows Year Ended December 31 (in millions)			
	2011	2010	2009
Operating Activities (details omitted)			
Net cash provided by operating activities	$ 9,474	$ 9,532	$ 8,186
Investing Activities			
Purchases of short-term investments	(4,057)	(4,579)	(2,130)
Proceeds from disposals of short-term investments	5,647	4,032	—
Acquisitions and investments	(977)	(2,511)	(300)
Purchases of other investments	(787)	(132)	(22)
Proceeds from disposals of bottling companies			
and other investments.	562	972	240
Purchases of property, plant, and equipment	(2,920)	(2,215)	(1,993)
Proceeds from disposals of property, plant, and equipment . .	101	134	104
Other investing activities	(93)	(106)	(48)
Net cash provided by (used in) investing activities	(2,524)	(4,405)	(4,149)
Financing Activities			
Issuances of debt	27,495	15,251	14,689
Payments of debt	(22,530)	(13,403)	(12,326)
Issuances of stock	1,569	1,666	664
Purchases of stock for treasury.	(4,513)	(2,961)	(1,518)
Dividends	(4,300)	(4,068)	(3,800)
Other financing activities	45	50	(2)
Net cash provided by (used in) financing activities	(2,234)	(3,465)	(2,293)
Effect of Exchange Rate Changes on			
Cash and Cash Equivalents	(430)	(166)	576
Cash and Cash Equivalents			
Net increase (decrease) during the year	4,286	1,496	2,320
Balance at beginning of the year.	8,517	7,021	4,701
Balance at end of year.	$12,803	$ 8,517	$ 7,021

Required:

a. Briefly review the consolidated statements of cash flows, and then provide an overall evaluation of the "big picture" during the three years presented for Coca-Cola. Have operating cash flows been sufficient to meet investing needs and to pay dividends?

b. Were there significant changes to any of the specific line-item details that you think would require further explanation or analysis?

Answers to Self-Study Material

Matching I: 1. e, 2. k, 3. p, 4. g, 5. l, 6. b, 7. q, 8. i, 9. f, 10. h
Matching II: 1. s, 2. g, 3. c, 4. n, 5. r, 6. d, 7. k, 8. p, 9. e, 10. l
Multiple choice: 1. c, 2. d, 3. a, 4. c, 5. c, 6. a, 7. c, 8. d, 9. c, 10. b

10 Corporate Governance, Notes to the Financial Statements, and Other Disclosures

The principal objectives of this chapter are to help you understand the issues of **corporate governance** and to enable you to make sense of the notes and other financial information found in most corporate annual reports.

A brief discussion of several recent corporate governance developments is provided to give you a sense of the current regulatory environment and to help establish the background necessary for your study of the notes. The role of the Public Company Accounting Oversight Board (PCAOB) as the watchdog of the accounting and auditing profession is examined in the context of financial reporting. Yet despite the heightened awareness of corporate governance issues in recent years, a wide variety of financial reporting misstatements continue to escape the attention of independent auditors; some of the reasons for these misstatements will be explored.

Because of the complexities related to financial reporting and because of the number of alternative generally accepted accounting principles that can be used, **notes to the financial statements** are included as an integral part of the financial statements. As explained in Chapter 2, the full disclosure concept means that companies are required to report all necessary information to prevent a reasonably astute user of the financial statements from being misled. The notes, or **financial review,** are referred to on each page of the individual financial statements and are presented immediately following the financial statements. In the Campbell Soup Company 2011 annual report in the appendix, the notes to the consolidated financial statements are on pages 715–750.

At first glance the notes to the financial statements can appear quite intimidating because they frequently require more pages than the financial statements themselves, contain a great deal of detailed information, and include much financial management terminology. However, the reader cannot fully understand the financial statements without referring to the notes.

Financial statements of companies whose securities are publicly traded must be audited by independent auditors, and the annual report of such a company must include disclosures required by the Securities and Exchange Commission. An understanding of the auditors' report and a review of the note disclosures lead to a more complete picture of a company's financial condition, results of operations, and cash flows.

LEARNING OBJECTIVES (LO)

After studying this chapter you should understand and be able to

LO 10-1   Discuss the significance of corporate governance.

LO 10-2   Identify the types of financial reporting misstatements that have occurred in recent years.

LO 10-3   Explain why the notes are an integral part of the financial statements.

LO 10-4   Discuss the kinds of significant accounting policies that are explained in the notes.

LO 10-5   Describe the nature and content of various note disclosures.

LO 10-6   Explain the role of the Securities and Exchange Commission and some of its reporting requirements.

LO 10-7   Explain why a statement of management's responsibility is included with the notes.

LO 10-8   Describe the significance of management's discussion and analysis of the firm's financial condition and results of operations.

LO 10-9   Identify what is included in the five-year (or longer) summary of financial data.

LO 10-10   Discuss the meaning and content of the independent auditors' report.

Corporate Governance

In addition to the numbers presented in the financial statements, the strategies, behaviors, and actions of the company and its directors, managers, and employees affect the success or lack thereof of the entity. Governance activities and the signals they send to the marketplace form the public's perception of the entity's acknowledgment and performance of its citizenship responsibilities. However, corporate governance is more than simply a set of structures, control mechanisms, rules, and regulations that directors, officers, and employees must follow. At the core of the governance concept are issues of business ethics, social responsibility, equitable treatment of stakeholders, full and fair disclosure, and the responsibilities of the board of directors and its various committees.

> **LO 1**
> Discuss the significance of corporate governance.

The focus on corporate governance has been heightened since the global stock market meltdown of the late 1980s. The unusual number of high-level corporate failures during the late 1980s and early 1990s initiated significant discussion and movement toward legislative and regulatory reform, including efforts by Congress, the SEC, and the FASB to strengthen financial disclosure requirements and clarify auditor independence issues. Although such efforts contributed to a management focus on ethical behavior, the cycle of business failures was repeated again in the late 1990s and early 2000s with some of the largest corporate bankruptcies in history. The size of failed organizations such as Enron and WorldCom, Inc., and the intensity of the fallout of these failures in the United States and overseas resulted in a perceived legitimacy challenge to the accounting profession and a general deterioration in investor confidence.

The failure of corporations to self-control, self-regulate, and fully disclose financial information to the marketplace and to investors in particular was a failure of corporate governance that led to a series of governmental and quasi-governmental reform measures, as well as private sector initiatives to help improve the financial reporting process. The most powerful legislation to date has been the Sarbanes–Oxley Act (SOX) of 2002, which created the Public Company Accounting Oversight Board (PCAOB) as the authoritative watchdog over the accounting and auditing profession. The SOX legislation was aimed primarily to curtail the misbehavior of senior management of corporate entities: Chief executive officers (CEOs) and chief financial officers (CFOs) are required under SOX to attest (in front of a notary) to the correctness of their company's financial statements. (See pages 757–760 in the appendix for examples of these disclosures.) Companies registered with the SEC must also report in a separate section of their annual 10-K report any "Changes in and Disagreements with Accountants on Accounting and Financial Disclosure" as an added measure of transparency and management accountability. *The simple answer provided by Campbell Soup Company for this required disclosure in its 2011 annual report was "None" (see Item 9 on page 754).*

During the years leading up to the SOX legislation, the question of whether accounting firms should be allowed to provide certain nonaudit services to their audit clients prompted considerable controversy. Many viewed the provision of consulting services by a company's independent auditor as constituting a conflict of interest and thus urged an outright ban on such services. Rather than taking such a severe approach, SOX prohibited specific nonaudit services, including financial information systems design and implementation (information technology work), performance of internal auditing, and "expert" services. Beyond these prohibited services, SOX required companies retaining their independent auditor to perform nonaudit services to get preapproval from the audit committee of the board of directors and to adequately disclose the details of any nonaudit services performed by the independent auditor.

In 2004, a rather strict interpretation of Section 404 of SOX was implemented. As a result, all public registrants have since been required to thoroughly document, test, and take responsibility for the effectiveness of their accounting and financial reporting safeguards. A separate "Management's Report on Internal Control over Financial Reporting" must be included with all 10-K filings. Likewise, in addition to expressing an audit opinion on the company's financial statements and related note disclosures, independent auditors are required to express an opinion on the effectiveness of the company's internal control systems. A separate internal controls report may be presented immediately after the report on the financial statements, or both reports may be combined into a single auditors' report. (See page 753 in the appendix for an example of the combined report format.)

In response to the financial crisis of 2007–2008, Congress passed the Wall Street Reform and Consumer Protection Act of 2010 (referred to as the *Dodd–Frank Act*). Although most of the act deals with financial regulation, several Dodd–Frank provisions impose new corporate governance rules not just on Wall Street banks but also on Main Street public corporations. For instance, the "say on pay" mandate requires periodic shareholder advisory votes on executive compensation and golden parachute provisions. Likewise, all board compensation committees must now be comprised solely of independent directors. Moreover, companies are now required to have clawback policies in place to recoup executive compensation in the event of financial reporting restatements (even absent misconduct). Another Dodd–Frank provision requires companies to disclose the reasons that they have chosen to have either the same person or separate people serve as the CEO and chairman of the board. The act also authorizes, but does not require, the SEC to implement rules to permit shareholders to use management's proxy materials for the purpose of nominating their own directors.

With the Dodd–Frank Act , the tenor of federal regulation in corporate governance matters has shifted from a focus on systems and safeguards (such as the internal controls and auditor independence rules created under SOX) to a focus on eliminating or at least greatly reducing any temptations for wrongdoing on the part of board members and senior management. Yet, while many of the Dodd–Frank provisions are aimed squarely at regulating executive compensation, shareholder empowerment represents another shift in focus, with several provisions aimed at enhancing voting rights and access to information. Considering the magnitude of the LIBOR rate-fixing scandal revealed in 2012, it seems likely that the corporate governance provisions enacted under both SOX and Dodd–Frank will get a heavy workout in the federal court system in the years to come.

In addition to adhering to enhanced reporting requirements, many companies have become more active in recent years in communicating their corporate governance policies and related social responsibility matters. Campbell's devotes a section of its website to governance-related issues, clearly demonstrating the company's commitment to a "best-practices" approach to corporate citizenship (see www.campbellsoup .com; then click on *Our Company* and *Governance*). Campbell's 2011 annual report also contains useful corporate governance disclosures (see page 754 in Campbell's 2011 annual report). Similar examples can be found for nearly every large U.S.-based corporation. Yet, despite the increased attention paid to governance and related matters in recent years, a variety of financial reporting problems continue to exist today.

---

1. What does it mean to state that corporate governance issues have become increasingly important in recent years?

What Does It Mean?

Answer on page 412

Financial Reporting Misstatements

Financial reporting misstatements requiring companies to issue revisions of financial statements previously filed with the Securities and Exchange Commission rose significantly between 2001 and 2006, but then rapidly declined between 2007 and 2010. In 2006, a total of 1,795 amended SEC filings for financial restatements were made because of accounting errors, as compared to only 613 such filings in 2001 and 735 in 2010. What's going on?

The full answer to that question is larger than the WorldCom, Inc., Enron, and Arthur Andersen scandals dating back to 2001, although researchers will study and report about these and other incidents for years to come. Suffice it to say that the stock market boom of the late 1990s was fueled by the greed and arrogance of certain CEOs and CFOs, auditors, investors, investment bankers, and others; greed and arrogance led them, in some instances, to engage in fraud and make inappropriate decisions that stretched the financial accounting and reporting processes beyond the limits of general acceptability. Increased regulation, in the form of the Sarbanes–Oxley Act of 2002, forced a rising tide of financial restatements from 2004 to 2006; SOX also led to an improvement in the reliability of financial reporting, which the more recent downward trend in reported misstatements appears to be attributable to. Yet, despite these positive strides witnessed in the post-SOX era, the temptation to "cook the books" will always exist.

Exhibit 10-1

Financial Shenanigans

LO 2

Identify the types of financial reporting misstatements that have occurred in recent years.

Earnings Manipulation Shenanigans

1. Recording revenue too soon.

- Recording revenue before completing any obligations under the contract.
- Recording revenue far in excess of work completed on the contract.
- Recording revenue before the buyer's final acceptance of the product.
- Recording revenue when the buyer's payment remains uncertain or unnecessary.

2. Recording bogus revenue.

- Recording revenue from transactions that lack economic substance.
- Recording revenue from transactions that lack a reasonable arm's-length process.
- Recording revenue on receipts from non-revenue-producing transactions.
- Recording revenue from appropriate transactions, but at inflated amounts.

3. Boosting income using one-time or unsustainable activities.

- Boosting income using one-time events.
- Boosting income through misleading classifications.

4. Shifting current expenses to a later period.

- Improperly capitalizing normal operating expenses.
- Amortizing costs too slowly.
- Failing to write down assets with impaired value.
- Failing to record expenses for uncollectible receivables and devalued investments.

5. Employing other techniques to hide expenses or losses.

- Failing to record an expense from a current transaction.
- Failing to record an expense for a necessary accrual or reversing a past expense.
- Failing to record or reducing expenses by using aggressive accounting assumptions.
- Reducing expenses by releasing bogus reserves from previous charges.

6. Shifting current income to a later period.

- Creating reserves (often in conjunction with an acquisition) and releasing them into income in a later period.
- Improperly accounting for derivatives in order to smooth income.
- Recording current-period sales in a later period.

7. Shifting future expenses to an earlier period.

- Improperly writing off assets in the current period to avoid expenses in a future period.
- Improperly recording charges to establish reserves used to reduce future expenses.

Cash Flow Shenanigans

1. Shifting financing cash inflows to the operating section.

- Recording bogus cash flows from operations from a normal bank borrowing.
- Boosting cash flows from operations by selling receivables before the collection date.
- Inflating cash flows from operations by faking the sale of receivables.

2. Shifting normal operating cash outflows to the investing section.

- Inflating cash flows from operations with boomerang transactions.
- Improperly capitalizing normal operating costs.
- Recording the purchase of inventory as an investing outflow.

(continued)

Exhibit 10-1

3. Inflating operating cash flow using acquisitions or disposals.
- Inheriting operating inflows in a normal business acquisition.
- Acquiring contracts or customers rather than developing them internally.
- Boosting cash flows from operations by creatively structuring the sale of a business.

4. Boosting operating cash flow using unsustainable activities.
- Boosting cash flows from operations by paying vendors more slowly.
- Boosting cash flows from operations by collecting from customers more quickly.
- Boosting cash flows from operations by purchasing less inventory.
- Boosting cash flows from operations with one-time benefits.

Key Metrics Shenanigans
1. Showcasing misleading metrics that overstate performance.
- Highlighting a misleading metric as a surrogate for revenue.
- Highlighting a misleading metric as a surrogate for earnings.
- Highlighting a misleading metric as a surrogate for cash flow.

2. Distorting balance sheet metrics to avoid showing deterioration.
- Distorting accounts receivable metrics to hide revenue problems.
- Distorting inventory metrics to hide profitability problems.
- Distorting financial asset metrics to hide impairment problems.
- Distorting debt metrics to hide liquidity problems.

Source: Howard Schilit and Jeremy Perler, *Financial Shenanigans: How to Detect Accounting Gimmicks and Fraud in Financial Reports,* 3rd ed. (New York: McGraw-Hill, 2010).

Howard Schilit, founder of the Financial Shenanigans Detection Group, LLC, and his coauthor, Jeremy Perler, have identified 13 financial shenanigans.[1] Many of their findings have been supported by Arthur Levitt, former chairman of the SEC, in an address titled "What the Numbers Mean." Typically these behaviors included inappropriate reporting of revenues and expenses and manipulation of liability numbers, but they also included manipulation of cash flow information and other key metrics. The 13 types of manipulative behaviors ("shenanigans") are listed in Exhibit 10-1.

Most of the shenanigans identified by Schilit and Perler are clearly contrary to the generally accepted accounting principles discussed in preceding chapters. Some of the examples they provide relate to managers' judgments concerning whether to include the effect of a particular transaction as a recurring item or as a nonrecurring item. In some cases the amounts involved are subject to managers' estimates of future amounts based on various assumptions. In any event, as explained in earlier chapters, a careful review of the statement of cash flows, the notes to the financial statements, and management's discussion and analysis may help to warn financial statement users about financial difficulties being experienced by the company issuing the statements.

The fundamentals of financial accounting that have been explained in Chapters 2–9 will continue to apply to business transactions for years to come even though some specific changes in accounting and reporting will occur. Efforts by operating and financial executives to have their company's financial statements reflect as favorable a picture as possible of the entity's financial position, results of operations, and cash flows will continue. Therefore, as it has always been, it will continue to be the responsibility of financial statement users to dig into the financial statements, notes,

---

[1] *Financial Shenanigans: How to Detect Accounting Gimmicks and Fraud in Financial Reports,* 3rd ed. (New York: McGraw-Hill, 2010).

and other financial information and to perform financial statement analysis to achieve an understanding of what the numbers mean. The material presented in the balance of this chapter, along with that in Chapter 11, will assist you in this process.

General Organization of Notes to the Financial Statements

LO 3

Explain why the notes are an integral part of the financial statements.

The notes that refer to specific financial statement items generally are presented in the same sequence as the financial statements and in the same sequence that items appear within the individual statements. The financial statement sequence usually is:

1.   Income statement.
2.   Balance sheet.
3.   Statement of cash flows.

Placement of the statement of changes in stockholders' equity usually depends on the complexity of that statement. If paid-in capital has not changed during the year, a statement of changes in retained earnings may be presented following the income statement and may even be combined with it because net income is the principal item affecting retained earnings. If there have been several capital stock transactions during the year, a full statement of changes in stockholders' equity, which includes changes in paid-in capital, retained earnings, and other comprehensive income, would normally be presented separately following the balance sheet, although it sometimes follows the statement of cash flows instead. Some companies present the statement of changes in stockholders' equity as part of the accompanying notes rather than as a separate financial statement.

The notes are an integral part of the financial statements because they contain important disclosures that are not contained in the financial statements themselves. Thus, for the financial statements to be relevant, reliable, and understandable, users must read and interpret the notes to make informed decisions and judgments.

In addition to the notes, sometimes called the *financial review,* annual reports include a narrative section called **management's discussion and analysis (MD&A).** This is a description of the firm's activities for the year, including comments about its financial condition and results of operations. Also included in most annual reports is a comparative summary of key financial data for several years. Both of these components can be quite helpful to users of the annual report.

What Does It Mean?
Answer on page 412

2.   What does it mean when a note at the bottom of the financial statements states, "The accompanying notes are an integral part of these statements"?

Notes to the Financial Statements
Significant Accounting Policies

LO 4

Discuss the kinds of significant accounting policies that are explained in the notes.

As emphasized in earlier chapters, management must make a number of choices among alternative accounting practices that are generally acceptable. Because these choices differ among firms, disclosure of the specific practices being followed by any given firm is necessary for readers to make sense of that firm's financial statements. Users also need information about **significant accounting policies** to make intelligent comparisons of the financial position and results of operations of different firms in the same industry. The following discussion highlights the importance of many of these accounting policy disclosures. The comments in italics refer to the 2011 annual report of Campbell Soup Company in the appendix.

Depreciation method.   The method (straight-line, units-of-production, sum-of-the-years'-digits, or declining-balance) being used for financial reporting purposes and the range of useful lives assumed for broad categories of asset types are usually disclosed. The amount of depreciation expense may also be disclosed in the notes, although it is also reported in the statement of cash flows as an add-back to net income. *Campbell's uses straight-line depreciation for financial reporting purposes (see page 715 in the appendix). How much depreciation and amortization expense did Campbell's report for 2011? (This amount is reported in the statement of cash flows on page 713.)*

Inventory valuation method.   The method (weighted-average, FIFO, or LIFO) being used is disclosed. If different methods are being used for different categories of inventory, the method used for each category is disclosed. When LIFO is used, a comparison of the cumulative difference in the balance sheet inventory valuation under LIFO with what it would have been under FIFO usually is disclosed. *All of Campbell's inventories are "valued at the lower of average cost or market."*

Basis of consolidation.   A brief statement confirms the fact that the consolidated financial statements include the financial data of all subsidiaries—or if not, why not.

Income taxes.   A reconciliation of the statutory income tax rate (35 percent for 2012) with the effective tax rate (indicated by the firm's income tax expense as a percentage of pretax income) is provided. Reasons for this difference include the effects of state taxes, non-U.S. income taxed at different rates, export sales benefits, and other special treatment given certain items for income tax purposes. This disclosure is especially pertinent for firms having a substantial business presence in a foreign country. In the United Kingdom, for example, the normal corporate income tax rate is 24 percent (for 2012). Because of the U.S. tax loss carryover rules, the effective tax rate can also differ from the statutory rate for a firm that has reported a net loss in a recent year. *Campbell's reports its effective tax rate for each of the past three years (see page 735). You can verify these calculations by dividing the "Taxes on earnings" reported on the statements of earnings by the "Earnings before taxes." Try this with the statements of earnings data reported on page 711. For 2011, this calculation should reconcile with the reported 31.3 percent effective tax rate.*

An explanation is also made of the deferred taxes resulting from differences between the fiscal year in which an expense (or revenue) is reported for book purposes and the fiscal year in which it is reported for tax purposes. As already discussed, the principal factor in deferred taxes for most firms is the use of straight-line depreciation for book purposes and accelerated depreciation for tax purposes. However, many firms also report significant deferred tax amounts for a variety of other items (as discussed in Chapter 7). *Campbell's reports a detailed table of deferred income tax assets and liabilities for the past two years (see page 736).*

Employee benefits.   The cost of employee benefit plans included as an expense in the income statement will be disclosed. The significant actuarial assumptions made with respect to funding pension plans may be discussed, and certain estimated future pension liabilities may be disclosed. The key to understanding the funded status of a defined benefit pension plan is to compare the *projected benefit obligation* (the present value of expected future payments to retirees) to the *fair value of plan assets* that are currently held in the pension fund.

An additional schedule is provided to show the components of **net pension expense** for each of the past three years if this amount is material. Several elements of pension expense will be reported, including the service cost, interest cost of the projected benefit obligation, and the expected return on plan assets. The latter item is treated as a reduction of pension expense because future funding requirements will decrease as income is earned on invested assets. Service costs represent the actuarially determined cost to provide future pension benefits based on employees' earnings and service in the current and prior years. Although the accounting for pension plans is complex, these key items are easy to identify in the schedules provided by most firms. *Campbell's provides a detailed discussion of its pension and postretirement benefit plans, including schedules that reconcile the changes during 2011 and 2010 in the benefit obligation and the fair value of plan assets. Details concerning the "net periodic benefit cost" (pension expense) are also provided (see page 728).*

Goodwill and other acquisition-related intangibles. If the balance sheet contains the intangible asset goodwill, the method of recognizing its initial cost (arising from business acquisitions) will be described. Further details will be provided concerning reductions in the cost of goodwill due to impairment losses and other similar adjustments. The cost of acquisition-related intangibles (other than goodwill) and the amortization methods used for these assets will also be disclosed. As discussed in Chapter 6, the accounting for goodwill is a sticky problem for accountants and is likely to generate further debate for many years to come. *Campbell's discloses its accounting policies concerning goodwill on page 715 and provides further discussion of goodwill and intangible assets on pages 719–720.*

Earnings per share of common stock. An explanation of the calculation will be provided, perhaps including details of the calculation of the weighted-average number of shares outstanding and the adjustments to net income for preferred stock dividends. The potential dilution of the earnings per share (EPS) figure resulting from convertible bonds or convertible preferred stock if conversions had taken place during the year, and the potential dilution from stock option plans, will also be explained. *Campbell's provides a schedule detailing its EPS calculation process in a note on page 727.*

Stock option and stock purchase plans. Many firms have a **stock option plan** under which directors, officers, and key employees are given an option to buy a certain number of shares of stock *at some time in the future* but at a price equal to the market value of the stock when the option is granted. The stock option presumably provides an incentive to increase the profitability of the firm so that the stock price will rise.

Stock options are accounted for under the *fair value* method, which requires the use of an option-pricing model (usually the Black-Scholes model) for estimation purposes. The Black-Scholes model calculates the present value of the stock option at the grant date, based upon specific information about the terms of the option and assumptions about future stock price performance. Once the fair value of the stock options has been determined, this amount is amortized to expense over the service periods presumed to apply to the group of executives and other employees who received the options.

During 2006 it was determined that some publicly owned corporations had engaged in a practice of backdating stock option grants. For example, options granted on May 20 were dated as of March 10, when the market price of the stock was lower. This resulted in an immediate advantage to the grantee as long as the market price did not fall before the option was exercised because the difference between the respective market prices resulted in additional gain to the grantee. In addition, because the market price on the false grant date was lower than the market price on the actual grant date, the compensation expense recognized by the corporation and the amount received from the option holder were both less than they should have been. More than 100 companies were involved in this scandal, and several chief executive officers and chief financial officers lost their jobs. The companies involved were required to restate previously reported earnings to reflect the additional compensation expense related to these backdating practices. In addition, in May 2007 the SEC announced that several of the companies involved had been fined. While not a scandal on the scope of the Enron Corporation or WorldCom, Inc., affairs, let alone the LIBOR rate-fixing debacle that came to light in 2012, stock option backdating represents another breakdown in the ethical behavior of some managers.

When stock options are exercised, the owner has an immediate profit that is in effect additional compensation for a job well done. The effect on the issuer's financial statements is the same as that of an ordinary common stock issuance (the cash, common stock, and additional paid-in capital accounts will each be increased) except that the issue price will be less than the prevailing market price of the stock at the date of exercise.

Under a *stock purchase plan,* employees can purchase shares of their company's common stock at a slight discount from market value. The objective is to permit the employees to become part owners of the firm and thus to have more of an owner's attitude about their jobs and the company. Stock purchase plans are also accounted for under the fair value method. *Campbell's has a long-term incentive plan that authorizes the issuance of shares of common stock to satisfy awards of stock options, stock appreciation rights, and total shareowner return (TSR) performance restricted stock/units. Details of the company's share-based compensation are discussed on pages 743–746.*

From the employees' point of view, stock option and stock purchase plans are usually good fringe benefits. From the investors' point of view, the shares that are issuable under these plans represent potential dilution of equity. Thus, the nature of these plans is described, and the potential dilution is disclosed.

Details of Other Financial Statement Amounts

Many firms will include in the notes to the financial statements the details of amounts that are reported as a single item in the financial statements. For example, details may be provided for the amount of research and development expenses included in a broader operating expense category on the income statement, the "other income" category of the income statement, or the cost and accumulated depreciation of plant and equipment that are reported in total on the balance sheet. Long-term debt, frequently reported as a single amount on the balance sheet, is usually made up of several obligations. A descriptive listing of the obligations, including a schedule of the principal payments required for each of the next five years, is a mandatory reporting requirement if the amounts involved are material. The extent of such detail to be reported is decided by the financial officers of the firm and is generally based on their judgment of the benefit of such detail to the broad user audience that will receive the financial statements. In some cases, disclosure requirements of the Securities and Exchange Commission and the desire to conform the stockholders' report with the Form 10-K report required to be filed with the SEC result in these details (see Business in Practice—Reporting to the Securities and Exchange Commission on page 403).

LO 5
Describe the nature and content of various note disclosures.

Other Disclosures

Accounting changes.   An **accounting change** is a change in the application of an accounting principle that has a material effect on the comparability of the current period financial statements with those of prior periods. The effects of recently adopted accounting changes must be disclosed. For example, if a firm changes its inventory cost flow assumption from FIFO to LIFO, this fact and the dollar effects of the change on both the income statement and balance sheet must be disclosed. Likewise, a change in depreciation methods, a change in the method of accounting for pension costs, or any other change having a significant effect on the financial statements must be disclosed.

Sometimes accounting changes are the result of recent FASB codification updates. The most common changes reported in the AICPA survey of the year 2010 annual reports of 500 corporations were of this variety and involved business combinations, noncontrolling interests, and fair value measurements.[2]

Business combinations.   If the firm has been involved in a **business combination** (a merger, acquisition, or disposition), the transaction(s) involved will be described and the effect on the financial statements will be explained. Recall that in the case of the disposition of part of the business, the income statement will segregate the impact of discontinued operations on the current year's results.

Mergers and acquisitions are accounted for using the **acquisition method.** Under the acquisition method, the net assets acquired are recorded by the acquiring company at their *fair value* at the date of acquisition. Any amount paid for the acquired net assets (or company) in excess of the fair value of the net assets is recorded as goodwill—an intangible asset that is evaluated annually for possible impairment losses but is *not* amortized, as discussed in Chapter 6.

Contingencies and commitments.   It is not unusual for a firm to be involved in litigation, the results of which are not known when the financial statements are prepared. If the firm is denying liability in a lawsuit in which it is a defendant, it is appropriate to disclose the fact of the lawsuit to readers of the financial statements. Of course the concept of matching revenue and expense requires the recognition of any anticipated cost of verdicts that the company expects to have to pay. An expense or a loss and a related liability should be reported in the period affected. Even if the lawsuit is one that management and legal counsel believe will not result in any liability to the company, the fact of the potential loss and liability should be disclosed. The nature of the legal action, the potential damages, and a statement to the effect that the claims against the company are not likely to be sustained are included in the notes. *Campbell's very brief "Contingencies" note does not describe any particular lawsuits pending against the company, but it does acknowledge that the company is party to legal proceedings and claims arising out of the ordinary course of business. In management's opinion, these proceedings and claims "will not have a material adverse effect" on the company's financial statements (see page 746).*

In some cases a firm or one of its subsidiaries may act as a guarantor of the indebtedness of another entity. In such cases it is appropriate for the amount of the potential liability and a brief description of the circumstances to be disclosed in the notes. Under certain circumstances a liability may actually need to be recorded for such guarantees. It was the lack of this type of disclosure by Enron Corporation that caused a great

---

[2]AICPA, *Accounting Trends and Techniques* (New York, 2011), Table 1–6.

Reporting to the Securities and Exchange Commission

The Securities and Exchange Commission (SEC) was created by the Securities and Exchange Act of 1934 to administer the provisions of that act and the Securities Act of 1933. Subsequently Congress assigned to the SEC the authority and responsibility for administering other securities laws. Securities issued by corporations (principally stocks and bonds) that are offered for sale to more than a very few investors must be registered with the SEC. The basic objective of this registration is to provide to potential investors a full and fair disclosure of the securities being issued, the issuer's business activities and financial position, and an explanation of the use to be made of the proceeds of the security issue. Registration does not result in a "seal of approval" or a guarantee against loss. It is up to investors to decide whether their objectives are likely to be achieved. Registration is required for additional issues of previously unregistered securities (for example, if the corporation wants to raise capital by selling additional shares of stock) and for issues of newly created securities (for example, bonds that will be offered to the public). A **prospectus** summarizing the complete registration statement must be provided to investors prior to, or concurrently with, their purchase of the security. A prospectus is provided by the company or the broker through whom the securities are being sold.

Registered securities can be traded publicly on a stock exchange or in the over-the-counter market. Firms that issue these securities are required to file an annual report with the SEC. This report is referred to as *Form 10-K.* The requirements of Form 10-K have had a significant impact on the scope of material included in the annual report to stockholders. Most companies include in their annual report to stockholders all of the financial statement information required in the Form 10-K, and some companies even send a copy of the Form 10-K, along with a separate brochure describing the company and its products/services, to their shareholders as the annual report.

Form 10-K requires some information not usually found in the financial statements, including data about executive compensation and ownership of voting stock by directors and officers. This information is also included in the *proxy statement* sent to stockholders along with the notice of the *annual general meeting (AGM)* and a description of the items expected to be acted upon by the stockholders at that meeting. Stockholders who do not expect to attend the AGM are invited to return a **proxy.** Although the proxy gives another person (usually a director of the corporation) the right to vote the stockholder's shares, the owner can indicate her or his preference for how the shares are to be voted on the indicated issues.

The registration statement, prospectus, Form 10-K, and proxy statement are public documents, and copies can be obtained from the corporation or from the SEC. Try the website of a corporation in which you are interested, or access the Electronic Data Gathering, Analysis, and Retrieval (EDGAR) system on the SEC's website at www.sec.gov.edgar.shtml.

Business in
Practice

LO 6
Explain the role of the Securities and Exchange Commission and some of its reporting requirements.

deal of criticism of the company's management and auditors after Enron's bankruptcy. *Campbell's guarantees certain bank loans made to Pepperidge Farm independent sales distributors that could potentially obligate the company for up to $162 million (see page 746).*

If the firm has made commitments to purchase a significant amount of plant and equipment or has committed to pay significant amounts of rent on leased property for several years into the future, these commitments will be disclosed. This is done because the commitment is like a liability but is not recorded on the balance sheet because the actual purchase transaction has not yet occurred. *Campbell's provides a schedule of rental payments that will be owed over the next several years under operating lease agreements for warehouse and office facilities and retail store space (see page 746).*

A firm may have quite a few other kinds of **contingencies** and **commitments;** most will have an adverse effect on the financial position of the firm and its results of operations if they materialize. The purpose of disclosing these items is to provide full disclosure to the user of the financial statements.

Events subsequent to the balance sheet date.   If, subsequent to the balance sheet date, a significant event occurs that has a material impact on the balance sheet or income statement, it is appropriate to provide an explanation of the probable impact of the subsequent event on future financial statements. Examples of such significant events include the issuance of a large amount of long-term debt, the restructuring of long-term debt, the issuance of a large amount of capital stock, the sale of a significant part of the company's assets, and the agreement to enter into a business combination.

Impact of inflation.   It has been emphasized that the financial statements do not reflect the impact of inflation. The original cost concept and the objectivity principle result in assets being recorded at their historical cost to the entity, based on current dollars at the time the transactions are initially recorded. The FASB encourages, but does not require, companies to provide supplementary information on the effects of changing prices (inflation) in the notes to the financial statements; in practice, very few companies voluntarily do so. However, the SEC's Regulation S-K requires registrants to "discuss" the effects of inflation and other changes in prices in the Management's Discussion and Analysis (MD&A) section of the 10-K if such effects are considered material; in practice, most companies discuss inflation briefly in their MD&A but do not provide specific financial data. These lax reporting requirements with respect to the effects of inflation are largely due to the fact that inflation has not been an issue of grave importance in the United States for several decades. If the U.S. economy experiences high rates of inflation in the future, the present SEC disclosure requirements are likely to be reexamined and enhanced.

Segment information.   Most large corporations operate in several lines of business and in several international geographic areas. In addition, some firms have major customers (frequently other large corporations or the U.S. government) that account for a significant part of the total business. A **business segment** is a group of the firm's business activities that has a common denominator. The components of each business segment are identified and defined by management. Segments may reflect the company's organizational structure, manufacturing processes, product line groups, or industries served. The required disclosure of segment, geographic, and major customer information is designed to permit the financial statement user to make judgments about the impact on the firm of factors that might influence specific lines of business, geographic areas, or specific major customers.

As you have learned, a company presents only one set of financial statements, regardless of how many industries or countries it serves. Segment data disaggregate one company into smaller components so that readers can have more useful information for decision making. Data shown for each segment include sales to unaffiliated customers, operating profit, capital expenditures, depreciation and amortization expense, and identifiable assets. Note that from these data it is possible to make a DuPont model return-on-investment calculation and to prepare for each segment a simple statement of cash flows showing cash flows from operating activities (net income plus depreciation expense) minus cash used for investing activities (capital expenditures). This simple statement of cash flows omits financing activities (such as long-term debt and dividend transactions), but it does highlight the principal cash flows related to each segment. Although these segment measures cannot be combined to equal the total company's ROI or cash flows (because assets and expenses applicable to the corporation as a whole have not been arbitrarily allocated to segments), segment trends over time can be determined. *Campbell's has 10 operating segments based on product type and geographic location, but it has aggregated the operating segments into five reportable business segments, based on a number of factors as described on page 720 in the appendix. (See pages 721–722 for the reported business segment amounts).*

Sales to unaffiliated customers, operating profits, and identifiable assets are also reported by geographic areas in which the firm operates. For example, the areas in the geographic breakdown used by *Campbell's* are the United States, Europe, Australia/Asia Pacific, and Other Countries. ROI calculations can also be made based on geographic areas, but cash flow information cannot be approximated because the required geographic disclosures do not include capital expenditures or depreciation and amortization expense.

If a firm has a major customer that accounts for more than 10 percent of its consolidated sales, it is appropriate to disclose this fact to the financial statement user so that a judgment can be made about the influence of this customer on the firm's continued profitability. However, the name of the major customer is not required to be disclosed. *Campbell's reports, "The company's largest customer, Wal-Mart Stores, Inc., and its affiliates, accounted for approximately 17% of consolidated net sales in 2011 and 18% in 2010 and 2009."*

Management's Statement of Responsibility

Many firms include in the notes **management's statement of responsibility,** which explains that the responsibility for the financial statements lies with the management of the firm, not the external auditor and certified public accountants who express an opinion about the fairness with which the financial statements present the financial condition and results of operations of the company. The statement of responsibility usually refers to the internal audit function, the audit committee of the board of directors, the company's code of conduct, and other policies and procedures designed to ensure that the company operates at a high level of ethical conduct. In addition to these voluntary disclosures, SOX requires management to include in its annual report an assessment of the effectiveness of the company's internal control over financial reporting.

LO 7
Explain why a statement of management's responsibility is included with the notes.

Management's Discussion and Analysis (MD&A)

For many years the Securities and Exchange Commission has required companies that must file a Form 10-K annual report with the commission to include in the report a section entitled "Management's Discussion and Analysis of Financial Condition and Results of Operations" (referred to as *MD&A*). MD&A is being included in more and more annual reports to stockholders, and most publicly traded companies now provide links to downloadable versions of their full 10-K reports on their websites. MD&A is designed to enhance public disclosure of information about the corporation and is a part of the annual report that should be read by current and potential investors.

Of particular interest to investors and potential investors are disclosures often provided in MD&A concerning non-GAAP financial measures and key performance indicators that are used to assess the company's financial and operating results. The reporting entity may use several non-GAAP financial measures, not to replace the presentation of financial results in accordance with U.S. generally accepted accounting principles but to supplement other metrics used by management to internally evaluate

LO 8
Describe the significance of management's discussion and analysis of the firm's financial condition and results of operations.

its businesses and to facilitate the comparison of past and present operations. Any reported non-GAAP measures must be reconciled with the most directly comparable GAAP measures in a table included with the disclosures.

In the Campbell Soup Company report in the appendix, the pages devoted to MD&A have been omitted from those selected for inclusion in this text (see pages 13–33 in the full version of Campbell's 2011 annual report, which can be downloaded from the company's website).

What Does It Mean?

Answer on page 412

3. What does it mean to state that management's discussion and analysis are essential to understanding the firm's activities and financial statements?

LO 9

Identify what is included in the five-year (or longer) summary of financial data.

Five-Year (or Longer) Summary of Financial Data

Most corporate annual reports will present a summary of financial data for at least the five most recent years. Many firms report these data for longer periods, and at least one firm reports these data for every year since it was organized. Included in the summary are key income statement data or even the entire income statement in condensed form. In addition to amounts, significant ratios such as earnings as a percentage of sales, average assets, and average stockholders' equity may also be included. Earnings and dividends per share, the average number of shares outstanding each year, and other operating statistics may be reported. Year-end data from the balance sheet such as working capital; property, plant, and equipment (net of accumulated depreciation); long-term debt; and stockholders' equity usually are reported. Book value per share of common stock (explained in Chapter 11) and the year-end market price of common stock frequently are reported. When stock dividends or stock splits have occurred, the per share data of prior years are adjusted retroactively so that the per share data are comparable.

As an illustration of the adjustment of per share data for stock dividends or stock splits, assume that Cruisers, Inc., reported basic earnings per share and cash dividends per share of $4.50 and $2.00, respectively, for fiscal 2012. Assume also that in 2013 the firm had a 2-for-1 stock split. In the annual report for 2013, earnings and dividends for 2012 should reflect the fact that because of the split there are now twice as many shares of common stock outstanding as there were when 2012 amounts were first reported. Therefore, in the 2013 annual report, 2012 basic earnings per share and dividends per share will be reported at $2.25 and $1.00, respectively. Assume further that in 2014, Cruisers had a 10 percent stock dividend that resulted in 110 shares outstanding for every 100 shares that were outstanding before the stock dividend. The 2014 annual report will report 2012 basic earnings per share and dividends per share as $2.05 ($2.25/1.10) and $0.91 ($1.00/1.10), respectively. Diluted earnings per share data (if required to be reported) would also be adjusted.

The **five-year (or longer) summary** is not included in the scope of the independent auditors' work, nor does their opinion relate to the summary. Likewise, the summary is not a part of the notes to the financial statements; it is a supplementary disclosure that may appear before or after the financial statements and notes. Campbell's annual report includes a five-year financial summary on page 709 in the appendix.

4. What does it mean to review the trends in the five-year (or longer) summary of financial data?

What Does It Mean?
Answer on page 413

Independent Auditors' Report

The independent auditors' report is a brief (usually four paragraphs), often easily overlooked report that relates to the financial statements and the accompanying explanatory notes. The SEC requires an audit of the financial statements of a publicly owned company. Many privately owned firms will have an audit of their financial statements to support their bank loan negotiations.

The independent auditors' report (officially referred to as the "Report of Independent Registered Public Accounting Firm") for The Coca-Cola Company for the period ended December 31, 2011, is reproduced in Exhibit 10-2. This report format,

LO 10
Discuss the meaning and content of the independent auditors' report.

Exhibit 10-2
Report of Independent Registered Public Accounting Firm

Board of Directors and Shareowners

The Coca-Cola Company

We have audited the accompanying consolidated balance sheets of The Coca-Cola Company and subsidiaries as of December 31, 2011 and 2010, and the related consolidated statements of income, shareowners' equity, and cash flows for each of the three years in the period ended December 31, 2011. These financial statements are the responsibility of the Company's management. Our responsibility is to express an opinion on these financial statements based on our audits.

We conducted our audits in accordance with the standards of the Public Company Accounting Oversight Board (United States). Those standards require that we plan and perform the audit to obtain reasonable assurance about whether the financial statements are free of material misstatement. An audit includes examining, on a test basis, evidence supporting the amounts and disclosures in the financial statements. An audit also includes assessing the accounting principles used and significant estimates made by management, as well as evaluating the overall financial statement presentation. We believe that our audits provide a reasonable basis for our opinion.

In our opinion, the financial statements referred to above present fairly, in all material respects, the consolidated financial position of The Coca-Cola Company and subsidiaries at December 31, 2011 and 2010, and the consolidated results of their operations and their cash flows for each of the three years in the period ended December 31, 2011, in conformity with U.S. generally accepted accounting principles.

We also have audited, in accordance with the standards of the Public Company Accounting Oversight Board (United States), The Coca-Cola Company and subsidiaries' internal control over financial reporting as of December 31, 2011, based on criteria established in Internal Control—Integrated Framework issued by the Committee of Sponsoring Organizations of the Treadway Commission and our report dated February 23, 2012, expressed an unqualified opinion thereon.

Ernst & Young, LLP

Atlanta, Georgia
February 23, 2012

which has been standardized by the Auditing Standards Board of the AICPA (as amended by the Public Company Accounting Oversight Board), is almost universal. Note that Coca-Cola received an *unqualified,* or "clean," audit opinion, meaning that its financial statements were "present[ed] fairly, in all material respects . . . in conformity with U.S. generally accepted accounting principles." This is by far the most commonly presented opinion in annual reports because most firms would prefer to make the necessary "auditor-suggested adjustments" to financial statement amounts and note disclosures than to receive a *qualified* audit opinion.

The report usually is addressed to the board of directors and stockholders of the corporation. The first paragraph, or *introductory paragraph,* identifies the financial statements that were audited and briefly describes the responsibilities of both management and the auditors with respect to the financial statements. It is important to note here that management is responsible for the financial statements; the auditors' task is to express an opinion about them.

The second paragraph is the *scope paragraph,* and it describes the nature and extent of the auditors' work. Note that their concern is with obtaining reasonable assurance about whether the financial statements are free of material misstatements and that their work involves tests. Auditors give no guarantee that the financial statements are free from fraudulent transactions or from the effects of errors. Remember that the accuracy of the financial statements is the responsibility of management, not of the auditors. However, the standards of the PCAOB do require extensive audit procedures as a means of obtaining reasonable assurance that the financial statements are free of material misstatements.

The third paragraph is the *opinion paragraph,* and in that sense it is the most important. The benchmark for fair presentation is U.S. generally accepted accounting principles. Again, note the reference to materiality. If during the audit the auditor determines that the financial statements taken as a whole do not "present fairly," the auditor will require a change in the presentation or withdraw from the audit. The latter action is very rare.

The fourth paragraph, now required by the PCAOB, refers to the audit of the effectiveness of the company's internal control over financial reporting and to the nature of the opinion (unqualified, qualified, or adverse) expressed thereon. An internal control audit is now conducted in conjunction with the audit of financial statements, and an internal control audit opinion is normally presented on a separate page immediately following the financial statements audit opinion.[3] An alternative presentation approach is to combine the financial statements audit opinion and the internal controls audit opinion into a single auditors' report. This was the approach taken by Campbell Soup Company's auditors (see page 753 in the appendix).

The name of the auditing firm, sometimes presented as a facsimile signature, and the date of the report are shown. The date of the report is the date the audit work was completed, and a required audit procedure is to review transactions subsequent to the balance sheet date up to the date of the report. As discussed earlier in this chapter, unusual transactions that occur during this period must be disclosed in the financial statements or in the notes.

---

[3]Public Company Accounting Oversight Board (PCAOB), *Auditing Standard No. 2,* "An Audit of Internal Control over Financial Reporting Performed in Conjunction with an Audit of Financial Statements," March 9, 2004. [Effective pursuant to SEC Release No. 34-49884; File No. PCAOB-2004-03, June 17, 2004.]

Occasionally the auditors' report will include additional language and/or an explanatory paragraph that describes a situation that does not affect fair presentation but that should be disclosed to keep the financial statements from being misleading. Examples of circumstances requiring departures from the standard auditors' report include the following:

1. Basing the opinion in part on the work of another auditor.
2. Uncertainties about the outcome of a significant event that would have affected the presentation of the financial statements if the outcome could have been estimated.
3. Substantial doubt about the entity's ability to continue as a going concern.
4. A material change from a prior accounting period in the application of an accounting principle.

The auditor can issue a qualified opinion if the scope of the audit was restricted and essential audit work could not be performed or if there is a material departure from generally accepted accounting principles that affects only part of the financial statements. The reason for the qualification is explained in the report, and the opinion about fair presentation is restricted to the unaffected parts of the financial statements. Qualified opinions rarely occur in practice.

It is appropriate for the financial statement reader to review the independent auditors' report and determine the effect of any departure from the standard report.

---

5. What does it mean to say that the auditors have given a clean opinion about the financial statements?

What Does It Mean?
Answer on page 413

Financial Statement Compilations

Accounting firms also perform services for client organizations whose debt and equity securities are not publicly traded (and whose financial statements are not required to be audited). Many small businesses use an outside accounting firm to prepare the necessary tax returns and to assemble financial information into conventional financial statements. The accounting firm may prepare financial statements to submit to banks and other major suppliers for purposes of obtaining commercial credit. Because the accounting firm is not engaged in an audit or review, it is necessary that a report be issued that clearly communicates to the user that the accounting firm is not providing any form of assurance about the fairness of the financial statements. Such a report, called a *compilation report,* is shown in Exhibit 10-3.

The user of the financial statements should be aware that the compilation means exactly what it says. If the firm's need for capital is great and it borrows substantial amounts from its bank, it is not uncommon for the bank to reject a compilation and insist on financial statements that have been audited by an independent accountant. Having an audit will cause the firm's accounting costs to rise significantly.

| **Exhibit 10-3** | The Board of Directors and Shareholders, |
| Compilation Report | Cruisers, Inc.: |

We have compiled the accompanying balance sheet of Cruisers, Inc., as of December 31, 2013, and the related statements of income, retained earnings, and cash flows for the year then ended. We have not audited or reviewed the accompanying financial statements and, accordingly, do not express an opinion or provide any assurance about whether the financial statements are in accordance with accounting principles generally accepted in the United States of America.

Management is responsible for the preparation and fair presentation of the financial statements in accordance with accounting principles generally accepted in the United States of America and for designing, implementing, and maintaining internal control relevant to the preparation and fair presentation of the financial statements.

Our responsibility is to conduct the compilation in accordance with Statements on Standards for Accounting and Review Services issued by the American Institute of Certified Public Accountants. The objective of a compilation is to assist management in presenting financial information in the form of financial statements without undertaking to obtain or provide any assurance that there are no material modifications that should be made to the financial statements.

Management has elected to omit substantially all of the disclosures required by accounting principles generally accepted in the United States of America. If the omitted disclosures were included in the financial statements, they might influence the user's conclusions about Cruisers, Inc.'s financial position, results of operations, and cash flows. Accordingly, the financial statements are not designed for those who are not informed about such matters.

[Accounting firm's signature, address, and date]

Summary

Corporate governance issues continue to command increased attention of legislators, regulators, investors, and the senior management teams of publicly traded companies. The Sarbanes–Oxley Act (SOX) of 2002 and the creation of the Public Company Accounting Oversight Board (PCAOB) have led to significant improvements in the development of a workable corporate financial reporting model. Further refinements to the reporting requirements now in place for U.S.-based companies are expected in the near future.

Notes to the financial statements are an integral part of the statements and result from the application of the full disclosure concept discussed in Chapter 2. The notes disclose details of amounts summarized for financial statement presentation, explain which permissible alternative accounting practices have been used by the entity, and provide detailed disclosure of information needed for a full understanding of the financial statements.

Accounting policies disclosed include the depreciation method, inventory cost flow assumption, and basis of consolidation. Accounting for the entity's income taxes, employee benefits, and amortization of intangible assets is described. Details of the calculation of earnings per share of common stock are sometimes provided. There is a discussion of employee stock option and stock purchase plans. The materiality concept is applied to the extent of each of these disclosures.

If there have been changes in the accounting for a material item, the consistency concept requires disclosure of the effect of the change on the financial statements. Sometimes accounting or reporting changes are required as a result of recent FASB codification updates.

There is a full discussion of any business combinations in which the entity has been involved.

Significant contingencies and commitments, such as litigation or loan guarantees, as well as significant events that have occurred since the balance sheet date, are described. This is a specific application of the full disclosure concept.

The impact of inflation on the historical cost amounts used in the financial statements may be reported; although this information is not currently required to be shown in the notes to the financial statements, most companies are required to discuss the impact of inflation in their MD&A.

Segment information summarizes some financial information for the principal activity areas of the firm. The intent of this disclosure is to permit judgment about the significance to the entity's overall results of its activities in certain business segments and geographic areas.

The financial statements are the responsibility of management, not the auditors, and management's statement of responsibility acknowledges this. This acknowledgment usually includes a reference to the system of internal control.

Management's discussion and analysis (MD&A) of the firm's financial condition and results of operations provides an important and useful summary of the firm's activities.

Although not usually a part of the notes to the financial statements, most annual reports include a summary of key financial data for a period of several years. This summary permits financial statement users to make trend evaluations easily.

The independent auditors' report includes their opinion about the fair presentation of the financial statements in accordance with U.S. generally accepted accounting principles and calls attention to special situations. Auditors do not guarantee that the company will be profitable, nor do they give assurance that the financial statements are absolutely accurate.

The Securities and Exchange Commission is responsible for administering federal securities laws. One of its principal concerns is that investors have full disclosure about securities and the companies that issue them. The reporting requirements of the SEC have led to many of the disclosures contained in corporate annual reports.

Refer to the notes to the consolidated financial statements in the Campbell Soup Company annual report in the appendix and to the comparable parts of other annual reports that you may have. Observe the organization of this part of the financial statements and the comprehensive explanation of the material discussed. Read management's discussion and analysis of the firm's financial condition and results of operations. Find the summary of key financial data for several years and evaluate the trends disclosed for sales, profits, total stockholders' equity, and other items reported in the summary. The next chapter will describe and illustrate some of the ways of analyzing financial statement data to support the informed judgments and decisions made by users of financial statements.

Key Terms and Concepts

accounting change (p. 402)   A change in the application of an accounting principle.

acquisition method (p. 402)   The method of accounting for the purchase of another company that records as the cost of the investment the fair value of the cash and/or securities paid, less the liabilities assumed in the transaction.

business combination (p. 402)   A merger between two or more firms, or the purchase of one firm by another.

business segment (p. 404)   A group of the firm's similar business activities; most large firms have several segments.

commitment (p. 404)   A transaction that has been contractually agreed to but that has not yet occurred and is not reflected in the financial statements.

contingency (p. 404)   An event that has an uncertain but potentially significant effect on the financial statements.

corporate governance (p. 392)   The strategies, behaviors, and structures that support the fulfillment by the board of directors and management of an entity's citizenship responsibilities and the achievement of its economic performance.

financial review (p. 392)   Another name for the notes to the financial statements.

five-year (or longer) summary (p. 406)   A summary of key financial data included in an organization's annual report; it is not a financial statement included in the scope of the independent auditors' report.

management's discussion and analysis (MD&A) (p. 398)   A narrative description of the firm's activities for the year, including comments about its financial condition and results of operations.

management's statement of responsibility (p. 405)   A discussion included in the notes to the financial statements describing management's responsibility for the financial statements.

net pension expense (p. 400)   The estimated annual cost of providing pension-related benefits to current and former employees based on certain actuarial assumptions. Normally reported in a detailed schedule in the notes to the financial statements.

notes to the financial statements (p. 392)   An integral part of the financial statements that contains explanations of accounting policies and descriptions of financial statement details.

prospectus (p. 403)   A summary of the characteristics of a security being offered for sale, including a description of the business and financial position of the firm selling the security.

proxy (p. 403)   An authorization given by a stockholder to another person to vote the shares owned by the stockholder.

significant accounting policies (p. 399)   A brief summary or description of the specific accounting practices followed by the entity.

stock option plan (p. 400)   A plan for compensating directors, officers, and key employees by providing an option to purchase a company's stock at a future date at the market price of the stock when the option is issued (granted).

ANSWERS TO What Does It Mean?

1. It means that as a result of the Sarbanes–Oxley Act (SOX) of 2002, the creation of the Public Company Accounting Oversight Board (PCAOB), and the additional requirements imposed by the Dodd–Frank Act of 2010, corporate governance–related issues have become more highly regulated and controlled. These developments have resulted in an improved level of financial disclosure and transparency in annual reports, improved systems of internal control, more effective monitoring of executive compensation arrangements, and enhanced shareholder rights.

2. It means that to understand the financial statements it is necessary to review the related notes to learn about the accounting policies that were followed, details of summary amounts reported in the financial statements, and unusual or significant transactions that affected the financial statements.

3. It means that this part of the annual report contains information that adds substance to the amounts reported in the financial statements.

4. It means that a picture of the firm's recent financial history can be readily obtained by reviewing these data and using them in various calculations (such as ROI and ROE) if those results are not included in the summary.

5. It means that in the opinion of an independent third party, the financial statements (of a public company) present fairly in all material respects, in accordance with the standards of the Public Company Accounting Oversight Board (United States), the financial position, results of operations, and cash flows of the entity for the period. It does not mean that there have not been any fraudulent transactions, that the company has been given an absolute "clean bill of health," or that investors are guaranteed that they will not suffer losses from investing in the company's securities.

Self-Study Material

Visit the text website at www.mhhe.com/marshall10e to take an online self-study quiz for this chapter.

Matching Following are a number of the key terms and concepts introduced in the chapter, along with a list of corresponding definitions. Match the appropriate letter for the key term or concept to each definition provided (items 1–8). Note that not all key terms and concepts will be used. Answers are provided at the end of this chapter.

a. Notes to financial statements
b. Five-year summary
c. Significant accounting policies
d. Stock option plan
e. Accounting change
f. Business combination
g. Proxy
h. Prospectus
i. Acquisition method
j. Corporate governance
k. Contingencies and commitments
l. Business segment
m. Management's statement of responsibility

_____ 1. A plan for compensating directors, officers, and key employees by providing the option of purchasing a company's stock at a future date at the market price of the stock when the option is issued.

_____ 2. A method of accounting for the purchase of another company that records as the cost of the investment the value of the cash and/or securities paid, less the liabilities assumed in the transaction.

_____ 3. A group of the firm's similar business activities.

_____ 4. An integral part of the financial statements that contains explanations of accounting policies and descriptions of financial statement details.

_____ 5. The strategies, behaviors, and structures that support the fulfillment by the board of directors and management of an entity's citizenship responsibilities and the achievement of its economic performance.

_____ **6.** A switch between two alternative generally accepted accounting principles for recording certain transactions (switching from FIFO to LIFO, for example).

_____ **7.** An authorization given by a stockholder to another person to vote the shares owned by the stockholder.

_____ **8.** A summary of the characteristics of a security being offered for sale, including a description of the business and financial position of the firm selling the security.

_____

Multiple Choice For each of the following questions, circle the best response. Answers are provided at the end of this chapter.

1. The notes to the financial statements contained in the annual report include descriptions of all of the following *except*

   a. accounting changes.

   b. employee productivity statistics.

   c. events subsequent to the balance sheet date.

   d. contingencies and commitments.

   e. segment information.

2. Required segment information disclosures do *not* include data concerning

   a. major customers that account for more than 10% of the company's consolidated sales.

   b. sales made to subsidiaries by each segment.

   c. identifiable assets of each segment.

   d. operating profits of each segment.

   e. capital expenditures of each segment.

3. Contingencies and commitments are disclosed as notes to the financial statements rather than being directly included in the financial statements because

   a. the obligation to make payments has not yet materialized.

   b. litigation losses and purchase commitments do not have to be paid within a year.

   c. reporting additional expenses and liabilities would have a negative effect on the income statement and balance sheet.

   d. investors prefer to see the details in the notes rather than in the financial statements.

   e. these items relate only to specific segments of the firm's operations.

4. "Significant accounting policy" disclosures normally provide detailed information in relation to all of the following *except*

   a. income taxes.

   b. employee benefits.

   c. stock option plans.

   d. depreciation methods.

   e. sales returns and allowances.

5. Earnings per share calculations are *not* adjusted to account for the

   a. past service cost element of pension expense.

   b. weighted-average number of shares outstanding.

    c. preferred stock dividend requirements.

    d. dilutive effects of convertible bonds.

    e. dilutive effects of stock option plans.

6. Which of these disclosures is unaudited and may appear either before or after the financial statements and notes?

    a. Segment information.

    b. Significant accounting policies.

    c. Contingencies and commitments.

    d. Five-year summary of financial data.

    e. Events subsequent to the balance sheet date.

7. Earnings per share for Carr Company were $4.80 in fiscal 2012. In 2013, a 20% stock dividend was issued, and in 2014, a 4-for-1 stock split was made. Earnings per share for 2012, to be reported in 2014, are

    a. $1.00.

    b. $1.20.

    c. $1.44.

    d. $4.00.

    e. $4.80.

8. Adequacy of disclosure in the financial statements and notes is the primary responsibility of the

    a. management of the company presenting the statements.

    b. public accounting firm auditing the statements.

    c. internal auditors of the company presenting the statements.

    d. attorneys of the company presenting the statements.

    e. financial analysts using the statements to make investment decisions for their clients.

Mini-Exercises

All applicable Mini-Exercises are available with McGraw-Hill's *Connect™ Accounting*.

Calculate restated EPS after stock split For the year ended December 31, 2013, Spike, Inc., reported earnings per share of $1.16. During 2014, the company had a 4-for-1 stock split.

Mini-Exercise 10.1

LO 9

Required:

Calculate the 2013 earnings per share that will be reported in Spike, Inc.'s 2014 annual report for comparative purposes.

Calculate originally reported EPS before stock split During the fiscal year ended June 30, 2014, Jones Co. had a 3-for-1 stock split. In its annual report for 2014, the company reported earnings per share for the year ended June 30, 2013, on a restated basis, of $0.90.

Mini-Exercise 10.2

LO 9

Required:

Calculate the originally reported earnings per share by Jones Co. for the year ended June 30, 2013.

ACCOUNTING

Exercises

All applicable Exercises are available with McGraw-Hill's *Connect*™ *Accounting.*

Exercise 10.3
LO 1, 2

Read and interpret corporate governance statement Refer to the "Governance" disclosures provided under the *Our Company* link on Campbell Soup Company's website. Identify the principal topics covered in those disclosures. Are there other topics that you believe would be appropriate to have included in those disclosures? Explain your answer.

Exercise 10.4
LO 2, 3

Campbell's

Scan the notes to the financial statements and read other annual report disclosures Refer to the Campbell Soup Company annual report for 2011 in the appendix or to the most recent full annual report that you have downloaded from Campbell's website. Find and scan the notes to consolidated financial statements. Read the independent auditors' report and management's discussion and analysis of financial condition and results of operations. What is your general impression regarding the adequacy of the company's financial disclosures?

Exercise 10.5
LO 10

Interpret auditors' opinion It is impossible for an auditor to "guarantee" that a company's financial statements are free of all error because the cost to the company to achieve absolute accuracy (even if that were possible) and the cost of the auditor's verification would be prohibitively expensive. How does the auditors' opinion recognize this absence of absolute accuracy?

Exercise 10.6
LO 10

Interpret auditors' opinion To what extent is the auditors' opinion an indicator of a company's future financial success and future cash dividends to stockholders?

Exercise 10.7
LO 9

Effects of stock split and stock dividend on EPS

Required:

a. For the year ended December 31, 2012, Finco, Inc., reported earnings per share of $3.12. During 2013, the company had a 3-for-1 stock split. Calculate the 2012 earnings per share that will be reported in Finco's 2013 annual report for comparative purposes.

b. During 2014, Finco had a 2-for-1 stock split. Calculate the 2012 earnings per share that will be reported in Finco's 2014 annual report for comparative purposes.

c. If Finco had issued a 10% stock dividend in 2013 and did not have a stock split, calculate the 2012 earnings per share that will be reported in Finco's 2013 annual report for comparative purposes. Round your answer to two decimal places.

Exercise 10.8
LO 9

Calculate EPS and effect of stock split on EPS During the year ended December 31, 2014, Gluco, Inc., split its stock on a 3-for-1 basis. In its annual report for 2013, the firm reported net income of $7,407,840 for 2013, with an average 1,073,600 shares of common stock outstanding for that year. There was no preferred stock.

Required:

a. What amount of net income for 2013 will be reported in Gluco's 2014 annual report?

b. Calculate Gluco's earnings per share for 2013 that would have been reported in the 2013 annual report.

c. Calculate Gluco's earnings per share for 2013 that will be reported in the 2014 annual report for comparative purposes.

Calculate EPS reported before stock split and stock dividend During the fiscal year ended September 30, 2014, Worrell, Inc., had a 2-for-1 stock split and a 5% stock dividend. In its annual report for 2014, the company reported earnings per share for the year ended September 30, 2013, on a restated basis, of $2.40.

Exercise 10.9
LO 9

Required:
Calculate the originally reported earnings per share for the year ended September 30, 2013.

Calculate EPS and dividends per share before stock split For several years Orbon, Inc., has followed a policy of paying a cash dividend of $0.75 per share and having a 10% stock dividend. In the 2014 annual report, Orbon reported restated earnings per share for 2012 of $3.60.

Exercise 10.10
LO 9

Required:
a. Calculate the originally reported earnings per share for 2012. Round your answer to two decimal places.
b. Calculate the restated cash dividend per share for 2012 reported in the 2014 annual report for comparative purposes. Round your answer to two decimal places.

Problems

All applicable Problems are available with McGraw-Hill's *Connect™ Accounting.*

Understanding note disclosures and financial summary data This problem is based on the 2011 annual report of Campbell Soup Company in the appendix. Find in the Selected Financial Data (also known as the Five-Year Review), or calculate, the following data:

Problem 10.11
LO 2, 4, 9

a. Net sales in 2008.
b. Operating income (earnings before interest and taxes) in 2007.
c. Difference between operating income and net income (net earnings) in 2009.
d. Year(s) in which net income decreased compared to the previous year.

Find the following data for 2011 in the Notes to Consolidated Financial Statements:

e. Amount of interest paid.
f. Number of stock options exercisable at July 31, 2011.
g. Net sales to customers outside the United States.
h. Cost of products sold for the third quarter of 2011.

Understanding note disclosures and financial summary data This problem is based on the 2011 annual report of Campbell Soup Company in the appendix. Find in the Selected Financial Data (also known as the Five-Year Review), or calculate, the following data:

Problem 10.12
LO 2, 4, 9

a. Dividends per share declared in 2011.
b. Capital expenditures in 2010.

c. Year in which total equity grew by the greatest amount over the previous year.

d. Change in total debt from 2007 to 2011.

Find the following data for 2011 in the Notes to Consolidated Financial Statements:

e. Amount of finished products inventory.

f. The company's effective income tax rate.

g. Total assets of the Global Baking and Snacking segment.

h. Market price range of common stock for the fourth quarter of 2011.

Cases

All applicable Cases are available with McGraw-Hill's _Connect_™ _Accounting_.

Case 10.13

LO 4

Focus company—find various accounting policy disclosures In Exercise 1.1, you were asked to obtain the most recent annual report of a company that you were interested in reviewing throughout this term. Please read the "significant accounting policies" and review other note disclosures as necessary to answer the following questions:

Required:

a. What are the principal components included in the firm's receivables (or accounts and notes receivable, or trade receivables)?

b. What inventory valuation method(s) is (are) being used for financial reporting purposes? How much more would ending inventory have been if it were reported on a total FIFO basis? *(Hint: This disclosure is sometimes referred to as the "LIFO Reserve.")*

c. Does the firm report a reconciliation of the statutory income tax rate with the effective tax rate? If so, what are these rates, and what principal temporary differences caused them to differ?

d. Have any significant subsequent events occurred since the balance sheet date? If so, describe the effects that these items will have on future financial statements.

e. What are the principal components included in the firm's cash (or cash and equivalents, or cash and short-term investments)?

f. What depreciation method(s) is (are) being used for financial reporting purposes? How much total depreciation and amortization expense did the firm report?

g. Does the firm have any stock options outstanding? If so, how many option shares are exercisable at the end of the year?

h. Does the firm have any significant contingencies or commitments that have not been reported as liabilities on the balance sheet? If so, describe the potential effects of these items from the perspective of a common stockholder.

Case 10.14

LO 5

Calculate ROI for geographic segments; analyze results—McDonald's Corp. McDonald's conducts operations worldwide and is managed in three primary geographic segments: America, Europe, and Asia/Pacific, Middle East and Africa (APMEA). A hybrid geographic/corporate segment (Other Countries and Corporate) reports on the results of Canada and Latin America as well as any unallocated amounts. McDonald's allocates resources to, and evaluates the performance of, its segments based on operating income. The asset totals disclosed by geography are directly managed by those regions and include accounts receivable, inventory, certain fixed assets, and certain other assets. Corporate assets primarily include cash and cash equivalents, investments, deferred tax assets, and other assets. Refer to the following geographic segment data (in millions) from the 2011 annual report of McDonald's Corp.:

		U.S.	Europe	APMEA	Other Countries & Corporate	Total Company
Revenues	2011	$ 8,528	$10,886	$6,020	$1,572	$27,006
	2010	8,112	9,569	5,066	1,328	24,075
	2009	7,944	9,274	4,337	1,190	22,745
Operating income	2011	$ 3,666	$ 3,227	$1,526	$ 111	$ 8,530
	2010	3,446	2,797	1,200	30	7,473
	2009	3,232	2,588	989	32	6,841
Depreciation and amortization expense	2011	$ 446	$ 570	$ 268	$ 131	$ 1,415
	2010	433	501	232	110	1,276
	2009	424	483	203	106	1,216
Assets	2011	$10,866	$12,015	$5,824	$4,285	$32,990
	2010	10,467	11,361	5,374	4,773	31,975
	2009	10,429	11,495	4,409	3,892	30,225

Required:

a. Based on a cursory review of the data, can you identify any significant trends in the consolidated totals? Are there any notable trends in the data for specific business segments?

b. Using the DuPont model to show margin and turnover, calculate ROI for each of the three primary geographic segments for 2011. Round your percentage answers to one decimal place.

c. Looking only at the data presented here, which business segment appears to offer McDonald's Corp. the greatest potential for high returns in the future?

d. Comment about the difficulties you may encounter when attempting to interpret the Other Countries and Corporate segment results.

e. Can you think of any ways in which McDonald's could improve upon its classification of geographic segment data?

Answers to Self-Study Material

Matching: 1. d, 2. i, 3. l, 4. a, 5. j, 6. e, 7. g, 8. h
Multiple choice: 1. b, 2. b, 3. a, 4. e, 5. a, 6. d, 7. a, 8. a

11

Financial Statement Analysis

The process of interpreting an entity's financial statements can be facilitated by certain ratio computations, and if one entity's financial condition and results of operations are to be compared to those of another entity, ratio analysis of the financial statements is essential. In Chapter 3 you learned about some of the fundamental interpretations made from financial statement data. The importance of financial statement ratios and the significance of *trends* in the ratio results were explained. The calculation of return on investment (ROI) and the use of the DuPont model, which recognizes margin and turnover in the ROI calculation, were described. In addition, the calculation and significance of return on equity (ROE) and the liquidity measures of working capital, current ratio, and acid-test ratio were explained. It would be appropriate for you to review Chapter 3 if you don't thoroughly understand these analytical tools. In Chapters 5 through 10 you learned about the business, accounting, and financial reporting aspects of most of the transactions that an entity may experience. The effects of these transactions on the financial statements were described and explained. Your understanding of the accounting process and the alternative choices that management must make for financial reporting purposes will permit you to make sense of an entity's financial statements. This chapter builds on the material presented in Chapter 3 and provides a comprehensive discussion of financial statement analysis concepts. The objective of this chapter is to expand your ability to read and interpret financial statements so that you can make decisions and informed judgments about an entity's financial condition and results of operations.

What Does It Mean?
Answer on page 443

1. What does it mean to use the trend of financial statement ratios to compare the financial position and results of operations of one firm with another firm?

LEARNING OBJECTIVES (LO)

After studying this chapter you should understand and be able to

LO 11-1   Explain how liquidity measures can be influenced by the inventory cost flow assumption used.

LO 11-2   Explain how suppliers and creditors use a customer's payment practices to judge liquidity.

LO 11-3   Discuss the influence of alternative inventory cost flow assumptions and depreciation methods on turnover ratios.

LO 11-4   Discuss how the number of days' sales in both accounts receivable and inventory are used to evaluate the effectiveness of the management of receivables and inventory.

LO 11-5   Discuss the significance of the price/earnings ratio in the evaluation of the market price of a company's common stock.

LO 11-6   Discuss how dividend yield and the dividend payout ratio are used by investors to evaluate a company's common stock.

LO 11-7   Explain what financial leverage is and why it is significant to management, creditors, and owners.

LO 11-8   Explain what book value per share of common stock is, describe how it is calculated, and discuss why it is not a very meaningful amount for most companies.

LO 11-9   Discuss how common size financial statements can be used to evaluate a firm's financial position and results of operations over a number of years.

LO 11-10   Generalize about how operating statistics using physical, or nonfinancial, data can be used to help management evaluate the results of the firm's activities.

Financial Statement Analysis Ratios

The ratios used to facilitate the interpretation of an entity's financial position and results of operations can be grouped into four categories that have to do with:

1. Liquidity.
2. Activity.
3. Profitability.
4. Debt or financial leverage.

Liquidity Measures

The liquidity measures of working capital, current ratio, and acid-test ratio were discussed in Chapter 3. One point that deserves reemphasis is the **effect of the inventory cost flow assumption on working capital**. The balance sheet carrying value of inventories will depend on whether the weighted-average, FIFO, or LIFO assumption is used. In periods of rising prices, a firm using the FIFO cost flow assumption will report

LO 1
Explain how liquidity measures can be influenced by the inventory cost flow assumption used.

a relatively higher asset value for inventories than a similar firm using the LIFO cost flow assumption. Thus, even though the firms may be similar in all other respects, they will report different amounts of working capital, and they will have different current ratios. Therefore, a direct comparison of the liquidity of the two firms by using these measures is not possible. To ease this reporting difficulty, many firms using the LIFO method will disclose a *LIFO reserve* amount in the notes to the financial statements. The LIFO reserve is the difference between the inventory valuation as reported under the LIFO basis and the amount that would have been reported under the FIFO basis.

LO 2
Explain how suppliers and creditors use a customer's payment practices to judge liquidity.

Even more significant to suppliers or potential suppliers/creditors of the firm than the aggregate working capital or liquidity ratios is the firm's current and recent payment experience. Suppliers/creditors want to know whether or not the firm is paying its bills promptly. One indication of this is whether all cash discounts for prompt payment (e.g., for payment terms of 2/10, net 30) are being taken. Information about current and recent payment practices can be obtained by contacting other suppliers or credit bureaus and by reviewing Dun & Bradstreet reports (see Business in Practice—Credit Rating and Financial Analysis Services).

What Does It Mean?
Answer on page 443

2. What does it mean to assess the liquidity of an entity?

Activity Measures

The impact of efficient use of assets on the firm's return on investment was explained in Chapter 3 in the discussion of the asset turnover component of the DuPont model (ROI = Margin × Turnover). Activity measures focus primarily on the relationship between asset levels and sales (i.e., turnover). Recall that the general model for calculating turnover is:

$$\text{Turnover} = \text{Sales} / \text{Average assets}$$

Recall also that average assets are used in the turnover calculation (rather than year-end assets) because the amount invested is compared to sales, which are generated over a period of time. The average assets amount is ordinarily determined by using the balance sheet amounts reported at the beginning and end of the period; however, if appropriate and available, monthly or quarterly balance sheet data can be used in the calculation. Turnover is frequently calculated for:

Accounts receivable.
Inventories.
Plant and equipment.
Total operating assets.
Total assets.

LO 3
Discuss the influence of alternative inventory cost flow assumptions and depreciation methods on turnover ratios.

Alternative inventory cost flow assumptions and depreciation methods will affect the comparability of turnover between companies. For example, a company using LIFO and an accelerated depreciation method would report lower amounts for inventory

Credit Rating and Financial Analysis Services

To help potential creditors and investors evaluate the financial condition and investment prospects of companies, a credit rating and financial analysis industry has developed. Firms in this industry gather and report data about individual companies, industries, segments of the economy, and the economy as a whole.

Credit-rating firms such as Dun & Bradstreet and credit bureaus collect data from companies and their creditors and sell credit history data to potential suppliers and others. These firms usually have a rating system and assign a credit risk value based on that system. A company being reported on can request to see the data in its file so that erroneous data can be eliminated or corrected.

The financial statements of larger firms whose stock or bonds have been issued to the public are analyzed and reported on by firms such as Standard & Poor's Corporation or Moody's Investors Service, Inc. A rating is assigned to bonds to reflect the rating firm's assessment of the risk associated with the security. The ratings range from AAA to C, or no rating at all for a speculative bond. Summary financial statements, ratio calculation results, and bond ratings are published in manuals that are available in many libraries. In addition to rating bonds, these firms and many others (such as Value Line Publishing, Inc., and stock brokerage firms) evaluate the common and preferred stock issues of publicly owned companies. They report summary financial data and trends in key ratios, along with their opinions about the investment prospects for the stocks. A potential investor will likely use reports from one or more of these sources as well as the company's annual report to support an investment decision.

Business in *Practice*

and net book value of depreciable assets than would a company using FIFO and the straight-line method. Although the sales volume of the two companies may be identical, the company reporting lower asset values would show a higher asset turnover. Of more significance than intercompany or company—industry comparisons as of a given date is the trend of turnover for the company relative to the trend of turnover for other companies or the industry. Even if the company's turnover data are not directly comparable to industry data because of accounting method choices, the patterns exhibited in the respective trends can be meaningfully compared.

When calculating inventory turnover, most analysts substitute the cost of goods sold amount for the sales amount in the calculation because inventories are reported at cost, not at selling prices. This approach eliminates distortions that could be caused by sales mix changes between product categories with different gross profit ratios or markup percentages. Even if sales are used in the numerator consistently, the inventory turnover trend will not be significantly affected unless there are major relative markup differences and major sales mix changes.

Some analysts use the cost of plant and equipment rather than the net book value (cost minus accumulated depreciation) when calculating plant and equipment turnover. This removes the impact of different depreciation calculation methods and may make intercompany and industry turnover data more comparable. This may be an illusory improvement, however, because the assets of each firm are reported at original cost, not current value or replacement cost. If they were acquired over different periods of time, the cost data are not likely to be comparable.

Exhibit 11-1 illustrates some turnover calculations for Campbell Soup Company with data from the company's 2011 annual report. Note that the calculation results usually are not carried beyond one decimal place because aggregate financial statement data are being used, and the accuracy implied by additional decimal places is not warranted.

Accounts receivable turnover for 2011 ($ millions):

Sales for 2011	$ 7,719
Accounts receivable at 7/31/11	560
Accounts receivable at 8/1/10	512

$$\text{Accounts receivable turnover} = \frac{\text{Sales}}{\text{Average accounts receivable}}$$

$$= \frac{\$7,719}{(\$512 + \$560) / 2}$$

$$= 14.4 \text{ times}$$

Inventory turnover for 2011 ($ millions):

Cost of goods sold for 2011	$ 4,616
Inventories at 7/31/11	767
Inventories at 8/1/10	724

$$\text{Inventory turnover} = \frac{\text{Cost of goods sold}}{\text{Average inventories}}$$

$$= \frac{\$4,616}{(\$724 + \$767) / 2}$$

$$= 6.2 \text{ times}$$

Plant and equipment turnover for 2011 ($ millions):

Sales for 2011	$ 7,719
Plant and equipment (net) at 7/31/11	2,103
Plant and equipment (net) at 8/1/10	2,051

$$\text{Plant and equipment turnover} = \frac{\text{Sales}}{\text{Average plant and equipment}}$$

$$= \frac{\$7,719}{(\$2,051 + \$2,103) / 2}$$

$$= 3.7 \text{ times}$$

Two other activity measures that permit assessment of the efficiency of asset management are the **number of days' sales in accounts receivable** and the **number of days' sales in inventory.** The sooner that accounts receivable can be collected, the sooner cash is available to use in the business or to permit temporary investment, and the less cash needs to be borrowed for prompt payment of liabilities. Likewise, the lower that inventories can be maintained relative to sales, the less inventory needs to be financed with debt or stockholders' equity, and the greater the return on investment. However, the risk of having minimum inventories is that an unanticipated increase in demand or a delay in receiving raw materials or finished product can result in an out-of-stock situation that may result in lost sales. Inventory management is a very important activity for many firms, and many quantitative and operational techniques have been developed to assist in this activity. The just-in-time (JIT) inventory management system was pioneered by some Japanese firms several decades ago and subsequently has been adopted by many firms in the United States and elsewhere throughout the world. The primary objective of a JIT system is to keep the investment in inventories at a minimum by forecasting needs and having suppliers deliver components as they are needed in the production process.

Each of the number of days' sales calculations involves calculating an average day's sales (or cost of sales) and dividing that average into the year-end balance sheet amount. A 365-day year is usually assumed for the average day's sales (or cost of sales) calculation. As in the calculation of inventory turnover, it is more appropriate to use cost of sales data in the days' sales in inventory calculation. Year-end asset values are used instead of average amounts because the focus here is on the number of days' sales (or cost of sales) in the ending balance sheet amounts. The results of these calculations also can be referred to, for receivables, as the *average collection period for accounts receivable* or the *number of days' sales outstanding,* and for inventories, as the *average sales period for inventories*. It must be stressed again that the inventory cost flow assumption will influence the result of the inventory activity calculations. Exhibit 11-2 illustrates these calculations for Campbell Soup Company for 2011.

LO 4

Discuss how the number of days' sales in both accounts receivable and inventory are used to evaluate the effectiveness of the management of receivables and inventory.

Number of days' sales in accounts receivable for 2011 ($ millions):

Sales for 2011 . . . . $7,719

Accounts receivable at 7/31/11   560

$$\text{Average day's sales} = \frac{\text{Annual sales}}{365}$$

$$= \frac{\$7,719}{365}$$

$$= \$21.148$$

$$\text{Days' sales in accounts receivable} = \frac{\text{Accounts receivable at year-end}}{\text{Average day's sales}}$$

$$= \frac{\$560}{\$21.148}$$

$$= 26.5 \text{ days}$$

The result of this calculation also can be expressed as the *average age of accounts receivable,* the *number of days' sales outstanding,* or the *average collection period for accounts receivable.*

Number of days' sales in inventory for 2011 ($ millions):

Cost of goods sold for 2011 . . . . $4,616

Inventories at 7/31/11   767

$$\text{Average day's cost of goods sold} = \frac{\text{Annual cost of goods sold}}{365}$$

$$= \frac{\$4,616}{365}$$

$$= \$12.647$$

$$\text{Days' sales in inventory} = \frac{\text{Inventory at year-end}}{\text{Average day's cost of goods sold}}$$

$$= \frac{\$767}{\$12.647}$$

$$= 60.6 \text{ days}$$

The result of this calculation also can be expressed as the *average age of the inventory* or the *average sales period for inventory.*

Exhibit 11-2

Campbell Soup Company, Number of Days' Sales Calculations Illustrated

Again, in evaluating the firm's operating efficiency, it is the trend of these calculation results that is important. A single year's days' sales in receivables or inventory is not very useful. Campbell Soup Company's 26.5 days' sales in accounts receivable would make sense if its credit terms are a combination of 2/10, net 30, and net 30 (without a discount), as is the case for many manufacturing firms. In addition, perhaps certain concessions are granted to major customers (e.g., Walmart) to enhance the market penetration and product placement of Campbell's products. In any event, it is difficult to assess the job performance of Campbell's credit managers without knowing about the firm's credit policies and the details of its accounts receivable balance by customer category. In fact, if the credit manager wanted to know how many days' sales were in receivables at any time, the most accurate result could be determined by doing the following:

1. Obtaining the daily sales amounts for the period ending with the date of the total accounts receivable.

2. Adding the daily sales amounts (working backward by day) until the sum equals the total accounts receivable.

3. Counting the number of days' sales that had to be included to reach this total.

Because of the different operating characteristics of various industries, rules of thumb for activity measures are difficult to develop. In general, the higher the turnover or the fewer the number of days' sales in accounts receivable and inventory, the greater the efficiency. Again, it should be emphasized that the answer from any financial statement analysis calculation is not important by itself; the *trend* of the result over time is most meaningful. An increase in the age of accounts receivable, an increase in inventory relative to sales, or a reduction in plant and equipment turnover are all early warning signs that the liquidity and profitability of a firm may be weakening.

What Does It Mean?
Answers on page 443

3. What does it mean to assess the activity measures of an entity?
4. What does it mean to state that total asset turnover has improved?

Profitability Measures

Two of the most significant measures of profitability, *return on investment* and *return on equity,* were explained and illustrated in Chapter 3. Each of these measures relates net income, or an income statement subtotal (e.g., operating income), to an element of the balance sheet. Operating income, which excludes other income and expense (principally interest expense) and income taxes, is frequently used in the ROI calculation because it is a more direct measure of the results of management's activities than is net income. Interest expense is a function of the board of directors' decisions about capital structure (the relationship between debt and stockholders' equity); income taxes are a function of the tax laws. Thus, ROI based on operating income becomes an evaluation of the operating activities of the firm. The balance sheet elements for these calculations are average total assets (or average operating assets) for ROI, and average common stockholders' equity for ROE. You know enough about accounting principles and how financial statement data are developed to have some healthy skepticism about the relationship of these rates of return to what a "true" rate of return based on real economic profit related to fair values would be.

Of course, the problem is that there is no agreement among managers, accountants, or financial analysts about what constitutes real economic profit or how to objectively determine fair values of the balance sheet data. In addition, the unique characteristics of individual companies and industries make the development of benchmark or target profitability ratios difficult if not impossible. Although many valid exceptions exist, a very broad rule of thumb useful for putting ROI in perspective is that average ROI based on net income for most U.S. merchandising and manufacturing companies is normally between 7% and 10%. Average ROI based on operating income (earnings before interest and taxes) for the same set of firms is between 10% and 15%. Average margin based on net income ranges from about 7% to 10%. Using operating income, average margin ranges from 10% to 15%. Asset turnover is usually about 1.0 to 1.5. A rule of thumb useful for putting ROE in perspective is that average ROE, for most U.S. merchandising and manufacturing companies, is normally between 12 and 20% during times of relative prosperity. Of course, during recessionary times, these averages decline significantly, making such generalizations even more problematic. Do not draw firm conclusions based on these rules of thumb. Profitability evaluations are likely to be more valid when they are based on the *trend* of one company's ROI and ROE relative to the *trend* of industry and competitors' rates of return.

---

5. What does it mean when ROI has decreased even though net income has increased?
6. What does it mean to use the DuPont model to help explain a decrease in ROI?

What Does It Mean?
Answers on page 443

The **price/earnings ratio**, or simply the P/E ratio, is calculated by dividing the market price of a share of common stock by the earnings per share of common stock (discussed in detail in Chapter 9). The P/E ratio is used extensively by investors to evaluate the market price of a company's common stock relative to that of other companies and relative to the market as a whole. **Earnings multiple** is another term for the price/earnings ratio. This term merely reflects the fact that the market price of stock is equal to the earnings per share multiplied by the P/E ratio. Diluted earnings per share is normally used in the P/E calculation, as illustrated by the following example using data for Campbell Soup Company, as of July 31, 2011.

$$\text{Price / earnings ratio (or earnings multiple)} = \frac{\text{Market price of common stock}^1}{\text{Diluted earnings per share of common stock}^2}$$

$$= \$33.05 \, / \, \$2.42$$

$$= 13.7$$

LO 5

Discuss the significance of the price/earnings ratio in the evaluation of the market price of a company's common stock.

Campbell's P/E ratio of 13.7 for 2011 is well within a range that would be regarded as normal for a firm supported by strong investor confidence.

To understand the significance of the P/E ratio, think about the reason an individual invests in the common stock of a company. The obvious objective is to "make money" (i.e., to achieve the investor's desired return on the investment). It is anticipated that return on investment will be realized in two ways: (1) The firm will pay cash dividends, and (2) the market price of the firm's stock will increase. The change in market value is usually called a *capital gain* or *loss*. A number of factors can cause the market price to change. One of the most significant of these is the prospect for future cash dividends. Both present and future cash dividends are a function of earnings. So, in a very real sense, the market price of a company's common stock reflects investors' expectations about the firm's future earnings. The greater the probability of increased earnings, the more investors are willing to pay for a claim to those earnings. Relating market price and earnings per share in a ratio is a way to express investors' expectations without confusing the issue by focusing on just market price per share. To illustrate, assume the following market price per share of common stock for each of two companies:

	Company A	**Company B**
Market price per share	$45.00	$63.00

Based on market price alone, the tempting conclusion is that the stock of Company B is more expensive than the stock of Company A. However, when earnings per share are considered, the table looks like this:

	Company A	**Company B**
Market price per share	$45.00	$63.00
Diluted earnings per share	1.80	3.50

The price/earnings ratio can now be calculated by dividing the market price per share by the earnings per share:

	Company A	**Company B**
Market price per share	$\dfrac{\$45.00}{1.80} = 25$	$\dfrac{\$63.00}{3.50} = 18$
Diluted earnings per share		

Company A's stock is more expensive because investors are willing to pay 25 times earnings for it, but they will pay only 18 times earnings for the stock of Company B. In essence, investors are showing that they expect greater future earnings growth and dividend payments from Company A than from Company B; therefore, they are willing to pay relatively more for a given amount of current earnings.

---

[1]Campbell's actual year-end closing price of $33.05 can be confirmed by visiting www.campbellsoup .com and then clicking on *Our Company; Investor Center; Stock Information; Historical Price Lookup.* Note that July 29, 2011, was the last trading day before the end of Campbell's fiscal year.

[2]Bottom of consolidated statements of earnings on page 711 of 2011 annual report in the appendix.

The price/earnings ratio, or earnings multiple, is one of the most important measures used by investors to evaluate the market price of a firm's common stock. This is one reason that earnings per share is reported prominently on the face of the income statement. As explained in Chapter 9, the effect of extraordinary items and potential dilution of EPS from any convertible long-term debt and/or convertible preferred stock and stock options is also disclosed separately on the income statement. It is usually the diluted earnings per share amount that is used to calculate the P/E ratio associated with a company's stock. Because of its significance, the P/E ratio is disclosed in the stock listing tables of *The Wall Street Journal* and other periodicals. Although the preceding illustration of the P/E ratio calculation was based on earnings for the past year, analysts sometimes use expected future earnings per share and the current market price in the calculation to evaluate the prospects for changes in the stock's market price. Another approach to forecast market price is to use expected future earnings per share and the current (or expected future) earnings multiple. It should be noted, however, that the P/E ratio applies only to common stock. A rule of thumb for putting the price/earnings ratio in perspective is that for the common stock of most merchandising and manufacturing companies, average P/E ratios have historically ranged from 12 to 18. Since the preferred stock dividend does not fluctuate as earnings change, it would not be meaningful to calculate a preferred stock P/E ratio.

The interpretation of P/E ratios for individual firms is fairly straightforward. An above-average P/E ratio indicates that the common stock price is high relative to the firm's current earnings, probably because investors anticipate relatively favorable future developments, such as increased earnings per share or higher dividends per share. Low P/E ratios usually indicate poor earnings expectations. Keep in mind, however, that P/E ratios are significantly influenced by the company's reported earnings. For example, assume that Cruisers, Inc., reported diluted earnings per share of $2.42 in 2013 and $5.27 in 2014. Assume also that the year-end market price per share of common stock was $40 in 2013 and $60 in 2014. Thus, the P/E ratio for Cruisers, Inc., would have fallen from 16.5 ($40/$2.42) to 11.4 ($60/$5.27) even though net income doubled (from $764,000 in 2013 to $1,527,000 in 2014 as illustrated in Exhibit 9-7) and the market price per share of common stock increased by 50 percent, in just one year! In this type of situation, the relatively low P/E ratio at the end of 2014 probably would reflect investors' recognition that 2014 earnings were exceptionally high relative to the company's recent experience. Although the market price per share has increased significantly, it has not adjusted as quickly as earnings have grown. What this demonstrates is that the P/E ratio should not be the sole, or even principal, consideration in an investment decision. Financial analysts might consider a low P/E ratio for a well-established company to be an indicator that the company's stock merits further analysis.

---

7. What does it mean when the price/earnings ratio of a firm's common stock is significantly higher than the P/E ratio for the overall stock market?

What Does It Mean?
Answer on page 443

Another ratio used by both common stock investors and preferred stock investors is the **dividend yield**. This is calculated by dividing the annual dividend per

LO 6

Discuss how dividend
yield and the dividend
payout ratio are used
by investors to evaluate
a company's common
stock.

share by the current market price of the stock. This calculation is illustrated here, using assumed amounts for the per share data for Cruisers, Inc., for the year ended August 31, 2014:

$$\text{Dividend yield} = \frac{\text{Annual dividend per share}}{\text{Market price per share of stock}}$$

$$\text{Dividend yield on}$$
$$\text{Common stock} = \frac{\$1.60}{\$60.00} = 2.7\%$$

$$\text{Preferred stock} = \frac{\$3.50}{\$56.00} = 6.25\%$$

The dividend yield would be compared to the yield available on alternative investments to help the investor evaluate the extent to which her investment objectives were being met. In many cases, investors will accept a low current dividend yield from a common stock if they believe that the firm is reinvesting the earnings retained for use in the business at a relatively high ROI because investors anticipate that future earnings will permit higher future dividends. In the case of preferred stock, investors will compare the yield to that available on other fixed-income investments with comparable risk to determine whether or not to continue holding the preferred stock as an investment. You may have noticed that the dividend yield on Cruisers, Inc.'s preferred stock is lower than the 7 percent stated dividend rate on its $50 par value preferred stock (refer to the EPS illustration on page 358 in Chapter 9). Since preferred dividends are linked to the par value per share, the dividend yield for preferred shareholders decreases as the market price per share increases. The average dividend yield on common stocks has historically been in the range of 3% to 6%; for preferred stocks, the yield is usually somewhat greater, in the range of 5% to 8%.

What Does It Mean?

Answer on page 443

8. What does it mean when the dividend yield on a firm's common stock is less than the average dividend yield for all common stocks?

Another ratio involving the dividend on common stock is the **dividend payout ratio.** This ratio, computed by dividing the dividend per share of common stock by the earnings per share of common stock (usually diluted earnings per share), reflects the dividend policy of the company. Most firms have a policy of paying dividends that are a relatively constant proportion of earnings (e.g., 40 to 50 percent, or 10 to 15 percent). Knowing the dividend payout ratio permits the investor to project dividends from an assessment of the firm's earnings prospects. Cruisers, Inc.'s dividend payout ratio for fiscal 2014, using assumed amounts, would be:

$$\text{Dividend payout ratio} = \frac{\text{Annual dividend per share}}{\text{Earnings per share}}$$

$$= \frac{\$1.60}{\$5.27}$$

$$= 30.4\%$$

Most firms try to avoid having significant fluctuations in the amount of the cash dividend per share because investors prefer to be relatively assured of the dividend amount. Therefore, very few firms use the payout ratio as the sole, or even the principal, determinant of the dividend amount. To help communicate its dividend policy to the stockholders, a firm refers to its dividends in two ways: **Regular dividends** are the stable, or gradually changing, periodic (i.e., quarterly, semiannual, or annual) dividends; **extra dividends** are additional dividends that may be declared and paid after an especially profitable year. The significance of the extra dividend is that it indicates to stockholders that they should not expect to receive the larger amount every year. The most dramatic example of this practice was Microsoft's payment of a one-time dividend of $3 per share toward the end of 2004, which represented a whopping $32.6 billion extra dividend!

As a rule of thumb, the dividend payout ratio for most merchandising and manufacturing companies is usually in the range of 30% to 50%. Keep in mind, however, that this range can vary significantly—especially when a firm has a low (or even negative) earnings year but wishes to maintain its dividend per share amount.

From the preferred stockholders' point of view, the ratio of net income to the total preferred stock dividend requirement indicates the margin of safety of the preferred dividend. If net income is less than three or four times the preferred dividend requirement and has been falling over time, the preferred stockholders would become concerned about the firm's ability to generate enough earnings and cash to be able to pay the preferred dividend. This **preferred dividend coverage ratio** for Cruisers, Inc., for fiscal 2014 (data from Chapter 9) was a somewhat healthy 5.5, calculated as follows:

$$\text{Preferred dividend coverage ratio} = \frac{\text{Net income}}{\text{Preferred dividend requirement}}$$

$$= \frac{\$1,527,000}{\$280,000}$$

$$= 5.5 \text{ times}$$

Financial Leverage Measures

Financial leverage (frequently called just *leverage*) refers to the use of debt (and, in the broadest context of the term, preferred stock) to finance the assets of the entity. Leverage adds risk to the operation of the firm because if the firm does not generate enough cash to pay principal and interest payments, creditors may force the firm into bankruptcy. However, because the cost of debt (i.e., interest) is a fixed charge regardless of the amount of earnings, leverage also magnifies the return to the owners (ROE) relative to the return on assets (ROI). The magnification effect of financial leverage is illustrated in Exhibit 11-3 on pages 432–433; please study the exhibit before reading the following discussion.

As Exhibit 11-3 illustrates, borrowing money at an interest rate that is less than the rate of return that can be earned on that money increases (or magnifies) the return on stockholders' equity. This makes common financial sense; who wouldn't borrow money at a 9% interest cost if the money could be invested to earn substantially more than 9% (20% in this illustration)? Of course, if the return on investment were less than the cost of borrowing, the result would be a reduction of stockholders' equity (a loss) at best, and bankruptcy at worst. This is the risk of leverage—the magnification works both ways! Highly leveraged firms or individuals (that is, those with lots of debt relative to stockholders' equity) are exposed to the risk of losses or bankruptcy if the return on investment falls below the cost of borrowing.

LO 7

Explain what financial leverage is and why it is significant to management, creditors, and owners.

Exhibit 11-3

Financial Leverage

I. Without financial leverage:

Assume the following balance sheet and income statement:

Balance Sheet		Income Statement	
Assets	$10,000	Earnings before interest and taxes.	$2,000
		Interest	0
Liabilities.	$ 0	Earnings before taxes	$2,000
Stockholders' equity.	10,000	Income taxes (40%).	800
Total liabilities and stockholders' equity	$10,000	Net income	$1,200

$$\text{Return on investment (assets) before interest and taxes} = \text{Earnings before interest and taxes / Total assets}$$
$$= \$2,000 / \$10,000$$
$$= 20\%$$

$$\text{Return on equity, after taxes} = \text{Net income / Stockholders' equity}$$
$$= \$1,200 / \$10,000$$
$$= 12\%$$

Return on investment measures the efficiency with which management has used the operating assets to generate operating income. Note that the return on investment calculation is based on earnings before interest and taxes (operating income) and total assets, rather than net income and total assets. Earnings before interest and taxes (operating income) are used because the interest expense reflects a financing decision, not an operating result, and income taxes are beyond the control of operating management. Thus, ROI becomes an evaluation of the operating activities of the firm. Return on equity measures the rate of return that net income provides to the owners/stockholders. ROI and ROE differ for the firm without financial leverage only because income taxes have been excluded from ROI but have been included in ROE.

(continued)

This does happen in economic recessions and industry business cycles. Accordingly, most nonfinancial firms try to limit the debt in their capital structure to no more than 50 percent of total capital (debt plus stockholders' equity).

 The effect of leverage can be seen in the graphs of Exhibit 3-2 (see page 83), on which are plotted ROI and ROE for Campbell Soup Company, for the period 2007–2012. Notice that ROE is several multiples of ROI for each year presented. By looking at the vertical difference between the ROI and ROE graphs in Exhibit 3-2 (keeping the scale in mind), you can see that Campbell's use of leverage has been fairly consistent over the period presented.

Debt and preferred stock provide leverage because the interest cost (or dividend rate) is fixed. When debt is issued, the interest rate is set and remains unchanged for the life of the debt issue. If the interest rate on the debt were to fluctuate as a function of the firm's ROI, or as a result of inflation or deflation in the economy, the magnification of ROE would be diminished or eliminated.

Another feature of debt illustrated in Exhibit 11-3 is the deductibility of interest as an expense in determining income subject to income taxes. The after-tax cost of debt is its interest rate multiplied by the complement of the firm's tax rate. In this example, the

II. With financial leverage:

Exhibit 11-3

Assume the following balance sheet and income statement:

Balance Sheet		Income Statement	
Assets	$10,000	Earnings before interest and taxes	$2,000
Liabilities (9% interest)	$ 4,000	Interest	360
Stockholders' equity	6,000	Earnings before taxes	$1,640
Total liabilities and		Income taxes (40%)	656
stockholders' equity	$10,000	Net income	$ 984

$$\text{Return on investment (assets) before interest and taxes} = \frac{\text{Earnings before interest and taxes}}{\text{Total assets}}$$
$$= \$2,000 / \$10,000$$
$$= 20\%$$
$$\text{Return on equity, after taxes} = \text{Net income / Stockholders' equity}$$
$$= \$984 / \$6,000$$
$$= 16.4\%$$

The use of financial leverage has not affected ROI; *financial leverage* refers to how the assets are financed, not how efficiently the assets are used to generate operating income.

The use of financial leverage has caused the ROE to increase from 12% to 16.4% because ROI (20%) exceeds the cost of the debt (9%) used to finance a portion of the assets.

assumed tax rate is 40 percent, so the after-tax cost of the debt is 9% × (1 − 40%) = 5.4%. Since preferred stock dividends are not deductible as an expense, financial managers prefer to use debt, rather than preferred stock, as the source of fixed-cost capital.

Two **financial leverage measures,** the debt ratio and the debt/equity ratio, are used to indicate the extent to which a firm is using financial leverage. Each ratio expresses the relationship between debt and equity in a slightly different manner. The **debt ratio** is the ratio of total liabilities to the total of liabilities and stockholders' equity. The **debt/equity ratio** is the ratio of total liabilities to total stockholders' equity. Thus, a debt ratio of 50% would be the same as a debt/equity ratio of 1 (or 1:1). To illustrate these ratios, assume the following *capital structure* (i.e., right side of the balance sheet) for a firm:

Liabilities	$ 40,000
Stockholders' equity	60,000
Total liabilities and stockholders' equity	$100,000

$$\text{Debt ratio} = \frac{\text{Total liabilities}}{\text{Total liabilities and stockholders' equity}}$$
$$= \frac{\$40,000}{\$100,000}$$
$$= 40\%$$

The Leveraged Buyout

In 2006 through mid-2008 the activities of hedge funds and private equity firms marked a period of relatively high corporate ownership rearrangement activity featuring friendly and unfriendly mergers and acquisitions, as well as leveraged buyouts. In a merger or acquisition one firm acquires another, either by issuing stock of the surviving company to the stockholders of the firm being acquired (usually on a merger) or by buying the stock of the company being acquired by paying cash (and sometimes other securities) to the stockholders of the other firm. This is referred to as a *takeover*. Changes in top management and operations of the acquired company frequently result. A leveraged buyout is a transaction in which the present top management of a publicly held firm buys the stock of the nonmanagement stockholders, and the firm becomes "privately owned" (i.e., its shares are no longer traded in the public market). Neither management nor the operations of the firm change significantly. Some firms that have been takeover targets have "gone private" through a leveraged buyout in order to avoid being acquired by another firm.

The leveraged buyout transaction gets its label from the fact that the company goes heavily into debt in order to obtain the funds needed to buy the shares of the public stockholders. In many cases the debt ratio will be substantially higher than is usually considered prudent, but investors are willing to invest in the firm's bonds because of their confidence in management's proven ability to operate the firm profitably.

The debt issued in a leveraged buyout is usually considered speculative or high risk (the term *junk bond* has been applied to much of it). Investors are often concerned about the impact of a major economic recession on the ability of these firms to meet their interest and principal payment requirements. During the recession of the early 1990s, many firms were forced into bankruptcy or mergers with other firms, and some of the firms that survived were forced to sell off many of their assets. Other financially healthier firms took advantage of rising stock market values to realign their capital structure by selling stock (going public again) and using the proceeds to reduce high-cost long-term debt. This cycle has shown signs of repeating itself as the world's economy slowly continues to recover from the global economic crisis that hit hard in late 2008.

$$\text{Debt / equity ratio} = \frac{\text{Total liabilities}}{\text{Total stockholders' equity}}$$
$$= \frac{\$40,000}{\$60,000}$$
$$= 66.7\%$$

As already indicated, most nonfinancial firms usually will have a debt ratio below 50%—a debt/equity ratio of less than 1—because of the risk associated with having a greater proportion of debt in the capital structure. However, many firms have been forced into unusually high financial leverage positions in recent years in order to survive competitive pressures (see Business in Practice—The Leveraged Buyout).

Since the deferred income tax liability and most of an entity's current liabilities are not interest-bearing, many financial analysts exclude these items from the numerator of the debt ratio and the debt/equity ratio. This allows analysts to get a better sense of what proportion of the entity's capital structure is financed by long-term, interest-bearing debt. Other liabilities that do not add risk to the entity's operations may also be excluded from these calculations.

Holders of a company's long-term debt will frequently want to know the **times interest earned ratio** for the firm. This measure is similar to the preferred dividend coverage ratio previously explained; it shows the relationship of earnings before interest and taxes (operating income) to interest expense. The greater the ratio, the more confident the debtholders can be about the firm's prospects for continuing to have enough earnings to cover interest expense, even if the firm experiences a decline in the demand for its products or services. Using data from Cruisers, Inc.'s, income statement for fiscal 2014, as shown in Exhibit 9-7, the calculation of times interest earned is:

Earnings before income taxes....................	$2,777 million
Add back interest expense.....................	3,378 million
Earnings before interest and taxes...............	$6,155 million

$$\text{Times interest earned} = \frac{\text{Earnings before interest and taxes}}{\text{Interest expense}}$$

$$= \frac{\$6,155}{\$3,378}$$

$$= 1.8 \text{ times}$$

The debtholders of Cruisers, Inc., would be concerned about the company's ability to continue to earn enough to cover its interest expense. As a general rule of thumb, a times interest earned ratio of 5 or higher is considered by creditors to indicate a relatively low risk that a firm will not be able to pay interest in the future. Campbell's times interest earned for 2011 was a very healthy 10.5 and was even higher in 2010 and 2009. This can be verified by reference to the consolidated statements of earnings on page 711 in the appendix.

---

9. What does it mean to state that a firm is highly leveraged?
10. What does it mean that the more financial leverage a firm has, the greater the risk to stockholders and creditors?

What Does It Mean?

Answers on page 443

Other Analytical Techniques

Book Value per Share of Common Stock

The **book value per share of common stock** is a frequently cited ratio in the financial press that can be easily misunderstood by investors who do not carefully interpret its meaning. Book value per share is calculated by dividing the total common stockholders' equity by the number of shares of common stock outstanding. If there is preferred stock in the capital structure of the firm, the liquidating value of the preferred stock is subtracted from total stockholders' equity to get the common stockholders' equity. *Net asset value per share of common stock* is another name for this measure.

The following illustration using data as of July 31, 2011, for Campbell Soup Company, illustrates the calculation (in millions of dollars):

LO 8

Explain what book value per share of common stock is, describe how it is calculated, and discuss why it is not a very meaningful amount for most companies.

$$\text{Book value per share of common stock}^3 = \frac{\text{Common stockholders' equity}}{\text{Number of shares of common stock outstanding}}$$

$$= \frac{\$1,088 \text{ million}}{320 \text{ million}}$$

$$= \$3.40$$

---

[3]The numerator is reported as "Total Campbell Soup Company shareowners' equity" in the consolidated balance sheets on page 712 in the appendix; the denominator is reported at the bottom of the consolidated statements of equity on page 714 as 542 million shares of capital stock issued less 222 million shares held as treasury stock.

Because total common stockholders' equity reflects the application of generally accepted accounting principles and the specific accounting policies that have been selected, book value per share is not a number that can be meaningfully compared to the market value per share of stock for most companies, especially if the market value is greater than the book value (which is usually the case). For Campbell's, the 2011 year-end market price per share was $33.05, which was obviously unrelated to its $3.40 book value per share. Although book value per share is not a very useful measure most of the time, you should be aware of how it is calculated and understand its limitations.

What Does It Mean?
Answer on page 443

11. What does it mean to state that a company's book value per share of common stock is less than its market value per share of common stock?

Common Size Financial Statements

LO 9
Discuss how common size financial statements can be used to evaluate a firm's financial position and results of operations over a number of years.

When comparing and evaluating the operating results of a company over a number of years, many analysts like to express the balance sheet and income statement in a percentage format. This type of presentation is referred to as a **common size statement.** To prepare a common size balance sheet, each asset is expressed as a percentage of total assets, and each liability and stockholders' equity amount is expressed as a percentage of that total. For the income statement, the sales amount is set at 100 percent, and each item on the income statement is expressed as a percentage of sales. This type of percentage analysis makes spotting trends in the composition of balance sheet and income statement items much easier than looking at dollar amounts. For example, inventories that represent an increasing percentage of total assets may indicate a weakness in inventory control procedures. An increase in the ratio of cost of goods sold to sales (which would be a decrease in the gross profit ratio) would indicate that management is either unable or unwilling to increase selling prices in response to cost increases, thus causing downward pressure on operating income. Of course, a well-designed graphical display of key balance sheet and income statement percentage data can also greatly help a reader interpret the data.

Exhibit 11-4 presents common size income statements for Campbell Soup Company for each of the years 2007 through 2011. When analyzing common size financial statement data, you should look first at the "big picture" items and make quick comparisons from year to year. By glancing at the trends for earnings before interest and taxes and net earnings, you will see that Campbell's had a relatively stable earnings pattern from 2007 to 2011. Check this out by scanning across each of the lines shown in bold in Exhibit 11-4. A line-by-line analysis of a company's common size data often will reveal additional information in support of a reader's basic interpretation of major trends. The actual dollar amounts associated with each of the common size percentage representations should also be considered. A wise investor or financial analyst will make appropriate use of all available information and refrain from drawing quick conclusions.

As mentioned at the beginning of this section, common size balance sheets can also be prepared using total assets as 100 percent. For any given year, each of the individual asset, liability, and stockholders' equity captions would be compared to total assets to determine its relative percentage. This process, illustrated in Exhibit 11-4 with Campbell's income statement data, is often referred to as *vertical* common size

CAMPBELL SOUP COMPANY Common Size Income Statements For the Five Years Ended July 31, 2011					
	2011	**2010**	**2009**	**2008**	**2007**
Net sales	100.0%	100.0%	100.0%	100.0%	100.0%
Costs and expenses:					
Cost of products sold	59.8	59.0	60.1	60.4	59.4
Marketing and selling expenses................................	13.0	13.8	14.2	14.5	15.0
Administrative expenses............	7.9	7.9	7.8	7.6	7.7
Research and development expenses................................	1.7	1.6	1.5	1.4	1.5
Other expenses (income)	0.2	0.0	0.8	0.2	(0.4)
Restructuring charges...............	0.8	0.1	0.0	2.2	0.0
Total costs and expenses	83.4%	82.4%	84.4%	86.3%	83.2%
Earnings before interest and taxes..................................	**16.6**	**17.6**	**15.6**	**13.7**	**16.8**
Interest expense, net	1.5	1.4	1.4	2.0	1.9
Earnings before taxes...................	15.1	16.2	14.2	11.7	14.9
Taxes on earnings.........................	4.7	5.2	4.6	3.3	4.2
Earnings from continuing operations.................................	10.4	11.0	9.6	8.4	10.7
Earnings from discontinued operations.................................	0.0	0.0	0.1	6.2	0.9
Net earnings................................	**10.4%**	**11.0%**	**9.7%**	**14.6%**	**11.6%**

Exhibit 11-4

Common Size Income Statements

analysis because each financial statement is examined from top to bottom on an annual basis. It is likewise possible, and often useful, to prepare *horizontal* common size financial statements. With horizontal analysis, several years' financial data are stated in terms of a base year. The amount reported for *each* item on the income statement or balance sheet in the base year is equal to 100 percent, and the amounts reported for all other years are stated as a percentage of this base. To illustrate, consider the sales and earnings results that Campbell's has reported in recent years:

	2011	**2010**	**2009**	**2008**	**2007**
Net sales (millions)...........................	$7,719	$7,676	$7,586	$7,998	$7,385
Net earnings (millions)	802	844	736	1,165	854

In Campbell's case, the net sales trend shows more stability than the net earnings trend, which is to be expected. Unfortunately, these raw data do not answer all of the questions you may have. For example, how rapidly have sales been increasing, and has net earnings kept pace with sales? Horizontal analysis answers these questions directly:

	2011	**2010**	**2009**	**2008**	**2007**
Net sales..	105%	104%	103%	108%	100%
Net earnings...................................	94%	99%	86%	136%	100%

Note that the selection of the base year influences the presentation of horizontal analysis trend results. With 2007 selected as the base year, the trends from 2009 through

2011 are shown in a more favorable light than they would be had 2008 been selected as the base year. Why? Simply because Campbell's reported higher dollar amounts for net sales and net earnings in 2008 than in 2007.

Other Operating Statistics

LO 10

Generalize about how operating statistics using physical, or nonfinancial, data can be used to help management evaluate the results of the firm's activities.

Physical measures of activity, rather than the financial measures included in the financial statements, are frequently useful. For example, reporting sales in units provides a perspective that may be hidden by price changes when only sales dollars are reported. Likewise, reporting the total number of employees (or employees by division or department) may be more useful for some purposes than reporting payroll costs.

Many analysts combine physical and financial measures to develop useful statistics to show trends or make comparisons between firms. For example, both sales dollars per employee and operating income per employee indicate a type of productivity measure. Plant operating expenses per square foot of plant space or gross profit per square foot of selling space might also be useful indicators of efficiency. There is no "cookbook" of quantitative measures for management to follow; the challenge is to understand the firm's objectives and procedures, and then to develop measurement and reporting techniques to help people accomplish their goals.

What Does It Mean?

Answers on page 444

12. What does it mean to prepare common size financial statements?
13. What does it mean to use more than financial ratios to evaluate a company's financial position and/or performance?

Demonstration Problem

Visit the text website at www.mhhe.com/marshall10e to view a demonstration problem for this chapter.

Summary

Financial statement analysis using ratio measurements and trend analysis assists the user of financial statements in making informed judgments and decisions about an entity's financial condition and results of operations. Keep in mind, however, that an analysis of an entity's financial data should be tempered by the fact that all of the data reviewed are historical. As a result, the analyst is making decisions about future events based primarily on past events. Without diminishing the value of financial ratio computations, it must be recognized that they do little to foretell the future. Therefore, the analyst must give due consideration to many other factors before making a decision about the entity.

Creditors especially are interested in the entity's liquidity. Working capital and the calculation of the current ratio and acid-test ratio were also discussed in Chapter 3.

Because alternative accounting methods affect financial statement data differently, it is important that readers know which alternatives (e.g., FIFO versus LIFO for inventory) have been used in the financial statements being analyzed.

Activity measures reflect the efficiency with which assets have been used to generate sales revenue. Most activity ratios focus on turnover. Activity also can be expressed in terms of the number of days of activity (e.g., sales) in the year-end balance (e.g., accounts receivable).

Rate of return calculations in general, and the return on investment (ROI) and return on equity (ROE) measures in particular, are essential in evaluating profitability. These measures were discussed in detail in Chapter 3.

The trend of a ratio over time contains much more information than a single ratio at one point in time. Trend comparisons between the entity and broad industry averages are also useful.

In addition to ROI and ROE based on total data, certain per share ratios are also important. The price/earnings ratio, dividend yield, dividend payout ratio, and preferred dividend coverage ratios are examples.

Leverage ratios focus on the financial leverage of the firm. Financial leverage magnifies ROE relative to ROI and adds risk to the securities issued by the firm.

Book value per share of common stock is frequently reported, but because it is based on the financial statement value of the firm's assets instead of their market value, book value is not very useful in most circumstances.

An effective way to compare the financial condition and results of operations of different size firms is to express balance sheet data as percentages of total assets and income statement data as percentages of sales. This process results in *vertical* common size financial statements. It is also useful to prepare *horizontal* common size financial statements that show trends in individual items over several years in comparison to a base year.

Investors, managers, employees, and others are frequently interested in other operating statistics that use data not contained in the financial statements. More than financial data are needed to develop a complete picture about a company.

Financial statement analysis ratios are summarized here by category of ratio:

I. Liquidity measures

A. Working capital

$$\text{Working capital} = \text{Current assets} - \text{Current liabilities}$$

The arithmetic relationship between current assets and current liabilities is a measure of the firm's ability to meet its obligations as they come due.

B. Current ratio

$$\text{Current ratio} = \frac{\text{Current assets}}{\text{Current liabilities}}$$

This ratio permits an evaluation of liquidity that is more comparable over time and between firms than the amount of working capital.

C. Acid-test ratio

$$\text{Acid-test ratio} = \frac{\text{Cash (including temporary cash investments)} + \text{Accounts receivable}}{\text{Current liabilities}}$$

By excluding inventories and other nonliquid current assets, this ratio gives a conservative assessment of the firm's bill-paying ability.

II. Activity measures

  A. Turnover

  1. Total asset turnover

$$\text{Total asset turnover} = \frac{\text{Sales}}{\text{Average total assets}}$$

Turnover shows the efficiency with which assets are used to generate sales. Refer also to the DuPont model under profitability measures.

  2. Variations include turnover calculations for accounts receivable, plant and equipment, and total operating assets. Each variation uses sales in the numerator and the appropriate average amount in the denominator.

  3. Inventory turnover

$$\text{Inventory turnover} = \frac{\text{Cost of goods sold}}{\text{Average inventories}}$$

Inventory turnover focuses on the efficiency of the firm's inventory management practices. Cost of goods sold is used in the numerator because inventories are carried at cost, not selling price.

  B. Number of days' sales in

  1. Accounts receivable

$$\frac{\text{Number of days' sales in}}{\text{accounts receivable}} = \frac{\text{Accounts receivable at year-end}}{\text{Average day's sales}}$$

$$\text{Average day's sales} = \frac{\text{Annual sales}}{365}$$

This measure shows the average age of the accounts receivable and reflects the efficiency of the firm's collection policies relative to its credit terms.

  2. Inventory

$$\frac{\text{Number of days'}}{\text{sales in inventory}} = \frac{\text{Inventory at year-end}}{\text{Average day's cost of goods sold}}$$

$$\frac{\text{Average day's cost}}{\text{of goods sold}} = \frac{\text{Annual cost of goods sold}}{365}$$

This measure shows the number of days' sales that could be made from the inventory on hand. The trend of this measure reflects management's ability to control inventories relative to sales.

III. Profitability measures

  A. Return on investment (ROI)

  1. General model

$$\text{ROI} = \frac{\text{Return}}{\text{Investment}}$$

Return is frequently net income, and investment is frequently average total assets. This ratio gives the rate of return that has been earned on the assets invested and is the key measure of profitability.

  2. DuPont model

$$\text{ROI} = \text{Margin} \times \text{Turnover}$$

$$= \frac{\text{Net income}}{\text{Sales}} \times \frac{\text{Sales}}{\text{Average total assets}}$$

Margin expresses the net income resulting from each dollar of sales. Turnover shows the efficiency with which assets are used to generate sales.

3. Variations of the general model use operating income, income before taxes, or some other intermediate income statement amount in the numerator and average operating assets in the denominator to focus on the rate of return from operations before taxes.

B. Return on equity (ROE)

1. General model

$$\text{ROE} = \frac{\text{Net income}}{\text{Average total stockholders' equity}}$$

This ratio gives the rate of return on that portion of the assets provided by the owners/stockholders of the entity.

2. A variation of the general model occurs when there is preferred stock. Net income is reduced by the amount of the preferred stock dividend requirement, and only common stockholders' equity is used in the denominator. This distinction is made because the ownership rights of the preferred and common stockholders differ.

C. Price/earnings ratio (P/E ratio)

$$\frac{\text{Price / earnings ratio}}{\text{(or earnings multiple)}} = \frac{\text{Market price per share}}{\text{Earnings per share}}$$

This ratio expresses the relative expensiveness of a share of a firm's common stock because it shows how much investors are willing to pay for the stock relative to earnings. Generally speaking, the greater a firm's ROI and rate of earnings growth, the higher the P/E ratio of its common stock will be. Most of the time the *diluted* earnings per share amount is used in this calculation.

D. Dividend yield

$$\text{Dividend yield} = \frac{\text{Annual dividend per share}}{\text{Market price per share of stock}}$$

The dividend yield expresses part of the stockholder's ROI: the rate of return represented by the annual cash dividend. The other part of the stockholder's total ROI comes from the change in the market value of the stock during the year; this is usually called the *capital gain* or *loss*.

E. Dividend payout ratio

$$\text{Dividend payout ratio} = \frac{\text{Annual dividend per share}}{\text{Earnings per share}}$$

The dividend payout ratio expresses the proportion of earnings paid as dividends to common stockholders. It can be used to estimate dividends of future years if earnings can be estimated. The diluted earnings per share amount is usually used in this calculation.

F. Preferred dividend coverage ratio

$$\frac{\text{Preferred dividend}}{\text{coverage ratio}} = \frac{\text{Net income}}{\text{Preferred dividend requirement}}$$

The preferred dividend coverage ratio expresses the ability of the firm to meet its preferred stock dividend requirement. The higher this coverage ratio, the lower the probability that dividends on common stock will be discontinued because of low earnings and failure to pay dividends on preferred stock.

IV. Financial leverage measures

A. Debt ratio

$$\text{Debt ratio} = \frac{\text{Total liabilities}}{\text{Total liabilities and stockholders' equity}}$$

B. Debt / equity ratio

$$\text{Debt / equity ratio} = \frac{\text{Total liabilities}}{\text{Total stockholders' equity}}$$

Each of these measures shows the proportion of debt in the capital structure. Note that a debt ratio of 50% is the same as a debt/equity ratio of 100%. These ratios reflect the risk caused by the interest and principal requirements of debt. Variations of these models involve the definition of total liabilities. Current liabilities and deferred tax liabilities are excluded by some analysts because they are not interest-bearing and do not add as much risk as does long-term debt.

C. Times interest earned

$$\text{Times interest earned} = \frac{\text{Earnings before interest and taxes}}{\text{Interest expense}}$$

This is a measure of the firm's ability to earn enough to cover its annual interest requirement.

Key Terms and Concepts

book value per share of common stock (p. 435)   The quotient of total common stockholders' equity divided by the number of shares of common stock outstanding. Sometimes called *net asset value per share of common stock*. Not a very useful measure most of the time.

common size statement (p. 436)   A financial statement in which amounts are expressed in percentage terms. In a *vertical* common size balance sheet, total assets are 100 percent, and all other amounts are expressed as a percentage of total assets each year; for an income statement, sales are 100 percent each year. *Horizontal* common size financial statements are side-by-side comparisons of several years' data in relation to the selected base year data.

debt/equity ratio (p. 433)   The ratio of total liabilities to total stockholders' equity. Sometimes only long-term debt is used for the numerator of the ratio.

debt ratio (p. 433)   The ratio of total liabilities to the sum of total liabilities and total stockholders' equity. Sometimes long-term debt is the only liability used in the calculation.

dividend payout ratio (p. 430)   The ratio of the annual dividend per share of common stock to the earnings per share.

dividend yield (p. 429)   The ratio of the annual dividend per share of common stock to the market price per share.

earnings multiple (p. 427)   Another term for *price/earnings ratio;* an indicator of the relative expensiveness of a firm's common stock.

effect of the inventory cost flow assumption on working capital (p. 421)   When the cost of items being purchased for inventory is changing, the inventory cost flow assumption used (e.g., FIFO or LIFO) influences the inventory account balance, total current assets, and working capital.

extra dividend (p. 431)   A dividend that is not likely to be incorporated as part of the regular dividend in the future.

financial leverage measures (p. 433)   The debt ratio and debt/equity ratio that indicate the extent to which financial leverage is being used.

number of days' sales in accounts receivable (p. 424) An indicator of the efficiency with which accounts receivable are collected.

number of days' sales in inventory (p. 424) An indicator of the efficiency with which inventories are managed.

preferred dividend coverage ratio (p. 431) The ratio of net income to the annual preferred stock dividend requirement.

price/earnings ratio (p. 427) An indicator of the relative expensiveness of a firm's common stock.

regular dividend (p. 431) A dividend that is likely to be declared on a repetitive, periodic (i.e., quarterly, semiannual, or annual) basis.

times interest earned ratio (p. 434) The ratio of earnings before interest and taxes to interest expense. An indicator of the risk associated with financial leverage.

ANSWERS TO
What Does It Mean?

1. It means that comparing the results of a particular ratio over a period of time permits a more valid comparison of the direction of relative performance than a comparison of that ratio at a single point in time. However, it is necessary to understand how alternative accounting practices have affected the financial statement amounts reported for each firm.

2. It means that working capital, the current ratio, and the acid-test ratio are calculated and interpreted to determine whether the entity is likely to be able to pay its current obligations when they come due.

3. It means that to determine how efficiently the firm's assets are being used and/or managed, various turnover ratios are calculated and evaluated.

4. It means that the ratio of sales for the period to average total assets used during the period has risen, indicating that assets were used more efficiently relative to sales generated. Perhaps this was accomplished by producing more product with the same amount of plant and equipment and/or by reducing inventories.

5. It means that the firm is less profitable in the sense of earnings related to assets used to generate earnings.

6. It means to break ROI into its margin and turnover components to help determine whether the decrease in ROI is due to reduced profitability or less efficient use of assets, or both.

7. It means that investors are willing to pay more, in relative terms, for a share of the firm's common stock than for a share of common stock of most other firms. This may be caused by investor expectations for much higher growth in profitability in the immediate future for the firm relative to expectations for other firms.

8. It means that the firm is retaining and reinvesting proportionately more of its earnings than other companies. This may be because the firm anticipates needing more capital for expansion and the board of directors prefer to retain earnings for that use rather than raise capital by selling more stock or issuing debt.

9. It means that the firm has a relatively high proportion of debt to equity in its capital structure.

10. It means that if the firm cannot earn a greater rate of return than the interest rate being paid on borrowed funds, its chances of not being able to meet its obligations and of going bankrupt are greater than if it had less financial leverage.

11. It doesn't mean much at all because book value is based on balance sheet values, which are not market values or replacement values.

12. It means that instead of using currency amounts in the statements, elements of the financial statements are expressed as a percentage of total assets (for the balance sheet) or as a percentage of sales (for the income statement). This is an easy and effective way of making comparisons over time for a single company and of comparing one company with another—as long as consideration is given to the effects of different accounting practices that may have been used.

13. It means that other statistics, such as rate of employee turnover, market share, and/or sales per employee, are frequently relevant and useful to the evaluator.

Self-Study Material

Visit the text website at www.mhhe.com/marshall10e to take an online self-study quiz for this chapter.

Matching Following are a number of the key terms and concepts introduced in the chapter, along with a list of corresponding definitions. Match the appropriate letter for the key term or concept to each definition provided (items 1–10). Note that not all key terms and concepts will be used. Answers are provided at the end of this chapter.

a.	Return on investment (ROI)	m.	Number of days' sales in accounts receivable
b.	DuPont model		
c.	Margin	n.	Earnings per share
d.	Turnover	o.	Price/earnings (P/E) ratio
e.	Return on equity (ROE)	p.	Earnings multiple
f.	Working capital	q.	Dividend yield
g.	Current ratio	r.	Dividend payout ratio
h.	Acid-test ratio	s.	Regular dividend
i.	Debt ratio	t.	Extra dividend
j.	Leverage ratios	u.	Preferred dividend coverage ratio
k.	Times interest earned ratio	v.	Debt/equity ratio
l.	Common size statement	w.	Book value per share

_____ 1. The ratio of earnings before interest and taxes to interest expense.

_____ 2. An indicator of the relative expensiveness of a firm's common stock.

_____ 3. The ratio of net income to the annual preferred stock dividend requirement.

_____ 4. An indicator of the efficiency with which accounts receivable are collected.

_____ 5. The ratio of the annual dividend per share to the market price per share of the stock.

_____ 6. The quotient of total common stockholders' equity divided by the number of shares of common stock outstanding.

_____ 7. A dividend that is not likely to be incorporated as part of the regular dividend in the future.

_____ **8.** A financial statement in which amounts are expressed in percentage terms.

_____ **9.** The ratio of total liabilities to total stockholders' equity.

_____**10.** The percentage of net income to sales.

Multiple Choice For each of the following questions, circle the best response. Answers are provided at the end of this chapter.

 1. Activity measures are designed to quantify the impact of a firm's ability to efficiently utilize its assets. Turnover ratios are the most common activity measures and are generally calculated for each of the following assets *except*
    a. accounts receivable.
    b. inventory.
    c. cash.
    d. plant and equipment.

 2. Which basis of ratio evaluation would you expect to produce the most meaningful comparisons?
    a. Within-company comparisons as of a given date.
    b. Company-to-industry comparisons as of a given date.
    c. Within-company trends over a period of time.
    d. Company-to-industry comparisons over a period of time.

 3. Many financial analysts substitute one amount for another in making ratio analysis comparisons in order to better achieve intercompany or company-to-industry data comparability. Which of the substitutions described here would *not* achieve better data comparability (for the ratio indicated) under any situation?
    a. Cost of goods sold for sales—in the numerator of the inventory turnover ratio.
    b. Cost of plant and equipment for net book value—in the numerator of the plant and equipment turnover ratio.
    c. Expected future earnings per share for current earnings per share—in the denominator of the price/earnings ratio.
    d. Average net assets for average total assets—in the denominator of the return on investment ratio.

 4. If the trend of the current ratio is increasing while the trend of the acid-test ratio is decreasing over a period of time, this could be a warning that the firm is
    a. carrying excess inventories.
    b. depleting its inventories.
    c. having trouble collecting its receivables.
    d. purchasing too much property, plant, and equipment.

 5. If current assets exceed current liabilities, payments of accounts payable will
    a. decrease the current ratio.
    b. increase the current ratio.
    c. decrease working capital.
    d. increase working capital.

Use the following information for Questions 6–8.

Information concerning O'Sadnick, Inc., on December 31, 2013, is as follows:

Book value per share	$ 6.00
Dividends per share	1.00
Earnings per share	4.00
Par value per share.	2.00
Market price per share	16.00

6. What is O'Sadnick, Inc.'s price/earnings ratio for 2013?

    a. 0.25   *c.* 4.0

    b. 1.5   *d.* 8.0

7. What is O'Sadnick, Inc.'s dividend payout ratio for 2013?

    a. 4.16%   *c.* 25%

    b. 6.25%   *d.* 50%

8. What is O'Sadnick, Inc.'s dividend yield for 2013?

    a. 4.16%   *c.* 25%

    b. 6.25%   *d.* 50%

Use the following information for Questions 9–10.

Porter Co. reported the following on its December 31, 2013, balance sheet:

Liabilities and Stockholders' Equity:	
Accounts payable.	$ 3,000
Notes payable.	22,000
Bonds payable	45,000
Common stock.	110,000
Preferred stock	20,000
Additional paid-in capital.	70,000
Retained earnings.	32,000
Treasury stock.	12,000

9. The debt/equity ratio for Porter Co. in 2013 (rounded) is

    a. 20.5%   *c.* 28.7%

    b. 24.1%   *d.* 31.8%

10. The debt ratio for Porter Co. in 2013 (rounded) is

    a. 20.5%   *c.* 28.7%

    b. 24.1%   *d.* 31.8%

Mini-Exercises

All applicable Mini-Exercises are available with McGraw-Hill's *Connect*™ *Accounting*.

(Note: Where no specific learning objective is identified, the requirements involve calculating and using several ratios, including those discussed in Chapter 3.)

Calculate liquidity measures The following amounts were reported on the December 31, 2013, balance sheet:

**Mini-Exercise
11.1**

Cash	$ 8,000	Accounts payable	$ 15,000
Accounts receivable	22,000	Bonds payable	120,000
Common stock	40,000	Merchandise inventory	30,000
Wages payable	5,000	Buildings and equipment, net of	
Retained earnings	80,000	accumulated depreciation	180,000
Land	20,000		

Required:

a. Calculate working capital at December 31, 2013.

b. Calculate the current ratio at December 31, 2013.

c. Calculate the acid-test ratio at December 31, 2013.

Calculate activity measures The following information was available for the year ended December 31, 2013:

**Mini-Exercise
11.2**

Net sales	$730,000	Average accounts receivable	
Cost of goods sold	584,000	for the year	$29,200
Average inventories for the year	146,000	Accounts receivable at	
Inventories at year-end	156,800	year-end	32,000

Required:

a. Calculate the inventory turnover for 2013.

b. Calculate the number of days' sales in inventory for 2013, using year-end inventories.

c. Calculate the accounts receivable turnover for 2013.

d. Calculate the number of days' sales in accounts receivable for 2013, using year-end accounts receivable.

Calculate profitability measures The following information was available for the year ended December 31, 2013:

**Mini-Exercise
11.3**

Sales	$200,000	Dividends per share	$ 1.20
Net income	30,000	Earnings per share	3.00
Average total assets	500,000	Market price per share	
Average total stockholders'		at year-end	48.00
equity	300,000		

Required:

a. Calculate margin, turnover, and ROI for the year ended December 31, 2013.

b. Calculate ROE for the year ended December 31, 2013.

c. Calculate the price/earnings ratio for 2013.

d. Calculate the dividend payout ratio for 2013.

e. Calculate the dividend yield for 2013.

**Mini-Exercise
11.4**

Calculate financial leverage measures The following information was available for the year ended December 31, 2013:

Earnings before interest and taxes (operating income)	$60,000	Net income	$ 35,000
Interest expense	10,000	Total assets at year-end	200,000
Income tax expense	15,000	Total liabilities at year-end	120,000

Required:

a. Calculate the debt ratio at December 31, 2013.

b. Calculate the debt/equity ratio at December 31, 2013.

c. Calculate the times interest earned for the year ended December 31, 2013.

connect
ACCOUNTING

Exercises

All applicable Exercises are available with McGraw-Hill's *Connect™ Accounting.*

Exercise 11.5

Identify information used in an investment decision Look forward to the day when you will have accumulated $5,000, and assume that you have decided to invest that hard-earned money in the common stock of a publicly owned corporation. What data about that company will you be most interested in, and how will you arrange those data so they are most meaningful to you? What information about the company will you want on a weekly basis, on a quarterly basis, and on an annual basis? How will you decide whether to sell, hold, or buy some more of the firm's stock?

Exercise 11.6

Obtain an annual report and discuss information sources If your library has a common stock investment advisory service such as *Moody's Handbook of Common Stocks* or online access to an investment advisory service such as *Value Line Research Center: Historical Reports,* use one of those sources to locate a report about a company you have heard about or in which you have an interest. Alternatively, visit a brokerage firm office and ask for a report from one of the above sources or a report prepared by the brokerage firm's research division. Review the report and notice the analytical data that it contains. What other data besides those in the report would you like to obtain? Why do you want these other data? How would you get them?

Exercise 11.7

Effect of transactions on various financial ratios Indicate the effect that each transaction/event listed here will have on the financial ratio listed opposite it, and provide an explanation for your answer. Use + for increase, − for decrease, and (NE) for no effect. Assume that current assets exceed current liabilities in all cases, both before and after the transaction/event.

Transaction/Event	Financial Ratio
a. Split the common stock 2 for 1.	Book value per share of common stock
b. Collected accounts receivable.	Number of days' sales in accounts receivable
c. Issued common stock for cash.	Total asset turnover
d. Sold treasury stock.	Return on equity
e. Accrued interest on a note receivable.	Current ratio
f. Sold inventory on account.	Acid-test ratio
g. Wrote off an uncollectible account.	Accounts receivable turnover
h. Declared a cash dividend.	Dividend yield
i. Incurred operating expenses.	Margin
j. Sold equipment at a loss.	Earnings per share

Effect of transactions on various financial ratios Indicate the effect that each transaction/event listed here will have on the financial ratio listed opposite it, and provide an explanation for your answer. Use + for increase, − for decrease, and (NE) for no effect. Assume that current assets exceed current liabilities in all cases, both before and after the transaction/event.

Exercise 11.8

Transaction/Event	Financial Ratio
a. Purchased inventory on account.	Number of days' sales in inventory
b. Sold inventory for cash, at a profit.	Inventory turnover
c. Issued a 10% stock dividend.	Earnings per share
d. Issued common stock for cash.	Debt ratio
e. Sold land at a gain.	Return on investment
f. Purchased treasury stock for cash.	Debt/equity ratio
g. Accrued interest on a note payable.	Times interest earned
h. Accrued wages that have been earned by employees.	Current ratio
i. Purchased equipment for cash.	Plant and equipment turnover
j. Issued bonds at an interest rate that is less than the company's ROI.	Return on equity

Problems

All applicable Problems are available with McGraw-Hill's *Connect™ Accounting.*

Prepare a common size balance sheet, 2010 Refer to the consolidated balance sheets on page 712 of the Campbell Soup Company annual report in the appendix.

Problem 11.9

LO 9

Required:

Prepare a common size balance sheet at August 1, 2010, using the following captions:

> Total current assets
> Plant assets, net of depreciation
> Goodwill
> Total other long-term assets

Total assets
Total current liabilities
Total long-term liabilities (including deferred taxes)
Total equity
Total liabilities and equity

Problem 11.10
LO 9
Prepare a common size balance sheet, 2011 Solve the requirements of Problem 11.9 for the year ended July 31, 2011.

Problem 11.11
LO 1
Review problem—understanding liquidity measures Assume that the current ratio for Arch Company is 2.0, its acid-test ratio is 1.5, and its working capital is $300,000. Answer each of the following questions *independently,* always referring to the original information.

a. How much does the firm have in current liabilities?

b. If the only current assets shown on the balance sheet for Arch Company are Cash, Accounts Receivable, and Merchandise Inventory, how much does the firm have in Merchandise Inventory?

c. If the firm collects an account receivable of $100,000, what will its new current ratio and working capital be?

d. If the firm pays an account payable of $100,000, what will its new current ratio and working capital be?

e. If the firm sells inventory that was purchased for $50,000 at a cash price of $60,000, what will its new acid-test ratio be?

Problem 11.12
LO 1
Effect of transactions on liquidity measures Selected balance sheet accounts for Tibbetts Company on September 30, 2013, are as follows:

Cash	$ 96,000
Marketable securities	174,000
Accounts receivable, net	258,000
Inventory	270,000
Prepaid expenses	42,000
Total current assets	$840,000
Accounts payable	$294,000
Other accrued liabilities	66,000
Short-term debt	120,000
Total current liabilities	$480,000

Required:

a. Calculate the working capital, current ratio, and acid-test ratio for Tibbetts Company as of September 30, 2013.

b. Summarized here are the transactions/events that took place during the fiscal year ended September 30, 2014. Indicate the effect of each item on Tibbetts Company's working capital, current ratio, and acid-test ratio. Use + for increase, – for decrease, and (NE) for no effect. *(Hint: It may be helpful to use the horizontal model or to record the journal entry(ies) for each item before considering the effects on liquidity measures.)*

Transaction/Event	Working Capital	Current Ratio	Acid-Test Ratio
0. Example: Paid accounts payable, $585,000.	NE	+	+
1. Credit sales for the year amounted to $720,000. The cost of goods sold was $468,000.			
2. Collected accounts receivable, $756,000.			
3. Purchased inventory on account, $504,000.			
4. Issued 500 shares of common stock for $54 per share.			
5. Wrote off $21,000 of uncollectible accounts using the allowance for bad debts.			
6. Declared and paid a cash dividend, $60,000.			
7. Sold marketable securities costing $78,000 for $93,000 in cash.			
8. Recorded insurance expense for the year, $36,000. The premium for the policy was paid in June 2013.			
9. Borrowed cash on a short-term bank loan, $30,000.			
10. Repaid principal of $120,000 and interest of $9,000 on a long-term bank loan.			

Ratio analysis—comprehensive problem Presented here are summarized data from the balance sheets and income statements of Wiper, Inc.:

Problem 11.13

WIPER, INC. Condensed Balance Sheets December 31, 2014, 2013, 2012 (in millions)			
	2014	**2013**	**2012**
Current assets.	$ 677	$ 891	$ 736
Other assets	2,413	1,920	1,719
	$3,090	$2,811	$2,455
Current liabilities	$ 562	$ 803	$ 710
Long-term liabilities	1,521	982	827
Stockholders' equity	1,007	1,026	918
	$3,090	$2,811	$2,455

WIPER, INC. Selected Income Statement and Other Data For the Years Ended December 31, 2014 and 2013 (in millions)		
	2014	**2013**
Income statement data:		
Sales	$3,050	$2,913
Operating income.	296	310
Interest expense.	84	65
Net income	192	187
Other data:		
Average number of common shares outstanding	41.3	46.7
Total dividends paid	$ 50.0	$ 52.3

Required:

a. Calculate return on investment, based on net income and average total assets, for 2014 and 2013. Show both margin and turnover in your calculation.

b. Calculate return on equity for 2014 and 2013.

c. Calculate working capital and the current ratio for each of the past three years.

d. Calculate earnings per share for 2014 and 2013.

e. If Wiper's stock had a price/earnings ratio of 13 at the end of 2014, what was the market price of the stock?

f. Calculate the cash dividend per share for 2014 and the dividend yield based on the market price calculated in part **e**.

g. Calculate the dividend payout ratio for 2014.

h. Assume that accounts receivable at December 31, 2014, totaled $309 million. Calculate the number of days' sales in receivables at that date.

i. Calculate Wiper's debt ratio and debt/equity ratio at December 31, 2014 and 2013.

j. Calculate the times interest earned ratio for 2014 and 2013.

k. Review the results of these calculations, evaluate the profitability and liquidity of this company, and state your opinion about its suitability as an investment for a young, single professional with funds to invest in common stock.

Problem 11.14

Ratio analysis—comprehensive problem, 2011 data This problem is based on the 2011 annual report of Campbell Soup Company in the appendix.

Required:

a. Compute the following profitability measures for the year ended July 31, 2011:
   1. Return on investment, based on net earnings (perform a DuPont analysis).
   2. Return on equity, based on net earnings and total equity.
   3. Price/earnings ratio. Use $33.05 as the year-end market price.
   4. Dividend yield.
   5. Dividend payout ratio.

b. Compute the following liquidity measures at July 31, 2011:
   1. Working capital.
   2. Current ratio.
   3. Acid-test ratio.

c. Compute the following activity measures for the year ended July 31, 2011:
   1. Number of days' sales in accounts receivable, based on a 365-day year.
   2. Number of days' sales in inventory, based on a 365-day year.
   3. Accounts receivable turnover.
   4. Inventory turnover.
   5. Turnover of net property, plant, and equipment.

d. Compute the following financial leverage measures at July 31, 2011:
   1. Debt ratio.
   2. Debt/equity ratio.

e. Compute the following physical measures of Campbell's profitability at July 31, 2011:

1. Net sales per employee.
2. Operating income per employee. *(Note: In a page not reproduced in the appendix, Campbell's 2011 annual report disclosed that on July 31, 2011, the company had approximately 17,500 employees.)*

Cases

All applicable Cases are available with McGraw-Hill's *Connect™ Accounting.*

Focus company—comprehensive financial statement analysis In Exercise 1.1, you were asked to obtain the most recent annual report of a company that you were interested in reviewing throughout this term.

Case 11.15

Required:

Liquidity:

a. Calculate working capital, the current ratio, and the acid-test ratio as of the most recent balance sheet date.

b. Based on your calculations in part **a,** assess the company's overall liquidity position. Explain which ratios indicate particular strengths and/or weaknesses within the company. Assume the following industry averages: current ratio = 2.0; acid-test ratio = 1.6.

c. Explain how working capital and the current ratio are related. Would you expect a company with a large amount of working capital to always have a high current ratio?

Profitability:

d. Calculate ROI, showing margin and turnover, for the most recent year.

e. Calculate ROE for the most recent year.

f. Calculate the price/earnings ratio for the most recent year, using the company's year-end market price per share of common stock in the numerator and diluted earnings per share in the denominator.

g. Calculate the dividend payout and dividend yield ratios for the most recent year.

h. Based on the results of your calculations in parts **d, e,** and **f,** assess the company's overall profitability. Explain which ratios indicate particular strengths and/or weaknesses within the company. Assume the following industry averages: ROI = 15%; margin = 10%; turnover = 1.5; ROE = 20%; price/earnings = 14.0; dividend payout = 40%; dividend yield = 5%.

i. As an investor in this company's stock, would you be pleased with this year's dividend yield? How would your dividend yield "expectations" change, if at all, if the company's ROI was 5% higher? Explain.

Financial leverage:

j. Calculate the debt ratio and the debt/equity ratio as of the most recent balance sheet date.

k. Based on the results of your calculations in part **j,** assess the company's overall leverage position. What would you estimate the industry averages to be for the debt ratio and debt/equity ratio? Explain.

l. Explain the relationship between ROI and ROE, and the concept of financial leverage. Would you expect the percentage difference between ROI and ROE to be high or low for a firm that makes substantial use of financial leverage?

Activity measures:

m. Calculate the accounts receivable turnover and number of days' sales in accounts receivable (based on a 365-day year) for the most recent year.

n. Based on your analysis in part **m,** do you believe that the company is doing an effective job at managing accounts receivable? What would you estimate the industry averages to be for the accounts receivable turnover and number of days' sales in accounts receivable? Explain.

o. Calculate the inventory turnover and number of days' sales in inventory (based on a 365-day year) for the most recent year.

p. Based on your analysis in part **o,** to what extent does the company need to be concerned about its inventory management policies? In assessing the inventory management policies, would you be more interested in knowing current ratio or acid-test ratio information? Explain.

Overall assessment:

q. Assume that you have $5,000 that you would like to invest in a single company. Evaluate the common stock of your focus company as a potential investment. From the data available in your focus company's financial statements, identify the five most important criteria that you would use to make your investment decision, and explain why each is important.

Case 11.16   Analytical case—comparative analysis of profitability and financial leverage measures The annual reports of the Coca-Cola Co. and PepsiCo, Inc., indicate the following for the year ended December 31, 2011 (amounts in millions):

	Coca-Cola Co.	PepsiCo, Inc.
Net revenues	$46,452	$66,504
Net income	8,634	6,462
Total assets, January 1, 2011	72,921	68,153
Total liabilities, January 1, 2011	41,607	46,667
Total liabilities, December 31, 2011	48,053	51,983
Total stockholders' equity, December 31, 2011	31,921	20,899

Required:

a. Calculate ROI and ROE for each company for 2011. *(Hint: You will need to calculate some of the numbers used in the denominator of these ratios.)*

b. Based on the results of your ROI and ROE analysis in part **a,** do you believe that either firm uses financial leverage more effectively than the other? Explain your answer. *(Hint: Compare the percentage differences between ROI and ROE for each firm. Is there a significant difference that would suggest that one firm uses leverage more effectively than the other?)*

c. Calculate the debt ratio and debt/equity ratio for each firm at the end of 2011.

d. Compare the results of your analysis in part **c** to your expectations concerning the relative use of financial leverage in part **b.** Do the debt and debt/equity ratios calculated in part **c** make sense relative to your expectations? Explain your answer.

Case 11.17

Analytical case—complete an income statement and balance sheet using financial ratio data Partially completed financial statements for Whittaker, Inc., follow:

WHITTAKER, INC.
Income Statement
For the Year Ended December 31, 2014

Sales...	$?
Cost of goods sold	?
Gross profit	$?
Operating expenses	?
Income from operations..	$?
Interest expense	?
Income before taxes	$?
Income taxes (20%)...	?
Net income	$?

WHITTAKER, INC.
Balance Sheet
December 31, 2014

Current assets:	
Cash	$?
Accounts receivable, net	?
Inventory	?
Total current assets	$171,000
Property, plant, and equipment, net.........................	?
Total assets.......................................	$?
Current liabilities	$?
Bonds payable, 15%...	70,000
Total liabilities......................................	$?
Stockholders' equity:	
Common stock, $2 par value...............................	$ 10,000
Additional paid-in capital	15,000
Retained earnings	?
Total stockholders' equity.............................	$?
Total liabilities and stockholders' equity...............	$?

Additional information:

- Financial ratios computed from these financial statements include the following:

Current ratio	1.9 to 1
Acid-test ratio	1.3 to 1
Debt/equity ratio	2.0 to 1
Inventory turnover	4.0 times
Accounts receivable turnover..............................	6.8 times
Times interest earned	4.45 times
Gross profit ratio	40%
Return on investment	12%
Earnings per share.......................................	$5.52

- All sales during the year were made on account. Cash collections during the year exceeded sales by $14,000, and no uncollectible accounts were written off.
- The balance of the accounts receivable account was $57,000 on January 1, 2014.
- No common stock was issued during the year.
- Dividends declared and paid during the year were $7,600.
- The balance of the inventory account was $48,000 on January 1, 2014.
- Interest expense on the income statement relates to the 15% bonds payable; $10,000 of these bonds were issued on May 1, 2014; the remaining amount of bonds payable were outstanding throughout the year. All bonds were issued at face amount.

Required:

a. Complete the income statement and balance sheet for Whittaker, Inc. Show how each amount was determined.

b. After completing part **a,** use your answers to recompute each of the financial ratios provided as additional information.

Case 11.18   **Capstone analytical review of Chapters 9–11. Calculate selected financial ratios and explain financial reporting issues**

(Note: Please refer to Case 4.30 on pages 145–146 for the financial statement data needed for the analysis of this case. You should also review the solution to Case 4.30, provided by your instructor, before attempting to complete this case.)

Required:

a. Case 4.30 presents the 2013 income statement and balance sheet for Gerrard Construction Co. What other financial statements are required? What information would these statements communicate that could not be determined by reviewing only the income statement and balance sheet?

b. Briefly describe the note disclosures that should be provided by Gerrard Construction Co., and explain why note disclosures are considered an integral part of the financial statements.

c. Assume that the balance of "Accounts Receivable, net" at December 31, 2012, was $8,200. Calculate the following activity measures for Gerrard Construction Co. for the year ended December 31, 2013:

    1.   Accounts receivable turnover.

    2.   Number of days' sales in accounts receivable.

d. Calculate the following financial leverage measures for Gerrard Construction Co. at December 31, 2013:

    1.   Debt ratio.

    2.   Debt/equity ratio.

e. Gerrard Construction Co. wishes to lease some new earthmoving equipment from Caterpillar on a long-term basis. What impact (increase, decrease, or no effect) would a capital lease of $4 million have on the company's debt ratio and debt/equity ratio? *(Note that these items were computed in part **b** and do not need to be recomputed for this requirement.)*

f. Review the answer to Case 4.30 part **i** at this time. Assume that Gerrard Construction Co. had 2,400,000 shares of $1 par value common stock outstanding throughout 2013, and that the market price per share of common stock at December 31, 2013, was $18.75. Calculate the following profitability measures for the year ended December 31, 2013:

    1.   Earnings per share of common stock.

    2.   Price/earnings ratio.

    3.   Dividend yield.

    4.   Dividend payout ratio.

Answers to Self-Study Material

Matching: 1. k, 2. o *or* p, 3. u, 4. m, 5. q, 6. w, 7. t, 8. l, 9. v, 10. c
Multiple choice: 1. c, 2. d, 3. d, 4. a, 5. b, 6. c, 7. c, 8. b, 9. d, 10. b

12

Managerial Accounting and Cost–Volume–Profit Relationships

You have learned in Part 1 of *Accounting: What the Numbers Mean* that financial accounting refers to the process that results in the preparation of the financial statements for an entity. These financial statements are oriented to the external user who is not in a position to be aware of the day-to-day financial and operating activities of the entity. In Part 2 of the book, you will learn about accounting for managers of the entity, which will provide yet additional insight to the phrase "what the numbers mean." When asked by the marketing or production manager what a certain item or activity costs, the management accountant who responds "Why do you want to know?" is not being disrespectful. Costs used for assigning a value to the inventory produced are different from the costs that should be considered when analyzing a modification to the product or a potential new product.

In **managerial accounting,** sometimes called *management accounting,* economic and financial information is used to plan and control many activities of the entity and to support the management decision-making process. Managerial accounting has an internal orientation, as opposed to the primarily external orientation of financial accounting. The transactions generated by the accounting information system and used for financial reporting also are used in managerial accounting; but the latter are more likely to have a future orientation, such as in the preparation of budgets or decision making. As with financial accounting, managerial accounting has special terminology or, as many would say, *jargon.* Most of these terms relate to different types of costs. An important early lesson about managerial accounting is that *there are different costs for different purposes.*

In this chapter we will look briefly at the management process, identify several contributions that management accounting makes to that process, and then introduce a model for classifying costs. Subsequent chapters will describe these costs and illustrate how they are used in the planning, control, and decision-making processes.

Cost–volume–profit (CVP) analysis involves using cost behavior patterns to interpret and forecast the changes in operating income that result from changes in revenues, costs, or volume of activity. One especially important application of CVP analysis is the determination of the break-even point for a company (or one of its units or products). Because CVP analysis emphasizes the cost behavior pattern of various costs and the impact on costs and profits of changes in the volume of activity, it is useful for planning and for evaluating the results of actual operations.

1. What does it mean to state that there are different costs for different purposes?

What Does It Mean?
Answer on page 486

LEARNING OBJECTIVES (LO)

After studying this chapter you should understand and be able to

LO 12-1   Explain the management planning and control cycle.

LO 12-2   Identify the major differences between financial accounting and managerial accounting.

LO 12-3   Describe the difference between variable and fixed cost behavior patterns and the simplifying assumptions made in this classification method.

LO 12-4   Demonstrate why expressing fixed costs on a per unit of activity basis is misleading and may result in faulty decisions.

LO 12-5   Explain what types of costs are likely to have a variable cost behavior pattern and what types of costs are likely to have a fixed cost behavior pattern.

LO 12-6   Use the high–low method to determine the cost formula for a cost that has a mixed behavior pattern.

LO 12-7   Explain and illustrate the difference between the traditional income statement format and the contribution margin income statement format.

LO 12-8   Use the contribution margin format to analyze the impact of cost and sales volume changes on operating income.

LO 12-9   Calculate the contribution margin ratio and explain how it can be used in CVP analysis.

LO 12-10   Analyze how changes in the sales mix can affect projections using CVP analysis.

LO 12-11   Describe the meaning and significance of the break-even point and illustrate how the break-even point is calculated.

LO 12-12   Use operating leverage to evaluate cost structures.

Managerial Accounting Contrasted to Financial Accounting

Managerial accounting supports the internal planning (future-oriented) decisions made by management. Financial accounting has more of a scorekeeping, historical orientation, although data produced by the financial accounting process form some of the foundation on which plans are based. Planning is a key part of the **management**

LO 1
Explain the management planning and control cycle.

process; and although there are many descriptions of that process, a generally acceptable definition would include reference to the process of planning, organizing, and controlling an entity's activities so that the organization can achieve its desired outcomes. A general model of the process looks like this:

The model suggests that control is achieved through feedback. Actual results are compared to planned results; if a difference exists between the two, then either the plan or the actions, or perhaps both, are changed. Management decision making occurs in each phase of the planning and control cycle using information provided by the accounting information system in an effort to continuously improve organizational performance.

Not all of a firm's objectives are stated in financial terms by any means. For example, market share, employee morale, absence of layoffs, and responsible corporate citizenship are all appropriate objectives that are expressed in nonfinancial terms. However, many of the firm's goals will be financial (ROI, ROE, growth in sales, earnings, and dividends, to name just a few). The management accountant plays a major role in identifying these goals, helping to achieve them, and measuring the degree to which they have been accomplished.

Emphasis on the future is a principal characteristic that makes managerial accounting different from financial accounting. Anticipating what revenues will be and forecasting the expenses that will be incurred to achieve those revenues are critical activities of the budgeting process. Another difference between managerial accounting and financial accounting that is emphasized in planning is breadth of focus. Financial accounting deals primarily with the financial statements for the organization as a whole; managerial accounting is more concerned with operating units within the organization. Thus, even though an overall company ROI objective is established, effective planning requires that the planned impact of the activities and results of each unit (division, product line, plant, sales territory, and so on) of the organization be considered.

Measuring results involves using the historical data of financial accounting; and because of the time required to perform financial accounting and auditing procedures, there is usually a time lag of weeks or months between the end of an accounting period and the issuance of financial statements. However, for performance feedback to be most effective, it should be provided as quickly as possible after action has been completed. Management accounting is not constrained by generally accepted accounting principles, so approximate results can be quickly generated for use in the control process. In other words, relevant data, even though not absolutely accurate in a financial accounting sense, are useful for evaluating performance soon after an activity has been completed.

LO 2

Identify the major differences between financial accounting and managerial accounting.

Characteristic	Managerial Accounting	Financial Accounting
Service perspective	Internal to managers.	External to investors and creditors.
Time frame	Present and future for planning and control.	Past—financial statements are historical.
Breadth of concern	Micro—individual units of the organization plan and act.	Macro—financial statements are for the organization as a whole.
Reporting frequency and promptness	Control reports issued frequently (e.g., daily) and promptly (e.g., one day after period-end).	Most financial statements issued monthly, a week or more after month-end.
Degree of precision of data used	Reasonable accuracy desired, but "close counts"—relevance is often more important than reliability.	High accuracy desired, with time usually available to achieve it—reliability is of utmost importance.
Reporting standards	None imposed because of internal and pragmatic orientation.	Imposed by generally accepted accounting principles and the FASB.

Exhibit 12-1

Managerial Accounting Compared to Financial Accounting

Exhibit 12-1 summarizes the principal differences between managerial accounting and financial accounting.

If time and effort have been devoted to developing a plan, it is appropriate to attempt to control the activities of the organization so that the desired outcomes of the plan are achieved. Many activities of the management accountant are related to cost control; this control emphasis will be seen in most of the managerial accounting ideas that are explained in these chapters.

Another management concept relevant to the control process is that if an individual is to be held accountable, or responsible, for the results of an activity, that individual also must have the authority to influence those results. If a manager is to be held responsible for costs incurred by a unit of the organization, the financial results reported for that unit should not include costs incurred by other units that have been arbitrarily assigned to the unit being evaluated. In other words, performance results should not reflect costs that the manager being held responsible cannot control.

Management accountants work extensively with people in other functional areas of the organization. For example, industrial engineers and management accountants work together to develop **production standards,** which are the expected or allowed times and costs to make a product or perform an activity. Management accountants help production managers interpret performance reports, which compare actual and planned production and costs. Sales personnel, the marketing staff, and management accountants are involved in estimating a future period's sales. Human resource professionals and management accountants work together to determine the cost effect of compensation changes. And the management accountant will play a significant role in the firm's systems development life cycle process by providing key insights into the planning, analysis, design, and implementation phases of an organization's information systems projects. These few key examples illustrate the need for management accountants to have a breadth of knowledge and interest about the organization and its operating environment. The examples also suggest that it is appropriate for people in other functional areas to have a general understanding of managerial accounting. Helping you achieve that general understanding is the primary objective of the remaining chapters in this book.

2. What does it mean that the time frame for managerial accounting is different from that for financial accounting?
3. What does it mean to have feedback for control purposes?

Cost Classifications

The term *cost* means different things to different people, and in the management planning and decision-making process, it is important to use costs that are appropriate to the situation. Likewise, management accountants should make sure that everyone participating in a given planning or decision-making activity understands the costs involved. Exhibit 12-2 presents a model for the cost classifications most frequently encountered and highlights the cost topics covered in this chapter.

Cost classifications are not mutually exclusive; you will learn that a cost might be identified as a "controllable, variable, direct, product cost," for example. Overall, this basic concept of *different costs for different purposes* is so fundamental to an understanding of the planning, control, and decision-making process that the cost classification model will be presented again in each managerial accounting chapter that follows. From the perspective of this model you will be introduced to these cost concepts as

Exhibit 12-2   Cost Classifications—The Big Picture

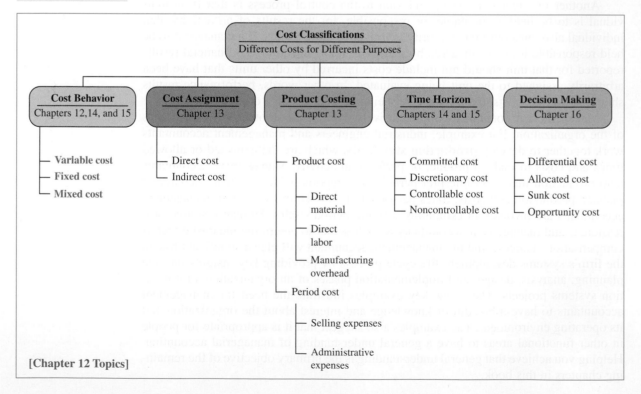

[Chapter 12 Topics]

they relate to the planning, control, or decision-making theme being developed. The cost classification concepts discussed in each chapter will explain:

- Relationships between total cost and volume of activity for understanding cost behavior (Chapters 12, 14, and 15).
- Product or activity relationships for cost assignment purposes (Chapter 13).
- Cost accounting to determine the cost of products produced (Chapter 13).
- A time-frame perspective for understanding cost planning and control (Chapters 14 and 15).
- Other analytical purposes to support decision making (Chapter 16).

Relationship of Total Cost to Volume of Activity

The relationship of total cost to volume of activity describes the **cost behavior pattern,** one of the most important cost classification techniques to understand. A **variable cost** is one that changes *in total* as the volume of activity changes. A cost that does not change *in total* as the volume of activity changes is a **fixed cost.** For example, raw material cost incurred to manufacture a product has a variable cost behavior pattern because the more units produced, the higher the total raw material costs incurred. On the other hand, factory building depreciation expense is a fixed cost because total depreciation expense will not change regardless of the level of production (unless, of course, a units-of-production method is used to calculate depreciation, in which case this cost would be variable). The distinction between fixed and variable cost behavior patterns is illustrated graphically in Exhibit 12-3.

Here are several additional examples of variable and fixed costs:

Variable Costs	Fixed Costs
Manufacturing labor wages	Supervisor's salary
Supplies used in production	Factory rent
Shipping costs	Advertising
Sales commissions	Property taxes
Warranty costs	Sales manager's salary

The fixed or variable label refers to the behavior of *total* cost relative to a change in activity. When referring to the behavior of unit costs, however, the labels may be confusing because variable costs are constant if expressed on a per unit basis but fixed costs per unit will change as the level of activity changes. Thus, it is necessary to understand the behavior pattern on both a total cost basis and a per unit basis as illustrated on the next page. Variable costs change in total as activity changes but are

LO 3

Describe the difference between variable and fixed cost behavior patterns and the simplifying assumptions made in this classification method.

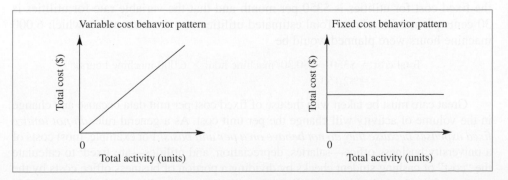

Exhibit 12-3

Cost Behavior Patterns

constant on a per unit basis. Fixed costs do not change in total as activity changes but will vary if expressed on a per unit of activity basis.

	As Activity Changes	
	---	---
	Total	**Per Unit**
Fixed Cost	*Remains constant*	Changes inversely
Variable Cost	Changes directly	*Remains constant*

Knowledge of the cost behavior pattern is important to the planning process, and several simplifying assumptions are usually made to facilitate the use of this analytical tool. The most fundamental assumption has to do with the range of activity over which the identified or assumed cost behavior pattern exists. This is the **relevant range** assumption, and it is most applicable to fixed costs. Returning to the depreciation expense example, it is clear that at some point an increase in the volume of production would require more plant capacity, and depreciation expense would increase. On the other hand, if substantially lower production volumes were anticipated in the future, some of the factory would be closed down or converted to another use, and depreciation expense would decrease. To say that depreciation expense is fixed is to say that over some relevant range of production activity, the total cost will not change. Different fixed expenses will have different relevant ranges over which they have a fixed cost behavior pattern. When a cost is identified as fixed and cost projections are made based on that cost behavior pattern classification, the limits of the relevant range assumption must be considered. The other major simplifying assumption is that the cost behavior pattern is *linear,* not curvilinear. This assumption relates primarily to variable costs. Because of economies of scale, quantity discounts, and other factors, variable costs will change slightly when expressed on a per unit basis. These changes are usually not significant; but if they are, appropriate adjustments in unit costs should be made in analyses based on cost behavior patterns. These assumptions are illustrated and described in more detail later in this chapter.

It is clear that not all costs can be classified as either variable or fixed. Some costs are partly fixed and partly variable. Sometimes costs with this mixed behavior pattern are called **semivariable costs.** Utilities for the factory, for example, have a mixed behavior pattern because when the plant isn't operating, some lights must be kept on for safety and security, but as production increases more electricity is required. Analytical techniques can break this type of cost into its fixed and variable components, and a **cost formula** can be developed:

$$\text{Total cost} = \text{Fixed cost} + \text{Variable cost}$$
$$= \text{Fixed cost} + (\text{Variable rate per unit of activity} \times \text{\# units of activity})$$

This cost formula then can be used to forecast the total cost expected to be incurred at various levels of activity. For example, assume that it has been determined that the fixed cost for utilities is $350 per month and that the variable rate for utilities is 30 cents per machine hour. Total estimated utilities cost for a month in which 6,000 machine hours were planned would be

$$\text{Total cost} = \$350 + (\$0.30/\text{machine hour} \times 6,000 \text{ machine hours})$$
$$= \$2,150$$

LO 4
Demonstrate why expressing fixed costs on a per unit of activity basis is misleading and may result in faulty decisions.

Great care must be taken with the use of fixed cost per unit data because any change in the volume of activity will change the per unit cost. As a general rule, *do not unitize fixed expenses because they do not behave on a per unit basis!* For example, most costs of a university business office—salaries, depreciation, and utilities—are fixed; to calculate the "cost" of cashing student checks by dividing a portion of business office costs by the number of checks cashed in a period of time will give a misleading result, as illustrated in overhead (see the discussion of manufacturing overhead in Chapter 13 for more detail) will have a variable cost behavior pattern. For example, maintenance and housekeeping materials used, as well as the variable portion of factory utilities, will be a function of the quantity of product made. Other manufacturing overhead costs are fixed, including depreciation expense, supervisory salaries, and the fixed portion of utility costs.

Selling, general, administrative, and other operating expenses also fit both patterns. Sales commissions, for example, vary in proportion to sales revenue or the quantity of product sold. The wages associated with employees who process orders from customers, or who handle payments from customers, may be variable if those functions are organized so that the number of workers can be expanded or contracted rapidly in response to changes in sales volume. On the other hand, advertising costs usually are fixed in the short run; once approved, the money is spent, and it is difficult to relate sales volume changes directly to advertising expenditures.

LO 5
Explain what types of costs are likely to have variable and fixed cost behavior patterns, respectively.

Estimating Cost Behavior Patterns

A particular cost's estimated behavior pattern is determined by analyzing cost and activity over time. One analytical technique involves using a scattergram to identify high and low cost–volume data relationships; then simple arithmetic is used to compute the variable rate and cost formula. This "high–low" method is illustrated in Exhibit 12-5. More complex techniques, including simple and multiple regression analysis, also can be used; but at some point the perceived increase in accuracy is offset by the simplifying assumptions involved in using the cost formula for planning and control purposes.

LO 6
Use the high–low method to determine the cost formula for a cost that has a mixed behavior pattern.

A Modified Income Statement Format

The traditional income statement format classifies costs according to the reason they were incurred: cost of goods sold, selling expenses, administrative expenses, research and development expenses, and so on. This format is used for financial statements prepared for external use, prepared according to generally accepted accounting principles. For internal purposes, however, managers need an income statement that can serve decision makers' needs. Therefore, the income statement format used in CVP analysis, frequently referred to as the **contribution margin format,** classifies costs according to their cost behavior pattern—variable or fixed. Here are the comparative formats with assumed amounts for illustration:

LO 7
Explain and illustrate the difference between the traditional income statement format and the contribution margin income statement format.

Traditional Format **(Expenses Classified by Function)**		**Contribution Margin Format** **(Expenses Classified** **by Cost Behavior Pattern)**	
Revenues	$100,000	Revenues	$100,000
Cost of goods sold	50,000	Variable expenses	60,000
Gross profit	$ 50,000	Contribution margin	$ 40,000
Operating expenses	40,000	Fixed expenses	30,000
Operating income	$ 10,000	Operating income	$ 10,000

Revenues and operating income (income before interest and taxes) are the same under either alternative. The difference is in the classification of expenses: functional in the traditional format and according to cost behavior pattern in the contribution margin format. Although the behavior pattern classification could be carried beyond operating income to other income and expense and income taxes, it usually isn't because the

Assumption:
During the months of January through June, the following utility costs were incurred at various production volumes:

Month	Total Utility Cost	Total Production Volume
January	$2,500	8,000 units
February	3,500	13,000 units
March	4,000	16,000 units
April	5,500	12,000 units
May	**2,000**	**6,000 units**
June	**5,000**	**18,000 units**

I. The scattergram:

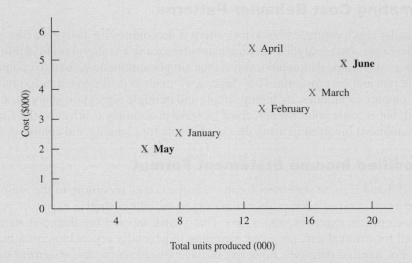

It can be observed in the scattergram that a cost–volume relationship does exist because of the approximate straight-line pattern of most of the observations. However, the April data do not fit the pattern. This condition may be due to an error or some unusual condition that caused cost for the month of April to be exceptionally high relative to the level of production activity for April. This observation is an *outlier* and should be investigated for pertinent information about the unusually high cost. However, it will be ignored in the calculation of the cost formula because of its variation from the cost–volume relationship that exists among other data.

II. Calculating the variable cost behavior pattern:
The high–low method of calculating the variable cost behavior pattern, or variable cost rate, relates the change in cost to the change in activity, using the highest and lowest relevant observations:

$$\text{Variable rate} = \frac{\text{High cost} - \text{Low cost}}{\text{High activity} - \text{Low activity}}$$

$$= \frac{\$5,000 - \$2,000}{18,000 \text{ units} - 6,000 \text{ units}}$$

$$= \$3,000/12,000 \text{ units}$$

$$= \$0.25 \text{ per unit}$$

(continued)

Exhibit 12-5

III. Calculating the fixed cost behavior pattern:

With the variable rate known, the fixed cost element can be calculated at either the high or low set of data, and the cost formula can then be developed because total cost is equal to variable cost plus fixed cost.

At 18,000 units of activity, the total variable cost is 18,000 units × $0.25 per unit = $4,500.

Fixed cost calculation:

$$\begin{aligned}
\text{Total cost at 18,000 units} &= \$5,000 \\
\text{Variable cost at 18,000 units} &= \underline{4,500} \\
\text{Fixed cost} &= \underline{\underline{\$500}}
\end{aligned}$$

At 6,000 units of activity, the total variable cost is 6,000 units × $0.25 per unit = $1,500.

Fixed cost calculation:

$$\begin{aligned}
\text{Total cost at 6,000 units} &= \$2,000 \\
\text{Variable cost at 6,000 units} &= \underline{1,500} \\
\text{Fixed cost} &= \underline{\underline{\$500}}
\end{aligned}$$

IV. The cost formula:

Using the calculated variable and fixed cost behavior patterns, the cost formula for utilities is

$$\begin{aligned}
\text{Total cost} &= \text{Fixed cost} + \text{Variable cost} \\
&= \$500 + \$0.25 \text{ per unit produced}
\end{aligned}$$

V. Using the cost formula:

This cost formula now can be used to estimate total utility costs at any level of activity (within the relevant range). For example, if production volume for the month of July was expected to be 14,000 units, the estimated total utility cost would be

$$\begin{aligned}
\text{Total cost} &= \text{Fixed cost} + \text{Variable cost} \\
&= \$500 + (\$0.25 \, / \, \text{unit} \times 14,000 \text{ units}) = \$4,000
\end{aligned}$$

Note that it is considered a coincidence if the cost formula explains total cost accurately at points not used in the high–low calculation. This is so because the calculation assumes a linear relationship between the observations used, and in practice exact linearity will not exist.

greatest benefits of the contribution margin approach are realized in the planning and control/evaluation processes applied to a firm's operations.

The contribution margin format derives its name from the difference between revenues and variable expenses (in managerial accounting, the terms *costs* and *expenses* are often used interchangeably). **Contribution margin** means that this amount is the contribution to fixed expenses and operating income from the sale of products or provision of services. The key to this concept lies in understanding cost behavior patterns. As revenues increase as a result of selling more products or providing more services, variable expenses will increase proportionately, and so will contribution margin. However, *fixed expenses will not increase* because they are not a function of the level of revenue-generating activity.

Use of the traditional income statement model can result in misleading and erroneous conclusions when changes in activity levels are being considered because it is assumed that all expenses change in proportion to changes in activity. This error is made because cost behavior patterns are not disclosed. The error is avoided when the

LO 8

Use the contribution margin format to analyze the impact of cost and sales volume changes on operating income.

Business in
Practice

Estimating Cost Behavior Patterns Using Microsoft Excel

Now that you understand the process by which cost behavior patterns are determined using the high–low method, Microsoft Excel can be used to quickly and easily create the cost formula. Several different functions in Excel can do this; all of them mathematically calculate the "best fit" of the data to a linear equation that is generated. The data from Exhibit 12-5 are illustrated below. Two functions are highlighted: INTERCEPT, which solves for the fixed cost; and SLOPE, which solves for the variable rate. Recall the discussion from Exhibit 12-5 regarding the April "outlier" and notice how different the solution is when the data are included on the left rather than excluded on the right. Also notice how close the mathematically precise results are when April is excluded from the analysis determined by the high–low method used in Exhibit 12-5.

contribution margin model is used correctly. For example, assume again that the firm illustrated in the income statement presentations on page 467 currently has revenues of $100,000 and operating income of $10,000. If revenues were to drop by 20 percent to $80,000, a quick conclusion would be that operating income also would decline by 20 percent to $8,000. However, analysis using the contribution margin format results in a much more accurate, and disturbing, result:

	Current Results	Results Assuming a 20% Decline in Revenue
Revenues	$100,000	$80,000
Variable expenses (60%)	60,000	48,000
Contribution margin (40%)	$ 40,000	$32,000
Fixed expenses	30,000	30,000
Operating income	$ 10,000	$ 2,000

Because fixed expenses did not change (the firm did not move into a different relevant range), the $8,000 reduction in contribution margin resulting from the 20 percent reduction in revenues carried right through to reduce operating income by the same dollar amount. This is an example of why it is misleading to think of fixed costs on a per unit basis. Although fixed costs (and especially the relevant range assumption) should not be overlooked by the manager, it must be recognized that they behave differently from variable costs.

The **contribution margin ratio** is the ratio of contribution margin to revenues. Think of this ratio as the portion of each sales dollar that remains after covering the variable costs and is available to cover fixed costs or provide profits. This ratio can be used to calculate directly the change in contribution margin given a change in revenues. Continuing with the same data, a $12,000 increase in revenue would result in a $4,800 (40% × $12,000) increase in contribution margin and a $4,800 increase in operating income since fixed costs will remain unchanged.

LO 9

Calculate the contribution margin ratio and explain how it can be used in CVP analysis.

---

6. What does it mean to rearrange the income statement model from the traditional format to the contribution margin format?
7. What does it mean to state that the contribution margin model is more useful than the traditional model for determining the effect of changes in activity on operating income?

What Does It Mean?
Answers on page 486

An Expanded Contribution Margin Model

The benefits of using the contribution margin model for planning and decision making can be best understood and illustrated by applying the model to a single product. For analytical purposes, an expanded version of the model, using the captions already illustrated, but adding some columns, is helpful. Here is the expanded model:

	Per Unit	×	**Volume**	=	**Total**	**%**
Revenue	$ Step 1					
Variable expenses	Step 1					
Contribution margin.	$ Step 1	×	Step 2	=	$ Step 3	Step 6 %
Fixed expenses					Step 4	
Operating income					$ Step 5	

The following steps highlight the preferred path through the model:

Step 1   Express revenue, variable expense, and contribution margin on a per unit basis.

Step 2   Enter volume.

Step 3   Multiply contribution margin per unit by volume to get total contribution.

Step 4   Enter fixed expenses.

Step 5   Subtract fixed expenses for the relevant period from total contribution margin to get operating income. Note that *fixed expenses are never entered on a per unit basis*.

Step 6   Calculate the contribution margin ratio by dividing contribution margin per unit by the per unit selling price. Essentially, you are setting the

Study

Suggestion

Understanding the relationships in the expanded contribution margin model may be the single most important concept developed in managerial accounting. The model presented here provides a structure for explaining, in a consistent manner, the effect on operating income of changes in selling price, variable expenses, fixed expenses, or the volume of activity. As you study these examples, you will notice that four relationships are constantly interacting with one another:

1. Revenue – Variable expenses = Contribution margin.

2. Contribution margin/Revenue = Contribution margin ratio.

3. Total contribution margin depends on the volume of activity.

4. Contribution margin must cover fixed expenses before an operating income is earned.

Your goals are to identify these relationships in every cost–volume–profit question and appreciate their interaction as a way of thinking that becomes second nature for you. Once you can visualize this interaction of these relationships, you are well on your way to becoming a successful decision maker.

selling price equal to 100 percent and then expressing the contribution margin as a percentage of the selling price.

Understanding these relationships will allow many what-if questions to be answered when analyzing changes to revenue.

Contribution margin in action—Example 1.   To illustrate the use of the model, assume management wants to know the operating income from a product that has the following revenue, cost, and volume characteristics:

Selling price per case	$ 15
Variable expenses per case	9
Fixed expenses associated with the product for the relevant period	$40,000
Sales volume in cases	8,000 cases

Using these data in the model results in the following analysis:

	Per Unit	**×**	**Volume**	**=**	**Total**	**%**
Revenue	$ 15					
Variable expenses	9					
Contribution margin.	$ 6	×	8,000	=	$48,000	40%
Fixed expenses					40,000	
Operating income					$ 8,000	

Contribution margin in action—Example 2.   Now suppose management wants to know what would happen to operating income if a $3 per unit price cut were to result in a volume increase of 5,000 units, to a total of 13,000 units. The solution:

	Per Unit	**×**	**Volume**	**=**	**Total**	**%**
Revenue	$ 12					
Variable expenses	9					
Contribution margin.	$ 3	×	13,000	=	$39,000	25%
Fixed expenses					40,000	
Operating income					$ (1,000)	

Based on the analysis, the price reduction would not be made.

Contribution margin in action—Example 3.   Next, suppose management proposes the same $3 per unit price cut in conjunction with a $3,000 increase in advertising, with the expectation that volume will increase to 18,000 units. Here is the analysis of the effect on operating income:

	Per Unit	×	**Volume**	=	**Total**	**%**
Revenue	$ 12					
Variable expenses	9					
Contribution margin.	$ 3	×	18,000	=	$54,000	25%
Fixed expenses					43,000	
Operating income					$11,000	

Note that the advertising expense increase is reflected in fixed expenses. The analysis suggests that if the volume increase can be achieved with the price cut and increased advertising combination, operating income will increase from its present level. But watch out for the relevant range assumption: The impact on fixed expenses of such a large increase in sales volume should be questioned.

Contribution margin in action—Example 4.   The expanded contribution margin model can also be used to calculate the volume of activity required to achieve a target level of operating income. For example, using the original data for selling price and variable expenses, suppose management wanted to know the sales volume required to have operating income of $23,000. The solution involves entering the known data in the model and working to the middle to obtain the required volume:

	Per Unit	×	**Volume**	=	**Total**	**%**
Revenue	$ 15					
Variable expenses	9					
Contribution margin.	$ 6	×	?	=	$63,000	40%
Fixed expenses					40,000	
Operating income					$23,000	

The required sales volume is $63,000/$6 = 10,500 units.

Contribution margin ratio in action—Example 5.   The contribution margin *ratio* is used to directly calculate the effect on contribution margin and operating income when the change in operations is expressed in terms of total revenues. For example, if the contribution margin ratio is 40 percent, and total revenues are expected to increase by $12,000, a $4,800 ($12,000 × 40%) increase in contribution margin and operating income would result, assuming that fixed expenses didn't change.

Contribution margin ratio in action—Example 6.   Another use of the contribution margin ratio is to determine the increase in revenues and sales volume that would be necessary to cover an increase in fixed expenses. For example, if fixed expenses were to increase by $9,000, contribution margin would have to increase by the same amount to keep operating income constant. If the contribution margin ratio is 40 percent, revenues would have to increase by $22,500 ($9,000/40%) to generate a $9,000 increase in contribution margin. The sales volume increase needed to generate the additional revenue is determined by dividing $22,500 by the $15 selling price per unit. (Of course we could also calculate the volume increase of 1,500 units by dividing the increased contribution margin required, $9,000, by the contribution margin of $6 per unit.)

Contribution margin ratio in action—Example 7.   The contribution margin ratio also is used to determine revenue and contribution margin changes when per unit data are not available or not applicable. For example, the contribution margin model is frequently used to analyze the impact on the operating income of an entire product line (perhaps a candy bar brand) that is sold in a variety of package or size configurations, assuming that each configuration has the same, or very nearly the same, contribution margin ratio. Thus, if a product line had a contribution margin ratio of 30 percent, would an advertising program costing $21,000 be cost-effective if it generated an additional $80,000 of revenue?

Increase in contribution margin ($80,000 × 30%)	$24,000
Increase in advertising	21,000
Increase in operating income	$ 3,000

So yes, the program would be cost-effective. Alternatively, dividing the increased fixed expenses by the contribution margin ratio ($21,000/30%) shows that an additional $70,000 of revenue would be needed to cover the increased fixed expense. Because the revenue increase is estimated to be $80,000, which is $10,000 more than required, an operating income increase of $3,000 (30% × $10,000) can be expected.

Contribution margin ratio in action—Example 8.   Although all of the examples used so far have expressed volume as units of product, the contribution margin model is also useful for organizations that provide services rather than sell products. For example, a day care center could identify variable expenses by type of activity and then set charges to achieve a target contribution margin to cover fixed expenses and operating income. Using the expanded contribution margin model, expected variable expenses of $18 per week per child, and a target contribution margin ratio of 40 percent, the revenue needed per week per child is calculated as follows:

	Per Child	×	Volume	=	Total	%
Revenue	$?					100%
Variable expenses	18					?
Contribution margin.	$?	×	?	=	$?	40%

If the contribution margin ratio is 40 percent, the variable expense ratio is 60 percent (revenues = 100%); 60 percent of revenue per child = $18; revenue per child = $18/0.60 = $30. This process is virtually the same as that described in Chapter 9 to calculate a required selling price when the cost of the item and the desired gross profit ratio are known.

What Does It Mean?

Answers on page 486

8. What does it mean to expand the contribution margin model?
9. What does it mean to state that the contribution model provides better support for decision making?

LO 10

Analyze how changes in the sales mix can affect projections made with CVP analysis.

Multiple Products or Services and Sales Mix Considerations

When the contribution margin model is applied using data for more than one product or service, the *sales* mix issue must be considered. **Sales mix** refers to the relative proportion of total sales accounted for by different products or services. Because different products or services are likely to have different contribution margin ratios, the average contribution margin ratio for a given mix of products or services will change if the sales mix of the products or services changes.

The effect of a sales mix change is illustrated in Exhibit 12-6. Sales mix is an important concept to understand because almost all firms have multiple products or services. When there is a range of quality to a firm's products (good, better, best), the higher-quality products generally have higher contribution margin ratios, so marketing efforts frequently focus on those products. On the other hand, a strategy that some firms try to follow is to price their products to achieve a contribution margin ratio that is about the same for all products. A company that can achieve this approximate parity in contribution margin ratios among its products doesn't have to be concerned, from a product profitability standpoint, about sales mix changes. Thus, marketing efforts can be more broadly based than if sales mix were a consideration.

---

10. What does it mean that fixed expenses should not be unitized because they don't behave that way?
11. What does it mean to state that contribution margin ratio is frequently a more useful measurement than contribution margin per unit?

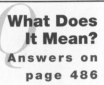

What Does It Mean?
Answers on page 486

Break-Even Point Analysis

The **break-even point** is usually expressed as the amount of revenue that must be realized for the firm (or product or activity or group of products or activities) to have neither profit nor loss (that is, operating income equal to zero). The break-even point is useful to managers because it expresses a minimum revenue target, and managers frequently find it easier to think in terms of revenues rather than variable and fixed expenses. In addition, the amount of sales (or revenues) generated by the firm is easily determined daily from the accounting system.

The contribution margin model is used to determine the break-even point by setting operating income equal to zero and solving the model for the revenue or physical sales volume that will cause that result. The calculation of break-even point in terms of units and total revenues is illustrated here:

LO 11

Describe the meaning and significance of the break-even point and illustrate how the break-even point is calculated.

Selling price per unit	$ 12
Variable expenses per unit	8
Total fixed expenses	$45,000

	Per Unit	×	**Volume**	=	**Total**	**%**
Revenue	$ 12					
Variable expenses	8					
Contribution margin	$ 4	×	?	=	?	33.3%
Fixed expenses					45,000	
Operating income					$ 0	

Exhibit 12-6   Multiple Products and Sales Mix

I. Assume that a company has two products. Per unit revenue, variable expenses, and product volumes for present operations follow:

	Product A					Product B					Total Company	
	Per Unit	×	Volume	=	Total	%	Per Unit	×	Volume	=	Total	%	Total	%
Revenue	$ 40	×	2,000	=	$80,000		$ 30	×	2,000	=	$60,000		$140,000	100%
Variable expenses	30						18							
Contribution margin	$ 10	×	2,000	=	$20,000	25%	$ 12	×	2,000	=	$24,000	40%	$ 44,000	31.4%
Fixed expenses													30,000	
Operating income													$ 14,000	

Note that fixed expenses are shown only in the Total Company column because they apply to the company as a whole, not to individual products.

II. Now assume that the sales mix changes and that, instead of sales volume of 2,000 units of each product, sales volume becomes 2,500 units of product A and 1,500 units of product B. The company's contribution margin format income statement becomes this:

	Product A					Product B					Total Company	
	Per Unit	×	Volume	=	Total	%	Per Unit	×	Volume	=	Total	%	Total	%
Revenue	$ 40	×	2,500	=	$100,000		$ 30	×	1,500	=	$45,000		$145,000	100%
Variable expenses	30						18							
Contribution margin	$ 10	×	2,500	=	$ 25,000	25%	$ 12	×	1,500	=	$18,000	40%	$ 43,000	29.7%
Fixed expenses													30,000	
Operating income													$ 13,000	

Note that even though total sales volume remained 4,000 units in both examples, total revenues increased, but total contribution margin and operating income decreased. This is due to the fact that proportionately more units of product A, with its relatively lower contribution margin ratio, were sold than product B, which has a relatively higher contribution margin ratio. As a result, the company's average contribution margin ratio also decreased.

According to the model, contribution margin must be equal to fixed expenses of $45,000.

$$\text{Volume in units at break-even} = \frac{\text{Fixed expenses}}{\text{Contribution margin per unit}}$$

$$= \$45,000/\$4$$

$$= 11,250 \text{ units}$$

$$\text{Total revenues at break-even} = \frac{\text{Fixed expenses}}{\text{Contribution margin ratio}}$$

$$= \$45,000/33.3\%$$

$$= \$135,000$$

or

$$\text{Volume in units at break-even} = \frac{\text{Total revenues required}}{\text{Revenue per unit}}$$

$$= \$135,000/\$12$$

$$= 11,250 \text{ units}$$

Most firms plan for certain desired levels of operating income and would not be satisfied to simply break even. As illustrated earlier, we can use the contribution margin model to determine total revenues and sales volume in units for any amount of desired operating income. The break-even formula also can be easily modified to determine these amounts by adding the desired operating income to the numerator. To illustrate, assume the same information and a desired operating income of $10,000:

$$\genfrac{}{}{0pt}{}{\text{Volume in units for desired}}{\text{level of operating income}} = \frac{\text{Fixed expenses} + \text{Desired operating income}}{\text{Contribution margin per unit}}$$

$$= (\$45,000 + \$10,000)/\$4$$

$$= 13,750 \text{ units}$$

$$\genfrac{}{}{0pt}{}{\text{Total revenues for desired}}{\text{level of operating income}} = \frac{\text{Fixed expenses} + \text{Desired operating income}}{\text{Contribution margin ratio}}$$

$$= (\$45,000 + \$10,000)/33.3\%$$

$$= \$165,000$$

Recall the discussion of multiple products and sales mix. Exhibit 12-6 illustrated the negative effect on operating income when the sales mix shifted by selling more units of product A, with its lower contribution margin, relative to product B, with its higher contribution margin. Break-even analysis can be performed when multiple products exist by using the average contribution margin ratio generated from the current sales mix.

$$\text{Total revenues at break-even} = \frac{\text{Fixed expenses}}{\text{Average contribution margin ratio}}$$

To illustrate using the sales mix information from Exhibit 12-6, Part I:

$$\text{Total revenues at break-even} = \$30,000/31.4\%$$

$$= \$95,541$$

To compare using the sales mix information from Exhibit 12-6, Part II:

$$\text{Total revenues at break-even} = \$30,000/29.7\%$$

$$= \$101,010$$

Just as the shifting of unit sales away from product B to product A produced a negative effect on operating margin, the same negative result is observed with break-even revenues.

Exhibit 12-7

Break-Even Graph

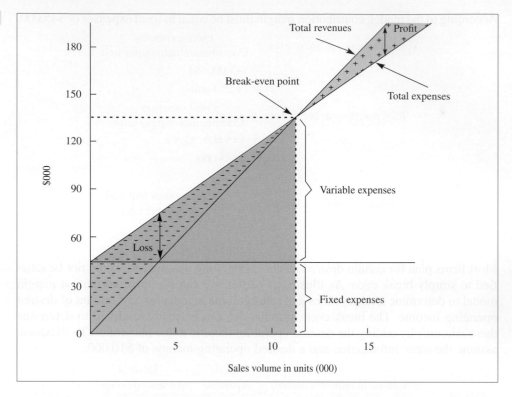

Break-even analysis is frequently presented in graphical format, as illustrated in Exhibits 12-7 and 12-8 with data from the preceding example. Note that in these graphs, the horizontal axis is sales volume in units, and the vertical axis is total dollars. In Exhibit 12-7 the horizontal line represents fixed expenses of $45,000, and variable expenses of $8 per unit are added to fixed expenses to produce the total expense line. Revenues start at the origin and rise at the rate of $12 per unit in proportion to the sales volume in units. The intersection of the total expense line and the total revenue line is the break-even point. The sales volume required to break even (11,250 units) is on the horizontal axis directly below this point, and total revenues required to break even ($135,000) can be read on the vertical axis opposite the intersection. The amount of operating income or loss can be read as the dollar amount of the vertical distance between the total revenue line and total expense line for the sales volume actually achieved. Sometimes the area between the two lines is marked as "profit area" or "loss area." Note that the loss area begins with an amount equal to total fixed expenses of $45,000 (at a sales volume of 0 units). As unit sales increase, the loss decreases by the contribution margin per unit of $4 for each unit sold until the break-even point is achieved; then the profit increases by the $4 contribution margin per unit.

Exhibit 12-8 is another version of the break-even graph. The variable expense line begins at the origin, with fixed expenses added to total variable expenses. Although expenses are rearranged compared to Exhibit 12-7, the total expense line stays the same, and the break-even point and the profit and loss areas are the same. This version permits identification of contribution margin and shows how contribution margin grows as volume increases.

The **margin of safety** is a measure of risk that describes a company's current sales performance relative to its break-even sales. This measure informs the manager about the amount of sales decline that a company can withstand before a loss would

Exhibit 12-8

Break-Even Graph
Featuring Contribution
Margin

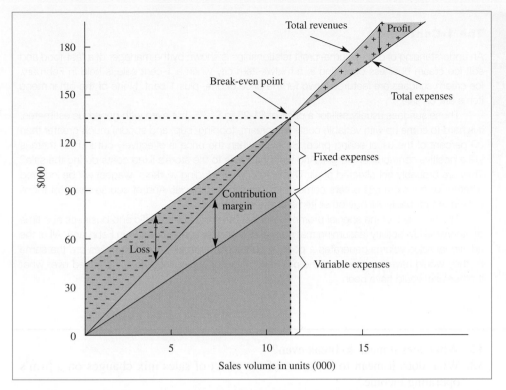

be incurred. Assuming sales revenue is currently $150,000 and break-even sales have been calculated to be $135,000, the margin of safety is calculated as

$$\text{Margin of safety} = \text{Total sales} - \text{Break-even sales}$$
$$= \$150,000 - \$135,000$$
$$= \$15,000$$

Sales can drop by no more than $15,000 before the company would begin to experience a loss. Perhaps expressing the margin of safety as a ratio rather than an absolute dollar amount would be even more meaningful. The margin of safety ratio is calculated as

$$\text{Margin of safety ratio} = \frac{\text{Margin of safety}}{\text{Total sales}}$$
$$= \$15,000/\$150,000$$
$$= 10\%$$

This margin of safety ratio informs the manager that if sales drop by 10 percent the company will be operating at its break-even point.

The key to the break-even point calculation (and graphic presentation) is that fixed expenses remain fixed in total regardless of the level of activity, subject to the relevant range assumption. In addition to that assumption, the linearity and constant sales mix assumptions also must be considered. In spite of these simplifications, the contribution margin model and cost behavior pattern concepts are among the most important management accounting ideas to understand and be able to apply. The manager encounters many situations in which cost–volume–profit analysis supports decisions that help the organization achieve its objective. One of these applications is described in Business in Practice—The 1-Cent Sale.

The 1-Cent Sale

An understanding of cost–volume–profit relationships is shown by the manager of a fast-food and soft ice cream business operating in a midwestern city when a 1-cent sale is held in February. Ice cream sundaes are featured—two for the price of one, plus 1 cent. None of the other menu items are on sale.

Those sundaes usually sell for a price of $1.25 to $1.75, but even with generous estimates, it is hard to come up with variable costs (ice cream, topping, cup, and spoon) much greater than 30 percent of the usual selling price. So even when the price is effectively cut in half, there is still a positive contribution margin. And what happens to the store's fixed costs during the sale? They are probably not affected at all. The fixed costs (including workers' wages) will be incurred whether or not extra customers come in for the sundae special. And of course many of those customers probably will buy other items at the regular price.

The net result of the special promotion is that the store builds traffic and business at a time of otherwise low activity (assuming that normal demand for sundaes is low in February). All of the additional sales volume generates a positive contribution margin; fixed expenses are the same as they would have been without the promotion; and operating income is increased over what it otherwise would have been.

What Does It Mean?

Answers on page 486

12. What does it mean to break even?
13. What does it mean to be aware of the effect of sales mix changes on a firm's operating income?

Operating Leverage

LO 12
Use operating leverage to evaluate cost structures.

When an entity's revenues change because the volume of activity changes, variable expenses and contribution margin will change proportionately. But the presence of fixed expenses, which do not change as the volume of activity changes, means that operating income will change proportionately more than the change in revenues. This magnification of the effect on operating income resulting from a change in revenue is called **operating leverage.** This concept was illustrated in the discussion of the contribution margin format income statement example earlier in this chapter (pages 469–471). It showed a 20 percent decline in volume, with revenues, variable expenses, and contribution margin also declining by 20 percent; but operating income declined 80 percent (from $10,000 to $2,000). Note the similarity of operating leverage to the discussion of financial leverage, explained in Chapter 11, in which fixed interest expense causes a proportionately larger change in ROE than the percentage change in ROI resulting from any given change in operating income.

Just as high financial leverage increases the risk that a firm may not be able to meet its required interest payments, high operating leverage increases the risk that a small percentage decline in revenues will cause a relatively larger percentage decline in operating income. *The higher a firm's contribution margin ratio, the greater its operating leverage*. Management can influence the operating leverage of a firm by its decisions about incurring variable versus fixed costs. For example, if a firm substitutes automated production equipment for employee labor, it has changed a variable cost (assuming the employees could be laid off if demand for the firm's products declined) to a fixed cost (the machine will depreciate, be insured, and be included in the property tax base whether or not it is being used); and it has increased its contribution margin ratio and operating leverage. If the management of a firm anticipates a decline in demand for the firm's products or services, it may be reluctant to change its cost structure by shifting variable costs to fixed costs, even though productivity increases could be attained, because the equipment has to be operating to realize the benefits of productivity gains.

The effect of different cost structures on operating leverage is illustrated in Exhibit 12-9. Observe in Part I that with alternative cost structures and a volume of 10,000 units, Company A and Company B achieved an identical amount of operating income of $100,000. This exhibit illustrates an important element of the decision-making process involving the trade-off between fixed cost (capital-intensive) and variable cost (labor-intensive) alternatives and is referred to as the **indifference point.** The indifference point is found by setting the cost structure (total cost) of each alternative (Company A and Company B in this example) equal to one another and solving for the volume of activity that equates total cost:

$$\frac{\text{Company A}}{\begin{array}{c}\text{Fixed costs} + \\ (\text{Variable cost per unit} \times \text{Volume})\end{array}} = \frac{\text{Company B}}{\begin{array}{c}\text{Fixed costs} + \\ (\text{Variable cost per unit} \times \text{Volume})\end{array}}$$

$$\$50,000 + (\$35 \times \text{Volume}) = \$200,000 + (\$20 \times \text{Volume})$$

$$\$15 \times \text{Volume} = \$150,000$$

$$\text{Volume} = 10,000 \text{ units}$$

Parts II and III of Exhibit 12-9 illustrate that as a change in volume moves each company away from the indifference point, the effect on operating income is more dramatic with Company B's higher proportion of fixed cost to variable cost relative to Company A. The relatively higher operating leverage provides faster accumulation of operating income for increases in volume but also indicates that operating income will

Operating Leverage **Exhibit 12-9**

I. Assume that two companies make similar products but that the companies have adopted different cost structures. Company A's product is made in a labor-intensive operation with relatively high variable costs but relatively low fixed costs, and Company B's product is made in a capital-intensive operation with relatively low variable costs but relatively high fixed costs. Each firm presently sells 10,000 units of product. A contribution margin model for each firm is presented here.

	Company A— Lower Operating Leverage				Company B— Higher Operating Leverage			
	Per Unit	× Volume =	Total	%	Per Unit	× Volume =	Total	%
Revenue.......	$ 50				$ 50			
Variable expenses	35				20			
Contribution margin.......	$ 15	× 10,000 =	$150,000	30%	$ 30	× 10,000 =	$300,000	60%
Fixed expenses			50,000				200,000	
Operating income			$100,000				$100,000	

(continued)

Exhibit 12-9

II. Effect on operating income of an increase in volume from 10,000 to 11,000 units:

	Company A— Lower Operating Leverage				Company B— Higher Operating Leverage			
	Per Unit	× Volume	= Total	%	Per Unit	× Volume	= Total	%
Contribution margin......	$ 15	× 11,000	= $165,000	30%	$ 30	× 11,000	= $330,000	60%
Fixed expenses ...			50,000				200,000	
Operating income			$115,000				$130,000	
Percentage change in volume		+10%				+10%		
Percentage change in operating income		+15%				+30%		

Note that Company B's operating income increased at a much higher rate, and to a considerably higher amount, than Company A's operating income. Operating leverage resulted in the operating income of each firm increasing proportionately more than the change in volume of activity. With an increase in volume, the greater contribution margin per unit and contribution margin ratio of Company B's product resulted in a greater increase in its operating income than experienced by Company A.

III. Effect on operating income of a decrease in volume from 10,000 units to 9,000 units:

	Company A— Lower Operating Leverage				Company B— Higher Operating Leverage			
	Per Unit	× Volume	= Total	%	Per Unit	× Volume	= Total	%
Contribution margin......	$ 15	× 9,000	= $135,000	30%	$ 30	× 9,000	= $270,000	60%
Fixed expenses....			50,000				200,000	
Operating income......			$ 85,000				$ 70,000	
Percentage change in volume......		−10%				−10%		
Percentage change in operating income......		−15%				−30%		

Note that Company B's operating income decreased at a much higher rate, and to a considerably lower amount, than Company A's operating income. Operating leverage resulted in the operating income of each firm decreasing proportionately more than the change in volume of activity. With a decrease in volume, the greater contribution margin per unit and contribution margin ratio of Company B's product resulted in a greater reduction of its operating income than experienced by Company A.

Cost Structures of Emerging Technologies

As illustrated in the accompanying discussion of operating leverage, relatively small changes in sales volume can lead to relatively large changes in operating income when a company has a high degree of operating leverage. This is often the reason for the disproportionate change frequently observed in these items between two accounting periods in a company's publicly reported earnings even though press reports generally don't mention operating leverage. Operating leverage has also influenced entire industries, as the following historical account illustrates.

In the 1880s there were more miles of railroad track laid than in any other decade in American history. By the 1890s there were more miles in bankruptcy than in any other decade.

Why do we always seem to overinvest in new technologies? In the case of railroads, the major economic force at work was economies of scale. The primary costs associated with a railroad are the fixed costs—the cost of servicing the debt incurred in laying the track and buying the rolling stock. In the late 1880s, about two-thirds of the total costs of operating a railroad were fixed.

When fixed costs are high, large companies have an inherent advantage, since (as volume increases) they have a lower total cost per shipment. The railroads recognized this and invested heavily in building capacity. But once the capacity was installed, there was inevitable cutthroat competition for freight. There was no way around the fact that there was just too much rail stock relative to demand. Companies went bankrupt, wiping out their obligation to make debt payments, leading to even more aggressive pricing. The industry sank into a slump from which it took decades to recover.

(What can be learned from this episode?) The railroad boom and bust arose because there were large fixed costs and a commodity product—freight transportation. Since there were many providers, price wars were all too likely. The cost structure of this industry bears a remarkable resemblance to long-haul fiber optics. The big fixed cost comes from laying the fiber cable, with (variable) operating expenses being relatively small. This is a recipe for price wars, and indeed, the cost of long-distance telephony—especially in negotiated contracts for large business—has been plummeting.

The demise of numerous Internet-based dot-com companies early this century provides a similar lesson. Many of these dot-com start-up companies invested heavily in building a technology infrastructure to support their business-to-consumer activities. The resulting cost structures provided a high degree of operating leverage and the opportunity for a very big payoff once the revenues from their venture produced enough contribution margin to exceed fixed costs. Of course, generating enough revenue proved to be a major challenge for many dot-com start-ups. The large number of business failures illustrates the high risk of high operating leverage.

Source: www.nytimes.com, "Economic Scene: Technology Rise and Fall Is as American as the Model T," December 14, 2000, by Hal R. Varian. Copyright ©2000, by the New York Times Co. Reprinted by permission.

decrease faster when volume decreases. Microsoft's performance during the 1990s is a good example of the effect that operating leverage can have on an organization's profit. During this period, Microsoft's profits grew by an average annual rate of 47 percent, which was much faster than the 38 percent average annual rate of growth in sales. Another example is described in Business in Practice—Cost Structures of Emerging Technologies. The effect of operating leverage on operating income is a key information component in the selection of a cost structure.

14. What does it mean to state that a firm has a relatively high degree of operating leverage?

What Does It Mean?

Answer on page 486

Demonstration Problem

Visit the text website at www.mhhe.com/marshall10e to view a demonstration problem for this chapter.

Summary

Management is the process of planning, organizing, and controlling an organization's activities to accomplish its goals. Managerial accounting (sometimes called *management accounting*) supports the management process.

Managerial accounting differs from financial accounting in several ways. Managerial accounting has an internal orientation and a future perspective, and it often focuses on individual units within the firm rather than on the organization as a whole. Reasonably accurate data are acceptable for internal analysis, and performance reports tend to be issued frequently for managerial control and decision making.

Costs are classified differently for different purposes, and cost terminology is important to understand if cost data are to be used appropriately. The behavior pattern of a cost relates to the change in total cost given a change in activity. Variable costs change, in total, as activity changes. Fixed costs remain constant in total as activity changes. Assumptions about linearity and relevant range are implicit when a cost is described as variable or fixed. Many costs have a mixed behavior pattern (they are partly variable and partly fixed). A cost formula expresses the total amount of a cost for a given level of activity by combining the fixed and variable elements of the total cost. It is inappropriate, and may be misleading, to express a fixed cost on a per unit basis because by definition a fixed cost is constant over a range of activity.

Cost–volume–profit (CVP) analysis uses knowledge about cost behavior patterns to interpret and forecast changes in operating income resulting from changes in revenue, cost, or the volume of activity.

When a particular cost is partly fixed and partly variable, the high–low method can be used to develop a cost formula that recognizes both the variable and fixed elements of the cost.

The contribution margin format income statement reclassifies the functional cost categories of the traditional income statement to cost behavior pattern categories. Contribution margin is the difference between revenues and variable expenses. Unless there are changes in the composition of variable expenses, contribution margin changes in proportion to the change in revenues.

The expanded contribution margin format model provides a framework for analyzing the effect of revenue, cost, and volume changes on operating income. A key to using this model is that fixed costs are recognized only in total; they are never expressed on a per unit basis.

The contribution margin ratio sometimes can be used to determine the effect of a volume change on operating income more quickly and more easily than using unit revenue and variable expense and volume.

Sales mix describes the relative proportion of total sales accounted for by specific products. When different products or product lines have significantly different contribution margin ratios, changes in the sales mix will cause the percentage change in total contribution margin to differ from the percentage change in revenues.

The break-even point is the total sales volume (in units or dollars) at which operating income is zero. With the contribution margin model, the break-even point is achieved when total contribution margin is equal to fixed expenses. Break-even analysis also can be illustrated graphically to provide a visual representation of profit and loss areas and to demonstrate the impact of the contribution margin per unit on operating income (or loss).

Operating leverage describes the percentage change in operating income for a given percentage change in revenues. The higher a firm's fixed expenses relative to its variable expenses, the greater the operating leverage and the greater the risk that a change in the level of activity will cause a relatively larger change in operating income than with less leverage. Operating leverage should inform management's decisions about whether to incur variable costs or fixed costs.

Key Terms and Concepts

break-even point (p. 475)   The amount of revenue required to have neither operating profit nor operating loss.

contribution margin (p. 469)   The difference between revenues and variable costs.

contribution margin format (p. 467)   An income statement format in which variable costs are subtracted from revenues to show contribution margin, from which fixed costs are subtracted to determine operating income.

contribution margin ratio (p. 471)   The ratio of contribution margin to revenues.

cost behavior pattern (p. 463)   Identification of whether a cost is fixed or variable.

cost formula (p. 464)   An algebraic expression that reflects the fixed and variable elements of a cost.

cost–volume–profit (CVP) analysis (p. 458)   Analysis of the impact on profit of volume and cost changes using knowledge about the behavior pattern of the costs involved.

fixed cost (p. 463)   A cost that does not change in total as the level of activity changes within the relevant range.

indifference point (p. 481)   The activity level that produces the same total cost when two different cost formulas or cost structures exist.

management process (pp. 459–460)   Planning, organizing, and controlling the activities of an organization so it can accomplish its purpose.

managerial accounting (p. 458)   Accounting that uses economic and financial information to plan and control many activities of the entity and to support the management decision-making process. Sometimes called *management accounting*.

margin of safety (p. 478)   the amount by which current sales exceed break-even sales, providing a relative measure of risk before an operating loss would be incurred.

operating leverage (p. 480)   The concept that operating income changes proportionately more than revenues for any change in the level of activity given the relative trade-off of variable versus fixed costs in a firm's cost structure.

production standard (p. 461)   Expected or allowed times and costs to make a product or perform an activity.

relevant range (p. 464)   The range of activity over which the fixed or variable cost behavior pattern exists.

sales mix (p. 474)   The proportion of total sales represented by various products or categories of products.

semivariable cost (p. 464)   A cost that has both fixed and variable elements—a mixed cost.

variable cost (p. 463)   A cost that changes in total as the volume of activity changes.

1. It means that *cost* is a very broad term that must be qualified so communication about cost is clear. It is important to understand cost terminology.

2. It means that managerial accounting is more future-oriented whereas financial accounting is concerned primarily with reporting events that have already occurred.

3. It means that planned results are compared to actual results, and either actions or plans are changed so future results come closer to planned results.

4. It means that classification of a cost as fixed or variable is based on the simplifying assumptions of linearity and relevant range.

5. It means that a formula for predicting the total cost at some level of activity has been developed and that it recognizes both the fixed and variable elements of the cost's behavior pattern.

6. It means that instead of using cost of goods sold and operating expense functional categories, expenses are classified according to their cost behavior pattern as variable or fixed; then variable expenses are subtracted from sales to arrive at contribution margin, from which fixed expenses are subtracted to arrive at operating income.

7. It means that because costs are classified based on behavior patterns (contribution margin format), the effect of changes in activity on expenses and operating income can be more easily and accurately determined.

8. It means that contribution per unit (revenue less variable expenses) is multiplied by volume to obtain total contribution margin, and fixed costs are subtracted to arrive at operating income.

9. It means that by organizing the relationships between revenues, variable expenses, fixed expenses, and volume into a model which provides a consistent way to better understand the interaction of these items, improved decision making should occur.

10. It means that because total fixed expenses don't change as the volume of activity changes, to express fixed expenses on a per unit basis doesn't make sense.

11. It means that because many firms have multiple products, overall planning and control are more easily accomplished by focusing on contribution margin ratio rather than the contribution margin of individual products.

12. It means that revenues equal expenses, so operating income is zero.

13. It means that because different products have different contribution margin ratios, changes in the proportion of sales of one product to total sales compared to the proportion of sales of another product to total sales—that is, a change in the sales mix—will affect operating income based on the products' relative contribution margin ratios.

14. It means that the firm has a relatively high proportion of fixed to variable costs, so the effect of changes in sales volume on contribution margin and operating income will be magnified relative to a firm with a lower operating leverage.

Self-Study Material

Visit the text website at www.mhhe.com/marshall10e to take an online self-study quiz for this chapter.

Matching Following are a number of key terms and concepts introduced in the chapter, along with a list of corresponding definitions. Match the appropriate letter for the key term or concept to each definition provided (items 1–12). Note that not all key terms and concepts will be used. Answers are provided at the end of this chapter.

a. Cost–volume–profit analysis
b. Cost formula
c. Contribution margin
d. Contribution margin format income statement
e. Linearity assumption
f. Contribution margin ratio
g. Operating leverage
h. Sales mix

i. Break-even point
j. High–low technique
k. Managerial accounting
l. Management process
m. Variable cost
n. Fixed cost
o. Relevant range
p. Mixed (semivariable) cost
q. Cost behavior pattern

_____ 1. The proportion of total sales represented by various products or categories of products.

_____ 2. The difference between revenues and variable costs.

_____ 3. The concept that operating income changes proportionately more than revenues for any given change in revenues.

_____ 4. The amount of revenue required to have neither operating income nor operating loss.

_____ 5. The percentage of each dollar in revenues that is available to cover fixed expenses; revenues minus variable costs, divided by revenues.

_____ 6. An income statement presentation in which variable costs are subtracted from revenues to show contribution margin, from which fixed costs are subtracted to determine operating income.

_____ 7. Analysis of the impact on profit of volume and cost changes using knowledge about the behavior patterns of the costs involved.

_____ 8. An arithmetic expression that reflects the fixed and variable elements of a cost.

_____ 9. The range of activity over which the fixed or variable cost behavior pattern exists.

____10. A cost that has both fixed and variable elements.

____11. A cost that does not change in total as the level of activity changes within a relevant range.

____12. Planning, organizing, and controlling the activities of an organization so it can accomplish its purpose.

Multiple Choice For each of the following questions, circle the best response. Answers are at the end of this chapter.

1. Managerial accounting, as opposed to financial accounting, is primarily concerned with
   a. the financial condition of the organization as a whole.
   b. meeting the requirements of generally accepted accounting principles.

c. emphasizing the future.

d. providing data for investors and creditors.

e. determining exact results.

2. Contribution margin can be expressed as

a. sales minus variable expenses.

b. sales minus cost of goods sold.

c. sales minus fixed expenses.

d. the level of sales required to cover variable expenses.

e. the level of sales required to cover fixed and variable expenses.

3. If the percentage change in operating income resulting from a given percentage change in sales is higher than the percentage change in sales itself, then

a. an increase in the selling price would not alter the contribution margin per unit.

b. variable costs per unit have increased.

c. variable costs have decreased in total.

d. the company has operating leverage.

e. the company has no fixed costs.

4. Chamberlain Music Studios seeks your help in analyzing the cost behavior pattern of its utility costs. At an activity level of 7,000 direct labor hours, total utility costs were $16,800; at 5,000 hours, total utility costs were only $14,300. Using the high–low method, the estimated total utility costs at an activity level of 6,500 direct labor hours would be

a. $15,600.

b. $16,175.

c. $16,300.

d. $18,590.

e. none of the above.

5. Seabold Interiors sold 18,400 yards of wallpaper last year at a contribution margin of $3.50 per yard and incurred $49,400 in total fixed costs. This year, contribution margin per yard is expected to increase to $4, and fixed costs are expected to increase to $58,000. How many units must be sold this year to earn the same operating income as was earned last year? (*Hint: Use the expanded contribution margin model described in this chapter.*)

a. 16,900.

b. 17,500.

c. 18,250.

d. 20,200.

e. None of the above.

6. With the following data, how many units must be sold to generate an operating income of $20,000?

Fixed expenses	$40,000
Selling price	$50 per unit
Contribution margin ratio	30%

   a. 800.
   b. 1,000.
   c. 2,500.
   d. 3,500.
   e. 4,000.

7. If both the fixed costs associated with a product and the variable costs (as a percentage of sales dollars) decrease, what will be the effect on the contribution margin ratio and the break-even point, respectively?

   a. Decrease, increase.
   b. Increase, decrease.
   c. Decrease, decrease.
   d. Increase, increase.

8. The contribution margin income statement

   a. reports expenses based on cost behavior pattern rather than cost function.
   b. unitizes fixed costs.
   c. shows contribution margin rather than operating income as the bottom line.
   d. is sometimes used for financial reporting purposes.
   e. none of the above.

Use the following information for Questions 9 and 10.
O'Brien, Inc.'s, 2013 contribution margin income statement shows the following:

Sales @ $10 per unit	$ 160,000
Less: Variable expense	(128,000)
Contribution margin.	$ 32,000
Less: Fixed expenses	(44,000)
Operating income (loss).	$ (12,000)

9. If O'Brien, Inc.'s, advertising costs increased by $8,000, by how much would sales have to increase for the company to achieve an operating income of $6,000?

   a. $66,000.
   b. $96,000.
   c. $102,000.
   d. $130,000.
   e. None of the above.

10. What would O'Brien, Inc.'s, operating income (or loss) be if fixed costs were increased by 10% and sales volume increased by 30%?

   a. $1,290.
   b. $2,650.
   c. $(6,800).
   d. $(9,680).
   e. None of the above.

Mini-Exercises

All applicable Mini-Exercises are available with McGraw-Hill's *Connect*™ *Accounting*.

Mini-Exercise
12.1
LO 3, 5

Using cost behavior patterns MFG Company experiences the following cost behavior patterns each week:

Fixed costs: supervisor's salary $1,000; factory rent $2,500

Mixed costs: utilities $1,500 + $5.25 per unit

Variable costs per unit: manufacturing labor wages $20; supplies used in production $8.50; packaging cost $2.25; warranty cost $4

Required:
Compute total costs to be incurred for a week with 2,750 units of activity.

Mini-Exercise
12.2
LO 6

High–low method During a year, Teri's monthly sales compensation ranged between $12,000 and $16,000 per month and units sold ranged between 1,600 and 2,400 units for those same months.

Required:
Use the high–low method to determine Teri's monthly salary and commission rate per unit sold and then calculate the total number of units sold in a year when Teri's total compensation amounted to $158,000.

Mini-Exercise
12.3
LO 7

Prepare a contribution margin format income statement China Imports, Inc., sold 18,000 units in May. Per unit selling price and variable expense were $25 and $17, respectively. Fixed expense incurred for May totaled $120,000.

Required:
Prepare the May income statement for China Imports, Inc., in the contribution margin format.

Mini-Exercise
12.4
LO 8

CVP analysis Current operating income for Bay Area Cycles Co. is $70,000. Selling price per unit is $100, the contribution margin ratio is 35%, and fixed expense is $280,000.

Required:
Calculate Bay Area Cycle's per unit variable expense and contribution margin. How many units are currently being sold? How many additional unit sales would be necessary to achieve operating income of $105,000?

Mini-Exercise
12.5
LO 9, 11

Break-even analysis Refer to the current information for Bay Area Cycle Co. in Mini-Exercise 12.4.

Required:
Calculate Bay Area Cycle's break-even point in units and total sales dollars. Calculate Bay Area Cycle's margin of safety and margin of safety ratio.

Mini-Exercise
12.6
LO 12

Operating leverage The cost structure of two firms competing in the same industry is represented by the following cost formulas: Company X = $1,420,000 + $34/unit; Company Z = $860,000 + $66/unit. The selling price is $120 per unit for both companies.

Required:
Calculate the indifference point between the two cost structures, that is, the amount of unit sales that produce exactly the same operating income for Company X and Company Z. If sales volume were expected to increase by 25% over the next two years, which cost structure would you prefer? Why?

Exercises

All applicable Exercises are available with McGraw-Hill's *Connect™ Accounting.*

Cost classifications For each of the following costs, check the column(s) that most likely apply:

Exercise 12.7
LO 3

Cost	Variable	Fixed
Wages of assembly-line workers	_____	_____
Depreciation—plant equipment	_____	_____
Glue and thread	_____	_____
Shipping costs	_____	_____
Raw materials handling costs	_____	_____
Salary of public relations manager	_____	_____
Production run setup costs	_____	_____
Plant utilities	_____	_____
Electricity cost of retail stores	_____	_____
Research and development expense	_____	_____

Cost classifications For each of the following costs, check the column(s) that most likely apply:

Exercise 12.8
LO 3

Cost	Variable	Fixed
Raw materials	_____	_____
Staples used to secure packed boxes of product	_____	_____
Plant janitors' wages	_____	_____
Order processing clerks' wages	_____	_____
Advertising expenses	_____	_____
Production workers' wages	_____	_____
Production supervisors' salaries	_____	_____
Sales force commissions	_____	_____
Maintenance supplies used	_____	_____
President's salary	_____	_____
Electricity cost	_____	_____
Real estate taxes for:		
Factory	_____	_____
Office building	_____	_____

Estimating costs based on behavior patterns Terry estimates that the costs of insurance, license, and depreciation to operate his car total $430 per month and that the gas, oil, and maintenance costs are 80 cents per mile. Terry also estimates that, on average, he drives his car 2,000 miles per month.

Exercise 12.9
LO 3

Required:

a. How much cost would Terry expect to incur during July if he drove the car 2,342 miles?

b. Would it be meaningful for Terry to calculate an estimated average cost per mile for a typical 2,000-mile month? Explain your answer.

Exercise 12.10

LO 3

Estimating costs based on behavior patterns The following information provides the amount of cost incurred in August for the cost items indicated. During August, 8,000 units of the firm's single product were manufactured.

Raw materials	$41,600
Factory depreciation expense	40,500
Direct labor	99,200
Production supervisor's salary	6,100
Computer rental expense	4,200
Maintenance supplies used	800

Required:

a. How much cost would you expect to be incurred for each of these items during September when 9,600 units of the product are planned for production?

b. Calculate the average total cost per unit for the 8,000 units manufactured in August. Explain why this figure would not be useful to a manager interested in predicting the cost of producing 9,600 units in September.

Exercise 12.11

LO 7, 9

Understanding CVP relationships Calculate the missing amounts for each of the following firms:

	Sales	Variable Costs	Contribution Margin Ratio	Fixed Costs	Operating Income (Loss)
Firm A	$320,000	?	32%	?	$38,300
Firm B	?	$465,050	?	$118,000	71,950
Firm C	134,000	?	26%	36,700	?
Firm D	?	59,000	20%	?	(4,920)

Exercise 12.12

LO 7, 9

Understanding CVP relationships Calculate the missing amounts for each of the following firms:

	Units Sold	Selling Price	Variable Costs per Unit	Contribution Margin	Fixed Costs	Operating Income (Loss)
Firm A	11,200	$24.00	?	$100,800	$41,300	?
Firm B	8,400	?	$18.20	?	64,500	$32,940
Firm C	?	7.30	4.20	10,850	?	(6,750)
Firm D	4,720	?	51.25	41,064	48,210	?

Exercise 12.13

LO 8, 9

Calculate selling price of new product with a target CM ratio Jackman, Inc., makes and sells many consumer products. The firm's average contribution margin ratio is 30%. Management is considering adding a new product that will require an additional $21,000 per month of fixed expenses and will have variable expenses of $7 per unit.

Required:

a. Calculate the selling price that will be required for the new product if it is to have a contribution margin ratio equal to 30%.

b. Calculate the number of units of the new product that would have to be sold if the new product is to increase the firm's monthly operating income by $9,000.

Calculate selling price of new product; what-if questions; breakeven D&R Corp. has annual revenues of $275,000, an average contribution margin ratio of 34%, and fixed expenses of $100,000.

Exercise 12.14
LO 8, 9, 10, 11

Required:

a. Management is considering adding a new product to the company's product line. The new item will have $8.25 of variable costs per unit. Calculate the selling price that will be required if this product is not to affect the average contribution margin ratio.

b. If the new product adds an additional $30,600 to D&R's fixed expenses, how many units of the new product must be sold at the price calculated in part **a** to break even on the new product?

c. If 20,000 units of the new product could be sold at a price of $13.75 per unit, and the company's other business did not change, calculate D&R's total operating income and average contribution margin ratio.

d. Describe how the analysis of adding the new product would be complicated if it were to "steal" some volume from existing products.

Special promotion—effects of a two-for-one sale Sam and Denny's ice cream shop charges $2.50 for a cone. Variable expenses are $0.80 per cone, and fixed costs total $3,200 per month. A "sweetheart" promotion is being planned for the second week of February. During this week, a person buying a cone at the regular price would receive a free cone for a friend. It is estimated that 750 additional cones would be sold and that 950 cones would be given away. Advertising costs for the promotion would be $350.

Exercise 12.15
LO 8, 9

Required:

a. Calculate the effect of the promotion on operating income for the second week of February.

b. Do you think the promotion should occur? Explain your answer.

Special promotion—effects of a 1-cent sale The management of Rocko's Pizzeria is considering a special promotion for the last two weeks of May, which is normally a relatively low-demand period. The special promotion would involve selling two medium pizzas for the price of one, plus 1 cent. The medium pizza normally sells for $9.99 and has variable expenses of $3. Expected sales volume without the special promotion is 400 medium pizzas per week.

Exercise 12.16
LO 8, 9

Required:

a. Calculate the total contribution margin generated by the normal volume of medium pizzas in a week.

b. Calculate the total number of medium pizzas that would have to be sold during the 1-cent sale to generate the same amount of contribution margin that results from the normal volume.

c. What other factors should management consider in evaluating the pros and cons of the special promotion?

ACCOUNTING

Problems

All applicable Problems are available with McGraw-Hill's *Connect*™ *Accounting.*

Problem 12.17
LO 6

High–low method A department of Alpha Co. incurred the following costs for the month of September. Variable costs, and the variable portion of mixed costs, are a function of the number of units of activity:

Activity level in units.............................	5,000
Variable costs	$10,000
Fixed costs	30,000
Mixed costs....................................	20,000
Total costs....................................	$60,000

During October the activity level was 8,000 units, and the total costs incurred were $70,500.

Required:

a. Calculate the variable costs, fixed costs, and mixed costs incurred during October.

b. Use the high–low method to calculate the cost formula for mixed cost.

Problem 12.18
LO 6

High–low method—missing amounts The following data have been extracted from the records of Puzzle, Inc.:

e**X**cel

	February	**August**
Production level, in units	12,000	18,000
Variable costs	$21,000	$?
Fixed costs	?	31,000
Mixed costs...........................	18,000	?
Total costs............................	$70,000	$88,000

Required:

a. Calculate the missing costs.

b. Calculate the cost formula for mixed cost using the high–low method.

c. Calculate the total cost that would be incurred for the production of 20,000 units.

d. Identify the two key cost behavior assumptions made in the calculation of your answer to part **c.**

Prepare a contribution margin format income statement; answer what-if questions Shown here is an income statement in the traditional format for a firm with a sales volume of 20,000 units. Cost formulas also are shown:

Revenues	$200,000
Cost of goods sold ($36,000 + $5.20/unit)	140,000
Gross profit	$ 60,000
Operating expenses:	
Selling ($9,200 + $0.30/unit)	15,200
Administration ($18,800 + $0.50/unit)	28,800
Operating income	$ 16,000

Required:

a. Prepare an income statement in the contribution margin format.

b. Calculate the contribution margin per unit and the contribution margin ratio.

c. Calculate the firm's operating income (or loss) if the volume changed from 20,000 units to

1. 28,000 units.

2. 12,000 units.

d. Refer to your answer to part **a** for total revenues of $200,000. Calculate the firm's operating income (or loss) if unit selling price and variable expenses per unit do not change and total revenues

1. Increase $60,000.

2. Decrease $52,000.

Prepare a contribution margin format income statement; answer what-if questions Shown here is an income statement in the traditional format for a firm with a sales volume of 15,000 units:

Revenues	$105,000
Cost of goods sold ($8,000 + $3.60/unit)	62,000
Gross profit	$ 43,000
Operating expenses:	
Selling ($1,500 + $0.80/unit)	13,500
Administration ($4,000 + $0.50/unit)	11,500
Operating income	$ 18,000

Required:

a. Prepare an income statement in the contribution margin format.

b. Calculate the contribution margin per unit and the contribution margin ratio.

c. Calculate the firm's operating income (or loss) if the volume changed from 15,000 units to

1. 20,000 units.

2. 10,000 units.

d. Refer to your answer to part **a** when total revenues were $105,000. Calculate the firm's operating income (or loss) if unit selling price and variable expenses do not change and total revenues

    1. Increase by $15,000.

    2. Decrease by $10,000.

Problem 12.21

LO 7, 8, 9, 11

Prepare a contribution margin format income statement; calculate break-even point Presented here is the income statement for Big Surf, Inc., for the month of May:

Sales..	$ 65,000
Cost of goods sold	53,500
Gross profit	$ 11,500
Operating expenses	14,000
Operating loss..	$ (2,500)

Based on an analysis of cost behavior patterns, it has been determined that the company's contribution margin ratio is 30%.

Required:

a. Rearrange the preceding income statement to the contribution margin format.

b. If sales increase by 10%, what will be the firm's operating income?

c. Calculate the amount of revenue required for Big Surf, Inc., to break even.

Problem 12.22

LO 7, 8, 9, 11

Prepare a contribution margin format income statement; calculate break-even point Presented here is the income statement for Fairchild Co. for March:

Sales...	$80,000
Cost of goods sold	42,000
Gross profit	$38,000
Operating expenses	32,000
Operating income	$ 6,000

Based on an analysis of cost behavior patterns, it has been determined that the company's contribution margin ratio is 30%.

Required:

a. Rearrange the preceding income statement to the contribution margin format.

b. Calculate operating income if sales volume increases by 8%. (*Note: Do not construct an income statement to get your answer.*)

c. Calculate the amount of revenue required for Fairchild to break even.

Problem 12.23

LO 7, 8, 9, 10

CVP analysis—what-if questions; breakeven Monterey Co. makes and sells a single product. The current selling price is $15 per unit. Variable expenses are $9 per unit, and fixed expenses total $27,000 per month.

Required:

(Unless otherwise stated, consider each requirement separately.)

a. Calculate the break-even point expressed in terms of total sales dollars and sales volume.

b. Calculate the margin of safety and the margin of safety ratio. Assume current sales are $75,000.

c. Calculate the monthly operating income (or loss) at a sales volume of 5,400 units per month.

d. Calculate monthly operating income (or loss) if a $2 per unit reduction in selling price results in a volume increase to 8,400 units per month.

e. What questions would have to be answered about the cost–volume–profit analysis simplifying assumptions before adopting the price cut strategy of part **d**?

f. Calculate the monthly operating income (or loss) that would result from a $1 per unit price increase and a $6,000 per month increase in advertising expenses, both relative to the original data. Assume a sales volume of 5,400 units per month.

g. Management is considering a change in the sales force compensation plan. Currently each of the firm's two salespeople is paid a salary of $2,500 per month. Calculate the monthly operating income (or loss) that would result from changing the compensation plan to a salary of $400 per month, plus a commission of $0.80 per unit, assuming a sales volume of

  1. 5,400 units per month.

  2. 6,000 units per month.

h. Assuming that the sales volume of 6,000 units per month achieved in part **g** could also be achieved by increasing advertising by $1,000 per month instead of changing the sales force compensation plan, which strategy would you recommend? Explain your answer.

CVP analysis—what-if questions; sales mix issue Miller Metal Co. makes a single product that sells for $32 per unit. Variable costs are $20.80 per unit, and fixed costs total $47,600 per month.

Problem 12.24
LO 7, 8, 9, 10, 11

Required:

a. Calculate the number of units that must be sold each month for the firm to break even.

b. Assume current sales are $160,000. Calculate the margin of safety and the margin of safety ratio.

c. Calculate operating income if 5,000 units are sold in a month.

d. Calculate operating income if the selling price is raised to $33 per unit, advertising expenditures are increased by $7,000 per month, and monthly unit sales volume becomes 5,400 units.

e. Assume that the firm adds another product to its product line and that the new product sells for $20 per unit, has variable costs of $14 per unit, and causes fixed expenses in total to increase to $63,000 per month. Calculate the firm's operating income if 5,000 units of the original product and 4,000 units of the new product are sold each month. For the original product, use the selling price and variable cost data given in the problem statement.

f. Calculate the firm's operating income if 4,000 units of the original product and 5,000 units of the new product are sold each month.

g. Explain why operating income is different in parts **e** and **f,** even though sales totaled 9,000 units in each case.

Problem 12.25
LO 7, 8, 9, 10, 11

CVP application—expand existing product line? Nautical Canvas Co. currently makes and sells two models of a boat cover. Data applicable to the current operation are summarized in the following columns labeled Current Operation. Management is considering adding a Value model to its current Luxury and Economy models. Expected data if the new model is added are shown in the following columns labeled Proposed Expansion:

	Current Operation		**Proposed Expansion**		
	Luxury	**Economy**	**Luxury**	**Economy**	**Value**
Selling price per unit	$2,000	$1,200	$2,000	$1,200	$1,500
Variable expenses per unit	800	700	800	700	800
Annual sales volume—units	1,000	2,000	600	1,700	800
Fixed expenses for year	Total of $700,000		Total of $840,000		

Required:

a. Calculate the company's current total contribution margin and the current average contribution margin ratio.

b. Calculate the company's current amount of operating income.

c. Calculate the company's current break-even point in dollar sales.

d. Explain why the company might incur a loss, even if the sales amount calculated in part **c** was achieved and selling prices and costs didn't change.

e. Calculate the company's total operating income under the proposed expansion.

f. Based on the proposed expansion data, would you recommend adding the Value model? Why or why not?

g. Would your answer to part **f** change if the Value model sales volume were to increase to 1,000 units annually, and all other data remained the same? Why or why not?

Problem 12.26
LO 8, 9, 10, 11

CVP application—eliminate product from operations? Muscle Beach, Inc., makes three models of high-performance weight-training benches. Current operating data are summarized here:

	MegaMuscle	**PowerGym**	**ProForce**
Selling price per unit	$ 170	$ 220	$ 310
Contribution margin per unit	51	77	62
Monthly sales volume—units	4,000	3,000	1,000
Fixed expenses per month		Total of $468,000	

Required:

a. Calculate the contribution margin ratio of each product.

b. Calculate the firm's overall contribution margin ratio.

c. Calculate the firm's monthly break-even point in sales dollars.

d. Calculate the firm's monthly operating income.

e. Management is considering the elimination of the ProForce model due to its low sales volume and low contribution margin ratio. As a result, total fixed expenses can be reduced to $420,000 per month. Assuming that this change would not affect the other models, would you recommend the elimination of the ProForce model? Explain your answer.

f. Assume the same facts as in part e. Assume also that the sales volume for the PowerGym model will increase by 500 units per month if the ProForce model is eliminated. Would you recommend eliminating the ProForce model? Explain your answer.

CVP analysis—effects of changes in cost structure; breakeven Riveria Co. makes and sells a single product. The current selling price is $32 per unit. Variable expenses are $20 per unit, and fixed expenses total $43,200 per month. Sales volume for May totaled 4,100 units.

Problem 12.27
LO 8, 9, 11

Required:

a. Calculate operating income for May.

b. Calculate the break-even point in terms of units sold and total revenues.

c. Management is considering installing automated equipment to reduce direct labor cost. If this were done, variable expenses would drop to $14 per unit, but fixed expenses would increase to $67,800 per month.

 1. Calculate operating income at a volume of 4,100 units per month with the new cost structure.

 2. Calculate the break-even point in units with the new cost structure. (Round your answer.)

 3. Why would you suggest that management seriously consider investing in the automated equipment and accept the new cost structure?

 4. Why might management not accept your recommendation but decide instead to maintain the old cost structure?

CVP analysis—effects of change in cost structure; breakeven Austin, Inc., produces small-scale replicas of vintage automobiles for collectors and museums. Finished products are built on a 1/20 scale of originals. The firm's income statement showed the following:

Problem 12.28
LO 8, 9, 11, 12

Revenues (1,500 units)	$840,000
Variable expenses	462,000
Contribution margin	$378,000
Fixed expenses	290,000
Operating income	$ 88,000

An automated stamping machine has been developed that can efficiently produce body frames, hoods, and doors to the desired scale. If the machine is leased, fixed expenses will increase by $30,000 per year. The firm's production capacity will increase, which is expected to result in a 20% increase in sales volume. It is also estimated that labor costs of $28 per unit could be saved because less polishing and finishing time will be required.

Required:

a. Calculate the firm's current contribution margin ratio and break-even point in terms of revenues. (Round your answer.)

b. Calculate the firm's contribution margin ratio and break-even point in terms of revenues if the new machine is leased.

c. Calculate the firm's operating income assuming that the new machine is leased.

d. Do you believe that management of Austin, Inc., should lease the new machine? Explain your answer.

Cases

All applicable Cases are available with McGraw-Hill's *Connect™ Accounting.*

Case 12.29
LO 8, 9, 11

CVP application—allow special discount? Assume you are a sales representative for Sweet Tooth Candy Company. One of your customers is interested in buying some candy that will be given to the members of a high school Substance Abuse Awareness Club. The club members will be marching in a community parade and will give the candy to children who are watching the parade. Your customer has asked that you discount the normal selling price of the candy to be given to the club by 30%. You know that the contribution margin ratio of the candy, based on the regular selling price, is 40%.

Required:

Identify the pros and cons of complying with the customer's request, and state the recommendation you would make to your sales manager.

Case 12.30
LO 5, 8, 9

CVP application—determine offering price Tommy Appleton is in charge of arranging the "attitude adjustment" period and dinner for the monthly meetings of the local chapter of the Management Accountants Association. Tommy is negotiating with a new restaurant that would like to have the group's business, and Tommy wants to apply some of the cost–volume–profit analysis concepts he has learned. The restaurant is proposing its regular menu prices of $4 for a before-dinner drink and $22 for dinner. Tommy has determined that, on average, the people attending the meeting have 1.5 drinks before dinner. He also believes that the contribution margin ratios for the drinks and dinner are 50% and 40%, respectively.

Required:

Prepare a memo to Tommy outlining the possible offers he might make to the restaurant owner, and recommend which offer he should make.

Comparison of operating leverage and financial leverage The concept of financial leverage was introduced in Chapter 7 and expanded on in Chapter 11. In Exercise 7.20 you were asked to describe the risks associated with financial leverage.

Case 12.31
LO 12

Required:

a. Describe the risks associated with operating leverage.

b. Outline the similarities and differences between operating leverage and financial leverage. *(Hint: Compare Exhibit 12-9 to the discussion and analysis in Exhibits 7-2 and 11-3.)*

Understanding the effects of operating leverage HighTech, Inc., and OldTime Co. compete within the same industry and had the following operating results in 2012:

Case 12.32
LO 12

	HighTech, Inc.	OldTime Co.
Sales	$2,100,000	$2,100,000
Variable expenses	420,000	1,260,000
Contribution margin	$1,680,000	$ 840,000
Fixed expenses	1,470,000	630,000
Operating income	$ 210,000	$ 210,000

Required:

a. Calculate the break-even point for each firm in terms of revenue.

b. What observations can you draw by examining the break-even point of each firm given that they earned an equal amount of operating income on identical sales volumes in 2012?

c. Calculate the amount of operating income (or loss) that you would expect each firm to report in 2013 if sales were to

   1. Increase by 20%.

   2. Decrease by 20%.

d. Using the amounts computed in requirement **c,** calculate the increase or decrease in the amount of operating income expected in 2013 from the amount reported in 2012.

e. Explain why an equal percentage increase (or decrease) in sales for each firm would have such differing effects on operating income.

f. Calculate the ratio of contribution margin to operating income for each firm in 2012. *(Hint: Divide contribution margin by operating income.)*

g. Multiply the expected increase in sales of 20% for 2013 by the ratio of contribution margin to operating income for 2012 computed in requirement **f** for each firm. *(Hint: Multiply your answer in requirement **f** by 0.2.)*

h. Multiply your answer in requirement **g** by the operating income of $210,000 reported in 2012 for each firm.

i.   Compare your answer in requirement **h** with your answer in requirement **d.** What conclusions can you draw about the effects of operating leverage from the steps you performed in requirements **f, g,** and **h**?

Case 12.33

LO 11

Break-even analysis; CVP application using Internet tools You have recently been engaged by Dominic's Italian Cafe to evaluate the financial impact of adding gourmet pizza items to the menu. A survey of the clientele indicates that demand for the product exists at an average selling price of $18 per pizza. Fixed costs related to new equipment would be $12,000 per month. Variable costs for ingredients, labor, and electricity for the oven would average $6 per pizza. You decide that a good starting point is to conduct an initial break-even analysis on the new project.

Knowing that many commercial Internet companies provide free downloads or online demos of their products for your evaluation and testing pleasure, you decide to conduct the break-even analysis using break-even calculators that have been located at several websites.

Required:

a.   Calculate the break-even point in pizzas per month and print your results using the online break-even analysis tools at each of the following websites:

1.   www.entrepreneur.com/calculators/breakeven.html

2.   http://fast4cast.com/break-even-calculator.aspx

3.   www.anz.com/aus/Small-Business/Tools-Forms-And-Guides/Benchmark-Your-Business/Breakeven-Analyser/default.asp

4.   www.dinkytown.net/java/BreakEven.html

b.   Write a comparative analysis of each of the four tools that you used to calculate the break-even point. You might discuss strengths, weaknesses, usefulness, and user interaction for each tool.

c.   Dominic's now is interested in the amount of operating income available from the gourmet pizza operation if sales are initially expected to be 2,000 pizzas each month. Calculate the operating income and print your results using the "View Report" button available with the www.dinkytown.net breakeven analysis tool.

d.   Dominic's now would like to understand the effect on operating income if certain changes in costs or volume occur. Use the www.dinkytown.net "View Report" results to present and evaluate each of the following independent cases assuming sales are initially expected to be 2,000 pizzas each month:

1.   Selling price is decreased by 10%, and pizza sales are expected to increase by 5%.

2.   Selling price is increased to $20, and pizza sales are expected to decrease by 20%.

3.   Higher-quality ingredients are used at a cost increase of $2 to $8 per pizza, and pizza sales are expected to increase to 2,200 pizzas per month.

4.   A more efficient pizza oven is available that would reduce the electricity used in baking each pizza. Variable costs would be reduced to $5 per pizza. The more efficient oven would increase the fixed costs to $15,000 per month.

e.   Write a memo to Dominic's explaining the results of your analysis.

Answers to Self-Study Material

Matching: 1. h, 2. c, 3. g, 4. i, 5. f, 6. d, 7. a, 8. b, 9. o, 10. p, 11. n, 12. l
Multiple choice: 1. c, 2. a, 3. d, 4. b, 5. c, 6. e, 7. b, 8. a, 9. d, 10. c

13

Cost Accounting and Reporting

"What does it cost?" may be the single most important question addressed by an organization's accounting information system. As you will come to realize, accurate cost information is necessary to guide managers in making pricing decisions, evaluating productivity and efficiency, developing operating budgets, determining if component product parts/services will be manufactured/performed internally or outsourced, analyzing whether production technology will replace human efforts, and appraising performance—in addition to helping address many other questions that will be explored throughout the remaining chapters of this text. **Cost accounting** is a subset of managerial accounting that relates primarily to the accumulation and determination of product, process, or services costs. The costing system used to accumulate, assign, and report these costs must be flexible enough to provide answers to support the broad array of internal questions for planning, control, and decision making.

The economic recession of 2008–2009 led many managers to seek more effective and less costly ways of performing their activities. These include seeking more efficient methods of processing and manufacturing, an activity frequently labeled "continuous improvement," or making the organization "leaner." This trend has led to the development of "lean accounting." Lean accounting refers to a system that focuses on product or process cost accumulation by element of the value chain (page 506). The development of lean accounting reflects the need for managers to have increasingly relevant cost data and illustrates the need for cost accounting to evolve in order to meet decision-making needs more effectively.

LO 1

Explain the role of cost accounting as it relates to financial and managerial accounting.

Cost accounting plays a very important role in the income measurement and inventory valuation aspects of financial accounting. You will recall that the fundamental focus of financial accounting is external to the organization: providing information to stockholders, creditors, the government, and others about the financial position and results of operations of the organization in accordance with generally accepted principles of accounting. To that end, the cost accounting system will report the cost of goods manufactured and sold, as well as the cost of goods manufactured and not sold—inventory valuation—along with other costs that are carried in the accounts of a manufacturing company. Exhibit 13-1 presents these relationships.

In this chapter we explore the cost accounting and reporting systems that serve the needs of both financial and managerial accounting.

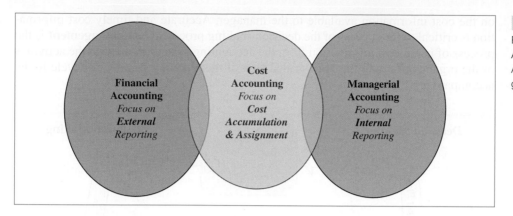

Exhibit 13-1

Relationship of Cost Accounting to Financial Accounting and Managerial Accounting

1. What does it mean to state that cost accounting serves both financial and managerial accounting?

What Does It Mean?
Answer on page 532

LEARNING OBJECTIVES (LO)

After studying this chapter you should understand and be able to

LO 13-1   Explain the role of cost accounting as it relates to financial and managerial accounting.

LO 13-2   Describe how cost management plays a strategic role in the organization's value chain.

LO 13-3   Contrast direct and indirect costs and illustrate how they relate to a product or activity.

LO 13-4   Distinguish between product costs and period costs, and identify the three components of product cost.

LO 13-5   Explain the general operation of a product costing system and illustrate how costs flow through the inventory accounts to cost of goods sold.

LO 13-6   Calculate predetermined overhead application rates and demonstrate how they are used.

LO 13-7   Prepare and interpret a statement of cost of goods manufactured.

LO 13-8   Explain and illustrate the difference between absorption and direct (or variable) costing.

LO 13-9   Perform activity-based costing and describe activity-based management.

Cost Management

Recall from the planning and control cycle that management attention is given to planning, executing, and controlling the entity's activities so that the organization can achieve its strategic goals. Along each step of that process decisions are made based on the cost information available to the manager. Accurate and timely cost information is critical to the success of the decision-making process. **Cost management** is the process of using cost information from the accounting system to manage the activities of the organization (see the gray shaded area of the planning and control cycle in the accompanying figure).

Considering the broad scope and function of an organization's activities helps one to appreciate how important quality cost information is to the manager. Too often, cost accounting is viewed in its traditional role of determining the cost of producing products or providing services and the related accounting for those activities—a results-oriented, short-term view of cost. A more contemporary view is that costs must be understood and managed at each stage of an organization's value chain in order to provide an awareness of cost over the entire life cycle of a product or service—a prescriptive, long-term view of cost where cost management clearly becomes a strategic initiative. The **value chain** is the sequence of functions and related activities that, over the life of a product or service, can ultimately make a difference to the customer. The significance of seeing each function as a link in a chain is that each is crucial to managing the firm's activities for each product or service to achieve management's desired quantitative and qualitative goals, and a weakness in any element of the value chain could impair that outcome. The sequence of functions that compose the value chain and examples of cost management initiatives at each stage are shown in Exhibit 13-2.

Viewing the organization's value chain highlights many questions that can be answered about activities by analyzing their cost. For example, focusing cost control questions independently on the production activity may be too late, from a cost incurrence perspective, because the current product design will provide only marginal opportunities to improve cost performance. Costs that will be incurred during production are effectively "locked in" during the product design process. Therefore, the objective is to improve or sustain any competitive advantage the firm may have in the marketplace while maintaining an appropriate level of product or service quality and to provide for an appropriate return on investment. Later in this chapter, activity-based costing is introduced as a technique for analyzing activities within the value chain to improve the relevance and accuracy of the costing process.

As can be seen in the example of value chain functions in Exhibit 13-2, there exists an emphasis on "different costs for different purposes," as was explained in Chapter 12.

LO 2

Describe how cost management plays a strategic role in the organization's value chain.

Exhibit 13-2

Value Chain Functions

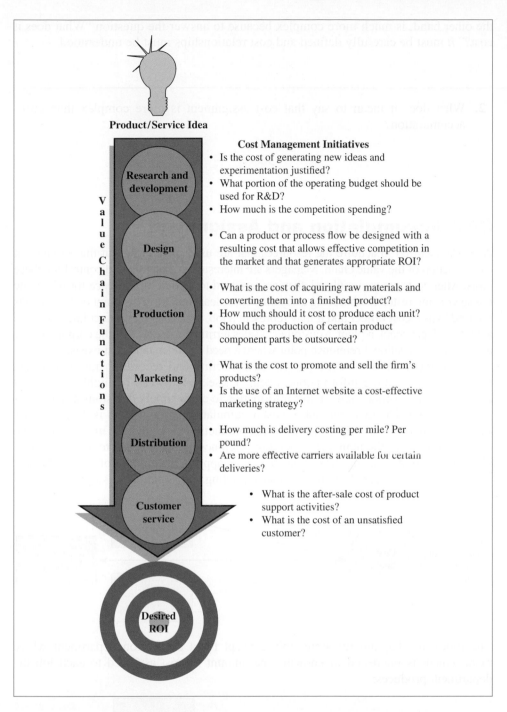

Value Chain Functions

Product/Service Idea

Cost Management Initiatives

Research and development
- Is the cost of generating new ideas and experimentation justified?
- What portion of the operating budget should be used for R&D?
- How much is the competition spending?

Design
- Can a product or process flow be designed with a resulting cost that allows effective competition in the market and that generates appropriate ROI?

Production
- What is the cost of acquiring raw materials and converting them into a finished product?
- How much should it cost to produce each unit?
- Should the production of certain product component parts be outsourced?

Marketing
- What is the cost to promote and sell the firm's products?
- Is the use of an Internet website a cost-effective marketing strategy?

Distribution
- How much is delivery costing per mile? Per pound?
- Are more effective carriers available for certain deliveries?

Customer service
- What is the after-sale cost of product support activities?
- What is the cost of an unsatisfied customer?

Desired ROI

An entire course could be devoted to developing cost management initiatives across the entire value chain. Thus, our focus throughout the remaining chapters of this text is primarily on the production stage and explaining the process for cost accumulation and assignment. Cost accumulation is the easy part; accounting systems always have focused on the collection and recording of transactions, and automated data collection systems are available for manufacturing environments today. Cost assignment, on the other hand, is much more complex because to answer the question "What does it cost?" *it* must be carefully defined and cost relationships must be understood.

What Does It Mean?

Answer on page 532

2. What does it mean to say that cost assignment is more complex than cost accumulation?

Cost Accumulation and Assignment

A cost is incurred to acquire the resources that are used in carrying out the activities in each function of the value chain. Managers are interested in planning and controlling these costs. After costs are accumulated, they are assigned to a point of reference for which the manager is interested in observing a separate cost measurement. This point of reference is referred to as a **cost object** and it may represent a job, a machine, a product line, a service activity, a department, a plant, a customer, a sales territory, a division of the corporation, or any other organizational reference point where a need to understand cost exists.

Cost accumulation is the process of collecting and recording transaction data through the accounting information system. These systems can be highly automated and provide a real-time view of cost information to allow timely decisions as the activity is occurring. The total amount of cost accumulated by the system is then logically categorized in different ways, such as by the production department. This classification of cost emphasizes the managerial point of reference and is referred to as a **cost pool**. **Cost assignment** is the process of attributing an appropriate amount of cost in the cost pool to each cost object. The process of cost pooling and assignment is illustrated here:

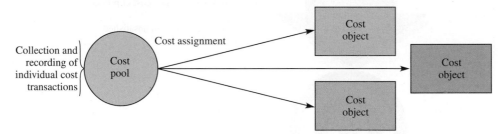

The following diagram illustrates this concept for a production department where management is interested in knowing the amount of cost assigned to each job the department produces:

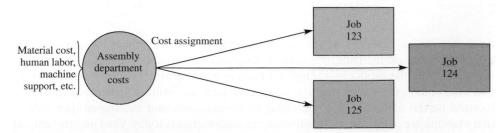

Cost Classifications—The Big Picture   **Exhibit 13-3**

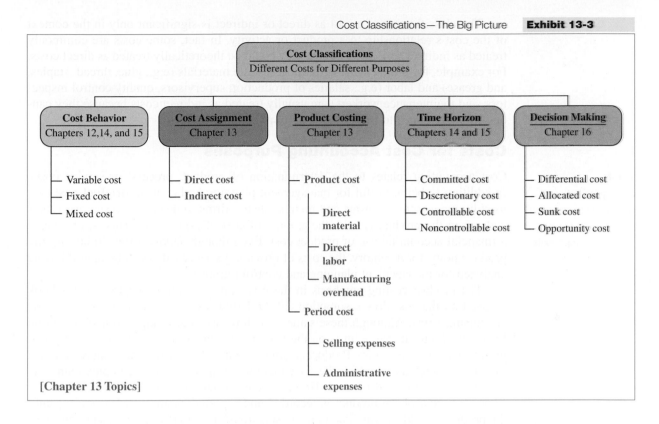

Cost Classifications
Different Costs for Different Purposes

| **Cost Behavior** Chapters 12,14, and 15 | **Cost Assignment** Chapter 13 | **Product Costing** Chapter 13 | **Time Horizon** Chapters 14 and 15 | **Decision Making** Chapter 16 |

Cost Behavior:
— Variable cost
— Fixed cost
— Mixed cost

Cost Assignment:
— Direct cost
— Indirect cost

Product Costing:
— Product cost
  — Direct material
  — Direct labor
  — Manufacturing overhead
— Period cost
  — Selling expenses
  — Administrative expenses

Time Horizon:
— Committed cost
— Discretionary cost
— Controllable cost
— Noncontrollable cost

Decision Making:
— Differential cost
— Allocated cost
— Sunk cost
— Opportunity cost

[Chapter 13 Topics]

Does the illustrated sequence seem simple enough? The answer is yes for some costs; but *let's think about this more carefully* is the more operative response. Certain costs in the cost pool, such as a raw material, are clearly traceable to the cost object, but common costs such as machine depreciation will need to be allocated to the cost object. The term *cost* means different things to different people depending upon one's point of reference. This chapter develops cost terminology further as two additional paths of the cost classification model introduced in Chapter 12 are explored. These are highlighted in Exhibit 13-3.

Cost Relationship to Products or Activity

Direct cost and **indirect cost** are terms used to relate a cost to a product or activity (i.e., a cost object). Whether a cost is direct or indirect depends on the context within which the term is being used. When we describe the cost of a specific product such as a book, the amount of paper used is clearly traceable to each book and is a direct cost, but the amount of electricity used by the printing press is not as obviously traceable to each book and therefore is an indirect cost. However, when we evaluate the profitability of the printing press, the amount of electricity used by the press would now be a direct cost, as would other costs traceable to the operation of the printing press. The cost of a training program designed to make all press operators more efficient would be an indirect cost. One way of distinguishing between a direct and an indirect cost is to think of a direct cost as a cost that would *not* be incurred if the product or activity were discontinued. An indirect cost is one that would continue to be incurred even if the product or activity were discontinued.

LO 3

Contrast direct and indirect costs and illustrate how they relate to a product or activity.

The classification of a cost as direct or indirect is significant only in the context of the cost's relationship to a product or activity. In fact, some costs are commonly treated as indirect costs even though they could be theoretically treated as direct costs. For example, for product costing purposes, some materials (e.g., glue, thread, staples, and grease) and labor (e.g., salaries of production supervisors, quality control inspectors, and maintenance workers) are usually treated as indirect costs because they cannot be easily traced to individual units of production.

Costs for Cost Accounting Purposes

Cost accounting relates to the determination of product, process, or service costs. In addition to being useful for management planning and control, **product costs** are used by manufacturing firms and merchandising firms to determine inventory values and, when the product is sold, the amount of cost of goods sold. This is, of course, a financial accounting use of product cost. Even though service firms do not usually produce items for inventory, the costs of providing services also will be identified and analyzed for management planning and control purposes.

The product costing emphasis in the financial accounting chapters of this book focused on the cost flow assumption (FIFO, LIFO, weighted-average) used by merchandising firms. Although these same cost flow issues also apply to manufacturing firms, our focus at this point is on the components of product cost for an entity that produces its own inventory. Product costing for a manufacturing firm is more complex than for a merchandising firm because making a product is more complex than buying an already finished product. However, the accounting concepts involved are the same. The cost of the product is recorded and reported as an asset (inventory) until the product is sold, at which point the cost is transferred to the income statement (cost of goods sold) as an expense to be matched with the revenue that resulted from the sale. The difference between a manufacturer and a merchandiser is illustrated in the following diagram:

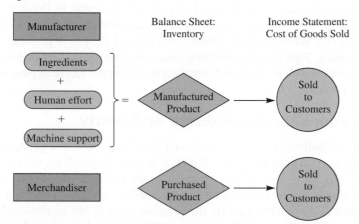

The cost associated with each of the manufacturing inputs is classified as raw materials, direct labor, or manufacturing overhead.

Raw materials are the ingredients of the product—the materials that are put into the production process and from which the finished product is made. The cost of raw materials includes the same items as the product cost of a merchandiser. The finished product of one process or company may be the raw material of another process or company. For example, corn is the raw material of a corn processor, and one of the processor's finished products may be corn syrup. The candy manufacturer uses the corn syrup as a raw material of its products.

Direct labor is the effort provided by workers who are directly involved with the manufacture of the product. For example, workers who perform machine operations on raw materials, workers who operate or control raw material conversion equipment (e.g., melters, mixers, heat treaters, coolers, and evaporators), and workers who assemble or package the product are directly involved in manufacturing activities. Their compensation costs would be considered direct labor costs.

Manufacturing overhead, or **overhead**, includes all manufacturing costs except those for raw materials and direct labor. Overhead is an indirect cost because it is not feasible to specifically relate overhead items to individual products. Examples of overhead costs include factory utilities, indirect materials for the product, maintenance and housekeeping costs (both materials and labor), depreciation expense for the factory building and production equipment, and compensation of production managers and supervisors.

As the manufacturing process becomes more complex and technology-driven, overhead costs generally become more significant. For example, the development of robotic production methods has resulted in increased overhead costs. Thus, planning and controlling overhead has become an increasingly important activity in many manufacturing firms.

Costs not included in inventory as product costs are reported in the income statement as incurred. These are the selling, general, and administrative costs (or operating expenses) of the firm that are not related to production activities. These items are called **period costs** because they are recorded as expenses in the accounting period in which they are incurred. Accounting for product and period costs is illustrated in Exhibit 13-4. Section I of the exhibit illustrates the effect of product and period costs on the financial statements when viewed as transactions in the horizontal model. Section II provides a cost flow view of the differences in accounting for product and period costs and their impact on the financial statements.

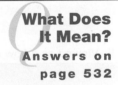

3. What does it mean that a cost is a direct, product, and variable cost?
4. What does it mean that product costs flow through inventory on their way to the income statement?

What Does It Mean?
Answers on page 532

Cost Accounting Systems

Cost Accounting Systems—General Characteristics

Every manufacturing firm uses a cost accounting system to accumulate the cost of products made. Although some firms manufacture a single, unique product, one unit at a time, most firms produce large quantities of identical products in a more or less continuous process (i.e., production runs). As you can imagine, cost accounting systems vary considerably in terms of complexity because they are designed for the specific needs of individual companies, but virtually all systems have the general characteristics described here.

A manufacturing cost accounting system involves three inventory accounts: *Raw Materials, Work in Process, and Finished Goods.* The **Raw Materials Inventory** account holds the cost of parts, assemblies, and materials (for example, for a sailboat

LO 5
Explain the general operation of a product costing system and illustrate how costs flow through the inventory accounts to cost of goods sold.

Exhibit 13-4   Accounting for Product and Period Costs

I. Viewed as transactions in the horizontal model:

	Balance Sheet	Income Statement
	Assets = Liabilities + Stockholders' equity	←Net income = Revenues − Expenses
Product costs: Become an asset until the product is sold		
Raw Materials	+ Inventory + Accounts (when Payable incurred)	
Direct Labor	+ Inventory + Accrued (when Wages incurred) Payable	
Manufacturing Overhead	+ Inventory + Other (when Accrued incurred) Liabilities	
	− Inventory (when sold)	− Cost of Goods Sold
Period costs: Nonproduct costs such as selling expense, advertising expense, and interest expense are recognized as expenses when incurred	+ Accounts Payable	− Selling Expense
	+ Other Accrued Liabilities	− Advertising Expense
	+ Interest Payable	− Interest Expense

II. Viewed as a flow of costs:

Cost	Balance Sheet	Income Statement
Product costs: Raw materials Direct labor Manufacturing overhead	Become an asset until the product is sold	
	When the cost is transferred to the income statement as ⟶	Cost of goods sold (an expense)
Period costs: Nonproduct costs such as Selling expenses Advertising Interest expense		Are recognized as expense when incurred

manufacturer—glass fiber cloth, epoxy resin, wood, sailcloth, deck fittings, and rope) that will be used in the manufacturing process. The **Work in Process Inventory** account is used to accumulate all of the manufacturing costs, including raw materials, direct labor, and manufacturing overhead while the product is being manufactured. When the manufacturing process is complete, the cost of the items made is transferred to the **Finished Goods Inventory** account. At the end of the accounting period, each of these inventory accounts may have a balance. For Raw Materials and Finished Goods, the balance represents the cost of the items on hand at the end of the period. For Work in Process, the balance represents the sum of the costs incurred for products that were started in production but have not been completed at the end of the period. The Work in Process Inventory account balance will be relatively small (or zero) for production processes that are of short duration or that are cleared out at the end of the period (e.g., candy manufacturing or food processing). Work in Process Inventory is likely to exist for firms that have relatively long-duration manufacturing processes, but the account balance will usually be low relative to Raw Materials and Finished Goods. For Campbell Soup Company, Work in Process Inventory does not exist in the 2010 and 2011 balance sheets, which illustrates their relatively short manufacturing process (see page 747 in the appendix). When a manufactured item is sold, its cost is transferred from the balance sheet Finished Goods Inventory account to cost of goods sold in the income statement. Exhibit 13-5 illustrates and compares the flow of product costs for a manufacturing firm and a merchandising firm. Section I of the exhibit illustrates the transaction effect of the cost flows on the financial statements when viewed in the horizontal model. Section II provides a cost flow view and presents a logical way to think about the sequence of activities involved in the conversion of raw materials into a finished product that is ultimately sold.

The cost of a single unit of a manufactured product is determined by averaging the total material, labor, and overhead costs incurred in the manufacture of some quantity of the product (for example, the average cost per unit in a production run). Determining the raw material and direct labor costs is usually fairly easy; raw material inventory usage records and time records for direct labor workers provide these data. It is the assignment of overhead costs that presents the challenge. Most cost systems apply overhead to production by using a single surrogate measure of overhead behavior—or at most very few. One commonly used measure of activity has been direct labor hours. Other bases include direct labor cost, machine hours, raw material usage, and the number of units made. The simplifying assumption is that overhead is incurred because products are being made, and the number of direct labor hours (or other base) used on a particular production run is a fair indicator of the overhead incurred for that production run. Given this relationship, at the beginning of the year an estimate is made of both the total overhead expected to be incurred during the year and the total direct labor hours (or other base) expected to be used. Estimated total overhead cost is divided by the estimated total direct labor hours (or other base) to get a **predetermined overhead application rate** per direct labor hour (or other base).

LO 6

Calculate predetermined overhead application rates and demonstrate how they are used.

To illustrate product costing and other cost and managerial accounting concepts, the hypothetical firm Cruisers, Inc., a manufacturer of fiberglass sailboats, will be used. Exhibit 13-6 illustrates how the cost of a boat (the cost object) made during the month of April is calculated. Note that the first step is the determination of the predetermined overhead application rate. This is shown in Section I of Exhibit 13-6. Then overhead is assigned to specific production runs based on this predetermined overhead application rate. This cost assignment is illustrated in Section II of Exhibit 13-6. If multiple overhead application bases are used, the estimated overhead cost associated

Exhibit 13-5 Flow of Cost Comparison—Manufacturer and Merchandiser

I. Viewed as transactions in the horizontal model:

A. Manufacturer:

Balance Sheet					Income Statement			
Assets	=	Liabilities	+	Stockholders' equity	← Net income	= Revenues	− Expenses	

Raw Materials Inventory
+ The cost of raw materials *purchased* is recorded as an asset

+ Accounts Payable

− The cost of raw materials *used* in production is transferred to →

Work in Process Inventory
+ Raw materials *used*
+ Direct labor *incurred*

+ Accrued Wages Payable

+ Manufacturing overhead costs *applied*

+ Other Accrued Liabilities

− The cost of products *manufactured* and transferred to the warehouse is added to →

Finished Goods Inventory
+ Cost of goods manufactured

− Cost of products sold   − Cost of Goods Sold

B. Merchandiser:

Merchandise Inventory
+ The cost of products *purchased*

+ Accounts Payable

− Cost of products sold   − Cost of Goods Sold

(continued)

Exhibit 13-5

II. Viewed as a flow of costs:

A. Manufacturer:

Balance Sheet			Income Statement
Raw Materials Inventory	**Work in Process Inventory**	**Finished Goods Inventory**	**Cost of Goods Sold**
The cost of raw materials *purchased* is recorded as an asset in raw materials inventory	The cost of raw materials *used* in production is moved from raw materials inventory to work in process inventory → Raw materials *used*, direct labor *incurred,* and manufacturing overhead costs *applied* are recorded as an asset in work in process inventory	The cost of products *manufactured* and transferred to the warehouse is removed from work in process inventory and added to finished goods inventory as → Cost of goods manufactured → The cost of manufactured products *sold* is removed from finished goods inventory to become	Cost of goods sold—an expense in the income statement

B. Merchandiser:

Balance Sheet		Income Statement
Merchandise Inventory		**Cost of Goods Sold**
The cost of products *purchased* is recorded as an asset in merchandise inventory	The cost of *products* sold *is removed* from merchandise inventory to become → Cost of goods sold—an expense in the income statement	

Exhibit 13-6

Product Costing
Illustration

I. Calculation of predetermined overhead application rate:

Assumptions:

Cruisers, Inc., incurs overhead costs in proportion to the number of direct labor hours worked; therefore, the predetermined overhead application rate is based on direct labor hours.

The estimated annual production level is 1,250 sailboats, and each sailboat should require 240 direct labor hours to complete.

Estimated total overhead cost to be incurred for the year: $4,200,000.

Estimated total direct labor hours to be worked in the year: 300,000.

$$\text{Overhead application rate} = \frac{\text{Estimated total overhead cost}}{\text{Estimated total direct labor hours}}$$

$$= \$4{,}200{,}000/300{,}000 \text{ hours}$$

$$= \$14/\text{direct labor hour}$$

II. Calculation of product cost:

Assumptions:

Cruisers, Inc., produced 86 SeaCruiser sailboats during April; a total of 20,640 labor hours were worked, and the following costs were incurred:

Raw materials	$368,510
Direct labor	$330,240

The cost of each boat is determined by dividing the total manufacturing costs incurred by the number of boats produced:

Raw materials	$368,510
Direct labor	330,240
Overhead (20,640 direct labor hours × the overhead application rate of $14/hour)	288,960
Total manufacturing cost incurred	$987,710
Cost per boat ($987,710/86 boats)	$ 11,485

with each base must be divided by the estimated usage of each base to develop the separate **overhead application rates.** For example, overhead may be applied based on 140 percent of direct labor cost, plus $3.10 per pound of a certain raw material used in the production process. Study Exhibit 13-6 to see how cost components are accumulated and then averaged to get the cost of a single unit.

Although the costing process involves estimates and provides an overall average, many firms do an excellent job of estimating both total overhead costs and total activity, resulting in quite accurate overhead application and product costing. Because the predetermined overhead application rate calculation is based on estimates, at the end of the year there will be a difference between the total overhead costs actually incurred and the costs applied to production during the year. This difference is called **overapplied overhead** or **underapplied overhead.** At the end of the year, if the overapplied or underapplied overhead is small relative to total overhead costs incurred, it is transferred to cost of goods sold. If it is material in amount, it is allocated between inventories and cost of goods sold in proportion to the total overhead included in each. On a monthly basis, the overapplied or underapplied overhead is carried forward in the Manufacturing Overhead account. The reason for this is that estimates for the whole year were used to calculate the predetermined overhead application rate, and

Working with manufacturing overhead for product costing can be confusing. Thinking of this process as one of cost pooling and assignment, as illustrated earlier in the chapter, will help you. The purpose is to assign an appropriate amount of overhead cost (otherwise indirect and therefore not traceable) to each sailboat (a cost object) that Cruisers, Inc., manufactures. Direct labor hours (the cost driver) incurred to produce each sailboat style will determine the amount of overhead (from the cost pool) that will be assigned to each sailboat.

Study
Suggestion

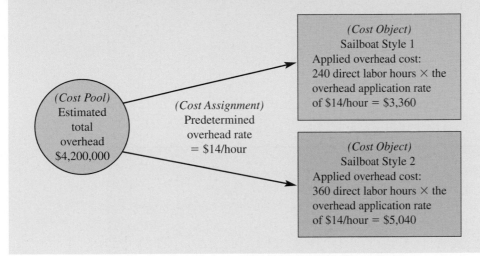

variations in cost and activity that occur in one month may be offset in a subsequent month. Thus, a better matching of revenue and expense occurs if the overapplied or underapplied overhead adjustment is made only at the end of the year.

Exhibit 13-7 illustrates the flow of these product costs through the accounts of Cruisers, Inc., for April. Note the use of the Manufacturing Overhead account—this is an account that functions as an asset-type clearing account. *Actual* manufacturing overhead costs incurred are recorded as increases (debits) in this account, and the manufacturing overhead *applied* to Work in Process is a reduction (credit) to the account. The Manufacturing Overhead account will not have any balance at the beginning or end of the year because, as already stated, overapplied or underapplied overhead is transferred to Cost of Goods Sold or allocated between Work in Process, Finished Goods, and Cost of Goods Sold. However, at month-ends during the year, the account is likely to have a relatively small overapplied or underapplied balance. This case is illustrated in Exhibit 13-7.

---

5. What does it mean that manufacturing overhead is applied to inventory?
6. What does it mean when there is underapplied overhead at the end of the year?

What Does
It Mean?
Answers on
page 532

Manufacturing costs can be summarized and reported in a **statement of cost of goods manufactured.** Such a statement using amounts for Cruisers, Inc., for April is illustrated in Exhibit 13-8. Although it was assumed that there were no beginning or

Exhibit 13-7 Cruisers, Inc., Flow of Costs for April

I. Viewed as transactions in the horizontal model:

Balance Sheet

Assets = Liabilities + Stockholders' equity

Income Statement

← Net income = Revenues − Expenses

Raw Materials Inventory

(1) Beginning balance 126,900
Cost of raw materials *purchased* in April +347,860   + Accounts Payable 347,860

(2) Cost of raw materials *used* −368,510
Ending balance 106,250

Manufacturing Overhead

Beginning balance (overapplied balance at March 31) (1,873)

(4) Actual manufacturing costs *incurred* during April +292,518   + Various Liabilities 292,518*

(5) Manufacturing overhead costs *applied* at a predetermined overhead application rate −288,960
Ending balance (underapplied) 1,685

Work in Process Inventory

Beginning balance 0

(2) Raw materials *used* +368,510

(3) Direct labor *incurred* +330,240   + Accrued Wages Payable 330,240*

(5) Manufacturing overhead costs *applied* +288,960

(continued)

Balance Sheet

Assets	= Liabilities + Stockholders' equity

Income Statement

←Net income = Revenues − Expenses

(6) Cost of goods *manufactured* and transferred to finished goods −987,710

    Ending balance 0

Finished Goods Inventory

    Beginning balance 243,820

(6) Cost of goods *manufactured* +987,710

(7) Cost of products *sold* −1,103,930   − Cost of Goods Sold 1,103,930

    Ending balance 127,600

Explanation of transactions:

(1) Purchase of raw materials on account.

(2) Cost of raw materials used is transferred to Work in Process.

(3) Direct labor costs for the month increase Work in Process and increase Wages Payable.*

(4) Actual manufacturing overhead costs incurred for the month increase Manufacturing Overhead and increase Accounts Payable, Accrued Wages Payable, or Other Accrued Liabilities.*

(5) Manufacturing Overhead is applied to Work in Process using the predetermined overhead application rate and the actual activity base (direct labor hours, for example).

(6) Cost of goods manufactured is transferred from Work in Process to Finished Goods.

(7) Cost of goods sold is transferred from Finished Goods Inventory to Cost of Goods Sold.

*Some transactions may result in a decrease of Cash if cash payment occurs at the time of the transaction.

(continued)

Exhibit 13-7

II. Viewed as a flow of costs:

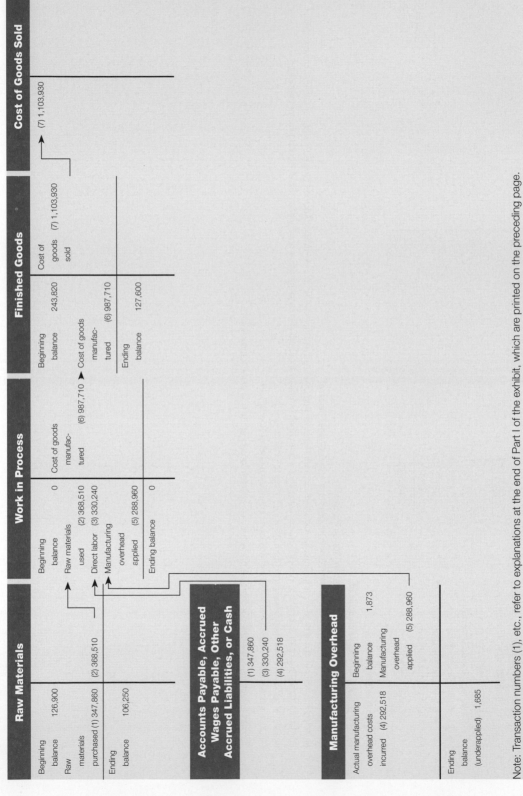

Note: Transaction numbers (1), etc., refer to explanations at the end of Part I of the exhibit, which are printed on the preceding page.

Exhibit 13-8

Statement of Cost of
Goods Manufactured

CRUISERS, INC.
Statement of Cost of Goods Manufactured
For the Month of April

Raw materials:

Inventory, March 31	$ 126,900	
Purchases during April	347,860	
Raw materials available for use	$ 474,760	
Less: Inventory, April 30	(106,250)	
Cost of raw materials used		$368,510
Direct labor cost incurred during April		330,240
Manufacturing overhead applied during April		288,960
Total manufacturing costs incurred during April		$987,710
Add: Work in process inventory, March 31		-0-
Less: Work in process inventory, April 30		-0-
Cost of goods manufactured during April		$987,710

ending inventories for work in process, Exhibit 13-8 illustrates how work in process balances would be reported in this statement.

LO 7

Prepare and interpret
a statement of cost of
goods manufactured.

To calculate cost of goods sold for April, the cost of goods manufactured is added to the beginning inventory of finished goods to get the cost of goods available for sale. The cost of the ending inventory of finished goods is then subtracted from goods available for sale to arrive at cost of goods sold.

The determination of cost of goods sold for April will depend on the type of inventory system in use. If the periodic system is used, the cost of ending inventory will be determined using the cost of goods sold model:

Beginning inventory	$ 243,820
Cost of goods manufactured	987,710
Cost of goods available for sale	$1,231,530
Less: Ending inventory	(127,600)
Cost of goods sold	$1,103,930

If the perpetual system is used, the cost of each unit of product will be calculated, and cost of goods sold will be the number of units sold multiplied by the cost of each. Recall that under the perpetual system, the cost of goods sold is recorded throughout the year as sales are made, whereas under the periodic system, cost of goods sold is determined at the end of the year when a physical inventory count is taken.

To summarize, product costs are attached to the product being manufactured and are treated as an expense when the product is sold (or is lost, becomes worthless from obsolescence, or is otherwise no longer an asset to the firm). Period costs—selling, general, and administrative expenses—are reported in the income statement of the period in which such costs are incurred. *Another way to distinguish between product and period costs is to think of product costs as manufacturing costs and period costs as nonmanufacturing costs.*

In the Exhibit 13-7 illustration of the flow of product costs for Cruisers, Inc., the end result was that cost of goods sold was $1,103,930 for the month of April.

Exhibit 13-9

Income Statement

CRUISERS, INC. Income Statement For the Month of April	
Sales	$2,012,400
Cost of goods sold	(1,103,930)
Gross profit	$ 908,470
Selling, general, and administrative expenses	(562,110)
Income from operations	$ 346,360
Interest expense	(78,420)
Income before taxes	$ 267,940
Income tax expense	(93,779)
Net income	$ 174,161

Revenues and nonmanufacturing (i.e., period) costs were omitted from the transaction data in Exhibit 13-7 for the sake of clarity. An income statement for Cruisers, Inc., using assumed amounts, is presented in Exhibit 13-9. Notice that selling, general, and administrative expenses represent a significant portion of the total expenses. Nonoperating expenses reported for interest and income taxes also are significant. You should keep these relationships in mind as you study the next two sections of this chapter. Each of the alternative cost accounting systems (job order costing and process costing) described in these sections emphasizes the flow of product costs and determination of cost of goods sold. Although cost of goods sold represents the largest expense for most manufacturing firms, overall profitability depends on the firm's ability to control all costs. This point is illustrated in Campbell Soup Company's consolidated statements of earnings, which appear in the appendix. In 2009, cost of products sold represented 60.1 percent of net sales; for 2010 it was down to 59.0 percent. Over the same two years, however, operating income improved from 15.6 percent of net sales to 17.6 percent, indicating that other nonmanufacturing expenses were better controlled, and it improved from 24.3 percent of net sales in 2009 to 23.5 percent in 2010. Interestingly, in 2011 the nonmanufacturing expenses remained relatively stable at 23.6 percent of net sales, but cost of product sold slipped to 59.8 percent and the resulting operating income dropped to 16.6 percent. A three-year change in operating income as a percent of net sales from 15.6 to 17.6 to 16.6 percent may not seem all that impressive at first glance, but the 2 percent cost savings experienced in 2010 amounted to a $163 million improvement in operating income, and the drop of 1 percent in 2011 amounted to a $69 million decline in operating income.

Cost Accounting Systems—Job Order Costing, Process Costing, and Hybrid Costing

The general cost accounting system illustrated in the prior section must be adapted to fit the manufacturing environment of the entity. A **job order costing system** is used when discrete products, such as sailboats, are manufactured. Each production run is treated as a separate "job." Costs are accumulated for each job, as illustrated in Exhibit 13-6 for Cruisers' production of 86 SeaCruiser sailboats, and the cost per unit is determined by dividing the total costs incurred by the number of units produced. During any accounting period, a number of jobs, or production runs of different products, may be worked on. For any job or production run, costs are accumulated, and the cost per unit of product made is calculated as illustrated for the SeaCruiser sailboat.

When the manufacturing environment involves essentially homogeneous products that are made in a more or less continuous process, frequently involving several departments, it is not feasible to accumulate product cost by job, so a **process costing system** is used. The processing of corn into meal, starch, and syrup is an example of an activity for which process costing would be applicable. The objectives of process costing and job order costing are the same: to assign raw material, direct labor, and manufacturing overhead costs to products and to provide a means to compute the unit cost of each item produced. In process costing, costs are accumulated by department (rather than by job) and are assigned to the products that are processed through the department.

The accumulation of costs by department is relatively straightforward, but the existence of partially completed work in process inventories adds a complexity to the determination of the number of units of product over which departmental costs are to be spread. For example, assume that during the month 100,000 units were transferred from the first department in the manufacturing sequence to the next department, and at the end of the month an additional 15,000 units in inventory were 50 percent completed. For process costing, production during the month is stated in **equivalent units of production**—the number of units that would have been produced if all production efforts during the month had resulted in completed products. In this example, the costs incurred by the first department during the period (including costs in the beginning inventory) would be spread over 107,500 units—the 100,000 units completed plus 50% × 15,000 ending inventory units—to get the weighted-average cost per equivalent unit for this department. This is the cost per unit for items transferred to the next department and the cost used to value the first department's ending inventory. Costs of subsequent departments include costs transferred in from prior departments. Ultimately, all production costs are transferred to Finished Goods Inventory after the final department completes the production cycle.

As manufacturing firms have sought to increase efficiency and to lower costs in recent years, production processes have been developed that mix elements of job order and continuous process manufacturing environments. Whether labeled flexible manufacturing, batch manufacturing, just-in-time manufacturing, or something else, most of these processes involve streamlined work flow, tighter inventory controls, and extensive use of automated equipment. Hybrid costing systems have evolved for these processes. Hybrid cost accounting systems mix elements of job order and process costing systems to accomplish the objective of assigning manufacturing costs to units produced. It is important to recognize that cost accounting systems will change, as illustrated with the evolution of lean accounting described in the Chapter 13 introduction, in response to changes in the production process; the opposite should not be true.

Cost Accounting Methods—Absorption Costing and Direct Costing

The cost accounting method described thus far is that of **absorption costing** because all manufacturing costs incurred are absorbed into the cost of the product. An alternative method, called **direct costing** or **variable costing,** assigns only variable costs to products; fixed manufacturing costs are treated as operating expenses of the period in which they are incurred. (Variable and fixed costs were described in Chapter 12.) Absorption costing must be used for financial reporting and income tax purposes because fixed manufacturing overhead is considered part of the cost of a product. However, some managers are willing to incur the additional expense of using direct (or variable) costing for internal planning and control purposes because it results in product and inventory values that reflect the relationship between total cost and volume of activity, which is important in CVP analysis and decision making.

LO 8

Explain and illustrate the difference between absorption and direct (or variable) costing.

Exhibit 13-10   Cost Flows—Absorption Costing and Direct (Variable) Costing

Balance Sheet			Income Statement

I. Absorption costing

Manufacturing Overhead		Work in Process	Operating Expenses
Variable and fixed overhead incurred	Variable and fixed overhead applied to work in process	Direct material used Direct labor incurred → Variable and fixed overhead applied	Selling, general, and administrative expenses

II. Direct (variable) costing

Manufacturing Overhead		Work in Process	Operating Expenses
Variable overhead incurred	Variable overhead applied to work in process	Direct material used Direct labor incurred → Variable overhead applied	Selling, general, and administrative expenses **Fixed overhead incurred**

The distinction between absorption costing and direct costing focuses on *manufacturing overhead* costs only. Raw material and direct labor are always product costs, and selling, general, and administrative expenses are always treated as operating expenses of the period in which they are incurred. Under absorption costing *both* variable and fixed manufacturing overhead are considered product costs and are applied to work in process. Under direct costing, however, only variable manufacturing overhead is a product cost applied to work in process; fixed manufacturing overhead is treated as a period cost and recorded as an operating expense when incurred. Exhibit 13-10 provides a cost flow illustration of these alternative methods.

The significance of the distinction between absorption costing and direct costing is a function of any change in ending inventory. If inventories have increased, under absorption costing the fixed manufacturing overhead related to the inventory increase is an asset in the balance sheet, but under direct costing it is an expense in the income statement. Thus, when inventories increase, expenses are lower and profits are higher under absorption costing than under direct costing. The opposite is true when inventories decrease. Direct costing advocates point out that absorption costing gives an erroneous profit signal to managers. These advocates maintain that higher profits should result in periods when the firm's sales result in inventory decreases rather than in periods when production has exceeded sales and inventories increase.

For financial reporting and income tax purposes, firms that use direct costing must make a year-end adjustment to reclassify that part of the fixed manufacturing overhead incurred during the year that relates to the ending inventory. The effect of this reclassification is to decrease the balance of the Operating Expense account on the income statement and to increase the Work in Process and Finished Goods Inventory account balances on the balance sheet. The amount of fixed manufacturing overhead to be reclassified can be calculated fairly easily based on the proportion of the variable cost of ending inventory to the total variable manufacturing costs incurred during the year.

Do not confuse the product costing procedure with what you may have experienced in a repair shop where the price you pay is based on material cost plus labor hours multiplied by a rate that includes the labor cost, overhead cost, and an amount to cover administrative costs and profit. This is a technique for arriving at the price a customer is to be charged and, although similar in concept to product costing, the result is selling price, not product cost.

Cost Accounting Systems in Service Organizations

The discussion of cost accounting systems has emphasized the need to collect and assign costs in manufacturing environments. But the reality of competing in today's service- and information-oriented economy is that nonmanufacturing businesses also have a fundamental need to accurately determine the cost of the services they provide. Think about the unique sequence of service activities represented by each of the following examples when trying to answer the question "What does it cost?"

- The accounting firm of Ernst & Young provides audit services for clients, and many professionals from the firm participate in these engagements.
- FedEx delivers your priority package to a client by 10 A.M. tomorrow morning.
- The emergency room at County General Hospital treats an auto accident victim.
- Tony's Auto Repair replaces the transmission of a Chrysler Sebring.
- American Airlines operates a St. Louis–Chicago route that carries passengers multiple times every day between the two cities.
- ADP processes a small business's payroll checks every two weeks.

Regardless of the type of services a company provides, the basic cost accounting principles are identical to those of manufacturing firms—certain costs will be direct to a particular service activity being measured and other costs will be common to all services provided by the organization. For Tony's Auto Repair, a system similar to job order costing described earlier in the chapter would be utilized to capture the cost of parts (direct materials) and the mechanic's time (direct labor) as well as to apply a share of the shop's indirect costs (overhead) to each repair order. Many software companies specialize in providing cost accounting solutions for specific service industries that not only efficiently collect direct time and materials costs and provide a basis for applying overhead but also automate many other important activities such as estimating job costs and job scheduling.

Activity-Based Costing

In recent years, overhead costs have become an increasingly significant part of product cost, and managers have needed higher-quality cost information to permit greater control and better responses to the pressures of increased competition. R&D, design, marketing, distribution, and customer service costs in each stage of the value chain have become as important as product costs in this environment. As a result, the application of overhead on the basis of a few broad rates based on direct labor hours and/or machine hours has been replaced in many firms by an **activity-based costing (ABC)** system.

An ABC system involves identifying the activity that causes the incurrence of a cost; this activity is known as a **cost driver.** Examples of cost drivers are

LO 9

Perform activity-based costing and describe activity-based management.

Exhibit 13-11

Activity-Based Costing
Illustration

I. Manufacturing overhead cost drivers, and estimated annual costs and activity levels, for Cruisers, Inc.:

Activity (Cost Driver)	Estimated Annual Cost	Estimated Total Activity	Predetermined Rate per Unit of Activity
Production order preparation	$ 135,000	180 orders	$ 750/order
Hull and deck mold setup	2,140,000	1,000 setups	2,140/setup
Raw material acquisition	650,000	2,600 receipts	250/receipt
Material handling	450,000	9,000 moves	50/move
Quality inspection	750,000	6,000 inspections	125/inspection
Cleanup and waste disposal	75,000	250 loads	300/load
Total manufacturing overhead	$4,200,000		

II. Actual activity levels required to produce 86 SeaCruiser sailboats in April and manufacturing overhead applied:

Activity (Cost Driver)	Activity Required	Rate per Unit of Activity	Overhead Applied
Production order preparation	11 orders	$750/order	$ 8,250
Hull and deck mold setup	86 setups	2,140/setup	184,040
Raw material acquisition	185 receipts	250/receipt	46,250
Material handling	610 moves	50/move	30,500
Quality inspection	340 inspections	125/inspection	42,500
Cleanup and waste disposal	17 loads	300/load	5,100
Total manufacturing overhead applied			$316,640

machine setup, quality inspection, production order preparation, and materials handling activities. The number of times each activity is performed and the total cost of the activity are estimated, and a predetermined cost per activity is calculated. These activity-based costs are applied to products, manufacturing processes, and even administrative and marketing efforts. There are likely to be significantly more cost drivers than direct labor hours or machine hours. The development of an ABC system is a complex process involving considerable analysis and a significant investment. Comprehensive computerized databases are virtually a prerequisite to effective activity-based costing.

ABC systems have led to more accurate costing than traditional overhead application methods and have supported more effective management of the production, administrative, and marketing functions. Exhibit 13-11 presents an example of activity-based costing for the manufacturing overhead related to the SeaCruiser sailboats previously costed in Exhibit 13-6. Notice that the $316,640 of manufacturing overhead applied to the production of the 86 SeaCruiser sailboats in April using activity-based costing is different from the $288,960 applied (using a rate based on direct labor hours) in Exhibit 13-6.

Activity-based costing should be especially emphasized in organizations where multiple products require differing amounts of manufacturing and other value chain activities. Given a basic difference in the complexity of each product, the more diverse an organization's product mix is, the more inaccurate it will be to utilize an overhead application rate based on a single cost driver such as direct

I. Manufacturing overhead applied on the basis of direct labor hours:

Assumptions (as modified from Exhibit 13-6):

Cruisers, Inc., estimates its production level at 1,250 sailboats and 5,000 canoes. The canoes are produced five times during the year in production runs of 1,000 canoes.

Each sailboat requires 240 direct labor hours and each canoe requires 13 direct labor hours to complete.

Overhead is applied at the rate of $14/direct labor hour. (Assumes total overhead is now estimated to be $5,110,000.)

During May, 100 sailboats were produced, requiring 24,000 labor hours, and 1,000 canoes were produced, requiring 13,000 labor hours.

Calculation of applied overhead:

Sailboats (24,000 direct labor hours × $14/hour)	$336,000
Canoes (13,000 direct labor hours × $14/hour).	182,000
Total overhead applied.	$518,000

II. Manufacturing overhead applied using activity-based costing:

(Activity rates calculated in Exhibit 13-11 are used):

Calculation of applied overhead for 100 sailboats:

Activity (Cost Driver)	Activity Required	Rate per Unit of Activity	Overhead Applied
Production order preparation	13 orders	$ 750/order	$ 9,750
Hull deck and mold setup	103 setups	2,140/setup	220,420
Raw material acquisition	222 receipts	250/receipt	55,500
Material handling	732 moves	50/move	36,600
Quality inspection	408 inspections	125/inspection	51,000
Cleanup and waste disposal	20 loads	300/load	6,000
Overhead applied to sailboats			$379,270

Calculation of applied overhead for 1,000 canoes:

Activity (Cost Driver)	Activity Required	Rate per Unit of Activity	Overhead Applied
Production order preparation	1 order	$ 750/order	$ 750
Production run setup	1 setup	2,140/setup	2,140
Raw material acquisition	10 receipts	250/receipt	2,500
Material handling	50 moves	50/move	2,500
Quality inspection	1,000 inspections	125/inspection	125,000
Cleanup and waste disposal	20 loads	300/load	6,000
Overhead applied to canoes			$138,890
Total overhead applied			$518,160

Exhibit 13-12

Cost Distortion
Illustration

labor hours. Cost distortions will likely occur because a single cost driver too narrowly defines the overhead application process. Products that are less complex to manufacture will likely be assigned a larger share of overhead as compared to products that are more complex, which in turn will likely be assigned a smaller share of overhead.

To illustrate the risk of **cost distortion** when applying overhead by using a single cost driver, information from Cruisers, Inc., will be revisited and the cost for a second product, canoes, will be analyzed. Exhibit 13-12 extends the examples presented earlier in Exhibit 13-6, which calculated an overhead application rate of $14/direct labor hour, and Exhibit 13-11, which developed activity-based rates for applying manufacturing overhead. Notice in Exhibit 13-12 that a considerable shift takes place in the amount of manufacturing overhead applied to sailboats when Cruisers, Inc., moves from a single cost driver (direct labor hours) to activity-based costing rates. Using direct labor hours, sailboats are assigned $336,000 of the manufacturing overhead and canoes receive $182,000, which represent 65 percent and 35 percent of the total $518,000. Exhibit 13-12 illustrates how activity-based costing reflects the difference in activity required for the production of the more complex sailboats and correspondingly assigns $43,270 more, or a total of 73 percent, of the manufacturing overhead cost pool to the sailboats produced. This difference is significant for both product lines and has important implications when considering how this cost information will ultimately be used by the management team at Cruisers to set selling prices, calculate ROI, evaluate the performance of the production managers, and more.

The advantage of ABC is that it more clearly focuses on the activities causing cost and directs management attention to those activities. For example, in analyzing the makeup of what appears to be a very high setup cost, management of Cruisers, Inc., might develop alternative setup methods that would be less costly. It also might be fruitful to study the material acquisition system to try to make that system more efficient or reduce the number of times raw materials need to be received. To the extent that management can determine cost drivers and understand why and how costs are incurred, the effectiveness of cost controls and the efficiency with which the organization operates can be increased.

Activity-based management (ABM) is the use of activity-based costing information to support the decision-making process. Managers seeking to achieve the broad range of organizational objectives encompassed in the value chain use ABM. The application of this tool is limited only by the collective imagination of the management team and can be relevant to efforts focusing on customer satisfaction, operational productivity and efficiency, product or process design, product mix, and profit and performance measurement, to name just a few. The extension of ABC to these value chain efforts has led to better decisions, and many nonmanufacturing organizations such as banks, professional organizations, technology firms, health care providers, and the government have realized the benefits of ABC as described in Business in Practice—ABC and the U.S. Fish and Wildlife Service.

ABC and the U.S. Fish and Wildlife Service

Numerous software providers dot the technology landscape offering activity-based costing/management (ABC/M) solutions. SAS is one of the world's leaders in business analytic software, with a goal of providing breakthrough technology to help organizations transform the way they do business. SAS compares its ABC/M solution to traditional accounting systems that are geared for external reporting, suggesting that SAS activity-based management provides financial information in a form that mirrors the day-to-day activities of the people, equipment, and processes that directly impact an organization's bottom line. The SAS website (www.sas.com) presents many descriptions of how SAS activity-based management has helped organizations maximize profits, contain costs, and improve operational efficiencies. Following are excerpts from the Success Story titled "Getting to Green," which explains how the U.S. Fish and Wildlife Service benefits from activity-based cost management:

Business in
Practice

> Using SAS, the U.S. Fish and Wildlife Service is set to become the first Department of Interior agency to meet a mandate designed to help federal agencies make better decisions about how to spend taxpayers' dollars. SAS Activity-Based Management is helping the Fish and Wildlife Service better integrate cost and performance data.
>
> With a $2 billion budget and a mission to conserve, protect and enhance fish, wildlife, plants and their habitats for the continuing benefit of the American people, the Fish and Wildlife Service delivers this mission at each regional office through five core programs:

- Operation of the National Wildlife Refuge System.
- Restoration of fisheries and conservation of habitat.
- Recovery of threatened or endangered species.
- Conservation of migratory birds and support of state fish and wildlife programs.
- Conservation of international fish and wildlife species.

In the past, budgetary data was viewed only to determine how much money was budgeted for specific program expenses and in specific categories, such as equipment, human resources and improvements in each area. Unfortunately, this traditional budget perspective does not reveal the relationships or strategies that are shared between programs or offices, or the similar types of work that each program completes in conjunction with sister programs. Nor does a traditional budget compare the costs of similar tasks carried out in different groups or regions.

> Using SAS software, the agency can track every expense and every hour of work back to those individual programs and to hundreds of activities carried out in the various subcategories within each program. Now, the Fish and Wildlife Service also can integrate those program costs as multiple contributions to products or services delivered to the public. As a result, agency leaders can better understand the full cost of business operations and make better assessments about acceptable levels of cost for each activity.

---

7. What does it mean when an activity-based costing system is used?

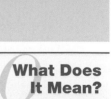

What Does It Mean?
Answer on page 532

Demonstration Problem

Visit the text website at www.mhhe.com/marshall10e to view a demonstration problem for this chapter.

Summary

Cost management is the process of using cost information from the accounting system to manage the activities of the organization. Accurate and timely cost information is critical to the success of the decision-making process. The value chain of the organization is the sequence of functions and related activities that adds value for the customer over the life of a product or service. Viewing the organization in terms of its value chain highlights many questions that must be answered about activities through the analysis and management of the activity cost.

Cost accumulation is the process of collecting and recording transaction data through the accounting system. The total amount of cost accumulated by the system is then logically categorized in different ways, such as by production department, which is referred to as a cost pool. Cost assignment is the process of attributing an appropriate amount of cost in the cost pool to each cost object. Costs can be classified as direct or indirect, relative to a particular product or activity (a cost object).

Cost accounting systems distinguish between product costs and period costs. Product costs for a merchandising firm are the costs associated with products held for sale. Product costs for a manufacturing firm include raw materials, direct labor, and manufacturing overhead. Period costs, such as selling, general, and administrative expenses, are reported as expenses in the fiscal period in which they are incurred.

Cost accounting systems account for the flow of product costs into Work in Process Inventory, the transfer of cost of goods manufactured out of Work in Process Inventory into Finished Goods Inventory, and finally to Cost of Goods Sold when the product is sold. One of the especially challenging objectives of the cost accounting system is to assign manufacturing overhead to products produced. The cost of a single unit of product is the sum of the costs incurred to produce a quantity of units divided by the number of units produced.

The difference between absorption costing and direct (or variable) costing is in the accounting for fixed manufacturing overhead. In absorption costing, fixed manufacturing overhead is a product cost. In direct (or variable) costing, fixed manufacturing overhead is a period cost.

The increased significance of overhead costs has led to the development of activity-based costing as a means of more accurately assigning overhead to production by relating costs to the activities that drive them.

Key Terms and Concepts

absorption costing (p. 523)   A product costing method by which both variable and fixed manufacturing costs are included in product costs.

activity-based costing (ABC) (p. 525)   The process of accumulating manufacturing overhead costs by production support activity (for example, machine setup) and then applying manufacturing overhead to production based on the activity required for each job or product.

activity-based management (ABM) (p. 529)   Use of activity-based costing information by managers to support the decision-making process.

cost accounting (p. 504)   A subset of managerial accounting that relates to the accumulation and determination of product, process, or service costs.

cost accumulation (p. 508)   The process of collecting and recording transaction data through the accounting system.

cost assignment (p. 508)   The process of allocating an amount of cost to a cost object.

cost distortion (p. 527)   A shift in the relative amount of manufacturing overhead costs applied to the mix of products produced that occurs because a single cost driver application rate is used instead of activity-based costing rates.

cost driver (p. 525)   An activity that causes the incurrence of a cost.

cost management (p. 506)   The process of using cost information to assess and manage the activities of the organization.

cost object (p. 508)   Any reference point for which cost is measured.

cost pool (p. 508)   Costs that have been accumulated for assignment to a cost object.

direct cost (p. 509)   A cost directly related to a product or activity; the cost would not be incurred if the product or activity were discontinued.

direct costing (p. 523)   A product costing method in which only variable manufacturing costs are included in product cost. Sometimes called *variable costing.*

direct labor (p. 511)   Effort provided by workers who are directly involved in the manufacture of a product.

equivalent units of production (p. 523)   In a process costing system, the number of units that would have been produced if all production efforts during the period had resulted in completed products.

Finished Goods Inventory (p. 513)   Inventory account applicable to goods available for sale to customers.

indirect cost (p. 509)   A cost that is indirectly related to the product or activity under consideration; the cost would continue to be incurred if the product or activity were discontinued.

job order costing system (p. 522)   A product costing system used when discrete products, or "jobs," are manufactured.

manufacturing overhead (p. 511)   All manufacturing costs except those classified as raw materials or direct labor.

overapplied overhead (p. 516)   A credit balance in the Manufacturing Overhead account that results from applied overhead in excess of actual overhead costs.

overhead (p. 511)   Another term for *manufacturing overhead.*

overhead application rate (p. 516)   The rate used to allocate overhead to specific production runs. See *predetermined overhead application rate.*

period costs (p. 511)   Noninventoriable costs, including *selling, general, and administrative expenses,* that relate to an accounting period.

predetermined overhead application rate (p. 513)   The rate per unit of activity (for example, direct labor hour) used to apply manufacturing overhead to work in process.

process costing system (p. 523)   A costing system used to accumulate costs for a production process that is more or less continuous, frequently involving several departments.

product costs (p. 510)   Inventoriable costs including raw materials, direct labor, and manufacturing overhead.

raw materials (p. 510)   The ingredients of a product.

Raw Materials Inventory (p. 511)   Inventory account applicable to materials ready for the production process.

statement of cost of goods manufactured (p. 517)   A supplementary financial statement that supports cost of goods sold, which is an element of the income statement. This statement summarizes raw material, direct labor, and manufacturing overhead costs during the period.

underapplied overhead (p. 516)   A debit balance in the Manufacturing Overhead account that results from actual overhead costs in excess of applied overhead.

value chain (p. 506)   The sequence of functions (R&D, design, production, marketing, distribution, and customer service) and related activities that, over the life of a product or service, adds value for the customer.

variable costing (p. 523)   A product costing method in which only variable manufacturing costs are included in product cost. Sometimes called *direct costing*.

Work in Process Inventory (p. 513)   Inventory account for the costs (raw material, direct labor, and manufacturing overhead) of items that are in the process of being manufactured.

ANSWERS to
What Does It Mean?

1. It means that cost accounting provides product cost and inventory value information for financial reporting purposes and provides planning, control, and decision-making information for managerial purposes.

2. It means that after costs are collected and recorded (cost accumulation), an understanding of cost relationships is necessary to complete the costing process (cost assignment) in which an appropriate portion of cost is assigned to a product or activity to determine its costs.

3. It means that the cost is either direct material or direct labor incurred in making a product; as such, total cost will vary with the quantity of product made.

4. It means that these costs are initially recorded as an inventory asset and that when the related product is eventually sold, the cost of the product is recognized as cost of goods sold.

5. It means that a way of assigning these indirect costs to inventory has been developed and used as a means of including manufacturing overhead in product cost.

6. It means that actual overhead incurred during the year is more than overhead applied to work in process by using the predetermined overhead application rate because actual overhead and/or actual production activity was different from the estimates used at the beginning of the year to develop the overhead application rate.

7. It means that there has been an extensive effort to refine the method of assigning overhead costs to products and processes so cost data are more accurate than was the case with earlier cost systems.

Self-Study Material

Visit the text website at www.mhhe.com/marshall10e to take an online self-study quiz for this chapter.

Matching Following are a number of key terms and concepts introduced in the chapter, along with a list of corresponding definitions. Match the appropriate letter for the key term or concept to each definition provided (items 1–14). Note that not all key terms and concepts will be used. Answers are provided at the end of this chapter.

a.	Cost accounting	f.	Cost assignment
b.	Cost management	g.	Direct cost
c.	Value chain	h.	Indirect cost
d.	Cost object	i.	Product costs
e.	Cost pool	j.	Period costs

k. Statement of cost of goods
    manufactured
l. Production standards
m. Raw material
n. Direct labor
o. Overhead

p. Overhead application rate
q. Job order costing system
r. Process costing system
s. Absorption costing
t. Direct (or variable) costing
u. Activity-based costing

_____ **1.** A product costing method by which only variable manufacturing costs are included in product cost.

_____ **2.** Any reference point for which management wants to measure cost.

_____ **3.** A supplementary financial statement that supports the cost of goods sold figure on the income statement by summarizing raw materials, direct labor, and manufacturing overhead costs incurred during the period.

_____ **4.** Noninventoriable costs, including selling, general, and administrative expenses, that relate to an accounting period.

_____ **5.** The process of allocating an amount of cost to a cost object.

_____ **6.** The rate used to allocate overhead to specific production runs.

_____ **7.** A cost incurred because of the product or activity under consideration; the cost would not be incurred if the product or activity were discontinued.

_____ **8.** A product costing method by which both variable and fixed manufacturing costs are included in product cost.

_____ **9.** A product costing system used when discrete products, such as sailboats tailored to the buyer's specifications, are manufactured.

_____ **10.** Effort provided by workers who are directly involved in the manufacture of a product.

_____ **11.** The sequence of functions (R&D, design, production, marketing, distribution, and customer service) and related activities that, over the life of a product or service, adds value for the customer.

_____ **12.** Inventoriable costs including raw materials, direct labor, and manufacturing overhead.

_____ **13.** A cost related to the product or activity under consideration but not incurred solely because of the product or activity; the cost would continue to be incurred if the product or activity were discontinued.

_____ **14.** Expected or allotted times and costs to make a product or perform an activity.

Multiple Choice For each of the following questions, circle the best response. Answers are provided at the end of this chapter.

1. Overhead is most often applied to production on the basis of
    a. direct labor hours.
    b. machine hours.
    c. raw material usage.
    d. number of units made.
    e. direct labor costs.

2. An example of a period cost is
    a. the salary of a production supervisor.
    b. the raw materials used in production.
    c. the property taxes on a factory building.
    d. advertising and promotion expenditures.
    e. none of the above.

3. A job order costing system would probably be appropriate for a firm that produces
    a. automobiles.   d. microcomputers.
    b. stained glass windows.   e. none of the above.
    c. DVDs.

4. Cost objects can be
    a. a product.   d. the computer center.
    b. a service.   e. all of the above.
    c. the machining department.

5. Suppose that your accounting textbook is the cost object of concern. The paper used to print the textbook is a(n)
    a. fixed cost.   d. indirect cost.
    b. labor cost.   e. period cost.
    c. direct cost.

6. Costs may be both
    a. direct and indirect.   d. period and product.
    b. indirect and fixed.   e. none of the above.
    c. raw material and labor.

7. Sterner Company computes its predetermined overhead application rate using direct labor hours as the activity base. Estimated and actual overhead costs and direct labor hours for the year were as follows:

	Estimated	**Actual**
Manufacturing overhead costs	$126,000	$118,020
Direct labor hours	10,000	9,200

Based on this information, manufacturing overhead was
    a. underapplied by $2,100.
    b. underapplied by $3,420.
    c. overapplied by $3,420.
    d. overapplied by $5,580.
    e. none of the above.

Use the following data for Questions 8–10.

Information obtained from Blue Heron, Inc.'s accounts on December 31 included:

	2013	**2012**
Raw materials inventory	$22,000	$18,000
Work in process inventory	38,000	26,000
Finished goods inventory	66,000	84,000

	For the Year Ended December 31, 2013
Sales	$420,000
Depreciation, factory	24,000
Direct labor costs	76,000
Purchase of raw materials	88,000
Advertising expense	20,000

Note: Assume that actual and applied overhead were equal
(i.e., not overapplied or underapplied at year-end).

8. The cost of raw materials used in production for Blue Heron, Inc., in 2013 was
   a. $22,000.
   b. $84,000.
   c. $88,000.
   d. $106,000.
   e. $128,000.

9. The cost of goods manufactured for Blue Heron, Inc., in 2013 was
   a. $172,000.
   b. $180,000.
   c. $192,000.
   d. $196,000.
   e. $202,000.

10. The cost of goods sold for Blue Heron, Inc., in 2013 was
    a. $154,000.
    b. $190,000.
    c. $198,000.
    d. $210,000.
    e. $214,000.

Mini-Exercises

All applicable Mini-Exercises are available with McGraw-Hill's *Connect*™ *Accounting*.

Total manufacturing costs Acme, Inc., incurs the following costs during May:

Sales expense.	$11,500	Administrative expense	$ 21,500
Direct labor	26,000	Plant depreciation	6,200
Factory supplies	2,500	Indirect labor	8,000
Advertising	2,800	Utilities.	10,000*
Raw material used	18,000		
*75% of this amount relates to the factory.			

Mini-Exercise 13.1
LO 3, 4

Required:
Calculate Acme's total manufacturing costs for May.

Calculate predetermined overhead rate and unit cost Bentley estimates manufacturing overhead of $1,800,000 for 2013 and will apply overhead to units produced based on 720,000 machine hours. During 2013, Bentley used $1,450,000 of raw materials, paid $2,282,500 of direct labor, generated 715,000 machine hours, and produced 2,000,000 units.

Mini-Exercise 13.2
LO 5, 6

Required:
Calculate Bentley's predetermined overhead rate and cost per unit of production for 2013.

Mini-Exercise
13.3
LO 6

Underapplied overhead analysis Tyler Company applies manufacturing overhead to production at the rate of $4 per direct labor hour and ended August with $12,000 underapplied overhead. Actual manufacturing overhead incurred for August amounted to $88,000.

Required:

How many direct labor hours did Tyler Company incur during August?

Mini-Exercise
13.4
LO 7

Statement of cost of goods manufactured The following information is from ABC Company's general ledger: Beginning and ending inventories, respectively, for raw materials were $8,000 and $10,000 and for work in process were $20,000 and $22,000. Raw material purchases and direct labor costs incurred were $36,000 each, and manufacturing overhead applied amounted to $20,000.

Required:

Prepare a statement of cost of goods manufactured for ABC Company.

Mini-Exercise
13.5
LO 8

Variable versus absorption costing The following cost behavior patterns describe anticipated manufacturing costs for 2013: raw material, $7/unit; direct labor, $10/unit; and manufacturing overhead, $240,000 + $8/unit.

Required:

If anticipated production for 2013 is 30,000 units, calculate the unit cost using variable costing and absorption costing. Explain the difference.

Mini-Exercise
13.6
LO 9

Activity-based costing Brooklyn Cycles produces custom bicycles and has used a traditional manufacturing overhead application rate based on direct labor hours. Currently, overhead is applied at the rate of $26/DLH. Brooklyn is now considering using activity-based driver rates to improve manufacturing overhead costing accuracy. Budgeted manufacturing overhead costs for expected driver activity are:

	Budgeted Cost	Budgeted Activity
Machining time	$250,000	10,000 hours
Direct labor time	$280,000	20,000 hours
Inspection time	$ 32,000	4,000 hours

Required:

Calculate manufacturing overhead rates that would be applied to bicycles produced using activity-based costing, and explain how Brooklyn Cycles could achieve improved costing accuracy.

Exercises

All applicable Exercises are available with McGraw-Hill's *Connect™ Accounting.*

Exercise 13.7
LO 2

Value chain classifications Match each of the following cost items with the value chain business function where you would expect the cost to be incurred:

Business Function	Cost Item	Answer
a. Research and development	1. Purchase of raw materials	_____
b. Design	2. Advertising	_____
c. Production	3. Salary of research scientists	_____
d. Marketing	4. Shipping expenses	_____
e. Distribution	5. Reengineering of product assembly process	_____
f. Customer service	6. Replacement parts for warranty repairs	_____
	7. Manufacturing supplies	_____
	8. Sales commissions	_____
	9. Purchase of CAD (computer-aided design) software	_____
	10. Salary of website designer	_____

Value chain classifications

Exercise 13.8
LO 2

Match each of the following cost items with the value chain business function where you would expect the cost to be incurred:

Business Function	Cost Item	Answer
a. Research and development	1. Labor time to repair products under warranty	_____
b. Design	2. TV commercial spots	_____
c. Production	3. Labor costs of filling customer orders	_____
d. Marketing	4. Testing of competitor's product	_____
e. Distribution	5. Direct manufacturing labor costs	_____
f. Customer service	6. Development of order tracking system for the Internet	_____
	7. Printing cost of new product brochures	_____
	8. Hours spent designing childproof bottles	_____
	9. Training costs for representatives to staff the customer call center	_____
	10. Installation of robotics equipment in manufacturing plant	_____

Cost classifications

Exercise 13.9
LO 3, 4

For each of the following costs, check the columns that most likely apply (both variable and fixed might apply for some costs).

Costs	Product Direct	Product Indirect	Period	Variable	Fixed
Wages of assembly-line workers	_____	_____	_____	_____	_____
Depreciation of plant equipment	_____	_____	_____	_____	_____
Glue and thread	_____	_____	_____	_____	_____
Outbound shipping costs	_____	_____	_____	_____	_____
Raw materials handling costs	_____	_____	_____	_____	_____
Salary of public relations manager	_____	_____	_____	_____	_____
Production run setup costs	_____	_____	_____	_____	_____
Plant utilities	_____	_____	_____	_____	_____
Electricity cost of retail stores	_____	_____	_____	_____	_____
Research and development expense	_____	_____	_____	_____	_____

Exercise 13.10

LO 3, 4

Cost classifications For each of the following costs, check the columns that most likely apply (both variable and fixed might apply for some costs).

	Product				
Costs	**Direct**	**Indirect**	**Period**	**Variable**	**Fixed**
Raw materials	____	____	____	____	____
Staples used to secure packed boxes of product	____	____	____	____	____
Plant janitors' wages	____	____	____	____	____
Order processing clerks' wages	____	____	____	____	____
Advertising expenses	____	____	____	____	____
Production workers' wages	____	____	____	____	____
Production supervisors' salaries	____	____	____	____	____
Sales force commissions	____	____	____	____	____
Maintenance supplies used	____	____	____	____	____
President's salary	____	____	____	____	____
Electricity cost for office building	____	____	____	____	____
Real estate taxes for					
Factory	____	____	____	____	____
Office building	____	____	____	____	____

Exercise 13.11

LO 4

Cost classifications Aussie Corp. manufactures rugby jerseys for collegiate sports teams and sells its merchandise through university bookstores.

Required:

Identify a specific item in the company's manufacturing, selling, or administrative processes for which the cost would be classified as

a. Raw material.
b. Direct labor.
c. Variable manufacturing overhead.
d. Fixed manufacturing overhead.
e. Fixed administrative expense.
f. Fixed indirect selling expense.
g. Variable direct selling expense.

Exercise 13.12

LO 4

Cost classifications College Carriers manufactures backpacks that are sold to students for use as book bags.

Required:

Identify a specific item in this company's manufacturing, selling, or administrative processes for which the cost would be classified as

a. Raw material.
b. Direct labor.
c. Variable manufacturing overhead.
d. Fixed manufacturing overhead.
e. Fixed administrative expense.

f. Fixed indirect selling expense.

g. Variable direct selling expense.

Product costing—various issues Clay Co. produces ceramic coffee mugs and pencil holders. Manufacturing overhead is assigned to production using an application rate based on direct labor hours.

Exercise 13.13
LO 5

Required:

a. For 2013, the company's cost accountant estimated that total overhead costs incurred would be $420,000 and that a total of 50,000 direct labor hours would be worked. Calculate the amount of overhead to be applied for each direct labor hour worked on a production run.

b. A production run of 400 coffee mugs used raw materials that cost $432 and used 40 direct labor hours at a cost of $10 per hour. Calculate the cost of each coffee mug produced.

c. At the end of October 2013, 280 coffee mugs made in the production run in part **b** had been sold and the rest were in ending inventory. Calculate (1) the cost of the coffee mugs sold that would have been reported in the income statement and (2) the cost included in the October 31, 2013, finished goods inventory.

Product costing—manufacturing overhead Nautical Accessories, Inc., manufactures women's boating hats. Manufacturing overhead is assigned to production on a machine-hour basis. For 2013, it was estimated that manufacturing overhead would total $359,520 and that 21,400 machine hours would be used.

Exercise 13.14
LO 5

Required:

a. Calculate the predetermined overhead application rate that will be used for absorption costing purposes during 2013.

b. During April, 3,900 hats were made. Raw materials costing $6,240 were used, and direct labor costs totaled $9,165. A total of 780 machine hours were worked during the month of April. Calculate the cost per hat made during April.

c. At the end of April, 1,050 hats were in ending inventory. Calculate the cost of the ending inventory and the cost of the hats sold during April.

Manufacturing overhead—over/underapplied Checker, Inc., produces automobile bumpers. Overhead is applied on the basis of machine hours required for cutting and fabricating. A predetermined overhead application rate of $18.50 per machine hour was established for 2013.

Exercise 13.15
LO 5, 6

Required:

a. If 12,000 machine hours were expected to be used during 2013, how much overhead was expected to be incurred?

b. Actual overhead incurred during 2013 totaled $229,400, and 12,200 machine hours were used during 2013. Calculate the amount of over- or underapplied overhead for 2013.

c. Explain the accounting necessary for the over- or underapplied overhead for the year.

Manufacturing overhead—over/underapplied Creative Lighting, Inc., makes specialty table lamps. Manufacturing overhead is applied to production on a direct

Exercise 13.16
LO 5, 6

labor hours basis. During June, the first month of the company's fiscal year, $56,520 of manufacturing overhead was applied to Work in Process Inventory using the predetermined overhead application rate of $6 per direct labor hour.

Required:

a. Calculate the number of hours of direct labor used during June.

b. Actual manufacturing overhead costs incurred during June totaled $49,340. Calculate the amount of over- or underapplied overhead for June.

c. Identify two possible explanations for the over- or underapplied overhead.

d. Explain the accounting appropriate for the over- or underapplied overhead at the end of June.

Exercise 13.17
LO 5, 6

Manufacturing overhead—multiple application bases Eddie Lander Tie Co. manufactures neckties and scarves. Two overhead application bases are used; some overhead is applied on the basis of raw material cost at a rate of 120% of material cost, and the balance of the overhead is applied at the rate of $8 per direct labor hour.

Required:

Calculate the cost per unit of a production run of 1,800 neckties that required raw materials costing $6,620 and 200 direct labor hours at a total cost of $2,240.

Exercise 13.18
LO 5, 6

Manufacturing overhead—multiple application bases Staley Toy Co. makes toy flutes. Two manufacturing overhead application bases are used; some overhead is applied on the basis of machine hours at a rate of $5.60 per machine hour, and the balance of the overhead is applied at the rate of 240% of direct labor cost.

Required:

a. Calculate the cost per unit of October production of 4,200 toy flutes that required

   1. Raw materials costing $490.
   2. 21 direct labor hours costing $357.
   3. 36 machine hours.

b. At the end of October, 3,870 of these toy flutes had been sold. Calculate the ending inventory value of the toy flutes still in inventory at October, 31.

Exercise 13.19
LO 8

Variable versus absorption costing Brent, Inc., manufactures wool sweaters. Costs incurred in making 55,000 sweaters in August included $330,000 of fixed manufacturing overhead. The total absorption cost per sweater was $38.60.

Required:

a. Calculate the variable cost per sweater.

b. The ending inventory of sweaters was 7,200 units lower at the end of the month than at the beginning of the month. By how much and in what direction (higher or lower) would cost of goods sold for the month of August be different under variable costing than under absorption costing?

c. Express the sweater cost in a cost formula.

Exercise 13.20
LO 8

Variable versus absorption costing Colorado Business Tools, manufactures calculators. Costs incurred in making 9,500 calculators in February included 29,450 of fixed manufacturing overhead. The total absorption cost per calculator was $10.25.

Required:

a. Calculate the variable cost per calculator.

b. The ending inventory of pocket calculators was 750 units higher at the end of the month than at the beginning of the month. By how much and in what direction (higher or lower) would operating income for the month of February be different under variable costing than under absorption costing?

c. Express the pocket calculator cost in a cost formula.

Problems

All applicable Problems are available with McGraw-Hill's *Connect*™ *Accounting.*

Activity-based costing MedTech, Inc., manufactures and sells diagnostic equipment used in the medical profession. Its job costing system was designed using an activity-based costing approach. Direct materials and direct labor costs are accumulated separately, along with information concerning four manufacturing overhead cost drivers (activities). Assume that the direct labor rate is $25 per hour and that there were no beginning inventories. The following information was available for 2013, based on an expected production level of 100,000 units for the year:

Problem 13.21
LO 9

Activity (Cost Driver)	Budgeted Costs for 2013	Cost Driver Used as Allocation Base	Cost Allocation Rate
Materials handling	$1,200,000	Number of parts used	$ 2.00 per part
Milling and grinding	2,200,000	Number of machine hours	11.00 per hour
Assembly and inspection	1,500,000	Direct labor hours worked	5.00 per hour
Testing	300,000	Number of units tested	3.00 per unit

The following production, costs, and activities occurred during the month of August:

Units Produced/Tested	Direct Materials Costs	Number of Parts Used	Machine Hours	Direct Labor Hours
10,000	$900,000	62,000	18,000	35,000

Required:

a. Calculate the total manufacturing costs and the cost per unit produced and tested during the month of August for MedTech, Inc.

b. Explain the advantages of the ABC approach relative to using a single predetermined overhead application rate based on direct labor hours. *(Note: You do not have to calculate the overhead that would be applied for the month of August using this alternative method.)*

Activity-based costing versus traditional overhead allocation methods
Woodland Industries manufactures and sells custom-made windows. Its job costing system was designed using an activity-based costing approach. Direct materials and direct labor costs are accumulated separately, along with information concerning three manufacturing overhead cost drivers (activities). Assume that the direct labor

Problem 13.22
LO 9

rate is $15 per hour and that there were no beginning inventories. The following information was available for 2013, based on an expected production level of 50,000 units for the year, which will require 200,000 direct labor hours:

Activity (Cost Driver)	Budgeted Costs for 2013	Cost Driver Used as Allocation Base	Cost Allocation Rate
Materials handling	$ 250,000	Number of parts used	$ 0.20 per part
Cutting and lathe work	1,750,000	Number of parts used	1.40 per part
Assembly and inspection	4,000,000	Direct labor hours	20.00 per hour

The following production, costs, and activities occurred during the month of July:

Units Produced	Direct Materials Costs	Number of Parts Used	Direct Labor Hours
3,200	$107,200	70,400	13,120

Required:

a. Calculate the total manufacturing costs and the cost per unit of the windows produced during the month of July (using the activity-based costing approach).

b. Assume instead that Woodland Industries applies manufacturing overhead on a direct labor hours basis (rather than using the activity-based costing system previously described). Calculate the total manufacturing cost and the cost per unit of the windows produced during the month of July. *(Hint: You will need to calculate the predetermined overhead application rate using the total budgeted overhead costs for 2013.)*

c. Compare the per unit cost figures calculated in parts **a** and **b**. Which approach do you think provides better information for manufacturing managers? Explain your answer.

Problem 13.23

LO 8

Variable versus absorption costing TroutPro Co. manufactures fishing equipment. During 2013, total costs associated with manufacturing 35,000 fly-cast fishing rods (a new product introduced this year) were as follows:

Raw materials	$372,500
Direct labor	99,000
Variable manufacturing overhead.	67,500
Fixed manufacturing overhead.	105,000

Required:

a. Calculate the cost per fishing rod under both variable costing and absorption costing.

b. If 750 of these fishing rods were in finished goods inventory at the end of 2013, by how much and in what direction (higher or lower) would 2013 operating income be different under variable costing than under absorption costing?

c. Express the fishing rod cost in a cost formula. What does this formula suggest the total cost of making an additional 500 fishing rods would be?

Problem 13.24

LO 8

Variable versus absorption costing Williamson, Inc., manufactures digital voice recorders. During 2013, total costs associated with manufacturing 32,000 of the new EZ 9900 model (introduced this year) were as follows:

Raw materials	$275,000
Direct labor	454,000
Variable manufacturing overhead	115,200
Fixed manufacturing overhead	108,800

Required:

a. Calculate the cost per recorder under both variable costing and absorption costing.

b. If 4,200 of these recorders were in finished goods inventory at the end of 2013, by how much and in what direction (higher or lower) would 2013 cost of goods sold be different under variable costing than under absorption costing?

c. Express the digital voice recorder cost in a cost formula. What does this formula suggest the total cost of making an additional 500 recorders would be?

Cost of goods manufactured, cost of goods sold, and income statement

Richards, Inc., incurred the following costs during May:

Problem 13.25

LO 4, 5, 7

Raw materials used	$ 662,000
Direct labor	1,304,000
Manufacturing overhead, actual	896,000
Selling expenses	534,000
Administrative expenses	388,000
Interest expense	182,000

Required:

During the month, 59,625 units of product were manufactured and 54,000 units of product were sold. On May 1, Richards, Inc., carried no inventories. On May 31, there were no inventories other than finished goods.

a. Calculate the cost of goods manufactured during May and the average cost per unit of product manufactured.

b. Calculate the cost of goods sold during May.

c. Calculate the difference between cost of goods manufactured and cost of goods sold. How will this amount be reported in the financial statements?

d. *(Optional)* Prepare a traditional (absorption) income statement for Richards, Inc., for the month of May. Assume that sales for the month were $4,896,000 and the company's effective income tax rate was 35%.

Cost of goods manufactured, cost of goods sold, and income statement

GrandSlam, Inc., incurred the following costs during March:

Problem 13.26

LO 4, 5, 7

Selling expenses	$25,340
Direct labor	37,752
Interest expense	7,135
Manufacturing overhead, actual	32,760
Raw materials used	61,464
Administrative expenses	19,675

Required:

During the month, 2,600 units of product were manufactured and 1,450 units of product were sold. On March 1, GrandSlam, Inc., carried no inventories. On March 31, there were no inventories for raw materials or work in process.

a. Calculate the cost of goods manufactured during March and the average cost per unit of product manufactured.

b. Calculate the cost of goods sold during March.

c. Calculate the difference between cost of goods manufactured and cost of goods sold. How will this amount be reported in the financial statements?

d. *(Optional)* Prepare a traditional (absorption) income statement for GrandSlam, Inc., for the month of March. Assume that sales for the month were $138,040 and the company's effective income tax rate was 35%.

Problem 13.27

LO 5, 7

Cost of goods manufactured and cost of goods sold The following table summarizes the beginning and ending inventories of Decatur Manufacturing, Inc., for the month of March:

	Feb. 28	Mar. 31
Raw materials	$ 53,600	$ 44,160
Work in process	114,080	103,680
Finished goods	75,520	67,040

Raw materials purchased during the month of March totaled $198,240. Direct labor costs incurred totaled $499,520 for the month. Actual and applied manufacturing overhead costs for March totaled $301,440 and $307,680, respectively. Over/ underapplied overhead is written off to cost of goods sold at the end of the year in December.

Required:

a. Calculate the cost of goods manufactured for March.

b. Calculate the cost of goods sold for March.

Problem 13.28

LO 4, 5, 7

Cost of goods manufactured, cost of goods sold, and income statement Buck & Company incurred the following costs during August:

Raw materials purchased	$ 44,140
Direct labor ($12.50 per hour)	57,500
Manufacturing overhead (actual)	90,300
Selling expenses	31,800
Administrative expenses	14,700
Interest expense	6,400

Manufacturing overhead is applied on the basis of $20 per direct labor hour. Assume that overapplied or underapplied overhead is transferred to cost of goods sold only at the end of the year. During the month, 4,200 units of product were manufactured and 4,400 units of product were sold. On August 1 and August 31, Buck & Company carried the following inventory balances:

	August 1	August 31
Raw materials	$19,600	$17,900
Work in process	53,200	57,400
Finished goods	41,800	32,700

Required:

a. Prepare a statement of cost of goods manufactured for the month of August and calculate the average cost per unit of product manufactured.

b. Calculate the cost of goods sold during August.

c. Calculate the difference between cost of goods manufactured and cost of goods sold. How will this amount be reported in the financial statements?

d. *(Optional)* Prepare a traditional (absorption) income statement for Buck & Company for the month of August. Assume that sales for the month were $272,800 and the company's effective income tax rate was 34%.

Cases

All applicable Cases are available with McGraw-Hill's *Connect™ Accounting.*

Cost of goods manufactured, cost of goods sold, and income statement   **Case 13.29**
Determine each of the following missing amounts: **LO 4, 5, 7**

	Firm A	Firm B	Firm C
Beginning raw materials inventory	$ 17,000	$?	$ 42,000
Purchases of raw materials during the year	?	96,000	226,000
Raw materials available for use	?	119,000	?
Ending raw materials inventory	12,000	?	51,000
Cost of raw materials used	90,000	101,000	?
Direct labor costs incurred	130,000	?	318,000
Variable manufacturing overhead applied	?	34,000	72,000
Fixed manufacturing overhead applied	100,000	60,000	?
Total manufacturing costs incurred	370,000	?	?
Beginning work in process	15,000	7,000	19,000
Ending work in process	25,000	11,000	16,000
Cost of goods manufactured	$?	266,000	$?
Sales	$?	410,000	$?
Beginning finished goods inventory	$ 30,000	?	61,000
Cost of goods manufactured	?	266,000	?
Cost of goods available for sale	?	303,000	761,000
Ending finished goods inventory	50,000	?	48,000
Cost of goods sold	?	273,000	?
Gross profit	140,000	?	198,000
Selling, general, and administrative expenses	68,000	?	?
Income from operations	$?	32,000	$ 89,000

Product costing—various issues Custom Granite, Inc., uses an absorption cost   **Case 13.30**
system for accumulating product cost. The following data are available for the past year: **LO 4, 5, 7**

- Raw materials purchases totaled $240,000.
- Direct labor costs incurred for the year totaled $480,000.

- Variable manufacturing overhead is applied on the basis of $6 per direct labor hour.
- Fixed manufacturing overhead is applied on the basis of machine hours used.
- When plans for the year were being made, it was estimated that total fixed overhead costs would be $312,000, and that 96,000 machine hours would be used during the year.
- The direct labor rate is $16 per hour.
- Actual machine hours used during the year totaled 88,000 hours.
- Actual general and administrative expenses for the year totaled $320,000.

Inventory balances at the beginning and end of the year were as follows:

	Beginning of Year	End of Year
Raw materials	$ 39,000	$ 27,000
Work in process	33,000	51,500
Finished goods	104,000	122,000

Required:

a. Calculate the predetermined fixed manufacturing overhead rate and explain how it will be used during the year.

b. Draw a graph for fixed manufacturing overhead showing two lines. The first line should illustrate cost behavior and how Custom Granite's management expects total fixed costs to be incurred for the year. The second line should illustrate product costing and how fixed costs are to be assigned to Custom Granite's production. Comment on your graph.

c. Repeat requirement **b** for variable manufacturing overhead.

d. Prepare a T-account for Raw Materials to calculate the cost of raw materials used. Explain the relationship between raw material purchased and raw material used.

e. Calculate the variable manufacturing overhead applied to work in process. Could the applied amount of variable overhead differ from the actual amount of variable overhead incurred by Custom Granite, Inc., for the year? If so, why might this occur?

f. Calculate the fixed manufacturing overhead applied to work in process. Could the applied amount of fixed overhead differ from the actual amount of fixed overhead incurred by Custom Granite, Inc., for the year? Why or why not?

g. Prepare a T-account for Work in Process to calculate the cost of goods manufactured.

h. Prepare a T-account for Finished Goods to calculate the cost of goods sold. Identify the cost of goods manufactured and *not sold*.

i. Custom Granite, Inc., estimated that it would use 96,000 machine hours during the year, but actual machine hours used totaled 88,000. Refer to the graph you prepared in requirement **b** and explain the implications for the product costing system of the 8,000 machine hours that Custom Granite failed to generate during the year. What are the implications for Custom Granite's balance sheet and income statement?

Case 13.31
LO 5, 7

Financial reporting, manufacturing firm—Internet assignment Campbell Soup Company provides access to its annual reports online at www.campbellsoup.com.

The annual reports are found in the "Our Company/Investor Center/Financial Information/Annual Reports" area of its website. Locate the following information in the annual reports provided for 2011, 2010, and 2009:

1. From the notes to consolidated financial statements, find the composition of the beginning and ending inventory for each of the following accounts: Raw Material, Work in Process, and Finished Goods.
2. From the consolidated statements of income, find the amount for Cost of Sales.
3. From the consolidated balance sheets, find the amount for Inventories.
4. From the management's discussion and analysis, find the overview section that explains Gross Profit.

Required:

a. Calculate the cost of goods manufactured for 2011, 2010, and 2009.
b. Calculate the total amount of combined cost incurred in 2011, 2010, and 2009 for raw material, direct labor, and manufacturing overhead.
c. From the 2011 "Management's Discussion and Analysis of Financial Condition and Results of Operations," identify the ratio of cost of sales to net sales. Comment on the overall trend.
d. Review Chapter 11 if necessary and calculate the inventory turnover and day's sales in inventory for 2011, 2010, and 2009. Comment on the overall trend.

Activity-based management—Internet assignment SAS is a world leader in business analytics software, delivering breakthrough technology to transform the way organizations do business. For SAS, the mission is to empower organizations around the world with superior software, solutions, and services and give them *The Power to Know*. At www.sas.com many activity-based management success stories are presented from a variety of firms in different industries.

Case 13.32

LO 9

Required:

a. Locate the product fact sheet about SAS's activity-based management solution. Read the product overview and information and write a summary report detailing your findings.
b. Locate the Success Stories for activity-based management. Choose an organization and read its testimonial. Write a summary report describing how that organization is using activity-based management.

Answers to Self-Study Material

Matching: 1. t, 2. d, 3. k, 4. j, 5. f, 6. p, 7. g, 8. s, 9. q, 10. n, 11. c, 12. i, 13. h, 14. l
Multiple choice: 1. a, 2. d, 3. b, 4. e, 5. c, 6. b, 7. a, 8. b, 9. a, 10. b

14

Cost Planning

Have you ever defined a personal goal which you deemed so important that you prepared a road-map to guide you toward your goal? Perhaps your goal was to purchase a new car and the road-map identified the portion of your paycheck that, given your other current responsibilities, needed to be set aside for the initial down payment and subsequent monthly payments. Or perhaps your goal involved more than a financial component, such as law school, where an academic roadmap was necessary in addition to a financial roadmap. And at the various stages defined in your road-map did you ask yourself the important question "How well am I doing?" These questions about goals, roadmaps, and performance, from a business perspective, are presented in Chapters 14 and 15 as we explore the management planning and control cycle.

Planning is an essential part of the management process, and it represents the initial activity in the planning and control cycle (see gray shaded area in the planning and control cycle model). A **budget** quantifies financial plans; *budgeting* is the process of financial planning. It involves the use of financial accounting concepts because ultimately the results of the organization's activities will be reported in terms of income, cash flows, and financial position—the financial statements. Budgeting also involves the use of managerial accounting concepts, especially cost behavior patterns,

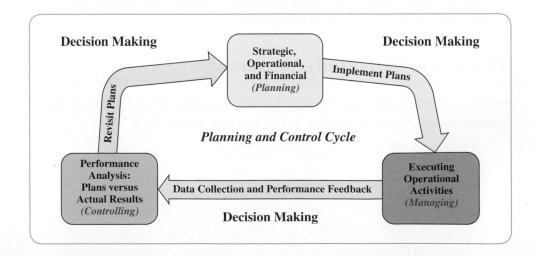

because the aggregate financial plan of an organization is the sum of all plans for individual products and units. Budgets are useful because the preparation of a budget forces management to plan. In addition, the budget provides a benchmark against which to compare actual results.

The budget preparation process requires communication and coordination of activities among the different functional areas of the firm—finance, production, marketing, and human resources—if organizational goals are to be aligned. Although it may seem that these benefits should be achieved even without a budget, often they are not realized without a budgeting process because each functional area gets so wrapped up in its own activities that its impact on other functions is overlooked or given secondary significance. When budgets are properly developed and administered, they also serve as motivational tools. Operating managers can focus on the specific goals that will help them achieve their budget objectives, knowing that their success will contribute to the overall success of the firm.

A **standard cost** is a unit budget allowance for a single component—material, labor, or overhead—of a product or service. Standard costs are used in the planning and control processes of manufacturing and service firms that perform repetitive operations in the production of goods or performance of services. Although usually associated with manufacturing, standard costs are being used with greater frequency in financial and consumer service organizations.

LEARNING OBJECTIVES (LO)

After studying this chapter you should understand and be able to

LO 14-1   Describe cost terminology that relates to the budgeting process.

LO 14-2   Explain why budgets are useful and how management philosophy can influence the budget process.

LO 14-3   Compare how alternative budget time frames can be used.

LO 14-4   Demonstrate the impact of the sales forecast (or revenue budget) on the overall operating budget.

LO 14-5   Prepare a purchases/production budget.

LO 14-6   Illustrate the importance of cost behavior patterns in developing the operating expense budget.

LO 14-7   Explain why and how a budgeted income statement and balance sheet are prepared.

LO 14-8   Prepare a cash budget.

LO 14-9   Explain why and how standards are useful in the planning and control process.

LO 14-10   Determine how the standard cost of a product is developed.

LO 14-11   Describe how standard costs are used in the cost accounting system.

Cost Classifications

Relationship of Total Cost to Volume of Activity

LO 1

Describe cost terminology that relates to the budgeting process.

For planning purposes, it is necessary to review and understand how costs are expected to change as the level of planned activity changes. For example, the raw material or direct labor requirements will depend on the planned level of production. Similarly, the planned level of production will depend on the planned level of sales. Raw material and direct labor, as discussed in Chapter 12, are **variable costs** that increase or decrease in total with the volume of activity but remain constant when expressed on a per unit basis. Many individual items classified within manufacturing overhead or selling and administrative costs are variable, and the amount of total cost expected will be a function of the amount of cost driver activity. Exhibit 14-1 highlights cost classification topics covered in this chapter.

Costs such as property taxes, executive salaries, and plant depreciation will not change (within the relevant range of activity) with plans for sales and related production requirements because these items represent **fixed costs.** The idea that a cost is classified as a fixed cost does not necessarily suggest that the amount to plan for in the budget will not change from year to year. The important point is that fixed costs will not change as the volume of activity changes (within the relevant range) but could change as a result of the managerial decision-making process as explained in the next section of this chapter.

Other costs such as utilities, maintenance, and compensation of salespeople who receive a salary plus commission suggest that a certain amount of cost can be expected

Exhibit 14-1   Cost Classifications—The Big Picture

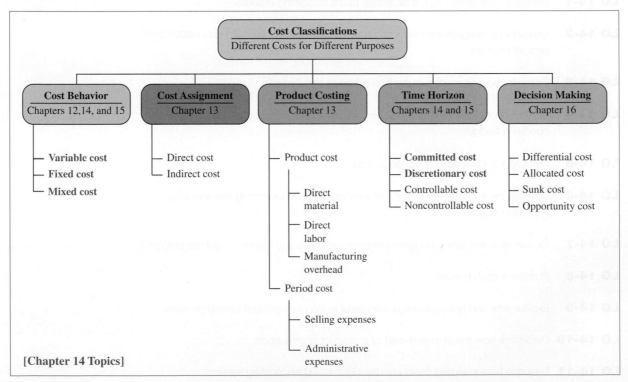

regardless of the level of activity, but these costs also will change as activity changes. These behavior patterns were referred to as **mixed costs** in Chapter 12, and the high–low method was illustrated as a simple technique for separating the variable and fixed components of the mixed cost. Knowing the cost behavior pattern for each line item of the operating budget is an essential prerequisite for effective planning.

Cost Classification According to a Time Frame Perspective

Whereas planning for exclusively variable cost items is strictly a function of the amount of cost driver activity expected each period, planning for many fixed cost items becomes more a function of the time horizon. Fixed costs classified according to a time frame perspective are known as *committed costs* and *discretionary costs*. A committed cost is one that will be incurred to execute long-range policy decisions to which the firm has "committed." Collectively, these **committed cost** investments provide the organization with the capacity resources necessary to carry out the basic activities along its value chain—R&D, design, production, marketing, distribution, and customer service. A **discretionary cost** is one that can be adjusted in the short run (usually on an annual basis) as management evaluates the organization's available resources and prioritizes the annual budget requests. Examples include:

Committed Costs	**Discretionary Costs**
Salaries of top management	Company softball team
Real estate taxes	Public relations
Advertising (especially for a consumer products company)	Charitable contributions
	Management development programs
Quality control	Internships for college students
Depreciation	Employee tuition reimbursement program
Insurance	Copy machine upgrades

With respect to committed costs, the control issue for managers is whether the cost is appropriate for the value received from the expenditure. On the other hand, when beginning or curtailing discretionary costs, managers do have short-term discretion about the level of cost to be incurred. As suggested by the preceding examples, significant nonfinancial considerations also must be evaluated with respect to discretionary costs.

Budgeting
The Budgeting Process in General

Many organizations commit substantial time and resources to the budgeting process. A useful budget is not prepared in a few hours or a few days; usually several months and the efforts of many people are devoted to the process. Once developed, a budget is not put on the shelf; it should become a practical tool to help managers accomplish the goals that have been established.

How the budget is used in an organization will depend on the management philosophy of the organization's top executives. In a highly structured, autocratically managed firm, the budget may be seen as being "carved in stone," and managers may develop dysfunctional practices to avoid being criticized for failing to meet budgeted results. For example, the sales force may defer entering customer orders in a month in which the sales target has already been achieved, sacrificing customer service levels and sales in order to get a head start on the next month's quota. Or a manager may

LO 2
Explain why budgets are useful and how management philosophy can influence the budgeting process.

commit funds for supplies that aren't really needed in order to use the full budget allowance, on the premise that doing so will facilitate justifying a budget allowance of at least an equal amount for the next period. These and other budget "games" waste valuable time and resources.

The budget should be seen as a guide that reflects management's best thinking at the time it is prepared. However, the plan may need to change if circumstances differ from those envisioned when the budget was prepared. Otherwise, large differences between budgeted amounts and actual amounts may have to be anticipated and accepted. The objective of the organization should not be to have actual results equal budgeted results; the objective should be to operate profitably, as expressed and measured by rate of return, growth in profits, market share, levels of service, and other metrics that reflect the mission and strategy of the organization.

Management philosophy is reflected in whether the budget is prepared using **top-down budgeting** (an authoritarian approach) or an interactive, participative approach in which lower-level managers provide significant input to the budgeting process. One approach is not necessarily better than the other in all situations. The **participative budgeting** approach should result in lower-level managers identifying more closely with the budget objectives; but there may be times, as when a firm is under heavy pressure to survive, that dictated objectives are appropriate.

The beginning point for most budgets is the actual performance for the current period. The manager first determines what the revenues and/or costs have been recently and then adjusts these amounts for changes that are expected to occur in the next period. The disadvantage of this incremental approach is that inefficiencies in the present way of doing things tend to be carried into the future. At the other extreme, **zero-based budgeting** is a technique that became popular in the 1970s. Zero-based budgeting involves identifying and prioritizing the activities carried out by a department, determining the costs associated with each, and then authorizing for the future only those activities that satisfy certain priority constraints. Some firms and organizations—especially governmental and social service agencies—embarked on a zero-based budgeting program but discontinued it because of the heavy administrative and record-keeping burdens it required.

What Does It Mean?

Answer on page 574

1. What does it mean to have a participative budgeting process?

The Budget Time Frame

LO 3

Compare how alternative budget time frames can be used.

Budgets can be prepared for a single period or for several periods. A **single-period budget** for a fiscal year would be prepared in the months preceding the beginning of the year and used for the entire year. The disadvantage of this approach is that some budget estimates must be made more than a year in advance. For example, a firm operating on a calendar year basis will prepare its 2013 budget during the last few months of 2012; November and December 2013 activities are being planned before actual results for those months of 2012 are known.

Exhibit 14-2

Budget Time Frames

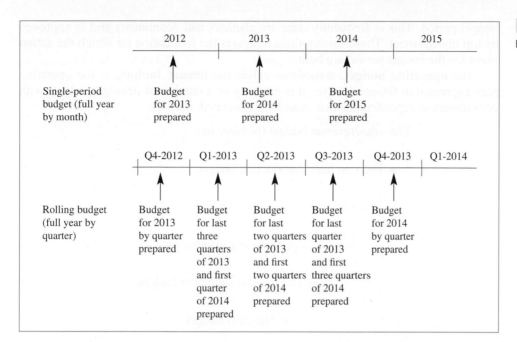

A multiperiod or **rolling budget** involves planning for segments of a year on a repetitive basis. For example, in a three-month/one-year rolling budget, a budget for each quarter of 2013 will be prepared late in 2012. During the first quarter of 2013, a budget for the next four quarters will be prepared. This will be the second budget prepared for each of the last three quarters of 2013 and the first budget for the first quarter of 2014. This process will continue each quarter, as illustrated in Exhibit 14-2.

The advantage of such a **continuous budget** is that the final budget for any quarter should be much more accurate because it has been prepared more recently. The obvious disadvantage to this process is the time, effort, and cost required. However, in a rapidly changing environment, the benefit of a budget that requires frequent assessment of the organization's plans may be worth the cost. The multiperiod budget can be prepared with any reporting frequency that makes sense for the organization and for the activity being budgeted. Thus, full financial statements may be budgeted on a six-month/one-year cycle, but cash receipt and disbursement details may be budgeted on a one-week/four-week cycle, or even a daily/one-week/four-week cycle (i.e., every day a budget by day for the next several days is prepared, and every week a budget by week for the next four weeks is prepared).

2. What does it mean to have a rolling or continuous budget?

What Does It Mean?

Answer on page 574

The Budgeting Process

The first step in the budgeting process is to develop and communicate a set of broad assumptions about the economy, the industry, and the organization's strategy for the budget period. This is frequently done by planners and economists and is approved by top management. These assumptions represent the foundation on which the action plans for the budget period are built.

The **operating budget,** sometimes called the **master budget,** is the operating plan expressed in financial terms; it is made up of a number of detailed budgets with commonsense dependencies that must be appreciated, such as

The sales/revenue budget (or forecast).

↳ The purchases/production budget.

   ↳ The cost of goods sold budget.

      ↳ The operating expense budget.

         ↳ The income statement budget.

            ↳ The cash budget.

               ↳ The balance sheet budget.

LO 4

Demonstrate the impact of the sales forecast (or revenue budget) on the overall operating budget.

The key to every budget is the forecast of "activity" that is expected during the budget period. This is usually a sales or revenue forecast developed using an estimate of the physical quantity of goods or services to be sold multiplied by the expected selling price per unit. Merchandising firms may develop a **sales forecast** using expected revenues from groups of products. Commodity processing firms may forecast expected activity (e.g., bushels of corn to be processed) because revenues are based on the commodity price plus a "spread" or markup, and the commodity price can fluctuate widely. Service organizations forecast expected activity based on the expected number of clients to be served and the quantity of service likely to be required by each client. Based on these activity measures and an anticipated revenue per service, total revenues can be estimated.

The sales forecast is the most challenging part of the budget to develop accurately because the organization has little or no control over a number of factors that influence revenue-producing activities. These include the state of the economy, regulatory restrictions, seasonal demand variations, and competitors' actions. A variety of computerized tools, including regression analysis and forecasting models, are available to assist in developing the sales forecast. The past experience of managers provides valuable input to the forecast. Information provided by the sales force and market research studies is also important. The firm's pricing policies, advertising effectiveness, and production capacity also may be considered. But in the final analysis, the sales forecast is only an educated guess resulting from a great deal of effort. Although the rest of the budgeting process flows from it, managers must remember that variations from the sales forecast will occur, and good managers will be prepared to respond quickly to those variations.

Once the sales forecast has been developed, the other budgets can be prepared because the items being budgeted are a function of sales (or a similar measure of activity). For example, the quantity of product to purchase or manufacture depends on planned sales and desired inventory levels. Selling expenses will be a function of sales, and other operating expenses depend on quantities purchased (or manufactured) and sold. After revenues and expenses have been forecast, an income statement can

Exhibit 14-3

Overview of the
Operating Budget
Development Sequence

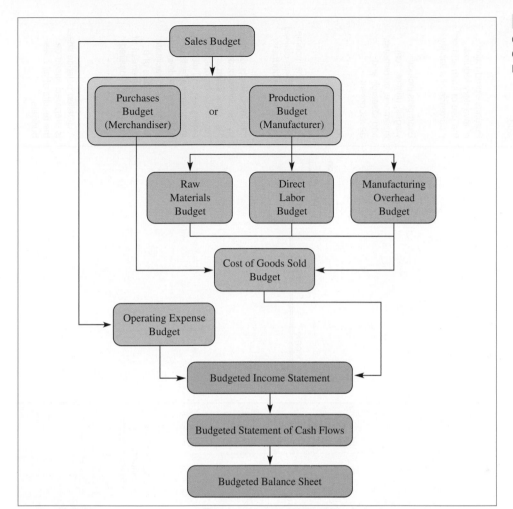

be completed. Next the cash budget (or projected statement of cash flows) can be prepared, given the budgeted operating results and plans for investing and financing activities. Finally, by considering all of these expectations, a balance sheet as of the end of the period can be prepared. This hierarchy of budgets is illustrated in Exhibits 14-3 and 14-4. An overview of the overall operating budget is presented in Exhibit 14-3 to illustrate the sequencing dependencies in the budget development process. Exhibit 14-4 illustrates the way each budget relates to the income statement and balance sheet and illustrates their effect on the horizontal model. Keep in mind that the key assumption in the entire budgeting process is the sales forecast.

3. What does it mean to say that the key to the entire budget (e.g., the sales budget) is the forecast of operating activity?

What Does It Mean?

Answer on page 574

Exhibit 14-4 Hierarchy of Budgets and Financial Statement Relationships

Budgets (in Order of Preparation)	Balance Sheet: Assets	=	Liabilities	+	Stockholders' equity	Income Statement: ← Net income	=	Revenues	−	Expenses	Explanation
1. Sales forecast	+ Cash + Accounts Receivable − Inventories							+ Revenues (i.e., sales)	−	Cost of Goods Sold	Assets are increased by the difference between sales and cost of goods sold.
2. Purchases/ production	+ Inventories − Cash		+ Accounts Payable								Purchase/production of inventory requires the use of cash and/or incurrence of a liability.
3. Operating expenses	− Cash		+ Other Accrued Liabilities						−	Operating Expenses	Examples include wages, utilities, rent, insurance, advertising, and research and development.
	− Accumulated Depreciation								−	Depreciation Expense	
4. Budgeted income statement					+ Retained Earnings	← Net income	=	Revenues	−	Expenses	Summarizes the income statement effects caused by the above budgets.
5. Cash: (Operating) (Investing) (Financing)	+/− Cash +/− Accounts Receivable +/− Inventories +/− Cash +/− Plant and Equipment +/− Cash		+/− Accounts Payable +/− Other Accrued Liabilities +/− Long-term Debt		+ Capital Stock − Dividends − Treasury Stock						Includes effects caused by the above budgets (i.e., cash sales and payments for operating expenses) and all other anticipated effects on cash. Broken down by categories to facilitate the preparation of a budgeted statement of cash flows, if desired.
6. Budgeted balance sheet	Assets	=	Liabilities	+	Owners' equity						A detailed balance sheet is prepared based on the results of all other budgets.

Calculations involving inventory accounts are sometimes easier to understand when viewed graphically. The key to understanding inventory is to think of "goods available" by looking at where those goods available come from and where they end up. Goods available come from two sources: beginning inventory and goods purchased (or produced) during the period. Goods available end up being sold or left unsold as ending inventory. Knowing any three of these components allows you to solve for the remaining item. This concept is illustrated here:

The Purchases/Production Budget

Recall that the following model was used to determine cost of goods sold under a periodic inventory system:

LO 5
Prepare a purchases/
production budget.

Beginning inventory	$
Add: Purchases	
Goods available for sale	$
Less: Ending inventory	( )
Cost of goods sold	$

By changing dollars to physical quantities, the same model can be used to determine the quantity of merchandise to be purchased or manufactured. The captions change slightly, and the model would be revised as follows:

Beginning inventory	units
Add: Purchases (or production)	units
Goods available for sale	units
Less: Ending inventory	( ) units
Quantity of goods sold	units

To use the model, first enter the beginning and ending inventory quantities based on the firm's inventory management policies and the quantity of goods sold from the sales forecast. The goods available for sale amount in units is calculated by working from the bottom up (the quantity of goods sold is added to ending inventory), and then beginning inventory is subtracted from goods available for sale to get the purchase or production quantity. Of course, the model could be rearranged to permit calculation of the purchase or production quantity in a traditional equation format:

$$\text{Purchases or production} = \text{Quantity sold} - \text{Beginning inventory} + \text{Ending inventory}$$

A firm's inventory management policies should recognize the average lead time to receive or make finished goods and/or raw materials. Likewise, these policies will ordinarily provide an allowance for forecast errors. For example, a finished goods inventory policy might be to have a desired ending inventory equal to 1.4 times the quantity expected to be sold in the subsequent month (or period). Remember that one period's ending inventory is the next period's beginning inventory. The beginning inventory for the first budget period could be estimated using the firm's inventory policy or the estimated ending inventory of the current period.

The results of the production and purchases budget model will frequently be adjusted to reflect production efficiencies or appropriate order quantities. For example, if the production budget calls for significantly different quantities of production each month for several months, management may elect to plan a constant production level and ignore the ending inventory policy because the benefits of production efficiencies are greater than the costs of carrying any excess inventory. Likewise, if the purchases budget indicates that 38,400 units of raw material should be purchased but standard shipping containers contain 2,000 units each, the actual quantity ordered will be either 38,000 or 40,000 units. Inventories will absorb the difference between the budget calculation and the practical order quantity. Remember that in most cases, the budget calculations result in a guide to action; they do not produce absolute amounts to be followed at all costs.

To complete a budgeted income statement, physical quantities developed in the model must be converted to dollars. This conversion is done by multiplying the cost of a unit by the budgeted quantity for each element of the model. When the number of units to be produced is known, the quantity of each raw material input to be purchased would be forecast using the same model. Of course, the quantity of each raw material used per unit of production must be substituted into the model, as follows:

Beginning inventory	units
Add: Purchases (or production)	_____ units
Raw materials available for use	units
Less: Ending inventory	(_____) units
Quantity of materials used in production	_____ units

Exhibit 14-5 illustrates the development of a manufacturing firm's production budget to support the sales forecast, and the raw materials purchases budget to support the budgeted level of production. A merchandising firm's purchases budget would be similar to a manufacturer's production budget. The computations involved are not complex, but they are numerous, and computer applications are widely used in the process.

If quantity forecast data are not desired because the cost of using the preceding approach is greater than its benefit, the approach can be easily modified to provide a dollar amount forecast for purchases or production. This is accomplished by using the complement of the budgeted gross profit ratio to calculate budgeted cost of goods sold. Beginning and ending inventories can be expressed as a function of budgeted cost of

Production Budget and Raw Materials Purchases Budget Illustration | **Exhibit 14-5**

I. Assumptions:

A. Sales forecast in units per month:

January	10,000 units
February	12,000 units
March	15,000 units
April	11,000 units

B. Inventory policy:

Finished goods ending inventory should equal 1.4 times the subsequent month's forecasted sales. Raw materials ending inventory should equal 50% of the subsequent month's budgeted raw material usage.

C. Three pounds of raw materials are required for each unit of finished product.

II. Production budget calculations:

A. Ending inventory of finished goods required:

	December	January	February	March
Ending inventory units required (1.4 × sales forecast for subsequent month)	14,000	16,800	21,000	15,400

B. Production budget using the cost of goods sold model (assuming that December 31 inventory is equal to that required by the finished goods inventory policy):

	January	February	March
Beginning inventory (units)	14,000	16,800	21,000
Add: Production (units)	?	?	?
Goods available for sale (units)	?	?	?
Less: Ending inventory (units)	(16,800)	(21,000)	(15,400)
Quantity of goods sold (units)	10,000	12,000	15,000
By working from the bottom up, the quantity of goods available for sale is calculated first, and then beginning inventory is subtracted from goods available for sale to get production in units of	12,800	16,200	9,400

(continued)

goods sold, and the dollar amount of budgeted purchases can then be determined. This process is illustrated in Exhibit 14-6 on page 561.

The cost of goods manufactured budget will include budgeted amounts for direct labor and manufacturing overhead. Determining these budget amounts frequently involves the use of a standard cost system (discussed later in this chapter), which is based on an analysis of the labor and overhead inputs required per unit of product.

Many manufacturing firms increase the accuracy of their cost of production and cost of goods sold forecasts by using the contribution margin model for manufacturing costs. (Note that in a merchandising firm, the cost of goods sold is a variable expense.) Variable costs of manufacturing (raw materials, direct labor, and variable overhead) are determined, and the variable cost ratio (variable manufacturing costs as a percentage of selling price) is calculated. This ratio is then used instead of the cost of goods sold ratio, as illustrated in Exhibit 14-6. Fixed manufacturing expenses are budgeted separately because they are not a function of the quantity produced or sold.

Exhibit 14-5

III. Raw materials purchases budget calculations:

	January	February	March
A. Quantity of raw material used each month to produce the number of units called for by the production budget (3 pounds of raw materials per unit of finished product)	38,400	48,600	28,200
B. Ending inventory required (equal to 50% of next month's usage in pounds)	24,300	14,100	———*

C. Purchases budget using cost of goods sold model with known data (assuming that December 31 inventory is equal to that required by the raw materials inventory policy):

	January	February
Beginning inventory (pounds)	19,200	24,300
Add: Purchases	?	?
Raw materials available for use (pounds).	?	?
Less: Ending inventory (pounds)	(24,300)	(14,100)
Quantity of materials used (pounds)	38,400	48,600

By working from the bottom up, the quantity of raw materials available for use is calculated first, and then beginning inventory is subtracted from raw materials available for use to get purchases in pounds of	43,500	38,400

Note that the purchases budget for March cannot be established until the sales budget for May is available because the inventory of finished goods at the end of March is a function of April production requirements.

*Won't be known until the April production budget is established.

The Cost of Goods Sold Budget

The cost of goods sold budget summarizes changes in the Merchandise Inventory account for the merchandising firm and changes in the Finished Goods Inventory account for the manufacturing firm as indicated by the results of the sales budget, the purchases/production budget, and the required ending inventory levels determined by management. For the merchandising firm, the cost of goods available for sale is determined by adding the beginning merchandise inventory and the purchases planned in the purchases budget. Ending inventory requirements are then subtracted from goods available for sale to calculate the budgeted cost of goods sold. This process is identical for the manufacturing firm except the merchandising firm has purchases and the manufacturing firm has the cost of goods manufactured as determined by the budgeted costs of each component of the production budget—the raw materials budget, the direct labor budget, and the manufacturing overhead budget.

The Operating Expense Budget

LO 6

Illustrate the importance of cost behavior patterns in developing the operating expense budget.

The cost behavior patterns of selling, general, administrative, and other operating expenses are determined, and these expenses are budgeted accordingly. For example, sales commissions will be a function of the forecast of either sales dollars or units. The historical pattern of some expenses will be affected by changes in strategy that management may plan for the budget period. In a participative budgeting system, the manager of each department or cost responsibility center will submit the anticipated cost of the

Budgeted Purchases Using the Gross Profit Ratio   **Exhibit 14-6**

I. Assumptions:
Sales forecast as shown below.
Gross profit ratio budgeted at 30%.
Ending inventory planned to be 80% of next month's cost of goods sold.

II. Required:
Calculate the budgeted purchases for April, May, and June.

III. Budget calculations:

	March	**April**	**May**	**June**	**July**
Sales forecast	$75,000	$55,000	$70,000	$80,000	$90,000
Cost of goods sold (Sales × (1 − 0.3))	52,500	38,500	49,000	56,000	63,000
Ending inventory (equal to 80% of next month's cost of goods sold)	30,800	39,200	44,800	50,400	
Beginning inventory		$30,800	$39,200	$44,800	
Add: Purchases.		?	?	?	
Goods available for sale.		$?	$?	$?	
Less: Ending inventory.		(39,200)	(44,800)	(50,400)	
Cost of goods sold		$38,500	$49,000	$56,000	
By working from the bottom up, the amount of goods available for sale is calculated first, and then beginning inventory is subtracted from goods available for sale to get purchases of.		$46,900	$54,600	$61,600	

department's planned activities, along with descriptions of the activities and explanations of significant differences from past experience. After review by higher levels of management, and perhaps negotiation, a final budget will be established. Exhibit 14-7 illustrates the significance of cost behavior patterns on the operating expense budget.

Operating managers have a natural tendency to submit budget estimates that are slightly higher than what the costs are really expected to be. This practice gives the manager some **budget slack** for contingencies or cost increases that may not have been anticipated. Adding budget slack or "padding the budget" can result in a significantly misleading budget for the organization as a whole. In spite of budget managers' pleas and/or threats that padding be eliminated, the practice probably continues in virtually all organizations. Some budget managers deal with the problem by judgmentally reducing the grand total of all departmental expense budgets when the company budget is prepared.

The Budgeted Income Statement

The sales forecast, cost of goods sold budget, and operating expense budget data are used by management accountants to prepare a budgeted income statement. This process is complex but necessary if the anticipated overall results of the budget period are to be evaluated in a meaningful way.

In many cases, if the budgeted income statement shows unacceptable results, top management will request that operating departments review their budget proposals and make appropriate adjustments so that profitability goals can be achieved.

LO 7

Explain why and how a budgeted income statement is prepared.

Exhibit 14-7

Operating Expense
Budget

I. Assumptions:

	January	February	March
Sales units	10,000	12,000	15,000
Sales revenue	$50,000	$60,000	$75,000

II. Budget calculations:

	Variable Activity Rate	January	February	March
Selling expenses:				
Variable selling expenses:				
Sales commissions	5% of sales	$ 2,500	$ 3,000	$ 3,750
Delivery expense	$0.25 per unit ...	2,500	3,000	3,750
Marketing promotions. ...	$0.50 per unit ...	5,000	6,000	7,500
Bad debt expense	1% of sales	500	600	750
Total variable expense		$10,500	$12,600	$15,750
Fixed selling expenses:				
Sales salaries		$ 2,000	$ 2,000	$ 2,000
Advertising		3,000	3,000	3,000
Depreciation		960	960	960
Other fixed expenses		520	520	520
Total fixed expense		$ 6,480	$ 6,480	$ 6,480
Total selling expense		$16,980	$19,080	$22,230
Administrative expenses:				
Administrative salaries		$ 5,000	$ 5,000	$ 5,000
Facility expense		8,000	8,000	8,000
Depreciation.		1,680	1,680	1,680
Property taxes		300	300	300
Other fixed expenses		480	480	480
Total administrative expense		$15,460	$15,460	$15,460
Budgeted operating expense.		$32,440	$34,540	$37,690

The Cash Budget

LO 8

Prepare a cash budget.

The cash budget is very much like a budgeted statement of cash flows but with a relatively short time frame. The financial manager must be able to anticipate short-term borrowing requirements because arrangements for borrowing must be made in advance of the date the cash is needed. When considering a loan proposal, the bank lending officer will want to know how much cash will be needed, how soon it will be needed, and when the borrower expects to repay the loan. A potential borrower who cannot answer these questions because a cash budget has not been prepared may be denied an otherwise reasonable loan request or may be charged a higher interest rate because of the perceived risk caused by these uncertainties. The financial manager also must know when temporarily excess cash is available for investment and when it will be needed, so that cash can be invested to earn interest income.

A number of assumptions about the timing of cash receipts and disbursements must be made when the cash budget is prepared. For example, how long after the sale will an account receivable be collected? The days' sales in receivables statistic will help answer this question. Again, the sales forecast comes into play. For example, assume that, based on past experience, the entity expects that 25 percent of a month's sales will be collected in the month of sale, 60 percent will be collected in the month following the month of sale, and 12 percent will be collected in the second month following the month of sale. (The last 3 percent will be collected over several months but is ignored in the budgeting process because of its relatively small amount and uncertain collection pattern. Some of these accounts may eventually be written off as uncollectible.) A cash receipts analysis for March and April might look like this:

	January	February	March	April
Sales forecast	$50,000	$60,000	$75,000	$55,000
Collections:				
25% of current month's sales			$18,750	$13,750
60% of prior month's sales			36,000	45,000
12% of second prior month's sales			6,000	7,200
Total collections			$60,750	$65,950

If this cash receipts forecast were being made in late December for the next four months, collections of sales made prior to January probably would be based on an estimate of when the accounts receivable at the end of December would be collected. This approach, and an alternative format for the cash receipts forecast analysis, would look like this:

	January	February	March	April
Sales forecast	$50,000	$60,000	$75,000	$55,000
Collections:				
From December 31 accounts receivable of $68,423 (amounts assumed)	$38,000	$25,000	$ 3,000	$ 1,000
From January sales	12,500	30,000	6,000	
From February sales		15,000	36,000	7,200
From March sales			18,750	45,000
From April sales				13,750
Total collections	$50,500	$70,000	$63,750	$66,950

Note that the difference between the budgeted cash receipts for March and April in the two formats is the estimated collections of December 31 accounts receivable. Even though the estimated collections from sales occur over three months, the estimated collections of December 31 accounts receivable are more realistically spread over a longer period, and it has been recognized that not all of the receivables are likely to be collected. It should be apparent that the keys to an accurate cash receipts forecast are the accuracy of the sales forecast and the accuracy of the collection percentage estimates.

On the cash disbursement side, the payment pattern for purchases must be determined. If suppliers' terms are 2/10, net 30, the financial manager will assume that two-thirds of a month's purchases will be paid for in the same month as the purchase, and one-third will be paid for in the subsequent month. The format of the analysis of payments of accounts payable will be similar to that illustrated for cash receipts. As was the case for the cash receipts forecast, the accuracy of the cash payments forecast is a function of the accuracy of the sales forecast and the payment pattern estimates. (Remember that the sales forecast impacts the finished goods budget and the raw materials purchases budget. Therefore, cash disbursements also will be impacted by the sales forecast.) A cash disbursements forecast for purchases budgeted for the months of April through June as calculated in Exhibit 14-6 would look like this:

	April	**May**	**June**
Purchases forecast	$46,900	$54,600	$61,600
Payments:			
From March purchases	$13,766		
From April purchases.	31,267	$15,633	
From May purchases		36,400	$18,200
From June purchases			41,067
Total payments.	$45,033	$52,033	$59,267

In addition to the payments for purchases, a number of other cash disbursements must be estimated. For example, the frequency with which the company pays its employees will be related to projected payroll expense to determine this significant disbursement. All other operating expense outlays need to be included in cash disbursements. Capital expenditure plans and anticipated dividend payments will also need to be considered. Of course, projected depreciation and amortization expenses are ignored in cash budgeting because these are not expenses requiring the use of cash.

Once the assumptions about the timing of cash receipts and disbursements have been made, the preparation of the cash budget is a straightforward process. Budgeted cash receipts are added to the beginning cash balance, budgeted disbursements are subtracted, and a preliminary ending balance is determined. The organization will have an established minimum cash balance to be maintained. This "inventory" of cash serves the same purpose as an inventory of product; it is a cushion that can absorb forecast errors. If the cash forecast indicates a preliminary balance that is less than the desired minimum, temporary investments must be liquidated or a loan must be planned to bring the forecast balance up to the desired level. If the preliminary balance is greater than the minimum desired working balance, the excess is available for repayment of loans or for investment. The cash budget will be prepared for monthly periods at least; many organizations forecast cash flows on a daily basis for a week or two, and then weekly for a month or two, so optimum cash management results can be achieved. Exhibit 14-8 illustrates a cash budget format and shows sources of the budget amounts.

The Budgeted Balance Sheet

LO 7

Explain why and how a budgeted balance sheet is prepared.

The impact of all of the other budgets on the balance sheet is determined, and a budgeted balance sheet is prepared. This hierarchy is illustrated in Exhibits 14-3 and 14-4. For example, the production and purchases budgets include inventory budget estimates. The operating expense budget is the source of the depreciation and amortization impact on the balance sheet. The budgeted income statement indicates the effect of net income or loss on retained earnings. The cash budget, with its assumptions about collections of accounts receivable and payments of accounts payable and other liabilities, purchases of equipment, and payment of dividends and other financing activities, is the source of many budgeted balance sheet amounts. All of the current assets (except inventories) are derived from the cash budget, as are the budgeted amounts for plant assets, liabilities, paid-in capital, treasury stock, and the dividend impact on retained earnings. In effect, the financial accounting process is applied using planned transaction amounts to generate an anticipated balance sheet. This balance sheet will be analyzed to determine that all of the appropriate financial ratios are within the limits established by top management. The reasons for any discrepancies

Cash Budget Illustration and Assumptions   **Exhibit 14-8**

CRUISERS, INC.
Cash Budget
For the Months of March and April

Date Budget Prepared: February 25

Activity	March	April	Source/Comments
Beginning cash balance	$19,425	$ 8,842	March: Forecast balance for March 1. April: Indicated cash balance at end of March.
Cash Receipts:			
From sales made in prior periods	45,000	53,200	Analysis of accounts receivable detail when budget prepared, and sales forecast for subsequent periods with collection estimates based on past experience.
From sales made in current period	18,750	13,750	Sales forecast and estimates based on past experience.
From investing activities	1,000	—	Plans for sale of assets.
From financing activities	5,000	—	Plans for new borrowings or sale of stock.
Total cash available	$89,175	$ 75,792	
Cash Disbursements:			
To suppliers for inventory purchases	$44,333	$ 45,033	Analysis of accounts payable detail for purchases that have been made and of purchases budget for subsequent periods with estimates based on supplier terms and past payment practices.
To other creditors and employees for operating expenses and wages	20,000	24,000	Analysis of accrued liability detail for transactions that have occurred and of production budget and operating expense budget for subsequent periods, and knowledge of past payment practices.
For investing activities	8,000	17,000	Plans for purchase of plant and equipment, and other investments.
For financing activities	3,000	—	Plans for dividend payments, debt repayments, or purchases of treasury stock.
Total disbursements	$75,333	$ 86,033	
Indicated cash balance	$13,842	$(10,241)	
Desired cash balance	5,000	5,000	Based on financial operating needs and amount of "cushion" for error that is desired.
Excess (deficiency)	$ 8,842	$(15,241)	Excess available for temporary investment or repayment of loans. Deficiency indicates a need to liquidate temporary investments or arrange financing.

will be determined, and appropriate changes in plans will be considered. This process may very well require modifications to some of the other budgets, and if so, the entire budgeting process may have to be repeated. Although this may seem like a tedious and frustrating thing to do, it is better done in the planning process than after the company has already acted. Recovery at that stage may be very difficult to accomplish, and the firm's financial condition may have been adversely affected.

If desired, a budgeted statement of cash flows can be prepared from the budgeted income statement and balance sheet data. The process for doing this is the same as illustrated in Chapter 9. Many organizations prepare cash budgets on a monthly basis, along with an overall annual cash budget, which serves the same purpose as a statement of cash flows.

The most challenging parts of the budgeting process are developing the sales forecast, coming up with the assumptions related to the timing of cash receipts and disbursements, and establishing policies for ending inventory quantities, the minimum desired cash balance, and other targets. The budget calculations are easily made for most organizations using computer spreadsheet models or software products designed to provide comprehensive budgeting support. These tools make it feasible for planners to change various assumptions and quickly and easily see the effect on budgeted results.

What Does It Mean?

Answer on pages 574–575

4. What does it mean when the cash budget forecasts a cash deficiency?

Standard Costs

Using Standard Costs

LO 9
Explain why and how standards are useful in the planning and control process.

Standard costs are budgets for a single unit of product which are used in the planning and control phases of the management process and in financial accounting to value the inventory of a manufacturing firm. A standard cost has two elements: the quantity of input and the cost per unit of input. The quantity of input could be weight or volume of raw materials, hours of labor, kilowatt hours of electricity, number of welding rods, or any other measure of physical input use. Standard cost systems are traditionally and most extensively used in the manufacturing environment, but their use in the service sector of the economy is growing rapidly.

Because the standard represents a unit budget (i.e., the expected quantity and cost of the resources required to produce a unit of product or provide a unit of service), standards are used extensively in the budget preparation process. Once the sales forecast has been developed and expressed in units, standards are used to plan for the inputs that will need to be provided to make the product or provide the service.

As the budget period proceeds, actual inputs used can be compared to the standard inputs that should have been used to make or service the actual output achieved. This comparison, which helps managers focus their efforts on achieving goals, is made in a performance report that will be discussed in detail in Chapter 15.

Frequently, control focuses on the quantity dimensions of the standard cost rather than the dollar amount of the standard cost (the product of quantity multiplied by unit cost) because the supervisor responsible can relate more easily to the physical quantity than to the dollar cost. For example, the supervisor responsible for raw material use and the supervisor responsible for order-processing activity probably relate more easily to pounds used and number of orders processed per employee, respectively, than they would to the costs of those inputs used during a reporting period.

Standard costs that have been appropriately developed (see the following discussion) can be used in the cost accounting system described in Chapter 13. This approach results in a cost system that is easier to use than one involving actual costs because when it comes to valuing inventory, standard costs have been developed prior to the accounting period, whereas actual costs aren't known until after the accounting period has been completed.

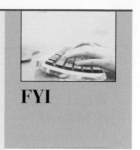

Developing Standards

Because standards are unit budgets, all of the management philosophy and individual behavior considerations identified in the discussion of the budgeting process also apply to standards. The three approaches to developing standards are

> Ideal, or engineered, standards.
>
> Attainable standards.
>
> Past experience standards.

LO 10
Determine how the standard cost of a product is developed.

An **ideal standard** assumes that operating conditions will be ideal and that material and labor inputs will be provided at maximum levels of efficiency at all times. One of the work measurement techniques used by industrial engineers is called *motion and time study*. This technique involves a very detailed analysis of the activities involved in performing a task, with the objective of designing workstation layout and operator movements so that the task can be performed most efficiently. Industrial engineers recognize that individual fatigue and other factors will result in actual performance over a period of time that will be less than 100 percent efficient, as defined by motion and time study analysis. However, these factors are ignored when an ideal standard is established. The principal disadvantage of ideal standards is that the standard will almost never be achieved, and as a result, supervisors and employees will not employ the standard as a realistic performance target.

An **attainable standard** recognizes that there will be some operating inefficiencies relative to ideal conditions. Actual performance will not always meet the standard, but employees are more likely to strive to achieve this type of standard than an ideal standard because of the sense of accomplishment that comes from meeting a legitimate goal. An attainable standard may present varying degrees of "tightness" or "looseness," depending on management philosophy and operating circumstances. For example, some firms create a highly competitive work environment and establish tight standards that require considerable effort to achieve. Once an attainable standard is established, it is not set forever. Changes in worker efficiency and/or changes in the work environment may call for changes in the standard.

A **past experience standard** has the disadvantage of including all of the inefficiencies that have crept into the operation over time. Such a standard is typically not challenging, and performance is not likely to improve over time. Such a standard reflects current performance but is not likely to provide much incentive for improvement.

Establishing performance standards for an organization that has not used them before is a significant management challenge. It is only natural for workers to be uncomfortable with the idea that someone will now be measuring and watching their efficiency. The usefulness of standards for planning and control purposes will increase over time as those affected by them learn and become accustomed to how supervisors and managers use the resulting performance reports. Many organizations have experienced productivity and profitability increases, and workers have experienced increases in job satisfaction and compensation as a result of well-designed and carefully implemented standard cost systems.

What Does It Mean?

Answers on page 575

5. What does it mean to develop a standard cost?
6. What does it mean to have an attainable standard?

Costing Products with Standard Costs

LO 11

Describe how standard costs are used in the cost accounting system.

The process of establishing a standard cost for a product involves aggregating the individual standard costs for each of the inputs to the product: raw materials, direct labor, and manufacturing overhead. Once the standard quantities allowed have been developed, as explained in the prior section, a standard cost for each unit of input is developed, and finally the standard cost for a unit of product is determined.

Developing the standard cost for each unit of input involves estimating costs for the budget period. The purchasing agent will provide input for raw material costs; the human resources department will be involved in establishing standard labor rates; and the production, purchasing, and human resources departments will provide data for estimating overhead component costs. Because of the necessity to recognize cost behavior patterns for planning and control purposes, overhead costs will be classified as variable or fixed. Variable overhead usually will be expressed in terms of direct labor hours, machine hours, or some other physical measure that reflects the causes of overhead expenditures. Fixed overhead is expressed as a total cost per accounting period for planning and control purposes, and it is allocated to individual products for product costing purposes. Recall from Chapter 13 that this allocation is made by developing a fixed overhead application rate that is established by dividing the total fixed overhead budget amount by an estimated total volume of activity (such as direct labor hours, machine hours, or some other measure of activity). But remember, since fixed overhead does not behave on a per unit basis, this approach is not valid for planning and controlling fixed overhead: It is used only to allocate fixed overhead to individual products for product costing purposes.

The result of this process is a standard cost calculation that might look like this for a SeaCruiser sailboat hull manufactured by Cruisers, Inc.:

Variable costs:	
Raw materials:	
218 yd of fiberglass cloth @ $2.10/yd	$ 457.80
55 gal of epoxy resin @ $0.92/gal	50.60
1 purchased keel plate @ $132.16	132.16
Total raw materials	$ 640.56
Direct labor:	
26 hours of "build-up" labor @ $12.80/hr	$ 332.80
8 hours of finishing labor @ $19.30/hr	154.40
Total direct labor	$ 487.20
	(continued)

Variable overhead (based on total direct labor hours):

34 hours @ $3.20/hr	$ 108.80
Total standard variable cost per unit	$1,236.56

Fixed costs:

    Fixed overhead (the $10.80 rate is based on total budgeted fixed overhead for the
    year divided by total estimated direct labor hours to be worked during the year):

34 hours @ $10.80/hr	$ 367.20
Total standard cost per unit	$1,603.76

Note: For consistency purposes, the total variable and fixed manufacturing overhead cost equals $14 per direct labor hour, as shown in Exhibit 13-6. This is the predetermined overhead application rate used for cost accounting. The fixed overhead component of that rate is determined as explained in Exhibit 13-6; the variable component is developed by building a standard based on the relationship between the elements of variable overhead (e.g., utilities and maintenance) and the chosen activity base. In this example, that activity base is direct labor hours, but it can be any other physical measure that has a causal relationship with the cost.

In a similar fashion, the standard cost of every component of the boat would be developed. The standard cost of the SeaCruiser is the sum of the standard costs for all of its components. The standard cost of all other models would be compiled in the same way. A great deal of effort and organizational resources are involved in implementing a standard cost system; but the benefit/cost ratio is positive because of the planning, control, and product costing uses of the system. Many firms revise standard quantities allowed when necessary because of performance and operating changes, and they revise standard costs per unit of input on an annual basis. However, some large firms with many products involving hundreds of raw material and direct labor inputs have adopted a different strategy. Standards may be reviewed and revised on a cyclical basis over a two- or three-year period, or they may be retained for several years, anticipating and accepting differences between standard and actual cost that result from quantity or price changes. Managers of any firm using standards must weigh the trade-offs involved in keeping the standards current compared to revising them periodically.

Other Uses of Standards

In addition to being used for product costing in a manufacturing environment, standards can be developed and used for planning and control of period costs and for qualitative goals in both manufacturing and service organizations. For example, a day care center could develop a standard cost for the food provided to its clients and/or a standard for the number of staff required for a given number of clients of a given age.

Both manufacturing firms and service organizations are seeking to respond to increased competitive pressures by becoming more efficient. One outcome of this effort has been the development of goals, which can be expressed as standards, for such activities as these:

- Quality control, including total quality management programs and statistical quality control measures.
- Inventory control, including just-in-time inventory management systems and flexible manufacturing environments.
- Machine usage, including downtime for setup, preventive maintenance, and unscheduled repairs.
- Service levels, including customer/client response times, out-of-stock frequencies, and delivery times.

Planning and Sarbanes–Oxley Compliance

The purpose of Sarbanes–Oxley Act's Section 404, management assessment of internal controls, is to promote greater corporate control and make it difficult for individuals to commit fraud that has a materially adverse impact on the company. Section 404 requires that a company's annual report contain an "internal control report," which shall (1) state the responsibility of management for establishing and maintaining an adequate internal control structure and procedures for financial reporting; and (2) contain an assessment, as of the end of the issuer's fiscal year, of the effectiveness of the internal control structure and procedures of the issuer for financial reporting. Companies with relatively mature control environments will have completed their initial 404 compliance initiatives and should begin implementing the next level of financial process and systems improvements that will facilitate audits and improve the effectiveness of financial performance management systems. As auditors steadily raise the bar for Section 404 compliance, companies that want to minimize their audit costs and enhance their control environment should expect to refine their processes on an ongoing basis.

Planning and budgeting do not play explicit roles in Sarbanes–Oxley compliance, but auditors will likely pay closer attention to this function once companies pass the initial round of Section 404 certification, for two reasons. First, companies that execute the forecasting, planning, and review cycle typically have a more mature control infrastructure, which was the prime motivation for Section 404. Second, managers that plan and forecast accurately have less reason to commit fraud than those that fall short of their projections. As part of their overall assessment of the maturity of a company's financial controls, auditors will expect (or hope to find) several outcomes in forecasting, planning, and budgeting systems:

- Operating units have predictive business models that identify and track the key factors driving business results for both revenues and costs. Companies with many projects or business lines with significant variability frequently reforecast, as well as track and assess, the relationship between drivers and results.

- Operating units use predictive business models to forecast profitability in future quarters on a rolling basis.

- Operating units can quickly identify the drivers of variances during the periodic review process (i.e., they can drill down to elements of original plans).

- Finance organizations that manage the planning process solicit sales and expense projections from the lowest level of budget authority on a bottom-up basis to promote accuracy.

- Finance/treasury organizations integrate operating plans into rolling cash flow forecasts.

- Treasury groups frequently measure sensitivity of profits to changes in exchange rates and interest rates for both on- and off-balance-sheet items.

In conclusion, companies should evaluate their forecasting, planning, and reporting processes to determine the maturity of these systems. The goal of this evaluation will be to have a system that first improves corporate performance by doing more effective planning and budgeting and second facilitates ongoing Section 404 compliance. The payoff from improved planning is greater control and more consistent, predictable results.

Source: Intelligent Enterprise, May 2004; www.intelligententerprise.com/showArticle.jhtml?articleID=20300931; and Robert D. Kugel, "Planning and Sarbanes–Oxley Compliance," *VentanaView*.

Few of these standards are expressed in terms of dollars per unit of product; they need not be expressed in dollars to be useful for management planning and control.

For manufacturing firms, standards often are developed to express organizational goals based on the notion of *continuous improvement* (e.g., "zero defects" or

"100 percent on-time deliveries"). Even though absolute perfection cannot be realistically achieved, many firms use this type of standard to emphasize the importance of making progress and showing improvement rather than simply meeting standards. To monitor progress toward such goals, performance must be measured in *real time*—as production occurs—so that feedback can be provided continually. Machine adjustments and/or changes in the work flow can be made as the need arises, and many problems can be solved on the factory floor. Management's feedback loop is shortened significantly under this approach, which has the effect of increasing *throughput* (i.e., the output rate or cycle time) in the manufacturing process and reducing machine *downtime*.

A similar approach can be taken to monitor the "quality" of production and/or customer service. For production quality, an important measure is the first-time pass rate for each process, as indicated by the number (or percentage) of defective units per batch inspected. The higher the first-time pass rate, the less rework and scrap, which in turn reduces labor and material costs, respectively. Perhaps more important, poor production quality leads to unhappy customers and lost sales opportunities. To monitor customer service quality, procedures must be established to ensure that immediate and appropriate actions will be taken to resolve all of those customer complaints that management deems it feasible to resolve. The true "cost" of losing a valued customer may be unknown, but it is likely to exceed many of the readily measurable costs for which standards traditionally have been developed.

Budgeting for Other Analytical Purposes

Although this chapter emphasizes the budgeting of dollars and units of production for manufacturing firms, many organizations in the service sector of the economy also use budgeting techniques for other important resources such as personnel time or for nonfinancial measures such as the utilization of productive capacity. Consider the following examples:

- Law firms and public accounting firms often are concerned with "time" budgets and the ability of professional staff to generate "billable hours."
- Merchandising firms, especially large retail organizations, may be concerned with budgeted "sales dollars per square foot" of floor space.
- State and municipal governments must determine the best use of tax and other revenues and budget these resources to provide services or operate certain social programs, which are measured on a "per capita" basis.
- NFL teams must budget player contracts to operate within the "salary cap" requirement.
- Universities may make resources available to academic units based on budgeted "credit hours" for which they expect students to enroll.
- Not-for-profit agencies funded by the United Way may attempt to demonstrate the outreach achieved by their programs when seeking a share of annual campaign contributions.

Within a manufacturing firm, budgets also can be developed to meet the needs of other functional areas, such as the research and development, marketing, or customer service departments. Likewise, activity-based costing principles (discussed in Chapter 13) can be extended to the budgeting process. *Activity-based budgeting* is an attempt to relate the cost of performing each unit of activity (cost driver) to the demand for that activity. The budgeted cost per unit of activity (e.g., cost per part handled or cost per unit inspected) can be compared to the actual cost incurred for the level of activity performed during the period, and corrective action can be taken if necessary.

Standard costs for raw materials, direct labor, and manufacturing overhead, as budgets for a single unit of product, provide benchmarks for evaluating actual performance. This control process, which is referred to as *variance analysis,* will be developed in Chapter 15. Capital budgeting (discussed in Chapter 16) involves long-term strategic planning and the commitment of a significant amount of the firm's resources for extended periods of time. Whereas the operating budget reflects the firm's strategic plans to achieve current-period profitability, the capital budget provides an overall blueprint to help the firm meet its long-term growth objectives.

Demonstration Problem

Visit the text website at www.mhhe.com/marshall10e to view a demonstration problem for this chapter.

Summary

A budget is a financial plan. Many organizations have a policy to require budgets because budgets force planning, provide a benchmark against which performance can be compared, and require coordination between the functional areas of the organization.

To a large extent, the budgeting process is influenced by behavioral considerations. How the budget is used by management will influence the validity of the budget as a planning and control tool. In most instances, an interactive, participative approach to budget preparation, together with an attitude that the budget is an operating plan, results in a most useful budget document.

Budgets can be prepared for a single period or on a multiperiod, rolling basis. Which is most appropriate for any activity depends on the degree of control over the activity and the speed with which the environment of the activity changes. Different activities may have different budget time frames.

Fixed costs classified according to a time frame perspective are known as *committed costs* and *discretionary costs*. A committed cost is one that will be incurred to execute long-range policy decisions to which the firm has committed. A discretionary cost is one that can be adjusted in the short run at management's discretion.

An operating budget is made up of several component budgets. The sales forecast (or revenue budget) is the starting point for all of the other budgets that become part of the operating budget. The operating budget consists of a hierarchy of budgets, and the results of one budget will provide input for the preparation of another budget.

The purchases/production budget is prepared once the sales forecast has been determined and an inventory policy has been established. Ending inventory is expressed as a function of the expected sales or usage of the subsequent period. One period's ending inventory is the next period's beginning inventory.

Operating managers have a natural tendency to build slack into their budget estimates. When budget managers combine departmental budgets into an overall organizational budget, the cumulative slack can cause the overall budget to lose significance. Budget managers must be aware of the slack issue and deal with it in ways that promote organizational goals.

The operating expense budget is a function of the sales forecast, cost behavior patterns, and planned changes from past levels of advertising, administrative, and other activities.

A budgeted income statement shows planned operating results for the entity as a whole. If top management is not satisfied with budgeted net income, changes in operations may be planned and/or various elements of the operating budget may be returned to operating managers for revision.

Once the income statement budget has been settled, a cash budget can be prepared. Cash flows from operating activities are forecast by adjusting net income for noncash items included in the income statement, as well as expectations about cash receipts and disbursements related to revenues and expenses. Cash flows from investing and financing activities are estimated, and the estimated cash balance at the end of the fiscal period is determined. Cash in excess of a minimum operating balance is available for investment. A deficiency in cash means that plans should be made to liquidate temporary investments or borrow money, or that cash payment assumptions must be revised.

The budgeted balance sheet uses data from all of the other budgets. Management uses this budget to evaluate the entity's projected financial position. If the result is not satisfactory, appropriate operating, investing, and financing plans will be revised.

The challenge to accurate budgeting is having an accurate estimate of activity and assumptions and policies that reflect what is likely to happen in the future. Computer spreadsheet models can make the budget calculation a relatively easy process that can be repeated many times to determine the impact of changes in estimates and assumptions.

A standard cost is a unit budget for a single component of a product or service. As such, standards are used like any budget in planning and controlling. Standards can also facilitate the calculation of product costs for inventory valuation purposes.

Because a standard is a unit budget, it can be used in the process of building the various component budgets of the operating budget. Standards also provide a benchmark for evaluating performance. Standards are usually expressed in monetary terms ($/unit) but can also be useful when expressed in physical quantities (lb/unit).

Standards are usually established on the basis of engineering studies and should be attainable. Ideal standards and past experience standards are less useful because they are not likely to serve as positive motivators.

The standard cost for a product is the sum of the standard costs for raw materials, direct labor, and manufacturing overhead used in making the product. A fixed manufacturing overhead standard is a unitized fixed expense and therefore must be used carefully because fixed expenses do not behave on a per unit basis.

Standards are useful for the entire range of planning and control activities; they are not restricted to use in product costing. Thus, many service organizations and manufacturing firms have developed standards for period costs. Standards can also be developed for qualitative goals that may not be expressed in financial terms.

Key Terms and Concepts

attainable standard (p. 567)   A standard cost or production standard that is achievable under actual operating conditions.

budget (p. 548)   A financial plan.

budget slack (p. 561)   Allowances for contingencies built into a budget. Sometimes called *padding* or *cushion*.

committed cost (p. 551) A cost that is incurred because of a long-range policy decision.

continuous budget (p. 553) A budget that is prepared for several periods in the future and then revised several times prior to the budget period. Sometimes called a *rolling budget*.

discretionary cost (p. 551) A cost that can be raised or lowered in the short run.

fixed cost (p. 550) A cost that does not change in total as the level of activity changes within the relevant range.

ideal standard (p. 567) A standard cost or a production standard that assumes ideal operating conditions and maximum efficiency at all times.

master budget (p. 554) An operating plan comprising the sales forecast (or revenue budget), the purchases/production budget, the operating expense budget, the income statement budget, the cash budget, and the budgeted balance sheet. Sometimes called an *operating budget*.

mixed cost (p. 551) A cost that has both fixed and variable elements.

operating budget (p. 554) An operating plan comprising the sales forecast (or revenue budget), the purchases/production budget, the operating expense budget, the income statement budget, the cash budget, and the budgeted balance sheet. Sometimes called a *master budget*.

participative budgeting (p. 552) A budgeting process that involves the input and negotiation of several layers of management.

past experience standard (p. 567) A standard cost or production standard that is based on historical data.

planning (p. 548) The management process of identifying and quantifying the goals of the organization.

rolling budget (p. 553) A budget that is prepared for several periods in the future and then revised several times prior to the budget period. Sometimes called a *continuous budget*.

sales forecast (p. 554) Expected sales for future periods; a key to the budgeting process.

single-period budget (p. 552) A budget that has been prepared only once prior to the budget period. This contrasts with a *continuous budget*.

standard cost (p. 549) A unit budget allowance for a cost component of a product or activity.

top-down budgeting (p. 552) A budgeting approach that implies little or no input from lower levels of management.

variable cost (p. 550) A cost that changes in total as the volume of activity changes.

zero-based budgeting (p. 552) A budgeting process that involves justifying resource requirements based on an analysis and prioritization of unit objectives without reference to prior period budget allowances.

**ANSWERS TO
What Does
It Mean?**

1. It means that the final budget results from the joint efforts of people at every level of management.

2. It means that the budget is prepared for several periods in the future, so subsequent budgeting involves refining the budgets previously prepared for subsequent periods, plus preparing the first budget for a new period added at the end of the budget horizon.

3. It means that the level of planned operating activity determines the quantity of product or the capacity for services needed to fulfill the plan, and that this in turn influences the level of operating expenses and other costs that will be incurred as well as the level of cash and other resources that will be needed to support fulfillment of the plan.

4. It means that the amount of cash available for the period (beginning cash balance + cash receipts) is exceeded by the cash requirements (cash disbursements +

desired ending cash balance) for the period. Having an understanding of this situation allows management to take the steps necessary to secure borrowings from its bank to ensure that all cash requirements will be fulfilled.

5. It means that a budgeted unit cost for material, labor, and overhead is developed to facilitate the determination of a product or process cost and for use in the planning and control activities of the firm.

6. It means that barring unusual circumstances, workers should be able to acquire and use materials, perform direct labor, and support the manufacturing process at the standard.

Self-Study Material

Visit the website at www.mhhe.com/marshall10e to take an online self-study quiz for this chapter.

Matching Following are a number of key terms and concepts introduced in the chapter, along with a list of corresponding definitions. Match the appropriate letter for the key term or concept to each definition provided (items 1–12). Note that not all key terms and concepts will be used. Answers are provided at the end of this chapter.

a.	Budgeting	i.	Cash budget
b.	Top-down budgeting	j.	Committed cost
c.	Participative budgeting	k.	Discretionary cost
d.	Zero-based budgeting	l.	Standard cost
e.	Single-period budget	m.	Ideal (or engineered) standard
f.	Rolling (or continuous) budget	n.	Attainable standard
g.	Operating budget	o.	Past experience standard
h.	Budget slack (or budget padding)	p.	Predetermined overhead application rate

_____ 1. A budgeting process that involves justifying resource requirements based on an analysis and prioritization of unit objectives without reference to prior period budget allowances.

_____ 2. A budgeting approach that implies little or no input from lower levels of management.

_____ 3. A budget that is prepared for several periods in the future and that is revised several times prior to the budget period.

_____ 4. A plan comprised of the sales budget (or sales forecast), the purchases/production budget, the operating expense budget, the income statement budget, the cash budget, and the budgeted balance sheet.

_____ 5. A budgeting process that involves input and negotiation at several management layers.

_____ 6. Allowances for contingencies built into a budget.

_____ 7. A cost that is incurred because of a long-range policy decision.

_____ 8. A unit budget allowance for a cost component of a product or an activity.

_____ **9.** A standard cost or production standard that is based on historical data.

_____**10.** A standard cost or production standard that assumes optimal operating conditions and maximum efficiency at all times.

_____**11.** The rate per unit of activity (e.g., direct labor hour) used to apply manufacturing overhead to work in process.

_____**12.** A standard cost or production standard that is achievable under actual operating conditions.

Multiple Choice For each of the following questions, circle the best response. Answers are provided at the end of this chapter.

1. The cash budget is prepared

    a. concurrently with the sales forecast.

    b. based upon the purchases/production budget.

    c. after the budgeted income statement.

    d. from the budgeted balance sheet.

    e. independently from the other budgets.

2. The operating budget requires the preparation of many detailed budgets, including the following: (1) cash budget, (2) balance sheet budget, (3) sales budget, (4) income statement budget, and (5) purchases budget. In which order must these budgets be prepared?

    a. 5, 3, 1, 2, 4.

    b. 1, 3, 4, 5, 2.

    c. 3, 5, 4, 1, 2.

    d. 1, 2, 3, 5, 4.

    e. 3, 5, 1, 4, 2.

3. Zero-based budgeting

    a. drops one period (i.e., week, month, or quarter) and adds another at the end of each successive period.

    b. presents a statement of expectations for a period of time but does not present a firm commitment.

    c. presents a plan for a range of activity so that the plan can be adjusted to the actual activity level.

    d. classifies budget requests by activity and estimates the benefits arising from each activity.

    e. none of the above.

4. Which of the following is *not* a benefit of budgeting?

    a. Budgeting provides benchmarks against which performance can be measured.

    b. Budgeting forces managers to concentrate on planning and to formalize their planning efforts.

    c. Budgeting helps managers build favorable variances into the performance evaluation process.

    d. Budgeting requires different functional areas of the firm to communicate and coordinate activities.

    e. All of the above are benefits of budgeting.

5. Seebold, Inc., has budgeted sales and production over the next quarter as follows:

	July	August	September	October
Sales in units	15,000	18,000	?	22,000
Production in units ..	15,900	18,900	21,300	—

On July 1, Seebold, Inc., has 4,500 units in finished goods. Ending inventory of finished goods for each month is budgeted to be 30% of the next month's budgeted sales in units. Calculate the budgeted unit sales for September. *(Hint: Use the cost of goods sold model.)*

a. 20,000.

b. 21,000.

c. 21,400.

d. 22,100.

6. Long Company's budgeted sales are as follows:

	January	February	March	April
Units sales	1,500	1,250	1,625	1,375

The ending inventory of finished goods for each month must be equal to 40% of the next month's budgeted unit sales. Finished goods inventory on January 1 was 600 units. Calculate the number of units scheduled for production in March. *(Hint: Use the cost of goods sold model.)*

a. 1,275.

b. 1,400.

c. 1,525.

d. 1,625.

7. Dax, Inc., collects its accounts receivable as follows: 30% in the month of sale, 60% in the next month, and 8% in the second month after the sale; 2% are uncollectible. Budgeted sales for the next four months are March, $16,000; April, $22,000; May, $19,000; and June, $23,000. Budgeted collections for June are

a. $20,060.

b. $20,380.

c. $21,260.

d. $21,380.

8. Under a standard cost system

a. fixed overhead applied to production should always equal budgeted fixed overhead.

b. past experience standards are normally used to estimate the cost per unit of input.

c. attainable standards are more likely to be achieved by workers than are ideal standards.

d. actual raw material prices and actual direct labor rates are charged to production.

9. Attainable standards, as compared to ideal standards,
   a. do not allow for operating inefficiencies.
   b. are more likely to elicit employee enthusiasm.
   c. are more difficult to adjust for changes in worker efficiency.
   d. are more difficult to achieve.

10. Budget slack is the situation in which
    a. there is an intentional overstatement of expenses.
    b. there is an intentional overstatement of revenues.
    c. the company is ahead of schedule in preparing the budget.
    d. sales are slow during certain budget periods.

connect |ACCOUNTING   Mini-Exercises

All applicable Mini-Exercises are available with McGraw-Hill's *Connect*™ *Accounting*.

Mini-Exercise 14.1
LO 5

Production budget ABC Company's budgeted sales for June, July, and August are 12,000, 16,000, and 14,000 units, respectively. ABC requires 30% of the next month's budgeted unit sales as finished goods inventory each month. Budgeted ending finished goods inventory for May is 3,600 units.

Required:
Calculate the number of units to be produced in June and July.

Mini-Exercise 14.2
LO 5

Purchases budget In addition to the information presented in Mini-Exercise 14.1, each unit that ABC Company produces uses 3 pounds of raw material. ABC requires 25% of the next month's budgeted production as raw material inventory each month.

Required:
Calculate the number of pounds of raw material to be purchased in June.

Mini-Exercise 14.3
LO 6

Operating expense budget In addition to the information presented in Mini-Exercise 14.1, the following cost behavior patterns are budgeted for ABC Company's operating expenses each month:

Fixed costs: salaries, $2,000; rent, $5,000; depreciation, $2,400; advertising, $3,200
Mixed costs: utilities, $3,000 + $0.50 per unit
Variable costs per unit sold: sales commissions, $2.00; marketing promotions, $1.00; supplies, $0.75; bad debt expense, $0.25

Required:
Prepare ABC Company's operating expense budget for June, July, and August.

Mini-Exercise 14.4
LO 8

Cash receipts analysis In addition to the information presented in Mini-Exercise 14.1, the selling price for each unit is $18. Based on past experience, ABC expects that 30% of a month's sales will be collected in the month of sale, 60% in the following month, and 8% in the second month following the sale.

Required:

Prepare an analysis of cash receipts from sales for ABC Company for August.

Cash budget In addition to the information presented in Mini-Exercise 14.4, ABC Company has a cash balance of $25,000 on August 1 and requires a minimum ending cash balance of $20,000. Cash disbursements budgeted for August include inventory purchases, $40,000; other manufacturing expenses, $98,000; operating expenses, $76,200; bond retirements, $50,000; and dividend payments, $15,000.

Mini-Exercise 14.5
LO 8

Required:

Prepare a cash budget for ABC Company for August.

Standard product cost In addition to the information presented in Mini-Exercises 14.1 and 14.2, ABC Company currently pays a standard rate of $1 per pound for raw materials. Each unit should be produced in 15 minutes of direct labor time at a standard direct labor rate of $12 per hour. Manufacturing overhead is applied at the standard rate of $16 per direct labor hour.

Mini-Exercise 14.6
LO 10

Required:

Calculate the standard cost per unit for ABC Company.

Exercises

All applicable Exercises are available with McGraw-Hill's *Connect*™ *Accounting*.

Production and purchases budgets Olympia Productions, Inc., makes award medallions that are attached to ribbons. Each medallion requires 18 inches of ribbon. The sales forecast for February is 8,000 medallions. Estimated beginning inventories and desired ending inventories for February are:

Exercise 14.7
LO 4, 5

	Estimated Beginning Inventory	Desired Ending Inventory
Medallions	4,000	3,200
Ribbon (yards)	200	80

Required:

a. Calculate the number of medallions to be produced in February.
b. Calculate the number of yards of ribbon to be purchased in February.

Production and purchases budgets Gillman Co. is forecasting sales of 62,000 units of product for August. To make one unit of finished product, 5 pounds of raw materials are required. Actual beginning and desired ending inventories of raw materials and finished goods are:

Exercise 14.8
LO 4, 5

	August 1 (Actual)	August 31 (Desired)
Raw materials (pounds)	74,700	68,200
Finished goods (units)	5,900	8,300

Required:

a. Calculate the number of units of product to be produced during August.

b. Calculate the number of pounds of raw materials to be purchased during August.

Exercise 14.9

LO 5

Purchases budget Each gallon of Old Guard, a popular aftershave lotion, requires 6 ounces of ocean scent. Budgeted *production* of Old Guard for the first three quarters of 2013 is:

Quarter I	10,000 gallons
Quarter II	18,000 gallons
Quarter III	11,000 gallons

Management's policy is to have on hand at the end of every quarter enough ocean scent inventory to meet 30% of the next quarter's production needs. At the beginning of Quarter I, 18,000 ounces of ocean scent were on hand.

Required:

a. Calculate the number of ounces of ocean scent to be purchased in each of the first two quarters of 2013.

b. Explain why management plans for an ending inventory instead of planning to purchase each quarter the amount of raw materials needed for that quarter's production.

Exercise 14.10

LO 4, 5

Production and purchases budgets Osage Inc. has actual sales for May and June and forecast sales for July, August, September, and October as follows:

Actual:	
May	5,900 units
June	6,200 units
Forecast:	
July	6,000 units
August	6,800 units
September	5,600 units
October	3,700 units

Required:

a. The firm's policy is to have finished goods inventory on hand at the end of the month that is equal to 70% of the next month's sales. It is currently estimated that there will be 4,400 units on hand at the end of June. Calculate the number of units to be produced in each of the months of July, August, and September.

b. Each unit of finished product requires 6.5 pounds of raw materials. The firm's policy is to have raw material inventory on hand at the end of each month that is equal to 60% of the next month's estimated usage. It is currently estimated that 26,000 pounds of raw materials will be on hand at the end of June. Calculate the number of pounds of raw materials to be purchased in each of the months of July and August.

Exercise 14.11

LO 4, 8

Cash receipts budget Kiel Center's sales are all made on account. The firm's collection experience has been that 35% of a month's sales are collected in the month the sale is made, 55% are collected in the month following the sale, and 8% are collected in the second month following the sale. The sales forecast for the months of June through September is:

June	$140,000
July	160,000
August	170,000
September	195,000

Required:

Calculate the cash collections that would be included in the cash budgets for August and September.

Cash receipts budget Scottsdale Co. has actual sales for July and August and forecast sales for September, October, November, and December as follows:

Exercise 14.12
LO 4, 8

Actual:	
July	$ 98,000
August	105,000
Forecast:	
September	114,000
October	94,000
November	122,000
December	107,000

Based on past experience, it is estimated that 30% of a month's sales are collected in the month of sale, 55% are collected in the month following the sale, and 10% are collected in the second month following the sale.

Required:

Calculate the estimated cash receipts for September, October, and November.

Developing direct labor cost standards Brass Creations Co. makes decorative candle pedestals. An industrial engineer consultant developed ideal time standards for one unit of the Cambridge model pedestal. The standards follow, along with the cost accountant's determination of current labor pay rates:

Exercise 14.13
LO 9, 10

Worktype 1	0.20 hour @ $18.40 per hour
Worktype 2	0.30 hour @ $16.50 per hour
Worktype 3	0.42 hour @ $28.00 per hour

Required:

a. Using the preceding data, calculate the direct labor cost for a Cambridge model pedestal.

b. Would it be appropriate to use the cost calculated in part **a** as a standard cost for evaluating direct labor performance and valuing inventory? Explain your answer.

Developing raw material cost standards Lakeway Manufacturing Co. manufactures and sells household cleaning products. The company's research department has developed a new cleaner for which a standard cost must be

Exercise 14.14
LO 9, 10

determined. The new cleaner is made by mixing 11 quarts of triphate solution and 4 pounds of sobase granules and boiling the mixture for several minutes. After the solution has cooled, 2 ounces of methage are added. This "recipe" produces 10 quarts of the cleaner, which is then packaged in 1-quart plastic dispenser bottles. Raw material costs are:

Triphate solution	$0.30 per quart
Sobase granules	0.74 per pound
Methage	1.20 per ounce
Bottle	0.12 each

Required:

a. Using the preceding data, calculate the raw material cost for one bottle of the new cleaner.

b. Assume that the preceding costs are the current best estimates of the costs at which required quantities of the raw material can be purchased. Would you recommend that any other factors be considered in establishing the raw material cost standard for the new cleaner?

c. Explain the process that would be used to develop the direct labor cost standard for the new product.

Exercise 14.15
LO 10, 11

Standard absorption cost per unit DMA, Inc., processes corn into corn starch and corn syrup. The company's productivity and cost standards follow:

From every bushel of corn processed, 12 pounds of starch and 6 pounds of syrup should be produced.

Standard direct labor and variable overhead total $0.86 per bushel of corn processed.

Standard fixed overhead (the predetermined fixed overhead application rate) is $0.66 per bushel processed.

Required:

a. Calculate the standard absorption cost per pound for the starch and syrup produced from the processing of 15,000 bushels of corn if the average cost per bushel is $5.68.

b. Comment about the usefulness of this standard cost for management planning and control purposes.

Exercise 14.16
LO 10, 11

Standard absorption cost per unit A cost analyst for Stamper Manufacturing Co. has assembled the following data about the Model 24 stamp pad:

The piece of sheet metal from which eight pad cases can be made costs $0.14. This amount is based on the number of sheets in a 3,000-pound bundle of sheet metal, which is the usual purchase quantity.

The foam pad that is put in the case costs $0.02, based on the number of pads that can be cut from a large roll of foam.

Production standards, based on engineering analysis recognizing attainable performance, provide for the manufacture of 1,800 pads by two workers in an eight-hour shift. The standard direct labor pay rate is $11 per hour.

Manufacturing overhead is applied to units produced using a predetermined overhead application rate of $16 per direct labor hour, of which $7 per hour is fixed manufacturing overhead.

Required:

a. Calculate the standard absorption cost of a package of 12 stamp pads.

b. Stamper Manufacturing Co.'s management is considering a special promotion that would result in increased sales of 2,000 packages of 12 pads per package. Calculate the cost per package that is relevant for this analysis.

Problems

All applicable Problems are available with McGraw-Hill's *Connect*™ *Accounting.*

Purchases budget Brooklyn Furniture, a retail store, has an average gross profit ratio of 42%. The sales forecast for the next four months follows:

Problem 14.17
LO 4, 5

May.	$100,000
June	88,000
July	124,000
August	160,000

Management's inventory policy is to have ending inventory equal to 80% of the cost of sales for the subsequent month, although it is estimated that the cost of inventory at April 30 will be $45,000.

Required:

Calculate the purchases budget, in dollars, for the months of May and June.

Purchases budget—analytical Precious Stones, Ltd., is a retail jeweler. Most of the firm's business is in jewelry and watches. The firm's average gross profit ratio for jewelry and watches is 60% and 37.5%, respectively. The sales forecast for the next two months for each product category is as follows:

Problem 14.18
LO 4, 5

	Jewelry	Watches
May.	$124,000	$60,000
June	96,000	51,000

The company's policy, which is expected to be achieved at the end of April, is to have ending inventory equal to 200% of the next month's cost of goods sold.

Required:

a. Calculate the cost of goods sold for jewelry and watches for May and June.

b. Calculate a purchases budget, in dollars, for each product for the month of May.

Cash budget—part 1 PrimeTime Sportswear is a custom imprinter that began operations six months ago. Sales have exceeded management's most optimistic projections. Sales are made on account and collected as follows: 50% in the month after the sale is made and 45% in the second month after sale. Merchandise purchases and operating expenses are paid as follows:

Problem 14.19
LO 4, 8

In the month during which the merchandise is purchased or the cost is incurred	75%
In the subsequent month.	25%

PrimeTime Sportswear's income statement budget for each of the next four months, newly revised to reflect the success of the firm, follows:

	September	October	November	December
Sales	$ 42,000	$ 54,000	$ 68,000	$ 59,000
Cost of goods sold:				
Beginning inventory	$ 6,000	$ 14,400	$ 20,600	$ 21,900
Purchases	37,800	44,000	48,900	33,100
Cost of goods available for sale	$ 43,800	$ 58,400	$ 69,500	$ 55,000
Less: Ending inventory	(14,400)	(20,600)	(21,900)	(20,000)
Cost of goods sold	$ 29,400	$ 37,800	$ 47,600	$ 35,000
Gross profit	$ 12,600	$ 16,200	$ 20,400	$ 24,000
Operating expenses	10,500	12,800	14,300	16,100
Operating income	$ 2,100	$ 3,400	$ 6,100	$ 7,900

Cash on hand August 31 is estimated to be $40,000. Collections of August 31 accounts receivable were estimated to be $20,000 in September and $15,000 in October. Payments of August 31 accounts payable and accrued expenses in September were estimated to be $24,000.

Required:

a. Prepare a cash budget for September.

b. What is your advice to management of PrimeTime Sportswear?

Problem 14.20
LO 4, 8

Cash budget—part 2 Refer to the PrimeTime Sportswear data presented in Problem 14.19.

Required:

a. Prepare a cash budget for October and November. What are the prospects for this company if its sales growth continues at a similar rate?

b. Assume now that PrimeTime Sportswear is a mature firm, and that the September–November data represent a seasonal peak in business. Prepare a cash budget for December, January, and February, assuming that the income statements for January and February are the same as December's. Explain how the cash budget would be used to support a request to a bank for a seasonal loan.

Problem 14.21
LO 8

Cash budget The monthly cash budgets for the second quarter of 2013 follow ($000 omitted) for Morrison Mfg. Co. A minimum cash balance of $30,000 is required to start each month, and a $100,000 line of credit has been arranged with a local bank at a 8% interest rate.

	April	May	June	Total
Cash balance, beginning	$ 26	$?	$?	$ 26
Add collections from customers	?	108	?	?
Total cash available	$ 94	$?	$166	$338
Less disbursements:				
Purchase of inventory	$?	$ 60	$ 48	$?
Operating expenses	30	?	?	?
Capital additions	34	8	?	44
Payment of dividends	–	–	?	8
Total disbursements	$?	$108	$ 82	$304
Excess (deficiency) of cash available				
over disbursements.	$(20)	$?	$ 84	$?
Borrowings	?	–	–	?
Repayments (including interest)	–	–	?	?
Cash balance, ending.	$?	$ 30	$?	$ 33

Required:

Calculate the missing amounts. *(Hint: The total cash available includes collections from customers for all three months, plus the beginning cash balance from April 1, 2013.)*

Cash budget—comprehensive Following are the budgeted income statements for the second quarter of 2013 for SeaTech, Inc.:

Problem 14.22

LO 8

	April	May	June
Sales	$140,000	$170,000	$190,000
Cost of goods sold*	96,000	114,000	126,000
Gross profit.	$ 44,000	$ 56,000	$ 64,000
Operating expenses†	22,000	25,000	27,000
Operating income.	$ 22,000	$ 31,000	$ 37,000

*Includes all *product costs* (i.e., direct materials, direct labor, and manufacturing overhead).

†Includes all *period costs* (i.e., selling, general, and administrative expenses).

The company expects about 30% of sales to be cash transactions. Of sales on account, 60% are expected to be collected in the first month after the sale is made, and 40% are expected to be collected in the second month after sale. Depreciation, insurance, and property taxes represent $12,000 of the estimated monthly cost of goods sold and $8,000 of the estimated monthly operating expenses. The annual insurance premium is paid in January, and the annual property taxes are paid in August. Of the remainder of the cost of goods sold and operating expenses, 80% are expected to be paid in the month in which they are incurred, and the balance is expected to be paid in the following month.

Current assets as of April 1, 2013, consist of cash of $14,000 and accounts receivable of $149,800 ($105,000 from March credit sales and $44,800 from February credit sales). Current liabilities as of April 1 consist of $18,000 of accounts payable for product costs incurred in March; $4,600 of accrued liabilities for operating expenses incurred in March; and a $40,000, 12%, 120-day note payable that is due on April 17, 2013.

An estimated income tax payment of $40,000 will be made in May. The regular quarterly dividend of $16,000 is expected to be declared in May and paid in June. Capital expenditures amounting to $17,200 will be made in April.

Required:

a. Complete the monthly cash budgets for the second quarter of 2013 using the following format. Note that the ending cash balance for June is provided as a check figure.

b. Assume that management of SeaTech, Inc., desires to maintain a minimum cash balance of $10,000 at the beginning of each month and has arranged a $50,000 line of credit with a local bank at an interest rate of 10% to ensure the availability of funds. Borrowing transactions are to occur only at the end of months in which the budgeted cash balance would otherwise fall short of the $10,000 minimum balance. Repayments of principal and interest are to occur at the end of the earliest month in which sufficient funds are expected to be available for repayment. Explain how this minimum cash balance requirement would affect the monthly cash budgets prepared in part **a.**

SEATECH, INC. Cash Budget For the Months of April, May, and June, 2013			
	April	May	June
Beginning cash balance	$14,000	$	$
Cash Receipts:			
From cash sales made in current month.			
From credit sales made in:			
February.			
March.			
April			
May			
Total cash available.	$	$	$
Cash Disbursements:			
For cost of goods sold and operating expenses incurred in:			
March.	$	$	$
April			
May.			
June			
For payment of note payable and interest.			
For capital expenditures			
For payment of income taxes			
For payment of dividends			
Total disbursements	$	$	$
Ending cash balance	$	$	$22,400

Sales, production, purchases, and cash budgets Soprano Co. is in the process of preparing the second quarter budget for 2013, and the following data have been assembled:

Problem 14.23
LO 4, 5, 8

- The company sells a single product at a selling price of $40 per unit. The estimated sales volume for the next six months is as follows:

March	6,000 units	June	8,000 units
April	7,000 units	July	9,000 units
May	10,000 units	August	6,000 units

- All sales are on account. The company's collection experience has been that 40% of a month's sales are collected in the month of sale, 55% are collected in the month following the sale, and 5% are uncollectible. It is expected that the net realizable value of accounts receivable (i.e., accounts receivable less allowance for uncollectible accounts) will be $132,000 on March 31, 2013.
- Management's policy is to maintain ending finished goods inventory each month at a level equal to 50% of the next month's budgeted sales. The finished goods inventory on March 31, 2013, is expected to be 3,500 units.
- To make one unit of finished product, 3 pounds of materials are required. Management's policy is to have enough materials on hand at the end of each month to equal 40% of the next month's estimated usage. The raw materials inventory is expected to be 10,200 pounds on March 31, 2013.
- The cost per pound of raw material is $6, and 80% of all purchases are paid for in the month of purchase; the remainder is paid in the following month. The accounts payable balance for raw material purchases is expected to be $26,280 on March 31, 2013.

Required:

a. Prepare a sales budget in units and dollars, by month and in total, for the second quarter (April, May, and June) of 2013.

b. Prepare a schedule of cash collections from sales, by month and in total, for the second quarter of 2013.

c. Prepare a production budget in units, by month and in total, for the second quarter of 2013.

d. Prepare a materials purchases budget in pounds, by month and in total, for the second quarter of 2013.

e. Prepare a schedule of cash payments for materials, by month and in total, for the second quarter of 2013.

Sales, production, purchases, and cash budgets Freese, Inc., is in the process of preparing the fourth quarter budget for 2013, and the following data have been assembled:

Problem 14.24
LO 4, 5, 8

e**X**cel

- The company sells a single product at a price of $60 per unit. The estimated sales volume for the next six months is as follows:

September	13,000 units
October	12,000 units
November	14,000 units
December	20,000 units
January	9,000 units
February	10,000 units

- All sales are on account. The company's collection experience has been that 32% of a month's sales are collected in the month of sale, 64% are collected in the month following the sale, and 4% are uncollectible. It is expected that the net realizable value of accounts receivable (i.e., accounts receivable less allowance for uncollectible accounts) will be $499,200 on September 30, 2013.
- Management's policy is to maintain ending finished goods inventory each month at a level equal to 40% of the next month's budgeted sales. The finished goods inventory on September 30, 2013, is expected to be 4,800 units.
- To make one unit of finished product, 5 pounds of materials are required. Management's policy is to have enough materials on hand at the end of each month to equal 30% of the next month's estimated usage. The raw materials inventory is expected to be 19,200 pounds on September 30, 2013.
- The cost per pound of raw material is $4, and 70% of all purchases are paid for in the month of purchase; the remainder is paid in the following month. The accounts payable for raw material purchases is expected to be $75,960 on September 30, 2013.

Required:

a. Prepare a sales budget in units and dollars, by month and in total, for the fourth quarter (October, November, and December) of 2013.

b. Prepare a schedule of cash collections from sales, by month and in total, for the fourth quarter of 2013.

c. Prepare a production budget in units, by month and in total, for the fourth quarter of 2013.

d. Prepare a materials purchases budget in pounds, by month and in total, for the fourth quarter of 2013.

e. Prepare a schedule of cash payments for materials, by month and in total, for the fourth quarter of 2013.

connect |ACCOUNTING   Cases

All applicable Cases are available with McGraw-Hill's *Connect*™ *Accounting*.

Case 14.25

LO 10

Standard-setting process Canada Printing Group, Inc. (CPGI), has recently begun the process of acquiring small to medium-size local and regional printing firms across the country to facilitate its corporate strategy of becoming the low-cost provider of graphic arts and printing services in Canada. To emphasize the importance of cost control, CPGI uses a standard cost system in all of its printing plants. Most of the smaller firms that CPGI has acquired have never used a standard cost system before. Therefore, when CPGI acquires a new printing plant, its first task is to evaluate the operation and set standards for the printing presses.

One such recent acquisition was Pierre's Lithographing of Montreal. Pierre has a five-year-old, 40-inch, four-color press that is in very good condition. Specifications provided by the manufacturer of the press indicate that under ideal conditions, the press should be able to produce 10,000 impressions per hour. CPGI has many similar presses throughout its organization, and in most locations the standard has been set at 9,000 impressions per hour. Many of Pierre's jobs have been for smaller run quantities, which means that the presses are stopped many times during the day as the press operator sets up the press for each new job. Additionally, the jobs that Pierre attracts are very complex and require high-quality results. Pierre suggests that even if everything ran perfectly throughout a day, the most he could expect the press to run would be 8,000 impressions per hour.

As usual with new acquisitions, CPGI has prepared a time study of the press for the past six months to determine how productive each of the operators has been. The results of the time study are as follows:

Press Operator	Average Impressions per Hour
M. Lemieux	6,800
G. LeFleur	5,700
M. Richard	7,400
P. Roy	6,100
P. Turgeon	6,500
Overall average	6,500

Required:

a. CPGI is considering five possibilities for setting the press standard for impressions per hour: 10,000, 9,000, 8,000, 7,400, or 6,500. Discuss the appropriateness, including a list of pros and cons, of setting the press standard at each level identified.

b. What qualitative factors should CPGI consider when setting a standard for the same model press at other sites across Canada?

c. Which level would you choose for the press standard at Pierre's Lithographing of Montreal? Explain your answer.

Budget of the United States government: Internet assignment The Office of Management and Budget (OMB) provides access to the budget of the United States government through the U.S. Government Printing Office's Federal Digital System (FDsys) at www.gpo.gov/fdsys. As the "Featured Collections" description states, "The Budget of the United States Government is a collection of documents that contains the budget message of the President, information about the President's budget proposals for a given fiscal year, and other budgetary publications that have been issued throughout the fiscal year. Other related and supporting budget publications are included, which may vary from year to year."

One particularly useful supporting publication that appeared from 1996 through 2002 was "A Citizen's Guide to the Federal Budget," which provided information about the budget and the budget process for the general public. This guide was

Case 14.26

designed to give the reader a walking tour of the budget of the United States. Access the guide for fiscal year 2002, and complete the following requirements:

Required:

a. Why was the guide designed, and what information is presented at this site?

b. What is the federal budget?

c. What percentage of the gross domestic product does spending for federal programs represent? What percentage does state and local government spending represent?

d. What was the amount of total receipts? Where did they come from?

e. What was the amount of total outlays? Where did they go?

f. Explain the process used by the government to create a budget.

g. How is the federal budget monitored?

h. What is meant by a *budget surplus?* A *budget deficit?*

i. Why is a budget deficit important? A budget surplus?

j. How does the government's budget process compare to the operating budgeting process described in the chapter? What are the similarities and differences?

Case 14.27 **Budgeting software review, collaborative project: Internet assignment**
Form a group of three or four students to research, evaluate, and report on software solutions available to support the budgeting needs of an organization. Choose three planning/budgeting products from the following list of company websites, and review the information about the software solutions available on each company's website. The list provided is meant to serve only as a starting point for this case; it is not a comprehensive listing of all budgeting software tools on the market. In fact, you are encouraged to search for other products and include them in your analysis.

Your information gathering should focus on things such as company history, product features and functionality, for what size organization the product is designed, product scalability, technology requirements, budgeting process employed by the system, customer references and/or testimonials, product demos, training, and/or other services available for implementation. After you have compiled information about each product, write a summary report that provides a comparative assessment of the three products.

Software Company	Website Address
A3 Solutions, Inc.	www.a3solutions.com
Centage Corporation	www.centage.com
financetrails.com	www.financetrails.com
GoHagit, Inc.	www.upyourcashflow.com
HCG Software, LLC	www.hcgsoftware.com
Host Analytics, Inc.	www.hostanalytics.com
Markitsoft Limited	www.budgeting4business.com
New Horizon Software Technologies, Inc.	www.planguru.com
Prophix Software Inc.	www.prophix.com
Questica Inc.	www.questica.com

Answers to Self-Study Material

Matching: 1. d, 2. b, 3. f, 4. g, 5. c, 6. h, 7. j, 8. l, 9. o, 10. m, 11. p, 12. n
Multiple choice: 1. c, 2. c, 3. d, 4. c, 5. b, 6. c, 7. a, 8. c, 9. b, 10. a

15 Cost Control

Answering the question "How well am I doing?" is a fundamental extension of the planning process and an important dimension of managerial accounting. Every strategic plan is, or should be, accompanied by an appropriate set of metrics that identify success. Every operational budget has a related analysis activity that compares actual performance to the budget. And every daily to-do list either receives a checkmark indicating completion or grows longer when tasks fail to be completed on time.

Performance reporting is a controlling activity that involves comparing actual results with planned results, with the objective of highlighting those activities for which actual and planned results differ, favorably or unfavorably, so appropriate action can be taken by either changing the way activities are carried out or adjusting goals (see the gray shaded area of the planning and control cycle). Ideally, a well-designed control system will provide leading indicators that identify when performance begins to drift from expectations so that corrective actions can be initiated as soon as possible.

Performance reporting tools, such as effectively designed measurement systems and the technology to deliver timely performance information to managers, are necessary for a successful control environment. This chapter will review the process of performance analysis as an extension of the planning and managing activities described in Chapters 13 and 14. It will then explain how variances (the differences between planned and actual results) are analyzed so that managers can identify why they occurred and plan appropriate response actions.

As you study the material presented in this chapter, remember that budgets and standards should be used in conjunction with a performance reporting system that is designed to meet the information needs of management but also serves to motivate those whose performance is being evaluated to achieve the goals defined in the plan. When appropriately designed and implemented, a control system establishes performance targets and provides benchmarks against which actual results can be compared to answer the question "How well am I doing?"

LEARNING OBJECTIVES (LO)

After studying this chapter you should understand and be able to

LO 15-1   Explain why all costs are controllable by someone at some time but in the short run some costs may be classified as noncontrollable.

LO 15-2   Discuss how performance reporting facilitates the management by exception process.

LO 15-3   Construct a flexible budget and describe how it is used.

LO 15-4   Calculate and explain the two components of a standard cost variance.

LO 15-5   Name and compare the specific variances assigned to different product inputs.

LO 15-6   Analyze and explain how the control of fixed overhead variances and that of variable cost variances differ.

LO 15-7   Illustrate the alternative methods of accounting for variances.

LO 15-8   Demonstrate how the operating results of segments of an organization can be reported most meaningfully.

LO 15-9   Explain and compare how return on investment and residual income are used to evaluate investment center performance.

LO 15-10   Explain the benefits of a balanced scorecard.

Cost Classifications

Relationship of Total Cost to Volume of Activity

Exhibit 15-1 highlights cost classification topics covered in this chapter. Chapter 14 emphasized that for planning purposes, it is necessary to understand how costs are expected to change as the level of planned activity changes. For control purposes, understanding the behavior patterns of fixed and variable cost items is equally important. Rarely, if ever, does an organization perform *exactly* as planned. In the process of analyzing performance, any differences between planned and actual costs should be evaluated. Actual cost is compared to expected cost for the level of activity achieved based on the fixed and/or variable cost behavior pattern of each cost item. As activity

Exhibit 15-1   Cost Classifications—The Big Picture

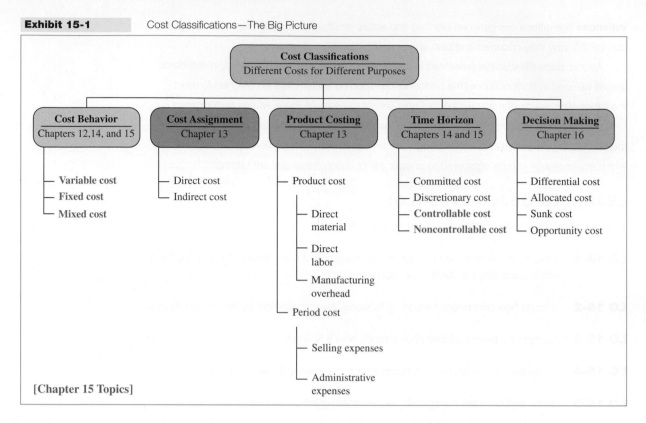

[Chapter 15 Topics]

changes from that originally planned, the expected total amount of variable cost would also be expected to change to an amount determined by multiplying the variable rate for that activity by the amount of activity achieved—just as the total variable amount would have been determined in the original budget. The total amount of fixed cost expected would not change if the actual and expected level of activity were different. Later in this chapter, a flexible budget will be introduced to implement this concept.

Cost Classification According to a Time Frame Perspective

LO 1

Explain why all costs are controllable by someone at some time but in the short run some costs may be classified as noncontrollable.

Frequently, reference is made to a "noncontrollable" cost, which implies that there is really nothing the manager can do to influence the amount of the cost. This may be true in the short run (e.g., for the coming quarter or year), but in the long run every cost incurred by the organization is controllable by someone at some time. For example, real estate taxes on a firm's plant and office facilities usually cannot be influenced by management in the short run because the assessed valuation and tax rates are established by taxing authorities. However, when the decision was made to build or buy the facilities, the relative level of property taxes was established. Land in a prime location and a fancy building with plenty of space for possible expansion could be expected to result in higher property taxes over the years than more modest facilities. The point is not whether appropriate facilities were obtained but that the decision makers (top management or the board of directors) had control over the general level of property taxes when the decision was being made. It is not appropriate to think of any cost as being noncontrollable over all time frames.

Performance Reporting

Characteristics of the Performance Report

The performance report compares actual results to budgeted amounts. The performance reporting system is an integral part of the control process because those activities that are performing differently from expectations are highlighted, and the managers responsible for achieving goals are provided with information about activities that need attention.

The general format of a performance report is:

(1)	(2)	(3)	(4)	(5)
Activity	Budget Amount	Actual Amount	Variance (2) – (3)	Explanation

The variance usually is described as *favorable* or *unfavorable*, depending on the nature of the activity and the relationship between the budget and actual amounts. For revenues, a **favorable variance** is the excess of actual revenues over the budget amount. An actual expense that is greater than a budgeted expense causes an **unfavorable variance.** Similarly, actual revenues that fall short of the budgeted amount cause an unfavorable variance, and when actual expenses are less than budgeted expenses, a favorable variance exists. Sometimes the favorable or unfavorable nature of the variance must be determined based on the relationship of one variance to another. For example, if a favorable variance in advertising expense resulted from not placing as many ads as planned, and this caused lower sales than were forecast, the variance is not really favorable to the company.

The explanation column of the performance report is used to communicate to upper-level managers concise explanations of significant variances. Because top management probably doesn't want to be inundated with details, a system of responsibility reporting is used by many organizations. **Responsibility reporting** involves successive degrees of summarization, such that each layer of management receives detailed performance reports for the activities directly associated with that layer but summaries of the results of activities of lower layers in the chain of command.

The principal concern of a manager should be with the actions that are going to be taken to eliminate unfavorable variances and to capture favorable ones. Performance reports should not be used to find fault or place blame; such uses are likely to result in dysfunctional behavior when developing budget amounts and/or reporting actual results.

Management by exception is frequently used in connection with performance reporting to permit managers to concentrate their attention on only those activities that are not performing according to plan. The presumption is that management time is scarce and that if a thorough job of planning is completed, a manager's attention need be devoted only to those areas not performing according to plan. To facilitate the use of management by exception, the variance is frequently expressed as a percentage of the budget, and only those variances in excess of a predetermined percentage (e.g., 10 percent) are investigated. The objective of this analysis is to understand why an unusual variance occurred and, if appropriate, to take action to eliminate unfavorable variances and capture favorable variances.

LO 2

Discuss how performance reporting facilitates the management by exception process.

Performance reports must be issued soon after the period in which the activity takes place if they are to be useful for influencing future activity. Otherwise, it would be difficult to link results to the actions that caused those results. If the time lag is too long between the activity and the analysis, the actions are forgotten or confused with later activities. Not all performance reports need to be issued with the same frequency. Thus, production supervisors might receive weekly cost and volume reports, a supervisor responsible for the use of a high-cost raw material might receive a daily usage report, and the advertising manager might receive only a monthly expenditure report.

An issue that arises in the design of a performance report is the extent of the cost-generating activities listed for a particular responsibility area relative to the degree of short-term control that the manager has over those activities. For example, should the performance report for a production line show the depreciation expense, property taxes, insurance cost, and other "noncontrollable" expenses associated with that production line? Or should the performance report be limited to those expenses over which the supervisor has real short-term control? Advocates of the all-inclusive report format suggest that it is appropriate for the supervisor to be aware of all costs, even though she or he may not be able to influence them in the short run. Advocates of the limited format believe that the report should focus only on those costs that the supervisor can control. They argue that the inclusion of other costs causes confusion and may focus attention on the wrong costs (i.e., those that can't be controlled in the short run). There is no "right" answer to this issue. One middle-ground solution is to periodically provide the supervisor with all cost data but to focus the performance report on those costs that can be controlled in the short run. Notice that at the heart of the issue is the allocation of fixed costs, and recall the previously discussed warning not to allocate fixed costs arbitrarily because "they don't behave that way."

A performance report for the April 2013 production of SeaCruiser sailboats made by Cruisers, Inc., is presented in Exhibit 15-2. (Actual costs in this exhibit have been brought forward from Exhibit 13-6.) Note that the manufacturing overhead has been classified according to cost behavior. This classification is appropriate because the efforts made to control these costs will be a function of their cost behavior pattern. The performance report in Exhibit 15-2, although interesting and perhaps helpful to top management's determination of why budgeted results were not achieved, is not very useful for operating managers and supervisors. Here are some questions raised by this report:

1. Were there significant but offsetting variances within raw materials?
2. Which workers were not efficient?
3. Were any new workers being paid a lower-than-budget wage rate until they became proficient?

Exhibit 15-2 Performance Report Illustration

	CRUISERS, INC. Performance Report—SeaCruiser Sailboats April 2013			
Activity	**Budget**	**Actual**	**Variance***	**Explanation**
Raw materials	$370,300	$368,510	$ 1,790 F	Variance not significant in total.
Direct labor	302,680	330,240	27,560 U	New workers not as efficient as planned.
Manufacturing overhead:				
Variable	89,400	103,160	13,760 U	Related to additional hours caused by labor inefficiency.
Fixed	193,200	185,800	7,400 F	Plant fire insurance premium credit received.
Totals	$955,580	$987,710	$32,130 U	

*F is favorable, U is unfavorable.

4. Is the training program for new workers effective?

5. How does the manufacturing overhead variance affect the validity of the predetermined overhead application rate used to apply overhead to production?

A method for answering these questions, and others, and for preparing a performance report that is useful for the cost-controlling efforts of operating managers and supervisors will be discussed later in this chapter.

---

1. What does it mean to use a performance report to evaluate the results achieved during a period?

2. What does it mean to have a favorable variance?

3. What does it mean to capture favorable variances and eliminate unfavorable variances?

What Does It Mean?

Answers on page 616

The Flexible Budget

Consider the following partial performance report for the hull manufacturing department of Cruisers, Inc., for the month of March:

Activity	Budget Amount	Actual Cost	Variance	Explanation
Raw materials	$ 54,936	$ 46,125	$ 8,811 F	Produced fewer boats than planned.
Direct labor	39,936	32,893	7,043 F	Same as above.
Variable overhead	9,984	8,128	1,856 F	Same as above.
Fixed overhead	36,720	37,320	600 U	Immaterial.
Total	$141,576	$124,466	$17,110 F	

Now suppose you find out that the budget amount was based on the expectation that 120 hulls would be built during March but that 100 hulls were actually built. Because we know that some of these product costs are variable and would change in total as more or less activity occurs, does it make sense to compare costs that were budgeted for 120 hulls to actual costs incurred to produce 100 hulls? What could be done to make this performance report more useful for managers?

The purpose of a flexible budget is to highlight the significance of cost behavior for planning and control purposes and to avoid the potential risk associated with comparing actual performance for the period with a budget that was constructed sometime earlier. A flexible budget can be prepared for any level of activity, as illustrated here:

LO 3

Construct a flexible budget and describe how it is used.

Activity	Variable Rate/Hull	Flexible Budget Allowance		
		100 Hulls	120 Hulls	140 Hulls
Raw materials	$ 457.80	$ 45,780	$ 54,936	$ 64,092
Direct labor	332.80	33,280	39,936	46,592
Variable overhead	83.20	8,320	9,984	11,648
	$873.80	$ 87,380	$104,856	$122,332
Fixed overhead		36,720	36,720	36,720
Total		$124,100	$141,576	$159,052

Notice that the variable rates for direct materials, direct labor, and variable overhead are used to calculate a budget allowance for any level of activity—but in particular for the level of activity achieved this period—so that a valid comparison can be made against actual costs incurred for that level of activity. (Why isn't the fixed overhead budget amount also adjusted?) Adjusting the original budget so it reflects budgeted amounts for actual activity is called *flexing the budget*.

The performance report using the **flexible budget** approach would look like this:

Activity	Budget Allowance	Actual Cost	Variance	Explanation
Raw materials	$ 45,780	$ 46,125	$345 U	Immaterial.
Direct labor	33,280	32,893	387 F	Immaterial.
Variable overhead	8,320	8,128	192 F	Immaterial.
Fixed overhead	36,720	37,320	600 U	Immaterial.
Total	$124,100	$124,466	$366 U	

The variances now are relatively insignificant, and the initial conclusion made from this report is the correct one: The production manager is performing according to plan for the number of hulls that were actually produced.

Of course, there is a question about why 100 hulls were produced when the original budget called for production of 120 hulls. The answer to that question, however, is not relevant to controlling costs for the number of hulls actually produced.

Using a flexible budget approach does not affect the predetermined overhead application rate used to apply overhead to production. To the extent that the actual level of production differs from the activity estimate used in developing the predetermined overhead application rate, fixed manufacturing overhead will be overapplied or underapplied. However, this is not a cost control issue. It is an accounting issue, usually resolved by closing the amount of overapplied or underapplied overhead to Cost of Goods Sold.

Flexible budgeting means that *the budget allowance for variable costs should be flexed to show the costs that should have been incurred for the level of activity actually experienced*. As illustrated with the Cruisers, Inc., example, this is done by multiplying the variable cost per unit of *each* variable cost item (i.e., direct materials, direct labor, and variable manufacturing overhead) by the actual activity level (e.g., number of units produced in a month) to determine the *budget allowance* against which actual costs can be meaningfully compared. The variance in the level of activity should be investigated and explained so that improvements in activity forecasting can be achieved, but this is a separate and distinct issue from the analysis of cost performance.

What Does It Mean?

Answers on page 617

4. What does it mean to do flexible budgeting?
5. What does it mean to state that budgeted fixed expenses are not flexed?

Standard Cost Variance Analysis

Analysis of Variable Cost Variances

LO 4

Calculate and explain the two components of a standard cost variance.

To achieve the control advantages associated with the standard cost system discussed in Chapter 14, performance reports must be provided to individuals responsible for incurring costs. Remember, the term *standard cost* was described as a budget for a single unit of product for its related components—raw materials, direct labor, and manufacturing overhead. The total variance for any particular cost component is referred to as the **budget variance** because it represents the difference between actual cost and standard cost. The budget variance is caused by two factors: the difference between actual and standard *unit costs* of the input, and the difference between actual and standard *quantities* of the input. Even if the same individual were responsible for both price and quantity, it would be desirable to break the budget variance into the **cost per unit of input variance** and the **quantity variance**. However, since different managers are usually responsible for each component of the total variance, it is essential to separate the two components so that each manager can take the appropriate action to eliminate unfavorable variances or capture those that are favorable. A summary overview of the budget variance is illustrated here:

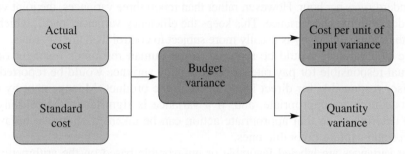

As is the case with much of managerial and financial accounting, different organizations use different terms for these variances. In the discussion that follows, the cost per unit of input variance will be referred to as a *price, rate,* or *spending variance*, and the quantity variance will be referred to as a *usage* or *efficiency* variance. These terms are generally, but not exclusively, used in practice. In addition, variances will be referred to here as *favorable* or *unfavorable*. In some organizations, a favorable variance is shown as a positive but otherwise unlabeled amount, and an unfavorable variance is shown as a negative amount. Whether a variance is favorable or unfavorable is determined in the context of the item being evaluated and the goals of the organization. Thus spending less for raw materials because lower-than-specified-quality materials were purchased may give rise to an arithmetically favorable variance (actual cost was less than standard cost) that is not desirable because of the negative impact on product quality.

To illustrate the two components of the budget variance, we will focus on the "build-up" labor of the SeaCruiser hull for which the standard cost was summarized on page 568. Assume that 100 hulls were made last month. The following table summarizes the actual and standard labor hours and the hourly rates for build-up labor inputs. Note that variances are also indicated (F is favorable, U is unfavorable).

Actual	2,540 hours @ $12.95/hr	$32,893
Standard	2,600 hours @ $12.80/hr	33,280
Budget variance	60 F $ 0.15 U	$ 387 F

The analysis of the budget variance into the quantity variance and the cost per unit of input variance is:

Variance due to rate difference:	
$0.15/hr × 2,540 hours (actual hours)	$381 U
Variance due to hours difference:	
60 hours × $12.80 (standard rate)	$768 F
Budget variance	$387 F

The cost per unit of input variance (due to the difference between the actual and standard hourly pay rates) is called the **direct labor rate variance.** In this case, the rate variance is unfavorable because workers were paid a higher rate than allowed at standard. The quantity variance (due to the difference between the actual hours worked and the standard hours allowed) is called the **direct labor efficiency variance** because it relates to the efficiency with which labor was used. In this case, the efficiency variance is favorable because the 100 hulls were produced in fewer build-up labor hours than were allowed at standard. Note that standard quantities for variable cost inputs are based on the flexible budgeting concept described earlier in this chapter; the standard quantity allowed is adjusted in response to the number of units produced. Part of the budget variance is really a joint variance due to the fact that there was a difference between both actual and standard *hours* and the actual and standard *rates* per hour. However, rather than report three variances, the joint variance is included with the rate variance. This keeps the efficiency variance "pure," which is appropriate because efficiency is usually more subject to control than are pay rates.

The rate variance would be reported to the human resources manager or other individual responsible for pay rates. The efficiency variance would be reported to the supervisor responsible for direct labor inputs to the product. Management by exception procedures are appropriate, and, if a variance is significant, the reasons for it will be determined so that appropriate action can be taken to eliminate unfavorable variances and capture favorable ones.

The variances are labeled favorable or unfavorable based on the arithmetic difference between actual and standard, but these labels are not necessarily synonymous with "good" and "bad," respectively. This example illustrates a trade-off that can frequently be made. Even though the workers were paid more than the standard rate, the work was performed efficiently enough to more than make up for the unfavorable rate variance. If this occurred because of a conscious decision by the production supervisor, it may be appropriate to make a permanent change in the way the work is done and to change the standards accordingly. Alternatively, achieving a favorable rate variance by using less skilled employees may result in a more-than-offsetting unfavorable efficiency variance.

LO 5

Name and compare the specific variances assigned to different product inputs.

The budget variance for raw materials and variable overhead can also be analyzed and separated into two components, as illustrated for direct labor. The label assigned to each of the components varies from input to input, but the calculations are similar. The labels generally used are **raw materials price variance, raw materials usage variance, variable overhead spending variance,** and **variable overhead efficiency variance.** These variances are summarized here:

	Variance due to Difference between Standard and Actual	
Input	**Cost per Unit of Input**	**Quantity**
Raw materials	Price	Usage
Direct labor	Rate	Efficiency
Variable overhead	Spending	Efficiency

The terms used for cost per unit of input variances are consistent with the way costs are usually referred to: *price* for raw materials and *rate* for employee wages. "Spending" is used for variable overhead because of the number of different cost items that comprise overhead; although an overall spending rate is calculated, the variance simply reflects the fact that actual overhead costs differ from the spending that was anticipated when the rate was established. The terms *usage* and *efficiency* refer to quantity of input; from the perspective of direct labor, efficiency relates to the quantity of hours actually used relative to the quantity called for by the standard. The variable overhead quantity variance is called the *efficiency variance* because variable overhead is, in most cases, assumed to be related to direct labor hours.

The general model for calculating each variance is:

$$\begin{array}{c} \textbf{Cost per unit} \\ \textbf{of input} \\ \textbf{variance} \end{array} = \left(\begin{array}{c} \text{Standard} \\ \text{cost per} \\ \text{unit} \end{array} - \begin{array}{c} \text{Actual} \\ \text{cost per} \\ \text{unit} \end{array} \right) \times \begin{array}{c} \text{Actual} \\ \text{quantity} \\ \text{used} \end{array}$$

$$\textbf{Quantity variance} = \left(\begin{array}{c} \text{Standard} \\ \text{quantity} \\ \text{allowed} \end{array} - \begin{array}{c} \text{Actual} \\ \text{quantity} \\ \text{used} \end{array} \right) \times \begin{array}{c} \text{Standard} \\ \text{cost per} \\ \text{unit} \end{array}$$

This model can also be expressed in the following way:

Actual quantity used × Actual cost per unit	Actual quantity used × Standard cost per unit	Standard quantity allowed × Standard cost per unit

Cost per unit
of input variance   Quantity variance

The arithmetic sign of the variance calculated using either of the preceding versions of the model indicates whether the variance is favorable (+) or unfavorable (−). Variance calculation examples for some of the SeaCruiser hull costs are illustrated in Exhibit 15-3.

Although the total budget variance of $234 F calculated in Exhibit 15-3 is easily considered immaterial, some of the individual variances are much more significant. It just happens that they are largely offsetting. This emphasizes the need to analyze the variances for each standard. Thus, although not illustrated in Exhibit 15-3, variances for the other raw material, direct labor, and variable overhead components of the Sea-Cruiser hulls would also be computed.

Integrate your knowledge! When studying the analysis of standard cost variances, realizing that the model is an application of the flexible budget concept presented earlier in the chapter is useful. Actual costs are at one end of the model. In order to evaluate actual results (cost × quantity), the question is "*How much cost should have been incurred* (standard cost × standard quantity) *given the actual units produced?*" Calculating total standard cost as the standard quantity allowed × standard cost per unit is simply flexing the budget *for the actual units produced* during the period.

Study

Suggestion

Actual Results: Actual quantity used × Actual cost per unit	Actual quantity used × Standard cost per unit	**Flexible Budget:** Standard quantity allowed × Standard cost per unit

Cost per unit
of input variance   Quantity variance

Total flexible budget variance

Exhibit 15-3

Calculation of Standard
Cost Variances

I. Assumptions:

The following performance report summarizes budget and actual usage and costs for the items shown for a month in which 100 SeaCruiser hulls were produced:

	Budget	**Actual**	**Variance**
Raw materials:			
Glass fiber cloth:	$45,780	$46,125	$345 U
Budget: Standard/hull of 218 yd			
@ $2.10/yd × 100 hulls			
Actual: 22,500 yd @ $2.05/yd			
Direct labor:			
Build-up labor:	33,280	32,893	387 F
Budget: Standard/hull of 26 hr			
@ $12.80/hr × 100 hulls			
Actual: 2,540 hr @ $12.95/hr			
Variable overhead:			
Related to build-up labor:	8,320	8,128	192 F
Budget: Standard/hull of 26 hr			
@ $3.20/hr × 100 hulls			
Actual: 2,540 hr @ $3.20/hr			
Totals...	$87,380	$87,146	$234 F

II. Required:

Analyze the budget variance for each item by calculating the cost per unit of input and quantity variances.

III. Solution:

$$\text{Cost per unit of input variance} = \left(\begin{array}{c}\text{Standard cost per unit} - \text{Actual cost per unit}\end{array}\right) \times \text{Actual quantity used}$$

$$\begin{aligned}\text{Raw materials price variance} &= (\$2.10/\text{yd} - \$2.05/\text{yd}) \times 22,500 \text{ yd} \\ &= \$1,125 \text{ F}\end{aligned}$$

$$\begin{aligned}\text{Direct labor rate variance} &= (\$12.80/\text{hr} - \$12.95/\text{hr}) \times 2,540 \text{ hr} \\ &= \$381 \text{ U}\end{aligned}$$

$$\begin{aligned}\text{Variable overhead spending variance} &= (\$3.20/\text{hr} - \$3.20/\text{hr}) \times 2,540 \text{ hr} \\ &= 0\end{aligned}$$

(continued)

What use will be made of the information in Exhibit 15-3? Remember that the objectives of variance analysis are to highlight deviations from planned results. With respect to raw materials, it is possible that the favorable price variance of $1,125 was caused by buying lower-quality fiberglass that resulted in the unfavorable usage variance of $1,470. As a result of the performance report, there should be communication between the purchasing agent and the raw materials supervisor to resolve the issue. Without this analysis and communication, the purchasing agent, being unaware that the price savings were more than offset by higher usage, might continue to buy lower-quality material. Likewise, the favorable labor efficiency variance of $768 might be the

Exhibit 15-3

$$\begin{matrix} \text{Quantity} \\ \text{variance} \end{matrix} = \begin{pmatrix} \text{Standard} & & \text{Actual} \\ \text{quantity} & - & \text{quantity} \\ \text{allowed} & & \text{used} \end{pmatrix} \times \begin{matrix} \text{Standard} \\ \text{cost per} \\ \text{unit} \end{matrix}$$

Raw materials
usage variance $= [(218 \text{ yd} \times 100 \text{ hulls}) - 22,500 \text{ yd}] \times \$2.10$
            $= \$1,470 \text{ U}$

Direct labor
efficiency variance $= [(26 \text{ hr} \times 100 \text{ hulls}) - 2,540 \text{ hr}] \times \$12.80$
            $= \$768 \text{ F}$

Variable overhead
efficiency variance $= [(26 \text{ hr} \times 100 \text{ hulls}) - 2,540 \text{ hr}] \times \$3.20$
            $= \$192 \text{ F}$

IV. Recap of variances:

	Price/Rate/Spending	Usage/Efficiency	Total
Raw materials	$1,125 F	$1,470 U	$345 U
Direct labor	381 U	768 F	387 F
Variable overhead .	0	192 F	192 F
Totals	$ 744 F	$ 510 U	$234 F

result of using more experienced and higher-paid employees this month, which in turn caused a $381 unfavorable rate variance. After analysis and discussion, the direct labor supervisor, production superintendent, and human resources manager might decide to continue this trade-off. Variance analysis information should result in actions to maintain or increase the profitability of the company. If the benefit of calculating variances is not greater than the cost of doing so, there isn't much sense in making the calculations.

As is the case with any performance reporting, variances should be communicated to the individuals responsible as promptly as possible after the activity has occurred. This way, the causes of the variances can be easily remembered and appropriate action can be taken. All variances need not be reported with the same frequency. In most organizations, the usage of raw materials and the efficiency of direct labor are most subject to short-term control, so these variances will be reported more frequently than the cost per unit of input variances. In many situations, it is appropriate to report raw materials usage variances and direct labor efficiency variances in physical terms because supervisors are more accustomed to thinking in terms of pounds, square feet, and direct labor hours as opposed to dollars. For example, using the data in Exhibit 15-3, and eliminating standard cost per unit from the model, the quantity variances would be calculated and expressed as follows:

$$\begin{matrix} \text{Quantity} \\ \text{variance} \end{matrix} = \begin{pmatrix} \text{Standard} & & \text{Actual} \\ \text{quantity} & - & \text{quantity} \\ \text{allowed} & & \text{used} \end{pmatrix}$$

Raw materials
usage variance $= (218 \text{ yd} \times 100 \text{ hulls}) - 22,500 \text{ yd}$
            $= 700 \text{ yd U}$

Direct labor
efficiency variance $= (26 \text{ hr} \times 100 \text{ hulls}) - 2,540 \text{ hr}$
            $= 60 \text{ hr F}$

Some organizations calculate and report the raw materials price variance at the time materials are purchased rather than when they are used. This variance is called the **raw materials purchase price variance.** This is especially appropriate if raw materials inventories are maintained, as opposed to having material purchases put directly into production, because it shows the purchasing manager any price variance soon after the purchase is made rather than later when the material is used. For example, if 25,000 yards of glass fiber cloth were purchased at a cost of $2.05 per yard, and the standard cost was $2.10 per yard, the purchase price variance would be calculated as follows:

General Model

$$\begin{matrix} \text{Cost per unit} \\ \text{of input} \\ \text{variance} \end{matrix} = \left(\begin{matrix} \text{Standard} \\ \text{cost per} \\ \text{unit} \end{matrix} - \begin{matrix} \text{Actual} \\ \text{cost per} \\ \text{unit} \end{matrix} \right) \times \begin{matrix} \text{Actual} \\ \text{quantity} \\ \text{used} \end{matrix}$$

Modification for Purchase Price Variance

$$\begin{matrix} \text{Cost per unit} \\ \text{of input} \\ \text{variance} \end{matrix} = \left(\begin{matrix} \text{Standard} \\ \text{cost per} \\ \text{unit} \end{matrix} - \begin{matrix} \text{Actual} \\ \text{cost per} \\ \text{unit} \end{matrix} \right) \times \begin{matrix} \text{Actual} \\ \text{quantity} \\ \textit{purchased} \end{matrix}$$

$$= (\$2.10 - \$2.05) \times 25,000 \text{ yd}$$
$$= \$1,250 \text{ F}$$

What Does It Mean?

Answers on page 617

6. What does it mean to have an unfavorable raw materials usage variance?
7. What does it mean to analyze the direct labor budget variance to determine the efficiency variance and rate variance components?
8. What does it mean to state that a favorable usage variance may not really be favorable?
9. What does it mean to state that for variance analysis to be effective, it should result in better communication between managers?

Analysis of Fixed Overhead Variance

LO 6

Analyze and explain how the control of fixed overhead variances and that of variable cost variances differ.

The fixed manufacturing overhead variance is analyzed differently from the variable cost variances because of the cost behavior pattern difference. For control purposes, the focus is on the difference between the actual fixed overhead expenditures and the fixed overhead that was budgeted for the period. This difference is labeled a *budget variance* (the same term used to identify the difference between actual and budgeted variable costs). A variance also arises if the number of units of product made differs from planned production. The reason for this is that fixed overhead is applied to production using a predetermined application rate (see Exhibit 13-6) based on planned activity. If actual activity is different, the amount of fixed overhead applied to production will be different from that planned to be applied. This variance is called a **volume variance.** *And remember that since fixed costs do not behave on a per unit basis, it is not appropriate to make any per unit fixed overhead variance calculations.*

To illustrate the calculation of fixed overhead variances, we return to the production of SeaCruiser sailboats by Cruisers, Inc. The predetermined fixed overhead application rate shown in the standard cost calculation on page 569 is $10.80 per direct labor hour. To recap from Chapter 13, this rate would have been determined as follows:

Total estimated (budgeted) fixed manufacturing overhead for the year	$3,240,000
Total estimated (budgeted) direct labor hours for the year (1,250 sailboats @ 240 hours each).	300,000 hours
Predetermined fixed overhead application rate ($3,240,000/300,000 hours).	$10.80/direct labor hour

Now assume that the actual fixed manufacturing overhead for the year totaled $3,327,500, and that the actual level of production was 1,288 sailboats. The standard direct labor hours allowed for actual production during the year would be 309,120 hours (1,288 actual sailboats × 240 standard hours allowed per sailboat). The Fixed Manufacturing Overhead account would appear as follows:

Fixed Manufacturing Overhead	
Actual costs incurred 3,327,500	Fixed manufacturing overhead *applied* to production (309,120 direct labor hours × $10.80/direct labor hr) 3,338,496
	Balance (overapplied overhead) $10,996

The overapplied overhead is made up of a budget variance and a volume variance, as follows:

Budget variance:		
Actual fixed manufacturing overhead		$3,327,500
Budgeted fixed manufacturing overhead		3,240,000
Budget variance		$ 87,500 U
Volume variance:		
Budgeted direct labor hours for year	300,000 hr	
Standard direct labor hours allowed for actual production during year	309,120 hr	
Excess of standard hours allowed for volume of production actually achieved over estimated hours . . .	9,120 hr	
Predetermined fixed overhead application rate	× $10.80/hr	
Volume variance		98,496 F
Net variance (overapplied overhead)		$ 10,996 F

This is another situation in which the net variance is small, but it results from significantly larger offsetting variances that may deserve investigation. The amount of fixed overhead actually incurred versus the amount applied to production during the year could be different for a variety of reasons. The cost category of fixed overhead comprises many individual cost items (e.g., supervisor salaries, depreciation, property taxes, and maintenance), and each line item should be evaluated to understand its individual effect on the budget variance. One possibility is that responsible managers could have paid more or less to acquire a particular fixed overhead item during the year. Conversely, property taxes, which are beyond management's control, may have increased. And just because a variance is favorable does not necessarily mean it is good for the company. For example, a favorable maintenance variance could indicate a manager's attempt to improve his or her performance by delaying or completely ignoring scheduled maintenance of equipment—a savings today that will likely require much higher costs in the long term.

The volume variance explains the effect of treating fixed overhead costs differently for planning and control purposes as opposed to product costing purposes. For planning purposes, fixed costs are expected to total $3,240,000, but for product costing purposes, fixed costs are unitized over 300,000 estimated direct labor hours of activity (at the rate of $10.80/direct labor hour) in order to allow each unit produced to absorb a share of the total budgeted fixed costs. Note that only when Cruisers, Inc., generates exactly 300,000 direct labor hours will the units produced exactly absorb budgeted fixed costs of $3,240,000. If the company generates more or less than 300,000 direct labor hours, too much or too little fixed overhead will be applied to production. The following graph demonstrates this concept:

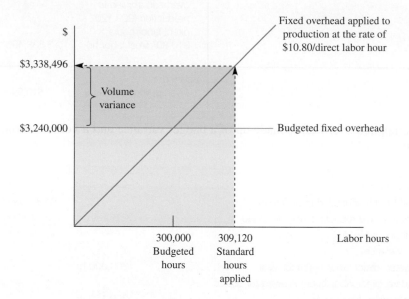

The graph illustrates that when Cruisers, Inc., generates more than 300,000 direct labor hours, it will apply more than the $3,240,000 amount of expected fixed overhead for the year. Likewise, if Cruisers, Inc., fails to generate the 300,000 direct labor hours, it will apply less than the $3,240,000 expected fixed overhead. By generating 9,120 more direct labor hours than planned, Cruisers, Inc., overapplied fixed overhead costs to the units produced in the amount of $98,496 (9,120 direct labor hours × $10.80 per direct labor hour). This volume variance means that work in process and finished goods inventories as well as cost of goods sold would have been overstated as a result of achieving a larger number of direct labor hours than estimated.

The preceding illustration uses annual data; in practice, the analysis is likely to be made monthly or with a frequency that leads to the most effective control of fixed overhead. As stated earlier, by its very nature, fixed overhead is difficult to control on a short-term basis. Yet, for many firms, it has become a significant cost that may be greater than all of the variable costs combined, so it does receive much management attention.

10. What does it mean to state that the analysis of fixed manufacturing overhead variance is not likely to be done with the same frequency as the analysis of variable cost variances?

What Does It Mean?
Answer on page 617

Accounting for Variances

Some interesting issues arise in connection with accounting for variances. Usually, if the net total of all of the favorable and unfavorable variances is not significant relative to the total of all production costs incurred during the period, the net variance will simply be included with cost of goods sold in the income statement. Since standard costs were used in valuing inventories during the period, standard costs were also released to cost of goods sold; classifying the net variance with this amount has the effect of reporting cost of goods sold at the actual cost of making those items. However, if the net variance is significant relative to total production costs, it may be allocated between inventories and cost of goods sold in proportion to the standard costs included in these accounts.

LO 7

Illustrate the alternative methods of accounting for variances.

How Well Am I Doing?

Performance reporting is a critical component of the planning and control cycle; it helps managers identify those activities for which actual and planned results differ so appropriate action can be taken. This process ranges from the evaluation of a single raw material used in the production cycle to an analysis of the entire operating budget and provides a yardstick against which further comparisons may be made. To fully appreciate how well a company is performing, however, the dimensions of time and industry should be examined.

The time dimension suggests that the current performance evaluation results be compared with results of prior periods to establish performance trends within the company. This perspective gives managers a longer-run internal view of the effectiveness of their planning strategy to support an objective of continuous improvement. The industry dimension suggests that the current performance evaluation results should be compared with those of similar organizations to establish performance benchmarks within the industry. This perspective gives managers a bigger-picture external view of their performance in the marketplace.

To facilitate evaluation, industry organizations and trade associations provide many sources of specific information. For example, Printing Industries of America, Inc. (PIA) at www.printing.org is a portal to the industry's largest knowledge resource. For more than 80 years, PIA *Ratios* reports have been the printing industry's premier tool for measuring individual company performance and benchmarking it against industry averages and the performance of industry profit leaders—printers in the top 25 percent of profitability. See the Industry Profile and Economics section for related content and information about best practices, benchmarks, PIA ratios, and industry statistics and surveys.

Agile Manufacturing Benchmarking Consortium at www.ambcbenchmarking.org is a group of manufacturing process improvement professionals who identify best practices surrounding manufacturing issues for the overall operations of the members. The organization's mission is to identify "Best in Class" business processes, which, when implemented, lead member companies to exceptional performance.

The American Productivity & Quality Center (APQC) at www.apqc.org is a resource for process and performance improvement for organizations of all sizes across all industries. APQC works with organizations to improve productivity and quality. This center provides the tools, information, and support needed to discover and implement best practices.

Business in Practice

On the other hand, if the standards represent currently attainable targets, then a net unfavorable variance can be interpreted as the cost of production inefficiencies that should be recognized as an expense of the current period. If this is the case, none of the net variance should be assigned to inventory because doing so results in postponing the income statement recognition of the inefficiencies until the product is sold. A net variance that is favorable would indicate that the standards were too loose, and so it would be appropriate to allocate the variance between inventory and cost of goods sold. In any event, the financial statements and explanatory notes are not likely to contain any reference to the standard cost system or accounting for variances because disclosures about these details of the accounting system do not increase the usefulness of the statements as a whole.

Analysis of Organizational Units

Reporting for Segments of an Organization

LO 8

Demonstrate how the operating results of segments of an organization can be reported most meaningfully.

A **segment** of an organization is a division, product line, sales territory, or other organizational unit. Management frequently reports company results by segment in such a way that the total income for each segment equals the total company net income. For example, assume that Cruisers, Inc., has three divisions: sailboats, motorboats, and repair parts. The following income statement might be prepared:

CRUISERS, INC. Segmented Income Statement Quarter Ended July 31, 2013				
	Total Company	**Sailboat Division**	**Motorboat Division**	**Repair Parts Division**
Sales.	$560,000	$320,000	$160,000	$80,000
Variable expenses . . .	240,000	128,000	72,000	40,000
Contribution margin. . .	$320,000	$192,000	$ 88,000	$40,000
Fixed expenses.	282,000	164,000	72,000	46,000
Operating income. . . .	$ 38,000	$ 28,000	$ 16,000	$ (6,000)

From an analysis of this segmented income statement, management might consider eliminating the repair parts division because it is operating at a loss. In fact, one might think that operating income would increase by $6,000 if this division were eliminated.

Now suppose that, as a result of a detailed analysis of the fixed expenses, it's learned that the fixed expenses assigned to each division represent the sum of the fixed expenses incurred in each division (**direct fixed expenses**) plus an allocated share of the corporate fixed expenses (**common fixed expenses**) that would continue to be incurred even if one of the divisions were to be closed. (Would the president's salary—a common fixed expense—be reduced if one of the divisions were closed?) An analysis of fixed expenses might reveal the following:

	Total Company	**Sailboat Division**	**Motorboat Division**	**Repair Parts Division**
Direct fixed expenses	$170,000	$100,000	$40,000	$30,000
Common fixed expenses allocated in proportion to sales	112,000	64,000	32,000	16,000
Total fixed expenses	$282,000	$164,000	$72,000	$46,000

Since the common fixed expenses will continue to be incurred even if the repair parts division is closed, Cruisers, Inc., would be worse off by $10,000 if the division were eliminated. Why? Because that division's contribution to common fixed expenses and profits (referred to as **segment margin**) would also be eliminated. This is illustrated clearly in a more appropriately designed segmented income statement:

	Total Company	Sailboat Division	Motorboat Division	Repair Parts Division
CRUISERS, INC.				
Segmented Income Statement				
Quarter Ended July 31, 2013				
Sales.	$560,000	$320,000	$160,000	$80,000
Variable expenses	240,000	128,000	72,000	40,000
Contribution margin.	$320,000	$192,000	$ 88,000	$40,000
Direct fixed expenses.	170,000	100,000	40,000	30,000
Segment margin.	$150,000	$ 92,000	$ 48,000	$10,000
Common fixed expenses. . .	112,000			
Operating income.	$ 38,000			

The key feature of the corrected segmented income statement is that common fixed expenses have not been *arbitrarily allocated* to the segments. The corrected statement reflects the contribution of each segment to the common fixed expenses and company profit. Using this approach should avoid analytical errors like the one that would have resulted in closing the repair parts division.

The same statement format separating direct and common fixed expenses should be used whenever both classifications of fixed expenses exist. For example, if the sailboat division's segment margin of $92,000 were to be broken down by sales territory, that division's $100,000 of direct fixed expenses would be analyzed, and the portion that is direct *to each territory* would be subtracted from the territory contribution margin to arrive at the territory's segment margin. The division's fixed expenses that are common from a territory perspective *would not* be allocated to the territories; they would be subtracted as a single amount from the total territory segment margin to arrive at the division's segment margin of $92,000.

Sometimes the segments of an organization are referred to as *responsibility centers, cost centers, profit centers*, or *investment centers*. A **responsibility center** is an element of the organization over which a manager has been assigned responsibility and authority, and for which performance is evaluated. A **cost center** does not directly generate any revenue for the organization. For example, the industrial engineering department would be a cost center. An organization segment that is responsible for selling a product, like the sailboat division of Cruisers, Inc., could be either a **profit center** or an **investment center.** The methods used to evaluate the performance of each type of center (or segment) are summarized in Exhibit 15-4.

Segment	How Performance Is Evaluated
Cost center	Actual costs incurred compared to budgeted costs.
Profit center	Actual segment margin compared to budgeted segment margin.
Investment center	Comparison of actual and budgeted return on investment (ROI) based on segment margin and assets controlled by the segment.

Exhibit 15-4

Methods of Evaluating Responsibility Centers (Segments)

Because individuals would like to think of their efforts in terms of profits rather than costs, sometimes an effort is made to convert cost centers to profit centers or investment centers by establishing a **transfer price** at which products, components, or services are "sold" from one segment of the organization to another. Since the revenue of one segment becomes the cost of another segment, it is difficult to establish a transfer price that is considered fair by all concerned. This issue, plus the increased bookkeeping costs, means that significant behavioral and other qualitative benefits must be expected to warrant transfer pricing at the cost center level of the organization. Transfer pricing is commonly applied to intersegment transactions between major divisions of a company and to affiliates organized as separate legal entities. These transfer prices can influence bonuses, source of supply decisions, and state and national income tax obligations. The determination of an appropriate transfer price in these situations is often quite complex.

What Does It Mean?

Answers on page 617

11. What does it mean to have a responsibility reporting system?
12. What does it mean to state that common fixed expenses should never be arbitrarily allocated to segments (for example, products or organizational units)?

LO 9

Explain and compare how return on investment and residual income are used to evaluate investment center performance.

The Analysis of Investment Centers

The manager of an investment center has a much higher level of responsibility for decision making in the organization than does the manager of a cost center or profit center. Not only is the investment center manager responsible for the incurrence of cost and the generation of revenue, but she also has autonomy for investing in the assets that will be used in conducting the operating activities of the organizational unit. Because of this additional dimension of responsibility, appropriate measures of performance are important for evaluating investment center managers across the organization. Many times the performance evaluation system is directly related to a manager's compensation or other bonus opportunities, and logically so; the evaluation system should motivate managers to maximize their individual performance, which, in turn, should contribute to maximizing the performance of the organization as a whole.

Exhibit 15-4 identified the comparison of actual and budgeted return on investment (ROI) based on income (segment margin) and assets controlled by the investment center manager as the primary method of evaluating performance. The DuPont model for separating ROI into margin and turnover presented in Chapter 3 is a particularly useful tool for this analysis because it gives a manager insight into the various factors within the numerator and denominator of the ROI calculation that can affect the overall ratio. Selected relevant information from the segmented income statement for the year ended July 31, 2013, for Cruisers, Inc., and information on the amount of operating assets in each division are presented here to illustrate this performance analysis technique:

	Total Company	Sailboat Division	Motorboat Division	Repair Parts Division
Sales	$ 560,000	$320,000	$160,000	$ 80,000
Segment margin	$ 150,000	$ 92,000	$ 48,000	$ 10,000
Divisional operating assets	$1,200,000	$600,000	$500,000	$100,000

	Total Company	Sailboat Division	Motorboat Division	Repair Parts Division
DuPont Performance Analysis:				
Margin (Segment margin/Sales)	26.8%	28.8%	30.0%	12.5%
Turnover (Sales/ Operating assets).	0.47 turns	0.53 turns	0.32 turns	0.80 turns
ROI (Segment margin/ Operating assets) or (Margin × Turnover).	12.5%	15.3%	9.6%	10.0%

With the information from a DuPont analysis, division managers can focus their attention on those activities that would increase profit margin without sacrificing sales, such as increasing revenues and/or reducing expenses, or that would increase turnover by increasing sales while holding operating assets constant and/or while holding sales constant and decreasing operating assets. Also notice how a performance ranking of each division manager changes with the details provided by the DuPont analysis. This information provides each division manager with an understanding of his or her relative performance within the organization:

	Sailboat Division	Motorboat Division	Repair Parts Division
DuPont Performance Analysis:			
Margin.	28.8%	30.0%	12.5%
Performance ranked by margin	2	1	3
Turnover	0.53 turns	0.32 turns	0.80 turns
Performance ranked by turnover	2	3	1
ROI.	15.3%	9.6%	10.0%
Performance ranked by ROI.	1	3	2

If the performance evaluation system is not carefully designed, it will lead to dysfunctional behavior on the part of the investment center manager. *Dysfunctional behavior* means that a manager will act in his or her own best interest without regard to the effect of his or her decision on the organization. For example, what would happen if the sailboat division manager were faced with an opportunity for a new sailboat line that would generate an ROI of 13.5 percent? If the only measure of performance used by Cruisers, Inc., to evaluate the manager's performance is ROI, and especially if his performance is tied to compensation, you can be assured that the manager of the sailboat division will reject the opportunity since his current ROI would be lowered if he invested in this sailboat line. But is this decision good for Cruisers, Inc.? The answer is no because its overall ROI is 12.5 percent and a new sailboat line earning a return of 13.5 percent would enhance the overall ROI. For this reason, known as **suboptimization,** ROI should not be the sole measure of investment center performance.

Another approach used to evaluate the performance of an investment center, which eliminates this risk of suboptimization, is known as **residual income.** This technique evaluates the manager's ability to generate a minimum required ROI. Therefore, the investment center manager's goal is to maximize the dollar amount of earnings above this minimum requirement rather than to maximize a percentage amount of ROI. Residual income is calculated as follows:

Residual income = Operating income − Required ROI $ (Operating assets × Required ROI %)

To illustrate, we will continue with the information from the segmented income statement at July 31, 2013, for Cruisers, Inc., and assume that the required ROI has been set at 10 percent:

	Total Company	Sailboat Division	Motorboat Division	Repair Parts Division
Divisional operating assets	$1,200,000	$600,000	$500,000	$100,000
Residual Income Analysis:				
Segment margin	$ 150,000	$ 92,000	$ 48,000	$ 10,000
ROI required (Operating assets × 10%)	120,000	60,000	50,000	10,000
Residual income	$ 30,000	$ 32,000	$ (2,000)	$ 0
Performance ranked by residual income		1	3	2

Residual income is positive when the investment center is earning an ROI greater than the required ROI, 10 percent in this example. A negative residual income means that a division is losing organization value by not earning the minimum required ROI, and viewing this underachievement brings greater emphasis to its significance. Notice in the preceding illustration that a performance ranking based on residual income produces the same order as using ROI, but using residual income would now allow the manager of the sailboat division to invest in the new sailboat line with an expected return of 13.5 percent because any opportunity that provides at least a 10 percent ROI would increase the division's residual income. It is clear that no single measure of performance will satisfy all information analysis needs of an organization at the same time while providing the behavioral incentive for managers to act in the best interest of the company as a whole.

What Does It Mean?

Answers on page 617

13. What does it mean when an investment center manager suboptimizes company performance?

14. What does it mean when residual income is zero?

The Balanced Scorecard

LO 10

Explain the benefits of a balanced scorecard.

A high-level approach to measuring and reporting organizational performance is accomplished by using a balanced scorecard. The **balanced scorecard** is a set of integrated financial and operating performance measures that highlight and communicate an organization's strategic goals and priorities. Developed by Harvard Professor Robert S. Kaplan and David P. Norton, this concept promotes the use of a few key financial and nonfinancial measures of performance. Too often, performance analysis is so intensely focused on financial measures, such as operating income, segment margin, or ROI, that managers lose sight of other key indicators that can provide additional insight to understanding performance. The balanced scorecard approach takes

(Assumed Data for Illustrative Purposes)	Budget	Actual
Return on investment *Organizational investment*		
Financial Perspective		
Return on investment	12%	12.5%
Contribution margin per sailboat	$950	$925
Revenue growth	10%	15%
Customer Perspective		
Market share	40%	44%
Customer satisfaction index	90	93
Number of new customers	25	22
Internal Business Process Perspective		
Percentage of systems automated	65%	60%
Percentage of on-time deliveries	95%	88%
Sailboat manufacturing time (days)	5	5.5
Learning and Growth Perspective		
Training hours per employee	30	33
Percentage of employees on project teams	50%	45%
Employee satisfaction index	90	86

Exhibit 15-5

Balanced Scorecard for Cruisers, Inc.

a "big picture" outlook and provides an analytical framework to support an organizationally integrated planning and performance measurement system.

The balanced scorecard framework is integrated through four key perspectives: the financial perspective, which is concerned with financial performance and improvements; the customer perspective, which is concerned with customer satisfaction and the organization's ability to serve the customer in a timely manner; the internal business process perspective, which is concerned with improvements in key operating areas to achieve greater efficiency and productivity; and the learning and growth perspective, which is concerned with empowering employees with new knowledge resources. Within each perspective, the organization will define several key objectives and related performance measurement targets, as illustrated in Exhibit 15-5.

The organizational investment flow and return on investment flow in Exhibit 15-5 illustrate the integrative nature of this measurement and reporting concept. As Cruisers, Inc., invests in programs and activities that focus on improving customer satisfaction, business processes, and organizational learning, the rewards will be upward flowing and

The Balanced Scorecard Institute provides training and consulting services to assist companies, nonprofit organizations, and government agencies in applying best practices in balanced scorecard (BSC) and performance measurement for strategic management and organizational transformation. At www.balancedscorecard.org, you will find a vast resource designed for managers and analysts to obtain information, ideas, tools, and lessons learned in building strategic management and performance measurement systems as they use balanced scorecard concepts. As the institute focuses on the needs of managers involved in deploying strategic plans and improving their organizations' strategic performance, many areas of the website are particularly interesting and provide useful information such as frequently asked questions, the nine steps to success, performance measurement, and examples of company success stories.

FYI

will result in improved financial strength. Talented and happy employees will work toward improvements in business activities and operations, which should add value for the customer and ultimately provide for a greater return on investment for the organization.

Demonstration Problem

Visit the text website at www.mhhe.com/marshall10e to view a demonstration problem for this chapter.

Summary

All costs are controllable by someone at some time; but in the short run some costs may be classified as noncontrollable because there is really nothing a manager can do to influence the amount of cost in the short run.

Part of the payoff of the budgeting process involves comparing actual results with planned results. This is accomplished in a performance report. The variance shown in the performance report is the difference between the actual and budgeted amounts. Management by exception involves focusing attention on those activities that have a significant variance, with the objective of understanding why the variance occurred and, if appropriate, taking action to eliminate unfavorable variances and capture favorable variances.

Flexible budgeting recognizes cost behavior patterns. The original budget amount for variable items based on planned activity is adjusted by calculating a budget allowance based on actual activity for the period. This results in a variable cost variance that is meaningful because the effect of a difference between actual and budgeted volumes of activity is removed from the variance. Only variable cost budgets are flexed.

Variances from standard can be caused by a difference between actual and standard costs per unit of input and by a difference between actual and standard quantities. Variance analysis breaks the total variance into the amounts caused by each difference. This is necessary because different managers are responsible for each component of the total variance. The objective of reporting variances is to have the appropriate manager take action to eliminate unfavorable variances and to capture favorable variances. Communication between managers is essential to achieve this objective.

Variances can be labeled in many ways, but a generally used classification is the following:

| | Variance due to Difference between Standard and Actual | |
Input	Cost per Unit of Input	Quantity
Raw materials	Price	Usage
Direct labor	Rate	Efficiency
Variable overhead	Spending	Efficiency

Quantity variances for raw materials and direct labor are frequently expressed by quantity as well as dollar amount because the manager responsible for controlling the variance usually thinks in quantity terms.

Fixed manufacturing overhead variances are analyzed differently from variable cost variances because the cost behavior pattern is different. The fixed overhead budget variance is the difference between total actual and total budgeted fixed overhead. The fixed overhead volume variance arises because the actual level of activity differed from that used in calculating the fixed overhead application rate.

In most standard cost systems, standard costs are recorded in Work in Process Inventory and Finished Goods Inventory. Variances are usually taken directly to the income statement in the fiscal period in which they arise as an adjustment of Cost of Goods Sold.

Segment reporting for an organization involves assigning revenues and expenses to divisions, product lines, geographic areas, or other responsibility centers. In this process, costs that are common to a group of segments should not be arbitrarily allocated to individual segments in that group.

Investment center performance is measured by return on investment and is separated into margin and turnover as defined by the DuPont model. Managers are then able to focus on each component of the DuPont formula in order to understand where performance improvements may be achieved. Residual income is an ROI alternative that measures the amount of income an investment center generates above a minimum required return on investment. This method seeks to maximize dollar amounts and eliminates the risk of suboptimization—decisions that result when an investment center manager rejects an opportunity to invest in a project that would increase the ROI of the company as a whole but would lower the ROI of the investment center.

A balanced scorecard communicates the set of integrated financial and operating performance measures that highlight an organization's priorities in achieving its strategic goals.

Key Terms and Concepts

balanced scorecard (p. 612)   A set of integrated financial and operating performance measures that communicates an organization's priorities associated with achieving strategic goals.

budget variance (p. 599)   The difference between actual and budgeted amounts.

common fixed expense (p. 608)   An expense that is not assigned to an organizational segment in a segmented income statement because the expense would be incurred even if the segment were eliminated.

cost center (p. 609)   A responsibility center for which performance is evaluated by comparing actual cost with budgeted cost.

cost per unit of input variance (p. 599)   That part of a variable cost budget variance due to a difference between the actual and standard costs per unit of input. See also *raw materials price variance, direct labor rate variance,* and *variable overhead spending variance.*

direct fixed expense (p. 608)   An expense assigned to an organizational segment in a segmented income statement that would not be incurred if the segment were eliminated.

direct labor efficiency variance (p. 600)   That part of the direct labor budget variance due to the difference between actual hours required and standard hours allowed for the work done.

direct labor rate variance (p. 600)   That part of the direct labor budget variance due to the difference between the actual hourly wage rate paid and the standard rate.

favorable variance (p. 595)   The excess of actual revenue over budgeted revenue, or budgeted cost over actual cost.

flexible budget (p. 598)   A budget adjusted to reflect a budget allowance based on the actual level of activity, rather than the planned level of activity used to establish the original budget.

investment center (p. 609)   A responsibility center for which performance is evaluated by comparing actual return on investment with budgeted return on investment.

management by exception (p. 595) A management concept that involves thorough planning and then corrective effort only in those areas that do not show results consistent with the plan.

performance reporting (p. 592) Comparing actual and planned activities or costs.

profit center (p. 609) A responsibility center for which performance is evaluated by comparing actual profit with budgeted profit.

quantity variance (p. 599) The part of a variable cost budget variance due to a difference between the actual and standard quantities of inputs. See also *raw material usage variance, direct labor efficiency variance,* and *variable overhead efficiency variance.*

raw materials price variance (p. 600) That part of the raw materials budget variance due to the difference between actual cost and standard cost of raw materials *used.*

raw materials purchase price variance (p. 604) A variance recognized soon after the purchase of raw materials that is caused by the difference between actual cost and standard cost of raw materials *purchased.*

raw materials usage variance (p. 600) That part of the raw materials budget variance due to the difference between actual usage and standard usage of raw material.

residual income (p. 611) The amount of income an investment center generates above a minimum required return on investment.

responsibility center (p. 609) An element of the organization over which a manager has been assigned responsibility and authority.

responsibility reporting (p. 595) A system of performance reporting that involves successive degrees of summarization as the number of management responsibility levels being reported about increases.

segment (p. 608) A unit of the organization, such as a product line, sales territory, or group of related activities.

segment margin (p. 609) The contribution of a segment of an organization to the common fixed expenses and operating income of the organization.

suboptimization (p. 611) The result of an investment center manager rejecting an opportunity to invest in a project that would increase the ROI of the company as a whole but would lower the ROI of the investment center.

transfer price (p. 610) A price established for the "sale" of goods or services from one segment of the organization to another segment of the organization.

unfavorable variance (p. 595) The excess of budgeted revenue over actual revenue, or actual cost over budgeted cost.

variable overhead efficiency variance (p. 600) That part of the variable overhead budget variance due to the difference between actual hours required and standard hours allowed for the work done.

variable overhead spending variance (p. 600) That part of the variable overhead budget variance due to the difference between actual variable overhead cost and the standard cost allowed for the actual inputs used (based on direct labor hours, for example).

variance (p. 593) The difference between actual and budget; variances are labeled as "favorable" or "unfavorable," usually on the basis of the arithmetic difference between actual and budget.

volume variance (p. 604) A fixed manufacturing overhead variance caused by actual activity being different from the estimated activity used in calculating the predetermined overhead application rate.

ANSWERS TO What Does It Mean?

1. It means that actual results are compared to planned or budgeted results, and explanations for variances are determined.
2. It means that actual results are better than planned results; for example, actual sales are greater than forecast sales, or actual expenses are less than budgeted expenses.
3. It means that managers usually should work to repeat activities that have resulted in favorable variances and to eliminate activities that have caused unfavorable variances.

4. It means that when the performance report is prepared, the budgeted amounts reflect expected costs at the actual level of activity achieved, rather than originally budgeted costs for the expected level of activity.

5. It means that because fixed expenses are not expected to change if the level of activity changes within the relevant range, it is not appropriate to change the budget for fixed expenses even though actual activity differs from planned activity.

6. It means that more than the standard amount of raw material allowed was used for the production achieved.

7. It means that the variance associated with each cost element—rate paid and hours used—is determined separately and reported to the individuals who are responsible for the rate paid and hours used.

8. It means that the variance may have resulted from an undesirable activity, such as purposely not putting enough ingredients into a batch, that could adversely affect the quality of the product.

9. It means that responsible managers don't operate in a vacuum and that their control activities have to be coordinated to achieve optimum results.

10. It means that because costs are fixed, this type of overhead is difficult to control on a short-term basis by shift or by week. But because fixed costs are becoming increasingly significant for many firms, they are likely to receive a lot of attention.

11. It means that a performance report for a particular area of responsibility reflects those items over which the managers of that area have control.

12. It means that because these expenses would not decrease in total even if the segment disappeared, erroneous conclusions can result from an analysis that includes arbitrarily allocated common fixed expenses.

13. It means that the manager has rejected an opportunity to invest in a project that would increase the ROI of the company as a whole because it would lower the ROI of the investment center.

14. It means that the investment center is earning an ROI exactly equal to the minimum required ROI used to calculate residual income.

Self-Study Material

Visit the text website at www.mhhe.com/marshall10e to take an online self-study quiz for this chapter.

Matching Following are a number of key terms and concepts introduced in the chapter, along with a list of corresponding definitions. Match the appropriate letter for the key term or concept to each definition provided (items 1–20). Note that not all key terms and concepts will be used. Answers are provided at the end of this chapter.

a. Performance report
b. Flexible budget
c. Organization segment

d. Direct fixed expenses
e. Common fixed expenses
f. Management by exception

g.   Segment margin
h.   Responsibility reporting
i.   Overapplied overhead
j.   Underapplied overhead
k.   Favorable variance
l.   Unfavorable variance
m.   Direct labor rate variance
n.   Direct labor efficiency variance
o.   Volume variance

p.   Raw materials usage variance
q.   Raw materials price variance
r.   Variable overhead efficiency variance
s.   Variable overhead spending variance
t.   Variance
u.   Residual income
v.   Balanced scorecard

_____ **1.** The excess of actual cost over budgeted cost.

_____ **2.** The contribution of a segment of an organization to the common fixed expenses and operating income of the organization.

_____ **3.** A system of performance reporting that involves successive degrees of summarization as the number of management levels being reported about increases.

_____ **4.** A management concept that involves thorough planning and then exerting corrective effort only in those areas that do not show results consistent with the plan.

_____ **5.** A report comparing actual and planned activities or costs.

_____ **6.** A budget that has been adjusted to reflect a budget allowance based on actual level of activity rather than the planned level of activity used to establish the original budget.

_____ **7.** An expense assigned to an organizational segment in a segmented income statement that would not be incurred if the segment were eliminated.

_____ **8.** The excess of budgeted cost over actual cost.

_____ **9.** An expense that is not assigned to an organizational segment in a segmented income statement because the expense would be incurred even if the segment were eliminated.

_____ **10.** A set of integrated financial and operating performance measures that communicate an organization's strategic goals and priorities.

_____ **11.** That part of the variable overhead variance due to the difference between actual hours required and standard hours allowed for the work done.

_____ **12.** A fixed manufacturing overhead variance caused by actual activity being different from the estimated activity used in calculating the predetermined overhead application rate.

_____ **13.** That part of the direct labor variance due to the difference between actual hours required and standard hours allowed for the work done.

_____ **14.** A debit balance in the manufacturing overhead account that results from actual overhead costs in excess of applied overhead.

_____ **15.** That part of the total raw materials variance due to the difference between actual usage and standard usage of raw materials.

_____ **16.** That part of the variable overhead variance due to the difference between actual variable overhead cost per hour and the standard rate used to apply overhead.

_____ **17.** The difference between actual amount and budgeted amount.

_____ **18.** That part of the direct labor variance due to the difference between the actual hourly wage rate paid and the standard rate used to cost a product.

_____ **19.** That part of the total raw materials variance due to the difference between actual cost and standard cost of raw materials used.

_____**20.** The amount of income an investment center generates above a minimum required return on investment.

_____

Multiple Choice For each of the following questions, circle the best response. Answers are provided at the end of this chapter.

1. To be most effective, performance reports should be

   a. issued to all managers within the organization at the level of summarization or detail most appropriate to their needs.

   b. controlled by the management by exception concept, which highlights only those variances that are significant.

   c. designed to avoid dysfunctional behavior by reporting positive as well as negative variances.

   d. issued soon after the period in which the activity took place so that results can be meaningfully linked to the actions that caused the results.

   e. all of the above.

2. Zona Company's income statement for 2013 for brands A and Z and for the company as a whole follows:

	Total	Brand A	Brand Z
Sales.	$450,000	$250,000	$200,000
Variable expenses	(322,000)	(160,000)	(162,000)
Contribution margin	$128,000	90,000	38,000
Direct fixed expenses	(53,000)	(22,000)	(31,000)
Segment margin	$ 75,000	$ 68,000	$ 7,000
Common fixed expenses	(45,000)		
Operating Income	$ 30,000		

If brand Z's sales increase by $25,000 and its direct fixed expenses increase by $3,000, operating income for the company as a whole would increase by

   a. $875.

   b. $1,167.

   c. $1,750.

   d. $4,167.

   e. $1,900.

Use the following data for Questions 3 through 6.
Precision Inc.'s standard cost per unit, based on a budgeted level of production of 400 units, is as follows:

Raw materials (200 pounds @ 30 cents per pound)	$60.00
Direct labor (3 hours @ $15.00 per hour)	45.00

The actual results for the 380 units produced were as follows:

Raw materials cost for 76,300 pounds used	$25,942
Direct labor cost for 1,200 hours worked	16,200

3. Raw material price variance is
   a. $2,905 U.
   b. $3,052 U.
   c. $3,075 U.
   d. $3,052 F.
   e. $3,075 F.
4. Raw material usage variance is
   a. $300 U.
   b. $180 U.
   c. $90 U.
   d. $300 F.
   e. $90 F.
5. Labor rate variance is
   a. $1,200 U.
   b. $1,800 U.
   c. $1,200 F.
   d. $1,800 F.
6. Labor efficiency variance is
   a. $0.
   b. $900 U.
   c. $300 U.
   d. $900 F.

Use the following data for Questions 7 through 10.
Air Fresh Industries uses a standard overhead costing system for the production of its EnergyPro cooling systems. Based on a capacity of 120,000 direct labor hours, the standard costs per unit of EnergyPro are applied to production as follows:

Variable overhead portion	2 hours @ $16 = $32
Fixed overhead portion	2 hours @ $10 = $20

During August, 30,000 units of EnergyPro were scheduled for production, but only 27,000 units were actually produced. Actual direct labor cost incurred was $885,600 for 55,350 actual hours of work. Actual variable overhead cost incurred was $863,450, and actual fixed overhead cost was $622,000.

7. The variable overhead spending variance was
   a. $540 U.
   b. $21,600 F.
   c. $22,140 F.
   d. $24,000 F.
   e. $96,540 F.
8. The variable overhead efficiency variance was
   a. $540 U.
   b. $21,600 U.

  c. $20,700 U.

  d. $74,400 F.

  e. $72,540 F.

9. The fixed overhead budget variance was

  a. $22,000 U.

  b. $46,500 U.

  c. $60,000 U.

  d. $46,500 F.

  e. $60,000 F.

10. The fixed overhead volume variance was

  a. $22,000 U.

  b. $46,500 U.

  c. $60,000 U.

  d. $46,500 F.

  e. $60,000 F.

Mini-Exercises

All applicable Mini-Exercises are available with McGraw-Hill's *Connect™ Accounting*.

Flexible budget Acme Company's production budget for August is 17,500 units and includes the following component unit costs: direct materials, $8; direct labor, $10; variable overhead, $6. Budgeted fixed overhead is $32,000. Actual production in August was 18,000 units.

Mini-Exercise 15.1
LO 3

Required:

Prepare a flexible budget that would be used to compare against actual production costs for August.

Flexible budget and performance reporting In addition to the information for Acme Company in Mini-Exercise 15.1, actual unit component costs incurred during August include direct materials, $8.25; direct labor, $9.45; variable overhead, $6.82. Actual fixed overhead was $33,500.

Mini-Exercise 15.2
LO 3, 4

Required:

Prepare a performance report, including each cost component, using the following headings:

Cost Component	Original Budget	Flexed Budget	Actual Cost	Budget Variance

Direct material variances In addition to the information for Acme Company in Mini-Exercises 15.1 and 15.2, the standard direct material cost per unit consists of 10 pounds of raw material at $0.80 per pound. During August, 198,000 pounds of raw material were used that were purchased at $0.75 per pound.

Mini-Exercise 15.3
LO 4, 5

Required:

Calculate the materials price variance and materials usage variance for August.

Mini-Exercise 15.4
LO 4, 5

Direct labor variances In addition to the information for Acme Company in Mini-Exercises 15.1 and 15.2, the standard direct labor cost per unit consists of 0.5 hour of labor time at $20 per hour. During August, $170,100 of actual labor cost was incurred for 8,100 direct labor hours.

Required:

Calculate the labor rate variance and labor efficiency variance for August.

Mini-Exercise 15.5
LO 4, 5, 6

Variable overhead variances In addition to the information for Acme Company in Mini-Exercises 15.1 and 15.2, the standard variable overhead rate per unit consists of $6 per machine hour and each unit is allowed a standard of 1 hour of machine time. During August, $122,760 of actual variable overhead cost was incurred for 19,800 machine hours.

Required:

Calculate the variable overhead spending variance and the variable overhead efficiency variance.

Mini-Exercise 15.6
LO 4, 5, 6

Fixed overhead variances In addition to the information for Acme Company in Mini-Exercises 15.1 and 15.2, the standard fixed overhead application rate per unit consists of $2 per machine hour and each unit is allowed a standard of 1 hour of machine time.

Required:

Calculate the fixed overhead budget variance and the fixed overhead volume variance.

Exercises

All applicable Exercises are available with McGraw-Hill's *Connect™ Accounting*.

Exercise 15.7
LO 3

Flexible budgeting The cost formula for the maintenance department of Rainbow, Ltd., is $12,600 per month plus $4.50 per machine hour used by the production department.

Required:

a. Calculate the maintenance cost that would be budgeted for a month in which 15,200 machine hours are planned to be used.

b. Prepare an appropriate performance report for the maintenance department assuming that 16,120 machine hours were actually used in the month of June and that the total maintenance cost incurred was $83,650.

Exercise 15.8
LO 3

Flexible budgeting Western Manufacturing produces a single product. The original budget for April was based on expected production of 14,000 units; actual production for April was 13,300 units. The original budget and actual costs incurred for the manufacturing department follow:

	Original Budget	Actual Costs
Direct materials	$220,500	$216,600
Direct labor	170,800	165,400
Variable overhead	86,100	78,100
Fixed overhead	68,000	69,000
Total	$545,400	$529,100

Required:

Prepare an appropriate performance report for the manufacturing department.

Performance reporting and flexible budgeting Following is a partially completed performance report for a recent week for direct labor in the binding department of a book publisher:

Exercise 15.9
LO 4, 5

	Original Budget	Flexed Budget	Actual	Budget Variance
Direct labor	$4,800		$5,330	

The original budget is based on the expectation that 8,000 books would be bound; the standard is 20 books per hour at a pay rate of $12 per hour. During the week, 7,600 books were actually bound. Employees worked 410 hours at an actual total cost of $5,330.

Required:

a. Calculate the flexed budget amount against which actual performance should be evaluated and then calculate the budget variance.
b. Calculate the direct labor efficiency variance in terms of hours.
c. Calculate the direct labor rate variance.

Performance reporting and flexible budgeting For the stamping department of a manufacturing firm, the standard cost for direct labor is $12 per hour, and the production standard calls for 2,000 stampings per hour. During February, 121 hours were required for actual production of 230,000 stampings. Actual direct labor cost for the stamping department for June was $1,573.

Exercise 15.10
LO 4, 5

Required:

a. Complete the following performance report for February:

	Flexed Budget	Actual	Budget Variance
Direct labor			

b. Analyze the budget variance by calculating the direct labor efficiency and rate variances for February.
c. What alternatives to the preceding monthly report could improve control over the stamping department's direct labor?

Exercise 15.11

LO 4, 5

Direct labor variances—solving for unknowns Ackerman's Garage uses standards to plan and control labor time and expense. The standard time for an engine tune-up is 3 hours, and the standard labor rate is $25 per hour. Last week, 42 tune-ups were completed. The labor efficiency variance was 14 hours unfavorable, and the labor rate variance totaled $140 favorable.

Required:

a. Calculate the actual direct labor hourly rate paid for tune-up work last week.

b. Calculate the dollar amount of the labor efficiency variance.

c. What is the most likely explanation for these two variances? Is this a good trade-off for the management of the garage to make? Explain your answer.

Exercise 15.12

LO 4, 5

Direct labor variances—solving for unknowns Four Seasons Industries has established direct labor performance standards for its maintenance and repair shop. However, some of the labor records were destroyed during a recent fire. The actual hours worked during August were 2,500, and the total direct labor budget variance was $1,300 unfavorable. The standard labor rate was $16 per hour, but recent resignations allowed the firm to hire lower-paid replacement workers for some jobs, and this produced a favorable rate variance of $3,500 for August.

Required:

a. Calculate the actual direct labor rate paid per hour during August.

b. Calculate the dollar amount of the direct labor efficiency variance for August.

c. Calculate the standard direct labor hours allowed for the actual level of activity during August. *(Hint: Use the formula for the quantity variance and solve for the missing information.)*

Exercise 15.13

LO 4, 5

Direct material variances—solving for unknowns Birchwood, Inc., manufactures end tables, armchairs, and other wood furniture products from high-quality materials. The company uses a standard costing system and isolates variances as soon as possible. The purchasing manager is responsible for controlling direct material price variances, and production managers are responsible for controlling usage variances. During August, the following results were reported for the production of Knotty Birch armchairs:

Units produced	1,000 armchairs
Direct materials purchased	12,000 board feet
Direct materials issued into production	11,500 board feet
Standard cost per unit (12 board feet × $12)	$144 per unit produced
Purchase price variance	$2,500 unfavorable

Required:

a. Calculate the actual price paid per board foot purchased.

b. Calculate the standard quantity of materials allowed (in board feet) for the number of units produced.

c. Calculate the direct materials usage variance.

d. What is the most likely explanation for the price and usage variances? Is this a good trade-off for management of Birchwood, Inc., to make? Explain your answer.

Direct material variances—solving for price and usage variances
Fiberworks Company is a manufacturer of fiberglass toy boats. The company has recently implemented a standard cost system and has designed the system to isolate variances as soon as possible. During the month of May, the following results were reported for the production of 100,000 toy boats:

Exercise 15.14
LO 4, 5

Direct materials (fiberglass) purchased	200,000 pounds
Direct materials issued into production	180,000 pounds
Standard pounds allowed per boat	1.75 pounds
Standard price per pound	$7.00
Cost of fiberglass purchased	$1,420,000

Required:
a. Calculate the actual cost per pound of fiberglass purchased during May.
b. Calculate the direct materials purchase price variance for May.
c. Calculate the direct materials usage variance for May.
d. Comment on calculating the material price variance based on pounds purchased rather than pounds issued into production.

Segmented income statement The president of Truman, Inc., attended a seminar about the contribution margin model and returned to her company full of enthusiasm about it. She requested that last year's traditional model income statement be revised, and she received the following report:

Exercise 15.15
LO 8

	Total Company	Division A	Division B	Division C
Sales.	$400,000	$160,000	$100,000	$140,000
Variable expenses	240,000	104,000	60,000	76,000
Contribution margin.	$160,000	$ 56,000	$ 40,000	$ 64,000
Fixed expenses	120,000	40,000	44,000	36,000
Net income (loss).	$ 40,000	$ 16,000	$ (4,000)	$ 28,000

The president was told that the fixed expenses of $120,000 included $84,000 that had been split evenly between divisions because they were general corporate expenses. After looking at the statement, the president exclaimed, "I knew it! Division B is a drag on the whole company. Close it down!"

Required:
a. Evaluate the president's remark.
b. Calculate what the company's net income would be if Division B were closed down.
c. Write a policy statement related to the allocation of fixed expenses.

Exercise 15.16

LO 8

Segmented income statement Vogel Co. produces three models of heating and air conditioning thermostat components. The following table summarizes data about each model:

	BV19	HV41	MV12
Selling price per unit	$ 12	$ 20	$ 10
Contribution margin per unit	4	6	2
Units sold per month	3,000	1,500	4,500
Total contribution margin	$12,000	$9,000	$ 9,000
Direct fixed expenses.	5,200	3,700	6,100
Segment margin	$ 6,800	$5,300	$ 2,900
Allocated company fixed expenses	3,333	1,667	5,000
Operating income (loss).	$ 3,467	$3,633	$(2,100)

Required:

a. Criticize the preceding presentation. On what basis does the $10,000 of company fixed expenses appear to be allocated?

b. Calculate the effect on total company net income if the MV12 model were discontinued.

c. Calculate the contribution margin ratio for each model.

d. If an advertising campaign focusing on a single model were to result in an increase of 5,000 units in the quantity of units sold, which model should be advertised? Explain your answer.

e. If an advertising campaign focusing on a single model were to result in an increase of $15,000 in revenues, which model should be advertised? Explain your answer.

Exercise 15.17

LO 9

Investment center analysis; ROI and residual income The Central Division of American, Inc., has operating income of $19,200 on sales revenue of $160,000. Divisional operating assets are $100,000, and management of American has determined that a minimum return of 16% should be expected from all investments.

Required:

a. Using the DuPont model, calculate The Central Division's margin, turnover, and ROI.

b. Calculate The Central Division's residual income.

Exercise 15.18

LO 9

Investment center analysis; ROI and residual income Romano Corporation has three operating divisions and requires a 12% return on all investments. Selected information is presented here:

	Division X	Division Y	Division Z
Revenues	$1,000,000	?	?
Operating income	$ 120,000	?	$100,000
Operating assets	$ 500,000	$300,000	?
Margin.	?	12%	?
Turnover	?	1 turn	2 turns
ROI	?	?	?
Residual income	?	?	$25,000

Required:

a. Calculate the missing amounts for each division.

b. Comment on the relative performance of each division.

c. Provide an example to show how residual income improves decision making at the divisional level.

Problems

All applicable Problems are available with McGraw-Hill's *Connect™ Accounting*.

Calculate variable cost variances—explain results The standards for one case of Springfever Tonic are:

Problem 15.19

LO 4, 5

Direct materials	6 lb @ $5.00/lb	= $30
Direct labor	5 hr @ $12.00/hr	= 60
Variable overhead (based on direct labor hours).	5 hr @ $6.00/hr	= 30

During the week ended March 28, the following activity took place:

16,000 lb of raw materials were purchased for inventory at a cost of $4.95 per pound.

2,500 cases of finished product were produced.

15,600 lb of raw materials were used.

12,200 direct labor hours were worked at a total cost of $152,500.

$76,860 of actual variable overhead costs were incurred.

Required:

Calculate each of the following variances and provide plausible explanations for the results:

a. Price variance for raw materials purchased.

b. Raw materials usage variance.

c. Direct labor rate variance.

d. Direct labor efficiency variance.

e. Variable overhead spending variance.

f. Variable overhead efficiency variance.

Calculate variable cost variances—explain results The standards for one case of liquid weed killer are:

Problem 15.20

LO 4, 5

Direct materials	5 lb @ $ 6.80/lb
Direct labor	2.4 hr @ $14.00/hr
Variable overhead (based on machine hours)	1.5 hr @ $ 4.50/hr

During the week ended May 6, the following activity took place:

2,910 machine hours were worked.

11,400 lb of raw material were purchased for inventory at a total cost of $80,940.

1,900 cases of finished product were produced.

9,260 lb of raw material were used.

4,420 labor hours were worked at an average rate of $14.35 per hour.

$12,513 actual variable overhead costs were incurred.

Required:

Calculate each of the following variances and provide plausible explanations for the results:

a. Price variance for raw materials purchased.

b. Raw materials usage variance.

c. Direct labor rate variance.

d. Direct labor efficiency variance.

e. Variable overhead spending variance.

f. Variable overhead efficiency variance.

Problem 15.21

LO 4, 5

Direct labor variances—insurance company application The Foster Insurance Company developed standard times for processing claims. When a claim was received at the processing center, it was first reviewed and classified as simple or complex. The standard time for processing was:

Simple claim	36 minutes
Complex claim	1.25 hours

Employees were expected to be productive 7.5 hours per day. Compensation costs were $135 per day per employee. During July, which had 20 working days, the following number of claims were processed:

Simple claims	3,000 processed
Complex claims.	960 processed

Required:

a. Calculate the number of workers that should have been available to process July claims.

b. Assume that 23 workers were actually available throughout the month of July. Calculate a labor efficiency variance expressed as both a number of workers and a dollar amount for the month.

Problem 15.22

LO 4, 5

Direct labor variances—banking application Founders State Bank developed a standard for teller staffing that provided for one teller to handle 12 customers per hour. During June, the bank averaged 50 customers per hour and had five tellers on duty at all times. (Relief tellers filled in during lunch and rest breaks.) The teller compensation cost is $12 per hour. The bank is open eight hours a day, and there were 21 working days during June.

Required:

a. Calculate the teller efficiency variance during June expressed in terms of number of tellers and cost per hour.

b. Now assume that in June, during the 11 A.M. to 1 P.M. period every day, the bank served an average of 80 customers per hour. During the other six hours of the day, an average of 40 customers per hour were served.

    1. Calculate a teller efficiency variance for the 11 to 1 period expressed in terms of number of tellers per hour and total cost for the month.

    2. Calculate a teller efficiency variance for the other six hours of the day expressed in terms of number of tellers per hour and total cost for the month.

    3. As teller supervisor, explain the significance of the variances calculated in 1 and 2, and explain how you might respond to the uneven work flow during each day.

Fixed overhead variances—various issues Silverstone's production budget for March called for making 200,000 units of a single product. The firm's production standards allow one-quarter of a machine hour per unit produced. The fixed overhead budget for March was $108,000. Silverstone uses an absorption costing system. Actual activity and costs for March were:

Problem 15.23
LO 5, 6

Units produced	195,000
Fixed overhead costs incurred	$111,000

Required:

a. Calculate the predetermined fixed overhead application rate that would be used in March.

b. Calculate the number of machine hours that would be allowed for actual March production.

c. Calculate the fixed overhead applied to work in process during March.

d. Calculate the over- or underapplied fixed overhead for March.

e. Calculate the fixed overhead budget and volume variances for March.

Variable and fixed overhead variances—various issues Presented here are the original overhead budget and the actual costs incurred during April for Piccolo, Inc. Piccolo's managers relate overhead to direct labor hours for planning, control, and product costing purposes. The original budget is based on budgeted production of 15,000 units in 5,000 standard direct labor hours. Actual production of 16,200 units required 5,600 actual direct labor hours.

Problem 15.24
LO 5, 6

	Original Budget	Actual Costs
Variable overhead	$21,000	$23,600
Fixed overhead	32,000	33,200

Required:

a. Calculate the flexed budget allowances for variable and fixed overhead for April.

b. Calculate the direct labor efficiency variance for April expressed in terms of direct labor hours.

c. Calculate the predetermined overhead application rate for both variable and fixed overhead for April.

d. Calculate the fixed and variable overhead applied to production during April if overhead is applied on the basis of standard hours allowed for actual production achieved.

e. Calculate the fixed overhead budget and volume variances for April.

f. Calculate the over- or underapplied fixed overhead for April.

connect ACCOUNTING   Cases

All applicable Cases are available with McGraw-Hill's *Connect*™ *Accounting.*

Case 15.25
LO 3

Performance reporting The chair of the Science Department of State University has a budget for laboratory supplies. Supplies have a variable cost behavior pattern that is a function of the number of students enrolled in laboratory courses. For planning purposes, when the budget was prepared in March 2013, it was estimated that there would be 300 students enrolled in laboratory courses during the fall 2013 semester. Actual enrollment for the fall semester was 318 students.

Required:

a. Explain what action should be taken with respect to the supplies budget when the actual enrollment is known.

b. Would your answer to part **a** be any different if the actual enrollment turned out to be 273 students? Explain your answer.

c. Suppose the budget item in question was the salary for the lab assistant. How would your answer to part **a** and part **b** change, if at all? Explain your answer.

Case 15.26
LO 3

Flexible budgeting One of the significant costs for a nonpublic college or university is student aid in the form of gifts and grants awarded to students because of academic potential or performance, and/or financial need. Gifts and grants are only a part of a financial aid package, usually accounting for no more than 20% of the total package. Federal and state grants, other scholarships, loans, and income from work constitute the rest of financial aid, but these funds are not provided by the institution. Assume that for the 2013–2014 academic year, Wonder College had a gift and grant budget of $900,000 and that all of these funds had been committed to students by May 15, 2013. The college had capacity to enroll up to 200 additional students.

Required:

Explain why and how flexible budgeting should be applied by the management of Wonder College in administering its gift and grant awards budget.

Case 15.27
LO 4

Frequency of performance reporting If a company uses a standard cost system, should all variances be calculated with the same frequency (e.g., monthly) and should they always be expressed in dollar amounts? Explain your answer and include in it the reason for calculating variances.

Rank the importance of eight variances Assume that you are the production manager of a small branch plant of a large manufacturing firm. The central accounting control department sends you monthly performance reports showing the flexed budget amount, actual cost and variances for raw materials, direct labor, variable overhead (which is expressed on a direct labor hour basis), and fixed overhead. The variable cost budget variances are separated into quantity and cost per unit of input variances, and the fixed overhead budget and volume variances are shown. All variances are expressed in dollars.

Required:

a.   Rank the eight variances in descending order of their usefulness to you for planning and controlling purposes. Explain your ranking.

b.   Given the usefulness ranking in part **a**, explain how the frequency of reporting and the units in which each variance is reported might make the performance reports more useful.

Direct material variances—the price versus usage trade-off Williamson, Inc., manufactures quality replacement parts for the auto industry. The company uses a standard costing system and isolates variances as soon as possible. The purchasing manager is responsible for controlling the direct material price variances for hundreds of raw material items that are used in the company's various production processes. Recent experience indicates that, in the aggregate, direct material price variances have been favorable. However, several problems have occurred. Direct material usage variances have become consistently unfavorable for many items, and the company's total budget variance for direct materials has been unfavorable during each of the past six months. Direct laborers have complained about the quality of certain raw material items, and major customers have canceled purchase orders. In the meantime, the company's raw materials inventory has increased by nearly 240%.

Required:

a.   Give a probable explanation of why these results have occurred. *(Hint: What might the purchasing manager be doing that is dysfunctional for the company as a whole?)*

b.   How could the performance reporting system be improved to encourage more appropriate behavior on the part of the purchasing manager?

Evaluate the effects of erroneous standards During the year ended May 31, 2012, Teller Register Co. reported favorable raw material usage and direct labor and variable overhead efficiency variances that totaled $285,800. Price and rate variances were negligible. Total standard cost of goods manufactured during the year was $1,905,340.

Required:

a.   Comment about the effectiveness of the company's standards for controlling material and labor usage.

b.   If standard costs are used for valuing finished goods inventory, will the ending inventory valuation be higher or lower than if actual costs are used? Explain your answer.

c. Assume that the ending inventory of finished goods valued at standard cost is $158,780. Calculate the adjustment to finished goods inventory that would be appropriate because of the erroneous standards.

Case 15.31

LO 7 **Using standard costs to record inventory transactions** York Co. uses a standard cost system. When raw materials are purchased, the standard cost of the raw materials purchased is recorded as an increase in the Raw Materials Inventory account. When raw materials are used, the standard cost of the materials allowed for the units produced is recorded as an increase in the Work in Process Inventory account. Likewise, the standard cost of direct labor and variable manufacturing overhead is recorded as an increase in Work in Process Inventory.

Required:

a. Explain where in the financial statements the difference between the actual and standard cost of raw materials purchased will be recorded.

b. In this system, under what circumstances will the increases and decreases in the Finished Goods Inventory account (due to production and sales, respectively) represent the actual cost of products made and sold?

c. How does the accounting for overapplied or underapplied overhead, originally discussed in Chapter 13, differ from York Co.'s cost accounting system?

Case 15.32 **The planning and control environment: Internet assignment** The Consortium for Advanced Manufacturing—International (CAM-I) is an international consortium of companies, consultancies, and academics that have elected to work cooperatively in a precompetitive environment to solve problems common to the group. Its sole purpose is to support member companies in their quest for excellence in today's highly competitive global marketplace. This case requires you to use the CAM-I website at www.cam-i.org to complete the following requirements.

Assume that a start-up manufacturing company has recently hired you, and your first task is to develop a cost planning and control environment for the firm.

Required:

a. Review CAM-I's executive overview. Summarize the history of the organization and describe how CAM-I's "participative model" produces value for its members.

b. Read CAM-I's most recent annual report to members. Prepare a one-page summary emphasizing important accomplishments described in the letter from the president and the interest group highlights.

c. Read CAM-I's value proposition, and review its membership options (corporate, smaller, and subscription based). Choose a membership option that you expect will be beneficial, and write a memo to your new supervisor describing your rationale to justify the cost of joining this organization.

d. Review CAM-I's online bookstore. Identify two items from the list of publications that would help you with your new responsibility. Explain your choices.

e. Review CAM-I's wiki. Read the main-page overview of CAM-I's Cost Management Systems (CMS) interest group; then choose one of the related topics presented in the topics list, and write a brief summary of your findings. How will the use of wiki technology enable collaboration and growth of this content?

Answers to Self-Study Material

Matching: 1. l, 2. g, 3. h, 4. f, 5. a, 6. b, 7. d, 8. k, 9. e, 10. v, 11. r, 12. o, 13. n, 14. j, 15. p, 16. s, 17. t, 18. m, 19. q, 20. u
Multiple choice: 1. e, 2. c, 3. b, 4. c, 5. d, 6. b, 7. c, 8. b, 9. a, 10. c

16 Costs for Decision Making

American cartoonist Scott Adams, creator of the *Dilbert* comic strip, once declared that "informed decision-making comes from a long tradition of guessing and then blaming others for inadequate results." Dilbert's satirical view of planning and control perhaps holds more truth about the art of decision making than one would care to admit as he typically portrays the corporate office culture as an inefficient political environment where mismanagement spawns ridiculous decisions. In Chapter 16, however, a more systematic approach to the decision-making process is examined for both short- and long-term decisions.

Decision making encompasses the entire planning and control cycle and involves members from all functional areas of the organization. Some decisions required in the planning process are short-term in nature and include the allocation of company resources for those discretionary cost items discussed in Chapter 14 such as advertising, charitable contributions, and employee development programs. Implementing the operational and financial budgets discussed in Chapter 14 requires decisions from those managers responsible for executing the activities defined by those budgets. Once feedback information is available from the performance reporting system discussed in Chapter 15, decisions will be required to enhance or correct operational plans and/or activities.

Decisions regarding the long-run competitive strategy for product markets and prices are made in conjunction with the investment in physical capacity resources necessary to meet the objectives of the firm's strategy. **Capital budgeting** is the process of analyzing proposed capital expenditures—investments in plant, equipment, new products, and so on—to determine whether the investment will generate a large enough return on investment (ROI) over time to contribute to the organization's overall ROI objective.

This chapter will examine several examples of short- and long-run decisions—and establish a way of thinking about the costs involved in the decision-making process. The analysis necessary for those unique opportunities that present themselves on a random basis, such as special discounted price offers a firm receives for a one-time sale of its product, will be significantly different from the analysis required for the investment in additional plant capacity.

LEARNING OBJECTIVES (LO)

After studying this chapter you should understand and be able to

LO 16-1   Explain and illustrate the following cost terms: *differential, allocated, sunk,* and *opportunity*.

LO 16-2   Explain how costs are determined to be relevant for short-run decisions.

LO 16-3   Analyze relevant costs for the following decisions: sell or process further, special pricing, target costing, make or buy, continue or discontinue a segment, and product mix.

LO 16-4   Describe the attributes of capital budgeting that make it a significantly different activity from operational budgeting.

LO 16-5   Explain why present value analysis is appropriate and use it in capital budgeting.

LO 16-6   Define the cost of capital and demonstrate its use in capital budgeting.

LO 16-7   Illustrate the use of and differences between various capital budgeting techniques: net present value, present value ratio, and internal rate of return.

LO 16-8   Describe how issues concerning estimates, income taxes, and the timing of cash flows and investments are treated in the capital budgeting process.

LO 16-9   Calculate the payback period of a capital expenditure project.

LO 16-10   Calculate the accounting rate of return of a project and explain how it can be used most appropriately.

LO 16-11   Explain why not all management decisions are made strictly on the basis of quantitative analysis techniques.

Cost Classifications

Cost Classifications for Other Analytical Purposes

LO 1

Explain and illustrate the following cost terms: *differential, allocated, sunk,* and *opportunity*.

Exhibit 16-1 highlights the final branch of the cost classification model and presents the cost terminology and concepts used in the decision-making process.

Differential costs are brought into focus when possible future activities are analyzed. A **differential cost** is one that will differ according to the alternative activity being considered. For example, if a modification of an existing product is being considered, only the changes in cost resulting from the modification need to be considered relative to the additional revenues expected to result from the modification. Those costs that will continue to be incurred whether or not the modification is made are not germane to the decision.

Allocated costs are those that have been assigned to a product or activity (a "cost object") using some sort of systematic process. For example, overhead costs are allocated to production runs using the overhead application rate, for which the process was described in Chapter 13. At this point a reminder about cost allocations is appropriate. Many cost allocation methods are arbitrary and do not result in assigning costs in a way that reflects the reason why the costs were incurred. (Recall the discussion about common fixed expenses in Chapter 15.) Therefore, managers must be very careful about the conclusions made from any analysis that includes allocated costs. A general rule, similar to the warning against expressing fixed cost on a per unit basis, is appropriate to learn: *Do not arbitrarily allocate costs to a responsibility center because the allocated costs may not behave the way assumed in the allocation method.*

A **sunk cost** is a cost that has been incurred and cannot be unincurred, or reversed, by some future action. For example, if a firm has acquired a special purpose asset that

Exhibit 16-1   Cost Classifications—The Big Picture

As you review the various examples presented in this chapter to illustrate the analysis of relevant costs in decision making, focus more on a *way of thinking* about relevant costs rather than trying to memorize a particular formula or problem-solving format. The analysis in each example will be presented differently, but the underlying concepts are exactly the same—determining which costs make a difference and are relevant to the decision versus those costs that are irrelevant to the decision.

Study

Suggestion

would not be useful to any other organization, the cost of the asset represents a sunk cost. If the asset is put in use, its cost will be shown as depreciation expense over its life; if scrapped, its net book value will be recorded as a loss. Either way, the cost of the asset will be reflected in the income statement. When a new car is driven out of the dealer's lot, a sunk cost has been incurred that is equal to the loss in value because the car is now "used." *Sunk costs are never relevant to the analysis of alternative future actions (i.e., they are never differential costs) because they have been incurred and will not change.*

Opportunity cost is an economic concept that is too frequently overlooked in accounting analyses. Opportunity cost is the income forgone because an asset was not invested at a rate of return that could have been earned. For example, assume that you keep a $200 minimum balance in a noninterest-bearing checking account for which no service charge is assessed regardless of balance. If your next best alternative is to invest the $200 in a 6 percent savings account, the opportunity cost of your decision is $12 per year (6% $\times$ $200). Because opportunity cost relates to a transaction that did not occur, no record of it is made in the financial accounting process; thus, it is often overlooked. Awareness of opportunity cost raises the question, what other alternatives are there for earning a return on a particular asset?

---

1. What does it mean to state that a cost is a sunk cost?

What Does It Mean?

Answer on page 662

Short-Run Decision Analysis
Relevant Costs

While executing their daily responsibilities of managing the operations of an organization, managers are faced with decisions that may affect only the next few days, weeks, or months. These short-run decisions could involve the utilization of resources not otherwise active or the opportunity to reduce costs by outsourcing the production of certain components that will be used in production. Or a manager might have the ability to improve profits by choosing to sell a product at a special price or at a certain point in the production process or by choosing to refine the product further and in doing so attract a higher selling price. **Relevant costs** are those *future* costs that represent differences between these decision alternatives, and they are the key to effective decision making. Past transaction costs, while appropriately recorded in the accounting system as a result of the financial accounting process, represent costs that are never relevant

LO 2

Explain how costs are determined to be relevant for short-run decisions.

for the decision-making process and can only confuse the manager presented with the challenge of correctly analyzing costs for a particular decision.

Discussion of the many cost classification concepts presented in Chapters 12 through 15 has emphasized the theme of *different costs for different purposes* by describing how costs are viewed from different perspectives for planning and control purposes. Those same costs are now analyzed as being relevant or irrelevant for decision making depending on the question being addressed by the decision alternatives. Variable or fixed costs may or may not be relevant to a decision; it simply depends on whether or not they represent a difference between the alternatives.

Relevant Costs in Action—The Sell or Process Further Decision

LO 3

Analyze relevant costs for the sell or process further decision.

The sell or process further decision will be used to introduce relevant cost analysis. Suppose that Air Comfort, Inc., produces a heating and cooling system that sells for $7,200 and requires the following production costs:

Direct materials	$2,400
Direct labor	1,600
Variable overhead	800
Fixed overhead	1,200

Next, assume that Air Comfort's design engineers have developed a more efficient air filtration system that would increase the efficiency of the current model. The only changes to the cost structure to produce the more efficient model would be direct materials that would now cost $3,400. Air Comfort's marketing vice president suggests that the more efficient version of the system could sell for $8,000 in the current marketplace for similar systems. What are the relevant costs to consider in deciding whether to sell the current system as is or to produce the more efficient system?

The relevant costs are those costs that are different between the current system and the more efficient system: direct materials in the amount of $1,000 ($3,400 new material cost – $2,400 current material cost). Note that the analysis requires the decision maker to think independently about each cost item presented; one cannot rely on the general cost classifications presented earlier for planning and control purposes. Costs in this example can be classified as direct (materials and labor) and indirect (overhead); or costs can be classified as variable (materials, labor, and variable overhead) and fixed (fixed overhead). But simply because a cost is direct rather than indirect or variable instead of fixed does not necessarily mean it will be relevant or irrelevant in a decision. Costs for decision-making purposes presented in this chapter are viewed as a *way of thinking* about their relevance to any decision by asking the fundamental question "Does it make a difference?"

Should Air Comfort sell the system as is or produce the more efficient system? The relevant cost of producing the more efficient system has been identified as $1,000, but before making the final decision the $1,000 must be compared to the difference in selling price that would be available from the more efficient system. The following relevant cost analysis indicates that it would not be wise to produce and sell the more efficient system given the current marketplace.

Difference in selling price ($8,000 − $7,200)	$ 800
Difference in materials cost ($3,400 − $2,400)	1,000
Difference in profit	$ (200)

In the Air Comfort example, the direct material cost is a differential cost and the selling price of the more efficient model is an opportunity cost; both items are considered relevant. The fixed overhead in the product cost is an allocated cost and the design engineering cost is a sunk cost; both costs are considered irrelevant. These cost classification concepts presented earlier in this chapter are used in decision analysis:

Relevant	**Irrelevant**
Differential cost—will differ according to alternative activities being considered.	Allocated cost—a common cost that has been arbitrarily assigned to a product or activity.
Opportunity cost—income forgone by choosing one alternative over another.	Sunk cost—has already been incurred and will not change.

2. What does it mean to state that a cost is a relevant cost?

What Does It Mean?
Answer on page 662

Relevant Costs in Action—The Special Pricing Decision

While many examples illustrate relevant cost analysis for short-run decision making, the special pricing decision offers several compelling issues. The product or service pricing decision, in general, is a long-run decision. In the long run, the product or service price must be adequate to recover all costs identified in the organization's value chain (R&D, design, production, marketing, distribution, and customer service), as well as provide for the necessary ROI. In many situations the marketplace and those firms competing in the marketplace determine the product or service price. If an organization wants to compete, the key issue is whether the firm can strategically manage costs within the value chain over the life of the product or service to produce the desired ROI. This cost management concept is referred to as **target costing.** The target cost is the maximum cost that can be incurred, which—when added to the desired amount of ROI—results in an amount equal to the marketplace selling price.

On certain occasions the firm may be presented with a special offer for its product or service at a price below the normal selling price. In addition to an assessment of relevant costs, the special pricing decision requires an understanding of where the firm is operating relative to its capacity. Assume MicroTech, Inc. (MTI), produces a high-end laptop computer that normally sells in the marketplace for $2,400. Also assume that World University (WU) wants to provide each of its MBA students with a laptop computer so they may participate in online courses with faculty and other students from all over the world. WU estimates that in July it will need to acquire 500 laptops for its MBA students and therefore makes an offer to MTI for 500 laptops at the price of $1,800 each.

MTI has the capacity to produce 5,000 laptop computers each month and uses this capacity as the denominator activity for computing predetermined fixed overhead rates. For the month of July the operating budget calls for the sale and production of 4,400 laptops. In addition to a standard sales commission of 5 percent paid on the sale

LO 3
Analyze relevant costs for the special pricing decision.

of each laptop, which would not be paid on the WU special order, standard manufacturing costs are as follows:

Manufacturing costs:	
Direct materials	$ 800
Direct labor	450
Variable overhead	250
Fixed overhead	500
Total unit cost	$2,000

At first glance, it appears that MTI should reject an offer of $1,800 when the cost of each laptop is $2,120 [$2,000 manufacturing cost plus $120 commission ($2,400 × 5%)]. But the important question is this: "What are the relevant costs for MTI in the decision to accept or reject this special pricing offer?" Exhibit 16-2 presents a relevant cost analysis for this special pricing decision. Notice in Section I that in the month of July, MTI has **idle capacity** of 600 units (5,000 units total capacity less 4,400 units in the current production budget). This unscheduled capacity allows MTI to consider adding 500 units of production without adding production capacity. Note that the analysis is presented in the contribution margin format that highlights cost behavior as activity changes. The current selling price of $2,400 generates $780 of contribution margin per unit toward covering total fixed costs of $2,500,000 and toward providing a profit.

An examination of the relevant costs for the special order of 500 laptops at a price of $1,800 each reveals that the variable cost items of direct material, direct labor, and variable overhead are relevant costs because they represent the additional productive resources necessary to produce 500 additional laptop computers. Variable sales commission, however, is not relevant to the special order because commissions will not be paid on the 500 laptops. Variable costs that can be avoided in the special pricing decision are never relevant costs. The special offer price of $1,800 generates a contribution margin of $300 per unit, and this positive contribution margin flows directly to the bottom line as $150,000 additional operating income since no additional fixed costs were incurred, given the idle capacity. Fixed overhead, assigned for accounting purposes at the predetermined overhead rate of $500 per unit, is not relevant to the special pricing offer but is often incorrectly included in an analysis that does not focus on relevant costs. It should be apparent from Exhibit 16-2 that any price offered above the relevant variable costs of $1,500 will generate a positive contribution margin and should be accepted as long as no other more profitable opportunity for the 600 units of idle capacity can be identified. MicroTech, by accepting the offer of $1,800 per laptop from World University, improved operating income by 16 percent for the month of July.

How would the analysis of relevant costs change if the firm were operating at **full capacity?** Sections II and III of Exhibit 16-2 assume that MTI is currently producing and selling at full capacity of 5,000 laptops in July. Illustrating the option of rejecting the special offer, Section II determines the maximum operating income that MTI can expect to earn with a selling price of $2,400 per laptop. When operating at full capacity, there is no reasonable explanation for considering any price less than the normal selling price unless an opportunity is provided to avoid more cost than the related decrease in price. At full capacity, any combination of price minus variable cost that produces less than $780 of contribution margin will lower total operating income.

Section III of Exhibit 16-2 illustrates the effect on operating income of accepting the special offer when operating at full capacity. Note that operating income has decreased

Relevant Cost Analysis for Special Pricing Decisions | **Exhibit 16-2**

I. Idle capacity = 600 laptops, special offer accepted:

	Current Sales 4,400 Laptops		Special Offer 500 Laptops		July Total 4,900 Laptops
	Unit	Total	Unit	Total	Total
Sales	$2,400	$10,560,000	$1,800	$900,000	$11,460,000
Less: Variable costs:					
Direct material	800	3,520,000	800	400,000	3,920,000
Direct labor	450	1,980,000	450	225,000	2,205,000
Variable overhead	250	1,100,000	250	125,000	1,225,000
Sales commission	120	528,000	—	—	528,000
Contribution margin	$ 780	$ 3,432,000	$ 300	$150,000	$ 3,582,000
Less: Fixed costs*		2,500,000		—	2,500,000
Operating income		$ 932,000		$150,000	$ 1,082,000
Percentage change in operating income				+ 16 %	

II. Full capacity, special offer rejected:

	Current Sales 5,000 Laptops		July Total 5,000 Laptops
	Unit	Total	Total
Sales	$2,400	$12,000,000	$12,000,000
Less: Variable costs:			
Direct material	800	4,000,000	4,000,000
Direct labor	450	2,250,000	2,250,000
Variable overhead	250	1,250,000	1,250,000
Sales commission	120	600,000	600,000
Contribution margin	$ 780	$ 3,900,000	$ 3,900,000
Less: Fixed costs*		2,500,000	2,500,000
Operating income		$ 1,400,000	$ 1,400,000

III. Full capacity, special offer accepted:

	Current Sales 4,500 Laptops		Special Offer 500 Laptops		July Total 5,000 Laptops
	Unit	Total	Unit	Total	Total
Sales	$2,400	$10,800,000	$1,800	$900,000	$11,700,000
Less: Variable costs:					
Direct material	800	3,600,000	800	400,000	4,000,000
Direct labor	450	2,025,000	450	225,000	2,250,000
Variable overhead	250	1,125,000	250	125,000	1,250,000
Sales commission	120	540,000	—	—	540,000
Contribution margin	$ 780	$ 3,510,000	$ 300	$150,000	$ 3,660,000
Less: Fixed costs*		2,500,000		—	2,500,000
Operating income		$ 1,010,000		$150,000	$ 1,160,000
Percentage change in operating income					−17 %

*Total fixed costs for month (5,000 units × $500).

by $240,000 ($1,400,000 − $1,160,000) as a result of generating $480 ($780 − $300) less contribution margin on the 500 special offer laptops ($480 × 500 = $240,000) than earned on sales at full capacity. The difference in contribution margin of $480 per laptop is a relevant opportunity cost—the operating profit forgone by choosing to accept rather than reject the special offer. As discussed in Chapter 12, contribution margin analysis is a powerful tool for managers to use to determine the effects on profits of decisions involving changes in selling prices, variable or fixed costs, or the volume of operating activity.

To summarize, MTI has an opportunity to maximize operating income regardless of whether it is operating at full or idle capacity, and the decision to accept or reject the special offer from World University hinges on the proper interpretation of relevant costs. By accepting the $1,800 offer when operating with idle capacity, MTI will improve its bottom line by 16 percent and put inactive resources to work. On the other hand, by rejecting the $1,800 offer when operating at full capacity, MTI will avoid an unnecessary 17 percent decline in profits.

Relevant cost analysis provides a quantitative framework for the special pricing decision. However, every quantitatively indicated decision should also be evaluated against a qualitative framework that could result in not executing the decision outcome. For example, the special order may not be accepted when operating with idle capacity even though the special price more than covers incremental costs because regular customers might learn of the special price and demand it for their "regular" business. Another example could be related to unanticipated increased volume in the near future; sales at a special price less than the regular price would absorb capacity that could be used for new regular sales. Additionally, management must be certain the special price is not in violation of the Robinson–Patman Act, which does not allow products to be priced differently unless those prices reflect related cost differences. To learn more about this law, see the FYI box on this page.

What Does It Mean?
Answer on page 662

3. What does it mean when a firm has an offer to sell its product or service at a special price and is operating with idle capacity?

LO 3
Analyze relevant costs for the target costing question.

Relevant Costs in Action—The Target Costing Question

Earlier in this chapter, *target costing* was described generally as a long-term concept. Given that the market price for a particular product or service may be a function of the firms competing in that market, the question becomes whether a potential entrant into the market can compete at the established market price and earn a desired amount of profit, thereby requiring the entrant to provide the product or service at the target cost.

This target cost is the minimum cost that can be incurred, which when subtracted from the selling price allows for a desired profit to be earned:

$$\text{Target cost} = \text{Market price} - \text{Desired profit}$$

Target costing analysis is primarily used to identify cost reduction initiatives in an organization's value chain when it becomes apparent that the firm is no longer competitive and is unable to achieve a desired level of profit at the current marketplace selling price for its products or services. The firm must find a way to reduce cost, or it will eventually be driven out of the market. However, in the short term, the target costing model can be used in a relevant cost analysis to effectively evaluate opportunities that may present themselves. Suppose that MTI is operating under conditions of idle capacity, as described earlier in the chapter, and is looking for opportunities to use that capacity. One of its customers is interested in acquiring 200 "tablet"-style laptops over the next year, a style that MTI has not produced to date. The marketplace selling price, given a standard configuration and basic features, is already well established at $2,600 per unit. The decision for MTI centers on the question of a target cost: Can MTI produce the 200 tablet laptops at a target cost that will allow it to earn a desired profit, given the selling price of $2,600?

The basic difference in producing the tablet-style laptop compared to MTI's standard laptop is the swivel screen architecture and the notepad user interface, which allows the user to transcribe handwritten notes directly on the tablet screen. What costs are relevant to this decision for MTI? The analysis is in many ways similar to the special pricing decision—the difference being that in the special pricing decision, costs were known up front and in this example some costs that will be new to MTI are not presently known. Obviously these new costs will be differential costs and certainly relevant to the analysis. New costs would likely include design and engineering time, raw material components for the swivel screen user interface, and software enhancements. Another potentially relevant cost could be a labor cost differential if the tablet laptop required more assembly or testing time than the standard laptop. How about equipment? Would new manufacturing equipment, equipment retooling, or other capacity-related costs be necessary?

Assume that MTI requires a 30 percent profit margin to be earned on all laptop products. What is the target cost for the new tablet laptop model?

$$\text{Target cost} = \$2,600 - (\$2,600 \times 30\%)$$
$$\text{Target cost} = \$2,600 - \$780$$
$$\text{Target cost} = \$1,820$$

MTI must be able to produce the tablet laptop at the target cost of $1,820, or less, if it wants to earn its required profit margin of 30 percent. At this point, MTI might consider this opportunity as an opening to compete in the tablet laptop market on a permanent basis; if so, a more long-term life cycle cost analysis would be appropriate. Or MTI's decision may simply focus on its currently available idle capacity and the 200 tablet-style laptops the customer has asked it to consider. In either case, the importance of understanding costs relevant to the decision is significant.

Relevant Costs in Action—The Make or Buy Decision

Another decision-making situation that illustrates the use of relevant costs is the make or buy decision. For example, how does a manager evaluate the alternatives of producing a component part of a product internally versus buying that component from an outside source? Any number of reasons could exist that might create an advantage for buying from outside the company. This question of **outsourcing** is prevalent in organizations looking to add value to the products and services they provide. The goal is to reduce costs while simultaneously improving the quality and/or functionality of the product or service.

LO 3

Analyze relevant costs for the make or buy decision.

Producing a component part internally may be more costly if other organizations specialize in producing that component and it is considered within their core competencies. As
such, these outside sources may provide an advantage in terms of newer, more specialized
equipment and technologies or certain skilled labor. Alternatively, being presented with a
more profitable use of the capacity needed to produce a component part internally might
make it desirable to outsource that part's production. Organizational services such as
payroll, tax return preparation, information technology, or the operation of the employee
cafeteria also could be candidates for the outsourcing decision.

What are the relevant costs in a make or buy decision? Suppose that MicroTech, Inc.,
currently produces the motherboards used in the laptop computers that were described in
the special pricing decision. As such, MTI incurs the following production costs:

Manufacturing costs:	
Direct materials	$120
Direct labor	80
Variable overhead	50
Fixed overhead	100
Total unit cost	$350

The laptop product manager has determined that a motherboard of comparable quality is now available and could be acquired from Integrated Technologies, Inc., at a
purchase cost of $300 plus a $5 shipping charge per motherboard. At first glance this
appears to be a simple decision, but until the analysis of relevant costs is performed,
the risk of an incorrect decision is considerable.

In a make or buy decision, the relevant cost of making a component or providing
a service internally is the cost that can be avoided by acquiring the resource or service
from a source outside the company. Therefore, avoidable costs are the relevant costs for
this decision. In evaluating each item of cost the important question to ask is, "Will this
cost continue if the resource is purchased from the outside?" If the cost will continue regardless of whether the resource is produced internally or purchased from outside, then
it is not relevant to the decision. Using the MTI information to illustrate this concept,
assume that 20 percent of the fixed overhead amount that has been allocated to each
unit represents the cost (in terms of salary) of the motherboard production manager who
would not be retained if the motherboards were not produced by MTI. Also assume
that at the present time there is no other use for the production resources being used to
produce the motherboards. An analysis of avoidable costs for this decision follows:

	Avoidable Cost to Make	Cost to Buy
Purchase costs:		
Motherboard cost		$300
Shipping cost		5
Manufacturing costs:		
Direct material	$120	
Direct labor	80	
Variable overhead	50	
Fixed overhead ($100 × 20%)	20	
Total unit cost	$270	$305
Advantage to make	$ 35	

It should be clear that the variable production costs will not be necessary if the motherboards are purchased, but notice that only 20 percent of the fixed overhead is included in the relevant cost analysis because the remainder of these fixed costs are sunk, unavoidable, and provide no alternative use. How would the analysis change if there were alternative uses for the capacity resources currently being used to produce the motherboards? Suppose that MTI could apply the resource capacity being used to produce the motherboards to expand production of flat screen monitors, which provide a contribution margin of $50 per unit. In this scenario, an opportunity cost has been introduced into the scenario, and we must remember that opportunity costs are always relevant for decision making. A revised relevant cost analysis follows:

	Avoidable Cost to Make	Cost to Buy
Purchase costs:		
Motherboard cost		$300
Shipping cost		5
Manufacturing costs:		
Direct material	$120	
Direct labor	80	
Variable overhead	50	
Fixed overhead ($100 × 20%)	20	
Total unit cost	$270	
Opportunity cost of not using available		
capacity to produce monitors	$ 50	
Total relevant costs	$320	$305
Advantage to buy		$ 15

A final decision to outsource a product component or other service should not be made merely on the basis of the quantitative analysis without considering important qualitative factors. Important dependencies will exist with suppliers, and the need to manage the supplier relationship will be ever important. Concerns about the quality of parts or services received should be addressed, and testing and measurement systems should be defined to ensure the necessary quality. Delivery times and having products or services when they are needed could also be a risk. On the other hand, it is possible that even higher quality and service could be achieved through outsourcing because of the unique expertise or technology that the outside resource or service provider can bring to the organization.

---

4. What does it mean when a cost is avoidable in the make or buy decision?

What Does It Mean?
Answer on page 662

Relevant Costs in Action—The Continue or Discontinue a Segment Decision

LO 3

Analyze relevant costs for the continue or discontinue a segment decision.

Consider next the question of whether to continue or discontinue a particular segment of the organization. You might recall from Chapter 15 that a *segment* is a division, a product or service line, a sales territory, or any other organizational unit. Since management frequently disaggregates total company operating results into segment results, it is possible that a segment will appear to be operating at a loss. When this occurs, the inevitable question arises as to whether to continue or discontinue the segment. The following illustration of a segmented income statement was presented in Chapter 15 for Cruisers, Inc., which showed three divisions: sailboats, motor-boats, and repair parts. However, this example assumes annual revenue and expense amounts:

CRUISERS, INC.
Segmented Income Statement
For the Year Ended December 31, 2013

	Total Company	Sailboat Division	Motorboat Division	Repair Parts Division
Sales.	$2,240,000	$1,280,000	$640,000	$320,000
Variable expenses	960,000	512,000	288,000	160,000
Contribution margin.	$1,280,000	$ 768,000	$352,000	$160,000
Fixed expenses	1,128,000	656,000	288,000	184,000
Operating income	$ 152,000	$ 112,000	$ 64,000	$ (24,000)

It appears that if the repair parts division were discontinued, operating income for Cruisers, Inc., would increase by $24,000. How does an analysis of relevant cost guide the decision maker to the correct outcome? In this type of decision, the relevant cost focus is on those costs that can be eliminated if the segment is eliminated. Otherwise, if a cost will continue even if a segment is discontinued, the cost is not a differential cost and, therefore, not relevant to the decision.

If the repair parts division is discontinued, it should be obvious that sales of $320,000, variable expenses of $160,000, and contribution margin of $160,000 would all be eliminated—these items would be relevant to this decision. What's not so obvious is what happens to the fixed expenses. Cruisers, Inc., would be willing to discontinue the repair parts division if the company could eliminate more fixed expenses than the amount of contribution margin it would be losing, in this example $160,000.

Now suppose that, as a result of a detailed analysis of fixed expenses, it is learned that the fixed expenses assigned to each division represent the sum of the fixed expenses incurred in each division plus an allocated share of the corporate fixed expenses. The corporate fixed expenses would continue to be incurred even if one of the divisions were to be closed. This analysis of fixed expenses reveals the following:

	Total Company	Sailboat Division	Motorboat Division	Repair Parts Division
Direct fixed expenses	$ 680,000	$400,000	$160,000	$120,000
Common fixed expenses allocated in proportion to sales . . .	448,000	256,000	128,000	64,000
Total fixed expenses	$1,128,000	$656,000	$288,000	$184,000

If Cruisers were to discontinue the repair parts division, $120,000 of direct fixed expenses could be eliminated. Direct fixed expenses would, therefore, be relevant to this decision. However, the $64,000 of corporate fixed expenses allocated to the repair parts division would continue regardless of whether the repair parts division were continued or discontinued. Remember, allocated costs are never relevant. The relevant cost analysis would look like this:

Relevant Cost Analysis of
Discontinuing the Repair Parts Division

Decrease in contribution margin	$(160,000)
Decrease in direct fixed expenses	120,000
Net decrease in segment margin	$ (40,000)

The relevant cost analysis indicates that if the repair parts division is discontinued, Cruisers, Inc., will experience a $40,000 decrease in company segment margin and, therefore, operating income. It is not logical to give up the $160,000 of contribution margin being generated by the repair parts division if the only benefit is the ability to avoid $120,000 of direct fixed expenses attributable to that division. The following illustration presents a revised segmented income statement for Cruisers, Inc., assuming the repair parts division is discontinued and the remaining $64,000 of corporate fixed expenses is reallocated to the sailboat and motorboat divisions:

CRUISERS, INC. Segmented Income Statement For the Year Ended December 31, 2013		
	Total Company	**Sailboat Division**	**Motorboat Division**
---	---	---	---
Sales.	$1,920,000	$1,280,000	$640,000
Variable expenses	$ 800,000	512,000	288,000
Contribution margin.	$1,120,000	$ 768,000	$352,000
Fixed expenses	1,008,000	698,667	309,333
Operating income	$ 112,000	$ 69,333	$ 42,667

The revised segmented income statement for Cruisers, Inc., shows the decrease in operating income of $40,000 ($152,000 − $112,000) by discontinuing the repair parts division that was suggested by the relevant cost analysis. A careful review and understanding of fixed expenses, as illustrated in this example, emphasizes an important point made earlier in the discussion of relevant costs—just because a cost is classified as fixed (or variable) does not mean that it is always relevant or irrelevant to the decision.

One final note here: Had the original segmented income statement been organized in the preferred format illustrated in Chapter 15, the decision would have been obvious from the beginning. The repair parts division is generating $40,000 of segment margin (sales less variable and direct fixed expenses); by eliminating the segment, the company as a whole would experience a decrease in operating income equal to the

$40,000 segment margin. The preferred segmented income statement organization is illustrated here:

	Total Company	Sailboat Division	Motorboat Division	Repair Parts Division
CRUISERS, INC. **Segmented Income Statement** **For the Year Ended December 31, 2013**				
Sales	$2,240,000	$1,280,000	$640,000	$320,000
Variable expenses	960,000	512,000	288,000	160,000
Contribution margin	$1,280,000	$ 768,000	$352,000	$160,000
Direct fixed expenses	680,000	400,000	160,000	120,000
Segment margin	$ 600,000	$ 368,000	$192,000	$ 40,000
Common fixed expenses . . .	448,000			
Operating income	$ 152,000			

What Does It Mean?

Answer on page 662

5. What does it mean when fixed expenses allocated to a segment are considered to be common corporate expenses?

Relevant Costs in Action—The Short-Term Allocation of Scarce Resources

LO 3

Analyze relevant costs for the product mix decision.

As a final example of how relevant costs are used in decision making, consider how production resources might be allocated to a mix of products when product demand exceeds the currently available production capacity. The next part of the chapter will explain the decision-making tools used to analyze long-term investments in additional production capacity; but in the short term, capacity constraints may force a decision about which product(s) should be produced next. The objective is to maximize contribution margin given the demand and capacity constraints. To illustrate, assume that Integrated Technologies, Inc. (ITI), produces the following items, which use the same circuitry production line. Demand is such that ITI can produce and sell as much of either product as it can process through the circuitry production line. Selling prices, variable costs, and contribution margins per unit follow:

	Motherboards	Video Circuit Boards
Selling price	$300	$200
Variable costs	150	100
Contribution margin per unit	$150	$100

It would appear that the motherboards are the more profitable product and should be a production priority. However, when capacity constraints exist, it is important to view the contribution margin of each product in terms of the capacity constraint.

Assume that one hour is required to produce a video circuit board and two hours are required to produce a motherboard on the circuitry production line, which has only 120 hours available each week. Does this information about the production time requirements of each product relative to the constrained resource change your view of profitability? Expressing the contribution margin of each product in terms of circuitry production line hours would generate the following results:

	Motherboards	Video Circuit Boards
Selling price	$300	$200
Variable costs	150	100
Contribution margin per unit	$150	$100
Circuitry line hours required	2	1
Contribution margin per hour	$ 75	$100

The contribution margin per circuitry line hour, the scarce resource, indicates that profit will be maximized with the production of video circuit boards. If all 120 available hours were used to produce video circuit boards, the contribution margin generated would be $12,000 ($100 × 120 hours). Only to the extent that any hours were unused for video circuit boards should any motherboards be produced. Of course, an appropriate question to pose at this point, given the current high demand for both products produced on the circuitry production line, is whether additional production capacity should be added. This question presents interesting new considerations that depend on a longer-run view of decision making. These considerations will be discussed in the remainder of this chapter.

Long-Run Investment Analysis

Capital Budgeting

Capital budgeting is the process of analyzing proposed capital expenditures— investments in plant, equipment, new products, and so on—to determine whether the investment will generate a large enough return on investment (ROI) over time to contribute to the organization's overall ROI objectives.

Capital budgeting differs from operational budgeting in the time frame being considered. Whereas operational budgeting involves planning for a period that is usually not longer than one year, capital budgeting concerns investments and returns that are spread over a number of years. Thus, the operating budget reflects the firm's strategic plans to achieve current period profitability, and the capital budget provides an overall blueprint to help the firm meet its long-term growth and profitability objectives.

LO 4

Describe the attributes of capital budgeting that make it a significantly different activity from operational budgeting.

Investment Decision Special Considerations

Investment decisions involve committing financial resources now in anticipation of a return that will be realized over an extended period of time. This extended time frame, which can be many years, adds complexity to the analysis of whether or not to make the investment because of compound interest/present value considerations. The time value of money can be ignored for most operating expenditure decisions because the benefit of an expenditure will be received soon after the expenditure is made, and a simple cost/benefit relationship can be determined. This is not so for capital expenditures because the benefits of the expenditure will be received over several years, and $100 of benefit to be received five years from now is not the same as $100 of benefit to be received one year from now.

LO 5

Explain why present value analysis is appropriate and use it in capital budgeting.

Most business firms and other organizations have more investment opportunities than resources available for investment. Capital budgeting procedures, especially those applying present value analysis techniques, are useful in helping management identify the alternatives that will contribute most to the future profitability of the firm. However, as is the case with most quantitative techniques, the quantitative "answer" will not necessarily dictate management's decision. The quantitative result will be considered along with qualitative factors in the decision-making process. Examples of qualitative factors include the willingness to assume competitive risks associated with expanding (or not expanding) into a new market area, the implications for a board of directors retaining control if more stock must be sold to raise funds for the expansion, and, of course, top management's personal goals for the organization. Because capital budgeting involves projections into the future, top management attitudes about the risk of forecasting errors have a major impact on investment decisions.

Most firms involve the board of directors in capital budgeting by having the board approve all capital expenditures above a certain minimum amount. Depending on the company and its financial circumstances, this amount may range from $5,000 to $1 million or more. High-level approval is required because the capital expenditure represents a major commitment of company resources, and it involves a multiyear period of time.

What Does It Mean?
Answer on page 662

6. What does it mean to have a capital budget?

Cost of Capital

LO 6
Define the cost of capital and demonstrate its use in capital budgeting.

The principal financial objective of a firm organized for profit is to earn a return on the assets invested that will permit payment of all borrowing costs (interest) and provide the owners a return on their investment (ROE—return on equity) that compensates them fairly for the financial risks being taken. To meet the requirements of these resource providers, whose claims are shown on the right side of the balance sheet, attention must be focused on the assets that are reported on the left side of the balance sheet. Thus, return on assets (ROI—return on investment) becomes a primary concern of financial managers who evaluate proposed capital expenditures.

The **cost of capital** is the rate of return on assets that must be earned to permit the firm to meet its interest obligations and provide the expected return to owners. Determining the cost of capital of a company is a complex process that is beyond the scope of this text. Suffice it to say here that the cost of capital is a composite of borrowing costs and stockholder dividend and earnings' growth rate expectations. The cost of capital is most useful as a "worry point" guide to management (i.e., an indication of an approximate *minimum* ROI that creditors and owners are expecting). Most firms set a cost of capital rate for investment analysis purposes that is somewhat greater than the "true" economic cost of acquiring funds. This allows for estimation errors in the calculation and provides some cushion for estimation errors in the data used in the investment analysis itself. The cost of capital used for analyzing proposed capital expenditures is also influenced by the perceived riskiness of the proposal being evaluated. More risky proposals (e.g., new product development or expansion into a new activity) will be required to earn a higher rate of return than less risky proposals (e.g., equipment replacement or expansion of an existing activity). This risk difference is related to the uncertainties associated with operating in a somewhat different environment than that in which the firm is experienced.

The cost of capital is the *discount rate* (i.e., the interest rate at which future period **cash flows** are discounted) used to determine the present value of the investment proposal being analyzed. For most firms, the cost of capital is probably in the range of 10 to 20 percent. In the capital budgeting illustrations presented in this chapter, the cost of capital will be a given. However, you should recognize that in practice the development of the cost of capital rate is a complex but important process.

Capital Budgeting Techniques

Of the four generally recognized capital budgeting techniques, two use present value analysis, and two do not. Because money does have value over time, the two methods that recognize this fact are clearly superior, at least conceptually, to those that ignore the time value of money.

Methods That Use Present Value Analysis

Net present value (NPV) method.

Internal rate of return (IRR) method.

Methods That Do Not Use Present Value Analysis

Payback method.

Accounting rate of return method.

Each of these methods uses the amount to be invested in the capital project. The net present value, internal rate of return, and payback methods use the amount of *cash* generated by the investment each year. The accounting rate of return method uses accrual accounting net income resulting from the investment. For most investment projects, the difference between the cash generated each year and accrual accounting net income is depreciation expense—a noncash item that reduces accrual accounting net income. Again, because they recognize the time value of money and focus on cash flows, the NPV and IRR methods are considered more appropriate than either payback or accounting rate of return.

Net present value.   The **net present value (NPV) method** involves calculating the present value of the expected cash flows from a project using the cost of capital as the discount rate, and comparing the total present value of the cash flows to the amount of investment required.

Based on this analysis, the following conclusions can be drawn:

LO 7

Illustrate the use of and differences between various capital budgeting techniques: net present value, present value ratio, and internal rate of return.

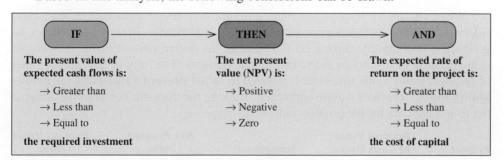

The discount rate used in net present value analysis is sometimes referred to as the *hurdle rate* because it represents the minimum rate of return required for an investment to yield a positive NPV. The net present value method is illustrated in Exhibit 16-3.

Exhibit 16-3   Net Present Value (NPV) Analysis of a Proposed Investment

I. Assumptions:

A. A new packaging machine costing $100,000, including installation, has an estimated useful life of five years and an estimated salvage value of $6,000 after five years. The new machine will be purchased at the end of 2013.

B. Installation and use of the machine in the firm's operations will result in labor savings during each of the next five years as follows:

2014	$26,000
2015	27,000
2016	31,000
2017	35,000
2018	38,000

C. The firm's cost of capital is 16%.

II. Time line presentation of cash flows from the investment:

	12/31/13	2014	2015	2016	2017	2018
Cash flows from investment:						
Savings		$26,000	$27,000	$31,000	$35,000	$38,000
Salvage						6,000
Total		$26,000	$27,000	$31,000	$35,000	$44,000

III. Net present value calculation at 16%:

	12/31/13	2014	2015	2016	2017	2018
Present value factors (Table 6-4, 16%)		0.8621	0.7432	0.6407	0.5523	0.4761
Present value of cash flows from investment		$22,415	$20,066	$19,862	$19,331	$20,948

Total present value of cash flows from investment $102,622

Investment . . . .   (100,000)

Net present value at 16% . . . $ 2,622

IV. Conclusion from analysis:

The net present value is positive; therefore the projected rate of return on this investment is greater than the 16% cost of capital. Based on this quantitative analysis, the investment should be made.

When alternative projects involving different investment amounts are being considered, the NPV approach must be carried one step further. Projects should not be assigned a profitability ranking on the basis of the dollar amount of the net present value because of disparities in the investment amounts. The ratio of the present value of the cash flows to the investment, referred to as the **present value ratio** (or **profitability index**), provides a more appropriate ranking mechanism. For example, assume the following data for the projects indicated:

Project	Present Value of Cash Flows	Investment	Net Present Value	Present Value Ratio
A	$22,800	$20,000	$2,800	1.14
B	34,000	30,000	4,000	1.13

Even though project B has a greater net present value, it is clear from looking at the present value ratios that project A has a higher present value for every dollar invested and is thus a more desirable investment. When the NPV approach to investment analysis is used, it is appropriate to take this second step and calculate the present value ratio, especially when a selection must be made from several positive NPV projects.

7. What does it mean to state that present value analysis is appropriate for capital budgeting?
8. What does it mean to calculate the net present value of a proposed capital investment?
9. What does it mean if the net present value of a proposed capital expenditure is positive?

What Does It Mean?

Answers on page 662

Internal rate of return. The **internal rate of return (IRR) method** and the NPV method differ in that the discount (interest) rate—the cost of capital—is a given in the NPV approach, whereas the IRR approach solves for the actual rate of return that will be earned by the proposed investment. This is the discount rate at which the present value of cash flows from the project will equal the investment (i.e., the discount rate at which the NPV equals zero). Thus, the IRR method may require several calculations using different discount rates. Once the project's internal rate of return is known, a conclusion about the suitability of the investment is made by comparing the IRR to the cost of capital. If the IRR is greater than the cost of capital, the investment will be recommended. If the IRR is less than the cost of capital, the investment will not be recommended.

With respect to the investment proposal illustrated in Exhibit 16-3, the IRR must be greater than 16 percent because the NPV is positive. Determination of the actual IRR requires another set of present value calculations using a higher discount rate (18 percent is the next higher rate in the Chapter 6 tables) and then **interpolating** to determine the actual discount rate at which the present value of cash flows would equal the investment. The IRR method is illustrated in Exhibit 16-4.

There are some theoretical advantages to the NPV approach to evaluate proposed capital expenditures, but many managers use both approaches because they are more comfortable knowing the actual rate of return. Computer applications make the calculations easy; estimating the amount and timing of future cash flows associated with a proposal is the more challenging part of the process.

10. What does it mean to state that the net present value calculation technique is easier to use than the internal rate of return calculation method?

What Does It Mean?

Answer on page 662

Exhibit 16-4   Internal Rate of Return (IRR) Analysis of a Proposed Investment

I. **Assumptions:**
Same as in Exhibit 16-3.
The NPV of the proposed investment at a discount rate of 16% is $2,622 (from Exhibit 16-3).

II. **Time line presentation of cash flows from the investment:**

	12/31/13	2014	2015	2016	2017	2018
Cash flows from investment:						
Savings		$26,000	$27,000	$31,000	$35,000	$38,000
Salvage						6,000
Total		$26,000	$27,000	$31,000	$35,000	$44,000

III. **Net present value calculation at 18%:**

	12/31/13	2014	2015	2016	2017	2018
Present value factors (Table 6-4, 18%)		0.8475	0.7182	0.6086	0.5158	0.4371
Present value of cash flows from investment		$22,035	$19,391	$18,867	$18,053	$19,232
Total present value of cash flows from investment	$ 97,578					
Investment	(100,000)					
Net present value at 18% . . .	$ (2,422)					

IV. **Interpolation:**

Discount rate	16%	17%	18%
Net present value	$2,622	$0	$(2,422)

The discount rate at an NPV of $0 is approximately 17%.

V. **Conclusion from analysis:**
The internal rate of return of the project is the discount rate at which the NPV = $0, so the IRR is 17%. The expected IRR is more than the firm's 16% cost of capital. Based on this quantitative analysis, the investment should be made.

LO 8

Describe how issues concerning estimates, income taxes, and the timing of cash flows and investments are treated in the capital budgeting process.

Some analytical considerations.

Estimates.   The validity of present value calculations will be a function of the accuracy with which future cash flows can be estimated. A great deal of effort will be expended in making estimates. When the project involves a replacement machine, the estimates of future cash flows (inflows from expense savings, and outflows for preventive and periodic maintenance) can be made relatively easily. When the project involves an investment in a new product or a major capacity expansion, the most important (and hardest) data to estimate are revenues. Most firms will require a **post-audit** of the project to determine whether or not the anticipated benefits are actually being realized. While it may be too late to affect a project already completed, knowledge about past estimating errors should permit analysts to improve future estimates.

Cash flows far in the future.   Given the challenges of estimating, many capital budgeting analysts will not consider probable cash flows that are expected to occur more than 10 years in the future. In essence, their position is that if the project will not have a satisfactory return considering the cash flows in the first 10 years, then the project is too risky to accept even if later cash flows will give it a satisfactory rate of return. For example, the present value of $100 to be received in 11 years, at a discount rate of 20 percent, is $13.46, so far-distant cash flows will not add significantly to the total present value of cash flows.

Timing of cash flows within the year.   The present value factors in Tables 6-4 and 6-5 assume that all of the cash flows each year are received at the end of the year. It is more likely that the cash flows will be received fairly evenly throughout the year; and although present value can be calculated using that assumption, it is not uncommon for the end-of-the-year assumption to be used because it results in a slightly lower, more conservative present value amount.

Investment made over a period of time.   Capital expenditure projects involving new products, new plants, and capacity expansion usually require expenditures to be made over a period of time. For example, payments are usually made to a building contractor every month during construction, and for a major project, construction may extend over several years. When this is going to occur, the investment amount used in the present value analysis should be determined as of the point at which the project is expected to be put into service. This means that interest on cash disbursements made during the construction or preoperating period should be considered, so the investment amount will include the time value of money invested during that period.

Income tax effect of cash flows from the project.   The cash flows identified with a proposed capital expenditure should include all of the associated inflows and outflows, including income taxes. The model for making this calculation is essentially the same as that used in the statement of cash flows to determine cash generated from operating activities. For example, assume that a capital expenditure proposal for a new product reflects the following makeup of operating income, income taxes, and net income for the first year the product is sold:

Revenues	$240,000
Variable expenses	100,000
Contribution margin	$140,000
Direct fixed expenses:	
Requiring cash disbursements	85,000
Depreciation of equipment	20,000
Operating income	$ 35,000
Income taxes @ 40%	14,000
Net income	$ 21,000

To calculate the amount of cash flow from this product, it is necessary to add back the depreciation expense to net income. Remember that depreciation is a deduction for income tax purposes but is not a cash expenditure. Therefore, the cash flow during the first year for this new product would be:

Net income	$21,000
Add: Depreciation expense	20,000
Cash flow from the product	$41,000

In addition, any other differences between accrual basis earnings and cash flows would be recognized when using the NPV and IRR methods.

Working capital investment.   Capital expenditure proposals that involve new products or capacity expansion will usually require a working capital increase because accounts receivable and inventories will increase. The working capital increase required is treated as additional investment (i.e., it is a cash outflow at the beginning of the project or later). If the new product or capacity expansion has a definite life, the investment in working capital will be recovered after the product is discontinued or the expansion is reversed. The expected recovery of the working capital investment should be treated as a cash inflow.

Least cost projects.   Not all capital expenditures are made to reduce costs or increase revenues. Some expenditures required by law—environmental controls, for example—will increase operating costs. (The benefit may include the avoidance of a fine.) Alternative expenditures in this category should also be evaluated using present value analysis; however, instead of seeking a positive NPV or IRR, the objective is to have the least negative result. Even though the present value ratio will be less than 1.0, the most desirable alternative is still the one with the highest present value ratio.

LO 9

Calculate the payback period of a capital expenditure project.

Payback.   The **payback method** to evaluate proposed capital expenditures answers this question: How many years will it take to recover the amount of the investment? The answer to this question is determined by adding up the cash flows (beginning with the first year) until the total cash flows equal the investment and then counting the number of years of cash flow required. For example, using the data from Exhibit 16-3, for a machine costing $100,000, the projected annual and cumulative cash flows were:

Year	Cash Flow	Cumulative Cash Flow
2014 (1st year)	$26,000	$ 26,000
2015 (2nd year)	27,000	53,000
2016 (3rd year)	31,000	84,000
2017 (4th year)	35,000	119,000
2018 (5th year)	44,000	163,000

The investment will be recovered during the fourth year after $16,000 of that year's $35,000 has been realized. Expressed as a decimal, 16/35 is 0.46, so the project's payback period would be expressed as 3.46 years.

The obvious advantage of the payback method is its simplicity. Present value analysis is confusing to some people, but anyone can understand payback period. There are two major disadvantages to the payback method. First, it does not consider the time value of money, and this is a serious flaw. Second, as traditionally used, the payback method does not consider cash flows that continue after the investment has been recovered. Thus, a project having a payback period of three years and no subsequent cash flows would appear to be more desirable than a project that has a payback period of four years and cash flows that continue for five more years.

In spite of its flaws, the payback method is used by many firms, especially in connection with equipment replacement decisions. The widespread use of the payback method is due to the clarity of its meaning and the fact that in a rapidly changing technological environment, the speed with which an investment is recovered is critical. Many firms require early and significant cash flows from an investment in new plant and equipment because they don't have the capacity to finance their activities while waiting for the payoff from an investment to begin. Some analysts report the payback

I. **Assumption:**
Same as in Exhibit 16-3.

II. **Calculation:**

$$\frac{\text{Accounting}}{\text{rate of return}} = \frac{\text{Operating income}}{\text{Average investment}}$$

$$= \frac{\text{Savings} - \text{Depreciation expense}}{\text{Average investment}}$$

For 2014:

$$= \frac{26,000 - 18,800^*}{(100,000 + 81,200^{\dagger})/2}$$

$$= \frac{7,200}{90,600}$$

$$= 7.9\%$$

*Straight-line depreciation expense:

(Cost − Salvage value)/Estimated life
(100,000 − 6,000)/5 years = 18,800

†Net book value at end of 2014:

Cost − Accumulated depreciation
100,000 − 18,800 = 81,200

period along with NPV (or present value ratio) and IRR just to answer the question "How long until the investment is recovered?"

Accounting rate of return.   The **accounting rate of return method** focuses on the impact of the investment project on the financial statements. Accounting operating income (or net income) is related to the effect of the investment on the balance sheet. This is done on a year-by-year basis. The calculation for 2014, using data from Exhibit 16-3, is illustrated in Exhibit 16-5.

As explained with the payback method, a serious flaw of the accounting rate of return approach is that the time value of money is not considered. Some financial managers will make the accounting rate of return calculation not for investment evaluation purposes but to anticipate the effect that the investment will have on the financial statements. Large start-up costs for a new product line or new production facility may adversely affect reported results for a year or two. Management should be aware of this and should put stockholders on notice in advance to minimize the impact of the start-up costs on the market price of the firm's common stock.

LO 10
Calculate the accounting rate of return of a project and explain how it can be used most appropriately.

11. What does it mean to state that both the payback method and the accounting rate of return method are flawed because they do not recognize the time value of money?

What Does It Mean?
Answer on page 662

The Investment Decision

As is the case with virtually every management decision, both quantitative and qualitative factors are considered. After the results of the quantitative models just illustrated have been obtained, the project with the highest NPV or IRR may not be selected. Overriding qualitative factors could include the following:

- Commitment to a segment of the business that requires capital investment to achieve or regain competitiveness even though that segment does not have as great an ROI as others.
- Regulations that mandate investment to meet safety, environmental, or access requirements. Fines and other enforcement incentives aside, management's citizenship goals for the organization may result in a high priority for these investments.
- Technological developments within the industry may require new facilities to maintain customers or market share at the cost of lower ROI for a period of time.
- The organization may have limited resources to invest in capital projects, and as a result of the capital rationing process, less ambitious, lower-ROI projects may be approved instead of large-scale, higher-ROI projects for which resources cannot be obtained.

In addition to considering issues such as these, management's judgments about the accuracy of the estimates used in the capital budgeting model may result in the selection of projects for which the estimates are believed to be more accurate.

The important point to be remembered here is that although the use of appropriate quantitative models can significantly improve the management decision-making process, most decisions are significantly influenced by top management's values and experiences—qualitative factors. Whether the decision involves the use of time value of money calculations, cost behavior pattern information, analysis of variances, or other applications you have learned, all important managerial decisions involve uncertainty and require the use of judgment. This is one reason top managers receive top salaries—their jobs are at risk if they make the wrong decisions.

Integration of the Capital Budget with Operating Budgets

Several aspects of the capital budget interact with the development of the operating budget. Contribution margin increases and cost savings from anticipated capital expenditure projects must be built into the expenditure and income statement budgets. Cash disbursements for capital projects must be included in the cash budget. The impact of capital expenditures on the balance sheet forecast must also be considered. Most important, you should understand that capital budgeting expenditures impact the level at which the firm will be able to operate in future years. Investments in equipment, new plant facilities, and other long-term operational assets are necessary to support the firm's growth objectives. Thus, the development of the capital budget is an integral part of the overall budgeting and strategic planning process. To learn how Microsoft Excel provides financial functions for capital budgeting techniques, see Business in Practice—Internal Rate of Return Using Microsoft Excel.

---

12. What does it mean to integrate the capital budget into the operating budget?

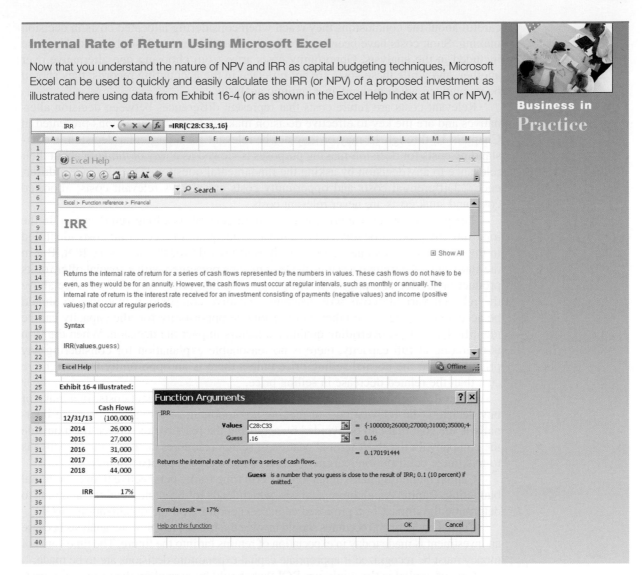

Internal Rate of Return Using Microsoft Excel

Now that you understand the nature of NPV and IRR as capital budgeting techniques, Microsoft Excel can be used to quickly and easily calculate the IRR (or NPV) of a proposed investment as illustrated here using data from Exhibit 16-4 (or as shown in the Excel Help Index at IRR or NPV).

Demonstration Problem

Visit the text website at www.mhhe.com/marshall10e to view a demonstration problem for this chapter.

Summary

Important cost classifications for analyzing decision alternatives include differential costs, allocated costs, sunk costs, and opportunity costs. Differential costs are those costs that differ between alternatives and must be considered in the analysis. Sometimes costs are allocated for analytical purposes; but if the allocation is made on an arbitrary basis rather than by recognizing causal factors, users of the data must be very careful about the conclusions they reach when considering allocated costs in decision making. Sunk costs have been incurred and cannot be reversed, so they should not be included in the analysis. Opportunity costs arise from choosing one alternative over another, and while these costs are not reflected in the accounting records, they should be recognized when making an economic analysis.

Relevant costs are future costs that represent differences between decision alternatives and are the key to effective decision making. Cost classifications presented in Chapters 12 through 15 may or may not be relevant for a particular decision. Understanding costs for decision-making purposes is viewed as a *way of thinking* about their relevance to any decision by asking the fundamental question "Does it make a difference?" Differential costs and opportunity costs are always relevant costs; allocated costs and sunk costs are never relevant costs.

The product or service pricing decision, in general, is a long-run decision. In the long run, the product or service price must be adequate to recover all costs identified in the organization's value chain, as well as to provide for the necessary ROI. But in the short run, on certain occasions the firm may be presented with a special offer for its product or service at a price below the normal selling price. Any offered price above the relevant variable costs will generate a positive contribution margin and should be accepted as long as no other more profitable opportunity for idle capacity can be identified, or unless overriding qualitative factors impact the decision. When the firm is operating at full capacity, there is no reasonable explanation for considering any price less than the normal selling price unless there is an opportunity to avoid more cost than the related decrease in selling price.

Other decision-making situations illustrate the use of relevant costs. In a make or buy decision, the relevant cost of making a component or providing a service internally is the cost that can be avoided by acquiring the resource or service from outside the company. In the short-term allocation of scarce resources decision, the objective is to maximize contribution margin in terms of the scarce capacity resource.

Capital budgeting has a much longer-term time frame perspective than operational budgeting. Capital expenditure analysis, which leads to the capital budget, attempts to determine the impact of a proposed capital expenditure on the organization's ROI.

Capital budgeting procedures should involve the use of present value analysis because an investment is made today in expectation of returns far into the future. The time value of money must be recognized if appropriate capital expenditure decisions are to be made.

Cost of capital is the minimum ROI that should be earned on the proposed investment. The risk associated with the proposal will affect the cost of capital, or desired ROI, used to evaluate the investment.

Net present value and internal rate of return are two investment analysis methods that recognize the time value of money. The net present value approach uses the cost of capital as the discount rate to calculate a difference between the present value of future cash flows from the investment and the amount invested. If the net present value is zero or positive, the proposed investment's ROI is equal to or greater than the cost of capital, and the investment is an appropriate one to make. The present value ratio, or profitability index, provides a means of ranking alternative proposals. The internal rate of return approach solves for the proposal's ROI, which is then compared to the cost of capital. The investment is an appropriate one to make if the ROI of the proposed investment equals or exceeds the cost of capital.

Some analytical considerations related to capital budgeting include estimating accuracy, the timing of cash flows within a year, and investments made over a period of time. Many firms require a postaudit of a capital project to evaluate the estimates made in the initial analysis. Some projects will require an increase in working capital, which is considered part of the investment.

Payback and accounting rate of return are two investment analysis methods that do not recognize the time value of money and are thus inappropriate analytical techniques. Nevertheless, many analysts and managers use the results of these methods along with the results of the NPV and IRR methods.

In addition to considering the results of the various quantitative models used to evaluate investment proposals, management also identifies and considers qualitative factors when deciding whether or not to proceed with an investment. These qualitative factors are frequently more significant than the quantitative model results.

The capital budget is integrated into the operating budget. Production capacity, depreciation expense, and cash outflows for purchases of new plant and equipment are directly affected by the capital budget.

Key Terms and Concepts

accounting rate of return method (p. 657) A capital budgeting technique that calculates the rate of return on the investment based on the impact of the investment on the financial statements.

allocated cost (p. 636) A cost that has been assigned to a product or activity using some sort of systematic process.

capital budgeting (p. 635) The process of analyzing proposed investments in plant and equipment and other long-lived assets.

cash flows (p. 651) In capital budgeting, the cash receipts and disbursements associated with a capital expenditure over its life.

cost of capital (p. 650) The ROI that must be earned to permit the firm to meet its interest obligations and provide the owners their expected return; the discount rate used in the present value calculations of capital budgeting.

differential cost (p. 636) A cost that will differ based on the selection of an alternative activity.

full capacity (p. 640) The operating condition when all available production resources are being utilized.

idle capacity (p. 640) The operating condition when some available production resources are not being utilized.

internal rate of return (IRR) method (p. 653) A capital budgeting technique that solves for the time-adjusted rate of return on an investment over its life.

interpolating (p. 653) A mathematical term that describes the process of interpreting and relating two factors from a (present value) table to approximate a third factor not shown in the table.

net present value (NPV) method (p. 653) A capital budgeting technique that uses a given cost of capital to relate the present value of the returns from an investment to the present value of the investment.

opportunity cost (p. 637) An economic concept relating to income forgone because an opportunity to earn income was not pursued.

outsourcing (p. 643) The acquisition of resources or services from outside the organization as opposed to producing those resources or services internally.

payback method (p. 656) A capital budgeting technique that calculates the length of time for the cash flows from an investment to equal the investment.

postaudit (p. 654) The process of comparing the assumptions used in a capital project analysis with the actual results of the investment.

present value ratio (p. 652)   The ratio of the present value of the cash flows from an investment to the investment. See *profitability index*.

profitability index (p. 652)   The ratio of the present value of the cash flows from an investment to the investment; used for ranking proposed capital expenditures by profitability.

relevant cost (p. 637)   A cost classification used in analyzing costs of decision alternatives; costs are relevant when they represent future differences between the alternatives.

sunk cost (p. 636)   A cost that has been incurred and that cannot be unincurred, or reversed, by some future action.

target costing (p. 639)   A cost management technique in which the firm determines the required cost for a product or service to earn a desired profit when the selling price is determined by the marketplace.

ANSWERS TO What Does It Mean?

1. It means that the cost has been incurred, and nothing will happen to affect that cost.

2. It means that the cost is a future cost that will represent a difference between the decision alternatives, and the cost must be included in the analysis.

3. It means that as long as there is no other more profitable use of the idle capacity, any price offered that exceeds the relevant costs and provides a positive contribution margin should be accepted in the short run because it will increase current operating income.

4. It means that it is a relevant cost of making the product or component part internally because it is a cost that would not be incurred if it were purchased from outside the company.

5. It means that these expenses are irrelevant for the decision to continue or discontinue a segment of the organization because they are arbitrarily allocated to the segments—these common corporate expenses will not decrease if a segment is eliminated.

6. It means that there is a plan for making capital expenditures (i.e., investments in new plant and equipment).

7. It means that because expenditures and/or benefits are likely to extend over a period of several years, it is appropriate to recognize the time value of money when determining the economic viability of an investment.

8. It means that the present value of the future cash flows expected from the investment, discounted at an appropriate interest rate (i.e., the cost of capital), is compared to the present value of the investment—also discounted at the cost of capital if necessary because the investment is made over several periods.

9. It means that the present value of the future inflows is greater than the present value of the investment, and if this actually occurs, the rate of return on the investment will be greater than the cost of capital.

10. It means that with the net present value technique, the discount rate (cost of capital) is given so that only one set of calculations needs to be made; but with the internal rate of return method, the discount rate (actual rate of return) must be solved for, sometimes on a trial-and-error basis.

11. It means that they ignore the vital economic fact that money does have value over time and that the pattern of returns from an investment has a major effect on its real rate of return.

12. It means that the additional productive capacity of new plant and equipment will affect activity and expense levels planned in the operating budget.

Self-Study Material

Matching Following are a number of key terms and concepts introduced in the chapter, along with a list of corresponding definitions. Match the appropriate letter for the key term or concept to each definition provided (items 1–15). Note that not all key terms and concepts will be used. Answers are provided at the end of this chapter.

a.	Differential cost	j.	Present value
b.	Allocated cost	k.	Cost of capital
c.	Sunk cost	l.	Net present value (NPV)
d.	Opportunity cost	m.	Internal rate of return (IRR)
e.	Relevant cost	n.	Payback method
f.	Full capacity	o.	Accounting rate of return
g.	Idle capacity	p.	Profitability index
h.	Capital budgeting	q.	Postaudit
i.	Cash flow	r.	Outsourcing

_____ **1.** The level of ROI that must be earned to permit the firm to meet its interest obligations and provide the owners their expected return; the discount rate used in the present value calculations of capital budgeting.

_____ **2.** A cost that has been incurred and that cannot be unincurred, or reversed, by some future action.

_____ **3.** A capital budgeting technique that calculates the length of time for the cash flows from an investment to equal the investment.

_____ **4.** The process of comparing the assumptions used in a capital budgeting analysis with the actual results of the investment.

_____ **5.** The operating condition when some available production resources are not being utilized.

_____ **6.** The process of analyzing proposed investments in plant and equipment and other long-lived assets.

_____ **7.** An economic concept relating to income forgone because an alternative to earn income was not pursued.

_____ **8.** A capital budgeting technique that solves for the time-adjusted rate of return on an investment over its life.

_____ **9.** The ratio of the present value of cash flows to the investment; used to rank proposed capital expenditures by profitability.

_____**10.** The acquisition of resources or services from outside the organization as opposed to producing those resources or services internally.

_____**11.** A capital budgeting technique that calculates the rate of return on the investment based on the financial statement impacts of the investment.

_____**12.** A cost that has been assigned to a product or activity using some sort of systematic process.

_____**13.** A cost that will differ based on the selection of an alternative activity.

_____**14.** A capital budgeting technique that relates the present value of the returns (cash inflows) from an investment to the present value of the cost (cash outflows) of the investment, given a cost of capital.

_____**15.** A cost classification used in analyzing costs of decision alternatives.

Multiple Choice For each of the following questions, circle the best response. Answers are provided at the end of this chapter.

1. A sunk cost is a cost that

  a. is always relevant in decision making.

  b. can be relevant in decision making depending on the circumstances.

  c. is never relevant in decision making.

  d. can be recovered in the future.

  e. none of the above.

2. An opportunity cost is

  a. income forgone because an opportunity to earn income was not pursued.

  b. never relevant in decision making.

  c. a cost that cannot be avoided.

  d. a cost that has been incurred and that cannot be reversed by some future action.

  e. present in every decision-making situation.

3. In considering whether to accept a special order at a price that is less than the normal selling price of the product when the additional sales will use present idle capacity, which of the following costs will *not* be relevant?

  a. Fixed manufacturing overhead that can be avoided.

  b. Direct materials.

  c. Variable overhead.

  d. Depreciation of the manufacturing plant.

  e. Direct labor.

4. In a make or buy decision, management should consider all of the following *except*

  a. opportunity costs of making internally.

  b. costs that are avoidable by buying outside the company.

  c. costs common to making internally or buying outside the company.

  d. other qualitative factors.

5. Chuck's investment proposal would be inferior to Edna's proposal if it was expected to have a

  a. longer payback period.

  b. higher accounting rate of return.

  c. higher internal rate of return.

  d. higher profitability index.

  e. larger net present value.

6. The payback method attempts to measure

  a. how soon an investment is recovered.

  b. the net cash inflow from an investment.

  c. the estimated life of an investment.

  d. the ROI of an investment.

7. Kafka, Inc., estimates that it can generate $4,600 per year in additional cash inflows for the next five years if it modernizes its equipment at a cost of $15,000. The company's minimum desired rate of return is 10%. Using the present value factors in your text (Tables 6-4 and 6-5), the net present value of the project is (rounded)

  a. $(12,562).

  b. $(2,438).

  c. $2,438.

  d. $8,000.

  e. $23,000.

8. Using the present value factors in your text, the estimated annual cash inflow from the following investment proposal would be (rounded)

Investment cost	$13,000
Net present value	$ 3,300
Life of the project	6 years
Cost of capital	14%

  a. $3,800.

  b. $3,900.

  c. $4,000.

  d. $4,100.

  e. $4,200.

Use the following data for Questions 9 and 10.

Antonio, Inc., has invested in new production equipment at a cost of $24,000. The equipment has an estimated useful life of eight years. The estimated annual sales and operating expense related to the equipment are as follows:

Annual sales	$44,000
Labor costs	(36,000)
Depreciation of equipment.	(3,000)
Operating income	$ 5,000
Income taxes (40%)	(2,000)
Net income	$ 3,000

9. The payback period of the investment in equipment is approximately

  a. 3.0 years.

  b. 4.0 years.

  c. 4.8 years.

  d. 8.0 years.

10. The accounting rate of return is approximately
   a. 12.5%.
   b. 20.8%.
   c. 25.0%.
   d. 33.3%.

connect
|ACCOUNTING **Mini-Exercises**

All applicable Mini-Exercises are available with McGraw-Hill's *Connect*™ *Accounting*.

Mini-Exercise 16.1

LO 2, 3

Sell or process further? Lakeside, Inc., produces a product that currently sells for $36 per unit. Current production costs per unit include direct materials, $10; direct labor, $12; variable overhead, $5; and fixed overhead, $5. Product engineering has determined that certain production changes could refine the product quality and functionality. These new production changes would increase material and labor costs by 20% per unit.

Required:

If Lakeside could sell the refined version of its product for $40 per unit, should it be processed further?

_____

Mini-Exercise 16.2

LO 2, 3

Accept special sales order? In addition to the product cost information for Lakeside, Inc., in Mini-Exercise 16.1, Lakeside has received an offer from a nonprofit organization to buy 5,000 units at $30 per unit. Lakeside currently has unused production capacity.

Required:

Should Lakeside accept this special sales order?

_____

Mini-Exercise 16.3

LO 2, 3

The make or buy decision In addition to the product cost information for Lakeside, Inc., in Mini-Exercise 16.1, product engineering has determined that a certain part of the product conversion process could be outsourced. Raw material costs would not be affected, but direct labor and variable overhead costs would be reduced by 30%. No other opportunity is currently feasible for unused production capacity.

Required:

Should Lakeside outsource part of the conversion process at a cost of $4 per unit?

_____

Mini-Exercise 16.4

LO 7

Net present value Lakeside, Inc., is considering replacing old production equipment with state-of-the-art technology that will allow production cost savings of $10,000 per month. The new equipment will have a five-year life and cost $450,000, with an estimated salvage value of $30,000. Lakeside's cost of capital is 10%.

Required:

Calculate the net present value of the new production equipment.

_____

Mini-Exercise 16.5

LO 7

Net present ratio and IRR Use the information presented for Lakeside, Inc., in Mini-Exercise 16.4 and your calculation of the net present value of the new production equipment.

Required:

Calculate the present value ratio of the new production equipment, and comment on the internal rate of return of this investment relative to the cost of capital.

Net present ratio and IRR Use the information presented for Lakeside, Inc., in Mini-Exercise 16.4.

Mini-Exercise 16.6
LO 9, 10

Required:

Calculate the payback period and the accounting rate of return for the new production equipment.

Exercises

All applicable Exercises are available with McGraw-Hill's *Connect™ Accounting.*

Application of cost terminology Assume that you have decided to drive your car to Florida for the spring break. A classmate learns about your plans and asks about riding along with you. Explain how you would apply each of the following cost concepts to the task of determining how much, if any, cost you would take into consideration for the purposes of setting a price to be charged for taking the classmate with you.

Exercise 16.7
LO 1

a. Differential cost.
b. Allocated cost.
c. Sunk cost.
d. Opportunity cost.

Give examples of various costs Attending college involves incurring many costs. Give an example of a college cost that could be assigned to each of the following classifications. Explain your reason for assigning each cost to the classification.

Exercise 16.8
LO 1

a. Sunk cost.
b. Discretionary cost.
c. Committed cost.
d. Opportunity cost.
e. Differential cost.
f. Allocated cost.

Sell or process further? National Chemical Company manufactures a chemical compound that is sold for $58 per gallon. A new variant of the chemical has been discovered, and if the basic compound were processed into the new variant, the selling price would be $72 per gallon. National expects the market for the new compound variant to be 5,600 gallons initially and determines that processing costs to refine the basic compound into the new variant would be $72,800.

Exercise 16.9
LO 2, 3

Required:

Should National produce the new compound variant? Explain your answer.

Sell or process further? ADP Mining Company mines an iron ore called Alpha. During the month of August, 175,000 tons of Alpha were mined and processed at a

Exercise 16.10
LO 2, 3

cost of $525,000. As the Alpha ore is mined, it is processed into Delta and Pi, where 60% of the Alpha output becomes Delta and 40% becomes Pi. Each product can be sold as is or processed into the refined products Super Delta and Precision Pi. Selling prices for these products are:

	Delta	Super Delta	Pi	Precision Pi
Selling price	$12/ton	$18/ton	$25/ton	$35/ton

Processing costs to refine Delta into Super Delta are $840,000; processing costs to refine Pi into Precision Pi are $560,000.

Required:

a. Should Delta and Pi be sold as is or refined into Super Delta and Precision Pi?

b. Identify any costs in the problem that are not relevant to this decision.

c. What is the maximum profit that ADP Mining Company can expect to earn from the production of the 175,000 tons of Alpha?

Exercise 16.11

LO 2, 3

Accept special sales order? Circuit Masters, Inc. (CMI), is presently operating at 80% of capacity and manufacturing 120,000 units of a patented electronic component. The cost structure of the component is as follows:

Raw materials	$ 6.00 per unit
Direct labor	6.00 per unit
Variable overhead	8.00 per unit
Fixed overhead	$480,000 per year

An Italian firm has offered to purchase 20,000 of the components at a price of $24 per unit, FOB CMI's plant. The normal selling price is $32 per component. This special order will not affect any of CMI's "normal" business. Management calculated that the cost per component is $24, so it is reluctant to accept this special order.

Required:

a. Show how management came up with a cost of $24 per unit for this component.

b. Evaluate this cost calculation. Explain why it is or is not appropriate.

c. Should the offer from the Italian firm be accepted? Why or why not?

Exercise 16.12

LO 2, 3

Accept special sales order? SureLock Manufacturing Co. makes and sells several models of locks. The cost records for the ZForce lock show that manufacturing costs total $19.62 per lock. An analysis of this amount indicates that $11.90 of the total cost has a variable cost behavior pattern, and the remainder is an allocation of fixed manufacturing overhead. The normal selling price of this model is $29.00 per lock. A chain store has offered to buy 14,000 ZForce locks from SureLock at a price of $15.75 each to sell in a market that would not compete with SureLock's regular business. SureLock has manufacturing capacity available and could make these locks without incurring additional fixed manufacturing overhead.

Required:

a. Calculate the effect on SureLock's operating income of accepting the order from the chain store.

b. If SureLock's costs had not been classified by cost behavior pattern, is it likely that a correct special order analysis would have been made? Explain your answer.

c. Identify the key qualitative factors that SureLock managers should consider with respect to this special order decision.

Target costing Canton Company, a manufacturer of digital cameras, is considering entry into the digital binocular market. Canton Company currently does not produce binoculars of any style, so this venture would require a careful analysis of relevant manufacturing costs to correctly assess its ability to compete. The market price for this binocular style is well established at $49 per unit. Canton has enough square footage in its plant to accommodate the new production line, although several pieces of new equipment would be required; their estimated cost is $2,500,000. Canton requires a minimum ROI of 10% on any product line investment and estimates that if it enters this market with its digital binocular product at the prevailing market price, it is confident of its ability to sell 20,000 units each year.

Exercise 16.13
LO 2, 3

Required:

a. Describe, in general terms, any costs that Canton Company would consider relevant to the decision of entering the digital binocular market.

b. Calculate the target cost per unit for entry into the digital binocular market.

Target costing Rainbow Cruises operates a week-long cruise tour through the Hawaiian Islands. Passengers currently pay $2,700 for a two-person cabin, which is an all-inclusive price that includes food, beverages, and entertainment. The current cost to Rainbow per two-person cabin is $2,160 for the week-long cruise, and at this cost, Rainbow is able to earn the minimum profit margin needed to operate the business. Rainbow competes with two other cruise lines and, to date, $2,700 has been the prevailing market price for the week-long cruises. Each cruise line provides exactly the same services to their passengers, but recently one of Rainbow's competitors found a way to permanently lower its price to $2,250 per two-person cabin.

Exercise 16.14
LO 2, 3

Required:

a. At a new market price of $2,250 per two-person cabin, calculate the target cost that will allow Rainbow to earn the same profit margin percentage it currently earns.

b. Calculate the target cost reduction that Rainbow must achieve if it expects to remain competitive.

c. Describe several cost reduction initiatives that Rainbow might explore to achieve its target cost reduction requirements.

The make or buy decision Eldon Engine, Inc., produces engines for the watercraft industry. An outside manufacturer has offered to supply several component parts used in the engine assemblies, which are currently being produced by Eldon. The supplier will charge Eldon $620 per engine for the set of parts. Eldon's current costs for those part sets are direct materials, $360; direct labor, $180; and manufacturing overhead applied at 100% of direct labor. Variable manufacturing overhead is considered to be 30% of the total, and fixed overhead will not change if the part sets are acquired from the outside supplier.

Exercise 16.15
LO 2, 3

Required:

Should Eldon Engine, Inc., continue to make the part sets or accept the offer to purchase them for $620?

Exercise 16.16

LO 2, 3

The make or buy decision Redbud Company uses a certain part in its manufacturing process that it buys from an outside supplier for $44 per part plus another $6 for shipping and other purchasing-related costs. The company will need 10,000 of these parts in the next year and is considering making the part internally. After performing a capacity analysis, Redbud determined that it has sufficient unused capacity to manufacture the 10,000 parts but would need to hire a manager at an annual salary of $40,000 to oversee this production activity. Estimated production costs are determined to be:

Direct material	$28
Direct labor	12
Variable overhead	6
Fixed overhead (includes manager at $4 per unit)	10
Total unit cost	$56

Required:

a. Identify the relevant costs to make this part internally.

b. Should Redbud produce the part or continue to buy it from the outside supplier?

c. What other factors are important to this decision?

Exercise 16.17

LO 2, 3

The product mix decision Product S has a contribution margin of $150 per unit and requires three hours of machine time. Product T requires four hours of machine time and provides $200 of contribution margin per unit.

Required:

If the capacity of machine time is limited to 600 hours and only one product can be produced, what is the maximum amount of contribution that could be generated?

Exercise 16.18

LO 2, 3

The product mix decision ABC Company produces product X, product Y, and product Z. All three products require processing on specialized finishing machines. The capacity of these machines is 1,200 hours per month. ABC Company wishes to determine the product mix that should be achieved to meet the high demand for each product and provide the maximum profit. Following is information about each product:

	Product X	**Product Y**	**Product Z**
Selling price	$100	$80	$25
Variable costs	70	40	20
Machine time per unit	3 hours	2 hours	1 hour
Monthly demand (units)	300	200	500

Required:

Determine how the 1,200 hours of machine time should be allocated to the three products to provide the most profitable product mix.

Review problem—time value of money applications An investor has asked for your help with the following time value of money applications. Use the appropriate factors from Table 6-4 or Table 6-5 to answer the following questions.

Exercise 16.19

Required:

a. What is the present value of $50,000 to be received in five years using a discount rate of 8%?

b. How much should be invested today at a return on investment of 8% compounded annually to have $50,000 in five years?

c. If the return on investment was greater than 8% compounded annually, would the amount to be invested today to have $50,000 in five years be more or less than the answer to part **b**? Explain your answer.

Review problem—time value of money applications Use the appropriate factors from Table 6-4 or Table 6-5 to answer the following questions.

Exercise 16.20

Required:

a. Spencer Co.'s common stock is expected to have a dividend of $10 per share for each of the next eight years, and it is estimated that the market value per share will be $92 at the end of eight years. If an investor requires a return on investment of 10%, what is the maximum price the investor would be willing to pay for a share of Spencer Co. common stock today?

b. Mario bought a bond with a face amount of $1,000, a stated interest rate of 7%, and a maturity date 10 years in the future for $985. The bond pays interest on an annual basis. Three years have gone by and the market interest rate is now 6%. What is the market value of the bond today?

c. Alexis purchased a U.S. Series EE savings bond for $75, and six years later received $106.38 when the bond was redeemed. What average annual return on investment did Alexis earn over the six years?

Present value analysis—effects of estimation errors Capital budgeting analysis involves the use of many estimates.

Exercise 16.21
LO 7

Required:

For each of the following estimation errors, state whether the net present value of the project will be too high or too low:

a. The investment is too high.

b. The cost of capital is too low.

c. The cash flows from the project are too high.

d. The number of years over which the project will generate cash flows is too low.

Present value analysis—cost of capital National Leasing is evaluating the cost of capital to use in its capital budgeting process. Over the recent past, the company has averaged a return on equity of 12% and a return on investment of 9%. The company can currently borrow short-term money for 6%.

Exercise 16.22
LO 6

Required:

a. Which of the preceding rates is most relevant to deciding the cost of capital to use? Explain your answer.

b. Without prejudice to your answer to part **a**, explain why the company might choose to use a cost of capital of 13% to evaluate capital expenditure opportunities.

Exercise 16.23
LO 7

Calculate NPV—compare to IRR South Bay Manufacturing Ltd. is considering the investment of $230,000 in a new machine. The machine will generate cash flow of $40,000 per year for each year of its eight-year life and will have a salvage value of $26,000 at the end of its life. The company's cost of capital is 10%.

Required:

a. Calculate the net present value of the proposed investment. (Ignore income taxes.)

b. What will the internal rate of return on this investment be relative to the cost of capital? Explain your answer.

Exercise 16.24
LO 7, 9

Calculate NPV—compare to IRR A task force of capital budgeting analysts at Morrison Ltd. collected the following data concerning the drilling and production of known petroleum reserves at an offshore location:

Investment in rigging equipment and related personnel costs required to pump the oil	$6,700,000
Net increase in inventory and receivables associated with the drilling and production of the reserves. Assume this investment will be recovered at the end of the project	1,200,000
Net cash inflow from operations for the expected life of the reserves, by year:	
2013	2,000,000
2014	3,600,000
2015	1,700,000
Salvage value of machinery and equipment at the end of the well's productive life	1,000,000
Cost of capital	8%

Required:

a. Calculate the net present value of the proposed investment in the drilling and production operation. Assume that the investment will be made at the beginning of 2013, and the net cash inflows from operations will be received in a lump sum at the end of each year. Ignore income taxes, and round answers to the nearest $1.

b. What will the internal rate of return on this investment be relative to the cost of capital? Explain your answer.

c. Differences between estimates made by the task force and actual results would have an effect on the actual rate of return on the project. Identify the significant estimates made by the task force. For each estimate, state the effect on the actual ROI if the estimate turns out to be less than the actual amount finally achieved.

Exercise 16.25
LO 6, 7, 9

Interpretation of present value analysis and payback The CarCare Garage is considering an investment in a new tune-up computer. The cost of the computer is $48,000. A cost analyst has calculated the discounted present value of the expected cash flows from the computer to be $52,650, based on the firm's cost of capital of 12%.

Required:

a. What is the expected return on investment of the machine, relative to 12%? Explain your answer.

b. The payback period of the investment in the machine is expected to be 4.25 years. How much weight should this measurement carry in the decision about whether or not to invest in the machine? Explain your answer.

Interpretation of present value analysis—calculate annual cash flow
Memorial Hospital is considering the acquisition of a new diagnostic scanning machine. The investment required to get the machine operational will be $2,466,840. The machine will be capable of performing 7,500 scanning procedures per year, but based on the experience of other hospitals, management estimates that the machine will be used at 80% of its capacity. The hospital's cost of capital is 12%; the machine has an estimated useful life of six years and no salvage value.

Exercise 16.26
LO 6, 7

Required:

a. Assuming a constant cash flow every year, calculate the annual net cash flow required from the scanner if the IRR of the investment is to equal 12%.
(Hint: The annual net cash flow requirement is an annuity.)

b. If the direct cash costs of operating the scanner equal 50% of the annual net cash flow requirement calculated in part **a,** what price should the hospital charge per scanning procedure in order to achieve a 12% ROI?

Problems

All applicable Problems are available with McGraw-Hill's *Connect™ Accounting*.

Relevant costs, special sales order—idle versus full capacity The Delmar Beverage Co. produces a premium root beer that is sold throughout its chain of restaurants in the Midwest. The company is currently producing 4,000 gallons of root beer per day, which represents 80% of its manufacturing capacity. The root beer is available to restaurant customers by the mug, in bottles, or packaged in six-packs to take home. The selling price of a gallon of root beer averages $10, and cost accounting records indicate the following manufacturing costs per gallon of root beer:

Problem 16.27
LO 2, 3

Raw materials	$3.20
Direct labor	1.60
Variable overhead	1.00
Fixed overhead	2.20
Total absorption cost	$8.00

In addition to the manufacturing costs just described, Delmar Beverage incurs an average cost of $0.50 per gallon to distribute the root beer to its restaurants.

SaveMore, Inc., a chain of grocery stores, is interested in selling the premium root beer in gallon jugs throughout its stores in the St. Louis area during holiday periods and has offered to purchase root beer from Delmar Beverage at a price of $7.70

per gallon. SaveMore believes it could sell 600 gallons per day. If Delmar Beverage agrees to sell root beer to SaveMore, it estimates the average distribution cost will be $0.70 per gallon.

Required:

a. Identify all the relevant costs that Delmar Beverage should consider in evaluating the special sales order from SaveMore.

b. How would Delmar Beverage's daily operating income be affected by the acceptance of this offer?

c. Assume that Delmar Beverage is currently producing 5,000 gallons of root beer daily. Repeat requirements **a** and **b**.

d. Explain why your answers are different when Delmar Beverage is producing 4,000 gallons per day versus 5,000 gallons per day.

Problem 16.28
LO 2, 3

Relevant costs, special sales order—idle versus full capacity Petro Motors, Inc. (PMI), produces small gasoline-powered motors for use in lawn mowers. The company has been growing steadily over the past five years and is operating at full capacity. PMI recently completed the addition of new plant and equipment at a cost of $6,000,000, thereby increasing its manufacturing capacity to 100,000 motors annually. The addition to plant and equipment will be depreciated on a straight-line basis over 10 years.

Sales of motors were 75,000 units prior to the completion of the additional capacity. Cost records indicated that manufacturing costs had totaled $76 per motor, of which $60 per motor was considered to be variable manufacturing costs. PMI has used the volume of activity at full capacity as the basis for applying fixed manufacturing overhead. The normal selling price is $100 per motor, and PMI pays a 10% commission on the sale of its motors.

LawnPro.com offered to purchase 20,000 motors at a price of $75 per unit to test the viability of distributing lawn mower replacement motors through its website. PMI would be expected to produce the motors, store them in its warehouse, and ship individual motors to LawnPro.com customers. As orders are placed directly through the LawnPro.com website, they would be forwarded instantly to PMI. No commissions will be paid on this special sales order, and freight charges will be paid by the customer purchasing a motor.

Required:

a. Calculate the cost per motor, for cost accounting purposes, after completion of the additional plant capacity.

b. Identify all the relevant costs that PMI should consider in evaluating the special sales order from LawnPro.com.

c. Should the offer from LawnPro.com be accepted? Why or why not?

d. If relevant cost analysis was not considered, is it likely that a correct special order analysis would have been made? Explain your answer.

e. Identify the key qualitative factors that PMI management should consider with respect to this special order.

f. Assume that with the additional plant capacity, sales of motors in PMI's regular market are expected to increase by 20% in the coming 12 months. Identify all the relevant costs that PMI should consider in evaluating the special sales order from LawnPro.com. Why is your answer different than in requirement **b**?

g. Assume that sales of motors in PMI's regular market are expected to increase by 20% in the coming 12 months. Should the offer from LawnPro.com be accepted? Why or why not?

Continue or discontinue a segment? MMV Inc., opened a chain of businesses several years ago that provide quick oil changes and other minor services in conjunction with a convenience operation consisting of a soup, sandwich, and snack bar. The strategy was that as customers brought autos in for oil changes, they would likely use the convenience operation to purchase a sandwich, bowl of soup, beverage, or some other snack while they were waiting for the work to be completed on their autos. The oil change operation occupies 75% of the facility and includes three service bays. The soup, sandwich, and snack bar occupies the remaining 25%. A general manager is responsible for the entire operation, but each segment also has a manager responsible for its individual operation.

Recently, the following annual operating information for the soup, sandwich, and snack bar at one of MMV's locations caught the general manager's attention. Sales for the year were $250,000, and cost of sales (food, beverages, and snack items) are 50% of sales revenue. Operating expense information for the convenience operation follows:

Problem 16.29
LO 2, 3

Food service items (spoons, napkins, etc.)	$ 3,600
Utilities	7,200
Wages for part-time employees	48,000
Convenience operation manager's salary	60,000
General manager's salary	18,000
Advertising	20,000
Insurance	12,000
Property taxes	3,000
Food equipment depreciation	5,000
Building depreciation	15,000

While investigating these operating expenses, MMV Inc. determines the following:

- Utilities are allocated to each segment based on square footage; however, 50% of the amount allocated to the soup, sandwich, and snack bar results from operating the food equipment.
- The general manager's salary is allocated between the segments based on estimated time spent with each operation. It is determined that 20% of the general manager's time is spent with the convenience operation.
- Advertising is allocated to each segment equally but could be reduced by $3,000 if MMV decided to advertise only the auto services.
- Insurance is allocated to each segment based on square footage, but only 25% of the amount allocated to the soup, sandwich, and snack bar results directly from its operation.
- Property taxes and building depreciation are allocated to each segment based on square footage.

Required:

a. From the preceding information, calculate the operating income from the soup, sandwich, and snack bar operation that has caught the general manager's attention.

b. Identify whether each of these operating expenses is relevant to the decision of discontinuing the soup, sandwich, and snack bar operation.

c. If MMV Inc. discontinues the soup, sandwich, and snack bar operation, how much will operating income increase or decrease for this location?

d. Should MMV continue or discontinue the soup, sandwich, and snack bar operation at this location? Consider possible opportunities for the use of this space in your response.

Problem 16.30
LO 2, 3

Continue or discontinue a segment? The segmented income statement for XYZ Company for the year ended December 31, 2013, follows:

	Total Company	Product A	Product B	Product C
XYZ COMPANY				
Segmented Income Statement				
For the Year Ended December 31, 2013				
Sales	$2,400,000	$1,200,000	$480,000	$720,000
Variable expenses	1,104,000	600,000	216,000	288,000
Contribution margin	$1,296,000	$ 600,000	$264,000	$432,000
Fixed expenses.	1,128,000	656,000	184,000	288,000
Operating income	$ 168,000	$ (56,000)	$ 80,000	$144,000

The company is concerned about the performance of product A, and you have been asked to analyze the situation and recommend to the president whether to continue or discontinue the product. During your investigation, you discover that certain fixed expenses are traceable directly to each product line as indicated here:

	Total Company	Product A	Product B	Product C
Direct fixed expenses	$408,000	$296,000	$40,000	$72,000

The remaining fixed expenses are considered to be corporatewide expenses that have been allocated to each product line based on sales revenue.

Required:

a. Prepare a relevant cost analysis for the decision to continue or discontinue product A. Comment on your analysis.

b. Assume that product A is discontinued. Prepare a segmented income statement for the remaining products. Allocate corporatewide fixed expenses as described.

c. Starting with the segmented income statement, use the information you discovered during your investigation to present a more appropriately designed segmented income statement. *(Hint: Refer to Chapter 15.)*

d. Explain to the president why the redesigned segmented income statement is more appropriate than the current one.

Calculate NPV, present value ratio, and payback Duncan Company is considering the investment of $140,000 in a new machine. It is estimated that the new machine will generate additional cash flow of $21,000 per year for each year of its 12-year life and will have a salvage value of $15,000 at the end of its life. Duncan's financial managers estimate that the firm's cost of capital is 12%.

Problem 16.31

LO 7, 9

Required:

a. Calculate the net present value of the investment.
b. Calculate the present value ratio of the investment.
c. What is the internal rate of return of this investment, relative to the cost of capital?
d. Calculate the payback period of the investment.

Calculate NPV, present value ratio, and payback TopCap Co. is evaluating the purchase of another sewing machine that will be used to manufacture sport caps. The invoice price of the machine is $88,000. In addition, delivery and installation costs will total $6,000. The machine has the capacity to produce 10,000 dozen caps per year. Sales are forecast to increase gradually, and production volumes for each of the five years of the machine's life are expected to be:

Problem 16.32

LO 7, 8, 9

e**X**cel

2013	3,000 dozen
2014	4,700 dozen
2015	7,100 dozen
2016	9,400 dozen
2017	10,000 dozen

The caps have a contribution margin of $4.20 per dozen. Fixed costs associated with the additional production (other than depreciation expense) will be negligible. Salvage value and the investment in working capital should be ignored. TopCap Co.'s cost of capital for this capacity expansion has been set at 8%.

Required:

a. Calculate the net present value of the proposed investment in the new sewing machine.
b. Calculate the present value ratio of the investment.
c. What is the internal rate of return of this investment relative to the cost of capital?
d. Calculate the payback period of the investment.

Present value ratios index Information about four investment proposals is summarized here:

Problem 16.33

LO 7

Proposal	Investment Required	Net Present Value
1	$60,000	$36,000
2	24,000	9,600
3	72,000	36,000
4	72,000	14,400

Required:

Calculate the present value ratio of each proposal and indicate which proposal is the most desirable investment.

Problem 16.34

LO 6

Calculate NPV—rank projects using present value ratios The following capital expenditure projects have been proposed for management's consideration at Scott, Inc., for the upcoming budget year:

		Project				
	Year(s)	A	B	C	D	E
Initial investment	0	$(100,000)	$(100,000)	$(200,000)	$(200,000)	$(400,000)
Amount of net cash return	1	17,000	0	58,000	18,000	105,000
. . . .	2	17,000	0	58,000	36,000	105,000
. . . .	3	17,000	32,000	58,000	54,000	52,000
. . . .	4	17,000	32,000	58,000	72,000	52,000
. . . .	5	17,000	32,000	58,000	90,000	52,000
Per year	6–10	17,000	20,000	0	0	52,000
NPV (10% discount rate)		$ 4,458	$?	$?	$?	$ 11,501
Present value ratio		1.04	?	?	?	?

Required:

a. Calculate the net present value of projects B, C, and D, using 10% as the cost of capital for Scott, Inc.

b. Calculate the present value ratio for projects B, C, D, and E.

c. Which projects would you recommend for investment if the cost of capital is 10% and

1. $200,000 is available for investment?

2. $600,000 is available for investment?

3. $1,000,000 is available for investment?

d. What additional factors (beyond those considered in parts **a–c** might influence your project rankings?

Problem 16.35

LO 6, 7, 10, 11

Accounting rate of return and NPV Crichton Publications uses the accounting rate of return method to evaluate proposed capital investments. The company's desired rate of return is 18%. The project being evaluated involves a new product that will have a three-year life. The investment required is $300,000, which consists of a $240,000 machine, and inventories and accounts receivable totaling $60,000. The machine will have a useful life of three years and a salvage value of $150,000. The salvage value will be received during the fourth year, and the inventories and accounts receivable related to the product also will be converted back to cash in the fourth year. Accrual accounting net income from the product will be $87,000 per year, before depreciation expense, for each of the three years. Because of the time lag between selling the product and collecting the accounts receivable, cash flows from the product will be:

1st year	$42,000
2nd year	72,000
3rd year	87,000
4th year	60,000

Required:

a. Calculate the accounting rate of return for the first year of the product. Assume straight-line depreciation. Based on this analysis, would the investment be made? Explain your answer.

b. Calculate the net present value of the product using a discount rate of 18% and assuming that cash flows occur at the end of the respective years. Based on this analysis, would the investment be made? Explain your answer.

c. Which of these two analytical approaches is the more appropriate to use? Explain your answer.

Accounting rate of return, payback, and NPV Tablerock Corp. is interested in reviewing its method of evaluating capital expenditure proposals using the accounting rate of return method. A recent proposal involved a $100,000 investment in a machine that had an estimated useful life of five years and an estimated salvage value of $10,000. The machine was expected to increase net income (and cash flows) before depreciation expense by $28,000 per year. The criteria for approving a new investment are that it have a rate of return of 12% and a payback period of three years or less.

Problem 16.36
LO 7, 9, 10, 11

Required:

a. Calculate the accounting rate of return on this investment for the first year. Assume straight-line depreciation. Based on this analysis, would the investment be made? Explain your answer.

b. Calculate the payback period for this investment. Based on this analysis, would the investment be made? Explain your answer.

c. Calculate the net present value of this investment using a cost of capital of 12%. Based on this analysis, would the investment be made? Explain your answer.

d. What recommendation would you make to the management of Tablerock Corp. about evaluating capital expenditure proposals? Support your recommendation with the appropriate rationale.

Cases

All applicable Cases are available with McGraw-Hill's *Connect*™ *Accounting*.

Case study—NPV of opening a small business Jinny Buffett recently retired as a flight attendant and is interested in opening a fitness center and health spa exclusively for women in Grand Cayman, where she resides. After careful study, she is somewhat puzzled as to how to proceed. In her words, "I see my business going in one of two directions: Either I open the fitness center and health spa all at once, or I start with the health spa and hold off on the fitness center for a while. Either way, it should be a success because women on this island love to be pampered. My only concern about the fitness center is the initial cost, but if the projections look good

Case 16.37
LO 7

enough, I know some investors in Phoenix who can help me get started. In any event, I plan to retire permanently in 10 years."

The following information is available:

- Jinny has identified a suitable location for her business in a new shopping center in George Town, capital of the Cayman Islands. The developer has units of 1,000 square feet and 2,500 square feet available and is willing to sell either unit for CI$150 per square foot (CI$1.00 = US$1.25). Alternatively, the space can be leased at a cost of CI$1.80 per square foot per month, on an annual basis.

- Commercial real estate values have more than doubled in Grand Cayman during the past 10 years, with no slowdown in sight. As a result, Jinny is more attracted to the purchase option because she expects the price per square foot to be CI$300 by the time she is ready to sell her unit in 10 years.

- Exercise machines and other equipment necessary to open the fitness center would cost US$50,000. In addition, US$35,000 would need to be invested in equipment related to the health spa. The useful life for all such equipment is 10 years, and the expected salvage value is not large enough to be concerned about.

- In addition, US$8,000 would need to be invested in an inventory of cosmetics and skin care products necessary to operate the health spa. This level of inventory would need to be maintained throughout the 10-year period and will be given away to loyal customers when Jinny retires permanently.

- The health spa can be operated in the 1,000-square-foot unit. Variable operating costs would include CI$0.10 per square foot per month for cleaning and CI$0.40 per square foot per month for utilities. The 2,500-square-foot unit is large enough to operate both the fitness center and health spa, and the CI$0.10 rate per square foot for cleaning would not change. However, if the 2,500-square-foot unit were used, the health spa would be located in an open loft that would need to be air-conditioned at all times. As a result, utility costs are expected to be CI$0.60 per square foot per month under this option.

- Jinny is a certified aesthetician and expects to do most of the makeovers, facials, and peels herself, but she needs a qualified assistant for the health spa. She estimates that hiring an appropriate person will cost US$25,000 per year. Likewise, for the fitness center, two full-time aerobics instructors would be hired for US$20,000 each per year, and a physical trainer would be hired for US$30,000 per year.

- Additional fixed costs include US$3,000 per year for advertising and US$4,500 per year for maintenance, insurance, and other items. These costs will be incurred without respect to the size of operations.

- Annual membership fees to the fitness center will be CI$300, and a preliminary market survey shows a demand of approximately 500 initial members. Although members tend to come and go, the net change in membership from year to year is not expected to be significant. No additional fees will be charged to fitness center members.

- Health spa fees are assessed on a user basis, although the steam room facilities are available at no charge to fitness center members. The net cash inflow from cosmetics and skin care products (after deducting the cost of inventory used and sold) is expected to be CI$8,000 per month.

- Jinny's cost of capital is 12%, and there are no taxes in the Cayman Islands.

Required:

a. Calculate the net present value in US$ of an investment in the health spa *only,* assuming that the 1,000-square-foot unit is purchased and then resold at the end of 10 years. *(Hint: Before making your present value calculations, multiply all amounts expressed in CI$ by $1.25 to convert into US$.)*

b. Calculate the net present value in US$ of an investment in the fitness center and health spa, assuming that the 2,500-square-foot unit is purchased and then resold at the end of 10 years.

c. Jinny is quite concerned about possible forecasting errors and has asked you to prepare a more conservative estimate. Repeat part **b,** assuming that the fitness center attracts only 300 members per year (rather than 500); that the net cash inflow per month from cosmetics and skin care products is only CI$6,000 per month (rather than CI$8,000 per month); and that commercial real estate values in Grand Cayman at the end of 10 years are only CI$200 per square foot (rather than CI$300 per square foot).

d. Explain why it might be in Jinny's best interest to lease (rather than purchase) the 1,000-square-foot unit if she initially decides to open the health spa only. Although no calculations are required, you should consider both quantitative and qualitative factors in your response.

e. What is your overall recommendation? Include an explanation of any additional factors that you would consider in making your recommendation. Keep in mind that Jinny has not given herself a salary in her projections. Assume that a reasonable salary would be CI$4,000 per month.

Comprehensive problem—quantitative and qualitative analysis The following data have been collected by capital budgeting analysts at Sunset Beach, Inc., concerning an investment in an expansion of the company's product line. Analysts estimate that an investment of $150,000 will be required to initiate the project at the beginning of 2013. The estimated cash returns from the new product line are summarized in the following table; assume that the returns will be received in a lump sum at the end of each year:

Case 16.38
LO 6, 7, 8, 9, 11

*e***Xcel**

Year	Amount of Cash Return
2013	$40,000
2014	50,000
2015	64,000
2016	46,000

The new product line will also require an investment in inventory and receivables of $50,000; this investment will become available for other purposes at the end of the project. The salvage value of machinery and equipment at the end of the product line's life is expected to be $25,000. The cost of capital used in Sunset Beach, Inc.'s, capital budgeting analysis is 12%.

Required:

a. Calculate the net present value of the proposed investment. Ignore income taxes and round all answers to the nearest $1.

b. Calculate the present value ratio of the investment.

c. What will the internal rate of return on this investment be relative to the cost of capital? Explain your answer.

d. Calculate the payback period of the investment.

e. Based on the quantitative analysis, would you recommend that the product line expansion project be undertaken? Explain your answer.

f. Identify some qualitative factors that you would want to have considered with respect to this project before management proceeds with the investment.

Case 16.39

Capital budget expenditure analysis: Internet assignment Annual reports provide significant information about an organization's capital budget and capital budgeting process. Campbell Soup Company provides financial reports for several years at www.campbellsoup.com (*Our Company → Investor Center → Financial Information → Annual Reports*). This exercise will require you to use Campbell's consolidated statements of cash flows, management's discussion and analysis of financial condition and results of operations, and notes to the consolidated financial statements for the most recent year presented.

Required:

Using Campbell's most recent annual report, answer the following:

a. From Campbell's consolidated statements of cash flows:
   1. Identify the amount of cash used for capital expenditures from the Investing Activities section. How much cash was provided from the sale of capital assets?
   2. How do these amounts compare to the previous two years? Comment on the trend relative to the general cash flow position for each year.

b. Read Campbell's discussion of the "Business," and highlight the information provided about capital expenditures reported in 2011 and plans identified for 2012.

c. Read Campbell's discussion of the "Risk Factors." How may the company be adversely impacted by failure to execute acquisitions and divestitures successfully?

d. Read Campbell's management's discussion and analysis of financial condition and results of operations.
   1. In the Liquidity and Capital Resources section, how were investing cash flows used or provided for capital expenditures?
   2. In the Significant Accounting Estimates section, how are fixed assets reviewed for impairment? What role does management judgment play?

e. From Campbell's notes to the consolidated financial statements, determine the following:
   1. How does Campbell's value and depreciate property, plant, and equipment?
   2. If applicable, describe Campbell's acquisitions for the year.
   3. If applicable, describe Campbell's divestitures for the year.
   4. How were Campbell's capital expenditures distributed among its business segments?

f. From Campbell's selected financial data, do the following:

1. For the five years presented, calculate the ratio of capital expenditures to net sales.

2. For the five years presented, calculate the ratio of net plant assets to total assets.

3. Comment on the trends.

Answers to Self-Study Material

Matching: 1. k, 2. c, 3. n, 4. q, 5. g, 6. h, 7. d, 8. m, 9. p, 10. r, 11. o, 12. b, 13. a, 14. l, 15. e

Multiple choice: 1. c, 2. a, 3. d, 4. c, 5. a, 6. a, 7. c, 8. e, 9. b, 10. b

Accounting— The Future

The "Welcome" from the authors included in the preface stated that this text's broad learning objective is to enable students to achieve an understanding of the basics of financial reporting by corporations and other enterprises. We hope that this objective has been achieved. However, the financial reporting challenges related to the worldwide financial reporting crisis that came to a head in the Fall of 2008, in conjunction with the continuing disclosures of financial reporting misstatements and accounting errors made by major corporations, questionable auditor oversight of the accounting and financial reporting processes, dubious practices that more recently rocked the mortgage industry and financial markets, and even the unfolding Libor scandal, all serve to beg the question: "What's going on—is the material I've been learning from this text at all relevant to the real world?" The answer to that question is a resounding **yes;** accounting of the future will be built on the solid foundation presented in this text. Yet new and complex business transactions continue to appear on the horizon, and the accounting standards (both new and amended) that have been developed to deal with these complexities continue to have a gestation period of several years. Moreover, implementation of the Sarbanes–Oxley Act of 2002 has led to a retrospective analysis of certain accounting methodologies that may not have been appropriately applied by many companies in the recent past. In light of current pressures to avoid the taint of controversy concerning any and all financial reporting matters, the accounting profession, large public accounting firms, and individual practitioners are likely to continue to face challenges— considerable, but not insurmountable—in the years to come.

The authors believe that the following seven themes will help you build a bridge to the future of accounting. These themes are presented as characteristics that accountants and users of accounting and financial statement information will encounter:

1. Having insight and integrity.

2. Having a vision for the future.

3. Competing in a global economy.

4. Using technology effectively.

FYI

For a comprehensive collection of resources devoted to providing relevant information about the evolving regulatory environment under the Sarbanes Oxley Act of 2002, visit the American Institute of CPAs website at www.aicpa.org, and read "A Guide to Sarbanes–Oxley" at www.soxlaw.com.

5. Committing to lifelong learning.

6. Becoming business partners.

7. Turning vision into reality.

The Accounting Profession

Congress, the SEC and other regulatory agencies, and the public in general were rightly outraged by the corrupt and erroneous financial reporting and accounting practices that have drawn so much attention in the past several years. The valuation of subprime mortgages (the mark-to-market controversy), corporate bankruptcies, executive convictions, and collapse of the auditing firm Arthur Andersen resulted from the ethical breakdown, greed, and arrogance of a very few individuals. Unfortunately, their actions affected hundreds of thousands of employees and investors—and shook the confidence of the world's equity markets. The resulting congressional hearings and legislation, criminal indictments, guilty pleas, and convictions focused an intensely bright spotlight on the accounting profession. If anything, this attention has increased and will continue to increase the demand for bright, ethical, and straight-thinking accountants, managers, and executives.

THEME 1
Having insight and integrity.

In July 2012 the *New York Times* reported Gallup poll research findings indicating that corporate misconduct no longer surprises most Americans and that only about 20 percent of Americans have much trust in banks and 62 percent believe corruption is widespread across America. Nearly three in four Americans believe that corruption has increased over the last three years, and this begs the question: "Have corporations lost whatever ethical compass they once had?" Clearly, technical accounting issues will not become any easier to solve in the future, and seeking solutions to those issues requires competence built on a foundation of moral integrity. Evidence of sound ethical values and the ability to apply those values across economic, political, and social activities will become crucial to acceptance and recognition as a professional.

Building on a strong ethical foundation, tomorrow's accounting professionals will require enhanced skill sets in order to survive in a technology-driven global business economy in which their clientele will be seen as strategic business partners. The CPA designation has, since its inception, conveyed a prestigious image of technical competence and professional skill, but the CPA brand image may too narrowly define tomorrow's accounting professional. An MBA degree might provide the breadth of skills that will be required, but MBA programs typically lack the needed depth of accounting knowledge. The Certified Management Accountant (CMA) designation comes closest to testing for the knowledge, skills, and abilities that corporate America needs in its accounting and financial professionals. To be certain, a continuing hallmark of

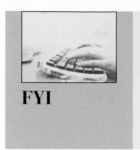

Information about the CPA examination process from the American Institute of CPAs can be found at www.aicpa.org—see the *Become a CPA* tab. Information about the CMA examination process from the Institute of Management Accountants can be found at www.imanet.org—see the *CMA Certification* tab.

FYI

tomorrow's accounting professional will be that services continue to be delivered with independent insight and a high degree of integrity.

THEME 2

Having a vision for the future.

In 1998 the AICPA published a Vision Project report titled "Focus on the Horizon: CPA Vision—2011 and Beyond," which proved enlightening for many accounting professionals. The Vision Project was an ongoing, professionwide initiative to understand, anticipate, and promote the requirements necessary for professional success in a new economy and to educate accounting professionals about changes. The following points summarize the CPA Vision:

Core purpose: CPAs . . . making sense of a changing and complex world.

Vision statement: CPAs are trusted professionals who enable people and organizations to shape their future. Combining insight with integrity, CPAs deliver value by

- Communicating the total picture with clarity and objectivity.
- Translating complex information into critical knowledge.
- Anticipating and creating opportunities.
- Designing pathways that transform vision into reality.

The AICPA's Vision Project identified five core competencies that are essential for CPAs to survive in the next decade: communication and leadership skills; strategic and critical thinking skills; a focus on the customer, client, and market; ability to interpret converging information; and technological proficiency.

In 2010, as an assessment of, and extension to, the original Vision Project, the AICPA embarked on a new visioning initiative, CPA Horizons 2025, which focused on leveraging the insights of CPAs, business leaders, regulators, thought leaders, and futurists on current and forecast trends that will impact the accounting profession operating in a technology-driven global economy. The research shows that the profession has a bright future and will need to respond quickly to

For more information and other resources describing the CPA Vision and the Vision Project, and CPA Horizons 2025, see www.aicpa.org/research/cpahorizons2025.

FYI

For the latest IASB and IFRS developments and information about projects in progress, active research, summaries of international accounting standards, and a look at what's happening with international accounting standards around the world, see www.ifrs.org.

FYI

ever-changing political, economic, social, technological, and regulatory environments. New insights about opportunities and challenges for CPAs and the profession over the next 15 years emerged and will serve as a road map to mold their future. Moreover, CPAs overwhelmingly agreed that the profession's core purpose, "making sense of a changing and complex world," remains relevant for today and the future.

The financial reporting breakdowns of the past decade caused by a relative handful of people who were responsible for major frauds, audit failures, or misapplication of generally accepted principles of accounting underscore the need for an ethical foundation on which business practices and competencies must be built. In some ways, the future seems quite certain—CPAs must be able to analyze traditional historical data and to provide forward-looking insights that create value for their client organizations (and ultimately these organizations' shareholders). Organizations will need financial professionals who can assume leadership roles and provide guidance and support. Increasingly, CPAs will be moving out of the accounting function and into the strategic and operational areas of the business.

Today's business environment is truly global in scope; the technology explosion has created a worldwide communications infrastructure that has played a major role in effectively shrinking the globe. Multinational corporations are common today and will continue to emerge as more companies seek strategic opportunities by combining with other companies as business partners to leverage their core competencies. Beyond needing people skills and the ability to perform effectively as a member of a cross-cultural team, what are the implications for an accounting professional working in a global marketplace? There will be continuing efforts toward the development of high-quality global accounting standards.

Although accounting is regarded as the language of business throughout the world, worldwide accounting rules have not existed historically. Accounting standards applied in one country may vary widely from those used in another country. Moreover, significant national differences still exist in the manner in which the accounting profession is regulated. Imagine an investor's frustration when attempting to compare the financial statements of Ford, Toyota, and Volkswagen without a clear understanding of the differences allowed in the financial reporting rules in the United States, Japan, and Germany. Or imagine the reporting costs and efforts required by a multinational corporation that operates in 100 countries and has to comply with the national accounting standards of each country. Fortunately efforts to unify the global accounting scene are currently under way.

The International Accounting Standards Committee (IASC), replaced by the International Accounting Standards Board (IASB) in 2001, was organized in 1973 as an independent, private-sector body with the objective of harmonizing the accounting

THEME 3
Competing in a global economy.

principles used by businesses and other organizations for financial reporting around the world. The objectives of the IASC, as stated in its constitution, were

1. To develop, in the public interest, a single set of high-quality, understandable, and enforceable global accounting standards that require high-quality, transparent, and *comparable* (emphasis added) information in financial statements and other financial reporting to help participants in the world's capital markets and other users make economic decisions.
2. To promote the use and rigorous application of those standards.
3. To bring about convergence of national accounting standards and international accounting standards to generate high-quality solutions.

The IASB's ability to bring convergence to the world's accounting standards will ultimately depend on the necessary acceptance of those standards by securities regulators and stock exchanges around the world, such as the Securities and Exchange Commission in the United States. The SEC has endorsed the efforts of the IASC and the IASB and has identified three key elements necessary for international accounting standards. The standards must

- Include a core set of accounting pronouncements that constitute a comprehensive, generally accepted basis of accounting.
- Be of high quality—they must result in comparability and transparency, and they must provide for full disclosure.
- Be rigorously interpreted and applied.

While the need for convergence of the world's accounting standards is clear and urgent, as of February 2012 the SEC reported that its decision on the use of IFRS by U.S. public companies was still a "few" months away from a final report.[1] It appears that the SEC will be using the term *endorsement* to describe a system in which the U.S. Financial Accounting Standards Board (FASB) would look at IFRS standards and consider how to implement and incorporate them in the United States. Whether to retain the idea of U.S. GAAP in an IFRS incorporation framework also remains an issue to be decided. It's also clear that if IFRS were adopted in the United States, ultimate responsibility for financial reporting standards in the United States would rest with a U.S. authority, presumably the FASB, which would also need to have a strong voice in the development of IFRS standards. By July 2012 the *Wall Street Journal* reported that the SEC's decision regarding IFRS adoption will be delayed even further, and possibly not issued until 2013, which demonstrates the continuing challenge of prescribing conformance.

IFRS accounting rules are now used by more than 100 countries, and when the United States adopts, other major economies like Japan will likely follow. For a current appreciation of IASB's convergence work, and the status of IFRS adoptions, see www.ifrs.org. Illustrated below is a summary from the document "Who We Are and What We Do" highlighting the major milestones and reporting for countries of the G20 regarding the use of IFRS worldwide.

---

[1] "IFRS Decision a 'Few' Months Away, Based on SEC Staff Report Timeline," www.journalofaccountancy.com, February 2012.

IFRSs around the world

Since 2001, almost 120 countries have required or permitted the use of IFRSs. All remaining major economies have established time lines to converge with or adopt IFRSs in the near future.

Current use of IFRSs in the countries of the G20	
COUNTRY	STATUS FOR LISTED COMPANIES
Argentina	Required for fiscal years beginning on or after 1 January 2012
Australia	Required for all private sector reporting entities and as the basis for public sector reporting since 2005
Brazil	Required for consolidated financial statements of banks and listed companies from 31 December 2010 and for individual company accounts progressively since January 2008
Canada	Required from 1 January 2011 for all listed entities and permitted for private sector entities including not-for-profit organisations
China	Substantially converged national standards
European Union	All member states of the EU are required to use IFRSs as adopted by the EU for listed companies since 2005
France	Required via EU adoption and implementation process since 2005
Germany	Required via EU adoption and implementation process since 2005
India	Converging with IFRSs, date to be determined
Indonesia	Convergence process ongoing; a decision about a target date for full compliance with IFRSs is expected to be made in 2012
Italy	Required via EU adoption and implementation process since 2005
Japan	Permitted from 2010 for a number of international companies; decision about mandatory adoption expected around 2012
Mexico	Required from 2012
Republic of Korea	Required since 2011
Russia	Required from 2012
Saudi Arabia	Required for banking and insurance companies. Full convergence with IFRSs currently under consideration
South Africa	Required for listed entities since 2005
Turkey	Required for listed entities since 2005
United Kingdom	Required via EU adoption and implementation process since 2005
United States	Allowed for foreign issuers since 2007; target date for substantial convergence with IFRSs is 2012 and decision about possible adoption for U.S. companies expected in 2012

Source: "Who We Are and What We Do," www.ifrs.org, February 2012.

Accounting and Technology

Computerized accounting systems handle much of the world's accounting today and will continue to do so in the future. Even inexpensive accounting systems, such as QuickBooks and Sage 50 (formerly Peachtree), provide fairly sophisticated transaction processing functionality to meet the basic bookkeeping needs of small businesses.

THEME 4
Using technology effectively.

At the other end of the business spectrum, enterprise-level systems, such as SAP and Oracle, provide automated solutions to support the business processes of the world's largest corporations.

Accounting was defined in Chapter 1 as a system of identifying, measuring, and communicating economic information about an entity for the purpose of making decisions and informed judgments. In its simplest form, any system is characterized by three essential flows, as illustrated here:

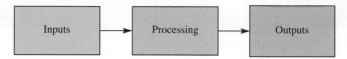

This systems view can be applied to the basics of accounting, and illustrated as an accounting information system:

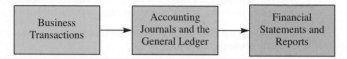

Today, and with a focus on the future, accounting has evolved into a complex, comprehensive business information system (as illustrated below)—and computer technology provides speed, power, accuracy, and more timely knowledge about an organization. Thus, users of such systems have a real-time window through which they can observe their organization's operations to support planning, control, and decision-making activities.

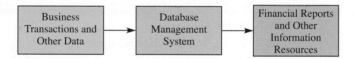

Inputs to the system will become increasingly automated as more than just the largest corporations leverage technology and the Internet by linking their systems to the systems of their customers and vendors. Physical copies of invoices, purchase orders, receiving reports, and remittance advices have served as source documents for accounting departments of the past; this type of paperwork is increasingly becoming obsolete as physical source documents are replaced by business-to-business electronic transaction flows (i.e., computer-to-computer communications). The purchaser can scan bar codes or read radio frequency identification tags as inventory items are received and, upon verification of the purchase order by the system, authorize an electronic funds transfer providing payment to the vendor. Likewise, data collection terminals located in strategic positions throughout the manufacturing plant can provide job costing input to the system for materials used, labor costs incurred, and manufacturing overhead applied. In some cases, the data collection technology can be wired directly into operating equipment to track speed, productivity, downtime, and other important production variables. These examples of technology's role in capturing and recording business events clearly define an important and ever-changing role for the accountant to play in the process of planning, analysis, design, implementation, use, and control of computerized transaction processing systems.

Once a business transaction has been captured by a system, it is maintained in a database—just as the general ledger provided a final resting place after transactions had been posted from the journals where they were initially recorded. *Database*

For a complete update on XBRL development activities and other technical information about XBRL, see www.xbrl.org. To see how XBRL works, go to the *xbrl basics* tab.

FYI

management systems store data in a manner that allows users to interact with the data either through online queries or by running predefined reports. The ability to cut, slice, and dice transactions in the database into a variety of enlightening views provides a powerful tool for the business analyst and decision maker to support his or her information needs. *Data warehouses* are large, refined collections of the organization's data resources—these super databases provide high-quality, easily retrievable data, thereby allowing users to manipulate and transform data in creative ways. *Data mining technology* allows organizations to search their data warehouses to find relationships in the data that provide new knowledge about the organization—a task that would be impossible without such technology.

In the future, there will continue to be an increased emphasis on the development of user-friendly technology tools that allow financial professionals to easily retrieve data for manipulation into meaningful information. *Structured Query Language (SQL)* is the interface language used today to interact with databases to produce predefined reports or to submit ad hoc requests for information. Tasks now done effortlessly with point-and-click and drag-and-drop techniques once involved cumbersome retrieval processes requiring programmers to write detailed source code to access the database and produce the desired information. With today's technology, any user with an understanding of the basic structure and relationships of the database can access and retrieve the data effectively. Moreover, powerful tools are evolving that allow users to easily manipulate retrieved data into finely tuned views and robust presentations of information. Examples include Microsoft Excel Pivot Tables and the emerging general category of data analytics and visualization tools.

In addition to supporting internal information users, databases also provide information for external financial reporting. Most major U.S. public companies provide some type of financial disclosure through their websites. To date, however, most financial information presented on the Internet has been relatively static, consisting mostly of quarterly and annual reports presented in a manner similar to the printed annual reports that communicate an organization's financial position and results of operations. Internet-based financial reporting is about to change dramatically with the development of *Extensible Business Reporting Language (XBRL),* a tool that will become the digital language of all business reporting. XBRL will format financial reports (based on generally accepted accounting principles) for transport across the Internet and viewing on web browsers by public and private companies, accounting professionals, investors, researchers, financial analysts, government agencies, banks, and others. The uniformity provided by XBRL will make it much easier for a multitude of users to prepare and analyze electronic financial information. Examples include printed financial statements, filings with regulatory agencies, credit and loan information required by banks, and the ability to search and extract detailed information from different forms of financial statements.

To conceptualize how XBRL will work, think of a balance sheet presented in a spreadsheet where you might find $20,000 to be the amount of inventory as of December 31, 2013. The $20,000 amount is meaningful because you can read the column heading "December 31, 2013," and the row label "Inventory." But what happens if you extract the $20,000 amount and move it to another spreadsheet or report? Without also extracting or reentering the column heading and row label, the $20,000 amount does not convey independent meaning. With XBRL, the $20,000 amount will retain the attributes of where it belongs in the financial statements as well as its label and dates. Therefore, data can be transported into spreadsheets, databases, printed reports, web pages, and more without the need to reenter attribute information. XBRL will likely be viewed as the most important technology developed for financial reporting since the spreadsheet, and it will revolutionize how business information is communicated.

The same power and speed of technology applications that can be so highly beneficial can also result in errors or even fraudulent activities in an environment of weak internal control. Part of the Sarbanes–Oxley Act of 2002 requires significant documentation, testing of internal controls, and auditor review and reporting about the effectiveness of internal controls. This is a complex, labor-intensive task, and it is not surprising that a number of software products have been developed to facilitate the process.

Students of Accounting Information

THEME 5

Committing to lifelong learning.

In today's rapidly changing business environment, business and accounting professionals must have a broad understanding of information technology and the role it plays in the 21st-century economy. It is critically important for players in this environment to understand what technology *can* and *cannot* accomplish; to possess the discipline to maintain the skills necessary to use technology to accomplish ever-changing business goals; and, finally, to integrate technology skills with leadership and communication skills to gain competitive advantages for themselves and their employers. Failure to do so will leave today's business and accounting graduates unprepared to function in a technology-driven information age.

THEME 6

Becoming business partners.

Today's accounting students and entry-level professionals must position themselves beyond the accountant's traditional role of financial historian. Traditional number-crunching transaction work and the preparation of financial statements is now left to computers to perform. Employers of accounting professionals will need to appreciate the new roles accounting graduates can perform today and leverage their knowledge and information skills by inviting these new hires to participate in the process of defining organizational strategy. While the *role* of accountants has changed dramatically in recent years, the *perception* of accountants (especially at lower levels of management) will take time to change because ingrained in that perception is the image of traditional scorekeepers, bean counters, watchdogs, and police. Viewed as business partners, accountants' work will be more analytical and less transactional, more decision oriented and less compliance oriented. In short, accountants will be more involved in running the business than ever before. These new accounting roles include financial modeling, strategic planning, business process improvement, internal consulting, financial analysis, systems implementation, and organizational education. To support these changing roles of financial professionals and users of accounting information, the educational process will need to focus less on number crunching (i.e., debits and credits) and more on developing communication skills, analytical skills, interpersonal skills, and technology skills. A serious problem could occur if today's business school graduates are disconnected from the needs of organizations in the new economy.

The accountant's new role in today's technology-driven economy is that of a strategic business partner with the responsibility of developing the information needed to support the organization's *value chain functions* (discussed in Chapter 13). This new role can be illustrated as follows:

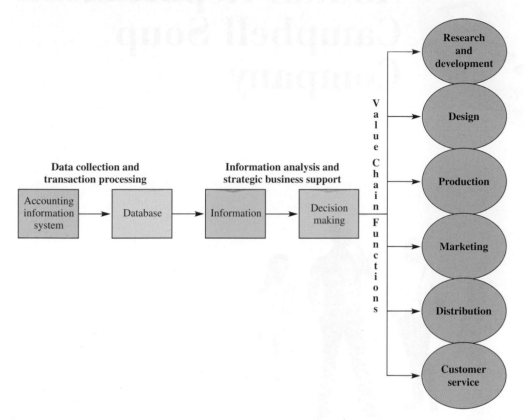

Tomorrow's accountant will play a pivotal role in enhancing long-term profitability by supporting managers at all levels within the organization's value chain in managing the resources under their control most effectively. To serve this important role, it will be essential to obtain a better understanding of the interaction between the organization's accounting information system, its information and decision-making needs, and each of the functional areas that are affected by strategic decision making.

Conclusion

To a large extent, what has been described as the future of accounting is already here—but not yet fully operational or widespread in application. Just as the technologies of the 20th century shaped industrial America's need for accounting information, so too will the technologies of the 21st century help to define accounting information needs in a global information age. Users of accounting information will include managers working on a team to plan, execute, and control the activities related to the entity's strategic plan. The objectives of this text have been to present a big-picture perspective of the financial statements and to show how management accounting information can be used effectively within an organization. To the extent that this epilogue provides insight into characteristics and activities of accounting professionals and future uses of accounting information, a further benefit has been achieved.

THEME 7
Turning vision into reality.

APPENDIX

Excerpts from 2011 Annual Report of Campbell Soup Company

FOCUS
FORWARD

CAMPBELL SOUP COMPANY
2011 ANNUAL REPORT

CONNECT WITH
CONSUMERS
DRIVE INNOVATION
DELIVER LONG TERM
PROFITABLE GROWTH

FOCUS
FORWARD

Campbell's

CAMPBELL SOUP COMPANY
2011 ANNUAL REPORT

CHART A NEW COURSE
EMBRACE CHANGE
EVOLVE
CREATE VALUE

Denise M. Morrison
President and Chief Executive Officer

Fellow Shareowners,

I am honored to begin my tenure as the twelfth Chief Executive Officer of Campbell Soup Company. In fiscal 2012, we are charting a new course for Campbell. Building on our distinguished history, we are pursuing new paths and new strategies to create a promising future.

In fiscal 2011, Campbell's new leadership team conducted a comprehensive strategic review of our business. We took a careful look at the competitive environment and the needs and preferences of today's consumers. We examined closely the forces that are driving growth in the global food industry and considered how our industry is likely to evolve in the next decade. We evaluated our opportunities with a fresh perspective, focusing on the choices that hold the greatest promise. Based on this important work, we have developed an exciting new strategic vision for our company.

The Foundation

Our overarching long-term goal is to deliver total shareowner returns that exceed the industry average on a sustainable basis. We know that the most important driver of above-average returns in the food industry is top-line growth. We also know that the key determinant of top-line performance is participation in high-growth spaces — in categories, consumer segments and geographies with strong growth momentum. This is good news for Campbell from a category perspective as we are in very good businesses.

In the United States and around the world, the three core categories in which we participate — Simple Meals, Baked Snacks and Healthy Beverages — are large and growing, and have strong prospects for continued growth. We are well positioned to seize the valuable opportunities that lie before us, but we have work to do to pursue them successfully.

Fiscal 2011 was an extremely challenging year for the economy and for Campbell. Sales increased 1 percent to $7.7 billion and adjusted net earnings per share rose 3 percent to $2.54.* Despite these challenges, there were notable bright spots in our performance. In our Global Baking and Snacking segment, which includes the Pepperidge Farm and Arnott's businesses, sales and operating earnings grew as we launched exciting new products and maintained the growth of core brands such as *Goldfish*, *Shapes* and *Tim Tam*. Our North America Foodservice segment also delivered sales and operating earnings gains. The company's fundamentals remained strong. We increased our cash flow from operations, announced a $1 billion share repurchase program and maintained a strong balance sheet.

But fiscal 2011 performance in our core Soup and Simple Meals business in North America was disappointing. Increased promotional spending in the first half of the year did not deliver expected volume lifts in U.S. Soup, and our U.S. Simple Meals segment saw sales, profit and share declines across our soup and sauce brands. These declines were not solely the result of the downturn in the economy. Today, consumer tastes and expectations are more diverse and variable than ever before. It is clear to us that in our Soup and Simple Meals business, we must respond more effectively to demographic changes and generational shifts in food preferences.

As we focus forward, we will have...

A More Innovative Company — We will be critically focused on consumer-driven innovation in products and packaging as the primary driver of organic growth.

A More Balanced Company — We will drive our company's growth by providing a wide array of delicious, nutritious and convenient products across a growing global consumer base.

A More Responsive Company — We will be far better positioned for engagement with new and growing consumer groups.

* This amount is adjusted for certain transactions not considered to be part of the ongoing business. For a reconciliation of non-GAAP financial measures, see page 706.

Growing Globally Campbell must also respond more effectively to the forces that are driving both the distribution of global economic growth and growth in the food industry. In the next 10 to 15 years, emerging markets will continue to transform the dynamics of the global economy, creating as many as a *billion* new consumers who will fuel as much as 75 percent of the growth in the food industry. The food preferences and choices of these consumers increasingly are driven by nutrition, taste, value and convenience. Campbell has many products well suited to meet their needs, and the capabilities to develop more. But to date, we have not seized the opportunities for our company in growing international markets.

Our new strategic plan seeks to correct our course in these critical respects.

A New Strategic Vision...

When you look at Campbell in a few years, you are likely to see a company that is focused in the same three core categories where we compete today. But we will have significantly broader category platforms, and our investments will be centered in segments and adjacencies with high-growth profiles and strong prospects for sustainable growth.

In North America, we will be better positioned for engagement with our loyal Baby Boomers and with growing consumer groups such as Millennials and Hispanics, whose needs and preferences our products currently do not adequately address. Elsewhere in the world, we will have a broader footprint, and a greater percentage of our total sales and earnings will come from markets outside the U.S. We will have expanded platforms and scale in our existing international markets, and we will have achieved a progressively increasing presence in fast-growing emerging markets.

From a strategic standpoint, we will be critically focused on consumer-driven innovation in products and packaging as the primary driver of organic growth. External development will be an integral component of our overall growth strategy, particularly in international markets. We believe

Campbell's Slow Kettle **Style soups in contemporary clear packaging were created by Campbell chefs to meet the changing tastes of consumers and be "better than homemade." These new soups offer the perfect combination of authentic ingredients and unique recipes in five different varieties.**

that these new strategic priorities will position our company well to deliver consistent above-average returns to our shareowners over the long term, driven by sustainable profitable top-line growth.

...And a New Strategic Plan

Today we are powered by three core business strategies and unwavering attention to the ways that people around the world want to shop, cook, eat and live. We plan to drive our company's growth by providing a wide array of delicious, nutritious and convenient products across a growing global consumer base.

Stabilize and then profitably grow North America Soup and Simple Meals

First, we will stabilize and then profitably grow our core Soup and Simple Meals business in North America. We will do so by rebalancing our marketing investments decisively toward the consumer to expand the equities of our brands, and by taking a noticeably different approach to innovation. While we will continue to invest in innovation designed to maintain the vitality of existing product lines and to reinforce their appeal to our core consumers, we will devote significantly greater resources to disruptive innovation that will expand our product and packaging platforms to reach new consumers and new eating occasions.

Our emphasis will be on choice. We know that many consumers take great interest in the impact of the foods they eat on their health and well-being. Yet the nutritional attributes of foods mean different things to different people. For many, weight loss and weight maintenance are of primary importance. For others, dietary objectives center on vegetable nutrition, sodium reduction, energy and stamina, or digestive health. In the future, lower

Culinary Inspiration

Campbell's Senior Executive Chef Tom Griffiths is a master chef certified by the American Culinary Federation. Chef Tom and his team members, like Chef Amanda Zimlich, seek to satisfy consumer cravings for new and different flavors by developing products that have a "wow" factor, yet are popular with the mainstream.

"Innovation is just as much about 'how' we create as it is about 'what' we create. Culinary innovation often requires us to embrace the classic, fundamental flavor combinations of foods, and find new, bold and exciting ways to showcase them," says Chef Amanda.

New on the menu this year are *Swanson Flavor Boost* concentrated broth packets. They are the secret ingredient for delicious meals.

Amanda Zimlich
Senior Research Chef, North America Foodservice Innovation

Tom Griffiths
Senior Executive Chef & Director of Campbell's Culinary & Baking Institute

sodium levels in our products will be just one component of Campbell's wellness strategy. We will continue to offer a wide range of lower-sodium products. We will also offer products that address a broad array of consumer tastes and lifestyles. In fiscal 2012, we will introduce 35 new products in North America, significantly more than in each of the past three years. You'll see some of these new products throughout this report, including *Campbell's Slow Kettle* Style soups in indulgent flavors, *Campbell's Select Harvest* soups in regionally inspired varieties, and *Swanson Flavor Boost* concentrated broth packets for more sophisticated cooks.

2

Expand our international presence

Second, we will expand our international presence. We will broaden the range and availability of our products in the international markets in which we currently do business. To grow our international Simple Meals business, we intend to strengthen our current Meal Maker platforms in European markets, appealing to a broader set of consumer demands within larger adjacent categories. We plan to drive category and share growth in Australia, New Zealand and Canada. We also will enter new geographies, particularly developing markets.

In fiscal 2011, Campbell entered into a joint venture with Swire Pacific Limited, a company with long and successful experience in the People's Republic of China and capabilities that are complementary to our own. While our business in China is small and will take time to develop, we see great potential for broadening our category platforms and building scale in China, the world's largest soup market. We plan to expand our product platforms in Latin America as well. It is a growing market where we have an established presence in soup and beverages. To reach beyond our current geographies, we have developed rigorous criteria for evaluating growth opportunities and a short list of priority markets.

We have partnered with Swire Pacific Limited in China, the world's largest soup market, to produce and sell soup and broth products, including a line of condensed soups. These convenient soups help ease and quicken meal preparation in Chinese households.

Continue to drive growth in Healthy Beverages and Baked Snacks

Third, we will continue to drive growth in Healthy Beverages and Baked Snacks. Over the past five years, we have achieved impressive success in our Healthy Beverages business, leveraging the differentiating credentials of the *V8* brand and expanding the brand platform through a steady stream of successful innovation. In fiscal 2011, however, growth in the U.S. business slowed as competitors entered the market. Through continuous innovation, improved marketing and investment to restore our competitiveness, we can and will reignite the growth of our U.S. Beverages business. In fiscal 2012, we are launching exciting new offerings, such as *V8 V-Fusion* Smoothies, *V8 V-Fusion + Energy* beverages and *V8* Energy Shots, which appeal to a wide range of consumers, especially the active Millennial generation.

In global Baked Snacks, we have a consistent track record of innovation, as well as a platform for future growth in existing and new geographies. Both Pepperidge Farm and Arnott's have strong potential to continue to grow beyond their current product and geographic borders.

Expanding the *Goldfish* Brand Within our Pepperidge Farm portfolio, the steady expansion of the *Goldfish* product range into adjacent segments exemplifies how smart and focused innovation can broaden brand scale and reach. In recent years, this brand has been extended from savory children's crackers to sweet products such as *Goldfish* Grahams, and from flavors centered on young children to those that appeal to tweens and beyond. In fiscal 2012, the franchise will expand from crackers to bakery, with new *Goldfish* sandwich breads that aim to delight kids and lunch-making parents.

The *Pepperidge Farm* brand has traced a similar course. Through continuous innovation, we've sustained the core equities of the brand in cookies and bakery, while extending them into the adult savory cracker segment with our

Pepperidge Farm Goldfish Flavor Blasted **Grahams, made with whole grain and no artificial preservatives, give parents a smart way to satisfy their kid's sweet tooth.**

The *V8* brand continues to satisfy consumers' thirst for new beverages. *V8 V-Fusion* Smoothies blend 100% fruit and vegetable juices and purees into a thick and creamy texture, providing a good-for-you and delicious snack.

successful *Baked Naturals* product line and capitalizing on the booming interest in wholesome alternatives to fried snacks with new products such as *Baked Naturals* cracker chips. Last year, we also enhanced our signature *Milano* cookie line with the introduction of delectable *Milano Melts*, which will be followed in fiscal 2012 by *Milano Slices*.

In Asia Pacific, our Arnott's biscuit business has posted impressive growth. In fiscal 2012, we will seek to continue its growth in the savory biscuit segment with the launch of *Arnott's Shapes Roadies*, a product with crispy textures and bigger flavors for young-adult-male consumers, and *Vita-Weat Lunch Slices* for health-conscious consumers. We are also creating new varieties of our signature *Arnott's Tim Tam* biscuit line.

A Year of Strategic Transition

Fiscal 2012 will be a year of transition and investment for Campbell. We will invest to ensure the competitiveness of our brands and fund enhanced brand-building activities across our portfolio. We will invest in external development as strategic opportunities arise. Most important, we will make a significant investment in innovation, as we develop new products and packaging formats to meet consumers where they are now and where we believe they will be in the future.

Successful execution of our new strategic imperatives will require strong and capable leadership. I am delighted with our new Campbell leadership team, and privileged to lead such a talented, accomplished and dedicated group of executives. We are committed to leveraging the exceptionally high engagement of Campbell employees to improve business performance, and to maintaining the powerful culture of our organization, which is rooted in Campbell's core values of Character, Competence and Teamwork. "The Way We Work" inspires us to continue to build a safe, diverse, inclusive, engaged and responsible company that conducts business and delivers strong results with the highest standards of integrity.

Baker's Bliss

Whenever employees would show a new product to Pepperidge Farm founder Margaret Rudkin, she would reply, "That's excellent, but what's next?"

Pepperidge Farm Master Baker and Chef Mark Fitch continues the quest to discover what's next. "That's the goal we work on every day," says Chef Mark.

Pepperidge Farm has a unique way of combining fun with wholesomeness, as shown by *Goldfish* sandwich breads. These unique breads mark the first time that a fresh-bakery product has adopted the iconic trademark shape or tapped into the massive brand equity of *Goldfish*.

To build on the hugely popular *Milano* cookies, we created *Milano Melts* — the first new style of cookie marketed under the *Milano* name since its inception in the 1950s.

Mark Fitch
Pepperidge Farm
Certified Master Baker

LEADERSHIP PERFORMANCE

OUR TEAM

1. **B. Craig Owens**
Senior Vice President —
Chief Financial
Officer and Chief
Administrative Officer

2. **Nancy A. Reardon**
Senior Vice President —
Chief Human Resources
and Communications
Officer

3. **David R. White**
Senior Vice President —
Global Supply Chain

4. **Irene Chang Britt**
Senior Vice President —
Chief Strategy Officer

5. **George Dowdie**
Senior Vice President —
Global Research &
Development and
Quality

6. **Denise M. Morrison**
President and Chief
Executive Officer

7. **Mark Alexander**
Senior Vice President
and President —
Campbell International

8. **Sean Connolly**
Senior Vice President
and President —
Campbell North
America

9. **Ellen Oran Kaden**
Senior Vice President —
Law and Government
Affairs

10. **Joseph C. Spagnoletti**
Senior Vice President
and Chief Information
Officer

11. **Patrick J. Callaghan**
Vice President
and President —
Pepperidge Farm

Our Corporate Citizenship

We believe corporate social responsibility and sustainability are integrated business platforms that build long-term shareowner value. These platforms foster innovation, drive operational efficiency, improve environmental performance, reduce costs, and strengthen our employees' relationships with our customers, suppliers, communities and each other.

Campbell's "Nourishing" Corporate Social Responsibility program continues to deliver measurable benefits to our communities, planet and consumers. In fiscal 2011, we launched a comprehensive, one-of-a-kind initiative to combat childhood hunger and obesity by joining Campbell's resources and expertise with powerful partners to improve the health of young people in Camden, N.J., and eventually, in all of our communities. Investments in improvements in environmental performance at our manufacturing plants and in product packaging significantly reduced our use of resources and delivered healthy returns on invested capital. Last year, construction was initiated on a 10-megawatt, 60-acre solar farm — the largest of its kind in the U.S. — at our plant in Napoleon, Ohio.

A New Campbell

Our employees around the world are working to build a Campbell of the future that will be meaningfully different from the company you know today. As we focus forward, you will see us create a company with a broader and stronger agenda for growth. We will be better balanced across our product portfolios and in our international presence, better positioned to compete based on our brand strengths and better equipped to respond to the evolving needs of both our loyal consumer base and other important consumer groups.

In fiscal 2012, these changes will require a reduction in earnings as we reinvest to rebuild important brands and jump-start a new innovation process, philosophy and pipeline. But we are confident that this course will enhance our ability to create shareowner value over the long term. Beyond fiscal 2012, our long-term targets are 3 to 4 percent net sales growth, 4 to 6 percent adjusted EBIT growth and 5 to 7 percent adjusted net earnings per share growth.

I am inspired by the opportunity to lead an exciting new era of growth at Campbell. In the years to come, I look forward to celebrating with you the ongoing success of our great company.

Best,

Denise M. Morrison
President and Chief Executive Officer

Campbell's

THE WAY WE WORK

We will positively contribute to building and sustaining a safe, diverse, inclusive, engaged and socially responsible workplace focused on delivering business results with integrity.

OUR VALUES

We will create a high-performance culture that lives our values.

Character
> Inspiring trust
> Acting with integrity
> Taking personal responsibility and driving our future with optimism

Competence
> Building a learning organization with diverse perspectives
> Developing new capabilities to drive growth and innovation
> Executing our plan with agility to deliver our business results

Teamwork
> Working together and operating as "One Team Plus" with an enterprise-wide mindset

Chairman's Message

 During fiscal 2011, management and the Board undertook an important process to forge a new path for our company while retaining its outstanding culture and strong traditions. Following a comprehensive review of Campbell's recent business performance and global trends in the food industry, we agreed on a new strategic framework and core strategic imperatives to build long-term shareowner value. The new strategy calls upon us to drive profitable growth through a carefully calibrated program of global expansion and a sharpened focus on innovation to meet the needs of today's consumers and expand Campbell's iconic brands and product offerings across our core categories of Simple Meals, Healthy Beverages and Baked Snacks. It is described in greater detail elsewhere in this report.

In June, the Board elected Denise Morrison as President and Chief Executive Officer, effective August 1, 2011. Denise is an exceptional leader with a comprehensive knowledge of Campbell's business and the food industry, and keen insights into the opportunities for driving profitable growth across Campbell's portfolio. We are confident that the company will flourish under her direction. The Board again thanks Doug Conant for a decade of superb leadership and for his assistance with a smooth and successful leadership transition. We are very pleased to have Denise at the helm, and look forward to the next exciting chapter at Campbell Soup Company.

After 15 years of distinguished service, including five years as Chairman, Harvey Golub will retire from the Board of Directors on November 17. Throughout his tenure, Harvey provided outstanding thought leadership and counsel to management and the Board. We are deeply grateful to him for his invaluable contributions. All other incumbent directors are standing for reelection at the Annual Meeting in November. The Board has nominated Tracey T. Travis, Senior Vice President of Finance and Chief Financial Officer of Ralph Lauren Corporation, to succeed Harvey. We believe that Tracey's business experience and financial expertise will be important assets to our company.

Paul R. Charron
Chairman of the Board

FINANCIAL HIGHLIGHTS

(dollars in millions, except per share amounts)	2011	2010
Results of Operations		
Net sales	$ 7,719	$ 7,676
Gross profit	$ 3,103	$ 3,150
Percent of sales	40.2%	41.0%
Earnings before interest and taxes	$ 1,279	$ 1,348
Net earnings attributable to Campbell Soup Company	$ 805	$ 844
Per share—diluted	$ 2.42	$ 2.42
Other Information		
Net cash provided by operating activities	$ 1,142	$ 1,057
Capital expenditures	$ 272	$ 315
Dividends per share	$ 1.145	$ 1.075

The 2011 Net earnings attributable to Campbell Soup Company were impacted by a $41 ($.12 per share) restructuring charge associated with initiatives announced in June 2011 to improve supply chain efficiency, reduce overhead costs across the organization and exit the Russian market.

The 2010 Net earnings attributable to Campbell Soup Company were impacted by the following: an $8 ($.02 per share) restructuring charge associated with the 2008 initiatives to improve operational efficiency and long-term profitability and $10 ($.03 per share) of deferred tax expense due to the enactment of U.S. health care legislation.

See below for a reconciliation of the impact of these items on reported results.

RECONCILIATION OF GAAP AND NON-GAAP FINANCIAL MEASURES

The following information is provided to reconcile certain non-GAAP financial measures disclosed in the Letter to Shareowners to reported earnings results. The company believes that financial information excluding certain transactions not considered to be part of the ongoing business improves the comparability of year-to-year earnings results. Consequently, the company believes that investors may be able to better understand its earnings results if these transactions are excluded from the results. These non-GAAP financial measures are measures of performance not defined by accounting principles generally accepted in the United States and should be considered in addition to, not in lieu of, GAAP reported measures.

	2011		2010		Earnings % Change	EPS % Change
(dollars in millions, except per share amounts)	Earnings Impact	Diluted EPS Impact	Earnings Impact	Diluted EPS Impact	2011/2010	2011/2010
Net earnings attributable to Campbell Soup Company, as reported	$ 805	$ 2.42	$ 844	$ 2.42		
Restructuring charges	41	0.12	8	0.02		
Tax expense from health care legislation	—	—	10	0.03		
Adjusted Net earnings attributable to Campbell Soup Company	$ 846	$ 2.54	$ 862	$ 2.47	(2)%	3%

UNITED STATES SECURITIES AND EXCHANGE COMMISSION
Washington, D.C. 20549

Form 10-K

ANNUAL REPORT PURSUANT TO SECTION 13 OR 15(d) OF THE SECURITIES EXCHANGE ACT OF 1934

For the Fiscal Year Ended	Commission File Number
July 31, 2011	1-3822

CAMPBELL SOUP COMPANY

New Jersey	21-0419870
State of Incorporation	*I.R.S. Employer Identification No.*

1 Campbell Place
Camden, New Jersey 08103-1799
Principal Executive Offices
Telephone Number: (856) 342-4800

Securities registered pursuant to Section 12(b) of the Act:

Title of Each Class	Name of Each Exchange on Which Registered
Capital Stock, par value $.0375	New York Stock Exchange

Securities registered pursuant to Section 12(g) of the Act: None

Indicate by check mark if the registrant is a well-known seasoned issuer, as defined in Rule 405 of the Securities Act. ☑ Yes   ☐ No

Indicate by check mark if the registrant is not required to file reports pursuant to Section 13 or 15(d) of the Act. ☐ Yes   ☑ No

Indicate by check mark whether the registrant: (1) has filed all reports required to be filed by Section 13 or 15(d) of the Securities Exchange Act of 1934 during the preceding 12 months (or for such shorter period that the registrant was required to file such reports), and (2) has been subject to such filing requirements for the past 90 days. ☑ Yes   ☐ No

Indicate by check mark whether the registrant has submitted electronically and posted on its corporate web site, if any, every Interactive Date File required to be submitted and posted pursuant to Rule 405 of Regulation S-T during the preceding 12 months (or for such shorter period that the registrant was required to submit and post such files). ☑ Yes   ☐ No

Indicate by check mark if disclosure of delinquent filers pursuant to Item 405 of Regulation S-K is not contained herein, and will not be contained, to the best of registrant's knowledge, in definitive proxy or information statements incorporated by reference in Part III of this Form 10-K or any amendment to this Form 10-K. ☐

Indicate by check mark whether the registrant is a large accelerated filer, an accelerated filer, a non-accelerated filer, or a smaller reporting company. See the definitions of "large accelerated filer," "accelerated filer" and "smaller reporting company" in Rule 12b-2 of the Exchange Act.

Large accelerated filer ☑   Accelerated filer ☐   Non-accelerated filer ☐   Smaller reporting company ☐
(Do not check if a smaller reporting company)

Indicate by check mark whether the registrant is a shell company (as defined in Rule 12b-2 of the Exchange Act). ☐ Yes   ☑ No

As of January 28, 2011 (the last business day of the registrant's most recently completed second fiscal quarter), the aggregate market value of capital stock held by non-affiliates of the registrant was approximately $6,343,490,643. There were 320,209,348 shares of capital stock outstanding as of September 15, 2011.

Portions of the Registrant's Proxy Statement for the Annual Meeting of Shareowners to be held on November 17, 2011, are incorporated by reference into Part III.

Table of Contents

Item 6. *Selected Financial Data*

FIVE-YEAR REVIEW — CONSOLIDATED

Fiscal Year	2011(1)	2010(2)	2009(3)	2008(4)	2007(5)
	(Millions, except per share amounts)				
Summary of Operations					
Net sales	$7,719	$7,676	$7,586	$7,998	$7,385
Earnings before interest and taxes	1,279	1,348	1,185	1,098	1,243
Earnings before taxes	1,168	1,242	1,079	939	1,099
Earnings from continuing operations	802	844	732	671	792
Earnings from discontinued operations	—	—	4	494	62
Net earnings	802	844	736	1,165	854
Net earnings attributable to Campbell Soup Company	805	844	736	1,165	854
Financial Position					
Plant assets — net	$2,103	$2,051	$1,977	$1,939	$2,042
Total assets	6,862	6,276	6,056	6,474	6,445
Total debt	3,084	2,780	2,624	2,615	2,669
Total equity	1,096	929	731	1,321	1,298
Per Share Data					
Earnings from continuing operations attributable to Campbell Soup Company — basic	$ 2.44	$ 2.44	$ 2.05	$ 1.77	$ 2.02
Earnings from continuing operations attributable to Campbell Soup Company — assuming dilution	2.42	2.42	2.03	1.75	1.99
Net earnings attributable to Campbell Soup Company — basic	2.44	2.44	2.06	3.06	2.18
Net earnings attributable to Campbell Soup Company — assuming dilution	2.42	2.42	2.05	3.03	2.14
Dividends declared	1.145	1.075	1.00	0.88	0.80
Other Statistics					
Capital expenditures	$ 272	$ 315	$ 345	$ 298	$ 334
Weighted average shares outstanding — basic	326	340	352	373	386
Weighted average shares outstanding — assuming dilution	329	343	354	377	392

In the first quarter of fiscal 2010, the company adopted and retrospectively applied new accounting guidance related to a noncontrolling interest in a subsidiary. The guidance requires a noncontrolling interest in a subsidiary to be classified as a separate component of total equity.

In the first quarter of fiscal 2010, the company adopted and retrospectively applied new accounting guidance related to the calculation of earnings per share. The retrospective application of the provision resulted in the following reductions to basic and diluted earnings per share:

	2009		2008		2007	
	Basic	Diluted	Basic	Diluted	Basic	Diluted
Earnings from continuing operations attributable to Campbell Soup Company	$(.03)	$(.01)	$(.03)	$(.01)	$(.03)	$(.01)
Net earnings attributable to Campbell Soup Company	$(.03)	$(.01)	$(.06)	$(.03)	$(.03)	$(.02)

(All per share amounts below are on a diluted basis)

The 2008 fiscal year consisted of fifty-three weeks. All other periods had fifty-two weeks.

(1) The 2011 earnings from continuing operations were impacted by a restructuring charge of $41 million ($.12 per share) associated with initiatives announced in June 2011 to improve supply chain efficiency, reduce overhead costs across the organization and exit the Russian market.

(2) The 2010 earnings from continuing operations were impacted by the following: a restructuring charge of $8 million ($.02 per share) for pension benefit costs associated with the 2008 initiatives to improve operational efficiency and long-term profitability and $10 million ($.03 per share) to reduce deferred tax assets as a result of the U.S. health care legislation enacted in March 2010.

(3) The 2009 earnings from continuing operations were impacted by the following: an impairment charge of $47 million ($.13 per share) related to certain European trademarks and $15 million ($.04 per share) of restructuring-related costs associated with the 2008 initiatives to improve operational efficiency and long-term profitability. The 2009 results of discontinued operations represented a $4 million ($.01 per share) tax benefit related to the sale of the Godiva Chocolatier business.

(4) The 2008 earnings from continuing operations were impacted by the following: a $107 million ($.28 per share) restructuring charge and related costs associated with initiatives to improve operational efficiency and long-term profitability and a $13 million ($.03 per share) benefit from the favorable resolution of a tax contingency. The 2008 results of discontinued operations included a $462 million ($1.20 per share) gain from the sale of the Godiva Chocolatier business.

(5) The 2007 earnings from continuing operations were impacted by the following: a $13 million ($.03 per share) benefit from the reversal of legal reserves due to favorable results in litigation; a $25 million ($.06 per share) benefit from a tax settlement of bilateral advance pricing agreements; and a $14 million ($.04 per share) gain from the sale of an idle manufacturing facility. The 2007 results of discontinued operations included a $24 million ($.06 per share) gain from the sale of the businesses in the United Kingdom and Ireland and a $7 million ($.02 per share) tax benefit from the resolution of audits in the United Kingdom.

Five-Year Review should be read in conjunction with the Notes to Consolidated Financial Statements.

Item 7. *Management's Discussion and Analysis of Financial Condition and Results of Operations*

Overview

Description of the Company

Campbell Soup Company is a global manufacturer and marketer of high-quality, branded convenience food products. Commencing with the fourth quarter of fiscal 2011, the company reports the results of operations in the following reportable segments: U.S. Simple Meals; U.S. Beverages; Global Baking and Snacking; International Simple Meals and Beverages; and North America Foodservice. Segment results of prior periods were modified to conform to the current presentation. See Note 6 to the Consolidated Financial Statements for additional information on segments.

Key Strategies

In fiscal 2011, management and the Board of Directors conducted a comprehensive review of the company's recent performance and business strategies. In July 2011, the company announced a new strategic framework focused on expansion of its brand and product platforms in its three core categories of simple meals, healthy beverages and baked snacks. The new framework is centered on three growth strategies:

- Stabilize and then profitably grow the company's North America soup and simple meals business.

- Expand the company's international presence.

- Continue to drive growth in the company's healthy beverages and baked snacks businesses.

The new growth strategies are intended to accelerate profitable net sales growth and build the foundation for delivery of sustainable above-average total shareholder returns.

Implementation of the company's new strategic framework will require substantial investment in 2012 to extend product platforms, re-invigorate consumer-focused marketing to expand the equities of its core brands, and drive global expansion. The company expects that these investments will negatively affect financial performance in 2012, but set the stage for profitable growth in 2013 and beyond.

Item 8. *Financial Statements and Supplementary Data*

CAMPBELL SOUP COMPANY

Consolidated Statements of Earnings

	2011	2010	2009
	(Millions, except per share amounts)		
Net sales	**$7,719**	$7,676	$7,586
Costs and expenses			
Cost of products sold	**4,616**	4,526	4,558
Marketing and selling expenses.	**1,007**	1,058	1,077
Administrative expenses	**612**	605	591
Research and development expenses	**129**	123	114
Other expenses / (income)	**13**	4	61
Restructuring charges	**63**	12	—
Total costs and expenses	**6,440**	6,328	6,401
Earnings before interest and taxes	**1,279**	1,348	1,185
Interest expense	**122**	112	110
Interest income	**11**	6	4
Earnings before taxes.	**1,168**	1,242	1,079
Taxes on earnings	**366**	398	347
Earnings from continuing operations.	**802**	844	732
Earnings from discontinued operations	**—**	—	4
Net earnings	**802**	844	736
Less: Net earnings (loss) attributable to noncontrolling interests	**(3)**	—	—
Net earnings attributable to Campbell Soup Company	**$ 805**	$ 844	$ 736
Per Share — Basic			
Earnings from continuing operations attributable to Campbell Soup Company	**$ 2.44**	$ 2.44	$ 2.05
Earnings from discontinued operations attributable to Campbell Soup Company	**—**	—	0.01
Net earnings attributable to Campbell Soup Company	**$ 2.44**	$ 2.44	$ 2.06
Weighted average shares outstanding — basic	**326**	340	352
Per Share — Assuming Dilution			
Earnings from continuing operations attributable to Campbell Soup Company	**$ 2.42**	$ 2.42	$ 2.03
Earnings from discontinued operations attributable to Campbell Soup Company	**—**	—	0.01
Net earnings attributable to Campbell Soup Company	**$ 2.42**	$ 2.42	$ 2.05
Weighted average shares outstanding — assuming dilution	**329**	343	354

The sum of individual per share amounts does not equal due to rounding.

See accompanying Notes to Consolidated Financial Statements.

CAMPBELL SOUP COMPANY

Consolidated Balance Sheets

	July 31, 2011	August 1, 2010
	(Millions, except per share amounts)	
Current assets		
Cash and cash equivalents	$ **484**	$ 254
Accounts receivable	**560**	512
Inventories	**767**	724
Other current assets	**152**	197
Total current assets	**1,963**	1,687
Plant assets, net of depreciation	**2,103**	2,051
Goodwill	**2,133**	1,919
Other intangible assets, net of amortization	**527**	509
Other assets	**136**	110
Total assets	**$ 6,862**	$ 6,276
Current liabilities		
Short-term borrowings	$ **657**	$ 835
Payable to suppliers and others	**585**	545
Accrued liabilities	**619**	560
Dividend payable	**95**	95
Accrued income taxes	**33**	30
Total current liabilities	**1,989**	2,065
Long-term debt	**2,427**	1,945
Deferred taxes	**367**	258
Other liabilities	**983**	1,079
Total liabilities	**5,766**	5,347
Campbell Soup Company shareowners' equity		
Preferred stock; authorized 40 shares; none issued	**—**	—
Capital stock, $.0375 par value; authorized 560 shares; issued 542 shares	**20**	20
Additional paid-in capital	**331**	341
Earnings retained in the business	**9,185**	8,760
Capital stock in treasury, at cost	**(8,021)**	(7,459)
Accumulated other comprehensive loss	**(427)**	(736)
Total Campbell Soup Company shareowners' equity	**1,088**	926
Noncontrolling interests	**8**	3
Total equity	**1,096**	929
Total liabilities and equity	**$ 6,862**	$ 6,276

See accompanying Notes to Consolidated Financial Statements.

CAMPBELL SOUP COMPANY

Consolidated Statements of Cash Flows

	2011	2010	2009
		(Millions)	
Cash flows from operating activities:			
Net earnings	$ 802	$ 844	$ 736
Adjustments to reconcile net earnings to operating cash flow			
Impairment charge	—	—	67
Restructuring charges	63	12	—
Stock-based compensation	87	88	84
Depreciation and amortization	268	251	264
Deferred income taxes	46	54	144
Other, net	108	99	57
Changes in working capital			
Accounts receivable	(15)	21	27
Inventories	(14)	105	(14)
Prepaid assets	19	(9)	28
Accounts payable and accrued liabilities	(26)	(34)	(125)
Pension fund contributions	(144)	(284)	(13)
Receipts from/(payments of) hedging activities	3	(20)	(44)
Other	(55)	(70)	(45)
Net cash provided by operating activities	**1,142**	1,057	1,166
Cash flows from investing activities:			
Purchases of plant assets	(272)	(315)	(345)
Sales of plant assets	9	13	1
Business acquired	—	—	(66)
Sale of business, net of cash divested	—	—	38
Other, net	2	2	(6)
Net cash used in investing activities	**(261)**	(300)	(378)
Cash flows from financing activities:			
Net short-term borrowings (repayments)	495	(265)	(320)
Long-term borrowings	500	400	600
Repayments of notes payable	(700)	—	(300)
Dividends paid	(378)	(365)	(350)
Treasury stock purchases	(728)	(472)	(527)
Treasury stock issuances	96	139	72
Excess tax benefits on stock-based compensation	11	11	18
Contribution from noncontrolling interest	10	—	—
Other, net	(6)	(4)	(7)
Net cash used in financing activities	**(700)**	(556)	(814)
Effect of exchange rate changes on cash	**49**	2	(4)
Net change in cash and cash equivalents	**230**	203	(30)
Cash and cash equivalents — beginning of period	**254**	51	81
Cash and cash equivalents — end of period	**$ 484**	$ 254	$ 51

See accompanying Notes to Consolidated Financial Statements.

CAMPBELL SOUP COMPANY

Consolidated Statements of Equity

	Campbell Soup Company Shareowners' Equity							
	Capital Stock				Additional Paid-in Capital	Earnings Retained in the Business	Accumulated Other Comprehensive Income (Loss)	Noncontrolling Interests	Total Equity
	Issued		In Treasury						
	Shares	Amount	Shares	Amount					
	(Millions, except per share amounts)								
Balance at August 3, 2008	542	$20	(186)	$(6,812)	$337	$7,909	$(136)	$ 3	$1,321
Comprehensive income (loss)									
Net earnings (loss).						736		—	736
Foreign currency translation adjustments, net of tax.							(148)	—	(148)
Cash-flow hedges, net of tax							(25)		(25)
Pension and postretirement benefits, net of tax							(409)		(409)
Other comprehensive income (loss) . . .							(582)	—	(582)
Total comprehensive income (loss)									154
Dividends ($1.00 per share)						(357)			(357)
Treasury stock purchased			(17)	(527)					(527)
Treasury stock issued under management incentive and stock option plans			4	145	(5)				140
Balance at August 2, 2009	542	20	(199)	(7,194)	332	8,288	(718)	3	731
Comprehensive income (loss)									
Net earnings (loss).						844		—	844
Foreign currency translation adjustments, net of tax.							39	—	39
Cash-flow hedges, net of tax							2		2
Pension and postretirement benefits, net of tax							(59)		(59)
Other comprehensive income (loss) . . .							(18)	—	(18)
Total comprehensive income (loss)									826
Dividends ($1.075 per share).						(372)			(372)
Treasury stock purchased			(14)	(472)					(472)
Treasury stock issued under management incentive and stock option plans			7	207	9				216
Balance at August 1, 2010	542	20	(206)	(7,459)	341	8,760	(736)	3	929
Contribution from noncontrolling interest								8	8
Comprehensive income (loss)									
Net earnings (loss)						805		(3)	802
Foreign currency translation adjustments, net of tax.							264	—	264
Cash-flow hedges, net of tax							(2)		(2)
Pension and postretirement benefits, net of tax.							47		47
Other comprehensive income (loss). .							309	—	309
Total comprehensive income (loss)									1,111
Dividends ($1.145 per share).						(380)			(380)
Treasury stock purchased			(21)	(728)					(728)
Treasury stock issued under management incentive and stock option plans			5	166	(10)				156
Balance at July 31, 2011	542	$20	(222)	$(8,021)	$331	$9,185	$(427)	$ 8	$1,096

See accompanying Notes to Consolidated Financial Statements.

NOTES TO CONSOLIDATED FINANCIAL STATEMENTS
(currency in millions, except per share amounts)

1. Summary of Significant Accounting Policies

Campbell Soup Company, together with its subsidiaries (the company), is a global manufacturer and marketer of high-quality, branded convenience food products.

Basis of Presentation — The consolidated financial statements include the accounts of the company and entities in which the company maintains a controlling financial interest. Intercompany transactions are eliminated in consolidation. Certain amounts in prior-year financial statements were reclassified to conform to the current-year presentation. The company's fiscal year ends on the Sunday nearest July 31. There were 52 weeks in 2011, 2010 and 2009.

Use of Estimates — Generally accepted accounting principles require management to make estimates and assumptions that affect assets and liabilities, contingent assets and liabilities, and revenues and expenses. Actual results could differ from those estimates.

Revenue Recognition — Revenues are recognized when the earnings process is complete. This occurs when products are shipped in accordance with terms of agreements, title and risk of loss transfer to customers, collection is probable and pricing is fixed or determinable. Revenues are recognized net of provisions for returns, discounts and allowances. Certain sales promotion expenses, such as feature price discounts, in-store display incentives, cooperative advertising programs, new product introduction fees and coupon redemption costs, are classified as a reduction of sales. The recognition of costs for promotion programs involves the use of judgment related to performance and redemption estimates. Estimates are made based on historical experience and other factors. Costs are recognized either upon sale or when the incentive is offered, based on the program.

Cash and Cash Equivalents — All highly liquid debt instruments purchased with a maturity of three months or less are classified as cash equivalents.

Inventories — All inventories are valued at the lower of average cost or market.

Property, Plant and Equipment — Property, plant and equipment are recorded at historical cost and are depreciated over estimated useful lives using the straight-line method. Buildings and machinery and equipment are depreciated over periods not exceeding 45 years and 20 years, respectively. Assets are evaluated for impairment when conditions indicate that the carrying value may not be recoverable. Such conditions include significant adverse changes in business climate or a plan of disposal. Repairs and maintenance are charged to expense.

Goodwill and Intangible Assets — Goodwill and indefinite-lived intangible assets are not amortized but rather are tested at least annually for impairment. Goodwill and indefinite-lived intangible assets are also tested for impairment as events or changes in circumstances occur indicating that the carrying value may not be recoverable. Intangible assets with finite lives are amortized over the estimated useful life and are also reviewed when appropriate for possible impairment. Goodwill impairment testing first requires a comparison of the fair value of each reporting unit to the carrying value. A reporting unit is an operating segment or a component of an operating segment. If the carrying value of the reporting unit exceeds fair value, goodwill is considered impaired. The amount of the impairment is the difference between the carrying value of goodwill and the "implied" fair value, which is calculated as if the reporting unit had just been acquired and accounted for as a business combination. Impairment testing for indefinite-lived intangible assets requires a comparison between the fair value and carrying value of the asset. If carrying value exceeds the fair value, the asset is reduced to fair value. Fair values are primarily determined using discounted cash flow analyses. See Note 5 for information on goodwill and other intangible assets.

Derivative Financial Instruments — The company uses derivative financial instruments primarily for purposes of hedging exposures to fluctuations in foreign currency exchange rates, interest rates, commodities and equity-linked employee benefit obligations. These derivative contracts are entered into for periods consistent with the related underlying exposures and do not constitute positions independent of those exposures. The company does not enter into derivative contracts for speculative purposes and does not use leveraged instruments. The company's derivative programs include strategies that both qualify and do not qualify for hedge accounting treatment. To

NOTES TO CONSOLIDATED FINANCIAL STATEMENTS — (Continued)

qualify for hedge accounting, the hedging relationship, both at inception of the hedge and on an ongoing basis, shall be expected to be highly effective in achieving offsetting changes in the fair value of the hedged risk during the period that the hedge is designated.

All derivatives are recognized on the balance sheet at fair value. For derivatives that qualify for hedge accounting, on the date the derivative contract is entered into, the company designates the derivative as a hedge of the fair value of a recognized asset or liability or a firm commitment (fair-value hedge), a hedge of a forecasted transaction or of the variability of cash flows to be received or paid related to a recognized asset or liability (cash-flow hedge), or a hedge of a net investment in a foreign operation. Some derivatives may also be considered natural hedging instruments (changes in fair value act as economic offsets to changes in fair value of the underlying hedged item) and are not designated for hedge accounting.

Changes in the fair value of a fair-value hedge, along with the gain or loss on the underlying hedged asset or liability (including losses or gains on firm commitments), are recorded in current-period earnings. The effective portion of gains and losses on cash-flow hedges are recorded in other comprehensive income (loss), until earnings are affected by the variability of cash flows. If the underlying hedged item ceases to exist, all changes in the fair value of the derivative are included in earnings each period until the instrument matures. If a derivative is used as a hedge of a net investment in a foreign operation, its changes in fair value, to the extent effective as a hedge, are recorded in other comprehensive income (loss). Any ineffective portion of designated hedges is recognized in current-period earnings. Changes in the fair value of derivatives that are not designated for hedge accounting are recognized in current-period earnings.

Cash flows from derivative contracts are included in Net cash provided by operating activities.

Advertising Production Costs — Advertising production costs are expensed in the period that the advertisement first takes place.

Research and Development Costs — The costs of research and development are expensed as incurred. Costs include expenditures for new product and manufacturing process innovation, and improvements to existing products and processes. Costs primarily consist of salaries, wages, consulting, and depreciation and maintenance of research facilities and equipment.

Income Taxes — Deferred tax assets and liabilities are recognized for the future impact of differences between the financial statement carrying amounts of assets and liabilities and their respective tax bases, as well as for operating loss and tax credit carryforwards. Deferred tax assets and liabilities are measured using enacted tax rates expected to apply to taxable income in the years in which those temporary differences are expected to be recovered or settled. The effect on deferred tax assets and liabilities of a change in tax rates is recognized in income in the period that includes the enactment date. Valuation allowances are recorded to reduce deferred tax assets when it is more likely than not that a tax benefit will not be realized.

2. Recent Accounting Pronouncements

In December 2007, the Financial Accounting Standards Board (FASB) issued authoritative guidance which establishes accounting and reporting standards for the noncontrolling interest in a subsidiary and for the deconsolidation of a subsidiary. It requires a noncontrolling interest in a subsidiary, which was formerly known as minority interest, to be classified as a separate component of total equity in the consolidated financial statements. The company retrospectively adopted the new noncontrolling interest guidance in the first quarter of fiscal 2010. The adoption did not have a material impact on the financial statements. See Note 10 for additional information.

In December 2007, the FASB issued authoritative guidance for business combinations, which establishes the principles and requirements for how an acquirer recognizes the assets acquired, the liabilities assumed, and any noncontrolling interest in the acquiree at the acquisition date, measured at their fair values as of that date with limited exceptions. The guidance requires acquisition-related transaction costs to be expensed as incurred rather than capitalized as a component of the business combination. The provisions as revised were effective as of the first quarter of fiscal 2010 and will be applied to any business combinations entered into thereafter.

NOTES TO CONSOLIDATED FINANCIAL STATEMENTS — (Continued)

In September 2006, the FASB issued authoritative guidance for fair value measurements, which establishes a definition of fair value, provides a framework for measuring fair value and expands the disclosure requirements about fair value measurements. This guidance does not require any new fair value measurements but rather applies to all other accounting pronouncements that require or permit fair value measurements. In February 2008, the FASB issued authoritative guidance which delayed by a year the effective date for certain nonfinancial assets and liabilities. The company adopted the provisions of the guidance for financial assets and liabilities in the first quarter of fiscal 2009. The adoption did not have a material impact on the consolidated financial statements. The company adopted the remaining provisions in the first quarter of fiscal 2010 for nonfinancial assets and liabilities, including goodwill and intangible assets. The adoption likewise did not have a material impact on the consolidated financial statements. See Note 15 for additional information.

In June 2008, the FASB issued authoritative guidance related to the calculation of earnings per share. The guidance provides that unvested share-based payment awards that contain non-forfeitable rights to dividends or dividend equivalents (whether paid or unpaid) are participating securities and shall be included in the computation of earnings per share pursuant to the two-class method. Upon adoption, a company is required to retrospectively adjust its earnings per share data (including any amounts related to interim periods, summaries of earnings and selected financial data) to conform with the new provisions. The company adopted the guidance in the first quarter of fiscal 2010. Prior periods have been restated. See Note 9 for additional information.

In December 2008, the FASB issued additional authoritative guidance related to employers' disclosures about the plan assets of defined benefit pension or other postretirement plans. The required disclosures include a description of how investment allocation decisions are made, major categories of plan assets, valuation techniques used to measure the fair value of plan assets, the impact of measurements using significant unobservable inputs and concentrations of risk within plan assets. The disclosures about plan assets required by this additional guidance must be provided for fiscal years ending after December 15, 2009. The company adopted the provisions in fiscal 2010. See Note 11 for additional information.

In January 2010, the FASB issued additional authoritative guidance related to fair value measurements and disclosures. The guidance requires disclosure of details of significant transfers in and out of Level 1 and Level 2 fair value measurements. Level 1 fair value measurements are based on unadjusted quoted market prices. Level 2 fair value measurements are based on significant inputs, other than Level 1, that are observable for the asset/liability through corroboration with observable market data. The guidance also clarifies the existing disclosure requirements for the level of disaggregation of fair value measurements and the disclosures on inputs and valuation techniques. The company adopted these provisions in the third quarter of fiscal 2010. The adoption did not have a material impact on the consolidated financial statements. In addition, the guidance requires a gross presentation of the activity within the Level 3 roll forward, separately presenting information about purchases, sales, issuances and settlements. The roll forward information must be provided by the company for the first quarter of fiscal 2012, as the provision is effective for annual reporting periods beginning after December 15, 2010 and for interim reporting periods within those years.

In June 2009, the FASB issued authoritative guidance that changed the consolidation model for variable interest entities. The provisions were effective for the first quarter of fiscal 2011. The adoption did not have a material impact on the company's consolidated financial statements.

In November 2010, the FASB issued additional authoritative guidance clarifying the required disclosures of supplementary pro forma information for business combinations. The guidance is effective prospectively for business combinations for which the acquisition date is on or after the beginning of the first annual reporting period beginning on or after December 15, 2010.

In December 2010, the FASB issued additional authoritative guidance on accounting for goodwill. The guidance clarifies the impairment test for reporting units with zero or negative carrying amounts. The guidance is effective for fiscal years and interim periods within those years beginning after December 15, 2011. The company does not expect the adoption to have a material impact on the company's consolidated financial statements.

NOTES TO CONSOLIDATED FINANCIAL STATEMENTS — (Continued)

In May 2011, the FASB issued further additional authoritative guidance related to fair value measurements and disclosures. The new guidance results in a consistent definition of fair value and common requirements for measurement of and disclosure about fair value between accounting principles generally accepted in the United States (U.S. GAAP) and International Financial Reporting Standards (IFRS). The guidance is effective for fiscal years and interim reporting periods within those years beginning after December 15, 2011. The company is assessing the impact of the guidance.

In June 2011, the FASB issued authoritative guidance requiring entities to present net income and other comprehensive income (OCI) in one continuous statement or two separate, but consecutive, statements of net income and comprehensive income. The option to present items of OCI in the statement of changes in equity has been eliminated. The new requirements are effective for annual reporting periods beginning after December 15, 2011 and for interim reporting periods within those years.

3. Divestitures

Discontinued Operations

On March 18, 2008, the company completed the sale of its Godiva Chocolatier business for $850. The purchase price was subject to certain post-closing adjustments, which resulted in an additional $20 of proceeds. The company has reflected the results of this business as discontinued operations in the consolidated statements of earnings. The company used approximately $600 of the net proceeds to purchase company stock. The company recognized a $4 benefit in 2009 as a result of an adjustment to the tax liability associated with the sale.

Other Divestitures

In July 2008, the company entered into an agreement to sell its sauce and mayonnaise business comprised of products sold under the *Lesieur* brand in France. The company recorded a pre-tax impairment charge of $2 to adjust the net assets to estimated realizable value in 2008. The sale was completed on September 29, 2008 and resulted in $36 of proceeds. The purchase price was subject to working capital and other post-closing adjustments, which resulted in an additional $6 of proceeds. The business was historically included in the International Simple Meals and Beverages segment.

The company has provided certain indemnifications in connection with the divestitures. Known exposures related to such matters are not material.

4. Comprehensive Income

Total comprehensive income is comprised of net earnings, net foreign currency translation adjustments, pension and postretirement benefit adjustments (see Note 11), and net unrealized gains and losses on cash-flow hedges (see Note 14). Total comprehensive income for the twelve months ended July 31, 2011, August 1, 2010, and August 2, 2009 was $1,111, $826, and $154, respectively.

The components of Accumulated other comprehensive income (loss), as reflected in the Statements of Equity, consisted of the following:

	2011	2010
Foreign currency translation adjustments, net of tax(1)	$ 396	$ 132
Cash-flow hedges, net of tax(2)	(20)	(18)
Unamortized pension and postretirement benefits, net of tax(3):		
Net actuarial loss	(809)	(856)
Prior service credit	6	6
Total Accumulated other comprehensive loss	$(427)	$(736)

NOTES TO CONSOLIDATED FINANCIAL STATEMENTS — (Continued)

(1) Includes a tax expense of $4 in 2011 and a tax benefit of $1 in 2010. The amount related to noncontrolling interests was not material.

(2) Includes a tax benefit of $11 in 2011 and $10 in 2010.

(3) Includes a tax benefit of $459 in 2011 and $489 in 2010.

5. Goodwill and Intangible Assets

The following table shows the changes in the carrying amount of goodwill by business segment:

	U.S. Simple Meals	U.S. Beverages	Global Baking and Snacking	International Simple Meals and Beverages	North America Foodservice	Total
Balance at August 2, 2009	$322	$112	$700	$621	$146	$1,901
Foreign currency translation adjustment	—	—	54	(36)	—	18
Balance at August 1, 2010	$322	$112	$754	$585	$146	$1,919
Foreign currency translation adjustment	—	—	160	54	—	214
Balance at July 31, 2011	**$322**	**$112**	**$914**	**$639**	**$146**	**$2,133**

The following table sets forth balance sheet information for intangible assets, excluding goodwill, subject to amortization and intangible assets not subject to amortization:

	2011	2010
Intangible Assets:		
Non-amortizable intangible assets	$515	$496
Amortizable intangible assets	21	21
	536	517
Accumulated amortization	(9)	(8)
Total net intangible assets	$527	$509

Non-amortizable intangible assets consist of trademarks, which mainly include *Pace, Royco, Liebig, Blå Band* and *Touch of Taste*. Amortizable intangible assets consist substantially of process technology and customer intangibles.

Amortization was less than $1 in 2011, 2010, and 2009. The estimated aggregated amortization expense for each of the five succeeding fiscal years is less than $1 per year. Asset useful lives range from ten to twenty years.

In 2011, as part of the company's annual review of intangible assets, an impairment charge of $3 was recognized related to the *Heisse Tasse* trademark used in the International Simple Meals and Beverages segment. The trademark was determined to be impaired as a result of a decrease in the fair value of the brand, resulting from reduced expectations for future sales and discounted cash flows. The impairment charge was recorded in Other expenses/(income) in the Consolidated Statements of Earnings. As of July 2011, certain European trademarks have a carrying value of approximately $100, which approximates fair value. Fair value is determined based on discounted cash flow analyses that include significant management assumptions such as revenue growth rates, weighted average cost of capital, and assumed royalty rates. Actual cash flows could differ from management's estimates due to changes in business performance, operating performance, and economic conditions. Holding all other assumptions constant, a 100-basis-point increase in the weighted average cost of capital would reduce fair value of all trademarks and result in impairment charges of approximately $21.

NOTES TO CONSOLIDATED FINANCIAL STATEMENTS — (Continued)

In 2009, as part of the company's annual review of intangible assets, an impairment charge of $67 was recognized related to certain European trademarks used in the International Simple Meals and Beverages segment, including *Heisse Tasse*, *Blå Band* and *Royco*. The trademarks were determined to be impaired as a result of a decrease in the fair value of the brands, resulting from reduced expectations for discounted cash flows. The reduction was due in part to a deterioration in market conditions and an increase in the weighted average cost of capital. The impairment charge was recorded in Other expenses/(income) in the Consolidated Statements of Earnings.

In May 2009, the company acquired Ecce Panis, Inc. Intangible assets from the acquisition totaled $16. See Note 8 for additional information.

6. Business and Geographic Segment Information

Commencing with the fourth quarter of fiscal 2011, the company reports the results of operations in the following reportable segments: U.S. Simple Meals; U.S. Beverages; Global Baking and Snacking; International Simple Meals and Beverages; and North America Foodservice. Segment results of prior periods were modified to conform to the current presentation. The company has ten operating segments based on product type and geographic location and has aggregated the operating segments into the appropriate reportable segment based on similar economic characteristics; products; production processes; types or classes of customers; distribution methods; and regulatory environment. The segments are discussed in greater detail below.

The U.S. Simple Meals segment aggregates the following operating segments: U.S. Soup and U.S. Sauces. The U.S. Soup retail business includes the following products: *Campbell's* condensed and ready-to-serve soups; and *Swanson* broth and stocks. The U.S. Sauces retail business includes the following products: *Prego* pasta sauce; *Pace* Mexican sauce; *Swanson* canned poultry; and *Campbell's* canned gravies, pasta and beans.

The U.S. Beverages segment represents the U.S. retail beverages business, including the following products: *V8* juices and beverages; and *Campbell's* tomato juice.

The Global Baking and Snacking segment aggregates the following operating segments: *Pepperidge Farm* cookies, crackers, bakery and frozen products in U.S. retail; and *Arnott's* biscuits in Australia and Asia Pacific.

The International Simple Meals and Beverages segment aggregates the simple meals and beverages operating segments outside of the United States, including Europe, Latin America, the Asia Pacific region and the retail business in Canada. See Note 3 for information on the sale of the sauce and mayonnaise business comprised of products sold under the *Lesieur* brand in France. This business was historically included in this segment.

The North America Foodservice segment represents the distribution of products such as soup, specialty entrees, beverage products, other prepared foods and Pepperidge Farm products through various food service channels in the United States and Canada.

The company's accounting policies for measuring segment assets and earnings before interest and taxes are substantially consistent with those described in Note 1. The company evaluates segment performance before interest, taxes, and beginning in fiscal 2011, costs associated with restructuring activities. Segment operating earnings of prior periods were modified to conform to the current presentation. The manufacturing, warehousing, distribution and selling activities of the company's U.S. retail business are operated as an integrated platform in order to maximize efficiency and productivity. As a result, assets and capital expenditures of the U.S. Simple Meals and U.S. Beverages are not discretely maintained. Depreciation expense associated with the integrated operations, however, is allocated to the U.S. Simple Meals and U.S. Beverages segments based on production hours. North America Foodservice products are principally produced by the tangible assets of the company's other segments, except for refrigerated soups, which are produced in a separate facility, and certain other products, which are produced under contract manufacturing agreements. Tangible assets of the company's other segments are not allocated to the North America Foodservice operations. Depreciation, however, is allocated to North America Foodservice based on production hours.

NOTES TO CONSOLIDATED FINANCIAL STATEMENTS — (Continued)

The company's largest customer, Wal-Mart Stores, Inc. and its affiliates, accounted for approximately 17% of consolidated net sales in 2011 and 18% in 2010 and 2009. All of the company's segments sold products to Wal-Mart Stores, Inc. or its affiliates.

Business Segments

	2011	2010	2009
Net sales			
U.S. Simple Meals	$2,751	$2,938	$3,049
U.S. Beverages	759	762	735
Global Baking and Snacking	2,156	1,975	1,846
International Simple Meals and Beverages	1,463	1,423	1,357
North America Foodservice	590	578	599
Total	$7,719	$7,676	$7,586

	2011	2010	2009(3)
Earnings before interest and taxes			
U.S. Simple Meals	$ 657	$ 737	$ 749
U.S. Beverages	182	206	178
Global Baking and Snacking	355	322	265
International Simple Meals and Beverages	185	161	69
North America Foodservice	82	55	53
Corporate(1)	(119)	(121)	(107)
Restructuring charges and related costs(2)	(63)	(12)	(22)
Total	$1,279	$1,348	$1,185

	2011	2010	2009
Depreciation and Amortization			
U.S. Simple Meals	$ 87	$ 86	$ 86
U.S. Beverages	20	21	15
Global Baking and Snacking	82	75	71
International Simple Meals and Beverages	42	35	41
North America Foodservice	13	13	28
Corporate(1)	24	21	23
Total	$ 268	$ 251	$ 264

	2011	2010	2009
Capital Expenditures			
U.S. Simple Meals and U.S. Beverages	$ 126	$ 139	$ 177
Global Baking and Snacking	73	81	58
International Simple Meals and Beverages	36	26	34
North America Foodservice	3	3	17
Corporate(1)	34	66	59
Total	$ 272	$ 315	$ 345

NOTES TO CONSOLIDATED FINANCIAL STATEMENTS — (Continued)

	2011	2010	2009
Segment Assets			
U.S. Simple Meals and U.S. Beverages	$2,129	$2,146	$2,168
Global Baking and Snacking	1,982	1,710	1,628
International Simple Meals and Beverages	1,539	1,396	1,474
North America Foodservice	350	360	377
Corporate(1)	862	664	409
Total	$6,862	$6,276	$6,056

(1) Represents unallocated corporate expenses and unallocated assets.

(2) See Note 7 for additional information.

(3) Earnings before interest and taxes of the International Simple Meals and Beverages segment included a $67 impairment charge on certain European trademarks. See Note 5 for additional information.

The company's global net sales based on product categories are as follows:

	2011	2010	2009
Net sales			
Simple Meals	$4,437	$4,594	$4,674
Baked Snacks	2,321	2,129	1,995
Beverages	961	953	917
Total	$7,719	$7,676	$7,586

Simple meals include condensed and ready-to-serve soups, broths and sauces. Baked snacks include cookies, crackers, biscuits and other baked products.

Geographic Area Information

Information about operations in different geographic areas is as follows:

	2011	2010	2009
Net sales			
United States	$5,309	$5,436	$5,548
Europe	596	601	608
Australia/Asia Pacific	1,138	978	816
Other countries	676	661	614
Total	$7,719	$7,676	$7,586

	2011	2010	2009
Long-lived assets			
United States	$1,281	$1,279	$1,388
Europe	102	104	119
Australia/Asia Pacific	384	326	283
Other countries	109	105	108
Corporate(1)	227	237	79
Total	$2,103	$2,051	$1,977

(1) Represents primarily corporate offices.

NOTES TO CONSOLIDATED FINANCIAL STATEMENTS — (Continued)

7. Restructuring Charges

2011 Initiatives

On June 28, 2011, the company announced a series of initiatives to improve supply chain efficiency and reduce overhead costs across the organization to help fund plans to drive the growth of the business. The company also announced its intent to exit the Russian market. The company expects to eliminate approximately 750 positions in connection with these initiatives. Details of the plans include:

- In Australia, the company will invest in a new system to automate packing operations at its biscuit plant in Virginia. This investment will occur over an 18-month period and will result in the elimination of approximately 190 positions, subject to union and employee consultations. Further, the company will improve asset utilization in the U.S. by shifting production of ready-to-serve soups from Paris, Texas, to other facilities in 2012. In addition, the manufacturing facility in Marshall, Michigan, was closed in 2011, and manufacturing of *Campbell's Soup at Hand* microwavable products will be consolidated at the Maxton, North Carolina, plant in 2012.

- The company streamlined its salaried workforce by approximately 510 positions around the world, including approximately 130 positions at its world headquarters in Camden, New Jersey. These actions were substantially completed in 2011. As part of this initiative, the company outsourced a larger portion of its U.S. retail merchandising activities to its current retail sales agent, Acosta Sales and Marketing, and eliminated approximately 190 positions. The company expects that this action will enhance merchandising effectiveness and coverage for its U.S. customers.

- In connection with exiting the Russian market, the company will eliminate approximately 50 positions. The exit process commenced in 2011 and is expected to be completed in fiscal 2012.

In 2011, the company recorded a restructuring charge of $63 ($41 after tax or $.12 per share) related to these initiatives. A summary of the pre-tax charge and remaining costs associated with the initiatives is as follows:

	Total Program	Recognized as of July 31, 2011	Remaining Costs to be Recognized
Severance pay and benefits	$40	$(37)	$ 3
Asset impairment/accelerated depreciation	25	(22)	3
Other exit costs....................................	10	(4)	6
Total...	$75	$(63)	$12

Of the aggregate $75 of pre-tax costs, the company expects approximately $50 will be cash expenditures, the majority of which will be spent in 2012. In addition, the company expects to invest approximately $40 in capital expenditures in connection with the actions. The initiatives are expected to be completed by the end of fiscal 2013.

A summary of restructuring activity and related reserves associated with these initiatives at July 31, 2011 is as follows:

	Accrued Balance at August 1, 2010	2011 Charges	2011 Cash Payments	Accrued Balance at July 31, 2011
Severance pay and benefits.................	$—	$37	$ (2)	$35
Asset impairment/accelerated depreciation	—	22	—	—
Other exit costs	—	4	—	4
Total	$—	$63	$ (2)	$39

NOTES TO CONSOLIDATED FINANCIAL STATEMENTS — (Continued)

A summary of restructuring charges associated with each segment is as follows:

	U.S. Simple Meals	U.S. Beverages	Global Baking and Snacking	International Simple Meals and Beverages	North America Foodservice	Corporate	Total
Severance pay and benefits	$10	$ 3	$12	$10	$ 1	$ 1	$37
Asset impairment/accelerated depreciation	20	—	—	2	—	—	22
Other exit costs.............	1	—	—	—	—	3	4
	$31	$ 3	$12	$12	$ 1	$ 4	$63

The company expects to incur additional pre-tax costs of approximately $12 by segment as follows: U.S. Simple Meals — $2, Global Baking and Snacking — $3, International Simple Meals and Beverages — $6 and Corporate — $1. Segment operating results do not include restructuring charges as segment performance is evaluated excluding such charges.

2008 Initiatives

On April 28, 2008, the company announced a series of initiatives to improve operational efficiency and long-term profitability, including selling certain salty snack food brands and assets in Australia, closing certain production facilities in Australia and Canada, and streamlining the company's management structure.

As a result of these initiatives, in 2009, the company recorded approximately $22 ($15 after tax or $.04 per share) of costs in Cost of products sold. Approximately $17 ($12 after tax) of the costs represented accelerated depreciation on property, plant and equipment; approximately $4 ($2 after tax) related to other exit costs; and approximately $1 related to employee severance and benefit costs, including other pension charges.

As a result of these initiatives, in 2010, the company recorded a restructuring charge of $12 ($8 after tax or $.02 per share) for pension benefit costs, which represented the final costs associated with the 2008 initiatives.

In the aggregate, the company incurred $216 of pre-tax costs for the total program in 2008 through 2010. Approximately $40 of the costs were cash expenditures, the majority of which was spent in 2009.

A summary of the pre-tax costs is as follows:

	Total Program	Change in Estimate(1)	Recognized 2008-2010
Severance pay and benefits	$ 62	$ (4)	$ 58
Asset impairment/accelerated depreciation	158	(4)	154
Other exit costs.....................................	10	(6)	4
Total...	$230	$(14)	$216

(1) Primarily due to foreign currency translation.

Details of the impact of the initiatives on fiscal 2010 and 2009 results are as follows:

- In April 2008, as part of the initiatives, the company announced plans to close the Listowel, Ontario, Canada food plant. The Listowel facility produced primarily frozen products, including soup, entrees, and Pepperidge Farm products, as well as ramen noodles for North America Foodservice. The facility employed approximately 500 people. The company closed the facility in April 2009. Production was transitioned to its network of North American contract manufacturers and to its Downingtown, Pennsylvania, plant. In connection with this action, in 2009, the company recorded $1 of employee severance and benefit costs, including other pension charges; $16 ($11 after tax) in accelerated depreciation of property, plant and

NOTES TO CONSOLIDATED FINANCIAL STATEMENTS — (Continued)

equipment; and $2 ($1 after tax) of other exit costs. In 2010, the company recorded a restructuring charge of $12 ($8 after tax) for pension benefit costs, which represented the final costs associated with the initiatives.

- In April 2008, as part of the initiatives, the company also announced plans to discontinue the private label biscuit and industrial chocolate production at its Miranda, Australia, facility, which was part of Global Baking and Snacking. The company closed the Miranda facility, which employed approximately 150 people, in the second quarter of 2009. In connection with this action, in 2009, the company recorded $1 in accelerated depreciation of property, plant, and equipment, and $2 ($1 after tax) in other exit costs.

A summary of restructuring activity and related reserves of the 2008 initiatives is as follows:

	Severance Pay and Benefits	Asset Impairment/ Accelerated Depreciation	Other Exit Costs	Total
Accrued balance at July 29, 2007	$ —			
2008 charge(1)	45	137	—	$182
Cash payments	(4)			
Pension termination benefits(2)	(4)			
Accrued balance at August 3, 2008	37			
2009 charge	1	17	4	$ 22
Cash payments	(26)			
Pension termination benefits(2)	(2)			
Foreign currency translation adjustment	(6)			
Accrued balance at August 2, 2009	4			
2010 charge	12	—	—	$ 12
Cash payments	(3)			
Pension termination benefits(2)	(12)			
Accrued balance at August 1, 2010	1			
Cash payments	**(1)**			
Accrued balance at July 31, 2011	**$ —**			

(1) In 2008, as part of the initiatives, the company sold certain Australian salty snack food brands and assets, which were part of Global Baking and Snacking, and recorded a pre-tax net loss of $120 on the sale. The company streamlined its management structure and eliminated certain overhead costs. These actions began in the fourth quarter of 2008 and were substantially completed in 2009. In connection with this action, the company recorded $17 in employee severance and benefit costs in 2008. The company also recognized $45 in costs associated with the closures of the Listowel, Canada, and Miranda, Australia, facilities.

(2) Pension termination benefits are recognized in Other Liabilities and Accumulated Other Compensation Income/(Loss). See Note 11.

A summary of restructuring charges incurred in 2008 through 2010 by segment follows:

	Global Baking and Snacking	International Simple Meals and Beverages	North America Foodservice	Total
Severance pay and benefits	$ 14	$ 9	$35	$ 58
Asset impairment/accelerated depreciation	131	—	23	154
Other exit costs.	2	—	2	4
	$147	$ 9	$60	$216

NOTES TO CONSOLIDATED FINANCIAL STATEMENTS — (Continued)

8. Acquisitions

On May 4, 2009, the company acquired Ecce Panis, Inc., an artisan bread maker, for $66. The results of operations of Ecce Panis, Inc. are included in the Global Baking and Snacking segment and were not material to 2009 results. The pro forma impact on sales, net earnings or earnings per share for the prior periods would not have been material. As part of the purchase price allocation, $46 was allocated to intangible assets, primarily consisting of goodwill, trade secret process technology, trademarks and customer relationships.

The following table presents the purchase price allocation of Ecce Panis, Inc.:

	May 4, 2009
Accounts receivable	$ 2
Inventories	1
Other current assets	1
Total current assets	$ 4
Plant assets	$12
Goodwill	30
Other intangible assets	16
Other assets	14
Total assets acquired	$76
Current liabilities	$ 3
Non-current liabilities	7
Total liabilities assumed	$10
Net assets acquired	$66

9. Earnings per Share

In June 2008, the FASB issued accounting guidance related to the calculation of earnings per share. The guidance provides that unvested share-based payment awards that contain non-forfeitable rights to dividends or dividend equivalents (whether paid or unpaid) are participating securities and shall be included in the computation of earnings per share pursuant to the two-class method. Share-based payment awards granted prior to fiscal 2011 contained non-forfeitable rights to dividends or dividend equivalents. The two-class method is an earnings allocation formula that determines earnings per share for each class of common stock and participating security according to dividends declared and participation rights in undistributed earnings. The company adopted and retrospectively applied the new guidance in the first quarter of fiscal 2010. The retrospective application of the provisions resulted in a reduction of basic and diluted earnings per share:

	2009	
	Basic	Diluted
Earnings from continuing operations attributable to Campbell Soup Company	$(.03)	$(.01)
Net earnings attributable to Campbell Soup Company	$(.03)	$(.01)

NOTES TO CONSOLIDATED FINANCIAL STATEMENTS — (Continued)

The computation of basic and diluted earnings per share attributable to common shareowners is as follows:

	2011	2010	2009
Earnings from continuing operations attributable to Campbell Soup Company	$ 805	$ 844	$ 732
Less: Allocation of earnings to participating securities	(9)	(14)	(12)
Available to Campbell Soup Company common shareowners	$ 796	$ 830	$ 720
Earnings from discontinued operations attributable to Campbell Soup Company	$ —	$ —	$ 4
Less: Allocation of earnings to participating securities	—	—	—
Available to Campbell Soup Company common shareowners	$ —	$ —	$ 4
Net earnings attributable to Campbell Soup Company	$ 805	$ 844	$ 736
Less: Allocation of earnings to participating securities	(9)	(14)	(12)
Available to Campbell Soup Company common shareowners	$ 796	$ 830	$ 724
Weighted average shares outstanding — basic	326	340	352
Effect of dilutive securities: stock options and other share-based payment awards	3	3	2
Weighted average shares outstanding — diluted	329	343	354
Earnings from continuing operations attributable to Campbell Soup Company per common share:			
Basic	$2.44	$2.44	$2.05
Diluted	$2.42	$2.42	$2.03
Earnings from discontinued operations attributable to Campbell Soup Company per common share:			
Basic	$ —	$ —	$ .01
Diluted	$ —	$ —	$ .01
Net earnings attributable to Campbell Soup Company per common share(1):			
Basic	$2.44	$2.44	$2.06
Diluted	$2.42	$2.42	$2.05

(1) The sum of the individual per share amounts does not equal due to rounding.

There were no antidilutive stock options in 2011. Stock options to purchase less than 1 million shares of capital stock in 2010, and 3 million shares of capital stock in 2009 were not included in the calculation of diluted earnings per share because the exercise price of the stock options exceeded the average market price of the capital stock and, therefore, would be antidilutive.

10. Noncontrolling Interests

The company owns a 60% controlling interest in a joint venture formed with Swire Pacific Limited to support the development of the company's business in China. The joint venture began operations on January 31, 2011, the beginning of the third fiscal quarter. At the inception of the joint venture, the joint venture partner contributed net assets of $7, including $9 of cash contributions, and the company made an $11 cash contribution. In July 2011, the

NOTES TO CONSOLIDATED FINANCIAL STATEMENTS — (Continued)

company and joint venture partner contributed additional cash of $2 and $1, respectively. The noncontrolling interest's share in the net loss was included in Net earnings (loss) attributable to noncontrolling interests in the Consolidated Statements of Earnings.

The company owns a 70% controlling interest in a Malaysian manufacturing company. The earnings attributable to the noncontrolling interest have historically been less than $1 annually and were previously included in Other expense/(income) in the Consolidated Statements of Earnings. Beginning in the third quarter of fiscal 2011, the earnings attributable to the noncontrolling interest were included in Net earnings (loss) attributable to noncontrolling interests in the Consolidated Statements of Earnings. The earnings were not material in 2011.

The noncontrolling interests in these entities were included in Total equity in the Consolidated Balance Sheets and Consolidated Statements of Equity.

11. Pension and Postretirement Benefits

Pension Benefits — The company sponsors a number of noncontributory defined benefit pension plans to provide retirement benefits to all eligible U.S. and non-U.S. employees. The benefits provided under these plans are based primarily on years of service and compensation levels. In 1999, the company implemented significant amendments to certain U.S. pension plans. Under a new formula, retirement benefits are determined based on percentages of annual pay and age. To minimize the impact of converting to the new formula, service and earnings credit continues to accrue for active employees participating in the plans under the old formula prior to the amendments through the year 2014. Employees will receive the benefit from either the new or old formula, whichever is higher. Benefits become vested upon the completion of three years of service. Benefits are paid from funds previously provided to trustees and insurance companies or are paid directly by the company from general funds. Effective as of January 1, 2011, the company's U.S. pension plans were amended so that employees hired or rehired on or after that date and who are not covered by collective bargaining agreements will not be eligible to participate in the plans.

Postretirement Benefits — The company provides postretirement benefits including health care and life insurance to substantially all retired U.S. employees and their dependents. The company established retiree medical account benefits for eligible U.S. retirees. The accounts were intended to provide reimbursement for eligible health care expenses on a tax-favored basis. Effective as of January 1, 2011, the retirement medical program was amended to eliminate the retiree medical account benefit for employees not covered by collective bargaining agreements. To preserve the benefit for employees close to retirement age, the retiree medical account will be available to employees who were at least age 50 with at least 10 years of service as of December 31, 2010, and who satisfy the other eligibility requirements for the retiree medical program.

The company uses the fiscal year end as the measurement date for the benefit plans.

Components of net periodic benefit cost:

	Pension		
	2011	2010	2009
Service cost	$ 58	$ 55	$ 46
Interest cost	121	121	122
Expected return on plan assets	(178)	(170)	(163)
Amortization of prior service cost	1	1	1
Recognized net actuarial loss	70	49	19
Settlement (gains)/costs	(1)	12	—
Special termination benefits	—	—	2
Net periodic pension expense	$ 71	$ 68	$ 27

NOTES TO CONSOLIDATED FINANCIAL STATEMENTS — (Continued)

The settlement costs in 2010 are related to the closure of a plant in Canada. The settlement costs are included in Restructuring charges in the Consolidated Statements of Earnings. See Note 7 for additional information.

The estimated net actuarial loss that will be amortized from Accumulated other comprehensive loss into net periodic pension cost during 2012 is $75.

	Postretirement		
	2011	**2010**	**2009**
Service cost.	**$ 3**	$ 3	$ 3
Interest cost.	**18**	19	22
Amortization of prior service cost/(credit)	**(1)**	1	1
Recognized net actuarial loss	**7**	1	—
Net periodic postretirement expense	**$27**	$24	$26

The estimated prior service credit and net actuarial loss that will be amortized from Accumulated other comprehensive loss into net periodic postretirement expense during 2012 are $1 and $9, respectively.

Change in benefit obligation:

	Pension		Postretirement	
	2011	**2010**	**2011**	**2010**
Obligation at beginning of year	**$2,275**	$2,077	**$362**	$340
Service cost	**58**	55	**3**	3
Interest cost	**121**	121	**18**	19
Actuarial loss	**61**	181	**15**	50
Participant contributions	**—**	—	**5**	4
Benefits paid.	**(146)**	(148)	**(34)**	(39)
Medicare subsidies	**—**	—	**5**	3
Other	**(4)**	(2)	**—**	—
Plan amendments	**(1)**	—	**—**	(18)
Settlement	**(8)**	(21)	**—**	—
Foreign currency adjustment	**32**	12	**—**	—
Benefit obligation at end of year	**$2,388**	$2,275	**$374**	$362

Change in the fair value of pension plan assets:

	2011	**2010**
Fair value at beginning of year	**$1,767**	$1,415
Actual return on plan assets	**266**	222
Employer contributions.	**144**	284
Benefits paid	**(139)**	(142)
Settlement	**(6)**	(21)
Foreign currency adjustment	**27**	9
Fair value at end of year.	**$2,059**	$1,767

NOTES TO CONSOLIDATED FINANCIAL STATEMENTS — (Continued)

Amounts recognized in the Consolidated Balance Sheets:

	Pension		Postretirement	
	2011	2010	2011	2010
Accrued liabilities	$ (10)	$ (8)	$ (30)	$ (30)
Other liabilities	(319)	(500)	(344)	(332)
Net amount recognized	$ (329)	$ (508)	$(374)	$(362)
Amounts recognized in accumulated other comprehensive loss consist of:				
Net actuarial loss	$1,179	$1,263	$ 95	$ 87
Prior service credit	(3)	(1)	(9)	(10)
Total	$1,176	$1,262	$ 86	$ 77

The changes in other comprehensive loss associated with pension benefits included the reclassification of actuarial losses into earnings of $70 and $49 in 2011 and 2010, respectively. The remaining changes in other comprehensive loss associated with pension benefits were primarily due to net actuarial losses arising during the period and the impact of foreign currency.

The change in other comprehensive loss associated with postretirement benefits in 2011 was primarily due to net actuarial losses arising during the period. The change in other comprehensive loss associated with postretirement benefits in 2010 included $50 of net actuarial losses arising during the period and $18 of prior service credit.

The following table provides information for pension plans with accumulated benefit obligations in excess of plan assets:

	2011	2010
Projected benefit obligation	$2,194	$2,261
Accumulated benefit obligation	$2,131	$2,140
Fair value of plan assets	$1,891	$1,757

The accumulated benefit obligation for all pension plans was $2,299 at July 31, 2011 and $2,148 at August 1, 2010.

Weighted-average assumptions used to determine benefit obligations at the end of the year:

	Pension		Postretirement	
	2011	2010	2011	2010
Discount rate	5.41%	5.46%	5.00%	5.25%
Rate of compensation increase	3.31%	3.29%	3.25%	3.25%

Weighted-average assumptions used to determine net periodic benefit cost for the years ended:

Pension	2011	2010	2009
Discount rate	5.46%	6.00%	6.87%
Expected return on plan assets	8.15%	8.13%	8.60%
Rate of compensation increase	3.29%	3.29%	3.97%

The discount rate is established as of the company's fiscal year-end measurement date. In establishing the discount rate, the company reviews published market indices of high-quality debt securities, adjusted as appropriate for duration. In addition, independent actuaries apply high-quality bond yield curves to the expected benefit payments of the plans. The expected return on plan assets is a long-term assumption based upon historical experience and expected future performance, considering the company's current and projected investment mix.

NOTES TO CONSOLIDATED FINANCIAL STATEMENTS — (Continued)

This estimate is based on an estimate of future inflation, long-term projected real returns for each asset class, and a premium for active management.

The discount rate used to determine net periodic postretirement expense was 5.25% in 2011, 6.00% in 2010, and 7.00% in 2009.

Assumed health care cost trend rates at the end of the year:

	2011	2010
Health care cost trend rate assumed for next year	**8.25%**	8.25%
Rate to which the cost trend rate is assumed to decline (ultimate trend rate)	**4.50%**	4.50%
Year that the rate reaches the ultimate trend rate	**2019**	2018

A one-percentage-point change in assumed health care costs would have the following effects on 2011 reported amounts:

	Increase	Decrease
Effect on service and interest cost	$ 1	$ (1)
Effect on the 2011 accumulated benefit obligation	$20	$(18)

Pension Plan Assets

The fundamental goal underlying the investment policy is to ensure that the assets of the plans are invested in a prudent manner to meet the obligations of the plans as these obligations come due. The primary investment objectives include providing a total return which will promote the goal of benefit security by attaining an appropriate ratio of plan assets to plan obligations, to provide for real asset growth while also tracking plan obligations, to diversify investments across and within asset classes, to reduce the impact of losses in single investments, and to follow investment practices that comply with applicable laws and regulations.

The primary policy objectives will be met by investing assets to achieve a reasonable tradeoff between return and risk relative to the plans' obligations. This includes investing a portion of the assets in funds selected in part to hedge the interest rate sensitivity to plan obligations.

The portfolio includes investments in the following asset classes: fixed income, equity, real estate and alternatives. Fixed income will provide a moderate expected return and partially hedge the exposure to interest rate risk of the plans' obligations. Equities are used for their high expected return. Additional asset classes are used to provide diversification.

Asset allocation is monitored on an ongoing basis relative to the established asset class targets. The interaction between plan assets and benefit obligations is periodically studied to assist in the establishment of strategic asset allocation targets. The investment policy permits variances from the targets within certain parameters. Asset rebalancing occurs when the underlying asset class allocations move outside these parameters, at which time the asset allocation is rebalanced back to the policy target weight.

The company's year-end pension plan weighted-average asset allocations by category were:

	Strategic Target	2011	2010
Equity securities	51%	**50%**	49%
Debt securities	35%	**35%**	34%
Real estate and other	14%	**15%**	17%
Total	100%	**100%**	100%

NOTES TO CONSOLIDATED FINANCIAL STATEMENTS — (Continued)

The company is required to categorize pension plan assets based on the following fair value hierarchy:

- Level 1: Observable inputs that reflect quoted prices (unadjusted) for identical assets in active markets.

- Level 2: Inputs other than quoted prices included in Level 1 that are observable for the asset through corroboration with observable market data.

- Level 3: Unobservable inputs that reflect the reporting entity's own assumptions.

The following table presents the company's pension plan assets by asset category at July 31, 2011 and August 1, 2010:

	Fair Value as of July 31, 2011	Fair Value Measurements at July 31, 2011 Using Fair Value Hierarchy			Fair Value as of August 1, 2010	Fair Value Measurements at August 1, 2010 Using Fair Value Hierarchy		
		Level 1	Level 2	Level 3		Level 1	Level 2	Level 3
Asset category								
Short-term investments	$ 65	$ 5	$ 60	$ —	$ 60	$ 5	$ 55	$ —
Equities:								
U.S.	396	396	—	—	308	308	—	—
Non-U.S.	267	267	—	—	245	245	—	—
Corporate bonds:								
U.S.	414	—	414	—	357	—	357	—
Non-U.S.	88	—	88	—	89	—	89	—
Government and agency bonds:								
U.S.	9	—	9	—	21	—	21	—
Non-U.S.	31	—	31	—	21	—	21	—
Municipal Bonds	42	—	42	—	17	—	17	—
Commingled funds:								
Equities	366	—	366	—	298	—	298	—
Fixed Income	73	—	73	—	46	—	46	—
Mortgage and asset backed securities	27	—	27	—	26	—	26	—
Real estate	70	7	44	19	60	4	38	18
Limited partnerships	20	—	—	20	24	—	—	24
Hedge funds	196	—	196	—	174	—	174	—
Guaranteed insurance contracts	—	—	—	—	8	—	—	8
Total	$2,064	$675	$1,350	$ 39	$1,754	$562	$1,142	$ 50
Other items to reconcile to fair value of plan assets	(5)				13			
Total pension assets at fair value	$2,059				$1,767			

Short-term investments — Investments include cash and cash equivalents, and various short-term debt instruments and short-term investment funds. Institutional short-term investment vehicles valued daily are classified as Level 1 at cost which approximates market value. Other investment vehicles are valued based upon a net asset value and are classified as Level 2.

Equities — Common stocks and preferred stocks are classified as Level 1 and are valued using quoted market prices in active markets.

NOTES TO CONSOLIDATED FINANCIAL STATEMENTS — (Continued)

Corporate bonds — These investments are valued based on quoted market prices, yield curves and pricing models using current market rates.

Government and agency bonds — These investments are generally valued based on bid quotations and recent trade data for identical or similar obligations.

Municipal bonds — These investments are valued based on quoted market prices, yield curves and pricing models using current market rates.

Commingled funds — Investments in commingled funds are classified as Level 2 assets as the funds are not traded in active markets. Commingled funds are valued based on the unit values of such funds. Unit values are based on the fair value of the underlying assets of the funds derived from inputs principally based on quoted market prices in an active market or corroborated by observable market data by correlation or other means.

Mortgage and asset backed securities — Fair value is based on prices obtained from third party pricing sources. The prices from third party pricing sources may be based on bid quotes from dealers and recent trade data. Mortgage backed securities are traded in the over-the-counter market.

Real estate — Real estate investments consist of real estate investment trusts and property funds. Real estate investment trusts are classified as Level 1 and are valued based on quoted market prices. Property funds are classified as either Level 2 or Level 3 depending upon whether liquidity is limited or there are few observable market participant transactions. Fair value is based on third party appraisals.

Limited partnerships — Investments in limited partnerships are valued based upon valuations provided by the general partners of the funds. The values of limited partnerships are based upon an assessment of each underlying investment, incorporating valuations that consider the evaluation of financing and sales transactions with third parties, expected cash flows, and market-based information, including comparable transactions and performance multiples among other factors. The investments are classified as Level 3 since the valuation is determined using unobservable inputs.

Hedge funds — Hedge fund investments include hedge funds valued based upon a net asset value derived from the fair value of underlying securities and are therefore classified as Level 2 assets. Hedge fund investments may include long and short positions in equity and fixed income securities, derivative instruments such as futures and options, commodities, and other types of securities.

Guaranteed insurance contracts — These assets are classified as Level 3 assets as they are valued using unobservable inputs. Guaranteed insurance contracts are valued based on the discounted stream of guaranteed benefit payments at a market rate increased for expected future profit sharing. The expected excess return is equal to expected indexation granted to participants. The discounted stream of guaranteed benefit payments is calculated based on the expected mortality rates of plan participants.

Other items to reconcile to fair value of plan assets included net accrued interest and dividends receivable, amounts due for securities sold, amounts payable for securities purchased, and other payables.

NOTES TO CONSOLIDATED FINANCIAL STATEMENTS — (Continued)

The following table summarizes the changes in fair value of Level 3 investments for the years ended July 31, 2011 and August 1, 2010:

	Real Estate	Limited Partnerships	Guaranteed Insurance Contracts	Total
Fair value at August 1, 2010	$18	$24	$ 8	$ 50
Actual return on plan assets	**4**	**4**	**(2)**	**6**
Purchases	—	—	—	—
Sales	(3)	(8)	—	(11)
Settlements	—	—	(6)	(6)
Transfers out of Level 3	—	—	—	—
Fair value at July 31, 2011	**$19**	**$20**	**$ —**	**$ 39**

	Real Estate	Limited Partnerships	Guaranteed Insurance Contracts	Total
Fair value at August 2, 2009	$ 32	$31	$ 5	$ 68
Actual return on plan assets.	(2)	(4)	2	(4)
Purchases	—	—	1	1
Sales	(1)	(3)	—	(4)
Settlements	—	—	—	—
Transfers out of Level 3	(11)	—	—	(11)
Fair value at August 1, 2010	$ 18	$24	$ 8	$ 50

The company contributed $55 to U.S. plans in the first quarter of 2012. Additional contributions to U.S. plans are not expected in 2012. Contributions to non-U.S. plans are expected to be approximately $10 in 2012.

Estimated future benefit payments are as follows:

	Pension	Postretirement
2012	$147	$ 30
2013	$150	$ 31
2014	$150	$ 31
2015	$154	$ 32
2016	$158	$ 32
2017-2021	$856	$163

The benefit payments include payments from funded and unfunded plans.

Estimated future Medicare subsidy receipts are approximately $3 annually from 2012 through 2016, and $15 cumulatively for the period 2017 through 2021.

Savings Plan — The company sponsors employee savings plans which cover substantially all U.S. employees. Effective January 1, 2011, the company provides a matching contribution of 100% of employee contributions up to 4% of compensation for employees who are not covered by collective bargaining agreements. Employees hired or rehired on or after January 1, 2011 who will not be eligible to participate in the defined benefit plans and who are not covered by collective bargaining agreements receive a contribution equal to 3% of compensation regardless of their participation in the Savings Plan. Prior to January 1, 2011, the company provided a matching contribution of 60% (50% at certain locations) of the employee contributions up to 5% of compensation after one year of continued service. Amounts charged to Costs and expenses were $20 in 2011, $17 in 2010, and $18 in 2009.

NOTES TO CONSOLIDATED FINANCIAL STATEMENTS — (Continued)

12. Taxes on Earnings

The provision for income taxes on earnings from continuing operations consists of the following:

	2011	2010	2009
Income taxes:			
Currently payable			
Federal	$ 215	$ 253	$ 145
State	27	46	12
Non-U.S.	78	45	46
	320	344	203
Deferred			
Federal	47	38	142
State	(2)	1	9
Non-U.S.	1	15	(7)
	46	54	144
	$ 366	$ 398	$ 347
Earnings from continuing operations before income taxes:			
United States	$ 944	$1,051	$ 976
Non-U.S.	224	191	103
	$1,168	$1,242	$1,079

The following is a reconciliation of the effective income tax rate on continuing operations with the U.S. federal statutory income tax rate:

	2011	2010	2009
Federal statutory income tax rate	35.0%	35.0%	35.0%
State income taxes (net of federal tax benefit)	1.4	2.5	1.7
Tax effect of international items	(2.1)	(2.5)	(0.8)
Settlement of tax contingencies	(0.5)	(0.7)	(1.0)
Federal manufacturing deduction	(1.8)	(1.3)	(1.0)
Other	(0.7)	(1.0)	(1.7)
Effective income tax rate	31.3%	32.0%	32.2%

During 2011, the company recorded a tax benefit of $8 following the finalization of tax audits.

In the third quarter of 2010, the company recorded deferred tax expense of $10 due to the enactment of U.S. health care legislation in March 2010. The law changed the tax treatment of subsidies to companies that provide prescription drug benefits to retirees. Accordingly, the company recorded the non-cash charge to reduce the value of the deferred tax asset associated with the subsidy.

In 2010, the company recorded a tax benefit of $9 following the finalization of tax audits. The company recorded an additional tax benefit of $2 during the year related to the resolution of other tax contingencies.

In 2009, the company recorded a tax benefit of $11 following the finalization of tax audits.

NOTES TO CONSOLIDATED FINANCIAL STATEMENTS — (Continued)

Deferred tax liabilities and assets are comprised of the following:

	2011	2010
Depreciation	$ 253	$ 221
Amortization	474	449
Other	14	13
Deferred tax liabilities	741	683
Benefits and compensation	307	319
Pension benefits	93	134
Tax loss carryforwards	84	67
Capital loss carryforwards	122	101
Other	83	76
Gross deferred tax assets	689	697
Deferred tax asset valuation allowance	(156)	(123)
Net deferred tax assets	533	574
Net deferred tax liability	$ 208	$ 109

At July 31, 2011, U.S. and non-U.S. subsidiaries of the company have tax loss carryforwards of approximately $395. Of these carryforwards, $163 expire between 2012 and 2028, and $232 may be carried forward indefinitely. The current statutory tax rates in these countries range from 20% to 35%. At July 31, 2011, deferred tax asset valuation allowances have been established to offset $132 of these tax loss carryforwards. Additionally, at July 31, 2011, non-U.S. subsidiaries of the company have capital loss carryforwards of approximately $406, which are fully offset by deferred tax asset valuation allowances.

The net change in the deferred tax asset valuation allowance in 2011 was an increase of $33. The increase was primarily due to the impact of currency and recognition of additional valuation allowances on foreign loss carryforwards. The net change in the valuation allowance in 2010 was an increase of $15. The increase was primarily due to the impact of currency and the recognition of additional valuation allowances on foreign loss carryforwards that are not expected to be utilized prior to the expiration date. The net change in the valuation allowance in 2009 was a decrease of $7, primarily due to currency.

As of July 31, 2011, U.S. income taxes have not been provided on approximately $420 of undistributed earnings of non-U.S. subsidiaries, which are deemed to be permanently reinvested. It is not practical to estimate the tax liability that might be incurred if such earnings were remitted to the U.S.

A reconciliation of the activity related to unrecognized tax benefits follows:

	2011	2010	2009
Balance at beginning of year	$36	$ 42	$ 54
Increases related to prior-year tax positions	6	14	—
Decreases related to prior-year tax positions	(4)	(11)	(11)
Increases related to current-year tax positions	9	4	4
Settlements	—	(11)	(2)
Lapse of statute	(4)	(2)	(3)
Balance at end of year	$43	$ 36	$ 42

As of July 31, 2011, August 1, 2010, and August 2, 2009, there were $17, $22, and $28, respectively, of unrecognized tax benefits that if recognized would affect the annual effective tax rate. The total amount of unrecognized tax benefits can change due to audit settlements, tax examination activities, statute expirations and the

NOTES TO CONSOLIDATED FINANCIAL STATEMENTS — (Continued)

recognition and measurement criteria under accounting for uncertainty in income taxes. The company is unable to estimate what this change could be within the next twelve months, but does not believe it would be material to the financial statements.

The company's accounting policy with respect to interest and penalties attributable to income taxes is to reflect any expense or benefit as a component of its income tax provision. The total amount of interest and penalties recognized in the Consolidated Statements of Earnings was a benefit of $1 in 2011, an expense of $2 in 2010 and a benefit of $1 in 2009. The total amount of interest and penalties recognized in the Consolidated Balance Sheets as of July 31, 2011, and August 1, 2010, was $8 and $9, respectively.

None of the unrecognized tax benefit liabilities, including interest and penalties, are expected to be settled within the next twelve months. The $51 and $45 of unrecognized tax benefit liabilities, including interest and penalties, were reported as other non-current liabilities in the Consolidated Balance Sheets as of July 31, 2011, and August 1, 2010, respectively.

The company does business globally and, as a result, files income tax returns in the U.S. federal jurisdiction and various state and non-U.S. jurisdictions. In the normal course of business, the company is subject to examination by taxing authorities throughout the world, including such major jurisdictions as the United States, Australia, Canada, Belgium, France and Germany. The 2011 tax year is currently under audit by the IRS. In addition, several state income tax examinations are in progress for fiscal years 2001 to 2009.

With limited exceptions, the company has been audited for income tax purposes in Canada and France through fiscal year 2005, in Germany through fiscal year 2007, and in Belgium and Australia through fiscal year 2009.

13. Short-term Borrowings and Long-term Debt

Short-term borrowings consist of the following:

	2011	2010
Commercial paper	$563	$ 96
Current portion of long-term debt	—	700
Variable-rate bank borrowings	92	34
Fixed-rate borrowings	1	1
Capital leases	1	1
Other(1)	—	3
	$657	$835

(1) Other includes unamortized net premium/discount on debt issuances and unamortized gain on a terminated interest rate swap.

As of July 31, 2011, the weighted-average interest rate of commercial paper, which consisted of U.S. borrowings, was 0.33%. As of August 1, 2010, the weighted-average interest rate of commercial paper, which consisted of U.S. borrowings, was 0.24%.

At July 31, 2011, the company had $45 of standby letters of credit issued on behalf of the company. The company had a $975 committed 364-day revolving credit facility that matured in September 2011, and a $975 revolving credit facility that was due to mature in September 2013. In September 2011, the company entered into committed revolving credit facilities totaling $2,000. The facilities are comprised of a $1,500 facility that matures in September 2016, and a $500, 364-day facility that contains a one-year term-out feature. These facilities replaced the two $975 revolving credit facilities.

NOTES TO CONSOLIDATED FINANCIAL STATEMENTS — (Continued)

Long-term Debt consists of the following:

Type	Fiscal Year of Maturity	Rate	2011	2010
Notes	2011	6.75%	$ —	$ 700
Notes	2013	5.00%	400	400
Notes	2014	4.88%	300	300
Notes	2015	3.38%	300	300
Notes	2017	3.05%	400	400
Notes	2019	4.50%	300	300
Notes	2021	4.25%	500	—
Debentures	2021	8.88%	200	200
Fixed-rate borrowings			—	1
Capital leases			—	1
Other(1)			27	43
Total			2,427	2,645
Less current portion			—	700
Total long-term debt			$2,427	$1,945

(1) Other includes unamortized net premium/discount on debt issuances and amounts related to interest rate swaps designated as fair-value hedges. For additional information on fair-value interest rate swaps, see Note 14.

In April 2011, the company issued $500 of 4.25% notes which mature on April 15, 2021. Interest on the notes is due semi-annually on April 15 and October 15, commencing on October 15, 2011. The company may redeem the notes in whole or in part at any time at a redemption price of 100% of the principal amount plus accrued interest or an amount designed to ensure that the note holders are not penalized by the early redemption.

In July 2010, the company issued $400 of 3.05% notes which mature on July 15, 2017. Interest on the notes is due semi-annually on January 15 and July 15, commencing on January 15, 2011. The company may redeem the notes in whole or in part at any time at a redemption price of 100% of the principal amount plus accrued interest or an amount designed to ensure that the note holders are not penalized by the early redemption.

The fair value of the company's long-term debt, including the current portion of long-term debt in Short-term borrowings, was $2,603 at July 31, 2011 and $2,829 at August 1, 2010.

Principal amounts of debt mature as follows: none in 2012; $400 in 2013; $300 in 2014; $300 in 2015; none in 2016; and beyond a total of $1,400.

14. Financial Instruments

The carrying value of cash and cash equivalents, accounts receivable, accounts payable and short-term borrowings, excluding the current portion of long-term debt, approximate fair value. The fair value of long-term debt as indicated in Note 13 is based on quoted market prices or pricing models using current market rates.

The principal market risks to which the company is exposed are changes in foreign currency exchange rates, interest rates, and commodity prices. In addition, the company is exposed to equity price changes related to certain deferred compensation obligations. In order to manage these exposures, the company follows established risk management policies and procedures, including the use of derivative contracts such as swaps, forwards and commodity futures and option contracts. These derivative contracts are entered into for periods consistent with the related underlying exposures and do not constitute positions independent of those exposures. The company does not enter into derivative contracts for speculative purposes and does not use leveraged instruments. The company's derivative programs include strategies that both qualify and do not qualify for hedge accounting treatment.

NOTES TO CONSOLIDATED FINANCIAL STATEMENTS — (Continued)

The company is exposed to the risk that counterparties to derivative contracts will fail to meet their contractual obligations. The company minimizes counterparty credit risk on these transactions by dealing only with leading, credit-worthy financial institutions having long-term credit ratings of "A" or better. In addition, the contracts are distributed among several financial institutions, thus minimizing credit-risk concentration. The company does not have credit-risk-related contingent features in its derivative instruments as of July 31, 2011.

Foreign Currency Exchange Risk

The company is exposed to foreign currency exchange risk related to its international operations, including non-functional currency intercompany debt and net investments in subsidiaries. The company is also exposed to foreign exchange risk as a result of transactions in currencies other than the functional currency of certain subsidiaries. Principal currencies hedged include the Australian dollar, Canadian dollar, euro, Swedish krona, New Zealand dollar, British pound and Japanese yen. The company utilizes foreign exchange forward purchase and sale contracts as well as cross-currency swaps to hedge these exposures. The contracts are either designated as cash-flow hedging instruments or are undesignated. The company typically hedges portions of its forecasted foreign currency transaction exposure with foreign exchange forward contracts for up to 18 months. To hedge currency exposures related to intercompany debt, the company enters into cross-currency swap contracts for periods consistent with the underlying debt. As of July 31, 2011, cross-currency swap contracts mature in fiscal 2012 through fiscal 2015. The notional amount of foreign exchange forward and cross-currency swap contracts accounted for as cash-flow hedges was $287 and $261 at July 31, 2011 and August 1, 2010, respectively. The effective portion of the changes in fair value on these instruments is recorded in other comprehensive income (loss) and is reclassified into the Consolidated Statements of Earnings on the same line item and same period in which the underlying hedge transaction affects earnings. The notional amount of foreign exchange forward and cross-currency swap contracts that are not designated as accounting hedges was $861 and $757 at July 31, 2011 and August 1, 2010, respectively.

Interest Rate Risk

The company manages its exposure to changes in interest rates by optimizing the use of variable-rate and fixed-rate debt and by utilizing interest rate swaps in order to maintain its variable-to-total debt ratio within targeted guidelines. Receive fixed rate/pay variable rate interest rate swaps are accounted for as fair-value hedges. The notional amount of outstanding fair-value interest rate swaps totaled $500 at July 31, 2011 and at August 1, 2010.

During fiscal 2010, the company entered into forward starting interest rate swap contracts accounted for as cash-flow hedges with a combined notional value of $200 to hedge a July 2010 anticipated debt offering. These swaps were settled concurrent with the July 2010 debt issuance of $400 seven-year 3.05% notes at a loss of $14, which was recorded in other comprehensive income (loss). The loss on the swap contracts will be amortized over the life of the debt as additional interest expense.

In June 2008, the company entered into two forward starting interest rate swap contracts accounted for as cash-flow hedges with a combined notional value of $200 to hedge an anticipated debt offering in fiscal 2009. These swaps were settled as of November 2, 2008, at a loss of $13, which was recorded in other comprehensive income (loss). In January 2009, the company issued $300 ten-year 4.50% notes. The loss on the swap contracts will be amortized over the life of the debt as additional interest expense.

Commodity Price Risk

The company principally uses a combination of purchase orders and various short- and long-term supply arrangements in connection with the purchase of raw materials, including certain commodities and agricultural products. The company also enters into commodity futures and options contracts to reduce the volatility of price fluctuations of diesel fuel, wheat, natural gas, soybean oil, aluminum, sugar, cocoa, and corn, which impact the cost of raw materials. Commodity futures and option contracts are typically accounted for as cash-flow hedges or are not designated as accounting hedges. The company enters into commodity futures and option contracts to hedge a portion of commodity requirements for periods typically up to 12 months. The notional amount of commodity contracts accounted for as cash-

NOTES TO CONSOLIDATED FINANCIAL STATEMENTS — (Continued)

flow hedges was $6 at July 31, 2011 and $7 at August 1, 2010. The notional amount of commodity contracts that were not designated as accounting hedges was $81 at July 31, 2011 and $43 at August 1, 2010.

Equity Price Risk

The company hedges a portion of exposures relating to certain deferred compensation obligations linked to the total return of the Standard & Poor's 500 Index, the total return of the company's capital stock and the total return of the Puritan Fund, or beginning in January 2011, the total return of the Vanguard International Stock Index. Under these contracts, the company pays variable interest rates and receives from the counterparty either the total return of the Standard & Poor's 500 Index, the total return on company capital stock, the total return of the Puritan Fund, or the total return of the iShares MSCI EAFE Index, which is expected to approximate the total return of the Vanguard International Index. The contracts related to the Puritan Fund matured in January 2011. The contracts were not designated as hedges for accounting purposes and are typically entered into for periods not exceeding 12 months. The notional amounts of the contracts were $71 as of July 31, 2011 and $75 as of August 1, 2010.

The following table summarizes the fair value of derivative instruments recorded in the Consolidated Balance Sheets as of July 31, 2011 and August 1, 2010:

	Balance Sheet Classification	2011	2010
Asset Derivatives			
Derivatives designated as hedges:			
Foreign exchange forward contracts	Other current assets	$ —	$ 1
Commodity derivative contracts	Other current assets	—	1
Cross-currency swap contracts	Other assets	—	3
Interest rate swaps	Other assets	33	46
Total derivatives designated as hedges		$ 33	$51
Derivatives not designated as hedges:			
Foreign exchange forward contracts	Other current assets	$ —	$ 1
Commodity derivative contracts	Other current assets	3	3
Cross-currency swap contracts	Other current assets	—	13
Cross-currency swap contracts	Other assets	1	1
Total derivatives not designated as hedges		$ 4	$18
Total asset derivatives		$ 37	$69
Liability Derivatives			
Derivatives designated as hedges:			
Foreign exchange forward contracts	Accrued liabilities	$ 7	$ 1
Commodity derivative contracts	Accrued liabilities	—	1
Cross-currency swap contracts	Accrued liabilities	8	—
Cross-currency swap contracts	Other liabilities	30	24
Total derivatives designated as hedges		$ 45	$26
Derivatives not designated as hedges:			
Foreign exchange forward contracts	Accrued liabilities	$ 2	$ 1
Commodity derivative contracts	Accrued liabilities	2	—
Cross-currency swap contracts	Accrued liabilities	17	—
Deferred compensation derivative contracts	Accrued liabilities	3	2
Cross-currency swap contracts	Other liabilities	74	14
Total derivatives not designated as hedges		$ 98	$17
Total liability derivatives		$143	$43

NOTES TO CONSOLIDATED FINANCIAL STATEMENTS — (Continued)

The derivative assets and liabilities are presented on a gross basis in the table. Certain derivative asset and liability balances, including cash collateral, are offset in the balance sheet when a legally enforceable right of offset exists.

The following table shows the effect of the company's derivative instruments designated as cash-flow hedges for the years ended July 31, 2011 and August 1, 2010 on other comprehensive income (loss) (OCI) and the Consolidated Statements of Earnings:

Derivatives Designated as Cash-Flow Hedges

		Total Cash-Flow Hedge OCI Activity	
	Location in Earnings	2011	2010
OCI derivative gain/(loss) at beginning of year		$(28)	$(31)
Effective portion of changes in fair value recognized in OCI:			
Foreign exchange forward contracts.		(12)	(5)
Cross-currency swap contracts.		—	4
Forward starting interest rate swaps.		—	(14)
Commodity derivative contracts.		—	1
Amount of (gain) or loss reclassified from OCI to earnings:.			
Foreign exchange forward contracts.	Other expenses/income	2	(1)
Foreign exchange forward contracts.	Cost of products sold	4	17
Forward starting interest rate swaps.	Interest expense	3	1
OCI derivative gain/(loss) at end of year		$(31)	$(28)

The amount expected to be reclassified from other comprehensive income into earnings within the next 12 months is a loss of $11. The ineffective portion and amount excluded from effectiveness testing were not material.

The following table shows the effect of the company's derivative instruments designated as fair-value hedges on the Consolidated Statements of Earnings:

Derivatives Designated as Fair-Value Hedges	Location of Gain or (Loss) Recognized in Earnings	Amount of Gain or (Loss) Recognized in Earnings on Derivatives		Amount of Gain or (Loss) Recognized in Earnings on Hedged Item	
		2011	2010	2011	2010
Interest rate swaps	Interest expense	$(13)	$8	$13	$(8)

The following table shows the effects of the company's derivative instruments not designated as hedges in the Consolidated Statements of Earnings:

Derivatives not Designated as Hedges	Location of Gain or (Loss) Recognized in Earnings	Amount of Gain or (Loss) Recognized in Earnings on Derivatives	
		2011	2010
Foreign exchange forward contracts	Other expenses/income	$ —	$ (8)
Foreign exchange forward contracts	Cost of products sold	(1)	—
Cross-currency swap contracts	Other expenses/income	(88)	(12)
Commodity derivative contracts	Cost of products sold	7	—
Deferred compensation derivative contracts.	Administrative expenses	1	9
Total		$(81)	$(11)

NOTES TO CONSOLIDATED FINANCIAL STATEMENTS — (Continued)

15. Fair Value Measurements

The company is required to categorize financial assets and liabilities based on the following fair value hierarchy:

- Level 1: Observable inputs that reflect quoted prices (unadjusted) for identical assets or liabilities in active markets.

- Level 2: Inputs other than quoted prices included in Level 1 that are observable for the asset or liability through corroboration with observable market data.

- Level 3: Unobservable inputs that reflect the reporting entity's own assumptions.

Fair value is defined as the exit price, or the amount that would be received to sell an asset or paid to transfer a liability in an orderly transaction between market participants as of the measurement date. When available, the company uses unadjusted quoted market prices to measure the fair value and classifies such items as Level 1. If quoted market prices are not available, the company bases fair value upon internally developed models that use current market-based or independently sourced market parameters such as interest rates and currency rates.

Financial Assets and Financial Liabilities Measured at Fair Value on a Recurring Basis

The following table presents the company's financial assets and liabilities that are measured at fair value on a recurring basis at July 31, 2011 and August 1, 2010, consistent with the fair value hierarchy:

	Fair Value as of July 31, 2011	Fair Value Measurements at July 31, 2011 Using Fair Value Hierarchy			Fair Value as of August 1, 2010	Fair Value Measurements at August 1, 2010 Using Fair Value Hierarchy		
		Level 1	Level 2	Level 3		Level 1	Level 2	Level 3
Assets								
Interest rate swaps(1)	$ 33	$ —	$ 33	$ —	$ 46	$ —	$46	$ —
Foreign exchange forward contracts(2)	—	—	—	—	2	—	2	—
Cross-currency swap contracts(3)	1	—	1	—	17	—	17	—
Commodity derivative contracts(5)	3	3	—	—	4	4	—	—
Total assets at fair value	$ 37	$ 3	$ 34	$ —	$ 69	$ 4	$65	$ —
Liabilities								
Foreign exchange forward contracts(2)	$ 9	$ —	$ 9	$ —	$ 2	$ —	$ 2	$ —
Cross-currency swap contracts(3)	129	—	129	—	38	—	38	—
Deferred compensation derivative contracts(4)	3	—	3	—	2	—	2	—
Commodity derivative contracts(5)	2	2	—	—	1	1	—	—
Deferred compensation obligation(6)	144	97	47	—	149	95	54	—
Total liabilities at fair value	$287	$ 99	$188	$ —	$192	$ 96	$96	$ —

(1) Based on LIBOR swap rates.

(2) Based on observable market transactions of spot currency rates and forward rates.

NOTES TO CONSOLIDATED FINANCIAL STATEMENTS — (Continued)

(3) Based on observable local benchmarks for currency and interest rates.

(4) Based on LIBOR and equity index swap rates.

(5) Based on quoted futures exchanges.

(6) Based on the fair value of the participants' investments.

Items Measured at Fair Value on a Nonrecurring Basis

In addition to assets and liabilities measured at fair value on a recurring basis, the company is required to measure certain assets at fair value on a nonrecurring basis, generally as a result of an impairment charge. In 2011, as part of the company's annual review of intangible assets, an impairment charge of $3 was recognized related to the *Heisse Tasse* trademark used in the International Simple Meals and Beverages segment. The fair value of the trademark was $11 at July 31, 2011 based on Level 3 inputs. Fair value was determined based on discounted cash flow analyses that include significant management assumptions such as revenue growth rates, weighted average cost of capital, and assumed royalty rates.

16. Shareowners' Equity

The company has authorized 560 million shares of Capital stock with $.0375 par value and 40 million shares of Preferred stock, issuable in one or more classes, with or without par as may be authorized by the Board of Directors. No Preferred stock has been issued.

Share Repurchase Programs

In June 2008, the company's Board of Directors authorized the purchase of up to $1,200 of company stock through fiscal 2011. This program began in fiscal 2009 and was completed in fiscal 2011. In June 2011, the Board authorized the purchase of up to $1,000 of company stock. This program has no expiration date. In addition to these publicly announced programs, the company repurchases shares to offset the impact of dilution from shares issued under the company's stock compensation plans.

In 2011, the company repurchased 21 million shares at a cost of $728. Of the 2011 repurchases, approximately 16 million shares at a cost of $550 were made pursuant to the company's June 2008 publicly announced share repurchase program, which was completed in the fourth quarter of fiscal 2011.

In 2010, the company repurchased 14 million shares at a cost of $472. Of the 2010 repurchases, approximately 7 million shares at a cost of $250 were made pursuant to the company's June 2008 publicly announced share repurchase program.

In 2009, the company repurchased 17 million shares at a cost of $527. Of the 2009 repurchases, approximately 13 million shares at a cost of $400 were made pursuant to the company's June 2008 publicly announced share repurchase program.

17. Stock-Based Compensation

In 2003, shareowners approved the 2003 Long-Term Incentive Plan, which authorized the issuance of 28 million shares to satisfy awards of stock options, stock appreciation rights, unrestricted stock, restricted stock/units (including performance restricted stock) and performance units. Approximately 3.2 million shares available under a previous long-term plan were rolled into the 2003 Long-Term Incentive Plan, making the total number of available shares approximately 31.2 million. In November 2005, shareowners approved the 2005 Long-Term Incentive Plan, which authorized the issuance of an additional 6 million shares to satisfy the same types of awards.

Awards under the 2003 and 2005 Long-Term Incentive Plans may be granted to employees and directors. The term of a stock option granted under these plans may not exceed ten years from the date of grant. Options granted

NOTES TO CONSOLIDATED FINANCIAL STATEMENTS — (Continued)

under these plans vest cumulatively over a three-year period at a rate of 30%, 60% and 100%, respectively. The option price may not be less than the fair market value of a share of common stock on the date of the grant.

Pursuant to the 2003 Long-Term Incentive Plan, in July 2005 the company adopted a long-term incentive compensation program which provides for grants of total shareowner return (TSR) performance restricted stock/units, EPS performance restricted stock/units, and time-lapse restricted stock/units. Initial grants made in accordance with this program were approved in September 2005. Under the program, awards of TSR performance restricted stock/units will be earned by comparing the company's total shareowner return during a three-year period to the respective total shareowner returns of companies in a performance peer group. Based upon the company's ranking in the performance peer group, a recipient of TSR performance restricted stock/units may earn a total award ranging from 0% to 225% of the initial grant. Awards of EPS performance restricted stock/units will be earned based upon the company's achievement of annual earnings per share goals. During the three-year vesting period, a recipient of EPS performance restricted stock/units may earn a total award ranging from 0% to 100% of the initial grant. Awards of time-lapse restricted stock/units will vest ratably over the three-year period. In addition, the company may issue special grants of time-lapse restricted stock/units to attract and retain executives which vest ratably over various periods. Awards are generally granted annually in October. Annual stock option grants are not part of the long-term incentive compensation program for 2009, 2010, and 2011. However, stock options may still be granted on a selective basis under the 2003 and 2005 Long-Term Incentive Plans.

Total pre-tax stock-based compensation expense recognized in Earnings from continuing operations was $87 for 2011, $88 for 2010, and $84 for 2009. Tax related benefits of $32 were recognized for 2011, $33 were recognized for 2010 and $31 were recognized for 2009.

Information about stock options and related activity is as follows:

	2011	Weighted-Average Exercise Price	Weighted-Average Remaining Contractual Life	Aggregate Intrinsic Value
	(Options in thousands)		(In years)	
Beginning of year	12,473	$26.47		
Granted	—	$ —		
Exercised	(3,737)	$26.97		
Terminated	(30)	$33.82		
End of year	8,706	$26.23	2.2	$59
Exercisable at end of year	8,706	$26.23	2.2	$59

The total intrinsic value of options exercised during 2011, 2010, and 2009 was $29, $33, and $30, respectively. As of January 2009, compensation related to stock options was fully expensed. The company measured the fair value of stock options using the Black-Scholes option pricing model.

NOTES TO CONSOLIDATED FINANCIAL STATEMENTS — (Continued)

The following table summarizes time-lapse restricted stock/units and EPS performance restricted stock/units activity:

	Shares/Units (Restricted stock/units in thousands)	Weighted-Average Grant-Date Fair Value
Nonvested at August 1, 2010	2,395	$35.05
Granted	1,585	$35.64
Vested	(1,113)	$35.74
Forfeited	(157)	$35.11
Nonvested at July 31, 2011	2,710	$35.11

The fair value of time-lapse restricted stock/units and EPS performance restricted stock/units is determined based on the number of shares granted and the quoted price of the company's stock at the date of grant. Time-lapse restricted stock/units are expensed on a straight-line basis over the vesting period, except for awards issued to retirement-eligible participants, which are expensed on an accelerated basis. EPS performance restricted stock/units are expensed on a graded-vesting basis, except for awards issued to retirement-eligible participants, which are expensed on an accelerated basis.

On July 1, 2011, the company issued approximately 400,000 special retention time-lapse restricted stock units to certain executives to support the successful execution of the company's shift in strategic direction and leadership transition. The awards vest over a two-year period. The grant-date fair value was $34.65 and is included in the table above.

As of July 31, 2011, total remaining unearned compensation related to nonvested time-lapse restricted stock/units and EPS performance restricted stock/units was $46, which will be amortized over the weighted-average remaining service period of 1.7 years. The fair value of restricted stock/units vested during 2011, 2010, and 2009 was $40, $32, and $47, respectively. The weighted-average grant-date fair value of restricted stock/units granted during 2010 and 2009 was $32.25 and $39.50, respectively.

The following table summarizes TSR performance restricted stock/units activity:

	Shares/Units (Restricted stock/units in thousands)	Weighted-Average Grant-Date Fair Value
Nonvested at August 1, 2010	3,581	$38.02
Granted	1,255	$43.18
Vested	(1,062)	$34.65
Forfeited	(343)	$39.74
Nonvested at July 31, 2011	3,431	$40.78

The company estimates the fair value of TSR performance restricted stock/units at the grant date using a Monte Carlo simulation. Assumptions used in the Monte Carlo simulation were as follows:

	2011	2010	2009
Risk-free interest rate	0.59%	1.27%	2.06%
Expected dividend yield	3.00%	3.06%	2.46%
Expected volatility	23.71%	24.83%	18.57%
Expected term	3 yrs.	3 yrs.	3 yrs.

NOTES TO CONSOLIDATED FINANCIAL STATEMENTS — (Continued)

Compensation expense is recognized on a straight-line basis over the service period. As of July 31, 2011, total remaining unearned compensation related to TSR performance restricted stock/units was $53, which will be amortized over the weighted-average remaining service period of 1.7 years. In the first quarter of fiscal 2011, recipients of TSR performance restricted stock/units earned 100% of their initial grants based upon the company's TSR ranking in a performance peer group during a three-year period ended July 30, 2010. The total fair value of TSR performance restricted stock/units vested during 2011, 2010 and 2009 was $38, $31 and $58, respectively. The grant-date fair value of TSR performance restricted stock/units granted during 2010 and 2009 was $33.84 and $47.20, respectively. In the first quarter of 2012, recipients of TSR performance restricted stock/units will receive 0% of the initial grant based upon the company's TSR ranking in a performance peer group during the three-year period ended July 31, 2011.

Prior to fiscal 2009, employees could elect to defer all types of restricted stock awards. These awards were classified as liabilities because of the possibility that they may be settled in cash. The fair value was adjusted quarterly. As of October 2010, these awards were fully vested. The total cash paid to settle the liabilities in 2011, 2010, and 2009 was not material.

The excess tax benefits on the exercise of stock options and vested restricted stock presented as cash flows from financing activities were $11 in 2011 and 2010 and $18 in 2009. Cash received from the exercise of stock options was $96, $139, and $72, for 2011, 2010, and 2009, respectively, and is reflected in cash flows from financing activities in the Consolidated Statements of Cash Flows.

18. Commitments and Contingencies

The company is a party to legal proceedings and claims arising out of the normal course of business.

Management assesses the probability of loss for all legal proceedings and claims and has recognized liabilities for such contingencies, as appropriate. Although the results of these matters cannot be predicted with certainty, in management's opinion, the final outcome of legal proceedings and claims will not have a material adverse effect on the consolidated results of operations or financial condition of the company.

The company has certain operating lease commitments, primarily related to warehouse and office facilities, retail store space and certain equipment. Rent expense under operating lease commitments was $50 in 2011, $48 in 2010, and $47 in 2009. Future minimum annual rental payments under these operating leases are as follows:

2012	2013	2014	2015	2016	Thereafter
$45	$34	$29	$24	$22	$52

The company guarantees approximately 2,000 bank loans made to Pepperidge Farm independent sales distributors by third party financial institutions for the purchase of distribution routes. The maximum potential amount of future payments the company could be required to make under the guarantees is $162. The company's guarantees are indirectly secured by the distribution routes. The company does not believe it is probable that it will be required to make guarantee payments as a result of defaults on the bank loans guaranteed. The amounts recognized as of July 31, 2011 and August 1, 2010 were not material.

In connection with the sale of certain Australian salty snack food brands and assets, the company agreed to provide a loan facility to the buyer of AUD $10, or approximately USD $10. The facility was drawn down in AUD $5 increments in 2009. Borrowings under the facility are to be repaid in 2013.

The company has provided certain standard indemnifications in connection with divestitures, contracts and other transactions. Certain indemnifications have finite expiration dates. Liabilities recognized based on known exposures related to such matters were not material at July 31, 2011.

NOTES TO CONSOLIDATED FINANCIAL STATEMENTS — (Continued)

19. Supplemental Financial Statement Data

Balance Sheets

	2011	2010
Accounts receivable		
Customer accounts receivable	$ 530	$ 483
Allowances	(11)	(17)
Subtotal	519	466
Other	41	46
	$ 560	$ 512
Inventories		
Raw materials, containers, and supplies	$ 261	$ 261
Finished products	506	463
	$ 767	$ 724
Other current assets		
Deferred taxes	$ 112	$ 128
Fair value of derivatives	1	16
Other	39	53
	$ 152	$ 197
Plant assets		
Land	$ 64	$ 61
Buildings	1,224	1,182
Machinery and equipment	3,896	3,651
Projects in progress	179	149
Total cost	5,363	5,043
Accumulated depreciation(1)	(3,260)	(2,992)
	$ 2,103	$ 2,051
Other assets		
Fair value of derivatives	$ 20	$ 34
Deferred taxes	47	21
Other	69	55
	$ 136	$ 110
Accrued liabilities		
Accrued compensation and benefits	$ 231	$ 229
Fair value of derivatives	37	2
Accrued trade and consumer promotion programs	132	129
Accrued interest	32	47
Restructuring	39	1
Other	148	152
	$ 619	$ 560

NOTES TO CONSOLIDATED FINANCIAL STATEMENTS — (Continued)

	2011	2010
Other liabilities		
Pension benefits	$ 319	$ 500
Deferred compensation(2)	144	149
Postretirement benefits	344	332
Fair value of derivatives	90	22
Unrecognized tax benefits	51	45
Other	35	31
	$ 983	$ 1,079

(1) Depreciation expense was $265 in 2011, $251 in 2010, and $264 in 2009. Buildings are depreciated over periods ranging from 7 to 45 years. Machinery and equipment are depreciated over periods generally ranging from 2 to 20 years.

(2) The deferred compensation obligation represents unfunded plans maintained for the purpose of providing the company's directors and certain of its executives the opportunity to defer a portion of their compensation. All forms of compensation contributed to the deferred compensation plans are accounted for in accordance with the underlying program. Deferrals and company contributions are credited to an investment account in the participant's name, although no funds are actually contributed to the investment account and no investments are actually purchased. Six investment choices are available, including: (1) a book account that tracks the total return on company stock; (2) a book account that tracks the performance of the Vanguard Institutional Index; (3) a book account that tracks the performance of the Vanguard Extended Market Index; (4) a book account that tracks the performance of the Vanguard Total International Stock Fund; (5) a book account that tracks the performance of the Vanguard Total Bond Market Index; and (6) a book account that tracks the performance of Charles Schwab Stable Value Fund. Participants can reallocate investments daily and are entitled to the gains and losses on investment funds. The company recognizes an amount in the Consolidated Statements of Earnings for the market appreciation/depreciation of each fund.

Statements of Earnings

	2011	2010	2009
Other Expenses/(Income)			
Foreign exchange (gains)/losses	$ 5	$ 1	$ (7)
Amortization/impairment of intangible and other assets(1)	3	—	67
Other	5	3	1
	$ 13	$ 4	$ 61
Interest expense			
Interest expense	$123	$116	$114
Less: Interest capitalized	1	4	4
	$122	$112	$110

(1) In 2011, a $3 impairment charge was recognized related to a trademark. In 2009, a $67 impairment charge was recognized on certain trademarks. See also Note 5.

NOTES TO CONSOLIDATED FINANCIAL STATEMENTS — (Continued)

Statements of Cash Flows

Cash Flows From Operating Activities	2011	2010	2009
Other non-cash charges to net earnings			
Non-cash compensation/benefit related expense	$104	$ 90	$ 59
Other	4	9	(2)
	$108	$ 99	$ 57
Other			
Benefit related payments	$ (48)	$ (58)	$ (52)
Other	(7)	(12)	7
	$ (55)	$ (70)	$ (45)
Other Cash Flow Information			
Interest paid	$142	$118	$120
Interest received	$ 11	$ 6	$ 4
Income taxes paid	$304	$333	$144

20. Quarterly Data (unaudited)

	2011			
	First	Second	Third	Fourth
Net sales	$2,172	$2,127	$1,813	$1,607
Gross profit	894	838	732	639
Net earnings attributable to Campbell Soup Company(1)	279	239	187	100
Per share — basic				
Net earnings attributable to Campbell Soup Company	0.82	0.72	0.58	0.31
Dividends	0.275	0.29	0.29	0.29
Per share — assuming dilution				
Net earnings attributable to Campbell Soup Company(1)	0.82	0.71	0.57	0.31
Market price				
High	$37.59	$36.99	$35.00	$35.66
Low	$35.32	$33.44	$32.66	$32.80

NOTES TO CONSOLIDATED FINANCIAL STATEMENTS — (Continued)

	2010			
	First	**Second**	**Third**	**Fourth**
Net sales	$2,203	$2,153	$1,802	$1,518
Gross profit	923	871	743	613
Net earnings attributable to Campbell Soup Company(2)	304	259	168	113
Per share — basic				
Net earnings attributable to Campbell Soup Company	0.87	0.74	0.49	0.33
Dividends	0.25	0.275	0.275	0.275
Per share — assuming dilution				
Net earnings attributable to Campbell Soup Company(2)	0.87	0.74	0.49	0.33
Market price				
High	$33.98	$35.80	$36.25	$37.50
Low	$29.81	$30.96	$32.18	$34.18

(1) Includes a $41 ($.12 per diluted share) restructuring charge in the fourth quarter related to the 2011 initiatives to improve supply chain efficiency, reduce overhead costs, and exit the Russian market. See also Note 7.

(2) Includes an $8 ($.02 per diluted share) restructuring charge in the third quarter for pension benefit costs related to the 2008 initiatives to improve operational efficiency and long-term profitability. See also Note 7.

A $10 ($.03 per diluted share) deferred tax expense to reduce deferred tax assets as a result of the U.S. health care legislation enacted in March 2010 was recorded in the third quarter. See also Note 12.

Reports of Management

Management's Report on Financial Statements

The accompanying financial statements have been prepared by the company's management in conformity with generally accepted accounting principles to reflect the financial position of the company and its operating results. The financial information appearing throughout this Annual Report is consistent with the financial statements. Management is responsible for the information and representations in such financial statements, including the estimates and judgments required for their preparation. The financial statements have been audited by PricewaterhouseCoopers LLP, an independent registered public accounting firm, as stated in their report, which appears herein.

The Audit Committee of the Board of Directors, which is composed entirely of Directors who are not officers or employees of the company, meets regularly with the company's worldwide internal auditing department, other management personnel, and the independent registered public accounting firm. The independent registered public accounting firm and the internal auditing department have had, and continue to have, direct access to the Audit Committee without the presence of other management personnel, and have been directed to discuss the results of their audit work and any matters they believe should be brought to the Committee's attention. The internal auditing department and the independent registered public accounting firm report directly to the Audit Committee.

Management's Report on Internal Control Over Financial Reporting

The company's management is responsible for establishing and maintaining adequate internal control over financial reporting. Internal control over financial reporting is a process designed to provide reasonable assurance regarding the reliability of financial reporting and the preparation of financial statements for external purposes in accordance with generally accepted accounting principles in the United States of America.

The company's internal control over financial reporting includes those policies and procedures that:

- pertain to the maintenance of records that, in reasonable detail, accurately and fairly reflect the transactions and dispositions of the assets of the company;

- provide reasonable assurance that transactions are recorded as necessary to permit preparation of financial statements in accordance with generally accepted accounting principles, and that receipts and expenditures of the company are being made only in accordance with authorizations of management and Directors of the company; and

- provide reasonable assurance regarding prevention or timely detection of unauthorized acquisition, use, or disposition of the company's assets that could have a material effect on the financial statements.

Because of its inherent limitations, internal control over financial reporting may not prevent or detect misstatements. Also, projections of any evaluation of effectiveness to future periods are subject to the risk that controls may become inadequate because of changes in conditions, or that the degree of compliance with the policies or procedures may deteriorate.

The company's management assessed the effectiveness of the company's internal control over financial reporting as of July 31, 2011. In making this assessment, management used the criteria set forth by the Committee of Sponsoring Organizations of the Treadway Commission (COSO) in *Internal Control — Integrated Framework*. Based on this assessment using those criteria, management concluded that the company's internal control over financial reporting was effective as of July 31, 2011.

The effectiveness of the company's internal control over financial reporting as of July 31, 2011 has been audited by PricewaterhouseCoopers LLP, an independent registered public accounting firm, as stated in their report, which appears herein.

/s/   Denise M. Morrison
_____
Denise M. Morrison
President and Chief Executive Officer

/s/   B. Craig Owens
_____
B. Craig Owens
Senior Vice President — Chief Financial Officer
and Chief Administrative Officer

/s/   Anthony P. DiSilvestro
_____
Anthony P. DiSilvestro
Senior Vice President — Finance
(Principal Accounting Officer)

September 28, 2011

Report of Independent Registered Public Accounting Firm

To the Shareowners and Directors of Campbell Soup Company

In our opinion, the accompanying consolidated balance sheets and the related consolidated statements of earnings, of equity, and of cash flows present fairly, in all material respects, the financial position of Campbell Soup Company and its subsidiaries at July 31, 2011 and August 1, 2010, and the results of their operations and their cash flows for each of the three fiscal years in the period ended July 31, 2011 in conformity with accounting principles generally accepted in the United States of America. In addition, in our opinion, the financial statement schedule listed in the index appearing under Item 15(a)(2) presents fairly, in all material respects, the information set forth therein when read in conjunction with the related consolidated financial statements. Also in our opinion, the Company maintained, in all material respects, effective internal control over financial reporting as of July 31, 2011, based on criteria established in *Internal Control — Integrated Framework* issued by the Committee of Sponsoring Organizations of the Treadway Commission (COSO). The Company's management is responsible for these financial statements and financial statement schedule, for maintaining effective internal control over financial reporting and for its assessment of the effectiveness of internal control over financial reporting, included in the accompanying Management's Report on Internal Control over Financial Reporting. Our responsibility is to express opinions on these financial statements, on the financial statement schedule, and on the Company's internal control over financial reporting based on our integrated audits. We conducted our audits in accordance with the standards of the Public Company Accounting Oversight Board (United States). Those standards require that we plan and perform the audits to obtain reasonable assurance about whether the financial statements are free of material misstatement and whether effective internal control over financial reporting was maintained in all material respects. Our audits of the financial statements included examining, on a test basis, evidence supporting the amounts and disclosures in the financial statements, assessing the accounting principles used and significant estimates made by management, and evaluating the overall financial statement presentation. Our audit of internal control over financial reporting included obtaining an understanding of internal control over financial reporting, assessing the risk that a material weakness exists, and testing and evaluating the design and operating effectiveness of internal control based on the assessed risk. Our audits also included performing such other procedures as we considered necessary in the circumstances. We believe that our audits provide a reasonable basis for our opinions.

As discussed in Note 9 to the consolidated financial statements, the Company changed the manner in which it accounts for unvested share-based payment awards that contain non-forfeitable rights to dividends or dividend equivalents in the computation of earnings per share pursuant to the two-class method in 2010.

A company's internal control over financial reporting is a process designed to provide reasonable assurance regarding the reliability of financial reporting and the preparation of financial statements for external purposes in accordance with generally accepted accounting principles. A company's internal control over financial reporting includes those policies and procedures that (i) pertain to the maintenance of records that, in reasonable detail, accurately and fairly reflect the transactions and dispositions of the assets of the company; (ii) provide reasonable assurance that transactions are recorded as necessary to permit preparation of financial statements in accordance with generally accepted accounting principles, and that receipts and expenditures of the company are being made only in accordance with authorizations of management and directors of the company; and (iii) provide reasonable assurance regarding prevention or timely detection of unauthorized acquisition, use, or disposition of the company's assets that could have a material effect on the financial statements.

Because of its inherent limitations, internal control over financial reporting may not prevent or detect misstatements. Also, projections of any evaluation of effectiveness to future periods are subject to the risk that controls may become inadequate because of changes in conditions, or that the degree of compliance with the policies or procedures may deteriorate.

/s/ PricewaterhouseCoopers LLP

PricewaterhouseCoopers LLP
Philadelphia, Pennsylvania

September 28, 2011

Item 9. *Changes in and Disagreements with Accountants on Accounting and Financial Disclosure*

None.

Item 9A. *Controls and Procedures*

The company, under the supervision and with the participation of its management, including the President and Chief Executive Officer and Senior Vice President — Chief Financial Officer and Chief Administrative Officer, has evaluated the effectiveness of the company's disclosure controls and procedures (as such term is defined in Rules 13a-15(e) and 15d-15(e) under the Securities Exchange Act of 1934, as amended (the Exchange Act)) as of July 31, 2011. Based on such evaluation, the President and Chief Executive Officer and the Senior Vice President — Chief Financial Officer and Chief Administrative Officer have concluded that, as of July 31, 2011, the company's disclosure controls and procedures are effective.

The annual report of management on the company's internal control over financial reporting is provided under "Financial Statements and Supplementary Data" on pages 751-2. The attestation report of PricewaterhouseCoopers LLP, the company's independent registered public accounting firm, regarding the company's internal control over financial reporting is provided under "Financial Statements and Supplementary Data" on page 753.

There were no changes in the company's internal control over financial reporting that materially affected, or were reasonably likely to materially affect, such internal control over financial reporting.

Item 9B. *Other Information*

None.

PART III

Item 10. *Directors, Executive Officers and Corporate Governance*

The sections entitled "Election of Directors," "Security Ownership of Directors and Executive Officers" and "Director and Executive Officer Stock Ownership Reports" in the company's Proxy Statement for the Annual Meeting of Shareowners to be held on November 17, 2011 (the 2011 Proxy) are incorporated herein by reference. The information presented in the section entitled "Corporate Governance — Board Committee Structure" in the 2011 Proxy relating to the members of the company's Audit Committee and the Audit Committee's financial expert is incorporated herein by reference.

Certain of the information required by this Item relating to the executive officers of the company is set forth under the heading "Executive Officers of the Company."

The company has adopted a Code of Ethics for the Chief Executive Officer and Senior Financial Officers that applies to the company's Chief Executive Officer, Chief Financial Officer, Principal Accounting Officer, Controller and members of the Chief Financial Officer's financial leadership team. The Code of Ethics for the Chief Executive Officer and Senior Financial Officers is posted on the company's website, www.campbellsoupcompany.com (under the "Governance" caption). The company intends to satisfy the disclosure requirement regarding any amendment to, or a waiver of, a provision of the Code of Ethics for the Chief Executive Officer and Senior Financial Officers by posting such information on its website.

The company has also adopted a separate Code of Business Conduct and Ethics applicable to the Board of Directors, the company's officers and all of the company's employees. The Code of Business Conduct and Ethics is posted on the company's website, www.campbellsoupcompany.com (under the "Governance" caption). The company's Corporate Governance Standards and the charters of the company's four standing committees of the Board of Directors can also be found at this website. Printed copies of the foregoing are available to any shareowner requesting a copy by:

- writing to Investor Relations, Campbell Soup Company, 1 Campbell Place, Camden, NJ 08103-1799;

- calling 1-800-840-2865; or

- e-mailing the company's Investor Relations Department at investorrelations@campbellsoup.com.

Item 11. *Executive Compensation*

The information presented in the sections entitled "Compensation Discussion and Analysis," "Fiscal 2011 Summary Compensation Table," "Grants of Plan-Based Awards in Fiscal 2011," "Outstanding Equity Awards at 2011 Fiscal Year-End," "Option Exercises and Stock Vested in Fiscal 2011," "Pension Benefits — Fiscal 2011," "Nonqualified Deferred Compensation — Fiscal 2011," "Potential Payments Upon Termination or Change in Control," "Fiscal 2011 Director Compensation," "Corporate Governance — Compensation and Organization Committee Interlocks and Insider Participation" and "Compensation and Organization Committee Report" in the 2011 Proxy is incorporated herein by reference.

Item 12. *Security Ownership of Certain Beneficial Owners and Management and Related Shareowner Matters*

The information presented in the sections entitled "Security Ownership of Directors and Executive Officers" and "Security Ownership of Certain Beneficial Owners" in the 2011 Proxy is incorporated herein by reference.

Securities Authorized for Issuance Under Equity Compensation Plans

The following table provides information about the company's stock that could have been issued under the company's equity compensation plans as of July 31, 2011:

Plan Category	Number of Securities to be Issued Upon Exercise of Outstanding Options, Warrants and Rights(a)	Weighted-Average Exercise Price of Outstanding Options, Warrants and Rights(b)	Number of Securities Remaining Available For Future Issuance Under Equity Compensation Plans (Excluding Securities Reflected in the First Column)(c)
Equity Compensation Plans Approved by Security Holders(1)	14,842,965	$26.23	12,099,132
Equity Compensation Plans Not Approved by Security Holders	N/A	N/A	N/A
Total	14,842,965	$26.23	12,099,132

---

(1) Column (a) represents stock options and restricted stock units outstanding under the 2005 Long-Term Plan, the 2003 Long-Term Plan and the 1994 Long-Term Plan. No additional awards can be made under the 1994 Long-Term Plan. Future equity awards under the 2005 Long-Term Plan and the 2003 Long-Term Plan may take the form of stock options, SARs, performance unit awards, restricted stock, restricted performance stock, restricted stock units or stock awards. Column (b) represents the weighted-average exercise price of the outstanding stock options only; the outstanding restricted stock and restricted stock units are not included in this calculation. Column (c) represents the maximum aggregate number of future equity awards that can be made under the 2005 Long-Term Plan and the 2003 Long-Term Plan as of July 31, 2011. The maximum number of future equity awards that can be made under the 2005 Long-Term Plan as of July 31, 2011 is 10,500,021. The maximum number of future equity awards that can be made under the 2003 Long-Term Plan as of July 31, 2011 is 1,599,111 (the 2003 Plan Limit). Each stock option or SAR awarded under the 2003 Long-Term Plan reduces the 2003 Plan Limit by one share. Each restricted stock unit, restricted stock, restricted performance stock unit, restricted performance stock or stock award under the 2003 Long-Term Plan reduces the 2003 Plan Limit by four shares. In the event any award (or portion thereof) under the 1994 Long-Term Plan lapses, expires or is otherwise terminated without the issuance of any company stock or is settled by delivery of consideration other than company stock, the maximum number of future equity awards that can be made under the 2003 Long-Term Plan automatically increases by the number of such shares.

CAMPBELL SOUP COMPANY
Valuation and Qualifying Accounts

For the Fiscal Years ended July 31, 2011, August 1, 2010, and August 2, 2009

	Balance at Beginning of Period	Charged to/ (Reduction in) Costs and Expenses	Deductions	Balance at End of Period
		(Dollars in millions)		
Fiscal year ended July 31, 2011				
Cash discount	$ 5	$113	$(113)	$ 5
Bad debt reserve	4	2	(4)	2
Returns reserve(1)	8	(2)	(2)	4
Total Accounts receivable allowances	$17	$113	$(119)	$11
Fiscal year ended August 1, 2010				
Cash discount	$ 5	$116	$(116)	$ 5
Bad debt reserve	3	2	(1)	4
Returns reserve(1)	11	(3)	—	8
Total Accounts receivable allowances	$19	$115	$(117)	$17
Fiscal year ended August 2, 2009				
Cash discount	$ 5	$116	$(116)	$ 5
Bad debt reserve	5	1	(3)	3
Returns reserve(1)	11	—	—	11
Total Accounts receivable allowances	$21	$117	$(119)	$19

(1) The returns reserve is evaluated quarterly and adjusted accordingly. During each period, returns are charged to net sales in the Consolidated Statements of Earnings as incurred. Actual returns were approximately $145 in 2011, $130 in 2010, and $140 in 2009, or less than 2% of net sales.

EXHIBIT 31(a)

CERTIFICATION PURSUANT
TO RULE 13a-14(a)

I, Denise M. Morrison, certify that:

1. I have reviewed this Annual Report on Form 10-K of Campbell Soup Company;

2. Based on my knowledge, this report does not contain any untrue statement of a material fact or omit to state a material fact necessary to make the statements made, in light of the circumstances under which such statements were made, not misleading with respect to the period covered by this report;

3. Based on my knowledge, the financial statements, and other financial information included in this report, fairly present in all material respects the financial condition, results of operations and cash flows of the registrant as of, and for, the periods presented in this report;

4. The registrant's other certifying officer(s) and I are responsible for establishing and maintaining disclosure controls and procedures (as defined in Exchange Act Rules 13a-15(e) and 15d-15(e)) and internal control over financial reporting (as defined in Exchange Act Rules 13a-15(f) and 15d-15(f)) for the registrant and have:

    a) designed such disclosure controls and procedures, or caused such disclosure controls and procedures to be designed under our supervision, to ensure that material information relating to the registrant, including its consolidated subsidiaries, is made known to us by others within those entities, particularly during the period in which this report is being prepared;

    b) designed such internal control over financial reporting, or caused such internal control over financial reporting to be designed under our supervision, to provide reasonable assurance regarding the reliability of financial reporting and the preparation of financial statements for external purposes in accordance with generally accepted accounting principles;

    c) evaluated the effectiveness of the registrant's disclosure controls and procedures and presented in this report our conclusions about the effectiveness of the disclosure controls and procedures, as of the end of the period covered by this report based on such evaluation; and

    d) disclosed in this report any change in the registrant's internal control over financial reporting that occurred during the registrant's most recent fiscal quarter (the registrant's fourth fiscal quarter in the case of an annual report) that has materially affected, or is reasonably likely to materially affect, the registrant's internal control over financial reporting; and

5. The registrant's other certifying officer(s) and I have disclosed, based on our most recent evaluation of internal control over financial reporting, to the registrant's auditors and the audit committee of the registrant's board of directors (or persons performing the equivalent functions):

    a) all significant deficiencies and material weaknesses in the design or operation of internal control over financial reporting which are reasonably likely to adversely affect the registrant's ability to record, process, summarize and report financial information; and

    b) any fraud, whether or not material, that involves management or other employees who have a significant role in the registrant's internal control over financial reporting.

Date: September 28, 2011

By: /s/   Denise M. Morrison
_____
Name: Denise M. Morrison
Title: President and Chief Executive Officer

EXHIBIT 31(b)

CERTIFICATION PURSUANT
TO RULE 13a-14(a)

I, B. Craig Owens, certify that:

1. I have reviewed this Annual Report on Form 10-K of Campbell Soup Company;

2. Based on my knowledge, this report does not contain any untrue statement of a material fact or omit to state a material fact necessary to make the statements made, in light of the circumstances under which such statements were made, not misleading with respect to the period covered by this report;

3. Based on my knowledge, the financial statements, and other financial information included in this report, fairly present in all material respects the financial condition, results of operations and cash flows of the registrant as of, and for, the periods presented in this report;

4. The registrant's other certifying officer(s) and I are responsible for establishing and maintaining disclosure controls and procedures (as defined in Exchange Act Rules 13a-15(e) and 15d-15(e)) and internal control over financial reporting (as defined in Exchange Act Rules 13a-15(f) and 15d-15(f)) for the registrant and have:

a) designed such disclosure controls and procedures, or caused such disclosure controls and procedures to be designed under our supervision, to ensure that material information relating to the registrant, including its consolidated subsidiaries, is made known to us by others within those entities, particularly during the period in which this report is being prepared;

b) designed such internal control over financial reporting, or caused such internal control over financial reporting to be designed under our supervision, to provide reasonable assurance regarding the reliability of financial reporting and the preparation of financial statements for external purposes in accordance with generally accepted accounting principles;

c) evaluated the effectiveness of the registrant's disclosure controls and procedures and presented in this report our conclusions about the effectiveness of the disclosure controls and procedures, as of the end of the period covered by this report based on such evaluation; and

d) disclosed in this report any change in the registrant's internal control over financial reporting that occurred during the registrant's most recent fiscal quarter (the registrant's fourth fiscal quarter in the case of an annual report) that has materially affected, or is reasonably likely to materially affect, the registrant's internal control over financial reporting; and

5. The registrant's other certifying officer(s) and I have disclosed, based on our most recent evaluation of internal control over financial reporting, to the registrant's auditors and the audit committee of the registrant's board of directors (or persons performing the equivalent functions):

a) all significant deficiencies and material weaknesses in the design or operation of internal control over financial reporting which are reasonably likely to adversely affect the registrant's ability to record, process, summarize and report financial information; and

b) any fraud, whether or not material, that involves management or other employees who have a significant role in the registrant's internal control over financial reporting.

Date: September 28, 2011

By: /s/   B. Craig Owens
_____

Name: B. Craig Owens
Title: Senior Vice President — Chief Financial
Officer and Chief Administrative Officer

EXHIBIT 32(a)

CERTIFICATION PURSUANT TO
18 U.S.C. SECTION 1350

In connection with the Annual Report of Campbell Soup Company (the "Company") on Form 10-K for the fiscal year ended July 31, 2011 (the "Report"), I, Denise M. Morrison, President and Chief Executive Officer of the Company, hereby certify, pursuant to 18 U.S.C. Section 1350, as adopted pursuant to Section 906 of the Sarbanes-Oxley Act of 2002, that, to my knowledge:

(1) The Report fully complies with the requirements of Section 13(a) or 15(d) of the Securities Exchange Act of 1934; and

(2) The information contained in the Report fairly presents, in all material respects, the financial condition and results of operations of the Company.

Date: September 28, 2011

By: /s/ Denise M. Morrison
        Name: Denise M. Morrison
        Title: President and Chief Executive Officer

EXHIBIT 32(b)

CERTIFICATION PURSUANT TO
18 U.S.C. SECTION 1350

In connection with the Annual Report of Campbell Soup Company (the "Company") on Form 10-K for the fiscal year ended July 31, 2011 (the "Report"), I, B. Craig Owens, Senior Vice President — Chief Financial Officer and Chief Administrative Officer of the Company, hereby certify, pursuant to 18 U.S.C. Section 1350, as adopted pursuant to Section 906 of the Sarbanes-Oxley Act of 2002, that, to my knowledge:

(1) The Report fully complies with the requirements of Section 13(a) or 15(d) of the Securities Exchange Act of 1934; and

(2) The information contained in the Report fairly presents, in all material respects, the financial condition and results of operations of the Company.

Date: September 28, 2011

By: /s/   B. Craig Owens
       Name: B. Craig Owens
       Title: Senior Vice President —
                Chief Financial Officer and
                Chief Administrative Officer

SHAREOWNER INFORMATION

World Headquarters
Campbell Soup Company
1 Campbell Place
Camden, NJ 08103
(856) 342-4800
(856) 342-3878 (Fax)

Stock Exchange Listings
New York
Ticker Symbol: CPB

Transfer Agent and Registrar
Computershare Trust Company, N.A.
P.O. Box 43078
Providence, RI 02940-3078
1-800-780-3203

Independent Accountants
PricewaterhouseCoopers LLP
Two Commerce Square
Suite 1700
2001 Market Street
Philadelphia, PA 19103-7042

Dividends
Campbell has paid dividends since the company became public in 1954. Dividends are normally paid quarterly, near the end of January, April, July and October.

A dividend reinvestment plan is available to shareowners. For information about dividends or the dividend reinvestment plan, write to Dividend Reinvestment Plan Agent, Campbell Soup Company, P.O. Box 43078, Providence, RI 02940-3078. Or call (781) 575-2723 or 1-800-780-3203.

Annual Meeting
The Annual Meeting of Shareowners will be held on November 17, 2011, at 2:00 p.m. Eastern Time at the Hilton Stamford Hotel and Executive Meeting Center, One First Stamford Place, Stamford, CT 06902.

Publications
For copies of the Annual Report or the SEC Form 10-K or other financial information, write to Investor Relations at the World Headquarters address, or call 1-800-840-2865 or visit our investor website at www.investor.campbellsoupcompany.com.

For copies of Campbell's Corporate Social Responsibility Report, write to Dave Stangis, Vice President – Corporate Social Responsibility, at csr_feedback@campbellsoup.com.

Information Sources
Inquiries regarding our products may be addressed to Campbell's Consumer Response Center at the World Headquarters address or by calling 1-800-257-8443.

Investors and financial analysts may contact Jennifer Driscoll, Vice President – Investor Relations, at the World Headquarters address or by calling (856) 342-6081.

Media and public relations inquiries should be directed to Anthony Sanzio, Vice President – External and Internal Communications, at the World Headquarters address or by calling (856) 968-4390.

Communications concerning share transfer, lost certificates, dividends and change of address should be directed to Computershare Trust Company, N.A., 1-800-780-3203.

Shareowner Information Service
For the latest quarterly business results, or other information requests such as dividend dates, shareowner programs or product news, call 1-800-840-2865. Shareowner information is also available on our worldwide website at www.campbellsoupcompany.com.

Campbell Brands
Product trademarks owned or licensed by Campbell Soup Company and/or its subsidiaries appearing in the narrative text of this report are italicized.

MIX
Paper from responsible sources
FSC® C020268

The papers, paper mills and printer utilized in the production of this Annual Report are all certified for Forest Stewardship Council (FSC) standards, which promote environmentally appropriate, socially beneficial and economically viable management of the world's forests. The report is printed on Mohawk Navajo, a 20% post-consumer waste recycled paper, manufactured with certified, nonpolluting, wind-generated electricity. This report was printed by Sandy Alexander, Inc., which uses 100% renewable wind energy. Additionally, Sandy Alexander has implemented technologies and processes to substantially reduce the volatile organic compound (VOC) content of inks, coatings and solutions, and invested in equipment to capture and recycle virtually all VOC emissions from its press operations.

Design: Sequel Studio, New York

Index